1890
Reconstructed Census
of
Harford County,
Maryland

Volume 2: K-Z

Henry C. Peden, Jr.

Heritage Books
2023

HERITAGE BOOKS

AN IMPRINT OF HERITAGE BOOKS, INC.

Books, CDs, and more—Worldwide

For our listing of thousands of titles see our website
at
www.HeritageBooks.com

Published 2023 by
HERITAGE BOOKS, INC.
Publishing Division
5810 Ruatan Street
Berwyn Heights, MD 20740

International Standard Book Number
Paperbound: 978-0-7884-3040-4

INTRODUCTION

Census records are very important research tools for genealogists and cultural historians. In the United States, beginning in 1790, the census was taken every ten years. The 1890 census, however, was lost in a fire in 1921 and only fragments survived, but none for Maryland. This two-volume book is a reconstruction of that census for Harford County.

The Aegis & Intelligencer reported on 23 May 1890 that the census takers had been appointed and the following men were required to take the census in June of that year: E. B. Ambler, Upper Cross Roads Precinct; Robert Jason Gilbert, Abingdon Precinct; Bonfield Gorrell, Level Precinct; Charles F. Harry, Stearns Precinct; William Dallam Lee, Churchville Precinct; Laban Lowe, Norrisville Precinct; Israel Griffith Mathews, Havre de Grace; Millard F. Minnick, Bel Air; Carrollton Pennington, Jarrettsville Precinct; William Hicks Rawhouser, Hall's Cross Roads [Aberdeen]; James M. Reynolds, Bel Air Precinct; Holliday Hicks Spicer, Fallston Precinct; and, Charles Y. Thomas, Dublin Precinct.

Taking the census was not without its problems. James M. Reynolds notified the authorities that it would be impossible to complete his work on time without assistance. No assistance was furnished, so he had to take two weeks extra time, although he was employed 47½ days of ten hours each. Had he sent in his returns when directed to do so he would have left 1,500 names unreported in the Bel Air Precinct. This matter was reported in the *Harford Democrat* on 25 Jul 1890 and also in *The Aegis & Intelligencer* on 1 Aug 1890. One can only wonder how many people were missed by the other census takers in order to meet the deadline and, therefore, raising the question of their completeness.

I took on the daunting task and monumental challenge of identifying as many of the people in 1890 as I possibly could, realizing that the result would be inherently incomplete. The original census takers probably faced this same dilemma; nevertheless, I felt it was an assignment well worth undertaking. Information was gleaned from a variety of sources, including newspapers, death records, church records, Bible records, cemetery records, tombstone inscriptions, funeral home records, court records, probate records, naturalizations, school records, marriage records, military records (including the *1890 Special Census of Civil War Veterans* compiled by my friend L. Tilden Moore), business records, local histories, family histories, and Find a Grave online. A considerable amount of time was also spent researching and correcting errors discovered in many primary and secondary sources.

My compilation is actually more than a reconstructed census of names, dates, and places. It is also a directory that includes businesses, churches, and civic, social, and political organizations, i.e., a snapshot of the life activities and experiences of many of the citizens in 1890, including vocations, avocations, and more. Unlike the census, it includes full names, maiden names, married names, and nicknames in many cases. In addition to places of origin and family relationships, it also includes places of residence, dates of birth and death, and places of burial for most of them, and baptisms and divorces for some of them.

With regards to family names, it should be noted that an African American woman sometimes gave her maiden surname to her children and not the father's surname. Keep this in mind when looking for an ancestor and also search for any woman under both her maiden and married names. Also, the 1890 newspapers and other records referred to African Americans as colored most of the time and sometimes as black or negro. In keeping with historical accuracy and the vernacular of the times they are referred to as colored in my book.

Since the original 1890 census for Harford County was lost by fire in 1921, every scrap of information about it is like mining for gold, and digging into the enumeration of the census uncovered some interesting nuggets. The *Havre de Grace Republican* reported on 25 Apr 1890 that "these questions must be answered by all, or a fine will be imposed upon such as refuse to comply. Read the questions over carefully and be prepared to give prompt answers:

1. Give Christian name, surname
2. Whether a soldier, sailor or marine during the civil war (United States or Confederate) or widow of such person
3. Relations to heads of family
4. Whether white or black, mulatto, quadroon, octoroon, Chinese. Japanese or Indian
5. Sex
6. Age at nearest birthday. If under one year give age in months
7. Whether single, married, widowed or divorced
8. Whether married during the census year (June 1, 1889, to May 31, 1890)
9.Number of or how many children, and number of children living
10. Place of birth
11. Place of birth of father
12. Place of birth of mother-in-law
13. Number of years in the United States
14. Whether naturalized
15. Whether naturalization papers have been taken out
16. Profession, trade or occupation
17. Months unemployed during the census year
18. Attendance at school (in months) during the census year
19. Able to read
20. Able to write
21. Able to speak English. If not, the language or dialect spoken
22. Whether suffering from acute or chronic disease, with the name of disease and length of time afflicted
23. Whether defective in mind, sight, hearing or speech, or whether crippled, maimed or deformed, with name of defect
24. Whether a prisoner, convict, homeless child, or pauper
25 and 26. Is the home you live in hired or is it owned by the head or a member of family, is the home free of a mortgage encumbrance?
27 and 28. If the head of the family is a farmer, is the farm which he cultivates hired; or is it owned by him or a member of his family?
29. If owned by head or member of family, is the farm free from mortgage encumbrance?
30. If the home or farm is owned by head or member of family, and mortgaged, give the post office address of owner."

On 25 Aug 1890 the *Harford Democrat* published the following two census articles.

"Very Ancient. The oldest person in Harford is beyond a doubt Milly Harris, an old lady of African descent, who lives with her daughter, Keziah Bond, near Glen Cove. Mrs. Harris' age, as reported by Mr. Chas. Y. Thomas, census enumerator for Dublin precinct, is 112 years. She is of course very feeble but wonderfully well preserved for one who has seen so many years' flow into the mighty ocean of the past. Mr. Jas. M. Reynolds, enumerator for Bel Air precinct, reports two centenarians living in his territory, neither so old as the ancient of Glen Cove, but both older than the Constitution of the United States. Like, Mrs. Harris, both are colored. One is a Mrs. Tasker, living near Kalmia post office. She is 100 years old and is the mother of twenty-two children, nearly all of whom are not dead.

She lives with a son, Robert Tasker, who has himself seen sixteen years more that the allotted age of three-score-and-ten. The other is a Mrs. Jarrett, who lives with her son, a 'boy' of seventy-six years, near the Hickory. One hundred and six years of storm and sunshine have passed over her head, The oldest man reported in Hopewell precinct is Mr. John Mitchell, who lived near Havre de Grace. His age is 91 years. In the first district the oldest person is Mr. Lawrence Whaland, who lives on the 'Mountain,' and whose age is reported as 87. Next to him was an old colored man, aged 85, who lived at the "Mount," near Creswell, but who died last Wednesday. His name was Isaac Dawes. He leaves a sister aged 83 years."

"Census Returns. To the courtesy of Messrs. H. H. Spicer, Carroll Pennington and Chas. Y. Thomas, enumerators, we are indebted for the following interesting census notes. Under the strict rules of the Census Department it is not possible as yet to give our readers the complete returns for the county, but we hope to do so next week. (*Note:* They did publish the total census figures as promised, but no people were mentioned. The newspaper quality was so poor anyway that it could not be completely transcribed.)

"Third District - Fallston Precinct - Population, 1,430 [in 1880 it was 1,672, but the precinct has been reduced in size since that year]; farms, 129; deaths in past year, 4; veterans, 19; manufacturing establishments, 23.

"Fourth District - Jarrettsville Precinct - Population, 2,611 [in 1880, 2,573]; dwellings, 501; families, 502; farms, 350; deaths in past year, 23; Union veterans, 34; Confederate veterans, 2; manufacturing establishments, 23.

"Fifth District - Dublin Precinct - Population, 2,924 [in 1880, 2,931]; farms, 142; deaths in past year, 17; Union veterans, 33; manufacturing establishments, 14. The village Darlington contains 227 inhabitants, comprising 48 families; Berkley has 48 inhabitants, 9 families; Dublin has 91 inhabitants, 18 families.

"Second District - Hall's X Roads (Aberdeen) - Population, 3,550 [in 1880, 3,562]; dwellings, about 610; families, about 620; farms, 250; deaths in past year, 13; Union veterans, 28; Confederate veterans, 4; manufacturing establishments, 62; tomato packers, 32; corn packers, 27; cases tomatoes packed last year, 120,800; cases corn packed last year, 197,800. Population - Spesutia Island, white 42, colored, 42, total 84.

"Hopewell Precinct - Population, 2,275 [in 1880, 2,263]; dwelling houses and families, each over 400; Union veterans, 39; Confederate veterans, 3; canning houses, 29. The total population of the Second District is 5,825, exactly the same that it was in 1880.

"The population of the first district is between 2,700 and 2,800. In 1880 it was 2,887. The population of Poole's Island is 13.

"The figures given above are not official. but may be relied on as accurate. Where there has been any doubt, from lack of notes, the figures have been marked as approximated."

On 22 Aug 1890 the *Havre de Grace Republican* reported the same information as the "Very Ancient" article above, but added the following: "Havre de Grace cannot boast of a centenarian, but we have a number of aged people. Mrs. Nancy Mahan is the oldest. She is a cousin of Mr. Mitchell, and ranks him in age by over two years. Mrs. Mahan was born here, and has lived in Harford all her life. Her health is good, and there is every indication of her living some years yet. Her memory is excellent, and her mental powers seem to be unimpaired. She resides with her son, Robert, who is comparatively young, about 50."

Also, on 22 Aug 1890, the *Harford Democrat* reported the following: "Mr. Laban Lowe, census enumerator for Norrisville precinct, informs us that the population of that precinct is 1,200. That is 329 more than the approximate number reported last week, and 111 more than the population of 1880. The number of dwellings in the precinct is 250; families, 256; farms, 180; deaths in past year, 15; Union veterans, 19; Confederate veterans, 1; manufacturing establishments, 12."

On 5 Sep 1890 the *Havre de Grace Republican* reported the following: "According to the report of census enumerator Laban Lowe, Norrisville precinct has two women the mother of 32 children, one having 17 to her credit and the other 15."

Finally, on 22 Sep 1890 the *Havre de Grace Republican* reported that the first official census enumeration for Maryland's population had been released and Harford's population was set down at 28,980, an increase of 938 since 1880.

My book identifies over 26,000 (approximately 90%) of the 28,980 people in Harford County in 1890. They have been arranged alphabetically by last name and cross-referenced within the text, thus precluding the necessity for a separate index. All sources have been cited within the text.

Henry C. Peden, Jr.
Bel Air, Maryland

1890 Reconstructed Census of Harford County, Maryland
Volume 2: K-Z

Kack, Kate, age 18 in 1890 (Marriage License Applications Book ALJ No. 2, 1891)

Kahoe, Helen A., 1869-1959 (St. Ignatius Catholic Church Cemetery)

Kahoe, James, 1867-1948 (St. Mary's Catholic Church Cemetery)

Kahoe, John H., 1865-1836 (St. Ignatius Catholic Church Cemetery)

Kahoe, Lawrence, see Michael Kahoe, Pauline Angela Kahoe and Lawrence Kehoe, q.v.

Kahoe, Margaret (Haviland), 1828-1908 (St. Ignatius Catholic Church Cemetery)

Kahoe, Mary (Crowe), 1870-1939 (St. Ignatius Catholic Church Cemetery)

Kahoe, Mary G., 1858-1938 (St. Ignatius Catholic Church Cemetery)

Kahoe, Michael, 1827-1915 (St. Ignatius Catholic Church Cemetery); resided at Berkley (*Harford Democrat*, 3 Jan 1890); father of Lawrence Kehoe *(sic)* (*The Aegis & Intelligencer*, 3 Jan 1890)

Kahoe, Pauline Angela, born -- June 1883, baptized 11 Aug 1883, daughter of Lawrence F. Kahoe, native of County Wexford, Ireland, and Sarah Tole, native of County Armagh, Ireland (St. Ignatius Catholic Church Baptism Register, p. 67)

Kahoe, Pauline L. (Crew), 1864-1894 (St. Ignatius Catholic Church Cemetery)

Kahoe, Rose L., 1862-1948 (St. Mary's Catholic Church Cemetery)

Kahoe, Thomas J., 1862-1940 (St. Ignatius Catholic Church Cemetery)

Kaiser, Margaret Elizabeth, 1883-1926 (Cokesbury Memorial Methodist Church Cemetery - married name Loughlin); native of Maryland, born 29 Mar 1883, daughter of Valentine Kaiser, of Germany, and Dorcas Carrick, of Maryland, resided at Edgewood (Death certificate misfiled as Coughlin)

Kalal, Barbara, 1856-1944 (St. Francis de Sales Catholic Church Cemetery)

Kalal, John, 1861-1938, farmer and resident of Belcamp, son of James Kalal and Mary Brejcha, all natives of Czechoslovakia (St. Francis de Sales Catholic Church Cemetery)

Kalal, John, c1834-1900, native of Germany, farmer, resided at Belcamp (Death certificate spelled it Klal)

Kalb, Conrad Henry, 1868-1931 (West Nottingham Cemetery, Cecil Co., MD); native of Germany, came to Havre de Grace in 1883 and later managed a hotel and tavern called the Lamm House (*Biographical Dictionary of Harford County, Maryland, 1774-1974*, by Henry C. Peden, Jr. and William O. Carr, 2021, p. 152)

Kalb, Mary Eldora (Phillips) (Lamm), 1868-1945 (West Nottingham Cemetery, Cecil Co., MD); wife of Conrad Henry Kalb, q.v.

Kalmbacher, Alexander, 1876-1952 (St. Paul's Lutheran Church Cemetery)

Kalmbacher, Anna Barbara (Schanz), 1845-1926 (St. Paul's Lutheran Church Cemetery); native of Germany, resided near Aberdeen (Death certificate); wife of John George Kalmbacher, q.v.

Kalmbacher, Elizabeth, 1874-1893, daughter of John G. and Anna B. Kalmbacher (St. Paul's Lutheran Church Cemetery)

Kalmbacher, Ella Nora W., 1876-1932 (Mt. Zion Methodist Church Cemetery)

Kalmbacher, George J, 1883-1960 (Baker Cemetery)

Kalmbacher, John G., 1872-1942 (Mt. Zion Methodist Church Cemetery)

Kalmbacher, John George, 1843-1914, born in Germany (St. Paul's Lutheran Church Cemetery)

Kalmbacher, Louise E., 1880-1951 (Baker Cemetery)

Kalmbacher, Mary E., 1880-1968 (St. Paul's Lutheran Church Cemetery); wife of Alexander C. Kalmbacher, q.v.

Kalmia Colored Public School No. 4, at Kalmia, Third District (*Harford County, Maryland Teachers and the Schools They Served, 1774-1900*, by Henry C. Peden, Jr., 2022, p. 370)

Kammerer, Ada Reed, 1856-1920 (William Watters Church Cemetery, Cooptown)

Kammerer, Charles H, 1856-1931 (Trinity Evangelical Lutheran Church Cemetery)

Kammerer, Christiana, 1819-1891 (Trinity Evangelical Lutheran Church Cemetery)

Kammerer, Ernestina Minnie (Ulrich), 1857-1900, native of Germany, resided at Magnolia, Harford Co. (Death certificate; Trinity Evangelical Lutheran Church Cemetery); wife of John Peter Kammerer, q.v.

Kammerer, John Peter, 1853-1927, native of Germany, resided at Joppa, Harford Co. (Death certificate; Trinity Evangelical Lutheran Church Cemetery)

Kammerer, Mary E., 1856-1931 (Trinity Evangelical Lutheran Church Cemetery)

Kane, Ellen Nora (colored), 1871-1942, daughter of Helen Kane and ---- (Death certificate)

Kane, G. W., member, Independent Social Club, Havre de Grace (*Havre de Grace Republican*, 28 Mar 1890)

Kane, Helen (colored), see Ellen Nora Kane (colored), q.v.

Kane, Jennie (colored), wife of William Kane (colored), q.v.

Kane, Patrick, 1834-1904 (Death certificate; Alms House Record Book); Mr. & Mrs. Ptrick Kane, residents of Big Branch (*The Aegis & Intelligencer*, 28 Nov 1890)

Kane, Rose (colored), 1846-1918, native of Maryland, daughter of Henry Giles and Mary Keithley (Death certificate)

Kane, T., member, Independent Social Club, Havre de Grace (*Havre de Grace Republican*, 28 Mar 1890)

Kane, William (colored), 1819-1899, native of Harford Co. (Death certificate)

Karr, John, farmer, Thomas Run (*The Aegis & Intelligencer*, 4 Apr 1890)

Katenkamp, Rowland W., 1890-1935 (Union Chapel Methodist Church Cemetery)

Kauffman, Henry, 1848-1920 (Death certificate; Alms House Record Book)

Kauffman, Margaret P. (Parry), 1887-1965 (Slate Ridge Cemetery, York Co., PA); native of Cardiff, Harford Co., born 2 Feb 1887, daughter of Thomas Parry and Carrie Stull)

Kazmaier, Andrew, livery stable, corner of Baltimore and Bond Streets, Bel Air (*The Aegis & Intelligencer*, 18 Apr 1890)

Kazmyer, Kate, student, Third District (*The Aegis & Intelligencer*, 24 Oct 1890)

Kean, Annie, student, Bynum School (*The Aegis & Intelligencer*, 7 Feb 1890)

Kean, Betty (colored), born 20 Feb 1874, daughter of ---- and Eliza Kean (Holy Trinity Episcopal Church Register of Baptisms, p. 82)

Kean, Cornelia (Bryant), 1853-1938 (Christ Episcopal Church Cemetery)

Kean, Eliza (colored), see Betty Kean (colored), q.v.

Kean, Frances W., 1875-1959 (Old Brick Baptist Church Cemetery)

Kean, J. Humphrey Wilson, 1839-1924 (St. Ignatius Catholic Church Cemetery); native of Maryland, farmer, resided at Forest Hill (Death certificate)

Kean, John, 1836-1913 (Christ Episcopal Church Cemetery); moved into Jacob A. Grafton's house in Forest Hill in 1890 (*Harford Democrat*, 21 Mar 1890)

Kean, Lorinda (Streett), 1836-1917 (Christ Episcopal Church Cemetery); see James Devoe, q.v.

Kean, William, 1833-1895 (St. Ignatius Catholic Church Cemetery); carpenter and barn builder (*Harford Democrat*, 10 Oct 1890); see James Devoe, q.v.

Keane, Thomas, member, St. Patrick's Catholic Church, Havre de Grace (*Havre de Grace Republican*, 13 Jun 1890)

Keane, Timothy ("Captain Tim"), 1854-1899 (Mt. Erin Cemetery); unmarried fisherman, native of Havre de

Grace (Death certificate; *The Aegis & Intelligencer*, 31 Mar 1899)

Kearney, Alice, born 7 Mar 1879, daughter of Patrick and Sarah Kearney (Holy Trinity Episcopal Church Register of Baptisms, p. 82)

Kearney, Patrick, see Alice Kearney and Sarah Ann Kearney, q.v.

Kearney, Sarah Ann, born 25 May 1884, daughter of Patrick and Sarah Kearney (Holy Trinity Episcopal Church Register of Baptisms, p. 86); twin of Thomas Patrick Kearney who died in infancy (Holy Trinity Episcopal Church Cemetery)

Kearney, Thomas Patrick, see Sarah Ann Kearney, q.v.

Kearns, Clara (Wiley), 1859-1910 (Highland Presbyterian Church Cemetery); native of Maryland, resided at Street, wife of Thomas C. Kearns (Death certificate)

Kearns, Thomas C., see Clara Kearns, q.v.

Kearns, William Walter, 31 Oct 1889 - 16 Nov 1890 (Highland Presbyterian Church Cemetery)

Keating, Bridget, 1833-1901 (St. Ignatius Catholic Church Cemetery); native of Ireland, resided at VanBibber, wife of John Keating (Death certificate

Keating, John, 1820-1890, native of County Clare, Ireland (St. Ignatius Catholic Church Cemetery); see Bridget Keating, q.v.

Keating, John, farmer on J. Kent Worthington's farm, near Shure's Landing (*The Aegis & Intelligencer*, 29 Aug 1890; bass violin, Darlington Orchestra (*Havre de Grace Republican*, 7 Mar 1890); actor, musical entertainment, at Darlington (*The Aegis & Intelligencer*, 30 May 1890)

Keating, Margaret, see Margaret H. McGuigan, wife of Sylvester A. McGuigan, q.v.

Keating, Margaret M., 1846-1896 (St. Ignatius Catholic Church Cemetery)

Keck, Annie (Miss), principal, Public School No. 1, First District (*The Aegis & Intelligencer*, 10 Jan 1890)

Kee, Pearl V., 1890-1960 (Jarrettsville Cemetery)

Keech, Betty Wharton Constance, 1880-1957 (Christ Episcopal Church Cemetery)

Keech, Blanche Franklin (Lee), 1867-1922 (Christ Episcopal Church Cemetery)

Keech, Edyth Lawrence, 1878-1934 (Christ Episcopal Church Cemetery); premium award winner, Class L - Children's Department, Harford County Fair, 1890 (*The Aegis & Intelligencer*, 24 Oct 1890)

Keech, Henry Hobart (born Dec 1869), piano and organ teacher, of Fallston (*Havre de Grace Republican*, 4 Jul 1890; *The Aegis & Intelligencer*, 8 Aug and 17 Oct 1890); age 21 in 1890 (Marriage License Applications Book ALJ No. 2, 1891); conducted religious services for inmates at the Almshouse (*Harford Democrat*, 10 Oct 1890)

Keech, James K., 1829-1905 (Christ Episcopal Church Cemetery); justice of the peace, Third District (*Havre de Grace Republican*, 21 Feb 1890); vestryman, Christ Church, Rock Spring (*Havre de Grace Republican*, 18 Apr 1890)

Keech, Rachel A. (Johns), 1842-1915 (Christ Episcopal Church Cemetery); wife of James K. Keech, q.v.

Keen, ----, right fielder, Bel Air Victors Baseball Club (*The Aegis & Intelligencer*, 25 Jul 1890)

Keen, Amanda (Sutton), 1830-1893 (Grove Presbyterian Church Cemetery)

Keen, Annie L., 1861-1913 (Wesleyan Chapel Methodist Church Cemetery); wife of William J. Keen, q.v.

Keen, Aquila, see Bennett Aquila Keen, q.v.

Keen, Aquilla W., see John Robert Keen, q.v.

Keen, B. Franklin, see Roderick Dorsey Keen, q.v.

Keen, Bennett Aquila, 1862-1961 (Angel Hill Cemetery); native of Aberdeen, Harford Co., born 18 Feb1862, son of Aquila Keen and Mary Tigner (Pennington Funeral Home Records); Bennett Keen, sink boat duck hunter, 1890 (*Havre de Grace Republican*, 7 Nov 1890); see Oden Bennett Keen, q.v.

Keen, Benedict Hall, 1825-1892 (St. George's Episcopal Church Cemetery); vestryman, Spesutia Church, St.

George's Parish, Perryman (*Havre de Grace Republican*, 11 Apr 1890); also see Ella Keen, q.v.

Keen, Corinne H., 1863-1928 (Grove Presbyterian Church Cemetery)

Keen, Ella, age 23, daughter of B. H. Keen, married Dr. Alexander Shaw Porter, age 22, of Lonaconing, MD, on 10 Jun 1890 in Perryman (*The Aegis & Intelligencer*, 13 Jun 1890; Marriage License Applications Book ALJ No. 2, 1890)

Keen, Enola W., 1884-1951 (Wesleyan Chapel Methodist Church Cemetery)

Keen, Fannie (Miss), member, Bel Air M. P. Church Sunday School (*The Aegis & Intelligencer*, 27 Jun 1890)

Keen, Frank, 1870-1910 (St. George's Episcopal Church Cemetery); choir member, Bel Air M. P. Church (*The Aegis & Intelligencer*, 27 Jun 1890); member, Bel Air Cornet Band (*The Aegis & Intelligencer*, 1 Aug 1890)

Keen, H., third baseman, Bel Air Victors Baseball Club (*The Aegis & Intelligencer*, 27 Jun 1890)

Keen, Harry (master), resident near Fallston (*The Aegis & Intelligencer*, 11 Apr 1890)

Keen, Harry, clerk at Trundle's Store in Joppa (*The Aegis & Intelligencer*, 11 Jul 1890)

Keen, Henrietta (Dorsey), 1864-1942 (St. George's Episcopal Church Cemetery); see Roderick Dorsey Keen, q.v.

Keen, Howard, choir member, Bel Air M. P. Church (*The Aegis & Intelligencer*, 27 Jun 1890); pitcher, Bel Air Victors Baseball Club (*The Aegis & Intelligencer*, 30 May 1890)

Keen, Ida Viola (Cain), 1878-1975 (Grove Presbyterian Church Cemetery)

Keen, John Robert, 1858-1942 (Grove Presbyterian Church Cemetery); native of Lapidum, Harford Co., born 2 Feb 1858, son of Aquilla W. Keen and Mary Tignor, the latter of Virginia (Pennington Funeral Home Records); J. R. Keen, sink boat and sneak boat duck hunter, 1890 (*Havre de Grace Republican*, 7 Nov 1890); see Katherine M. Keen, q.v.

Keen, Katharine E. "Kate" (Horner), 1865-1901, native of Maryland, resided on Spesutia Island (Death certificate)

Keen, Katherine M., 1889-1969, native of Havre de Grace, born 13 May 1889, daughter of John R. Keen and Jenny Horner (Pennington Fnneral Home Records - married name Vandiver)

Keen, Lilly, 1861-1940 (Grove Presbyterian Church Cemetery)

Keen, Lycurgus, 1849-1923, native of Maryland, storekeeper in Havre de Grace (Death certificate; Angel Hill Cemetery)

Keen, Martha P., 1868-1958 (Fallston Methodist Church Cemetery)

Keen, Mary (Tigner), 1832-1915 (Grove Presbyterian Church Cemetery)

Keen, Mary Catherine, 1836-1926 (St. George's Episcopal Church Cemetery)

Keen, Mary Eleanor (Poplar), 1886-1979 (Angel Hill Cemetery)

Keen, Mary Jane (Holland), 1851-1925, native of Maryland, resided at Fulford (Death certificate misfiled with the J's; Mt. Zion Methodist Church Cemetery)

Keen, Mary K., 1837-1916 (Rock Run Methodist Church Cemetery); wife of Samuel M. Keen, q.v.

Keen, Mary P. (Keen), born 1885, died ---- (Grove Presbyterian Church Cemetery)

Keen, Michael & Co., storekeepers, Perryman (*Havre de Grace Republican*, 20 Jun 1890)

Keen, Nicholas T., 1856-1935 (Grove Presbyterian Church Cemetery)

Keen, Oden Bennett, 1889-1965 (Angel Hill Cemetery); native of Oakington, Harford Co., born 21 Sep 1889, son of Bennett A. Keen and Charlotte Johnson (Pennington Funeral Home Records)

Keen, Roderick Dorsey, born 23 Aug 1889, died 26 Jul 1890, son of B. Franklin and Henrietta Keen (St. George's Episcopal Church Cemetery and Church Register of Baptisms, p. 9; *The Aegis & Intelligencer*, 1 Aug 1890)

Keen, Samuel M., 1832-1900 (Rock Run Methodist Church Cemetery)

Keen, Sarah A., 1816-1895 (Grove Presbyterian Church Cemetery)

Keen, Sarah E., 1844-1923 (Fallston Methodist Church Cemetery)

Keen, Susanna, 1859-1934 (Grove Presbyterian Church Cemetery)

Keen, Thomas E., and Maggie J., acquired land in November 1890 (*The Aegis & Intelligencer*, 5 Dec 1890)

Keen, Timothy Littleton, 1829-1896 (Grove Presbyterian Church Cemetery)

Keen, W. Frank, 1866-1960 (Fallston Methodist Church Cemetery)

Keen, William A., 1881-1915 (Grove Presbyterian Church Cemetery)

Keen, William J., 1837-1912 (Fallston Methodist Church Cemetery); resident on Broadway in Bel Air, 1890 (*The Aegis & Intelligencer*, 29 Aug 1890)

Keen, William J., 1854-1907 (Grove Presbyterian Church Cemetery); trustee, Oakington School No. 16, Second District (*Havre de Grace Republican*, 30 May 1890)

Keen, William J., 1859-1912 (Wesleyan Chapel Methodist Church Cemetery)

Keenan, Alexander, Civil War veteran, Havre de Grace (*1890 Special Census of the Civil War Veterans of the State of Maryland*, by L. Tilden Moore, Volume III, p. 89)

Keene, Anna (Hanna?) Catherine (Bradfield), 1863-1950, native of Level, Harford Co., born 8 Apr 1863, daughter of James F. Bradfield and Catherine Hughes (Pennington Funeral Home Records); see Beulah Keene and Harry E. Keene, q.v.

Keene, Arthur Ramsey, 1858-1950 (Angel Hill Cemetery); born 29 Jul 1858, son of James Keene and Lydia Kincaid (*The Hughes Genealogy, 1636-1953*, by Joseph Lee Hughes, 1953, p. 128)

Keene, Beulah, born 2 Jul 1889, daughter of Arthur Ramsey Keene and Hannah *(sic)* Catherine Bradfield (*The Hughes Genealogy, 1636-1953*, by Joseph Lee Hughes, 1953, p. 128)

Keene, Harry Elwood, born 16 Oct 1885, son of Arthur Ramsey Keene and Hannah *(sic)* Catherine Bradfield (*The Hughes Genealogy, 1636-1953*, by Joseph Lee Hughes, 1953, pp. 128, 151)

Keene, James, see Arthur Ramsey Keene, q.v.

Keene, John M., member, Young Men's Pleasure Club, Havre de Grace (*Havre de Grace Republican*, 21 Nov 1890); charter member, Havre de Grace Gunning Club (*Havre de Grace Republican*, 14 Nov 1890)

Keene, Mabel V. (Rogers), 1880-1960 (Slate Ridge Cemetery, York Co., PA); native of Fallston, Harford Co., born 20 Jan 1880, daughter of George Rogers and Ella Force (Harkins Funeral Home Records)

Kegley, Eliza Jane (Catron), 1871-1923 (Bethel Presbyterian Church Cemetery Records); wife of George L. Kegley, q.v.

Kegley, Emma A. (Cassady), 1870-1941, second wife of Lemuel Eddley Kegley (Bethel Presbyterian Church Cemetery Records)

Kegley, George L., born 11 Feb 1880, son of Lemuel Eddley Kegley and Margaret Leedy (Bethel Presbyterian Church Cemetery Records)

Kehoe, Charles, born -- Dec 1889, baptized 4 Jan 1889, son of John Kehoe and Pauline Crew (St. Ignatius Catholic Church Baptism Register, p. 110)

Kehoe, Edward, born -- Dec 1889, baptized 13 Jan 1890, son of Edward Kehoe, native of Harford Co., and Johanna Lynch, native of Baltimore Co. (St. Ignatius Catholic Church Baptism Register, p. 110, wrote "Edwin M. Lynch" in the margin)

Kehoe, Henry Ignatius, born -- Mar 1887, baptized 20 Apr 1887, son of Lawrence Kehoe, of County Wexford, Ireland, and Sarah Toal, of County Armagh, Ireland (St. Ignatius Catholic Church Baptism Register, p. 91)

Kehoe, Irene Celeste, born -- Jan 1885, baptized 7 Feb 1885, daughter of Lawrence Kehoe, of County Wexford, Ireland, and Sarah Toal, of County Armagh, Ireland (St. Ignatius Catholic Church Baptism Register, p. 77)

Kehoe, Lawrence, son of Michael Kehoe (*The Aegis & Intelligencer*, 3 Jan 1890); see Irene C. Kehoe and Pauline A. Kahoe, q.v.

Kehoe, Mary Josephine, born -- Sep 1888, baptized 7 Oct 1888, daughter of John Kehoe and Pauline Crew (St. Ignatius Catholic Church Baptism Register, p. 99)

Keighler, John Chickley, Jr., died in 1890 (Priestford Cemetery)

Keighler, Rosa Neilson, 1848-1913 (Priestford Cemetery)

Keim, N. M. (Mrs.), millinery, Havre de Grace (*Havre de Grace Republican*, 4 Apr 1890)

Keith's Boot and Shoemaking Shop, Main & Bond Streets, Bel Air, B. F. Keith, prop. (*Harford Democrat*, 10 Jan 1890)

Keith, Anna L. (Berry), 1873-1918 (Fallston Methodist Church Cemetery)

Keith, Benjamin F., 1845-1917 (Fallston Methodist Church Cemetery)

Keith, D. Clarkson, 1876-1946 (Fallston Methodist Church Cemetery); Clarkson Keith, student, Bel Air Academy and Graded School (*The Aegis & Intelligencer*, 23 May 1890)

Keith, John H., 1827-1903, native of Pennsylvania, shoemaker in Bel Air (Death certificate; Cokesbury Memorial Methodist Church Cemetery)

Keith, Margie (Miss), postmistress, Kirkwood (*Harford Democrat*, 28 Mar 1890)

Keith, Martha, see Dora V. Howlett, q.v.

Keith, Mary L. (Anderson), 1828-1904, native of Pennsylvania, resided in Fallston (Death certificate; Fallston Methodist Church Cemetery)

Keith, Mary M. (Burgoyne), 1812-1903, native of Cecil Co., MD, resided at Prospect, Harford Co. (Death certificate; Emory Methodist Church Cemetery)

Keith, Sarah M., 1847-1901 (Fallston Methodist Church Cemetery)

Keithley, Anna, 1884-1964, native of Harford Co., born 7 Sep 1884, daughter of Samuel Thomas Keithley and Elizabeth Baldwin (Pennington Funeral Home Records - married name Burt)

Keithley, Arthur A., 1880-1907 (Baker Cemetery)

Keithley, Belle, 1861-1950 (Smith Chapel Methodist Church Cemetery)

Keithley, C. Alonzo, 1877-1959 (St. Paul's Lutheran Church Cemetery)

Keithley, Carrie G., 1882-1928 (Smith Chapel Methodist Church Cemetery)

Keithley, Carroll F., 1888-1953, native of Hopewell, Harford Co., born 24 Apr 1888, son of S. Thomas Keithley and Elizabeth A. Baldwin (Pennington Funeral Home Records; Angel Hill Cemetery)

Keithley, Elizabeth A. (Baldwin), 1864-1905 (Baker Cemetery)

Keithley, Elizabeth A. (Cullum), 1835-1911, native of Harford Furnace, resided at Carsins (Death certificate)

Keithley, Emma Frances, 1850-1931 (Smith Chapel Methodist Church Cemetery)

Keithley, Fannie C., wife of Christmas Day Coale, q.v.

Keithley, George T., 1870-1961 (Baker Cemetery)

Keithley, Harry Gallow, 1888-1972 (Baker Cemetery)

Keithley, Harry Moore, 1873-1919 (Baker Cemetery tombstone inscribed 1872-1918); native of Harford Co., resided near Aberdeen, born 10 Feb 1873, son of Jonathan Keithley and Elizabeth Cullum (Death certificate states 1873-1919); second baseman, Carsins Run Baseball Club, near Aberdeen (*Havre de Grace Republican*, 8 Aug 1890)

Keithley, James, catcher, Carsins Run Baseball Club, near Aberdeen (*Havre de Grace Republican*, 8 Aug 1890); also see Christmas Day Coale, q.v.

Keithley, James M., 1832-1905 (Smith Chapel Methodist Church Cemetery)

Keithley, Jane E., 1838-1930 (Baker Cemetery); Miss Jennie Keitley *(sic)*, tent holder, Carsins Run Camp Meeting of the East Harford Circuit, P. E. Church, 1890 (*The Aegis & Intelligencer*, 1 Aug 1890)

Keithley, John T., 1834-1913 (Baker Cemetery)

Keithley, Lillie Belle, 1889-1974 (Angel Hill Cemetery)

Keithley, Lily, born 1878, died ---- (Grove Presbyterian Church Cemetery)

Keithley, Margaret Jane 1842-1911 (Smith Chapel Methodist Church Cemetery)

Keithley, Mary (colored), see Rose Kane (colored), q.v.

Keithley, Mary Agnes (Lee), see Henry Reed Coale, Norris Wenster Coale and William Watson Coale, q.v.

Keithley, Mary C., 1837-1923 (Smith Chapel Methodist Church Cemetery)

Keithley, Mary E., 1877-1948 (Baker Cemetery)

Keithley, Pauline "Lena" K., 1886-1973 (St. Paul's Lutheran Church Cemetery)

Keithley, Samuel Thomas, 1862-1948 (Baker Cemetery); see Anna Keithley and Carroll F. Keithley, q.v.

Keithley, T., right fielder, Carsins Run Baseball Club, near Aberdeen (*Havre de Grace Republican*, 8 Aug 1890)

Keithley, Viola M., 1882-1955 (Baker Cemetery)

Keithley, William Jacob, 1838-1892 (Calvary Methodist Church Cemetery)

Kell, Basil, county out-pensioner [welfare recipient], Third District (*Havre de Grace Republican*, 4 Jul 1890)

Kell, Benjamin Franklin "Frank" (colored), 1841-1934 (Fairview AME Church Cemetery); native of Forest Hill, Harford Co. (Death certificate); see Maggie M. Kell and John E. Kell, q.v.

Kell, Bessie Amanda (colored), age 19 in 1890 (Marriage License Applications Book ALJ No. 2, 1891)

Kell, Bond (colored), c1842-1922 (Death certificate; Alms House Record Book; *The Aegis & Intelligencer*, 10 Mar 1922)

Kell, Bowan, c1842-1922 (Heavenly Waters Cemetery)

Kell, Edward (colored), see Josephine Kell (colored), q.v.

Kell, Eliza (colored), c1861-1912 (Death certificate; St. James United Cemetery)

Kell, Emily L. (colored), 1883-1960 (Union Methodist Church Cemetery, Aberdeen); wife of Robert A. Kell, q.v.

Kell, Frank (colored), employed by Haviland Hull near Forest Hill (*Harford Democrat*, 20 Jun 1890)

Kell, George E. (colored), 1861-1921 (Union Methodist Church Cemetery, Aberdeen)

Kell, Henry (colored), 1840-1906, native of Maryland (Death certificate)

Kell, John Edward (colored), 1875-1917, native of Harford Co., born 17 Feb 1875, son of Benjamin Franklin Kell and Darcus Ann Johnson (Death certificate)

Kell, Josephine (colored), died 8 Aug 1906, age not given, native of Maryland, wife of Edward Kell and daughter of Gabriel Hill and Phoebe Bond (Death certificate)

Kell, Maggie Margarete (colored), 1870-1936, native of Forest Hill, Harford Co., born 1 Apr 1870, daughter of Benjamin Franklin "Frank" Kell and Darcus Ann Johnson (Death certificate)

Kell, Mary (colored), county out-pensioner [welfare recipient], Second District, 1890 (*Havre de Grace Republican*, 4 Jul 1890)

Kell, Mary E. (Rice) (colored), 1860-1932 (Death certificate); wife of Robert A. Kell, q.v.

Kell, Mary Ellen (colored), age 37 in 1890 (Marriage License Applications Book ALJ No. 2, 1891); see Mary Ellen Fisher and Jeremiah Fisher, q.v.

Kell, Mary Olivia (colored), 1888-1916, native of Harford Co., born 2 Sep 1888, daughter of Robert A. Kell and Mary Rice (Death certificate - maried name Hoke)

Kell, Robert A. (colored), c1864-1919 (Death certificate); trustee, Sydney Park Colored School No. 3, Second District, 1890 (*Havre de Grace Republican*, 30 May 1890); see Mary E. Kell and Mary Olivia Kell, q.v.

Kell, Robert A. (colored), 1890-1970 (Union Methodist Church Cemetery, Aberdeen); see Emily L. Kell, q.v.

Kell, Susie E. (colored), born 1866, died ---- [sunken tombstone] (Union Methodist Church Cemetery,

Aberdeen)

Keller, Andrew W., 1876-1936 (Baker Cemetery)

Keller, Clara T., 1888-1942 (Baker Cemetery)

Keller, Leah Eva 1880-1908 (Emory Methodist Church Cemetery)

Keller, Louis, 1866-1939 (Death certificate; Heavenly Waters Cemetery); native of Germany, parents unknown (Bailey Funeral Home Records)

Kelley, Annie M., 1863-1920 (St. Ignatius Catholic Church Cemetery)

Kelley, Carrie B., 1886-1927 (Baker Cemetery)

Kelley, Elizabeth (Armstrong), 1874-1928 (St. Ignatius Catholic Church Cemetery)

Kelley, Howard M., 1868-1893 (Highland Presbyterian Church Cemetery)

Kelley, Jacob B., 1823-1894 (Highland Presbyterian Church Cemetery)

Kelley, James M., 1869-1936 (St. Ignatius Catholic Church Cemetery)

Kelley, Johanna V., 1878-1959 (Baker Cemetery)

Kelley, Rudolph T., 1876-1953 (Baker Cemetery)

Kelley, Thomas H., farmer, Carsins Run (*Havre de Grace Republican*, 5 Dec 1890)

Kellie, Joseph H., Civil War veteran, Thomas Run (*1890 Special Census of the Civil War Veterans of the State of Maryland*, by L. Tilden Moore, Volume III, p. 70)

Kelling, John, postmaster, at Wheel (*Havre de Grace Republican*, 21 Feb 1890)

Kellogg, Alethia (Wilson), 1846-1927 (Bethel Presbyterian Church Cemetery Records); wife of Zachary T. Kellogg, q.v.; also see Marian Kellogg, q.v.

Kellogg, Eliza (Streett), 1817-1903 (Centre Methodist Church Cemetery)

Kellogg, Marian (Miss), 1882-1939, born 16 Apr 1882, daughter of Zachary T. and Alethia (Wilson) Kellogg (Bethel Presbyterian Church Cemetery Records)

Kellogg, Mary, 1855-1932 (Centre Methodist Church Cemetery)

Kellogg, Maud (Miss), member of the Asbury M. E. Church, Jarrettsville (*The Aegis & Intelligencer*, 28 Feb 1890); secretary, Co. D., Loyal Temperance League, of Jarrettsville (*Havre de Grace Republican*, 21 Mar 1890); daughter of Zachary T. Kellogg, q.v.

Kellogg, Sarah, see Howard E. Wallis, q.v.

Kellogg, Zachary T., 1849-1922 (Bethel Presbyterian Church Cemetery Records); delegate, Fourth District, Republican Party Convention, 1890 (*The Aegis & Intelligencer*, 26 Sep 1890); see Marian Kellogg, q.v.

Kellum, Emma E. (Sherron), 1873-1936 (Highland Presbyterian Church Cemetery); native of Harford Co., born 6 Dec 1873, daughter of William E. and Elizabeth Sherron (Bailey Funeral Home Records)

Kelly, Alice (Arkwright), 1853-1905, native of Philadelphia, resident of Havre de Grace, wife of Richard Kelly (Death certificate)

Kelly, Alice Mary, 1888-1902, native of Maryland, resided at Fallston, born 16 Oct 1888, daughter of Michael J. Kelly and Sarah E. Burns (Death certificate)

Kelly, Anderson, trustee, Trappe School No. 14, Fifth District, 1890 (*Havre de Grace Republican*, 30 May 1890); see Bessie E. Scarborough, q.v.

Kelly, Andrew, 1865-1923 (Heavenly Waters Cemetery; Alms House Record Book)

Kelly, Annie (Miss), member, Havre de Grace Reading Circle (*Havre de Grace Republican*, 7 Feb 1890)

Kelly, Annie (Moore), 1889-1979 (Angel Hill Cemetery)

Kelly, Annie C. (Crowl), 1854-1923, native of Pennsylvania (Bailey Funeral Home Records)

Kelly, Bessie E., see Bessie E. Scarborough, q.v.

Kelly, Catherine, see Francis J. McGuigan, q.v.

Kelly, Catherine(Keough), 1831-1912 (St. Ignatius Catholic Church Cemetery)

Kelly, Charles R., see Theodosia Kelly, q.v.

Kelly, Clara B., 1854-1931 (Angel Hill Cemetery)

Kelly, Cornelia Stackhouse (Miss), 1851-1931, native of, and dry goods storekeeper in, Havre de Grace (Death certificate)

Kelly, E. Russell, 1883-1934 (Angel Hill Cemetery)

Kelly, Edgar Cooper, 1855-1937 (Angel Hill Cemetery); member, Susquehanna Lodge No. 130, A.F. & A. M., Havre de Grace (*Havre de Grace Republican*, 11 Jul 1890)

Kelly, Elbert C., 1884-1954 (Angel Hill Cemetery); native of Havre de Grace, born 27 Oct 1884, son of Joseph Kelly and Clara Birely (Pennington Funeral Home Records)

Kelly, Ellen, 1825-1900 (St. Ignatius Catholic Church Cemetery)

Kelly, Florence L. (Glackin), 1883-1969 (St. Mary's Catholic Church); native of Harford Co., born 25 Apr 1883, daughter of Charles R. Glackin and Caroline R. Sweeney (Harkins Funeral Home Records)

Kelly, George J., 1827-1910, native of Harford Co., resided at Whiteford (Death certifcate)

Kelly, Gertrude R., 1877-1953 (Fallston Methodist Church Cemetery)

Kelly, Grace L., see Grace L. Scarborough, q.v.

Kelly, Howard A., 1871-1950 (Mt. Zion Methodist Church Cemetery)

Kelly, James, 1833-1903 (St. Ignatius Catholic Church Cemetery)

Kelly, James, 1858-1934 (St. Ignatius Catholic Church Cemetery)

Kelly, James Calvin, 1877-1946 (William Watters Memorial Methodist Church Cemetery, Thomas Run); native of Harford Co., born 10 Feb 1877, son of Robert A. Kelly and Annie Crowl (Bailey Funeral Home Records)

Kelly, James M., 1859-1894 (St. Ignatius Catholic Church Cemetery); James Kelly and sold land in April 1890 (*The Aegis & Intelligencer*, 9 May 1890)

Kelly, John, farmer on Lawrence Penniman's farm at Thomas Run (*The Aegis & Intelligencer*, 29 Aug 1890)

Kelly, John, 1815-1901 (St. Ignatius Catholic Church Cemetery); native of County Wexford, Ireland, resided at Chestnut Hill (Death certificate)

Kelly, John L., 1867-1919 (St. Ignatius Catholic Church Cemetery); age 24 in 1891 (Marriage License Applications Book ALJ No. 2)

Kelly, Joseph, 1848-1919 (Angel Hill Cemetery); businessman (trader's license), Havre de Grace (*Havre de Grace Republican*, 30 May 1890); delegate, Sixth District, to the Republican Party Convention (*The Aegis & Intelligencer*, 26 Sep 1890); vice president, Republican Club (*Havre de Grace Republican*, 7 Nov 1890); see Elbert C. Kelly and Leslie B. Kelly, q.v.

Kelly, Joseph A., 1888-1972 (Angel Hill Cemetery)

Kelly, Joseph F., 1850-1919 (Fallston Methodist Church Cemetery)

Kelly, Joseph W., 1881-1960 (Fallston Methodist Church Cemetery)

Kelly, Julia M., 1828-1906 (St. Ignatius Catholic Church Cemetery)

Kelly, Julia M., 1872-1938 (St. Ignatius Catholic Church Cemetery)

Kelly, Laura Joann, born -- Nov 1890, baptized 14 Dec 1890, daughter of John and Sarah (Burns) Kelly, natives of Baltimore (St. Ignatius Catholic Church Baptism Register, p. 116)

Kelly, Lavinia R., 1879-1961 (Fallston Methodist Church Cemetery)

Kelly, Leslie Birely, 1882-1974 (Angel Hill Cemetery); native of Maryland, born 2 Nov 1882, son of Joseph Kelly and Clara Birely (Pennington Funeral Home Records)

Kelly, Louisa, 1828-1897 (Angel Hill Cemetery)

Kelly, Mabel C., 1877-1953 (Mt. Zion Methodist Church Cemetery)

Kelly, Margaret A., 1859-1924 (St. Ignatius Catholic Church Cemetery)

Kelly, Margaret T, 1882-1904, native of Maryland, resided at Upper Cross Roads, born 6 Aug 1882, daughter of William J. Kelly and Ellen Lynch (Death certificate)

Kelly, Martha Jeanette (Scarff), 1860-1924 (Angel Hill Cemetery); wife of Edgar Cooper Kelly, q.v.

Kelly, Martin J., 1886-1965 (St. Mary's Catholic Church Cemetery); baptized 17 Feb 1886, son of James and Bridget (Martin) Kelly (St. Ignatius Catholic Church Baptism Register, p. 86; Harkins Funeral Home Records stated his mother was Annie Martin)

Kelly, Mary A., (Golden), 1835-1924 (St. Ignatius Catholic Church Cemetery); native of Ireland, resident of Bel Air (Death certificate); wife of John Kelly (1815-1901), q.v.

Kelly, Mary A. (Tollinger), 1840-1902, native of Harford Co., resided at Lapidum, widow of Thomas Kelly (Death certificate and Rock Run Methodist Church Cemetery tombstone have different dates)

Kelly, Mary Catherine (Trout), c1875-1950 (Death certificate; Angel Hill Cemetery)

Kelly, Mary E. (Elliott), 1840-1917, native of Harford Co., resided at Gibson, wife of Smith Kelly (Death certificate; Mt. Zion Methodist Church Cemetery)

Kelly, Mary G., born -- May 1888, baptized 20 May 1888, daughter of James and Bridget (Martin) Kelly (St. Ignatius Catholic Church Baptism Register, p. 98)

Kelly, Mary J. (Cooper), 1827-1910 (Death certificate); millinery (trader's license), Washington Street, Havre de Grace (*Havre de Grace Republican*, 24 Jan 1890, 30 May 1890, 28 Nov 1890 and 23 Apr 1910)

Kelly, Mary Jane, 1843-1909 (Highland Presbyterian Church Cemetery)

Kelly, Mary M., 1861-1900 (Mt. Erin Cemetery)

Kelly, Mary V., 1850-1943 (Mt. Erin Cemetery)

Kelly, R. Anderson, 1871-1949 (Mt. Zion Methodist Church Cemetery)

Kelly, Richard, Civil War veteran, Havre de Grace (*1890 Special Census of the Civil War Veterans of the State of Maryland*, by L. Tilden Moore, Volume III, p. 91); sneak boat duck hunter, 1890 (*Havre de Grace Republican*, 7 Nov 1890)

Kelly, Richard, 1881-1916, native and resident of Havre de Grace, son of Richard Kelly, of London, England, and Alice Arkwright, of Philadelphia (Death certificate)

Kelly, Robert Anderson, 1838-1912 (William Watters Memorial Methodist Church Cemetery, Thomas Run); native of Maryland, farmer (Death certificate); R. A. Kelly, resident of *Indian Spring Farm*, near Priestford Bridge, Deer Creek, 1890 (*The Aegis & Intelligencer*, 25 Apr 1890); superintendent, Thomas Run M. E. Church Sunday School (*The Aegis & Intelligencer*, 13 Jun 1890); see James C. Kelly and Grace L. Scarborough, q.v.

Kelly, Sarah, see Jesse A. Price, q.v.

Kelly, Sarah C., 1862-1924 (Mt. Erin Cemetery)

Kelly, Smith, see Mary E. Kelly, q.v.

Kelly, Susanna B., 1874-1954 (Mt. Zion Methodist Church Cemetery)

Kelly, Theodosia, 1871-1959, native of Pennslyvania, resident of Havre de Grace, born 14 Oct 1871, daughter of Charles R. Kelly and Ella Amanda Miller (Pennington Funeral Home Records - married name Trench)

Kelly, Thomas J., 1849-1917, native of Maryland, blacksmith at Upper Cross Roads (Death certificate); associate judge of elections, Upper Cross Roads Precinct, 1890 (*Havre de Grace Republican*, 17 Oct 1890)

Kelly, Timothy, 1825-1900, native of County Galway, Ireland (Mt. Erin Cemetery)

Kelly, Timothy, 1840-1903, native of London, England, single, seaman, of Havre de Grace (Death certificate)

Kelly, William A., 1853-1918, native of Harford Co., single, farmer at Whiteford (Death certificate; St. Mary's Catholic Church Cemetery)

Kelly, William F., 1875-1961 (Fallston Methodist Church Cemetery)

Kelly, William J., see Margaret T. Kelly, q.v.

Kelly, William Scarff, 1887-1967 (Angel Hill Cemetery)

Kemp, Lizzie, daughter of Thomas Kemp. q.v.

Kemp, Mary Ellen, daughter of Thomas Kemp, q.v.

Kemp, Nicholas, tenant on William Davis' farm near Bel Air (*The Aegis & Intelligencer*, 9 May 1890)

Kemp, Thomas, 1802-1890 (Little Falls Quaker Cemetery); farmer near Wilna (*The Aegis & Intelligencer*, 14 Mar 1890)

Kemp, Thomas William (colored), 1880-1931 (Death certificate; St. James United Cemetery)

Kenard, George (colored), died 11 Oct 1900, no age given (Alms House Record Book)

Kenchel, Anthony, Civil War veteran, Bel Air (*1890 Special Census of the Civil War Veterans of the State of Maryland*, by L. Tilden Moore, Volume III, p. 71)

Kenley, Anna E. (colored), 1874-1940, native of Darlington, Harford Co., born 15 Apr 1874, daughter of William Kenley and ---- (Death certificate - married named Paca)

Kenley, Annie (colored), see Susie M. Christy (colored), q.v.

Kenley, Edward (colored), age 7, son of George Kenley, indentured to George W. Jones to learn farming on 4 Jun 1890 (Harford County Indentures Book WSB No. 1)

Kenley, George (colored), see Edward Kenley (colored), q.v.

Kenley (Kenly), Harriet (colored), 1830-1905 (Death certificate)

Kenley, John (colored), see Susie M. Christy (colored), q.v.

Kenley (Kenly), Mary J. (colored), see Mary J. Webster (colored) and Mary A. Snowden (colored), q.v.

Kenley, Mary S. (colored), 1875-1937, native of Michaelsville, Harford Co., born 22 Jan 1875, daughter of William Kenley and Rebecca Peaco (Death certificate - married name Peaco)

Kenley (Kenly), Richard (colored), 1849-1916, native of Maryland, son of William Kenly and Phebe Aikens (Death certificate)

Kenley, Richard Edward (colored), age 10 years and 7 months on 6 Jan 1891, indentured to Robert J. Walker (Harford County Indentures Book WSB No. 1, 1891)

Kenley, Susie M. (colored), see Susie M. Christy (colored), q.v.

Kenley (Kenly), William (colored), see Richard Kenley, Mary S. Kenley, and Mary J. Webster, q.v.

Kenly, Annie (Hollingsworth) (colored), 1820-1901, native of Harford Co., servant, resided at Cole (Death certificate)

Kenly, Annie E. (colored), c1875-1925, daughter of William Kenly and Milky Griffith (Death certificate - married name Wilmore)

Kenly, Carrie (colored), 1879-1951, native of Maryland, born 19 May 1879, daughter of William Kenly and Rebecca Paca (Death certificate - married name Harris)

Kenly, Charles B., see Margaret (Kenly) Rigdon, q.v.

Kenly, Charles Sherwood, born 16 Nov 1890, son of James B. and Emma Louise (Bay) Kenly (Bethel Presbyterian Church Cemetery Records)

Kenly, Christina Rebecca "Teny" (Paca) (colored), 1843-1915, native of Maryland (Death certificate; *The Aegis*, 23 Apr 1915)

Kenly, Clarence C., treasurer, Harford Lodge No. 54, of Aberdeen, Order of the Golden Chain (*Havre de Grace Republican*, 28 Nov 1890)

Kenly, Edward C., see Edward Larkin, q.v.

Kenly, Elsie Bay, born 13 Feb 1884, daughter of James B. and Emma Louise (Bay) Kenly (Bethel Presbyterian Church Cemetery Records)

Kenly, Emma Louise (Bay), 1858-1933 (Bethel Presbyterian Church Cemetery Records); wife of James B. Kenly, q.v.

Kenly, George W., 1814-1892 (Rock Run Methodist Church Cemetery); farmer, near Glenville (*The Aegis & Intelligencer*, 12 Sep 1890; *Deaths and Marriages in Harford County, Maryland, and Vicinity, 1873-1904, from the Diaries of Albert Peter Silver*, transcribed by Glenn Randers-Pehrson, 1995, p. 15, mistakenly stated he was age 8)

Kenly, George W. (colored), 1883-1946, native of Perryman, Harford Co., born 22 May 1883, son of William Kenly and Sadie ---- (Death certificate)

Kenly, George, farmer, near Level (*Havre de Grace Republican*, 12 Sep 1890)

Kenly, Hattie J. (Mrs.) (colored), 1889-1986 (*The Aegis*, 13 Nov 1986)

Kenly, J. T. C., vestryman and junior warden, St. John's Episcopal Church, Havre de Grace (*Havre de Grace Republican*, 11 Apr 1890)

Kenly, James Buchanan, 1856-1928 (Bethel Presbyterian Church Cemetery Records); resident near Level (*The Aegis & Intelligencer*, 12 Sep 1890); member of Susquehanna Lodge No. 130, A.F. & A. M., in Havre de Grace (*Havre de Grace Republican*, 11 Jul 1890); secretary, Deer Creek Farmers' Club (*Havre de Grace Republican*, 9 May 1890)

Kenly, James F., trustee, Locust Hill School No. 19, Second District (*Havre de Grace Republican*, 30 May 1890)

Kenly, John (colored), 1876-1904, son of Henry Lee and Mary Jane Kenly, resided at Cedars (Death certificate)

Kenly, John B., senior deacon, Susquehanna Lodge No. 130, A. F. & A. M. (*Havre de Grace Republican*, 26 Dec 1890)

Kenly, Julia (colored), c1822-1912, resided at Castleton (Death certificate)

Kenly, Leroy, high school student, Second District (*Havre de Grace Republican*, 31 Oct 1890)

Kenly, Lillie (Miss), president, Young Folks' Band of Churchville Presbyterian Church (*Havre de Grace Republican*, 1 Aug 1890)

Kenly, Margaret L. (colored), 1888-1966 (Union Methodist Church Cemetery, Aberdeen)

Kenly, Mary Jane (colored), see John Kenly (colored), q.v.

Kenly, Susie Ann (colored), see Annie G. Williams (colored), q.v.

Kenly, W. E., vestryman and senior warden, St. John's Episcopal Church, Havre de Grace (*Havre de Grace Republican*, 11 Apr 1890)

Kenly, William (colored), see Annie E. Kenly, Carrie Kenly and George W. Kenly, q.v.

Kenly, William F. (colored), 1843-1925 (Death certificate)

Kennard, Affie (Mrs.) (colored), 1818-1893 (John Wesley Methodist Church Cemetery, Abingdon; *The Aegis & Intelligencer*, 21 Apr 1893, spelled her name Effie)

Kennard, David Richard (colored), 1867-1943, native of Harford Co., son of John Kennard and Hannah Jones (Death certificate)

Kennard, John Thomas (colored), 1841-1914, native of Maryland (Death certificate); Civil War veteran, of Calvary (*1890 Special Census of the Civil War Veterans of the State of Maryland*, by L. Tilden Moore, Volume III, p. 70); see David Richard Kennard, q.v.

Kennard, Mamie (Butler) (colored), 1870-1944, native of Abingdon, Harford Co., daughter of Samuel Butler and Annie Harris (Death certificate); wife of David R, Kennard, q.v.

Kennedy Baseball Club, of Havre de Grace (*Havre de Grace Republican*, 11 Jul 1890)

Kennedy, Ada Belle, 1879-1971 (Baker Cemetery); born 18 Aug 1879, daughter of William Thomas Kennedy and Mary Ann Gorrell (Churchville Presbyterian Church Register Roll of Infant Church Members or Baptized Children, No. 305)

Kennedy, Alonzo L., 1877-1961 (Rock Run Methodist Church Cemetery)

Kennedy, Ann Eliza, 1828-1904 (Churchville Presbyterian Church Cemetery)

Kennedy, Annie M., 1874-1935 (Baker Cemetery)

Kennedy, Augustus, farmer, near Fountain Green (*The Aegis & Intelligencer*, 31 Oct 1890)

Kennedy, Catherine 1826-1892, mother of Denis John Shanahan, q.v.

Kennedy, Charles F., 1854-1937 (Highland Presbyterian Church Cemetery); native of Harford Co., born 24 Jul 1854, son of Philip G. Kennedy, of Harford Co., and Mary T. Findley, of Delaware (Harkins Funeral Home Records)

Kennedy, Chester Boyd, 1883-1945 (Angel Hill Cemetery); native of Havre de Grace, born 15 Apr 1883, son od George Kennedy, of Havre de Grace, and Lillian Malone, of Pennsylvania (Pennington Funeral Home Records)

Kennedy, Clara Offutt (Hayes), 1880-1957 (Angel Hill Cemetery)

Kennedy, Clarence W., 1884-1952 (Baker Cemetery)

Kennedy, Cora, 1880-1900, daughter of George F. and Lizzie C. Kenendy (Bethel Presbyterian Church Cemetery Records)

Kennedy, Douglas Elliott, 1886-1949 (St. George's Episcopal Church Cemetery); born 17 Apr 1886, son of James H. and Ione E. Kennedy (St. George's Episcopal Church Register of Baptisms, pp. 12-13)

Kennedy, E. (Mrs.), and Jane, treated by unidentified doctor in 1890 ("Medical Account Book – 1890," Historical Society of Harford County Archives Folder)

Kennedy, Elise, 1878-1918, native of Maryland, resident of Aberdeen, born 26 Nov 1878, daughter of J. H. Kennedy and Ione Elliott (Death certificate)

Kennedy, Eliza E., 1823-1911 (Ebenezer Methodist Church Cemetery)

Kennedy, Eliza Jane (Miss), 1834-1927 (Death certificate), native of Ireland, resided near Havre de Grace (Bailey Funeral Home Records)

Kennedy, Ella "Ellie" (Miss), 1870-1890 (Mt. Erin Cemetery); member, St. Patrick's Women's Total Abstinence Society, Havre de Grace (*Havre de Grace Republican*, 31 Jan 1890)

Kennedy, Elmira (Miss), 1849-1924 (Ebenezer Methodist Church Cemetery); native of Harford Co., resided at Upper Cross Roads (Death certificate)

Kennedy, Ethel, born 2 Dec 1880, daughter of James H. and Ione E. Kennedy (St. George's Episcopal Church Register of Baptisms, pp. 12-13)

Kennedy, George F., 1850-1899 (Bethel Presbyterian Church Cemetery Records); served on a petit jury, Fifth District (*The Aegis & Intelligencer*, 14 Nov 1890); resided near Macton (Death certificate)

Kennedy, George H., 1857-1928 (Angel Hill Cemetery); native of Maryland, laborer, resided near Havre de Grace (Death certificate); farmer, near Havre de Grace (*Havre de Grace Republican*, 13 Jun 1890); husband of Lillian DeMoss Kennedy, q.v.; also see Chester Boyd Kennedy, q.v.

Kennedy, Harry E., 1873-1893, son of George F. and Lizzie C. Kennedy (Bethel Presbyterian Church Cemetery Records)

Kennedy, Harry M., 1886-1907 (Highland Presbyterian Church Cemetery)

Kennedy, Howard Wilson, 1877-1936 (Union Chapel Methodist Church Cemetery); son of Jacob C. Kennedy, q.v.

Kennedy, Ida Bell, born 1882, daughter of Jacob C. and Sarah Elizabeth (Harkins) Kennedy (*Harkins and Related Families of Harford County, Maryland*, by Henry C. Peden, Jr., 2003, p. 32)

Kennedy, Ida E. (Miller), 1875-1931 (Rock Run Methodist Church Cemetery); native of Maryland, born 14 Apr 1875, daughter of James H. Miller and Mary E. Baker (Bailey Funeral Home Records)

Kennedy, Ione (Elliott), 1854-1939, native of Harford Co., resident of Aberdeen (Death certificate; Grove Presbyterian Church Cemetery); wife of James H. Kennedy, q.v.; also see Douglas Elliott Kennedy, Elise Kennedy and Ethel Kennedy, q.v.

Kennedy, Ivory Pearl, 1883-1958 (Mt. Tabor Methodist Church Cemetery)

Kennedy, Jacob C., 1842-1933 (Centre Methodist Church Cemetery); blacksmith, Bel Air (*The Aegis & Intelligencer*, 1 Aug 1890)

Kennedy, James Bay, 1871-1949 (Baker Cemetery); born 10 Sep 1871, son of William Thomas Kennedy and Mary Ann Gorrell (Churchville Presbyterian Church Register Roll of Infant Church Members or Baptized Children, No. 249)

Kennedy, James Henry (Dr.), 1846-1933 Grove Presbyterian Church Cemetery); native of Upper Cross Roads, resident of Aberdeen (Death certificate); president, Harford County Medical Society (*Havre de Grace Republican*, 16 May 1890); trustee, Aberdeen School No. 1, Second District (*Havre de Grace Republican*, 30 May 1890); also see Douglas Elliott Kennedy, Elise Kennedy and Ethel Kennedy, q.v.

Kennedy, James J., 1882-1945 (Mt. Erin Cemetery)

Kennedy, Jane Ann (Miss), 1822-1908 (Death certificate); see Mrs. E. Kennedy, q.v.

Kennedy, Jane Belle (Moore), 1876-1920 (Union Chapel Methodist Church Cemetery); wife of Howard Wilson Kennedy, q.v.

Kennedy, John, premium award winner, Class I - Agricultural Productions, Harford County Fair (*The Aegis & Intelligencer*, 24 Oct 1890)

Kennedy, John Elwyn, born 7 Aug 1875, son of William Thomas Kennedy and Mary Ann Gorrell (Churchville Presbyterian Church Register Roll of Infant Church Members or Baptized Children, No. 290)

Kennedy, John Scott, 1854-1929, farmer near Wesleyan Chapel and Aberdeen (Death certificate; Wesleyan Chapel Cemetery; *The Aegis*, 15 Nov 1929)

Kennedy, John T., 1865-1914 (Mt. Erin Cemetery); committeeman and deputy, Knights of St. Leo, Havre de Grace (*Havre de Grace Republican*, 11 Jul 1890 and 19 Sep 1890); member, St. Patrick's Catholic Church, Havre de Grace (*Havre de Grace Republican*, 13 Jun 1890); musician, Bayside Cornet Band, Havre de Grace (*Havre de Grace Republican*, 31 Jan 1890)

Kennedy, John Thomas, 1839-1901 (Mt. Tabor Methodist Church Cemetery)

Kennedy, Joseph, farmer near Upper Cross Roads, brother of P. Kennedy (*The Aegis & Intelligencer*, 15 Aug 1890)

Kennedy, Lillian DeMoss (Malone), 1860-1946 (Angel Hill Cemetery), native of Havre de Grace, born 19 Oct 1860, daughter of Dennis Malone and Anne Reese, natives of Pennsylvania (Pennington Funeral Home Records); wife of George H. Kennedy, q.v.

Kennedy, Lydia Ann, born 1874, daughter of Jacob C. and Sarah Elizabeth (Harkins) Kennedy (*Harkins and Related Families of Harford County, Maryland*, by Henry C. Peden, Jr., 2003, p. 32)

Kennedy, Margaret (Folk), 1846-1908 (Mt. Tabor Methodist Church Cemetery)

Kennedy, Marie E., 1871-1954 (Mt. Erin Cemetery)

Kennedy. Mary (Mrs.), c1827-1907 (Old Brick Baptist Church Cemetery; *The Aegis*, 28 Jun 1907)

Kennedy, Mary Ann (Gorrell), 1839-1917 (Churchville Presbyterian Church Cemetery); wife of William Thomas Kennedy, q.v.

Kennedy, Maud, 1884-1907 (Highland Presbyterian Church Cemetery)

Kennedy, Michael, 1866-1938, native of Maryland, carpenter, single, resided in Bel Air, born 16 Jun 1866, son of Patrick Kennedy and Anna Fitzgerald, natives of Ireland (Death certificate)

Kennedy, Mollie E. (Hanson), born 1876, died ---- (Churchville Presbyterian Church Cemetery; www.findagrave.com)

Kennedy, Oscar W., 1886-1910 (Angel Hill Cemetery)

Kennedy, P., farmer near Upper Cross Roads, brother of Joseph Kennedy (*The Aegis & Intelligencer*, 15 Aug 1890)

Kennedy, Patrick, see Michael Kennedy, q.v.

Kennedy, Philip G., see Charles F. Kennedy, q.v.

Kennedy, Rosa M. (Bradford), 1869-1931 (Death certificate; Wesleyan Chapel Cemetery)

Kennedy, Samuel L., 1852-1933 (Ebenezer Methodist Church Cemetery)

Kennedy, Sarah Cole, born 6 Aug 1890, died ---- (St. George's Episcopal Church Cemetery)

Kennedy, Sarah E. (Rigdon), 1864-1948 (Highland Presbyterian Church Cemetery); native of Harford Co., born 7 Dec 1864, daughter of Benjamin Rigdon and Sarah J. Amos (Harkins Funeral Home Records)

Kennedy, Sarah Elizabeth (Harkins), 1840-1896 (Centre Methodist Church Cemetery); wife of Jacob C. Kennedy, q.v.

Kennedy, Silas, 1806-1892 (Ebenezer Methodist Church Cemetery)

Kennedy, Thomas, farmer, near Hickory (*The Aegis & Intelligencer*, 8 Aug 1890)

Kennedy, Thomas, of J., trustee, Hickory School No. 7, Third District (*Havre de Grace Republican*, 30 May 1890)

Kennedy, W., second baseman, Kennedy Baseball Club, of Havre de Grace (*Havre de Grace Republican*, 25 Jul 1890)

Kennedy, William, 1845-1920 (Rock Run Methodist Church Cemetery); juror, Second District, 1890 (*Havre de Grace Republican*, 2 May 1890); see Annie E. Miller, q.v.

Kennedy, William B., 1870-1941 (Mt. Tabor Methodist Church Cemetery)

Kennedy, William T., 1863-1950 (Churchville Presbyterian Church Cemetery)

Kennedy, William Thomas, c1825-1898 (Churchville Presbyterian Church Cemetery); treated by unidentified doctor in 1890 ("Medical Account Book – 1890," Historical Society of Harford County Archives Folder); husband of Mary Ann Gorrell and father of John Elwyn Kennedy and Ada Bell (Kennedy) Whiteford, q.v.

Kennett, Harriett C. R. (Hamilton) (colored), 1847-1940, native of Harford Co., wife of John Kennett (Death certificate)

Kennett, John T., see Alberta Harris and Harriett C. R. Kennett, q.v.

Kennett, Walberga, see Margaret Taylor, q.v.

Kenney, Anna C., 1873-1948 (Grove Presbyterian Church Cemetery)

Kenney, Daniel C., 1868-1906 (Mt. Erin Cemetery); new name on the Havre de Grace voter registration list, 1890 (*Havre de Grace Republican*, 19 Sep 1890) committeeman, Knights of St. Leo, Havre de Grace (*Havre de Grace Republican*, 19 Sep 1890); member, Independent Social Club, Havre de Grace (*Havre de Grace Republican*, 28 Feb 1890 and 28 Mar 1890); member, St. Patrick's Catholic Church, Havre de Grace (*Havre de Grace Republican*, 13 Jun 1890); member, Merry Ten Social Club, Havre de Grace (*Havre de Grace Republican*, 25 Jul 1890)

Kenney, James A., 1867-1913 (Ebenezer Methodist Church Cemetery)

Kenny, Mary A., died in 1890 and her will named "my son Benjamin Amos Thompson" and daughters Mary M. Tracy, Rebecca E. Devoe, Ariel J. Duncan (wife of James H. Duncan) and Jerusah C. Kunkel (Harford County Will Book JMM 11:176-177)

Kent, Annie (Whiteford), wife of Grier Kent, q.v.

Kent, Grier (Greer, Grear), 1821-1900, native of Maryland, resided at Harkins, Harford Co. (Death certificate) see Irene C. Pennington and Mary Ellen Richardson, q.v.

Kent, Irene C., see Irene C. Pennington, q.v.

Kent, M. Letitia, 1870-1945 (Slate Ridge Cemetery, York Co., PA); native of Harford Co., born 1 Apr 1870, daughter of William Kent and Mary Jane Gibson (Harkins Funeral Home Records)

Kent, Mary Ellen, see Mary Ellen Richardson, q.v.

Kent, William, see M. Letitia Kent, q.v.

Kentner, Katherine (Martin), 18873-1957 (St. Francis de Sales Catholic Church Cemetery)

Keough, James, 1841-1891 (St. Ignatius Catholic Church Cemetery)

Kerchoff, Ernest E., died 18 Sep 1890, age 29, of Bel Air, foreman of the woodwork department, Bulett Carriage Factory, native of Pennsylvania (*The Aegis & Intelligencer*, 26 Sep 1890)

Kernan, Eugene and Ruth, see E. Maude Richardson, q.v.

Kerr, Alice May, baptized 21 Jan 1883, daughter of John Kerr, of Harford County, and Ellen Dadey, of County Kerry, Ireland (St. Ignatius Catholic Church Baptism Register, p. 62, spelled the name Karr)

Kerr, Bridget Anna ("Annie") (Doyle), 1855-1919 (St. Ignatius Catholic Church Cemetery and Baptismal Register, p. 55; Death certificate); widow of Charles Edward Kerr, q.v.

Kerr, Catharine Roberta, born -- Jan 1889, baptized 13 Mar 1889, daughter of Charles E. Kerr, native of Harford Co., and Bridget Ann Doyle, native of Baltimore Co. (St. Ignatius Catholic Church Baptism Register, p. 104)

Kerr, Charles E., 1876-1956 (St. Ignatius Catholic Church Cemetery)

Kerr, Charles Edward, 1843-1917, resident of Bel Air (St. Ignatius Catholic Church Cemetery; Death certificate); juror, Third District (*Havre de Grace Republican*, 2 May 1890); see Catharine R. Kerr, Clara F. Kerr, Dora E. Kerr, Margaret L. Kerr and Mary E. Kerr, q.v.

Kerr, Clara Frances, born -- Sep 1886, baptized 1 Nov 1886, daughter of Charles Edward Kerr, native of Harford Co., and [Bridget] Ann Doyle, native of Baltimore Co. (St. Ignatius Catholic Church Baptism Register, p. 89, spelled the name Karr)

Kerr, Dora Elizabeth, born -- Sep 1890, baptized 8 Nov 1890, daughter of Charles Edward Kerr, native of Harford Co., and Bridget Ann Doyle, native of Baltimore Co. (St. Ignatius Catholic Church Baptism Register, p. 116)

Kerr, Elizabeth, 1882-1931 (St. Ignatius Catholic Church Cemetery)

Kerr, Elizabeth J., 1845-1919 (Tabernacle Cemetery)

Kerr, Ellen (Dadey), 1840-1931, native of County Kerry, Ireland (St. Ignatius Catholic Church Cemetery)

Kerr, George N., 1876-1931 (Tabernacle Cemetery)

Kerr, George S., 1839-1913 (Tabernacle Cemetery)

Kerr, Ida, see Ida Jones, q.v.

Kerr, James, 1889-1963 (Slateville Cemetery, York Co., PA); native of Whiteford, Harford Co., born 2 Jan 1889, son of James H. Kerr and Elizabeth Proctor (Harkins Funeral Home Records)

Kerr, James H., 1837-1909 (Tabernacle Cemetery); native of Lancaster Co., PA, resident of Cooper, Harford Co. (Death certificate); James Kerr, assistant superintendent, Susquehanna Hall Sabbath School, Fifth District, 1890 (*Havre de Grace Republican*, 6 Jun 1890); see Jamer Kerr, Roxie Tennant and Ida K. Jones, q.v.

Kerr, James McD., 1879-1918 (St. Ignatius Catholic Church Cemetery)

Kerr, John, 1838-1922 (St. Ignatius Catholic Church Cemetery); see John Edward Kerr and Stephen M. Kerr, q.v.

Kerr, John Edward, born -- Feb 1881, baptized 24 Apr 1881, son of John Kerr, of Harford Co., and Ellen Dadey, of County Kerry, Ireland (St. Ignatius Catholic Church Baptismal Register,. p. 52)

Kerr, Matilda, see Matilda Heimiller and William Henry Heimiller, q.v.

Kerr, Margaret A., 1877-1921 (St. Ignatius Catholic Church Cemetery)

Kerr, Margaret L., born -- Feb 1885, baptized 19 Apr 1885, daughter of C. Edward Kerr and Bridget Anna Doyle (St. Ignatius Catholic Church Baptism Register, p. 79)

Kerr, Mary (Wilson), 1879-1936 (St. Ignatius Catholic Church Cemetery)

Kerr, Mary Ellen, born 25 Feb 1883, baptized 3 May 1883, daughter of Charles E. Kerr and Bridget Anna Doyle (St. Ignatius Catholic Church Baptism Register, p. 65)

Kerr, Mary Stephenson (Miss), 1827-1901, native of Cecil Co., MD, resident of Havre de Grace (Death certificate)

Kerr, Nannie, 1822-1907 (St. George's Episcopal Church Cemetery)

Kerr, Nannie R., 1874-1891 (St. Ignatius Catholic Church Cemetery)

Kerr, Rosa, graduated from Thomas Run Public School (*The Aegis & Intelligencer*, 4 Jul 1890)

Kerr, Stephen M., 1884-1966 (St. Ignatius Catholic Church Cemetery; *The Aegis*, 10 Mar 1966); born 22 Oct 1884, baptized 14 Dec 1884, son of John Kerr, of Harford Co., and Ellen Dadey, of County Kerry, Ireland (St. Ignatius Catholic Church Baptism Register, p. 76, listed him as Stephen Charles Karr, but his tombstone and obituary stated Stephen M. Kerr)

Kesler, H. (Mrs.), premium award winner, Class J - Domestic Products, Harford County Fair (*The Aegis & Intelligencer*, 24 Oct 1890)

Kesner, William, died 10 Jan 1906, no age given (Alms House Record Book)

Kessler, Henry, Mr. & Mrs., residents near Schuck's Corner and Churchville (*The Aegis & Intelligencer*, 4 Apr and 27 Jun 1890)

Kessling, William, resided on Bel Air turnpike near the tollgate (*The Aegis & Intelligencer*, 19 Sep 1890)

Kesterson, James R. (colored), c1869-1926 (Union Methodist Church Cemetery, Aberdeen); native of Virginia; laborer, resided in Havre de Grace (Death certificate)

Keuchel, Anthony, watchmaker and jeweler Main St., Bel Air (*The Aegis & Intelligencer*, 21 Feb 1890); wrote his will in 1890 and died in 1891, naming Mrs. Amanda Born, of Konigsburg, Prussia. in the Empire of Germany, as his only heir and friend David Openheimer, of Baltimore City, as executor (Harford County Will Book JMM 11:183)

Keys, Jennie (Miss), pianist, resident of Bel Air (*The Aegis & Intelligencer*, 19 Sep 1890)

Keys, Mary A. (Reed), died 11 Feb 1901, age not stated (*Deaths and Marriages in Harford County, Maryland, and Vicinity, 1873-1904, from the Diaries of Albert Peter Silver*, transcribed by Glenn Randers-Pehrson, 1995, p. 15)

Keyser, Blanche (Rumsey), 1864-1956 (St. John's Episcopal Church, Kingsville); wife of Newberry Kesyer, q.v.

Keyser, Ellen F., 1849-1926 (Mountain Christian Church Cemetery)

Keyser, George Washington, 1864-1919 (St. George's Episcopal Church Cemetery)

Keyser, Irene Estelle (Gill), 1868-1926 (St. George's Episcopal Church Cemetery)

Keyser, Laura A. (McComas), 1825-1903 (Mountain Christian Church Cemetery)

Keyser, Mary (Claypoole), 1839-1895 (St. George's Episcopal Church Cemetery)

Keyser, Newberry Allen Smith, 1860-1922 (St. John's Episcopal Church, Kingsville); physician, Kellville (*The Aegis & Intelligencer*, 2 May 1890)

Keyworth, Thomas, native of England, died in Bel Air on 26 Jan 1890, age 63 (*The Aegis & Intelligencer*, 31 Jan 1890)

Kidd, Charles M., 1852-1914 (Holy Cross Church Cemetery); native of Maryland, resided at Rocks, farm hand, unmarried (Death certificate)

Kidd, Emma (Schissler), 1863-1922 (Grove Presbyterian Church Cemetery)

Kidd, Eugenia M. (Miss), 1839-1909, resided at Creswell (Death certificate)

Kidd, Ferdinand T., 1852-1944 (Grove Presbyterian Church Cemetery)

Kidd, Harry P., 1889-1949 (Fallston Methodist Church Cemetery)

Kidd, John, 1819-1901 (Churchville Presbyterian Church Cemetery); resident of Churchville (*The Aegis & Intelligencer*, 13 Jun 1890); cattle agent for James Sawdon, Jr, (*Harford Democrat*, 5 Sep 1890)

Kidd, Mary Slee (Evans), 1824-1905 (Churchville Presbyterian Church Cemetery); native and resident of Churchville (Death certificate)

Kieffer, William Miles, born 13 Aug 1882, son of Rev. William Thompson Linn Kieffer and Elizabeth Gould Miles (Churchville Presbyterian Church Register Roll of Infant Church Members or Baptized Children, No. 320)

Kiefierle, Henry H., member, Young Men's Pleasure Club, Havre de Grace (*Havre de Grace Republican*, 21 Nov 1890)

Kilgore, Elizabeth Holland ("Lizzie" and "Hollie"), born 1868, daughter of James Robert Kilgore (1829-1917)and Susan Elizabeth Whiteford (1841-1889); teacher, Aberdeen Graded School and/or Carsins Run School, 1888-1890 (*Harford County, Maryland Teachers and the Schools They Served, 1774-1900*, by Henry C. Peden, Jr., 2021, p. 180; *The Aegis & Intelligencer*, 17 Oct 1890, mistakenly listed her as Hallie)

Kilgore, Georgianna (Webb), 1855-1929 (Highland Presbyterian Church Cemetery)

Kilgore, Harry C., 1858-1929 (Highland Presbyterian Church Cemetery)

Kilgore, Ida, wife of Elmer E. Ramsay; also see Robert Ralph Ramsay, q.v.

Kilgore, James F., tanner, near Five Forks (*Havre de Grace Republican*, 17 Jan 1890)

Kilgore, James M., bark mill, Pylesville (*The Aegis & Intelligencer*, 17 Jan 1890)

Kilgore, James R. trustee, School No. 18, Fifth District (*Havre de Grace Republican*, 30 May 1890); tannery, near Fishel's Mill, burned down (*Harford Democrat*, 17 Jan 1890); father of Elizabeth Holland Kilgore, q.v.

Killingsworth, Annie P. (Price), 1845-1923 (Bailey Funeral Home Records)

Killingsworth, Julia (Miss), actress, musical entertainment, at Darlington (*The Aegis & Intelligencer*, 30 May 1890)

Kilroy, Anastatia, born -- Apr 1884, baptized 22 May 1884, daughter of Patrick and Rose (Armstrong) Kilroy, both natives of Ireland (St. Ignatius Catholic Church Baptism Register, p. 72)

Kilroy, Catherine Mary, born -- Feb 1887, baptized 20 Mar 1887, daughter of Patrick and Rose (Armstrong) Kilroy, both natives of Ireland (St. Ignatius Catholic Church Baptism Register, p. 91)

Kilroy, Patrick J., 1841-1912 (St. Ignatius Catholic Church Cemetery); farmer, Forest Hill (Death certificate); sold land in May 1890 (*The Aegis & Intelligencer*, 6 Jun 1890)

Kilroy, Rose (Armstrong), c1842-1928 (St. Ignatius Catholic Church Cemetery); wife of Patrick J. Kilroy, q.v.

Kilroy, Rose Elizabeth, born -- Jan 1882, baptized 26 Feb 1882, daughter of Patrick and Rose (Armstrong) Kilroy, both natives of Ireland (St. Ignatius Catholic Church Baptism Register, p. 58)

Kimball, Elizabeth, see Guy Morris, q.v.

Kimball, Ethel May (Ritter), 1890-1965 (Angel Hill Cedmetery); wife of Samuel M. Kimball, q.v.

Kimball, Lucy, 1890-1975 (Darlington Cemetery)

Kimball, Mary Elizabeth, baptized 4 Jan 1887, daughter of Samuel C. and Anna R. Kimball (Holy Trinity Episcopal Church Register of Baptisms, p. 92)

Kimball, Maude A., 1880-1944 (Angel Hill Cemetery)

Kimball, Maude E. (Heagy), 1885-1957, wife of Robert H. Kimball (St. Paul's Lutheran Church Cemetery)

Kimball, Samuel M., 1882-1971 (Angel Hill Cemetery)

Kimball, Violet (Wrigley), 1869-1942 (Darlington Cemetery)

Kimble, Alfred W., 1817-1894 (Calvary Methodist Church Cemetery)

Kimble, Eliza E., 1826-1899 (St. George's Episcopal Church Cemetery)

Kimble, F., right fielder, Perryman Baseball Club (*The Aegis & Intelligencer*, 18 Jul 1890)

Kimble, George A., 1845-1894 (Calvary Methodist Church Cemetery); associate judge of elections, Abingdon Precinct (*Havre de Grace Republican*, 17 Oct 1890); George Kimble, and family, residents near Hall's Shop, Abingdon District (*The Aegis & Intelligencer*, 5 Sep 1890)

Kimble, George C., 1890-1945 (St. George's Episcopal Church Cemetery)

Kimble, George Finney, born 15 Dec 1889, son of George A. and Phoebe Kimble (George A. Kimble Bible, *Maryland Bible Records, Volume 1*, by Henry C. Peden, Jr., 2003, p. 140)

Kimble, Harry Kirk, 1879-1935 (Calvary Methodist Church Cemetery; George A. Kimble Bible, *Maryland Bible Records, Volume 1*, by Henry C. Peden, Jr., 2003, p. 140)

Kimble, Harvey W., 1887-1906 Calvary Methodist Church Cemetery)

Kimble, Hattie Semelia, born 19 Jun 1882, daughter of George A. and Phoebe Kimble (George A. Kimble Bible, *Maryland Bible Records, Volume 1*, by Henry C. Peden, Jr., 2003, p. 140)

Kimble, John H., 1889-1916 (St. George's Episcopal Church Cemetery)

Kimble, Lillian Pearl, born 20 Mar 1884, daughter of George A. and Phoebe Kimble (George A. Kimble Bible, *Maryland Bible Records, Volume 1*, by Henry C. Peden, Jr., 2003, p. 140)

Kimble. Phoebe Elizabeth, 1853-1913 (Calvary Methodist Church Cemetery; George A. Kimble Bible, *Maryland Bible Records, Volume 1*, by Henry C. Peden, Jr., 2003, p. 140)

Kimble, Phoebe Loflin, born 7 Jun 1886, daughter of George A. and Phoebe Kimble (George A. Kimble Bible, *Maryland Bible Records, Volume 1*, by Henry C. Peden, Jr., 2003, p. 140)

Kimble, Robert E., 1848-1926 (Calvary Methodist Church Cemetery; George A. Kimble Bible, *Maryland Bible Records, Volume 1*, by Henry C. Peden, Jr., 2003, p. 140); native of Maryland, farmer, single, resided near Perryman (Death certificate)

Kimble, Ross Wilkinson, 1860-1948 (Mt. Zion Methodist Church Cemetery)

Kimble, Samuel Alfred, 1876-1944 (St. Paul's Lutheran Church Cemetery); son of George A. and Phoebe Kimble (George A. Kimble Bible, *Maryland Bible Records, Volume 1*, by Henry C. Peden, Jr., 2003, p. 140); resident near Harford Furnace (*The Aegis & Intelligencer*, 28 Mar 1890)

Kimble, Samuel Z., 1854-1919 (St. George's Episcopal Church Cemetery); blacksmith, Michaelsville (*The Aegis & Intelligencer*, 4 Apr 1890)

Kimble, Sarah, county out-pensioner [welfare recipient], Second District (*Havre de Grace Republican*, 4 Jul 1890)

Kimble, William D., 1850-1926 Calvary Methodist Church Cemetery)

Kimble, William F., 1813-1892 Calvary Methodist Church Cemetery)

Kimes, Frederick J., 1880-1934 (Old Brick Baptist Church Cemetery)

Kimes, Nettie L. (Grafton), 1879-1943 (Old Brick Baptist Church Cemetery); widow of Frederick J. Kimes, q.v.

Kimmell, Neva M., born -- Oct 1887 (1900 Aberdeen Census)

Kincaid, Annie Laura, born 19 Apr 1873, daughter of Charles P. and Sarah A.(Knight) Kincaid (*The Hughes Genealogy, 1636-1953*, by Joseph Lee Hughes, 1953, p. 106)

Kincaid, Cecilia E., 1887-1964 (McKendree Methodist Church Cemetery)

Kincaid, Charles Herman, born 19 Feb 1876, son of Charles P. and Sarah A.(Knight) Kincaid (*The Hughes Genealogy, 1636-1953*, by Joseph Lee Hughes, 1953, p. 106)

Kincaid, Charles Parker, 1837-1890 (Grove Presbyterian Church Cemetery; *The Hughes Genealogy, 1636-1953*, by Joseph Lee Hughes, 1953, p. 106); juror, Second District (*Havre de Grace Republican*, 2 May 1890); senior warden, Stephenson Masonic Lodge, Lapidum (*The Aegis & Intelligencer*, 21 Nov 1890)

Kincaid, Jane "Jennie" Emerick, 1878-1956 (Rock Run Methodist Church Cemetery), born 23 May 1878, daughter of Charles P. and Sarah A.(Knight) Kincaid (*The Hughes Genealogy, 1636-1953*, by Joseph Lee Hughes, 1953, p. 106; *The Aegis*, 28 Jun 1956; Pennington Funeral Home Records gave her name as Jennie Elizabeth Kincaid)

Kincaid, Katherine Silver, native of Harford Co., born 15 Jan 1881, daughter of Charles P. and Sarah A.(Knight) Kincaid (*The Hughes Genealogy, 1636-1953*, by Joseph Lee Hughes, 1953, p. 106; Pennington Funeral Home Records, 1955 - married name Lee)

Kincaid, Lydia, see Arthur Ramsey Keene, q.v.

Kincaid, Mary Elizabeth, 1875-1950 (Grove Presbyterian Church Cemetery); native of Harford Co., born 28 Aug 1875, daughter of Charles P. and Sarah A.(Knight) Kincaid (*The Hughes Genealogy, 1636-1953*, by Joseph Lee Hughes, 1953, p. 106; Pennington Funeral Home Records)

Kincaid, Sarah Ann (Knight), 1844-1918 (Grove Presbyterian Church Cemetery), wife of Charles Parker Kincaid, q.v.

Kincaid, William Edward, 1885-1948 (McKendree Methodist Church Cemetery); born 27 Nov 1885, son of Charles P. and Sarah A.(Knight) Kincaid (*The Hughes Genealogy, 1636-1953*, by Joseph Lee Hughes, 1953, p. 106, states born in 1884)

Kindley, Bradley Wilson (Rev.), 1862-1937 (Union Chapel Methodist Church Cemetery); pastor of Deer Creek M. P. Circuit (*Havre de Grace Republican*, 30 May 1890), married Fannie H. Robinson, daughter of Mr. & Mrs. Alphonso Robinson, of Fallston, on 27 May 1890 at the Bel Air M. P. Church (*The Aegis & Intelligencer*, 23 May 1890; Bel Air Methodist Charge Marriage Records, p. 238)

Kindley, Frances "Fannie" Helen (Robinson), 1868-1929 (Union Chapel Methodist Church Cemetery), wife of Rev. Bradley Wilson Kindley, q.v.

King's Daughters, Willing and Obedient Circle (*Harford Democrat*, 3 Jan 1890)

King, Alfred, 1851-1924 (Calvary Methodist Church Cemetery); native of Harford Co., farmer, resided near Jarrettsville (Death certificate; *Havre de Grace Republican*, 7 Mar 1890)

King, Amanda A., age 17 in 1890 (Marriage License Applications Book ALJ No. 2, 1891); see Frederick Eichholtz, q.v.

King, B. Franklin, 1841-1909 (Bethel Presbyterian Church Cemetery Records)

King, Charles W., new name on the voter registration list at Abingdon, First District (*Havre de Grace Republican*, 26 Sep 1890)

King, Christopher, c1848-1918 (Death certificate; Alms House Record Book)

King, Elizabeth, c1830-1899, age not stated, resided near Bradenbaugh (Death certificate); wife of John R. King, q.v.

King, John R., 1830-1895 (*The Aegis & Intelligencer*, 2 Aug 1895); see Elizabeth King, q.v.

King, Lena Rigdon (Daughton), 1888-1970 (Emory Methodist Church Cemetery); native of Whiteford, Harford Co., born 4 Mar 1888, daughter of George Daughton and Cecelia Day (Harkins Funeral Home Records)

King, Lewis, 1807-1892 (Bethel Presbyterian Church Cemetery Records); Louis King resided at Chrome Hill (*Harford Democrat*, 24 Jan 1890)

King, Martha E., 1839-1910 (William H. Ward Bible, *Maryland Bible Records, Volume 2*, by Henry C. Peden, Jr., 2003, p. 166)

King, Mary (Markline), 1864-1956 (Bethel Presbyterian Church Cemetery Records); wife of Philip J. King, q.v.

King, Mason, c1879-1939 (Death certificate; Heavenly Waters Cemetery)

King, Philip J., 1865-1945 (Bethel Presbyterian Church Cemetery Records)

King, Timothy, transferred from the voter registration list in the Sixth District (*Havre de Grace Republican*, 17 Oct 1890)

King, William, 1839-1891 (Bethel Presbyterian Church Cemetery Records); county out-pensioner [welfare recipient], Fourth District (*Havre de Grace Republican*, 4 Jul 1890)

King, William H., businessman (trader's license), Havre de Grace (*Havre de Grace Republican*, 30 May 1890); merchant, Havre de Grace (*Havre de Grace Republican*, 16 May 1890); vice president, Republican Club (*Havre de Grace Republican*, 7 Nov 1890); drug store, Havre de Grace (*Havre de Grace Republican*, 7 Mar 1890); greenhouses and nursery, Ontario and Juniata Streets, Havre de Grace (*Havre de Grace Republican*, 18 Apr 1890); president and charter member, Havre de Grace Gunning Club (*Havre de Grace Republican*, 14 Nov 1890)

Kinhart, Andrew, 1848-1930 (Bethel Presbyterian Church Cemetery Records); former farmer of Pennsylvania, he acquired land near Madonna in May 1890 (*The Aegis & Intelligencer*, 6 Jun 1890; *Biographical Dictionary of Harford County, Maryland, 1774-1974*, by Henry C. Peden, Jr. and William O. Carr, 2021, p. 155)

Kinhart, Andrew Cleveland, 1884-1957, son of Andrew and Catherine (Heil) Kinhart (Bethel Presbyterian Church Cemetery Records)

Kinhart, Catharine (Heil), 1845-1921 (Bethel Presbyterian Church Cemetery Records); wife of Andrew Kinhart, q.v.

Kinhart, David John, 1870-1942, resided at Madonna, born 27 Dec 1870, son of Andrew and Catherine (Heil) Kinhart (Bethel Presbyterian Church Cemetery Records)

Kinhart, Dora Jane (Crowl), 1886-1963 (Bethel Presbyterian Church Cemetery Records); wife of Andrew C. Kinhart, q.v.

Kinhart, Emma M., born 10 Sep 1875, daughter of Andrew and Catherine (Heil) Kinhart (Bethel Presbyterian Church Cemetery Records)

Kinhart, Frances Olivia "Fannie" (Turner), 1872-1951 (Bethel Presbyterian Church Cemetery Records); wife of David John Turner, q.v.

Kinhart, Harry Martin, 1878-1926, son of Andrew and Catherine (Heil) Kinhart (Bethel Presbyterian Church Cemetery Records)

Kinhart, Ida Elizabeth, born 19 Aug 1873, daughter of Andrew C. and Catherine (Heil) Kinhart (Bethel Presbyterian Church Cemetery Records)

Kinhart, Viola A. (Edie), 1879-1968 (Bethel Presbyterian Church Cemetery Records); wife of Harry M. Kinhart, q.v.

Kinnier, Blanche (Mitchell), 1876-1968 (Angel Hill Cemetery)

Kinnier, Robert, 1871-1922 (Angel Hill Cemetery)

Kinsey, Clark C., dairyman (*Harford Democrat*, 14 Feb 1890); delegate, Fifth District, Republican Party Convention (*The Aegis & Intelligencer*, 26 Sep 1890); director, Mutual Fire Insurance Company in Harford County (*The Aegis & Intelligencer*, 10 Jan 1890); member, Agricultural and Mechanical Society (*Havre de Grace Republican*, 23 May 1890); member, Maryland Central Dairymen's Association (*Havre de Grace Republican*, 28 Feb 1890); trustee, School No. 18, Fifth District (*Havre de Grace Republican*, 30 May 1890); committeeman, Harford County Fair (*The Aegis & Intelligencer*, 5 Sep 1890); sold land in November 1890 (*The Aegis & Intelligencer*, 5 Dec 1890)

Kinsey, Elam and Seth L., trading as Elam Kinsey & Son, Fifth District; insolvent, 1890 (*Havre de Grace Republican*, 29 Aug 1890); sold land in August 1890 (*The Aegis & Intelligencer*, 12 Sep 1890)

Kinsey, Howard, see Leslie Kinsey, q.v.

Kinsey, Leslie, son of Howard Kinsey, and nephew of William M. Scarborough, of Mill Green (*The Aegis & Intelligencer*, 25 Jul 1890)

Kinsey, Seth L., 1857-1948 (Eastland Friends Cemetery, Lancaster Co., PA); carriage maker, Graceton (*Carriages Back in the Day: Harford County's Rural Heritage*, by Jack L. Shagena, Jr. and Henry C. Peden, Jr., 2016, pp. 86-87); postmaster, Graceton (*Havre de Grace Republican*, 25 Jul 1890); sold land in August 1890 (*The Aegis & Intelligencer*, 12 Sep 1890); see Elam Kinsey, q.v.

Kinsler, Maude M. (Day), 1877-1964 (Slate Ridge Cemetery, York Co., PA); native of Harford Co., born 22 Apr 1877, daughter of Matthew Day and Sarah Jones Coates (Harkins Funeral Home Records)

Kinzer, William M., 1882-1954 (Darlington Cemetery)

Kirby, Charles A., 1877-1969 (Mt. Erin Cemetery)

Kirby, Charles A., 1881-1944 (Mt. Zion Methodist Church Cemetery)

Kirby, Edward, age 23 in 1890 (Marriage License Applications Book ALJ No. 2, 1891)

Kirby, Ella E., 1870-1933 (Mt. Erin Cemetery)

Kirby, Harry, 1863-1935 (St. George's Episcopal Cburch Cemetery); H. Kirby, sneak boat duck hunter (*Havre de Grace Republican*, 7 Nov 1890)

Kirby, James H., see Mary Louisa Kirby, q.v.

Kirby, Mary, 1844-1919 (Mt. Erin Cemetery)

Kirby, Mary Estelle, 1873-1944 (St. George's Episcopal Cburch Cemetery)

Kirby, Mary Louisa, died 2 Mar 1890 in her 45th year, wife of Capt. James H. Kirby and daughter of James Love (*The Aegis & Intelligencer*, 7 Mar 1890)

Kirby, Thomas E., 1838-1905 (Mt. Erin Cemetery); Thomas E. Kirby & Sons, tomato canners, Bush River Neck (*The Aegis & Intelligencer*, 5 Sep 1890)

Kirchoff, E., wood room foreman, Bulett Carriage Factory, Bel Air (*The Aegis & Intelligencer*, 31 Jan 1890)

Kirk, A. Raymond, 1889-1949 (Fallston Methodist Church Cemetery)

Kirk, Allen Hoffman, born 18 Jan 1879, son of Elijah Kirk son of Elijah Kirk (Caleb G. Kirk Bible, *Maryland Bible Records, Volume 5*, by Henry C. Peden, Jr., 2004, p. 102); premium award winner, Class M - Miscellaenous, Harford County Fair (*The Aegis & Intelligencer*, 24 Oct 1890); student, Bel Air Graded School (*The Aegis & Intelligencer*, 26 Dec 1890)

Kirk, Annie D. (Bailey), 1872-1910 (Fallston Methodist Church Cemetery); wife of Henry C. Kirk, q.v.

Kirk, B., right fielder, Havre de Grace Ash Alleys Baseball Club (*The Aegis & Intelligencer*, 27 Jun 1890)

Kirk, Bertram Sheridan, 1869-1937 (Mt. Zion Methodist Church Cemetery); son of Elijah Kirk and ---- (Caleb G. Kirk Bible, *Maryland Bible Records, Volume 5*, by Henry C. Peden, Jr., 2004, p. 102); general manager, Bel Air Victors Baseball Club (*The Aegis & Intelligencer*, 27 Jun 1890); private, Jackson Guards [Co. D, 1st Regiment, Maryland National Guard], 1889-1890 (*The Aegis & Intelligencer*, 11 Jan 1889)

Kirk, Caleb, see John P. Kirk and William J. Kirk, q.v.

Kirk, E. (Mrs.), premium award winner, Class N - Floral Decorations, Harford County Fair (*The Aegis & Intelligencer*, 24 Oct 1890)

Kirk, Edwin Perry, 1865-1923 (Western Cemetery, Baltimore); son of Elijah Kirk and ---- (Caleb G. Kirk Bible, *Maryland Bible Records, Volume 5*, by Henry C. Peden, Jr., 2004, pp. 102-103); private, Jackson Guards, 1889-1890 [Co. D, 1st Regiment, Maryland National Guard] (*The Aegis & Intelligencer*, 11 Jan 1889, listed him as Edward Kirk)

Kirk, Elijah, 1841-1923 (Mt. Zion Methodist Church Cemetery; Caleb G. Kirk Bible, *Maryland Bible Records, Volume 5*, by Henry C. Peden, Jr., 2004, pp. 102-103)

Kirk, Eudocia Elizabeth (Day), 1868-1943 (Fallston Methodist Church Cemetery)

Kirk, George J., 1863-1908 (Fallston Methodist Church Cemetery)

Kirk, George W., 1813-1896 (Fallston Methodist Church Cemetery); associate judge of elections, Fallston Precinct (*Havre de Grace Republican*, 17 Oct 1890)

Kirk, Henry C., 1859-1928 (Fallston Methodist Church Cemetery); native of Harford Co., farmer, resided at Fallston (Death certificate)

Kirk, J. Hall, 1857-1913 (Union Chapel Methodist Church Cemetery)

Kirk, Jacob, 1809-1894 (Union Chapel Methodist Church Cemetery)

Kirk, Janie J., 1845-1929 (Fallston Methodist Church Cemetery)

Kirk, John P., 1834-1924 (Darlington Cemetery); native of Delaware, son of Caleb Kirk and Hannah Peach (Caleb G. Kirk Bible, *Maryland Bible Records, Volume 5*, by Henry C. Peden, Jr., 2004, p. 102; Bailey Funeral Home Records); house painter, Darlington (*The Aegis & Intelligencer*, 26 Sep 1890); actor, musical entertainment, at Darlington (*The Aegis & Intelligencer*, 30 May 1890)

Kirk, John R., 1826-1892 (Churchville Presbyterian Church Cemetery)

Kirk, Josiah P., 1844-1929, native of Maryland (Bailey Funeral Home Records)

Kirk, Lemuel A., 1853-1940 (Fallston Methodist Church Cemetery); blacksmith, Fallston (*The Aegis & Intelligencer*, 28 Nov 1890)

Kirk, Lillian M., 1865-1952 (Darlington Cemetery)

Kirk, Malinda P., 1811-1893 (Fallston Methodist Church Cemetery)

Kirk, Margaret, see Andrew C. Smith and Emma J. Scotten, q.v.

Kirk, Margaret (Wilson), 1868-1948, native of Harford Co. (Bailey Funeral Home Records); wife of Walter B. Kirk, q.v.

Kirk, Mary, see Clyde S. Pyle, q.v.

Kirk, Mary E., 1848-1936 (Union Chapel Methodist Church Cemetery)

Kirk, Milton U., 1866-1925 (Fallston Methodist Church Cemetery); age 24 in 1890 (Marriage License Applications Book ALJ No. 2, 1891)

Kirk, Olivia O., 1864-1920 (Fallston Methodist Church Cemetery)

Kirk, Samuel J., 1832-1913 (Baker Cemetery); son of Caleb and Hannah Kirk son of Elijah Kirk (Caleb G. Kirk Bible, *Maryland Bible Records, Volume 5*, by Henry C. Peden, Jr., 2004, p. 102); juror, Second District (*Havre de Grace Republican*, 31 Jan 1890)

Kirk, Sarah M., 1842-1909 (Darlington Cemetery)

Kirk, Susie J. (Miss), 1857-1929 (Fallston Methodist Church Cemetery); actress, musical entertainment, at Darlington (*The Aegis & Intelligencer*, 30 May 1890)

Kirk, Walter B. (Dr.), 1868-1934 (Darlington Cemetery); native of Cecil Co., MD, son of J. P. Kirk and Annie Reynolds (Bailey Funeral Home Records)

Kirk, William J., 1840-1926 (Darlington Cemetery); native of Delaware, farmer, single, resided near Darlington son of Caleb G. Kirk and Hannah Peach (Death certificate; Bailey Funeral Home Records); juror, Fifth District (*Havre de Grace Republican*, 31 Jan 1890, listed him as William P. Kirk)

Kirkwood Public School No. 20, at Kirkwood, Fourth District (*Harford County, Maryland Teachers and the Schools They Served, 1774-1900*, by Henry C. Peden, Jr., 2022, p. 370)

Kirkwood, Andrew (Mrs.), see Cora Poteet, q.v.

Kirkwood, Andrew Wilson, 1810-1907 (Bethel Presbyterian Church Cemetery Records)

Kirkwood, Ann (Miss), 1807-1894 (Bethel Presbyterian Church Cemetery Records)

Kirkwood, Anna Blanche, born 9 Sep 1882, daughter of Robert and Mary Elizabeth (Robinson) Kirkwood (Bethel Presbyterian Church Cemetery Records)

Kirkwood, Carl Bradenbaugh, born 8 Nov 1877, son of Robert J. and Caroline (Bradenbaugh) Kirkwood (*Kirkwoods and Their Kin, 1731-1971*, by Anna Lee Kirkwood Smith, 1972, p. 104; Bethel Presbyterian Church Cemetery Records)

Kirkwood, Caroline (Bradenbaugh), 1845-1910 (Bethel Presbyterian Church Cemetery Records); wife of Robert J. Kirkwood, q.v.

Kirkwood, Catherine J. (Miss), 1842-1902, daughter of Richard and Arravilla (Ruhl) Kirkwood (*Kirkwoods and Their Kin, 1731-1971*, by Anna Lee Kirkwood Smith, 1972, p. 94; Bethel Presbyterian Church Cemetery Records)

Kirkwood, Clinton, born 21 Dec 1869, son of Joseph and Elizabeth (Stritehoff) Kirkwood (*Kirkwoods and Their Kin, 1731-1971*, by Anna Lee Kirkwood Smith, 1972, p. 76)

Kirkwood, Daniel Henderson, 1851-1921 (Bethel Presbyterian Church Cemetery Records); Daniel Kirkwood, of John, served as a juror, Fourth District, 1890 (*Havre de Grace Republican*, 31 Oct 1890)

Kirkwood, Elizabeth (Stritehoff), 1825-1910 (Bethel Presbyterian Church Cemetery Records); wife of Joseph Kirkwood, q.v.

Kirkwood, Hannah, 1835-1905 (Bethel Presbyterian Church Cemetery Records)

Kirkwood, Hannah A., 1848-1929 (Bethel Presbyterian Church Cemetery Records); wife of James H. Kirkwood, q.v.

Kirkwood, Harriett (Henry) (Miskimmon), 1822-1901 (Bethel Presbyterian Church Cemetery Records); second wife of Andrew Wilson Kirkwood, q.v.

Kirkwood, Hope, 1855-1924, daughter of Andrew Wilson and Margaret (Brierly) Kiekood (Bethel Presbyterian Church Cemetery Records)

Kirkwood, Ida Virginia (Luckey), 1859-1917 (Bethel Presbyterian Church Cemetery Records); wife of Samuel M. Kirkwood, q.v.

Kirkwood, Irwin, 1875-1927, son of Robert Jabez and Caroline (Bradenbaugh) Kirkwood (*Kirkwoods and Their Kin, 1731-1971*, by Anna Lee Kirkwood Smith, 1972, p. 104)

Kirkwood, Irwin G., born 1881, son of James Hope and Hannah (Davis) Kirkwood (Bethel Presbyterian Church Cemetery Records;*Kirkwoods and Their Kin, 1731-1971*, by Anna Lee Kirkwood Smith, 1972, p. 84)

Kirkwood, J. Luckey, born 6 Jun 1886, son of Samuel M. and Ida Virginia (Luckey) Kirkwood (Bethel Presbyterian Church Cemetery Records)

Kirkwood, James, of George, served on a grand jury, Fourth District (*The Aegis & Intelligencer*, 14 Nov 1890)

Kirkwood, James Hope, 1845-1916 (Bethel Presbyterian Church Cemetery Records)

Kirkwood, James LeRoy, born 1877, son of James Hope and Hannah (Davis) Kirkwood (Bethel Presbyterian Church Cemetery Records)

Kirkwood, James Richard Hope, 1868-1954, son of George C. and Isabella (Cairnes) Kirkwood (*Kirkwoods and Their Kin, 1731-1971*, by Anna Lee Kirkwood Smith, 1972, p. 53; Bethel Presbyterian Church Cemetery Records)

Kirkwood, John Richard, 1846-1922 (Bethel Presbyterian Church Cemetery Records); trustee, Kirkwood School No. 20, Fourth District (*Havre de Grace Republican*, 30 May 1890)

Kirkwood, Joseph, 1837-1923 (Bethel Presbyterian Church Cemetery Records)

Kirkwood, Joseph R., 1884-1890 (Bethel Presbyterian Church Cemetery)

Kirkwood, Lena Almira, born 9 Oct 1873, daughter of Joseph and Elizabeth (Stritehoff) Kirkwood (*Kirkwoods and Their Kin, 1731-1971*, by Anna Lee Kirkwood Smith, 1972, pp. 76-77)

Kirkwood, Lula (Anderson), 1889-1965 (Bethel Presbyterian Church Cemetery Records); wife of J. Luckey Kirkwood, q.v.

Kirkwood, Margaret A., 1839-1914, daughter of Richard and Arravilla (Ruhl) Kirkwood (*Kirkwoods and Their Kin, 1731-1971*, by Anna Lee Kirkwood Smith, 1972, p. 94; Bethel Presbyterian Church Cemetery Records)

Kirkwood, Margaret Elizabeth, 1863-1952, daughter of George C. and Isabella (Cairnes) Kirkwood (*Kirkwoods and Their Kin, 1731-1971*, by Anna Lee Kirkwood Smith, 1972, p. 53; Bethel Presbyterian Church Cemetery Records)

Kirkwood, Marion (Anderson), 1877-1949 (Bethel Presbyterian Church Cemetery Records); wife of Stuart R. Kirkwood, q.v.

Kirkwood, Martha A. (Rodgers), 1830-1899 (Bethel Presbyterian Church Cemetery Records); wife of John Richard Kirkwood, q.v.

Kirkwood, Martha Ann (McComas), 1868-1946 (Bethel Presbyterian Church Cemetery Records); wife of James R. H. Kirkwood, q.v.

Kirkwood, Mary Belle (Bevard), 1856-1905 (Bethel Presbyterian Church Cemetery Records); wife of Robert E. C. Kirkwood, q.v.

Kirkwood, Mary Elizabeth (Robinson), 1844-1903 (Bethel Presbyterian Church Cemetery Records); wife of Robert Kirkwood, q.v.

Kirkwood, Mary Margaret, 1872-1908, daughter of Robert and Mary E. (Robinson) Kirkwood (Bethel Presbyterian Church Cemetery Records)

Kirkwood, Mary Ruth, born 15 Feb 1884, daughter of Samuel M. and Virginia (Luckey) Kirkwood (Bethel Presbyterian Church Cemetery Records); see Mary Ruth Anderson, q.v.

Kirkwood, Nathaniel C., 1816-1902 (Bethel Presbyterian Church Cemetery Records)

Kirkwood, Nathaniel Calvin, born 25 Mar 1887, son of Robert and Mary Elizabeth (Robinson) Davis (*Kirkwoods and Their Kin, 1731-1971*, by Anna Lee Kirkwood Smith, 1972, p. 67)

Kirkwood, Ozella, born 6 Nov 1871, daughter of Joseph and Elizabeth (Stritehoff) Kirkwood (*Kirkwoods and Their Kin, 1731-1971*, by Anna Lee Kirkwood Smith, 1972, p. 76)

Kirkwood, Rebecca Emily (Miss), 1845-1911 (Bethel Presbyterian Church Cemetery Records)

Kirkwood, Robert, 1839-1895 (Bethel Presbyterian Church Cemetery Records)

Kirkwood, Robert Edwin C., 1860-1933 (Bethel Presbyterian Church Cemetery Records)

Kirkwood, Robert Jabez, 1849-1929 (Bethel Presbyterian Church Cemetery Records)

Kirkwood, Samuel Miskimmon, 1859-1917 (Bethel Presbyterian Church Cemetery Records)

Kirkwood, Sarah Ann, see Joshua Augustus Anderson, q.v.

Kirkwood, Stuart Robinson, born 5 Jul 1876, son of Robert and Mary E. (Robinson) Kirkwood (Bethel Presbyterian Church Cemetery Records; *Kirkwoods and Their Kin, 1731-1971*, by Anna Lee Kirkwood Smith, 1972, p. 67)

Kirkwood, Thone B., born c1879, son of Robert Jabez and Caroline (Bradenbaugh) Kirkwood (*Kirkwoods and Their Kin, 1731-1971*, by Anna Lee Kirkwood Smith, 1972, p. 104)

Kirkwood, Wakeman B., 1889-1892, son of Robert E. C. and Mary B. (Bevard) Kirkwood (Bethel Presbyterian Church Cemetery Records)

Kirkwood, Wiletta, born 23 Aug 1875, daughter of Joseph and Elizabeth (Stritehoff) Kirkwood (*Kirkwoods and Their Kin, 1731-1971*, by Anna Lee Kirkwood Smith, 1972, p. 76)

Kirwan, Etta Virginia, 1881-1891 (Grove Presbyterian Church Cemetery)

Klair's General Store, Havre de Grace, Vesta B. Klair, prop. (*Country Stores: Harford County's Rural Heritage*, by Henry C. Peden, Jr. and Jack L. Shagena, Jr., 2015, p. 155)

Klair, Ann D., 1818-1911 (Dublin Southern Cemetery)

Klair, Annie, see Frederick K. Smith, Anna L. Walker and Martha L. Wise, q.v.

Klair, Cora Belle (Werner), 1872-1954 (Angel Hill Cemetery), wife of Louis Harry Klair, q.v.

Klair, Edwin H., 1853-1930 (Darlington Cemetery); farmer and native of Pennsylvania (Bailey Funeral Home Records); see Etta W. Harkins, q.v.

Klair, Etta W., see Etta W. Harkins, q.v.

Klair, Hiram Goldsborough, born 23 Dec 1876, son of Pierson D. and Vesta B. Klair (Pierson D. Klair Bible, *Maryland Bible Records, Volume 1*, by Henry C. Peden, Jr., 2003, p. 144)

Klair, Howard O., 1867-1954 (Angel Hill Cemetery); son of Pierson D. and Vesta B. Klair (Pierson D. Klair Bible, *Maryland Bible Records, Volume 1*, by Henry C. Peden, Jr., 2003, p. 144)

Klair, Jesse B., born 22 Oct 1872, son of Pierson D. and Vesta B. Klair (Pierson D. Klair Bible, *Maryland Bible Records, Volume 1*, by Henry C. Peden, Jr., 2003, p. 144)

Klair, Louis Harry, 1870-1952 (Angel Hill Cemetery); son of Pierson D. and Vest B. Klair (Pierson D. Klair Bible, *Maryland Bible Records, Volume 1*, by Henry C. Peden, Jr., 2003, p. 144)

Klair, Maggie, born 15 Mar 1874, daughter of Pierson D. and Vesta B. Klair (Pierson D. Klair Bible, *Maryland Bible Records, Volume 1*, by Henry C. Peden, Jr., 2003, p. 144); student, of Havre de Grace (*The Aegis & Intelligencer*, 23 May 1890, misspelled her name Klaire)

Klair, Margaret (Curry), 1860-1954 (Angel Hill Cemetery)

Klair, Pierson D., 1845-1912 (Angel Hill Cemetery); alias Aquilla Jones, Civil War veteran, Havre de Grace (*1890 Special Census of the Civil War Veterans of the State of Maryland*, by L. Tilden Moore, Volume III, p. 89)

Klair, Sarah B., 1849-1933 (Darlington Cemetery)

Klair, Vesta (Baldwin), 1839-1909 (Angel Hill Cemetery); Mrs. Pierson D. Klair, superintendent of work among colored people, Women's Christian Temperance Union, of Havre de Grace (*Havre de Grace Republican*, 19 Sep 1890); wife of Pierson D. Klair, q.v.; also see Klair's General Store, q.v.

Kline, Frank M., fox hunter, near Bel Air (*The Aegis & Intelligencer*, 14 Feb 1890)

Kline, Mary, died 24 Nov 1901, no age given (Alms House Record Book)

Klinefelter, H. H. & W. E., bone and fertilizer manufacturers, Havre de Grace (*Havre de Grace Republican*, 30 May 1890)

Klinger, Charles B., 1873-1936 (Death certificate)

Knee, Edward J., 1868-1919 (Bethel Presbyterian Church Cemetery Records)

Knee, Sophia A. (Wiley), 1868-1931 (Bethel Presbyterian Church Cemetery Records)

Knell, J. Henry, 1839-1899, lumber dealer at Jarrettsville, native of Baltimore (Death certificate)

Knell, Mary E., wife of J. Henry Knell, q.v.

Knellinger, Carl Edward, 1856-1945 (Mountain Christian Church Cemetery)

Knellinger, Elizabeth, 1836-1921 (Mountain Christian Church Cemetery)

Knellinger, Frances V. (Carr), 1858-1915 (Mountain Christian Church Cemetery)

Knellinger, Ollie, fifth grade student, Prospect Hill School (*The Aegis & Intelligencer*, 21 Feb 1890)

Knight, Anne (Hughes), died 14 Jun 1898, age not given (John Hughes Bible, *Maryland Bible Records, Volume 1*, by Henry C. Peden, Jr., 2003, pp. 123-124)

Knight, Annie, 1876-1941 (Emory Methodist Church Cemetery)

Knight, Annie E., 1809-1998 (St. George's Episcopal Church Cemetery)

Knight, Austin, 1886-1956 (Smith Chapel Methodist Church Cemetery)

Knight, B. Andrews, president, Susquehanna and Tidewater Canal Company (*Havre de Grace Republican*, 11 Apr 1890)

Knight, Belle E. age 22 in 1890 (Marriage License Applications Book ALJ No. 2, 1891)

Knight, Bessie (Love), 1867-1943 (Darlington Cemetery)

Knight, C. H., chaplain, Camp Dallam, Sons of [Confederate] Veterans, at Minefield Station, Maryland Central Railroad (*Havre de Grace Republican*, 5 Dec 1890)

Knight, Catharine (Murphy), 1855-1905 (St. Ignatius Catholic Church Cemetery); wife of Robert A. Knight, q.v.; also see Esther Crow Knight and Robert Bernard Knight, q.v.

Knight, Charles, resident near Black Horse (*The Aegis & Intelligencer*, 8 Aug 1890)

Knight, Charles H., 1864-1938 (Emory Methodist Church Cemetery)

Knight, Clarence, student, Public School No. 1, First District (*The Aegis & Intelligencer*, 10 Jan 1890)

Knight, Edwin W., 1849-1921 (Cokesbury Memorial Methodist Church Cemetery)

Knight, Elizabeth, see Annie E. Miller, q.v.

Knight, Elsie, 1866-1965 (Rock Run Methodist Church Cemetery)

Knight, Esther Crow, baptized 7 May 1882, daughter of Robert Knight and Catharine Murphy (St. Ignatius Catholic Church Baptism Register, p. 60)

Knight, Eva L. (Orr), 1886-1964 (Dublin Southern Cemetery); native of Darlington, Harford Co., born 2 Feb 1886, daughter of Robert Orr and JoAnn Sampson (Harkins Funeral Home Records)

Knight, Florence O., 1871-1938 (Rock Run Methodist Church Cemetery); wife of H. Archer Knight, q.v.

Knight, Frances A., 1886-1962 (Baker Cemetery)

Knight, George A., 1870-1936 (Emory Methodist Church Cemetery)

Knight, George Archer, 1865-1947 (Rock Run Methodist Church Cemetery), native of Harford Co., born 10 Apr 1865, son of William Knight, of Kent Co., MD, and Jane Scott, of Ireland (Death certificate; Bailey Funeral Home Records; William Knight Bible, *Maryland Bible Records, Volume 1*, by Henry C. Peden, Jr., 2003, p. 145, gave his name as George A. B. Knight)

Knight, George Leon, 1890-1925 (Wesleyan Chapel Methodist Church Cemetery); native of Maryland, born 16 Aug 1890, son of John W. Knight and Mary Eleanor Pearthree (Bailey Funeral Home Records; William Knight Bible, *Maryland Bible Records, Volume 1*, by Henry C. Peden, Jr., 2003, p. 145)

Knight, H. Archer, 1879-1963 (Rock Run Methodist Church Cemetery)

Knight, Hannah (Wilson), 1848-1901, native of Cecil Co., MD, resided at Webster, Harford Co. (Death certificate; Rock Run Methodist Church Cemetery); wife of Joseph W. Knight, q.v.

Knight, Hannah E., 1855-1899 (Grove Presbyterian Church Cemetery)

Knight, Howard Raphael, born -- Feb 1892, baptized 15 May 1887, son of Robert and Catharine (Murphy) Knight (St. Ignatius Catholic Church Baptism Register, p. 92)

Knight, Hugh Rufus, 1859-1920, native of Maryland, born 7 Nov 1859, son of James F. Knight and Martha J. Smith (Bailey Funeral Home Records; Darlington Cemetery); see Staton W. Knight, q.v.

Knight, Hugh S., 1888-1955 (Darlington Cemetery)

Knight, Ida Bell, age 20 in 1890 (Marriage License Applications Book ALJ No. 2, 1890), married George Reynolds on 19 Nov 1890 at her parents' home (*The Aegis & Intelligencer*, 28 Nov 1890)

Knight, Isabelle, 1872-1934 (Rock Run Methodist Church Cemetery); parents unknown, wife of Oliver Knight, q.v. (Bailey Funeral Home Records)

Knight, J. Ernest, 1887-1920 (Darlington Cemetery)

Knight, J. Glover, member, Harford Bicycle Club, of Havre de Grace (*Havre de Grace Republican*, 1 Aug 1890)

Knight, J. Graham, 1859-1959 (Darlington Cemetery)

Knight, J. Thomas, 1866-1900 (Baker Cemetery)

Knight, James F., 1826-1890 (Darlington Cemetery); flint quarry owner, near Castleton (*Havre de Grace Republican*, 10 Jan 1890); see Martha J. Jones and Hugh R. Knight, q.v.

Knight, James T., 1826-1890 (Darlington Cemetery); see William Wilson Knight, q.v.

Knight, James T., 1861-1937 (Darlington Cemetery); farmer and native of Harford Co. (Bailey Funeral Home Records)

Knight, Jane Ann (Scott), died 17 Jan 1898 (William Knight Bible, *Maryland Bible Records, Volume 1*, by Henry C. Peden, Jr., 2003, p. 145); wife of William Knight, q.v.

Knight, John, road mender, at Webster (*The Aegis & Intelligencer*, 13 Jun 1890)

Knight, John O., born -- Jan 1884, baptized 24 May 1884, son of Robert and Catherine (Murphy) Knight (St. Ignatius Catholic Church Baptism Register, p. 73)

Knight, John W., 1858-1928 (Wesleyan Chapel Methodist Church Cemetery); son of William and Jane Knight (William Knight Bible, *Maryland Bible Records, Volume 1*, by Henry C. Peden, Jr., 2003, p. 145); see George Leon Knight, q.v.

Knight, John Wesley, 1873-1948 (Cokesbury Memorial Methodist Church Cemetery)

Knight, Joseph E., 1868-1934 (Darlington Cemetery)

Knight, Joseph Lybrand, 1858-1921 (Smith Chapel Methodist Church Cemetery)

Knight, Joseph T., transferred from the voter registration list at Hopewell, Second District (*Havre de Grace Republican*, 17 Oct 1890)

Knight, Joseph W., 1842-1907 (Rock Run Methodist Church Cemetery); Civil War veteran, of Harford County (*1890 Special Census of the Civil War Veterans of the State of Maryland*, by L. Tilden Moore, Volume III, p. 67)

Knight, Joshua T., 1842-1921 (Darlington Cemetery); new name on the voter registration list at Abingdon, First

District (*Havre de Grace Republican*, 17 Oct 1890)

Knight, "Josue Andream" [Joshua Andrew?] born -- Jan 1889, baptized 19 May 1889, son of Robert and Catharine (Murphy) Knight (St. Ignatius Catholic Church Baptism Register, p. 105)

Knight, Juliet Sarah, 1872-1936 (Holy Trinity Episcopal Church Cemetery)

Knight, Kate C., 1855-1939 (Rock Run Methodist Church Cemetery)

Knight, Laura, wife of William Foster; also see Ada Foster, q.v.

Knight, Laura Jane, wife of James W. Foster, q.v.; also see Rebecca E. Foster, q.v.

Knight, Lola Estelle, born 10 Mar 1889, daughter of John and Mary Eleanor Knight (William Knight Bible, *Maryland Bible Records, Volume 1*, by Henry C. Peden, Jr., 2003, p. 145)

Knight, Lorenzo, student, Public School No. 1, First District (*The Aegis & Intelligencer*, 10 Jan 1890)

Knight, Margaret, 1877-1967, native of Lapidum, Harford Co., born 31 Jan 1877, daughter of William C. Knight and Margaret Daugherty (Pennington Funeral Home Records - married name Chandlee, and stated her mother was named Mary)

Knight, Margaret A., 1867-1954 (Darlington Cemetery); native of Ireland, born 20 Dec 1867, daughter of John Stuart or Stewart and Margaret Graham (Bailey Funeral Home Records); wife of James T. Knight, q.v.

Knight, Margaret A., 1869-1944 (Emory Methodist Church Cemetery)

Knight, Margaret C., 1840-1919 (Rock Run Methodist Church Cemetery)

Knight, Mary, see William A. Wilson, q.v.

Knight, Mary A., age 24 in 1889 (Marriage License Applications Book ALJ No. 2, 1889); also see Mary Jane Hopkins, q.v.

Knight, Mary E. (Miss), 1855-1935 (Darlington Cemetery)

Knight, Mary Ellen (James), 1880-1927 (Darlington Cemetery)

Knight, Maude V., wife of W. Scott Knight, q.v.; also see Maude V. Bowman, q.v.

Knight, May H. (Hopkins), 1864-1946 (Bailey Funeral Home Records); wife of George Archer Knight, q.v.

Knight, Myrtle, 1864-1952, native of Lapidum, Harford Co., born 12 Nov 1864, daughter of William C. Knight and Margaret J. Daugherty (Pennington Funeral Home Records -married name Jones)

Knight, Oliver, 1868-1931 (Rock Run Methodist Church Cemetery); native of Maryland, born 10 Sep 1868, son of William C. Knight and Margaret Daugherty (Bailey Funeral Home Records); age 22 in 1890 (Marriage License Applications Book ALJ No. 2, 1891); new name on the voter registration list at Hopewell, Second District, 1890 (*Havre de Grace Republican*, 26 Sep 1890); see Isabelle Knight, q.v.

Knight, Philema Woolston (Jourdan), 1861-1941 (Smith Chapel Methodist Church Cemetery)

Knight, Robert Bernard, 1880-1939 (Darlington Cemetery; www.findagrave.com); native of Harford Co., born 2 Sep 1880, son of Robert A. Knight and Catherine Murphy (Bailey Funeral Home Records)

Knight, Robert A., 1850-1920 (St. Ignatius Catholic Church Cemetery); see Robert Bernard Knight, q.v.

Knight, Robert H. L., born 23 Mar 1863, son of William and Jane Knight (William Knight Bible, *Maryland Bible Records, Volume 1*, by Henry C. Peden, Jr., 2003, p. 145); incorporator and director, Guardian Star Council No. 9, Junior Order of United American Mechanics, Havre de Grace (*The Aegis & Intelligencer*, 17 Jan 1890); juror, Sixth District (*Havre de Grace Republican*, 2 May 1890); member, Guiding Star Council No. 9, Jr. O. U. A. M., Havre de Grace (*Havre de Grace Republican*, 11 Jul 1890)

Knight, Sarah, see Stella F. Knight, q.v.

Knight, Sarah Jane (Troutner), 1862-1940, native of Harford Co. (Bailey Funeral Home Records)

Knight, Staton W., 1886-1920 (Darlington Cemetery); native of Maryland, born 25 Feb 1886, son of Hugh R. Knight and Sarah J. Troutner (Bailey Funeral Home Records)

Knight, Stella F. (Fink), 1886-1955 (Rock Run Methodist Church Cemetery); native of Harford Co., born 21 Jan 1886, daughter of Harrison Fink and Sarah Knight (Bailey Funeral Home Records)

Knight, Susan Beatrice (Main), 1869-1936, native of York Co., PA (Bailey Funeral Home Records; Darlington Cemetery); wife of William James Knight, q.v.

Knight, Thomas W., 1872-1952 (Rock Run Methodist Church Cemetery); native of Harford Co., born 22 Sep 1872, son of William and Margaret Knight (Bailey Funeral Home Records)

Knight, Violet S. (Gallion), 1888-1942 (Darlington Cemetery); native of Harford Co., born 1 Nov 1888, daughter of James K. Gallion and Emma M. Sheppard (Bailey Funeral Home Records)

Knight, Warren J., 1889-1967 (Darlington Cemetery); native of Darlington, Harford Co., born 13 Sep 1889, son of Wilson Knight and Bessie Love (Harkins Funeral Home Records)

Knight, W. Scott, 1874-1974 (Rock Run Methodist Church Cemetery)

Knight, Wesley, 1840-1914 (Jarrettsville Cemetery)

Knight, William, 1815-1898 (Wesleyan Chapel Methodist Church Cemetery)

Knight, William, see George Archer Knight, q.v.

Knight, William C., 1836-1919 (Rock Run Methodist Church Cemetery); see Margaret Knight, Oliver Knight and Myrtle Knight, q.v.

Knight, William Fristoe, 1819-1907 (Holy Trinity Episcopal Church Cemetery)

Knight, William H., 1839-1922 (Emory Methodist Church Cemetery); Civil War veteran, Chestnut Hill (*1890 Special Census of the Civil War Veterans of the State of Maryland*, by L. Tilden Moore, Volume III, p. 86)

Knight, William H., delegate, Fifth District, Republican Party Convention, 1890 (*The Aegis & Intelligencer*, 26 Sep 1890)

Knight, William James, 1866-1951 (Darlington Cemetery); married Susan B. Main, of York Co., PA, on 13 Feb 1890 (*The Aegis & Intelligencer*, 21 Feb 1890)

Knight, William T., born 11 Sep 1854, son of William and Jane Knight (William Knight Bible, *Maryland Bible Records, Volume 1*, by Henry C. Peden, Jr., 2003, p. 145)

Knight, William Wilson, 1869-1940 (Darlington Cemetery); native of Harford Co., born 18 Oct 1869, son of James T. Knight and Martha Smith (Bailey Funeral Home Records); see Warren J. Knight, q.v.

Knights of Pythias, Harford Lodge No. 54, Havre de Grace (*Havre de Grace Republican*, 11 Jul 1890; *Havre de Grace: Its Historic Past, Its Charming Present and Its Promising Future: Harford County's Rural Heritage.* by Jack L. Shagena, Jr. and Henry C. Peden, Jr., 2018, p. 267)

Knights of St. Leo, Havre de Grace (*Havre de Grace Republican*, 11 Jul 1890)

Knoble, Fred, "night work at the tower" in Aberdeen (*The Aegis & Intelligencer*, 9 May 1890); night operator, P.W.&B. Railroad, Aberdeen (*Havre de Grace Republican*, 17 Jan 1890)

Knoble, Mary M., age 21 in 1889 (Marriage License Applications Book ALJ No. 2, 1889)

Knoff, Joseph E., premium award winner, Class I - Agricultural Productions, Harford County Fair (*The Aegis & Intelligencer*, 24 Oct 1890)

Knofler, August, 1834-1910 (Christ Episcopal Church Cemetery); incorporator, Bel Air Water and Light Company (*Havre de Grace Republican*, 14 Feb 1890); proprietor of the Bel Air Boot and Shoe Store, and former town commissioner (*Biographical Dictionary of Harford County, Maryland, 1774-1974*, by Henry C. Peden, Jr. and William O. Carr, 2021, p. 157); also see Florence Knofler, q.v.

Knofler, Florence, daughter of A. Knofler, graduated from Bel Air Academy and Graded School (*The Aegis & Intelligencer*, 23 May and 4 Jul 1890)

Knofler, Mary Berugin, 1839-1905, wife of August Knofler, q.v.

Knopp, Amanda Jane (Frey), 1867-1923 (William Watters Memorial Church Cemetery, Cooptown; Joseph Enos Knopp Bible, *Maryland Bible Records, Volume 2*, by Henry C. Peden, Jr., 2003, pp. 79-81)

Knopp, Amelia (Eck), 1851-1927 (William Watters Memorial Church Cemetery, Cooptown; *Knopp Family*, by Pauline Knopp Smith, 1990, p. 7); wife of Dennis C. Knopp, q.v.

Knopp, Annie Mary, 1890-1892 (William Watters Memorial Church Cemetery, Cooptown); daughter of Joseph Enos and Amanda (Frey) Knopp (Joseph Enos Knopp Bible, *Maryland Bible Records, Volume 2*, by Henry C. Peden, Jr., 2003, pp. 79-81; *Knopp Family*, by Pauline Knopp Smith, 1990, p. 2)

Knopp, Charles Edward, 1888-1961 (William Watters Memorial Church Cemetery, Cooptown); born 17 Aug 1888, son of Joseph Enos and Amanda (Frey) Knopp (Joseph Enos Knopp Bible, *Maryland Bible Records, Volume 2*, by Henry C. Peden, Jr., 2003, pp. 79-81)

Knopp, Christiana, 1886-1942 (William Watters Memorial Methodist Church Cemetery, Cooptown - married name Gardner); born 24 May 1886, daughter of Joseph Enos and Amanda (Frey) Knopp (Joseph Enos Knopp Bible, *Maryland Bible Records, Volume 2*, by Henry C. Peden, Jr., 2003, pp. 79-81; *Knopp Family*, by Pauline Knopp Smith, 1990, p. 2)

Knopp, Christopher E., 1878-1964 (William Watters Memorial Church Cemetery, Cooptown); born 29 Dec 1878, son of Dennis Knopp and Amelia Eck (*Knopp Family*, by Pauline Knopp Smith, 1990, pp. 8, 8A)

Knopp, Daniel R., 1875-1956 (St. Paul's Methodist Church Cemetery); born 22 Apr 2875, son of Dennia Knopp and Amelia Eck (*Knopp Family*, by Pauline Knopp Smith, 1990, p. 7)

Knopp, Dennis C., 1841-1932 (William Watters Memorial Church Cemetery, Cooptown; *Knopp Family*, by Pauline Knopp Smith, 1990, p. 7); see Noah E. Knopp, q.v.

Knopp, George W., 1876-1937 (William Watters Memorial Church Cemetery, Cooptown); born 18 Sep 1876, son of Dennis Knopp and Amelia Eck (*Knopp Family*, by Pauline Knopp Smith, 1990, p. 8, mistakenly stated 1871)

Knopp, Grace S. (Boyd), 1874-1960 (William Watters Memorial Church Cemetery, Cooptown; *Knopp Family*, by Pauline Knopp Smith, 1990, p. 8A); wife of George W. Knopp, q.v.

Knopp, Harry Clifford, 1884-1963 (William Watters Memorial Church Cemetery, Cooptown); born 28 Oct 1884, son of Joseph Enos Knopp and Amanda Frey (*Knopp Family*, by Pauline Knopp Smith, 1990, p. 1)

Knopp, Henrietta (Reynolds), 1882-1962 (William Watters Memorial Church Cemetery, Cooptown); wife of Harry Clifford Knopp, q.v.

Knopp, Joseph Enos, 1860-1948 (William Watters Memorial Church Cemetery, Cooptown; Joseph Enos Knopp Bible, *Maryland Bible Records, Volume 2*, by Henry C. Peden, Jr., 2003, pp. 79-81)

Knopp, Joseph L., 1880-1936 (Highland Presbyterian Church Cemetery); born 1 Aug 1880, son of Joseph Enos Knopp and Amanda Jane Frey (*Knopp Family*, by Pauline Knopp Smith, 1990, pp. 10, 10A)

Knopp, Lillie Mirl, 1880-1968 (St. Paul's Methodist Church Cemetery; *Knopp Family*, by Pauline Knopp Smith, 1990, p. 7); wife of Daniel Knopp, q.v.

Knopp, Mamie Ellen (McCann), wife of Noah E. Knopp, q.v.

Knopp, Minnie Luella (Horn), 1880-1967 (William Watters Memorial Church Cemetery, Cooptown; *Knopp Family*, by Pauline Knopp Smith, 1990, p. 8); wife of Christopher E. Knopp, q.v.

Knopp, Noah E., 1873-1961 (Bel Air Memorial Gardens); native of Rocks, Harford Co., born 6 Dec 1873, son of Dennis Knopp and Amelia Eck (Harkins Funeral Home Records)

Knopp, Olive Mary, 1890-1964 (Highland Presbyterian Church Cemetery; *Knopp Family*, by Pauline Knopp Smith, 1990, p. 10A, states Mary Olive); wife of Joseph Knopp, q.v.

Knopp, Samuel, born 1851, died ----, son of John George Knopp and Elizabeth Harmon (*Knopp Family*, by Pauline Knopp Smith, 1990, p. 11)

Knopp, Samuel, student, LaGrange School No. 14, Fourth District (*The Aegis & Intelligencer*, 25 Apr 1890); son of Samuel Knopp (b. 1851) and Mary Elizabeth Saunders (*Knopp Family*, by Pauline Knopp Smith, 1990, p. 11)

Knopp, Sarah Jane (Harmon), 1841-1926 (Ashland Presbyterian Church Cemetery, Cockeysville, MD; widow of Joseph Enos Knopp (*Knopp Family*, by Pauline Knopp Smith, 1990, p. 1)

Knopp, Wilhelmina M., 1888-1977 (William Watters Memorial Church Cemetery, Cooptown)

Koendres, Catharine M. ("Kate"), businesswoman (trader's license), Havre de Grace (*Havre de Grace Republican*, 30 May 1890; *The Aegis & Intelligencer*, 9 May 1890)

Koendres, Ella Louise, 1873-1914, native of Havre de Grace, born 18 Jan 1873, daughter of John Koendres and Annie C. Hindermann, both natives of Germany (Death certificate - married name Foley; Mt. Erin Cemetery)

Koendres, John, died 30 Sep 1890, age about 27 (Mt. Erin Cemetery); member, Knights of St. Leo, St. Patrick's Catholic Church, Havre de Grace (*Havre de Grace Republican*, 3 Oct 1890); removed from the voter registration list in the Sixth District (*Havre de Grace Republican*, 17 Oct 1890)

Koendres, John, Jr., died 1896, age not stated (Mt. Erin Cemetery)

Koendres, Mary Florence, 1886-1913 (Mt. Erin Cemetery)

Koendres, William R., 1887-1960, native of Havre de Grace, born 6 Sep 1887, son of John Koendres and Catherine Hollahan (Pennington Funeral Home Records)

Koendries, Eva Katherine (Bodt), 1860-1924 (St. Paul's Lutheran Church Cemetery)

Koendries, Henry, 1862-1915 (St. Paul's Lutheran Church Cemetery)

Kohlbus, George, 1886-1962 (Highland Presbyterian Church Cemetery); native of Street, Harford Co., born 5 Mar 1886, son of William H. Kohlbus and Elizabeth Nicholas (Harkins Funeral Home Records)

Kohlbus, Henrietta, see Henrietta Muth, q.v.

Kohlbus, Minnie E., see Minnie E. Smith, q.v.

Kohlbus, William H., see George Kohlbus, Minnie E. Smith and Henrietta Muth, q.v.

Koin, Adele Jane (colored), born -- Aug 1881, daughter of Rachel Koin (Holy Trinity Episcopal Church Register of Baptisms, p. 86)

Kolk, Adam, farmer near Fallston (*The Aegis & Intelligencer*, 3 Jan 1890)

Kolk, Annie, student, School No. 1, Third District (*The Aegis & Intelligencer*, 11 Jul 1890)

Kolk, George, student, School No. 1, Third District (*The Aegis & Intelligencer*, 11 Jul 1890)

Kolk, Godfrey, fourth grade student, School No. 1, Third District (*The Aegis & Intelligencer*, 11 Jul 1890)

Kolk, Paul F., architect and builder, Bel Air (*Harford Democrat*, 3 Jan 1890; *The Aegis & Intelligencer*, 19 Sep 1890); juror, Third District, 1890 (*Havre de Grace Republican*, 2 May 1890)

Kolmeyer, William, c1827-1892, resided near Bell's Mill, Abingdon District (*The Aegis & Intelligencer*, 30 Dec 1892)

Kolson, Joseph, 1865-1931 (Death certificate; Alms House Record Book)

Koser, ----, wife of Dr. Koser, member, Havre de Grace Reading Circle (*Havre de Grace Republican*, 7 Feb 1890)

Koser, J. S. (Dr.), dentist, Havre de Grace (*Havre de Grace Republican*, 10 Jan 1890 and 7 Feb 1890); member, Harford Bicycle Club, of Havre de Grace (*Havre de Grace Republican*, 1 Aug 1890)

Kragel (Kraigle), Henry, 1862-1930 (Death certificate; Alms House Record Book)

Kramer, Elizabeth, 1827-1902 (Salem Evangelical Lutheran Church Cemetery)

Kramer, Jacob, 1824-1898 (Salem Evangelical Lutheran Church Cemetery)

Krause, Joseph Milton, 1844-1913 (St. Ignatius Catholic Church Cemetery)

Krause, Lillie A., 1878-1905 (St. Ignatius Catholic Church Cemetery)

Krebs, Sarah C., businesswoman (trader's license), Havre de Grace (*Havre de Grace Republican*, 30 May 1890)

Kreider, Gertrude Octavia, 1833-1913 (Baker Cemetery)

Krein, Joseph A., merchant tailor, Main St., Bel Air (*Harford Democrat*, 21 Feb 1890); member, Division No. 2, Bel Air Fire and Salvage Corps (*The Aegis & Intelligencer*, 10 Oct 1890)

Kreiss, George H., widower, of Abingdon District, age 42 in 1891, illegally married a colored woman named Elizabeth Bishop, age 33, in 1891 ("News of Long Ago: News of 1891," *Havre de Grace Republican*, 19 Jan

1935; Marriage License Applications Book ALJ No. 2, 1891, incorrectly stated she was white)

Kretlow, Henry C., 1886-1960 (Baker Cemetery)

Kriete, Charles Henry, 1870-1946, physician (Baker Cemetery; 1900 Aberdeen Census)

Kriete, Elizabeth Richardson (Neale), 1877-1965 (Baker Cemetery)

Krig, Ernestine widow, age 38 in 1890 (Marriage License Applications Book ALJ No. 2, 1890), married Frederick Bechtold on 3 Jul 1890 (*The Aegis & Intelligencer*, 4 Jul 1890)

Krill, Charles, new name on the voter registration list at Magnolia, First District (*Havre de Grace Republican*, 26 Sep 1890)

Kroh, Amy P., 1890-1977 (Mountain Christian Church Cemetery)

Kroh, Christopher, died 24 Dec 1899 at New Park, married adult, age not given (Death certificate)

Kroh, Elizabeth "Eliza" M. (Leight), 1858-1933 (Mountain Christian Church Cemetery; *The Aegis*, 10 Feb 1933); wife of Franklin A. Kroh, q.v.

Kroh, Ella, sixth grade student, Prospect Hill School (*The Aegis & Intelligencer*, 21 Feb 1890)

Kroh, Frank, worshipful master, Charity Lodge No. 134, A. F. & A. M., Norrisville (*The Aegis & Intelligencer*, 26 Dec 1890)

Kroh, Franklin Albert, 1856-1943 (Mountain Christian Church Cemetery)

Kroh, George H., 1884-1962 (Trinity Evangelical Lutheran Church Cemetery)

Kroh, George L., of Harford County, incorporator, Gunpowder Permanent Building Association of Baltimore County (*The Aegis & Intelligencer*, 23 May 1890)

Kroh, George W., 1880-1956 (Mountain Christian Church Cemetery)

Kroh, Philip H., 1824-1913 (Mountain Christian Church Cemetery)

Krouse, Agnes (Gallagher), 1844-1899, resident of Forest Hill, native of American, wife of Joseph Krouse (Death certificate)

Krouse, Annie (Drechsler), see Mary Annie Krouse, q.v.

Krouse, Conrad, 1844-1905 (Mt. Erin Cemetery); farmer, near Aberdeen (*Havre de Grace Republican*, 4 Jul 1890)

Krouse, Elizabeth, see Emma J. Duncan, q.v.

Krouse, Emma, fourth grade honor student, Bel Air Graded School (*The Aegis & Intelligencer*, 4 Jul 1890)

Krouse, Grover Cleveland, born Dec 1884, son of Conrad and Annie (Drechsler) Krouse (1900 Aberdeen Census; Baker Cemetery)

Krouse, Joseph Albert, 1875-1942, native of Havre de Grace, born 6 Jan 1875, son of Conrad Krouse, of Germany, and Annie Drechsler, of Baltimore (Death certificate; Mt. Erin Cemetery; Pennington Funeral Home Records)

Krouse, Joseph Milton, Civil War veteran, Forest Hill (*1890 Special Census of the Civil War Veterans of the State of Maryland*, by L. Tilden Moore, Volume III, p. 74); officer of the guard, Wann Post No. 49, G. A. R., of Forest Hill (*Havre de Grace Republican*, 25 Jul 1890)

Krouse, Katie E., born -- Apr 1876, daughter of Conrad and Annie (Drechsler) Krouse (1900 Aberdeen Census stated she was born in April 1875, but her brother Joseph was born in Jan 1875)

Krouse, Margaret J., 1882-1940 (Baker Cemetery)

Krouse, Mary Annie (Dreschler), 1855-1911 (Mt. Erin Cemetery); wife of Conrad Krouse, q.v.

Krouse, Paul Conrad, born -- May 1878, son of Conrad and Annie (Drechsler) Krouse (1900 Aberdeen Census; Baker Cemetery inscribed 1877-1956)

Krouse, Pearl V., 1888-1957 (Baker Cemetery)

Krouse, Thomas M., born -- Mar 1883, son of Conrad and Annie (Drechsler) Krouse (1900 Aberdeen Census;

Baker Cemetery inscribed 1882-1965)

Krouse, William W., born -- Feb 1880, son of Conrad and Annie (Drechsler) Krouse (1900 Aberdeen Census)

Krozier, William, 1842-1928, native of Germany, resided at Joppa (Death certificate)

Kulp, Alfred W., 1883-1962 (St. Mary's Catholic Church Cemetery)

Kulp, Teresa C. (Welch), 1882-1963 (St. Mary's Catholic Church Cemetery); native of Whiteford, Harford Co., born 13 Jan 1882, daughter of Thomas Welch and Rebecca Dick (Harkins Funeral Home Records)

Kunkel, Clara Wellsetta, born 29 Jan 1881, daughter of Michael J. and Margaret J. B. (Shamberger) Kunkel (Bethel Presbyterian Church Cemetery Records)

Kunkel, Jerusha C., see Mary A. Kenny, q.v.

Kunkel, John T., 1864-1938 (St. Paul's Methodist Church Cemetery)

Kunkel, Sarah M. (Rampley), 1863-1943 (St. Paul's Methodist Church Cemetery)

Kurtz Funeral Home (Cabinet Making and Undertaking), Jarrettsville (*1953 Harford County Directory*, p. 301)

Kurtz, Almira Virginia (Miss), 1854-1928 (Bethel Presbyterian Church Cemetery Records); native of Maryland, resided at Jarrettsville (Death certificate)

Kurtz, Adam E., 1862-1932 (Centre Methodist Church Cemetery)

Kurtz, Bessie L., born 1886, died ---- (Deer Creek Methodist Church Cemetery)

Kurtz, Blanch, student, Forest Hill School, 1890 (*The Aegis*, 2 Jul 1965, school picture)

Kurtz, Carrie H., 1890-1969 (Centre Methodist Church Cemetery)

Kurtz, Clara H., 1868-1953, daughter of Martin Kurtz and Sarah Elenor Mead (Jarrettsville Cemetery); former teacher at Jarrettsville and member of Asbury M. E. Church in Jarrettsville (*Havre de Grace Republican*, 14 Feb 1890 and 28 Feb 1890); married Joshua B. Ward on 6 Mar 1890 (*The Aegis & Intelligencer*, 14 Mar 1890; Marriage License Applications Book ALJ No. 2, 1890)

Kurtz, Edmund Grove, 1859-1928 (Jarrettsville Cemetery); farmer Jarrettsville (*The Aegis & Intelligencer*, 2 May 1890 and 4 Jul 1890, mistakenly listed him as Edward); native of Maryland, resided in Jarrettsville, married, funeral director (Death certificate)

Kurtz, John, 1883-1947 (Deer Creek Methodist Church Cemetery); student, Forest Hill School, 1890 (*The Aegis*, 2 Jul 1965, school picture)

Kurtz, Margaret E., 1853-1931 (Mt. Erin Cemetery)

Kurtz, Martha, see Joseph Henry Moore, q.v.

Kurtz, Martha Elizabeth (McIntire), 1830-1890 (Mt. Erin Cemetery); died testate in Havre de Grace and her named heirs were son John C. Kurtz and daughters Martha J. Moore, Mary Alice Finnan, Harriet V. Frederick and Margaret Elizabeth Kurtz (Harford County Will Book JMM 11:107-109)

Kurtz, Mary A., 1861-1953 (Jarrettsville Cemetery)

Kurtz, Ralph Hess, 1884-1985 (Centre Methodist Church Cemetery); student, Forest Hill School, 1890 (*The Aegis*, 2 Jul 1965, school picture)

Kurtz, Rebecca, student, Forest Hill School, 1890 (*The Aegis*, 2 Jul 1965, school picture)

Kurtz, Sarah Ellen or Elenor (Meads), 1827-1920 (Bethel Presbyterian Church Cemetery Records)

Kutchie, Michael, 1870-1950 (Death certificate; Heavenly Waters Cemetery)

Kyle, Anna Evelyn ("Annie"), born 22 Jul 1882, daughter of Samuel A. S. and Ella V. (Harward) Kyle (Holy Trinity Episcopal Church Register of Baptisms, p. 86); premium award winner, Class L - Children's Department, Harford County Fair (*The Aegis & Intelligencer*, 24 Oct 1890)

Kyle, Beulah S., 1886-1971 (Darlington Cemetery); native of Darlington, Harford Co., born 22 Nov 1886, daughter of Lee H. Kyle and Rachel Hughes (Harkins Funeral Home Records)

Kyle, Ella V., see Anna Evelyn Kyle, q.v.

Kyle, Grace Harwood, 1879-1958 (Holy Trinity Episcopal Church Cemetery); premium award winner, Class L - Children's Department, Harford County Fair (*The Aegis & Intelligencer*, 24 Oct 1890)

Kyle, Josephine, see Fannie L. Brinkman, q.v.

Kyle, Lee H. 1865-1939 (Darlington Cemetery); see Beulah S. Kyle, q.v.

Kyle, Rachel J., 1860-1930 (Darlington Cemetery)

Kyle, Samuel (Mrs.), premium award winner, Class J - Domestic Products, and Class N - Flora Decorations, Harford County Fair (*The Aegis & Intelligencer*, 24 Oct 1890)

Kyle, Samuel Alexander. Stuart, 1815-1893 (Holy Trinity Episcopal Church Cemetery); farmer, at Fountain Green (*The Aegis & Intelligencer*, 7 Feb 1890); vestryman, Holy Trinity Church, Churchville (*Havre de Grace Republican*, 18 Apr 1890); also see Anna Evelyn Kyle, q.v.

LaBree, Benjamin, 1855-1945 (Churchville Presbyterian Church Cemetery)

LaBree, Benjamin, Jr., 1884-1966 (Churchville Presbyterian Church Cemetery)

LaBree, Lucy (Jeffery), 1845-1910 (Churchville Presbyterian Church Cemetery)

Labruler, Edward, moved to Churchville (*Harford Democrat*, 4 Nov 1890)

Lachmann, George J., born 21 Sep 1879, son of John and Caroline (Beiler) Lachmann (Bethel Presbyterian Church Cemetery Records)

Lackey, Amy Ross (Warner), 1882-1961 (Deer Creek Methodist Church Cemetery); native of Harford Co., born 13 Feb 1882, daughter of Silas and Mary E. Warner (Bailey Funeral Home Records); wife of Augustus Lackey, q.v.

Lackey, August, 1874-1962 (Deer Creek Methodist Church Cemetery); native of Forest Hill, Harford Co., born 12 Sep 1874, parents unknown (Harkins Funeral Home Records)

Lackey, Charles E., 1885-1927 (Christ Episcopal Church Cemetery)

Lackey, Ernest, 1870-1956 (Christ Episcopal Church Cemetery)

Lackey, Henry J., 1843-1932, Civil War veteran (Christ Episcopal Church Cemetery)

Lackey, Joe, student, Forest Hill School, 1890 (*The Aegis*, 2 Jul 1965, school picture)

Lackey, Mary J., 1845-1911 (Christ Episcopal Church Cemetery)

Lackey, Mary L., 1868-1936 (Christ Episcopal Church Cemetery)

Lacey, Mildred E. (colored), 1889-1972 (Union Methodist Church Cemetery, Aberdeen)

Lacey, William R. (colored), 1889-1952 (Union Methodist Church Cemetery, Aberdeen)

Laconey, Joseph, born 14 Jun 1877, son of Joseph W. and ---- Laconey (St. George's Episcopal Church Register of Baptisms, pp. 4-5)

Laddy, Susan (colored), died 13 Mar 1925, old age, native of Maryland, parents unknown (Death certificate)

Ladies' Relief Association, Havre de Grace (*Havre de Grace: Its Historic Past, Its Charming Present and Its Promising Future: Harford County's Rural Heritage.* by Jack L. Shagena, Jr. and Henry C. Peden, Jr., 2018, p. 268)

Ladies' Sewing Society of Darlington (*Harford Democrat*, 7 Feb 1890)

Lafferty, Margaret (Homes), 1861-1902 (Mt. Erin Cemetery)

Lagan, Andrew, see John S. Lagan, q.v.

Lagan, John Steven (1866-1946 (St. Mary's Catholic Church Cemetery tombstone inscribed John F. Lagan, 1867-1946); son of Andrew Lagan, married Sarah A. Terry on 8 Oct 1890 (St. Ignatius Catholic Church Marriage Register, p. 19; Lagan Bible gave his name as John Steven Lagan John and Mary Eleanor Knight (John S. Lagan Bible, *Maryland Bible Records, Volume 1*, by Henry C. Peden, Jr., 2003, pp. 145-146, but his death certificate gave his name as John Francis Lagan; Marriage License Applications Book ALJ No. 2, 1890, gave his name as John S. Lagan and his age as 21)

Lagan, Maggie, fourth grade student, Bynum School (*The Aegis & Intelligencer*, 7 Feb 1890)

Lagan, Sarah A. (Terry), 1862-1937 (Fallston Methodist Church Cemetery)

LaGrange Colore Public School No. 3, near Rocks, Fourth District (*Harford County, Maryland Teachers and the Schools They Served, 1774-1900*, by Henry C. Peden, Jr., 2022, p. 370)

Laird, Florence W. (Famous), 1884-1969 (Emory Methodist Church Cemetery); native of Street, Harford Co., born 8 Oct 1884, daughter of Andrew J. Famous and Mary Ann Carr (Harkins Funeral Home Records)

Laird, Hugh M., see Samuel C. Laird, q.v.

Laird, Hugh M., Jr., 1878-1961 (St. Ignatius Catholic Church Cemetery)

Laird, May J. (Famous), 1876-1969 (St. Ignatius Catholic Church Cemetery); native of Glenville, Harford Co., born 4 Nov 1876, daughter of Joseph Famous and Sarah E. Murphy (Harkins Funeral Home Records)

Laird, Rebecca (Mrs.), resident of Glenville (*The Aegis & Intelligencer*, 19 Sep 1890)

Laird, Samuel C., 1883-1967 (Emory Methodist Church Cemetery); native of Harford Co., born 16 Mar 1883, son of Hugh M. Laird and Mary Ann Boyd (Harkins Funeral Home Records)

Lamar, E. Holmes, Jr. (Rev.), 1864-1921 (Ebenezer Methodist Church Cemetery); junior preacher, West Harford Circuit (*Havre de Grace Republican*, 14 Mar and 15 Aug 1890); pastor of West Harford Circuit, married Emma C. Scarff on 7 Aug 1890 (*The Aegis & Intelligencer*, 15 Aug 1890); reportedly age 30 in 1890 (Marriage License Applications Book ALJ No. 2)

Lamar, Ellen (Miss), treasurer, Fountain Green Women's Christian Temperance Union (*Havre de Grace Republican*, 2 May 1890)

Lamar, Emma C. (Scarff), 1858-1935 (Ebenezer Methodist Church Cemetery)

Lamar, Thomas, 1803-1894 (Mt. Zion Methodist Church Cemetery)

Lamb, ----, catcher, Baptist Baseball Club, of Fourth District (*Havre de Grace Republican*, 8 Aug 1890)

Lamb, Amanda L., age 23 in 1889 (Marriage License Applications Book ALJ No. 2, 1889)

Lamb, Annie M. (Liddell), 1873-1954 (Deer Creek Harmony Presbyterian Church Cemetery); native of Harford Co., born 15 Jan 1873, daughter of Thomas Liddell and Julia Russell (Bailey Funeral Home Records)

Lamb, Bessie H. E., 1866-1954 (Deer Creek Harmony Presbyterian Church Cemetery)

Lamb, Charles, c1853-1914 (Death certificate; Alms House Record Book)

Lamb, Charles H., 1861-1928 (Bethel Presbyterian Church Cemetery Records); native of Maryland, married, resided at Jarrettsville (Death certificate)

Lamb, Georgia H. (Streett), 1859-1937 (Bethel Presbyterian Church Cemetery Records); wife of John A. Lamb, q.v.

Lamb, Hannah Elizabeth (Miss), 1866-1954 (Deer Creek Presbyterian Church Cemetery); native of Harford Co., daughter of John Lamb and Jeanete Harper (Bailey Funeral Home Records)

Lamb, Helen, born 21 Apr 1889, daughter of Charles H. and Laura (Deets) Lamb (Bethel Presbyterian Church Cemetery Records); see Helen (Lamb) Talbott, q.v.

Lamb, James A., 1870-1947 (Deer Creek Harmony Presbyterian Church Cemetery)

Lamb, John, 1838-1915 (Deer Creek Harmony Presbyterian Church Cemetery); Civil War veteran, Darlington (*1890 Special Census of the Civil War Veterans of the State of Maryland*, by L. Tilden Moore, Volume III, p. 87); see Hannah E. Lamb and Ruth A. McDoon, q.v.

Lamb, John A., 1849-1898 (Bethel Presbyterian Church Cemetery Records); trustee, Baptist School No. 7, Fourth District (*Havre de Grace Republican*, 30 May 1890)

Lamb, John A., Jr., born 20 May 1884, son of John A. and Georgia H. (Streett) Lamb (Bethel Presbyterian Church Cemetery Records)

Lamb, Laura V., 1861-1934 (Bethel Presbyterian Church Cemetery Records); wife of Charles H. Lamb, q.v.

Lamb, Mary Genette (Harper), 1834-1921 (Deer Creek Harmony Presbyterian Church Cemetery)

Lambert, Jacob, 1861-1927, native of Maryland (Death certificate; Alms House Book; Heavenly Waters Cemetery)

Lambright, Mattie A., age 20 in 1889 (Marriage License Applications Book ALJ No. 2, 1889)

Lamm, Charles, businessman (liquor license), Havre de Grace (*Havre de Grace Republican*, 30 May 1890)

Lancaster, Charles F., 1881-1902 (Fallston Methodist Church Cemetery)

Lancaster, George L., 1879-1949 (Fallston Methodist Church Cemetery)

Lancaster, Georgia E., 1878-1946 (Fallston Methodist Church Cemetery)

Lancaster, Julia A., 1844-1917 (Little Falls Quaker Cemetery)

Lancaster, Leonard, member, Cleveland Junior Baseball Club, at Pleasantville (*The Aegis & Intelligencer*, 22 Aug 1890)

Lancaster, M. Rebecca (Patton), 1860-1940 (Old Brick Baptist Church Cemetery)

Lancaster, William E., 1845-1931 (Fallston Methodist Church Cemetery)

Lancaster, William O., 1882-1947 (Fallston Methodist Church Cemetery)

Lander, D. F., Civil War veteran, Line Bridge (*1890 Special Census of the Civil War Veterans of the State of Maryland*, by L. Tilden Moore, Volume III, p. 84)

Lane, Caroline (Jiles), 1844-1932 (Death certificate; St. James United Cemetery)

Lane, Elizabeth, see Bryan Donnan, Horace Lane and Paul R. Donnan, q.v.

Lane, Joseph W., sold land in November 1890 (*The Aegis & Intelligencer*, 5 Dec 1890)

Langley, ---- (Miss), art teacher, Archer Institute, Bel Air (*The Aegis & Intelligencer*, 20 Jun 1890)

Langreder, August, 1855-1910 (Trinity Lutheran Church Cemetery); native of Germany, naturalized on 13 Sep 1890 (Harford County Circuit Court Minute Book ALJ No. 5, p. 256); new name on the voter registration list at Magnolia, First District, 1890 (*Havre de Grace Republican*, 26 Sep 1890)

Langreder, Mary, 1858-1921 (Trinity Lutheran Church Cemetery)

Langreder, William H., 1890-1954 (Cokesbury Memorial Church Cemetery)

Lantz, Frederick, chief judge of elections, Magnolia Precinct (*Havre de Grace Republican*, 17 Oct 1890)

Lapidum Baseball Club, of Lapidum (*Havre de Grace Republican*, 11 Jul 1890)

Lapidum Methodist Protestant Church (Lapidum, near Havre de Grace)

Lapidum Public School No. 13, Second District (*Harford County, Maryland Teachers and the Schools They Served, 1774-1900*, by Henry C. Peden, Jr., 2022, p. 370)

Larkin, Edward, of Havre de Grace, wrote his will in 1883 and died in 1891 mentioning his mother (not named) and friend Edward C. Kenly (Harford County Will Book JMM 11:180-181)

Larkin, John Edward, 1831-1891, died at home in Havre de Grace; architect and railroad engineer from South Yarmouth, MA (*Biographical Dictionary of Harford County, Maryland, 1774-1974*, by Henry C. Peden, Jr. and William O. Carr, 2021, p. 160); also see Mary Grace Minnie Larkin, q.v.

Larkin, Mary Grace Minnie, born 14 Oct 1876, daughter of John and Mary Larkin (St. George's Episcopal Church Register of Baptisms, pp. 4-5)

Larner, Delia, 1839-1891 (Mt. Erin Cemetery)

Larner, James, 1834-1907 (Mt. Erin Cemetery)

Larner, John C., 1870-1928 (Mt. Erin Cemetery); native of Maryland, resided near Level, born 20 Jul 1870, son of James Larner and Delia Clancy, natives of Ireland (Death certificate)

Larner, Julie M., age 18 in 1890 (Marriage License Applications Book ALJ No. 2, 1891)

Larner, Margaret A., 1874-1966 (Mt. Erin Cemetery)

Larue, Catherine (Mrs.), 1858-1927 (Baker Cemetery)

Larue, Etta, 1866-1946 (Baker Cemetery)

Larue, Martin and Ellis, sold land in November 1890 (*The Aegis & Intelligencer*, 5 Dec 1890)

Larue, William (Mrs.), 1847-1894 (*Havre de Grace Republican*, 21 Sep 1894)

Larue, William H., 1856-1940 (Baker Cemetery)

Lasley, John P., 1886-1949 (Wesleyan Chapel Methodist Church Cemetery)

Last Chance Public School No. 18, near Pylesville (*Harford County, Maryland Teachers and the Schools They Served, 1774-1900*, by Henry C. Peden, Jr., 2022, p. 370)

Latter, Garmmond, Civil War veteran (Confederate), Aberdeen (*1890 Special Census of the Civil War Veterans of the State of Maryland*, by L. Tilden Moore, Volume III, p. 63)

Lauver, Samuel A., Civil War veteran, Perryman (*1890 Special Census of the Civil War Veterans of the State of Maryland*, by L. Tilden Moore, Volume III, p. 64)

Lavalle, Charles, Civil War veteran, Bel Air (*1890 Special Census of the Civil War Veterans of the State of Maryland*, by L. Tilden Moore, Volume III, p. 71); see Eugenia D. Levalley, q.v.

Lavery, John, c1836-1924 (Death certificate; Alms House Record Book)

Law, Robert C., see Viola A. Severs, q.v.

Law, Viola A., see Viola A. Severs, q.v.

Lawder's Meat and Grocery Store, Havre de Grace (*1953 Harford County Directory*, p. 264)

Lawder, Bessie, 1879-1963, native of Havre de Grace, born 12 Feb 1879, daughter of Henry Lawder and Roxanna Moore (Pennington Funeral Home Records - married name Rimmey)

Lawder, Charles W., 1863-1941, native of Havre de Grace, born 1 Jun 1863, son of Samuel Lawder and Caroline Miller (Pennington Funeral Home Records)

Lawder, Esther Rosanna, 1852-1935 (Angel Hill Cemetery); wife of Henry Clay Lawder, Sr., q.v.

Lawder, Frederick Carroll, 1877-1948, native of Havre de Grace, born 15 Jan 1877, son of Henry C. Lawder and Roxanna Moore, both natives of Havre de Grace (Pennington Funeral Home Records)

Lawder, Georgianna, see Robert Seneca Myers, q.v.

Lawder, Grace M., 1889-1964 (Angel Hill Cemetery)

Lawder, Henry [Harry] Clay, Jr., 1881-1964, native of Havre de Grace, born 13 Jun 1881, son of Harry Clay Lawder and Roxanna Moors (Pennington Funeral Home Records; Angel Hill Cemetery)

Lawder, Henry [Harry] Clay, Sr., 1842-1921 (Angel Hill Cemetery); butcher and green grocer, Washington and Green Streets, Havre de Grace (*Havre de Grace Republican*, 31 Jan and 30 May 1890); delegate, Sixth District, Democrat Party Convention (*The Aegis & Intelligencer*, 5 Sep 1890); organizer and vice president, Havre de Grace Democratic Club (*Havre de Grace Republican*, 31 Oct 1890); register of voters, Sixth District (*Havre de Grace Republican*, 21 Feb 1890); see Frederick C. Lawder, Bessie Lawder and Henry [Harry] Clay Lawder, Jr., q.v.

Lawder, Lillian Baldwin (Odell), 1884-1948 (Angel Hill Cemetery)

Lawder, Minnie E., 1861-1908 (Angel Hill Cemetery)

Lawder, Rosalie "Rose" E., see Rosalie E. Boyd, Caroline Boyd, Carroll E. Boyd and Nellie Boyd, q.v.

Lawder, Samuel, see Charles W. Lawder, q.v.

Lawder, Samuel W., 1860-1940 (Angel Hill Cemetery)

Lawder, William M., 1883-1919 (Angel Hill Cemetery)

Lawder, Winnie E., 1861-1908 (Angel Hill Cemetery)

Lawson, Anna (colored), see Robert I. Lawson (colored), q.v.

Lawson, Edward (colored), husband of Sarah Annie Lawson, q.v.

Lawson, Howard, uncalled for letter in Bel Air P. O. (*The Aegis & Intelligencer*, 14 Nov 1890)

Lawson, Mary E. (colored), 1888-1966 (Mt. Calvary Methodist Church Cemetery)

Lawson, Robert I. (colored), 1884-1946, native of Harford Co., son of Anna Lawson and ---- (Death certificate; Berkley Memorial Cemetery tombstone states born 1882)

Lawson, Sarah Annie (colored), 1869-1933, native of Lancaster, PA, resident of Darlington, parents unknown (Death certificate)

Lawson, Tate (colored), 1841-1920 (Death certificate; St. James United Cemetery)

Lay, Adaline (Mrs.), born 1873, died ---- (St. Paul's Lutheran Church Cemetery); wife of August Lay, q.v.

Lay, August, 1873-1932 (St. Paul's Lutheran Church Cemetery)

Lay, Ava Elizabeth, 1867-1902 (St. Paul's Lutheran Church Cemetery); wife of John Lay, q.v.

Lay, Catherine, born 1852, died ----, wife of Frank Lay (St. Paul's Lutheran Church Cemetery)

Lay, Charles, 1865-1932, son of Frank and Catherine Lay (St. Paul's Lutheran Church Cemetery)

Lay, Christine, 1885-1978, native of Havre de Grace, born 13 Sep 1885, daughter of Randolf Lay and Mary ---- (Pennington Funeral Home Records - married name Carroll)

Lay, Christopher, see Mary Lay, q.v.

Lay, Frank, 1860-1917 (St. Paul's Lutheran Church Cemetery)

Lay (Laye), Frank, 1888-1955, native of Perryman, Harford Co., born 28 Nov 1888, son of John C. Laye and Margaret Swope (Pennington Funeral Home Records)

Lay, George E., 1881-1918, native of Maryland, son of John C. Lay and Margaret Schrop [Swope?] (Angel Hill Cemetery; Death certificate)

Lay, John, 1869-1936 (St. Paul's Lutheran Church Cemetery)

Lay (Laye), John C., see Frank Lay (Laye), q.v.

Lay, Katherine (Salzig), 1852-1939, native of Baltimore, resident of Havre de Grace (Death certificate spelled her name Catherine); wife of Frank Lay, q.v.

Lay, Margaret, 1853-1928 (Angel Hill Cemetery)

Lay, Margaret (Thompson), 1876-1955 (Slate Ridge Cemetery, York Co., PA); native of Harford Co., born 20 Oct 1876, daughter of Henry S. Thompson and Frances C. Thompson (Harkins Funeral Home Records)

Lay, Mary, see Christine Lay, q.v.

Lay, Mary, 1863-1919, native of Baltimore, resident of Havre de Grace, born 2 Jan 1863, daughter of Christopher Lay and ---- (Death certificate; Angel Hill Cemetery)

Lay, Randolf, see Christine Lay, q.v.

Lay, Rudolph, 1833-1901 (St. Paul's Lutheran Church Cemetery); resident of Perryman (*The Aegis & Intelligencer*, 19 Sep 1890); trustee, Michaelsville School No. 6, Second District (*Havre de Grace Republican*, 30 May 1890)

Leager, Hannah Jane (Miss) (colored), c1850-1915, native of Maryland (Death certificate)

League, John Wesley, 1839-1928 (Ebenezer Methodist Church Cemetery, Chase, MD); native of Baltimore Co., fisherman, maried, resided at Perryman (Death certificate)

League, T. W., director, Maryland Central Dairymen's Association (*The Aegis & Intelligencer*, 28 Feb 1890)

Leamon, Robert John, 1889-1968 (Slate Ridge Cemetery, York Co., PA); native of Cardiff, Harford Co., born 3 Sep 1889, son of Strome Leamon and Annie Cash (Harkins Funeral Home Records)

Leamon, Strome, see Robert John Leamon, q.v.

Lear, Alice, 1869-1896 (St. George's Episcopal Church Cemetery)

Lear, George W., 1842-1920 (St. George's Episcopal Church Cemetery)

Lear, Mary C. (Shay), 1842-1924, native of Maryland (Death certificate; St. George's Episcopal Church Cemetery); Mrs. George W. Lear, resident of Bush River Neck, 1890 (*The Aegis & Intelligencer*, 24 Jan 1890)

Lear, Mary Martha (Michael), 1865-1961 (St. George's Episcopal Church Cemetery)

Lear, May E., 1885-1935 (Angel Hill Cemetery)

Leatherman, George, Civil War veteran, at Cole (*1890 Special Census of the Civil War Veterans of the State of Maryland*, by L. Tilden Moore, Volume III, p. 65)

Lee, ----, second baseman, Bel Air Victors Baseball Club (*The Aegis & Intelligencer*, 25 Jul 1890)

Lee, Addie Marilla (Swift), 1861-1953, native of Dublin, Harford Co. (Bailey Funeral Home Records); wife of Alexander D. Lee, q.v.

Lee, Addison (Mrs.), resident near Dublin (*The Aegis & Intelligencer*, 18 Jul 1890)

Lee, Addison W., 1860-1936 (Dublin Southern Cemetery); farmer, near Dublin (*The Aegis & Intelligencer*, 4 Apr 1890); W. Addison Lee, served on a petit jury, 1890 (*Havre de Grace Republican*, 14 Feb 1890) see William W. Lee, q.v.

Lee, Alexander D., 1857-1912 (Dublin Southern Cemetery); see Katie S. Temple and Bessie B. Orr, q.v.

Lee, Alice C. (Miss), singer and member, Emmanuel Episcopal Church, Bel Air (*The Aegis & Intelligencer*, 11 Apr 1890); third maid of honor, Bel Air jousting tournament (*Havre de Grace Republican*, 19 Sep 1890); member, Loyal Temperance Legion of Bel Air (*The Aegis & Intelligencer*, 2 May 1890)

Lee, Annie (colored), c1872-1924, daughter of William Lee and Jane Dorsey, all natives of Maryland (Death certificate)

Lee, Annie M., 187-1940 (Rock Run Methodist Church Cemetery); wife of Wade H. Lee, q.v.

Lee, Barbara Baltzell, 1802-1890 (Little Falls Quaker Cemetery); widow of David Lee, of Jerusalem Mills (*The Aegis & Intelligencer*, 24 Oct 1890)

Lee, Bessie, daughter of Otho Scott Lee, graduated from Bel Air Graded School (*The Aegis & Intelligencer*, 4 Jul 1890); singer and member, Emmanuel Episcopal Church, Bel Air (*The Aegis & Intelligencer*, 11 Apr 1890)

Lee, Bettie (Miss), daughter of Barbara Baltzell Lee, q.v.

Lee, Birdie (Miss), resident of Clayton (*The Aegis & Intelligencer*, 21 Feb 1890)

Lee, Blanch Franklin, age 21 in 1890 (Marriage License Applications Book ALJ No. 2, 1891)

Lee, Caroline Webster (Hunter), 1882-1979, wife of John L. G. Lee, q.v.

Lee, Cassie, student and actress, Bel Air Academy and Graded School (*The Aegis & Intelligencer*, 23 May and 26 Dec 1890); premium award winner, Class L - Children's Department, Harford County Fair (*The Aegis & Intelligencer*, 24 Oct 1890)

Lee, Charles, Civil War veteran, at Webster (*1890 Special Census of the Civil War Veterans of the State of Maryland*, by L. Tilden Moore, Volume III, p. 68)

Lee, Charles (colored), see William Lee (colored), q.v.

Lee, Charles (colored), age 21 in 1890 (Marriage License Applications Book ALJ No. 2, 1890)

Lee, Charles Benjamin, 1889-1944 (Dublin Southern Cemetery); native of Harford Co., born 23 Nov 1889, son of Alexander Lee and Addie M Swift (Bailey Funeral Home Records)

Lee, Charles W., constable, Second District (*Havre de Grace Republican*, 4 Jul 1890); Civil War veteran (Confederate), Aberdeen (*1890 Special Census of the Civil War Veterans of the State of Maryland*, by L. Tilden Moore, Volume III, p. 65)

Lee, Daniel H, acquired land in April 1890 (*The Aegis & Intelligencer*, 9 May 1890)

Lee, David (Mrs.), resident of Jerusalem Mills, died (*The Aegis & Intelligencer*, 24 Oct 1890)

Lee, Deliverance Hannah, 1814-1890 (Churchville Presbyterian Church Cemetery); died testate and her named heirs were husband James C. Lee, nieces Mary E. G. Harlan and Delia L. Wilson, nephews R. Harris Archer and George Archer, sister Susanna Archer, brothers James Glasgow and George R. Glasgow, and colored servants Samuel Gibson and Fred Gibson (Harford County Will Book JMM 11:93-95); daughter of Dr. James Glasgow and wife of James Carville Lee, q.v.

Lee, Dolly M. (colored), 1880-1948, native of Maryland, born 19 Oct 1880, daughter of William S. Lee and ---- (Death certificate - married name Cromwell)

Lee, E. Louisa (colored), 1856-1929 (Berkley Memorial Cemetery; Death certificate states Louisa E. Lee was born in 1861); wife of Jacob F. Lee, q.v.

Lee, Edward (colored), 1879-1899, resident of Bel Air (Death certificate)

Lee, Edward (colored), 1890-1890 (Berkley Memorial Cemetery)

Lee, Edward K., born -- Dec 1888, baptized 10 Mar 1889, son of Isaac and Sarah (Kehoe) Lee (St. Ignatius Catholic Church Baptism Register, p. 103)

Lee, Elizabeth G. (Mrs.), of Bel Air, sister of John Briarly, of Winchester, VA (*The Aegis & Intelligencer*, 3 Oct 1890); member, Loyal Temperance Legion of Bel Air (*The Aegis & Intelligencer*, 2 May 1890)

Lee, Elizabeth Olivia (colored), 1890-1990, native of Perryman, Harford Co. (*The Aegis*, 15 Aug 1990; *Havre de Grace Record*, 15 May 1990)

Lee, Ella (McCann), 1859-1926 (Darlington Cemetery); wife of Addison W. Lee, q.v.

Lee, Emma (colored), age 21 in 1890 (Marriage License Applications Book ALJ No. 2, 1891)

Lee, Francis Granville, 1890-1973 (Mountain Christian Church Cemetery)

Lee, Francis Lightfoot, 1879-1942 (Centre Methodist Church Cemetery); native of Maryland, born 22 Aug 1879, son of William Lee and Josephine Oren (Death certificate); Francis Lee, third grade honor student, Bel Air Academy and Graded School (*The Aegis & Intelligencer*, 4 Jul 1890)

Lee, George (colored), 1851-1921, native of Maryland, son of Bruce Bond and Georgeanna Lee (Death certificate); also see James Lee, q.v.

Lee, Georgeanna (colored), see Sarah Ann Brown (colored) and George Lee (colored), q.v.

Lee, Hannah (colored), 1883-1951, native of Rock Run, Harford Co., born 24 Sep 1883, daughter of Sidney Lee and Mary Peaco, natives of Maryland (Death certificate)

Lee, Hannah B., daughter of Col. Otho S. Lee, of Bel Air (*The Aegis & Intelligencer*, 24 Jan 1890)

Lee, Harrison (colored), husband of Nelle E. Lee, q.v.

Lee, Harrison C. (colored), 1890-1978, native of Maryland, born 2 Apr 1890, son of Sidney Lee and Ellen Pekoe [Peaco] (St. James United Cemetery; Pennington Funeral Home Records misakenly stated he was white)

Lee, Harry, student, Bel Air Academy and Graded School (*The Aegis & Intelligencer*, 23 May 1890)

Lee, Harry F., resident of Bel Air, and brother of Miss Virginia Lee (*The Aegis & Intelligencer*, 15 Aug 1890); member, Division No. 2, Bel Air Fire and Salvage Corps (*The Aegis & Intelligencer*, 10 Oct 1890); private, Jackson Guards, 1889-1890 [Co. D, 1st Regiment, Maryland National Guard] (*The Aegis & Intelligencer*, 11 Jan 1889)

Lee, Helen M., daughter of Otho Scott Lee, of Bel Air (*The Aegis & Intelligencer*, 6 Jun 1890)

Lee, Helene A. (Bradshaw) (Bateman), 1874-1929, second wife of Otho S. Lee, q.v.

Lee, Henry (colored), see John Kenly (colored), q.v.

Lee, Hezekiah (colored), 1884-1910 (Death certificate)

Lee, Isabella (colored), age 18 in 1890 (Marriage License Applications Book ALJ No. 2, 1891)

Lee, J. Frank (colored), 1880-1954, native of Havre de Grace, born -- Apr 1880, son of William Sidney Lee and Mary Ellen Peaco (Pennington Funeral Home Records)

Lee, Jacob Frank (colored), 1851-1928 (Berkley Memorial Cemetery); native of Maryland, farmer, married, resided at Darlington (Death certificate)

Lee, James (colored), 1873-1928, native of Harford Co., born 1 Apr 1873, son of Jube Lee and Betty Clark (Death certificate); see Jupiter Lee, q.v.

Lee, James (colored), c1874-1914, son of George Lee and Susan Hall (Death certificate)

Lee, James, 1847-1916 (Holy Trinity Episcopal Church Cemetery); farmer and cattle raiser at *Cool Spring Farm* in Thomas Run Valley and an organizer of the Harford National Bank (*Biographical Dictionary of Harford County, Maryland, 1774-1974*, by Henry C. Peden, Jr. and William O. Carr, 2021, p. 162); trustee, Thomas Run School No. 9, Third District (*Havre de Grace Republican*, 30 May 1890); vestryman, [Holy] Trinity Church, Churchville (*Havre de Grace Republican*, 18 Apr 1890); age 42 in 1889 (Marriage License Applications Book ALJ No. 2, 1889)

Lee, James C. (colored), 1890-1968 (Union Methodist Church Cemetery, Aberdeen)

Lee, James Carville (Mrs.), resident at Thomas Run (*The Aegis & Intelligencer*, 28 Mar 1890); see Deliverance Hannah Lee, q.v.

Lee, Jennie (colored), 1876-1958, native of Rock Run, Harford Co., born 30 Aug 1876, daughter of William S. Lee and Mary Ellen Peaco (Pennington Funeral Home Records - married name Daugherty)

Lee, Jennie (colored), age 20 in 1889 (Marriage License Applications Book ALJ No. 2, 1890), married James Henry Jamison on 6 Feb 1890 (marriage certificate)

Lee, Jane (colored), see Lucretia Lee (colored), q.v.

Lee, Jim (colored), resident of Bel Air (*The Aegis & Intelligencer*, 27 Jun 1890)

Lee, John H., Civil War veteran, Chestnut Hill (*1890 Special Census of the Civil War Veterans of the State of Maryland*, by L. Tilden Moore, Volume III, p. 74)

Lee, John Leypold Griffith, 1869-1952 (Christ Episcopal Church Cemetery); treasurer and executive committee, Bel Air Academy Association (*Havre de Grace Republican*, 11 Jul 1890)

Lee, John S. (colored), 1882-1964 (Cedars Chapel Cemetery)

Lee, Josiah (colored), 1852-1908 (Tabernacle Mt. Zion Methodist Church Cemetery); resident in or near Bel Air (*The Aegis & Intelligencer*, 25 Apr 1890); Josiah Lee, and wife, conveyed land in April 1890 (*The Aegis & Intelligencer*, 9 May 1890); see Lucretia Lee, q.v.

Lee, Jube, Jr. (colored), age 21 in 1890 (Marriage License Applications Book ALJ No. 2, 1891)

Lee, Jupiter "Jube" (colored), 1837-1919 (Death certificate); trustee, Colored School No. 4, Fourth District (*Havre de Grace Republican*, 30 May 1890); see James Lee, q.v.

Lee, Lillie (colored), 1884-1986 (Cedars Chapel Cemetery); wife of John S. Lee, q.v.

Lee, Loucinder (colored), 1889-1890 (Berkley Memorial Cemetery)

Lee, Louis (colored), 1849-1899, laborer in Lapidum, native of Virginia (Death certificate)

Lee, Louise (Mrs.), treated by unidentified doctor in 1890 ("Medical Account Book – 1890," Historical Society of Harford County Archives Folder)

Lee, Lucretia (colored), c1875-1950, native of Fallston, Harford Co., daughter of Josiah Lee and Jane ---- (Death certificate - married name Scott)

Lee, Mamie A. (Lowe), 1883-1967 (Slate Ridge Cemetery, York Co., PA); native of Street, Harford Co., born 15 Mar 1883, daughter of William Lowe and Mary Few (Harkins Funeral Home Records)

Lee, Mary, county out-pensioner [welfare recipient], Second District (*Havre de Grace Republican*, 4 Jul 1890)

Lee, Mary (colored), c1875-1931, daughter of Abraham Lee and ---- (Death certificate - married name Gould)

Lee, Mary Elizabeth (Whitaker), 1850-1938, wife of James Lee, q.v.

Lee, Mary Ellen (Peaco) (colored), 1863-1938, native of Harford Co. (Death certificate); wife of William Sidney Lee, q.v.

Lee, Mary H. (Peco) (colored), 1859-1890 (Berkley Memorial Cemetery)

Lee, Nellie E. (Mrs.) (colored), 1873-1976, native of Churchville (*The Aegis*, 5 Jul 1979)

Lee, Oliver, third grade student, Fallston School (*The Aegis & Intelligencer*, 21 Feb 1890)

Lee, Otho, student, Bel Air Graded School (*The Aegis & Intelligencer*, 11 Apr 1890)

Lee, Otho S. (Mrs.), premium award winner, Class I - Agricultural Productions, Harford County Fair (*The Aegis*

Lee, Otho Scott (colonel), 1840-1918 (Christ Episcopal Church Cemetery); attorney, Bel Air (*Havre de Grace Republican*, 10 Jan 1890); Civil War (Confederate Army) veteran (*Havre de Grace Republican*, 30 May 1890); delegate, Third District, Democrat Party Convention (*The Aegis & Intelligencer*, 5 Sep 1890); director, Bel Air Fire Company, Inc. (*Havre de Grace Republican*, 19 Sep 1890); incorporator and chairman, Bel Air Fire and Salvage Corps (*The Aegis & Intelligencer*, 19 Sep 1890); member, Division No. 1, Bel Air Fire and Salvage Corps (*The Aegis & Intelligencer*, 10 Oct 1890); president, Bel Air Water and Light Company (*Havre de Grace Republican*, 14 Feb 1890); trustee, Bel Air School No. 14, Third District (*Havre de Grace Republican*, 30 May 1890); also see Bessie Lee and Helen M. Lee, q.v.

Lee, Parker A., age 39 in 1890 (Marriage License Applications Book ALJ No. 2, 1890), married Martha J. Creswell, of Baltimore County, on 17 Dec 1890 at Jarrettsville M. E. Parsonage (*The Aegis & Intelligencer*, 26 Dec 1890)

Lee, Parker Hall, 1818-1896 (Holy Trinity Episcopal Church Cemetery)

Lee, R. Charles, son of Barbara Baltzell Lee, q.v.

Lee, R. H., manager, Bel Air Stars Baseball Club (*The Aegis & Intelligencer*, 9 May 1890)

Lee, R. Henry, student, Bel Air Graded School (*The Aegis & Intelligencer*, 11 Apr 1890)

Lee, Richard D. (Dr.), 1826-1890 (Christ Episcopal Church Cemetery); physician, Bel Air (*Havre de Grace Republican*, 7 Feb 1890)

Lee, Rosa Coale, 1890-1969 (Churchville Presbyterian Church Cemetery)

Lee, S. Cassie, student, Third District (*The Aegis & Intelligencer*, 24 Oct 1890)

Lee, Samuel M., farmer, Thomas Run (*The Aegis & Intelligencer*, 17 Jan 1890)

Lee, Sarah Biays (Griffith), 1840-1898, first wife of Otho Scott Lee, q.v.

Lee, Sidney (colored), see Hannah Lee (colored) and Harrison C. Lee (colored), q.v.

Lee, Susan, see Lillie Belle Griffith, q.v.

Lee, Thomas W. (colored), 1883-1973 (*The Aegis*, 19 Mar 1973)

Lee, Virginia, see Harry F. Lee, q.v.

Lee, Wade H., 1877-1953 (Rock Run Methodist Church Cemetery)

Lee, Walter W., captain and second baseman, Bel Air Victors Baseball Club (*The Aegis & Intelligencer*, 27 Jun 1890); W. Lee, left fielder, Bel Air Victors Baseball Club (*The Aegis & Intelligencer*, 30 May 1890)

Lee, William, 1825-1900, florist, Bel Air (*The Aegis & Intelligencer*, 15 Aug 1890; Death certificate incomplete)

Lee, William, see Francis Lightfoot Lee, q.v.

Lee, William (colored), 1869-1933, native of Harford Co., born 23 Jun 1869, son of Charles Lee, of Harford Co., and Mary J. Washington, of Philadelphia (Death certificate)

Lee, William (colored), see Annie Lee (colored), q.v.

Lee, William D. (Mrs.), premium award winner, Class J - Domestic Products, Harford County Fair (*The Aegis & Intelligencer*, 24 Oct 1890)

Lee, William Dallam, 1853-1902 (Holy Trinity Episcopal Church Cemetery); member, Deer Creek Farmers' Club (*Havre de Grace Republican*, 3 Oct 1890); warden, Holy Trinity Episcopal Church (*Havre de Grace Republican*, 18 Apr 1890); associate judge of elections, Churchville Precinct (*Havre de Grace Republican*, 17 Oct 1890); census taker for the Churchville Precinct: inhabitants 1,351; farms 159; establishments 30 of which 21 are canning houses; deaths past year 12; Union veterans 13; number of dwelling houses about 256; number of families about 259 (*The Aegis & Intelligencer*, 22 Aug 1890)

Lee, William Dean, born 10 Apr 1874 (*The Hughes Genealogy, 1636-1953*, by Joseph Lee Hughes, 1953, p. 117)

Lee, William Sidney (colored), 1853-1940, native of Harford Co. (Death certificate); see Dolly M. Lee, J. Frank

Lee, Jennie Lee and Mary Ellen Lee, q.v.

Lee, William W., 1883-1967 (Dublin Methodist Church Cemetery); native of Dublin, Harford Co., born 7 Nov 1883, son of Addison W. Lee and Ella P. McCann (Harkins Funeral Home Records)

Leedy, Clarence, 1868-1948 (Bethel Presbyterian Church Cemetery Records)

Leedy, Florence, 1870-1934 (Bethel Presbyterian Church Cemetery Records); wife of Clarence Leedy, q.v.

Leeper, John, uncalled for letter in Bel Air P. O. (*The Aegis & Intelligencer*, 14 Nov 1890)

Leffler, Albert, 1846-1909 (Angel Hill Cemetery); storekeeper, Union Ave. & St. Clair Street, Havre de Grace (*Havre de Grace Republican*, 4 Jul 1890); see Clara A. Leffler, Mervin J. Leffler and William A. Leffler, q.v.

Leffler, Anna L., 1871-1937 (Angel Hill Cemetery)

Leffler, Clara Augusta, 1879-1954, native of Havre de Grace, born 2 Aug 1879, daughter of Albert Leffler and Elizabeth Moseman (Pennington Funeral Home Records; Angel Hill Cemetery)

Leffler, Cornelia K., 1889-1973 (Angel Hill Cemetery)

Leffler, Edna M., 1881-1933 (St. George's Episcopal Church Cemetery)

Leffler, Elizabeth (Moseman), 1849-1932 (Angel Hill Cemetery); businesswoman (trader's license), Havre de Grace (*Havre de Grace Republican*, 30 May 1890); Mrs. A. Leffler, millinery, Union Avenue, Havre de Grace (*Havre de Grace Republican*, 21 Mar 1890); wife of Albert Leffler, q.v.

Leffler (Leiffler, Leissler?), George A., native of Germany, filed for naturalization on 14 May 1890 (Harford County Circuit Court Minute Book ALJ No. 5, p. 246)

Leffler, Joseph, 1810-1890, native of Wurtemburg, Germany (Mt. Erin Cemetery); deceased and removed from Havre de Grace voter registration list (*Havre de Grace Republican*, 19 Sep 1890)

Leffler, M. Josephine (Visitation Sister Mary James), 1875-1898 (Mt. Erin Cemetery)

Leffler, Mervin Jackson, 1884-1949, native of Havre de Grace, born 20 Sep 1884, son of Albert Leffler and Elizabeth Moseman (Pennington Funeral Home Records; Angel Hill Cemetery)

Leffler, Vesperina M., 1884-1942 (Angel Hill Cemetery)

Leffler, William Arthur, 1876-1961, native of Havre de Grace, born 24 Nov 1876, son of Albert Leffler and Elizabeth Moseman (Pennington Funeral Home Records; Angel Hill Cemetery)

Legal, Elizabeth (colored), see Charles Henry Osborne (Osborn) (colored), q.v.

Legatees, David H., Civil War veteran, Havre de Grace (*1890 Special Census of the Civil War Veterans of the State of Maryland*, by L. Tilden Moore, Volume III, p. 89)

Leger, Frances (colored), see Thomas G. Skinner (colored), q.v.

Leggar, Thomas Edward (colored), c1837-1915 (Death certificate; St. James United Cemetery)

Lego, Arthur, second grade student, Prospect Hill School (*The Aegis & Intelligencer*, 21 Feb 1890)

Lehman, Emma Jane (Brown) (colored), 1881-1978, resided in Havre de Grace, daughter of Zechariah and Cassie Brown (Berkley Memorial Cemetery; *The Aegis*, 2 Feb 1978)

Leib, Andrew, farmer, near Norrisville (*The Aegis & Intelligencer*, 4 Jul 1890)

Leib, Samuel Allen, 1853-1891 (Hopewell Cemetery, York Co., PA); teacher and principal, Norrisville Graded School No. 1, Fourth District, 1889-1891 (*The Aegis & Intelligencer*, 4 Jul 1890 and 29 Aug 1890); president, Harford County School Teachers' Association (*Havre de Grace Republican*, 19 Sep 1890)

Leight, Alice Elizabeth (Moulsdale), 1862-1896 (Cokesbury Memorial Methodist Church Cemetery; James B. Leight Bible, *Maryland Bible Records, Volume 2*, by Henry C. Peden, Jr., 2003, p. 85)

Leight, Dora May, 1867-1946 (Cokesbury Memorial Methodist Church Cemetery)

Leight, Edward Roy, born 19 Nov 1886, son of James B. and Alice E. (Moulsdale) Leight (James B. Leight Bible, *Maryland Bible Records, Volume 2*, by Henry C. Peden, Jr., 2003, p. 85)

Leight, Edna (Murphy), 1884-1950 (Angel Hill Cemetery)

Leight, Emma Louise, born 16 Aug 1883, daughter of James B. and Alice E. (Moulsdale) Leight (James B. Leight Bible, *Maryland Bible Records, Volume 2*, by Henry C. Peden, Jr., 2003, p. 85)

Leight, James Buchanan, 1856-1935 (Cokesbury Memorial Methodist Church Cemetery; James B. Leight Bible, *Maryland Bible Records, Volume 2*, by Henry C. Peden, Jr., 2003, p. 85)

Leight, James Henry, born 2 Feb 1882, son of James B. and Alice E. (Moulsdale) Leight (James B. Leight Bible, *Maryland Bible Records, Volume 2*, by Henry C. Peden, Jr., 2003, p. 85)

Leight, John, 1827-1901, native of Maryland, farmer at Joppa (Death certificate incomplete)

Leight, John Philip, 1850-1915 (Cokesbury Memorial Methodist Church Cemetery); proprietor, Otter Point Fishery on Bush River near Abingdon (*The Aegis & Intelligencer*, 4 Apr 1890, 25 Apr 1890 and 20 Jun 1890); juror, First District (*Havre de Grace Republican*, 31 Jan 1890)

Leight, Joseph T., 1861-1951 (Cokesbury Memorial Methodist Church Cemetery)

Leight, Levinia, 1852-1930 (Cokesbury Memorial Methodist Church Cemetery)

Leight, Nicholas H., of Harford County, incorporator, Gunpowder Permanent Building Association of Baltimore County (*The Aegis & Intelligencer*, 23 May 1890)

Leight, Thomas W., 1871-1915 (Highland Presbyterian Church Cemetery)

Lein, John, age 26 in 1890 (Marriage License Applications Book ALJ No. 2, 1891)

Leithiser, Anne W., born 2 Mar 1879, daughter of Isaac and Catherine Leithiser (Isaac I. Leithiser Bible, *Maryland Bible Records, Volume 1*, by Henry C. Peden, Jr., 2003, p. 151)

Leithiser, Bayard, born 8 Jul 1886, son of Isaac and Catherine Leithiser (Isaac I. Leithiser Bible, *Maryland Bible Records, Volume 1*, by Henry C. Peden, Jr., 2003, p. 151)

Leithiser, Claudia Louis, born 30 Apr 1875, daughter of Isaac and Catherine Leithiser (Isaac I. Leithiser Bible, *Maryland Bible Records, Volume 1*, by Henry C. Peden, Jr., 2003, p. 151)

Leithiser, Ella (Dobson), 1860-1946, daughter of William H. Dobson and Margaret Brown, all natives of Havre de Grace; wife of George S. Leithiser (Pennington Funeral Home Records)

Leithiser, Emma Oneida, 1880-1950, native of Havre de Grace, born 11 Nov 1880, daughter of Isaac I. Leithiser and Catherine A. Bayard (Isaac I. Leithiser Bible, *Maryland Bible Records, Volume 1*, by Henry C. Peden, Jr., 2003, p. 151; Pennington Funeral Home Records - married name Baldwin)

Leithiser, George S., husband of Ella (Dobson) Leithiser, q.v.

Leithiser, Hartman, born 29 Mar 1826 (Isaac I. Leithiser Bible, *Maryland Bible Records, Volume 1*, by Henry C. Peden, Jr., 2003, p. 151); Civil War veteran, Havre de Grace (*1890 Special Census of the Civil War Veterans of the State of Maryland*, by L. Tilden Moore, Volume III, p. 92); "Herman Leitheiser" was a government pensioner in 1890 (*The Aegis & Intelligencer*, 15 Aug 1890)

Leithiser, Isaac I., 1853-1923 (Angel Hill Cemetery); see Emma O. Leithiser and Richard H. Leithiser, q.v.

Leithiser, John W., 1828-1906 (Angel Hill Cemetery); waterman and duck hunter, of Havre de Grace (*The Aegis & Intelligencer*, 14 Nov 1890)

Leithiser, Lawrence Brett, born 6 Sep1884, son of Isaac and Catherine Leithiser (Isaac I. Leithiser Bible, *Maryland Bible Records, Volume 1*, by Henry C. Peden, Jr., 2003, p. 151)

Leithiser, Lydia E., businesswoman (trader's license), Havre de Grace (*Havre de Grace Republican*, 30 May 1890, spelled her name Leitheiser)

Leithiser, Myrtle Ruby, born 7 Apr 1889, daughter of Isaac and Catherine Leithiser (Isaac I. Leithiser Bible, *Maryland Bible Records, Volume 1*, by Henry C. Peden, Jr., 2003, p. 151)

Leithiser, Nathaniel, sneak boat duck hunter (*Havre de Grace Republican*, 7 Nov 1890)

Leithiser, Rebecca Eleanora (Foster), 1879-1957 (Angel Hill Cemetery)

Leithiser, Richard Henry, 1877-1961, native of Havre de Grace, born 19 Mar 1877, son of Isaac Leithiser and Katherine Bayard (Pennington Funeral Home Records; Angel Hill Cemetery; Isaac I. Leithiser Bible, *Maryland*

Bible Records, Volume 1, by Henry C. Peden, Jr., 2003, p. 151)

Leithiser, Sarah, 1832-1903 (Angel Hill Cemetery); wife of John W. Leithiser, q.v.

Lemmon, Austin, 1884-1890, son of Austin S. C. and Louisa (Bahr) Lemmon (Bethel Presbyterian Church Cemetery)

Lemmon, Austin S. C., 1858-1923 (Bethel Presbyterian Church Cemetery); trustee, Madonna School No. 9, Fourth District (*Havre de Grace Republican*, 30 May 1890)

Lemmon, Cleveland H., born 1884, son of George and Mollie (King) Lemmon (Bethel Presbyterian Church Cemetery Records)

Lemmon, Elizabeth, born 23 May 1883, daughter of Christopher Columbus and Annie (Hunter) Slade (Bethel Presbyterian Church Cemetery Records); see Elizabeth Anderson, q.v.

Lemmon, Estelle, born 11 Apr 1874, daughter of George and Mollie (King) Lemmon (Bethel Presbyterian Church Cemetery Records); see Estelle (Lemmon) Woodrow, q.v.

Lemmon, George Holmes, born 1882, son of George and Mollie (King) Lemmon (Bethel Presbyterian Church Cemetery Records)

Lemmon, George W., 1825-1898 (Bethel Presbyterian Church Cemetery Records); juror, Fourth District (*Havre de Grace Republican*, 31 Oct 1890)

Lemmon, Ida Lurretta (Brookhart), 1885-1961 (Bethel Presbyterian Church Cemetery Records); wife of Cleveland H. Lemmon, q.v.

Lemmon, Laura (Standiford), 1881-1959 (Bethel Presbyterian Church Cemetery Records); wife of George Holmes Lemmon, q.v.

Lemmon, Louisa (Bahr), 1858-1923 (Bethel Presbyterian Church Cemetery Records); wife of Austin S.C. Lemmon, q.v.

Lemmon, Mary Jane (King), 1844-1901 (Bethel Presbyterian Church Cemetery Records); wife of George W. Lemmon, q.v.

Lenoir, Andrew (colored), 1868-1922, native of Ohio (Death certificate)

Lenoir, Florence (colored), 1877-1940 (Death certificate); see Florence Peaker, q.v.

Lenord, Florence (colored), wife of William Lenord, q.v.

Lenord, William (colored), 1855-1935, native of Maryland (Death certificate)

Leonard, Amelia (colored), see John W. Morgan (colored), q.v.

Leonard, Charles J., age 31 in 1890 (Marriage License Applications Book ALJ No. 2, 1891); junior deacon, Susquehanna Lodge No. 130, A. F. & A. M. (*Havre de Grace Republican*, 11 Jul 1890 and 26 Dec 1890)

Leonard, William R., age 30 in 1890 (Marriage License Applications Book ALJ No. 2, 1890)

Leovott, W. B., uncalled for letter in Bel Air P. O., 1890 (*The Aegis & Intelligencer*, 14 Nov 1890)

Leslie, Earlene (Mrs.), 1890-1947 (Death certificate; St. James United Cemetery)

Lesse, Harry C., 1886-1890 (Cokesbury Memorial Methodist Church Cemetery)

Leucke, Christina (Horn), 1853-1928 (Trinity Evangelical Lutheran Church Cemetery); native of Maryland, resided at Joppa Death certificate)

Levalley, Eugenia D., born -- Apr 1889, baptized 30 May 1889, daughter of Charles Levalley, native of Canada, and Eliza Elizabeth *(sic)* Reilly (St. Ignatius Catholic Church Baptism Register, p. 106)

Level Colored Public School No. 1, near Level, Second District (*Harford County, Maryland Teachers and the Schools They Served, 1774-1900*, by Henry C. Peden, Jr., 2022, p. 370)

Levering, Emily (Miss), premium award winner, Class O - Discretionary, Harford County Fair (*The Aegis & Intelligencer*, 24 Oct 1890)

Levering, Sarah (Miss), donated land to the Baltimore Synod as a site for a boys industrial home (*Harford Democrat*, 21 Nov 1890)

Leviness, Joseph, 1859-1926 (Death certificate; Alms House Record Book)

Levy's Department Store, Havre de Grace (*1953 Harford County Directory*, p. 265)

Levy, Henry, businessman (trader's license), Havre de Grace (*Havre de Grace Republican*, 30 May 1890)

Lewin, Lydia L., 1818-1893 (Broad Creek Friends Cemetery)

Lewis, Addison Leroy, 1888-1985 (Angel Hill Cemetery)

Lewis, Adelaide H. (Schad), 1855-1916 (Little Falls Quaker Cemetery); native of Georgetown, DC, resided near Jerusalem Mill (Death certificate)

Lewis, Alvin M., 1871-1925 (Centre Methodist Church Cemetery)

Lewis, Ann Elmira, 1837-1895 (Little Falls Quaker Cemetery)

Lewis, Anna Belle Whaley (Jones), 1875-1907 (Wesleyan Chapel Methodist Church Cemetery); wife of Robert L. Lewis, q.v.

Lewis, Aura A., 1878-1953 (Emory Methodist Church Cemetery)

Lewis, Charles Morton, 1888-1950 (Mountain Christian Church Cemetery)

Lewis, Charlie (colored), 1849-1928 (Mt. Calvary Methodist Church Cemetery, Aberdeen); preacher, native of Maryland (Death certificate)

Lewis, Claude M., 1890-1929 (Centre Methodist Church Cemetery)

Lewis, David, 1850-1910 (Smith Chapel Methodist Church Cemetery)

Lewis, David J, 1819-1905 (Fallston Methodist Church Cemetery); Mr. & Mrs. David Lewis, residents of *Magnolia Heights* near Fallston (*The Aegis & Intelligencer*, 19 Dec 1890)

Lewis, Edna C., 1886-1947 (Mountain Christian Church Cemetery)

Lewis, Eloiza S., 1843-1918 (Little Falls Quaker Cemetery)

Lewis, Emma J. (Rutledge), 1842-1925 (Bethel Presbyterian Church Cemetery Records)

Lewis, Frank Spencer, 1852-1923 (Little Falls Quaker Cemetery)

Lewis, Genelia E., 1872-1944 (Centre Methodist Church Cemetery)

Lewis, Helen Amanda, 1885-1962 (Little Falls Quaker Cemetery)

Lewis, Henrietta M. (Cohen) (colored), 1881-1913, native of Harford Co., born 31 May 1881, daughter of William Cohen, of Harford Co., and Mary A. Price, of Boston, MA (Death certificate)

Lewis, Howard W., 1877-1946 (Mountain Christian Church Cemetery)

Lewis, Joseph Horace, 1889-1978 (Mountain Christian Church Cemetery)

Lewis, Maria (colored), see Sarah Holland (colored), q.v.

Lewis, Mary, see William M. Williams, q.v.

Lewis, Mary Elizabeth (colored), 1863-1938, native of Maryland, wife of John Wesley Grinage; see Charles Washington Grinage, q.v.

Lewis, Maud (Miss), member, Mountain Reading Circle (*The Aegis & Intelligencer*, 21 Feb 1890)

Lewis, Nelly, 1826-1891 (St. Mary's Episcopal Church Cemetery)

Lewis, Olevia S., 1885-1927 (Mountain Christian Church Cemetery)

Lewis, Oscar E., 1876-1958 (Emory Methodist Church Cemetery)

Lewis, Paul W., 1853-1927 (St. Francis de Sales Catholic Church Cemetery)

Lewis, Rainbow (colored), 1855-1933 (Chestnut Grove Church Cemetery)

Lewis, Robert Kendall, 1865-1919 (Wesleyan Chapel Methodist Church Cemetery)

Lewis, Rosetta (Douglas) (colored), 1868-1920 (Death certificate)

Lewis, Sarah Elizabeth, born 16 Apr 1874, daughter of George L. and Pamelia A. Lewis (Holy Trinity Episcopal Church Register of Baptisms, p. 82)

Lewis, Sarah L. (colored), see William P. Wilmore (colored), q.v.

Lewis, Sarah S., 1823-1902 (Fallston Methodist Church Cemetery)

Lidde, Thomas, see Annie M. Lamb, q.v.

Lieske, Frederick, 1868-1936 (St. Paul's Lutheran Church Cemetery)

Lieske, Lena, 1874-1907, born in Neuwiler, Wuertemburg, Germany, died at Perryman; first wife of Frederick Lieske (St. Paul's Lutheran Church Cemetery tombstone inscribed Leiske)

Lieske, Magdalena, born 1881, died ----, second wife of Frederick Lieske (St. Paul's Lutheran Church Cemetery)

Ligeo, Julia (colored), 1799-1899, resident of Clayton, native of Maryland (Death certificate)

Lilly, Adeline, see Edwin W. Davis, q.v.

Lilly, Alfred, student, Harford Furnace School (*The Aegis & Intelligencer*, 14 Feb 1890)

Lilly, Annette Isabel, born 15 Mar 1878, daughter of William and Mary Lilly (Holy Trinity Episcopal Church Register of Baptisms, p. 82)

Lilly, Bertha, student, Harford Furnace School, First District (*The Aegis & Intelligencer*, 14 Feb and 24 Oct 1890)

Lilly, Ellen, died 2 May 1890 in her 52nd year (St. Francis de Sales Catholic Church Cemetery); wife of Samuel Lilly (*The Aegis & Intelligencer*, 9 May 1890)

Lilly, Emma V., 1879-1960 (Baker Cemetery)

Lilly, George Harrison, 1890-1895 (Smith Chapel Methodist Church Cemetery)

Lilly, Laura V., 1851-1930 (St. Francis de Sales Catholic Church Cemetery)

Lilly, Martha Bertha, 1878-1966 (St. Francis de Sales Catholic Church Cemetery)

Lilly, Mary, see James Silas White, q.v.

Lilly, Mary Elizabeth, 1845-1928 (Holy Trinity Episcopal Church Cemetery), see Annette Isabel Lilly, q.v.

Lilly, Robert H., 1859-1934 (Smith Chapel Methodist Church Cemetery); native of Harford Co., farmer, near Havre de Grace (Death certificate)

Lilly, Samuel, see Ellen Lilly, q.v.

Lilly, Sarah E., 1863-1949 (Smith Chapel Methodist Church Cemetery)

Lilly, Susan, see Robert White, q.v.

Lilly, William T., 1844-1933 (Holy Trinity Episcopal Church Cemetery); Civil War veteran, Cburchville (*1890 Special Census of the Civil War Veterans of the State of Maryland*, by L. Tilden Moore, Volume III, p. 66); William Lily *(sic)*, treated by unidentified doctor in 1890 ("Medical Account Book – 1890," Historical Society of Harford County Archives Folder); also see Annette Isabel Lilly, q.v.

Lilly, Willie, student, Harford Furnace School (*The Aegis & Intelligencer*, 14 Feb 1890)

Lilly, Winfield Coale, 1887-1898 (Smith Chapel Methodist Church Cemetery)

Lincoln, George, see Inez Hopkins, q.v.

Lincoln, Inez, see Inez Hopkins, q.v.

Lingan, Alice Ann (Duff), 1810-1890, widow of Edward Lingan (1796-1885) and mother-in-law of John S. Quinn, of near Hickory (*The Aegis & Intelligencer*, 7 Nov 1890; St. Ignatius Catholic Church Cemetery); mother of James T. Lingan, q.v.

Lingan, Ann Elizabeth, born -- Dec 1889, baptized 5 Jan 1890, daughter of Edward and Mary (Lynch) Lingan (St. Ignatius Catholic Church Baptism Register, p. 110)

Lingan, Anna Mary (Mrs.), 1845-1926 (St. Ignatius Catholic Church Cemetery)

Lingan, David N., 1850-1930 (St. Ignatius Catholic Church Cemetery)

Lingan, Edward, see Thomas Henry Lingan and Alice Ann Lingan, q.v.

Lingan, Edward F., property owner adjacent to Broadway in Bel Air in 1890 (*The Aegis & Intelligencer*, 16 May 1890); member, Bel Air Cornet Band (*The Aegis & Intelligencer*, 1 Aug 1890); son of Alice Ann Lingan, q.v.

Lingan, Edward Herman Stump, born -- Jul 1890, baptized 7 Nov 1890, son of David and Harriet L. (Councilman) Lingan (St. Ignatius Catholic Church Baptism Register, p. 116)

Lingan, Elizabeth Ann (Wann), c1837-1892 (Christ Episcopal Church Cemetery); wife of John F. Lingan, q.v.

Lingan, Harriet L. (Counselman), 1859-1932 (Christ Episcopal Church Cemetery)

Lingan, James T., 1842-1926 (St. Ignatius Catholic Church Cemetery); member, Bel Air Cornet Band (*The Aegis & Intelligencer*, 1 Aug 1890); member, Division No. 1, Bel Air Fire and Salvage Corps (*The Aegis & Intelligencer*, 10 Oct 1890); private, later sergeant, Jackson Guards [Co. D, 1st Regiment, Maryland National Guard], 1889-1890 (*The Aegis & Intelligencer*, 11 Jan 1889 and 28 Nov 1890); son of Alice Ann Lingan, q.v.

Lingan, John Edward, born -- Jul 1885, baptized 16 Aug 1885, son of G. Edward and Mary E. (Lynch) Lingan (St. Ignatius Catholic Church Baptism Register, p. 82)

Lingan, John F., 1834-1913 (Christ Episcopal Church Cemetery); town commissioner, Bel Air (*The Aegis & Intelligencer*, 9 May 1890); master builder and contractor, Bel Air (*Havre de Grace Republican*, 1 Aug 1890); lieutenant, Jackson Guards [Co. D., First Regiment, Maryland National Guard] (*Havre de Grace Republican*, 5 Dec 1890); son of Alice Ann Lingan, q.v.

Lingan, John T., 1860-1931 (Christ Episcopal Church Cemetery)

Lingan, Margaret Teresa, born 30 Apr 1884, baptized 2 Jul 1884, daughter of Edward and Mary (Wright) Lingan (St. Ignatius Catholic Church Baptism Register, p. 73)

Lingan, Mary, student, Bel Air Graded School (*The Aegis & Intelligencer*, 26 Dec 1890)

Lingan, Mary E. (Lynch), 1858-1926, wife of William Edward Lingan, q.v.

Lingan, Mary Estella, born -- Apr 1887, baptized 22 May 1887, daughter of Edward and Mary (Wright) Lingan (St. Ignatius Catholic Church Baptism Register, p. 93)

Lingan, Robert (colored), drowned in the Chesapeake Bay near Havre de Grace on 25 May 1890 (*The Aegis & Intelligencer*, 30 May 1890)

Lingan, Robert Harry, 1873-1953 (Mt. Tabor Methodist Church Cemetery); Harry Lingan, member, Bel Air Cornet Band, 1890 (*The Aegis & Intelligencer*, 1 Aug 1890)

Lingan, Thomas Henry, baptized 16 Aug 1882, son of Edward and Mary (Wright) Lingan (St. Ignatius Catholic Church Baptism Register, p. 61)

Lingan, William Edward, 1860-1936 (New Cathedral Cemetery, Baltimore); member, Division No. 1, Bel Air Fire and Salvage Corps (*The Aegis & Intelligencer*, 10 Oct 1890)

Lingham, Amanda Jane (colored), 1854-1909, born at Stepney, Harford Co. (Death certificate; wife of Robert Lingham, q.v.

Lingham, Charles A. (colored), see Henrietta Lingham (colored), q.v.

Lingham, Charlotte (colored), see Annie R. Butler (colored), q.v.

Lingham, Henrietta (colored), widow of Charles A. Lingham, a Civil War veteran, Havre de Grace (*1890 Special Census of the Civil War Veterans of the State of Maryland*, by L. Tilden Moore, Volume III, p. 89)

Lingham, Jennie C. (Berry) (colored), 1874-1961 (John Wesley Methodist Church Cemetery, Abingdon); wife of Robert W. Lingham, q.v.

Lingham, Lillian R. (colored), 1886-1962 (John Wesley Methodist Church Cemetery, Abingdon)

Lingham, Mary A. (colored), c1873-1911, native of Maryland, daughter of Robert Lingham and Amanda Norris (Death certificate - married named Currington)

Lingham Robert (colored), see Amanda Jane Lingham, Mary A. Lingham and William Lingham, q.v.

Lingham, Robert W. (colored), 1870-1946 (John Wesley Methodist Church Cemetery, Abingdon)

Lingham, T. Edward (colored), 1879-1960 (John Wesley Methodist Church Cemetery, Abingdon)

Lingham, William (colored), 1877-1964, native of Abingdon, Harford Co., born 19 Jul 1877, son of Robert Lingham and Amanda Norton (Death certificate)

Linkous, Launa, 1876-1948 (Highland Presbyterian Church Cemetery)

Linkous, Sarah M. (Sparks), 1875-1933 (Highland Presbyterian Church Cemetery)

Linkous, William W., 1872-1955 (Highland Presbyterian Church Cemetery)

Lisbon, Adam (colored), c1837-1912, resident of Cooptown (Death certificate)

Lisby, Annie (Jones) (colored), c1868-1914, native of Harford Co. (Death certificate)

Lisby, Charlie H. (colored), 1854-1925, native of Maryland (Death certificate)

Lisby, Eliza (colored), see Frank Anna Hollingsworth, Nellie R. Jackson, Mary E. Johnson, and Emily A. Parker, q.v.

Lisby, Eliza Jane (colored), mother of Daniel Reese Stansbury and Mary (Stansbury) Smith, q.v.

Lisby, George (colored), c1857-1931, native of Maryland (Death certificate)

Lisby, John (colored), 1816-1900, laborer, native of Harford Co., resided at Gravelly Hill (Death certificate)

Lisby, John Wesley (colored), 1847-1939, native of Maryland (Death certificate)

Lisby, Joseph Henry (colored), 1837-1931, native of Maryland (Death certificate)

Lisby, Mary, of Havre de Grace, and of unsound mind, sent to Alms House, 1890 (*The Aegis & Intelligencer*, 5 Sep 1890); Mary Ellen Lisby died 10 Aug 1892, no age given (Alms House Record Book)

Lisby, Mary (Presbury) (colored), 1844-1925 (Death certificate)

Lisby, Phoebe (Hollis) (colored), 1854-1928, parents unknown (Death certificate)

Lisby, Solomon J. (colored), 1848-1911, native of Maryland (Death certificate)

Liskey, Emma, of Perryman, married Peter Wirsing, of Baltimore County, on 19 Oct 1890 in Perryman (*The Aegis & Intelligencer*, 7 Nov 1890)

List, Christian, Civil War veteran, Pylesville (*1890 Special Census of the Civil War Veterans of the State of Maryland*, by L. Tilden Moore, Volume III, p. 83)

List, Jacob, Civil War veteran, Pylesville (*1890 Special Census of the Civil War Veterans of the State of Maryland*, by L. Tilden Moore, Volume III, p. 83); see Emma J. Duncan, q.v.

Litchfield, George, see Martha Emily Litchfield, q.v.

Litchfield, George W., 1880-1953 (Trinity Evangelical Lutheran Church Cemetery)

Litchfield, Martha Emily, 1877-1902, native of Harford Co, born 28 Aug 1877, daughter of George Litchfield and Lizzie Parker (Death certificate - married name Chilcoat; Mountain Christian Church Cemetery)

Little Falls Friends Meeting House and Cemetery (Old Fallston Road, Fallston)

Little Gunpowder Colored School, First District (*Harford County, Maryland Teachers and the Schools They Served, 1774-1900*, by Henry C. Peden, Jr., 2022, p. 370)

Little, Amos, government pensioner, Fourth District (*Havre de Grace Republican*, 20 Jun 1890)

Little, Ann Eve (Main), 1871-1904 (Darlington Cemetery)

Little, Annie, 1856-1913 (Rock Run Methodist Church Cemetery); wife of Richard T. Little, q.v.

Little, Archibald, 1862-1935 (Darlington Cemetery)

Little, Archie W., 1888-1969 (Tabernacle Cemetery); native of Harford Co., born 12 Apr 1888, son of Hamilton Little and Mary A. Henry (Harkins Funeral Home Records)

Little, David A., 1870-1924, native of Maryland, born 8 Apr 1870, son of Robert Little and Elizabeth Hamilton, natives of Ireland (Death certificate; Bailey Funeral Home Records)

Little, Elizabeth (Hamilton), 1833-1917, native of Ireland (Darlington Cemetery; Bailey Funeral Home Records); wife of Robert Little, q.v.

Little, Elizabeth M., 1880-1948 (Angel Hill Cemetery)

Little, Hamilton, 1866-1930 (Tabernacle Cemetery); see Archie W. Little and Oliver N. Little, q.v.

Little, James, 1855-1908 (Darlington Cemetery); served on an inquest jury in the Fifth District in 1890 (*The Aegis & Intelligencer*, 1 Aug 1890)

Little, John, see Robert A. Little and Scott W. Little, q.v.

Little, John W., 1889-1971 (Angel Hill Cemetery)

Little, Laura B. (Bulle), 1864-1900, native of Maryland, resided at Dublin, Harford Co.. wife of David Little (Death certificate)

Little, Mary Amanda, 1868-1940 (Tabernacle Cemetery)

Little, Miriam Forwood (Hanway), 1866-1918 (Calvary Methodist Church Cemetery)

Little, Oliver N., 1889-1965 (Tabernacle Cemetery); native of Whiteford, Harford Co., born 29 Jul 1889, son of Hamilton Little and Maize Henry (Harkins Funeral Home Records)

Little, Rachael 1873-1900, native of Maryland, daughter of Robert and Elizabeth Little (Death certificate)

Little, Richard T., 1855-1911 (Rock Run Methodist Church Cemetery)

Little, Robert, 1824-1895 (Darlington Cemetery); see David A. Little and Rachael Little, q.v.

Little, Robert A., 1885-1943 (Darlington Cemetery); native of Harford Co, born 27 Nov 1885, son of John Little and Laura Duff (Bailey Funeral Home Records)

Little, Sarah E., 1888-1959 (Angel Hill Cemetery)

Little, Scott William, 1881-1930 (Dublin Cemetery); native of Maryland, born 14 May 1881, son of John Little and Laura Duff (Bailey Funeral Home Records)

Little, Susan, wife of John O. Orr, q.v.; also see Samuel M. Orr, q.v.

Little, William H., 1889-1973 (Tabernacle Cemetery)

Litzinger, Clarence O., new name on the voter registration list at Magnolia, First District (*Havre de Grace Republican*, 26 Sep 1890)

Litzinger, John E., 1890-1943 (St. George's Episcopal Church Cemetery)

Livesay, Myrtle O., 1872-1952 (Highland Presbyterian Church Cemetery)

Livesay, Robert L., 1867-1943 (Highland Presbyterian Church Cemetery)

Livezey, Annie Louise (Nagle), 1876-1930 (Baker Cemetery)

Livezey, Della May, 1882-1912 (Centre Methodist Church Cemetery)

Livezey, Elizabeth, 1870-1953 (Baker Cemetery)

Livezey, Elizabeth Riach (Hutcheson), 1850-1910 (Churchville Presbyterian Church Cemetery)

Livezey, Florence, born 12 Nov 1869, daughter of Thomas and Sylvana Livezey (Thomas N. Livezey Bible, *Maryland Bible Records, Volume 1*, by Henry C. Peden, Jr., 2003, p. 155)

Livezey, Frances E., 1839-1913 (Mt. Zion Methodist Church Cemetery)

Livezey, George Kessler, 1876-1953 (Baker Cemetery); born 20 Sep 1876, son of Thomas and Sylvana Livezey (Thomas N. Livezey Bible, *Maryland Bible Records, Volume 1*, by Henry C. Peden, Jr., 2003, p. 155)

Livezey, Isaac W., postmaster, Paradise, Second District (*Havre de Grace Republican*, 5 Sep 1890); storekeeper, Mechanicsville, Second District (*Havre de Grace Republican*, 7 Nov 1890)

Livezey, Jacob Ott, 1885-1951 (Mt. Carmel Methodist Church Cemetery); born 7 Aug 1885, son of Robert S. and Mary Ann Livezey (Robert S. Livezey Bible, *Maryland Bible Records, Volume 1*, by Henry C. Peden, Jr., 2003, p. 154)

Livezey, Jacob, Jr., 1850-1911 (Mt. Zion Methodist Church Cemetery); Jacob Livezey, and wife, sold land in April 1890 (*The Aegis & Intelligencer*, 9 May 1890)

Livezey, James S., 1890-1965 (Mt. Zion Methodist Church Cemetery); born 21 Aug 1890, son of Robert S. and

Mary Ann Livezey (Robert S. Livezey Bible, *Maryland Bible Records, Volume 1*, by Henry C. Peden, Jr., 2003, p. 154)

Livezey, John, 1834-1897 (Little Falls Quaker Cemetery)

Livezey, Joseph E., Jr., 1866-1899, resided at Watervale, son of Joseph and Fannie Livezey (Death certificate; Mt. Zion Methodist Church Cemetery)

Livezey, Joseph W., 1836-1908 (Churchville Presbyterian Church Cemetery); farmer, at Watervale (*The Aegis & Intelligencer*, 25 Jul 1890); road examiner, Third District (*Havre de Grace Republican*, 4 Jul 1890)

Livezey, Kate E. S., born 9 Jan 1871, daughter of Thomas and Sylvana Livezey (Thomas N. Livezey Bible, *Maryland Bible Records, Volume 1*, by Henry C. Peden, Jr., 2003, p. 155)

Livezey, Louise, 1876-1930 (Baker Cemetery)

Livezey, Mary Ann (Swartz), 1863-1939 (Little Falls Quaker Cemetery); wife of Robert S. Livezey, q.v.

Livezey, Mary J., born 16 Aug 1888, daughter of Robert S. and Mary Ann Livezey (Robert S. Livezey Bible, *Maryland Bible Records, Volume 1*, by Henry C. Peden, Jr., 2003, p. 154)

Livezey, Mary Jane (Roberts), 1863-1935 (Mt. Zion Methodist Church Cemetery)

Livezey, Maude Melicent, 1881-1962 (Mt. Carmel Methodist Church Cemetery); wife of Jacob Ott Livezey, q.v.

Livezey, Priscilla, 1842-1910 (Little Falls Quaker Cemetery)

Livezey, Robert H., 1886-1976 (Mt. Zion Methodist Church Cemetery); born 23 Dec 1886, son of Robert S. and Mary Ann Livezey (Robert S. Livezey Bible, *Maryland bible Records, Volume 1*, by Henry C. Peden, Jr., 2003, p. 154)

Livezey, Robert S., 1854-1927 (Little Falls Quaker Cemetery); "an extensice farmer of old Quaker stock," born 15 Aug 1854, son of Jacob Livezey (Robert S. Livezey Bible, *Maryland Bible Records, Volume 1*, by Henry C. Peden, Jr., 2003, pp. 153-154); Robert and Mary Ann, residents near Churchville, sold land in April 1890 (*The Aegis & Intelligencer*, 9 May 1890 and 29 Aug 1890)

Livezey, Sylvania (Stewart), 1849-1924 (Mt. Zion Methodist Church Cemetery); wife of Thomas Nice Livezey, q.v.

Livezey, Thomas Franklin, 1851-1923 (Churchville Presbyterian Church Cemetery); farmer, near Thomas Run (*The Aegis & Intelligencer*, 14 Nov 1890)

Livezey, Thomas Nice, 1839-1926 (Mt. Zion Methodist Church Cemetery); native of Pennsylvania, farmer, married, resided near Bel Air (Death certificate)

Livezey, Thomas Nice, Jr., 1880-1959 (Mt. Zion Methodist Church Cemetery); born 25 Nov 1880, son of Thomas and Sylvana Livezey (Thomas N. Livezey Bible, *Maryland Bible Records, Volume 1*, by Henry C. Peden, Jr., 2003, p. 155)

Livingston, John G., age 21 in 1890 (Marriage License Applications Book ALJ No. 2, 1890)

Liziere, William, died 7 May 1894, no age given (Alms House Record Book)

Lloyd's Singing School, Pylesville, Fifth District (*Harford County, Maryland Teachers and the Schools They Served, 1774-1900*, by Henry C. Peden, Jr., 2022, p. 370)

Lloyd, Agnes B. (Beattie), 1884-1969 (Slate Ridge Cemetery, York Co., PA); native of Whiteford, Harford Co., born 17 Nov 1884, daughter of John S. Beattie and Mary M. Norris (Harkins Funeral Home Records)

Lloyd, Benjamin, 1882-1947 (Slate Ridge Cemetery, York Co., PA); native of Harford Co., born 21 Feb 1882, son of Robert W. Lloyd and Mary Davis (Harkins Funeral Home Records)

Lloyd, Edward, Civil War veteran, Stearns Precinct (*1890 Special Census of the Civil War Veterans of the State of Maryland*, by L. Tilden Moore, Volume III, p. 85)

Lloyd, Edward R., Civil War veteran, Delta P. O. (*1890 Special Census of the Civil War Veterans of the State of Maryland*, by L. Tilden Moore, Volume III, p. 84)

Lloyd, Humphrey R. (1838-1919), native of Wales, and Jane H. Williams (1838-1915), sold land in February and April 1890 and removed to Delta, York Co., PA (*The Aegis & Intelligencer*, 7 Mar and 9 May 1890) (Slateville Presbyterian Church Cemetery)

Lloyd, Mamie (Miss), member, Aberdeen M. E. Church (*Havre de Grace Republican*, 21 Feb 1890)

Lloyd, Robert W., see Benjamin Lloyd and William A. Lloyd, q.v.

Lloyd, Sarah E. (Tarbert), 1886-1965 (Slate Ridge Cemetery, York Co., PA); native of Whiteford, Harford Co., born 2 May 1886, daughter of William Tarbert and Theresa Ellis (Harkins Funeral Home Records)

Lloyd, William A., 1876-1947 (Slate Ridge Cemetery, York Co., PA); native of Harford Co., born 1 May 1876, son of Robert Lloyd and Mary Davis, natives of Wales (Harkins Funeral Home Records)

Loan, Trust, Security and Insurance Company of Harford County, Inc. (*Harford Democrat*, 28 Feb 1890)

Lochary, Agnes, 1882-1955, daughter of Thomas H. and Cassandra (Wilson) Lochary (St. Ignatius Catholic Church Cemetery and Baptism Register, p.59)

Lochary, Anna W., 1878-1960 (St. Ignatius Catholic Church Cemetery)

Lochary, Caroline, baptized 15 Apr 1883, daughter of John and Mary (Wilson) Lochary (St. Ignatius Catholic Church Baptism Register, p. 64)

Lochary, Cassandra (Wilson), 1845-1910 (St. Ignatius Catholic Church Cemetery); wife of Thomas H. Lochary, q.v

Lochary, Cassandra "Cassie" A., 1872-1960 (St. Ignatius Catholic Church Cemetery); teacher, Locust Hill School No. 19, Second District (*The Aegis & Intelligencer*, 29 Aug 1890)

Lochary, Clara, born 4 Nov 1886, baptized 26 Dec 1886, daughter of Thomas H. and Cassandra (Wilson) Lochary (St. Ignatius Catholic Church Baptism Register, p. 90)

Lochary, Elizabeth, 1871-1956 (St. Ignatius Catholic Church Cemetery)

Lochary, Fannie, 1831-1913 (St. Ignatius Catholic Church Cemetery)

Lochary, Frances M., c1875-1952 (St. Ignatius Catholic Church Cemetery);, daughter of John and Mary Lochary (The Aegis, 31 Oct 1952); Fannie Lochary graduated from Thomas Run Public School, 1890 (*The Aegis & Intelligencer*, 4 Jul 1890)

Lochary, George, Jr., 1827-1898 (St. Ignatius Catholic Church Cemetery)

Lochary, George, Sr., 1805-1891 (St. Ignatius Catholic Church Cemetery)

Lochary, John, cattle farmer (*Havre de Grace Republican*, 20 Jun 1890); trustee, Thomas Run School No. 9, Third District (*Havre de Grace Republican*, 30 May 1890)

Lochary, Joseph G., 1877-1951 (*Harkins and Related Families of Harford County, Maryland*, by Henry C. Peden, Jr., 2003, p. 43)

Lochary, Mary (Wilson), 1847-1917 (St. Ignatius Catholic Church Cemetery); widow of John Lochary, q.v.

Lochary, Thomas H., 1843-1915 (St. Ignatius Catholic Church Cemetery)

Lochary, Thomas William, born -- Jun 1884, baptized 20 Jul 1884, son of Thomas and Cassandra (Wilson) Lochary (St. Ignatius Catholic Church Baptism Register, p. 74)

Lockard, Mary Eliza (Bull), 1826-1900, native of Harford Co., resided at High Point (Death certificate misfiled as Sockard); wife of William C. Lockard, q.v.

Lockard, Mary Eliza (colored), see Charles Barnes Robinson (colored), q.v.

Lockard, Samuel L., son of William L. Lockard, moved to Wilmington, DE in 1890 (*The Aegis & Intelligencer*, 5 Dec 1890)

Lockard, William C., farmer, Forest Hill (*The Aegis & Intelligencer*, 21 Mar 1890)

Lockard, William H., poultry farmer, Forest Hill (*The Aegis & Intelligencer*, 5 Dec 1890)

Lockard, William L., see Samuel L. Lockard, q.v.

Locust Hill Public School No. 19, Second District (*Harford County, Maryland Teachers and the Schools They*

Served, 1774-1900, by Henry C. Peden, Jr., 2022, p. 370)

Loehning, Louise, born 25 Dec 1882, daughter of Ansmiel(?) and Annie Loehning (St. George's Episcopal Church Register of Baptisms, pp. 14-15)

Loflin, Adeline (Courtney), died 1 Oct 1892, age 79, widow of Richard Loflin (*Deaths and Marriages in Harford County, Maryland, and Vicinity, 1873-1904, from the Diaries of Albert Peter Silver*, transcribed by Glenn Randers-Pehrson, 1995, p. 15)

Loflin, Albert, 1847-1915 (Rock Run Methodist Church Cemetery); widower, married Hattie A. Armstrong on 5 Nov 1890 at Level M. P. Parsonage (*The Aegis & Intelligencer*, 28 Nov 1890; Marriage License Applications Book ALJ No. 2, 1890); member, Division No. 2, Bel Air Fire and Salvage Corps (*The Aegis & Intelligencer*, 10 Oct 1890); see Horace Loflin, q.v.

Loflin, Cora E. (Dick), 1860-1941 (Smith Chapel Cemetery; *Barnes-Bailey Genealogy*, by Walter D. Barnes, 1939, p. H-46); wife of Edgar Loflin, q.v.

Loflin, Edgar P., 1851-1929 (Smith Chapel Methodist Church Cemetery); resident of Bel Air (*The Aegis & Intelligencer*, 25 Jul 1890)

Loflin, Emily B. (Bailey), 1812-1890 (Deer Creek Harmony Presbyterian Church; *Barnes-Bailey Genealogy*, by Walter D. Barnes, 1939, p. G-17); Mrs. William Loflin, age 78, widow, resident near Churchville (*The Aegis & Intelligencer*, 14 Mar 1890 and 11 Apr 1890)

Loflin, Ethel J., 1873-1938 (Baker Cemetery)

Loflin, H. Linwood, 1879-1940 (Baker Cemetery)

Loflin, Harry C., born 19 Oct 1888, son of Smith Loflin and Ellen Bailey (*Barnes-Bailey Genealogy*, by Walter D. Barnes, 1939, p. H-40)

Loflin, Hattie Jackson, born 4 Mar 1886, daughter of Smith Loflin and Ellen Bailey (*Barnes-Bailey Genealogy*, by Walter D. Barnes, 1939, p. H-40)

Loflin, Hattie A. (Armstrong), second wife of Albert Loflin, q.v.

Loflin, Herbert E., 1876-1932 (Baker Cemetery)

Loflin, Horace, 1879-1907, son of Albert Loflin and Hattie A. Armstrong (Rock Run Methodist Church Cemetery); see Albert Loflin, q.v.

Loflin, Mary Elizabeth, 1819-1896 (Deer Creek Harmony Presbyterian Church Cemetery)

Loflin, Phebe M., 1827-1897 (Wesleyan Chapel Methodist Church Cemetery)

Loflin, Smith, see Harry C. Loflin and Hattie J. Loflin, q.v.

Loflin, Sophia J. (James), 1844-1918 (Baker Cemetery)

Loflin, Susie S., 1880-1910 (Baker Cemetery)

Loflin, William P., 1842-1906 (Baker Cemetery); Civil War veteran, at Level (*1890 Special Census of the Civil War Veterans of the State of Maryland*, by L. Tilden Moore, Volume III, p. 67); also see Emily Loflin q.v.

Logan, Christean, see Lena M. Rumsey, q.v.

Logan, Jane, county out-pensioner [welfare recipient], Fifth District (*Havre de Grace Republican*, 4 Jul 1890); Mrs. Jane Logan died 15 Oct 1890 and was buried in Rock Run Methodist Church Cemetery (*The Aegis & Intelligencer*, 7 Nov 1890)

Logan, Malcolm B., 1890-1960 (Angel Hill Cemetery)

Logan, Mary A. (Miss), 1814-1900, native of Cecil Co., MD, resident of Havre de Grace (Death certificate)

Logue, Philip, 1813-1908 (Death certificate; Alms House Record Book)

Loker, Ellen E., 1847-1924 (Little Falls Quaker Cemetery)

Loker, John Ferris, 1840-1930 (Little Falls Quaker Cemetery)

Loker, Joseph, 1814-1901, native of Prussia, resided at Pleasantville, Harford Co. (Death certificate)

Loker, Laura L., 1866-1948 (Fallston Methodist Church Cemetery)

Loker, Martha Virginia, 1850-1931 (Little Falls Quaker Cemetery)

Loker, Mary Ann (Whitson), wife of Joseph Loker, q.v.

Loker, William A., 1853-1914 (Fallston Methodist Church Cemetery)

Lomis, Sidney (colored), see William Henry Crockson , q.v.

Lomyer, Elizabeth S., 1879-1930 (Holy Trinity Lutheran Church Cemetery)

Lomyer, John, first grade student, Prospect Hill School (*The Aegis & Intelligencer*, 21 Feb 1890)

Lomyer, Margaret (Herbert), 1849-1904, native of Maryland, resided at Joppa (Holy Trinity Lutheran Church Cemetery)

Lomyer, Robert, 1843-1914 (Holy Trinity Lutheran Church Cemetery)

Lomyer, William H., 1876-1970 (Holy Trinity Lutheran Church Cemetery)

Long, Eliza J. (Miss), 1852-1916 (Bethel Presbyterian Church Cemetery Records)

Long, Elizabeth M. "Betsy" (Miss), 1846-1910 (Bethel Presbyterian Church Cemetery Records); Misses Margaret and Betsy Long sold their house in Jarrettsville and moved to York, PA (*Harford Democrat*, 19 Dec 1890)

Long, Margaret B. (Miss), 1843-1929 (Bethel Presbyterian Church Cemetery Records); Misses Margaret and Betsy Long sold their house in Jarrettsville and moved to York, PA (*Harford Democrat*, 19 Dec 1890)

Long, William Shipley, 1840-1905 (Bethel Presbyterian Church Cemetery Records), juror, Fourth District (*Havre de Grace Republican*, 31 Jan 1890); resident of Jarrettsville, sick in Kentucky (*The Aegis & Intelligencer*, 7 Feb 1890)

Longley, Ella M., married John H. Hughes on 5 Jan 1890 (marriage certificate)

Loomis, Mary, 1877-1963 (Slate Ridge Cemetery, York Co., PA); native of Rocks, Harford Co., born 6 Aug 1877, daughter of Lorenzo Loomis and Eliza Boughter (Harkins Funeral Home Records)

Loomis, Lorenzo, see Mary Loomis, q.v.

Lord, Kate, 1890-1960 (St. Mary's Episcopal Church Cemetery)

Loring, James A., 1861-1937 (Heavenly Waters Cemetery)

Lort, Laura J., see Laura B. Tammany, q.v.

Loudon, Ann W., 1821-1907 (Mt. Vernon Methodist Church Cemetery)

Loughlin, Edward J., 1882-1929 (Cokesbury Memorial Methodist Church Cemetery)

Loughlin, M. Elizabeth, 1884-1926 (Cokesbury Memorial Methodist Church Cemetery); wife of Edward J. Loughlin; also see Margaret Elizabeth Kaiser, q.v.

Love, Amelia (McNamee), 1886-1982 (Mt. Carmel Methodist Church Cemetery)

Love, B. Alexander, 1872-1954 (Mt. Carmel Methodist Church Cemetery)

Love, Bessie, 1876-1943, native of Harford Co., born 2 Jan 1876, daughter of Oliver Love and Martha Hutchinson (Bailey Funeral Home Records; Darlington Cemetery - married name Knight)

Love, Clara L. (Miss), premium award winner, Class K - Household and Domestic Manufactures, Harford County Fair (*The Aegis & Intelligencer*, 24 Oct 1890)

Love, Elizabeth (Griest), 1888-1930 (Darlington Cemetery); native of Maryland, born 18 Oct 1888, daughter of Isaac Griest and Mary Caldwell (Bailey Funeral Home Records)

Love, Ella R. (Smith), 1877-1936 (Dublin Southern Cemetery); native of Maryland, born 18 Dec 1877, daughter of Hugh Smith and Henrietta Scarborough (Bailey Funeral Home Records)

Love, Esther A. (Smith) 1855-1900, native of England, resided at Castleton, Harford Co. (Death certificate; Darlington Cemetery); wife of Samuel T. Love, q.v.

Love, Henrietta (Scott), c1843-1922 (Death certificate; Angel Hill Cemetery)

Love, James, see Marion Love and Mary Louisa Kirby, q.v.

Love, John, see Oliver W. Love, q.v.

Love, Marion, 1844-1922, wife of James Love (Bethel Presbyterian Church Cemetery Records)

Love, Oliver, see Bessie Love, q.v.

Love, Oliver W., 1873-1941 (Dublin Southern Cemetery); native of Harford Co., born 19 Apr 1873, son of John Love and Margaret Gordon, natives of York Co., PA (Bailey Funeral Home Records)

Love, Rebecca L., 1856-1927 (Darlington Cemetery)

Love, Robert, died 24 Mar 1895, age 82 (*Deaths and Marriages in Harford County, Maryland, and Vicinity, 1873-1904, from the Diaries of Albert Peter Silver*, transcribed by Glenn Randers-Pehrson, 1995, p. 16); resident near Castleton, and brother of Mrs. Mary L. Reynolds (1806-1890) who was formerly of Cecil Co., MD (*The Aegis & Intelligencer*, 28 Feb 1890)

Love, Robert E., 1874-1950 (Mt. Carmel Methodist Church Cemetery)

Love, Samuel Taylor, 1849-1911 (Darlington Cemetery); trustee, Franklin School No. 9, Fifth District (*Havre de Grace Republican*, 30 May 1890); served on an inquest jury in the Fifth District (*The Aegis & Intelligencer*, 1 Aug 1890); husband of Esther A. Love, q.v.

Love, Sophia (Taylor), 1819-1908 (Darlington Cemetery)

Love, Wilfred Benjamin, 1885-1973 (Darlington Cemetery)

Lovel, William, of Black Horse, married Miss Lizzie Sanders on 20 May 1890 at Jarrettsville M. E. Church parsonage (*Harford Democrat*, 2 May 1890)

Lovelace, Charles B., 1865-1942 (St. Paul's Lutheran Church Cemetery)

Lovelace, Lula Josephine, 1872-1924 (St. Paul's Lutheran Church Cemetery)

Lovering, Harry C., Civil War veteran, Bel Air (*1890 Special Census of the Civil War Veterans of the State of Maryland*, by L. Tilden Moore, Volume III, p. 71)

Lovett, John H., sentinel, Perryman Lodge, Order of the Golden Chain (*Havre de Grace Republican*, 5 Dec 1890); served on a grand jury (*The Aegis & Intelligencer*, 14 Nov 1890); juror, Second District (*Havre de Grace Republican*, 31 Oct 1890)

Lovette, Annelisa, see Henry Lovette Mitchell, q.v.

Loving, Charles, member, Taylor Fox Hunting Club (*Havre de Grace Republican*, 24 Jan 1890)

Loving, William Rufus, age 22 in 1890 (Marriage License Applications Book ALJ No. 2, 1890)

Lowe, Amon D., Civil War veteran, Fawn Grove P. O. (*1890 Special Census of the Civil War Veterans of the State of Maryland*, by L. Tilden Moore, Volume III, p. 81)

Lowe, Benjamin Franklin, age 30 in 1890 (Marriage License Applications Book ALJ No. 2, 1890), married Sallie R. Wright on 19 Feb 1890 at the home of Joshua W. Wright (marriage certificate)

Lowe, Clayton, 1880-1968 (Fawn Grove Friends Cemetery, York Co., PA); native of Pylesville, Harford Co., born 9 Mar 1880, son of Laban R. Lowe and Margaret Taylor (Harkins Funeral Home Records)

Lowe, J. Stewart, 1849-1933 (Centre Methodist Church Cemetery); married Ella M. Ward (1863-1942) on 26 Feb 1890 in Baltimore (marriage certificate); acquired land in Harford County in February 1890 (*The Aegis & Intelligencer*, 7 Mar 1890); age 24 in 1890 (Marriage License Applications Book ALJ No. 2, 1890)

Lowe, Jeremiah, 1813-1890 (Fellowship Church Cemetery), resident of New Park; died testate in 1890 and his named heirs were daughter Olivia Ann Wilson, granddaughter Annie V. Wilson, and son-in-law John F. Wilson (Harford County Will Book JMM 11:86-87); also see Mrs.William A.Wilson, q.v.

Lowe, John George, 1876-1953 (Bel Air Memorial Gardens); native of Harford Co., born 24 Apr 1876, son of William A. Lowe and Mary Few (Harkins Funeral Home Records)

Lowe, Justice, Civil War veteran, Clermont (*1890 Special Census of the Civil War Veterans of the State of Maryland*, by L. Tilden Moore, Volume III, p. 80)

Lowe, Laban, 1838-1926 (Fawn Grove Friends Cemetery, York Co., PA); census taker, Norrisville Precinct (*Havre de Grace Republican*, 23 May 1890); trustee, Mt. Pleasant School No. 11, Fourth District (*Havre de Grace Republican*, 30 May 1890); see Clayton Lowe, q.v.

Lowe, Mamie A., see Mamie A. Lee, q.v.

Lowe, Sallie E., 1859-1891 (St. Paul's Methodist Church Cemetery)

Lowe (Low), Sarah V., see James W. Preston, q.v.

Lowe, William, Civil War veteran, resided at Street (*1890 Special Census of the Civil War Veterans of the State of Maryland*, by L. Tilden Moore, Volume III, p. 84); see Mamie A. Lee, q.v.

Lowe, William A., see John George Lowe, q.v.

Lowry, Ellen (colored), 1846-1930, native of Maryland (Death certificate); wife of Lewis Lowry, q.v.

Lowry, Grace Marie, born 5 Oct 1888 (Thomas W. Ricketts Bible states she married S. Davis Ricketts; *Maryland Bible Records, Volume 1*, by Henry C. Peden, Jr., 2003, pp. 210-211)

Lowry, Lewis (colored), 1851-1903, native of Talbot Co., MD, resided at Singer (Death certificate)

Loyal Temperance Legion of Bel Air (*Harford Democrat*, 21 Feb 1890)

Lubinska, Mary A., age 35 in 1890 (Marriage License Applications Book ALJ No. 2, 1890), married John H. Bowman on 19 Aug 1890 (marriage certificate)

Lucas, Samuel, 1854-1919 (Alms House Record Book)

Luciani, Augustus, new name on the voter registration list in the Sixth District (*Havre de Grace Republican*, 17 Oct 1890)

Luciani. John, new name on the voter registration list in the Sixth District (*Havre de Grace Republican*, 17 Oct 1890)

Luckey, Edwin T., 1858-1935 (Bethel Presbyterian Church Cemetery Records)

Luckey, Hannah Elizabeth (Nelson), 1856-1914 (Bethel Presbyterian Church Cemetery Records); wife of Edwin T. Luckey, q.v.

Luckey, Howard Watters, born 1886, son of James and Ida M. (Amos) Luckey (Bethel Presbyterian Church Cemetery Records)

Luckey, Ida M. (Amos), 1862-1917 (Bethel Presbyterian Church Cemetery Records); first wife of James B. Luckey, q.v.

Luckey, James B., 1855-1946 (Bethel Presbyterian Church Cemetery Records); board of directors, Agricultural and Mechanical Society (*Havre de Grace Republican*, 23 May 1890)

Luckey, Joshua G., 1825-1899 (Bethel Presbyterian Church Cemetery Records); magistrate, Fourth District (*The Aegis & Intelligencer*, 28 Feb 1890); see Mary Slade, q.v.

Luckey, Mary Susan (Lytle), 1835-1913 (Bethel Presbyterian Church Cemetery Records), wife of Joshua G. Luckey, q.v.

Lukens, Jesse C. (Mrs.), see L. Maud Riley, q.v.

Lusby, Ellen (colored), died -- Aug 1890, aged woman, resided near Webster (*The Aegis & Intelligencer*, 15 Aug 1890)

Luster, Levy (colored), c1881-1931, native of Maryland, parents unknown (Death certificate)

Lutz, Emma J., 1878-1959 (Angel Hill Cemetery)

Lutz, John W., 1871-1943 (Angel Hill Cemetery)

Lutz, Otto, 1833-1908, native of Berlin, Germany, tinsmith at Benson (Death certificate)

Lutz, Sarah, wife of Otto Lutz, q.v.

Lyle, Arthur (colored), 1873-1890, son of George M. and Margaret Lyle, of Bel Air (Hendon Hill Cemetery; *The Aegis & Intelligencer*, 4 Jul 1890)

Lyle, George, music supplies salesman in the Masonic Temple in Bel Air (*The Aegis & Intelligencer*, 13 Jun 1890)

Lyle, George M. (colored), 1843-1908, native of Maryland, parents unknown (Death certificate); see Margaret L. Lyle, William H. Lyle and Arthur Lyle, q.v.

Lyle, James A., 1854-1912 (Churchville Presbyterian Church Cemetery); justice of the peace, Third District (*Havre de Grace Republican*, 21 Feb 1890); resident of Bel Air, and brother-in-law of Gov. McKinney of Virginia (*The Aegis & Intelligencer*, 18 Jul 1890); Confederate Army veteran (*Havre de Grace Republican*, 30 May 1890)

Lyle, John T. (colored), age 21 in 1890 (Marriage License Applications Book ALJ No. 2, 1891)

Lyle, Lena (Miss), premium award winner, Class K - Household and Domestic Manufactures, Harford County Fair (*The Aegis & Intelligencer*, 24 Oct 1890)

Lyle, Margaret L. (Wilson) (colored), 1850-1906, native of Maryland (Death certificate); wife of George M. Lyle, q.v.; also see Arthur Lyle and William H. Lyle, q.v.

Lyle, William H. (colored), 1867-1903, son of George M. and Margaret Lyle (Hendon Hill Cemetery)

Lynch, Agnes B., 1870-1941 (St. Ignatius Catholic Church Cemetery)

Lynch, Alfred T., 1879-1925 (Jarrettsville Cemetery); native and resident of Jarrettsville, born 27 Dec 1879, son of William Hope Lynch, of Harford Co., and Charlotte Anderson Barber, of Pennsylvania (Death certificate)

Lynch, Amanda S., 1867-1944 (St. George's Episcopal Church Cemetery); wife of William B. Lynch, q.v.

Lynch, Amelia Catherine, born 24 Oct 1890, daughter of Edward and Amelia Lynch (Edward Lynch Bible, *Maryland Bible Records, Volume 2*, by Henry C. Peden, Jr., 2003, pp. 108-109)

Lynch, Anna, 1856-1932 (St. Ignatius Catholic Church Cemetery)

Lynch, Anna (Kelly), 1865-1935 (St. Ignatius Catholic Church Cemetery)

Lynch, Anna Louisa, born 10 Jun 1873, daughter of Edward and Amelia Lynch (Edward Lynch Bible, *Maryland Bible Records, Volume 2*, by Henry C. Peden, Jr., 2003, pp. 108-109)

Lynch, Charles B., 1872-1962 (Jarrettsville Cemetery)

Lynch, Charlotte Anderson (Barber), 1841-1906 (Jarrettsville Cemetery; Death certificate); wife of William Henry Lynch, q.v.

Lynch, Clara V., 1867-1899 (Jarrettsville Cemetery); daughter of William J. Lynch (Death certificate incomplete)

Lynch, Daniel E., 1830-1894 (St. Ignatius Catholic Church Cemetery)

Lynch, Daniel Joseph, 1858-1916 (St. Francis de Sales Catholic Church Cemetery); served on a petit jury in 1890 (*The Aegis & Intelligencer*, 14 Nov 1890)

Lynch, Daniel P., 1859-1923 (St. Ignatius Catholic Church Cemetery)

Lynch, Edward, 1841-1892 (Cokesbury Memorial Methodist Church Cemetery)

Lynch, Edward (Jr.), born 27 Dec 1878, son of Edward and Amelia Lynch (Edward Lynch Bible, *Maryland Bible Records, Volume 2*, by Henry C. Peden, Jr., 2003, pp. 108-109)

Lynch, Elizabeth "Lizzie" Dora, born 9 Aug 1876, daughter of Edward and Amelia Lynch (Edward Lynch Bible, *Maryland Bible Records, Volume 2*, by Henry C. Peden, Jr., 2003, pp. 108-109); Lizzie Lynch, student, Harford Furnace School (*The Aegis & Intelligencer*, 14 Feb 1890)

Lynch, Ellen, see Margaret T. Kelly, q.v.

Lynch, Hannorah E. (Sullivan), 1839-1900 (St. Francis de Sales Catholic Church Cemetery; www.findagrave.com); wife of James P. Lynch, q.v.

Lynch, James F., 1866-1907 (St. Francis de Sales Catholic Church Cemetery); born in Harford Co., farmer, single, resided a Belcamp, son of James Lynch and Hanora Sullivan (Death certificate)

Lynch, James P., 1839-1891, native of County Kerry, Ireland (St. Francis de Sales Catholic Church Cemetery)

Lynch, Jane Wade, born 10 Aug 1884, daughter of Edward and Amelia Lynch (Edward Lynch Bible, *Maryland Bible Records, Volume 2*, by Henry C. Peden, Jr., 2003, pp. 108-109)

Lynch, Jeremiah A., 1864-1935 (St. Francis de Sales Catholic Church Cemetery)

Lynch, Jeremiah "Jerry" J., 1867-1902 (St. Francis de Sales Catholic Church Cemetery; single, resided at Harford Furnace (Death certificate incomplete)

Lynch, Jeremiah J., 1874-1892 (St. Francis de Sales Catholic Church Cemetery)

Lynch, Johannah, 1849-1904 (St. Francis de Sales Catholic Church Cemetery); native of Ireland, single, resided at VanBibber (Death certificate)

Lynch, John, 1810-1901, native of Maryland, died in "country" (Death certificate)

Lynch, John, 1826-1892 (St. Francis de Sales Catholic Church Cemetery)

Lynch, John E., 1870-1899 (St. Francis de Sales Catholic Church Cemetery); unmarried farmer at Harford Furnace, son of John and Mary Lynch (Death certificate)

Lynch, John Lindsey, born 15 Sep 1887, son of Edward and Amelia Lynch (Edward Lynch Bible, *Maryland Bible Records, Volume 2*, by Henry C. Peden, Jr., 2003, pp. 108-109)

Lynch, John M., 1870-1923 (St. Ignatius Catholic Church Cemetery)

Lynch, Julia (Welsh), 1816-1911 (St. John's Catholic Church Cemetery, Long Green, Baltimore Co.); native of Ireland, resided at Taylor (Death certificate)

Lynch, Katherine M. ("Katie"), 1876-1897 (St. Francis de Sales Catholic Church Cemetery); student, Harford Furnace School (*The Aegis & Intelligencer*, 14 Feb 1890)

Lynch, Lottie, 1841-1906 (Jarrettsville Cemetery)

Lynch, Margaret E., 1867-1948 (St. Francis de Sales Catholic Church Cemetery)

Lynch, Mary, 1820-1903, native of Ireland, resided at Bagley (Death certificate)

Lynch, Mary, 1830-1910 (St. Ignatius Catholic Church Cemetery)

Lynch, Mary, 1835-1907 (St. Francis de Sales Catholic Church Cemetery)

Lynch, Mary, age 31, married Richard Daugherty on 12 Feb 1890 (Marriage License Applications Book ALJ No. 2, 1890, and marriage certificate)

Lynch, Mary A. (Smith), 1876-1906, native of Harford Co., wife of John Lynch, resided at Sharon (Death certificate)

Lynch, Mary H., 1869-1935 (St. Francis de Sales Catholic Church Cemetery); native of Harford Furnace, born 2 Feb 1868, resided at Emmorton, daughter of James Lynch and Hannorah Sullivan, natives of Ireland (Death certificate states born in 1868)

Lynch, Maude Louisa, 1880-1940 (Jarrettsville Cemetery)

Lynch, Sophia M., 1872-1958 (Jarrettsville Cemetery)

Lynch, Thomas H., 1840-1904, native of Ireland, married, farmer, resided at Upper Cross Roads (Death certificate)

Lynch, William, county out-pensioner [welfare recipient], First District (*Havre de Grace Republican*, 4 Jul 1890)

Lynch, William B., 1866-1912 (St. George's Episcopal Church Cemetery); native of Maryland, laborer, married, resided at Perryman (Death certificate)

Lynch, William Barber, 1877-1935 (Jarrettsville Cemetery)

Lynch, William Henry, 1834-1910 (Jarrettsville Cemetery); native of Baltimore Co., farmer, married, resided at Jarrettsville (Death certificate)

Lynch, William J., see Clara V. Lynch, q.v.

Lynch, William T., 1863-1920 (St. Francis de Sales Catholic Church Cemetery)

Lynn, Rachel (colored), 1880-1899, house girl, native of Havre de Grace, daughter of Rhemus Lynn and Carrie Thomas (Death certificate which stated on reverse side that her mother was Rachel Tillson)

Lyon, A. & G. T. & Co., merchants, Havre de Grace (*Havre de Grace Republican*, 16 May 1890)

Lyon, Andrew Lincoln, 1866-1943 (Angel Hill Cemetery); secretary, Republican Club (*Havre de Grace Republican*, 7 Nov 1890); A. & G. T. & Co., storekeepers, Havre de Grace (*Havre de Grace Republican*, 16 May 1890; *Biographical Dictionary of Harford County, Maryland, 1774-1974*, by Henry C. Peden, Jr. and William O. Carr, 2021, p. 170)

Lyon, Beulah W., 1875-1955, native of Havre de Grace, born 11 Mar 1875, daughter of George T. Lyon and Maria Pennington (Pennington Funeral Home Records - married name Spencer); member, Havre de Grace Reading Circle (*Havre de Grace Republican*, 7 Feb 1890); student, Havre de Grace High School (*Havre de Grace Republican*, 31 Oct 1890; *The Aegis & Intelligencer*, 24 Oct 1890)

Lyon, Eliza P., 1861-1924 (Angel Hill Cemetery)

Lyon, George Taylor, 1816-1891 (Angel Hill Cemetery); A. & G. T. Lyon & Co., storekeepers, Havre de Grace (*Havre de Grace Republican*, 16 May 1890); see Beulah W. Lyon, q.v.

Lyon, Georgia T., 1862-1924 (Angel Hill Cemetery)

Lyon, Louisa (Miss), member, Havre de Grace Reading Circle (*Havre de Grace Republican*, 7 Feb 1890)

Lyon, Maria Louisa (Pennington), 1834-1910 (Angel Hill Cemetery); see Beulah W. Lyon, q.v.

Lyon, Sarah (Magowan), 1866-1940 (Angel Hill Cemetery)

Lyons, Alois J., 1884-1938 (St. George's Episcopal Church Cemetery)

Lyons, Lida (Miss), member, Havre de Grace Reading Circle (*Havre de Grace Republican*, 7 Feb 1890)

Lytle's Oyster House, Bel Air, James S. Lytle, prop. (*Bel Air: An Architectural and Cultural History, 1782-1945*, by Marilynn M. Larew, 1995, p. 68)

Lytle, ----, third baseman, A. R. Walker Baseball Club, Havre de Grace (*Havre de Grace Republican*, 4 Jul 1890)

Lytle, Alice C., 1886-1973 (McKendree Methodist Church Cemetery)

Lytle, Amanda Victoria, born 17 Oct 1878, daughter of Nicholas D. and Amanda Lytle (Nicholas D. Lytle Bible, *Maryland Bible Records, Volume 2*, by Henry C. Peden, Jr., 2003, p. 112)

Lytle, Ann "Annie" Hughes, born 27 Jun 1871, daughter of Nicholas D. and Amanda Lytle (Nicholas D. Lytle Bible, *Maryland Bible Records, Volume 2*, by Henry C. Peden, Jr., 2003, p. 112)

Lytle, Anna "Annie" Elizabeth Webb, 1874-1957 (Bethel Presbyterian Church Cemetery Records); second wife of James Frank Lytle, q.v.

Lytle, Bertha (Miss), 1874-1941 (Cokesbury Memorial Methodist Church Cemetery); resident of Magnolia (*The Aegis & Intelligencer*, 19 Sep 1890)

Lytle, Charles, born 31 Jan 1869, son of Nicholas D. and Amanda Lytle (Nicholas D. Lytle Bible, *Maryland Bible Records, Volume 2*, by Henry C. Peden, Jr., 2003, p. 112)

Lytle, Edgar Hughes, born 9 Aug 1876, son of Nicholas D. and Amanda Lytle (Nicholas D. Lytle Bible, *Maryland Bible Records, Volume 2*, by Henry C. Peden, Jr., 2003, p. 112)

Lytle, Edward C., 1876-1941 (Mt. Zion Methodist Church Cemetery)

Lytle, Ethel, premium award winner, Class L - Children's Department, Harford County Fair (*The Aegis & Intelligencer*, 24 Oct 1890)

Lytle, Fannie W., 1866-1953 (Mt. Zion Methodist Church Cemetery)

Lytle, Florence T. (Miss), 1870-1960 (Cokesbury Memorial Methodist Church Cemetery); resident of Magnolia (*The Aegis & Intelligencer*, 19 Sep 1890)

Lytle, Harry Elmore, born 15 Mar 1867, son of Nicholas D. and Amanda Lytle (Nicholas D. Lytle Bible, *Maryland Bible Records, Volume 2*, by Henry C. Peden, Jr., 2003, p. 112)

Lytle, Ida V., 1879-1953 (St. Paul's Methodist Church Cemetery)

Lytle, J. Clarence, 1882-1966 (McKendree Methodist Church Cemetery)

Lytle, James Franklin ("Frank"), 1850-1923 (Bethel Presbyterian Church Cemetery Records)

Lytle, James S., 1832-1896 (Christ Episcopal Church Cemetery); see Lytle's Oyster House, q.v.

Lytle, John H., 1832-1896 (Cokesbury Memorial Methodist Church Cemetery)

Lytle, John (Mrs.), premium award winner, Class N - Floral Decorations, Harford County Fair (*The Aegis & Intelligencer*, 24 Oct 1890)

Lytle, Laura E., 1862-1937 (Holy Cross Church Cemetery)

Lytle, Margaret Anna, 1836-1906 (Holy Cross Church Cemetery)

Lytle, Margaret S., 1845-1928 (Cokesbury Memorial Methodist Church Cemetery)

Lytle, Maria S. (Mrs.), farm resident near Bel Air (*The Aegis & Intelligencer*, 7 Feb 1890)

Lytle, Mary Ridgley (Godd), 1810-1904 (Christ Episcopal Church Cemetery)

Lytle, Nicholas D., see Amanda V. Lytle, Ann H. Lytle, Charles Lytle, Harry E. Lytle, and Thomas G. Lytle, q.v.

Lytle, Nicholas McComas, born 1 Nov 1873, son of Nicholas D. and Amanda Lytle (Nicholas D. Lytle Bible, *Maryland Bible Records, Volume 2*, by Henry C. Peden, Jr., 2003, p. 112)

Lytle, Rachel H, 1813-1897 (Cokesbury Memorial Methodist Church Cemetery)

Lytle, Sarah M, 1838-1921 (Cokesbury Memorial Methodist Church Cemetery)

Lytle, Sue "Susie" (Miss), property owner adjacent to Broadway in Bel Air (*The Aegis & Intelligencer*, 16 May 1890); premium award winner, Class J - Domestic Products, Harford County Fair (*The Aegis & Intelligencer*, 24 Oct 1890)

Lytle, Thomas Grant, born 22 Sep 1864, son of Nicholas D. and Amanda Lytle (Nicholas D. Lytle Bible, *Maryland Bible Records, Volume 2*, by Henry C. Peden, Jr., 2003, p. 112)

Lytle, William K., 1830-1910 (Holy Cross Church Cemetery)

Lytle, Zannie Frances, age 26 in 1890 (Marriage License Applications Book ALJ No. 2, 1891)

Macatee's Public School, near Pylesville, Fourth District (*Harford County, Maryland Teachers and the Schools They Served, 1774-1900*, by Henry C. Peden, Jr., 2022, p. 370)

Macatee, Catherine (Jenkins), 1861-1923 (St. Mary's Catholic Church Cemetery)

Macatee, Charles M., 1876-1892 (St. Mary's Catholic Church Cemetery)

Macatee, Elizabeth O., 1889-1897 (St. Mary's Catholic Church Cemetery)

Macatee, Frank B., 1846-1936 (St. Mary's Catholic Church Cemetery); farmer, near The Rocks *The Aegis & Intelligencer*, 1 Jul 1890 and 12 Sep 1890); trustee, School No. 18, Fifth District (*Havre de Grace Republican*, 30 May 1890); son of Margaret Macatee, q.v.

Macatee, Henry, 1842-1918 (St. Mary's Catholic Church Cemetery); dairyman (*Harford Democrat*, 14 Feb 1890)

Macatee, Ignatius James, 1838-1896 (St. Mary's Catholic Church Cemetery); Civil War (Confederate) veteran (*Havre de Grace Republican*, 20 Jun 1890)

Macatee, J. Harry, 1878-1923 (St. Mary's Catholic Church Cemetery)

Macatee, J. Ramsay, 1869-1890 (St. Mary's Catholic Church Cemetery); son of Henry Macatee, of Pylesville (*The Aegis & Intelligencer*, 7 Feb 1890)

Macatee, Margaret, 1873-1924 (St. Mary's Catholic Church Cemetery); Maggie Macatee, young lady of near Pylesville (*The Aegis & Intelligencer*, 7 Feb 1890)

Macatee, Margaret (Johnson), 1806-1890 (St. Mary's Catholic Church Cemetery); widow of Ignatius G. Macatee, q.v.

Macatee, Mary (Glenn), 1851-1899, resided near Pylesville (St. Mary's Catholic Church Cemetery; Death certificate); wife of Frank B. Macatee, q.v.

Macatee, Mary Frances G., 1844-1905 (St. Mary's Catholic Church Cemetery)

Macatee, Mary J., 1871-1944, daughter of Frank B. and Mary (Glenn) Macatee (St. Mary's Catholic Church Cemetery; *The Aegis*, 15 Dec 1944); Mary Macatee, young lady of near Pylesville (*The Aegis & Intelligencer*, 7 Feb 1890)

Macatee, Mary Margaret (Ramsay), 1844-1901, native of Pennsylvania, resided near St. Mary's Church (Death certificate; St. Mary's Catholic Church Cemetery); wife of Henry Macatee, q.v.

Macatee, Rachel Ann, 1813-1895 (St. Mary's Catholic Church Cemetery)

Macatee, Samuel, 1846-1925, Civil War (Confederate) veteran (St. Mary's Catholic Church Cemetery; *Havre de Grace Republican*, 20 Jun 1890); son of Margaret Macatee, q.v.

Macatee, Samuel A., 1885-1918, World War I veteran, killed in action (St. Mary's Catholic Church Cemetery)

Macatee, Walter F., 1878-1930 (St. Mary's Catholic Church Cemetery)

Mackall, Joseph (colored), 1887-1900, son of Robert Mackall and ---- Williamson (Death certificate)

Mackay, John W., acquired land in November 1890 (*The Aegis & Intelligencer*, 5 Dec 1890)

Mackenzie, Lucie Tennelle (Emory), 1855-1900, native of Maryland, resident of Bel Air, wife of George N. Mackenzie (Death certificate)

Mackin, Ann, see Katherine Donnelly, q.v.

Mackin, Charles, sold land in April 1890 (*The Aegis & Intelligencer*, 9 May 1890)

Mackin, Cora S., native of Havre de Grace, born 2 Feb 1881, daughter of Thomas Mackin and Margaret Cloak (Pennington Funeral Home Records, 1955 - married name Beckman; Angel Hill Cemetery)

Mackin, James J., sold land in April 1890 (*The Aegis & Intelligencer*, 9 May 1890)

Mackin, John J., 1886-1951, native of Havre de Grace, born 8 Mar 1886, son of Joseph Mackin and Mary Crane (Pennington Funeral Home Records)

Mackin, Joseph, see John J. Mackin and Joseph G. Mackin, q.v.

Mackin, Joseph G., 1888-1955, native of Havre de Grace, born 15 Jun 1888, son of Joseph Mackin and Mary Crane (Pennington Funeral Home Records)

Mackin, Margaret R., 1864-1937 (Angel Hill Cemetery)

Mackin, Mary, and husband, sold land in February 1890 (*The Aegis & Intelligencer*, 7 Mar 1890)

Mackin, May, acquired land in April 1890 (*The Aegis & Intelligencer*, 9 May 1890)

Mackin, Michael, Jr., age 21 in 1890 (Marriage License Applications Book ALJ No. 2, 1891); new name on the Havre de Grace voter registration list (*Havre de Grace Republican*, 19 Sep 1890)

Mackin, P. J., committeeman, Knights of St. Leo, Havre de Grace (*Havre de Grace Republican*, 19 Sep 1890); hauling contractor, Havre de Grace (*Havre de Grace Republican*, 6 Jun 1890)

Mackin, Thomas H., 1862-1939 (Angel Hill Cemetery); constable, Sixth District (*Havre de Grace Republican*, 4 Jul 1890); see Cora S. Mackin, q.v.

Mackin, Thomas L., 1886-1918 (Angel Hill Cemetery)

Mackin, Violet, see Violet Whitney, q.v.

Mackison, William T., 1827-1899, merchant and farmer at Glenville, native of Maryland (Death certificate)

Macklem, Anna, born 16 Aug 1870, daughter of John Montgomery and Elizabeth Davies (Hayes) Hughes (*The Hughes Genealogy, 1636-1953*, by Joseph Lee Hughes, 1953, p. 109); Miss Annie Macklem, actress, Darlington Company (*Havre de Grace Republican*, 7 Mar 1890)

Macklem, Anna M. (Miss), 1835-1911, native of Delaware, resided in Bel Air (Death certificate)

Macklem, Bessie V., 1880-1955 (Rock Run Methodist Church Cemetery)

Macklem, Elizabeth (Davies), 1826-1915 (Rock Run Methodist Church Cemetery)

Macklem, Elizabeth T., age 26 in 1890 (Marriage License Applications Book ALJ No. 2, 1890)

Macklem, Jennie W., 1882-1967 (Rock Run Methodist Church Cemetery); wife of John M. Macklem, q.v.

Macklem, John Montgomery, 1837-1924 (Rock Run Methodist Church Cemetery); trustee, Harford Seminary, School No. 12, Second District (*Havre de Grace Republican*, 30 May 1890); see Mary Barrow, q.v.

Macklem, John W., 1875-1939 (Rock Run Methodist Church Cemetery)

Mackem, Lavinia D., 1869-1961 (Rock Run Methodist Church Cemetery)

Macklem, Lucy B., 1873-1944 (Rock Run Methodist Church Cemetery)

Macklem, Mary T., age 24 in 1890 (Marriage License Applications Book ALJ No. 2, 1890), married John B. Gordon on 2 Apr 1890 (marriage certificate)

Macklem, Rebecca J, 1872-1960 (Rock Run Methodist Church Cemetery); high school student, Second District (*Havre de Grace Republican*, 31 Oct 1890)

Macklem, Sadie (Miss), actress, Darlington Company (*Havre de Grace Republican*, 7 Mar 1890)

Macklem, W. (Master), actor, Darlington Company (*Havre de Grace Republican*, 7 Mar 1890)

MacLean, Abbie Lillie (Pennington), 1873-1950, wife of Thomas F. MacLean, q.v.

MacLean, Thomas Frank, 1869-1933 (Fallston Methodist Church Cemetery)

MacNabb, see McNabb, q.v.

Madden, Anna C. "Annie" (Miss), native of Utica, NY; teacher, St. Patrick's Catholic School, Havre de Grace (*Havre de Grace Republican*, 31 Jan 1890 and 5 Jun 1891)

Madden, M. T., member, Merry Ten Social Club, Havre de Grace (*Havre de Grace Republican*, 25 Jul 1890)

Maddox, Joshua M. (colored), see Sulena M. Maddox (colored), q.v.

Maddox, Romer (colored boy), resident of Bel Air (*The Aegis & Intelligencer*, 18 Apr 1890)

Maddox, Sophia (Ruff) (colored), 1854-1915, native of Harford Co. (Death certificate)

Maddox, Sulena M. (colored), 1887-1911, native of Harford Co., born 17 Feb 1887, daughter of Joshua M. Maddox, of Somerset Co., MD, and Sophia Ruff, of Harford Co. (Death certificate - married name Ruff; Tabernacle Mt. Zion Methodist Church Cemetery)

Madonna Public School No. 9, at Madonna near Jarrettsville (*Harford County, Maryland Teachers and the Schools They Served, 1774-1900*, by Henry C. Peden, Jr., 2022, p. 370)

Magaw, Frances Lillian, 1876-1947, native of Pennsylvania, born 20 Jun 1876, daughte of George Magaw and Martha G. Carr, natives of Pennsylvania, resided in Havre de Grace (Death certificate - married name Carr)

Magaw, George, see Frances Lillian Magaw, q.v.

Magaw, James W., trustee, School No. 16, Second District (*The Aegis & Intelligencer*, 22 Aug 1890)

Magaw, Martha G., see Frances Lillian Magaw, q.v.

Magness, Ada O., 1872-1906 (Mt. Carmel Methodist Church Cemetery)

Magness, Albert R., 1839-1902 (Death certificate; Mountain Christian Church Cemetery); juror, First District, 1890 (*Havre de Grace Republican*, 2 May 1890); see Bertha Mae Magness, q.v.

Magness, Albert Stanley, 1877-1943 (Mountain Christian Church Cemetery); son of Albert R. Magness, q.v.

Magness, Amanda (Demoss), 1844-1926 (Mountan Christian Church Cemetery); wife of Albert R. Magness, q.v.; also see Bertha Mae Magness, q.v.

Magness, Ann M., 1812-1890 (Mountain Christian Church Cemetery)

Magness, Arthur J., 1866-1945 (St. Francis de Sales Catholic Church Cemetery); age 24 in 1890 (Marriage License Applications Book ALJ No. 2, 1891)

Magness, Bertha Mae, born 17 Jun 1885, daughter of Albert Magness and Amanda ---- [Demoss] (Albert R.Magness Bible, *Maryland Bible Records, Volume 1*, by Henry C. Peden, Jr., 2003, p. 158)

Magness, Bessie S., 1872-1971 (Mountain Christian Church Cemetery)

Magness, Carrie H., 1866-1915 (Mountain Christian Church Cemetery)

Magness, Charles, resident at Bush (*The Aegis & Intelligencer*, 28 Mar 1890)

Magness, Charles E. 1819-1890, resided near Abingdon (*Baltimore Sun*, 29 Mar 1890); crier of the Circuit Court for Harford County (*Havre de Grace Republican*, 4 Apr 1890); deceased and removed from the voter registration list at Abingdon, First District (*Havre de Grace Republican*, 17 Oct 1890)

Magness, Charles H., 1850-1919 (Cokesbury Memorial Methodist Church Cemetery)

Magness, Charles H., 1882-1954 (Churchville Presbyterian Church Cemetery; *The Aegis*, 8 Jul 1954)

Magness, Christina (Unkart), 1888-1940 (Union Chapel Methodist Church Cemetery)

Magness, Clara (Pennington), 1881-1968 (Mountain Christian Church Cemetery)

Magness, Clarence T., 1879-1945 (William Watters Memorial Methodist Church Cemetery, Cooptown)

Magness, Edward W., 1880-1953 (Cokesbury Memorial Methodist Church Cemetery)

Magness, Effie C., 1877-1925 (Cokesbury Memorial Methodist Church Cemetery)

Magness, Fannie (Miss), resident of Emmorton (*The Aegis & Intelligencer*, 29 Aug 1890)

Magness, Florence, 1876-1948 (Mt. Carmel Methodist Church Cemetery)

Magness, Frances M., 1865-1911 (Mt. Carmel Methodist Church Cemetery)

Magness, Frank (Mrs.), premium award winner, Class J - Domestic Products, Harford County Fair (*The Aegis & Intelligencer*, 24 Oct 1890)

Magness, Franklin "Frank" H., mortising machine operator, Hollingsworth's Spoke Factory, at Wheel, injured at work (*The Aegis & Intelligencer*, 4 Jul 1890; *Harford Democrat*, 4 Jul 1890)

Magness, Frank J., 1882-1954 (St. Francis de Sales Catholic Church Cemetery)

Magness, Georgia Anna, born 29 Aug 1874, daughter of James M. and Mary Susan (DeMoss) Magness (Bethel Presbyterian Church Cemetery Records)

Magness, H. Minerva, 1837-1895, widow of William O. Magness, 1836-1877 (Mt. Carmel Methodist Church Cemetery)

Magness, Harry W., 1879-1961 (Mountain Christian Church Cemetery)

Magness, Irene, 1852-1915 (Union Chapel Methodist Church Cemetery)

Magness, Iola W., 1877-1902, daughter of W. O. and H. M. Magness (Mt. Carmel Methodist Church Cemetery)

Magness, James H., c1829-1899 (Mountain Christian Church Cemetery); resided near Bel Air (Death certificate)

Magness, James M., 1828-1899 (Mt. Carmel Methodist Church Cemetery); see L. Purnell Magness, q.v.

Magness, James R., 1879-1956 (Union Chapel Cemetery; *The Aegis*, 2 Aug 1956)

Magness, John Thomas, 1850-1931 (Union Chapel Methodist Church Cemetery)

Magness, John Thomas, Jr., 1880-1939 (Union Chapel Methodist Church Cemetery)

Magness, Joseph G., 1840-1898 (Mountain Christian Church Cemetery); son of Maria Magness, q.v.

Magness, Katherine E., 1870-1967 (St. Francis de Sales Catholic Church Cemetery)

Magness, L. Purnell, 1859-1917, son of James M. and Mary S. Magness (Mt. Carmel Methodist Church Cemetery)

Magness, Lawrence Farnandis, born 21 Aug 1888, son of Henry F. and Laura A. Magnes (Thomas H. Magness Bible, *Maryland Bible Records, Volume 1*, by Henry C. Peden, Jr., 2003, p. 161)

Magness, Lee, cornetist, Mt. Carmel M. P. Church, at Emmorton, 1890 (*The Aegis & Intelligencer*, 27 Jun 1890)

Magness, Lee A. (Mrs.), resident near Emmorton (*The Aegis & Intelligencer*, 15 Aug 1890)

Magness, Leonidas M., born 13 Nov 1881, son of Henry F. and Laura A. Magness (Thomas H. Magness Bible, *Maryland Bible Records, Volume 1*, by Henry C. Peden, Jr., 2003, p. 161)

Magness, Lizzie (Miss), member, Mountain Reading Circle (*The Aegis & Intelligencer*, 21 Feb 1890); organist, Mt. Carmel M. P. Church, at Emmorton (*The Aegis & Intelligencer*, 27 Jun 1890); student, Union Chapel Public

School (*The Aegis & Intelligencer*, 14 Mar 1890)

Magness, Mamie (Hopkins), 1877-1948 (Darlington Cemetery)

Magness, Margaret A., 1882-1910 (William Watters Memorial Methodist Church Cemetery, Cooptown)

Magness, Maria, died 13 May 1890, age 79, wife of Samuel Magness (*The Aegis & Intelligencer*, 16 May 1890)

Magness, Mary C., 1853-1919 (Cokesbury Memorial Methodist Church Cemetery)

Magness, Mary E., 1857-1949 (St. Francis de Sales Catholic Church Cemetery)

Magness, Mary L., 1861-1935 (Mt. Zion Methodist Church Cemetery)

Magness, Mary S., 1840-1906 (Mt. Carmel Methodist Church Cemetery); see L. Purnell Magness, q.v.

Magness, Mary Theresa, 1889-1958 (St. Francis de Sales Catholic Church Cemetery; *The Aegis*, 17 Jul 1958); wife of William L. Magness, q.v.

Magness, Oathman, 1824-1890 (St. George's Episcopal Church Cemetery)

Magness, Ramsey Lee, 1867-1946 (Mountain Christian Church Cemetery)

Magness, Rhea Sylva, born 14 Nov 1874, daughter of Henry F. and Laura A. Magnes (Thomas H. Magness Bible, *Maryland Bible Records, Volume 1*, by Henry C. Peden, Jr., 2003, p. 161)

Magness, Robert Lee, 1877-1949 (Mt. Carmel Methodist Church Cemetery)

Magness, Sally A., 1843-1893 (Mt. Carmel Methodist Church Cemetery)

Magness, Samuel, see Maria Magness, q.v.

Magness, Sarah H., 1888-1971 (Mountain Christian Church Cemetery)

Magness, Susie H., 1882-1938 (Churchville Presbyterian Church Cemetery)

Magness, Thomas N., born 13 Jun 1879, son of Henry F. and Laura A. Magness (Thomas H. Magness Bible, *Maryland Bible Records, Volume 1*, by Henry C. Peden, Jr., 2003, p. 161)

Magness, Walter Pinkney, 1874-1920 (Mountain Christian Church Cemetery); son of Albert and Amanda Magness (Albert R.Magness Bible, *Maryland Bible Records, Volume 1*, by Henry C. Peden, Jr., 2003, p. 158); student, Public School No. 1, First District (*The Aegis & Intelligencer*, 10 Jan 1890)

Magness, William Henry, born 20 Oct 1878, son of Albert and Amanda Magness (Albert R.Magness Bible, *Maryland Bible Records, Volume 1*, by Henry C. Peden, Jr., 2003, p. 158)

Magness, William L., 1889-1955 (St. Francis de Sales Catholic Church Cemetery)

Magnolia Baseball Club, First District (*The Aegis & Intelligencer*, 1 Aug 1890)

Magnolia Colored Public School No. 3, at Magnolia, First District (*Harford County, Maryland Teachers and the Schools They Served, 1774-1900*, by Henry C. Peden, Jr., 2022, p. 370)

Magnolia House, at Magnolia, George W. Brown, prop. (*Country Stores: Harford County's Rura Heritage*, by Henry C. Peden, Jr. and Jack L. Shagena, Jr., 2015, p. 66)

Magnolia Methodist Episcopal Church (Magnolia Road, near Joppa)

Magnolia Public School No. 6, at Magnolia, First District (*Harford County, Maryland Teachers and the Schools They Served, 1774-1900*, by Henry C. Peden, Jr., 2022, p. 370)

Magowan, Edward T., supreme past chancellor, Harford Lodge No. 54, Knights of Pythias, Havre de Grace (*The Aegis & Intelligencer*, 11 Jul 1890)

Magowan, Julia E., student, Havre de Grace High School (*Havre de Grace Republican*, 31 Oct 1890; *The Aegis & Intelligencer*, 24 Oct 1890)

Magowan, M. M., musician, Bayside Cornet Band, Havre de Grace (*Havre de Grace Republican*, 31 Jan 1890)

Magowan, Miranda, new name on the Havre de Grace voter registration list (*Havre de Grace Republican*, 19 Sep 1890)

Magowan, R. A., trustee, Equitable League of America, Court No. 70, Havre de Grace (*Havre de Grace Republican*, 11 Jul 1890)

Magraw, Elizabeth Neeper, born 4 Apr 1873, daughter of Dr. James Martin Magraw and Katherine Whiteley Stump (Churchville Presbyterian Church Register Roll of Infant Church Members or Baptized Children, No. 253)

Magraw, Katherine Whiteley (Stump), 1846-1936 (West Nottingham Cemetery, Cecil Co., MD); wife of Dr. James Mitchell Magraw, 1841-1889, lived at *Henrico* near Thomas Run, and died in Perryville, Cecil Co., MD (*The Aegis & Intelligencer*, 17 Jan 1936)

Magraw, Mary Maxwell, born 17 Mar 1870, daughter of Dr. James Martin Magraw and Katherine Whiteley Stump (Churchville Presbyterian Church Register Roll of Infant Church Members or Baptized Children, No. 252)

Magraw, Robert, honor student, third grade, Thomas Run Public School (*The Aegis & Intelligencer*, 4 Jul 1890)

Magruder, Andrew (colored), 1858-1939 (Death certificate; Heavenly Waters Cemetery)

Magruder, Willis N. (colored), 1860-1939, son of a slave named Lafayette and owned by George W. Magruder (Death certificate)

Maguire, Amanda (Demoss), 1844-1926 (Mountain Christian Church Cemetery); native of Maryland, resided at Emmorton (Death certificate)

Maguire, Elizabeth A. (Stine), 1851-1925 (St. Ignatius Catholic Church Cemetery); native of Harford Co., resided near Rocks (Death certificate)

Maguire, Francis, Civil War veteran, Fallston (*1890 Special Census of the Civil War Veterans of the State of Maryland*, by L. Tilden Moore, Volume III, p. 75)

Mahan, Angeline Virginia (Bailey), 1852-1924 (*Barnes-Bailey Genealogy*, by Walter D. Barnes, 1939, pp. H-43, I-62); wife of James P. Mahan, q.v.

Mahan, Charles A., 1856-1952 (Angel Hill Cemetery); also see Sarah A. Mahan and Charles Winfield Mahan, Ida May Mahan, and Fannie Rebecca Mahan, q.v.

Mahan, Charles Winfield, born 1 Mar 1887, son of Charles A. and Sarah A. Mahan (Holy Trinity Episcopal Church Register of Baptisms, p. 92)

Mahan, Clara O., born 1 Dec 1882, daughter of James P. and Angeline V. (Bailey) Mahan (*Barnes-Bailey Genealogy*, by Walter D. Barnes, 1939, p. I-62)

Mahan, Estella, student, Union School House, near Bush Chapel (*The Aegis & Intelligencer*, 14 Mar 1890, lspelled her name Mahen)

Mahan, Fannie, see Lida E. Hawkins, q.v.

Mahan, Fannie E. (Mahan), 1850-1924 (Smith Chapel Methodist Church Cemetery); native of Harford Co., resided near Aberdeen (Death certificate)

Mahan, Fannie Rebecca, born 21 Nov 1885, daughter of Charles A. and Sarah A. Mahan (Holy Trinity Episcopal Church Register of Baptisms, p. 92)

Mahan, Hattie P., 1889-1924 (Smith Chapel Methodist Church Cemetery - married name Sheridan); native of Harford Co., born 16 Jan 1889, daughter of James P. Mahan and Angie V. Bailey (Death certificate)

Mahan, Ida May, born 19 Nov 1883, daughter of Charles A. and Sarah A. Mahan (Holy Trinity Episcopal Church Register of Baptisms, p. 86); student, Union School House, near Bush Chapel (*The Aegis & Intelligencer*, 14 Mar 1890, listed her name was May Mahen)

Mahan, James Allen, born 28 Jun 1880, son of James P. and Angeline V. (Bailey) Mahan (*Barnes-Bailey Genealogy*, by Walter D. Barnes, 1939, p. I-62)

Mahan, James P., 1843-1898 (Smith Chapel Methodist Church Cemetery); see Hattie P. Mahan, q.v.

Mahan, John, 1827-1900, dealer in fish and ducks, Havre de Grace (Death certificate); organizer and vice president, Havre de Grace Democratic Club (*Havre de Grace Republican*, 31 Oct 1890)

Mahan, John E., resided on Romney Creek, Bush River Neck (*The Aegis & Intelligencer*, 20 Jun 1890)

Mahan, John H., proprietor of High House Fishing and Crabbing Resort, Romney Creek, Michaelsville, Bush

River Neck (*The Aegis & Intelligencer*, 11 Jul 1890 and 15 Aug 1890)

Mahan, Laura N., see Bessie L. Abbott, q.v.

Mahan, Nancy (Mrs.), enumerated as age 93 in the 1890 census, Havre de Grace (*Havre de Grace Republican*, 22 Aug 1890, listed a handful of names from the actual 1890 census and she was one of them)

Mahan, Robert, c1838-1919, Civil War veteran (Angel Hill Cemetery); enumerated as age 50 in the 1890 census, Havre de Grace (*Havre de Grace Republican*, 22 Aug 1890, listed a handful of names from the actual 1890 census and he was one of them); Robert B. F. Mahan, junior commander, Rodgers Post, G. A. R. Havre de Grace (*Havre de Grace Republican*, 11 Jul 1890)

Mahan, Robie, born 8 Dec 1887, daughter of James P. and Angeline V. (Bailey) Mahan (*Barnes-Bailey Genealogy*, by Walter D. Barnes, 1939, p. I-62)

Mahan, Sarah (Cantler), wife of John Mahan, q.v.

Mahan, Sarah A., 1860-1938 (Angel Hill Cemetery); wife of Charles A. Mahan, q.v.

Mahan, Thomas C., Civil War veteran, Chrome Hill (*1890 Special Census of the Civil War Veterans of the State of Maryland*, by L. Tilden Moore, Volume III, p. 80); government pensioner, Chrome Hill (*The Aegis & Intelligencer*, 25 Jul 1890)

Mahan, William H., farmer, near Avondale (*The Aegis & Intelligencer*, 3 Jan 1890); trustee, Avondale School No. 11, Second District (*Havre de Grace Republican*, 30 May 1890); treated by unidentified doctor in 1890 ("Medical Account Book – 1890," Historical Society of Harford County Archives Folder)

Mahan, William M., road mender, Second District (*Havre de Grace Republican*, 28 Mar 1890)

Maher, Katherine, wife of Andrew Gleason, q.v.; also see Katherine E. Gleason, q.v.

Mahoney, Ella Virginia (Harward) (Kyle), 1858-1847 (St. Ignatius Catholic Church Cemetery)

Mahoney, John F., 1852-1916 (St. Ignatius Catholic Church Cemetery)

Main, Mary Ellen, 1877-1919 (Darlington Cemetery)

Main, William H., 1873-1944 (Darlington Cemetery)

Maine, Hattie, high school student, Second District (*Havre de Grace Republican*, 31 Oct 1890)

Maisler, William, 1853-1932, born in Germany (Death certificate; Alms House Record Book also spelled his name Misner and Misier)

Makeson, Diana, born 31 May 1874, daughter of William and Hannah Makeson (Holy Trinity Episcopal Church Register of Baptisms, p. 84)

Makeson, John Howard, born 27 Jun 1879, son of William and Hannah Makeson (Holy Trinity Episcopal Church Register of Baptisms, p. 84)

Makeson, Rose, born 22 Mar 1872, daughter of William and Hannah Makeson (Holy Trinity Episcopal Church Register of Baptisms, p. 84)

Makinson & Ewing's General Store, at Level, William B. Makinson and Lawson Ewing, prop. (*Country Stores: Harford County's Rural Heritage*, by Henry C. Peden, Jr. and Jack L. Shagena, Jr., 2015, p. 163)

Makinson, Alice H., 1873-1932 (Deer Creek Harmony Presbyterian Church)

Makinson, Henry L, 1869-1930 (Deer Creek Harmony Presbyterian Church)

Makinson, Mary S., 1828-1913 (Deer Creek Harmony Presbyterian Church)

Makinson, William T., 1826-1899 (Deer Creek Harmony Presbyterian Church); William Mackinson, trustee, Glenville School No. 17, Second District (*Havre de Grace Republican*, 30 May 1890)

Malcolm, Amanda (Bush), 1887-1948 (St. George's Episcopal Church Cemetery)

Malcolm, Elizabeth A., 1835-1895 (Grove Presbyterian Church Cemetery)

Malcolm, Elsie, born 7 Dec 1882, daughter of William Edward Malcolm and Frances E. Johnson (Albert Kesyer Ford Bible, *Maryland Bible Records, Volume 2*, by Henry C. Peden, Jr., 2003, p. 40)

Malcolm, Florence, born 19 Sep 1884, daughter of William Edward Malcolm and Frances E. Johnson (Albert Kesyer Ford Bible, *Maryland Bible Records, Volume 2*, by Henry C. Peden, Jr., 2003, p. 40)

Malcolm, Frank, youngest son of Othman Malcolm, of Perryman, died 14 Jan 1890, in his 19th year (*The Aegis & Intelligencer*, 24 Jan 1890, but St. George's Episcopal Church Cemetery tombstone states died in his 22nd year)

Malcolm, Frank P., 1840-1912 (St. George's Episcopal Church Cemetery); Civil War veteran, Aberdeen (*1890 Special Census of the Civil War Veterans of the State of Maryland*, by L. Tilden Moore, Volume III, p. 63)

Malcolm, Georgia (Miss), resident of Perryman (*The Aegis & Intelligencer*, 19 Sep 1890)

Malcolm, Helen Elizabeth, born 16 Nov 1884, daughter of James W. and Mary E. Malcolm (St. George's Episcopal Church Register of Baptisms, pp. 4-5, misspelled her name as Hellen Elizabeth Malcombe)

Malcolm, Hugh Bush, 1889-1891 (St. George's Episcopal Cemetery); born 11 Nov 1889, son of James W. and Mary E. Malcolm (St. George's Church Register of Baptisms, p. 9)

Malcolm, J., shortstop, Perryman Baseball Club (*The Aegis & Intelligencer*, 18 Jul 1890)

Malcolm, James C., see Frank Malcolm and Oathman Malcolm, q.v.

Malcolm, James Emory, born 30 Aug 1887, son of James W. and Mary Ella Malcolm (St. George's Episcopal Church Register of Baptisms, p. 6)

Malcolm, James Walker, 1858-1931 (St. George's Episcopal Church Cemetery); see Hugh Bush Malcolm and Helen Elizabeth Malcolm, q.v.

Malcolm, Mary Ella, 1861-1938 (St. George's Episcopal Church Cemetery); see Hugh Bush Malcolm and Helen Elizabeth Malcolm, q.v.

Malcolm, Marion, 1856-1922 (St. George's Episcopal Church Cemetery)

Malcolm, Millie (Allen), 1855-1932 (St. George's Episcopal Church Cemetery)

Malcolm, Nellie (Michael), 1864-1938 (St. George's Episcopal Church Cemetery)

Malcolm, Nellie A., 1865-1952 (St. George's Episcopal Church Cemetery)

Malcolm, Oathman, 1824-1890 (St. George's Episcopal Church Cemetery); farmer at *Delph* near Michaelsville, died in his 67th year; brother of the late James C. Malcolm (*The Aegis & Intelligencer*, 31 Oct 1890); also see Frank Malcolm, q.v.

Malcolm, Sadie, high school student, Second District (*Havre de Grace Republican*, 31 Oct 1890)

Malcolm. Thomas J. J., 1884-1940 (St. George's Episcopal Church Cemetery)

Malcolm, William Edward, died 1896 (Albert Kesyer Ford Bible, *Maryland Bible Records, Volume 2*, by Henry C. Peden, Jr., 2003, p. 40); husband of Frances E. Johnson (married 1876, she died 1942)

Malcolm, Williana, born 23 Sep 1888, daughter of William Edward Malcolm and Frances E. Johnson (Albert Kesyer Ford Bible, *Maryland Bible Records, Volume 2*, by Henry C. Peden, Jr., 2003, p. 40)

Mallick, Fannie E., born -- Oct 1871, wife of Robert Mallick (1900 Aberdeen Census)

Mallick, George, treated by unidentified doctor in 1890 ("Medical Account Book – 1890," Historical Society of Harford County Archives Folder)

Mallick, George McClennon, age 23 in 1889 (Marriage License Applications Book ALJ No. 2, 1890; Holy Trinity Episcopal Church Register of Marriages, p. 216)

Mallick, Laura Virginia, 1869-1891 (Holy Trinity Episcopal Church Cemetery)

Mallick, Pearl (Miss), member, Aberdeen M. E. Church (*Havre de Grace Republican*, 21 Feb 1890); student, Aberdeen Public School (*The Aegis & Intelligencer*, 23 May 1890); born 1873, see Pearl Aaronson, q.v.

Mallick, Robert, born -- Feb 1862 (1900 Aberdeen Census)

Mallick, Susan A. (Cullum), 1829-1911, native of Harford Furnace, resided at Carsins (Death certificatet spelled her name Malack); Susan Mallick sold land in April 1890 (*The Aegis & Intelligencer*, 9 May 1890)

Mallock, Slade, mason, Bush River Neck (*The Aegis & Intelligencer*, 11 Jul 1890)

Malone, Dennis, see Lillian DeMoss Kennedy, q.v.

Malone, Frank D., name removed from the voter registration list in the Sixth District (*Havre de Grace Republican*, 17 Oct 1890)

Malone, Lillian, see Chester Boyd Kennedy, q.v.

Malone, Viola Cecelia, wife of John M. Scarborough; also see Guy Wilson Scarborough and Russell Kenneth Scarborough, q.v.

Maloney, Annie, age 21 in 1890 (Marriage License Applications Book ALJ No. 2, 1891)

Maloney, William, farmer, near Edgewood (*The Aegis & Intelligencer*, 7 Nov 1890)

Maloy, James E., new name on the voter registration list at Hopewell, Second District, 1890 (*Havre de Grace Republican*, 17 Oct 1890)

Maloy, Joseph G., new name on the voter registration list at Hopewell, Second District, 1890 (*Havre de Grace Republican*, 17 Oct 1890)

Mang, Bernhard, native of Germany, filed for naturalization in 1890 (*Harford Democrat*, 14 Mar 1890)

Manifold, A. Clarkson, resident near Norrisville (*The Aegis & Intelligencer*, 5 Dec 1890); husband of Mary Manifold, q.v.

Manifold, Mary (Wilson), 1824-1900, native of Pennsylvania, resident of Cambria, Harford Co. (Death certificate); wife of A. Clarkson Manifold, q.v.

Manifold, Myra, student, Bel Air Graded School (*The Aegis & Intelligencer*, 26 Dec 1890)

Manifold, Rebecca, see Rebecca J. Heaps, q.v.

Manifold, Rose, student, Bel Air Graded School (*The Aegis & Intelligencer*, 26 Dec 1890)

Manifold, S. M., road supervisor for the Maryland Central Railroad, moved to Bel Air in September, 1890 (*Harford Democrat*, 5 Sep 1890); second vice president, Survivors' Association of the 51st Pennsylvania Cavalry Regiment (*Havre de Grace Republican*, 31 Oct 1890)

Manifold, William, superintendent Prospect Sunday School (*Havre de Grace Republican*, 25 Apr 1890)

Manley AUMP Church (Havre de Grace)

Mann, Mary L., 1855-1915 (Angel Hill Cemetery)

Manning, T. W., member, Bel Air Cornet Band (*The Aegis & Intelligencer*, 1 Aug 1890)

Manning, Timothy, resident of Forest Hill (*The Aegis & Intelligencer*, 20 Jun 1890)

Mannix, Lawrence, 1870-1948 (Death certificate; Alms House Record Book)

Mansley, John, 1826-1899, merchant at Havre de Grace, native of England, widower of Elizabeth Mansley (Death certificate)

Marine, William Matthew, 1843-1904 (Loudon Park Cemetery, Baltimore City); trustee, Robin Hood School No. 18, Second District (*Havre de Grace Republican*, 30 May 1890; attorney-at-law, Marine & Bradford, Bel Air; officer in Susquehanna Lodge No. 130, A. F. & A.M. (*Biographical Dictionary of Harford County, Maryland, 1774-1974*, by Henry C. Peden, Jr. and William O. Carr, 2021, p. 173)

Maris, Samuel W., 1822-1891 (Darlington Cemetery)

Markel, Adam, mason, Havre de Grace (*Havre de Grace Republican*, 20 Jun 1890)

Marker (Marku?), Minnie (Roe), 1851-1899, resided near Reckord, native of Germany, wife of William Marker (Death certificate)

Markey, C. William, 1884-1957 (Jarrettsville Cemetery)

Markland's General Store, at Cedars or Cedarville, George A. Markland, prop. (*Country Stores: Harford County's Rural Heritage*, by Henry C. Peden, Jr. and Jack L. Shagena, Jr., 2015, p. 164)

Markland, George Augustus, 1843-1915 (Dublin Southern Cemetery); tomato farmer, near Dublin, Fifth District (*Havre de Grace Republican*, 25 Jul 1890; *The Aegis & Intelligencer*, 18 Jul 1890)

Markland, George Augustus, Jr., 1878-1935 (Dublin Southern Cemetery)

Markland, Jennie M. (McCann), 1855-1935 (Dublin Southern Cemetery)

Markley, C. William, 1884-1957 (Jarrettsville Cemetery)

Markley, John, 1858-1930 (Jarrettsville Cemetery)

Markley, Lehr Cordelia (Dixon), 1861-1928 (Death certificate)

Markley, Louisa, 1837-1900, native of Baltimore, resided near Creswell (Death certificate)

Markline, Benjamin, born 4 May 1886, son of John N. Markline and Mary C. Fieseler (Bethel Presbyterian Church Cemetery Records)

Markline, Catherine, born 1 Feb 1883, daughter of John N. Markline and Mary Fieseler (Bethel Presbyterian Church Cemetery Records)

Markline, John Jacob, 1806-1890 (Bethel Presbyterian Church Cemetery Records)

Markline, John Nicholas, 1854-1928 (Bethel Presbyterian Church Cemetery Records); native of Baltimore Co., married, farmer, resided at Madonna (Death certificate)

Markline, John Nicholas, Jr., born 24 Aug 1888, son of John N. Markline and Mary C. Fieseler (Bethel Presbyterian Church Cemetery Records)

Markline, Mary C. (Fieseler), 1858-1932 (Bethel Presbyterian Church Cemetery Records); wife of John N. Markline, q.v.

Markline, Philip, carriage and wagon maker, of Fourth District, near Black Horse (*Havre de Grace Republican*, 17 Jan 1890)

Markline, William, born 1884, son of John N. Markline and Mary C. Fieseler (Bethel Presbyterian Church Cemetery Records)

Marks, Rose L. (colored), see Rose L. Dunsen (colored), q.v.

Marll, John P., Civil War veteran, Joppa (*1890 Special Census of the Civil War Veterans of the State of Maryland*, by L. Tilden Moore, Volume III, p. 62)

Mars, Mary C., 1853-1938 (Rock Run Methodist Church Cemetery)

Mars, Elizabeth, see Casper Smith, q.v.

Marsh, Chester W., 884-1972 (Mt. Zion Methodist Church Cemetery)

Marsh, Grover Howard, 1890-1954 (Mt. Zion Methodist Church Cemetery)

Marsh, Lelia Evana, 1890-1954 (Mt. Zion Methodist Church Cemetery)

Marshall, Amanda C., 1853-1924 (Angel Hill Cemetery)

Marshall, Annie (Mrs.), 1872-1927 (Death certificate)

Marshall, Catherine (Washington) (colored), 1849-1914, native of Virginia, resided in Havre de Grace (Death certificate; St. James United Cemetery)

Marshall, Geoffrey, 1890-1966 (St. Mary's Episcopal Church Cemetery)

Marshall, J. Henry (colored), 1846-1934 (St. James United Cemetery tombstone inscribed 1846, but death certificate states 1843); farmer, of Hickory Ridge, near Stepney (*Havre de Grace Republican*, 5 Dec 1890)

Marshall, Laura, wife of William H. Fletcher, q.v., also see Lily M. Fletcher and Sarah Emma Fletcher, q.v.

Martin's General Store, at Chesney near Michaelsville on Bush River Neck, Samuel H. Martin, prop. (*Country Stores: Harford County's Rural Heritage*, by Henry C. Peden, Jr. and Jack L. Shagena, Jr., 2015, p. 165)

Martin, Agnes Ann, born -- May 1885, baptized 14 Jun 1885, daughter of William Martin, of New York, and Lucinda Burkholder, of Baltimore (St. Ignatius Catholic Church Baptism Register, p. 81)

Martin, Amanda C., 1866-1911 (Calvary Methodist Church Cemetery)

Martin, Anna E., 1876-1952 (St. Ignatius Catholic Church Cemetery)

Martin, Anna J., 1849-1914 (Fallston Methodist Church Cemetery)

Martin, Anna Virginia (Martin), 1869-1967 (St. Francis de Sales Catholic Church Cemetery); native of Havre de Grace, born 22 Jan 1869, daughter of J. Patrick Martin and Barbara Burkett (Pennington Funeral Home Records); wife of Walter L. Martin, q.v.

Martin, Annie, confirmed 26 Oct 1890 (Churchville Presbyterian Church Chronological Roll of Communicants, No. 552)

Martin, Annie M., born 1878, died ---- (Emory Methodist Church Cemetery)

Martin, August, 1847-1939 (Fallston Methodist Church Cemetery); farmer, Upper Cross Roads (*The Aegis & Intelligencer*, 22 Aug 1890); see Mollie A. Martin, q.v.

Martin, Berta C. (Miss), treasurer, Mountain Christian Church Sunday School (*Havre de Grace Republican*, 7 Feb 1890)

Martin, Bessie Courtney (Spencer), born 1887, died ---- (Grove Presbyterian Church Cemetery)

Martin, Catherine, 1827-1899 (St. Ignatius Catholic Church Cemetery); native of Ireland, resident of Chestnut Hill, widow of John Martin (Death certificate)

Martin, Catharine Lorretto, 1888-1891 (St. Ignatius Catholic Church Cemetery); daughter of Richard Martin, native of Harford Co., and Susannah "Susan" Smith, native of Anne Arundel Co., MD (St. Ignatius Catholic Church Baptism Register, p. 101)

Martin, Charles, student, Oakland School, 1890 (George G. Curtiss Ledger)

Martin, Christopher, 1872-1929 (Angel Hill Cemetery)

Martin, Clara E., 1887-1959 (Mt. Zion Methodist Church Cemetery)

Martin, Clarence W., 1870-1945 (St. George's Episcopal Church Cemetery)

Martin, Cornelia C., born -- Jun 1885, daughter of George C. and Cornelia S. Martin (1900 Aberdeen Census)

Martin, Cornelia S., 1849-1920 (St. George's Episcoal Church Cemetery); wife of George Chapman Martin, q.v.; also see Cornelia C. Martin and George E. Martin, q.v.

Martin, Della, 1867-1948, native of Harford Furnace, Harford Co., born 20 Jun 1867, daughter of John Martin and Lorenza Hitchcock, both natives of Cecil Co., MD (Pennington Funeral Home Records - married name Smith)

Martin, E. Jennie, 1842-1915 (St. George's Episcopal Church Cemetery)

Martin, E. M., incorporator and director, Guardian Star Council No. 9, Junior Order of United American Mechanics, Havre de Grace (*The Aegis & Intelligencer*, 17 Jan 1890); member, Guiding Star Council No. 9, Jr. O. U. A. M., Havre de Grace (*Havre de Grace Republican*, 11 Jul 1890); recording secretary, Venus Council No. 44, O. U. A. M., Havre de Grace (*Havre de Grace Republican*, 11 Jul 1890)

Martin, Edna H., born 1882, see Edna H. Grafton, q.v.

Martin, Edwin E., 1862-1925 (Centre Methodist Church Cemetery)

Martin, Elizabeth A., 1844-1913 (Centre Methodist Church Cemetery); see John D. Grafton, q.v.

Martin, Elizabeth Alice, born -- Apr 1883, baptized 10 Jun 1883, daughter of Patrick Martin, native of Ireland, and Frances Keywood (St. Ignatius Catholic Church Baptism Register, p. 66)

Martin, Elizabeth Christine, 1843-1899 (Mt. Zion Methodist Church Cemetery); resided near Fulford, wife of Samuel H. Martin, q.v. (Death certificate incomplete)

Martin, Ella C., born -- Jan 1880, daughter of George C. and Cornelia S. Martin (1900 Aberdeen Census)

Martin, Elwood D., 1878-1962 (Fallston Methodist Church Cemetery)

Martin, Emma C., 1867-1961 (Mt. Zion Methodist Church Cemetery)

Martin, Eugene F., 1885-1961 (Fallston Methodist Church Cemetery)

Martin, Fannie, student, Public School No. 1, First District (*The Aegis & Intelligencer*, 10 Jan 1890)

Martin, Francis, new name on the voter registration list in the Sixth District (*Havre de Grace Republican*, 17 Oct 1890)

Martin, Francis Michael ("Frank"), 1888-1918 (St. Ignatius Catholic Church Cemetery); born 27 Apr 1888, baptized 27 May 1888, son of John Martin, native of County Tipperary, Ireland, and Margaret Whaland, native of Harford Co. (St. Ignatius Catholic Church Baptism Register, p. 99)

Martin, Frank, 1866-1937 (St. Ignatius Catholic Church Cemetery); musician, Bayside Cornet Band, Havre de Grace, 1890 (*Havre de Grace Republican*, 31 Jan 1890)

Martin, G. Herbert, 1873-1897 (Centre Methodist Church Cemetery); son of J. K. Polk Martin, q.v. (*Deaths and Marriages in Harford County, Maryland, and Vicinity, 1873-1904, from the Diaries of Albert Peter Silver*, transcribed by Glenn Randers-Pehrson, 1995, p. 16, inadvertently stated J. R. Polk Martin)

Martin, George, student, Harford Furnace School (*The Aegis & Intelligencer*, 14 Feb 1890)

Martin, George Chapman, 1849-1931 (St. George's Episcopal Church Cemetery); see Cornelia C. Martin and George E. Martin, q.v.

Martin, George D., 1840-1900 (Little Falls Quaker Cemetery)

Martin, George D., 1857-1939 (Calvary Methodist Church Cemetery)

Martin, George Edwin, 1888-1960 (Grove Presbyterian Church Cemetery); born -- Oct 1888, son of George C. and Cornelia S. Martin (1900 Aberdeen Census)

Martin, George H., 1861-1940 (Mt. Zion Methodist Church Cemetery)

Martin, Gusteen H., 1885-1960 (St. Paul's Methodist Church Cemetery)

Martin, H. May (Pyle), 1874-1934 (Old Brick Baptist Church Cemetery)

Martin, Harry M., 1885-1954 (Mt. Zion Methodist Church Cemetery)

Martin, Henry Regester, 1875-1935 (St. George's Episcopal Church Cemetery)

Martin, Henry T., 1836-1904 (Cokesbury Memorial Methodist Church Cemetery)

Martin, Howard W., 1876-1963 (Old Brick Baptist Church Cemetery); student, Forest Hill School, 1890 (*The Aegis*, 2 Jul 1965, school picture)

Martin, J. C. (Mrs.), county out-pensioner [welfare recipient], Third District (*Havre de Grace Republican*, 4 Jul 1890)

Martin, J. Oliver, 1872-1925 (St. George's Episcopal Church Cemetery)

Martin, J. Patrick, see Anna Virginia Martin, q.v.

Martin, James, Civil War veteran, Norrisville (*1890 Special Census of the Civil War Veterans of the State of Maryland*, by L. Tilden Moore, Volume III, p. 81); see John D. Grafton, q.v.

Martin, James Alfred, 1879-1966 (St. Paul's Methodist Church Cemetery)

Martin, James H., 1846-1900 (St. Paul's Methodist Church Cemetery); see Samuel Oscar Martin, q.v.

Martin, James Knox Polk, 1844-1923 (Centre Methodist Church Cemetery); building contractor, Havre de Grace (*Havre de Grace Republican*, 7 Feb 1890; Bailey Funeral Home Records listed his name as James K. P. Martin and Death certificate gave it as James P. K. Martin; full name was most likely James Knox Polk Martin); see G. Herbert Martin, q.v.

Martin, James Walter, 1886-1911 (St. Ignatius Catholic Church Cemetery); born -- Apr 1886, baptized 30 May 1886, son of John C. Martin, native of County Tipperary, Ireland, and Margaret Whaland, native of Harford Co. (St. Ignatius Catholic Church Baptism Register, p. 87)

Martin, Jane, see Mollie A. Martin, q.v.

Martin, John, see Della Martin, q.v.

Martin, John, 1829-1897 (St. Ignatius Catholic Church Cemetery); see Catherine Martin, q.v.
Martin, John H. (Dr.), 1834-1903 (St. George's Episcopal Church Cemetery); native of Harford Co., resident of Aberdeen (Death certificate)

Martin, John T., 1863-1925 (St. Francis de Sales Catholic Church Cemetery)

Martin, John William, born -- Jan 1890, baptized 16 Feb 1890, son of William Martin, native of Harford Co., and Lucnda Burkholder, native of Pennsylvania (St. Ignatius Catholic Church Baptism Register, p. 111)

Martin, Julia Craig (Caldwell), 1871-1947 (Deer Creek Harmony Presbyterian Church Cemetery); native of Virginia, resided near Havre de Grace (Death certificate)

Martin, Kate (Miss), resident near Harford Furnace (*The Aegis & Intelligencer*, 9 May 1890); Bible class teacher, St. Francis de Sales Catholic Church Sunday School (*The Aegis & Intelligencer*, 10 Jan 1890)

Martin, Kate E., 1862-1945 (Centre Methodist Church Cemetery)

Martin, Katherine P., born -- Sep 1886, baptized 3 Oct 1886, daughter of William Martin, native of New York, and Lucinda Burkholder, native of York Co., PA (St. Ignatius Catholic Church Baptism Register, p. 89)

Martin, Livingston, 1880-1936 (Centre Methodist Church Cemetery); student, Forest Hill School, 1890 (*The Aegis*, 2 Jul 1965, school picture)

Martin, Lloyd R., 1836-1905 (Centre Methodist Church Cemetery)

Martin, Louis Gover (Rev.), 1839-1907 (St. George's Episcopal Church Cemetery); native of Poppler Hill *(sic)*, resided near Aberdeen, married son of Daniel Martain *(sic)* and Priscilla Hopkins (Death certificate)

Martin, Louis Henry, 1883-1959 (St. George's Episcopal Church Cemetery); born -- Sep 1883, son of George C. and Cornelia S. Martin (1900 Aberdeen Census)

Martin, Louis I., 1840-1917 (St. Mary's Catholic Church Cemetery)

Martin, Lucinda, acquired land in April 1890 (*The Aegis & Intelligencer*, 9 May 1890)

Martin, Lucinda, 1884-1919 (Churchville Presbyterian Church Cemetery)

Martin, Margaret E., 1861-1914 (St. Ignatius Catholic Church Cemetery)

Martin, Marion A., 1879-1963 (Fallston Methodist Church Cemetery)

Martin, Marion S., 1868-1925 (Churchville Presbyterian Church Cemetery)

Martin, Mary (Rumsey) (colored), 1863-1911, native of Harford Co. (Death certificate)

Martin, Mary (Mrs.), died 19 Feb 1899, age not stated, resided at Belcamp (Death certificate)

Martin, Mary Agnes, age 22 in 1889 (Marriage License Applications Book ALJ No. 2, 1889); also see John A. Shipley, q.v.

Martin, Mary E., 1848-1927 (St. Paul's Methodist Church Cemetery)

Martin, Mary Ellen, born -- Dec 1884, baptized 1 Feb 1885, daughter of John C. Martin, native of County Tipperary, Ireland, and Margaret Whaland, native of Harford Co. (St. Ignatius Catholic Church Baptism Register, p. 77)

Martin, Mary Frances, 1873-1960 (St. George's Episcopal Church Cemetery)

Martin, Mary J., 1886-1971 (St. Paul's Methodist Church Cemetery)

Martin, Mary Rebecca, born -- Jan 1863, baptized 14 Jan 1894 (ex-Presbyterian), daughter of Samuel and Elizabeth (Kilgore) Martin, natives of York Co., PA (St. Ignatius Catholic Church Baptism Register, p. 135)

Martin, May H. (Pyle), 1874-1934 (Old Brick Baptist Church Cemetery); native of Maryland, born 13 May 1874, daughter of William Pyle and Mary Famous (Bailey Funeral Home Records); wife of Howard W. Martin, q.v.

Martin, Mollie A., 1872-1900 (Fallston Methodist Church Cemetery); native of Maryland, resided at Fallston, daughter of August Martin and Jane ---- (Death certificate)

Martin, Mollie R., 1887-1957 (Fallston Methodist Church Cemetery)

Martin, Moses V. (colored), 1855-1917 (Skinner Ceetery, Havre de Grace); native of Harford Co (Death certificate)

Martin, Patrick (Mrs.), of Fallston, daughter of Catherine Burke, q.v.

Martin, Rebecca (Miss), 1852-1923 (Bethel Presbyterian Church Cemetery Records)

Martin, Richard, born -- Apr 1887, baptized 17 Apr 1887, son of Michael Martin, native of Harford Co., and

Ann Carroll, native of Baltimore Co. (St. Ignatius Catholic Church Baptism Register, p. 92)

Martin, Richard A., 1852-1945 (St. Ignatius Catholic Church Cemetery)

Martin, Robert, potato farmer, Fallston (*Havre de Grace Republican*, 5 Sep 1890)

Martin, Rosalie M. "Rosa" (Blake), 1867-1943 (St. Francis de Sales Catholic Church Cemetery)

Martin, Samuel Edwin, 1889-1898 (Mt. Zion Methodist Church Cemetery)

Martin, Samuel H., 1834-1902 (Mt. Zion Methodist Church Cemetery); juror, Second District, 1890 (*Havre de Grace Republican*, 31 Oct 1890); see Elizabeth C. Martin and Samuel H. Martin, q.v.

Martin, Samuel H., 1853-1899 (St. Francis de Sales Catholic Church Cemetery); resident of Michaelsville (Death certificate); see Martin's General Store, q.v.

Martin, Samuel H. ("Sammy"), died 18 Jul 1890, age 10 months (*The Aegis & Intelligencer*, 25 Jul 1890); Sam Martin treated by unidentified doctor in 1890 ("Medical Account Book – 1890," Historical Society of Harford County Archives Folder)

Martin, Samuel Oscar, 1881-1941 (Emory Methodist Church Cemetery); native of Harford Co., born 23 Aug 1881, son of James H. Martin and Mary Smithson (Bailey Funeral Home Records)

Martin, Sarah Jane, 1878-1945 (Centre Methodist Church Cemetery)

Martin, Sarah R. (Grafton), 1842-1914 (Centre Methodist Church Cemetery; Death certificate); wife of James Polk Martin, q.v.

Martin, Susan (Miss), 1846-1918 (Bethel Presbyterian Church Cemetery Records)

Martin, Susan M. (Smith), 1862-1938 (St. Ignatius Catholic Church Cdemetery); wife of Richard A. Smith, q.v.

Martin, Susie D. (Cole), 1844-1918 (St. George's Episcopal Church Cemetery)

Martin, Teresa Agnes, 1848-1928 (St. Mary's Catholic Church Cemetery)

Martin, Thomas, father of M. Agnes Martin; see John A. Shipley, q.v.

Martin, Thomas J., 1881-1949, of Bel Air (Death certificate)

Martin, Wakeman, resident near Harford Furnace (*The Aegis & Intelligencer*, 9 May 1890)

Martin, Walter, student, Forest Hill School, c1890 (*The Aegis*, 2 Jul 1965, school picture)

Martin, Walter Lee, 1871-1946 (Mt. Zion Methodist Church Cemetery); native of Harford Co., born 8 Sep 1871, son of Samuel H. Martin and ---- (Pennington Funeral Home Records); see Anna Virginia Martin, q.v.

Martin, William, sold land in April 1890 (*The Aegis & Intelligencer*, 9 May 1890)

Martin, William H., widower, age 31 in 1890 (Marriage License Applications Book ALJ No. 2, 1891)

Martin, William M., 1859-1923 (St. Francis de Sales Catholic Church Cemetery); station master at McGaw, 1890 (*Harford Democrat,* 24 Jan 1890)

Martin, William S., 1883-1944 (St. Paul's Methodist Church Cemetery)

Martin, William Virdin, born 6 Nov 1881, son of J. Polk and Sarah Martin (*The Hughes Genealogy, 1636-1953,* by Joseph Lee Hughes, 1953, p. 136)

Maryland & Pennsylvania Railroad ("Ma & Pa"), stations at Fallston, Watervale, Bel Air, Bynum, Forest Hill, Sharon, Fern Cliff, Rocks, Minefield, Highland [Street], Pylesville, Cambria [Whiteford], and South Delta (*Harford Democrat*, 31 Jan 1890)

Maryland Central Dairymen's Association of Harford and Baltimore Counties (*Harford Democrat*, 28 Feb 1890)

Maslin, Alice Anne (Allen), 1837-1895 (Angel Hill Cemetery); Mrs. Carville Maslin, third vice president, Women's Christian Temperance Union, Havre de Grace (*Havre de Grace Republican*, 19 Sep 1890)

Maslin, Carville H., 1832-1906 (Angel Hill Cemetery); Susquehanna & Tidewater Canal lock tender at Havre de Grace, 1865-190 (*Biographical Dictionary of Harford County, Maryland, 1774-1974*, by Henry C. Peden, Jr. and William O. Carr, 2021, p. 175)

Maslin, Catherine (Staublitz), 1875-1948 (Angel Hill Cemetery)

Maslin, Frank Smith, 1868-1914 (Angel Hill Cemetery); grocery store merchant, Washington Street, Havre de Grace (*Havre de Grace Republican*, 19 Dec 1890)

Maslin, Harry Carville, 1865-1953 (Angel Hill Cemetery); musician, Bayside Cornet Band, Havre de Grace (*Havre de Grace Republican*, 31 Jan 1890)

Maslin, Jackson Wickes, 1862-1943 (Angel Hill Cemetery); treasurer, The Philomathean Society, of Havre de Grace (*Havre de Grace Republican*, 21 Feb 1890); treasurer, Susquehanna Court No. 170, Equitable League of America, Court No. 70, Havre de Grace (*Havre de Grace Republican*, 28 Feb and 11 Jul 1890); worthy archon, Willard Section No. 58, Cadets of Temperance, Havre de Grace (*Havre de Grace Republican*, 11 Jul 1890); council treasurer, Beneficial Order of Equity, Havre de Grace (*Havre de Grace Republican*, 21 Nov 1890); organizer and secretary, Havre de Grace Democratic Club (*Havre de Grace Republican*, 31 Oct 1890)

Maslin, Kate A. (Bristow), 1863-1918 (Angel Hill Cemetery); wife of Jackson Wickes Maslin, q.v.

Maslin, Sallie Hopper (Rauscher), 1871-1952 (Angel Hill Cemetery); wife of Frank Smith Maslin, q.v.

Maslin, Samuel, watchman, Willard Section No. 58, Cadets of Temperance, Havre de Grace (*Havre de Grace Republican*, 11 Jul 1890)

Mason, Amanda V., 1847-1910 (Deer Creek Harmony Presbyterian Church Cemetery)

Mason, Anna "Annie" Elizabeth (Devoe), 1844-1909 (William Watters Memorial Church Cemetery, Cooptown); wife of Benjamin L. Moore, q.v.

Mason, Benjamin, 1812-1895 (William Watters Memorial Church Cemetery, Cooptown); postmaster at Jarrettsville, age 78 years old on 4 Feb 1890 (*Havre de Grace Republican*, 14 Feb 1890)

Mason, Benjamin L., 1840-1899 (William Watters Memorial Church Cemetery, Cooptown); carpenter at Cooptown (Death certificate incomplete); trustee, North Bend School No. 15, Fourth District (*Havre de Grace Republican*, 30 May 1890); see Bessie M. Baity and Mary Estelle Mason, q.v.

Mason, Cornelia L., 1883-1963 (William Watters Memorial Church Cemetery, Cooptown)

Mason, Frank, student, Jarrettsville Graded School (*The Aegis & Intelligencer*, 25 Apr 1890)

Mason, Harry Russell, 1879-1916 (William Watters Memorial Church Cemetery, Cooptown)

Mason, Henry C., uncalled for letter in Bel Air P. O. (*The Aegis & Intelligencer*, 4 Jul 1890)

Mason, James A., 1871-1909 (William Watters Memorial Church Cemetery, Cooptown)

Mason, John T., 1857-1914 (Deer Creek Harmony Presbyterian Church Cemetery)

Mason, Luther J. (Dr.), c1850-1892, dentist near Jarrettsville (William Watters Memorial Church Cemetery, Cooptown; *The Aegis & Intelligencer*, 15 Jan 1892); Board of County School Commissioners (*Havre de Grace Republican*, 7 Feb 1890); trustee, Sarah Furnace School No. 22, Fourth District (*Havre de Grace Republican*, 30 May 1890)

Mason, Mary A., 1844-1905 (William Watters Memorial Church Cemetery, Cooptown)

Mason, Mary Estelle, 1873-1944, native of Jarrettsville, Harford Co., born 10 Jul 1873, daughter of Benjamin L. Mason and Anna Elizabeth Devoe (Death certificate - married name Kirby)

Mason, Russell Steele, 1881-1901 (William Watters Memorial Church Cemetery, Cooptown)

Mason, Samuel, 1887-1957 (Darlington Cemetery)

Mason, T. Edwin, 1872-1940 (William Watters Memorial Church Cemetery, Cooptown)

Mason, Virginia Belle, 1869-1936 (William Watters Memorial Church Cemetery, Cooptown)

Masonic Library and Reading Room, Havre de Grace (*Havre de Grace: Its Historic Past, Its Charming Present and Its Promising Future: Harford County's Rural Heritage.* by Jack L. Shagena, Jr. and Henry C. Peden, Jr., 2018, p. 268)

Masonic Temple, Bel Air (*1953 Harford County Directory*, pp. 350-351)

Massey, Annie B., native of Maryland's Easten Shore; teacher, Mill Green School No. 7, Fifth District (*The Aegis & Intelligencer*, 29 Aug 1890; *Havre de Grace Republican*, 7 Nov 1890)

Massey, James Rigbie, 1840-1917 (Darlington Cemetery); farmer, Darlington (*The Aegis & Intelligencer*, 14 Mar 1890); acquired land in February 1890 (*The Aegis & Intelligencer*, 7 Mar 1890); member, Darlington Road League (*Havre de Grace Republican*, 6 Jun 1890)

Massey, Mary (Bayless), 1864-1949 (Deer Creek Harmony Presbyterian Church Cemetery)

Massey, William, 1843-1920 (Deer Creek Harmony Presbyterian Church Cemetery)

Masters, Virginia, 1829-1900, resident of Aberdeen, widow of James Masters (Death certificate)

Mather's General Store, at Garland, Thomas W. Mather, prop. (*Country Stores: Harford County's Rural Heritage*, by Henry C. Peden, Jr. and Jack L. Shagena, Jr., 2015, pp. 165-166)

Mather, Ellen Nora, age 19 in 1890 (Marriage License Applications Book ALJ No. 2, 1890)

Mather, Eva Augusta, 1883-1896, daughhter of Thomas W. and Mary E. Mather (Rock Run Methodist Church Cemetery)

Mather, Thomas. W., storekeeper, Garland (*Havre de Grace Republican*, 2 May 1890); trustee, Rock Run School No. 14, Second District (*Havre de Grace Republican*, 30 May 1890); see Mather's General Store, q.v.

Mathers, Mary K., acquired land in April 1890 (*The Aegis & Intelligencer*, 9 May 1890)

Mathew, Henry E., age 26 in 1889 (Marriage License Applications Book ALJ No. 2)

Mathews, Abiana B., 1865-1955 (Grove Presbyterian Church Cemetery)

Mathews, Abigail Helen, 1838-1901 (Grove Presbyterian Church Cemetery)

Mathews, Albert B., 1871-1936 (Grove Presbyterian Church Cemetery)

Mathews, Carrie Virginia, 1874-1900 (Wesleyan Chapel Methodist Church Cemetery); native of Maryland, resided at Paradise, Harford Co., daughter of Julius Mathews and Elizabeth ---- (Death certificate)

Mathews, Elizabeth S., 1843-1931 (Wesleyan Chapel Methodist Church Cemetery); wife of Julius H. Mathews, q.v.

Mathews, Henry, 1875-1959 (Grove Presbyterian Church Cemetery)

Mathews, Isabella, 1863-1940 (Angel Hill Cemetery)

Mathews, Israel Griffith, 1838-1923 (Grove Presbyterian Church Cemetery); census taker, Havre de Grace (*Havre de Grace Republican*, 30 May 1890); first patron and worthy patron, Willard Section No. 58, Order of the Cadets of Temperance, Havre de Grace (*Havre de Grace Republican*, 7 Feb 1890 and 11 Jul 1890); council chaplain, Beneficial Order of Equity, Havre de Grace (*Havre de Grace Republican*, 21 Nov 1890); member, Susquehanna Court No. 70, Equitable League of America, of Havre de Grace (*Havre de Grace Republican*, 11 Apr 1890); president, The Philomathean Society, of Havre de Grace (*Havre de Grace Republican*, 21 Feb 1890)

Mathews, Israel Griffith, Jr., 1877-1948 (Grove Presbyterian Church Cemetery)

Mathews, Jeremiah (colored), husband of Mary L. Mathews (colored), q.v.

Mathews, John E., 1853-1930 (Heavenly Waters Cemetery)

Mathews, Julius H., 1831-1925 (Wesleyan Chapel Methodist Church Cemetery)

Mathews, Mary L. (Johnson) (colored), 1868-1921, wife of Jeremiah Mathews (Tabernacle Mt. Zion Methodist Church Cemetery)

Mathews, Sarah M., 1832-1907 (Angel Hill Cemetery)

Mathias, Ida Caroline, 1851-1905 (Christ Episcopal Church Cemetery)

Mathias, Sarah Louise, see Bertha Arthur, q.v.

Matthews, Alphonso, resident near Michaelsville (*Havre de Grace Republican*, 27 Jun 1890); see George A. Matthews and Mamie Matthews, q.v.

Matthews, Athar R. (Miss), age 22 in 1890 (Marriage License Applications Book ALJ No. 2, 1891)

Matthews, Charles H. (colored), 1844-1919 (Death certificate)

Matthews, Clarence, student, Forest Hill School, 1890 (*The Aegis*, 2 Jul 1965, school picture)

Matthews, George (colored), see Jane Matthews (colored), q.v.

Matthews, George A., died 9 Dec 1890, age 9 months and 16 days, son of Al and Mary Matthews (*The Aegis & Intelligencer*, 19 Dec 1890)

Matthews, George W. (colored), age 22 in 1890 (Marriage License Applications Book ALJ No. 2, 1890)

Matthews, Henry, student, Havre de Grace High School (*Havre de Grace Republican*, 31 Oct 1890)

Matthews, Jane (colored), 1881-1967, native of Maryland, born -- Jul 1881, daughter of George Matthews and Sarah Reed (*The Aegis*, 20 Jul 1967 - married name Banks; 1900 Aberdeen Census)

Matthews, Jannie (colored), see Santa Banks (colored), q.v.

Matthews, John E., c1850-1930 (Death certificate; Alms House Record Book)

Matthews, Joshua H., 1864-1904 (Darlington Cemetery)

Matthews, Laura, sister of George A. Matthews, q.v.

Matthews, Lemuel E., peach farmer, near Perryman (*The Aegis & Intelligencer*, 29 Aug 1890); trustee, Bush River Neck School No. 9, Second District (*Havre de Grace Republican*, 30 May 1890)

Matthews, Mamie, died 6 Jun 1890, age 16, daughter of Mr. & Mrs. Alphonso Matthews, of near Perryman (*The Aegis & Intelligencer*, 20 Jun 1890)

Matthews, Mary, see George A, Matthews and Mamie Matthews, q.v.

Matthews, Mary E. (Coale), 1865-1941 (Darlington Cemetery); native of Harford Co., born 6 May 1865, daughter of Walter S. Coale and Rebecca M. Hutton (Bailey Funeral Home Records); wife of Joshua H. Matthews, q.v.

Matthews, Matilda (colored), see Samuel Buckham (colored), q.v.

Matthews, S. A., premium award winner, Class A - Horses, Harford County Fair (*The Aegis & Intelligencer*, 24 Oct 1890)

Matthews, Samuel (colored), 1842-1895 (Mt. Zion Church Cemetery, at Mountain)

Matthews, Samuel H., 1828-1902 (Darlington Cemetery)

Matthews, Tacy B., 1862-1955 (Darlington Cemetery inscription, but her obituary gave her name as Mrs. Tracy B. Matthews Swift); teacher, Thomas Run School No. 9, Third District (*The Aegis & Intelligencer*, 29 Aug 1890); executive committee, Harford County School Teachers' Association (*Havre de Grace Republican*, 19 Sep 1890); recording secretary, Women's Christian Temperance Union, of Bel Air (*Havre de Grace Republican*, 5 Sep 1890)

Mattingley, Angeline Wood, age 37 in 1890 (Marriage License Applications Book ALJ No. 2, 1890), married Henry Baker Courtney on 7 Oct 1890 (marriage certificate)

Mattingley, Elizabeth J. (Peters), 1827-1924, native of Maryland, resident of Havre de Grace (Death certificate; Angel Hill Cemetery)

Mattingley, John Frederick, 1862-1918 (Angel Hill Cemetery); secretary, The Advance Benevolent Society, Havre de Grace (*Havre de Grace Republican*, 12 Dec 1890); John F. Mattingly acquired land in November 1890 (*The Aegis & Intelligencer*, 5 Dec 1890)

Mattingley, Lillie W., 1872-1958 (Angel Hill Cemetery); wife of John Frederick Mattingley, q.v.

Maul, Rebecca Jane, wife of Joshua McComas; also see James B. McComas and Mary Edith McComas, q.v.

Maul, William, uncalled for letter in Bel Air P. O., 1890 (*The Aegis & Intelligencer*, 14 Nov 1890)

Mauldin, Edward Wilmer, c1860-1943 (Angel Hill Cemetery); husband of Mary Ella (Currier), Mauldin, q.v.

Mauldin, Ethel May, 1890-1913 (Angel Hill Cemetery)

Mauldin, Harry L., 1873-1940 (Baker Cemetery)

Mauldin, Mary Ella (Currier), 1863-1936, native of Nebraska, resided in Havre de Grace (Death certificate; Angel Hill Cemetery)

Mauldin, Sarah A., 1868-1933 (Baker Cemetery)

Maulsby, Florence Young, 1867-1958 (St. Mary's Episcopal Church Cemetery)

Maulsby, George Saunders, 1872-1915 (St. Mary's Episcopal Church Cemetery)

Maulsby, Mary A. (colored), age 22 in 1890 (Marriage License Applications Book ALJ No. 2, 1891)

Maulsby, Richard, name removed from the voter registration list in Sixth District, 1890 (*Havre de Grace Republican*, 17 Oct 1890)

Maurice, John Taylor, 1890-1956, native of Aberdeen, Harford Co., born 17 Sep 1890, son of Frank Maurice and Annie Thalman (Pennington Funeral Home Records)

Maxa, Frank, 1874-1953 (Baker Cemetery)

Max, Hannah, 1857-1944 (Baker Cemetery)

Maxfield, Callie (colored), see Jane Dutton (colored), q.v.

Maxfield, Caroline (colored), age 32 in 1890 (Marriage License Applications Book ALJ No. 2, 1891)

Maxfield, Eliza (colored), see Harry Jackson (colored), q.v.

Maxfield, Harriet (colored), see Harry Jackson (colored), q.v.

Maxfield, James (colored), 1883-1935, born at Preston Mill, Harford Co., son of Thomas Maxfield and ---- (Death certificate)

Maxfield, L. Mary (colored), 1871-1904 (Death certificate)

Maxfield, Laura (colored), 1881-1941, native of Rocks, Harford Co., born 10 Sep 1881, daughter of Thomas Maxfield and Fannie Rice (Death certificate - married name Buchanan)

Maxfield, Nancy (colored), see Harry Jackson (colored), q.v.

Maxfield, Samuel (colored), husband of L. Mary Maxfield (colored), q.v.

Maxfield, Thomas (colored), see James Maxfield (colored) and Laura Maxfield (colored), q.v.

Maxwell, Annie Elizabeth, 1889-1891 (Churchville Presbyterian Church Cemetery)

Maxwell, Belle (Mrs.), uncalled for letter in Bel Air P. O., 1890 (*The Aegis & Intelligencer*, 14 Nov 1890)

Maxwell, David, and Clara, residents of Bel Air (*The Aegis & Intelligencer*, 26 Dec 1890)

Maxwell, Eli Glenn, 1890-1953 (Emory Methodist Church Cemetery)

Maxwell, James M., farmer, near Avondale (*Havre de Grace Republican*, 21 Nov 1890)

Maxwell, John W., swine and poultry breeder, Carsins Run (*Havre de Grace Republican*, 17 Jan 1890); juror, Second District (*Havre de Grace Republican*, 2 May 1890)

Maxwell, Julia A. (colored), see Eva Moses (colored), q.v.

Maxwell, Mary Ann, see George Amos Courtney, q.v.

Maxwell, Mollie (Miss), choir member, Grove Presbyterian Church, Aberdeen (*Havre de Grace Republican*, 14 Feb 1890)

Maxwell, Walter, treated by unidentified doctor in 1890 ("Medical Account Book – 1890," Historical Society of Harford County Archives Folder)

May, Peter, resident near Dublin (*The Aegis & Intelligencer*, 18 Jul 1890)

Mayflower Club, Havre de Grace (*Havre de Grace: Its Historic Past, Its Charming Present and Its Promising Future: Harford County's Rural Heritage.* by Jack L. Shagena, Jr. and Henry C. Peden, Jr., 2018, p. 269)

Maynadier, Edith, 1889-1968 (William Watters Memorial Methodist Church Cemetery. Cooptown)

Maynadier, Elizabeth (Yellott), 1808-1891 (Christ Episcopal Church Cemetery)

Maynadier, Esther (Mitchell), 1882-1979 (Christ Episcopal Church Cemetery)

Maynadier, Frank W., delegate, Third District, Democrat Party Convention (*The Aegis & Intelligencer*, 5 Sep 1890); see Grace Estelle Maynadier, q.v.

Maynadier, George Yellott, 1839-1905 (Christ Episcopal Church Cemetery); attorney, Bel Air (*Biographical Dictionary of Harford County, Maryland, 1774-1974*, by Henry C. Peden, Jr. and William O. Carr, 2021, p. 1757); member, Bel Air Social, Literary, Musical and Dramatic Club (*Havre de Grace Republican*, 27 Jun 1890); member, Mt. Ararat Lodge No. 44, A. F. & A. M., Bel Air (*Havre de Grace Republican*, 11 Jul 1890); member, Democrat Party, and representative, Harford County Tariff Reform Club (*The Aegis & Intelligencer*, 5 Sep 1890); also see Henry Gustavus Maynadier, q.v.

Maynadier, Grace Estelle, 1885-1974, native of Maryland, born 13 Nov 1885, daughter of Frank W. Maynadier and Ida Laura Amos (Pennington Funeral Home Records - married name Steiner)

Maynadier, Henry Gustavus, born 1871, died ---- (Christ Episcopal Church Cemetery); clerk, Second National Bank, son of George Y. Maynadier, of Bel Air, 1890 (*The Aegis & Intelligencer*, 6 Jun 1890)

Maynadier, Ida Laura, 1857-1941 (William Watters Memorial Methodist Church Cemetery, Cooptown)

Maynadier, Joseph Ennals, 1820-1899 (Christ Episcopal Church Cemetery)

Maynadier, Paca Moores, 1873-1950 (Christ Episcopal Church Cemetery); Moores Maynadier, member, Bel Air Tennis Club, 1890 (*The Aegis & Intelligencer*, 18 Jul 1890)

Maynadier, Roberta, student, Bel Air Graded School (*The Aegis & Intelligencer*, 11 Apr 1890)

Maynadier, Rose (Gallego), 1824-1912 (Christ Episcopal Church Cemetery)

Mayo, George Upshur (Major), 1834-1896 (St. Mary's Episcopal Church Cemetery)

Mayo, Pattie W. (Jewell), 1846-1920 (St. Mary's Episcopal Church Cemetery)

McAbee, James, tomato farmer, near Bel Air (*Havre de Grace Republican*, 31 Oct 1890)

McAfee & Hanna, shoe store, Main St., Bel Air (*The Aegis & Intelligencer*, 14 Feb 1890)

McAfee Brothers & Cline, commission merchants at "Bel Air Exchange" on Main Street at the railroad station (*The Aegis & Intelligencer*, 24 Jan 1890)

McAllister, John S., see Ella Cira Boswell, q.v.

McAtee, Fannie, premium award winner, Class M - Miscellaenous, Harford County Fair (*The Aegis & Intelligencer*, 24 Oct 1890)

McAtee, George, young man of near Pylesville (*The Aegis & Intelligencer*, 7 Feb 1890)

McAtee, Henry, county out-pensioner [welfare recipient], Fourth District (*Havre de Grace Republican*, 4 Jul 1890)

McAuliff, Maggie (Miss), member, St. Patrick's Women's Total Abstinence Society, Havre de Grace (*Havre de Grace Republican*, 31 Jan 1890)

McBride, Evelyn B. (Scarborough), 1881-1955 (Highland Presbyterian Church Cemetery); native of Street, Harford Co., born 7 Oct 1881, daughter of Parker Scarborough and Belle V. Heaps (Harkins Funeral Home Records)

McCabe Bros., sub-contractors, Deer Creek and Susquehanna Railroad (*Harford Democrat*, 25 Jul 1890)

McCall, Joshua, 1861-1921 (Bailey Funeral Home Records)

McCall, Nellie, see Lewis Simpers, q.v.

McCall, Rachael J. (Mrs.) (colored), 1856-1922 (Death certificate)

McCall, Rebecca A., widow of Civil War veteran Thomas Wilson, Havre de Grace (*1890 Special Census of the Civil War Veterans of the State of Maryland*, by L. Tilden Moore, Volume III, p. 91)

McCallister, Alonzo, widower, age 37 in 1890 (Marriage License Applications Book ALJ No. 2, 1891)

McCallister, Mary, see Alonzo Wilson, q.v.

McCandlass, George, Civil War veteran, Delta P. O. (*1890 Special Census of the Civil War Veterans of the State of Maryland*, by L. Tilden Moore, Volume III, p. 83)

McCann, A, Bertha, 1868-1944 (Dublin Southern Cemetery)

McCann, A. Laura (Robinson), 1869-1968 (Dublin Southern Cemetery), wife of Wilbur McCann, q.v.

McCann, Albert L., 1854-1932 (Christ Episcopal Church Cemetery)

McCann, Amanda M. (Troutner), 1831-1915 (Dublin Methodist Church Cemetery)

McCann, C. Bingley, 1852-1936, native of Harford Co. (Bailey Funeral Home Records; Dublin Southern Cemetery)

McCann, Charles A., died 4 Mar 1900, adult, age not given (Death certificate incomplete) delegate, Fifth District, Democrat Party Convention, 1890 (*The Aegis & Intelligencer*, 5 Sep 1890); see Sallie Carroll Carr and Stella H. Dick, q.v.

McCann, Charles W., 1860-1925 (William Watters Memorial Methodist Church, Cooptown)

McCann, E. Virginia, c1855-1896 (William Watters Memorial Methodist Church, Cooptown)

McCann, Edward P., 1868-1943 (Dublin Methodist Church Cemetery), son of William E. McCann, of Dublin District (*The Aegis & Intelligencer*, 9 May 1890); resident of Muttonsburg, 1890 (*The Aegis & Intelligencer*, 28 Mar 1890)

McCann, Elizabeth R. "Bessie" (O'Donnell), 1881-1967 (Dublin Southern Cemetery)

McCann, Ella P., see William W. Lee, q.v.

McCann, Emma (Holland), 1854-1916 (Christ Episcopal Church Cemetery), wife of Albert L. McCann, q.v.

McCann, Emma V., 1888-1966 (Fallston Methodist Church Cemetery)

McCann, Ephraim, 1828-1904 (Fallston Methodist Church Cemetery); Civil War veteran, Fallston (*1890 Special Census of the Civil War Veterans of the State of Maryland*, by L. Tilden Moore, Volume III, p. 75); juror, Third District (*Havre de Grace Republican*, 2 May 1890)

McCann, John A., 1884-1965 (Fallston Methodist Church Cemetery)

McCann, John H., sold land in May 1890 (*The Aegis & Intelligencer*, 6 Jun 1890)

McCann, Lamar, see Louis L. McCann, q.v.

McCann, Louis Lamar, 1873-1939 (Dublin Southern Cemetery); native of Harford Co., born 5 Apr 1873, son of Lamar McCann and Sarah Bavington (Bailey Funeral Home Records spelled his name Lewis)

McCann, Mae (Thompson), 1881-1956 (Dublin Southern Cemetery); native of Harford Co., daughter of William Thompson and Margaret Russell (Bailey Funeral Home Records)

McCann, Mamie L., 1873-1956 (William Watters Memorial Methodist Church, Cooptown)

McCann, Mary Ann, 1830-1917 (Fallston Methodist Church Cemetery)

McCann, Mary E. (Taylor), 1876-1924 (Darlington Cemetery); native of Maryland, resided at Dublin, born 31 Jul 1876, daughter of Richard Taylor, of England, and Sarah M. Scarff, of Maryland (Death certificate; Bailey Funeral Home Records)

McCann, May, daughter of William E. McCann, of Muttonsburg (*The Aegis & Intelligencer*, 4 Apr 1890)

McCann, Mollie S., 1861-1925 (Dublin Southern Cemetery)

McCann, Nelson, 1871-1936 (Darlington Cemetery); native of Harford Co., born 14 Feb 1871, son of William E. McCann and Amanda Troutner, of Dublin District (Bailey Funeral Home Records; *The Aegis & Intelligencer*, 9 May 1890)

McCann, R. Lamar, 1826-1904 (Dublin Southern Cemetery)

McCann, S. Archer, 1870-1952 (Dublin Southern Cemetery)

McCann, Sarah D., 1830-1902 (Dublin Southern Cemetery)

McCann, Wilbur, 1863-1924 (Dublin Southern Cemetery); native of Harford Co., born 7 Sep 1863, son of William E. McCann and Amanda Troutner, of Muttonsburg (Bailey Funeral Home Records; *The Aegis & Intelligencer*, 4 Apr 1890); age 27 in 1890 (Marriage License Applications Book ALJ No. 2, 1891)

McCann, William A., 1816-1898 (West Liberty Church Cemetery); resident near Bradenbaugh (*The Aegis &*

McCann, William Everette, 1830-1891 (Dublin Methodist Church Cemetery); member and superintendent, Dublin M E. Church Sunday School (*Havre de Grace Republican*, 18 Apr 1890); trustee, Trappe School No. 14, Fifth District (*Havre de Grace Republican*, 30 May 1890); general road supervisor, Fifth District (*Havre de Grace Republican*, 28 Mar 1890); also see Edward P. McCann, Wilbur McCann, Nelson McCann and May McCann, q.v.

McCardell, William R., sold land in May 1890 (*The Aegis & Intelligencer*, 6 Jun 1890)

McCausland, Ellen J. (Cunningham), 1873-1951 (Darlington Cemetery); native of Harford Co., born 25 Mar 1873, daughter of Joseph Cunningham and Mary E. Chipman (Harkins Funeral Home Records); wife of Marcus H. McCausland, q.v.

McCausland, Inez (Miss), resident, of Macton (*Havre de Grace Republican*, 13 Jun 1890)

McCausland, Marcus H., 1869-1947 (Rock Run Methodist Church Cemetery); native of Harford Co., born 21 Oct 1869, son of Thomas Jefferson McCausland and ---- (Bailey Funeral Home Records)

McCausland, Robert, Jr., 1831-1907 (Darlington Cemetery)

McCausland, Thomas Jefferson, see Marcus H. McCausland, q.v.

McClafferty, A. J., name removed from the voter registration list in the Sixth District (*Havre de Grace Republican*, 17 Oct 1890)

McClain, Henry, 1866-1938 (Death certificate; Alms House Record Book)

McCleary, Louisa M. (Byrd), 1862-1936 (Darlington Cemetery)

McCleary, Robert, see William H. McCleary, q.v.

McCleary, William, age 12, stepson of William Swift, of Dublin [Fifth District] (*The Aegis & Intelligencer*, 27 Jun 1890); William McCleary, age 14, of Dublin, son of the late James McCleary fell from an apple tree and taken to the home of his mother Mrs. William Smith (*Harford Democrat*, 27 Jun 1890)

McCleary, William H., 1876-1953 (Darlington Cemetery); native of Kansas, born 28 Sep 1876, son of Robert McCleary and Ida Anderson (Bailey Funeral Home Records)

McClenahan & Brother, contractors, Havre de Grace (*Havre de Grace Republican*, 13 Jun 1890)

McClintock, Emma Norris (Bowman), 1876-1952 (Rock Run Methodist Church Cemetery)

McClintock, Frederick Stump, 1860-1932, son of James and Mary McClintock (*The Hughes Genealogy, 1636-1953*, by Joseph Lee Hughes, 1953, p. 131)

McClintock, Robert, charter member, Havre de Grace Gunning Club (*Havre de Grace Republican*, 14 Nov 1890)

McClung, Amanda Z. (Miss), member, Norrisville M. P. Church (*The Aegis & Intelligencer*, 7 Mar 1890)

McClung, Cora (Dunlap), 1872-1953 (Norrisville Methodist Church Cemetery)

McClung, Elsie (Miss), member, Norrisville M. E. Church Sunday School (*The Aegis & Intelligencer*, 20 Jun 1890)

McClung, Ephraim B., 1831-1918 (Norrisville Methodist Church Cemetery); trustee, Norrisville School No. 1, Fourth District (*Havre de Grace Republican*, 30 May 1890); incorporator, Norrisville Methodist Protestant Church (*Havre de Grace Republican*, 4 Apr 1890)

McClung, Hannah A., 1841-1921 (Norrisville Methodist Church Cemetery)

McClung, Hannah E., 1834-1916 (Norrisville Methodist Church Cemetery)

McClung, John Nelson, 1859-1926 (Norrisville Methodist Church Cemetery); native of Harford Co., farmer, married, resided near White Hall (Death certificate)

McClung, Mary E. J., (Gemmill), 1872-1905 (Norrisville Methodist Church Cemetery); wife of John Nelson McClung, q.v.

McClung, Mary G., 1879-1964 (Norrisville Methodist Church Cemetery)

McClung, Minnie (Miss), member, Norrisville M. P. Church (*The Aegis & Intelligencer*, 7 Mar 1890)

McClung, Morgan E., 1875-1964 (Norrisville Methodist Church Cemetery)

McClung, Pearl (Miss), member, Norrisville M. E. Church Sunday School (*The Aegis & Intelligencer*, 20 Jun 1890)

McClung, Thomas W., born 1867 died ---- (Norrisville Methodist Church Cemetery)

McClung, Webster C., 1858-1928 (Stewartstown Cemetery, York Co., PA); teacher, Summit Hill School No. 12, Fourth District (*The Aegis & Intelligencer*, 29 Aug 1890)

McClung, William R., born 1876, died ---- (Norrisville Methodist Church Cemetery)

McComas Funeral Home (Abingdon)

McComas' General Store, at Clayton, First District, George W. McComas, prop. (*Country Stores: Harford County's Rural Heritage*, by Henry C. Peden, Jr. and Jack L. Shagena, Jr., 2015, p. 168)

McComas Institute, Colored Public School No. 2, near Clayton, First District (*Harford County, Maryland Teachers and the Schools They Served, 1774-1900*, by Henry C. Peden, Jr., 2022, p. 370)

McComas, A. Grace (Timmons), 1877-1935 (McComas Memorial Methodist Church Cemetery)

McComas, Adele (Anderson), 1881-1956 (Bethel Presbyterian Church Cemetery Records); wife of Charles H. McComas, Jr., q.v.

McComas, Agnes G. (Beaumont), 1871-1961 (Bethel Presbyterian Church Cemetery Records); wife of William N. McComas, q.v.

McComas, Alexander, 1829-1894 (Bethel Presbyterian Church Cemetery Records); member, Taylor Fox Hunting Club (*Havre de Grace Republican*, 24 Jan 1890); trustee, School No. 5, Fourth District (*The Aegis & Intelligencer*, 8 Aug 1890); see Emory McComas, Marion Stanley McComas, and William N. McComas, q.v.

McComas, Alice (Deaver), 1841-1901, native of Harford Co., resided at Clermont Mills, wife of Thomas McComas (Death certificate)

McComas, Amanda (Miss), organist, Providence M. P. Church Sunday School (*The Aegis & Intelligencer*, 18 Jul 1890)

McComas, Amelia A., see Virginia C. Barton, q.v.

McComas, Ann (Hunter), 1815-1890 Cokesbury Memorial Methodist Church Cemetery); widow of [John] Calvin McComas, of Abingdon, and mother of Thomas, William and John McComas (*The Aegis & Intelligencer*, 28 Feb 1890); also see Thomas McComas, q.v.

McComas, Anna B., 1804-1892 (McKendree Methodist Church Cemetery)

McComas, Anna Maria (Rieger), 1882-1971 (Cokesbury Memorial Methodist Church Cemetery)

McComas, Caleb J. (colored), 1849-1943 (Death certificate)

McComas, Calvin, see Ann McComas and Thomas McComas, q.v.

McComas, Cardiff M., 1877-1936 (Mountain Christian Church Cemetery)

McComas, Charles Henry, born 25 Apr 1876, son of Alexander McComas and Hannah Cairnes (Bethel Presbyterian Church Cemetery Records)

McComas, Charlotte (colored), see Annie Rice, Hattie C. Rice and Emma A. Rice, q.v.

McComas, Elenora, 1813-1901 (McComas Memorial Methodist Church Cemetery)

McComas, Ella (Duvall), 1878-1969 (Mountain Christian Church Cemetery)

McComas, Emily, 1821-1899 (St. Paul's Methodist Church Cemetery)

McComas, Emory, born 1872, son of Alexander McComas and Hannah Cairnes (Bethel Presbyterian Church Cemetery Records)

McComas, Gabriel Jordan, 1869-1943 (Little Falls Quaker Cemetery); member, Providence M. P. Church Sunday School, 1890 (*The Aegis & Intelligencer*, 18 Jul 1890); jousting tournament rider, Knight of Delmar,

1890 (*Havre de Grace Republican*, 19 Sep 1890)

McComas, George William, 1841-1928 (Union Chapel Methodist Church Cemetery); trustee, School No. 9, First District (*Havre de Grace Republican*, 30 May 1890); resident near Clayton (*The Aegis & Intelligencer*, 14 Nov 1890); road examiner, First District (*Havre de Grace Republican*, 4 Jul 1890); incorporator and director, Wilna Library Association (*Havre de Grace Republican*, 9 May 1890)

McComas, Hannah E. (Cairnes), 1837-1920 (Bethel Presbyterian Church Cemetery Records), wife of Alexander McComas, q.v.

McComas, Harriet (Brown) (colored), 1855-1914 (Death certificate)

McComas, Harriett, 1845-1919 (Highland Presbyterian Church Cemetery)

McComas, Harry Preston, 1862-1917 (Bethel Presbyterian Church Cemetery Records)

McComas, Henry Gough, 1875-1946 (Union Chapel Methodist Church Cemetery)

McComas, Howard Kennard, 1876-1943 (Cokesbury Memorial Methodist Church Cemetery); student, Public School No. 1, First District, 1890 (*The Aegis & Intelligencer*, 10 Jan 1890)

McComas, Ida K. (Kenly) (colored), 1870-1937 (Death certificate)

McComas, J. Marche (captain), 1804-1896 (McKendree Methodist Church Cemetery)

McComas, Jacob, 1825-1903 (Cokesbury Memorial Methodist Church Cemetery)

McComas, James A., 1866-1948 (Bethel Presbyterian Church Cemetery Records)

McComas, James B., 1869-1966 (Parkwood Cemetery, Baltimore Co.); son of Joshua McComas and Rebecca Jane Maul; moved to Baltimore in Dec 1890; teacher, Hope's School No. 4, Fourth District (*The Aegis & Intelligencer*, 29 Aug 1890; *Harford County, Maryland Teachers and the Schools They Served*, by Henry C. Peden, Jr., 2021, p. 209); jousting tournament rider, Knight of Gunpowder (*Havre de Grace Republican*, 17 Oct 1890); secretary, Black Horse Singing School (*Havre de Grace Republican*, 28 Mar 1890); secretary, Shawsville Glee Club (*Havre de Grace Republican*, 7 Mar 1890)

McComas, Jemima (Beatty), 1810-1892, widow of James Benton McComas (Bethel Presbyterian Church Cemetery Records)

McComas, John, see Ann McComas, q.v.

McComas, John J., 1828-1916 (Bethel Presbyterian Church Cemetery Records)

McComas, Jordan G., born 9 Apr 1879, son of Mrs. Rachel McComas, of Upper Cross Roads (*Harford Democrat*, 11 Apr 1890)

McComas, Joshua, 1832-1896 (McKendree Methodist Church Cemetery); see James B. McComas and Mary Edith McComas, q.v.

McComas, Keziah A. (Mrs.), 1812-1899, resided near Singer (Death certificate)

McComas, Luella (Cathcart), 1869-1942 (Bethel Presbyterian Church Cemetery Records); wife of Harry P. McComas, q.v.

McComas, Mabel M. (Reckord), 1885-1963, wife of Walter R. McComas, q.v.

McComas, Margaret (Riley), 1868-1945 (Little Falls Quaker Cemetery)

McComas, Marion Stanley, born 1871, son of Alexander McComas and Hannah Cairnes (Bethel Presbyterian Church Cemetery Records)

McComas, Martha K., age 25 in 1890 (Marriage License Applications Book ALJ No. 2, 1890), married John Mulligan on 13 Feb 1890 (marriage certificate)

McComas, Mary, 1806-1901 (Holy Cross Cemetery)

McComas, Mary (colored), see Isaac L. Dennison (colored), q.v.

McComas, Mary Edith, born 6 Oct 1876, daughter of Joshua McComas and Rebecca Jane Maul (Bethel Presbyterian Church Cemetery Records); see Mary Edith (McComas) Wiley, q.v.

McComas, Mary Elizabeth (Miss), 1844-1925 (Bethel Presbyterian Church Cemetery Records)

McComas, Mary Ensor (Ross), 1881-1958 (Little Falls Quaker Cemetery)

McComas, Mary Martha (Long), 1840-1913 (Bethel Presbyterian Church Cemetery Records); wife of John J. McComas, q.v.

McComas, Mary N., 1854-1926 (McComas Memorial Methodist Church Cemetery)

McComas, Mary Winona, 1887-1962 (Union Chapel Methodist Church Cemetery)

McComas, Minnie Louisa (Emerick), 1868-1951 (Bethel Presbyterian Church Cemetery Records); wife of James A. McComas, q.v.

McComas, R. G., jousting tournament rider, Knight of Greenwood, 1890 (*Havre de Grace Republican*, 17 Oct 1890)

McComas, Rachel (Mrs.), see Jordan G. McComas, q.v.

McComas, Rachel (colored), see Sarah Ann Anderson (colored) and Adeline Williams (colored), q.v.

McComas, Rachel Ann (Miss), 1827-1909 (Bethel Presbyterian Church Cemetery Records)

McComas, Rebecca Jane, 1834-1916 (McKendree Methodist Church Cemetery)

McComas, Sarah E., 1872-1950 (Bethel Presbyterian Church Cemetery Records)

McComas, Sarah Ellen ("Nellie"), 1872-1907, daughter of John J. McComas and Mary M. Long (Bethel Presbyterian Church Cemetery Records; Death certificate)

McComas, Thomas, see Alice McComas, q.v.

McComas, Thomas, 1853-1917 (Cokesbury Memorial Methodist Church Cemetery; Death certificate); son of John Calvin McComas and Ann Hunter, q.v.

McComas, Virginia Ellen (Norris), 1851-1929 (Union Chapel Methodist Church Cemetery)

McComas, Walter R., 1879-1922, son of Alexander McComas and Hannah Cairnes (Bethel Presbyterian Church Cemetery Records)

McComas, William, 1832-1910 (Highland Presbyterian Church Cemetery); Civil War veteran, at McIntyre (*1890 Special Census of the Civil War Veterans of the State of Maryland*, by L. Tilden Moore, Volume III, p. 84); see Ann McComas, q.v.

McComas, William A., 1830-1900 (McComas Memorial Methodist Church Cemetery)

McComas, William N., 1867-1943 (Bethel Presbyterian Church Cemetery Records); insurance agent, born 28 Jul 1867, son of Alexander McComas and Hannah Cairnes (Bethel Presbyterian Church Cemetery Records; Death certificate)

McComas, William T., resident of Muttonsburg (*The Aegis & Intelligencer*, 11 Apr 1890)

McComas, Winona, age 3 *(sic)*, student, Bleak Height School, near Clayton (*The Aegis & Intelligencer*, 18 Jul 1890)

McCombs, Abram Prizer, 1824-1916 (Angel Hill Cemetery); native of Chester Co., PA; owner/editor, *Havre de Grace Republican* newspaper, and former town commissioner (*Havre de Grace Republican*, 7 Feb 1890; *Biographical Dictionary of Harford County, Maryland, 1774-1974*, by Henry C. Peden, Jr. and William O. Carr, 2021, p. 179); president, First National Bank of Havre de Grace (*Havre de Grace Republican*, 17 Jan 1890), and president, Havre de Grace Improvement Company (*Havre de Grace Republican*, 7 Feb 1890); also see Sallie McCombs, q.v.

McCombs, Maria C. (Schott), 1828-1916 (Angel Hill Cemetery), wife of Abram Prizer McCombs, q.v.

McCombs, Rachael Elizabeth (Wilson), 1850-1922 (Angel Hill Cemetery), wife of William S. McCombs, q.v.

McCombs, Sallie, daughter of Abram P. McCombs, of Havre de Grace, married William P. Jackson on 12 Feb 1890 (*The Aegis & Intelligencer*, 14 Feb 1890); age 22 in 1890 (Marriage License Applications Book ALJ No. 2, 1890)

McCombs, Vesta, student, Havre de Grace High School (*Havre de Grace Republican*, 31 Oct 1890); daughter of William Sivard McCombs, q.v.

McCombs, William Sivard, 1850-1928 (Angel Hill Cemetery); editor, *Havre de Grace Republican* newspaper (*Havre de Grace Republican*, 7 Feb 1890); incorporator, Havre de Grace Academy (*Havre de Grace Republican*, 15 Aug 1890); city councilman, Havre de Grace (*Havre de Grace Republican*, 10 Jan 1890); secretary, Susquehanna Lodge No. 130, A. F. & A. M. (*Havre de Grace Republican*, 26 Dec 1890); trustee, High School No. 20, Sixth District (*Havre de Grace Republican*, 30 May 1890); son of Abram P. McCombs, q.v.

McCommons, Ada, 1875-1973 (Rock Run Methodist Church Cemetery); wife of G. Milton McCommons, q.v.

McCommons, Anna, see Ernest H. McCommons, q.v.

McCommons, Annie, 1861-1891 (Wesleyan Chapel Methodist Church Cemetery)

McCommons, Annie R., 1853-1940 (Rock Run Methodist Church Cemetery); wife of George N. McCommons, q.v.

McCommons, Avarilla, see John Edward McCommons, q.v.

McCommons, Benjamin L., 1822-1899, cooper at Aldino, native of Harford Co. (Death certificate)

McCommons, Caroline W., 1844-1929 (St. George's Episcopal Church Cemetery)

McCommons, Charles Elmer, 1867-1957, native of Chestnut Hill, Harford Co., son of John McCommons and Phebe Grafton (Pennington Funeral Home Records; Deer Creek Methodist Church Cemetery)

McCommons, Charles N., born 1875, died ---- (St. George's Episcopal Church Cemetery); Charlie McCommons, student, Forest Hill School, 1890 (*The Aegis*, 2 Jul 1965, school picture)

McCommons, Clarence Arthur, 1884-1945 (Angel Hill Cemetery)

McCommons, Edward R. (Angel Hill Cemetery, no dates, Civil War veteran); deceased and removed from the voter registration list at Hopewell, Second District (*Havre de Grace Republican*, 26 Sep 1890); see Fannie Hoke McCommons, q.v.

McCommons, Eli F., 1856-1926 (Baker Cemetery); native of Maryland, farmer, married , resided near Aberdeen (Death certificate)

McCommons, Elizabeth, wife of Benjamin L. McCommons, q.v.

McCommons, Ernest H., 1884-1962, native of Harford Co., born 19 Jun 1884, son of William McCommons and Anna ---- (Pennington Funeral Home Records; Angel Hill Cemetery)

McCommons, Fannie Hoke, 1868-1951, native of Maryland, born 25 Aug 1868, daughter of Edward R. McCommons and Lydia A. Deaver (Pennington Funeral Home Records - married name Williams)

McCommons, G. Milton, 1870-1945 (Rock Run Methodist Church Cemetery); native of Harford Co., born 21 Feb 1870, son of William McCommons and Mary McMorris (Bailey Funeral Home Records)

McCommons, George N., 1848-1926 (Rock Run Methodist Church Cemetery)

McCommons, George N., 1890-1947 (Rock Run Methodist Church Cemetery)

McCommons, Hannah (Deaver), 1818-1899, resident of Aldino, native of Harford Co., widow of John McCommons (Death certificate)

McCommons, Harold A., 1871-1935 (Angel Hill Cemetery)

McCommons, Henry, see John Edward McCommons, q.v.

McCommons, J. V., farmer, near Aberdeen (*The Aegis & Intelligencer*, 28 Nov 1890); secretary, Aberdeen Can Factory (*Havre de Grace Republican*, 19 Dec 1890)

McCommons, James (Mrs.), daughter of Alice Ann Lingan, q.v.

McCommons, James, resident near Level (*The Aegis & Intelligencer*, 12 Dec 1890); Civil War veteran, at Level (*1890 Special Census of the Civil War Veterans of the State of Maryland*, by L. Tilden Moore, Volume III, p. 70)

McCommons, James F., 1870-1967 (Rock Run Methodist Church Cemetery)

McCommons, John, resident of Fallston (*The Aegis & Intelligencer*, 28 Nov 1890)

McCommons, John, died before 1899; see Hannah McCommons, q.v.; also see Charles Elmer McCommons, q.v.

McCommons, John A., resident of Singer (*The Aegis & Intelligencer*, 7 Nov 1890); juror, First District (*Havre de Grace Republican*, 31 Oct 1890); sold land in November 1890 (*The Aegis & Intelligencer*, 5 Dec 1890)

McCommons, John Edward, 1885-1946, native and resident of Havre de Grace, son of Henry and Avarilla McCommons (Death certificate; Angel Hill Cemetery)

McCommons, Joseph T., 1842-1916 (St. George's Episcopal Church Cemetery); Civil War veteran, Aberdeen (*1890 Special Census of the Civil War Veterans of the State of Maryland*, by L. Tilden Moore, Volume III, p. 63)

McCommons, Katherine W., 1886-1966 (Angel Hill Cemetery)

McCommons, Laura Jane, 1860-1942 (Cokesbury Memorial Methodist Church Cemetery)

McCommons, Lewis, 1824-1899 (Wesleyan Chapel Methodist Church Cemetery)

McCommons, Lula B., 1884-1971 (Mountan Christian Church Cemetery)

McCommons, Lydia A. (Deaver), 1851-1916 (Angel Hill Cemetery)

McCommons, Margaret, see David M. Bunce, q.v.

McCommons, Margaret Susan, 1886-1978 (Angel Hill Cemetery)

McCommons, Martha Ann, 1849-1911 (Rock Run Methodist Church Cemetery)

McCommons, Mary, see Mary R. Forwood, q.v.

McCommons, Mary Ann (McMorris), 1834-1894 (Rock Run Methodist Church Cemetery); wife of William McCommons, q.v.

McCommons, Mary C., 1866-1957 (Deer Creek Methodist Church Cemetery)

McCommons, Mary C., 1874-1959 (Angel Hill Cemetery)

McCommons, Minnie C., 1876-1900 (Rock Run Methodist Church Cemetery)

McCommons, Nannie C. (Ward), 1873-1928 (Deer Creek Methodist Church Cemetery)

McCommons, Oleita M., 1877-1966 (Rock Run Methodist Church Cemetery)

McCommons, Pearl E., 1887-1948, native of Forest Hill, Harford Co., born 28 May 1887, daughter of Stephen A. McCommons and Mary C. Banister (Death certificate - married name Roe); student, Forest Hill School (*The Aegis*, 2 Jul 1965, school picture)

McCommons, Roberta, 1851-1941 (Wesleyan Chapel Methodist Church Cemetery)

McCommons, Rose G., age 18 in 1890 (Marriage License Applications Book ALJ No. 2, 1890), married Joseph H. Pyle on 19 Mar 1890 (announcement in *The Aegis & Intelligencer*, 14 Mar 1890)

McCommons, Sarah A. (Moffet), 1862-1935 (Baker Cemetery)

McCommons, Stephen A., 1861-1927 (Deer Creek Methodist Church Cemetery); see Pearl E. McCommons, q.v.

McCommons, Thomas B., 1857-1952 (Cokesbury Memorial Methodist Church Cemetery)

McCommons, W. Herbert, 1878-1950 (Mountan Christian Church Cemetery)

McCommons, William, 1825-1898 (Rock Run Methodist Church Cemetery); treated by unidentified doctor in 1890 ("Medical Account Book – 1890," Historical Society of Harford County Archives Folder, misspelled name McCommins); see C. Milton McCommons, q.v.

McCommons, William T., 1848-1924 (Wesleyan Chapel Methodist Church Cemetery)

McComsey, Harry, sandpapering machine operator, Bulett Carriage Factory, Bel Air (*The Aegis & Intelligencer*, 28 Nov 1890)

McConkey, Annie H., sold land in February 1890 (*The Aegis & Intelligencer*, 7 Mar 1890)

McConkey, C. Oliver, acquired land in February 1890 (*The Aegis & Intelligencer*, 7 Mar 1890)

McConkey, Charles R., incorporator, The Loan, Trust, Security and Insurance Company of Harford County (*Havre de Grace Republican*, 28 Feb 1890); also see Harry A. McConkey, q.v.

McConkey, Harry A., principal, Bel Air Academy and Graded School, and son of Charles R. McConkey (*The Aegis & Intelligencer*, 15 Aug and 29 Aug 1890)

McConkey, Louisa (Mrs.), of Whiteford, granted a government pension (*Havre de Grace Republican*, 3 Oct 1890)

McConkey, Marian J., wife of W. Scott Whiteford; also see Clay P. Whiteford and Henry C. Whiteford, q.v.

McConkey, Mary Elizabeth (Davis), 1845-1924 (Slateville Cemetery, York Co, PA); native of Harford Co., resided at Street (Death certificate); see Elisha Davis, q.v.

McCope, Miles, new name on the Havre de Grace voter registration list in 1890 (*Havre de Grace Republican*, 19 Sep 1890)

McCormick, Alice E., see Elizabeth B. McCormick, q.v.

McCormick, Elizabeth B., died testate in 1890 and her named heirs were husband J. Lawrence McCormick, her brothers and sisters (names not given) and "my mother Alice E. McCormick" (Harford County Will Book JMM 11:156-157)

McCormick, James Lawrence, 1862-1957 (Christ Episcopal Church Cemetery); director, Maryland Central Dairymen's Association (*Havre de Grace Republican*, 14 Mar 1890); board of directors, Agricultural and Mechanical Society (*Havre de Grace Republican*, 23 May 1890); premium award winner, Class B - Cattle, and Class C - Sheep, Harford County Fair (*The Aegis & Intelligencer*, 24 Oct 1890); see Elizabeth B. McCormick, q.v.

McCormick, Martha S. "Meta" (Gilbert), 1874-1942 (Christ Episcopal Church Cemetery); wife of James Lawrence McCormick, q.v.

McCormick, Mary J. (Holland), 1823-1910 (Christ Episcopal Church Cemetery)

McCormick, Mary R, 1866-1949 (Christ Episcopal Church Cemetery)

McCormick, Norval, 1846-1911 (Christ Episcopal Church Cemetery)

McCormick, P. Henderson, 1857-1943 (Christ Episcopal Church Cemetery); director, Harford County Fair (*The Aegis & Intelligencer*, 5 Sep 1890); premium award winner, Class A - Horses, and Class B - Cattle, Harford County Fair (*The Aegis & Intelligencer*, 24 Oct 1890)

McCormick, Rachel (colored), see HattieTurner (colored), q.v.

McCourtney's General Store, Jerusalem Mills, Samuel O. McCourtney, prop. (*Country Stores: Harford County's Rural Heritage*, by Henry C. Peden, Jr. and Jack L. Shagena, Jr., 2015, p. 170)

McCourtney, Adelia (Mrs.), 1848-1916 (Deer Creek Methodist Church Cemetery)

McCourtney, Edna, age 4 *(sic)*, student, Bleak Height School, near Clayton (*The Aegis & Intelligencer*, 18 Jul 1890)

McCourtney, Emma J., 1858-1902 (Mountain Christian Church Cemetery)

McCourtney, Mary B. (Singer), 1854-1891 (St. Mary's Episcopal Church Cemetery)

McCourtney, Newton M., 1854-1922 (Deer Creek Methodist Church Cemetery); resident of Harford County, moved to Long Green Valley near Baldwin Station, Baltimore County, 1890 (*The Aegis & Intelligencer*, 21 Mar 1890)

McCourtney, Rachel May (Parker), 1864-1938 (Mountain Christian Church Cemetery)

McCourtney, Samuel J., 1873-1895 (Deer Creek Methodist Church Cemetery)

McCourtney, Samuel Oliver, 1848-1939 (Mountain Christian Church Cemetery); general store proprietor at Jerusalem Mill in Kellville (*Jerusalem: A Preserved Mill Village*, by Jack L. Shagena, Jr., 2005, pp. 100-102); trustee, Public School No. 9, First District (*Havre de Grace Republican*, 30 May 1890); delegate, First District, Republican Party Convention (*The Aegis & Intelligencer*, 26 Sep 1890)

McCoy, Andrew W., 1845-1899, resided near Castleton (Broad Creek Friends Cemetery; Death certificate states he died at age 50)

McCoy, Edna Grace, 1877-1905 (Broad Creek Friends Cemetery)

McCoy, H. Victorine, 1844-1912 (Broad Creek Friends Cemetery)

McCoy, Henry W., 1851-1920 (Fallston Methodist Church Cemetery)

McCoy, John W., 1869-1893 (Churchville Presbyterian Church Cemetery)

McCoy, Martha Ann, 1835-1894 (Broad Creek Friends Cemetery)

McCoy, Richard B., 1822-1902 (Broad Creek Friends Cemetery); farmer, Greenstone (*Havre de Grace Republican*, 3 Oct 1890); delegate, Fifth District, Republican Party Convention (*The Aegis & Intelligencer*, 26 Sep 1890)

McCoy, Richard G., 1832-1901 (Broad Creek Friends Cemetery)

McCoy, William G., 1833-1919 (Broad Creek Friends Cemetery)

McCrea, Ann S., 1853-1917 (Darlington Cemetery)

McCrea, Jennie R., 1876-1948 (Darlington Cemetery)

McCrea, Lewis, 1846-1922 (Darlington Cemetery); Lewis McCray *(sic)* served on an inquest jury in the Fifth District (*The Aegis & Intelligencer*, 1 Aug 1890)

McCrea, Mortimer B., 1878-1898 (Darlington Cemetery)

McCreary, Edward, uncalled for letter in Bel Air P. O., 1890 (*The Aegis & Intelligencer*, 4 Jul 1890)

McCrone, Ida, see Ida James and E. Roy James, q.v.

McCrone, Samuel B., 1856-1930 (Angel Hill Cemetery)

McCubbin, Jennie V., 1870-1940 (Baker Cemetery)

McCubbin, Martha A. (Ford), 1827-1899, resident on Swan Creek, native of Baltimore Co., widow of John H. McCubbin (Death certificate)

McCue, Leah, 1826-1910 (Emory Methodist Church Cemetery)

McCullough, Ellwood Leveing, 1895-1985 (Angel Hill Cemetery)

McCullough, Owen, c1846-1926 (St. Ignatius Catholic Church Cemetery); native of Ireland, single (Death certificate)

McCullough, William, waterman, drowned 23 Mar 1900, age not given (Death certificate incomplete)

McCummings, Alice B. (Lingan), 1837-1935 (St. Ignatius Catholic Church Cemetery; *The Aegis*, 26 Apr 1935)

McCummings, James, 1855-1904 (St. Ignatius Catholic Church Cemetery)

McCummings, James Morrison, born -- Sep 1883, baptized 14 Oct 1883, son of James and Alice (Lingan) McCummings (St. Ignatius Catholic Church Baptism Register, p. 68)

McCummings, John Edward, 1885-1960 (St. Ignatius Catholic Church Cemetery); born -- Sep 1885, baptized 11 Oct 1885, son of James and Alice (Lingan) McCummings (St. Ignatius Catholic Church Baptism Register, p. 83)

McCummings, Mary Lilia, born -- Aug 1883, baptized 21 Oct 1883, daughter of John and Henrietta (Grafton) McCummings (St. Ignatius Catholic Church Baptism Register, p. 69)

McCummings, Mary Lydia, 1881-1893 (St. Ignatius Catholic Church Cemetery); daughter of James and Alice (Lingan) McCummings (St. Ignatius Catholic Church Baptism Register, p. 58)

McCummings, Morris, first grade student, Bynum School (*The Aegis & Intelligencer*, 11 Jul 1890); son of James and Alice (Lingan) McCummings (*The Aegis*, 26 Apr 1935)

McCurdy, Augusta A., 1872-1946 (Bethel Presbyterian Church Cemetery)

McCurdy, H. J., egg dealer, of Prospect (*Havre de Grace Republican*, 21 Mar 1890)

McCurdy, Hannah A. (Stansbury), 1847-1915 (Bethel Presbyterian Church Cemetery Records); postmistress at Madonna (*Havre de Grace Republican*, 25 Apr and 25 Jul 1890); H. A. McCurdy, vice principal, Bel Air Graded School, 1890 (*The Aegis & Intelligencer*, 8 Aug 1890)wife of Dr. William C. McCurdy, q.v.

McCurdy, James, artist, of Prospect (*Havre de Grace Republican*, 21 Mar 1890)

McCurdy, Madonna S., born 1875, daughter of Dr. William C. McCurdy and Hannah A. Stansbury (Bethel Presbyterian Church Cemetery Records - married name Streett; *The Aegis & Intelligencer*, 18 Jul 1890)

McCurdy, William C., 1846-1922 (Bethel Presbyterian Church Cemetery Records); physician and merchant at Madonna and then in Bel Air (*The Aegis & Intelligencer*, 6 Jun 1890)

McCusker, John, uncalled for letter in Bel Air P. O., 1890 (*The Aegis & Intelligencer*, 14 Nov 1890)

McDaniel, Elizabeth M., 1884-1957 (Mountain Christian Church Cemetery)

McDaniel, Harry G., 1878-1933 (Mountain Christian Church Cemetery)

McDaniel, William (colored), 1865-1940, parents unknown (Death certificate)

McDermott, Constantine, 1840-1906, Civil War veteran (St. Mary's Catholic Church Cemetery)

McDermott, Elizabeth A., 1835-1900 (St. Mary's Catholic Church Cemetery)

McDermott, Melissa (Mrs.), resided near Highland, died 2 Apr 1890, age not given (*Harford Democrat*, 11 Apr 1890)

McDermott, Rachael, 1820-1894 (St. Mary's Catholic Church Cemetery)

McDermott, Sarah, 1819-1909 (St. Mary's Catholic Church Cemetery)

McDevitt, Francis, 1845-1917 (Mt. Erin Cemetery)

McDiarmid, Scott (colored), 1877-1956 (Community Baptist Church Cemetery)

McDonald's Singing School, Norrisville, Fourth District (*Harford County, Maryland Teachers and the Schools They Served, 1774-1900*, by Henry C. Peden, Jr., 2022, p. 371)

McDonald, Agness, see Joseph C. Bosley, q.v.

McDonald, Aquilla, and Sarah E. McDonald, daughter of the late Robert Gemmill, residents of Norrisville (*The Aegis & Intelligencer*, 19 Sep 1890); see Joseph C. Bosley, q.v.

McDonald, Catherine, 1846-1914 (Mt. Erin Cemetery)

McDonald, Catherine T. (O'Leary), 1852-1930, native of Ireland, resided at Perryman, Harford Co. (Death certificate; Mt. Erin Cemetery); wife fof Patrick McDonald, q.v.

McDonald, Cora V., 1878-1946 (Mt. Erin Cemetery)

McDonald, Daniel P., 1874-1940 (Mt. Erin Cemetery)

McDonald, Henry F., 1872-1946 (St. Francis de Sales Catholic Church Cemetery)

McDonald, James, confidential clerk for J. H. Emmord, of Perryman, moved to Baltimore (*Harford Democrat*, 18 Apr 1890)

McDonald, James, 1851-1904 (Mt. Erin Cemetery); resident of Havre de Grace (*The Aegis & Intelligencer*, 5 Sep 1890)

McDonald, John, 1832-1921 (Mt. Erin Cemetery)

McDonald, John C., 1879-1958 (Cranberry Methodist Church)

McDonald, John E, 1876-1903 (Mt. Erin Cemetery)

McDonald, John J., 1881-1940 (Mt. Erin Cemetery)

McDonald, Katherne C. (Moran), 1881-1914 (St. Francis de Sales Catholic Church Cemetery)

McDonald, Mamie A. (Mary Ann), 1885-1953 (St. Francis de Sales Catholic Church Cemetery)

McDonald, Margaret Ann (Whitcomb), 1856-1937 (St. Francis de Sales Catholic Church Cemetery)

McDonald, Margaret B., 1884-1944 (Mt. Erin Cemetery)

McDonald, Mary E., 1887-1977 (Mt. Erin Cemetery)

McDonald, Nellie (Miss), actress, musical entertainment, at Darlington (*The Aegis & Intelligencer*, 30 May 1890)

McDonald, Patrick, 1834-1900, native of Maryland (Death certificate; Mt. Erin Cemetery); railroad crossing watchman at Perryman (*Havre de Grace Republican*, 17 Jan 1890)

McDonald, Richard, treasurer, Black Horse Singing School (*Havre de Grace Republican*, 28 Mar 1890); also see Winfield Scott Morris, q.v.

McDonald, Robert, see Willis R. McDonald, q.v.

McDonald, Sarah C., 1874-1904 (Mt. Erin Cemetery)

McDonald, Thomas, 1871-1932 (St. Francis de Sales Catholic Church Cemetery)

McDonald, Thomas V., 1877-1938 (Mt. Erin Cemetery)

McDonald, William J., 1882-1905 (Mt. Erin Cemetery)

McDonald, William John, 1854-1935 (St. Francis de Sales Catholic Church Cemetery)

McDonald, Willis R., young son of Robert McDonald, of Norrisville (*The Aegis & Intelligencer*, 11 Jul 1890)

McDoon, Herman, 1880-1901 (Dublin Methodist Church Cemetery)

McDoon, John, 1839-1905 (Dublin Methodist Church Cemetery); blacksmith and former county commissioner (*Biographical Dictionary of Harford County, Maryland, 1774-1974*, by Henry C. Peden, Jr. and William O. Carr, 2021, p. 180); justice of the peace, Fifth District (*Havre de Grace Republican*, 21 Feb 1890); trustee, Dublin School No. 13, Fifth District (*Havre de Grace Republican*, 30 May 1890)

McDoon, Laura (Jones), 1845-1909 (Dublin Methodist Church Cemetery); wife of John McDoon, q.v.

McDoon, Rosa (Miss), 1867-1934 (Dublin Methodist Church Cemetery); native of Dublin, Harford Co., born 24 Nov 1865, daughter of John McDoon and Laura Jones (Bailey Funeral Home Records)

McDoon, Ruth Anna (Lamb), 1872-1955 (Dublin Methodist Church Cemetery); native of Harford Co., born 11 Nov 1872, daughter of John Lamb and Genett Harper (Bailey Funeral Home Records)

McDoon, Wesley, 1870-1902 (Dublin Methodist Church Cemetery)

McDowell, Elizabeth, see Elsie Susan Smith, q.v.

McDowell, Eugene Page, died 2 Jan 1893, adult, age not given (Mountain Christian Church Cemetery)

McElvain, William A., acquired land in February 1890 (*The Aegis & Intelligencer*, 7 Mar 1890)

McElroy, William Reed (D.D.), 1856-1934, pastor at Bethel Presbyterian Church (Bethel Presbyterian Church Cemetery Records)

McElwain, John, trustee, Mt. Pleasant School No. 11, Fourth District (*Havre de Grace Republican*, 30 May 1890)

McEwing, ----, left fielder, A. R. Walker Baseball Club, Havre de Grace (*Havre de Grace Republican*, 6 Jun 1890)

McEwing, Annie F., 1885-1956 (Angel Hill Cemetery)

McEwing, Annie Low (Cornell), 1841-1909, native of Virginia resident of Havre de Grace (Death cerificate); wife of Levanion McEwing, q.v.

McEwing, Charles B., 1871-1926 (Angel Hill Cemetery)

McEwing, Charlotte E. "Lottie" (Whitney), 1883-1937 (Angel Hill Cemetery), wife of Frederick W. McEwing, q.v.

McEwing, Frederick W., 1875-1926 (Angel Hill Cemetery), native of Maryland, resided in Havre de Grace, born 27 Feb 1875, son of Levanion McEwing and Annie Low (Death certificate); husband of Charlotte E. (Whitney) McEwing, q.v.

McEwing, James M., 1877-1958 (Angel Hill Cemetery)

McEwing, Levanion ("Levi"), 1839-1903, native of Virginia, resided in Havre de Grace (Angel Hill Cemetery; www.findagrave.com); vice president, Republican Club (*Havre de Grace Republican*, 7 Nov 1890); see Annie Low McEwing and Frederick W. McEwing, q.v.

McEwing, Mary A., born 1862, died ---- (Angel Hill Cemetery)

McFadden, Alvira T. (Thompson), 1874-1954 (Church of the Ascension Cemetery); native of Maryland, born 7 Feb 1874, daughter of William John Thompson and Sarah Rachel Huff (Bailey Funeral Home Records)

McFadden, Anna "Annie" S., 1850-1926 (Angel Hill Cemetery); businesswoman (trader's license), Havre de Grace (*Havre de Grace Republican*, 30 May 1890)

McFadden, Bertha Almira, 1885-1904 (St. Paul's Methodist Church Cemetery)

McFadden, Carrie B., 1876-1895 (Cokesbury Memorial Methodist Church Cemetery)

McFadden, Charles, 1868-1953 (Church of the Ascension Cemetery)

McFadden, Cora L., 1839-1913, of Churchville (Death certificate)

McFadden, Cora R., see Cora R. Sheridan, q.v.

McFadden, Elizabeth A., 1857-1908 (Cranberry Methodist Church Cemetery)

McFadden, Ethel F., 1885-1945 (Cokesbury Memorial Methodist Church Cemetery)

McFadden, Hannah E., see Hannah E. Hamilton, q.v.

McFadden, Harriet C., 1837-1923 (Rock Run Methodist Church Cemetery)

McFadden, Hugh B., 1865-1895 (Mt. Vernon Methodist Church Cemetery); secretary, Pleasant Hill Lyceum (*The Aegis & Intelligencer*, 3 Jan 1890); juror, Fifth District, 1890 (*Havre de Grace Republican*, 31 Oct 1890)

McFadden, John Wesley, 1841-1917 (Tabernacle Cemetery); resident of Fifth District, served on a grand jury, 1890 (*The Aegis & Intelligencer*, 14 Nov 1890); see Hannah E. Hamilton, q.v.

McFadden, Louisa Barbara (Jeffers), 1841-1930 (Tabernacle Cemetery)

McFadden, Lydia Almira, 1874-1954 (Church of the Ascension Cemetery)

McFadden, Mamie C., of Harford County, married William G. Cooper, of Pennsylvania, on 23 Dec 1890 at Dublin M. E. Church (*The Aegis & Intelligencer*, 2 Jan 1891); age 19 in 1890 (Marriage License Applications Book ALJ No. 2, 1890)

McFadden, Margaret, see Viola J. Williams, q.v.

McFadden, Martha, 1839-1917 (Rock Run Methodist Church Cemetery)

McFadden, Mary E. (Scotten), 1873-1963 (Fawn Grove Methodist Church Cemetery); native of Harford Co., born 6 Oct 1873, daughter of J. J. Scotten and Mary J. McGibney (Harkins Funeral Home Records)

McFadden, Minnie (Gross), 1864-1925, native of New York, resided at Priestford (Death certificate)

McFadden, R., road examiner, Fifth District (*Havre de Grace Republican*, 4 Jul 1890)

McFadden, Sarah E., see Samuel J. Neeper, q.v.

McFadden, Sophia, 1841-1916 (Rock Run Methodist Church Cemetery)

McFadden, William H., 1858-1932 (Cranberry Methodist Church Cemetery)

McFadden, William J., superintendent, Susquehanna Hall Sabbath School, Fifth District (*Havre de Grace Republican*, 6 Jun 1890); sold land in November 1890 (*The Aegis & Intelligencer*, 5 Dec 1890)

McFadden, William T., 1857-1916, of Prospect (Death certificate)

McFarland, Charles Henry (colored), 1853-1932, native of Pennsylvania, resident of Havre de Grace (Death certificate)

McFarland, Elizabeth, 1886-1955, native of Carlyle, PA, born 8 Jan 1886, daughter of Henry McFarland and ---- (Pennington Funeral Home Records - married name Osborne)

McFeely, Lucy E., 1886-1972 (Mt. Zion Methodist Church Cemetery)

McFeely, William James, 1889-1964 (Mt. Zion Methodist Church Cemetery)

McGavin, Sherman Sheridan, 1888-1967 (Angel Hill Cemetery)

McGaw, Abbie V., 1870-1954 (Grove Presbyterian Church Cemetery)

McGaw, Aquilla (colored), c1848-1918 (Death certificate); see Sadie V. Banks, q.v.

McGaw, Aquilla (colored), born -- Feb 1864, native of Maryland (1900 Aberdeen Census)

McGaw, Arthur (colored), born -- Apr 1890, native of Maryland, son of Aquilla and Frances McGaw (1900

Aberdeen Census)

McGaw, Charles Augustus, 1845-1926 (Cokesbury Memorial Methodist Church Cemetery); sheriff and member of Mt. Ararat Lodge No. 44, A. F. & A. M., Bel Air (*Havre de Grace Republican*, 11 Jul 1890); Confederate Army veteran (*Havre de Grace Republican*, 30 May 1890); fox hunter, near Bel Air (*The Aegis & Intelligencer*, 14 Feb 1890); stockholder, Aberdeen Can Factory (*Havre de Grace Republican*, 19 Dec 1890)

McGaw, Edward (colored), age 23 in 1889 (Marriage License Applications Book ALJ No. 2, 1890)

McGaw, Ella Jane (Griffin), 1857-1935 (Cokesbury Memorial Methodist Church Cemetery), wife of Charles Augustus McGaw, q.v.

McGaw, Ellen (colored), see Martha Rumsey (colored), q.v.

McGaw, Frances (colored), born -- Jan 1866, native of Maryland (1900 Aberdeen Census); wife of Aquilla McGaw, q.v.

McGaw, Frances (colored), 1880-1931 (Death certificate; St. James United Cemetery)

McGaw, George H., 1881-1892 (Grove Presbyterian Church Cemetery)

McGaw, George Keen, 1850-1919 (Grove Presbyterian Church Cemetery)

McGaw, Helen J., 1867-1951 (Grove Presbyterian Church Cemetery)

McGaw, Henry Martyn, 1840-1911 (Grove Presbyterian Church Cemetery)

McGaw, James W., 1840-1909 (Grove Presbyterian Church Cemetery); trustee, Oakington School No. 16, Second District (*Havre de Grace Republican*, 30 May 1890)

McGaw, John E., juror, Second District (*Havre de Grace Republican*, 2 May 1890)

McGaw, Julia, see Catherine Morrison, q.v.

McGaw, Louisa A., c1830-1899, resided at Bush, native of Maryland, widow of William Edward McGaw, 1830-1868 (Death certificate; Grove Presbyterian Church Cemetery)

McGaw, Lydia Stockham (Gallion), 1858-1926 (Grove Presbyterian Church Cemetery); wife of Robert Franklin McGaw, Jr., q.v.

McGaw, Margaret A. (Warden), 1861-1924 (Grove Presbyterian Church Cemetery)

McGaw, Mary (colored), see Lidie Whims (colored), q.v.

McGaw, Mary Bartol, 1877-1958 (Grove Presbyterian Church Cemetery)

McGaw, Mary M. (colored), age 22 in 1890 (Marriage License Applications Book ALJ No. 2, 1890; Holy Trinity Episcopal Church Register of Marriages, p. 216)

McGaw, Matilda E., 1834-1900 (Churchville Presbyterian Church Cemetery)

McGaw, P. A., former postmaster, McGaw (*Havre de Grace Republican*, 4 Apr 1890)

McGaw, Phoebe E., 1840-1909 (Grove Presbyterian Church Cemetery)

McGaw, Robert Franklin, III, 1879-1958 (Angel Hill Cemetery)

McGaw, Robert Franklin, Jr., 1846-1921 (Angel Hill Cemetery); juror, Second District (*Havre de Grace Republican*, 31 Oct 1890); resident of Havre de Grace (*The Aegis & Intelligencer*, 5 Dec 1890)

McGaw, Robert M., special ducking policeman, Havre de Grace (*Havre de Grace Republican*, 21 Feb 1890)

McGaw, Sadie V. (colored), see Sadie V. Banks (colored), q.v.

McGaw, Sarah (colored), married George Banks on 24 Aug 1890 (marriage certificate)

McGaw, Sarah (colored), c1850-1917 (Death certificate; St. James United Cemetery)

McGaw, Sarah "Sallie" J., 1880-1904 (Churchville Presbyterian Church Cemetery)

McGaw, Susan (Mrs.), resident of Spesutia Island (*The Aegis & Intelligencer*, 6 Jun 1890)

McGaw, Susan G. (Trigger-Maxwell), 1808-1891 (Grove Presbyterian Church Cemetery)

McGaw, Susanna B., 1856-1896 (Grove Presbyterian Church Cemetery)

McGaw, Virginia, 1863-1916 (Grove Presbyterian Church Cemetery)

McGaw, W. Martin, postmaster, at McGaw (*Havre de Grace Republican*, 4 Apr 1890)

McGaw, William, member, Guy Social Club, Aberdeen (*Havre de Grace Republican*, 31 Oct 1890)

McGaw, William Edward, see Lydia S. McGaw, q.v.

McGee, Anna, see Anna Healy, Mary Ellen Healy and Thomas J. Healy, q.v.

McGee, Mary, see Katherine Welsh, q.v.

McGibney, Emily Forwood (Holloway), 1890-1984 (Darlington Cemetery)

McGibney, H. Medford, 1871-1933 (Darlington Cemetery)

McGibney, John Wilton, 1883-1916 (Dublin Southern Cemetery)

McGibney, Lillian V. (Gallion), 1883-1944 (Darlington Cemetery); native of Harford Co., born 17 Aug 1883, daughter of James B. Gallion (Bailey Funeral Home Records)

McGibney, Mary, wife of Joshua Scotten; also see Amy Glasgow, Hugh J. Scotten and Bessie J. Wiley, q.v.

McGibney, Mary F., 1879-1899, resident of Stafford, daughter of Philip and Mary F. McGibney (Death certificate)

McGibney, Mary Frances (Smith), 1843-1932 (Dublin Southern Cemetery); native of Berkley, Harford Co., and wife of Philip F. McGibney, q.v. (Bailey Funeral Home Records); also see Mary F. McGibney and Maude E. Wilkinson, q.v.

McGibney, Mary J., see Mary E. McFadden, q.v.

McGibney, Minnie Alma, 1868-1917 (Dublin Southern Cemetery)

McGibney, Philip Farrell, 1845-1919 (Dublin Southern Cemetery); see Mary F. McGibney and Maude E. Wikinson, q.v.

McGibney, Philip Farrell, Jr., 1880-1947 (Darlington Cemetery; *The Aegis*, 5 Sep 1947)

McGinniss, Peter, caterer, Bel Air, 1890 (*Havre de Grace Republican*, 7 Mar 1890)

McGonigal, Albert, see Mary V. Rees, q.v.

McGonigal, Barney L., Jr., 1867-1947, native of Harford Co., born 27 Sep 1867, son of Barney L. McGonigal, Sr., of Ireland, and Margaret Herbert, of Scotland (Pennington Funeral Home Records; Angel Hill Cemetery)

McGonigal, John Thomas, 1871-1939 (Angel Hill Cemetery)

McGonigal, Martha, 1834-1918 (Angel Hill Cemetery)

McGonigal, Mary V., see Mary V. Rees, q.v.

McGonigal, Michael, 1844-1929 (Death certificate; Alms House Record Book)

McGonigall, J. Lesley, 1888-1973 (Rock Run Methodist Church Cemetery)

McGonigall, John Madison, 1840-1891 (Churchville Presbyterian Church Cemetery)

McGonigall, Josephine, 1874-1936 (Churchville Presbyterian Church Cemetery)

McGonigall, Marian (Miss), 1847-1930 (Churchville Presbyterian Church Cemetery)

McGonigall, Millard (Mrs.), resident near Webster (*The Aegis & Intelligencer*, 4 Jul 1890)

McGonigall, Sarah R. (Stillwell), 1860-1928, native of Delaware (Rock Run Methodist Church Cemetery; Death certificate)

McGrady, Delia M., 1868-1953 (Upper Cross Roads Baptist Church Cemetery)

McGrady, Jackson Lee, 1866-1943 (Upper Cross Roads Baptist Church Cemetery)

McGrady, Milford G., 1887-1978 (Grace Chapel Cemetery)

McGraw, Annie M., 1859-1894 (Angel Hill Cemetery)

McGreevy, Jennie, 18 May 1890 - 8 Oct 1890 (Holy Cross Church Cemetery)

McGreevy, M. Helen, 1883-1946 Holy Cross Church Cemetery)

McGreevy, Martha J., 1856-1927 Holy Cross Church Cemetery)

McGreevy, Sarah (Davis), 1873-1951 (Angel Hill Cemetery)

McGreevy, Thomas B., 1852-1917 (Holy Cross Church Cemetery), resided near Clermont Mills (*The Aegis & Intelligencer*, 31 Jan 1890); see Thomas H. McGreevy, q.v.

McGreevy, Thomas H., 1880-1954 (Holy Cross Church Cemetery); native of Harford Co., born 13 Apr 1880, son of Thomas B. McGreevy and Martha J. Daughton (Harkins Funeral Home Records)

McGuigan, A. Smith, 1883-1910 (St. Mary's Catholic Church Cemetery)

McGuigan, Anna M., 1889-1950 (St. Ignatius Catholic Church Cemetery)

McGuigan, Annie, 1835-1926 (St. Ignatius Catholic Church Cemetery)

McGuigan, Bernard Ignatius, 1880-1964 (St. Ignatius Catholic Church Cemetery); honor student, fourth grade, Thomas Run Public School (*The Aegis & Intelligencer*, 4 Jul 1890)

McGuigan, Elizabeth M., 1884-1966 (St. Ignatius Catholic Church Cemetery)

McGuigan, Florence M. (Adams), 1882-1951 (Dublin Southern Cemetery); native of Harford Co., born 1 Apr 1872, daughter of William T. Adams and Josephine Hopkins (Bailey Funeral Home Records)

McGuigan, Francis J., 1868-1900, native of Maryland, resident of Havre de Grace; son of John McGuigan, q.v., and Catherine Kelly (Death certificate; Mt. Erin Cemetery)

McGuigan, Harry, private, Jackson Guards [Co. D, 1st Regiment, Maryland National Guard], 1889-1890 (*The Aegis & Intelligencer*, 11 Jan 1889)

McGuigan, John, 1835-1906 (St. Ignatius Catholic Church Cemetery); juror, Second District (*Havre de Grace Republican*, 31 Jan 1890); treated by unidentified doctor in 1890 ("Medical Account Book – 1890," Historical Society of Harford County Archives Folder); see Francis J. McGuigan, q.v.

McGuigan, John James, 1880-1957, native of Darlington, Harford Co., born 4 Jan 1880, son of Sylvester A. McGuigan and Margaret Keating (Pennington Funeral Home Records gave his name as J. James McGuigan); Jimmie McGuigan, actor, musical entertainment, at Darlington (*The Aegis & Intelligencer*, 30 May 1890)

McGuigan, Joseph, 1838-1912 (St. Ignatius Catholic Church Cemetery); postmaster, Thomas Run (*Havre de Grace Republican*, 3 Oct 1890)

McGuigan, Joseph P., 1876-1933 (St. Ignatius Catholic Church Cemetery)

McGuigan, Margaret C. (McDonald), 1878-1939 (Mt. Erin Cemetery)

McGuigan, Margaret H. (Keating), 1852-1919 (Mt. Erin Cemetery); wife of Sylvester A. McGuigan, q.v.

McGuigan, Martin, 1870-1892 (St. Ignatius Catholic Church Cemetery)

McGuigan, Mary F., 1872-1951 (Dublin Southern Cemetery)

McGuigan, Oriscilla F., 1869-1939 (Mt. Erin Cemetery)

McGuigan, Peter T., 1865-1930 (Mt. Erin Cemetery); transferred from the voter registration list at Hopewell, Second District (*Havre de Grace Republican*, 17 Oct 1890)

McGuigan, Sylvester A., 1857-1935 (Mt. Erin Cemetery); see John James McGuigan, q.v.

McGurk, John, secretary of minutes, Franklin Sunday School (*Havre de Grace Republican*, 25 Apr 1890)

McGurk, William, farmer, near Prospect (*The Aegis & Intelligencer*, 9 May 1890)

McHenry's Mills (aka Monmouth Mill and Bell's Mill), on Winter's Run near Singer, Alexander Bell, prop. (*Mills: Grist, Saw, Bone, Flint, Fulling ... & More*, by Jack L. Shagena, Jr., Henry C. Peden, Jr. and John W. McGrain, 2009, pp. 212-213)

McHugh, Leah, see Henrietta Heaps, q.v.

McIlvain, Bernard Stump, 1871-1908 (Darlington Cemetery)

McIlvain, Jeremiah, 1808-1893 (Darlington Cemetery)

McIlvain, Rachel A. (Ramsey), 1842-1924 (Darlington Cemetery); native of Maryland (Bailey Funeral Home

Records)

McIntyre, John E., 1889-1943 (Angel Hill Cemetery)

McIntyre, William, 1868-1943 (Cokesbury Memorial Methodist Church Cemetery)

McJilton, Annie (Mrs.), see John Doyle Denham, q.v.

McKaig, William M., of Sixth District, Democrat candidate for Congress (*The Aegis & Intelligencer*, 26 Sep 1890)

McKee, Annie M., age 19 in 1890 (Marriage License Applications Book ALJ No. 2, 1890), married Fred J. Gorrell on 20 Mar 1890 (marriage certificate)

McKee, Charles, canner, Thomas Run (*The Aegis & Intelligencer*, 28 Mar 1890)

McKee, Charles A., 1851-1928, native of Maryland, farmer, married, resided at Cardiff (Death certificate)

McKee, Charles Edward, born 13 Jun 1883, baptized 1 Nov 1883, son of Joseph and Anne S. (O'Donnell) McKee (St. Ignatius Catholic Church Baptism Register, p. 69, in margin wrote McGee (McKee?)

McKee, Columbia Barrett, 1886-1931 (Churchville Presbyterian Church Cemetery)

McKee, David, canner, Thomas Run (*The Aegis & Intelligencer*, 28 Mar 1890)

McKee, Henry, born -- Oct 1885, baptized 29 May 1886, son of Joseph and Anne S. (O'Donnell) McKee (St. Ignatius Catholic Church Baptism Register, p. 87)

McKee, James, 1838-1909 (Churchville Presbyterian Church Cemetery); glass ball shooter (*Harford Democrat*, 24 Jan 1890)

McKee, James P., 1881-1932 (Churchville Presbyterian Church Cemetery)

McKee, John, 1842-1911 (Churchville Presbyterian Church Cemetery)

McKee, John T., c1881-1927 (St. Ignatius Catholic Church Cemetery)

McKee, Mary H., 1873-1954 (Churchville Presbyterian Church Cemetery)

McKee, Mary Jane (Ely), 1863-1909, of near Sharon (William Watters Memorial Church Cemetery; Death certificate)

McKee, Sara M., 1848-1923 (Churchville Presbyterian Church Cemetery)

McKee, William T., 1840-1908, of near Sharon (William Watters Memorial Church Cemetery; Death certificate)

McKendree Methodist Episcopal Church and Cemetery (Troyer Road, Black Horse)

McKenna, Mary, student, Fallston School (*The Aegis & Intelligencer*, 9 May 1890)

McKenna, Thomas, sixth grade student, Fallston School (*The Aegis & Intelligencer*, 21 Feb and 9 May 1890)

McKenzie, Captain, detailed by the census department to collect statistics on the fishing industries in Harford County (*The Aegis & Intelligencer*, 8 Aug 1890)

McKindless, Alice E. (Ewing), 1832-1893 (Rock Run Methodist Church Cemetery); wife of Richard S. McKindless, q.v.

McKindless, Elizabeth R., 1839-1897, wife of Rev. John A. McKindless (Rock Run Methodist Church Cemetery)

McKindless, Hilliard H., 1890-1892 (Rock Run Methodist Church Cemetery)

McKindless, J. A., merchant and vice president of the Havre de Grace Mutual Protection Society (*Havre de Grace Republican*, 31 Jan 1890); chancellor, Harford Lodge No. 54, Knights of Pythias, Havre de Grace (*The Aegis & Intelligencer*, 11 Jul 1890)

McKindless, Richard S., died 5 Nov 1891, age 85 (*Deaths and Marriages in Harford County, Maryland, and Vicinity, 1873-1904, from the Diaries of Albert Peter Silver*, transcribed by Glenn Randers-Pehrson, 1995, p. 17)

McKinney, Gov., see James A. Lyle, q.v.

McKoy, John, see Sarah McKoy, q.v.

McKoy, Sarah, widow of John McKoy, Civil War veteran, Bradenbaugh (*1890 Special Census of the Civil War*

Veterans of the State of Maryland, by L. Tilden Moore, Volume III, p. 82)

McLain, Alfred, Civil War veteran, Darlington (*1890 Special Census of the Civil War Veterans of the State of Maryland*, by L. Tilden Moore, Volume III, p. 88)

McLain, Charles (colored), 1890-1935, native of Maryland, born 2 Feb 1890, son of Walter Walters and Nellie McLain (Death certificate)

McLain, Nellie (colored), see Charles McLain (colored), q.v.

McLaughlin, Chester A., 1887-1962 (Slateville Cemetery, York Co., PA); native of Whiteford, Harford Co., born 18 Dec 1887, son of Theodore C. McLaughlin and Ida Wiley (Harkins Funeral Home Records)

McLaughlin, Duncan T., son of Mr. & Mrs. Joshua McLaughlin, of Line Bridge (*The Aegis & Intelligencer*, 17 Jan and 24 Jan 1890)

McLaughlin, Elizabeth, acquired land in August 1890 (*The Aegis & Intelligencer*, 12 Sep 1890)

McLaughlin, J. Clinton, 1862-1939 (Mt. Nebo Cemetery, York Co., PA); native of Harford Co., born 5 Mar 1862, son of Joshua McLaughlin and Mary Mc---- (Harkins Funeral Home Records)

McLaughlin, James, farmer, near Prospect (*Havre de Grace Republican*, 11 Apr 1890)

McLaughlin, James, 1839-1900, native of Ireland, resident of Havre de Grace (Death certificate)

McLaughlin, Joshua, see Duncan McLaughlin and J. Clinton McLaughlin, q.v.

McLaughlin, Maggie T., age 22 in 1889 (Marriage License Applications Book ALJ No. 2, 1889)

McLaughlin, Ruth, age 20 in 1889 (Marriage License Applications Book ALJ No. 2, 1890)

McLaughlin, Sarah A., 1818-1890 (Tabernacle Cemetery)

McLaughlin, Theodore C., see Chester A. McLaughlin, q.v.

McLean, Alice T., 1886-1968 (St. Mary's Episcopal Church Cemetery)

McLean, Sallie (colored), see Sarah (Dougherty) Walker (colored), q.v.

McLhinney, Alice, 1830-1895 (Mt. Erin Cemetery)

McLhinney, Elizabeth, 1890-1974, native of Havre de Grace, born 6 May 1890, daughter of John McLhinney and Sarah Fudge (Pennington Funeral Home Records - married name Hill)

McLhinney, James A., 1863-1933 (Mt. Erin Cemetery); member, St. Patrick's Catholic Church, Havre de Grace (*Havre de Grace Republican*, 13 Jun 1890); member, Young Men's Pleasure Club, Havre de Grace (*Havre de Grace Republican*, 21 Nov 1890); vice president, St. John the Baptist Beneficial Association, Havre de Grace (*Havre de Grace Republican*, 11 Jul 1890); see Margaret M. McIlhinney, q.v.

McLhinney, John M., 1859-1918 (Mt. Erin Cemetery); see Elizabeth McLhinney, q.v.

McLhinney, Margaret M. (Hollahan), 1865-1943, native of Maryland, wife of James A. McLhinney, q.v. (Pennington Funeral Home Records)

McLhinney, Sarah E. (Fudge), 1863-1919 (Mt. Erin Cemetery); wife of John M. McLhinney, q.v.

McManus, Mary (Miss), uncalled for letter in Bel Air P. O. (*The Aegis & Intelligencer*, 14 Nov 1890)

McMaster, Albert, member, inquest jury, Havre de Grace (*Havre de Grace Republican*, 6 Jun 1890)

McMaster, Elmer E., age 28 in 1890 (Marriage License Applications Book ALJ No. 2, 1890)

McMaster, George W., age 23 in 1889 (Marriage License Applications Book ALJ No. 2, 1889)

McMorris, Mary, see C. Milton McCommons, q.v.

McMullen, John, Civil War veteran, Allibone (*1890 Special Census of the Civil War Veterans of the State of Maryland*, by L. Tilden Moore, Volume III, p. 86); invalid pensioner, Allibone (*Havre de Grace Republican*, 6 Jun 1890)

McNabb (MacNabb), Charles H., 1877-1955 (Darlington Cemetery); mative of Harford Co., born 12 May 1876, son of J. Martin McNabb (MacNabb) and Sarah Savin (Harkins Funeral Home Records); C. H McNabb., student, Macton School, 1890 (*The Aegis & Intelligencer*, 4 Jul 1890)

McNabb, Charles, young nephew of James McNabb, of Fifth District (*The Aegis & Intelligencer*, 14 Nov 1890)

McNabb, David Graves, 1820-1899, of Macton, native of Harford Co. (Death certificate; Darlington Cemetery); resident of Fifth District (*The Aegis & Intelligencer*, 14 Nov 1890); brother of Isaac McNabb, q.v.

McNabb, Hannah J. (Scarborough), 1861-1943 (Slate Ridge Cemetery, York Co., PA); Mrs. James W. McNabb, premium award winner, Class J - Domestic Products, Harford County Fair (*The Aegis & Intelligencer*, 24 Oct 1890); second wife of James W. McNabb, q.v.

McNabb, Isaac, 1818-1890 (*The Aegis & Intelligencer*, 14 Nov 1890), but 1812-1892 are the dates inscribed on his tombstone (Dublin Southern Cemetery)

McNabb, James, see Charles McNabb, q.v.

McNabb, James C., road surveyor, Fifth District (*Havre de Grace Republican*, 4 Jul 1890)

McNabb, James W., 1850-1927 (Slate Ridge Cemetery, York Co., PA); teacher, lawyer and surveyor (*Biographical Dictionary of Harford County, Maryland, 1774-1974*, by Henry C. Peden, Jr. and William O. Carr, 2021, p. 185); committeeman, Harford County Fair (*The Aegis & Intelligencer*, 5 Sep 1890); counsel for the county commissioners (*Havre de Grace Republican*, 4 Jul 1890); secretary of the Agricultural and Mechanical Society (*Havre de Grace Republican*, 23 May 1890); see Hannah J. McNabb and Laura T. McNabb, q.v.

McNabb, John A., 1810-1897 (Dublin Southern Cemetery); brother of Isaac McNabb, q.v.

McNabb (MacNabb), Joseph Martin, 1847-1926 (Darlington Cemetery); attorney-at-law, married, native of Maryland (Death certificate); see Charles H. McNabb (MacNabb); q.v.

McNabb, Laura Thomas, died 11 Jun 1890, age about 35 (*The Aegis & Intelligencer*, 13 Jun 1890 and 20 Jun 1890); first wife of James W. McNabb, q.v.

McNabb, Luther H., justice of the peace, Fifth District (*Havre de Grace Republican*, 21 Feb 1890)

McNabb, Maggie E., witnessed an indenture on 4 Jun 1890 (Harford County Indentures Book WSB No. 1)

McNabb, Nancy Hutchinson (Martin), 1815-1877, wife of David Graves McNabb, q.v.

McNabb, Nannie, student, Macton School (*The Aegis & Intelligencer*, 4 Jul 1890)

McNabb (MacNabb), V. Catharine (Weitzel), 1871-1956 (Darlington Cemetery)

McNabb, William F., see Berkley Grist Mill, q.v.

McNamee, Alice M. 1861-1912 (Grove Presbyterian Church Cemetery)

McNamee, Delilah, 1870-1923 (Grove Presbyterian Church Cemetery

McNamee, Eli, 1841-1918 (Grove Presbyterian Church Cemetery); Civil War veteran, Aberdeen (*1890 Special Census of the Civil War Veterans of the State of Maryland*, by L. Tilden Moore, Volume III, p. 64)

McNamee, Nancy M., 1836-1911 (Grove Presbyterian Church Cemetery)

McNeal, Anna Mary (Watters), 1874-1950, daughter of James D. Watters and Fanny H. ---- (William Watters Memorial Methodist Church Cemetery, Thomas Run)

McNeal, J. Preston Wickham, 1878-1954, son of Joshua Van Sant McNeal and Mary Preston (William Watters Memorial Methodist Church Cemetery, Thomas Run)

McNeil, Ellen E., see Ellen E. Flavin, q.v.

McNeil, Joseph F., 1874-1899 (Mt. Erin Cemetery)

McNulty, Andrew J., Civil War veteran, Bel Air (*1890 Special Census of the Civil War Veterans of the State of Maryland*, by L. Tilden Moore, Volume III, p. 73); granted a government pensioner, 1890, Bel Air (*The Aegis & Intelligencer*, 21 Feb 1890)

McNulty, Catherine, see John L. Abbott, Joseph L. Abbott, Martin L. Abbott, and William F. Abbott, q.v.

McNutt's General Store, Glen Cove, John T. McNutt, prop. (*Country Stores: Harford County's Rural Heritage*, by Henry C. Peden, Jr. and Jack L. Shagena, Jr., 2015, p. 173)

McNutt's General Store, Berkley, Charles F. McNutt, prop. (*Country Stores: Harford County's Rural Heritage*,

by Henry C. Peden, Jr. and Jack L. Shagena, Jr., 2015, p. 173)

McNutt, Alfred B., 1849-1895 (Dublin Southern Cemetery)

McNutt, Alice L.(Enfield), 1863-1942, native of Maryland, parents unknown (Bailey Funeral Home Records; Darlington Cemetery); wife of William F. McNutt, q.v.

McNutt, Annie R. (Miss), 1864-1949 (Darlington Cemetery)

McNutt, Christie C. (Negela), 1882-1975 (Darlington Cemetery)

McNutt, Clara Jane, see Grafton Gover Roussey, q.v.

McNutt, David, see John T. McNutt, q.v.

McNutt, Edith, 1885-1947 (Darlington Cemetery); wife of Wilton G. McNutt, q.v.

McNutt, Edwin T., 1873-1954 (Darlington Cemetery); native of Harford Co., born 22 Apr 1873, son of Thomas A. McNutt and Julia Wilson (Bailey Funeral Home Records)

McNutt, Elizabeth Jane "Lizzie" (Day), 1856-1915 (Darlington Cemetery)

McNutt, Ella, 1860-1905 (Darlington Cemetery)

McNutt, Ella N. (Wills), c1859-1935 (Darlington Cemetery); native of Cecil Co., MD, wife of John T, McNutt, q.v. (Bailey Funeral Home Records)

McNutt, Elvira B., 1879-1945 (Darlington Cemetery)

McNutt, Elvira B. (Jones), 1874-1961 (Darlington Cemetery); native of Harford Co., born 26 Mar 1874, daughter of Lewis Jones and Elizabeth Hughes (Bailey Funeral Home Records); wife of R. Calvin McNutt, q.v.

McNutt, Ernest Thomas, 1872-1935 (Darlington Cemetery)

McNutt, Gover, blacksmith, near Line Bridge and Castleton (*Havre de Grace Republican*, 7 Mar 1890; *The Aegis & Intelligencer*, 21 Feb 1890)

McNutt, Hugh Jones, 1853-1910 (Darlington Cemetery); see Hugh Jones McNutt, Jr. and S. Gover McNutt, q.v.

McNutt, Hugh Jones, Jr., 1886-1957 (Darlington Cemetery); native of Harford Co., born 25 Mar 1886, son of Hugh J. McNutt and Elizabeth "Lizzie" Day (Bailey Funeral Home Records)

McNutt, Jesse S., 1858-1915 (Darlington Cemetery); see Wilton G. McNutt, q.v.

McNutt, John T., 1857-1933 (Darlington Cemetery); native of Berkley, Harford Co., born 7 Sep 1857, son of David McNutt and Susan Akers (Bailey Funeral Home Records); age 32 in 1889 (Marriage License Applications Book ALJ No. 2, 1889)

McNutt, Julia M., 1838-1928 (Darlington Cemetery)

McNutt, Katie May (Gorrell), 1873-1953 (Darlington Cemetery); native of Harford Co., born 13 Feb 1873, daughter of Joshua S. Gorrell and Esther Oldfield (Bailey Funeral Home Records)

McNutt, Lilly M., 1886-1956 (Darlington Cemetery)

McNutt, Margaret E., 1884-1985 (Darlington Cemetery)

McNutt, Martha R. (Scarborough), 1844-1923 (Darlington Cemetery)

McNutt, Mary (Miss), 1830-1906 (Darlington Cemetery)

McNutt, R. Calvin, 1861-1933 (Darlington Cemetery)

McNutt, Richard S., 1832-1900, resided at Darlington, native of Maryland (Death certificate misfiled with 1899 certificates); constable, Darlington, Fifth District (*The Aegis & Intelligencer*, 26 Sep 1890; *Havre de Grace Republican*, 4 Jul 1890); inspector of fish pots on the Susquehanna River (*Havre de Grace Republican*, 11 Jul 1890; trustee, Darlington Academy (*Havre de Grace Republican*, 26 Sep 1890)

McNutt, Richard S., 1869-1952 (Silver Br Cemetery, Newcastle, DE); native of Harford Co., born 20 Apr 1869, son of Thomas A. McNutt and Julia Wilson (Bailey Funeral Home Records)

McNutt, S. Gover, 1883-1954 (Darlington Cemetery); native of Harford Co, born 11 Jun 1883, son of Hugh J. McNutt and Elizabeth "Lizzie" Day (Bailey Funeral Home Records)

McNutt, Samuel G., 1861-1941 (Darlington Cemetery); see Annie O. Giffing, q.v.

McNutt, Samuel Gover, 1810-1892 (Dublin Southern Cemetery)

McNutt, Samuel J., 1834-1922 (Darlington Cemetery)

McNutt, Samuel T., 1865-1943 (Darlington Cemetery)

McNutt, Thomas A., 1838-1902 (Darlington Cemetery); see Edwin T. McNutt and Richard S. McNutt, q.v.

McNutt, William F., 1855-1921 (Darlington Cemetery)

McNutt, Wilton G., 1889-1965 (Darlington Cemetery); native of Darlington, Harford Co., born 18 Jun 1889, son of Jesse McNutt and ---- (Harkins Funeral Home Records)

McPherson, Irene T., 1888-1959 (Baker Cemetery)

McPherson, James H., 1876-1941 (Baker Cemetery)

McRoy, Annie M. B. (Gillespie), 1846-1918 (Mt. Zion Methodist Church Cemetery)

McRoy, Hester Lavinia, 1883-1959 (Mt. Zion Methodist Church Cemetery)

McRoy, John Lee, 1851-1930 (Mt. Zion Methodist Church Cemetery)

McRoy, Mary, student, Bel Air Graded School (*The Aegis & Intelligencer*, 11 Apr 1890)

McRoy, Minnie Belle, 1888-1901, native of Harford Co., resided in Bel Air, born 21 Oct 1881, daughter John L. and Annie M. McRoy (Death certificate; Mt. Zion Methodist Church Cemetery)

McRoy, Sarah Etta, 1881-1926 (Mt. Zion Methodist Church Cemetery)

McSparran, W. F., former canner (*Havre de Grace Republican*, 30 May 1890)

McVey & White's Carriage Shop, Havre de Grace. Joseph L. McVey and Thomas M. White, prop. (*Carriages Back in the Day: Harford County's Rural Heritage*, by Jack L. Shagena, Jr. and Henry C. Peden, Jr., 2016, pp. 97-98)

McVey, Benjamin Harrison, 1889-1949, son of Joseph Logan McVey, q.v.

McVey, Elizabeth (Miss), 1836-1927 (Smith Chapel Methodist Church Cemetery)

McVey, Gertrude B., born 7 Mar 1871, daughter of William Henry and Mary Elizabeth (Bailey) McVey (William Henry McVey Bible, *Maryland Bible Records, Volume 2*, by Henry C. Peden, Jr., 2003, p. 93)

McVey, Harvey, born 29 Dec 1886, son of John J. and Martha McVey (Holy Trinity Episcopal Church Register of Baptisms, p. 94)

McVey, Ida May (Coale), 1876-1959 (Smith Chapel Methodist Church Cemetery); wife of Nelson A. McVey, q.v.

McVey, Jessie Virginia, born 31 Oct 1882, daughter of John J. and Martha McVey (Holy Trinity Episcopal Church Register of Baptisms, p. 94)

McVey, Joseph Logan, 1846-1915 (Angel Hill Cemetery); blacksmith and owner of the Keystone Shop on Ontario Street in Havre de Grace; former city councilman (*Havre de Grace Republican*, 18 Apr 1890; *Biographical Dictionary of Harford County, Maryland, 1774-1974*, by Henry C. Peden, Jr. and William O. Carr, 2021, p. 186)

McVey, Mary Elizabeth (Bailey), 1843-1927 (William Henry McVey Bible, *Maryland Bible Records, Volume 2*, by Henry C. Peden, Jr., 2003, p. 93; Smith Chapel Cemetery); wife of William H. McVey, q.v.

McVey, Nelson Augustus, born 21 Oct 1877, son of William Henry and Mary Elizabeth (Bailey) McVey (William Henry McVey Bible, *Maryland Bible Records, Volume 2*, by Henry C. Peden, Jr., 2003, p. 93; Smith Chapel Cemetery)

McVey, Sarah Ann, see Eliza Kennedy Wakeland, q.v.

McVey, William Henry, 1840-1918 (William Henry McVey Bible, *Maryland Bible Records, Volume 2*, by Henry C. Peden, Jr., 2003, p. 93; Smith Chapel Cemetery)

Meads, Amanda J. (Fowler) (Brown) (Stall) (Nelson), 1825-1898 (Bethel Presbyterian Church Cemetery

Records); married in 1885 to her fourth husband John D. Meads, q.v.

Meads, Elizabeth H., 1867-1945 (McKendree Methodist Church Cemetery)

Meads, Emily J. (Hughes), 1839-1906 (Bethel Presbyterian Church Cemetery Records); wife of James B. Meads, q.v.

Meads, Hannah, 1818-1900 (McKendree Methodist Church Cemetery)

Meads, James B., 1834-1909 (Bethel Presbyterian Church Cemetery Records)

Meads, John D., sold land in May 1890 (*The Aegis & Intelligencer*, 6 Jun 1890)

Meads, L. Loretta, 1845-1927 (McKendree Methodist Church Cemetery)

Meads, T. Milton, 1867-1832 (McKendree Methodist Church Cemetery)

Meads, William L., 1838-1918 (McKendree Methodist Church Cemetery)

Mechem, Agnes, 1875-1898 (St. Ignatius Catholic Church Cemetery)

Mechem, Anna J., see Bertha Mechem, q.v.

Mechem, Bertha, born 14 Aug 1876, daughter of Jon. E. and Anna J. Mechem (Holy Trinity Episcopal Church Register of Baptisms, p. 82)

Mechem, Bertha Cecelia, born 19 May 1883, baptized 6 Jun 1883, daughter of Isaac and Cassandra (Kean) Mechem (St. Ignatius Catholic Church Baptism Register, p. 66); first grade student, Bynum School (*The Aegis & Intelligencer*, 11 Jul 1890)

Mechem, Casssandra M. (Kean), 1848-1936 (St. Ignatius Catholic Church Cemetery); widow of Isaac Mechem (1839-1888); also shown as M. Cassandra (Cain) Mechem (Death certificate)

Mechem, Clara, student, Third District (*The Aegis & Intelligencer*, 24 Oct 1890)

Mechem, Cynthia, 1818-1894 (Forest Hill Friends Cemetery)

Mechem, Edith Agatha, born -- Oct 1887, baptized 26 Nov 1887, daughter of Isaac and Cassandra (Kean) Mechem (St. Ignatius Catholic Church Baptism Register, p. 96)

Mechem, Isaac M., born -- Jul 1885, baptized 11 Sep 1885, son of Isaac and Casandra (Kean) Mechem (St. Ignatius Catholic Church Baptism Register, p. 83)

Mechem, Jon. E, see Bertha Mechem, q.v.

Mechem, M. Cassandra (Cain or Kean), 1848-1936, widow of Isaac Mechem, 1839-1888 (St. Ignatius Catholic Church Cemetery; Death certificate)

Mechem, Mary Estella, baptized 7 Dec 1880, daughter of Isaac and Cassandra (Kean) Mechem (St. Ignatius Catholic Church Baptism Register, p. 51); Stella Mechem, fourth grade student, Bynum School, 1890 (*The Aegis & Intelligencer*, 11 Jul 1890); born 20 Oct 1880 *(sic)*, native of Maryland (Death certificate - married name Spencer)

Mecklin, Alice, see Margaret (Kenly) Rigdon, q.v.

Mectling, William S., born -- May 1822, nephew of Conrad and Annie (Drechsler) Krouse (1900 Aberdeen Census)

Meehan, Henry, 1856-1930 (St. Francis de Sales Catholic Church Cemetery); native of Churchville, gardener, married, resided in Aberdeen (Death certificate)

Meehan, Joseph, 1839-1917 (St. Francis de Sales Catholic Church Cemetery)

Meehan, Mary A., 1836-1917 (St. Francis de Sales Catholic Church Cemetery)

Meehan, Mary A., 1863-1940 (St. Francis de Sales Catholic Church Cemetery); wife of Henry Meehan, q.v.

Meehan, Mary Ann, see Mary Ann Conway and John Lawrence Conway, q.v.

Meehan, Peter, born -- Feb 1888, son of Henry and Mary A. Meehan (1900 Aberdeen Census)

Meehan, William F., born -- Mar 1890, son of Henry and Mary A. Meehan (1900 Aberdeen Census)

Meeks, Hannah, see Margaret C. Hughes, q.v.

Meeks, Joanne, see Joanna Furlong, q.v.

Mehnert, E. G., Civil War Confederate Army veteran, Havre de Grace (*Havre de Grace Republican*, 30 May 1890)

Mehnert, Ernest, new name on the Havre de Grace voter registration list (*Havre de Grace Republican*, 19 Sep 1890)

Melhorn, George W., associate judge of elections, Magnolia Precinct (*Havre de Grace Republican*, 17 Oct 1890)

Mellor, Elizabeth A., see Albert Norman Mellor, q.v.

Mellor, Emma V. (Wiley), 1858-1904, wife of Thomas H. Mellor (Bethel Presbyterian Church Cemetery Records)

Mellor, Thomas H., died 6 Sep 1899, age not given, resided at Shawsville (Death certificate stated his wife was Florence); see Emma V. Mellor, q.v.

Meloy, J. E. (Rev.), Susquehanna Circuit (Wesleyan Chapel, Level and Lapidum) (*Havre de Grace Republican*, 11 Apr 1890)

Melvin, Chester (Master), member, Bel Air M. P. Church Sunday School (*The Aegis & Intelligencer*, 27 Jun 1890)

Melvin, Maud (Miss), member, Bel Air M. P. Church Sunday School (*The Aegis & Intelligencer*, 27 Jun 1890)

Melvin, Susie, member, Providence M. P. Church Sunday School (*The Aegis & Intelligencer*, 18 Jul 1890)

Melvin, Walton, member, Providence M. P. Church Sunday School (*The Aegis & Intelligencer*, 18 Jul 1890)

Merchant, William J. (colored), 1887-1949 (St. James United Cemetery)

Meredith, Mary E., sold land in April 1890 (*The Aegis & Intelligencer*, 9 May 1890)

Meredith's Ford and Jarrettsville Turnpike Company (*Harford Democrat*, 3 Jan 1890)

Mergler, Frank X., 1872-1921, native of Maryland, resided in Havre de Grace, born 15 Oct 1872, son of John L. Mergler and ---- (Death certifcate)

Mergler, John, new name on the voter registration list in Sixth District, 1890 (*Havre de Grace Republican*, 17 Oct 1890); see Frank X. Mergler, q.v.

Merkel, Henry, master at arms, Harford Lodge No. 54, Knight of Pythias, Havre de Grace (*Havre de Grace Republican*, 11 Jul 1890)

Merrell, Emeline (Miss), 1808-1900, native of Maryland, resided at Chapel (Death certificate)

Merry Ten Social Club, Havre de Grace (*Havre de Grace: Its Historic Past, Its Charming Present and Its Promising Future: Harford County's Rural Heritage.* by Jack L. Shagena, Jr. and Henry C. Peden, Jr., 2018, p. 269)

Merryman, E. Gittings, premium award winner, Class A - Horses, and Class B - Cattle, Harford County Fair (*The Aegis & Intelligencer*, 24 Oct 1890)

Merryman, N. O., superintendent, Cooptown Sunday School (*Havre de Grace Republican*, 18 Apr 1890)

Messenkop, Albert, general manager, Bel Air Specialty Company, an entertainment group mostly connected to the young men of the Bulett Carriage Factory (*The Aegis & Intelligencer*, 13 Jun 1890)

Metzel, Jacob B., Civil War veteran, Fawn Grove P. O. (*1890 Special Census of the Civil War Veterans of the State of Maryland*, by L. Tilden Moore, Volume III, p. 81); delegate, Fourth District, Democrat Party Convention (*The Aegis & Intelligencer*, 5 Sep 1890)

Metzger, Caroline, see Caroline Rogers and Clara L. Rogers, q.v.

Meyer, John B., merchant tailor, Havre de Grace (*Havre de Grace Republican*, 30 May 1890)

Meyers, Rachel J., age 22 in 1889 (Marriage License Applications Book ALJ No. 2, 1889)

Michael, Keen & Co., General Store, Perryman (*Country Stores: Harford County's Rural Heritage*, by Henry C. Peden, Jr. and Jack L. Shagena, Jr., 2015, pp. 175-176)

Michael's General Store, Michaelsville, F. Willis Michael, prop. (*Country Stores: Harford County's Rural Heritage*, by Henry C. Peden, Jr. and Jack L. Shagena, Jr., 2015, p. 175)

Michael's General Store, near Mulberry Point, James H. Michael, prop. (*Country Stores: Harford County's Rural Heritage*, by Henry C. Peden, Jr. and Jack L. Shagena, Jr., 2015, p. 175)

Michael's General Store, Perryman, William B. Michael, prop. (*Country Stores: Harford County's Rural Heritage*, by Henry C. Peden, Jr. and Jack L. Shagena, Jr., 2015, p. 176)

Michael, Alonzo (Rev.), Aberdeen (*Havre de Grace Republican*, 31 Jan 1890)

Michael, Ann Martha (Mitchell), 1831-1918 (Grove Presbyterian Church Cemetery; John M. Michael Bible, *Maryland Bible Records, Volume 1*, by Henry C. Peden, Jr., 2003, p. 169); wife of John Calvin Michael, q.v.; also see John Mitchell, Sr., q.v.

Michael, Annie Florence (Smith), 1859-1944, native and resident of Aberdeen, Harford Co. (Death certificate); wife of John M. Michael, q.v.

Michael, Avarilla Ann (Courtney), 1826-1912 (Grove Presbyterian Church Cemetery); wife of William Balcher Michael, q.v.

Michael, Belle (Mrs.), premium award winner, Class K - Household and Domestic Manufactures, Harford County Fair (*The Aegis & Intelligencer*, 24 Oct 1890)

Michael, Catherine (Tracey), 1845-1916 (Mt. Nebo Cemetery, York Co., PA), native of New Market, Baltimore Co., resided at Cardiff, Harford Co. (Death certificate)

Michael, Charles O., 1870-1934 (Centre Methodist Church Cemetery)

Michael, Charles Wesley, 1850-1915 (St. George's Episcopal Church Cemetery); farmer and attorney-at-law; an organizer of the Harford Historical Society in 1885; owner of Buttonwood near Perryman (*Biographical Dictionary of Harford County, Maryland, 1774-1974*, by Henry C. Peden, Jr. and William O. Carr, 2021, p. 187); owner of the *Bay Shore Farm*, near Michaelsville (*The Aegis & Intelligencer*, 6 Jun 1890); vestryman and treasurer, Spesutia Church, St. George's Parish, Perryman (*Havre de Grace Republican*, 11 Apr 1890); vice president of the Third Annual Convention, Farmers' Club of Harford County (*Havre de Grace Republican*, 5 Dec 1890); vice president, Harford County Farmers' Association (*The Aegis & Intelligencer*, 17 Jan 1890)

Michael, Charles Wesley, 1884-1952 (St. George's Episcopal Church Cemetery); born 9 Jan 1884, son of Dr. J. E. and S. R. Michael (St. George's Episcopal Church Register of Baptisms, pp. 4-5)

Michael, Clara V., 1868-1952 (St. George's Episcopal Church Cemetery)

Michael, Cora May (Harvey), 1879-1903 (Death certificate)

Michael. Daniel W., see Laura V. Michael, q.v.

Michael, Edwin Bonn, born 15 Nov 1890, son of Louis T. and Honora Michael (St. George's Episcopal Church Register of Baptisms, pp. 10-11)

Michael, Effie, see Mary Susanna Nelson, q.v.

Michael, Elizabeth (Keen), 1841-1925 (St. George's Episcopal Church Cemetery)

Michael, Emily A., see Robert Lee Michael and Frank Pusey Michael, q.v.

Michael, F. Willis, see Michael's General Store, q.v.

Michael, Fannie Cordelia, 1879-1956 (St. George's Episcopal Church Cemetery)

Michael, Florence M., 1884-1944 (Grove Presbyterian Church Cemetery)

Michael, Frances Cornelia (Courtney), 1829-1916 (Grove Presbyterian Church Cemetery; Henry C. Michael Bible, *Maryland Bible Records, Volume 1*, by Henry C. Peden, Jr., 2003, pp. 166-167)

Michael, Frank Pusey, born 5 Sep 1881, son of James W. and Emily A. Michael (St. George's Episcopal Church Register of Baptisms, pp. 4-5)

Michael, George C., 1890-1948 (St. George's Episcopal Church Cemetery)

Michael, George Mount, 1857-1928 (St. George's Episcopal Church Cemetery)

Michael, George T., husband of Margaret A. (Fitchett) Michael, q.v.

Michael, George W., 1831-1912 (Cokesbury Memorial Methodist Church Cemetery)

Michael, Georgeanna (Ward), c1860-1912 (Deer Creek Methodist Church Cemetery)

Michael, H. Dorsey, 1860-1933 (Cokesbury Memorial Methodist Church Cemetery)

Michael, Harriet Elizabeth (Keen) 1841-1925 (St. George's Episcopal Church Cemetery); wife of James Henry Michael, q.v.; also see Sarah Elizabeth Michael, q.v.

Michael, Harry, painter, son of J. H. Michael (*Harford Democrat*, 7 Mar 1890)

Michael, Henry Clay, 1828-1907 (Grove Presbyterian Church Cemetery; Henry C. Michael Bible, *Maryland Bible Records, Volume 1*, by Henry C. Peden, Jr., 2003, pp. 166-167); trustee, Paradise School No. 2, Second District (*Havre de Grace Republican*, 30 May 1890)

Michael, Henry J., husband of Cora May (Harvey) Michael, q.v.

Michael, Herbert Harlan, 1881-1948 (St. George's Episcopal Church Cemetery); born 18 Jul 1881, son of Dr. J. E. and S. R. Michael (St. George's Episcopal Church Register of Baptisms, pp. 2-3)

Michael, Honora B., 1868-1941 (St. George's Episcopal Church Cemetery); see Edwin Bonn Michael, q.v.

Michael, Honoria Blake, born 22 Jan 1889, daughter of Louis T. Michael and Honoria Blake (St. George's Episcopal Church Register of Baptisms, p. 8)

Michael, Ida Belle (Gilbert), 1858-1931 (Churchville Presbyterian Church Cemetery)

Michael, Ida M., 1854-1938 (Grove Presbyterian Church Cemetery)

Michael, J. C., tomato farmer, near Aberdeen, 1890 (*Havre de Grace Republican*, 22 Aug 1890); trustee, Oakington School No. 16, Second District (*Havre de Grace Republican*, 30 May 1890)

Michael, J. Edmund, 1876-1939, born 10 Oct 1876 near Aberdeen, Harford Co., son of J. Edwin Michael and Susanna R. Mitchell (Death certificate; St. George's Episcopal Church Cemetery)

Michael, Jackson E., 1865-1937 (Grove Presbyterian Church Cemetery); jousting tournament rider, Knight of Lone Star, 1890 (*The Aegis & Intelligencer*, 29 Aug 1890)

Michael, Jacob C., 1877-1953 (Deer Creek Methodist Church Cemetery)

Michael, Jacob Edwin (Dr.), 1848-1895 (St. George's Episcopal Church Cemetery); also see J. Edmund Michael, Charles Wesley Michael, Susan Rebecca Michael, Herbert Harlan Michael and William Howard Michael, q.v.

Michael, Jacob Jackson, 1816-1892 (St. George's Episcopal Church Cemetery); owner of *Gravelly Farm* below Michaelsville (*The Aegis & Intelligencer*, 31 Jan 1890)

Michael, James (colored), see James H. Stansbury(colored), q.v.

Michael, James Henry, 1839-1893 (St. George's Episcopal Church Cemetery); glass ball shooter, Bush River Neck, 1890 (*The Aegis & Intelligencer*, 24 Jan 1890); see Sarah Elizabeth Michael and Michael's General Store, q.v.

Michael, James W., see Robert Lee Michael and Frank Pusey Michael, q.v.

Michael, John Calvin, 1825-1895 (Grove Presbyterian Church Cemetery; John M. Michael Bible, *Maryland Bible Records, Volume 1*, by Henry C. Peden, Jr., 2003, p. 169); see John Mitchell, Sr., q.v.

Michael, John H., treated by unidentified doctor in 1890 ("Medical Account Book – 1890," Historical Society of Harford County Archives Folder)

Michael, John M., 1857-1921 (Grove Presbyterian Church Cemetery); son of John Calvin and Ann Martha Michael (John M. Michael Bible, *Maryland Bible Records, Volume 1*, by Henry C. Peden, Jr., 2003, p. 169); John M. Michael, and wife, sold land in November 1890 (*The Aegis & Intelligencer*, 5 Dec 1890)

Michael, Joseph V., 1887-1955 (St. George's Episcopal Church Cemetery)

Michael, Keen & Co., merchants, Perryman (*The Aegis & Intelligencer*, 20 Jun 1890)

Michael, Laura V. (Dorsey), 1861-1899 (Calvary Methodist Church Cemetery); resided at Calvary, wife of Daniel W. Michael (Death certificate)

Michael, Louis Taylor, 1864-1898 (St. George's Episcopal Church Cemetery); member, Order of the Golden Chain, at Perryman (*Havre de Grace Republican*, 14 Mar 1890, spelled his name Lewis); Lou Michael, catcher, Perryman Baseball Club (*The Aegis & Intelligencer*, 18 Jul 1890); also see Honoria Blake Michael and Edwin Bonn Michael, q.v.

Michael, Louisa E. (Mitchell), 1822-1896 (Calvary Methodist Church Cemetery)

Michael, Luther T., collector, Perryman Lodge, Order of the Golden Chain (*Havre de Grace Republican*, 5 Dec 1890)

Michael, M., pitcher, Perryman Baseball Club (*The Aegis & Intelligencer*, 18 Jul 1890)

Michael, M. Daisy (Miss), resident of Michaelsville (*The Aegis & Intelligencer*, 12 Dec 1890)

Michael, Margaret A. (Fitchett), 1838-1907 (Death certificate)

Michael, Martha S. (Richardson), 1863-1937 (Grove Presbyterian Church Cemetery)

Michael, Mary (Johnson), 1818-1905 (Deer Creek Methodist Church Cemetery)

Michael, Mary L., 1857-1925 (St. George's Episcopal Church Cemetery)

Michael, Mary M., see Isabelle Nelson, q.v.

Michael, May, 1878-1904 (Highland Presbyterian Church Cemetery)

Michael, Nannie (Miss), honor student, Archer Institute, Bel Air (*The Aegis & Intelligencer*, 20 Jun 1890); organist, Emmanuel Episcopal Church, Bel Air (*The Aegis & Intelligencer*, 20 Jun 1890)

Michael, Oleita Z. (Miss), member, Guy Social Club, Aberdeen (*Havre de Grace Republican*, 24 Oct 1890); choir member, Grove Presbyterian Church, Aberdeen (*Havre de Grace Republican*, 14 Feb 1890)

Michael, Orion Clay, 1861-1944 (Grove Presbyterian Church Cemetery); born 10 Apr 1861, son of Henry C. and Cornelia F. Michael (Henry C. Michael Bible, *Maryland Bible Records, Volume 1*, by Henry C. Peden, Jr., 2003, pp. 166-167); Orie Michael, actor, musical entertainment, at Darlington (*The Aegis & Intelligencer*, 30 May 1890)

Michael, Orion Clay, Jr., 1887-1940 (Grove Presbyterian Church Cemetery)

Michael, Robert Lee, 1879-1948 (St. George's Episcopal Church Cemetery); born 10 Jul 1879, son of James W. and Emily A. Michael (St. George's Episcopal Church Register of Baptisms, pp. 4-5)

Michael, Sarah E., see Carrie J. Grafton, q.v.

Michael, Sarah Elizabeth, born 1 Dec 1885, daughter of James H. and Harriet E. Michael (St. George's Episcopal Church Register of Baptisms, pp. 4-5)

Michael, Susan (Kimble) (Pritchard), 1810-1895, second wife of Jacob J. Michael, q.v.

Michael, Susan Rebecca, born 4 Dec 1877, daughter of Dr. J. E. and S. R. Michael (St. George's Episcopal Church Register of Baptisms, pp. 2-3); also see William Howard Michael, Susan Rebecca Michael, Herbert Harlan Michael and Charles Wesley Michael, q.v.

Michael, Walter Cook, 1878-1956 (Evergreen Burial Park, Roanoke, VA); born 6 Feb 1878, son of James Henry Michael and Harriet Elizabeth Keen (www.findagrave.com)

Michael, William, resident of Chestnut Hill (*The Aegis & Intelligencer*, 28 Nov 1890)

Michael, William Balcher, 1822-1917 (Grove Presbyterian Church Cemetery)

Michael, William C., 1848-1912 (St. George's Episcopal Church Cemetery)

Michael, William H., 1859-1933 (Deer Creek Methodist Church Cemetery)

Michael, William Howard, 1888-1961 (St. George's Episcopal Church Cemetery); born 26 Feb 1888, son of J. Edwin and Susan R. Michael (St. George's Episcopal Church Register of Baptisms, p. 7)

Michael, William Nagle, 1885-1956 (St. George's Episcopal Church Cemetery)

Michael, William Otho, 1860-1945 (Churchville Presbyterian Church Cemetery)

Michael, Willie, jousting tournament herald (*The Aegis & Intelligencer*, 8 Aug 1890)

Michaelsville Colored Public School No. 2, Second District (*Harford County, Maryland Teachers and the Schools They Served, 1774-1900*, by Henry C. Peden, Jr., 2022, p. 371)

Michaelsville Public School No. 6, Second District (*Harford County, Maryland Teachers and the Schools They Served, 1774-1900*, by Henry C. Peden, Jr., 2022, p. 371)

Middendorf, Anna "Annie" A., born 16 Oct 1867, daughter of John Henry Middendorf and Cassaandra Everett; teacher, Bleak Height School, near Clayton (*The Aegis &Intelligencer*, 18 Jul 1890; *Harford County, Maryland Teachers and the Schools They Served*, by Henry C. Peden, Jr., 2021, p. 219); secretary, Mountain Christian Church Sunday School (*Havre de Grace Republican*, 7 Feb 1890); member, Mountain Reading Circle (*The Aegis & Intelligencer*, 12 Sep 1890)

Middendorf, Cassandra (Everett), 1835-1923 (Mountain Christian Church Cemetery); wife of John Henry Middendorf, q.v.

Middendorf, Charles Albert, born 2 Jul 1872, son of John Henry Middendorf and Cassandra Everett *Harford County, Maryland Teachers and the Schools They Served*, by Henry C. Peden, Jr., 2021, pp. 219-220)

Middendorf, Emma Griselda, 1870-1952 (Mountain Christian Church Cemetery)

Middendorf, Emma L., born 29 Aug 1863, daughter of John Henry Middendorf and Cassandra Everett; teacher, Prospect Hill School No. 4, First District (*The Aegis & Intelligencer*, 21 Feb 1890 and 29 Aug 1890; *Harford County, Maryland Teachers and the Schools They Served*, by Henry C. Peden, Jr., 2021, p. 220); member, Mountain Reading Circle (*The Aegis & Intelligencer*, 21 Feb 1890)

Middendorf, George H., 1867-1953 (Mountain Christian Church Cemetery)

Middendorf, John Henry, 1836-1927 (Mountain Christian Church Cemetery); road mender, near Wheel P. O. (*The Aegis & Intelligencer*, 1 Aug 1890)

Middendorf, John W., 1874-1937 (Good Will Church Cemetery)

Middendorf, Lillie M., 1876-1940 (Mountain Christian Church Cemetery)

Middendorf, Rose M., 1877-1948 (Mountain Christian Church Cemetery)

Middleditch, John, Civil War veteran, Cooptown (*1890 Special Census of the Civil War Veterans of the State of Maryland*, by L. Tilden Moore, Volume III, p. 79)

Middleditch, Lena A., 1863-1913 (Old Brick Baptist Church Cemetery)

Middleditch, William T., 1857-1917 (Old Brick Baptist Church Cemetery); divorced, age 32 in 1890 and remarried in 1891 (Marriage License Applications Book ALJ No. 2, 1891)

Middleton, Bennett Baker, 1887-1963 (Baker Cemetery)

Middleton, Bertha Baker, 1881-1956 (Baker Cemetery)

Middleton, James Scott, 1881-1969 (Baker Cemetery)

Middleton, Samuel, 1856-1932 (Alms House Record Book; Heavenly Waters Cemetery)

Miers, Frank, new name on the voter registration list at Magnolia, First District, 1890 (*Havre de Grace Republican*, 17 Oct 1890)

Milburn, Emma (colored), 1855-1900, cook, native of Lancaster, PA, resident of Bel Air, wife of George Milburn (Death certificate)

Milburn, George (colored), see Emma Milburn (colored), q.v.

Milburn, Henrietta (colored), died 24 Apr 1893, age not given, wife of Joseph Milburn (*The Aegis & Intelligencer*, 28 Apr 1893)

Milburn, Henry (colored), trustee, Gunpowder Neck Colored School No. 3, First District (*Havre de Grace Republican*, 30 May 1890)

Milburn, Joseph (colored), see Henrietta Milburn (colored), q.v.

Mihlway, Sarah, 1820-1900, of Bel Air, wife of John Mihlway (Death certificate)

Mill Green Public School No. 7, at Mill Green, Fifth District (*Harford County, Maryland Teachers and the*

Schools They Served, 1774-1900, by Henry C. Peden, Jr., 2022, p. 371)

Miller, A. R. (Rev.), late of Virginia, now pastor of Avondale and Mountain Christian Churches, 1890 (*The Aegis & Intelligencer*, 7 Nov 1890)

Miller, Aaron 1823-1905 (Tabernacle Cemetery)

Miller, Alice C., 1875-1932 (Heaps Family Cemetery)

Miller, Alonzo J. (colored), 1885-1957 (Trinity AME Zion Church); native of Street, Harford Co., born 15 Nov1885, son of John C. Miller and Rebecca Jamison (Harkins Funeral Home Records)

Miller, Amelia, see Adda S. Walter, q.v.

Miller, Amelia (colored), see Hannah Thompson (colored), q.v.

Miller, Amelia S., 1871-1960 (Dublin Southern Cemetery)

Miller, Annie (colored), age 21 in 1889 (Marriage License Applications Book ALJ No. 2, 1889)

Miller, Annie E. (Kennedy), 1874-1951 (Rock Run Methodist Church Cemetery); native of Harford Co., born 10 Oct 1874, daughter of William Kennedy and Elizabeth Knight (Bailey Funeral Home Records)

Miller, Bessie P., 1889-1981 (Mt. Zion Methodist Church Cemetery)

Miller, Caroline, see Charles W. Lawder, q.v.

Miller, Caroline (colored), wife of Sidney H. Miller, q.v.

Miller, Delmer T., 1889-1965 (Slate Ridge Cemetery, York Co., PA); native of Harford Co., born 26 May 1889, son of Robert Miller and Matilda Morris, q.v.

Miller, Edward C., 1888-1921 (Mt. Zion Methodist Church Cemetery)

Miller, Elizabeth, see Florida White, q.v.

Miller, Ella Amanda, see Theodosia Kelly, q.v.

Miller, Elmira E., 1839-1915 (Norrisville Methodist Church Cemetery)

Miller, Emma (Barber), 1836-1896 (Jarrettsville Cemetery)

Miller, Emma C., 1870-1961 (St. Paul's Methodist Church)

Miller, Fannie A., wrote her will in 1890 and died in 1891, naming her sister Marion B. Miller as her only heir (Harford County Will Book JMM 11:182)

Miller, Frances Rebecca (Mrs.) (colored), 1854-1927, native of Maryland (Death certificate)

Miller, George E., 1888-1890 (Deer Creek Harmony Presbyterian Church Cemetery)

Miller, George F., 1885-1965 (St. Paul's Methodist Church)

Miller, George Franklin (colored), 1857-1911, native of Maryland (Death certificate)

Miller, George H., 1857-1927 (Angel Hill Cemetery)

Miller, George Henry (colored), 1872-1922, born in Maryland, parents unknown (Death certificate); age 29 in 1891 (Marriage License Applications Book ALJ No. 2)

Miller, Grace E., 1873-1959 (Jarrettsville Cemetery)

Miller, H. (colored), see Mary Elizabeth Monk (colored), q.v.

Miller, Hannon, see Talitha Turner, q.v.

Miller, Harry (colored), 1881-1959 (Death certificate; Alms House Record Book)

Miller, Harry C., college student, of Webster (*Havre de Grace Republican*, 14 Feb 1890)

Miller, Harry S., 1888-1933 (Angel Hill Cemetery)

Miller, Henry Clay, 1853-1916, native of Harford Co., can maker at Havre de Grace (Death certificate; Angel Hill Cemetery)

Miller, Herbert J., 1873-1959 (Mountain Christian Church Cemetery)

Miller, Irene (Miss), 1873-1963 (Jarrettsville Cemetery); resident of Jarrettsville, 1890 (*The Aegis &*

Miller, J. Harry, 1882-1959 (Wesleyan Chapel Methodist Church Cemetery); native of Harford Co., born 22 Feb 1882, son of James Miller and ---- (Bailey Funeral Home Records)

Miller, J. Raymond, 1863-1937 (St. Paul's Methodist Church)

Miller, James, see J. Harry Miller, q.v.

Miller, James H., see Ida E. Kennedy and James R. Miller, q.v.

Miller, James M., 1844-1901 (Wesleyan Chapel Methodist Church Cemetery)

Miller, James Robert, 1873-1952 (Rock Run Methodist Church Cemetery); native of Harford Co., born 6 Jan 1873, son of James Harrison Miller and Mary Ellen Baker (Bailey Funeral Home Records)

Miller, Jermiah (colored), 1843-1940, native of Harford Co. (Death certificate)

Miller, John, hotel keeper, Jarrettsville (*Havre de Grace Republican*, 16 May 1890)

Miller, John, 1829-1901, native of Harford Co., farmer at Chestnut Hill (Death certificate)

Miller, John, 1861-1936, native of Scotland, laborer in Aberdeen (Baker Cemetery; Death certificate)

Miller, John (colored), wood room machine operator, Susquehanna Paper Company (*The Aegis & Intelligencer*, 17 Oct 1890); see Mrs. James Giles, q.v.

Miller, John (Mrs.), county out-pensioner [welfare recipient], Second District (*Havre de Grace Republican*, 4 Jul 1890)

Miller, John A., native of Germany, naturalized on 1 Sep 1890 (Harford County Circuit Court Minute Book ALJ No. 5, p. 253)

Miller, John A., new name on the voter registration list at Magnolia, First District, 1890 (*Havre de Grace Republican*, 26 Sep 1890)

Miller, John C. (colored), see Alonzo J. Miller (colored), q.v.

Miller, Kate L. (Garrettson), 1874-1960 (Wesleyan Chapel Methodist Church Cemetery); native of Harford Co., born 1 Jun 1874, daughter of George Garrettson and Sallie Whitson (Bailey Funeral Home Records)

Miller, Kate Virginia (Charshee), 1856-1936 (Angel Hill Cemetery)

Miller, Katherine M., 1890-1967 (Angel Hill Cemetery)

Miller, Laura (Preston) (colored), c1859-1913, native of Harford Co. (Death certificate)

Miller, Lewis (colored), 1877-1922, native of Harford Co., parents unknown (Death certificate)

Miller, Lewis G., 1878-1961 (Angel Hill Cemetery)

Miller, Lizzie (Walker), 1879-1961 (Angel Hill Cemetery)

Miller, Lue, uncalled for letter in Bel Air P. O. (*The Aegis & Intelligencer*, 14 Nov 1890)

Miller, Marion B., see Fannie A. Miller, q.v.

Miller, Martha J. (Miss), premium award winner, Class K - Household and Domestic Manufactures, Harford County Fair (*The Aegis & Intelligencer*, 24 Oct 1890)

Miller, Martha M., 1854-1941 (Wesleyan Chapel Methodist Church Cemetery); wife of Robert L. Miller, q.v.

Miller, Mary E. (Baker), 1846-1935 (Wesleyan Chapel Methodist Church Cemetery); wife of James M. Miller, q.v.

Miller, Mary "Mollie" Eliza, born 18 Aug 1870, daughter of James Harrison and Mary Ellen (Baker) Miller (*The Hughes Genealogy, 1636-1953*, by Joseph Lee Hughes, 1953, p. 130)

Miller, Mitchell H., 1837-1910 (Fellowship Church Cemetery)

Miller, Myrtle A., 1887-1965 (Free Will Baptist Church Cemetery)

Miller, Peter, 1868-1926 (Darlington Cemetery)

Miller, Rachel Caroline (Ebaugh), 1840-1906 (Norrisville Methodist Church Cemetery)

Miller, Rebecca, see Caleb A. Beard, q.v.

Miller, Rebecca A., 1837-1920 (Mountain Christian Church Cemetery)

Miller, Rena M., 1867-1915 (Centre Methodist Church Cemetery)

Miller, Robert, see Delmer T. Miller, q.v.

Miller, Robert L., 1852-1893 (Wesleyan Chapel Methodist Church Cemetery)

Miller, Robert L, 1870-1961 (Jarrettsville Cemetery); resident of Jarrettsville, 1890 (*The Aegis & Intelligencer*, 18 Apr 1890)

Miller, Rose (Miss), member, Norrisville M. E. Church Sunday School (*The Aegis & Intelligencer*, 20 Jun 1890)

Miller, S. Streett, 1866-1934 (Jarrettsville Cemetery)

Miller, Sallie R., 1874-1943 (Providence Methodist Church Cemetery)

Miller, Sidney H. (colored), 1840-1936, native of Harford Co. (Death certificate)

Miller, Stevenson A., 1868-1913 (Providence Methodist Church Cemetery)

Miller, Tamyse Mae, 1887-1975 (Mountain Christian Church Cemetery)

Miller, Thomas, deceased and removed from the voter registration list at Hopewell, Second District, 1890 (*Havre de Grace Republican*, 26 Sep 1890)

Miller, Thomas 1833-1903 (Norrisville Methodist Church Cemetery)

Miller, Thomas D., 1860-1951 (Wesleyan Chapel Methodist Church Cemetery)

Miller, Thomas Hutchins, 1836-1920 (Jarrettsville Cemetery)

Miller, Virginia, 1830-1897 (Bethel Presbyterian Church Cemetery)

Miller, William, 1867-1925 (Angel Hill Cemetery)

Miller, William H., born 1874, died --- (Heaps Family Cemetery)

Miller, William J., born 1867, died --- (Mountain Christian Church Cemetery)

Milligan, Sue, see Mary B. Beattie, q.v.

Mills, Annie L. (colored), 1880-1971 (St. James United Cemetery)

Mills, Emma (Cullison), 1888-1928 (Angel Hill Cemetery)

Mills, Grover C., 1886-1959 (Darlington Cemetery)

Mills, J. Henry, 1885-1952 (Bel Air Memorial Gardens)

Mills, Samuel I. (colored), 1865-1937 (St. James United Cemetery); native of Somerset Co., MD (Death certificate states he died in 1937, but tombstone is inscribed 1936)

Milton, Griffin Taylor (1847-1904 (Deer Creek Harmony Presbyterian Church Cemetery); delegate, Fifth District, Democrat Party Convention, 1890 (*The Aegis & Intelligencer*, 5 Sep 1890)

Milton, Isabel Pannell (Silver), 1851-1922 (Deer Creek Harmony Presbyterian Church Cemetery; *Our Silver Heritage*, by Benjamin Stump Silver and Frances Aylette (Bowen) Silver, 1976, p. 3051); wife of Griffin Taylor Milton, q.v.

Milway, Joanna R., 1872-1945 (St. Mary's Episcopal Church Cemetery); wife of Kinsey D. Milway, q.v.

Milway, Kinsey D., 1863-1928 (St. Mary's Episcopal Church Cemetery; Death certificate);

Mink, Mary, wife of Michael Mink, q.v.

Mink, Michael, 1850-1925 (Angel Hill Cemetery)

Minnick's General Store, Mechanicsville, Benjamin F. Minnick, prop. (*Country Stores: Harford County's Rural Heritage*, by Henry C. Peden, Jr. and Jack L. Shagena, Jr., 2015, p. 177)

Minnick's General Store, Hickory, Martha C. Minnick, prop. (*Country Stores: Harford County's Rural Heritage*, by Henry C. Peden, Jr. and Jack L. Shagena, Jr., 2015, p. 177)

Minnick, Anna A., 1881-1969 (Christ Episcopal Church Cemetery)

Minnick, Benjamin Franklin, 1829-1900 (St. Ignatius Catholic Church Cemetery); property owner adjacent to Broadway in Bel Air (*The Aegis & Intelligencer*, 16 May 1890); treasurer, Harford County Agricultural Society (*Havre de Grace Republican*, 10 Oct 1890); premium award winner, Class E - Poultry, Harford County Fair (*The Aegis & Intelligencer*, 24 Oct 1890); see Mary Corinne Minnick and Florence M. Minnick, q.v.

Minnick, Cyrus, 1839-1895 (Emory Methodist Church Cemetery)

Minnick, Edith C., 1866-1945, wife of Millard F. Minnick, q.v.

Minnick, Edith Eliza, born in 1890, died ---- (Christ Episcopal Church Cemetery)

Minnick, Elizabeth C. (Martin), 1860-1961 (Christ Episcopal Church Cemetery)

Minnick, Elizabeth P., 1802-1898 (Christ Episcopal Church Cemetery)

Minnick, Elmer, clay pigeon shooter, Forest Hill (*The Aegis & Intelligencer*, 7 Feb 1890)

Minnick, Florence M., 1867-1942, native of Harford Co., born 12 Dec 1867, daughter of Benjamin F. Minnick and Martha Rider (Death certificate; St. Mary's Catholic Church Cemetery)

Minnick, George E., acquired land in February 1890 (*The Aegis & Intelligencer*, 7 Mar 1890)

Minnick, Harry (Henry) A., acquired land in February 1890 (*The Aegis & Intelligencer*, 7 Mar 1890); also see Laura A. Minnick, q.v.

Minnick, Howard Calender, 1881-1946 (Christ Episcopal Church Cemetery)

Minnick, Jacob J., 1837-1897 (Christ Episcopal Church Cemetery); Civil War veteran, resided at Hickory (*1890 Special Census of the Civil War Veterans of the State of Maryland*, by L. Tilden Moore, Volume III, p. 72)

Minnick, Laura A., died 4 Jul 1890, age 25 (Christ Episcopal Church Cemetery); wife of Henry A. Minnick, of Hickory (*The Aegis & Intelligencer*, 11 Jul 1890)

Minnick, Marjorie (Keith), 1855-1946 (Emory Methodist Church Cemetery)

Minnick, Martha C., 1832-1917 (St. Ignatius Catholic Church Cemetery); see Minnick's General Store, q.v.

Minnick, Mary Belle, 1884-1919 (Grace Chapel, Friendship Church)

Minnick, Mary Corinne, daughter of Mr. & Mrs. B. F. Minnick, married Frederick N. Ramsay on 30 Apr 1890 (*The Aegis & Intelligencer*, 2 May 1890)

Minnick, Millard F., 1863-1932 (Loudon Park Cemetery, Baltimore, MD), son of Uriah Minnick and Eliza Ann Callender (www.findagrave.com); attorney at law, Bel Air (*Harford Democrat*, 14 Feb 1890); census taker, Bel Air (*Havre de Grace Republican*, 17 Jan 1890); treasurer, Harford County Agricultural and Mechanical Society (*Havre de Grace Republican*, 31 Jan 1890); trustee, Hickory School No. 7, Third District (*Havre de Grace Republican*, 30 May 1890); vestryman, Christ Church, Rock Spring (*Havre de Grace Republican*, 18 Apr 1890)

Minnick, Owen M., 1882-1968 (Christ Episcopal Church Cemetery)

Minnick, Samuel J., acquired land in February 1890 (*The Aegis & Intelligencer*, 7 Mar 1890)

Minnick, Samuel P., 1825-1909 (Christ Episcopal Church Cemetery); sold land in February 1890 (*The Aegis & Intelligencer*, 7 Mar 1890)

Minnick, Sarah Jane, 1851-1948 (Christ Episcopal Church Cemetery)

Minnick, Stevenson Archer, 1869-1957 (Grace Chapel, Friendship Church)

Minnick, Susan E. (Wann), 1826-1898 (Christ Episcopal Church Cemetery)

Minnick, Susanna, age 19 in 1890 (Marriage License Applications Book ALJ No. 2, 1890)

Minnick, Thomas Alfred, 1854-1947 (Christ Episcopal Church Cemetery); acquired land in February 1890 (*The Aegis & Intelligencer*, 7 Mar 1890)

Minnick, Uriah, 1820-1906 (Green Mount Cemetery, Baltimore, MD); native of Lancaster or Dauphin Co., PA, resided at Hickory, Harford Co. (www.findagrave.com; *The Aegis & Intelligencer*, 4 Apr 1890)

Minnick, William Henry, 1846-1927 (Christ Episcopal Church Cemetery); Civil War veteran, Hickory (*1890 Special Census of the Civil War Veterans of the State of Maryland*, by L. Tilden Moore, Volume III, p. 72)

Minor, George (colored), 1888-1938 (Death certificate; St. James United Cemetery)

Mitchell's Corn Packing Plant, Aberdeen (*1953 Harford County Directory*, pp. 273-274)

Mitchell's General Store, Calvary, Joseph F. Mitchell, prop. (*Country Stores: Harford County's Rural Heritage*, by Henry C. Peden, Jr. and Jack L. Shagena, Jr., 2015, p. 178)

Mitchell, Addie S., 1867-1936 (Angel Hill Cemetery)

Mitchell, Adelia (Arnold), 1808-1898 (Rock Run Methodist Church Cemetery); mother of John Henry Mitchell, q.v.

Mitchell, Adeline, see Fannie Dye and Joseph E. Dye, q.v.

Mitchell, Agnes, 1864-1965, native of Havre de Grace, born 16 Sep 1874, daughter of Ezekiel Mitchell and Margaret Fogerty (Pennington Funeral Home Records - married name McDonald)

Mitchell, Alfred, farmer, near Aberdeen (*Havre de Grace Republican*, 17 Jan 1890)

Mitchell, Alice (Duvall), 1849-1945 (Christ Episcopal Church Cemetery)

Mitchell, Alice Virginia (Wakeland), 1857-1944 (Calvary Methodist Church Cemetery); mother of Oleita Virginia Mitchell, q.v.

Mitchell, Alitha, see Sarah Jane Warner, q.v.

Mitchell, Alonza Edward, 1879-1952 (Calvary Methodist Church Cemetery)

Mitchell, Amanda Louise (Raymond), 1881-1960 (Grove Presbyterian Church Cemetery)

Mitchell, Amos A., 1819-1901 (Wesleyan Chapel Methodist Church Cemetery)

Mitchell, Ann (Porter), 1808-1900 (Angel Hill Cemetery); native of Talbot Co., MD, resided in Havre de Grace (Death certificate)

Mitchell, Ann Eliza (Lovett), 1827-1899 (Angel Hill Cemetery); wife of John Mitchell, Jr., q.v.

Mitchell, Anna May, 1878-1916 (Grove Presbyterian Church Cemetery)

Mitchell, Annie (colored), born -- May 1855, native of Maryland, wife of William Mitchell (1900 Aberdeen Census)

Mitchell, Annie A., 1874-1946 (Mt. Zion Methodist Church Cemetery)

Mitchell, Annie E., 1822-1897 (Calvary Methodist Church Cemetery)

Mitchell, Annie E., 1880-1932 (Tabernacle Cemetery)

Mitchell, Annie Elvina, 1879-1957, native of Maryland, born 26 Jun 1879, daughter of John Thomas Mitchell and Eliza Bunce (Calvary Methodist Church Cemetery - married name Chesney; *The Aegis*, 21 Feb 1957)

Mitchell, Annie L., 1884-1928 (Rock Run Methodist Church Cemetery); native of Maryland, resided at Level, born 22 Dec 1884, daughter of William R. Mitchell and Hannah E. Sampson (Death certificate - married name Denham)

Mitchell, Annie Mary, 1876-1957 (Angel Hill Cemetery)

Mitchell, Annie V. (Evans), 1848-1921 (Angel Hill Cemetery); wife of Solomon T. Mitchell, q.v.

Mitchell, Arthur V., 1877-1962 (Grove Presbyterian Church Cemetery); native of Havre de Grace, born 11 Jul 1877, son of George V. Mitchell and Sarah Courtney (Pennington Funeral Home Records)

Mitchell, Aubrey (master), resided at Old Bay [near Havre de Grace] (*Harford Democrat*, 3 Jan 1890)

Mitchell, Aubrey Nelson, 1878-1964 (Grove Presbyterian Church Cemetery); premium award winner, Class O - Discretionary, Harford County Fair (*The Aegis & Intelligencer*, 24 Oct 1890)

Mitchell, Avarilla, 1810-1892 (Calvary Methodist Church Cemetery)

Mitchell, B. Silver, 1870-1950 (Grove Presbyterian Church Cemetery)

Mitchell, Bernard Morean, born 5 Jul 1884, son of C. P. and Mallie Mitchell (St. George's Episcopal Church Register of Baptisms, pp. 4-5); brother of Ethel Mitchell, q.v.

Mitchell, Bessie M., 1887-1979 (Angel Hill Cemetery)

Mitchell, Betsy (colored), see Rebecca E. Bond (colored), q.v.

Mitchell, Blanche, 1876-1968, native of Maryland, born 29 Nov 1876, daughter of Solomon T. Mitchell and Anna V. Jones (Pennington Funeral Home Records - married name Kinnier); student, Havre de Grace High School, 1890 (*Havre de Grace Republican*, 31 Oct 1890)

Mitchell, C. Emory, 1890-1968 (Churchville Presbyterian Church Cemetery)

Mitchell, C. P. (Mr.), see Bernard Morean Mitchell and Ethel Mitchell, q.v.

Mitchell, Caroline P., 1821-1910 (Calvary Methodist Church Cemetery)

Mitchell, Carrie (Cord), 1875-1913 (Grove Presbyterian Church Cemetery)

Mitchell, Carrie E., born 1876, died 19-- (Wesleyan Chapel Methodist Church Cemetery); wife of William E. Mitchell, q.v.

Mitchell, Carrie Gertrude, born 4 Aug 1871, daughter of Robert P. and Mary Cole (Hughes) Mitchell (*The Hughes Genealogy, 1636-1953*, by Joseph Lee Hughes, 1953, p. 107)

Mitchell, Charles H., new name on the voter registration list at Hopewell, Second District (*Havre de Grace Republican*, 17 Oct 1890)

Mitchell, Charles W., 1828-1900 (Fallston Methodist Church Cemetery)

Mitchell, Charles W., 1838-1891 (Angel Hill Cemetery); son of Parker Mitchell (*Havre de Grace Republican*, 9 Jan 1891)

Mitchell, Charles W., 1868-1961 (Angel Hill Cemetery); canner, Perryman (*Heavy Industries of Yesteryear; Harford County's Rural Heritage*, by Jack L. Shagena, Jr. and Henry C. Peden, Jr., 2015, p. 44)

Mitchell, D. E., member, Mt. Ararat Lodge No. 44, A. F. & A. M., Bel Air (*Havre de Grace Republican*, 11 Jul 1890)

Mitchell, Daniel Edward, 1840-1897 (Grove Presbyterian Church Cemetery); canner, Perryman (*Heavy Industries of Yesteryear; Harford County's Rural Heritage*, by Jack L. Shagena, Jr. and Henry C. Peden, Jr., 2015, p. 44)

Mitchell, David S., 1859-1924 (Mt. Zion Methodist Church Cemetery); blacksmith, Calvary, moved to Hagerstown, MD, 1890 (*The Aegis & Intelligencer*, 15 Aug 1890)

Mitchell, Dora E., age 21 in 1889, married Charles H. Chesney on 8 Jan 1890 (Marriage License Applications Book ALJ No. 2, 1890, and marriage certificate)

Mitchell, E. (capt.), sneak boat duck hunter (*Havre de Grace Republican*, 7 Nov 1890)

Mitchell, E. Madison, sink boat duck hunter (*Havre de Grace Republican*, 7 Nov 1890)

Mitchell, Edmund, 1817-1891 (St. George's Episcopal Church Cemetery); farmer and canner, near Short Lane Station of the P. W. & B. Railroad, Aberdeen (*Havre de Grace Republican*, 27 Nov 1891)

Mitchell, Edward. farmer on Middle Island, near Bush River Neck (*The Aegis & Intelligencer*, 1 Aug 1890)

Mitchell, Edward M., 1858-1935 (Angel Hill Cemetery)

Mitchell, Edwin Webster, 1862-1925 (*Ancestral Charts, Volume 2*, Harford County Genealogical Society, 1986, p. 76; Death certificate and obituary state Edward W., but family chart and Calvary Methodist Church Cemetery tombstone state Edwin W.)

Mitchell, Eleanora (colored), 1882-1957 (St. James United Cemetery)

Mitchell, Eliza A. (McGaw), 1844-1921 (Grove Presbyterian Church Cemetery); wife of Frederick O. Mitchell, q.v.

Mitchell, Eliza D., 1846-1933 (Calvary Methodist Church Cemetery)

Mitchell, Elizabeth, 1827-1899, resided at Aldino, native of Pennsylvania, widow of John Mitchell (Death certificate)

Mitchell, Elizabeth (Bechtold), 1882-1942 (Calvary Methodist Church Cemetery)

Mitchell, Elizabeth (Michael), 1885-1978, wife of Ryland Lee Mitchell, q.v.

Mitchell, Elizabeth (Rickey), 1844-1944 (Grove Presbyterian Church Cemetery)

Mitchell, Elizabeth F. (Mrs.), premium award winner, Class K - Household and Domestic Manufactures, Harford County Fair (*The Aegis & Intelligencer*, 24 Oct 1890); see Walter H. Mitchell, q.v.

Mitchell, Elsie Lillian "Lillie" (Hollis), 1874-1949 (Baker Cemetery); wife of Robert Henry Mitchell, q.v.

Mitchell, Elva M. (Cannon), 1856-1908 (Fallston Methodist Church Cemetery); first wife of Noble Lilly Mitchell, q.v.

Mitchell, Emily J., 1827-1916 (Wesleyan Chapel Methodist Church Cemetery); wife of Amos A. Mitchell, q.v.

Mitchell, Emma (colored), 1872-1913, native of Harford Co., born 8 Nov 1872, daughter of William Mitchell, native of Virginia, and Annie Brooks, native of Talbot Co., MD (Death certificate - married name Stansbury)

Mitchell, Emma C., 1842-1918 (Angel Hill Cemetery)

Mitchell, Emma W., 1845-1908 (Grove Presbyterian Church Cemetery); wife of George L. Mitchell, q.v.

Mitchell, Estelle Elizabeth, born 28 Dec 1884, daughter of Morgan and Hannah Mitchell (R. Morgan Mitchell Bible, *Maryland Bible Records, Volume 5*, by Henry C. Peden, Jr., 2004, pp. 122-123)

Mitchell, Estelle (Archer), 1861-1938, second wife of Noble Lilly Mitchell, q.v.

Mitchell, Ethel, born 20 Oct 1880, native of Maryland, daughter of C. P. Mitchell, of Maryland, and Malvaine Morean, of Delaware (St. George's Episcopal Church Register of Baptisms, pp. 2-3; Death certificate - married name Richardson); high school student, Second District, 1890 (*Havre de Grace Republican*, 31 Oct 1890)

Mitchell, Ethel (Kennedy), 1879-1968 (Grove Presbyterian Church Cemetery)

Mitchell, Eva G., born 1884, died ---- (Grove Presbyterian Church Cemetery)

Mitchell, Evan Lewis, 1845-1926 (Grove Presbyterian Church Cemetery); native of Maryland, farmer and canner, single, resided near Perryman and Aberdeen (Death certificate; *Heavy Industries of Yesteryear; Harford County's Rural Heritage*, by Jack L. Shagena, Jr. and Henry C. Peden, Jr., 2015, p. 44)

Mitchell, Evan Madison, 1846-1916 (*The Hughes Genealogy, 1636-1953*, by Joseph Lee Hughes, 1953, p. 111); see John Mitchell, Sr., q.v.

Mitchell, Ezekiel Thomas, 1836-1904 (Mt. Erin Cemetery); member, inquest jury, Havre de Grace (*Havre de Grace Republican*, 6 Jun 1890); see Agnes Mitchell, q.v.

Mitchell, F. P., farmer, Boothby Hill (*Havre de Grace Republican*, 4 Jul 1890); also see Silver Mitchell, q.v.

Mitchell, Flora, see Anna A. Streett, Catherine A. Streett, Ella V. Streett, Joseph McC. Streett and Anna A. Chester, q.v.

Mitchell, Florence (Miss), resident of Boothby Hill (*Harford Democrat*, 3 Jan 1890)

Mitchell, Florence O., 1868-1935 (Calvary Methodist Church Cemetery)

Mitchell, Francis, 1801-1894 (Calvary Methodist Church Cemetery); resident near Calvary (*The Aegis & Intelligencer*, 15 Aug 1890)

Mitchell, Frederick O'Neill, 1836-1900 (Grove Presbyterian Church Cemetery); owner of *Mulberry Point Farm* at the mouth of Spesutia Narrows (*The Aegis & Intelligencer*, 18 Apr 1890); stockholder, Aberdeen Can Factory (*Havre de Grace Republican*, 19 Dec 1890); trustee, Oakland School No. 7, Second District (*Havre de Grace Republican*, 30 May 1890); juror, Second District (*Havre de Grace Republican*, 31 Jan 1890); resided at Mulberry Point, Harford Co., "native of America" (Death certificate); canner, Perryman (*Heavy Industries of Yesteryear; Harford County's Rural Heritage*, by Jack L. Shagena, Jr. and Henry C. Peden, Jr., 2015, p. 44)

Mitchell, Frederick O'Neill, Jr., 1869-1919 (Grove Presbyterian Church Cemetery); born 1 Nov 1869, son of Frederick O. and Eliza Ann (McGaw) Mitchell (Frederick O'Neill Mitchell Bible, *Maryland Bible Records, Volume 5*, by Henry C. Peden, Jr., 2004, p. 12); jousting tournament rider, Knight of Shamrock, 1890 (*The Aegis & Intelligencer*, 29 Aug 1890)

Mitchell, George A. (colored), 1882-1969 (St. James United Cemetery)

Mitchell, George Alfred, 1857-1922 (St. George's Episcopal Church Cemetery); acquired land in February 1890

(*The Aegis & Intelligencer*, 7 Mar 1890)

Mitchell, George Hays, 1874-1944 (Grove Presbyterian Church Cemetery)

Mitchell, George Lewis, 1851-1922 (Grove Presbyterian Church Cemetery); canner, Perryman (*Heavy Industries of Yesteryear; Harford County's Rural Heritage*, by Jack L. Shagena, Jr. and Henry C. Peden, Jr., 2015, p. 44); see Lillian M. Mitchell and Rose Ella Mitchell, q.v.

Mitchell, George M., 1840-1909 (Grove Presbyterian Church Cemetery); see Mabel Hawkins, q.v.

Mitchell, George Nelson, 1889-1955 (Angel Hill Cemetery)

Mitchell, George S., 1872-1891 (Angel Hill Cemetery)

Mitchell, George V., 1835-1904 (Grove Presbyterian Church Cemetery); building contractor, Havre de Grace (*Havre de Grace Republican*, 14 Feb 1890); see Arthur V. Mitchell and Grace Mitchell, q.v.

Mitchell, George W., 1837-1913 (Angel Hill Cemetery), son of Solomon Mitchell; sink boat duck hunter (*Havre de Grace Republican*, 7 Nov 1890)

Mitchell, Georgia Anastatia, 1877-1905 (Mt. Erin Cemetery)

Mitchell, Grace, 1873-1938 (Grove Presbyterian Church Cemetery); native of Harford Co., born 12 Jul 1873, daughter of George V. Mitchell and Sarah Courtney (Death certificate - married name Botts)

Mitchell, Griffin W., 1869-1924 (Rock Run Methodist Church Cemetery); native of Maryland, born 4 Sep 1869, son of William Mitchell and Sarah A. Ewing (Bailey Funeral Home Records)

Mitchell, Hannah (Bodensick), 1811-1898 (Calvary Methodist Church Cemetery); mother of Noble Lilly Mitchell, q.v.

Mitchell, Hannah E. (Sampson), 1865-1946 (Bailey Funeral Home Records)

Mitchell, Hannah Silver (Morgan), 1856-1921 (Grove Presbyterian Church Cemetery); wife of Morgan Mitchell, q.v.

Mitchell, Harry, farmer, of Boothby Hill (*Havre de Grace Republican*, 10 Jan 1890)

Mitchell, Harry A., 1880-1958 (Calvary Methodist Church Cemetery)

Mitchell, Harry Edmund, 1851-1891 (St. George's Episcopal Church Cemetery); member, Order of the Golden Chain, at Aberdeen (*Havre de Grace Republican*, 14 Mar 1890); husband of Rosina Mitchell, q.v.

Mitchell, Helen (Miss), resided at Boothby Hill (*Harford Democrat*, 3 Jan 1890)

Mitchell, Henrietta Hughes, born 3 Jan 1879, daughter of Evan Madison and Virginia Elizabeth (Hughes) Mitchell (*The Hughes Genealogy, 1636-1953*, by Joseph Lee Hughes, 1953, p. 111)

Mitchell, Henry F., 1849-1920 (Fallston Methodst Church Cemetery)

Mitchell, Henry Lovette, 1872-1933 (Angel Hill Cemetery); native of Harford Co., born 2 Oct 1872, son of John Mitchell and Annelisa Lovette, both of Harford Co. (Death certificate)

Mitchell, Henry T., 1828-1894 (Angel Hill Cemetery)

Mitchell, Herbert H., 1884-1964 (Baker Cemetery)

Mitchell, Horace A., 1863-1926 (Angel Hill Cemetery)

Mitchell, Horace Beal, 21 Jun 1889 - 2 Feb 1890 (St. George's Episcopal Church Cemetery)

Mitchell, Howard Holmes, 1879-1933 (Grove Presbyterian Church Cemetery)

Mitchell, Howard K., 1851-1945 (Fallston Methodist Church Cemetery)

Mitchell, Ida W., born 1867, died ---- (Wesleyan Chapel Methodist Church Cemetery); wife of John T. Mitchell, q.v.

Mitchell, Ida B. (Whitson), 1860-1918 (Fallston Methodist Church Cemetery)

Mitchell, J. Alfred, member, Guy Social Club, Aberdeen (*Havre de Grace Republican*, 31 Oct 1890)

Mitchell, J. Franklin, 1885-1962 (Angel Hill Cemetery)

Mitchell, J. L., executive committee, Bel Air Academy Association (*Havre de Grace Republican*, 11 Jul 1890)

Mitchell, Jacob F., 1839-1906 (Fallston Methodist Church Cemetery)

Mitchell, James Farnandis, auctioneer and storekeeper, Calvary (*The Aegis & Intelligencer*, 24 Jan 1890 and 15 Aug 1890); executive committee, Bel Air Academy Association (*Havre de Grace Republican*, 11 Jul 1890); competitive bicycle rider, Harford County Fair (*Havre de Grace Republican*, 26 Sep 1890); member, Calvary Road League (*The Aegis & Intelligencer*, 17 Jan 1890)

Mitchell, James H., 1842-1923 (Grove Presbyterian Church Cemetery)

Mitchell, James R. (colored), 1874-1946 (Death certificate; St. James United Cemetery)

Mitchell, James Streett, see Lamar Mitchell, q.v.

Mitchell, Jane "Jennie," born 8 Apr 1877, daughter of Frederick O'Neill and Eliza Ann (McGaw) Mitchell (Frederick O'Neill Mitchell Bible, *Maryland Bible Records, Volume 5*, by Henry C. Peden, Jr., 2004, p. 12; *The Hughes Genealogy, 1636-1953*, by Joseph Lee Hughes, 1953, p. 116)

Mitchell, John, see Elizabeth Mitchell and Henry Lovette Mitchell, q.v.

Mitchell, John, Civil War veteran, Hopewell (*1890 Special Census of the Civil War Veterans of the State of Maryland*, by L. Tilden Moore, Volume III, p. 69)

Mitchell, John, Jr., 1824-1896 (Angel Hill Cemetery); served on a petit jury in 1890 (*The Aegis & Intelligencer*, 14 Nov 1890); see John Mitchell, Sr., q.v.

Mitchell, John, Sr., 1799-1891 (Grove Presbyterian Church Cemetery; *Havre de Grace Republican*, 9 Jan 1891); enumerated as age 91 in the 1890 census, Hopewell Precinct, near Havre de Grace (*Havre de Grace Republican*, 22 Aug 1890, listed a handful of names from the actual 1890 census and he was one of them); died testate and his named heirs were daughters Ann Martha Michael (wife of J. Calvin Michael), Sarah H. Mitchell (wife of John Archer Mitchell), Mary E. Mitchell (single), and Jerusia Gertrude Osborne (wife of Charles B. Osborne), and sons John Mitchell, Jr., Robert P. Mitchell and E. Madison Mitchell (Harford County Will Book JMM 11:162-163)

Mitchell, John A., 1847-1914 (St. George's Episcopal Church Cemetery)

Mitchell, John Archer, 1839-1931 (Grove Presbyterian Church Cemetery); see John Mitchell, Sr., q.v.

Mitchell, John Henry, 1835-1915 (Rock Run Methodist Church Cemetery); juror, Second District (*Havre de Grace Republican*, 2 May 1890)

Mitchell, John Otho, born 21 Dec 1873, son of Robert P. Mitchell and Mary Cole Hughes (*The Hughes Genealogy, 1636-1953*, by Joseph Lee Hughes, 1953, p. 107)

Mitchell, John P., of Aberdeen, agent for Western Washer (*The Aegis & Intelligencer*, 30 May 1890); member, Guy Social Club, Aberdeen (*Havre de Grace Republican*, 31 Oct 1890); also see William Osborn Mitchell, q.v.

Mitchell, John Parker, 1834-1910, canner, Perryman (*Heavy Industries of Yesteryear; Harford County's Rural Heritage*, by Jack L. Shagena, Jr. and Henry C. Peden, Jr., 2015, p. 44)

Mitchell, John Sappington, 1848-1907 (Grove Presbyterian Church Cemetery); canner, Perryman (*Heavy Industries of Yesteryear; Harford County's Rural Heritage*, by Jack L. Shagena, Jr. and Henry C. Peden, Jr., 2015, p. 44)

Mitchell, John T., 1863-1932 (Wesleyan Chapel Methodist Church Cemetery)

Mitchell, John Thomas, 1841-1912 (Calvary Methodist Church Cemetery); see Annie Elvina Mitchell, q.v.

Mitchell, John William, 1868-1944 (Angel Hill Cemetery)

Mitchell, Joseph, resided near Harford Furnace (*The Aegis & Intelligencer*, 9 May 1890); trustee, School No. 11, Third District (*The Aegis & Intelligencer*, 4 Jul 1890)

Mitchell, Joseph B., storekeeper at Calvary (*The Aegis & Intelligencer*, 16 May 1890)

Mitchell, Joseph F., 1822-1902 (Grove Presbyterian Church Cemetery)

Mitchell, Joseph Frederick, 1851-1923 (Calvary Methodist Church Cemetery); see Mitchell's General Store, q.v.

Mitchell, Joseph G., and wife, sold land in August 1890 (*The Aegis & Intelligencer*, 12 Sep 1890)

Mitchell, Julian Fairfax, 1888-1960 (Grove Presbyterian Church Cemetery); born 3 Mar 1887 *(sic)*, daughter of Morgan and Hannah Mitchell (R. Morgan Mitchell Bible, *Maryland Bible Records, Volume 5*, by Henry C. Peden, Jr., 2004, pp. 122-123)

Mitchell, L. G., private, Jackson Guards [Co. D, 1st Regiment, Maryland National Guard], 1889-1890 (*The Aegis & Intelligencer*, 11 Jan 1889)

Mitchell, Lamar, born 21 Jul 1889, daughter of James Streett and Mary Elizabeth Mitchell (St. George's Episcopal Church Register of Baptisms, p. 9)

Mitchell, Lewis, farmer, of Boothby Hill (*Havre de Grace Republican*, 10 Jan 1890); name removed from the voter registration list in Sixth District, 1890 (*Havre de Grace Republican*, 17 Oct 1890)

Mitchell, Lidia, age 22 in 1889 (Marriage License Applications Book ALJ No. 2, 1889)

Mitchell, Lillian M., 1886-1926 (Grove Presbyterian Church Cemetery - married name Bonnett); native of Maryland, resided in Aberdeen, daughter of George L.Mitchell and Emma Bowman (Death certificate)

Mitchell, Lillie N. (Courtney), 1883-1954 (Grove Presbyterian Church Cemetery)

Mitchell, Lizzie (Mrs.), resident of Level (*The Aegis & Intelligencer*, 15 Aug 1890)

Mitchell, Lydia A., 1842-1919 (Grove Presbyterian Church Cemetery)

Mitchell, Lydia (Singleton), wife of James Mitchell; see Martha J. Mitchell, q.v.

Mitchell, Mabel, born 2 Dec 1886, daughter of Oakley P. Mitchell and Mary Carroll (*The Hughes Genealogy, 1636-1953*, by Joseph Lee Hughes, 1953, p. 118)

Mitchell, Mahala, 1804-1890 (Grove Presbyterian Church Cemetery)

Mitchell, Malcolm (master), resided in Aberdeen (*Harford Democrat*, 3 Jan 1890)

Mitchell, Mallie, see Bernard Morean Mitchell and Ethel Mitchell, q.v.

Mitchell, Margaret J., 1881-1950 (Angel Hill Cemetery)

Mitchell, Martha J., 1883-1928 (Rock Run Methodist Church Cemetery - married name Zellman); native of Maryland, born 15 Aug 1883, resided at Level, daughter of James Mitchell and Lydia Singleton (Death certificate)

Mitchell, Martha Jane (Streett), 1823-1890 (St. George's Episcopal Church Cemetery); wife of Edmund Mitchell, of near Perryman (*The Aegis & Intelligencer*, 11 Jul 1890)

Mitchell, Martha Sophia (Webster), 1848-1932 (Calvary Methodist Church Cemetery)

Mitchell, Mary (Miss), member, St. Patrick's Women's Total Abstinence Society, Havre de Grace (*Havre de Grace Republican*, 31 Jan 1890)

Mitchell, Mary (Anthony), 1874-1927 (Calvary Methodist Church Cemetery)

Mitchell, Mary A., 1867-1939, daughter of Amos A. and Emily J. Mitchell (Wesleyan Chapel Methodist Church Cemetery)

Mitchell, Mary Amanda (Walker), 1863-1947 (Angel Hill Cemetery); wife of Robert Otho Mitchell, q.v.

Mitchell, Mary B., 1872-1961 (Grove Presbyterian Church Cemetery)

Mitchell, Mary Cole (Hughes), 1845-1901, native of Maryland, resided near Havre de Grace (Death certificate; Grove Presbyterian Church Cemetery); wife of Robert Parker Mitchell, q.v.

Mitchell, Mary E., see John Mitchell, Sr., q.v.

Mitchell, Mary Eliza, 1849-1913 (Grove Presbyterian Church Cemetery)

Mitchell, Mary Elizabeth "Mollie" (Nelson), 1856-1938 (Grove Presbyterian Church Cemetery),; wife of Robert Amos Mitchell, q.v.

Mitchell, Mary Elizabeth, see Lamar Mitchell, q.v.

Mitchell, Mary Emma (Bowman), 1858-1940 (Grove Presbyterian Church Cemetery); wife of George Lewis Mitchell, q.v.

Mitchell, Mary F., 1833-1910 (Angel Hill Cemetery); businesswoman (trader's license), Havre de Grace (*Havre de Grace Republican*, 30 May 1890)

Mitchell, Mary Florence, 1876-1952 (Grove Presbyterian Church Cemetery)

Mitchell, Mary Jane, born 29 Nov 1890, daughter of Edwin Webster Mitchell and Florence Oleita Swartz (*Ancestral Charts, Volume 2*, Harford County Genealogical Society, 1986, p. 76)

Mitchell, Mary Jane (colored), age 28 in 1889 (Marriage License Applications Book ALJ No. 2, 1889)

Mitchell, Mary M. (Miss), vice president, Helping Hand Society of Avondale Christian Church (*Havre de Grace Republican*, 7 Feb 1890)

Mitchell, Matilda (Reybold), 1850-1904 (St. George's Episcopal Church Cemetery)

Mitchell, Maude R., 1877-1949 (Grove Presbyterian Church Cemetery)

Mitchell, May (Miss), organist and member, Grove Presbyterian Church, Aberdeen (*The Aegis & Intelligencer*, 10 Jan 1890)

Mitchell, McHenry, 1879-1959 (St. Mary's Episcopal Church Cemetery)

Mitchell, Minnie (Gallup), 1876-1958 (St. George's Episcopal Church Cemetery)

Mitchell, Morgan, 1855-1927 (Grove Presbyterian Church Cemetery); sneak boat duck hunter (*Havre de Grace Republican*, 7 Nov 1890); canner, Perryman (*Heavy Industries of Yesteryear; Harford County's Rural Heritage*, by Jack L. Shagena, Jr. and Henry C. Peden, Jr., 2015, p. 44); name shown as R. Morgan Mitchell in his family Bible (*Maryland Bible Records, Volume 5*, by Henry C. Peden, Jr., 2004, p. 122)

Mitchell, Murray A., 1889-1953 (Smith Chapel Methodist Church Cemetery)

Mitchell, Nellie, daughter of Cornelius and Mollie Mitchell, baptized 7 Sep 1787 (St. George's Episcopal Church Register of Baptisms, p. 6, did not record the date of birth)

Mitchell, Noble Lilly, 1854-1932 (Fallston Methodist Church Cemetery); attorney-at-law, member of the House of Delegates, and an organizer of the Harford Historical Society in 1885 (*Biographical Dictionary of Harford County, Maryland, 1774-1974*, by Henry C. Peden, Jr. and William O. Carr, 2021, p. 189); secretary, Harford County Agricultural and Mechanical Society (*Havre de Grace Republican*, 31 Jan 1890); treasurer, Harford Hedge and Wire Fence Company of Harford County (*Havre de Grace Republican*, 7 Feb 1890)

Mitchell, Oaker (colored), born -- Apr 1885, native of Maryland, son of William and Annie Mitchell (1900 Aberdeen Census)

Mitchell, Oakley Perdy, 1859-1922 (St. George's Episcopal Church Cemetery); farmer, near Aberdeen (*Havre de Grace Republican*, 17 Jan 1890); sold land in February 1890 (*The Aegis & Intelligencer*, 7 Mar 1890); son-in-law of Mary K. Carroll, q.v.; also see Mabel Mitchell, q.v.

Mitchell, Oleita H., 1870-1951 (Angel Hill Cemetery)

Mitchell, Oleita Virginia, born 7 Jun 1877, daughter of Samuel Bryson Mitchell and Alice Virginia Mitchell (Churchville Presbyterian Church Register Roll of Infant Church Members or Baptized Children, No. 289)

Mitchell, Oliver A., Civil War veteran, Havre de Grace (*1890 Special Census of the Civil War Veterans of the State of Maryland*, by L. Tilden Moore, Volume III, p. 92)

Mitchell, Parker, see Charles W. Mitchell, q.v.

Mitchell, Parker, 1874-1958 (St. George's Episcopal Church Cemetery); born 17 Feb 1874, son of Frederick O. and Eliza Ann (McGaw) Mitchell (Frederick O'Neill Mitchell Bible, *Maryland Bible Records, Volume 5*, by Henry C. Peden, Jr., 2004, p. 12); jousting tournament rider, Knight of Mulberry Point (*Havre de Grace Republican*, 15 Aug 1890)

Mitchell, Pearl Sylvia, born 18 Mar 1882, daughter of George L. and Mary Emma (Bowman) Mitchell (*Barnes-Bailey Genealogy*, by Walter D. Barnes, 1939, p. I-64a)

Mitchell, Phebe Alice (Miss), 1856-1928 (Angel Hill Cemetery; Death certificate)

Mitchell, Rachel, 1810-1890 (Angel Hill Cemetery)

Mitchell, Ralph Morgan, 1882-1930 (Grove Presbyterian Church Cemetery); born 7 Oct 1882, son of Morgan and Hannah Mitchell, all natives of Maryland (Death certificate; R. Morgan Mitchell Bible, *Maryland Bible Records, Volume 5*, by Henry C. Peden, Jr., 2004, pp. 122-123)

Mitchell, Richard H., see Walter H. Mitchell, q.v.

Mitchell, Richard Parker, born 1 Mar 1875, son of ---- Mitchell and Sarah Ewing (Bethel Presbyterian Church Cemetery Records)

Mitchell, Robert, 1804-1890 (Calvary Methodist Church Cemetery); resided at Calvary resident of Perryman (*The Aegis & Intelligencer*, 26 Dec 1890); treated by unidentified doctor in 1890 ("Medical Account Book – 1890," Historical Society of Harford County Archives Folder)

Mitchell, Robert Amos, 1847-1929 (Grove Presbyterian Church Cemetery); tax collector in Second and Sixth Districts (*Havre de Grace Republican*, 4 Jul 1890); charter member, Havre de Grace Gunning Club (*Havre de Grace Republican*, 14 Nov 1890); sneak boat duck hunter (*Havre de Grace Republican*, 7 Nov 1890); tenant farmer on *Old Bay Farm* near Havre de Grace (*Havre de Grace Republican*, 4 Jul 1890); Mrs. R. A. Mitchell was a tent holder, Carsins Run Camp Meeting, East Harford Circuit, P. E. Church (*The Aegis & Intelligencer*, 1 Aug 1890)

Mitchell, Robert Henry, 1869-1942 (Baker Cemetery); born 29 Mar 1869, son of Robert P. Mitchell and Mary Cole Hughes (*The Hughes Genealogy, 1636-1953*, by Joseph Lee Hughes, 1953, p. 107)

Mitchell, Robert Lewis, 1847-1931 (Calvary Methodist Church Cemetery); son of Robert Mitchell, q.v.

Mitchell, Robert Otho, 1858-1931 (Angel Hill Cemetery); hauling contractor, Havre de Grace (*Havre de Grace Republican*, 20 Jun 1890)

Mitchell, Robert Parker, 1836-1904 (Grove Presbyterian Church Cemetery); farmer on the Robert Smith farm in Bush River Neck (*The Aegis & Intelligencer*, 1 Aug 1890); see Mary Cole Mitchel, John Otho Mitchell and John Mitchell, Sr., q.v.

Mitchell, Rose Ella, born 30 Mar 1884, daughter of George L. Mitchell and Mary Emma Bowman (*Barnes-Bailey Genealogy*, by Walter D. Barnes, 1939, p. I-64a)

Mitchell, Rosina (Badger), 1850-1911 (St. George's Episcopal Church Cemetery, and Register of Baptisms, p. 6, 1886)

Mitchell, Ryland Lee, 1884-1971 (Grove Presbyterian Church Cemetery)

Mitchell, S. A., 1858-1916 (Wesleyan Chapel Methodist Church Cemetery)

Mitchell, S. Houston, 1847-1923 (Fallston Methodist Church Cemetery)

Mitchell, Samuel Bryson, 1851-1934 (Calvary Methodist Church Cemetery); Samuel Mitchell and family, residents at Calvary (*The Aegis & Intelligencer*, 29 Aug 1890); son of Robert Mitchell, q.v., and father of Oleita Virginia Mitchell, q.v.

Mitchell, Sarah A., 1815-1895 (Calvary Methodist Church Cemetery); county out-pensioner [welfare recipient], Third District (*Havre de Grace Republican*, 4 Jul 1890)

Mitchell, Sarah H., 1844-1914 (Grove Presbyterian Church Cemetery); see John Mitchell, Sr., q.v.

Mitchell, Sarah J., 1870-1938, daughter of Amos A. and Emily J. Mitchell (Wesleyan Chapel Methodist Church Cemetery)

Mitchell, Sarah J. (Cantler), 1860-1930 (Rock Run Methodist Church Cemetery)

Mitchell, Sarah M., 1838-1944 (Grove Presbyterian Church Cemetery)

Mitchell, Sarah S., 1849-1904 (Grove Presbyterian Church Cemetery)

Mitchell, Shirley A., 1884-1940 (Grove Presbyterian Church Cemetery); native of Maryland, born -- Apr 1884, son of John A. and Sarah H. Mitchell (1900 Aberdeen Census)

Mitchell, Silver, son of Mr. & Mrs. F. P. Mitchell, of Boothby Hill (*The Aegis & Intelligencer*, 4 Jul 1890); farmer, Boothby Hill (*Havre de Grace Republican*, 4 Jul 1890); member, Guy Social Club, Aberdeen (*Havre de Grace Republican*, 31 Oct 1890)

Mitchell, Solomon, see George W. Mitchell, q.v.

Mitchell, Solomon T., 1843-1921 (Angel Hill Cemetery); city councilman, Havre de Grace (*The Aegis & Intelligencer*, 10 Jan 1890); director, The Seneca Hosiery Company of Havre de Grace (*Havre de Grace Republican*, 21 Mar 1890); vice president, Republican Club (*Havre de Grace Republican*, 7 Nov 1890); worshipful master, Susquehanna Lodge No. 130, A. F. & A. M. (*Havre de Grace Republican*, 26 Dec 1890); see Blanche Mitchell, q.v.

Mitchell, Susanna R., see J. Edmund Michael, q.v.

Mitchell, Thomas (master), resided at Boothby Hill (*Harford Democrat*, 3 Jan 1890)

Mitchell, Thomas J., Civil War veteran, Havre de Grace (*1890 Special Census of the Civil War Veterans of the State of Maryland*, by L. Tilden Moore, Volume III, p. 90)

Mitchell, Thomas P., 1840-1926 (Grove Presbyterian Church Cemetery); farmer, near Boothby Hill (*The Aegis & Intelligencer*, 2 May 1890); trustee, Boothby Hill School No. 4, Second District (*Havre de Grace Republican*, 30 May 1890)

Mitchell, Tillie R., see William Osborn Mitchell, q.v.

Mitchell, Virginia Elizabeth (Hughes), 1844-1890, wife of Evan Madison Mitchell, q.v.

Mitchell, Virginia S., see Virginia S. Osborn, Virginia M. Osborn and Walter C. Osborn, q.v.

Mitchell, Walter F., 1869-1944 (Angel Hill Cemetery); new name on the voter registration list in Sixth District, 1890 (*Havre de Grace Republican*, 17 Oct 1890)

Mitchell, Walter Hanson, 1865-1890, son of Richard H. and Elizabeth F. Mitchell, of Baltimore, died at the home of his uncle James Farnandis at *The Homestead* farm near Bel Air (*The Aegis & Intelligencer*, 27 Jun 1890; *Harford Democrat*, 27 Jun 1890)

Mitchell, William, see Griffin W. Mitchell, q.v.

Mitchell, William (colored), native of Virginia; see Emma Mitchell, q.v.

Mitchell, William (colored), 1858-1922, native of Maryland, parents unknown (Death certificate); see Annie Mitchell (colored), q.v.

Mitchell, William E., 1866-1943 (Wesleyan Chapel Methodist Church Cemetery)

Mitchell, William Grant, 1869-1940 (Angel Hill Cemetery)

Mitchell, William H., age 26 in 1889 (Marriage License Applications Book ALJ No. 2, 1889)

Mitchell, William Osborn, born 2 Aug 1881, son of John P. and Tillie R. Mitchell (St. George's Episcopal Church Register of Baptisms, pp. 2-3)

Mitchell, William R., 1860-1924 (Bailey Funeral Home Records); see Naomi C. Walstrum, q.v.

Mite Society, Level M. P. Church (*The Aegis & Intelligencer*, 7 Nov 1890)

Mite Society, Havre de Grace M. E. Church (*Havre de Grace: Its Historic Past, Its Charming Present and Its Promising Future: Harford County's Rural Heritage.* by Jack L. Shagena, Jr. and Henry C. Peden, Jr., 2018, p. 269)

Mitzel, Eva J. (Watson), 1878-1953 (Slate Ridge Cemetery, York Co., PA); native of Harford Co., born 18 Nov 1878, daughter of John Watson and Mary E. Connolly (Harkins Funeral Home Records)

Mobus, Frederick, see Frederick Morbus, q.v.

Moffet, Harriet A., widow of John T. Moffet, Civil War veteran, Aberdeen (*1890 Special Census of the Civil War Veterans of the State of Maryland*, by L. Tilden Moore, Volume III, p. 68)

Moffet, James A., Civil War veteran, Aberdeen (*1890 Special Census of the Civil War Veterans of the State of Maryland*, by L. Tilden Moore, Volume III, p. 68)

Moffet, John T., see Harriet A. Moffet, q.v.

Moffitt, Edward E., 1876-1948 (Bethel Presbyterian Church Cemetery Records)

Moitz, Adelina E. "Addie" 1866-1928 (Angel Hill Cemetery); native of Pennsylvania, resided in Havre de

Grace, married, later divorced (Death certificate)

Moitz, Charles Henry, 1868-1926 (Angel Hill Cemetery); native of Maryland, single, storekeeper at Havre de Grace, son of Gabriel and Bertha Moitz, of Prussia (Death certificate); businessman (trader's license), Havre de Grace (*Havre de Grace Republican*, 30 May 1890)

Monaghan, Rose, wife of Elisha Johnson, q.v.; also see Charles E. Johnson, q.v.

Monahan, Felix, resident of Bel Air (*The Aegis & Intelligencer*, 8 Aug 1890)

Monk, Abraham, 1857-1940 (Mountain Christian Church Cemetery)

Monk, Alfred (colored), 1874-1943, son of Lewis Henry Monk and Catherine Rice (Death certificate); brother of Thaddeus Monk, q.v.

Monk, Angiline (colored), 1879-1942, native of Perryman, Harford Co., born 24 Apr 1879, daughter of Philip G. Monk and Susan Christy, natives of Perryman (Death certificate - married name Collins)

Monk, Bazella, 1869-1926 (Deer Creek Methodist Church Cemetery)

Monk, Caroline (colored), see Mary Elizabeth Monk (colored), q.v.

Monk, Caroline K. (colored), 1890-1948, native of Maryland, born 15 Dec 1890, daughter of Jacob Monk and Elsie Williams (Death certificate - married name Bowser)

Monk, Charlotte (colored), see James Henry Warfield (colored), q.v.

Monk, Hampton (colored), see Mary Martha Monk (colored), q.v.

Monk, Harriet R. (Mrs.) (colored), 1866-1936, native of Aberdeen, Harford Co., parents unknown; wife of Philip Monk (Death certificate)

Monk, Jacob (colored), see Caroline K. Monk (colored), q.v.

Monk, Jacob H. (colored), age 21 in 1890 (Marriage License Applications Book ALJ No. 2, 1891)

Monk, James Henry (colored), 1848-1917 (Death certificate; Union Methodist Church Cemetery, Aberdeen)

Monk, John (colored), see Smaley C. Monk (colored), q.v.

Monk, John Andrew Dolphin (colored), see Sidney (Washington) Monk , q.v.

Monk, John D., 1868-1938 (Death certificate; Union Methodist Church Cemetery, Aberdeen)

Monk, John Thurmond, 1890-1964 (Mountain Christian Church Cemetery)

Monk, Josephine H. ("Josie"), 1886-1961 (Mountain Christian Church Cemetery); widoe of Lafayette A. Monk, q.v.

Monk, Lafayette A., 1882-1953 (Mountain Christian Church Cemetery)

Monk, Lewis Henry (colored), see Alfred Monk (colored) and Thaddeus Monk (colored), q.v.

Monk, Mary Elizabeth (colored), born 18 May 1882, daughter of Caroline Monk and H. Miller (St. George's Episcopal Church Register of Baptisms, pp. 2-3)

Monk, Mary Ethel, 1890-1955 (Mountain Christian Church Cemetery)

Monk, Mary Martha (colored), 1878-1938, native of Harford Co., born 1 Jan 1878, daughter of Hampton Monk and Lotta Ringgold (Death certificate - married name Stevens)

Monk, Peter G. (colored), 1856-1923, native of Harford Co., resided at Perryman (Union Methodist Church Cemetery, Aberdeen)

Monk, Philip (colored), husband of Harriet R. Monk (colored), q.v.

Monk, Philip G. (colored), see Angiline Monk (colored), q.v.

Monk, Robert (colored), see William S. Monk (colored), q.v.

Monk, Sidney (Washington) (colored), 1836-1901, "native of America," resident of Perryman, wife of John Andrew Dolphin Monk (Death certificate)

Monk, Smaley C. (colored), c1879-1917, native of Harford Co., daughter of John Monk and ---- (Death certificate)

Monk, Susie (colored), 1887-1918 (Union Methodist Church Cemetery, Aberdeen)

Monk, Thaddeus "Thad" (colored), 1873-1932, native of Perryman, Harford Co., born 18 Jul 1873, son of Lewis Henry Monk and Catherine Rice (Death certificate mistakenly spelled his name Thasseus); husband of Susie Monk and brother of Alfred Monk, q.v.

Monk, William S. (colored), 1882-1945, native of Maryland, born 16 Aug 1882, son of Robert Monk, of Maryland, and Elsie Williams, of Florida (Death certificate)

Monk, Zachariah T., 1863-1945 (Mountain Christian Church Cemetery); noted as Taylor C. Monk aka Zachariah T. Monk, born in Virginia (Pennington Funeral Home Book, p. 85)

Monks' General Store, Kalmia Road, Edward T. Monks, prop. (*Country Stores: Harford County's Rural Heritage*, by Henry C. Peden, Jr. and Jack L. Shagena, Jr., 2015, pp. 178-179; *Harford Democrat*, 10 Jan 1890)

Monks, Adaline, see Mary Margaret Morrison, q.v.

Monks, Amy Drucilla, 1868-1898, daughter of Edward T. and Ellen C. Monks, married William D. Jones (Edward T. Monks Bible, *Maryland Bible Records, Volume 1*, by Henry C. Peden, Jr., 2003, pp. 171-172)

Monks, Annie (Middendorf), 1867-1908 (Mt. Tabor Methodist Church Cemetery)

Monks, Edward Treadway, 1831-1924 (Mt. Tabor Methodist Church Cemetery; Edward T. Monks Bible, *Maryland Bible Records, Volume 1*, by Henry C. Peden, Jr., 2003, pp. 171-172); trustee, Mechanicsville School No. 8, Third District, 1890 (*Havre de Grace Republican*, 30 May 1890); see Monks' General Store, q.v.

Monks, Elizabeth H., 1871-1931 (Christ Episcopal Church Cemetery)

Monks, Elizabeth Virene, 1879-1909 (Mt. Tabor Methodist Church Cemetery)

Monks, George W., 1863-1890 (Mt. Tabor Methodist Church Cemetery); resident near Sandy Hook and wife of William Monks, of Mechanicsville, died 3 Aug 1890 (*The Aegis & Intelligencer*, 8 Aug 1890); age 26 in 1889 (Marriage License Applications Book ALJ No. 2, 1889)

Monks, Harry Scott, 1873-1951 (Christ Episcopal Church Cemetery); resident of Forest Hill (*The Aegis & Intelligencer*, 20 Jun 1890)

Monks, J. Lewis, 1867-1949 (Fallston Methodist Church Cemetery)

Monks, James H., see Carvil Treadway, q.v.

Monks, James Henry, 1836-1895 (Mt. Tabor Methodist Church Cemetery)

Monks, James P., 1869-1935 and (Mt. Tabor Methodist Church Cemetery)

Monks, John L., age 23 in 1890 (Marriage License Applications Book ALJ No. 2, 1890)

Monks, Laura B., see Sarah Jane Jourdan, q.v.

Monks, Lillie Ella, 1876-1900, native of Maryland, resided at High Point, daughter of James Monks and Gertrude ---- (Mt. Tabor Methodist Church Cemetery; Death certificate - married name shown as Lilly Whittaker)

Monks, Luella, student, Third District (*The Aegis & Intelligencer*, 24 Oct 1890)

Monks, Mary A., 1876-1940 (Mt. Tabor Methodist Church Cemetery); see Carvil Treadway, q.v.

Monks, Mary E., 1865-1938 (Mt. Tabor Methodist Church Cemetery)

Monks, Mary K., age 26 in 1890 (Marriage License Applications Book ALJ No. 2, 1890), married Harry D. Bannister on 2 Dec 1890 (marriage certificate)

Monks, Mattie H., 1869-1940 (Fallston Methodist Church Cemetery)

Monks, Olie (Harkins), 1885-1962 (Centre Methodist Church Cemetery)

Monks, Sallie Ann, 1871-1942, daughter of Edward T. and Ellen C. Monks, married Harry E. Harkins on 8 Oct 1890 (Edward T. Monks Bible, *Maryland Bible Records, Volume 1*, by Henry C. Peden, Jr., 2003, pp. 171-172; Marriage License Applications Book ALJ No. 2, 1890, and marriage certificate); organist, Mt. Tabor M. P. Church (*The Aegis & Intelligencer*, 4 Jul 1890)

Monks, Thomas A., 1862-1929 (Christ Episcopal Church Cemetery)

Monks, Virginia (Mrs.), married Jesse A. Carr on 4 Dec 1890 at Dublin M. E Parsonage (*The Aegis & Intelligencer*, 5 Dec 1890); widow, age 31 in 1890 (Marriage License Applications Book ALJ No. 2, 1890)

Monks, William, born -- Dec 1864, baptized 11 Oct 1885, son of John C. and Elizabeth (Stonebraker) Monks (St. Ignatius Catholic Church Baptism Register, p. 84, states he was an ex-Methodist)

Monks, William T., 1837-1916 (Mt. Tabor Methodist Church Cemetery); resident near Hickory (*The Aegis & Intelligencer*, 9 May 1890); trustee, Mechanicsville School No. 8, Third District (*Havre de Grace Republican*, 30 May 1890; *The Aegis & Intelligencer*, 8 Aug 1890); also see George W. Monks, q.v.

Monmouth Mills, see McHenry's Mill, q.v.

Monroe, Lillie J. (Harkins), 1868-1951 (Centre Methodist Church Cemetery); native of Forest Hill, Harford Co., born 18 Oct 1868, daughter of John T. Harkins and Sultana Grier (Harkins Funeral Home Records)

Monsees, Otto, shoemaker, Darlington (*The Aegis & Intelligencer*, 26 Sep 1890)

Montgomery, James, c1852-1922, native of Ireland (Cokesbury Memorial Methodist Church Cemetery)

Montgomery, Mamie J., 1872-1953 (Bethel Presbyterian Church Cemetery, married name Forder); teacher, Madonna School No. 9, Fourth District (*The Aegis & Intelligencer*, 29 Aug 1890)

Montgomery, Mary A. (Tammany), 1833-1929, native of Maryland (Death certificate)

Montgomery, Mary A., 1835-1908 (St. Mary's Catholic Church Cemetery)

Montgomery, Sarah E. (colored) teacher, Muttonsburg School, Dublin District (*The Aegis & Intelligencer*, 28 Feb 1890)

Montgomery, William T., age 22 in 1889 (Marriage License Applications Book ALJ No. 2, 1889)

Moobray, William Henry, 1879-1940 (Holy Trinity Episcopal Church Cemetery)

Moobrey, Susanna (Singleton), 1833-1926 (Deer Creek Harmony Presbyterian Church Cemetery); native of Maryland, resided at Level (Death certificate)

Moody, Emma (Oliver), 1886-1962 (St. Mary's Episcopal Church Cemetery)

Mooney, Richard, see Harriet Cager, q.v.

Moore's General Store, Woodville, Samue T. Moore, prop. (*Country Stores: Harford County's Rural Heritage*, by Henry C. Peden, Jr. and Jack L. Shagena, Jr., 2015, p. 180)

Moore, Ada J., 1889-1984 (St. George's Episcopal Church Cemetery)

Moore, Annie (colored), c1876-1931, native of Maryland, daughter of Joseph and Eliza Moore (Death certificate - married name Aikens)

Moore, Annie G., 1861-1946 (Grove Presbyterian Church Cemetery)

Moore, Annie H., see James Russell Riley, q.v.

Moore, Annie M. (Miss), member, Havre de Grace Reading Circle (*Havre de Grace Republican*, 7 Feb 1890)

Moore, Archer Hanson, 1868-1933 (Baker Cemetery); resident at Calvary (*The Aegis & Intelligencer*, 29 Aug 1890)

Moore, Belle, student, Bel Air Graded School (*The Aegis & Intelligencer*, 11 Apr 1890)

Moore, Benjamin, student, Third District (*The Aegis & Intelligencer*, 24 Oct 1890)

Moore, Benjamin N. (colored), c1839-1914, native of Baltimore Co., resided near Fallston (Death certificate); 23rd U.S.C.I., Civil War veteran, Fallston (*1890 Special Census of the Civil War Veterans of the State of Maryland*, by L. Tilden Moore, Volume III, p. 75; *The Aegis*, 6 Nov 1914)

Moore, Bertha G. (colored), 1884-1975, native of Bel Air, born 17 Sep 1884, daughter of Marcus Moore and Isabelle ---- [Cox] (Tabernacle Mt. Zion Methodist Church Cemetery - married name Gray; *The Aegis*, 18 Aug 1975)

Moore, Bessie May (Little), 1878-1928 (Death certificate; Union Chapel Cemetery)

Moore, Buchanan, age 27 in 1890 (Marriage License Applications Book ALJ No. 2, 1890)

Moore, Caleb J., 1843-1922 (Little Falls Quaker Cemetery); director, Bel Air Turnpike Company (*The Aegis & Intelligencer*, 17 Jan 1890); of Fallston, married Mary A. Dixon, of *Bloomfield*, near Easton, Talbot Co., MD, on 21 Oct 1890 (*The Aegis & Intelligencer*, 24 Oct 1890)

Moore, Carrie (colored), 1890-1974, native of Harford Co., born 2 Apr 1890, daughter of Marcus Westley Moore and Isabelle ---- [Cox] (Mt. Zion Methodist Church Cemetery, at Mountain; *The Aegis*, 9 Apr 1974 - married name Armstrong)

Moore, Cecelia E. (Tildon) (colored), wife of George Michael Moore, q.v.

Moore, Charles Byron, 1859-1928 (Angel Hill Cemetery; Death certificate)

Moore, Coley, treated by unidentified doctor in 1890 ("Medical Account Book – 1890," Historical Society of Harford County Archives Folder)

Moore, Cora (Rambo), 1869-1954 (Mt. Zion Methodist Church Cemetery)

Moore, Daniel, acquired land in August 1890 (*The Aegis & Intelligencer*, 12 Sep 1890)

Moore, Deborah H., 1830-1900 (Little Falls Quaker Cemetery), daughter of Benjamn P. Moore and ----, resided at Fallston (Death certificate incomplete)

Moore, E. Estelle (Nelson), 1853-1924 (Little Falls Quaker Cemetery)

Moore, E. Ross, 1881-1926 (St. Stephen's Catholic Church Cemetery, Bradshaw, MD), native of Maryland, resided at Joppa, born 13 Nov 1881, son of Samuel T. Moore and Sarah P. Shepperd (Death certificate)

Moore, Edna E., 1886-1906 (St. George's Episcopal Church Cemetery)

Moore, Edward E., charter member, Havre de Grace Gunning Club (*Havre de Grace Republican*, 14 Nov 1890)

Moore, Edward Gwynne, 24 Apr 1890 - 16 Jul 1890, son of Samuel Moore, native of Indiana, and Sarah Shepherd, native of Baltimore, residents of Scarborough (St. Ignatius Catholic Church Cemetery, and Baptism Register, p. 113; *The Aegis & Intelligencer*, 25 Jul 1890)

Moore, Elijah J. B., 1834-1902 (Union Chapel Methodist Church Cemetery); farmer near Bel Air (*The Aegis & Intelligencer*, 15 Aug 1890)

Moore, Elijah J. B., 1863-1953 (St. George's Episcopal Church Cemetery)

Moore, Eliza (colored), see Annie Moore (colored), q.v.

Moore, Elizabeth (colored), see Flora Christie (colored), q.v.

Moore, Emma (Miss), member, Mt. Carmel M. P. Church, at Emmorton (*The Aegis & Intelligencer*, 27 Jun 1890)

Moore, Evaleen, 1865-1957 (Angel Hill Cemetery)

Moore, Frank K., 1878-1961 (Union Chapel Methodist Church Cemetery)

Moore, George A .F., musician and secretary, Bayside Cornet Band, Havre de Grace (*Havre de Grace Republican*, 31 Jan 1890 and 24 Oct 1890); sneak boat duck hunter (*Havre de Grace Republican*, 7 Nov 1890)

Moore, George Michael (colored), 1869-1932, native of Harford Co., born 24 Dec 1869, son of Lloyd A. Moore and Mary Jane Paca (Death certificate; Union Methodist Church Cemetery, Aberdeen, tombstone inscribed "husband of Cecelia E. Moore")

Moore, George Victor, 1885-1908 (St. George's Episcopal Church Cemetery)

Moore, Harry O., 1864-1945 (Angel Hill Cemetery); member, Havre de Grace Gun Club, 1890 (*Havre de Grace Republican*, 26 Dec 1890)

Moore, Harry R., 1873-1941 (Smith Chapel Methodist Church Cemetery)

Moore, Hattie (colored), 1881-1919, native of Harford Co., born 12 Feb 1881, daughter of Richard Moore and Millie Griffin (Death certificate - married name Hall)

Moore, Henry (colored), see Malinda Bond (colored), q.v.

Moore, Isabelle "Belle" (Cox) (colored), c1856-1928, native of Maryland, storekeeper in Bel Air (Death certificate age about 65 is incorrect since she was married in 1874 to Marcus "Mark" Moore, later divorced

(Harford Co. Equity Court Records, 1904); also see Carrie Moore, Bertha G. Moore, and William O. Moore, q.v.

Moore, J. Cole, 1866-1891 (Smith Chapel Methodist Church Cemetery)

Moore, J. Wilson, 1844-1909 (Little Falls Quaker Cemetery); superintendent, Harford Hedge and Wire Fence Company of Harford County (*Havre de Grace Republican*, 7 Feb 1890)

Moore, Jacob, deceased and removed from the voter registration list at Hall's Cross Roads, Second District, 1890 (*Havre de Grace Republican*, 17 Oct 1890)

Moore, Jacob (colored), 1879-1949 (Death certificate stated parents unknown)

Moore, James (colored), see Josephine Gilbert (colored), q.v.

Moore, James Oscar, 1863-1938 (Bethel Presbyterian Church Cemetery Records)

Moore, James Thomas, 1829-1901 (Bethel Presbyterian Church Cemetery Records)

Moore, Jane (Hobbs), 1812-1895 , widow of Henry Moore (Angel Hill Cemetery)

Moore, Jarrett B., 1835-1918 (Smith Chapel Methodist Church Cemetery); treated by unidentified doctor in 1890 ("Medical Account Book – 1890," Historical Society of Harford County Archives Folder)

Moore, Jesse S., 1845-1924 (Grove Presbyterian Church Cemetery)

Moore, John, 1834-1907 (St. George's Episcopal Church Cemetery); vice president, Bel Air Academy Association, 1890 (*Havre de Grace Republican*, 11 Jul 1890)

Moore, John Leeds, 1889-1976 (Angel Hill Cemetery)

Moore, John R., 1848-1914 (St. Mary's Catholic Church Cemetery); native of Baltimore Co., farmer at Street, Harford Co. (Death certificate); born 3 Jan 1848, son of Joseph Moore and Mary A. Boarman, of Harford Co., married Sarah R. Stokes on 13 Mar 1890 (St. Ignatius Catholic Church Marriage Register, p. 18); age 35 *(sic)* in 1890 (Marriage License Applications Book ALJ No. 2); married and then moved to Dr. Harlan's farm near Churchville (*Harford Democrat*, 28 Mar 1890)

Moore, John T., 1834-1900 (Angel Hill Cemetery)

Moore, John T. (colored), trustee, Fairview Colored School No. 1, Fourth District (*Havre de Grace Republican*, 30 May 1890); vice president, Republican Club (*Havre de Grace Republican*, 7 Nov 1890)

Moore, John Thomas, 1866-1951 (Bethel Presbyterian Church Cemetery Records)

Moore, Joseph, see John R. Moore, q.v.

Moore, Joseph, 1878-1941 (St. Francis de Sales Catholic Church Cemetery)

Moore, Joseph (colored), see Annie Moore (colored), q.v.

Moore, Joseph Henry, 1872-1945 (Mt. Erin Cemetery), native of Maryland, born 30 Jun 1872, son of Michael Moore and Martha Kurtz, both natives of Maryland (Pennington Funeral Home Records)

Moore, Katie (colored), 1872-1949, native of Harford Co., born 1 Jan 1872, daughter of Wesley Moore and Jane Spriggs (Death certificate - married name Bishop); wife of Jacob Moore (colored), q.v.

Moore, Laura Archer (Keithley), 1844-1907 (Union Chapel Methodist Church Cemetery)

Moore, Lawson, 1880-1951 (Jarrettsville Cemetery)

Moore, Leo Michael, 1880-1946 (Mt. Erin Cemetery)

Moore, Levina Ellen (Grant), c1866-1959 (Bethel Presbyterian Church Cemetery Records); wife of John Thomas Moore, q.v.

Moore, Lida J., 1863-1957 (St. George's Episcopal Church Cemetery)

Moore, Lilliam "Lillie" M., 1865-1932 (Angel Hill Cemetery)

Moore, Lizzie (colored), wife of William Moore, q.v.

Moore, Lloyd A. (colored), see George Michael Moore (colored), q.v.

Moore Lois S., 1883-1977 (Baker Cemetery)

Moore, Louisa (McComas) (colored), 1864-1933, native of Bush, Harford Co., parents unknown, wife of Mark

Moore (Death certificate)

Moore, Louise (Whareham), 1836-1909 (Angel Hill Cemetery)

Moore, Lucy (Frost), 1856-1926 (St. George's Episcopal Church Cemetery)

Moore, M. Josephine, 1884-1975 (Union Chapel Methodist Church Cemetery)

Moore, Marcus "Mark" (colored), 1854-1929 (Death certificate); husband first of Isabelle Moore and then of Louisa Moore, q.v.; also see Carrie Moore, Bertha G. Moore and William O. Moore, q.v.

Moore, Margaret "Maggie" (Travers), 1872-1941 (Baker Cemetery); wife of Archer H. Moore, q.v.

Moore, Martha J. (Kurtz), 1850-1917 (Mt. Erin Cemetery); uncalled for letter in Bel Air P. O., 1890 (*The Aegis & Intelligencer*, 4 Jul 1890); wife of Michael Moore, q.v

Moore, Mary (Dixon), 1849-1911 (Little Falls Quaker Cemetery)

Moore, Mary (O'Neill), 1828-1912 (Angel Hill Cemetery)

Moore, Mary Breen (McPake), 1887-1967 (Mt. Erin Cemetery); wife of Joseph Henry Moore, q.v.

Moore, Mary Eleanor (Mansley), 1857-1931, native and resident of Havre de Grace (Death certificate; Angel Hill Cemetery); wife of William Edward Moore, q.v.

Moore, Mary Emma, 1868-1936, daughter of James Thomas and Mary James (Burns) Moore (Bethel Presbyterian Church Cemetery Records); teacher, Emmorton School No. 3, First District, 1890 (*The Aegis & Intelligencer*, 29 Aug 1890)

Morre, Mary G. (Jones), 1860-1896 (Little Falls Quaker Cemetery)

Moore, Mary M., 1850-1900 (Grove Presbyterian Church Cemetery)

Moore, Michael, 1846-1903 (Mt. Erin Cemetery); see Joseph Henry Moore, q.v.

Moore, Milton Floyd, 18872-1939 (Mt. Zion Methodist Church Cemetery)

Moore, Nathaniel (colored), 1880-1945, native of Harford Co., son of Robert Moore and Rachel---- (Death certificate)

Moore, Olevia, 1840-1913 (Darlington Cemetery)

Moore, Rachel (colored), see Nathaniel Moore (colored), q.v.

Moore, Rachel Elizabeth (Cameron), wife of Robert L. Moore, q.v.

Moore, Richard, 1864-1922 (Darlington Cemetery)

Moore, Richard (colored), see Hattie Moore (colored), q.v.

Moore, Richard H., 1860-1920 (Wesleyan Chapel Methodist Church Cemetery); native of Maryland, laborer, resided Webster, son of Patrick Moore, of Ireland, and Mary Wallace, of Scotland (Death certificate)

Moore, Robert (colored), see Nathaniel Moore (colored), q.v.

Moore, Robert L., 1835-1898 (Angel Hill Cemetery)

Moore, Roxanna, wife of Henry [Harry] Clay Lawder; also see Frederick Carroll Lawder, Bessie Lawder and Henry [Harry] Clay Lawder, Jr., q.v.

Moore, Ruth M., age 20 in 1889 (Marriage License Applications Book ALJ No. 2, 1889)

Moore, Sallie (colored), see Lula Dorsey (colored), q.v.

Moore, Samuel T., 1829-1893 (St. Ignatius Catholic Church Cemetery); served on an inquest jury in Havre de Grace (*Havre de Grace Republican*, 6 Jun 1890); see Edward Gwynne Moore, E. Ross Moore, and Sarah (Pearce) Moore, q.v.

Moore, Sarah (colored), see James Wesley Collins (colored), q.v.

Moore, Sarah Pearce (Shepperd), wife of Samuel T. Moore, died 1 Jan 1910, age 69 (St. Ignatius Catholic Church Cemetery); Mrs. S. T. Moore, resident of Scarborough (*The Aegis & Intelligencer*, 15 Aug 1890)

Moore, Sarah A. (Cole), 1837-1908 (Death certificate; Smith Chapel Cemetery)

Moore, Susanna (colored), see Thaddeus Stephens Brown (colored), q.v.

Moore, Theodore R. (Mrs.), member, Women's Christian Temperance Union, Fallston (*The Aegis & Intelligencer*, 3 Jan 1890); manager, Fallston Baseball Club (*The Aegis & Intelligencer*, 22 Aug 1890)

Moore, Varina D., 1887-1965 (Union Chapel Methodist Church Cemetery)

Moore, W. Clinton, age 23 in 1890 (Marriage License Applications Book ALJ No. 2, 1890), married Bertie Burkins on 29 Apr 1890 at Franklin M. E. Church (*The Aegis & Intelligencer*, 9 May 1890)

Moore, Wesley (colored), see Katie Moore (colored) and William Wesley Moore (colored), q.v.

Moore, William, 1870-1920, fisherman, native of Maryland, parents unknown (Death certificate; Alms House Record Book)

Moore, William (colored), 1864-1899, waiter in Bel Air, husband of Lizzie Moore (Death certificate); age 26 in 1890 (Marriage License Applications Book ALJ No. 2, 1891)

Moore, William Edward (captain), 1850-1932, fisherman and native of Harford Co. (Death certificate; Angel Hill Cemetery); famous one-and-a-half armed duck sink boat hunter, of Havre de Grace (*The Aegis & Intelligencer*, 14 Nov 1890; *Havre de Grace Republican*, 7 Nov 1890); member, Havre de Grace Gun Club (*Havre de Grace Republican*, 26 Dec 1890); husband of Mary Eleanor Moore, q.v.

Moore, William Frost. 1883-1932 (St. George's Episcopal Church Cemetery)

Moore, William J., 1836-1914 (Darlington Cemetery)

Moore, William N., 1879-1954 (Baker Cemetery)

Moore, William Osborne (colored), 1887-1934 (Tabernacle Mt. Zion Methodist Church Cemetery), native of Bel Air, born 17 Aug 1887, son of Mark Moore and Isabelle ---- [Cox] (Death certificate)

Moore, William Thomas (colored), c1859-1939, native of Harford Co. (Death certificate)

Moore, William Wesley "Uncle Wess" (colored), c1820-1908 (Death certificate; *The Aegis & Intelligencer*, 17 Jan 1908)

Moores' Mills (aka Moreland Mills), on Paca's Meadow near Bel Air, John Moores, prop. (*Mills: Grist, Saw, Bone, Flint, Fulling ... & More*, by Jack L. Shagena, Jr., Henry C. Peden, Jr. and John W. McGrain, 2009, p. 217)

Moores, Edward Paca, member, Deer Creek Farmers' Club (*Havre de Grace Republican*, 3 Oct 1890); son of John Moores, q.v.

Moores, Elizabeth, wife of Robert Harris Archer, q.v.

Moores, George Gover, 1860-1932 (Christ Episcopal Church Cemetery); son of John Moores, q.v.

Moores, John, 1829-1911 (Christ Episcopal Church Cemetery); farmer, at the Big Woods, near Bel Air (*The Aegis & Intelligencer*, 15 Aug 1890); director, Harford National Bank (*The Aegis & Intelligencer*, 2 May 1890); member, Deer Creek Farmers' Club (*Havre de Grace Republican*, 3 Oct 1890); member, Harford County Agricultural and Mechanical Society (*The Aegis & Intelligencer*, 10 Jan 1890); road commissioner, Third District (*Havre de Grace Republican*, 7 Feb 1890); road committee chairman, Farmers' Convention (*Havre de Grace Republican*, 14 Feb 1890); vestryman, Christ Church, Rock Spring (*Havre de Grace Republican*, 18 Apr 1890); premium award winner, Class C - Sheep, Harford County Fair (*The Aegis & Intelligencer*, 24 Oct 1890); see Moores' Mills, q.v.

Moran, Bridget, see Henry Riley, q.v.

Moran, Catherine, 1841-1891 (St. Francis de Sales Catholic Church Cemetery)

Moran, Frank, student, Harford Furnace School (*The Aegis & Intelligencer*, 14 Feb 1890)

Moran, James, 1845-1910 (Mt. Erin Cemetery)

Moran, Patrick, 1832-1890, resided near Harford Furnace (St. Francis de Sales Catholic Church Cemetery; *The Aegis & Intelligencer*, 5 Sep 1890); removed from voter registration list at Abingdon, First District (*Havre de Grace Republican*, 17 Oct 1890)

Morbus (Mobus), Frederick, acquired land in February 1890 (*The Aegis & Intelligencer*, 7 Mar 1890); native of Germany, applied for naturalization on 4 Dec 1890 (*The Aegis & Intelligencer*, 12 Dec 1890; *Harford Democrat*, 12 Dec 1890); Harford County Circuit Court Minute Book ALJ No. 5, p. 259)

Mordew, Jacob M., juror, Fourth District (*Havre de Grace Republican*, 31 Jan 1890); member, Almshouse Committee, Bel Air (*The Aegis & Intelligencer*, 28 Feb 1890)

Mordew, Martha Elizabeth (Holland), 1854-1926 (Good Will Church Cemetery); native of Harford Co., resided at Rutledge (Death certificate)

Mordew, Rebecca A., 1849-1923 (McKendree Methodist Church Cemetery)

Morean, Alexander C., 1835-1891 (St. George's Episcopal Church Cemetery); farmer at *Meadow Farm* near Perryman (*The Aegis & Intelligencer*, 31 Oct 1890)

Morean, Ellen (Kenney), 1836-1908 (St. George's Episcopal Church Cemetery)

Morean, Malvaine, see Ethel Mitchell, q.v.

Morgan & Brother, butchers and green grocers, St. John Street, Havre de Grace (*Havre de Grace Republican*, 18 Apr 1890)

Morgan, Annie (colored), 1887-1922, parents unknown (Death certificate)

Morgan, Annie (Haines) (Mrs.) (colored), 1845-1922 (Death certificate); wife of Jarrett Morgan, q.v.

Morgan, Annie C., 1858-1923 (Grove Presbyterian Church Cemetery); Mr. T. E. Morgan, resident of Aberdeen, formerly of Dorchester Co., MD (*The Aegis & Intelligencer*, 13 Jun 1890); wife of Thomas E. Morgan, q.v.; also see Oscar Leroy Morgan and W. Morgan Whiteford, q.v.

Morgan, Augusta F., 1890-1955 (St. Mary's Episcopal Church Cemetery)

Morgan, Benjamin (colored), divorced, age 57 in 1889 and remarried in 1890 (Marriage License Applications Book ALJ No. 2, 1890)

Morgan, Blanche (Worthington), 1853-1925 (Angel Hill Cemetery); wife of Francis Huntington Morgan, q.v.

Morgan, Charles B., 1874-1948 (Smith Chapel Methodist Church Cemetery)

Morgan, Clara M., 1882-1918 (Smith Chapel Methodist Church Cemetery)

Morgan, Cornelia, 1843-1921 (Angel Hill Cemetery)

Morgan, Dolly (Miss), member, Guy Social Club, Aberdeen, 1890 (*Havre de Grace Republican*, 31 Oct 1890)

Morgan, Dora, student, Aberdeen Public School (*The Aegis & Intelligencer*, 23 May 1890)

Morgan, Effie Lee (Salter), 1851-1917 (Grove Presbyterian Church Cemetery), native of Yorktown, VA, resident of Aberdeen (Death certificate); wife of William Elliott Morgan, q.v.

Morgan, Elizabeth E. (Miss), graduate of State Normal School, 1890 (*Havre de Grace Republican*, 6 Jun 1890)

Morgan, Esther Olevia, 1869-1944 (Fallston Methodist Church Cemetery)

Morgan, Esther R., age 18 in 1890 (Marriage License Applications Book ALJ No. 2, 1891)

Morgan, Florence V., 1872-1947 (Grove Presbyterian Church Cemetery); native of Aberdeen, Harford Co., born 9 Jan 1872, daughter of Thomas E. Morgan and Jennie Osborn (Death certificate); choir member, Grove Presbyterian Church, Aberdeen (*The Aegis & Intelligencer*, 10 Jan 1890); member, Guy Social Club, Aberdeen (*Havre de Grace Republican*, 31 Oct 1890); student, Aberdeen Public School (*The Aegis & Intelligencer*, 23 May 1890)

Morgan, Francis Huntington ("Frank"), 1951-1921 (Angel Hill Cemetery); butcher and green grocer on St. John Street, Havre de Grace; city councilman; member of Havre de Grace Presbyterian Church (*Biographical Dictionary of Harford County, Maryland, 1774-1974*, by Henry C. Peden, Jr. and William O. Carr, 2021, p. 194); incorporator, Havre de Grace Academy (*Havre de Grace Republican*, 15 Aug 1890); trustee, High School No. 20, Sixth District (*Havre de Grace Republican*, 30 May 1890)

Morgan, Francis Huntington ("Frank"), Jr., 1881-1917 (Angel Hill Cemetery)

Morgan, Frank, miller, Little Gunpowder River, Fourth District (*The Aegis & Intelligencer*, 18 Jul 1890)

Morgan, George C., 1866-1920 (Darlington Cemetery)

Morgan, Hannah (colored), see John W. Bond (colored), q.v.

Morgan, Hannah (colored), age 20 in 1890 (Marriage License Applications Book ALJ No. 2, 1890); see Hannah Thompson, q.v.

Morgan, Harriet (colored), age 20 in 1890 (Marriage License Applications Book ALJ No. 2, 1891)

Morgan, Henry (colored), 1853-1918 (Death certificate)

Morgan, Henry (colored), died 21 Dec 1894, age not given (Alms House Record Book)

Morgan, Jane (colored), see Robert Gibson (colored), q.v.

Morgan, Jarrett (colored), 1840-1934 (Green Spring Methodist Church Cemetery); Civil War veteran, at Level (*1890 Special Census of the Civil War Veterans of the State of Maryland*, by L. Tilden Moore, Volume III, p. 67); treated by unidentified doctor in 1890 ("Medical Account Book – 1890," Historical Society of Harford County Archives Folder); see Odie Morgan, q.v.

Morgan, John, farmer, at Upper Cross Roads (*The Aegis & Intelligencer*, 18 Jul 1890)

Morgan, John R. Wesley (colored), age 21 in 1890 (Marriage License Applications Book ALJ No. 2, 1891)

Morgan, John Thomas, 1857-1944 (Fallston Methodist Church Cemetery); age 33 in 1890 (Marriage License Applications Book ALJ No. 2, 1890)

Morgan, John W. (colored), 1876-1933, native of Harford Co., son of William Morgan and Amelia Leonard (Death certificate)

Morgan, Julia (colored), see Lavinia E. Dunsen (colored), q.v.

Morgan, Lizzie (Miss), member of the Guy Social Club in Aberdeen (*Havre de Grace Republican*, 31 Oct 1890)

Morgan, Mabel Leslie (Hopper), 1883-1959 (Angel Hill Cemetery); wife of Francis H. Morgan, Jr., q.v.

Morgan, Mary Ann (Johns), 1821-1916 (Highland Presbyterian Church Cemetery); wife of Robert E. Morgan, q.v.

Morgan, Mary Roberta (Anderson), 1867-1943 (Fallston Methodist Church Cemetery; *Harford Democrat*, 25 Apr 1890); wife of John T. Morgan, q.v.

Morgan, Mary V. (Simmons), 1849-1936 (Angel Hill Cemetery)

Morgan, Nannie, born -- Aug 1885, daughter of William E. and Effie L. Morgan (1900 Aberdeen Census)

Morgan, Nellie, 1886-1976, native of Havre de Grace, born 2 Dec 1886, daughter of Oliver A. Morgan and Sarah Ferry (Pennington Funeral Home Records - married name Knight)

Morgan, Odie (colored), 1870-1923, native of Maryland, born 20 Apr 1870, son of Jarrett Morgan and Caroline Billingsley (Death certificate)

Morgan, Oliver A., 1862-1941 (Angel Hill Cemetery); musician, Bayside Cornet Band, Havre de Grace, 1890 (*Havre de Grace Republican*, 31 Jan 1890); see Nellie Morgan, q.v.

Morgan, Oscar Leroy, born 30 Nov 1885, son of Thomas E. and Annie C. Morgan (St. George's Episcopal Church Register of Baptisms, pp. 4-5)

Morgan, Robert E., 1821-1903 (Highland Presbyterian Church Cemetery); ex-sheriff, Mill Green (*Havre de Grace Republican*, 4 Apr 1890)

Morgan, Robert Lytle, 1875-1931 (Grove Presbyterian Church Cemetery); son of Mr. & Mrs. W. E. Morgan, of Aberdeen (*Harford Democrat*, 3 Jan 1890); member, Guy Social Club, Aberdeen, 1890 (*Havre de Grace Republican*, 31 Oct 1890)

Morgan, Sarah, 1865-1892 (Angel Hill Cemetery)

Morgan, Sarah Ann (Hoskins), 1819-1901 (Little Falls Quaker Cemetery)

Morgan, Shirley C., born -- Dec 1878, son of William E. and Effie L. Morgan (1900 Aberdeen Census; *Harford Democrat*, 3 Jan 1890); jousting tournament herald, 1890 (*Havre de Grace Republican*, 17 Oct 1890)

Morgan, Susanna Elizabeth (Miss), 1847-1928 (Christ Episcopal Church Cemetery)

Morgan, Thomas C., 1890-1960 (St. Mary's Episcopal Church Cemetery)

Morgan, Thomas Elliott, 1843-1913 (Grove Presbyterian Church Cemetery); vice commander, Harford Lodge No. 54, of Aberdeen, Order of the Golden Chain (*The Aegis & Intelligencer*, 13 Jun 1890; *Havre de Grace Republican*, 28 Nov 1890); see Oscar Leroy Morgan and Florence V. Morgan, q.v.

Morgan, Timothy, see Jane M. Evans, q.v.

Morgan, Wakeman F., 1828-1892 (St. Ignatius Catholic Church Cemetery)

Morgan, William (colored), 1835-1909, native of Bel Air (Death certificate)

Morgan, William (colored), widower, age 51 in 1890 (Marriage License Applications Book ALJ No. 2, 1890); see John W. Morgan and Hannah Thompson, q.v.

Morgan, William B. (colored), 1835-1916, native of Maryland (Death certificate)

Morgan, William Edward, 1867-1955 (Fallston Methodist Church Cemetery)

Morgan, William Elliott, 1848-1925 (Grove Presbyterian Church Cemetery); canned goods broker, Aberdeen (*Havre de Grace Republican*, 11 Apr 1890); senior warden, Aberdeen Lodge No. 87, A. F. & A. M. (*Havre de Grace Republican*, 11 Jul 1890); past commander, Harford Lodge No. 54, of Aberdeen, Order of the Golden Chain (*Havre de Grace Republican*, 28 Nov 1890); judge of jousting tournament in Bel Air (*Havre de Grace Republican*, 17 Oct 1890)

Morgan, William Henry, 1839-1913 (Angel Hill Cemetery)

Morlok, Alexander, 1887-1891, son of J. G. F. and Katherina Morlok (St. Paul's Lutheran Cemetery)

Morlok, John Gottlieb Frederick, 1868-1935 (St. Paul's Lutheran Cemetery)

Morlok, Katherina, 1864-1891 (St. Paul's Lutheran Cemetery)

Morning Star Lodge No. 20, Independent Order of Odd Fellows (*Havre de Grace Republican*, 11 Jul 1890)

Morris, Abe (colored), died 22 Sep 1890, age not given (Alms House Record Book)

Morris, Albert, 1869-1939 (St. Mary's Catholic Church Cemetery)

Morris, Agusta ("Gussie"') (Fortner), 1862-1937 (Dublin Methodist Church Cemetery); native of Baltimore (Bailey Funeral Home Records); wife of Philip Morris, q.v.

Morris, Annie R. (Cantler), 1871-1941 (Dublin Southern Cemetery); native of Harford Co., born 22 Nov 1871, daughter of Henry Cantler and Elizabeth Russell (Bailey Funeral Home Records)

Morris, Bertha M., 1884-1979 (Bel Air Memorial Gardens)

Morris, Carrie, 1888-1970, native of Maryland, born 14 Aug 1888, daughter of William Morris and Anna Cantler (Pennington Funeral Home Records)

Morris, Charles A., 1869-1947 (Baker Cemetery)

Morris, Christena, 1889-1959 (Trinity Evangelical Lutheran Church Cemetery)

Morris, Clayton B., 1880-1956 (St. Paul's Methodist Church Cemetery)

Morris, Columbus S., 1866-1924 (Rock Run Methodist Church Cemetery)

Morris, Cylena C., 1887-1953 (Dublin Southern Cemetery)

Morris, David Alfred, age 17 in 1890 (Holy Trinity Episcopal Church Register of Marriages, p. 216, 1893)

Morris, E. Rebecca, see E. Rebecca Jones, q.v.

Morris, Edith G. (Boyle), 1889-1969 (Tabernacle Cemetery); native of Whiteford, Harford Co., born 13 Mar 1889, daughter of Hugh A. Boyle and Bertha Bennington (Harkins Funeral Home Records)

Morris, Eleanor, 1830-1906 (Tabernacle Cemetery)

Morris, Eliza (Wright), wife of Jarrett G. Morris, q.v.

Morris, Elizabeth J., 1854-1952 (St. Paul's Methodist Church Cemetery)

Morris, Guy, 1875-1944 (Dublin Southern Cemetery); native of Harford Co., born 30 Jul 1875, son of Henry Morris and Elizabeth Kimball (Bailey Funeral Home Records)

Morris, H. Raymond, 1889-1958 (Slate Ridge Cemetery, York Co., PA); native of Harford Co., born 26 Jul 1889, son of Isaac E. Morris and Lourena Watson (Harkins Funeral Home Records)

Morris, Hannah A., 1852-1927 (Highland Presbyterian Church Cemetery)

Morris, Harriett, see Sarah E. Singleton, q.v.

Morris, Henry, see Guy Morris, q.v.

Morris, Ida Belle, 1881-1911 (St. Paul's Methodist Church Cemetery)

Morris, Isaac E., 1862-1901 (Tabernacle Cemetery); see H. Raymond Morris and John C. Morris, q.v.

Morris, J. Melville, 1887-1971 (Dublin Southern Cemetery)

Morris, Jacob G., resident near Clermont Mills (*The Aegis & Intelligencer*, 31 Jan 1890)

Morris, James, see Philip Morris, q.v.

Morris, Jarrett G., 1824-1901, native of Harford Co. (Death certificate)

Morris, Jarrett J., see Walter Streett Morris, q.v.

Morris, John C., 1886-1954 (Tabernacle Cemetery); native of Whiteford, Harford Co., born 25 Jul 1886, son of Isaac E. Morris and Lourena Watson (Harkins Funeral Home Records)

Morris, John H., see E. Rebecca Jones, q.v.

Morris, John Richard, 1854-1936 (St. Paul's Methodist Church Cemetery)

Morris, John W., husband of Sallie A. Morris, q.v.

Morris, Kate (Patterson), 1872-1904 (Fallston Methodist Church Cemetery)

Morris, Leurenna, 1865-1936 (Tabernacle Cemetery)

Morris, Louisa K., 1877-1925 (Deer Creek Harmony Presbyterian Church Cemetery)

Morris, Marshall, 1886-1957 (Tabernacle Cemetery); native of Maryland, born 5 Sep 1886, son of Peter Morris and Rebecca ---- (Harkins Funeral Home Records)

Morris, Martha, see Martha E. Smith and Helen May Carr, q.v.

Morris, Mary, see Winfield Scott Morris, Philip Morris and Ulyseia K. Morris, q.v.

Morris, Mary Elizabeth, 1828-1899 (Cokesbury Memorial Methodist Church Cemetery); resided at Carsins Run, wife of William Morris (Death certificate)

Morris, Matilda, see Delmer T. Miller, q.v.

Morris, Nettie (Baker), 1883-1972 (Baker Cemetery)

Morris, Paul, 1886-1962 (Bel Air Memorial Gardens)

Morris, Peter, see Marshall Morris, q.v.

Morris, Philip, 1857-1898 (Dublin Methodist Church Cemetery); native of Maryland, farmer at Dublin, husband of Agusta Morris and son of James and Mary Morris (Death certificate)

Morris, Rebecca I., 1860-1893 (Tabernacle Cemetery); see Marshall Morris, Clinton M. Tayson and Philip C. Tayson, q.v.

Morris, Sallie A. (Wheeler), 1851-1900, native of Maryland, resident of Havre de Grace (Death certificate)

Morris, Sarah (Mrs.), of near Fellowship Church, age 95 in 1890, born 12 Jan 1795 (*The Aegis & Intelligencer*, 14 Feb 1890); mother of Mrs. Robert Jennings, of near Long Corner (*Harford Democrat*, 21 Feb 1890)

Morris, Sarah E., 1874-1943 (St. Mary's Catholic Church Cemetery)

Morris, Scott (Master), resident of Muttonsburg (*The Aegis & Intelligencer*, 4 Apr 1890)

Morris, Sheridan, age 24 in 1890 (Marriage License Applications Book ALJ No. 2, 1890)

Morris, Stanley E., 1889-1981 (Baker Cemetery)

Morris, Thomas (Master), resident of Muttonsburg (*The Aegis & Intelligencer*, 28 Mar 1890)

Morris, Thomas James Vincent, 1862-1931 (Fallston Methodist Church Cemetery)

Morris, Ulyseia K. (colored), daughter of Mary Morris, born 17 May 1873 and indentured to Richard McDonald in 1883 (Harford County Indentures Book WSB No. 1)

Morris, Walter, 1876-1951 (Fawn Grove Methodist Church Cemetery); native of Harford Co., born 7 Sep 1876, son of Walter S. Morris and Hannah Slade (Harkins Funeral Home Records)

Morris, Walter Streett, 1851-1935 (Highland Presbyterian Church Cemetery); native of Harford Co., born 10 Mar 1851, son of Jarrett J. Morris and Eliza Wright (Harkins Funeral Home Records); see Walter Morris and Florence D. Barton, q.v.

Morris, William, see Carrie Morris, q.v.

Morris, William, resident near Harford Furnace (*The Aegis & Intelligencer*, 28 Mar 1890)

Morris, William Payne (Mrs.), neé Grove, 1874-1899 (Death certificate)

Morris, William W., age 22 in 1890 (Marriage License Applications Book ALJ No. 2, 1890); new name on the voter registration list at Hopewell, Second District (*Havre de Grace Republican*, 17 Oct 1890)

Morris, William W., 1870-1935 (Dublin Cemetery); native of Harford Co., born 24 Jan 1870, son of James Morris and Sarah Flahart (Bailey Funeral Home Records)

Morris, Winfield Scott (colored), son of Mary Morris, born 17 May 1873 and indentured to Richard McDonald in 1883 (Harford County Indentures Book WSB No. 1)

Morrison, Annie F., 1888-1905 (Darlington Cemetery)

Morrison, Asa L., 1889-1948 (Darlington Cemetery)

Morrison, Catherine E., 1846-1901, native of Maryland, resident and nurse in Whiteford, daughter of Daniel Morrison and Julia McGaw (Death certificate; Mt. Vernon Methodist Church Cemetery)

Morrison, Celina, see Bertha Allison, q.v.

Morrison, Daniel, see Catherine Morrison, q.v.

Morrison, Ellen A., 1849-1919 (St. Mary's Catholic Church Cemetery)

Morrison, Ellis, 1823-1901, native of Maryland, single, resided at Emmorton (Death certificate incomplete)

Morrison, Emmor, 1826-1898 (Little Falls Quaker Cemetery)

Morrison, Frances L., 1822-1915 (Angel Hill Cemetery)

Morrison, George W., Civil War veteran, Havre de Grace (*1890 Special Census of the Civil War Veterans of the State of Maryland*, by L. Tilden Moore, Volume III, p. 64)

Morrison, George W., 1885-1918 (St. Mary's Catholic Church Cemetery)

Morrison, Harry H., 1887-1947 (Mt. Vernon Church Cemetery); native of Macton, Harford Co., born 13 May 1887, son of William J. Morrison and Hannah Sealor (Harkins Funeral Home Records)

Morrison, Isaac, road surveying chain man, Fifth District (*Havre de Grace Republican*, 4 Jul 1890)

Morrison, James R., house and carriage painter, Perryman (*Havre de Grace Republican*, 25 Jul 1890)

Morrison, John, c1840-1915 (Death certificate; Heavenly Waters Cemetery)

Morrison, Joseph A., 1890-1927 (St. Ignatius Catholic Church Cemetery)

Morrison, Joseph R., house and carriage painting shop, Perryman (*The Aegis & Intelligencer*, 25 Jul 1890)

Morrison, Julia A., 1811-1900 (Mt. Vernon Methodist Church Cemetery); see David Elwood Hughes and B. Elizabeth Jones, q.v.

Morrison, Margaret S., 1884-1934 (Darlington Cemetery)

Morrison, Mary Margaret (Smith), 1886-1934 (Darlington Cemetery); native of Harford Co., born 31 Jul 1886, daughter of William S. Smith and Adaline Monks (Bailey Funeral Home Records); wife of Asa L. Morrison, q.v.

Morrison, Mary E. (Love), 1845-1938 (Darlington Cemetery)

Morrison, Mary S., 1884-1983 (Oak Grove Baptist Church Cemetery)

Morrison, Selina, see George Eli Allison, q.v.

Morrison, Susan E., 1808-1891 (Little Falls Quaker Cemetery)

Morrison, Teresa E., 1883-1970 (St. Mary's Catholic Church Cemetery)

Morrison, Thomas E., 1886-1966 (Oak Grove Baptist Church Cemetery)

Morrison, Thomas S., 1846-1914 (St. Mary's Catholic Church Cemetery)

Morrison, Walter A., telegraph operator, Rocks of Deer Creek (*Havre de Grace Republican*, 25 Apr 1890)

Morrison, William H., 1859-1940 (Angel Hill Cemetery)

Morrison, William J., see Harry H. Morrison, q.v.

Morrison, William T., 1843-1922 (Darlington Cemetery)

Morse's Mills, on East Branch of Winter's Run near Jarrettsville, George W. Morse, prop. (*Mills: Grist, Saw, Bone, Flint, Fulling ... & More*, by Jack L. Shagena, Jr., Henry C. Peden, Jr. and John W. McGrain, 2009, pp. 218-219)

Morse, Eliza (colored), mother of Mary M. Chase, q.v.

Morse, Elizabeth, 1797-1890 (William Watters Memorial Methodist Church Cemetery); died testate and her named heirs were son George W. Morse and daughters Hannah C. Curry and Rebecca R. Morse (Harford County Will Book JMM 11:157-158)

Morse, G. Walter, 1876-1966 (William Watters Memorial Methodist Church Cemetery, Cooptown)

Morse, George W., 1834-1912 (William Watters Memorial Methodist Church Cemetery, Cooptown); see Elizabeth Morse amd Morse's Mills, q.v.

Morse, Harry L., 1879-1979 (William Watters Memorial Methodist Church Cemetery, Cooptown)

Morse, George M., 1868-1942 (William Watters Memorial Methodist Church Cemetery, Cooptown)

Morse, Laura J. (Green), 1838-1910 (William Watters Memorial Methodist Church Cemetery, Cooptown)

Morse, M. Adelia (Glenn), 1882-1911 (William Watters Memorial Methodist Church Cemetery, Cooptown)

Morse, Nelson W., 1882-1948 (William Watters Memorial Methodist Church Cemetery, Cooptown)

Morse, Rebecca R., see Elizabeth Morse, q.v.

Morsey, Easley Eva (colored), 1888-1973 (St. James United Cemetery)

Mortgage, Frank H., and wife, sold land in February 1890 (*The Aegis & Intelligencer*, 7 Mar 1890)

Morton, George D., 1845-1900, native of Des Moines, IA, resided at Laurel Brook, Harford Co. (Death certificate)

Moseman, Elizabeth, wife of Albert Leffler, q.v., also see Clara A. Leffler and William A. Leffler, q.v.

Moses, Eva (colored), 1887-1940, native of Havre de Grace, born 14 Jul 1887, daughter of Peter Moses, native of Virginia, and Julia A. Maxwell, native of Maryland (Death certificate - married name Durbin)

Moses, Hans, 1851-1925, born in Germany (Death certificate; Alms House Record Book)

Moses, Julia Ann (Pinion) (colored), 1855-1930, native of Maryland (St. James Church, Gravel Hill Cemetery tombstone inscribed 1855; Death certificate states she died about age 72)

Moses, Peter (colored), 1847-1890, U.S.C.T., Civil War, resident of Havre de Grace (*Havre de Grace Republican*, 18 Jul 1890); deceased and removed from the Havre de Grace voter registration list, 1890 (*Havre de Grace Republican*, 19 Sep 1890); see Eva Moses, q.v.

Moshenaud, Ben, c1867-1927, born in France (Death certificate)

Motson, Emma M., 1876-1944 (Darlington Cemetery)

Motson, Joseph E., 1875-1956 (Darlington Cemetery); native of Harford Co., born 20 Feb 1875, son of Thomas Motson and Blanche James (Bailey Funeral Home Records)

Motson, L. James, 1866-1897 (Churchville Presbyterian Church Cemetery)

Motson, Mary L., 1869-1891 (Churchville Presbyterian Church Cemetery)

Motson, Sarah, 1875-1973, native of Street, Harford Co., born 20 Feb 1875, daughter of Thomas H. Motson and ---- James (Pennington Funeral Home Records - married nae Johnson)

Motson, Thomas, 1851-1917 (Dublin Methodist Church Cemetery); uncalled for letter in Bel Air P. O., 1890 (*The Aegis & Intelligencer*, 14 Nov 1890); see Joseph E. Motson and Sarah Motson, q.v.

Moulsdale's General Store, Aberdeen, Mr. J. J. Moulsdale, prop. (*Country Stores: Harford County's Rural Heritage*, by Henry C. Peden, Jr. and Jack L. Shagena, Jr., 2015, p. 182)

Moulsdale, Alfred T., 1868-1933 (Cokesbury Memorial Methodist Church Cemetery)

Moulsdale, Annie, student, Public School No. 1, First District (*The Aegis & Intelligencer*, 10 Jan 1890)

Moulsdale, Charles, 1882-1908 (Angel Hill Cemetery)

Moulsdale, Christine, 1882-1931 (Cokesbury Memorial Methodist Church Cemetery)

Moulsdale, David, see George F. Moulsdale, q.v.

Moulsdale, David H., 1845-1918 (Baker Cemetery)

Moulsdale, David H., 1875-1954 (Cokesbury Memorial Methodist Church Cemetery)

Moulsdale, Edward A., 1880-1947 (Cokesbury Memorial Methodist Church Cemetery); Eddie Moulsdale, student, Abingdon School, 1890 (*The Aegis & Intelligencer*, 26 Dec 1890)

Moulsdale, Eleanor Louise, 1878-1911 (Cokesbury Memorial Methodist Church Cemetery)

Moulsdale, George F., 1888-1966 (Baker Cemetery); native of Maryland, born 12 Mar 1888, son of David Moulsdale and Elizabeth Thompson (Pennington Funeral Home Records)

Moulsdale, Jame H., 1877-1954 (Baker Cemetery)

Moulsdale, Jane M., 1841-1919 (Cokesbury Memorial Methodist Church Cemetery)

Moulsdale, John A., 1862-1923 (Cokesbury Memorial Methodist Church Cemetery)

Moulsdale, John J., wheelwright, coach painter and carriage maker, Hall's Cross Roads [Aberdeen] (*Carriages Back in the Day: Harford County's Rural Heritage*, by Jack L. Shagena, Jr. and Henry C. Peden, Jr., 2016, p. 81)

Moulsdale, Joseph Mark, 1866-1941 (Cokesbury Memorial Methodist Church Cemetery); son of Thomas Moulsdale, of Abingdon District (*The Aegis & Intelligencer*, 14 Nov 1890; Holy Trinity Episcopal Church Register of Marriages, p. 216)

Moulsdale, Joseph W., 1847-1897 (Cokesbury Memorial Methodist Church Cemetery); resident of Abingdon (*The Aegis & Intelligencer*, 12 Dec 1890)

Moulsdale, Kezia O. (Hackett), 1844-1931 (Cokesbury Memorial Methodist Church Cemetery); second wife of Thomas Moulsdale, q.v.

Moulsdale, Nora, student, Public School No. 1, First District (*The Aegis & Intelligencer*, 10 Jan 1890)

Moulsdale, Pearl (Miss), member, Aberdeen M. E. Church (*Havre de Grace Republican*, 21 Feb 1890)

Moulsdale, Sarah M., 1879-1940 (Baker Cemetery)

Moulsdale, Susanna Elizabeth (Miss), 1847-1928 (Death certificate)

Moulsdale, Thomas, 1829-1910 (Cokesbury Memorial Methodist Church Cemetery); delegate, First District, Democrat Party Convention, and vice president, Harford County Tariff Reform Club (*The Aegis & Intelligencer*, 5 Sep 1890); served on a grand jury foreman, First District (*The Aegis & Intelligencer*, 14 Nov 1890); public landing examiner on Otter Point Creek (*The Aegis & Intelligencer*, 11 Apr 1890); trustee, Abingdon School No. 1, First District (*Havre de Grace Republican*, 30 May 1890); vice president, Democratic Club (*Havre de Grace Republican*, 5 Sep 1890); resided at Harford Station (*Harford Democrat*, 24 Oct 1890); see Joseph M. Moulsdale, q.v.

Moulton, Alba, Jr. (colored), 1867-1950, native of Maryland, born 6 Aug 1867, son of Alba Moulton and Harriet Washington (Death certificate)

Moulton, Arthur J. (colored), born -- Jan 1882, native of Maryland, son of James and Harriett Moulton (1900 Aberdeen Census)

Moulton, Caroline (Wilkinson), 1829-1916 (Wesleyan Chapel Methodist Church Cemetery)

Moulton, Charles Lewis, 1860-19-- (Wesleyan Chapel Methodist Church Cemetery)

Moulton, Charles O., 1855-1923 (Broad Creek Friends Cemetery)

Moulton, Cora A. (colored), 1867-1939 (Union Methodist Church Cemetery, Aberdeen)

Moulton, Effie (colored), 1876-1933, native of Aberdeen, Harford Co., born 15 May 1876, daughter of James Moulton and Harriet Washington (Death certificate - married name Murphy)

Moulton, Elba N., age 25 in 1890 (Marriage License Applications Book ALJ No. 2, 1890)

Moulton, Emma R., 1861-1934 (Broad Creek Friends Cemetery)

Moulton, Gertrude (colored), 1880-1940, native of Maryland, born 17 Aug 1880, daughter of James Moulton and Harriet Washington, all born in Aberdeen, Harford Co. (Death certificate - married name Hardy)

Moulton, Harriet A. (Washington) (colored), 1847-1925 (Death certificate); wife of James Moulton, q.v.; also see Effie Moulton, q.v.

Moulton, Harriett (colored), born -- May 1849, native of Maryland (1900 Aberdeen Census); wife of James Moulton, q.v.; also see Arthur J. Moulton, q.v.

Moulton, Henrietta, c1816-1896 (Wesleyan Chapel Methodist Church Cemetery)

Moulton, James (colored), born -- Mar 1848, native of Maryland (1900 Aberdeen Census)

Moulton, James (colored), 1857-1932, native of Spotsylvania, VA, resided in Aberdeen (Death certificate); brother of Richard A. Moulton, q.v.; also see Effie Moulton and Gertrude Moulton, q.v.

Moulton, James Columbus, 1862-1936 (Wesleyan Chapel Methodist Church Cemetery)

Moulton, Laura Belle (Ruth), 1867-1911 (Wesleyan Chapel Methodist Church Cemetery); wife of James C. Moulton, q.v.

Moulton, Maria Ross (Harper), 1858-1938 (Wesleyan Chapel Methodist Church Cemetery); wife of Charles L. Moulton, q.v.

Moulton, Marion Thompson, 1872-1933 (Wesleyan Chapel Methodist Church Cemetery)

Moulton, Mary G., see Anna G. Touchstone, q.v.

Moulton, Rebecca Ann (Bailey), 1815-1900, resided at Level, Harford Co., "native of America" (Death certificate; *Barnes-Bailey Genealogy,* by Walter D. Barnes, 1939, p. G-23)

Moulton, Richard Anderson (colored), c1856-1913, native of Virginia, resided in Aberdeen (Death certificate); brother of James Moulton, q.v.

Mount, Annie E. (Mrs.), 1831-1908; resided on Bush River Neck (St. George's Episcopal Church Cemetery; *The Aegis & Intelligencer*, 29 Aug 1890)

Mount, Charles G., 1849-1902, farmer at Michaelsville, son of Thomas S. Mount and Sarah Gaskill (Death certificate; St. George's Episcopal Church Cemetery)

Mount, George H., 1857-1928 (St. George's Episcopal Church Cemetery); native of Pennsylvania, single, clerk, resided in Aberdeen (Death certificate)

Mount, Harry A., 1884-1969, native of Perryman, Harford Co., born 15 Dec 1884, son of James A. Mount and Laura Johnson (Pennington Fnneral Home Records; St. George's Episcopal Church Cemetery)

Mount, James Albert, 1861-1942 (St. George's Episcopal Church Cemetery); see Harry A. Mount and Laura B. Mount, q.v.

Mount, Laura B. (Mrs.), 1866-1953. native of Perryman, Harford Co., born 8 Oct 1866, daughter of ---- [James A. Mount] and Laura Johnson (Pennington Funeral Home Records)

Mount, Russell M., 1889-1912 (St. George's Episcopal Church Cemetery)

Mount, Thomas S., see Charles G. Mount, q.v.

Mountain Christian Church, formerly Jerusalem Christian Church (Mountain Road, at Wilna)

Mountain Colored Public School No. 2, near Clayton, First District (*Harford County, Maryland Teachers and the Schools They Served, 1774-1900*, by Henry C. Peden, Jr., 2022, p. 371)

Mowbray, William Henry, 1879-1940 (Holy Trinity Episcopal Church Cemetery; Death certificate); born 19 Apr 1879, baptized 3 Dec 1889, son of George M. and Susan A. Mowbray (Holy Trinity Episcopal Church Register of Baptisms, p. 98, spelled his name Moobary)

Mt. Ararat Lodge No. 44, A. F. & A. M., Bel Air (*Havre de Grace Republican*, 11 Jul 1890)

Mt. Calvary AME Church and Cemetery (Mt. Calvary Road, Aberdeen)

Mt. Calvary Colored Public School No. 4, First District (*Harford County, Maryland Teachers and the Schools They Served, 1774-1900*, by Henry C. Peden, Jr., 2022, p. 371)

Mt. Carmel Chapel Methodist Episcopal Church and Cemetery (Old Emmorton Road, Emmorton)

Mt. Pleasant Public School No. 11, near Ady, Fifth District (*Harford County, Maryland Teachers and the Schools They Served, 1774-1900*, by Henry C. Peden, Jr., 2022, p. 371)

Mt. Tabor Methodist Church and Cemetery (Conowingo Road, near Hickory)

Mt. Vernon Methodist Church and Cemetery (Deep Run Road, at Prospect)

Mt. Zion AME Church and Cemetery (Singer Road, near Clayton, First District)

Mt. Zion Methodist Church and Cemetery (Churchville Road, near Bel Air)

Mt. Zion Public School No. 12, Fountain Green, Third District (*Harford County, Maryland Teachers and the Schools They Served, 1774-1900*, by Henry C. Peden, Jr., 2022, p. 371)

Mulberry Point School, near Michaelsville, Second District (*Harford County, Maryland Teachers and the Schools They Served, 1774-1900*, by Henry C. Peden, Jr., 2022, p. 371)

Mulhearn, ----, center fielder, A. R. Walker Baseball Club, Havre de Grace (*Havre de Grace Republican*, 4 Jul 1890)

Mulherran, J. H., member, Merry Ten Social Club, Havre de Grace (*Havre de Grace Republican*, 25 Jul 1890)

Muller Brothers, saddles, harnesses, collars and horse blankets, Branch House, Main Street, Bel Air (*Harford Democrat*, 10 Jan 1890; *The Aegis & Intelligencer*, 4 Apr 1890)

Mulligan, John, age 37 in 1890 (Marriage License Applications Book ALJ No. 2, 1890), married Martha K. McComas on 13 Feb 1890 (marriage certificate); residents near Jarrettsville (*The Aegis & Intelligencer*, 28 Mar 1890)

Mullineaux's General Store, near Bradenbaugh P. O., Samuel Mullineaux, prop. (*Country Stores: Harford County's Rural Heritage*, by Henry C. Peden, Jr. and Jack L. Shagena, Jr., 2015, p. 182)

Mullineaux, Agnes Bell (Wiley), 1865-1950 (Ayres Chapel Methodist Church Cemetery)

Mullineaux, John Wesley, c1853-1938, native of St. Charles, MO, resided near White Hall (Death certificate; Ayres Chapel Cemetery)

Mullineaux, Joseph Claudius, born 8 Mar 1887, son of Samuel and Agnes Bell (Wiley) Mullineaux (*Kirkwoods and Their Kin, 1731-1971*, by Anna Lee Kirkwood Smith, 1972, p. 135)

Mullineaux, Joseph H., 1832-1905 (Ayres Chapel Methodist Church Cemetery)

Mullineaux, Leila Rebecca, born 1 Nov 1888, daughter of Samuel and Agnes Bell (Wiley) Mullineaux (*Kirkwoods and Their Kin, 1731-1971*, by Anna Lee Kirkwood Smith, 1972, p. 135)

Mullineaux, Levina, 1832-1916 (Ayres Chapel Methodist Church Cemetery)

Mullineaux, Marie Nelson, born 26 Mar 1890 of Samuel and Agnes Bell (Wiley) Mullineaux (*Kirkwoods and Their Kin, 1731-1971*, by Anna Lee Kirkwood Smith, 1972, p. 135)

Mullineaux, Myrtle Reed (Wright), 1890-1933 (Ayres Chapel Cemetery; *Kirkwoods and Their Kin, 1731-1971*, by Anna Lee Kirkwood Smith, 1972, p. 135)

Mullineaux, Samuel, 1863-1894 (Ayres Chapel Methodist Church Cemetery)

Munder, Lelia, see Mrs. M. L. Sewell, q.v.

Munnikhuysen, Ann (Lee), 1845-1932 (William Watters Memorial Church, Thomas Run)

Munnikhuysen, Annie (Farnandis), 1853-1925 (St. Mary's Episcopal Church Cemetery), wife of Wakeman B. Munnikhysen, q.v.

Munnikhuysen, Bryarly, 1888-1945 (St. Mary's Episcopal Church Cemetery)

Munnikhuysen, Cornelia (Miss), dancing student, Archer Institute, Bel Air (*The Aegis & Intelligencer*, 6 Jun 1890)

Munnikhuysen, Edward Pearce, 1884-1953 (Fallston Methodist Church Cemetery); native of Baltimore, born 4 May 1884, son of James Carvel Munnikhuysen and Ann Rosela Pearce (Bailey Funeral Home Records)

Munnikhuysen, Elizabeth D. (Miss), 1852-1928 (St. Mary's Episcopal Church Cemetery; Death certificate)

Munninkhuysen, Ella (Gover), 1858-1932 (Christ Episcopal Church Cemetery)

Munnikhuysen, Fannie Lee, born 16 Oct 1873, daughter of William and Louisa W. Munnikhuysen (Holy Trinity Episcopal Church Register of Baptisms, p. 82); graduated from Thomas Run Public School (*The Aegis & Intelligencer*, 4 Jul 1890)

Munnikhuysen, Frances (Miss), 1853-1935 (St. Mary's Episcopal Church Cemetery; Death certificate)

Munnikhuysen, Frances Lee, 1873-1956 (Christ Episcopal Church Cemetery)

Munnikhuysen, Francis William, 1889-1928 (St. Mary's Episcopal Church Cemetery); native of Maryland, born 13 Dec 1889, William T. Munnikhuysen and Ella Gove (Death certificate shows name as W. Francis Munnikhuysen)

Munnikhuysen, Hall Lee, 1875-1954 (Christ Episcopal Church Cemetery); born 10 Nov 1875, son of William and Louisa W. Munnikhuysen (Holy Trinity Episcopal Church Register of Baptisms, p. 82)

Munnikhuysen, Hannah Tunis, 1888-1981 (St. Mary's Episcopal Church Cemetery - married name Brookes)

Munnikhuysen, Howard, sold land in April 1890 (*The Aegis & Intelligencer*, 9 May 1890)

Munnikhuysen, Jane (Miss), 1842-1926 (St. Mary's Episcopal Church Cemetery' Death certificate)

Munnikhuysen, James Carvel, see Edward Pearce Munnikhuysen, q.v.

Munnikhuysen, Leila (Miss), 1855-1905 (St. Mary's Episcopal Church Cemetery; Death certificate)

Munnikhuysen, Loula (Amoss), 1886-1987 (Fallston Methodist Church Cemetery)

Munnikhuysen, Louisa (Wyatt), 1835-1812, wife of William Munnikhuysen, q.v.; also see Fannie Lee Munnikhuysen and Hall Lee Munnikhuysen, q.v.

Munnikhuysen, Louise Wyatt, 1877-1965 (Christ Episcopal Church Cemetery)

Munnikhuysen, Lutine (Keen), 1881-1978 (Christ Episcopal Church Cemetery)

Munnikhuysen, Mary (Howard), 1847-1921 (St. Mary's Episcopal Church Cemetery)

Munnikhuysen, Nannie (Miss), dancing student, Archer Institute, Bel Air (*The Aegis & Intelligencer*, 6 Jun 1890)

Munnikhuysen, Novilla (Paul), 1886-1965 (St. Mary's Episcopal Church Cemetery)

Munnikhuysen, Olivia Jane, 1844-1926 (St. Mary's Episcopal Church Cemetery)

Munnikhuysen, Robert Baker, 1879-1970 (Christ Episcopal Church Cemetery)

Munnikhuysen, Virginia (Reid), 1876-1960 (Christ Episcopal Church Cemetery), wife of Hall Lee Munnikhuysen, q.v.

Munnikhuysen, W. Francis, 1889-1928 (St. Mary's Episcopal Church Cemetery)

Munnikhuysen, W. T. (Mrs.), premium award winner, Class K - Household and Domestic Manufactures, Harford County Fair (*The Aegis & Intelligencer*, 24 Oct 1890)

Munnikhuysen, Wakeman Bryarly, 1845-1903, physician, Third District (*Havre de Grace Republican*, 4 Jul

1890)

Munnikhuysen, Wakeman Bryarly, Jr., 1890-1944 (St. Mary's Episcopal Church Cemetery)

Munnikhuysen, William, 1836-1917 (Christ Episcopal Church Cemetery); tax collector, First District (*The Aegis & Intelligencer*, 25 Jul 1890); see Fannie Lee Munnikhuysen and Hall Lee Munnikhuysen, q.v.

Munnikhuysen, William Temmick, 1860-1918 (Christ Episcopal Church Cemetery)

Murphy, Albert, sneak boat duck hunter, 1890 (*Havre de Grace Republican*, 7 Nov 1890)

Murphy, Alice P., see Mary Slade, q.v.

Murphy, Anna Marie, 1885-1965 (St. Ignatius Catholic Church Cemetery)

Murphy, Annie Lee, born 28 Nov 1885, daughter of John Thomas and Mary Alice (Kenly) Murphy (*Barnes-Bailey Genealogy,* by Walter D. Barnes, 1939, p. H-9)

Murphy, Benjamin D., 1840-1931 (St. George's Episcopal Church Cemetery)

Murphy, Bessie I. (Cathcart), 1873-1934 (St. Mary's Catholic Church Cemetery)

Murphy, Bridget M. (Furlong), 1849-1936 (St. Ignatius Catholic Church Cemetery); native of Ireland, born 17 Mar 1849, daughter of Nicholas Furlong and ---- (Bailey Funeral Home Records); second wife of Cornelius Murphy, q.v.

Murphy, Catherine, see Esther Crow Knight and Robert Bernard Knight, q.v.

Murphy, Catherine S., 1809-1893 (St. George's Episcopal Church Cemetery)

Murphy, Catherine T., 1867-1905 (St. Ignatius Catholic Church Cemetery)

Murphy, Cora, see Mary J. Walker, q.v.

Murphy, Cornelius, 1839-1909, native of County Kerry Ireland (St. Ignatius Catholic Church Cemetery); widower, age 45 *(sic)* in 1889 (Marriage License Applications Book ALJ No. 2, 1889); see Jeremiah J. Murphy, q.v.

Murphy, Cornelius F., 1877-1933 (St. Mary's Catholic Church Cemetery)

Murphy, Edna, 1885-1950, native of Havre de Grace, born 28 Feb 1885, daughter of Isaac D. Murphy and Alice Hamby (Pennington Funeral Home Records - married name Leicht)

Murphy, Ellen P. (Dignan), 1884-1928 (Angel Hill Cemetery); native of Maryland, born 25 Dec 1884, daughter of Patrick Dignan and ----, natives of Ireland (Death certificate)

Murphy, Frank, 1873-1952 (Mt. Erin Cemetery)

Murphy, Frank, born 17 May 1889, son of John Thomas and Mary Alice (Kenly) Murphy (*Barnes-Bailey Genealogy,* by Walter D. Barnes, 1939, p. H-9)

Murphy, Frank P., 1849-1890 (Angel Hill Cemetery); hotel keeper, Havre de Grace (*Havre de Grace Republican*, 9 May 1890); deceased and removed from the Havre de Grace voter registration list (*Havre de Grace Republican*, 19 Sep 1890)

Murphy, Frederick Francis, 1883-1951 (St. Mary's Catholic Church Cemetery); born -- Sep 1883, baptized 4 Nov 1883, son of James and Josephine (Kolling) Murphy (St. Ignatius Catholic Church Baptism Register, p. 69)

Murphy, George (colored), see Mary Liza Murphy (colored), q.v.

Murphy, Harry, 1880-1916, son of John Thomas and Mary Alice (Kenly) Murphy (*Barnes-Bailey Genealogy,* by Walter D. Barnes, 1939, p. H-9)

Murphy, Henry, employee at Pope's Mill (*The Aegis & Intelligencer*, 12 Dec 1890)

Murphy, Henry T., 1858-1929 (Darlington Cemetery)

Murphy, Hettie, 1871-1910 (St. Ignatius Catholic Church Cemetery)

Murphy, James, 1852-1929 (St. Mary's Catholic Church Cemetery)

Murphy, Isaac D., see Edna Murphy, q.v.

Murphy, James (colored), Civil War veteran, Carsins Run (*1890 Special Census of the Civil War Veterans of the*

State of Maryland, by L. Tilden Moore, Volume III, p. 66)

Murphy, James, 1852-1929 (St. Mary's Catholic Church Cemetery)

Murphy, James, baptized 27 Dec 1881, son of James and Josephine (Kolling) Murphy (St. Ignatius Catholic Church Baptismal Register, p. 57)

Murphy, Jeremiah Joseph, born 16 Feb 1883, baptized 6 May 1883, son of Cornelius and Deborah (Sullivan) Murphy (St. Ignatius Catholic Church Baptism Register, p. 65; Bethel Presbyterian Church Cemetery Records stated born 1882 and died 1937)

Murphy, John, 1820-1904 (St. Ignatius Catholic Church Cemetery)

Murphy, John, Jr., died 21 Jul 1890 (St. Ignatius Catholic Church Cemetery)

Murphy, John Thomas, 1851-1924 (Angel Hill Cemetery); member, Susquehanna Court No. 70, Equitable League of America, of Havre de Grace (*Havre de Grace Republican*, 11 Apr 1890)

Murphy, Josephine (Kolling), 1853-1932, native of Pennsylvania (St. Mary's Catholic Church Cemetery; St. Ignatius Catholic Church Baptismal Register, p. 57); wife of James Murphy, q.v.

Murphy, Lee L., 1877-1953, native of Maryland, born 10 May 1877, son of William Murphy and Phoebe Griffith (Pennington Funeral Home Records)

Murphy, Lemuel Whitaker, 1847-1925 (Angel Hill Cemetery); grocery store merchant, Fountain Street, Havre de Grace (*Havre de Grace Republican*, 19 Dec 1890); member, Susquehanna Lodge No. 130, A.F. & A. M., Havre de Grace (*Havre de Grace Republican*, 11 Jul 1890); organizer and vice president, Havre de Grace Democratic Club (*Havre de Grace Republican*, 31 Oct 1890); former city councilman, Havre de Grace (*Havre de Grace Republican*, 10 Jan 1890)

Murphy, Lulu Alice, (Miss), born 16 Mar 1883, daughter of John Thomas and Mary Alice (Kenly) Murphy (*Barnes-Bailey Genealogy*, by Walter D. Barnes, 1939, p. H-9)

Murphy, Margaret, sold land in May 1890 (*The Aegis & Intelligencer*, 6 Jun 1890)

Murphy, Margaret, see Henry T. Norris, q.v.

Murphy, Mary (colored), see Daniel Osborne (colored), q.v.

Murphy, Mary Alice (Kenly), 1855-1898 (St. Ignatius Catholic Church Cemetery)

Murphy, Mary Ann, see J. Elmer Heaps, q.v.

Murphy, Mary Liza (colored), 1878-1931, native of Hopewell, Harford Co., born 14 May 1878, daughter of George Murphy, of North Carolina, and Frances Bosley, of Georgia (Death certificate - married name Lee)

Murphy, Mary Louisa (Burke), 1850-1926 (Angel Hill Cemetery); wife of Lemuel Whitaker Murphy, q.v.

Murphy, Mary S., acquired land in November 1890 (*The Aegis & Intelligencer*, 5 Dec 1890)

Murphy, Michael, member, Independent Social Club, Havre de Grace (*Havre de Grace Republican*, 28 Mar 1890); council door keeper, Beneficial Order of Equity, Havre de Grace (*Havre de Grace Republican*, 21 Nov 1890); served on a petit jury (*The Aegis & Intelligencer*, 14 Nov 1890)

Murphy, Owen P., 1854-1924 (St. Ignatius Catholic Church Cemetery)

Murphy, Phoebe M. (Griffith), c1848-1920 (Death certificate)

Murphy, Sarah, 1797-1893 (St. Ignatius Catholic Church Cemetery)

Murphy, Sarah E., see May J. Laird, q.v.

Murphy, Susan A. (Miss), 1841-1925 (St. George's Episcopal Church Cemetery)

Murphy, Susannah, born -- Oct 1888, baptized 18 Nov 1888, daughter of James Murphy, native of Harford Co., and Josephine Kolling, native of Pennsylvania (St. Ignatius Catholic Church Baptism Register, p. 102)

Murphy, Thomas, student, LaGrange School No. 14, Fourth District (*The Aegis & Intelligencer*, 25 Apr 1890)

Murphy, Thomas F., 1873-1919 (St. Mary's Catholic Church Cemetery)

Murphy, William, see Lee L. Murphy, q.v.

Murphy, William H., 1844-1913 (*Barnes-Bailey Genealogy,* by Walter D. Barnes, 1939, p. H-9); sink boat duck hunter (*Havre de Grace Republican,* 7 Nov 1890)

Murphy, William J., Civil War veteran, Havre de Grace (*1890 Special Census of the Civil War Veterans of the State of Maryland,* by L. Tilden Moore, Volume III, p. 89)

Murray, Anna G., 1888-1918 (St. Francis de Sales Catholic Church Cemetery)

Murray, Annie, see Lida Poplar and William M. Poplar, q.v.

Murray, Bertha (colored), 1888-1921, native of Sharon, Harford Co., born 18 Dec 1888, daughter of Spencer Murray and Georgianna Turner (Death certificate)

Murray, Bertha F., 1883-1965 (Mt. Erin Cemetery)

Murray, Bertha (Magness), 1884-1949 (Union Chapel Methodist Church Cemetery)

Murray, Bridget, 1832-1918 (Mt. Erin Cemetery)

Murray, Catharine Theresa, 1872-1895 (Mt. Erin Cemetery)

Murray, Dennis, died 27 Jun 1890, adult, age not given (*The Aegis & Intelligencer,* 4 Jul 1890; St. Mary's Catholic Church Cemetery)

Murray, Ellis (colored), 1890-1928 (Federal Hill Cemetery); native of Harford Co., son of Spencer Murray and Georgeann Turner (Death certificate)

Murray, George (colored), see Jessie Murray (colored), q.v.

Murray, George C., 1884-1928 (Union Chapel Methodist Church Cemetery)

Murray, Hugh J., committeeman, Knights of St. Leo, Havre de Grace (*Havre de Grace Republican,* 19 Sep 1890); member, Young Men's Pleasure Club, Havre de Grace (*Havre de Grace Republican,* 21 Nov 1890)

Murray, James F., 1868-1932 (Mt. Erin Cemetery)

Murray, Jessie (colored), 1862-1926 (Abingdon Colored Cemetery); laborer, married, resided at Edgewood, son of George Murray, native of Georgia, and ---- (Death certificate)

Murray, John, 1832-1895, native of County Monohan, Ireland (Mt. Erin Cemetery)

Murray, Katie (colored), 1872-1932 (Death certificate; St. James United Cemetery)

Murray, Maria (Miss), 1869-1926 Churchville Presbyterian Church Cemetery); native of Pennsylvania, resided in Churchville and later in Havre de Grace (Death certificate); secretary, Young Folks' Band of Churchville Presbyterian Church, 1890 (*Havre de Grace Republican,* 1 Aug 1890)

Murray, Mary E., 1885-1907 (Mt. Erin Cemetery)

Murray, Mary Ellen, 1868-1935 (Mt. Erin Cemetery)

Murray, Mary L., 1855-1928 (Mt. Erin Cemetery)

Murray, Russell, and wife, resided at Waverly near Bel Air (*Harford Democrat,* 25 Jul 1890)

Murray, Samuel J. (colored), 1858-1932 (Death certificate; St. James United Cemetery)

Murray, Sarah, 1865-1952 (Mt. Erin Cemetery)

Murray, Spencer (colored), see Bertha Murray (colored) and Ellis Murray (colored), q.v.

Murrell, Emeline, 1807-1900 (Wesleyan Chapel Methodist Church Cemetery)

Musser, Hugh, age 31 in 1890 (Marriage License Applications Book ALJ No. 2, 1891)

Musser, Jacob, acquired and sold land in April 1890 (*The Aegis & Intelligencer,* 9 May 1890)

Muth, Henrietta (Kohlbus), 1888-1967 (Slate Ridge Cemetery, York Co., PA); native of Street, Harford Co., born 8 Mar 1888, daughter of William H. Kohlbus and Mary E. Nichols (Harkins Funeral Home Records)

Muth, Thomas, Civil War veteran, Aberdeen (*1890 Special Census of the Civil War Veterans of the State of Maryland,* by L. Tilden Moore, Volume III, p. 63)

Muttonburg Colored Public School No. 3, near Cedars, Third District (*Harford County, Maryland Teachers and the Schools They Served, 1774-1900,* by Henry C. Peden, Jr., 2022, p. 371)

Mutual Protection Society, Havre de Grace (*Havre de Grace: Its Historic Past, Its Charming Present and Its Promising Future: Harford County's Rural Heritage.* by Jack L. Shagena, Jr. and Henry C. Peden, Jr., 2018, p. 270)

Myer, Ira, young man, resided near Pylesville (*The Aegis & Intelligencer*, 7 Feb 1890)

Myer, Margaret J., 1839-1908 (St. Mary's Catholic Church Cemetery)

Myers, Bertie May, 1888-1958 (Angel Hill Cemetery)

Myers, Bertie S., 1882-1900 (Ange Hill Cemetery); daughter of George Myers and ----, of Havre de Grace (Death certificate)

Myers, Beulah (Ricketts), 1883-1979 (Angel Hill Cemetery)

Myers, Eliza R. (Lawder), 1840-1925 (Wesleyan Chapel Cemetery; Death certificate)

Myers, Elizabeth (Russell), 1863-1928 (Angel Hill Cemetery; Death certificate)

Myers, Elizabeth M., 1868-1944 (Angel Hill Cemetery)

Myers, Florence H., 1883-1958 (Ayres Chapel Methodist Church Cemetery)

Myers, Frances, wife of Henry Myers (1826-1901), q.v.

Myers, Frank, 1862-1926 (Angel Hill Cemetery); native of Italy, married, resided in Havre de Grace (Death certificate)

Myers, Fred Joseph, 1884-1961 (Baker Cemetery)

Myers, Frederick H., 1890-1960 (Trinity Evangelical Lutheran Church Cemetery)

Myers, George T., 1855-1918 (Angel Hill Cemetery); member, Guiding Star Council No. 9, Jr. O. U. A. M., Havre de Grace (*Havre de Grace Republican*, 11 Jul 1890); musician and president, Bayside Cornet Band, Havre de Grace (*Havre de Grace Republican*, 31 Jan and 24 Oct 1890); see Bertie Myers and Stephen C. Myers, q.v.

Myers, Georgianna L., 1848-1922 (Angel Hill Cemetery)

Myers, Grace, 1889-1964, native of Harford Co., born 23 Aug 1889, daughter of John Myers and ---- (Pennington Funeral Home Records - married name Lawder)

Myers, Harry E., 1868-1893 (St. George's Episcopal Church Cemetery); age 25 *(sic)* in 1890 (Marriage License Applications Book ALJ No. 2, 1891)

Myers, Henry, resident on Gunpowder Neck below Magnolia (*The Aegis & Intelligencer*, 18 Jul 1890)

Myers, Henry, 1826-1901, native of Lancaster Co., PA. laborer, resided at Harkins, Harford Co. (Death certificate)

Myers, Irene H., born 1889, died ---- (Trinity Evangelical Lutheran Church Cemetery)

Myers, John, see Grace Myers, q.v.

Myers, John Dorus, 1887-1978 (Angel Hill Cemetery)

Myers, John K., 1817-1906 (Angel Hill Cemetery)

Myers, Mabel M., 1889-1982 (Mt. Zion Methodist Church Cemetery)

Myers, Mary A. (Ergood), 1827-1890 (Angel Hill Cemetery); daughter of Jacob Ergood, of Havre de Grace (*The Aegis & Intelligencer*, 17 Jan 1890)

Myers, Mary E., 1829-1907 (Angel Hill Cemetery); businesswoman (trader's license), Havre de Grace (*Havre de Grace Republican*, 30 May 1890); Mrs. John Myers, first vice president, Women's Christian Temperance Union, of Havre de Grace (*Havre de Grace Republican*, 19 Sep 1890)

Myers, Mary Jane, see Charles Henry Glackin, q.v.

Myers, Mattie, county out-pensioner [welfare recipient], Third District (*Havre de Grace Republican*, 4 Jul 1890)

Myers, Rachel, see William Hildt, q.v.

Myers, Robert Seneca, 1881-1951, native of Havre de Grace, boern 17 Jan 1881, sonof William A. Myers and

Georgianna Lawder (Pennington Funeral Home Records)

Myers, Stephen Clyde, 1884-1951, native of Havre de Grace, born 17 Mar 1884, son of George T. Myers and Elizabeth Russell (Pennington Funeral Home Records)

Myers, Teny (Miss), age 16, of Havre de Grace (*The Aegis & Intelligencer*, 11 Jul 1890)

Myers, Vallie R., 1877-1915 (William Watters Memorial Church Cemetery, Cooptown)

Myers, W. Ransom, 1872-1933 (Angel Hill Cemetery)

Myers, Wallace T., 1884-1923 (Ayres Chapel Methodist Church Cemetery)

Myers, William A., 1836-1903 (Angel Hill Cemetery); waterman and sink boat duck hunter; native and resident of Havre de Grace (Death certificate; *Havre de Grace Republican*, 7 Nov 1890); see Robert S. Myers, q.v.

Nagle & Hanson's General Store, Churchville, John H. Nagle and Aquila B. Hanson, prop. (*Country Stores: Harford County's Rural Heritage*, by Henry C. Peden, Jr. and Jack L. Shagena, Jr., 2015, p. 783

Nagle, Albert Clinton, 1887-1932 (Centre Methodist Church Cemetery); born 17 Mar 1887, son of Samuel O. and Margaret Ann Nagle (Samuel O. Nagle Bible, *Maryland Bible Records, Volume 1*, by Henry C. Peden, Jr., 2003, p. 187)

Nagle, Anna Margaret, born 29 Sep 1883, daughter of Samuel O. and Margaret Ann Nagle (Samuel O. Nagle Bible, *Maryland Bible Records, Volume 1*, by Henry C. Peden, Jr., 2003, p. 187); student, Forest Hill School, 1890 (*The Aegis*, 2 Jul 1965, school picture)

Nagle, Charles Chapman, born 27 Jul 1870, son of Emanuel and Elizabeth Howe Nagle (John Nagle Bible, *Maryland Bible Records, Volume 1*, by Henry C. Peden, Jr., 2003, p. 184); employee of Bulett Carriage Factory, Bel Air (*The Aegis & Intelligencer*, 9 May 1890); competitive bicycle rider, Harford County Fair (*Havre de Grace Republican*, 26 Sep 1890; *The Aegis & Intelligencer*, 19 Sep 1890)

Nagle, Daniel S., Sr., of Harford County, moved to Sparrows Point, Baltimore County (*The Aegis & Intelligencer*, 21 Mar 1890)

Nagle, Della May, 1882-1912 (Samuel O. Nagle Bible, *Maryland Bible Records, Volume 1*, by Henry C. Peden, Jr., 2003, p. 187); student, Forest Hill School, 1890 (*The Aegis*, 2 Jul 1965, school picture)

Nagle, Elizabeth (Howe), 1827-1908, wife of Emanuel Nagle, q.v.

Nagle, Elizabeth Reich (Hutchinson), 1850-1910 (Churchville Presbyterian Church Cemetery); see Mary Hutchinson Nagle, q.v.

Nagle, Emanuel, 1822-1906 (Emory Methodist Church Cemetery; John Nagle Bible, *Maryland Bible Records, Volume 1*, by Henry C. Peden, Jr., 2003, pp. 184-185); resided on *Medical Hall* farm near Churchville (*Harford Democrat*, 8 Aug 1890)

Nagle, Esther Bateman, born 20 Apr 1879, daughter of Thomas Franklin Nagle and Elizabeth Reich Hutchinson (Churchville Presbyterian Church Register Roll of Infant Church Members or Baptized Children, No. 315)

Nagle, Florence (Livezey), 1869-1943 (Mt. Zion Methodist Church Cemetery); wife of John H. Nagle, q.v.

Nagle, John Henry, 1864-1951, son of Emanuel and Elizabeth Howe Nagle (John Nagle Bible, *Maryland Bible Records, Volume 1*, by Henry C. Peden, Jr., 2003, p. 184); storekeeper, Churchville, insolvent, 1889-1890 (*The Aegis & Intelligencer*, 13 Dec 1889, 14 Feb 1890 and 28 Mar 1890); moved to *Woodside* farm near Fountain Green (*Harford Democrat*, 30 May 1890)

Nagle, Laura Ellen, born 7 Sep 1866, daughter of Emanuel and Elizabeth Howe Nagle (John Nagle Bible, *Maryland Bible Records, Volume 1*, by Henry C. Peden, Jr., 2003, p. 184) age 23 in 1889 (Marriage License Applications Book ALJ No. 2, 1889)

Nagle, Linn Kieffer, born 24 Oct 1881, son of Thomas Franklin Nagle and Elizabeth Reich Hutchinson (Churchville Presbyterian Church Register Roll of Infant Church Members or Baptized Children, No. 316)

Nagle, Louise, student, Forest Hill School, 1890 (*The Aegis*, 2 Jul 1965, school picture)

Nagle, Margaret Ann, 1863-1947 (Centre Methodist Church Cemetery); wife of Samuel Owen Nagle, q.v.

Nagle, Margaret H., 1872-1949 (Good Will Church Cemetery)

Nagle, Mary Hutchinson, born 19 Dec 1888, baptized 29 Jan 1889, daughter of Thomas F. and Elizabeth R. Nagle (Holy Trinity Episcopal Church Register of Baptisms, p. 96)

Nagle, Millard Howe, 1890-1970 (Mt. Zion Methodist Church Cemetery); son of John H. and Florence Nagle (John H. Nagle Bible, *Maryland Bible Records, Volume 1*, by Henry C. Peden, Jr., 2003, p. 186)

Nagle, Oleita Harlan, born -- Aug 1883, daughter of Thomas Franklin Nagle and Elizabeth Reich Hutchinson (Churchville Presbyterian Church Register Roll of Infant Church Members or Baptized Children, No. 321)

Nagle, Rebecca J., died 20 Jan 1890, age 71 (William Watters Memorial Church Cemetery)

Nagle, Samuel Owen, born 8 Apr 1858, son of Emanuel and Elizabeth Howe Nagle (John Nagle Bible and Samuel O. Nagle Bible, *Maryland Bible Records, Volume 1*, by Henry C. Peden, Jr., 2003, pp. 184, 187, 188)

Nagle, Thomas Franklin, 1851-1908 (Churchville Presbyterian Church Cemetery); trustee, Thomas Run School No. 9, Third District (*Havre de Grace Republican*, 30 May 1890); also see Mary Hutchinson Nagle, q.v.

Nagle, Thomas H., farmer, Thomas Run (*The Aegis & Intelligencer*, 2 May 1890)

Nagle, Walter Chapman, 1889-1912 (Centre Methodist Church Cemetery); born 8 Dec 1889, son of Samuel O. and Margaret Ann Nagle (Samuel O. Nagle Bible, *Maryland Bible Records, Volume 1*, by Henry C. Peden, Jr., 2003, p. 187)

Nagle, William Stephenson, born 13 Jun 1880, son of Thomas Franklin Nagle and Elizabeth Reich Hutchinson (Churchville Presbyterian Church Register Roll of Infant Church Members or Baptized Children, No. 316)

Nash, Joseph W., new name on the voter registration list at Hall's Cross Roads, Second District (*Havre de Grace Republican*, 17 Oct 1890)

Neal, Harry, member, Mountain Reading Circle (*The Aegis & Intelligencer*, 21 Feb 1890)

Neal, Ella M. (Hopkins), 1860-1928, resided near Norrisville (Death certificate misfiled as Meal)

Neal, Lizzie, student, Aberdeen Public School (*The Aegis & Intelligencer*, 23 May 1890)

Neal, Mary (Healy), 1875-1955 (Church of the Ascension Cemetery); native of Harford Co., born 15 Jul 1875, daughter of William W. Neal and Martha Rigdon (Bailey Funeral Home Records)

Neal, William W., see Mary Neal, q.v.

Neeper, Charles R., 1875-1947 (Slateville Cemetery, York Co., PA); native of Maryland, born 24 Jun 1875, son of William K. Neeper and Sally Ann Davis (Harkins Funeral Home Records)

Neeper, Clara "Clair" (Beard), 1862-1953 (Tabernacle Cemetery); native of Harford Co., born 17 Oct 1862, daughter of James Beard and Mary Norris (Harkins Funeral Home Records)

Neeper, J. Edwin, 1868-1947 (Slateville Cemetery, York Co., PA); native of Harford Co., born 21 Nvov 1868, son of William K. Neeper and Sallie A. Davis (Harkins Funeral Home Records)

Neeper, James, see Louella (Neeper) Doyle, q.v.

Neeper, James K., see Samuel J. Neeper, q.v.

Neeper, Mary A., see Mary A. Bay, q.v.

Neeper, Nelson B., 1808-1910 (Tabernacle Cemetery)

Neeper, Sadie A., born 1882, died 19-- (North Bend Presbyterian Church Cemetery)

Neeper, Samuel J., 1867-1940 (Slate Ridge Cemetery, York Co., PA); native of Harford Co., born 17 Jul 1867, son of James K. Neeper and Sarah E. McFadden (Bailey Funeral Home Records); age 22 in 1889 (Marriage License Applications Book ALJ No. 2, 1890)

Neeper, William K., see Charles R. Neeper, J. Edwin Neeper and Mary A. Bay, q.v.

Neeper, William M., 1873-1923 (North Bend Presbyterian Church Cemetery)

Neeper, William Nelson, 1869-1932 (Tabernacle Cemetery)

Neidlein, Henry, 1858-1936 (Angel Hill Cemetery); juror, Sixth District, 1890 (*Havre de Grace Republican*, 31 Oct 1890)

Neidlein, John H., Jr., 1889-1980 (Angel Hill Cemetery)

Neidlein, John H., Sr., 1860-1942 (Angel Hill Cemetery)

Neidlein, Wilhelmina H. ("Minnie"), 1862-1923 (Angel Hill Cemetery)

Neild, Howard, former assistant railroad agent, Perryman (*Havre de Grace Republican*, 11 Apr 1890)

Neild, J. N., assistant agent. P. W. & B. Railroad, Perryman (*The Aegis & Intelligencer*, 2 May 1890)

Neilson, James Crawford, 1816-1900 (Priestford Cemetery)

Neilson, James Crawford, 1881-1942 (Darlington Cemetery)

Neilson, Louisa G. (Wright), died 1893 (Priestford Cemetery)

Neilson, Rosa (Williams), 1818-1904 (Priestford Cemetery)

Neiter, Conrad M., 1871-1903 (Mountain Christian Church Cemetery)

Neiter, Elizabeth Louisa, 1873-1901 (Mountain Christian Church Cemetery)

Neiter, Leonard, new name on the voter registration list at Magnolia, First District (*Havre de Grace Republican*, 26 Sep 1890)

Neilson, Nicholas, 1839-1895, native of Hemgundam, Hesse Darmstadt, Germany (Mountain Christian Church Cemetery)

Neilson, P. Leonard, 1860-1915 (Mountain Christian Church Cemetery)

Neilson, Regina Magdalena, 1845-1907, native of Schlnbach, Wunemburg, Germany (Mountain Christian Church Cemetery)

Neiper, Sarah A., see Elisha Davis, q.v.

Neiter, Conrad M., 1871-1903 (Mountain Christian Church Cemetery)

Neiter, Edward, telegraph operator, Edgewood (*Harford Democrat*, 21 Feb 1890)

Neiter, Elizabeth Louisa, 1873-1895 (Mountain Christian Church Cemetery)

Neiter, Nicholas, 1839-1905 (Mountain Christian Church Cemetery)

Neiter, P. Leonard, 1860-1915 (Mountain Christian Church Cemetery)

Neiter, Regina Magdalena, 1845-1907 (Mountain Christian Church Cemetery)

Nelson, Alverta, born 27 Jan 1873, daughter of William Nelson and Betsy Moore (Bethel Presbyterian Church Cemetery Records)

Nelson, Aquila H., 1841-1894 (St. George's Episcopal Church Cemetery); see Elizabeth Keen Nelson, Emily Cowan Nelson, Isabelle Nelson and Mary Ella Nelson, q.v.

Nelson, Augusta L., 1863-1934 (St. George's Episcopal Church Cemetery)

Nelson, Bennett V., 1853-1905 (St. George's Episcopal Church Cemetery)

Nelson, Bettie, see William Thomas Anderson, q.v.

Nelson, Blanche, age 23, married Benjamin F. Richardson on 30 Apr 1890 at the Aberdeen Southern Methodist Parsonage (Marriage License Applications Book ALJ No. 2, 1890; *The Aegis & Intelligencer*, 9 May 1890)

Nelson, C. Irvin, 1886-1952 (Oak Grove Baptist Church Cemetery)

Nelson, C. Leroy, 1886-1946, native of Maryland, born 8 Nov 1886, son of Nicholas Nelson and Charity Luella Luckey (Bethel Presbyterian Church Cemetery Records)

Nelson, Capitola B., see Samuel E. Thompson, Jr., q.v.

Nelson, Caroline Missouri (Wiley), 1840-1917 (Bethel Presbyterian Church Cemetery Records); wife of James H. Nelson, q.v.

Nelson, Charity Luella (Luckey), 1865-1934 (Bethel Presbyterian Church Cemetery Records); wife of Nicholas Nelson, q.v.; also see C. Leroy Nelson and Mary Nelson, q.v.

Nelson, Charles B., 1840-1891 (St. George's Episcopal Church Cemetery)

Nelson, Charles E., 1844-1910 (Christ Episcopal Church Cemetery); tobacco farmer, near Chestnut Hill (*The Aegis & Intelligencer*, 7 Nov 1890); member, Almshouse Committee, Bel Air (*The Aegis & Intelligencer*, 28 Feb 1890); juror (*Havre de Grace Republican*, 31 Jan 1890)

Nelson, Charles E., 1864-1890 (Cokesbury Memorial Methodist Church Cemetery)

Nelson, Effie Lizzie (Michael), 1862-1956 (St. George's Episcopal Church Cemetery); see Mary Susanna Nelson, q.v.

Nelson, Eliza S., 1852-1938 (Christ Episcopal Church Cemetery)

Nelson, Elizabeth, born 8 Jan 1883, daughter of Thomas H.Nelson and Isabelle Ashton (Bethel Presbyterian Church Cemetery Records)

Nelson, Elizabeth (Streett), 1866-1947 (Bethel Presbyterian Church Cemetery Records); second wife of Thomas Rush Nelson, q.v.

Nelson, Elizabeth A., 1828-1924 (St. George's Episcopal Church Cemetery)

Nelson, Elizabeth B., 1810-1894 (Bethel Presbyterian Church Cemetery Records); wife of cousin Robert Nelson, q.v.

Nelson, Elizabeth Keen, 1885-1981 (www.findagrave.com - married name Streett), born 22 Feb 1885, daughter of Aquila H. Nelson and Mary M. Michael (St. George's Episcopal Church Register of Baptisms, pp. 4-5)

Nelson, Elizabeth S., 1848-1931 (St. Mary's Catholic Church Cemetery)

Nelson, Ella, 1864-1899, dressmaker in Aberdeen, native of Maryland, daughter of Bennett Nelson and Elizabeth ---- (Death certificate)

Nelson, Ellen (Hope), 1822-1899 (Bethel Presbyterian Church Cemetery Records); wife of Joshua Nelson, q.v.

Nelson, Emily B., 1879-1958 (Christ Episcopal Church Cemetery)

Nelson, Emily Cowan, born 18 Apr 1889, daughter of A. H. Nelson and Mary ---- (St. George's Episcopal Church Register of Baptisms, p. 8)

Nelson, Estelle (Reppard), 1871-1902 (Bethel Presbyterian Church Cemetery Records); first wife of Thomas Rush Nelson, q.v.

Nelson, F. Arthur, 1877-1910 (Grove Presbyterian Church Cemetery)

Nelson, Fannie W., born 24 Sep 1876, daugter of John Thomas Nelson and Octavia Luckey (Bethel Presbyterian Church Cemetery Records)

Nelson, Florence M., 1855-1911 (St. George's Episcopal Church Cemetery)

Nelson, Frank M., 1881-1948 (Mt. Zion Methodist Church Cemetery)

Nelson, Frederick, 1849-1921 (St. George's Episcopal Church Cemetery); see Mary Susanna Nelson, q.v.

Nelson, George A., 1829-1904 (St. George's Episcopal Church Cemetery); see Sarah E. Cole, q.v.

Nelson Grace L., born 27 Sep 1885, daughter of John Thomas Nelson and Octavia Luckey (Bethel Presbyterian Church Cemetery Records)

Nelson, Harriet A., 1849-1898 (St. George's Episcopal Church Cemetery)

Nelson, Henry Clay, 1844-1911 (St. George's Episcopal Church Cemetery); farmer, *Skipper Hill Farm* on Romney Neck near Perryman (*The Aegis & Intelligencer*, 14 Mar 1890)

Nelson, Horatio, 1847-1904 (Bethel Presbyterian Church Cemetery Records)

Nelson, Horatio (Mrs.), resident of Federal Hill (*The Aegis & Intelligencer*, 7 Feb 1890)

Nelson, Isabel C., 1843-1926 (Bethel Presbyterian Church Cemetery Records)

Nelson, Isabelle, 1883-1922, native of Maryland, resided at Rocks, Harford Co., born 20 Dec 1883, daughter of Aquila H. Nelson and Mary M. Michael (Death certificate; St. George's Episcopal Church Register of Baptisms, pp. 2-3)

Nelson, J. Milton, 1877-1939 (St. Mary's Catholic Church Cemetery)

Nelson, James H., 1835-1913 (Bethel Presbyterian Church Cemetery Records)

Nelson, Jennie C., 1883-1966 (Mt. Erin Cemetery)

Nelson, John N., 1850-1925 (St. Mary's Catholic Church Cemetery)

Nelson, John S., 1882-1967 (Mt. Erin Cemetery)

Nelson, John Thomas, 1848-1924 (Bethel Presbyterian Church Cemetery Records)

Nelson, Luma E., 1881-1937 (Mt. Zion Methodist Church Cemetery)

Nelson, M. Ella, 1858-1899 (St. George's Episcopal Church Cemetery)

Nelson, Margaret Sim(?), 1863-1923 (Christ Episcopal Church Cemetery)

Nelson, Martha M., 1870-1904 (St. George's Episcopal Church Cemetery)

Nelson, Mary, born 10 Jul 1889, daughter of Nicholas Nelson and Charity Luella Luckey (Bethel Presbyterian Church Cemetery Records)

Nelson, Mary, see Elizabeth Keen Nelson, Emily Cowan Nelson, Mary Ella Nelson and Isabel Nelson, q.v.

Nelson, Mary A. (Henderson), 1816-1900, resided at Perryman (Death certificate; St. George's Episcopal Church Cemetery)

Nelson, Mary Ella, 1887-1969 (www.findagrave.com - married name Ford); born 23 Dec 1887, daughter of Aquila H. Nelson and Mary M Michael (St. George's Episcopal Church Register of Baptisms, p. 7)

Nelson, Mary M., 1851-1929 (St. Mary's Catholic Church Cemetery)

Nelson, Mary Susanna, 1883-1953, native of Harford Co., born 1 Dec 1883, daughter of Frederick Nelson and Effie L. Michael (St. George's Episcopal Church Register of Baptisms, pp. 2-3; St. George's Episcopal Church Cemetery - married name Smithson; Bailey Funeral Home Records)

Nelson, Mary Wilson (Dallam), 1859-1931 (Christ Episcopal Church Cemetery)

Nelson, Maude, born 1871, daughter of Thomas Hope Nelson and Isabella C. Ashton (Bethel Presbyterian Church Cemetery Records); see Maude (Nelson) Wiley, q.v.

Nelson, Milton, sixth grade student, Mount Horeb School (*The Aegis & Intelligencer*, 14 Feb 1890)

Nelson, Nicholas, 1861-1933 (Bethel Presbyterian Church Cemetery Records)

Nelson, Octavia (Luckey), 1854-1938 (Bethel Presbyterian Church Cemetery Records); wife of John Thomas Nelson, q.v.

Nelson, Olivia (Hutchins) (Hope), 1848-1940 (Bethel Presbyterian Church Cemetery Records); wife of first Joshua Hope and secondly of William H. Nelson, q.v.

Nelson, Robert A., 1840-1897, carriage maker, Bond Street, Bel Air (*Carriages Back in the Day: Harford County's Rural Heritage*, by Jack L. Shagena, Jr. and Henry C. Peden, Jr., 2016, p. 85)

Nelson, Sarah E. (Mrs.), mother-in-law of J. Fred Crew, of near Dublin (*The Aegis & Intelligencer*, 26 Dec 1890)

Nelson, Sarah H., 1831-1902 (Angel Hill Cemetery)

Nelson, Sarah N. (Kimble), 1839-1914 (St. George's Episcopal Church Cemetery)

Nelson, Susan R., 1847-1915 (Darlington Cemetery)

Nelson, Thomas Hope, 1839-1908 (Bethel Presbyterian Church Cemetery Records); director, Mutual Fire Insurance Company in Harford County (*The Aegis & Intelligencer*, 10 Jan 1890)

Nelson, Thomas Rush 1864-1948 (Bethel Presbyterian Church Cemetery Records); served on a petit jury, Third District (*The Aegis & Intelligencer*, 14 Nov 1890)

Nelson, Thomas W. (colored), trustee, School No. 9, Fourth District (*The Aegis & Intelligencer*, 22 Aug 1890)

Nelson, Tittle, alias Gray Nelson, Civil War veteran, Blakc Horsd (*1890 Special Census of the Civil War Veterans of the State of Maryland*, by L. Tilden Moore, Volume III, p. 79)

Nelson, W. Hervey, born 1886, son of Thomas Hope Nelson and Isabelle Ashton (Bethel Presbyterian Church

Cemetery Records)

Nelson, William Burrows, 1860-1921 (Christ Episcopal Church Cemetery)

Nelson, William Hope, 1848-1924 (Bethel Presbyterian Church Cemetery); native of Harford Co., resided at Taylor (Death certificate)

Nelson, William N., 1875-1941 (Christ Episcopal Church Cemetery)

Neuwiller, Eva V., age 19 in 1890 (Marriage License Applications Book ALJ No. 2, 1890), married John H. Foreman on 12 Feb 1890 (*The Aegis & Intelligencer*, 21 Feb 1890; marriage certificate)

Neuwiller, John C., Civil War veteran, Carsins Run (*1890 Special Census of the Civil War Veterans of the State of Maryland*, by L. Tilden Moore, Volume III, p. 66)

Neville, James, see Susan R. Neville, q.v.

Neville, Susan (Robinson), 1818-1890 (Dublin Southern Cemetery); widow of James Neville (*The Aegis & Intelligencer*, 16 May 1890); died testate and her named heirs were nieces Anna Laura Robinson, Mary Esabella Robinson and Olivia Wood, and Lillie May Cole (Harford County Will Book JMM 11:105-106)

Newbolt, Harry, treated by unidentified doctor in 1890 ("Medical Account Book – 1890," Historical Society of Harford County Archives Folder)

Newman, Augustus, member of the Bel Air Cornet Band (*The Aegis & Intelligencer*, 1 Aug 1890); member of Division No. 1, Bel Air Fire and Salvage Corps (*The Aegis & Intelligencer*, 10 Oct 1890)

Newmeyer's Department Store, Havre de Grace (*1953 Harford County Directory*, p. 267)

Newmeyer, Emanuel, 1884-1954, native of Havre de Grace, born 31 Dec 1884, son of Solomon Newmeyer and Hannah Blumenthal (Pennington Funeral Home Records)

Newmeyer, Hannah (Blumenthal), 1861-1945, native of Baltimore, resident of Havre de Grace (Pennington Funeral Home Records); wife of Solomon Newmeyer, q.v.

Newmeyer, Solomon, merchant and treasurer of the Havre de Grace Mutual Protection Society (*Havre de Grace Republican*, 31 Jan 1890); organizer and vice president, Havre de Grace Democratic Club (*Havre de Grace Republican*, 31 Oct 1890); Blumenthal & Newmeyer, businessmen (trader's license), Havre de Grace, 1890 (*Havre de Grace Republican*, 30 May 1890)

Newsom, Mary, see Louanna (Rigdon) Famous, q.v.

Nicholas, Elizabeth, see George Kohlbus, q.v.

Nicholas, Emory (colored), age 35 in 1889 (Marriage License Applications Book ALJ No. 2, 1889)

Nicholas, Mary, see Price Jones, Minnie E. Smith and Henrietta Muth, q.v.

Nichols, Belle (Miss), resident of Aberdeen (*The Aegis & Intelligencer*, 31 Jan 1890)

Nichols, Emory (colored), 1854-1929, native of Maryland (Death certificate)

Nichols, Henry, Civil War veteran, Upper Cross Roads (*1890 Special Census of the Civil War Veterans of the State of Maryland*, by L. Tilden Moore, Volume III, p. 78)

Nichols, Susan (Peaker) (colored), 1861-1930, native of Maryland (Death certificate)

Nicholson, J. C. (Rev.), Methodist minister, Havre de Grace (*Havre de Grace Republican*, 21 Feb 1890)

Nickenson, Ada (Mrs.) (colored), see King David Nickenson, Jr. (colored) and Ada Williams (colored), q.v.

Nickinson, David (colored), father of Lottie Carry, q.v.

Nickenson, King David, Jr. (colored), 1874-1934, native of Maryland, born 12 Apr 1874, son of King David Nickenson and Sarah Stansberry (Death certificate in 1934 and Ada Nickenson in 1919)

Nicoll, Selina "Lena" (Grafton), 1861-1927 (Old Brick Baptist Church Cemetery; Death certificate)

Nimmo, Frances (Gladden), 1886-1922 (Holy Cross Church Cemetery)

Nimmo, Rose (Miss), actress, musical entertainment, at Darlington (*The Aegis & Intelligencer*, 30 May 1890)

Nixon, James, 1832-1895 (Wesleyan Chapel Methodist Church Cemetery)

Nixon, Rachel, 1881-1954 (Emory Methodist Church Cemetery)

Noble's Mill, Nobles Mill Road at Deer Creek, Benjamin Noble, prop. (*Mills: Grist, Saw, Bone, Flint, Fulling ... & More*, by Jack L. Shagena, Jr., Henry C. Peden, Jr. and John W. McGrain, 2009, pp. 220-221)

Noble, Benjamin, 1820-1894 (Deer Creek Harmony Presbyterian Church Cemetery); see Noble's Mill, q.v.

Noble, John T., 1840-1912 (Wesleyan Chapel Methodist Church Cemetery); born 7 Aug 1840, son of James and Elizabeth Noble (James Noble Bible, *Maryland Bible Records, Volume 1*, by Henry C. Peden, Jr., 2003, p. 188)

Noble, Susannah ("Susan"), 1826-1914 (Deer Creek Harmony Presbyterian Church Cemetery)

Noble, William Henry, 1838-1892 (Wesleyan Chapel Cemetery; James Noble Bible, *Maryland Bible Records, Volume 1*, by Henry C. Peden, Jr., 2003, p. 188); see Chrome Valley Mills, q.v.

Noble, William Silver, 1853-1942 (Deer Creek Harmony Presbyterian Church Cemetery)

Nock, ----, shortstop, Bel Air Victors Baseball Club (*The Aegis & Intelligencer*, 25 Jul 1890)

Nock, Gamma (Long), 1862-1914 (Mt. Zion Methodist Church Cemetery); wife of Nicholas N. Nock, q.v.

Nock, Nicholas Norman, 1845-1911 (Mt. Zion Methodist Church Cemetery); owner and editor of the *Bel Air Times* (*The Aegis & Intelligencer*, 31 Oct 1890); member, Loyal Temperance Legion of Bel Air (*The Aegis & Intelligencer*, 2 May 1890); president, Harford County Temperance Alliance (*Havre de Grace Republican*, 18 Apr 1890); State delegate, National Republican League (*Havre de Grace Republican*, 9 May 1890);; Civil War veteran, Bel Air (*1890 Special Census of the Civil War Veterans of the State of Maryland*, by L. Tilden Moore, Volume III, p. 72); member, Division No. 2, Bel Air Fire and Salvage Corps (*The Aegis & Intelligencer*, 10 Oct 1890)

Nolan, Mary, see Catherine Agnes Casey and Elizabeth Casey, q.v.

Nolan, Mary Ellen (Quirk), 1875-1966 (Mt. Erin Cemetery)

Nolan, Patrick, c1838-1923, native of Ireland (Death certificate; Alms House Record Book)

Nonemaker, Abram P., age 32 in 1890 (Marriage License Applications Book ALJ No. 2, 1891)

Nonemaker, S., pitcher, Taylor Baseball Club (*The Aegis & Intelligencer*, 6 Jun 1890)

Nonpareil Baseball Club, of Aberdeen (*Havre de Grace Republican*, 6 Jun 1890)

Noonan, Floyd, 1877-1963 (Mt. Zion Methodist Church Cemetery)

Noonan, John C., 1850-1933 (Broad Creek Friends Cemetery)

Noonan, M. Roberta, 1879-1954 (Mt. Zion Methodist Church Cemetery)

Noonan, Martha, 1857-1921 (Broad Creek Friends Cemetery)

Norrington, Edith, born -- Feb 1890, native of Maryland, daughter of James Norrington and Martha V. ---- (1900 Aberdeen Census)

Norrington, James T., 1849-1900 (Grove Presbyterian Church Cemetery)

Norrington, Elizabeth "Lizzie" Cole, 1884-1900, native of Aberdeen, born 27 Sep 1884, daughter of James Norrington and Martha ---- (Death certificate; 1900 Aberdeen Census)

Norrington, Martha V., born -- Sep 1861, native of Maryland, wife of James Norrington (1900 Aberdeen Census)

Norrington, Mary S., born -- Sep 1886, native of Maryland, daughter of James Norrington and Martha V. ---- (1900 Aberdeen Census)

Norris' General Store, Fallston, Frank C. Norris, prop. (*Country Stores: Harford County's Rural Heritage*, by Henry C. Peden, Jr. and Jack L. Shagena, Jr., 2015, p. 185)

Norris' General Store, Cambria, Henry J. Norris, (*Country Stores: Harford County's Rural Heritage*, by Henry C. Peden, Jr. and Jack L. Shagena, Jr., 2015, p. 185)

Norris, Alexander, 1839-1905 (Cokesbury Memorial Methodist Church Cemetery); Confederate Army veteran (*Havre de Grace Republican*, 20 Jun 1890); delegate, Third District, Democrat Party Convention (*The Aegis & Intelligencer*, 5 Sep 1890); juror, Third District (*Havre de Grace Republican*, 31 Jan 1890)

Norris, Alexander P., 1845-1916 (Trinity Evangelical Lutheran Church Cemetery)

Norris, Alice, student, Union Chapel Public School (*The Aegis & Intelligencer*, 14 Mar 1890)

Norris, Alice Edna (Tipton), 1860-1938 (Cokesbury Memorial Methodist Church Cemetery)

Norris, Alice L. C., 1872-1910 (Mountain Christian Church Cemetery)

Norris, Amanda (colored), see Mary A. Lingham (colored), q.v.

Norris, Amanda J. (Beard), 1876-1954 (Slate Ridge Cemetery, York Co., PA); native of Harford Co., born 20 Feb 1876, daughter of James Beard and Mary Norris (Harkins Funeral Home Records)

Norris, Amanda Taylor (M.D.), 1849-1944 (Union Chapel Methodist Church Cemetery)

Norris, Amanda Z. (Hutchins), 1811-1894 (Norrisville Methodist Church Cemetery)

Norris, Amos, resident near Dublin (*The Aegis & Intelligencer*, 18 Jul 1890)

Norris, Andrew Jackson, 1843-1920 (St.George's Episcopal Church Cemetery)

Norris, Ann, 1809-1905 (Christ Episcopal Church Cemetery)

Norris, Anna Mary (Griffith), 1876-1943 (Union Chapel Methodist Church Cemetery)

Norris, Anna Mary, 1886-1926 (Slate Ridge Cemetery, York Co., PA - married name Miller); native of Maryland, born 6 Feb 1886, daughter of Reuben Norris and Amanda Duncan, resided near Whiteford (Death certificate)

Norris, Benjamin, 1821-1901 (William Watters Memorial Methodist Church Cemetery. Cooptown)

Norris, Benjamin, see Georgie Norris and Lida E. Norris, q.v.

Norris, Beulah J., 1890-1907, native of Maryland, resided at Whiteford, born 18 Nov 1890, daughter of Thomas N. Norris and Nancy J. Jones (Death certificate)

Norris, C., third baseman, Bel Air Victors Baseball Club (*The Aegis & Intelligencer*, 30 May 1890)

Norris, Carrie Irene (Ely), 1880-1915 (Mt. Zion Methodist Church Cemetery)

Norris, Charles P., 1860-1948, native of Harford Co. (Death certificate)

Norris, Charles W., 1840-1914 (Union Chapel Methodist Church Cemetery)

Norris, Charles W. (Mrs.), resident of Bel Air, and mother of Bessie Norris (*The Aegis & Intelligencer*, 15 Aug 1890)

Norris, Claiborne, 1882-1908 (Cokesbury Memorial Methodist Church Cemetery)

Norris, Clara Augusta, 1847-1927 (Union Chapel Methodist Church Cemetery)

Norris, Eli, resided at Hickory (*Harford Democrat*, 28 Feb 1890)

Norris, Elizabeth, 1850-1937 (Union Chapel Methodist Church Cemetery)

Norris, Elizabeth E., 1829-1907 (McKendree Methodist Church Cemetery)

Norris, Elizabeth K., 1875-1964 (Union Chapel Methodist Church Cemetery)

Norris, Elizabeth R., see Elizabeth R. Jones, q.v.

Norris, Ella (Norris), 1865-1958 (Slate Ridge Cemetery, York Co., PA); native of Whiteford, Harford Co., born 17 Sep 1865, daughter of James Norris and Sarah Wright (Harkins Funeral Home Records)

Norris, Ella (Miss), member, Union Chapel M. P. Church (*The Aegis & Intelligencer*, 10 Jan 1890)

Norris, Emma (Miss), treasurer, Union Chapel M. P. Church Sunday School (*Havre de Grace Republican*, 11 Apr 1890); see Mary Emma Norris, q.v.

Norris, Emma E., 1880-1953 (Darlington Cemetery)

Norris, Fannie, sold land in May 1890 (*The Aegis & Intelligencer*, 6 Jun 1890)

Norris, Florence L., 1860-1937 (Norrisville Methodist Church Cemetery); wife of George N. W. Norris, q.v.

Norris, Frances A. (Sanders), 1838-1924 (Union Chapel Methodist Church Cemetery), mother of James Thomas Norris, q.v.

Norris, Frank, member, Norrisville Silver Cornet Band (*The Aegis & Intelligencer*, 30 May 1890)

Norris, Frank C., 1845-1905 (Union Chapel Methodist Church Cemetery); storekeeper, Fallston (*Havre de Grace Republican*, 17 Jan 1890); see Norris' General Store, q.v.

Norris, G. Webster, 1876-1901 (Norrisville Methodist Church Cemetery)

Norris, George B., 1860-1945 (Mt. Carmel Methodist Church Cemetery)

Norris, George E., 1876-1936 (Mt. Zion Methodist Church Cemetery)

Norris, George Edgar, 1882-1933 (Cokesbury Memorial Methodist Church Cemetery)

Norris, George L., 1869-1934 (Tabernacle Cemetery); native of Cardiff, Harford Co., son of and ---- and Mary Norris (Bailey Funeral Home Records)

Norris, George N. W., 1855-1936 (Norrisville Methodist Church Cemetery); native of Baltimore Co., farmer and resident of Norrisville (Death certificate; *The Aegis & Intelligencer*, 11 Apr 1890, mistakenly reported name as George W. W. Norris)

Norris, George S., name stricken off the voter registration list at Magnolia, First District, 1890 (*Havre de Grace Republican*, 17 Oct 1890)

Norris, George S., c1850s-1928 (Cokesbury Memorial Methodist Church Cemetery); brother of Sydney (Mrs. Charles) Harward, q.v. (*The Aegis*, 9 Mar 1928)

Norris, George Smith, 1840-1912 (St. Mary's Episcopal Church Cemetery); Register of Wills, Bel Air (*Havre de Grace Republican*, 20 Jun 1890); Civil War (Confederate) veteran (*Havre de Grace Republican*, 20 Jun 1890); delegate, Democrat Convention, and president, Harford County Tariff Reform Club (*The Aegis & Intelligencer*, 5 Sep 1890); farmer near Bel Air (*The Aegis & Intelligencer*, 15 Aug 1890); president, Democratic Club (*Havre de Grace Republican*, 5 Sep 1890); warden and vestryman, Emmanuel Church, Bel Air (*Havre de Grace Republican*, 18 Apr 1890); chairman, Tariff Reform Club of Harford County (*Harford Democrat*, 5 Sep 1890)

Norris, George Washington (colored), c1839-1934 (West Liberty Church Cemetery); laborer at Upper Cross Roads, native of Harford Co., son of Henry Norris and Caroline Hicks (Death certificate)

Norris, Georgianna C. (Grey), 1823-1912 (Cokesbury Memorial Methodist Church Cemetery), wife of James Norris, q.v.

Norris, Georgie, daughter of Benjamin and Lizzie Norris, died 29 Apr 1890, age not stated (*The Aegis & Intelligencer*, 9 May 1890)

Norris, H. Mae, 1882-1935 (Norrisville Methodist Church Cemetery)

Norris, Hamilton, resided at Chrome Hill (*Harford Democrat*, 24 Jan 1890)

Norris, Hannah Elizabeth (Slade), c1824-1901, native of Maryland, resided at Cooptown (Death certificate; William Watters Memorial Methodist Church Cemetery. Cooptown)

Norris, Harriet Wharton, 1876-1894, daughter of G. Smith Norris and Mary J. --- (Mt. Carmel Methodist Church Cemetery)

Norris, Harry, c1844-1919, native of Harford Co., single, resided in Bel Air or Fountain Green, parents unknown (Death certificate; Alm House Record Book)

Norris, Henry (colored), see George Washington Norris (colored), q.v.

Norris, Henry James, 1868-1955 (Slate Ridge Cemetery, York Co., PA); native of Whiteford, Harford Co., born 8 Feb 1868, son of Matthew Norris and Susanna Giffing (Harkins Funeral Home Records)

Norris, Henry T., born -- Mar 1888, baptized 20 May 1888, son of William Norris and Margaret Murphy (St. Ignatius Catholic Church Baptism Register, p. 98)

Norris, Howard R., 1882-1954 (Good Will Church Cemetery)

Norris, Iris G., 1885-1941 (Mt. Zion Methodist Church Cemetery)

Norris, J. Payne (Miss), member, Norrisville M. E. Church Sunday School (*The Aegis & Intelligencer*, 20 Jun 1890)

Norris, J. W. Stump (Dr.), brother of Octavius J. Norris, resident of Holland's boarding house, Bel Air (*The Aegis & Intelligencer*, 30 May 1890)

Norris, J. Wiley, 1844-1929 (Norrisville Methodist Church Cemetery); farmer, near Norrisville (*The Aegis & Intelligencer*, 11 Apr 1890); incorporator, Norrisville Methodist Protestant Church (*Havre de Grace Republican*, 4 Apr 1890); vice president, Norrisville Branch, Young People's Society of Christian Endeavor (*Havre de Grace Republican*, 24 Oct 1890)

Norris, Jacob M., 1888-1890 (Darlington Cemetery)

Norris, James, see Ella Norris, q.v.

Norris, James, 1818-1900 (Cokesbury Memorial Methodist Church Cemetery)

Norris, James, Civil War veteran, Churchville (*1890 Special Census of the Civil War Veterans of the State of Maryland*, by L. Tilden Moore, Volume III, p. 70)

Norris, James Steven, 1857-1912 (Cokesbury Memorial Methodist Church Cemetery)

Norris, James Thomas, 1861-1942 (Union Chapel Methodist Church Cemetery); superintendent, Union Chapel M. P. Church Sunday School (*The Aegis & Intelligencer*, 10 Jan 1890; *Havre de Grace Republican*, 11 Apr 1890); see Elizabeth R. Jones, q.v.

Norris, Jesse, Civil War veteran, Bel Air (*1890 Special Census of the Civil War Veterans of the State of Maryland*, by L. Tilden Moore, Volume III, p. 72)

Norris, John, 1835-1897 (Union Chapel Methodist Church Cemetery)

Norris, John (Master), member, Union Chapel M. P. Church (*The Aegis & Intelligencer*, 10 Jan 1890)

Norris, John A., 1863-1913 (Mountain Christian Church Cemetery)

Norris, John A., 1863-1923 (Union Chapel Methodist Church Cemetery)

Norris, John N., 1875-1940 (McKendree Methodist Church Cemetery)

Norris, John W. (colored), 1861-1929 (Tabernacle Methodist Church Cemetery)

Norris, Joseph, acquired land in April 1890 (*The Aegis & Intelligencer*, 9 May 1890)

Norris, Laura, see Louella (Neeper) Doyle, q.v.

Norris, Libbie (Miss), member, Union Chapel M. P. Church (*The Aegis & Intelligencer*, 10 Jan 1890)

Norris, Lida E., daughter of Benjamin and Lizzie Norris, died 14 Sep 1889 (*The Aegis & Intelligencer*, 9 May 1890)

Norris, Liza J., see Alpha L. Payne, q.v.

Norris, Lizzie, see Georgie Norris and Lida E. Norris, q.v.

Norris, Lizzie F., 1858-1892 (Old Brick Baptist Church Cemetery; *The Aegis & Intelligencer*, 14 Oct 1892); wife of McComas Norris, q.v.

Norris, Lorena T. (Hawkins), 1885-1967 (Union Chapel Methodist Church Cemetery)

Norris, Maggie C., 1870-1916 (Norrisville Methodist Church Cemetery); wife of Nicholas N Norris, q.v.

Norris, Malinda Celeste, 1861-1944 (Union Chapel Methodist Church Cemetery)

Norris, Margaret, died 4 Jul 1890, age about 33 (Slate Ridge Presbyterian Church Cemetery); wife of William Norris, of Whiteford (*The Aegis & Intelligencer*, 11 Jul 1890)

Norris, Margaret F. (Murphy), 1860-1919 (St. Ignatius Catholic Church Cemetery)

Norris, Maria (Churchman), 1860-1946 (St. Mary's Episcopal Church Cemetery)

Norris, Maria (Crawford), 1833-1911, native of Baltimore, resided at Bel Air (Death certificate stated her name was A. Maria; St. Mary's Episcopal Church Cemetery); wife of George Smith Norris, q.v.

Norris, Martha E. (Dixon), 1837-1920 (Union Chapel Methodist Church Cemetery)

Norris, Martha M. (colored), 1854-1936 (Tabernacle Methodist Church Cemetery)

Norris, Mary, see George L. Norris, Amanda J. Norris and Clara Neeper, q.v.

Norris, Mary (Mansfield), 1864-1939 (St. Mary's Episcopal Church Cemetery)

Norris, Mary (Young), 1851-1909 (Union Chapel Methodist Church Cemetery)

Norris, Mary Amelia (Lantz), 1855-1945 (Trinity Evangelical Lutheran Church Cemetery)

Norris, Mary E., 1836-1897 (Norrisville Methodist Church Cemetery)

Norris, Mary E., 1856-1940 (Tabernacle Cemetery); also see Charles E. Beard, q.v.

Norris, Mary E. (colored), 1868-1956 (Tabernacle Methodist Church Cemetery)

Norris, Mary Emma, 1842-1916 (Union Chapel Methodist Church Cemetery); teacher, Union Chapel School No. 1, Third District (*The Aegis & Intelligencer*, 29 Aug 1890); see Emma Norris, q.v.

Norris, Mary J., 1835-1924 (St. Mary's Episcopal Church Cemetery)

Norris, Mary M., 1838-1913 (McKendree Methodist Church Cemetery); see Simon Beattie and Agnes B. Lloyd, q.v.

Norris, Matthew, see Henry James Norris, q.v.

Norris, Maud E., 1890-1944 (Good Will Church Cemetery)

Norris, McComas ("Mack"), 1856-1934 (Old Brick Baptist Church Cemetery)

Norris, Melissa J. (colored), 1843-1918 (Tabernacle Methodist Church Cemetery)

Norris, Moses (colored), 1837-1906 (Tabernacle Methodist Church Cemetery); resided at Prospect (*Harford Democrat,* 14 Mar 1890)

Norris, Moses D., resided near Greenstone (*The Aegis & Intelligencer*, 3 Jan 1890)

Norris, Nicholas N., 1867-1944 (Norrisville Methodist Church Cemetery; *The Aegis*, 26 Oct 1944)

Norris, Nancy J., see Beulah J. Norris, q.v.

Norris, Octavius J., brother of Dr. J. W. Stump Norris, resident of Holland's boarding house, Bel Air (*The Aegis & Intelligencer*, 30 May 1890)

Norris, Reuben, Civil War veteran, resided at Street (*1890 Special Census of the Civil War Veterans of the State of Maryland*, by L. Tilden Moore, Volume III, p. 84); sold land in August 1890 (*The Aegis & Intelligencer*, 12 Sep 1890); see Mrs. Burley J. Williams, q.v.; also see Anna Mary Norris, q.v.

Norris, Rhesa M. (Dr.), died 28 Feb 1890, age 38 (Union Chapel Methodist Church Cemetery)

Norris, Rhoda (Miss), member, Union Chapel M. P. Church (*The Aegis & Intelligencer*, 10 Jan 1890)

Norris, Robert R. (Dr.), 1851-1914 (Norrisville Methodist Church Cemetery)

Norris, Robert Wesley, 1822-1903 (Union Chapel Methodist Church Cemetery)

Norris, S. Elizabeth, 1885-1958 (Centre Methodist Church Cemetery)

Norris, Samuel, see Gertrude Baldwin, q.v.

Norris, Samuel Benson, 1881-1942 (Union Chapel Methodist Church Cemetery)

Norris, Samuel J. (colored), 1844-1933 (Tabernacle Methodist Church Cemetery)

Norris, Samuel John, 1870-1957 (Slate Ridge Cemetery, York Co., PA); native of Harford Co., born 6 Mar 1870, son of Samuel J. Norris and Melissa Singleton (Harkins Funeral Home Records)

Norris, Sarah J., 1824-1910 (Christ Episcopal Church Cemetery)

Norris, Sarah Jane, see Benjamin H. Jones, q.v.

Norris, Susan Elizabeth, 1840-1907 (Cokesbury Memorial Methodist Church Cemetery)

Norris, Susan Elizabeth (Miss), 1849-1926 (Union Chapel Methodist Church Cemetery; Death certificate)

Norris, Susan L. (colored), age 18 in 1890 (Marriage License Applications Book ALJ No. 2, 1891)

Norris, T. J., 1840-1907 (McKendree Methodist Church Cemetery)

Norris, Thomas, see Violetta V. Griffin, q.v.

Norris, Thomas (colored), 1841-1906 (Tabernacle Methodist Church Cemetery); resided at Upper Cross Roads in 1890, brother of John Norris (*Harford Democrat*, 7 Nov 1890)

Norris, Thomas E., age 32 in 1890 (Marriage License Applications Book ALJ No. 2, 1890); uncalled for letter in Bel Air P. O., 1890 (*The Aegis & Intelligencer*, 4 Jul 1890)

Norris, Thomas N., see Beulah J. Norris, q.v.

Norris, Thomas Nelson, 1875-1890 (Mt. Vernon Methodist Church Cemetery)

Norris, Tillie J., age 22 in 1890 (Marriage License Applications Book ALJ No. 2, 1890)

Norris, W. Payne, 1870-1954 (*The Aegis*, 15 Apr 1954); Payne Norris, member, Norrisville Silver Cornet Band, 1890 (*The Aegis & Intelligencer*, 30 May 1890)

Norris, William, Civil War veteran, Norrisville (*1890 Special Census of the Civil War Veterans of the State of Maryland*, by L. Tilden Moore, Volume III, p. 82); served on a petit jury (*Havre de Grace Republican*, 14 Feb 1890); trustee, Norrisville School No. 1, Fourth District (*Havre de Grace Republican*, 30 May 1890); see Margaret Norris, q.v.

Norris, William A., 1869-1946 (Darlington Cemetery)

Norris, William C., premium award winner, Class I - Agricultural Productions, Harford County Fair (*The Aegis & Intelligencer*, 24 Oct 1890); member, Bel Air Tennis Club (*The Aegis & Intelligencer*, 18 Jul 1890)

Norris, William H., delegate, Fifth District, Democrat Party Convention (*The Aegis & Intelligencer*, 5 Sep 1890)

Norris, William H. (colored), 1856-1920 (Tabernacle Methodist Church Cemetery)

Norris, William J., 1880-1917 (Centre Methodist Church Cemetery)

Norris, Willie (Master), member, Union Chapel M. P. Church (*The Aegis & Intelligencer*, 10 Jan 1890)

Norrisville Colored Public School, Norrisville, Fourth District (*Harford County, Maryland Teachers and the Schools They Served, 1774-1900*, by Henry C. Peden, Jr., 2022, p. 371)

Norrisville Cornet Band (*Harford Democrat*, 3 Oct 1890)

Norrisville Methodist Church and Cemetery (W. Church Lane, Norrisville)

Norrisville Public School No. 1, Norrisville, Fourth District (*Harford County, Maryland Teachers and the Schools They Served, 1774-1900*, by Henry C. Peden, Jr., 2022, p. 371)

North Bend Presbyterian Church and Cemetery (North Bend Road, near Federal Hill)

Norton, Amanda (colored), see William Lingham (colored), q.v.

Norton, Charles H. (colored), age 28 in 1889 (Marriage License Applications Book ALJ No. 2, 1889)

Norton, David (colored), 1846-1912, native of Harford Co. (Death certificate); Civil War veteran, of VanBibber (*1890 Special Census of the Civil War Veterans of the State of Maryland*, by L. Tilden Moore, Volume III, p. 61)

Norton, Emma J. (colored), age 18 in 1890 (Marriage License Applications Book ALJ No. 2, 1891); see Thomas P. Norton, q.v.

Norton, Eva V. (colored), age 21 in 1890 (Marriage License Applications Book ALJ No. 2, 1890); see Thomas P. Norton, q.v.

Norton, Howard (colored), 1890-1963 (John Wesley Methodist Church Cemetery, Abingdon)

Norton, Mary (Mrs.) (colored), 1821-1901, native of Maryland, cook, resided at Magnolia (Death certificate incomplete; *The Aegis & Intelligencer*, 15 Feb 1901)

Norton, Miriam A. (colored), 1863-1919, native of Maryland (Death certificate); wife of Thomas M. Norton, q.v.

Norton, Rachel S. (Evans) (colored), 1838-1915 (Cedars Chapel Cemetery)

Norton, Sarah J. (Bond) (colored), 1841-1914, native of Harford Co. (Death certificate)

Norton, Thomas M. (colored), 1861-1948 (Berkley Memorial Cemetery); see Thomas P. Norton, q.v.

Norton, Thomas P. (colored), died testate in 1890 and his named heirs were wife Rachel S. Norton, son Thomas Norton, and daughters Eva Norton and Emma Norton (Harford County Will Book JMM 11:152-154)

Norton, Howard (colored), 1890-1963 (John Wesley UM Church Cemetery)

Norwood, Lizzie (colored), c1861-1922 (Death certificate; St. James United Cemetery)

Notely, Thomas F., 1836-1917 (Mt. Erin Cemetery)

Notely, Viola S., 1838-1891 (Mt. Erin Cemetery)

Notely, William T., 1874-1925 (Mt. Erin Cemetery)

Nourse, William B., insolvent, 1890 (*The Aegis & Intelligencer,* 11 Apr 1890); transferred and removed from the voter registration list at Hall's Cross Road, Second District, 1890 (*Havre de Grace Republican*, 26 Sep 1890); Mrs. William B. Nourse, a daughter of Samuel W. Raymond (*The Aegis & Intelligencer*, 11 Jul 1890)

Nowell, William, member, St. Patrick's Catholic Church, Havre de Grace (*Havre de Grace Republican*, 13 Jun 1890)

Numbers, Georgeanna (Keen), born 1868, died ---- (St. George's Episcopal Church Cemetery)

Numbers, H., first baseman, Perryman Baseball Club (*The Aegis & Intelligencer*, 18 Jul 1890)

Numbers, John Reese, 1861-1944 (St. George's Episcopal Church Cemetery); vice commander, Perryman Lodge, Order of the Golden Chain (*Havre de Grace Republican*, 5 Dec 1890)

Numbers, Joseph H., 1865-1960 (Angel Hill Cemetery)

Numbers, Martha J., see Mary Emmaline Aaronson, q.v.

Numbers, Mary Augustus "Gussie" (Galloway), 1867-1948 (Angel Hill Cemetery); native and resident of Havre de Grace (Death certificate)

Numbers, Sally, see Belle J. Ivins, q.v.

Numbers, Sarah Jane, 1838-1917 (St. George's Episcopal Church Cemetery)

Nye, Sarah (colored), 1826-1891 (Hendon Hill Cemetery)

Nyssen, Rev. Father, of St. Mary's Catholic Church on Deer Creek (*Havre de Grace Republican*, 10 Jan 1890)

O'Brien, Albert Henri, 1846-1914 (Christ Episcopal Church Cemetery)

O'Brien, Ann Stella, born -- May 1887, baptized 15 Jun 1887, daughter of William O'Brien, native of County Tipperary, Ireland, and Hannah McCummings, native of County Galway, Ireland (St. Ignatius Catholic Church Baptism Register, p. 93)

O'Brien, Frances Elizabeth, born -- Apr 1882, baptized 18 Jun 1882, daughter of William O'Brien, native of County Tipperary, Ireland, and Hannah McCummings, native of County Galway, Ireland (St. Ignatius Catholic Church Baptism Register, p. 60)

O'Brien, Hannah (McCummings), 1850-1901, native of County Galway, Ireland (St. Ignatius Catholic Church Cemetery); wife of William O'Brien, q.v.

O'Brien, John, 1841-1916 (St. Ignatius Catholic Church Cemetery)

O'Brien, John J., 1889-1944 (Baker Cemetery)

O'Brien, John M., 1869-1900 (St. Ignatius Catholic Church Cemetery)

O'Brien, Katharine Cecelia, born 7 Mar 1885, baptized 12 Apr 1885, daughter of William O'Brien, native of County Tipperary, Ireland, and Hannah McCummings, native of County Galway, Ireland (St. Ignatius Catholic Church Baptism Register, p. 78)

O'Brien, Loulie (infant), died in 1890 (Christ Episcopal Church Cemetery)

O'Brien, Loulie (Dallam), 1854-1908 (Christ Episcopal Church Cemetery)

O'Brien, Phyllis (infant), died 1893 (Christ Episcopal Church Cemetery)

O'Brien, William, 1847-1916 (St. Ignatius Catholic Church Cemetery)

O'Conner, Patrick F., 1888-1968 (St. Francis de Sales Catholic Church Cemetery)

O'Conners, Belle (Mrs.), resident of First District, granted a permit to Mt. Hope Hospital (*Harford Democrat*, 7 Nov 1890)

O'Donald, Martha E., see Elizabeth V. Sadler, q.v.

O'Donnell, Annie, 1828-1906 (St. Ignatius Catholic Church Cemetery)

O'Donnell, Bessie, fourth grade student, Bynum School (*The Aegis & Intelligencer*, 11 Jul 1890)

O'Donnell, Clara, born -- Dec 1887, baptized 29 Jan 1888, daughter of Matthew and Bridget (McDonald) O'Donnell (St. Ignatius Catholic Church Baptism Register, p. 96)

O'Donnell, Elizabeth Rosalie, baptized 1 May 1881, daughter of Matthew and Bridget (McDonald) O'Donnell (St. Ignatius Catholic Church Baptism Register, p. 53)

O'Donnell, Frances, born -- Dec 1885, baptized 14 Feb 1886, daughter of Matthew and Bridget (McDonald) O'Donnell (St. Ignatius Catholic Church Baptism Register, p. 86)

O'Donnell, George, 1820-1897 (St. Ignatius Catholic Church Cemetery)

O'Donnell, Mamie, fourth grade student, Bynum School (*The Aegis & Intelligencer*, 11 Jul 1890)

O'Donnell, Margaret Mary, born -- May 1884, baptized 27 Jul 1884, daughter of Matthew and Bridget (McDonald) O'Donnell (St. Ignatius Catholic Church Baptism Register, p. 74); Maggie O'Donnell, student, Bynum School (*The Aegis & Intelligencer*, 11 Jul 1890)

O'Donnell, Mary E., 1871-1907 (St. Ignatius Catholic Church Cemetery)

O'Donnell, Matthew ("Matt"), resident near Frogtown (*The Aegis & Intelligencer*, 5 Sep 1890)

O'Donnell, Matthew, born 27 Jan 1883, baptized 14 Mar 1883, son of Matthew and Bridget (McDonald) O'Donnell (St. Ignatius Catholic Church Baptism Register, p. 63)

O'Neill, Elizabeth Jane (Latour), 1814-1896, wife of William O'Neill, 1809-1845 (Angel Hill Cemetery); novelties and goods store at Congress and Washington Streets, Havre de Grace (*Havre de Grace Republican*, 19 Dec 1890); businesswoman trader's license (*Havre de Grace Republican*, 30 May 1890); mother of John William O'Neill, q.v.

O'Leary, Julia, see Margaret C. Johnston, q.v.

O'Neill, Elizabeth Jane (Latour), 1814-1896 (Angel Hill Cemetery)

O'Neill, Frances (Kirby), 1841-1895 (Angel Hill Cemetery), wife of Henry Edward O'Neill, q.v.

O'Neill, Henry Edward, 1841-1919 (Angel Hill Cemetery); Civil War veteran, Havre de Grace (*1890 Special Census of the Civil War Veterans of the State of Maryland*, by L. Tilden Moore, Volume III, p. 91); senior vice commander and trustee, John Rodgers Post, G.A.R., of Havre de Grace (*Havre de Grace Republican*, 14 Feb and 12 Dec 1890); government pensioner, Havre de Grace (*Havre de Grace Republican*, 7 Nov 1890); Concord Point lighthouse keeper (*Biographical Dictionary of Harford County, Maryland, 1774-1974*, by Henry C. Peden, Jr. and William O. Carr, 2021, p. 204)

O'Neill, Harry F., 1872-1927 (Angel Hill Cemetery), native of Havre de Grace, born 15 Sep 1872, son of Henry O'Neill, of Maryland, and Frances Kirby, of England (Death certificate)

O'Neill, J. E., director, The Seneca Hosiery Company of Havre de Grace (*Havre de Grace Republican*, 21 Mar 1890)

O'Neill, J. H., member, Independent Social Club, Havre de Grace (*Havre de Grace Republican*, 28 Mar 1890)

O'Neill, John William, 1845-1931 (Angel Hill Cemetery); merchant and city councilman in Havre de Grace (*The Aegis & Intelligencer*, 10 Jan 1890); director, First National Bank of Havre de Grace (*Havre de Grace Republican*, 17 Jan 1890); organizer and vice president, Havre de Grace Democratic Club (*Havre de Grace Republican*, 31 Oct 1890); foreman, served on a grand jury, Sixth District (*Havre de Grace Republican*, 2 May and 16 May 1890); incorporator, Havre de Grace Academy (*Havre de Grace Republican*, 15 Aug 1890); vestryman and treasurer, St. John's Episcopal Church, Havre de Grace (*Havre de Grace Republican*, 11 Apr 1890)

O'Neill, Katherine, 1821-1903, native of Ireland, resided in Havre de Grace, wife of Owen O'Neill (Death certificate)

O'Neill, Lillian "Lillie" Augusta G., 1858-1921 (Angel Hill Cemetery)

O'Neill, Mary, wife of Millard F. Tydings, q.v.; also see Millard E. Tydings, q.v.

O'Neill, Michael, Civil War veteran, Havre de Grace (*1890 Special Census of the Civil War Veterans of the State of Maryland*, by L. Tilden Moore, Volume III, p. 68)

O'Neill, Owen, see Katherine O'Neill, q.v.

O'Neill, Warren Evelyn, 1868-1913 (Angel Hill Cemetery)

O'Toole, Michael, of Magnolia, P. W.& B. Railroad workman, 1890 (*Havre de Grace Republican*, 16 May 1890); prisoner in the county jail (*Harford Democrat*, 3 Jan 1890) charged with asssault, but was found not guilty (Harford County Criminal Docket, 1888-1892, p. 80; *Harford Democrat*, 21 Feb 1890)

Oakington Public School No. 16, near Aberdeen, Second District (*Harford County, Maryland Teachers and the Schools They Served, 1774-1900*, by Henry C. Peden, Jr., 2022, p. 371)

Oakland Boarding School, Fallston [Bagley's Corner], Third District, G. G. Curtiss, principal (*Harford County, Maryland Teachers and the Schools They Served, 1774-1900*, by Henry C. Peden, Jr., 2022, p. 371)

Oakland Public School No. 7, near Cole, Second District (*Harford County, Maryland Teachers and the Schools They Served, 1774-1900*, by Henry C. Peden, Jr., 2022, p. 371)

Oakley, Charles H., 1883-1960 (Cokesbury Memorial Methodist Church Cemetery)

Oakley, Fredericka (Rembold), 1888-1967 (Cokesbury Memorial Methodist Church Cemetery)

Oakley, Grover Cleveland, 1890-1971 (Cokesbury Memorial Methodist Church Cemetery)

Oakley, John Thomas, 1888-1959 (Cokesbury Memorial Methodist Church Cemetery)

Oakley, Laura Jane, 1860-1942 (Cokesbury Memorial Methodist Church Cemetery)

Oakley, Thomas B., 1857-1952 (Cokesbury Memorial Methodist Church Cemetery)

Obrum, S. C. (Rev.), acquired land in August 1890 (*The Aegis & Intelligencer*, 12 Sep 1890)

Odd Fellows Lodge, Bel Air (*Bel Air: An Architectural and Cultural History, 1782-1945*, by Marilynn M. Larew, 1995, p. 113); also see Independent Order of Odd Fellows, q.v.

Offley, Annie Edmondson, 1848-1919 (Friends Cemetery, Baltimore); teacher, Bel Air School No. 14, Third District (*The Aegis & Intelligencer*, 29 Aug 1890)

Offley, Margaret "Maggie" M., 1856-1917 (Friends Cemetery, Baltimore); teacher, Aberdeen School No. 1, Second District (*The Aegis & Intelligencer*, 29 Aug 1890)

Offley, Martha "Mattie" Milton 1852-1923 (Friends Cemetery, Baltimore); teacher, Havre de Grace High School, Sixth District (*The Aegis & Intelligencer*, 29 Aug 1890); superintendent of flower mission, Women's Christian Temperance Union (*Havre de Grace Republican*, 5 Sep 1890); president and superintendent of juvenile work, Women's Christian Temperance Union, of Havre de Grace (*Havre de Grace Republican*, 19 Sep 1890); third patron, Willard Section No. 58, Cadets of Temperance, Havre de Grace (*Havre de Grace Republican*, 11 Jul 1890)

Old Peach Bottom Slate Company of Harford County (*Havre de Grace Republican*, 27 Jun 1890)

Oldfield, Alice A. (Wilkinson), 1864-1950 (Mt. Zion Methodist Church Cemetery)

Oldfield, Edmund L., 1863-1938 (Mt. Zion Methodist Church Cemetery); dairy farmer at Rocks and active in Democrat Party; member, Mt. Ararat Lodge No. 44, A. F. & A. M. (*Biographical Dictionary of Harford County, Maryland, 1774-1974*, by Henry C. Peden, Jr. and William O. Carr, 2021, p. 203)

Oldfield, Esther, see Katie May McNutt, q.v.

Oldfield, Hannah (Carter), 1822-1907 (Mt. Zion Methodist Church Cemetery)

Oldfield, John F., 1855-1927 (Mt. Zion Methodist Church Cemetery)

Oldfield, Laura Esther (Miss), 1851-1938 (Mt. Zion Methodist Church Cemetery); member of the Methodist Protestant Church, vice president and secretary, Fountain Green Women's Christian Temperance Union (*Havre de Grace Republican*, 2 May 1890; *The Aegis & Intelligencer*, 25 Apr 1890)

Oldfield, Martha E., born 1855, died ---- (Mt. Zion Methodist Church Cemetery)

Oldfield, Nathan H, 1855-1910 (Mt. Zion Methodist Church Cemetery)

Oldfield, William, 1825-1901 (Mt. Zion Methodist Church Cemetery); served on the property committee for Mt. Zion Methodist Church (*The Aegis & Intelligencer*, 25 Apr 1890)

Oldfield, William L., 1889-1970 (Mt. Zion Methodist Church Cemetery)

Olford, Janie, student, Sixth District (*The Aegis & Intelligencer*, 24 Oct 1890)

Oliver's General Store, Harford Furnace, Thomsa J. Oliver, (*Country Stores: Harford County's Rural Heritage*, by Henry C. Peden, Jr. and Jack L. Shagena, Jr., 2015, p. 187)

Oliver, Belle, student, Harford Furnace School (*The Aegis & Intelligencer*, 14 Feb 1890)

Oliver, Caroline (colored), born -- Jan 1886, native of Maryland (1900 Aberdeen Census)

Oliver, Catherine (colored), see C. Augustus Boone (colored), q.v.

Oliver, Charles F., 1875-1961 (St. George's Episcopal Church Cemetery); Charlie Oliver, student, Harford Furnace School, 1890 (*The Aegis & Intelligencer*, 14 Feb 1890)

Oliver, Dorthea L., 1890-1943 (Baker Cemetery)

Oliver, Edith R., 1879-1968 (St. Mary's Episcopal Church Cemetery)

Oliver, George Frank, 1873-1943 (St. Mary's Episcopal Church Cemetery)

Oliver, Herbert, 1882-1950 (St. Mary's Episcopal Church Cemetery)

Oliver, James, 1859-1945 (St. Mary's Episcopal Church Cemetery); native of Harford Co., farmer, near Harford Furnace (Death certificate)

Oliver, James W., 1889-1944 (St. Mary's Episcopal Church Cemetery)

Oliver, Laura V. (colored), wife of Robert E. Oliver, q.v.

Oliver, Louise E., 1863-1938 (St. Mary's Episcopal Church Cemetery)

Oliver, Magdalene S., 1863-1951 (St. Mary's Episcopal Church Cemetery)

Oliver, Margaret, born 1884, died 19-- (St. Mary's Episcopal Church Cemetery)

Oliver, Mary M. (colored), 1875-1928, daughter of ----and Laura Gough (Death certificate)

Oliver, Matilda B., 1871-1891, daiughter of William and Sarah Oliver (St. Mary's Episcopal Church Cemetery)

Oliver, Matilda Isabelle, 1887-1931 (St. Mary's Episcopal Church Cemetery)

Oliver, Robert E. (colored), 1865-1937, native of Bel Air (Death certificate)

Oliver, Ruth A., 1863-1945 (St. Mary's Episcopal Church Cemetery)

Oliver, Sarah (Miss), of Harford Furnace, cousin of Miss Mary Andrew, of Paradise (*Harford Democrat,* 18 Apr 1890)

Oliver, Sarah (McCoy), 1837-1910 (St. Mary's Episcopal Church Cemetery)

Oliver, Thomas J., 1856-1947 (St. Mary's Episcopal Church Cemetery); wife of William Oliver, q.v.

Oliver, William, 1826-1912 (St. Mary's Episcopal Church Cemetery); tomato canner, Abingdon District (*The Aegis & Intelligencer*, 15 Aug 1890); trustee, Harford Furnace School No. 2, First District (*Havre de Grace Republican*, 30 May 1890)

Oliver, William E., 1858-1943 (St. Mary's Episcopal Church Cemetery)

Onent, John, 1873-1935 (Death certificate; Alms House Record Book)

Onion, Alice Hannah (Whitaker), 1864-1939, resided at Cooptown (Death certificate; William Watters Memorial Methodist Church Cemetery, Cooptown); wife of Lingan J. Onion, q.v.

Onion, Corbin J., 1819-1896 (William Watters Memorial Methodist Church Cemetery, Cooptown); resident near High Point (*The Aegis & Intelligencer*, 14 Feb 1890)

Onion, Erma Whitaker, 1886-1948, daughter of Lingan Onion and Alice W. ---- (*The Aegis*, 5 Mar 1948 - married name Myers)

Onion, Ida Jane, see Ida Jane Whitaker, q.v.

Onion, James B., 1868-1950 (William Watters Memorial Methodist Church Cemetery, Cooptown); second baseman, Baptist Baseball Club, of Fourth District (*Havre de Grace Republican*, 8 Aug 1890)

Onion, Lingan J., 1858-1939, resided at Cooptown (Death certificate; William Watters Memorial Methodist Church Cemetery, Cooptown); see Alice H. Onion and Erma W. Onion, q.v.

Onion, Samuel A., 1862-1935, native of Maryland, farmer and resident of Pylesville (Death certificate)

Onion, Sarah M., 1824-1906 (William Watters Memorial Methodist Church Cemetery, Cooptown)

Onion, William C., 1860-1928 (William Watters Memorial Methodist Church Cemetery, Cooptown); W. Onion, first baseman, Baptist Baseball Club, Fourth District (*Havre de Grace Republican*, 8 Aug 1890)

Only, Louisa (colored), widow, age 28 in 1890 (Marriage License Applications Book ALJ No. 2, 1891)

Openheimer, David, see Anthony Keuchel, q.v.

Opperman, Ida, student, Public School No. 1, First District (*The Aegis & Intelligencer*, 10 Jan 1890)

Opperman, R., physician, First District (*Havre de Grace Republican*, 4 Jul 1890)

Order of Red Men, Hiawatha Council, Havre de Grace, Tribe No. 82 (*Havre de Grace: Its Historic Past, Its Charming Present and Its Promising Future: Harford County's Rural Heritage.* by Jack L. Shagena, Jr. and Henry C. Peden, Jr., 2018, p. 272)

Order of the Golden Chain, see Harford Lodge No. 54 and Perryman Lodge No. 88, q.v.

Oren, Josephine, see Francis Lightfoot Lee, q.v.

Oriental Baseball Club, of Aberdeen (*Havre de Grace Republican*, 9 May 1890)

Oriole Gunning Club, Benson (*Harford Democrat*, 4 Apr 1890)

Orr, Annie E., see Annie E. Henry, q.v.

Orr, Annie J. (Sampson), 1864-1954 (Dublin Southern Cemetery)

Orr, Bessie Beulah (Lee), 1890-1967 (Dublin Southern Cemetery); native of Dublin, Harford Co., born 25 Dec 1890, daughter of Alexander R. Lee and Addie M. Swift (Harkins Funeral Home Records)

Orr, Emma, wife of George W. Orr, q.v.

Orr, Emmaline S., 1884-1942 (Broad Creek Friends Cemetery)

Orr, Evalyn S., 1890-1957 (Darlington Cemetery)

Orr, George W., 1864-1938 (Dublin Southern Cemetery); native of Harford Co. (Bailey Funeral Home Records)

Orr, Howard W., 1883-1941 (Tabernacle Cemetery); native of Darlington, Harford Co., born 26 Sep 1883, son of William H. Orr and Mary E. Sampson (Bailey Funeral Home Records)

Orr, Ella A., 1889-1976 (Dublin Southern Cemetery)

Orr, Eva L., see Eva L. Knight, q.v.

Orr, Ida Emma (Griest), 1866-1955 (Dublin Southern Cemetery); native of Lancaster Co., PA, born 4 Sep 1866, daughter of Isaac Griest and Ruth Harris (Bailey Funeral Home Records)

Orr, Irene S., 1888-1975 (Tabernacle Cemetery)

Orr, James Merton, 1887-1934 (Dublin Southern Cemetery); son of George W. Orr, q.v.

Orr, John K., age 36 in 1889 (Marriage License Applications Book ALJ No. 2, 1889)

Orr, John O., 1859-1910 (Darlington Cemetery); charged with assault in 1890, but no verdict was recorded in the docket book (Harford County Criminal Docket, 1888-1892, p. 90); also see Annie E. Henry and Samuel M. Orr, q.v.

Orr, Jonathon "John" K., 1853-1909 (Angel Hill Cemetery); born in Havre de Grace, blacksmith at Boothby Hill (Death certificate)

Orr, Joseph W., 1871-1896 (Tabernacle Cemetery)

Orr, Margaret Ann, 1832-1892 (Mt. Vernon Church Cemetery)

Orr, Mary Elizabeth (Sampson), 1858-1952 (Dublin Southern Cemetery)

Orr, Rebecca C. (Greenland), 1884-1946 (Angel Hill Cemetery)

Orr, Robert D., magistrate, Fifth District (*Havre de Grace Republican*, 4 Apr 1890); see Eva L. Knight, q.v.

Orr, Sallie A., 1890-1972 (Tabernacle Cemetery)

Orr, Samuel E., 1868-1922 (Dublin Southern Cemetery)

Orr, Samuel M., 1832-1901 (Tabernacle Cemetery); trustee, Boyle's School No. 5, Fifth District (*Havre de Grace Republican*, 30 May 1890); see Viola Mae Beard, q.v.

Orr, Samuel M., 1884-1962 (Broad Creek Friends Cemetery); native of Dublin, Harford Co., born 23 Aug 1884, son of John O. Orr and Susan Little (Harkins Funeral Home Records)

Orr, Sarah E., 1834-1908 (Tabernacle Cemetery)

Orr, Susan "Susie" A. (Little), 1862-1938 (Darlington Cemetery); wife of John O. Orr, q.v.; also see Annie E. Henry and Samuel M. Orr, q.v.

Orr, Susie M. (Heck), 1886-1956 (Slate Ridge Cemetery, York Co., PA); native of Harford Co., born 2 Aug 1886, daughter of Philip Heck and ---- (Harkins Funeral Home Records)

Orr, William H., see Howard W. Orr, q.v.

Orr, William Henry, 1853-1916 (Dublin Southern Cemetery)

Orsburn, Agnes, born 12 Jun 1881, daughter of J. Ramsey and Ella (Calhoun) Orsburn (Bethel Presbyterian Church Cemetery Records)

Orsburn, Clara, third grade student, Prospect Hill School (*The Aegis & Intelligencer*, 21 Feb 1890)

Orsburn, Emily Ella (Calhoun), 1854-1922, wife of John Ramsey Orsburn, q.v.

Orsburn, Harry Wade, 1886-1968 (Mountain Christian Church Cemetery)

Orsburn, John Ramsey, 1851-1925 (Mountain Christian Church Cemetery); served as superintendent of the Mountain Christian Church Sunday School (*Havre de Grace Republican*, 7 Feb 1890)

Osborn, ----, pitcher, Aberdeen Baseball Club (*The Aegis & Intelligencer*, 25 Jul 1890)

Osborn's Grocery Store, Hall's Cross Roads [Aberdeen], George B. Osborn, (*Country Stores: Harford County's Rural Heritage*, by Henry C. Peden, Jr. and Jack L. Shagena, Jr., 2015, p. 188)

Osborn, Ada H., born -- Jun 1865, sister of Cornelia S. Martin (1900 Aberdeen Census)

Osborn, Albert C., 1875-1898 (Cokesbury Memorial Methodist Church Cemetery)

Osborn, Alfred H., 1869-1937, farmer, son of Bennett Osborn (Baker Cemetery; 1900 Aberdeen Census)

Osborn, Annie J. (Flynn), 1849-1899, resident of Aberdeen, native of Govanstown, MD, wife of Bennett Osborn (Death certificate); acquired land in April 1890 (*The Aegis & Intelligencer*, 9 May 1890)

Osborn, B., third baseman, Carsins Run Baseball Club, near Aberdeen (*Havre de Grace Republican*, 8 Aug 1890)

Osborn, Barney, Civil War veteran, at Cole (*1890 Special Census of the Civil War Veterans of the State of Maryland*, by L. Tilden Moore, Volume III, p. 65)

Osborn, Benjamin H. (colored), 1868-1950, native of Harford Co., son of George Henry Osborn and Julia Ann Cooper (Death certificate)

Osborn, Bennett, 1832-1907 (St. George's Episcopal Church Cemetery); juror, Second District (*Havre de Grace Republican*, 31 Oct 1890); tent holder, Carsins Run Camp Meeting of the East Harford Circuit, P. E. Church (*The Aegis & Intelligencer*, 1 Aug 1890); widowed farmer (1900 Aberdeen Census)

Osborn, Bertie W., 1881-1972 (Baker Cemetery)

Osborn, C. Benjamin, 1864-1910 (Deer Creek Harmony Presbyterian Church Cemetery)

Osborn, Carrie E., 1867-1932 (Cokesbury Memorial Methodist Church Cemetery)

Osborn, Carroll S., 1887-1958 (Baker Cemetery)

Osborn, Charles, 1832-1910 (St. George's Episcopal Church Cemetery)

Osborn, Charles B., born -- May 1890, son of Charles B. and J. Gertrude Osborn (1900 Aberdeen Census)

Osborn, Charles Benjamin, 1856-1924 (Grove Presbyterian Church Cemetery); corn packer, Aberdeen (*Havre de Grace Republican*, 5 Sep 1890); captain and road mender, Swan Creek (*Havre de Grace Republican*, 31 Jan 1890); road examiner in the Second District (*Havre de Grace Republican*, 4 Jul 1890); stockholder, Aberdeen Can Factory (*Havre de Grace Republican*, 19 Dec 1890); tent holder, Carsins Run Camp Meeting of the East Harford Circuit, P. E. Church (*The Aegis & Intelligencer*, 1 Aug 1890)

Osborn, Cyrus, 1813-1895 (Grove Presbyterian Church Cemetery)

Osborn, Delia Matthews (Spencer), 1853-1932, native of Bel Air (Death certificate)

Osborn, Effie M., student, Union School House, near Bush Chapel (*The Aegis & Intelligencer*, 14 Mar 1890)

Osborn, Elizabeth Fletcher, born 2 Aug 1882, daughter of Henry A. and Frances Almira (Fletcher) Osborn (*Barnes-Bailey Genealogy*, by Walter D. Barnes, 1939, p. I-16)

Osborn, Eva G., born -- Oct 1884, daughter of Charles B. and J. Gertrude Osborn (1900 Aberdeen Census)

Osborn, Fannie C., wife of Benjamin W. Herring, q.v.; also see George R. Herring, q.v.

Osborn, Florence, age 20 in 1890, married Edmund D. Gallup in 1891 (Marriage License Applications Book ALJ No. 2, 1891)

Osborn, Frances Almira (Fletcher), 1845-1932 (Grove Presbyterian Church Cemetery); wife of Henry Amos Osborn, q.v.

Osborn, G. B. (colored), trustee, Michaelsville School No. 6, Second District (*Havre de Grace Republican*, 30 May 1890)

Osborn, Garrett, 1813-1894 (Grove Presbyterian Church Cemetery); Garrett Osborn & Son, coffin makers and undertakers, Michaelsville, Second District (*Havre de Grace Republican*, 4 Jul 1890; *The Aegis & Intelligencer*, 6 Jun 1890); see Sarah A. Osborne, q.v.

Osborn, George B., 1847-1921 (St. George's Episcopal Church Cemetery)

Osborn, George Henry (colored), see Benjamin H. Osborn (colored), q.v.

Osborn, George V., died 28 Mar 1903, age 71 (*Deaths and Marriages in Harford County, Maryland, and Vicinity, 1873-1904, from the Diaries of Albert Peter Silver*, transcribed by Glenn Randers-Pehrson, 1995, p. 18)

Osborn, Georgianna, see Abbie O. Burkins, q.v.

Osborn, Harry (colored), see Charles Henry Osborne (Osborn) (colored), q.v.

Osborn, Harry C., 1878-1963 (Baker Cemetery)

Osborn, Harry R. S., 1879-1955 (St. George's Episcopal Church Cemetery)

Osborn, Harry S., 1862-1929 (Deer Creek Harmony Presbyterian Church Cemetery)

Osborn, Harry S., a boy who served as a pall bearer, lived on Bush River Neck (*The Aegis & Intelligencer*, 1 Aug 1890); student, Union School House, near Bush Chapel (*The Aegis & Intelligencer*, 14 Mar 1890)

Osborn, Helen, student, Union School House, near Bush Chapel (*The Aegis & Intelligencer*, 14 Mar 1890)

Osborn, Henry Amos, 1841-1925 (Grove Presbyterian Church Cemetery); vice president, Harford County Farmers' Association (*The Aegis & Intelligencer*, 17 Jan 1890); vice president, Third Annual Convention, Farmers' Club of Harford County (*Havre de Grace Republican*, 5 Dec 1890)

Osborn, Henry Amos, Jr., 1884-1918 (Grove Presbyterian Church Cemetery); born 2 Oct 1884, son of Henry A. Osborn and Frances Almira Fletcher (*Barnes-Bailey Genealogy*, by Walter D. Barnes, 1939, p. I-16)

Osborn, Howard, 1875-1946 (St. George's Episcopal Church Cemetery); student, Union School House, near Bush Chapel, 1890 (*The Aegis & Intelligencer*, 14 Mar 1890)

Osborn, Inez Henry, 1880-1977 (Grove Presbyterian Church Cemetery); born 17 Oct 1880, daughter of Henry A. Osborn and Frances Almira Fletcher (*Barnes-Bailey Genealogy*, by Walter D. Barnes, 1939, p. I-16)

Osborn, J., first baseman, Webster Baseball Club, of Webster (*Havre de Grace Republican*, 25 Jul 1890)

Osborn, J. R., trustee, School No. 4, First District (*Havre de Grace Republican*, 9 May 1890)

Osborn, Jacob & Co., float fisherman, west of the Battery in the Chesapeake Bay (*The Aegis & Intelligencer*, 4 Apr 1890)

Osborn, Jacob Preston, 1834-1916, merchant tailor in Aberdeen (Death certificate)

Osborn, James Howard, 1880-1964 (Baker Cemetery)

Osborn, Jennie, wife of Thomas E. Morgan, q.v.; also see Florence V. Morgan, q.v.

Osborn, Jerusha Gertrude (Mitchell), 1854-1926 (Grove Presbyterian Church Cemetery); wife of Charles B. Osborn, q.v.

Osborn, John Amos, 1846-1902 (Grove Presbyterian Church Cemetery); judge, Bel Air jousting tournament (*Havre de Grace Republican*, 17 Oct 1890); secretary, Harford Lodge No. 54, of Aberdeen, Order of the Golden Chain (*Havre de Grace Republican*, 28 Nov 1890); member, Guy Social Club, Aberdeen (*Havre de Grace Republican*, 31 Oct 1890); see Theodora Osborn, q.v.

Osborn, Julia Ann (colored), 1848-1935, native of Churchville (Death certificate); wife of George Henry Osborn, q.v.

Osborn, Lavinia (Rawhouser), 1849-1905 (Grove Presbyterian Church Cemetery), wife of John Amos Osborn, q.v.

Osborn, Lotta E. "Lottie" (Jackson) (Wells), 1861-1946 (Baker Cemetery), wife of Alfred H. Osborn, q.v.

Osborn, Lucy (Loflin), 1882-1974 (Baker Cemetery)

Osborn, Luther S., 1837-1922 (Baker Cemetery); assistant manager and tent holder, Carsins Run Camp Meeting of the East Harford Circuit, P. E. Church (*The Aegis & Intelligencer*, 1 Aug 1890); trustee, Union School No. 10, First District (*Havre de Grace Republican*, 30 May 1890); served on a petit jury, Second District (*Havre de Grace Republican*, 31 Oct 1890; *The Aegis & Intelligencer*, 14 Nov 1890); see Effie M. Arthur, q.v.

Osborn, Mabel Streett, daughter of William G. and Virginia Osborn, baptized 11 Sep 1887 (St. George's Episcopal Church Register of Baptisms, p. 7, did not record the date of birth)

Osborn, Macie, born 1882, died ---- (Cokesbury Memorial Methodist Church Cemetery)

Osborn, Mamie W., 1871-1909 (Cokesbury Memorial Methodist Church Cemetery)

Osborn, Margaret L., 1887-1960 (Baker Cemetery)

Osborn, Marion T., 1864-1890 (Cokesbury Memorial Methodist Church Cemetery)

Osborn, Martha E. C., 1844-1935 (Grove Presbyterian Church Cemetery)

Osborn, Martha Jane (Grafton), 1886-1964 (Baker Cemetery)

Osborn, Mary A., born -- Jul 1886, daughter of Bennett Osborn (1900 Aberdeen Census)

Osborn, Mary C., 1853-1907 (Grove Presbyterian Church Cemetery)

Osborn, Mary E., 1857-1939 (St. George's Episcopal Church Cemetery)

Osborn, Mary M., 1821-1910 (St. George's Episcopal Church Cemetery)

Osborn, Moses, county out-pensioner [welfare recipient], Second District (*Havre de Grace Republican*, 4 Jul 1890)

Osborn, O. Percival, 1875-1960 (Baker Cemetery); Percy Osborn, student, Union School House, near Bush Chapel, 1890 (*The Aegis & Intelligencer*, 14 Mar 1890)

Osborn, Oleita W., 1883-1952 (Churchhville Presbyterian Church Cemetery)

Osborn, Phoebe (colored), c1831-1911 (Death certificate; St. James United Cemetery)

Osborn, Rachel (Hoopman), 1824-1918 (Grove Presbyterian Church Cemetery); tent holder, Carsins Run Camp Meeting of the East Harford Circuit, P. E. Church, 1890 (*The Aegis & Intelligencer*, 1 Aug 1890)

Osborn, Roberta A., 1830-1909 (St. George's Episcopal Church Cemetery)

Osborn, Sarah A. (Sumwalt), 1822-1900 (Grove Presbyterian Church Cemetery), wife of Garrett Osborn, resided at Michaelsville (Death certificate spelled her name Osborne)

Osborn, Sarah A. (Wells), 1848-1931 (Baker Cemetery)

Osborn, Silver Mitchell, 1880-1958 (Grove Presbyterian Church Cemetery); son of Charles B. and J. Gertrude Osborn (1900 Aberdeen Census)

Osborn, Susie S., 1880-1910 (Baker Cemetery)

Osborn, Susanna Silver (Miss), 1840-1900, native of Maryland, resided at Aberdeen (Death certificate; Deer Creek Harmony Presbyterian Church Cemetery); Miss Susie Osborn, choir member, Grove Presbyterian Church, Aberdeen, 1890 (*The Aegis & Intelligencer*, 10 Jan 1890)

Osborn, Theodora, born -- Mar 1873, niece of John A. and Venie Osborn (1900 Aberdeen Census)

Osborn, Thomas (colored), 1848-1926 (Death certificate); see Charles Henry Osborne (Osborn) and Joseph A. Spencer, q.v.

Osborn, Tom, treated by unidentified doctor in 1890 ("Medical Account Book – 1890," Historical Society of Harford County Archives Folder)

Osborn, Venie, see Theodora Osborn, q.v.

Osborn, Virginia Annie (Courtney), 1881-1946 (Grove Presbyterian Church Cemetery)

Osborn, Virginia Mitchell, born 1 Jun 1886, daughter of William D. Osborn and Virginia Mitchell (St. George's Episcopal Church Register of Baptisms, p. 6)

Osborn, Virginia S. (Mitchell), 1852-1929 (St. George's Episcopal Church Cemetery); wife of William Davis Osborn, q.v.; also see Walter Cochran Osborn, q.v.

Osborn, Walter Cochran, 1884-1957 (Churchville Presbyterian Church Cemetery); native of Swan Creek, Harford Co., born 11 Jan 1884, son of William Davis Osborn and Virginia S. Mitchell (St. George's Episcopal Church Register of Baptisms, pp. 4-5; Pennington Funeral Home Records)

Osborn, William Davis, 1846-1927 (St. George's Episcopal Church Cemetery); farmer, near Aberdeen (*Havre de Grace Republican*, 28 Feb 1890); trustee, Robin Hood School No. 18, Second District (*Havre de Grace Republican*, 30 May 1890); chief judge of elections, Hall's Cross Roads Precinct (*Havre de Grace Republican*, 17 Oct 1890); judge, Bel Air jousting tournament (*Havre de Grace Republican*, 17 Oct 1890); see Walter Cochran Osborn and Virginia Mitchell Osborn, q.v.

Osborn, William G., 1863-1956 (Grove Presbyterian Church Cemetery); juror, Second District (*Havre de Grace Republican*, 2 May 1890); superintendent, Garrettson Chapel Sunday School (*Havre de Grace Republican*, 27 Jun 1890)

Osborn, William O., 1851-1919 (St. George's Episcopal Church Cemetery)

Osborn, William S., 1834-1920 (Cokesbury Memorial Methodist Church Cemetery)

Osborn, Willie S., 1869-1929 (Cokesbury Memorial Methodist Church Cemetery)

Osborne, Angie (Peery), 1883-1948 (Churchville Presbyterian Church Cemetery)

Osborne, Charles B., see John Mitchell, Sr., q.v.

Osborne, Charles Franklin (colored), 1864-1931 (Death certificate)

Osborne (Osborn), Charles Henry (colored), aka Harry Osborn, 1872-1940, native of Churchville, born 19 Dec 1872, son of Thomas Osborn (Osborne) and Elizabeth Legal (Death certificate; *The Aegis*, 5 Jul 1940)

Osborne, Daniel (colored), c1882-1947, native of Harford Co., son of Henry Osborne and Mary Murphy (Death certificate)

Osborne, Elizabeth (McFarland), 1886=1955 (Mt. Calvary Methodist Church Cemetery)

Osborne, Garrett, see Sarah A. Osborn and Garrett Osborn & Son, q.v.

Osborne, George Howard, 1876-1946 (Deer Creek Harmony Presbyterian Church); native of Harford Co., born 29 Apr 1876, son of Robert A. Osborne and Mercy Silver (Bailey Funeral Home Records)

Osborne, Georgina, see Nellie Standiford, q.v.

Osborne, Harriet A. (Hilton) (colored), 1858-1924 (Death certificate)

Osborne, Harry S., 1861-1929 (Deer Creek Harmony Presbyterian Church Cemetery)

Osborne, Henry (colored), see Daniel Osborne (colored), q.v.

Osborne, Jerusia Gertrude, see John Mitchell, Sr., q.v.

Osborne, John, 1865-1943 (Death certificate; Heavenly Waters Cemetery)

Osborne, Luther S., see Effie M. Arthur, q.v.

Osborne, Mary J. (colored), 1827-1909 (St. James United Cemetery)

Osborne, Mary M. (Miss), 1858-1926 (Slate Ridge Cemetery, York Co., PA); born in Pennsylvania, resided in Whiteford (Death certificate)

Osborne, Robert A., see George Howard Osborne, q.v.

Osborne, Robert L. (colored), 1866-1939 (Green Spring Methodist Church Cemetery)

Osborne, William, 1851-1918 (Death certificate)

Osbourn, Sidney (colored), died 27 Sep 1894, age not give (Alms House Monthly Register)

Osburn, Margaret Rosan, 1872-1937 (Darlington Cemetery)

Osmond, Clara (Gallup), 1850-1915, wife of Herman Carroll Osmond, q.v.

Osmond, Clarence R., 1872-1941 (Angel Hill Cemetery), native and resident of Havre de Grace, born 14 Mar 1872, son of Herman Osmond and Elizabeth ---- (Death certificate; Pennington Funeral Home Records)

Osmond, David Monroe, 1860-1940 (Angel Hill Cemetery); coal business co-owner at the furnace wharf, Havre de Grace (*Havre de Grace Republican*, 6 Jun 1890); delegate, Sixth District, Republican Party Convention (*The Aegis & Intelligencer*, 26 Sep 1890); vice president, Republican Club (*Havre de Grace Republican*, 7 Nov 1890)

Osmond, Elizabeth, 1823-1893 (Angel Hill Cemetery)

Osmond, Elizabeth "Libbie" Carver (Chamberlain), 1856-1902 (Angel Hill Cemetery; www.findagrave.com)

Osmond, Herman Carroll, 1848-1916 (Angel Hill Cemetery; Death certificate spelled his middle name Carrylle); delegate, Sixth District, Republican Party Convention (*The Aegis & Intelligencer*, 26 Sep 1890); see Katie May Osmond, Mary E. Osmond and Clarence R. Osmond, q.v.

Osmond, Herman Caroll, Jr., 1876-1946 (Angel Hill Cemetery)

Osmond, J. & Co., fishing firm, Havre de Grace (*Havre de Grace Republican*, 21 Mar 1890)

Osmond, Jacob, Jr., 1850-1938 (Angel Hill Cemetery); coal business co-owner, at the furnace wharf, Havre de Grace (*Havre de Grace Republican*, 6 Jun 1890); city council candidate, Havre de Grace (*Havre de Grace Republican*, 10 Jan 1890); see Thomas Jacob Osmond, q.v.

Osmond, Jacob, Sr., 1818-1903 (Angel Hill Cemetery); vice president, Republican Club (*Havre de Grace Republican*, 7 Nov 1890)

Osmond, Jane, 1812-1891 (Wesleyan Chapel Methodist Church Cemetery)

Osmond, Katie May, 1879-1900 (Angel Hill Cemetery), native of Maryland resident of Havre de Grace, daughter of Herman C. Osmond and Clara Gallup (Death certificate)

Osmond, Margaret (Hammond), 1876-1947 (Death certificate); see Margaret Hammond, q.v.

Osmond, Mary E., 1870-1936 (Angel Hill Cemetery)

Osmond, Mary E., 1882-1951, native of Havre de Grace, born 17 Nov 1882, daughter of Herman Osmond and Clara Gallup (Pennington Funeral Home Records - married name Beck)

Osmond, Mary Elizabeth (Johnson), 1823-1893, wife of Jacob Osmond, Sr., q.v.

Osmond, Thomas Jacob, 1889-1974, native of Havre de Grace, born 7 Oct 1889, son of Jacob Osmond and Elizabeth Chamberlain (Pennington Funeral Home Records)

Osterkamp, Mary A., 1848-1921 (Ayres Chapel Methodist Church Cemetery)

Osterkamp, Theodore, 1886-1948 (Ayres Chapel Methodist Church Cemetery)

Ostheim, Henry, 1821-1898 (Little Falls Quaker Cemetery)

Ostheim. Mary, 1828-1895 (Little Falls Quaker Cemetery)

Ould, M. F., vestryman, Spesutia Church, St. George's Parish, Perryman (*Havre de Grace Republican*, 11 Apr 1890)

Owens, Ann, see Robert D. Roberts, q.v.

Owens, Clara B., 1877-1938 (Mt. Carmel Methodist Church Cemetery)

Owens, Clara Hayes, 1880-1958, native of Havre de Grace, born 20 Mar 1880, daughter of Franklin Owens and Mary M. Anderson (Pennington Funeral Home Records - married name Kennedy)

Owens, Franklin, see Clara H. Owens, q.v.

Owens, H. F., trustee and alternate delegate to department encampment, John Rodgers Post, G. A. R., Havre de Grace (*Havre de Grace Republican*, 12 Dec 1890)

Owens, Hannah, see Owen A Greider, q.v.

Owens, J. Herbert, 1874-1940 (St. George's Episcopal Church Cemetery)

Owens, John Henry, 1864-1925 (Angel Hill Cemetery); council secretary, Beneficial Order of Equity, Havre de Grace (*Havre de Grace Republican*, 21 Nov 1890); clerk, Susquehanna Court No. 70, Equitable League of America, of Havre de Grace (*Havre de Grace Republican*, 28 Feb and 11 Jul 1890)

Owens, John W. T., 1836-1899 (Angel Hill Cemetery)

Owens, Margaret (Huggins), 1827-1909 (Angel Hill Cemetery)

Owens, Mary Emma, 1847-1910 (Angel Hill Cemetery)

Owens, Mary [Maria] Louisa (Hays), 1860-1940 (Death certificate; Angel Hill Cemetery), wife of John Henry Owens, q.v.

Owens, Oliver W., 1875-1943 (Mt. Carmel Methodist Church Cemetery)

Owens, Verdine, sneak boat duck hunter (*Havre de Grace Republican*, 7 Nov 1890)

Owings, Alfred Raymond (colored), born 26 Jun 1880, son of William S. and Laura Owings (Holy Cross Episcopal Church Register of Baptisms, p. 84)

Oxford Lyceum of Havre de Grace, an association of the Havre de Grace M. E. Church (*Havre de Grace: Its Historic Past, Its Charming Present and Its Promising Future: Harford County's Rural Heritage.* by Jack L. Shagena, Jr. and Henry C. Peden, Jr., 2018, p. 270)

Oxford, John (colored), born -- May 1860, native of Maryland (1900 Aberdeen Census)

Oxford, William (colored), 1865-1940 (Death certificate; St. James United Cemetery)

Ozmon, Ann, 1808-1892 (Cokesbury Memorial Church Cemetery); widow of Capt. Henry Ozmon, 1818-1881, and mother-in-law of Henry C. Johnson, of near Fallston (*The Aegis & Intelligencer*, 21 Nov 1890)

Paca, A. Burns, 1862-1937 (Mt. Zion Methodist Church Cemetery)

Paca, Anna E. (colored), see Anna E. Kenley (colored) and John W. Paca (colored), q.v.

Paca, Burnet, student, Union Chapel Public School (*The Aegis & Intelligencer*, 14 Mar 1890)

Paca, Cassandra (Gilbert), 1821-1906, resided at Fulford Death certificate; Mt. Zion Methodist Church Cemetery)

Paca, Elizabeth G., 1859-1947 (Mt. Zion Methodist Church Cemetery)

Paca, James (colored), trustee, Abingdon Colored School No. 1, First District (*Havre de Grace Republican*, 30 May 1890)

Paca, James Wesley (colored), 1837-1916, native of Maryland, resided at Michaelsville (Death certificate); trustee, Michaelsville Colored School No. 2, Second District, 1890 (*Havre de Grace Republican*, 30 May 1890); husband of Martha C. Paca, q.v.

Paca, John H. (colored), husband of Susie A. Paca, q.v.

Paca, John P. (colored), 1867-1910 (Union Methodist Church Cemetery, Aberdeen)

Paca, John W., 1934-1921 (Mt. Zion Methodist Church Cemetery)

Paca, John W. (colored), 1864-1941; husband of Anna E. Paca (Death certificate); juror, Third District, 1890 (*Havre de Grace Republican*, 31 Jan 1890)

Paca, Lizzie G. (Miss), resident near Wilna (*The Aegis & Intelligencer*, 7 Feb 1890); student at the Union Chapel Public School (*The Aegis & Intelligencer*, 14 Mar 1890); Class J - Domestic Products, and Class N - Floral Decorations, Harford County Fair (*The Aegis & Intelligencer*, 24 Oct 1890); member, Mountain Reading Circle (*The Aegis & Intelligencer*, 12 Sep 1890)

Paca, Martha C. (Simms) (colored), 1842-1931 (Death certificate spelled her name Paco; Union Methodist Church Cemetery, Aberdeen); wife of James W. Paca, q.v.

Paca, Mary Jane (colored), see George Michael Moore (colored), q.v.

Paca, Rebecca (colored), see Carrie Kenly (colored), q.v.

Paca, Sarah A. (Giles) (colored), 1868-1927 (Death certificate spelled her name Paco; Union Methodist Church Cemetery, Aberdeen)

Paca, Stephen (colored), new name on the voter registration list at Abingdon, First District, 1890 (*Havre de Grace Republican*, 17 Oct 1890); see Stephen Peaco (colored) and Stephen Peaker (colored), q.v.

Paca, Susie A. (Meadow) (colored), 1867-1910, wife of John H. Paca (Death certificate; Union Methodist Church Cemetery, Aberdeen)

Padgett, Augustus J., 1884-1928 (Hickory Cemetery); native of Maryland, born 9 May 1884, son of Richard Padgett, origin unknown, and Annie Garnes, native of Scotland (Bailey Funeral Home Records; Death certificate)

Page, Anna E., 1866-1917, resided at Cardiff (Death certificate)

Page, Anna S. (Mrs.), uncalled for letter in Bel Air P. O., 1890 (*The Aegis & Intelligencer*, 14 Nov 1890)

Page, Clara J., age 27 in 1890 (Marriage License Applications Book ALJ No. 2, 1890)

Page, Grace (Street), 1873-1945 (Christ Episcopal Church Cemetery)

Page, Henry, of First District, Democrat candidate for Congress, 1890 (*The Aegis & Intelligencer*, 26 Sep 1890)

Page, Joseph M., 1835-1918, resided at Churchville (Rock Run Methodist Church Cemetery)

Page, Mabel Adair (Anderson), 1883-1967 (Churchville Presbyterian Church Cemetery)

Page, Robert Middleton, 1879-1977 (Churchville Presbyterian Church Cemetery)

Page, Robert S., 1874-1920 (Christ Episcopal Church Cemetery)

Page, Rufus E., 1871-1901, resided at Flintville (Death certificate); Master Rufus Page, member, Aberdeen M. E. Church, 1890 (*Havre de Grace Republican*, 21 Feb 1890)

Page, Sarah E. (Tollenger), 1845-1930 (Rock Run Methodist Church Cemetery); second wife of Joseph M. Page, q.v.

Paige, Andrew G., 1840-1904 (Death certificate); transferred from the voter registration list at Hopewell, Second District, 1890 (*Havre de Grace Republican*, 17 Oct 1890)

Paige, Joseph, farmer, of Deer Creek, later at Perryman (*The Aegis & Intelligencer*, 28 Mar 1890)

Paine & Eggleston, hardware store, Jarrettsville (*The Aegis & Intelligencer*, 11 Apr 1890)

Palbal, Ezra, uncalled for letter in Bel Air P. O., 1890 (*The Aegis & Intelligencer*, 14 Nov 1890)

Palmatary, Beulah (Miss), age 21 in 1890 (Marriage License Applications Book ALJ No. 2); former public school principal (*Havre de Grace Republican*, 11 Apr 1890)

Palmer, Benjamin D., see Robert McGill Palmer, q.v.

Palmer, Charles, boat captain, near Havre de Grace (*The Aegis & Intelligencer*, 30 May 1890); sink boat duck hunter (*Havre de Grace Republican*, 7 Nov 1890)

Palmer, Elizabeth G., 1814-1894 (St. George's Episcopal Church Cemetery); Mrs. Mahlon Palmer, resided near Aberdeen (*The Aegis & Intelligencer*, 17 Jan 1890)

Palmer, George M., 1886-1913, resided in Havre de Grace (Death certificate)

Palmer, Harriet L., 1853-1923 (St. George's Episcopal Church Cemetery)

Palmer, Harry W., 1884-1945 (Baker Cemetery)

Palmer, Helen (Groton), 1876-1953 (St. George's Episcopal Church Cemetery)

Palmer, Isabella (Coe), 1831-1906 (St. George's Episcopal Church Cemetery)

Palmer, Lillian G., born 1885, died ---- (Baker Cemetery); wife of Harry W. Palmer, q.v.

Palmer, M. Herbert, 1874-1955 (St. George's Episcopal Church Cemetery); Herbert Palmer, jousting tournament rider, Knight of Glanuskie, 1890 (*The Aegis & Intelligencer*, 29 Aug 1890)

Palmer, Mahlon, 1812-1895 (St. George's Episcopal Church Cemetery)

Palmer, Mary J. (Mackell), see Robert McGill Palmer, q.v.

Palmer, Robert, 1861-1920 (Mt. Erin Cemetery)

Palmer, Robert McGill, 1880-1928 (Loudon Park Cemetery, Baltimore); native of Maryland, resided in Bel Air, born 17 Oct 1880, son of Benjamin D. Palmer and Mary J. Mackell (Death certificate)

Palmer, Samuel Webster, 1851-1902 (St. George's Episcopal Church Cemetery); resided t Cole (Death certificate); Webster Palmer, trustee, Oakland School No. 7, Second District (*Havre de Grace Republican*, 30 May 1890)

Palmer, Thomas (colored), born -- Mar 1890, native of Maryland (1900 Aberdeen Census); grandson of Barney Butler, q.v.

Palmer, Walter M. H., 1814-1895 (St. George's Episcopal Church Cemetery)

Parke, Mary, wife of James Ross Scarborough, q.v.; also see Clarence P. Scarborough, R. Marshall Scarborough and N. Maxwell Scarborough, q.v.

Parker, ----, center fielder, Webster Baseball Club, of Webster (*Havre de Grace Republican*, 25 Jul 1890)

Parker, Albert (Rev.), pastor, Highland Presbyterian Church (*The Aegis & Intelligencer*, 18 Apr 1890, stated his name was Albert G. Parker; *Havre de Grace Republican*, 25 Apr 1890, stated Albert B. Parker, *Havre de Grace Republican*, 30 May 1890, stated A. J. Parker, and *The Aegis & Intelligencer*, 14 Nov 1890, stated J. A Parker)

Parker, Alice Lee, 1874-1952 (Christ Episcopal Church Cemetery)

Parker, Alice R. (colored), 1867-1891, daughter of James W. Parker and Rebecca J. Prigg (Berkley Memorial Cemetery)

Parker, Annie A. (Colbert), 1843-1938 (Angel Hill Cemetery); native of Baltimore, resided in Havre de Grace (Death certificate); wife of Charles J. Parker, q.v.; also see Joseph Colbert Parker, George Edward Parker, Harru Augustus Parker, and Levin Stephenson Parker, q.v.

Parker, Anna Elizabeth ("Annie"), 1867-1950 (Ebenezer Methodist Church Cemetery); teacher, Youth's Benefit School No. 6, Fourth District (*The Aegis & Intelligencer*, 29 Aug 1890)

Parker, Charles A., 1886-1890 (Churchville Presbyterian Church Cemetery)

Parker, Charles J., 1844-1926 (Angel Hill Cemetery); see Annie A. Parker, Joseph Colbert Parker, George Edward Parker, Harry Augustus Parker, and Levin Stephenson Parker, q.v.

Parker, Clara L., 1878-1966 (Angel Hill Cemetery)

Parker, Elizabeth, died 12 Sep 1893, adult, age not given (Pennington Funeral Home Records)

Parker, Elizabeth (colored), see Henry Brown (colored), q.v.

Parker, Elizabeth Annie (Miss), 1859-1939 (Old Brick Baptist Church Cemetery)

Parker, Elizabeth M. "Bettie" (Mattingley), 1864-1947 (Angel Hill Cemetery); native of Havre de Grace

(Pennington Funeral Home Records); wife of Joseph C. Parker, q.v.

Parker, Elmira, see Elmira James, q.v.

Parker, Emily A. (colored), 1874-1927, native of Maryland, born 19 Jan 1874, daughter of William Parker and Rebecca Prigg (Death certificate - married name Hollingsworth)

Parker, Fannie E. (Miss), 1852-1938 (Rock Run Methodist Church Cemetery)

Parker, George Edward Davis, born 2 May 1877, son of Charles J. and Anna A. Parker (Holy Trinity Episcopal Church Register of Baptisms, p. 82)

Parker, Georgia (colored), see Georgia Cain (colored), q.v.

Parker, Georgianna, age 21 in 1890 (Marriage License Applications Book ALJ No. 2, 1890)

Parker, Harriet (colored), age 25 in 1890 (Marriage License Applications Book ALJ No. 2, 1890)

Parker, Hannah (Scott), 1876-1972 (Rock Run Methodist Church Cemetery)

Parker, Hannah H., 1809-1893 (Parker Family Cemetery)

Parker, Harry Augustus, born 26 Jun 1878, son of Charles J. and Anna A. Parker (Holy Trinity Episcopal Church Register of Baptisms, p. 82)

Parker, James T. (colored), 1873-1926 (Berkley Memorial Cemetery); native of Maryland, born 2 Jan 1873, resided near Darlington, son of James W. Parker and Rebecca Taylor (Death certificate)

Parker, James N., 1861-1940 (Churchville Presbyterian Church Cemetery)

Parker, James W. (colored), see Elmira James, Alice R. Parker, James T. Parker and Rebecca J. Parker, q.v.

Parker, James William (colored), 1830-1913, native of Maryland (Death certificate)

Parker, Jennette Carpenter, 1882-1951 (Rock Run Methodist Church Cemetery); native of Harford Co., born 17 Nov 1882, daughter of William S. Parker and Emma Purdy (Bailey Funeral Home Records)

Parker, John Scott, 1873-1940 (Christ Episcopal Church Cemetery)

Parker, Joseph Colbert, 1875-1940 (Angel Hill Cemetery); native of Harford Co., born 6 Aug 1875, son of Charles J. Parker, native of Harford Co., and Annie A. Colbert, native of Baltimore (Holy Trinity Episcopal Church Register of Baptisms, p. 82; Death certificate)

Parker, Joseph Couden, 1804-1892 (Parker Family Cemetery)

Parker, Josephine (Miss), 1836-1917 (Parker Family Cemetery)

Parker, Levin Stephenson, 1874-1943 (Angel Hill Cemetery); born 17 May 1874, son of Charles J. and Annie A. Parker (Holy Trinity Episcopal Church Register of Baptisms, p 82)

Parker, Lizzie, see Martha Emily Litchfield, q.v.

Parker, Lloyd (colored), 1853-1954 (Mt. Calvary Methodist Church Cemetery); husband of Rose Etta Curtis, q.v.

Parker, Lucile (colored), 1871-1923 (Death certificate; St. James United Cemetery)

Parker, Lucy (Miss), 1847-1901 (Parker Family Cemetery; Death certificate misfiled as Jarker and stated she died at Garland on 1 Jan 1901, age 55)

Parker, Martha I., 1861-1927 (Churchville Presbyterian Church Cemetery)

Parker, Mary E. (McCourtney), 1833-1909 (Ebenezer Methodist Church Cemetery)

Parker, Mary J., see Lonnie W. Thompson, q.v.

Parker, Maud Stephenson, 1874-1966 (Rock Run Methodist Church Cemetery)

Parker, Nancy G., 1808-1891 (Parker Family Cemetery); Miss Nancy Parker, age 82, resident near Darlington, sister-in-law of Judge John H. Price (*The Aegis & Intelligencer*, 25 Apr 1890)

Parker, Nicholas, 1861-1931, son of Nicholas H. and Susan (Poteet) Parker (Old Brick Baptist Church Cemetery)

Parker, Rachel (Price), died 22 Apr 1897, age 88, widow of Robert Parker (*Deaths and Marriages in Harford*

County, Maryland, and Vicinity, 1873-1904, from the Diaries of Albert Peter Silver, transcribed by Glenn Randers-Pehrson, 1995, p. 19)

Parker, Rebecca J. (Prigg) (colored), 1845-1913, native of Maryland (Berkley Memorial Cemetery; Death certificate states born in 1844); wife of James William Parker, q.v.

Parker, Robert, see Rachel Parker, q.v.

Parker, Samuel O. (colored), 1873-1918, native of Harford Co., born 15 Aug 1873, son of William Parker and ---- (Death certificate)

Parker, Sarah, wife of Lewis Henry Barron, q.v.; also see Mary Penelope Barron, q.v.

Parker, Sarah H. (Stephenson), 1809-1893 (Parker Family Cemetery), wife of Joseph Couden Parker and Hettie G. Stephenson, q.v.

Parker, Sarah Jane (Jamison) (colored), 1860-1936 (Death certificate); wife of James T. Parker, q.v.

Parker, Susan Alice, 1856-1915, daughter of Nicholas H. and Susan (Poteet) Parker (Old Brick Baptist Church Cemetery)

Parker, Vera R., 1890-1972 (Churchville Presyterian Church Cemetery)

Parker, Walter A., 1888-1892 (Churchville Presyterian Church Cemetery)

Parker, William (colored), see Georgia Cain, Emily A. Parker, Samuel O. Parker and Willimina Parker, q.v.

Parker, William H. (colored), 1843-1919, native of Maryland (Death certificate); Civil War veteran, Havre de Grace (*1890 Special Census of the Civil War Veterans of the State of Maryland*, by L. Tilden Moore, Volume III, p. 88)

Parker, William Stephenson, 1840-1932 (Rock Run Methodist Church Cemetery); see Jennette Carpenter Parker and Hettie G. Stephenson, q.v.

Parker, Willimina (colored), 1878-1900, servant, native of Maryland, resided near Darlington, daughter of William Parker and Rebecca ---- (Death certificate)

Parks, Alice, 1880-1947 (Cokesbury Memorial Methodist Church Cemetery)

Parks, Mary A., 1871-1948 (Cokesbury Memorial Methodist Church Cemetery)

Parks, William E., new name on the voter registration list at Hall's Cross Road, Second District (*Havre de Grace Republican*, 26 Sep 1890)

Parlett, David W., age 22 in 1890 (Marriage License Applications Book ALJ No. 2, 1891)

Parlett, Martha Anne (Phelps), 1870-1934, native and resident of Taylor, Harford Co. (Death certificate)

Parlett, Sarah E. (Cochran), 1882-1963 (Pine Grove Church Cemetery); native of Harford Co., born 26 Apr 1882, daughter of Daniel Cochran and Margaret Turnbaugh (Harkins Funeral Home Records)

Parrish, Edward Moore, see Eliza P. Anderson, Lillian E. Parrish, and Lillian E. Wheeler, q.v.

Parrish, Lillian E., born 1877, daughter of Edward Moore Parrish and Sabra Ellen Henderson (Bethel Presbyterian Church Cemetery Records); see Eliza P. Anderson and Lillian E. Wheeler, q.v.

Parr, Edward, c1857-1933 (Death certificate)

Parrott, Carroll S. (colored), 1887-1925, son of Sarah Parrott and ---- (Death certificate)

Parrott, Eli (colored), 1842-1912, native of Virginia, resident near Thomas Run (Death certificate); Civil War veteran, Churchville (*1890 Special Census of the Civil War Veterans of the State of Maryland*, by L. Tilden Moore, Volume III, p. 70); see Adeline P. Banks, Joseph H. Parrott and William H. Parott, q.v.

Parrott, Elizabeth (Banks) (colored), 1887-1910 (Death certificate)

Parrott, Estella (Highland) (colored), 1884-1933, native of Maryland (Death certificate); wife of William H. Parrott, q.v.

Parrott, Joseph H. (colored), c1869-1939, born in Maryland, son of Eli Parrott and Hannah Chambers (Death certificate)

Parrott, Millie (Mrs.) (colored), 1853-1935 (Death certificate)

Parrott, Sarah (colored), see Virginia L. Hill, Carroll S. Parrott and William H. Parrott, q.v.

Parrott, Telitha (colored), 1884-1952 (*The Aegis*, 2 Jan 1953)

Parrott, William H. (colored), 1885-1948, native of Harford Co., born 22 Apr 1885, son of Eli and Sarah Parrott (Death certificate)

Parry, Anna, 1889-1967 (Slate Ridge Cemetery, York Co., PA); native of Cardiff, Harford Co., born 9 Jun 1889, daughter of Thomas Parry and Carrie Stull (Harkins Funeral Home Records)

Parry, Catharine (Evans), 1844-1926 (Slateville Cemetery, York Co., PA); native of Wales, resided at Cardiff, Harford Co. (Death certificate)

Parry, Eleanor, see Jane W. Thomas, q.v.

Parry, Ellan Jane, see Ellen Jane Roberts, q.v.

Parry, Horace, see Thomas J. Parry, q.v.

Parry, Margaret, see Margaret P. Kauffman, q.v.

Parry, Mary, see Margaret W. Wilson, q.v.

Parry, Mary E., see Mary E. Ross, q.v.

Parry, Thomas, 1852-1926 (Slateville Cemetery, York Co., PA); native of Wales, quarryman, resided at Cardiff, Harford Co. (Death certificate); Thomas and wife [Carrie] sold land in April 1890 (*The Aegis & Intelligencer*, 9 May 1890); see Margaret P. Kauffman, Ellen Jane Roberts, Mary E. Ross and Anna Parry, q.v.

Parry, Thomas J., 1879-1950 (Slate Ridge Cemetery, York Co., PA); native of Maryland, born 21 Sep 1879, son of Horace Parry and Anna Stull (Harkins Funeral Home Records)

Parson, Caleb, 32nd PA Regt., Civil War veteran, lost left arm; resident of Dublin, Harford Co., 1890 (*1890 Special Census of the Civil War Veterans of the State of Maryland*, by L. Tilden Moore, Volume III, p. 88)

Parson, Calvin (colored), 1870-1948 (Death certificate; St. James United Cemetery)

Parson, Ellen (colored), wife of Richard Bowser, q.v.; also see Mary B. Bowser, q.v.

Parson, Susie (colored), mother of Lucy C. Ringgold, q.v.

Parsons, Alfred, delegate, Fifth District, Republican Party Convention (*The Aegis & Intelligencer*, 26 Sep 1890); trustee, Muttonsburg Colored School No. 4, Fifth District (*Havre de Grace Republican*, 30 May 1890)

Parsons, Ella (colored), c1871-1918 (Death certificate; St. James United Cemetery)

Parsons, Henry, and wife, sold land in April 1890 (*The Aegis & Intelligencer*, 9 May 1890)

Parsons, Isaiah (colored), resident of the Fifth District (*The Aegis & Intelligencer*, 25 Apr 1890); trustee, Muttonsburg Colored School No. 4, Fifth District, later resigned (*Havre de Grace Republican*, 30 May 1890; *Harford Democrat*, 10 Oct 1890)

Parsons, Sarah, and husband, sold land in April 1890 (*The Aegis & Intelligencer*, 9 May 1890)

Patsel, Thomas, died 14 Apr 1890, age not given (Alms House Record Book)

Patterson, Abel W., 1862-1919 (Bethel Presbyterian Church Cemetery Records)

Patterson, Alice, see Alice Hall Smith, wife of Dr. Richard H. Smith, q.v.

Patterson, Amentus Thomas, 1829-1915 (Churchville Presbyterian Church Register); trustee, School No. 8, First District (*Havre de Grace Republican*, 30 May 1890); premium award winner, Class A - Horses, Harford County Fair (*The Aegis & Intelligencer*, 24 Oct 1890)

Patterson, Arthur Maynard, born 3 May 1876, son of Samuel H. and Martha N. Patterson (William Patterson Bible, *Maryland Bible Records, Volume 5*, by Henry C. Peden, Jr., 2005, p. 144)

Patterson, Augustus N., age 46 in 1890 (Marriage License Applications Book ALJ No. 2, 1890)

Patterson, E. Stanley, jousting tournament rider, Knight of Greenwood (*Havre de Grace Republican*, 19 Sep 1890)

Patterson, Elizabeth, 1825-1901 (Bethel Presbyterian Church Cemetery Records); wife of John N. Patterson (1819-1886)

Patterson, Ella J. (Vaughn), 1856-1943 (Bethel Presbyterian Church Cemetery Records); wife of John W. Patterson, q.v.

Patterson, Elmira Jane, see John Varnes, q.v.

Patterson, Emma Elizabeth, 1890-1970 (Churchville Presyterian Church Cemetery)

Patterson, George D., see Grace Hall Patterson, q.v.

Patterson, George L. N., born 25 Aug 1872, son of Samuel H. and Martha N. Patterson (William Patterson Bible, *Maryland Bible Records, Volume 5*, by Henry C. Peden, Jr., 2005, p. 144)

Patterson, Grace Hall (Gover), 1873-1940 (Holy Trinity Episcopal Church Cemetery); native of Harford Co., born 22 Mar 1873, daughter of Gerard Gover and Cassandra Smithson, and wife of George D. Patterson (Bailey Funeral Home Records)

Patterson, Hannah Ellen (Hanna), 1830-1904 (Churchville Presbyterian Church Register; Death certificate); Mrs. A. T. Patterson, premium award winner, Class O - Discretionary, Harford County Fair (*The Aegis & Intelligencer*, 24 Oct 1890); wife of Amentus T. Patterson, q.v.

Patterson, Harry W., 1855-1943 (Old Brick Baptist Church Cemetery)

Patterson, Isabella (Lee), 1834-1922, native of Maryland (Bailey Funeral Home Records)

Patterson, James, trustee, Mt. Horeb School No. 10, Fourth District (*Havre de Grace Republican*, 30 May 1890)

Patterson, John T., delegate, Fourth District, Democrat Party Convention (*The Aegis & Intelligencer*, 5 Sep 1890)

Patterson, John W., 1854-1904 (Bethel Presbyterian Church Cemetery Records); see John Varnes, q.v.

Patterson, Josephine B., born 4 Apr 1883, daughter of Samuel H. and Martha N. Patterson (William Patterson Bible, *Maryland Bible Records, Volume 5*, by Henry C. Peden, Jr., 2005, p. 144)

Patterson, Lizzie, second grade student, Mount Horeb School (*The Aegis & Intelligencer*, 14 Feb 1890)

Patterson, M. V., student, Fourth District (*The Aegis & Intelligencer*, 24 Oct 1890)

Patterson, Martha E., age 31 in 1890 (Marriage License Applications Book ALJ No. 2, 1891)

Patterson, Mary E. (Dance), 1857-1916 (Old Brick Baptist Church Cemetery); wife of Harry W Patterson, q.v.

Patterson, Nelly H., premium award winner, Class L - Children's Department, Harford County Fair (*The Aegis & Intelligencer*, 24 Oct 1890)

Patterson, Samuel, student, Mount Horeb School (*The Aegis & Intelligencer*, 14 Feb 1890)

Patterson, Samuel Hanson, 1831-1893 (William Patterson Bible, *Maryland Bible Records, Volume 5*, by Henry C. Peden, Jr., 2005, p. 144)

Patterson, Stanley (master), resident near Fallston (*The Aegis & Intelligencer*, 11 Apr 1890)

Patterson, William, 1851-1916 (Death certificate; Heavenly Waters Cemetery)

Patton, Annie V., age 23 in 1890 (Marriage License Applications Book ALJ No. 2, 1891)

Patton, Bertha A., 1876-1963 (William Watters Memorial Methodist Church Cemetery, Cooptown)

Patton, Harry, student, Jarrettsville Graded School (*The Aegis & Intelligencer*, 25 Apr 1890)

Patton, Howard W, 1877-1961 (William Watters Memorial Methodist Church Cemetery, Cooptown)

Patton, John, see Mary Ann Billingslea, q.v.

Patton, Lillian V., 1881-1964 (William Watters Memorial Methodist Church Cemetery, Cooptown)

Patton, Lulu M., age 27 in 1890 (Marriage License Applications Book ALJ No. 2, 1891)

Patton, Mary H., 1836-1908 (Old Brick Baptist Church Cemetery)

Patton, Rebecca, see Hannah Way Ely, q.v.

Patton, William R., 1870-1949 (William Watters Memorial Methodist Church Cemetery, Cooptown)

Paul, Annie M. E. (Mitchell), 1852-1936 (Wesleyan Chapel Methodist Church Cemetery); wife of William . Paul, q.v.

Paul,George W., 1813-1892 (Wesleyan Chapel Methodist Church Cemetery)

Paul, James C., new name on the voter registration list at Abingdon, First District, 1890 (*Havre de Grace Republican*, 26 Sep 1890)

Paul, Robert, member of the firm of Paul & Eggleston, Jarrettsville (*Havre de Grace Republican*, 12 Dec 1890)

Paul, William H., 1840-1911 (Wesleyan Chapel Methodist Church Cemetery); Civil War veteran, Havre de Grace (*1890 Special Census of the Civil War Veterans of the State of Maryland*, by L. Tilden Moore, Volume III, p. 69); trustee and commander, Rodgers Post, G.A.R., of Havre de Grace (*Havre de Grace Republican*, 14 Feb and 11 Jul and 12 Dec 1890); government pensioner, at Webster (*The Aegis & Intelligencer*, 30 May 1890); member, Stephenson Lodge No. 128, A. F. & A. M., Lapidum (*Havre de Grace Republican*, 11 Jul 1890); member, Lapidum Debating Society (*Havre de Grace Republican*, 7 Feb 1890)

Paxton, Annie E., 1862-1947 (Grove Presbyterian Church Cemetery)

Paxton, Charles, carpenter, near Black Horse (*The Aegis & Intelligencer*, 3 Jan 1890)

Paxton, Samuel S., 1853-1932 (Grove Presbyterian Church Cemetery)

Payne, Alice Maud, 1872-1939 (Christ Episcopal Church Cemetery, married name Thompson); teacher, Davis' Corner School No. 21, Fourth District (*The Aegis & Intelligencer*, 29 Aug 1890, listed her name as Alice V. Payne)

Payne, Alpha L., 1872-1960 (Norrisville Methodist Church Cemetery); native of Norrisville, Harford Co., born 13 Jun 1872, son of William F. Payne and Liza J. Norris (Harkins Funeral Home Records)

Payne, Annie M., 1868-1972 (Norrisville Methodist Church Cemetery); wife of C. Reed Payne, q.v.

Payne, C. Reed, 1874-1953 (Norrisville Methodist Church Cemetery)

Payne, Carrie C. (Stokes), 1880-1963 (Norrisville Methodist Church Cemetery); native of Harford Co., born 16 Feb 1880, daughter of Harvey S. Stokes and Mary A Streett (Harkins Funeral Home Records)

Payne, Eliza Jane, 1846-1905 (Norrisville Methodist Church Cemetery)

Payne, George W., jousting tournament rider, Knight of Perryman (*Havre de Grace Republican*, 15 Aug and 17 Oct 1890); guitar player, Perryman (*The Aegis & Intelligencer*, 9 May 1890)

Payne, J. Ross, teacher, North Bend School No. 15, Fourth District (*The Aegis & Intelligencer*, 29 Aug 1890)

Payne, Josiah T., physician, near Shawsville (*Havre de Grace Republican*, 6 Jun 1890); juror, Fourth District (*Havre de Grace Republican*, 31 Jan 1890)

Payne, William Finney, 1845-1920 (Norrisville Methodist Church Cemetery); resident of Norrisville (*The Aegis & Intelligencer*, 3 Oct 1890); see Alpha L. Payne, q.v.

Peach Bottom Slate Company, Harford County quarry (*Heavy Industries of Yesteryear; Harford County's Rural Heritage*, by Jack L. Shagena, Jr. and Henry C. Peden, Jr., 2015, p. 212)

Peaco, Abraham Henry (colored), 1868-1937 (Death certificate; St. James United Cemetery)

Peaco, Alice Lucinda Elizabeth, 1881-1901, native of Harford Co., resided near Pyesville, wife of Theodore B. Peaco and daughter of John Sands and Mary Peaco (Death certificate also spelled the name Pecoe)

Peaco, Ann (colored), see Sarah A. Webster (colored), q.v.

Peaco, Charles W. (colored), new name on the voter registration list at Hopewell, Second District, 1890 (*Havre de Grace Republican*, 17 Oct 1890)

Peaco, Elizabeth A. (colored), 1828-1908 (St. James United Cemetery)

Peaco (Pekoe), Ellen (colored), see Harrison C. Lee (colored), q.v.

Peaco, George (colored), died 7 Dec 1903, age not given (Alms House Record Book spelled his namer Pico)

Peaco, George (colored), 1868-1934 (Death certificate; St. James United Cemetery)

Peaco, Harriet (Shields) (colored), 1858-1918, native of Maryland (Death certificate)

Peaco, Hezekiah (colored), 1861-1914, native of Harford Co., born 22 May 1861, son of John Peaco and Mary Boyins (Death certificate)

Peaco, Howard (colored), 1889-1932 (Death certificate; St. James United Cemetery)

Peaco, Isaiah (colored), 1876-1937, native of Harford Co., born 9 Jul 1867, son of James Peaco and Martha Simms, natives of Harford Co. (Death certificate)

Peaco, Jacob (colored), 1872-1943, native of Harford Co., parents unknown (Death certificate); also see Mary L. Peaco, q.v.

Peaco, James (colored), see Isaiah Peaco (colored) and Charles Peaker (colored), q.v.

Peaco, John (colored), see Hezekiah Peaco (colored), q.v.

Peaco, Lonnie W. (colored), 1877-1952 (Fairvew AME Church Cemetery)

Peaco, Lydia A. (Dorsey) (colored), 1840-1920 (Death certificate)

Peaco, Madeline (colored), 1885-1980, daughter of Sarah E. Peaco and Melcar Harris (*The Aegis*, 11 Dec 1980 - married name Williams; St. James United Cemetery)

Peaco, Mary (colored), see Alice Lucinda Elizabeth Peaco, (colored) q.v.

Peaco, Mary (Mrs.) (colored), 1835-1919, native of Maryland (Death certificate); see Hannah Lee, q.v.

Peaco, Mary B. (colored), 1880-1957 (Fairvew AME Church Cemetery)

Peaco, Mary L. (colored), c1886-1939, native and resident of Havre de Grace, daughter of Jacob Peaco and Mary Liza ---- (Death certificate)

Peaco (Peco), Mary Eliza (colored), age 30 in 1890 (Marriage License Applications Book ALJ No. 2, 1890)

Peaco, Mary Ellen (colored), wife of William S. Lee; also see J. Frank Lee and Jennie Lee, q.v.

Peaco, Rebecca S. (colored), see Mary S. Kenley (colored), q.v.

Peaco, Sarah E. (colored), 1866-1918 (Death certificate; St. James United Cemetery); see Madeline Peaco, q.v.

Peaco, Sarah Elizabeth (colored), 1875-1959, native of Aberdeen, Harford Co. (*The Democratic Ledger,* 29 Jan 1959)

Peaco, Stephen (colored), resident of Third District (*The Aegis & Intelligencer*, 14 Nov 1890)

Peaco, Theodore B. (colored), see Alice Lucinda Elizabeth Peaco (colored), q.v.

Peaco, William H. (colored), 1887-1959 (St. James United Cemetery)

Peaco (Peaca), William T. (colored), c1866-1936, native of Harford Co. (Death certificate); age 24 in 1890 (Marriage License Applications Book ALJ No. 2)

Peaker, Anna Maria (Mrs.) (colored), 1843-1919, native of Maryland (Death certificate)

Peaker, Charles (colored), 1873-1949, native of Maryland, born 30 May 1873, son of James W. Peaker and Martha Simms (Death certificate)

Peaker, Eliza E. (Bishop) (colored), 1849-1927, native of Maryland (Death certificate)

Peaker, Emma Howard (colored), 1873-1971, native of Maryland, daughter of Stephen Peaker and Eliza Bishop (Death certificate - married name Bond)

Peaker, Florence (colored), 1877-1940, native of Maryland, born 9 Mar 1877, daughter of Stephen Peaker and Eliza Bishop (Death certificate - married name Lenoir)

Peaker, James W. (colored), see Charles Peaker (colored), q.v.

Peaker, John Clayton (colored), 1875-1937, native of Maryland, born 6 Sep 1875, son of Stevenson Peaker and Eliza Bishop (Death certificate)

Peaker, Lillian (colored), 1886-1918, native of Harford Co., born 19 Dec 1886, daughter of Stephen Peaker and Eliza Bishop (Death certificate misfiled as Teaker)

Peaker, Lloyd T. (colored), 1869-1951 (Mt. Zion Methodist Church Cemetery, at Mountain)

Peaker, Mary E. (colored), 1870-1923, native of Harford Co., born 1 Jan 1870, daughter of Stephen Peaker and Eliza Bishop (Death certificate - married name Wright)

Peaker, Rachel Ann (Cohen) (colored), 1885-1943, native of Maryland, daughter of William and Mary Cohen (Death certificate)

Peaker, Stephen (colored), 1867-1943, native of Harford Co. (Death certificate)

Peaker, Stephen [Stevenson] (colored), see John C. Peaker, Emma H. Peaker, Florence Peaker, Lillian Peaker and Mary E. Peaker, q.v.

Peaker, Susan (colored), age 35 in 1889 (Marriage License Applications Book ALJ No. 2, 1889)

Pearce, Ann Rosela, see Edward Pearce Munnikhuysen, q.v.

Pearce, Edwin Lawrence, married Flora Julia Scarff, daughter of the late Joshua Scarff, on 18 Feb 1890 (*The Aegis & Intelligencer*, 21 Feb 1890)

Pearce, Elizabeth, county out-pensioner [welfare recipient], Fifth District (*Havre de Grace Republican*, 4 Jul 1890)

Pearce, Francis G., 1843-1920 (Old Brick Baptist Church Cemetery)

Pearce, George, see Thomas Pearce and William W. Pearce, q.v.

Pearce, George K., 1837-1900, resided at Reckord, Harford Co. (Death certificate incomlete)

Pearce, Mary E. (Durham), 1853-1911 (Old Brick Baptist Church Cemetery); wife of Frances G. Pearce, q.v.

Pearce, Solomon, 1823-1899, resident at Fallston, native of Maryland (Death certificate)

Pearce, Thomas, 1880-1966 (Slate Ridge Cemetery, York Co., PA); native of Whiteford, Harford Co., born 11 Aug 1880, son of George Pearce and ---- [blank] (Harkins Funeral Home Records); for his mother's name see his brother William W. Pearce, q.v.

Pearce, William W., 1886-1958 (Slate Ridge Cemetery, York Co., PA); native of Cardiff, Harford Co., born 19 Jan 1886, son of George Pearce and Mary Roberts (Harkins Funeral Home Records)

Pearson, Alice A., 1883-1969 (St. Mary's Episcopal Church Cemetery)

Pearson, Edwin Ergood, 1859-1932 (Angel Hill Cemetery)

Pearson, Frank C., 1864-1944 (St. George's Episcopal Church Cemetery); sergeant at arms, Equitable League of America, Court No. 70, Havre de Grace (*Havre de Grace Republican*, 11 Jul 1890)

Pearson, Franklin D., 1828-1897 (St. George's Episcopal Church Cemetery); see Ada Kate Burns, q.v.

Pearson, Harriet, see Eliza Jones, q.v.

Pearson, Irene Lillian (Mahan), 1863-1929, wife of Edwin Ergood Pearson, q.v.

Pearson, Mollie (Miss), secretary, Willard Section No. 58, Cadets of Temperance, Havre de Grace (*Havre de Grace Republican*, 11 Jul 1890)

Pearson, Nellie (Miss), assistant secretary, Willard Section No. 58, Order of the Cadets of Temperance, of Havre de Grace (*Havre de Grace Republican*, 7 Feb 1890)

Pearthree, Mary Eleanor, see John W. Knight and George Leon Knight, q.v.

Peck, Matilda (colored), see Matilda Webster (colored), q.v.

Peerless Slate Company, Harford County quarry (*Heavy Industries of Yesteryear; Harford County's Rural Heritage*, by Jack L. Shagena, Jr. and Henry C. Peden, Jr., 2015, p. 212)

Peery, John Brown, 1872-1943 (St. Mary's Episcopal Church Cemetery)

Peery, Minnie P., 1873-1965 (St. Mary's Episcopal Church Cemetery)

Peevy, Frances R. (colored), 1889-1967 (Union Methodist Church Cemetery, Aberdeen)

Pennell, Hannah A., 1827-1891, sister of J. M. Withers (Providence M. P. Church Cemetery)

Penniman, A. L., of Thomas Run, Harford Co., married Miss Fannie Griffith, of Baltimore Co., on 10 Apr 1890 (*Harford Democrat,* 18 Apr 1890)

Penniman, Lawrence, farmer, Thomas Run (*The Aegis & Intelligencer*, 29 Aug 1890); also see John Kelly, q.v.

Penning, Alice Markland ("Elsie"), 1866-1942 (Old School Baptist Church Cemetery, Snow Hill, MD - married name Coulbourn); teacher, Churchville School No. 10, Third District (*The Aegis & Intelligencer*, 29 Aug 1890, listed her as Elsie E. Penning)

Penning, Blanche Dorsey (McGaw), 1882-1963 (Grove Presbyterian Church Cemetery; www.findagrave.com)

Penning, Oliver Parker, grocery store merchant at the "Old Market" in Havre de Grace (*Harford Democrat*, 28 Aug 1890; *Havre de Grace Republican*, 19 Dec 1890); secretary, Willard Section No. 58, Order of the Cadets of Temperance, of Havre de Grace (*Havre de Grace Republican*, 7 Feb 1890)

Penning, Sylvester E., merchant and secretary of the Havre de Grace Mutual Protection Society (*Havre de Grace Republican*, 31 Jan 1890); vice grand, Morning Star Lodge No. 20, I. O. O. F., Havre de Grace (*Havre de Grace Republican*, 11 Jul 1890); justice of the peace, Sixth District (*Havre de Grace Republican*, 21 Feb 1890)

Pennington & Son Funeral Home, Havre de Grace (*1953 Harford County Directory*, p. 155)

Pennington, Abbie Lilly, born 31 May 1873, daughter of Lambert and Hannah Ell64 Pennington, of Fallston (Pennington Family Records, *Maryland Bible Records, Volume 2*, by Henry C. Peden, Jr., 2003, pp. 108-109)

Pennington, Alverda, 1870-1896 (William Watters Memorial Methodist Church Cemetery, Cooptown); member, Asbury M. E. Church, Jarrettsville (*The Aegis & Intelligencer*, 28 Feb 1890); vice president, Co. D., Loyal Temperance League, of Jarrettsville (*Havre de Grace Republican*, 21 Mar 1890)

Pennington, Annie Jane, see Annie Jane Aaronson, q.v.

Pennington, Bedellah (Hollahan), 1838-1899, resident and native of Havre de Grace (Death certificate; Angel Hill Cemetery); wife of Joseph Atlee Pennington, q.v.

Pennington, Birdie, high school student, Second District (*Havre de Grace Republican*, 31 Oct 1890)

Pennington, C. Archie, 1886-1965 (William Watters Memorial Church Cemetery, Cooptown)

Pennington, Carrie (Boyd), 1870-1948 (Angel Hill Cemetery); wife of Robert Rice Pennington, q.v.

Pennington, Carrollton ("Carroll"), 1843-1934 (William Watters Memorial Church Cemetery, Cooptown; John Pennington Bible, *Maryland Bible Records, Volume 5*, by Henry C. Peden, Jr., 2005, p. 145); delegate, Fourth District, Republican Party Convention (*The Aegis & Intelligencer*, 26 Sep 1890); census taker, Jarrettsville Precinct (*Havre de Grace Republican*, 23 May 1890); Civil War veteran, Jarrettsville (*1890 Special Census of the Civil War Veterans of the State of Maryland*, by L. Tilden Moore, Volume III, p. 80); juror, Fourth District (*Havre de Grace Republican*, 31 Jan 1890); served on a petit jury (*Havre de Grace Republican*, 14 Feb 1890)

Pennington, Catharine (Mrs.), 1800-1894 (William Watters Memorial Church Cemetery, Cooptown); resident of Jarrettsville, age 90, born 7 Feb 1800 (*The Aegis & Intelligencer*, 14 Feb 1890)

Pennington, Catherine, 1873-1959 (William Watters Memorial Church Cemetery, Cooptown)

Pennington, Charles B., 1889-1988 (Mt Zion Methodist Church Cemetery)

Pennington, Clara E., born 3 Feb 1881, daughter of Lambert and Hannah Ellen Pennington, of Fallston (Pennington Family Records, *Maryland Bible Records, Volume 2*, by Henry C. Peden, Jr., 2003, pp. 108-109)

Pennington, Cora M., 1887-1968 (William Watters Memorial Church Cemetery, Cooptown)

Pennington, Eliza Ellen (Arthur), 1846-1927 (Bethel Presbyterian Church Cemetery Records), wife of Franklin Pennington, q.v.

Pennington, Elizabeth Florence (Streett), 1874-1949 (William Watters Memorial Church Cemetery, Cooptown)

Pennington, Ellie, student, Jarrettsville Graded School (*The Aegis & Intelligencer*, 25 Apr 1890)

Pennington, Ellis, 1871-1938 (William Watters Memorial Church Cemetery, Cooptown)

Pennington, Elmer C., 1878-1962 (William Watters Memorial Church Cemetery, Cooptown)

Pennington, Emily C., 1875-1966, native of Havre de Grace, born 7 Apr 1875, daughter of Joseph A. Pennington and Bedelia Hollahan (Pennington Funeral Home Records - married name James)

Pennington, Evalena S. ("Eva"), 1869-1901 (Fallston Methodist Church Cemetery, married name Bosley);

teacher, Trappe School No. 14, Fifth District, on Deer Creek (*The Aegis & Intelligencer*, 29 Aug 1890; *Havre de Grace Republican*, 11 Apr 1890)

Pennington, Franklin, 1834-1914 (Bethel Presbyterian Church Cemetery Records)

Pennington, George Thompson, 1871-1947, native of Havre de Grace, born 15 Apr 1871, son of Joseph A. Pennington and Bedelia Hollahan (Pennington Funeral Home Records; Angel Hill Cemetery); third baseman, Kennedy Baseball Club, of Havre de Grace, 1890 (*Havre de Grace Republican*, 25 Jul 1890)

Pennington, H. O., sneak boat duck hunter (*Havre de Grace Republican*, 7 Nov 1890)

Pennington, Hannah C., age 22 in 1890 (Marriage License Applications Book ALJ No. 2, 1891)

Pennington, Hannah Ellen (Wetherill), 1842-1915 (Fallston Methodist Church Cemetery; Pennington Family Records, *Maryland Bible Records, Volume 2*, by Henry C. Peden, Jr., 2003, pp. 108-109); wife of Lambert Pennington, q.v.

Pennington, Harry O., 1856-1895 (St. George's Episcopal Church Cemetery)

Pennington, Harry O. H., 1813-1892 (St. George's Episcopal Church Cemetery)

Pennington, Irene C. (Kent), 1875-1960 (Slate Ridge Cemetery, York Co., PA); native of Pylesville, Harford Co., born 27 Oct 1875, daughter of Grier Kent and Mary Alice Whiteford (Harkins Funeral Home Records)

Pennington, Jasper Lindamore, born 9 Jan 1885, son of Franklin and Eliza (Arthur) Pennington (Bethel Presbyterian Church Cemetery Records)

Pennington, John H., 1827-1892 (John Pennington Bible, *Maryland Bible Records, Volume 5*, by Henry C. Peden, Jr., 2005, p. 145)

Pennington, John L., 1871-1890 (Fallston Methodist Church Cemetery); son of Lambert and Hannah Ellen Pennington, of Fallston (*The Aegis & Intelligencer*, 14 Nov 1890; Pennington Family Records, *Maryland Bible Records, Volume 2*, by Henry C. Peden, Jr., 2003, pp. 108-109)

Pennington, Joseph Atlee, 1828-1895 (Angel Hill Cemetery); J. A. Pennington & Son, coffin makers and undertakers, Havre de Grace, Sixth District (*Havre de Grace Republican*, 4 Jul 1890); see Emily C. Pennington, George Thompson Pennington and Robert Rice Pennington, q.v.

Pennington, Lambert, 1840-1924, wheelwright, native of Maryland, resident of Fallston (Death certificate; Fallston Methodist Church Cemetery; John Pennington Bible, *Maryland Bible Records, Volume 5*, by Henry C. Peden, Jr., 2005, p. 145; *The Aegis & Intelligencer*, 28 Nov 1890)

Pennington, Lee Roberts (Dr.), 1864-1930 (Angel Hill Cemetery)

Pennington, Levi, 1825-1913 (John Pennington Bible, *Maryland Bible Records, Volume 5*, by Henry C. Peden, Jr., 2005, p. 145)

Pennington, Levi Sargent, 1875-1919, tea company agent, resident of Jarrettsville, native of Harford Co. (Death certificate; William Watters Memorial Church Cemetery, Cooptown)

Pennington, Mary E., 1824-1900 (St. George's Episcopal Church Cemetery)

Pennington, Mary E., 1838-1925 (William Watters Memorial Church Cemetery, Cooptown)

Pennington, Mary J. (Devoe), 1887-1949 (Slate Ridge Cemetery, York Co., PA); native of Pylesville, Harford Co., born 27 Jan 1887, daughter of Grafton Devoe and ---- (Harkins Funeral Home Records)

Pennington, Mary Lareine (Hulett), 1871-1946 (Angel Hill Cemetery)

Pennington, Mary Maslin (Green), 1873-1946, native of Havre de Grace, born 23 Sep 1873, daughter of Lyttleton Green and Sarah E. Gorrell (Pennington Funeral Home Records; Angel Hill Cemetery), wife of George T. Pennington, q.v.

Pennington, Nancy "Nannie" Sophia, 1844-1894 (William Watters Memorial Church Cemetery, Cooptown); wife of Carrollton Pennington, q.v.

Pennington, Nettie L., 1876-1965 (William Watters Memorial Church Cemetery, Cooptown)

Pennington, Robert Rice, 1867-1949 (Angel Hill Cemetery); native and resident of Havre de Grace, born 4 Oct

1867, son of Joseph Atlee Pennington and Bedellah Hollohan (Death certificate); charter member, Havre de Grace Gunning Club and sneak boat duck hunter (*Havre de Grace Republican*, 7 Nov 1890 and 14 Nov 1890)

Pennington, Sadye Elizabeth, 1888-1968 (Bethel Presbyterian Church Cemetery Records); wife of Jasper Lindamore Pennington, q.v.

Pennington, Samuel A., born 29 Oct 1876, son of Franklin and Eliza (Arthur) Pennington (Bethel Presbyterian Church Cemetery Records)

Pennington, Samuel W., born 2 Jul 1877, son of Lambert and Hannah Ellen Pennington, of Fallston (Pennington Family Records, *Maryland Bible Records, Volume 2*, by Henry C. Peden, Jr., 2003, pp. 108-109)

Pennington, William, c1854-1934 (Death certificate; Alms House Record Book)

Pennington, William C., 1860-1920 (Angel Hill Cemetery)

Penny, Harriett Ann (Wagge) (colored), c1844-1929 (Death certificate)

Pennypacker, Charlotte Whitaker, 1852-1937 (St. George's Episcopal Church Cemetery)

Pennypacker, Isaac Anderson, 1879-1950 (St. George's Episcopal Church Cemetery)

Pennypacker, Isaac Rusling, 1852-1935 (St. George's Episcopal Church Cemetery)

Pennypacker, Julia Elizabeth, 1888-1958 (St. George's Episcopal Church Cemetery)

Pennypacker, Mary Ramsay, born 28 Mar 1888, baptized 10 Jul 1892, daughter of Isaac R. and Charlotte Pennypacker (Holy Trinity Episcopal Church Register of Baptisms, p. 102)

Pennypacker, Nathaniel Ramsay, 1881-1911 (St. George's Episcopal Church Cemetery)

Pentland, James Rutledge Gilbert, born 29 May 1883, son of James J. D. and Ellen Elizabeth (Gilbert) Pentland (Bethel Presbyterian Church Cemetery Records)

Pentz, Annie L. (Miss), librarian, Fallston (*Havre de Grace Republican*, 17 Jan 1890)

Pentz, Lewis, allias Lewis Smith, resident of Upper Cross Road (*The Aegis & Intelligencer*, 14 Mar 1890)

Pentz, William Henry, 1866-1939 (St. George's Episcopal Church Cemetery)

Perigo, John C., Civil War veteran, Norrisville (*1890 Special Census of the Civil War Veterans of the State of Maryland*, by L. Tilden Moore, Volume III, p. 82)

Perkins, Nathan E., acquired land in May 1890 (*The Aegis & Intelligencer*, 6 Jun 1890)

Perry, Hannah Ann (colored), see Charity Wade (colored) and Stewart K. Wade (colored), q.v.

Perryman Colored Public School No. 2, at Perryman, Second District (*Harford County, Maryland Teachers and the Schools They Served, 1774-1900*, by Henry C. Peden, Jr., 2022, p. 371)

Perryman Lime Kiln Club (*The Aegis & Intelligencer*, 30 May 1890)

Perryman Little Stars Baseball Club (*The Aegis & Intelligencer*, 1 Aug 1890)

Perryman Lodge No. 88, Order of the Golden Chain (*Havre de Grace Republican*, 27 Jun 1890)

Perryman Public School No. 5, at Perryman, Second District (*Harford County, Maryland Teachers and the Schools They Served, 1774-1900*, by Henry C. Peden, Jr., 2022, p. 371)

Perryman Theatrical Club (*Harford Democrat*, 26 Dec 1890)

Peters, Daniel, see Missouri Peters, q.v.

Peters, Hannah (colored), 1890-1963 (Ebenezer Baptist Church Cemetery)

Peters, Joseph (colored), see Nathan Peters (colored), q.v.

Peters, Lettie (colored), see William H. Watters (colored), q.v.

Peters, Missouri, 1850-1900, resident of Edgewood, wife of Daniel Peters (Death certificate)

Peters, Nathan (colored), c1869-1929, son of Joseph Peters and Rachel Giles (Death certificate); Nathaniel Peters acquired land in May 1890 (*The Aegis & Intelligencer*, 6 Jun 1890)

Peters, Sarah, see Sarah Harris Carver, q.v.

Peters, T. E. (Rev.), Methodist minister for the West Harford Circuit (*Havre de Grace Republican*, 21 Feb 1890); incorporator and ex-officio trustee, Friendship M. E. Church, Third District (*Havre de Grace Republican*, 21 Nov 1890)

Peters, T. L. (Mrs.), organist, Asbury M. E. Church, Jarrettsville (*The Aegis & Intelligencer*, 28 Feb 1890)

Peters, Zora (colored), wife of Daniel Peters, of Gunpowder Neck, Abingdon District, gave birth to her third pair of twins on 7 Oct 1890; the first pair are 12 years old and the second pair are 4 years old; she also had a number of single births (*The Aegis & Intelligencer*, 10 Oct 1890)

Peterson, Anna Florence, born 27 Dec 1881, daughter of John Pere and Anna Wilhelmina (Johnson) Peterson (*The Hughes Genealogy, 1636-1953*, by Joseph Lee Hughes, 1953, p. 114)

Peterson, C. Wilson, 1890-1941 (Mt. Tabor Methodist Church Cemetery)

Peterson, Charles H. (colored), c1852-1912 (Death certificate)

Peterson, Elias J., 1824-1907 (St. Ignatius Catholic Church Cemetery)

Peterson, Frances, see Ellen Lavinia Jones, q.v.

Peterson, Grace Lee (Debow), 1872-1932 (Mt. Tabor Methodist Church Cemetery)

Peterson, Isaac, property owner adjacent to Broadway in Bel Air (*The Aegis & Intelligencer*, 16 May 1890)

Peterson, James, 1817-1911, native of England (Mt. Tabor Methodist Church Cemetery); resident near Hickory (*The Aegis & Intelligencer*, 9 May 1890)

Peterson, James W., 1862-1926 (Mt. Tabor Methodist Church Cemetery); native of Maryland, carpenter, married, resided near Darlington (Death certifiicate)

Peterson, John Eli, born -- Jul 1824, baptized 19 Oct 1891 (ex-Methodist), son of John Peterson, native of Connecticut, and Delilia Wilson, native of Baltimore (St. Ignatius Catholic Church Baptism Register, p. 122)

Peterson, John W., 1864-1947 (Mt. Tabor Methodist Church Cemetery)

Peterson, Julia M., 1834-1913 (St. Ignatius Catholic Church Cemetery)

Peterson, Lucie M., 1871-1962 (Mt. Tabor Methodist Church Cemetery)

Peterson, Mary E. (Mrs.), 1829-1899, resident of Aberdeen (Death certificate)

Peterson, Mathew M., 1870-1929 (Mt. Zion Methodist Church Cemetery)

Peterson, Rennis (Judd), 1822-1910 (Mt. Tabor Methodist Church Cemetery)

Peterson, Retta N., 1876-1944 (Mt. Zion Methodist Church Cemetery)

Peterson, Stella A., 1885-1935 (Fallston Methodist Church Cemetery)

Peterson, Walter E., 1880-1948 (Fallston Methodist Church Cemetery)

Pevey, Hattie (colored), see HattieTurner (colored), q.v.

Pevey, John (colored), see Rachel Pevey (Pever), Sarah Ann Anderson, Hattie Turner and Adeline Williams, q.v.

Pevey Rachel (McComas) (colored), 1886-1901, native of Maryland, resided at Calvary, daughter of ---- and Sarah McComas, wife of John Pevey (Death certificate spelled her name Rachael Pever); see Sarah Ann Anderson and Adeline Williams, q.v.

Peyton, Rosa Elizabeth, baptized 11 Feb 1883, daughter of George and ---- Peyton (St. George's Episcopal Church Register of Baptisms, pp. 2-3, did not record her date of birth)

Pfaffenbach, George, 1869-1950 (Angel Hill Cemetery); member, Merry Ten Social Club, Havre de Grace (*Havre de Grace Republican*, 25 Jul 1890)

Pfaffenbach, Mary Ann Martin (Pearson), 1867-1930, wife of George Pfaffenbach, q.v.

Phelps, John W., Civil War veteran, Pleasantville (*1890 Special Census of the Civil War Veterans of the State of Maryland*, by L. Tilden Moore, Volume III, p. 78)

Phelps, Josephine C., 1860-1935 (Ebenezer Methodist Church Cemetery)

Phelps, M. Anna "Annie" (Miss), organist, Ebenezer M. E. Church Sunday School (*Havre de Grace Republican*,

25 Apr 1890); age 19 in 1890 (Marriage License Applications Book ALJ No. 2, 1891)

Phelps, Maggie G., 1873-1902 (Emory Methodist Church Cemetery)

Phelps, Margaret Susan, 1873-1902 (Ebenezer Methodist Church Cemetery)

Phelps, Mary Virginia ("Mamie"), born 1879, daughter of Sylvester Phelps and Susanna Arthur (*Harford County, Maryland Teachers and the Schools They Served*, by Henry C. Peden, Jr., 2021, p. 251)

Phelps, Penrose Carr, 1879-1918 (Emory Methodist Church Cemetery)

Phelps, Robert W., 1868-1902 (Mt. Zion Methodist Church Cemetery)

Phelps, Rose M., 1869-1946 (Mt. Erin Cemetery)

Phelps, Susanna (Arthur), 1851-1915 (Ebenezer Methodist Church Cemetery); wife of Sylvester Phelps, q.v.

Phelps, Sylvester, 1841-1919 (Ebenezer Methodist Church Cemetery); trustee, Hope's School No. 4, Fourth District (*Havre de Grace Republican*, 30 May 1890); see Mary Virginia Phelps, q.v.

Phelps, Wesley, juror, Third District (*Havre de Grace Republican*, 2 May 1890); see Bertha I. Duff, q.v.

Phenix Carriage Works, Bond Street, Bel Air, Zacehus DeBow and John H. Heuer, prop. (*Carriages Back in the Day: Harford County's Rural Heritage*, by Jack L. Shagena, Jr. and Henry C. Peden, Jr., 2016, pp. 82-83)

Philadelphia, Wilmington & Baltimore Railroad, stations at Havre de Grace. Aberdeen, Perryman, Bush River, Edgewood and Magnolia (*Harford Democrat*, 31 Jan 1890)

Phillips, Albert McVey, 1855-1921 (William Watters Memorial Methodist Church Cemetery, Cooptown); native of Chester Co., PA, resided near Cooptown (Death certificate); see Ellis Eugene Phillips, q.v.

Phillips, Annie E., 1868-1942 (William Watters Memorial Methodist Church Cemetery, Cooptown)

Phillips, Callie (Poteet), 1871-1938 (William Watters Memorial Methodist Church Cemetery, Cooptown)

Phillips, Delia (Brown) (colored), c1867-1918 (Death certificate)

Phillips, Dora (Faidley), 1865-1961 (Jarrettsville Cemetery)

Phillips, Easter P. (colored), c1862-1925 (Death certificate)

Phillips, Ellis Eugene, 1883-1935 (William Watters Memorial Methodist Church Cemetery, Cooptown); native of Harford Co., born 5 Feb 1883, son of Albert M. Phillips and Mary Poteet (Bailey Funeral Home Records)

Phillips, Florence, 1879-1966 (Ayres Chapel Methodist Church Cemetery)

Phillips, G. Thomas, 1864-1942 (Ebenezer Methodist Church Cemetery)

Phillips, George Barclay, 1886-1961 (Old Brick Baptist Church Cemetery; *The Aegis*, 9 Feb 1961)

Phillips, Ida Belle, 1870-1913 (Ayres Chapel Methodist Church Cemetery)

Phillips, James R., 1868-1929 (Jarrettsville Cemetery)

Phillips, Jane E., 1886-1967 (Baker Cemetery)

Phillips, Katie E., 1870-1936 (Ebenezer Methodist Church Cemetery)

Phillips, Lucretia (Arthur), 1835-1912 (Ayres Chapel Methodist Church Cemetery)

Phillips, M. Luther, 1873-1958 (Ayres Chapel Methodist Church Cemetery)

Phillips, Martha A. E., 1856-1930 (William Watters Memorial Methodist Church Cemetery, Cooptown)

Phillips, Mary, age 14, student, Oakland School, 1890 (George G. Curtiss Ledger)

Phillips, Mary Elizabeth, 1833-1920 (Ebenezer Methodist Church Cemetery)

Phillips, Mary Zora (Poteet), 1882-1959 (Old Brick Baptist Church Cemetery); wife of George Barclay Phillips, q.v.

Phillips, Ralph K., 1877-1964 (Baker Cemetery)

Phillips, Stephen John, 1826-1899 (Ayres Chapel Methodist Church Cemetery)

Phillips, W., blacksmith, Mill Green (*Harford Democrat*, 4 Apr 1890)

Philomathean Society, Havre de Grace (*Havre de Grace: Its Historic Past, Its Charming Present and Its*

Promising Future: Harford County's Rural Heritage. by Jack L. Shagena, Jr. and Henry C. Peden, Jr., 2018, p. 271)

Phippen, Anna M., 1834-1897 (Baker Cemetery)

Phoenix Club, Havre de Grace (*Havre de Grace: Its Historic Past, Its Charming Present and Its Promising Future: Harford County's Rural Heritage.* by Jack L. Shagena, Jr. and Henry C. Peden, Jr., 2018, p. 271)

Phrisby, George (colored), see George Frisby (colored), q.v.

Pickelberg, Charles H., 1856-1929 (Angel Hill Cemetery); see Frederick Pickelberg, q.v.

Pickelberg, Frederick, shoemaker, Stokes Street; Havre de Grace (*Havre de Grace Republican*, 7 Feb 1890); died testate in 1890 and his named heirs were wife Wilhelmina Pickelberg, son Charles H. Pickelberg and daughter Augusta C. Drager (Harford County Will Book JMM 11:89-80)

Pickelberg, Wilhelmina, 1818-1899, resident and native of Havre de Grace (Death certificate); wife of Frederick Pickelberg, q.v.

Pieper, Bertha, 1868-1910, wife of Henry Pieper (Mt. Carmel Methodist Church Cemetery)

Pieper, Eliza, 1826-1910, wife of Henry A. Pieper (Mt. Carmel Methodist Church Cemetery)

Pieper, Henry, 1855-1908 (Mt. Carmel Methodist Church Cemetery); Henry Piper, Jr., acquired land in August 1890 (*The Aegis & Intelligencer*, 12 Sep 1890)

Pieper, Henry A., 1816-1896 (Mt. Carmel Methodist Church Cemetery); Henry Piper, hauling contractor, First District (*Havre de Grace Republican*, 4 Jul 1890)

Pierce, Annie B., 1813-1898 (Death certificate; Alms House Record Book)

Pierce, Frank, fourth grade student, Prospect Hill School (*The Aegis & Intelligencer*, 21 Feb 1890)

Pierce, George F., born 1890, died ---- (Trinity Evangelical Lutheran Church Cemetery)

Pierce, John Y., juror, First District, 1890 (*Havre de Grace Republican*, 31 Jan 1890)

Pierce, Mary A. (Miss), teacher, Angleside School No. 3, Third District (*The Aegis & Intelligencer*, 29 Aug 1890); premium award winner, Class M - Miscellaenous, Harford County Fair (*The Aegis & Intelligencer*, 24 Oct 1890)

Pierson, Cassandra (colored), wife of Wilson Bouldin, q.v., also see Henry Bouldin, q.v.

Pill, Samuel, county out-pensioner [welfare recipient], Fourth District (*Havre de Grace Republican*, 4 Jul 1890)

Pillsbury, Jennie T., teacher, Whiteford's School No. 2, Fifth District (*The Aegis & Intelligencer*, 25 Jul 1890 and 29 Aug 1890)

Pine, Lizzie (Miss), niece of Charles W. Roberts, near Emmorton, died 15 Mar 1890, age 17 (*The Aegis & Intelligencer*, 21 Mar 1890)

Pinion, Amanda (colored), c1865-1927 (Death certificate; St. James United Cemetery)

Pinion, Carrie J. (colored), born 1865, died ---- (Union Methodist Church Cemetery, Aberdeen); wife of John L. Pinion, q.v.

Pinion, Ellen (Mrs.) (colored), 1797-1903 (*Havre de Grace Republican*, 31 Jan 1903)

Pinion, Hannah (Stansbury) (colored), 1843-1912 (Death certificate)

Pinion, Henrietta (colored), see William H. Pinion (colored), q.v.

Pinion, Jacob Henry (colored), age 20 in 1890 (Marriage License Applications Book ALJ No. 2, 1891)

Pinion, John L. (colored), 1857-1958 (Union Methodist Church Cemetery, Aberdeen)

Pinion, Lewis (colored), see William H. Pinion (colored), q.v.

Pinion, Lillie Bowser (Mrs.) (colored), 1886-1922 (Union Methodist Church Cemetery, Aberdeen); resided near Perryman, native of Maryland, born 5 Dec 1886, daughter of Robert J. Pinion and Harriett Christy (Death certificate)

Pinion, Mary E. (Giddings) (colored), 1888-1949 (Death certificate; St. James United Cemetery)

Pinion, Mary Eliza (colored) age 24 in 1890 (Marriage License Applications Book ALJ No. 2, 1891)

Pinion, Mary G. (colored), born -- May 1876, native of Maryland (1900 Aberdeen Census)

Pinion, Philip S. (colored), 1861-1932 (Union Methodist Church Cemetery, Aberdeen); Philip Pinion, age 28 in 1890, married Mary M. Webster on 2 Oct 1890 at Perryman, MD (Marriage License Applications Book ALJ No. 2)

Pinion, Raymond A. (colored), 1884-1987 (Union Methodist Church Cemetery, Aberdeen)

Pinion, Robert J. (colored), see Lillie Bowser Pinion (colored), q.v.

Pinion, William (colored), born -- Feb 1876, native of Maryland (1900 Aberdeen Census)

Pinion, William H. (colored), 1884-1946, native of Havre de Grace, son of Lewis and Henrietta Pinion (Death certificate; St. James United Cemetery)

Pinkney, Annie M. (colored), 1881-1920, native of Harford Co., born 21 Nov 1881, daughter of James Pinkney and Cornelia Giles, natives of Harford Co. (Death certificate - married name Tasker)

Pinkney, Hester J. (colored), died 23 Aug 1907, young adult, age not given (*The Aegis & Intelligencer*, 23 Aug 1907)

Pinkney, James (colored), 1832-1918, native of Harford Co. (Death certificate); see Annie M. Pinkney, q.v.

Pinkney, Sarah Ann Cornelia (Giles), 1844-1919, native of Harford Co. (Death certificate)

Pitcock, Anna R., 1884-1951 (Mountain Christian Church Cemetery)

Pitcock, Arabella (Leight), 1855-1934, wife of Charles Henry Pitcock, q.v.; also see Mary Pitcock, q.v.

Pitcock, Charles E., Sr., 1883-1970 (Mountain Christian Church Cemetery)

Pitcock, Charles Henry, 1841-1900, engineer, native of Maryland, resided at Wheel (Death certificate; Mountain Christian Church Cemetery)

Pitcock, Elghie Marion, 1885-1972 (Mountain Christian Church Cemetery)

Pitcock, John Henry, 1878-1950 (Mountain Christian Church Cemetery)

Pitcock, Margaret A., 1882-1982 (Mountain Christian Church Cemetery)

Pitcock, Mary, 1886-1908, daughter of ---- and Arabella Pitcock, of Wheel, Harford Co. (Mountain Christian Church Cemetery; *The Aegis & Intelligencer*, 27 Mar 1908)

Pitt, Albert James (colored), see James Albert Pitt (colored), q.v.

Pitt, Cassie (colored), see Thomas Pitt (colored), q.v.

Pitt, Cora A., age 21 in 1890 (Marriage License Applications Book ALJ No. 2, 1890)

Pitt, Frances E. (colored), 1879-1926 (Union Methodist Church Cemetery, Aberdeen); native of Maryland, born 7 Feb 1879, daughter of John W. Pitt and Frances Harris (Death certificate)

Pitt, George, county out-pensioner [welfare recipient], Third District (*Havre de Grace Republican*, 4 Jul 1890)

Pitt, George A. (colored), c1870-1920, native of Harford Co., son of John A. Pitt and Grace Reid (Death certificate)

Pitt, Gertie Cordelia (colored), 1887-1901, resident of Michaelsville, daughter of J. Albert Pitt and Mary Stansbury (Death certificate)

Pitt, Hannah (colored), and child, died 12 Jun 1892 (Alms House Record Book)

Pitt, J. Albert (colored), see Gertie Cordelia Pitt (colored), q.v.

Pitt, James Albert (colored) 1882-1945, native of Perryman, Harford Co., born 2 Feb 1882, son of Albert James Pitt and Mary C. Stansbury (Death certificate)

Pitt, John A. (colored), see George A. Pitt (colored), q.v.

Pitt, John W. (colored), 1843-1939 (Death certificate); see Frances E. Pitt (colored), q.v.

Pitt, Josiah E. (colored), 1880-1964 (Union Methodist Church Cemetery, Aberdeen)

Pitt, Margaret S. (colored), 1867-1944 (Union Methodist Church Cemetery, Aberdeen)

Pitt, Martha C. (Mrs.) (colored), 1876-1967 (Union Methodist Church Cemetery, Aberdeen)

Pitt, Mary Frances (Harris) (colored), 1848-1926 (Death certificate; Union Methodist Church Cemetery, Aberdeen, tombstone inscribed Frances M. Pitt); wife of John W. Pitt, q.v.; also see Frances E. Pitt (colored), q.v.

Pitt, Mary Jane (colored), age 18 in 1889 (Marriage License Applications Book ALJ No. 2, 1889)

Pitt, Thomas (colored), 1876-1901, native of Maryland, single, farm hand at Cole, son of Casssie Pitt and Isaac Brown (Death certificate)

Pitt, William (colored), c1851-1918, native of Harford Co. (Death certificate)

Pitts, George (colored), 1858-1898 (Death certificate; Alms House Record Book)

Plaskitt, Sophia Catherine, died 15 Mar 1890 (St. George's P. E. Church Cemetery)

Plato, J. K. (Rev.) (colored), pastor of the African M. E. Church in Churchville (*The Aegis & Intelligencer*, 2 May 1890)

Platt, Samuel, see James H. Grafton, q.v.

Plowman, Henry F., 1805-1895 (Mountain Christian Church Cemetery)

Plowman, Ida Bernice, 1861-1909 (Mt. Carmel Methodist Church Cemetery), daughter of Jacob H. Plowman, q.v.

Plowman, Jacob H., 1836-1897 (Mt. Carmel Methodist Church Cemetery), farmer, of Emmorton, and Commodore of the State Oyster Navy; former county commissioner and Civil War veteran (*Havre de Grace Republican*, 27 Jun and 31 Oct 1890 (*Biographical Dictionary of Harford County, Maryland, 1774-1974*, by Henry C. Peden, Jr. and William O. Carr, 2021, p. 216); board of directors, Agricultural and Mechanical Society (*Havre de Grace Republican*, 23 May 1890)

Plowman, Joseph, 1848-1927 (Mountain Christian Church Cemetery)

Plowman, Martha R., 1864-1947 (Mountain Christian Church Cemetery)

Plowman, Martha S. (Hess), 1848-1926 (Mountain Christian Church Cemetery); native of Harford Co., resided at Joppa (Death certificate)

Plowman, Mary E., 1819-1899 (Mountain Christian Church Cemetery)

Plowman, Silas B., 1837-1902 (Grove Presbyterian Church Cemetery)

Plowman, Silas G., 1885-1952 (Baker Cemetery)

Pocock, Annie Johnson (Nelson), 1859-1936 (Bethel Presbyterian Church Cemetery Records; Death certificate); Mrs. C. W. Pocock, premium award winner, Class J - Domestic Products, Harford County Fair (*The Aegis & Intelligencer*, 24 Oct 1890); wife of Charles W. Pocock, q.v.

Pocock, Bertie, 1880-1891 (Bethel Presbyterian Church Cemetery Records); born 3 Sep 1880, daughter of Charles and Annie Pocock (Cornelius Garrison Bible, *Maryland Bible Records, Volume 5*, by Henry C. Peden, Jr., 2004, p. 78)

Pocock, Catherine Belle, born 17 May 1883, daughter of Charles W. and Annie (Nelson) Pocock (Bethel Presbyterian Church Cemetery Records)

Pocock, Charles Wesley, born 28 Apr 1854, son of Salem and Susannah Pocock (Cornelius Garrison Bible, *Maryland Bible Records, Volume 5*, by Henry C. Peden, Jr., 2004, p. 78; Bethel Presbyterian Church Cemetery Records); farmer, at the Big Woods near Bel Air (*The Aegis & Intelligencer*, 25 Jul 1890)

Pocock, Frances Anne (Jackson), 1852-1934 (Bethel Presbyterian Church Cemetery Records); wife of Jesse Pocock, q.v.

Pocock, Harry Gilmore, 1869-1955 (St. Mary's Catholic Church Cemetery)

Pocock, James, died 22 Jul 1890, in his 83rd year, at Taylor (*The Aegis & Intelligencer*, 25 Jul 1890)

Pocock, Jesse, 1845-1930 (Bethel Presbyterian Church Cemetery Records); see Frances Anne Pocock and Cora

A. Cockey, q.v.

Pocock, Jessie Mayfield, born 11 Aug 1881, daughter of Jesse and Frances (Jackson) Pocock (Bethel Presbyterian Church Cemetery Records)

Pocock, Katie B., born 17 May 1883, daughter of Charles and Annie Pocock (Cornelius Garrison Bible, *Maryland Bible Records, Volume 5*, by Henry C. Peden, Jr., 2004, p. 78)

Pocock, Margaret Reatha, born 13 Aug 1878, daughter of Charles W. and Annie Johnson (Nelson) Pocock (Bethel Presbyterian Church Cemetery Records); born 13 Aug 1878, daughter of Charles and Annie Pocock (Cornelius Garrison Bible, *Maryland Bible Records, Volume 5*, by Henry C. Peden, Jr., 2004, p. 78)

Pocock, Mary E., 1866-1946 (Ebenezer Methodist Church Cemetery)

Pocock, Mary Prisclla (Gladden), 1876-1965 (St. Mary's Cathlolic Church Cemetery); wife of Harry G. Pocock, q.v.

Pocock, Philip H., 1856-1927 (Ebenezer Methodist Church Cemetery); resident of Marshall's District (*The Aegis & Intelligencer*, 3 Oct 1890); son of James Pocock, q.v.

Poff, Henry A., see Hugh A. Poff, q.v.

Poff, Hugh A., 1860-1939 (Slate Ridge Cemetery, York Co., PA); native of Harford Co., born 30 Mar 1860, son of Henry A. Poff and Susan Curran (Harkins Funeral Home Records)

Poff, Mary J. (Jones), 1851-1939 (Slate Ridge Cemetery, York Co., PA); native of Harford Co., born 15 Jul 1851, daughter of John Jones and Mary Troutner (Harkins Funeral Home Records)

Pohl, Lambert C., 1879-1926 (Mt. Erin Cemetery); native of Germany, born 26 Jun 1879, son of Lambert Pohl and ----, resided in Havre de Grace (Death certificate)

Pohl, Margaret (Vincent), 1874-1955 (Mt. Erin Cemetery)

Poist, Charles S., 1884-1968 (Mt. Erin Cemetery)

Poist, Jacob H., formerly of Delta, PA, proprietor, Bel Air Meat and Produce Market, Bond St. and Pennsylvania Ave., near the Eagle Hotel (*Harford Democrat*, 24 Jan 1890; *The Aegis & Intelligencer*, 14 Feb 1890)

Poist, Jessie Jackson, 1884-1959 (Mt. Erin Cemetery)

Pokorny, Leopold, age 21 in 1890 (Marriage License Applications Book ALJ No. 2, 1891)

Polar, Jenie (Miss), resided in Dublin (*Harford Democrat*, 14 Mar 1890)

Pomeroy, Eugene H., 1840-1907 (St. Mary's Episcopal Church Cemetery)

Pomeroy, Elizabeth (Polk), 1845-1924 (St. Mary's Episcopal Church Cemetery)

Pontston, Eliza (colored), age 21 in 1889 (Marriage License Applications Book ALJ No. 2, 1889)

Poole, Clara Isabel, born -- Oct 1885, baptized 29 Nov 1885, daughter of James Poole, native of Cecil Co., MD, and Louisa Heuisler, native of Baltimore (St. Ignatius Catholic Church Baptism Register, p. 85)

Poole, Emily (colored), see Florence E. White (colored), q.v.

Poole, Georgia R. (Scarborough), 1868-1941, native of Harford Co. (Bailey Funeral Home Records)

Poole, Hattie Agnes, 1871-1950 (St. Ignatius Catholic Church Cemetery); daughter of Mrs. Lucinda Poole, of Forest Hill (*The Aegis & Intelligencer*, 18 Jul 1890); teacher, Thomas Run Public School, and sister of Miss Lillie Poole (*The Aegis & Intelligencer*, 4 Jul 1890); assistant teacher, Forest Hill School No. 5, Third District; trustee, School No. 1, Fourth District (*The Aegis & Intelligencer*, 8 Aug and 29 Aug 1890); teacher, Forest Hill School, 1890 (*The Aegis*, 2 Jul 1965, school picture)

Poole, Isabelle (Wright), 1834-1916 (St. Ignatius Catholic Church Cemetery); wife of Thomas M. Poole, q.v.

Poole, John Sprigg (Dr.), 1862-1904, moved from Poolesville, MD to Dublin, MD in 1888, was issued a ducking license in 1889-1890, married in 1891 and later returned (*Duck Hunters on the Susquehanna Flats, 1850-1930*, by Henry C. Peden, Jr. and Jack L. Shagena, Jr., 2014, p. 93); premium award winner, Class A - Horses, Harford County Fair (*The Aegis & Intelligencer*, 24 Oct 1890); age 28 in 1890 (Marriage License Applications Book ALJ No. 2, 1891)

Poole, James, 1843-1915 (St. Ignatius Catholic Church Cemetery)

Poole, James Thomas, baptized 21 Apr 1883, son of James and Louisa (Heuisler) Poole (St. Ignatius Catholic Church Baptism Register, p. 64)

Poole, Lillie, daughter of Mrs. Lucinda Poole, of Forest Hill (*The Aegis & Intelligencer*, 18 Jul 1890); premium award winner, Class J - Domestic Products, Harford County Fair (*The Aegis & Intelligencer*, 24 Oct 1890); also see Hattie Agnes Poole, q.v.

Poole, Louisa (Heuisler), 1851-1935 (St. Ignatius Catholic Church Cemetery); wife of James Poole, q.v.

Poole, Mary Ann (Mackey), 1811-1897 (St. Ignatius Catholic Church Cemetery)

Poole, Mary Catharine, born -- Jun 1889, baptized 26 Jul 1889, daughter of James Poole, native of Cecil Co., MD, and Louis Heuisler, native of Baltimore (St. Ignatius Catholic Church Baptism Register, p. 106)

Poole, Mary Lucinda (Clark), 1843-1927 (St. Ignatius Catholic Cemetery), mother of Hattie Agnes Poole, q.v.

Poole, Stuart B., 1890-1932 (Churchville Presbyterian Church Cemetery)

Poole, T. Howard, age 24 in 1890 (Marriage License Applications Book ALJ No. 2, 1891)

Poole, Thomas M., 1833-1922 (St. Ignatius Catholic Church Cemetery); farmer and county commissioner, Third District (*Havre de Grace Republican*, 14 Feb 1890 and 4 Jul 1890); trustee, Ward's School No. 6, Third District (*Havre de Grace Republican*, 30 May 1890)

Poole, William (Mrs.), premium award winner, Class M - Miscellaenous, Harford County Fair (*The Aegis & Intelligencer*, 24 Oct 1890)

Pope, Rennis Lee (Miss), 1839-1926 (Green Mount Cemetery, Baltimore); native of Maryland, resided at Forest Hill (Death certificate)

Poplar, Annie C. (Murray), 1861-1923 (Angel Hill Cemetery); wife of William H. Poplar, q.v.; also see William M. Poplar, q.v.

Poplar, Charles ("Charlie"), 1871-1892, son of William Poplar (*Havre de Grace Republican*, 9 Dec 1892); catcher, Kennedy Baseball Club, of Havre de Grace (*Havre de Grace Republican*, 25 Jul 1890)

Poplar, Carrie Virginia (Haines), 1871-1962 (Angel Hill Cemetery)

Poplar, Elizabeth, see Florence Hackney, q.v.

Poplar, Ephenea ("Effie"), 1840-1902 (Death certificate); wife of James Poplar, q.v.; also see John Henrie Poplar, q.v.

Poplar, Florence Ewing, 1869-1898 (Angel Hill Cemetery)

Poplar, Florence G., 1869-1898 (Death certificate)

Poplar, H. J., sink boat duck hunter, 1890 (*Havre de Grace Republican*, 7 Nov 1890)

Poplar, Ida A. (DeMars), 1875-1949 (Angel Hill Cemetery; *The Aegis*, 18 Feb 1949)

Poplar, James, captain of the boat *Geo. W. Jr.*, of Havre de Grace (*Havre de Grace Republican*, 4 Jul 1890); member, inquest jury, Havre de Grace (*Havre de Grace Republican*, 6 Jun 1890); see John Henrie Poplar, q.v.

Poplar, Jesse Dobson, 1864-1942 (Death certificate); age 25 in 1889 (Marriage License Applications Book ALJ No. 2, 1889)

Poplar, John, 1834-1911 (Death certificate); sink boat duck hunter (*Havre de Grace Republican*, 7 Nov 1890)

Poplar, John Henrie, 1864-1958 (Angel Hill Cemetery); native of Havre de Grace, born 15 Jul 1864, son of James Poplar and Effie Purnell (Pennington Funeral Home Records; Angel Hill Cemetery)

Poplar, Lida, 1884-1962, native of Havre de Grace, born 8 Jul 1884, daughter of William H. Poplar and Annie C. Murray (Pennington Funeral Home Records - married name Preston)

Poplar, William, deceased and removed from the voter registration list in Sixth District, 1890 (*Havre de Grace Republican*, 17 Oct 1890); see Charles Poplar, q.v.

Poplar, William H. ("Bill"), 1861-1933 (Angel Hill Cemetery); captain of the sloop-yacht *Carrie*, of Havre de Grace, 1890 (*Havre de Grace Republican*, 15 Aug 1890); committeeman, Knights of St. Leo, Havre de Grace

(*Havre de Grace Republican*, 19 Sep 1890); member, Havre de Grace Gun Club (*Havre de Grace Republican*, 26 Dec 1890); sink boat duck hunter (*Havre de Grace Republican*, 7 Nov 1890); charter member, Havre de Grace Gunning Club (*Havre de Grace Republican*, 14 Nov 1890); member, Independent Social Club, Havre de Grace (*Havre de Grace Republican*, 28 Mar 1890); see Lida Poplar and William M. Poplar, q.v.

Poplar, William Murray, 1889-1961 (Angel Hill Cemetery); native of Havre de Grace, born 10 Jan 1889, son of William H. Poplar and Annie Murray (Pennington Funeral Home Records)

Porter, Alexander Shaw (Dr.), married Ella Keen, daughter of B. H. Keen, of Perryman, on 10 Jun 1890 (*The Aegis & Intelligencer*, 13 Jun 1890)

Porter, Benjamin F., 1887-1972 (St. Mary's Catholic Church Cemetery)

Porter, Harry P., 1880-1934 (Union Chapel Methodist Church Cemetery)

Porter, Larue, student, Bel Air Graded School (*The Aegis & Intelligencer*, 11 Apr 1890)

Porter, Madison, young son of J. C. Porter, of Emmorton (*Harford Democrat*, 21 Mar 1890)

Post, Alfred Phillip, 1880-1940 (Darlington Cemetery)

Post, Ruth Lillian (Richmond), 1883-1952 (Darlington Cemetery)

Poteet, Cora, 1880-1900 (Death certificate incomplete); resided at Bradenbaugh, wife of Harry Poteet and granddaughter of Mrs. Andrew Kirkwood

Poteet, Harry, see Cora Poteet, q.v.

Poteet, James, 1828-1912 (Old Brick Baptist Church Cemetery)

Poteet, James Howard, 1871-1952 (Old Brick Baptist Church Cemetery); son of Thomas Howard Poteet and Mary A. Durham (*The Aegis*, 23 May 1952)

Poteet, Mary, see Ellis Eugene Phillips, q.v.

Poteet, Mary Ann (Durham), 1847-1899 (Old Brick Baptist Church Cemetery); resided at Cooptown, native of Maryland (Death certificate; ; wife of Thomas H. Poteet, q.v.

Poteet, Mary Zora, born 1882, daughter of Thomas Howard Poteet and Mary Durham (*The Aegis*, 15 Jan 1959); Zora Poteet, resided near High Point (*The Aegis & Intelligencer*, 8 Aug 1890); see Mary Zora Phillips, q.v.

Poteet, Sheffield T., 1866-1912 (William Watters Church Cemetery, Cooptown), son of Thomas H. Poteet, of Cooptown, married Callie J. Burkins, daughter of Charles Burkins, of Jarrettsville, on 5 Mar 1890 (Marriage License Applications Book ALJ No. 2, 1890, and marriage certificate; *The Aegis & Intelligencer*, 14 Mar 1890); farmer, at Cooptown (*The Aegis & Intelligencer*, 25 Jul 1890) [Some family records state his name was Thomas Sheffield Poteet and he was called Sheffield.]

Poteet, Thomas Howard, 1830-1915 (Old Brick Baptist Church Cemetery)

Potts, Annie May (Silver), 1870-1938 (Highland Presbyterian Church Cemetery; www.findagrave.com)

Potts, John Wesley, 1843-1916 (Highland Presbyterian Church Cemetery; www.findagrave.com)

Poulson, John (colored), 1840-1897 (*The Aegis*, 12 Feb 1897)

Poulton, Blanche E., 1872-1947 (Fallston Methodist Church Cemetery)

Pow, John T., 1835-1910 (*Barnes-Bailey Genealogy*, by Walter D. Barnes, 1939, p. G-13)

Pow, Lydia (Barnes), 1840-1917 (*Barnes-Bailey Genealogy*, by Walter D. Barnes, 1939, p. G-13)

Powell, James, died 7 Sep 1890, age about 50, of Cambria (*The Aegis & Intelligencer*, 12 Sep 1890' Slateville Presbyterian Church Cemetery)

Powell, John (colored), died 26 Apr 1919, married adult, age not given, resided near Reckord, parents unknown (Death certificate)

Powell, Lillian (Mrs.), 1878-1970 (Fawn Grove Methodist Church Cemetery); native of Whiteford, Harford Co., born 9 Jul 1878, parents unknown (Harkins Funeral Home Records)

Power, Amelia Elizabeth, born -- Oct 1886, baptized 1 May 1887, daughter of Philip Power, native of Prince George's Co., MD, and Mary Sonbiron, native of Baltimore (St. Ignatius Catholic Church Baptism Register, p.

92)

Power, Mary H., 1848-1914 (St. Francis de Sales Catholic Church Cemetery)

Power, Philip W., 1847-1903 (St. Francis de Sales Catholic Church Cemetery)

Powers, Ellen (Carney), 1856-1933 (Mt. Erin Cemetery)

Powers, Mary, 1822-1901 (Mt. Erin Cemetery)

Powers, Walter, 1816-1879 (Mt. Erin Cemetery)

Pratt, Edith (Miss), treasurer, Willard Section No. 58, Order of the Cadets of Temperance, Havre de Grace (*Havre de Grace Republican*, 7 Feb 1890 and 11 Jul 1890)

Pratt, Katherine, see Katherine Bauer and William Henry Bauer, q.v.

Presberry, Albert (colored), 1876-1941, native of Castleton, Harford Co., son of Henry Presberry and Kiziah Prigg (Death certificate spelled the name Presbury)

Presberry, Amelia (colored), see Eben P. Hill (colored), q.v.

Presberry, Amos (colored), age 23 in 1890 (Marriage License Applications Book ALJ No. 2, 1890)

Presberry, Annie (Webster) (colored), c1872-1940, native of Harford Co., daughter of William and Annie Webster (Death certificate); wife of John E. Presberry, q.v.

Presberry, Annie M. (colored), 1889-1988, native of Harford Co., daughter of Nelson Presberry and Eliza ---- (*The Aegis*, 21 Jul 1988 - married name Lisby; 1900 Aberdeen Census listed her as Mary A. Presberry, born in March 1889)

Presberry, Daisy (colored), wife of John M. Presberry (colored), q.v.

Presberry, Eliza (colored), born -- Jun 1858, native of Maryland (1900 Aberdeen Census); wife of Nelson Presberry (colored) and mother of Annie M. Presberry (coloed), q.v.

Presberry, Frances (colored), see Frances Jamison. Frances P. Jamison (colored) and George W. Jamsion (colored), q.v.

Presberry (Presbury), George (colored), see Lily P. Smith, Hannah J. Wilson and Priscilla P. Wilson, q.v.

Presberry, George (colored), 1872-1948, native of Harford Co., son of Henry Presberry and Kiziah Prigg (Death certificate)

Presberry, George W. (colored), 1852-1918, native of Harford Co. (Death certificate)

Presberry, Georgia (colored), see Dora Webster (colored), q.v.

Presberry, Grace (colored), see Granville Aikens (colored) and Malissie Aikens (colored), q.v.

Presberry, Hannah (colored), see Sarah W. Johnson (colored), q.v.

Presberry, Harriett K. (colored), 1848-1922 (Death certificate)

Presberry, Hazzard (colored), 1856-1929 (Berkley Memorial Cemetery)

Presberry, Henry (colored), see Albert Presberry, George Presberry, John M. Presberry, Henry J. Presberry, Jr. and William E. Presberry, q.v.

Presberry, Henry J., Jr. (colored), 1875-1946, native of Castleton, Harford Co., son of Henry J. Presberry and Kiziah Prigg (Death certificate; Berkley Memorial Cemetery)

Presberry, Ida E. (colored), born 1888, died ---- (Berkley Memorial Cemetery)

Presberry, Jane (Howard) (colored), 1844-1938 (Death certificate)

Presberry, John E. (colored), 1873-1944, native of Darlington, son of Robert Presberry and Jane Foreman (Death certificate)

Presberry, John M. (colored), 1881-1933, native of Castleton, Harford Co., son of Henry Presberry and Kiziah Prigg (Death certificate); see Bertha L. Presbury, q.v.

Presberry, Kiziah E. (colored), 1887-1952, native of Castleton, Harford Co. (Berkley Memorial Cemetery tombstone inscription)

Presberry, Mabel P. (colored), see Mabel P. Webster (colored), q.v.

Presberry, Mary (colored), see Nathaniel Ash, Benjamin Green and David A. Green, q.v.

Presberry, Nelson (colored), born -- May 1856, native of Maryland (1900 Aberdeen Census); father of Annie M. Presberry (colored), q.v.

Presberry, Robert (colored), 1846-1928 (Berkley Memorial Cemetery); native of Maryland, resided at Berkley (Death certificate); see John E. Presberry and Mabel P. Webster, q.v.

Presberry, Sarah (colored), see Hannah J. Wilson (colored), q.v.

Presberry, Sarah E. (Spriggs) (colored), 1863-1928 (Berkley Memorial Cemetery; Death certificate states born in 1864); wife of Hazzard Presberry, q.v.

Presberry, Susan (Washington), 1875-1939, native of Harford Co., daughter of Sylvester Washington and Mary E. Hill (Death certificate); wife of Henry J. Presberry, Jr., q.v.

Presberry, Susan V. (Wilson) (colored), 1864-1939, native of Harford Co., daughter of Edward Wilson and Mary A. Turner, and wife of George Presberry (Death certificate)

Presberry, William Edward, 1869-1940, native of Harford Co., son of Henry Presberry and Kiziah Prigg (Death certificate)

Presbury Methodist Church (Gunpowder Neck)

Presbury, Agnes (colored), see Alice Virgina Presbury (colored), q.v.

Presbury, Albert (colored), see Albert Presberry (colored), q.v.

Presbury, Alice Virginia, 1878-1900, native of Maryland, resided at Darlington, daughter of Hazzard Presbury and Agnes ---- (Death certificate - married name Cain)

Presbury, Amos (colored), husband of Hannah J. Presbury, q.v.

Presbury, Amous (colored), 1845-1925 (Death certificate)

Presbury, Annie E. (colored), 1886-1917, native of Harford Co., born 12 Feb 1886, daughter of William E. Presbury and Mary F. Jackson (Death certificate - married name Turner)

Presbury, Benjamin P. (colored), 1842-1912, native of Harford Co. (Death certificate); see George W. Presbury, q.v.

Presbury, Bertha L. (Wilson) (colored), 1876-1907, native of Cecil Co., MD, wife of John M. Presbury (Death certificate); see John M. Presberry, q.v.

Presbury, Buddy (colored), c1847-1922 (Alms House Record Book; *The Aegis & Intelligencer*, 2 Feb 1922)

Presbury, Cassie (colored), died 24 Apr 1900, old age; daughter of Robert and Sabina Presbury (Death certificate)

Presbury, David, proprietor, Enterprise Mills, Bush River Neck (*The Aegis & Intelligencer*, 1 Aug 1890)

Presbury, Eliza H. (Brooks) (colored), 1867-1941 (Death certificate)

Presbury George W. (colored), 1884-1915, native of Harford Co., born 22 May 1884, son of Benjamin Presbury and Ella Christy (Death certificate)

Presbury, Hannah (colored), see Charlotte A. Smith (colored) and Hannah J. Wilson (colored), q.v.

Presbury, Hannah J. (Hill) (colored), 1870-1900, native of Harford Co., resided at Gravel Hill (Death certificate)

Presbury, Hazzard (colored), see Alice Virginia Presbury, q.v.

Presbury, Jeremiah (colored), born -- Feb 1840, native of Maryland (1900 Aberdeen Census); Civil War veteran, of Aberdeen (*1890 Special Census of the Civil War Veterans of the State of Maryland*, by L. Tilden Moore, Volume III, p. 64); Jerry Presbury, trustee, Gravelly Hill Colored School No. 4, Second District (*Havre de Grace Republican*, 30 May 1890)

Presbury, John H. (colored), trustee, Cedars Colored School No. 2, Fifth District (*Havre de Grace Republican*, 30 May 1890)

Presbury, Martha (colored), age 23 in 1890 (Marriage License Applications Book ALJ No. 2, 1891)

Presbury, Mary (colored), 1852-1944 (Death certificate; Alms House Record Book)

Presbury, Mary F. (Jackson) (colored), 1868-1934, native of Harford Co. (Death certificate)

Presbury, Nelson F. (colored), 1859-1936, native of Camden, NJ, resided near Aberdeen (Death certificate); acquired land in February 1890 (*The Aegis & Intelligencer*, 7 Mar 1890)

Presbury, Priscilla (colored), see Harriet W. Berry (colored), q.v.

Presbury, Robert and Sabina (colored), see Cassie Presbury (colored), q.v.

Presbury, Stephen Henry (colored), c1832-1910, native of Harford Co. (Death certificate stated he died at age 74, but *The Aegis & Intelligencer*, 17 Jun 1910, stated he was 82); trustee, McComas Institute, Colored School No. 2, First District, 1890 (*Havre de Grace Republican*, 30 May 1890)

Presbury, William H. (colored), 1869-1946, native of Harford Co. (Death certificate)

Presby, Betty (colored), 1879-1891 (Hendon Hill Cemetery)

Presco, Amanda (colored), see Mary E. Dorsey (colored) and Laura Wells (colored), q.v.

Prescott, Charles E., 1870-1955 (Angel Hill Cemetery)

Prescott, Maud E., 1882-1950 (Angel Hill Cemetery)

Preston, A. Belle (Stephens), 1890-1976 (Wesleyan Chapel Methodist Church Cemetery)

Preston, Aaron (colored), died 5 Apr 1908, age not given(Alms House Record Book)

Preston, Abbie (Fletcher), 1872-1956 (Norrisville Methodist Church Cemetery)

Preston, Achsah (Carroll), 1871-1926 (St. George's Episcopal Church Cemetery)

Preston, Achsah (Ridgely), 1838-1917 (St. George's Episcopal Church Cemetery)

Preston, Agnes V., 1885-1959 (Rock Run Methodist Church Cemetery)

Preston, Alberta B., 1889-1973 (Mountain Christian Church Cemetery)

Preston, Alexander, 1859-1917 (Wesleyan Chapel Methodist Church Cemetery); son of James H. Preston and Eliza J. ---- (James H. Preston Bible, *Maryland Bible Records, Volume 2*, by Henry C. Peden, Jr., 2003, p. 110)

Preston, Alice C., 1848-1929 (Wesleyan Chapel Methodist Church Cemetery); wife of Alexander Preston, q.v.

Preston, Alice M., wife of Walter A. Aaronson, q.v.

Preston, Ann Louise (colored), born -- Dec 1887, baptized 12 Feb 1888, daughter of Harrison and Mary (Gordon) Preston (St. Ignatius Catholic Church Baptism Register, p. 97)

Preston, Anne E. (colored), 1834-1904 (Hendon Hill Cemetery); wife of Joshua Preston, q.v.

Preston, Annie A., 1861-1947 (Baker Cemetery)

Preston, Annie B., born 4 Apr 1865, daughter of James H. Preston and Eliza J. ---- (James H. Preston Bible, *Maryland Bible Records, Volume 2*, by Henry C. Peden, Jr., 2003, p. 110); age 25 in 1890 (Marriage License Applications Book ALJ No. 2, 1891)

Preston, Arthur, 1870-1938 (Baker Cemetery)

Preston, Augusta (Harris) (colored), c1864-1916, native of Aberdeen, Harford Co. (Death certificate)

Preston, Avarilla (colored), born -- Feb 1888, native of Maryland, daughter of Noah and Eliza Preston (1900 Aberdeen Census)

Preston, Belle Xenia (Carsins), 1886-1915 (Baker Cemetery)

Preston, Benjamin, 1855-1925 (Cokesbury Memorial Methodist Church Cemetery)

Preston, Benjamin Oscar (colored), born -- 1890, baptized 28 Jul 1890, son of Laura Preston, father unknown (St. Ignatius Catholic Church Baptism Register, p.115)

Preston, Benjamin Van Buren, 1840-1923 (Baker Cemetery); widower, age 50 in 1890 (Marriage License Applications Book ALJ No. 2, 1891)

Preston, Caroline, 1830-1922 (Christ Episcopal Church Cemetery)

Preston, Carrie Virginia (Preston), 1884-1965 (Wesleyan Chapel Methodist Church Cemetery)

Preston, Cecelia E. (Harward), 1882-1924 (Mt. Zion Methodist Church Cemetery); native of Harford Co., resided at Fulford, daughter of William D. Harward and Laura V. Jeffery (Death certificate)

Preston, Charles (colored), resident of Bel Air (*The Aegis & Intelligencer*, 27 Jun 1890)

Preston, Charles F., 1872-1948 (Norrisville Methodist Church Cemetery)

Preston, Charles R., 1854-1902 (Salem Evangelical Lutheran Church Cemetery); road surveying chain man, Fourth District, 1890 (*Havre de Grace Republican*, 4 Jul 1890); see James W. Preston, q.v.

Preston, Clara Wellsetta (Kunkle), 1881-1935 (Bethel Presbyterian Church Cemetery Records); wife of John W. Preston, q.v.

Preston, Columbus, 1861-1943 (Jarrettsville Cemetery); see James W. Preston, q.v.

Preston, Cora C. (Stansbury) (colored), 1869-1925 (Death certificate)

Preston, David, Jr., 1843-1900 (Little Falls Quaker Cemetery); druggist, native of Harford Co., resided at Fallston (Death certificate)

Preston, Deborah, 1817-1895 (Little Falls Quaker Cemetery)

Preston, Edmond, 1814-1893 (Little Falls Quaker Cemetery); son of David and Judith Preston, and wife Phoebe Hoskins, daughter of Nathaniel and Elizabeth Hoskins, resided at *Cecil's Adventure* near Fallston and celebrated their 50th anniversary in 1890 (*The Aegis & Intelligencer*, 14 Nov 1890)

Preston, Edmond, Jr., 1862-1894 (Little Falls Quaker Cemetery)

Preston, Edmond D., 1882-1907 (Little Falls Quaker Cemetery)

Preston, Edna (Standiford), 1887-1960 (Little Falls Quaker Cemetery)

Preston, Eliza J. (Hill) (colored), 1858-1926 (St. James Church, Gravel Hill Cemetery); native of Maryland, resided in Aberdeen (Death certificate); wife of Noah Preston (colored), q.v.

Preston, Eliza Jane, 1838-1918 (James H. Preston Bible, *Maryland Bible Records, Volume 2*, by Henry C. Peden, Jr., 2003, p. 110); wife of James Henry Preston, q.v.; also see Tilden Preston, q.v.

Preston, Elizabeth (Hollingsworth), 1848-1920 (Christ Episcopal Church Cemetery)

Preston, Ella, 1873-1956, daughter of James H. Preston and Eliza J. ---- (James H. Preston Bible, *Maryland Bible Records, Volume 2*, by Henry C. Peden, Jr., 2003, p. 110); assistant secretary, Helping Hand Society of Avondale Christian Church (*Havre de Grace Republican*, 7 Feb 1890)

Preston, Ella May, 1871-1949 (Baker Cemetery)

Preston, Ella O., 1872-1918 (Wesleyan Chapel Methodist Church Cemetery); wife of Samuel W. Preston, q.v.

Preston, Ephraim A. (colored), 1883-1938, native of Harford Co., born 12 May 1883. son of Wesley Preston and Hattie Brown (Death certificate)

Preston, F. Celia, 1879-1969 (Baker Cemetery)

Preston, F. Dicty (colored), 1873-1949, native of Kalmia, Harford Co., born 17 Oct 1873, son of Harrison Preston and Mary Gordon (Death certificate)

Preston, Franklin "Frank" A., 1874-1957 (Wesleyan Chapel Methodist Church Cemetery); son of James H. Preston and Eliza J. ----, born 23 Aug 1874 (James H. Preston Bible, *Maryland Bible Records, Volume 2*, by Henry C. Peden, Jr., 2003, p. 110); road surveying poleman, Fourth District, 1890 (*Havre de Grace Republican*, 4 Jul 1890)

Preston, Franklin I., 1846-1896 (Jarrettsville Cemetery)

Preston, Frederick J., see James W. Preston, q.v.

Preston, G. Howard, 1890-1973 (Baker Cemetery)

Preston, George, farmer, Jarrettsville (*The Aegis & Intelligencer*, 7 Nov 1890)

Preston, George Orman, 1886-1956 (Wesleyan Chapel Methodist Church Cemetery)

Preston, George W., road surveying chain man, Fourth District, 1890 (*Havre de Grace Republican*, 4 Jul 1890); see James W. Preston and John W. Preston, q.v.

Preston, George Washington (colored), 1879-1974, native of Perryman, Harford Co., born 15 Aug 1879, son of John W. Preston and Harriett ---- (*The Aegis*, 3 Jan 1975)

Preston, Georgia "Georgie" A. (Gallion), 1852-1926 (Wesleyan Chapel Methodist Church Cemetery); wife of Jesse E. Preston, q.v.; also see Winnie Smith Preston, q.v.

Preston, Grace, 1890-1900 (Baker Cemetery); daughter of Sylvester Preston and Ella ----, resided at Carsins Run (Death certificate)

Preston, Grover Cleveland, 1885-1958 (Rock Run Methodist Church Cemetery)

Preston, Hall S., 1873-1958 (Fallston Methodist Church Cemetery)

Preston, Hannah (colored), see George E. Rumsey (colored), q.v.

Preston, Hannah (Mooberry), 1821-1907 (Jarrettsville Cemetery); wife of James W. Preston, q.v.

Preston, Harriet (colored), see Ida Preston (colored) and George Washngton Preston (colored), q.v.

Preston, Harriet Andrews (Hoskins), 1844-1926 (Little Falls Quaker Cemetery); wife of David Preston (1843-1900), q.v.

Preston, Harriet P., 1828-1891 (Calvary Methodist Church Cemetery)

Preston, Harriett H. (Mrs.), (colored), died 27 Jun 1916, widow, age not given (Death certificate)

Preston, Harrison (colored), 1851-1920, native of Harford Co. (Death certificate); see Ann Louise Preston, F. Dicty Preston, Henry Edward Preston and Samuel William Preston, q.v.

Preston, Harry (colored), resident of Harford Co.,,, location not stated (*The Aegis & Intelligencer*, 14 Nov 1890)

Preston, Harry, tomato farmer, at Webster (*The Aegis & Intelligencer*, 30 May 1890)

Preston, Harry P., 1884-1955 (Wesleyan Chapel Methodist Church Cemetery)

Preston, Helen, county out-pensioner [welfare recipient], Fourth District, 1890 (*Havre de Grace Republican*, 4 Jul 1890)

Preston, Henry, charged with assault in 1890, but found not guilty (Harford County Criminal Docket, 1888-1892, p. 92)

Preston, Henry C., son of Edmund Preston, q.v.

Preston, Henry Edward (colored), born -- Aug 1882, baptized 15 Oct 1882, son of Harrison Preston and Mary Gordon (St. Ignatius Catholic Church Baptism Register, p. 61)

Preston, Ida V., 1863-1952 (Jarrettsville Cemetery)

Preston, Irene J., born 1890, died 19-- (Cokesbury Memorial Methodist Church Cemetery)

Preston, Irvin H., 1884-1958 (Wesleyan Chapel Methodist Church Cemetery)

Preston, Isaac (colored), 1849-1929 (Death certificate; Alms House Record Book)

Preston, J. Alexander, 1836-1904 (St. George's Episcopal Church Cemetery)

Preston, J. Ann (Mrs.) (colored), 1799-1911, native of Harford Co., born 11 Mar 1799, daughter of ---- and Hannah Tally (Death certificate)

Preston, J. Harry, 1869-1927 (Jarrettsville Cemetery)

Preston, James (colored), see Ora Preston (colored), q.v.

Preston, James (colored), age 35 in 1889 (Marriage License Applications Book ALJ No. 2, 1889)

Preston, James A. (colored), 1850-1916, native of Harford Co. (Death certificate)

Preston, James Bond, Jr., 1827-1902 (Christ Episcopal Church Cemetery); delegate, First District, Democrat Party Convention (*The Aegis & Intelligencer*, 5 Sep 1890); member, Democrat Party, and representative, Harford County Tariff Reform Club (*The Aegis & Intelligencer*, 5 Sep 1890); premium award winner, Class C -

Sheep, Harford County Fair (*The Aegis & Intelligencer*, 24 Oct 1890)

Preston, James H., 1872-1902 (Cokesbury Memorial Methodist Church Cemetery)

Preston, James H., see Alexander Preston and James W. Preston, q.v.

Preston, James Henry, 1830-1915 (Wesleyan Chapel Cemetery; James H. Preston Bible, *Maryland Bible Records, Volume 2*, by Henry C. Peden, Jr., 2003, p. 110); see John Henry Preston, q.v.

Preston, James Robinson, 1889-1944 (Little Falls Quaker Cemetery)

Preston, James W., 1820-1890 (Jarrettsville Cemetery); died testate and his named heirs were wife Hannah M. Preston, sons George W. Robinson, Frederick J. Robinson, Charles R. Preston, James H. Preston, Columbus Preston and John Preston, and daughters Mary E. Hess and Sarah V. Low (Harford County Will Book JMM 11:109-110)

Preston, Jane (colored), see Samuel Taylor (colored), q.v.

Preston, Jarrett Henry (colored), 1887-1934, native of Harford Co., born 12 May 1887, son of Wesley S. Preston and Hattie Brown (Death certificate)

Preston, Jennie May, 1882-1948 (Baker Cemetery)

Preston, Jeremiah Anthony (colored), born -- May 1890, baptized 20 Jul 1890, son of Harrison Preston and Mary Gordon (St. Ignatius Catholic Church Baptism Register, p. 113, misspelled his mother's name Goden)

Preston, Jesse, 1822-1890 (Rock Run Methodist Church Cemetery)

Preston, Jesse E., 1856-1945 (Wesleyan Chapel Methodist Church Cemetery); son of James H. Preston and Eliza J. ---- (James H. Preston Bible, *Maryland Bible Records, Volume 2*, by Henry C. Peden, Jr., 2003, p. 110; Death certificate); farmer, at Webster (*Havre de Grace Republican*, 13 Jun 1890); see Winnie Smith Preston, q.v.

Preston, John, see James W. Preston and Noah Preston, q.v.

Preston, John (colored), charged with disorderly conduct at Fallston in 1890, was found guilty and fined (*Harford Democrat*, 21 Feb 1890; Harford County Criminal Docket, 1888-1892, p. 82)

Preston, John A. (Dr.), see William Ringgold, q.v.

Preston, John Ellsworth, 1864-1922 (Calvary Methodist Church Cemetery)

Preston, John F., 1826-1895 (Calvary Methodist Church Cemetery)

Preston, John Henry, 1875-1961 (Angel Hill Cemetery); native of Harford Furnace, Harford Co., born 14 Mar 1875, son of James H. Preston and Eliza Jane Cullum (Pennington Funeral Home Records; James H. Preston Bible, *Maryland Bible Records, Volume 2*, by Henry C. Peden, Jr., 2003, p. 110)

Preston, John T. (colored), 1889-1934, native of Bel Air, parents unknown (Death certificate)

Preston, John W., see Rachel McClure Preston, q.v.

Preston, John W. (colored), see George Wasbington Preston (colored), q.v.

Preston, John Wesley, 1844-1925 (Fallston Methodist Church Cemetery)

Preston, John Wilbur, 1871-1936 (Mt. Zion Methodist Church Cemetery)

Preston, John Winfield, born 15 Nov 1875, son of George W. Preston and Rebecca C. Tucker (Bethel Presbyterian Church Cemetery Records)

Preston, Joseph T. (colored), born -- Mar 1886, baptized 1 May 1886, son of Benjamin Preston and Elizabeth Hollis (St. Ignatius Catholic Church Baptism Register, p. 86)

Preston, Joshua (colored), 1839-1891 (Hendon Hill Cemetery); husband of Anne E. Preston, q.v.

Preston, Laura A., born 1883, died ---- (Wesleyan Chapel Methodist Church Cemetery); wife of Irvin H. Preston, q.v.

Preston, Lena (Griest), 1863-1960 (Little Falls Quaker Cemetery)

Preston, Lida R., 1884-1962 (Angel Hill Cemetery)

Preston, Lizzie (colored), resident of Bel Air (*The Aegis & Intelligencer*, 27 Jun 1890); age 21, married Charles

Bradford on 30 Nov 1890 (Marriage License Applications Book ALJ No. 2, 1890, and marriage certificate)

Preston, Lydia B., 1886-1978 (Baker Cemetery)

Preston, M. Priscilla, 1855-1943, wife of Charles R. Preston (Salem Evangelical Lutheran Church Cemetery)

Preston, Marrie (colored), died 2 Aug 1891, age not given (Alms House Record Book)

Preston, Martha K., 1862-1908 (Wesleyan Chapel Methodist Church Cemetery); daughter of James H. Preston and Eliza J. ---- (James H. Preston Bible, *Maryland Bible Records, Volume 2*, by Henry C. Peden, Jr., 2003, p. 110)

Preston, Martha W., 1813-1901, native of Harford Co., resided at Mill Green, daughter of William Preston and ---- (Death certificate)

Preston, Mary (colored), resident of Fallston (*The Aegis & Intelligencer*, 28 Nov 1890)

Preston, Mary (Markland), 1866-1937 (Calvary Methodist Church Cemetery)

Preston, Mary C. (colored), born -- Jan 1886, native of Maryland, daughter of Noah and Eliza Preston (1900 Aberdeen Census)

Preston, Mary Corner (Robinson), 1864-1954 (Little Falls Quaker Cemetery); wife of Robert Stanley Preston, q.v.

Preston, Mary E., 1865-1940 (Cokesbury Memorial Methodist Church Cemetery)

Preston, Mary Elizabeth, see Maud Gallion, q.v.

Preston, Mary Elizabeth (Pue), 1859-1937, daughter of Michael E. and Elizabeth H. Pue, born at Woodview, resided in Emmorton (St. Mary's Episcopal Church Cemetery); wife of Walter Wilks Preston, q.v.

Preston, Mollie (Miss), uncalled for letter in Bel Air P. O., 1890 (*The Aegis & Intelligencer*, 14 Nov 1890)

Preston, Mollie V., 1877-1933 (Wesleyan Chapel Methodist Church Cemetery); wife of Franklin A. Preston, q.v.

Preston, Noah, son of John Preston, of Calvary (*The Aegis & Intelligencer*, 31 Oct 1890)

Preston, Noah (colored), 1857-1913, native of Harford Co. (1900 Aberdeen Census; Death certificate)

Preston, Ollie, born 2 May 1878, son of James H. Preston and Eliza J. ---- (James H. Preston Bible, *Maryland Bible Records, Volume 2*, by Henry C. Peden, Jr., 2003, p. 110)

Preston, Ora (Macall) (colored), 1881-1907, daughter of Jennie Macall and ----, and wife of James Preston (Death certificate)

Preston, Oscar L., 1865-1935 (Cokesbury Memorial Methodist Church Cemetery)

Preston, Priscilla (colored), born -- Apr 1883, baptized 2 Sep 1883, daughter of Benjamin Preston and Elizabeth Hollis (St. Ignatius Catholic Church Baptism Register, p. 68)

Preston, Rachel McClure, 1873-1930 (Cokesbury Memorial Methodist Church Cemetery); native of Maryland, born 13 Sep 1873, daughter of John W. Preston and ---- (Death certificate - married name Moore; Marriage License Applications Book ALJ No. 2, 1890)

Preston, Robert (colored), born -- Apr 1890, native of Maryland, son of Noah and Eliza Preston (1900 Aberdeen Census)

Preston, Robert Stanley, 1856-1932 (Little Falls Quaker Cemetery)

Preston, Roberta Jane (Gilbert), 1865-1936 (Baker Cemetery); wife of Benjamin V. Preston, q.v.

Preston, Salome E., 1846-1940 (Jarrettsville Cemetery)

Preston, Samuel Walter, 1868-1911 (Wesleyan Chapel Methodist Church Cemetery); son of James H. Preston and Eliza J. Cullum (James H. Preston Bible, *Maryland Bible Records, Volume 2*, by Henry C. Peden, Jr., 2003, p. 110; Death certificate)

Preston, Samuel William (colored), born 18 Mar 1884, baptized 18 May 1884, son of Harrison Preston and Mary Gordon (St. Ignatius Catholic Church Baptism Register, p. 72)

Preston, Sara (Fearon), 1885-1911 (Little Falls Quaker Cemetery)

Preston, Sarah (colored), see James Adams (colored), q.v.

Preston, Sarah E., 1851-1923 (Fallston Methodist Church Cemetery)

Preston, Sarah J., 1874-1955 (Jarrettsville Cemetery)

Preston, Sophia C., 1858-1972 (Mt. Zion Methodist Church Cemetery)

Preston, Stephen (colored), 1860-1935, native of Harford Co., son of Stephen Preston and Mary Wheeler (Death certificate; St. James Church, Gravel Hill Cemetery)

Preston, Stephen (colored), c1884-1916, born near Aberdeen, Harford Co., son of Noah Preston, born near Level, and Elizabeth Wheems [Whims], born near Churchville (Death certificate)

Preston, Sylvester, 1866-1946 (Baker Cemetery); see Grace Preston, q.v.

Preston, Thomas T., 1889-1979 (Mountain Christian Church Cemetery)

Preston, Tilden, born 28 Oct 1876, son of James H. Preston and Eliza J. ---- (James H. Preston Bible, *Maryland Bible Records, Volume 2*, by Henry C. Peden, Jr., 2003, p. 110)

Preston, W. Frank, 1885-1957 (Mt. Zion Methodist Church Cemetery)

Preston, Walter Stephen (colored), born -- Mar 1888, baptized 24 Apr 1888, son of Benjamin Preston and Elizabeth Hollis (St. Ignatius Catholic Church Baptism Register, p. 98)

Preston, Walter Wilks, 1863-1851 (St. Mary's Episcopal Church Cemetery); attorney-at-law, Bel Air (*Havre de Grace Republican*, 10 Jan 1890); incorporator, The Old Peach Bottom Slate Company of Harford County (*Havre de Grace Republican*, 27 Jun 1890); jousting tournament rider, Knight of Wayside (*Havre de Grace Republican*, 19 Sep 1890); lieutenant, Jackson Guards [Co. D, 1st Regt., Maryland National Guard] (*The Aegis & Intelligencer*, 11 Jan 1889 and 28 Nov and 26 Dec 1890); worshipful master, Mt. Ararat Lodge, A. F. & A. M., Bel Air (*Havre de Grace Republican*, 19 Dec 1890); House of Delegates, 1888-1892 (*Biographical Dictionary of Harford County, Maryland, 1774-1974*, by Henry C. Peden, Jr. and William O. Carr, 2021, p. 219)

Preston, Wesley (colored), see Ephraim A. Preston (colored) and Jarrett Henry Preston (colored), q.v.

Preston, William, 1857-1921, son of James H. Preston and Eliza J. ---- (James H. Preston Bible, *Maryland Bible Records, Volume 2*, by Henry C. Peden, Jr., 2003, p. 110)

Preston, William (colored), c1830-1900, resided at Hickory (Death certificate incomplete; *The Aegis & Intelligencer*, 1 Jun 1900)

Preston, William Edgar, 1879-1948 (Mt. Zion Methodist Church Cemetery)

Preston, William Silvester Bills, 1850-1904 (Little Falls Quaker Cemetery); William S. Preston, member, Maryland Central Dairymen's Association, 1890 (*Havre de Grace Republican*, 28 Feb 1890); trustee, Angleside School No. 3, Third District, 1890 (*Havre de Grace Republican*, 30 May 1890); son of Edmund Preston, q.v.

Preston, William T., 1857-1921 (Wesleyan Chapel Methodist Church Cemetery)

Preston, Winnie Smith, died 16 Sep 1890, age 13 months and 7 days, only son of Jesse E. Preston and Georgie A. ---- (*The Aegis & Intelligencer*, 24 Oct 1890)

Price, ----, catcher, Nonpareil Baseball Club, Aberdeen (*Havre de Grace Republican*, 6 Jun 1890)

Price's GeneralStore, Abingdon, Joseph A. Price, prop. (*Country Stores: Harford County's Rural Heritage*, by Henry C. Peden, Jr. and Jack L. Shagena, Jr., 2015, p. 194)

Price's General Store, Magnolia, Frank N. Price, prop. (*Country Stores: Harford County's Rural Heritage*, by Henry C. Peden, Jr. and Jack L. Shagena, Jr., 2015, p. 194)

Price's General Store, Price's Corner, at Mountain, William J. Price, prop. (*Country Stores: Harford County's Rural Heritage*, by Henry C. Peden, Jr. and Jack L. Shagena, Jr., 2015, p. 194)

Price, Adele (Spence), 1874-1961 (Darlington Cemetery)

Price, Alice (Lee), 1845-1928 (Union Chapel Methodist Church Cemetery); native of Harford Co., resided at Fallston (Death certificate)

Price, Anna T., 1878-1963 (Rock Run Methodist Church Cemetery); wife of George A. Price, q.v.

Price, Arthur G., 1882-1953 (Cokesbury Memorial Methodist Church Cemetery)

Price, Callender, 1847-1921 (Angel Hill Cemetery); native of Maryland, resident of Havre de Grace, single, boat captain (Death certificate); member, inquest jury, Havre de Grace (*Havre de Grace Republican*, 6 Jun 1890); sneak boat duck hunter (*Havre de Grace Republican*, 7 Nov 1890)

Price, Caroline H., 1819-1913 (Forest Hill Friends Cemetery)

Price, Cassandra (Magness), 1807-1894 (Mountain Christian Church Cemetery), wife of William J. Price, q.v.

Price, Charles Diffenderffer, born 29 Dec 1890, son of Henry A. and Laura Price (Reese-Price Bible, *Maryland Bible Records, Volume 1*, by Henry C. Peden, Jr., 2003, p. 204)

Price, Charles Henry, born 29 Mar 1885, son of Henry A. and Laura Price (Reese-Price Bible, *Maryland Bible Records, Volume 1*, by Henry C. Peden, Jr., 2003, p. 204)

Price, Charlotte A., 1848-1922 (Cokesbury Memorial Methodist Church Cemetery)

Price, Clara J. (Miss), premium award winner, Class J - Domestic Products, Harford County Fair (*The Aegis & Intelligencer*, 24 Oct 1890)

Price, Clifford W., c1885-1931 (Angel Hill Cemetery), native of Maryland, resident of Havre de Grace, son of James Price and ---- (Death certificate)

Price, David Elisha, 1851-1929 (Darlington Cemetery); juror, Fifth District, 1890 (*Havre de Grace Republican*, 2 May 1890); fox hunter and blue hound owner (*Harford Democrat*, 7 Feb 1890)

Price, Dollie, daughter of Jesse Price, q.v.

Price, Dora, daughter of Jesse Price, q.v.

Price, Edward C., 1824-1898 (Forest Hill Friends Cemetery)

Price, Elizabeth, see Elizabeth Cloak, Arthur Cloak, George H. Cloak and George A. Fadeley, q.v.

Price, Ella L. (Dorrell), 1843-1931 (Angel Hill Cemetery); see John Franklin Price and Henry Harrison Price, q.v.

Price, Ellen Ann (Roberts), wife of Griffith Price, q.v.

Price, Ellen J., 1848-1898 (Wesleyan Chapel Methodist Church Cemetery)

Price, Florence Bell, born 3 Dec 1868, daughter of George R. and Sarah A. (Hughes) Price (*The Hughes Genealogy, 1636-1953*, by Joseph Lee Hughes, 1953, p. 112); Florence Price acquired land in November 1890 (*The Aegis & Intelligencer*, 5 Dec 1890)

Price, Frances Davis (Quarles) (Hill), 1855-1915 (Darlington Cemetery; www.findagrave.com)

Price, Francis "Frank" N., 1841-1927 (Death certificate; Alms House Record Book)

Price, Frank Lee, 1875-1896 (Union Chapel Methodist Church Cemetery); age 15, student, Oakland School, 1890 (George G. Curtiss Ledger)

Price, G., warden, Venus Council No. 44, O. U. A. M., Havre de Grace (*Havre de Grace Republican*, 11 Jul 1890)

Price, George A., 1875-1961 (Rock Run Methodist Church Cemetery)

Price, George Albert, Jr., born 25 Feb 1871, son of George R. and Sarah A. (Hughes) Price (*The Hughes Genealogy, 1636-1953*, by Joseph Lee Hughes, 1953, pp. 112, 128)

Price, George R., see Robert Frederick Price, q.v.

Price, Griffith, 1867-1899, moulder, resided at Cardiff (Death certificate)

Price, H., first baseman, Havre de Grace Ash Alleys Baseball Club (*The Aegis & Intelligencer*, 27 Jun 1890)

Price, Harry G., 1868-1930 (Cokesbury Memorial Methodist Church Cemetery)

Price, Henry, juror, of the Fifth District (*The Aegis & Intelligencer*, 16 May 1890)

Price, Henry A., 1849-1941 (Cokesbury Memorial Methodist Church Cemetery)

Price, Henry Harrison, 1875-1938 (Angel Hill Cemetery); native of Maryland, resident of Havre de Grace, born

16 Oct 1875, son of James A. Price and Ella Dorrell (Death certificate)

Price, Howard L., 1869-1950 (Cokesbury Memorial Methodist Church Cemetery); new name on the voter registration list at Abingdon, First District, 1890 (*Havre de Grace Republican*, 17 Oct 1890)

Price, Hyland, see John G. Price, q.v.

Price, Ida G. (Mrs.), 1870-1925, native of Maryland, resided in Havre de Grace (Death certificate; Angel Hill Cemetery)

Price, Isabel, 1861-1946 (Darlington Cemetery)

Price, J. Scott, treasurer, Charity Lodge No. 134, A. F. & A. M., Norrisville (*The Aegis & Intelligencer*, 26 Dec 1890)

Price, James, 1851-1921 (Heavenly Waters Cemetery)

Price, James, see John Frankin Price and Henry Harrison Price, q.v.

Price, James H. (colored), age 28 in 1889 (Marriage License Applications Book ALJ No. 2, 1889)

Price, James W., died 17 Jul 1890, an aged citizen of Dublin, Fifth District (*The Aegis & Intelligencer*, 25 Jul 1890); died testate and his named heirs were Henry L. Jones and Gussie A. Jones, children of Emory and Lidia Jones (Harford County Will Book JMM 11:121-122)

Price, Jesse, 1822-1890 (Rock Run Methodist Church Cemetery); resided near Lapidum (*The Aegis & Intelligencer*, 24 Oct 1890); see Jesse A. Price and William John Price, q.v.

Price, Jesse A., 1870-1948 (Rock Run Methodist Church Cemetery), native of Lapidum, Harford Co., born 26 Jan 1870, son of Jesse Price and Sarah Kelly, natives of Maryland (Pennington Funeral Home Records); age 21 in 1891 (Marriage License Applications Book ALJ No. 2, 1891)

Price, John, canner, First District (*Havre de Grace Republican*, 20 Jun 1890); delegate, First District, Democrat Party Convention (*The Aegis & Intelligencer*, 5 Sep 1890)

Price, John, served on an inquest jury, Havre de Grace (*Havre de Grace Republican*, 6 Jun 1890)

Price, John B., resident of Clayton (*The Aegis & Intelligencer*, 18 Apr 1890); see William J. Price, q.v.

Price, John F., 1874-1936 (Cokesbury Memorial Methodist Church Cemetery)

Price, John Franklin, 1873-1958 (Angel Hill Cemetery), native of Havre de Grace, born 3 Jan 1873, son of James Price and Ella Dorrell (Pennington Funeral Home Records)

Price, John G., 1860-1941 (Angel Hill Cemetery); born 29 Feb 1860, native and resident of Havre de Grace, single, waterman, son of Hyland Price and Lacey Currier, natives of Cecil Co., MD (Death certificate)

Price, John H., resident of Abingdon District; see Mrs. Austin Standiford, q.v.

Price, John Henry (Honorable), 1808-1892 (Darlington Cemetery); vestryman, Grace Memorial Methodist Church, Darlington (*Havre de Grace Republican*, 18 Apr 1890); trustee, Darlington School No. 15, Fifth District (*Havre de Grace Republican*, 30 May 1890); former judge of the Sixth and later of the Ninth Judicial Circuit of Maryland (*Biographical Dictionary of Harford County, Maryland, 1774-1974*, by Henry C. Peden, Jr. and William O. Carr, 2021, p. 219)

Price, John Henry, 1877-1958 (Darlington Cemetery)

Price, John Henry, Jr., 1844-1916 (Darlington Cemetery)

Price, John R., member, Robinson Can Company of Harford County, at Fallston (*Havre de Grace Republican*, 24 Oct 1890)

Price, Joseph A., 1837-1912 (Cokesbury Memorial Methodist Church Cemetery); tax collector, First District (*Havre de Grace Republican*, 4 Jul 1890)

Price, Josephine (Stanford), 1873-1968 (Angel Hill Cemetery)

Price, Keturah, daughter of Jesse Price, q.v.

Price, Laura (Reese), 1850-1932 (Cokesbury Memorial Methodist Church Cemetery)

Price, Laura E. (Michael), 1839-1909 (Christ Episcopal Church Cemetery)

Price, Lettie E., 1879-1959, native of Harford Co. (Bailey Funeral Home Records)

Price, Lizzie, daughter of Jesse Price, q.v.

Price, Lottie L., 1876-1923 (Rock Run Methodist Church Cemetery); wife of Jesse A. Price, q.v.

Price, Martha Elizabeth (Amoss), 1879-1958 (Darlington Cemetery)

Price, Mary (Miller), 1853-1934, native of Howard Co. (Bailey Funeral Home Records); wife of David Elisha Price, q.v.

Price, Mary A. (colored), see Henrietta M. Lewis (colored), q.v.

Price, Mary Elizabeth, wife of B. Lewis Gallion, q.v.

Price, Mary Elizabeth, wife of William Moore Fadeley, q.v.

Price, Mary Estelle, 1889-1959 (Cokesbury Memorial Methodist Church Cemetery)

Price, Mary R. (Russell), 1887-1968 (Darlington Cemetery); native of Darlington, Harford Co., born 6 Oct 1887, daughter of John H. Russell and Martha E. Thompson (Harkins Funeral Home Records)

Price, Mary Ritchie (Parker), 1818-1912 (Darlington Cemetery), second wife of John Henry Price, q.v.

Price, Mary W., 1853-1917 (Darlington Cemetery)

Price, Minnie Madeline (Rimmey), c1871-1949 (Angel Hill Cemetery); native of Baltimore Co., resident of Havre de Grace (Death certificate)

Price, Mordecai, 1822-1902 (Little Falls Quaker Cemetery)

Price, Mordecai, of Fallston, married Sarah J. Dare, of Baltimore, on 4th day of 12th month, 1890, at Baltimore Monthly Meeting of Friends (*The Aegis & Intelligencer*, 5 Dec 1890)

Price, Ola, 1873-1926 (Angel Hill Cemetery)

Price, R. Adora, 1866-1933 (Rock Run Methodist Church Cemetery)

Price, Rebecca, 1804-1894 (Little Falls Quaker Cemetery)

Price, Robert E., 1852-1939 (Darlington Cemetery)

Price, Robert Frederick, 1878-1954 (Angel Hill Cemetery), native of Maryland, born 23 Mar 1878, son of George R. Price and Sarah Ann Hughes (*The Hughes Genealogy, 1636-1953*, by Joseph Lee Hughes, 1953, p. 112; Pennington Funeral Home Records)

Price, Rose E., 1872-1962, native of Pennsylvania (Angel Hill Cemetery)

Price, Roy Courtney, born 2 Apr 1887, son of William John and Sallie (Courtney) Price (*The Hughes Genealogy, 1636-1953*, by Joseph Lee Hughes, 1953, p. 115)

Price, S. Elizabeth, 1864-1943 (Rock Run Methodist Church Cemetery)

Price, Sadie H., 1870-1951 (Cokesbury Memorial Methodist Church Cemetery)

Price, Sarah A. (Kelly), 1831-1904 (Rock Run Methodist Church Cemetery)

Price, Sarah Anne (Hughes), 1832-1906 (Rock Run Methodist Church Cemetery; *The Hughes Genealogy, 1636-1953*, by Joseph Lee Hughes, 1953, p. 112); wife of George Albert Price (1826-1883)

Price, Sarah P. "Sallie" (Courtney), 1858-1928 (Rock Run Methodist Church Cemetey; Bailey Funeral Home Records; *The Hughes Genealogy, 1636-1953*, by Joseph Lee Hughes, 1953, p. 116); wife of William John Price, q.v.

Price, Thomas, son of Jesse Price, q.v.

Price, Thomas Emory, 1860-1933 (Cokesbury Memorial Methodist Church Cemetery)

Price, Thomas K., 1866-1943 (Rock Run Methodist Church Cemetery)

Price, Viola Boyd (Smith), 1883-1966 (Angel Hill Cemetery)

Price, W. Ingram, 1842-1916 (Union Chapel Methodist Church Cemetery)

Price, Webster, 1890-1953 (Darlington Cemetery)

Price, William, see William J. Price, q.v.

Price, William G., 1876-1955 (Wesleyan Chapel Methodist Church Cemetery)

Price, William J. (Mrs.), daughter of Barbara Baltzell Lee, q.v.

Price, William J., 1804-1891 (Mountain Christian Church Cemetery); incorporator and director, Wilna Library Association (*Havre de Grace Republican*, 9 May 1890); justice of the peace, First District (*Havre de Grace Republican*, 21 Feb 1890); wrote his will in 1886 and died in 1891, naming wife Cassandra Price, sons John B. Price and William Price, daughter Elizabeth T. Swartz, children of Sarah Demoss (wife of William Demoss) and children of John B. Price (Harford County Will Book JMM 11:185-186)

Price, William John 1858-1921 (Rock Run Methodist Church Cemetery; *The Hughes Genealogy, 1636-1953*, by Joseph Lee Hughes, 1953, p. 116); trustee of Lapidum School No. 13, Second District (*Havre de Grace Republican*, 30 May 1890); superintendent, Lapidum Sunday School (*Havre de Grace Republican*, 30 May 1890); son of Jesse Price, q.v. (*The Aegis & Intelligencer*, 24 Oct 1890)

Price, William Otho, 1874-1962 (Angel Hill Cemetery); born 13 Dec 1874, son of George R. Price and Sarah A. Hughes (*The Hughes Genealogy, 1636-1953*, by Joseph Lee Hughes, 1953, pp. 112, 128)

Price, Yura (Miss), actress, Darlington Company (*Havre de Grace Republican*, 7 Mar 1890)

Prigg's General Store, near Hickory, Edward H. Prigg, prop. (*Country Stores: Harford County's Rural Heritage*, by Henry C. Peden, Jr. and Jack L. Shagena, Jr., 2015, p. 195)

Prigg, Abraham (colored), born -- Nov 1848, native of Maryland (1900 Aberdeen Census); see Josephine Bond, Bertie Prigg, Jane Prigg, and Daniel Prigg, q.v.

Prigg, Albert L., 1853-1917 (Christ Episcopal Church Cemetery)

Prigg, Amanda Melvina, see John Smith Dallam and Charles Lee Dallam. q.v.

Prigg, Annie (colored), see Elisha Webster (colored), q.v.

Prigg, Bertha (colored), 1866-1897 (Green Spring Methodist Church Cemetery)

Prigg, Bertie (Miss) (colored), 1864-1900, native of Harford Co., daughter of Abraham Prigg and Jane ---- (Death certificate)

Prigg, Charles (colored), see Charles H. Prigg (colored) and William Prigg (colored), q.v.

Prigg, Charles H. (colored), 1861-1911, native of Harford Co., resident of Havre de Grace, born 23 Feb 1861, son of Charles Prigg, native of the West Indies, and Mary Warfield, native of Harford Co. (Death certificate); see Patience J. Prigg, q.v.

Prigg, Clara L. C., 1854-1931 (Darlington Cemetery); native of New Hampshire, maiden name VonCran, born 27 Apr 1853 *(sic)* (Bailey Funeral Home Records); wife of Robert E. Prigg, q.v.

Prigg, D. Sallie, see H. Kenton Whiteford, q.v.; wife of Hugh Clay Whiteford, q.v.

Prigg, Daniel (colored), c1875-1935, native of Harford Co., son of Abraham Prigg and Jane ----, natives of Harford Co. (Death certificate)

Prigg, Darius K., private, Jackson Guards [Co. D, 1st Regiment, Maryland National Guard], 1889-1890 (*The Aegis & Intelligencer*, 11 Jan 1889); house and sign painter, Bel Air (*Harford Democrat,* 17 Jan 1890); son of Ms. M. A. Prigg, of Bel Air, moved to Wilmington, DE by June 1890 (*Harford Democrat*, 4 Jul 1890)

Prigg, Devereaux S., 1867-1937 (Christ Episcopal Church Cemetery); telegraph officer, Bel Air (*The Aegis & Intelligencer*, 7 Nov 1890); competitive bicycle rider, Harford County Fair (*Havre de Grace Republican*, 20 Jun and 26 Sep 1890; *The Aegis & Intelligencer*, 19 Sep 1890); musician, Jackson Guards, 1889-1890 [Co. D, 1st Regiment, Maryland National Guard] (*The Aegis & Intelligencer*, 11 Jan 1889); organizer of Athletic Club No. 2 in Bel Air (*Harford Democrat*, 21 Feb 1890)

Prigg, Edward (colored), 1861-1892 (Green Spring Methodist Church Cemetery); resided near Glenville (*The Aegis & Intelligencer*, 22 Aug 1890)

Prigg, Edward H., 1825-1892 (St. Ignatius Catholic Church Cemetery; *The Aegis & Intelligencer*, 29 Apr 1892); see Laura A. Prigg, q.v.

Prigg, Elizabeth, see Millie Harris, q.v.

Prigg, Ellen (Miss), resided near Hickory (*The Aegis & Intelligencer*, 4 Apr 1890)

Prigg, Harriett (colored), 1821-1899, housekeeper at Berkley, native of Maryland. widow of Henry Prigg (Death certificate)

Prigg, Henry, and wife, conveyed land in April 1890 (*The Aegis & Intelligencer*, 9 May 1890); see Harriett Prigg, q.v.

Prigg, Horace (colored), 1854-1919, native of Maryland (Death certificate); trustee, Hosanna Colored School No. 1, Fifth District, 1890 (*Havre de Grace Republican*, 30 May 1890); see Lawrence S. Prigg and Oscar Prigg, q.v.

Prigg, Jane (Presbury) (colored), 1829-1912 (Death certificate; Green Spring Methodist Church Cemetery); resided near Glenville (*The Aegis & Intelligencer*, 22 Aug 1890); wife of Abraham Prigg; also see Bertie Prigg and Daniel Prigg, q.v.

Prigg, Jennie (colored), see Jennie Collins (colored), q.v.

Prigg, John (colored), 1854-1917 (Green Spring Methodist Church Cemetery); resided near Glenville (*The Aegis & Intelligencer*, 22 Aug 1890)

Prigg, Josephine (colored), see Verden Bond (colored), q.v.

Prigg, Kiziah (colored), see Albert Presberry, George Presberry, John M. Presberry, Henry J. Presberry, Jr. and William E. Prigg, q.v.

Prigg, Laura Augusta (Lytle), 1835-1899, wife of Edward H. Prigg, q.v. (Death certificate); Mrs. E. H. Prigg, resident of Hickory, 1890 (*The Aegis & Intelligencer*, 28 Feb 1890)

Prigg, Lawrence S. (colored), 1889-1939, native of Harford Co., son of Horace Prigg and Louisa Spriggs (Death certificate)

Prigg, Louisa (Sprigg) (colored), 1860-1911, native of Baltimore Co., (Death certificate)

Prigg, Margery A., 1837-1907 (Christ Episcopal Church Cemetery)

Prigg, Mark (colored), see Millie Harris (colored) and Rena Green (colored), q.v.

Prigg, Mary (colored), see Mary Martha Webster (colored) and Sarah Jane Webster (colored), q.v.

Prigg, Mary F. (Lee) (colored), 1859-1922, native of Maryland (Death certificate)

Prigg, Mazie A. (colored), 1886-1926 (Union Chapel Methodist Church Cemetery, Aberdeen); native of Maryland, resided in Havre de Grace, daughter of James Priggs *(sic)* and Cora Stansbury (Death certificate - married name Brown)

Prigg, Oscar (colored), 1882-1930, native of Maryland, son of Horace Prigg and Louisa Spriggs *(sic)* (Death certificate)

Prigg, Patience J. (colored), 1884-1943, native of Maryland, born 5 Jan 1884, daughter of Charles H. Prigg and Sarah Holland Death certificate - married name Wilmore)

Prigg, Rebecca (colored), see Georgia Cain, Alice R. Parker, Emily A. Parker and James W. Parker, q.v.

Prigg, Rena (colored), see Rena Green (colored), q.v.

Prigg, Robert Emmett, 1851-1939 (Darlington Cemetery); native of Lancaser Co, PA (Bailey Funeral Home Records); second violin, Darlington Orchestra (*Havre de Grace Republican*, 7 Mar 1890)

Prigg, Sarah (colored), see John Westly Bond (colored) and Sarah Holland (colored), q.v.

Prigg, Urith L., 1863-1951 (Christ Episcopal Church Cemetery)

Prigg, William (colored), 1884-1913, native of Harford Co., born 15 Apr 1884, son of Charles Prigg and Mary Holland (Death certificate)

Prigg, William W., 1855-1916 (Darlington Cemetery)

Pritchard, ----, right fielder, Aberdeen Baseball Club (*The Aegis & Intelligencer*, 25 Jul 1890)

Pritchard, Charles Arthur, 1874-1893 (Grove Presbyterian Church Cemetery); born 3 Jul 1874, son of William and Christianna Pritchard (William Pritchard Bible, *Maryland Bible Records, Volume 1*, by Henry C. Peden, Jr., 2003, p. 196)

Pritchard, Christianna (Rawhouser), 1837-1916 (Baker Cemetery; William Pritchard Bible, *Maryland Bible Records, Volume 1*, by Henry C. Peden, Jr., 2003, p. 196); wife of William G. Pritchard, q.v.

Pritchard, E., left fielder, Nonpareil Baseball Club, Aberdeen (*Havre de Grace Republican*, 4 Jul 1890)

Pritchard, Emily Isadore (Crevensten), born 24 Oct 1865, native of Maryland, wife of George Edwin Pritchard (George A. Crevensten Bible, *Maryland Bible Records, Volume 1*, by Henry C. Peden, Jr., 2003, pp. 69-70)

Pritchard, Fannie M., age 20 in 1890 (Marriage License Applications Book ALJ No. 2, 1891)

Pritchard, George Edwin, 1863-1947 (Grove Presbyterian Church Cemetery); born 22 Feb 1863, son of William and Christianna Pritchard (William Pritchard Bible, *Maryland Bible Records, Volume 1*, by Henry C. Peden, Jr., 2003, p. 196); G. Pritchard, shortstop, Nonpareil Baseball Club, Aberdeen (*Havre de Grace Republican*, 6 Jun and 4 Jul 1890)

Pritchard, George Ray, born 8 Mar 1889, son of George E. Pritchard and Emily Isadore Crevensten (George A. Crevensten Bible, *Maryland Bible Records, Volume 1*, by Henry C. Peden, Jr., 2003, pp. 69-70)

Pritchard, Guy Edwin, born 23 May 1887, son of George E. Pritchard and Emily Isadore Crevensten (George A. Crevensten Bible, *Maryland Bible Records, Volume 1*, by Henry C. Peden, Jr., 2003, pp. 69- 70)

Pritchard, James T., 1831-1922 (Grove Presbyterian Church Cemetery); justice of the peace, Second District (*The Aegis & Intelligencer*, 12 Sep 1890)

Pritchard, Joshua R., 1859-1918 (Grove Presbyterian Church Cemetery); born 6 Jan 1859, son of William and Christianna Pritchard (William Pritchard Bible, *Maryland Bible Records, Volume 1*, by Henry C. Peden, Jr., 2003, p. 196)

Pritchard, Morgan Elliott, 1872-1926 (Grove Presbyterian Church Cemetery); native of Maryland, resided in Aberdeen, born 17 Feb 1872, son of William and Christianna Pritchard (Death certificate; William Pritchard Bible, *Maryland Bible Records, Volume 1*, by Henry C. Peden, Jr., 2003, p. 196)

Pritchard, Ruth Silver (Forsythe), 1833-1898 (Grove Presbyterian Church Cemetery); native of Maryland, resident of Aberdeen, wife of James T. Pritchard, q.v., and daughter of Samuel and Amelia Forsythe (Death certificate)

Pritchard, Susan Ordella, born 27 Aug 1866, daughter of William G. and Christianna Pritchard (William Pritchard Bible, *Maryland Bible Records, Volume 1*, by Henry C. Peden, Jr., 2003, p. 196); Susie Pritchard, singer and member, member, Aberdeen M. E. Church (*The Aegis & Intelligencer*, 21 Feb 1890)

Pritchard, T. L., sneak boat duck hunter (*Havre de Grace Republican*, 7 Nov 1890)

Pritchard, William Alfred, 1861-1916 (Grove Presbyterian Church Cemetery); born 25 Nov 1861, son of William and Christianna Pritchard (William Pritchard Bible, *Maryland Bible Records, Volume 1*, by Henry C. Peden, Jr., 2003, p. 196)

Pritchard, William G., 1835-1905 (Baker Cemetery; William Pritchard Bible, *Maryland Bible Records, Volume 1*, by Henry C. Peden, Jr., 2003, p. 196); building contractor, Second District (*The Aegis & Intelligencer*, 4 Jul 1890); tent holder, Carsins Run Camp Meeting of the East Harford Circuit, P. E. Church (*The Aegis & Intelligencer*, 1 Aug 1890)

Proctor, ----, left fielder, Bel Air Victors Baseball Club (*The Aegis & Intelligencer*, 25 Jul 1890)

Proctor, Ada G., died 6 May 1890 (Tabernacle Evangelical Church Cemetery); wife of Walter Proctor, resident near Love's Mill, Fifth District (*The Aegis & Intelligencer*, 9 May 1890)

Proctor, Augustus, resident near Susquehanna Paper Company, and father of Percy Proctor (*The Aegis & Intelligencer*, 24 Oct 1890)

Proctor, Burton, age 15, graduated from Bel Air Academy and Graded School; son of Charles W. Proctor, of Bel Air (*The Aegis & Intelligencer*, 22 Aug 1890); center fielder and left fielder, Bel Air Victors Baseball Club (*The

Aegis & Intelligencer, 30 May and 30 Jun 1890); premium award winner, Class L - Children's Department, Harford County Fair (*The Aegis & Intelligencer*, 24 Oct 1890); member, Loyal Temperance Legion of Bel Air (*The Aegis & Intelligencer*, 2 May 1890); entered St. John's College, Annapolis (*Harford Democrat*, 19 Sep 1890)

Proctor, Charles Wesley, 1844-1904 (Christ Episcopal Church Cemetery); clerk and treasurer to the county commissioners (*Havre de Grace Republican*, 4 Jul 1890); justice of the peace, Third District (*Havre de Grace Republican*, 21 Feb 1890); member, Mt. Ararat Lodge No. 44, A. F. & A. M., Bel Air (*Havre de Grace Republican*, 11 Jul 1890); member, Board of Town Commissioners, Bel Air, 1889-1892 (*Biographical Dictionary of Harford County, Maryland, 1774-1974*, by Henry C. Peden, Jr. and William O. Carr, 2021, pp. 220, 338); see Burton Proctor, Dora B. Proctor. Sophia E. Proctor, and Mary Iola Silver, q.v.

Proctor, Dora B. (Miss), 1879-1904 (Christ Episcopal Church Cemetery); born 3 Jan 1879, native of Harford Co., daughter of Charles Wesley Proctor and Sophia E. Spencer (Death certificate; *The Aegis & Intelligencer*, 19 Aug 1904); student, Bel Air Graded School, 1890 (*The Aegis & Intelligencer*, 11 Apr 1890); dancing student, Archer Institute, Bel Air, 1890 (*The Aegis & Intelligencer*, 6 Jun 1890)

Proctor, Edward, c1820-1890 (Tabernacle Methodist Church Cemetery); resided near Line Bridge (*The Aegis & Intelligencer*, 24 Jan 1890 and 11 Jul 1890); died testate and his named heirs were wife Martha Jane Proctor, daughters Rebecca J. Whiteford (wife of Nelson Whiteford), Mary Guyton (wife of Joseph Guyton), Lida Dooley (wife of Hugh E. Dooley), Paulina Bennington (wife of John Bennington), and sons Thomas Edward Proctor, Jeremiah B. Proctor, Walter Proctor, George C. Proctor and Howard Proctor (Harford County Will Book JMM 11:125-126; *Harford Democrat*, 25 Jul 1890)

Proctor, Elizabeth, acquired land in November 1890 (*The Aegis & Intelligencer*, 5 Dec 1890); see James Kerr, Roxie Tennant and Ida Jones, q.v.

Proctor, Frank Brand (Dr.), 1852-1891 (St. Mary's Episcopal Church Cemetery)

Proctor, George C., see Edward Proctor, q.v.

Proctor, George E., 1889-1962 (Providence Methodist Church Cemetery)

Proctor, George M., 1858-1940 (Providence Methodist Church Cemetery)

Proctor, H. Raymond, 1887-1922 (Providence Methodist Church Cemetery)

Proctor, Howard, see Edward Proctor, q.v.

Proctor, Howard O., Sr., 1868-1938 (Slate Ridge Cemetery, York Co., PA); acquired land in Harford County in April 1890 (*The Aegis & Intelligencer*, 9 May 1890)

Proctor, Ida M., 1861-1920 (Providence Methodist Church Cemetery)

Proctor, Jeremiah B., see Edward Proctor, q.v.

Proctor, Lillie Whitney, 1869-1924, first wife of Howard O. Proctor, Sr., q.v.

Proctor, Lyda, see Ina D. Day, q.v.

Proctor, Martha Jane, see Edward Proctor, q.v.

Proctor, Mary Webb (Bulette), 1888-1971 (Fellowship Cemetery)

Proctor, Mary Zimmerman, 1890-1900 (Christ Episcopal Church Cemetery)

Proctor, Percy, see Augustua Proctor, q.v.

Proctor, Sadie L., premium award winner, Class L - Children's Department, Harford County Fair (*The Aegis & Intelligencer*, 24 Oct 1890)

Proctor, Sophia Elizabeth (Spencer), 1854-1949 (Christ Episcopal Church Cemetery); wife of Charles Wesley Proctor, q.v.; also see Dora B. Proctor, q.v.

Proctor, Thomas Edward, see Edward Proctor, q.v.

Proctor, Walter, see Ada G. Proctor and Edward Proctor, q.v.

Progressive Euchre Club, Havre de Grace (*Havre de Grace: Its Historic Past, Its Charming Present and Its*

Promising Future: Harford County's Rural Heritage. by Jack L. Shagena, Jr. and Henry C. Peden, Jr., 2018, p. 271)

Prospect Hill Public School No. 4, First District (*Harford County, Maryland Teachers and the Schools They Served, 1774-1900*, by Henry C. Peden, Jr., 2022, p. 371)

Prospect Public School No. 15, near Level, Second District (*Harford County, Maryland Teachers and the Schools They Served, 1774-1900*, by Henry C. Peden, Jr., 2022, p. 371)

Providence Methodist Protestant Church (Fallston Road, Upper Cross Roads)

Pruitt, Charlott Jane, 1890-1950 (Angel Hill Cemetery)

Pue, Caleb, see Michael E. Pue, q.v.

Pue, Cornelia "Corrie" Galmese, 161-1935, born in New Orleans, died at Woodview, Harford Co., wife of Edward Hill Dorsey Pue, q.v. (St. Mary's Episcopal Church Cemetery); also see Michael E. Pue, q.v.

Pue, Edward Hill Dorsey, 1841-1905 (St. Mary's Episcopal Church Cemetery); Civil War (Confederate Army) veteran (*Havre de Grace Republican*, 30 May 1890); premium award winner, Class C - Sheep, and Class J - Domestic Products, Harford County Fair (*The Aegis & Intelligencer*, 24 Oct 1890); see Michael E. Pue, q.v.

Pue, Elizabeth (Bull), 1819-1891, wife of Michael E. Pue (St. Mary's Episcopal Church Cemetery)

Pue, Michael E., 1817-1890, son of Caleb Pue and Emily Dorsey (St. Mary's Episcopal Church); farmer, near Bel Air (*Havre de Grace Republican*, 26 Sep 1890); died testate and his named heirs were daughter Mary E. Hall, son Edward H. D. Pue and Corrie Pue, wife of said Edward (Harford County Will Book JMM 11:145); see Mary Elizabeth Preston and Elizabeth (Bull) Pue, q.v.

Pugh, George Edward (colored), c1880-1934, native of Maryland, resided near Fallston, son of Henry Pugh and Julia Spencer (Death certificate)

Pugh, Henry (colored), see George Edward Pugh (colored), q.v.

Pugh, J. Howard, sold land in April 1890 (*The Aegis & Intelligencer*, 9 May 1890)

Pugh, William B., 1868-1900 (Union Chapel Methodist Church Cemetery); premium award winner, Class O - Discretionary, Harford County Fair, 1890 (*The Aegis & Intelligencer*, 24 Oct 1890)

Purcell's Ice Cream Parlor, Bel Air, Annie Purcell, prop. (*Bel Air: An Architectural and Cultural History, 1782-1945*, by Marilynn M. Larew, 1995, p. 68)

Purcell, Anna, 1828-1913 (St. Ignatus Catholic Church Cemetery)

Purcell, Anna R., 1887-1906 (Centre Methodist Church Cemetery)

Purcell, Annie M., 1867-1957 (St. Ignatus Catholic Church Cemetery)

Purcell, C. Coleman, 1871-1924 (Centre Methodist Church Cemetery), son of Martin J. and Hester (Harkins) Purcell, q.v.

Purcell, Clarence M., 1876-1942 (Centre Methodist Church Cemetery), son of Martin J. and Hester (Harkins) Purcell, q.v.

Purcell, Hester ("Hettie"), 1846-1917 (Centre Methodist Church Cemetery); wife of Martin J. Purcell, q.v.

Purcell, Lydia A., 1873-1936 (Centre Methodist Church Cemetery), daughter of Martin J. and Hester (Harkins) Purcell, q.v.

Purcell, Martin J., 1842-1926 (Centre Methodist Church Cemetery); native of New York and Civil War veteran, resided near Forest Hill (*1890 Special Census of the Civil War Veterans of the State of Maryland*, by L. Tilden Moore, Volume III, p. 74; *Harkins and Related Families of Harford County, Maryland*, by Henry C. Peden, Jr., 2003, pp. 14-15)

Purcell, William R., 1868-1894 (Centre Methodist Church Cemetery), son of Martin J. and Hester (Harkins) Purcell, q.v.

Purdy, Emma, see Jennette Carpenter Parker, q.v.

Purdy, George Warren, 1858-1926 (Angel Hill Cemetery)

Purdy, Kezia B., 1832-1922 (Angel Hill Cemetery)

Purnell, Effie, see John Henrie Poplar, q.v.

Purnell, Ellen (colored), 1858-1911 (St. James United Cemetery)

Purnell, Robert (colored), c1874-1934, parents unknown (Death certificate)

Purnell, Stephen (colored), 1845-1902 (St. James United Cemetery)

Pusey, Anna L. (Barron), 1861-1942 (Angel Hill Cemetery); wife of Charles J. Pusey, q.v.; also see Anna L. Barron, q.v.

Pusey, Charles Joel, 1861-1931 (Angel Hill Cemetery); age 24 in 1890 (Marriage License Applications Book ALJ No. 2, 1890); son of Mr. & Mrs. Joel Pusey, of Havre de Grace, married Anna L. Barron on 22 Apr 1890 (*The Aegis & Intelligencer*, 25 Apr 1890; *Harford Democrat*, 25 Apr 1890); tyler [outside guard], Susquehanna Lodge No. 130, A. F. & A. M. (*Havre de Grace Republican*, 26 Dec 1890)

Pusey, Clarence Crane, 1864-1922 (Angel Hill Cemetery); businessman (trader's license), Havre de Grace (*Havre de Grace Republican*, 30 May 1890); city council candidate, Havre de Grace (*Havre de Grace Republican*, 10 Jan 1890); charter member, Havre de Grace Gunning Club (*Havre de Grace Republican*, 14 Nov 1890); senior warden, Susquehanna Lodge No. 130, A. F. & A. M. (*Havre de Grace Republican*, 26 Dec 1890); juror, Sixth District (*Havre de Grace Republican*, 31 Oct 1890)

Pusey, Elizabeth J., 1873-1954 (Angel Hill Cemetery)

Pusey, Jesse L., 1863-1945 (Angel Hill Cemetery)

Pusey, Lida Langdon (Crane), 1840-1929 (Angel Hill Cemetery), wife of Clarence Crane Pusey, q.v.

Pusey, Mattie (Parker), 1868-1941 (Angel Hill Cemetery)

Putnam, Carrie Lee, 1877-1948 (Mt. Zion Methodist Church Cemetery)

Putnam, Walter A., 1880-1946 (Mt. Zion Methodist Church Cemetery)

Pyle, ----, catcher, Aberdeen Baseball Club (*The Aegis & Intelligencer*, 25 Jul 1890)

Pyle's General Store, Chestnut Hill, William H. Pyle, prop. (*Country Stores: Harford County's Rural Heritage*, by Henry C. Peden, Jr. and Jack L. Shagena, Jr., 2015, p. 197)

Pyle's General Store, Hickory, Herman T. Pyle, prop. (*Country Stores: Harford County's Rural Heritage*, by Henry C. Peden, Jr. and Jack L. Shagena, Jr., 2015, p. 197)

Pyle's General Store, Pylesville, Edward E. Pyle, prop. (*Country Stores: Harford County's Rural Heritage*, by Henry C. Peden, Jr. and Jack L. Shagena, Jr., 2015, p. 197)

Pyle's Grist Mill (aka Pylesville Mill), on Broad Creek at Pylesville, William O. Herrman, prop. (*Mills: Grist, Saw, Bone, Flint, Fulling ... & More*, by Jack L. Shagena, Jr., Henry C. Peden, Jr. and John W. McGrain, 2009, p. 235)

Pyle, A. Amanda (McComas), 1850-1934 (Mt. Zion Methodist Church Cemetery)

Pyle, Alfred, see Floyd Augustus Pyle and John D. Grafton, q.v.

Pyle, Amer, 1826-1906 (Union Chapel Methodist Church Cemetery)

Pyle, Ann Eliza, 1877-1904 (Broad Creek Friends Cemetery)

Pyle, Anna M., 1883-1963 (Centre Methodist Church Cemetery)

Pyle, Augustus, trustee, Hickory School No. 7, Third District (*Havre de Grace Republican*, 30 May 1890)

Pyle, Benjamin T., 1864-1943 (Angel Hill Cemetery)

Pyle, Bertha C. ("Bertie"), 1879-1962 (Mt. Zion Methodist Church Cemetery); student, Union Chapel Public School (*The Aegis & Intelligencer*, 14 Mar 1890); member, Mountain Reading Circle (*The Aegis & Intelligencer*, 21 Feb 1890); member, Union Chapel M. P. Church (*The Aegis & Intelligencer*, 10 Jan 1890)

Pyle, Bertha Lavinia (Alexander), 1890-1919 (Mt. Vernon Methodist Church Cemetery)

Pyle, Bessie S., 1889-1983 (Centre Methodist Church Cemetery)

Pyle, C. W., blacksmith, Perryman (*Havre de Grace Republican*, 12 Sep 1890)

Pyle, Carl L., 1890-1895 (Centre Methodist Church Cemetery)

Pyle, Cassandra D., 1817-1890 (Broad Creek Friends Cemetery); wife of Ely Pyle, q.v., of near Chestnut Hill (*The Aegis & Intelligencer*, 6 Jun 1890)

Pyle, Charles M., 1876-1893 (Mt. Zion Methodist Church Cemetery)

Pyle, Charles Wesley, 1846-1928 (Mt. Zion Methodist Church Cemetery)

Pyle, Clyde S., 1885-1956 (Slate Ridge Cemetery, York Co., PA); native of Maryland, born 19 Oct 1885, son of James Pyle and Mary Kirk (Harkins Funeral Home Records)

Pyle, Cordelia, 1876-1942 (Centre Methodist Church Cemetery)

Pyle, Edward E., acquired land in May 1890 (*The Aegis & Intelligencer*, 6 Jun 1890)

Pyle, Elisha Rutledge, 1850-1928 (Centre Methodist Church Cemetery); born 22 Apr 1850, son of Joshua H. and Gulielma E. Pyle (Joshua Harlan Pyle Bible, *Maryland Bible Records, Volume 1*, by Henry C. Peden, Jr., 2003, p. 200); farmer near Forest Hill in 1890 when he was burned by an exploding lantern (*Harford Democrat*, 14 Feb 1890)

Pyle, Elizabeth, see Corbin A. Grafton, q.v.

Pyle, Ella Dora (Sidwell), 1861-1903 (Broad Creek Friends Cemetery)

Pyle, Ella L., 1871-1950 (Centre Methodist Church Cemetery)

Pyle, Ellen F., 1849-1941 (Mt. Tabor Methodist Church Cemetery)

Pyle, Ely, 1822-1903 (Broad Creek Friends Cemetery); also see Cassandra Pyle, q.v.

Pyle, Esther (Lancaster), 1829-1901 (Centre Methodist Church Cemetery)

Pyle, Florence B. (Monks), 1860-1935 (Mt. Tabor Methodist Church Cemetery); native of Harford Co. (Bailey Funeral Home Records); wife of Herman T. Pyle, q.v.

Pyle, Floyd Augustus, 1880-1954 (Centre Methodist Church Cemetery); native of Harford Co, born 17 Jan 1880, son of Alfred Pyle and Hellen Grafton (Bailey Funeral Home Records)

Pyle, Frank C., 1870-1945 (Centre Methodist Church Cemetery)

Pyle, Frank H., 1880-1944 (Emory Methodist Church Cemetery)

Pyle, Frederick B., 1867-1944 (Union Chapel Methodist Church Cemetery); member, Union Chapel M. P. Church (*The Aegis & Intelligencer*, 10 Jan 1890)

Pyle, George, uncalled for letter in Bel Air P. O. (*The Aegis & Intelligencer*, 14 Nov 1890)

Pyle, George M., 1848-1932 (Mt. Tabor Methodist Church Cemetery); member, Deer Creek M. P. Church (*Havre de Grace Republican*, 21 Mar 1890); also see Milton Pyle, q.v.

Pyle, George Orville, 1886-1962 (Mt. Tabor Methodist Church Cemetery)

Pyle, Granville Putman, 1871-1950 (Baker Cemetery); born 9 Oct 1871, son of Isaac and Mary Pyle (Isaac C. Pyle Bible, *Maryland Bible Records, Volume 1*, by Henry C. Peden, Jr., 2003, p. 198)

Pyle, Gulielma E. (Rutledge), 1829-1911 (Forest Hill Friends Cemetery; Joshua Harlan Pyle Bible, *Maryland Bible Records, Volume 1*, by Henry C. Peden, Jr., 2003, p. 200)

Pyle, H. F. (Master), member, Union Chapel M. P. Church (*The Aegis & Intelligencer*, 10 Jan 1890)

Pyle, H. Harlan, 1886-1966 (Centre Methodist Church Cemetery)

Pyle, H. T., see Sarah Jane Jourdan, q.v.

Pyle, Hannah J., 1855-1927 (Mt. Tabor Methodist Church Cemetery); wife of Lewis A. Pyle, q.v.

Pyle, Harlan, student, Forest Hill School, 1890 (*The Aegis*, 2 Jul 1965, school picture)

Pyle, Harmon (Herman), 1819-1901 (Deer Creek Methodist Church Cemetery)

Pyle, Harry, 1880-1917 (Mt. Vernon Methodist Church Cemetery); student, Union Chapel Public School (*The Aegis & Intelligencer*, 14 Mar 1890); member, Mountain Reading Circle (*The Aegis & Intelligencer*, 21 Feb

1890)

Pyle, Harry S, 1863-1955 (Mountain Christian Church Cemetery)

Pyle, Helen V., 1851-1918 (Deer Creek Methodist Church Cemetery); see John D. Grafton, q.v.

Pyle, Herman B., 1875-1954 (Mt. Zion Methodist Church Cemetery)

Pyle, Herman Thomas, 1859-1914 (Mt. Tabor Methodist Church Cemetery); resident near Hickory (*The Aegis & Intelligencer*, 9 May 1890); also see Mary Pyle, q.v.

Pyle, Hester H., see John D. Grafton, q.v.

Pyle, Hudson, manager, Chestnut Hill Literary Club (*The Aegis & Intelligencer*, 6 Jun 1890); see S. Hudson Pyle and John D. Grafton, q.v.

Pyle, Isaac C., 1815-1909 (Centre Methodist Church Cemetery)

Pyle, Isaac L., postmaster, Abingdon (*Havre de Grace Republican*, 11 Jul 1890)

Pyle, Isaac W., resident near Forest Hill, and father of Charles T. Pyle, of Hayt, KS (*The Aegis & Intelligencer*, 3 Oct 1890)

Pyle, J. H., treasurer, Franklin Sunday School (*Havre de Grace Republican*, 25 Apr 1890)

Pyle, J. L., postmaster, Aberdeen (*The Aegis & Intelligencer*, 8 Aug 1890)

Pyle, James, see Clyde S. Pyle, q.v.

Pyle, Jessie J., 1881-1909 (Centre Methodist Church Cemetery)

Pyle, John R., 1854-1941 (Emory Methodist Church Cemetery)

Pyle, Joseph, 1845-1928 (Broad Creek Friends Cemetery); native of Pennsylvania, farmer near Dublin (Death certificate; Bailey Funeral Home Records)

Pyle, Joseph D., 1852-1914 (St. Mary's Catholic Church Cemetery)

Pyle, Joseph H., 1853-1924 (Centre Methodist Church Cemetery); married Rose G. McCommons on 19 Mar 1890 (Marriage License Applications Book ALJ No. 2, 1890, and announcement in *The Aegis & Intelligencer*, 14 Mar 1890)

Pyle, Joshua Harlan, 1813-1894 (Forest Hill Friends Cemetery; Joshua Harlan Pyle Bible, *Maryland Bible Records, Volume 1*, by Henry C. Peden, Jr., 2003, p. 200)

Pyle, Julia A. (Martin), 1858-1939 (St. Mary's Catholic Church Cemetery)

Pyle, Lewis A., 1855-1930 (Mt. Tabor Methodist Church Cemetery); farmer, near Hickory (*The Aegis & Intelligencer*, 18 Jul 1890)

Pyle, Lizzie Bell, 1879-1904 (Broad Creek Friends Cemetery)

Pyle, Lulie C., 1862-1950 (Mt. Zion Methodist Church Cemetery)

Pyle, Lydia S., 1840-1914 (Centre Methodist Church Cemetery)

Pyle, Margaret C., sold land in May 1890 (*The Aegis & Intelligencer*, 6 Jun 1890)

Pyle, Margaret E., 1886-1921 (Emory Methodist Church Cemetery)

Pyle, Martin W., acquired land in April 1890 (*The Aegis & Intelligencer*, 9 May 1890)

Pyle, Mary, 1817-1890 (Deer Creek Methodist Church Cemetery); sister of Hermon Pyle, of near Hickory (*The Aegis & Intelligencer*, 21 Feb 1890)

Pyle, Mary E., 1875-1939 (St. George's Episcopal Church Cemetery)

Pyle, Mary E. (Magness), 1869-1924 (Mountain Christian Church Cemetery); native of Harford Co., resided at Emmorton (Death certificate)

Pyle, Mary Ella, 1856-1923 (Joshua Harlan Pyle Bible, *Maryland Bible Records, Volume 1*, by Henry C. Peden, Jr., 2003, p. 200)

Pyle, Mary P. (Hoopes), 1851-1920 (Broad Creek Friends Cemetery)

Pyle, Mary R., 1834-1919 (Union Chapel Methodist Church Cemetery)

Pyle, Milton, young son of George M. Pyle, of Chestnut Hill (*The Aegis & Intelligencer*, 19 Dec 1890)

Pyle, Nathan, trustee, Enterprise School No. 19, Fourth District (*Havre de Grace Republican*, 30 May 1890); Nathan I. Pyle, and wife, sold land in May 1890 (*The Aegis & Intelligencer*, 6 Jun 1890)

Pyle, Octavia, see Octavio C. Bennington and William C. Pyle, q.v.

Pyle, Olie Baker, 1873-1949 (Baker Cemetery)

Pyle, Parker F., 1859-1930 (Baker Cemetery); clay pigeon shooter, Churchville (*The Aegis & Intelligencer*, 7 Feb 1890)

Pyle, Rebecca, 1824-1904 (Emory Methodist Church Cemetery)

Pyle, Rosa G., 1871-1960 (Centre Methodist Church Cemetery); wife of Joseph H. Pyle, q.v.

Pyle, Rosa R. (Grancel), 1886-1978 (St. Paul's Methodist Church Cemetery)

Pyle, S. Hudson, see Hudson Pyle and John D. Grafton, q.v.

Pyle, Samuel L., 1875-1950 (St. George's Episcopal Church Cemetery)

Pyle, Sarah Ann, 1821-1896 (Broad Creek Friends Cemetery)

Pyle, Sarah J. (Harkins), 1824-1904 (Centre Methodist Church Cemetery)

Pyle, Stanley (Master), member, Union Chapel M. P. Church (*The Aegis & Intelligencer*, 10 Jan 1890); fourth grade student, School No. 1, Third District (*The Aegis & Intelligencer*, 11 Jul 1890)

Pyle, Susan Emma, 1866-1938 (Joshua Harlan Pyle Bible, *Maryland Bible Records, Volume 1*, by Henry C. Peden, Jr., 2003, p. 200)

Pyle, Thomas, student, Oakland School, 1890 (George G. Curtiss Ledger)

Pyle, Thomas Walter, 1888-1967 (Broad Creek Friends Cemetery)

Pyle, Vinton, secretary, Union Chapel M. P. Church Sunday School (*Havre de Grace Republican*, 11 Apr 1890)

Pyle, Virginia S., 1880-1959 (Union Chapel Methodist Church Cemetery)

Pyle, Wilberta, 1865-1956 (Union Chapel Methodist Church Cemetery)

Pyle, Willard D., 1889-1966 (Baker Cemetery)

Pyle, William, see May H. Martin, q.v.

Pyle, William C., widower, age 34, married Octavia Bennington on 18 Dec 1890 at the Bel Air Parsonage (Bel Air Methodist Charge Marriage Records, p. 238, Marriage License Applications Book ALJ No. 2

Pyle, William H., juror, Fifth District (*Havre de Grace Republican*, 31 Oct 1890)

Pyle, William Stump, 1847-1937 (Broad Creek Friends Cemetery)

Pyle, Wilson Roby, 1857-1926 (Grove Presbyterian Church Cemetery; Death certificate)

Pyle, Woodley, student, Union Chapel Public School (*The Aegis & Intelligencer*, 14 Mar 1890)

Quarles, Alice (colored), 1879-19-- (Berkley Memorial Cemetery); wife of George H. Quarles, q.v.

Quarles, Edward ("Ned"), 1877-1932 (Darlington Cemetery); fifth grade honor student, Bel Air Academy and Graded School, 1890 (*The Aegis & Intelligencer*, 4 Jul 1890); premium award winner, Class L - Children's Department, Harford County Fair, 1890 (*The Aegis & Intelligencer*, 24 Oct 1890)

Quarles, George H. (colored), 1860-1940 (Berkley Memorial Cemetery)

Quarles, John ("Jack"), student, Bel Air Academy and Graded School (*The Aegis & Intelligencer*, 11 Apr 1890); premium award winner, Class L - Children's Department, Harford County Fair (*The Aegis & Intelligencer*, 24 Oct 1890)

Qui Vive Social Club, Havre de Grace (*Havre de Grace: Its Historic Past, Its Charming Present and Its Promising Future: Harford County's Rural Heritage.* by Jack L. Shagena, Jr. and Henry C. Peden, Jr., 2018, p. 272)

Quick, James, new name on the voter registration list in the Sixth District (*Havre de Grace Republican*, 17 Oct 1890)

Quickley, Amelia (colored), 1879-1961 (Quickley family records, bured at Tabernacle Mt. Zion Methodist Church Cemetery, no tombstone)

Quickley, Isaac (colored), 1871-1955 (Quickley family records, bured at Tabernacle Mt. Zion Methodist Church Cemetery, no tombstone)

Quinby, Cassie S., age 23 in 1889 (Marriage License Applications Book ALJ No. 2, 1889)

Quinby, Frances Elizabeth ("Lizzie"), 1860-1932 (Ebenezer Methodist Church Cemetery); Miss Lizzie Quinby, vice principal, Bel Air Graded School (*Havre de Grace Republican*, 23 May 1890)

Quinby, James F., member, Maryland Central Dairymen's Association (*Havre de Grace Republican*, 28 Feb 1890)

Quinby, James Houghton, 1826-1892 (Christ Episcopal Church Cemetery); resident of Bynum near Hickory (*The Aegis & Intelligencer*, 4 Jul 1890; *Harford Democrat*, 4 Jul 1890); premium award winner, Class A - Horses, Harford County Fair, 1890 (*The Aegis & Intelligencer*, 24 Oct 1890)

Quinby, Nancy Benedict (Farrand), 1831-1916 (Christ Episcopal Church Cemetery)

Quinby, Phoebe Adaline (Miss), 1808-1890 (Christ Episcopal Church Cemetery); sister of J. H. Quinby, of near the Hickory (*The Aegis & Intelligencer*, 8 Aug 1890)

Quinlan, Charles, student, Oakland School, 1890 (George G. Curtiss Ledger)

Quinlan, Laura S., born 3 Feb 1870, baptized 3 Mar 1885, daughter of Philip T. Quinlan, of Harford Co., and Elizabeth Taylor, of England (St. Ignatius Catholic Church Baptism Register, p. 78)

Quinlan, Lavinia M., 1820-1898 (St. Mary's Catholic Church Cemetery)

Quinlan, Philip T., 1814-1893 (Centre Methodist Church Cemetery)

Quinlan, Susannah (Miss), 1808-1890 (St. Ignatius Catholic Church Cemetery); resident near the Rocks of Deer Creek (*Havre de Grace Republican*, 4 Jul 1890)

Quinn, Anne M., 1859-1928 (Mt. Erin Cemetery)

Quinn, Catharine, 1831-1898 (Mt. Erin Cemetery)

Quinn, Ellen F., 1836-1936 (St. Ignatius Catholic Church Cemetery); widow of John S. Quinn and daughter of Alice Ann Lingan, q.v.

Quinn, Frank A., 1869-1924 (Angel Hill Cemetery)

Quinn, George, died 19 Jan 1893, no age given (Alms House Monthly Register)

Quinn, James (Mrs.), of Fallston, native of County Derry, Ireland, died 23 Jun 1890, age about 65 (*The Aegis & Intelligencer*, 27 Jun 1890)

Quinn, Jim, 1869-1939 (Heavenly Waters Cemetery)

Quinn, John H., name removed from the voter registration list in the Sixth District (*Havre de Grace Republican*, 17 Oct 1890); also see Phoebe Adaline Quinby, q.v.

Quinn, John S., 1838-1912 (St. Ignatius Catholic Church Cemetery); resident near Hickory (*The Aegis & Intelligencer*, 9 May 1890)

Quinn, Loretta, 1873-1936 (Angel Hill Cemetery)

Quirk, Agnes H., 1872-1936 (Mt. Erin Cemetery)

Quirk, Bridget, see Michael H. Quirk and Margare V. Quirk, q.v.

Quirk, Catherine B., 1878-1952, native of Havre de Grace, born 28 Oct 1878, daughter of Dennis Quirk and Margaret Hollahan (Pennington Funeral Home Records)

Quirk, Dennis, see Catherine B. Quirk and Mary Ellen Quirk, q.v.

Quirk, James J., 1868-1946 (Mt. Erin Cemetery); new name on the Havre de Grace voter registration list (*Havre de Grace Republican*, 19 Sep 1890)

Quirk, Jeremiah, see Michael Henry Quirk and Margaret Vincent Quirk, q.v.

Quirk, Johanna, see Anna Marua Fisher, q.v.

Quirk, Margaret (Hollahan), c1842-1920, native of Ireland (Mt. Erin Cemetery; Death certificate); see Catherine B. Quirk, q.v.

Quirk, Margaret Vincent, 1874-1955 (Mt. Erin Cemetery - married name Pohl); native of Havre de Grace, born 24 Jan 1874, daughter of Jeremiah Quirk and Bridget ---- (Pennington Funeral Home Records)

Quirk, Mary Ellen, 1875-1966 (Mt. Erin Cemetery - married name Nolan); native of Havre de Grace, born 25 Mar 1875, daughter of Dennis Quirk and Margaret Hollahan (Pennington Funeral Home Records)

Quirk, Michael Henry, 1870-1945 (Mt. Erin Cemetery); native of Havre de Grace, born 6 Aug 1870, son of Jeremiah Quirk and Bridget Wall, both natives of Ireland (Pennington Funeral Home Records)

Rahll, Andrew Walter 1879-1944 (Little Falls Quaker Cemetery)

Rahll, George, Civil War veteran, Fallston (*1890 Special Census of the Civil War Veterans of the State of Maryland*, by L. Tilden Moore, Volume III, p. 75)

Rahll, Phebe Alice (Preston), 1881-1968 (Little Falls Quaker Cemetery)

Rainbow, Louis (colored), 1855-1933, native of Maryland (Death certificate)

Rainbow, Phebe Leah (colored), 1861-1958 (Chestnut Grove Cemetery); wife of Louis Rainbow, q.v.

Rampley, Alverta R., see Alverta R. Streett, q.v.

Rampley, Anne Silestine, born 11 Feb 1880, daughter of James and Elizabeth (Nelson) Rampley (Bethel Presbyterian Church Cemetery Records)

Rampley, Annie Laurie (Bevard), 1866-1904 (Bethel Presbyterian Church Cemetery Records); first wife of Robert N. Rampley, q.v.

Rampley, Charles, born 1869, son of William and Elizabeth (Streett) Rampley (Bethel Presbyterian Church Cemetery Records)

Rampley, Eleanor (Turner), 1820-1901 (Bethel Presbyterian Church Cemetery Records); wife of James Rampley, q.v.

Rampley, Elizabeth, 1825-1907 (Bethel Presbyterian Church Cemetery Records)

Rampley, Frances R. (Maul), 1829-1900 (Bethel Presbyterian Church Cemetery Records); wife of Robert Nelson Rampley, q.v.

Rampley, Hannah Elizabeth (Deets), 1859-1941 (Bethel Presbyterian Church Cemetery Records); wife of William S. Rampley, q.v.

Rampley, Isabelle B. (Bevard), 1859-1947 (Bethel Presbyterian Church Cemetery Records); second wife of Robert N. Rampley, q.v.

Rampley, James, 1819-1901 (Bethel Presbyterian Church Cemetery Records); served as a juror, Fourth District, 1890 (*Havre de Grace Republican*, 31 Jan 1890); see Alverta R. Streett, q.v.

Rampley, Laura Augusts (Ensor), 1879-1964 (Bethel Presbyterian Church Cemetery Records); wife of Charles S. Rampley, q.v.

Rampley, Mary E. (Streett), 1856-1928 (Highland Presbyyterian Church Cemetery); native of Maryland, resided at Rocks (Death certificate); see Alverta R. Streett, q.v.

Rampley, Robert N., 1866-1941 (Bethel Presbyterian Church Cemetery Records)

Rampley, Robert Nelson, 1817-1899 (Bethel Presbyterian Church Cemetery Records); see Frances R. Rampley, q.v.

Rampley, Sarah M., age 26 in 1889 (Marriage License Applications Book ALJ No. 2, 1889)

Rampley, William N., 1825-1894 (Bethel Presbyterian Church Cemetery Records; *The Aegis & Intelligencer*, 12 Jan 1890)

Rampley, William Streett, 1859-1941 (Bethel Presbyterian Church Cemetery Records)

Ramsay's General Store, Highland, Frederick N. Ramsay and John R. Ramsay (brothers), prop. (*Country Stores: Harford County's Rural Heritage*, by Henry C. Peden, Jr. and Jack L. Shagena, Jr., 2015, pp. 199-200)

Ramsay, Corinne M. (Miss), 1857-1929 (St. Mary's Catholic Church Cemetery); premium award winner, Class K - Household and Domestic Manufactures, Harford County Fair (*The Aegis & Intelligencer*, 24 Oct 1890)

Ramsay, Elizabeth A. (colored), 1862-1890, wife of George Ramsay (St. James Church, Gravel Hill Cemetery)

Ramsay, Elmer E., 1861-1932 (Highland Presbyterian Church Cemetery); see Robert Ralph Ramsay, q.v.

Ramsay, Florence (colored), 1862-1918 (Death certificate)

Ramsay, Frederick "Fred" N., 1863-1954 (Slate Ridge Cemetery, York Co., PA); resident of Highland, son of Robert N. Ramsay, married Mary Corinne Minnick on 30 Apr 1890 (*The Aegis & Intelligencer*, 21 Feb 1890 and 2 May 1890); native of Maryland, born 28 Oct 1863, son of Robert Ramsay and Mary M. Heaps (Harkins Funeral Home Records); brother of John R. Ramsay, q.v.

Ramsay, George (colored), see Elizabeth A. Ramsay (colored), q.v.

Ramsay, H. Clarence, 1872-1935 (Slate Ridge Cemetery, York Co., PA); native of Street, Harford Co., born 8 Dec 1872, son of Robert E. Ramsay and Martha M. Heaps (Harkins Funeral Home Records)

Ramsay, Harry W., 1866-1896 (Rock Run Methodist Church Cemetery)

Ramsay, Hugh C., see Rena E. Ramsay, q.v.

Ramsay, John R., 1867-1932 (Highland Presbyterian Church Cemetery); merchant, of Highland, son of Robert N. Ramsay (*The Aegis & Intelligencer*, 21 Feb 1890 and 12 Dec 1890); brother of Frederick N. Ramsay, q.v.

Ramsay, Lloyd, deceased and removed from the Havre de Grace voter registration list, 1890 (*Havre de Grace Republican*, 19 Sep 1890)

Ramsay, Lloyd A. (colored), 1858-1924 (Death certificate)

Ramsay, Mary E. (Ramsay), 1861-1928 (Slateville Cemetery, York Co., PA); native of Pennsylvania, resided at Whiteford (Death certificate)

Ramsay, Rena E., died 8 Aug 1890, age 21 months, only child of Hugh C. and Bettie Ramsay (*The Aegis & Intelligencer*, 22 Aug 1890)

Ramsay, Robert E., see H, Clarence Ramsay, q.v.

Ramsay, Robert N. (Mrs.), resident of Highland, sister of Hugh T. Heaps (*The Aegis & Intelligencer*, 21 Feb 1890); delegate, Fifth District, Republican Party Convention (*The Aegis & Intelligencer*, 26 Sep 1890); also see Frederick N. Ramsay, q.v.

Ramsay, Robert Ralph, 1889-1905 (Highland Presbyterian Church Cemetery), born 10 Nov 1889, native of Maryland, resided at Street, son of Elmer Ramsay and Ida Kilgore (Death certificate)

Ramsay, Samuel J., see Susanna G. Ramsay, q.v.

Ramsay, Sarah (Hall), 1820-1899 (Angel Hill Cemetery)

Ramsay, Susannah G. (Stump), 1812-1901, native of Maryland, resided at Darlington, wife of Samuel J. Ramsay (Death certificate)

Ramsay, William (colored), c1880-1918, native of Maryland, single, laborer in Havre d Grace, son of William Ramsay and Mary Giles (Death certificate)

Ramsay, William White, 1827-1895 (Angel Hill Cemetery)

Ramsey, H. Anna (Rampley), 1857-1926 (Bethel Presbyterian Church Cemetery Records)

Ramsey, Hugh C., Jr., master of James Brown in 1883 (Harford County Indentures Book WSB No. 1)

Ramsey, Robert L. (colored), 1851-1929, native of Maryland, resident of Havre de Grace (Death certificate)

Ramsey, Sallie M., acquired land in November 1890 (*The Aegis & Intelligencer*, 5 Dec 1890)

Ramsey, Samuel (colored), died 29 Jun 1912, of old age, native of Maryland (Death certificate)

Ramsey, Wage, c1855-1935 (Heavenly Waters Cemetery)

Randall, Charlie, student, Mount Horeb School (*The Aegis & Intelligencer*, 14 Feb 1890)

Randall, Thomas O., died 27 Aug 1890, no age given, but the Randall family were residents near Fallston, being a wife and five children, three of whom recently died, one age 6 and the other under age 2, surviving (*The Aegis & Intelligencer*, 15 Aug 1890 and 29 Aug 1890); Civil War veteran, of High Point (*1890 Special Census of the Civil War Veterans of the State of Maryland*, by L. Tilden Moore, Volume III, p. 75); government pensioner, Pleasantville (*Havre de Grace Republican*, 4 Jul 1890)

Randall, Thomas, resident of near Fallston, died at the Almshouse, 1890 (*The Aegis & Intelligencer*, 29 Aug 1890)

Randow, Christian, see James L. Randow, q.v.

Randow, Amanda A., 1874-1946 (Dublin Southern Cemetery)

Randow, Frank H., 1858-1929 (Dublin Southern Cemetery); native of Germany (Bailey Funeral Home Records)

Randow, James L., 1874-1941 (Dublin Southern Cemetery); native of Harford Co., born 16 Oct 1874, son of Christian Randow, of Germany, and ---- (Bailey Funeral Home Records)

Randow, Mary C. (Rhoades), 1862-1929 (Dublin Southern Cemetery)

Ranson, Hattie (colored), see Mary Tildon(colored), q.v.

Ranstead, Lyman L., sink boat duck hunter (*Havre de Grace Republican*, 7 Nov 1890)

Ranstead's Saw Mill, Oakington, burned down (*Harford Democrat*, 17 Oct 1890)

Rasin, Alonzo (colored), age 23 in 1890 (Marriage License Applications Book ALJ No. 2, 1891)

Rasin, Sarah E., 1855-1938 (Wesleyan Chapel Methodist Church Cemetery); wife of Thomas F. Rasin, q.v.

Rasin, Thomas F., 1850-1934 (Wesleyan Chapel Methodist Church Cemetery)

Rather, Ella M., 1874-1949 (St. George's Episcopal Church Cemetery)

Rather, George E., 1880-1950 (St. George's Episcopal Church Cemetery)

Rather, Laura Victoria (Matthews), 1872-1904 (St. George's Episcopal Church Cemetery)

Rauscher, Anna ("Annie"), 1875-1960 (Angel Hill Cemetery)

Rauscher, Frederick, 1837-1902 (Angel Hill Cemetery)

Rauscher, Henry, 1864-1940 (Angel Hill Cemetery)

Ravenel, W., de C., chief of the U.S. government fish hatching operations, Havre de Grace, 1890 (*Havre de Grace Republican*, 11 Apr 1890 and 16 May 1890)

Rawhouser, ----, right fielder, Nonpareil Baseball Club, Aberdeen (*Havre de Grace Republican*, 6 Jun 1890)

Rawhouser, Elizabeth A. (Hicks), 1818-1900 (Baker Cemetery); wife of Joshua Rawhouser, q.v.

Rawhouser, Florence May (Mitchell), 1866-1923 (Baker Cemetery); wife of William Hicks Rawhouser and daughter of Frederick O. Mitchell, q.v.

Rawhouser, John, tent holder, Carsins Run Camp Meeting of the East Harford Circuit, P. E. Church (*The Aegis & Intelligencer*, 1 Aug 1890)

Rawhouser, Joshua, 1810-1892 (Baker Cemetery)

Rawhouser, William Hicks, 1854-1930 (Grove Presbyterian Church Cemetery); census taker, Hall's Cross Road Precinct (*Havre de Grace Republican*, 23 May 1890); delegate, First District, Republican Party Convention (*The Aegis & Intelligencer*, 26 Sep 1890); associate judge of elections, Hall's Cross Roads Precinct (*Havre de Grace Republican*, 17 Oct 1890); jousting tournament rider, Knight of My Maryland, and Knight of Aberdeen (*Havre de Grace Republican*, 15 Aug 1890; *The Aegis & Intelligencer*, 29 Aug 1890); member, Guy Social Club, Aberdeen (*Havre de Grace Republican*, 31 Oct 1890)

Ray, Bessie Virginia, 1885-1976, native of Jerusalem Mills, daughter of John Ray and Virginia Johnson (*The Aegis*, 15 Apr 1976 - married name Spicer)

Ray, Charles "Charlie" (colored), widower, age 37 in 1890 (Marriage License Applications Book ALJ No. 2, 1890); see George D. Ray and Matilda E. Ray, q.v.

Ray, Frank B., 1854-1936 (Mountain Christian Church Cemetery)

Ray, George D. (colored), 1886-1901, native of Maryland, son of Charles Ray and Sarah E. Williamson (Death certificate)

Ray, James Benjamin ("Ben"), 1886-1972 (Baker Cemetery)

Ray, John, see Bessie Virginia Ray, q.v.

Ray, John C., 1845-1911 (Mountain Christian Church Cemetery)

Ray, Lila "Lillie" M. (Jordan), 1857-1944 (Mountain Christian Church Cemetery)

Ray, Lucretia, see Emma Alverta Skillman, q.v.

Ray, Lucy (colored), see Matilda E. Ray (colored), q.v.

Ray, Matilda E. (colored), 1883-1978, daughter of Charlie Ray and Lucy ---- (*The Aegis*, 6 Apr 1978 - married name Hemore, widow of John Hemore)

Ray, Oscar Frank, 1889-1962 (Mountain Christian Church Cemetery)

Ray, Sarah E. (Williamson), 1859-1945, native of Maryland (Death certificate) wifeof Charles Ray, q.v.

Ray, Virginia A., 1861-1941 (Mountain Christian Church Cemetery)

Raymond, Amanda Louise, 1881-1960 (*The Aegis*, 3 Nov 1960); daughter of Fletcher Raymond, q.v.

Raymond, Fletcher, 1846-1905 (St. George's Episcopal Church Cemetery)

Raymond, Frank, 1873-1929 (Death certificate; Alms House Record Book)

Raymond, Harry H., 1880-1928 (St. George's Episcopal Church Cemetery)

Raymond, Henry A., 1843-1927 (St. George's Episcopal Church Cemetery); resident at Stepney and farmer on Bush River Neck (*The Aegis & Intelligencer*, 21 Mar 1890 and 11 Jul 1890); guardian, Perryman Lodge, Order of the Golden Chain (*Havre de Grace Republican*, 5 Dec 1890); son of Samuel Wilson Raymond, q.v.

Raymond, Martha Priscilla (Mitchell), 1846-1933 (Death certificate; St. George's Episcopal Church Cemetery); wife of Fletcher Raymond, q.v.

Raymond, Mary A., born -- Sep 1879, daughter of Fletcher and Mary M. Raymond (1900 Aberdeen Census)

Raymond, Mary Virginia (Osborn), 1850-1904 (Death certificate; St. George's Episcopal Church Cemetery); wife of Henry A. Raymond, q.v.

Raymond, Samuel Wilson, 1815-1890 (Cokesbury Memorial Church Cemetery); farmer and former county commissioner, Bush River Neck (*Havre de Grace Republican*, 4 Jul 1890)

Rayner, Isidor, of Fourth District, Democrat candidate for Congress (*The Aegis & Intelligencer*, 26 Sep 1890)

Read, Allisore, 1831-1901, resided at Macton (Death certificate incomplete)

Reading Circle, Havre de Grace women's literary group (*Havre de Grace: Its Historic Past, Its Charming Present and Its Promising Future: Harford County's Rural Heritage*. by Jack L. Shagena, Jr. and Henry C. Peden, Jr., 2018, p. 272)

Ready, David, 1836-1893 (St. Francis de Sales Catholic Church Cemetery)

Ready, Eleanora (Miss), 1828-1898, resident of Aberdeen (Death certificate)

Reamer, Abraham, 1865-1940, native of Russia, general store proprietor, Main Street, Whiteford (*Country Stores: Harford County's Rural Heritage*, by Henry C. Peden, Jr. and Jack L. Shagena, Jr., 2015, pp. 200-201)

Reasin, Alfred B., 1848-1917 (Angel Hill Cenetery); seeds and plants merchant, Otsego Street, Havre de Grace (*Havre de Grace Republican*, 17 Jan 1890); juror, Sixth District (*Havre de Grace Republican*, 31 Oct 1890); sneak boat duck hunter (*Havre de Grace Republican*, 7 Nov 1890)

Reasin, Claude Nelson, born 29 Mar 1889, son of William H. and Fannie N. Reasin (St. George's Episcopal Church Register of Baptisms, p. 9; William H. Reasin Bible, *Maryland Bible Records, Volume 1*, by Henry C.

Peden, Jr., 2003, p. 203)

Reasin, Elizabeth I. T., born 23 Jun 1877, daughter of of William J. and Esther (Russell) Reasin (*Barnes-Bailey Genealogy*, by Walter D. Barnes, 1939, p. I-9)

Reasin, Emily Barnes, born 17 Mar 1881, daughter of William J. and Esther (Russell) Reasin (*Barnes-Bailey Genealogy*, by Walter D. Barnes, 1939, p. I-9)

Reasin, Emma Alberta (Sheridan), 1864-1941 (Angel Hill Cemetery); wife of Frederick W. Reasin, q.v.

Reasin, Esther A. (Russell), 1846-1920 (Angel Hill Cemetery); wife of William J. Reasin, q.v.

Reasin, Fannie N. (Cole), 1854-1897 (St. George's Episcopal Church Cemetery; William H. Reasin Bible, *Maryland Bible Records, Volume 1*, by Henry C. Peden, Jr., 2003, p. 203); wife of William H. Reasin, q.v.

Reasin, Frederick W., 1859-1940 (Angel Hill Cemetery); member, Susquehanna Lodge No. 130, A.F. & A. M., Havre de Grace (*Havre de Grace Republican*, 11 Jul 1890)

Reasin, Gertrude, born -- Nov 1857 (1900 Aberdeen Census)

Reasin, Hannah E., born -- Feb 1825, widow (1900 Aberdeen Census)

Reasin, Jennie, born -- Mar 1867 (1900 Aberdeen Census)

Reasin, Rebecca (Townsley), 1856-1937 (Angel Hill Cemetery); wife of Alfred B. Reasin, q.v.

Reasin, Samuel Russell, born 23 Oct 1874, son of William J. and Esther (Russell) Reasin (*Barnes-Bailey Genealogy*, by Walter D. Barnes, 1939, p. I-9; Pennington Funeral Home Records gave his parents' names as William F. and Hester)

Reasin, William A., treated by unidentified doctor in 1890 ("Medical Account Book – 1890," Historical Society of Harford County Archives Folder)

Reasin, William F., served on a grand jury, Second District (*The Aegis & Intelligencer*, 14 Nov 1890); see Samuel R. Reasin, q.v.

Reasin, William F., 1882-1900, native of Havre de Grace, born 29 Mar 1882, son of William J. Reasin and Esther A. Russell (Death certificate; *Barnes-Bailey Genealogy*, by Walter D. Barnes, 1939, p. I-9)

Reasin, William F. (Mrs.), premium award winner, Class J - Domestic Products, Harford County Fair (*The Aegis & Intelligencer*, 24 Oct 1890); daughter of Abraham Cole, q.v.

Reasin, William H., 1855-1917 (St. George's Episcopal Church Cemetery); station agent, P. W. & B. Railroad, Aberdeen (*Havre de Grace Republican*, 17 Jan 1890); also see Claude Nelson Reasin, q.v.

Reasin, William J., 1842-1899, laborer at Havre de Grace (Death certificate; *Barnes-Bailey Genealogy*, by Walter D. Barnes, 1939, p. H-8); watchman, Susquehanna Bridge, P. W. & B. Railroad (*Havre de Grace Republican*, 16 Sep 1899); see Samuel R. Reasin, q.v.

Reckord's Mill, Bel Air, John Henry Reckord, prop. (*Bel Air: An Architectural and Cultural History, 1782-1945*, by Marilynn M. Larew, 1995, p. 80)

Reckord, Archie, small son of John H. Reckord, of Bel Air, 1890 (*Havre de Grace Republican*, 28 Nov 1890)

Reckord, Bessie Payne (Roe), 1883-1943 (Mountain Christian Church Cemetery), wife of Milton Atchison Reckord, q.v.

Reckord, Caroline S., 1878-1944 (Mountain Christian Church Cemetery)

Reckord, Clinton Lang 1886-1967 (Mountain Christian Church Cemetery)

Reckord, D. Burnett, 1867-1930 (Mountain Christian Church Cemetery); incorporator, Henry Reckord Manufacturing Company, 1890 (*Havre de Grace Republican*, 21 Feb 1890)

Reckord, Henry Herman, 1878-1837 (Mountain Christian Church Cemetery); Master Herman Reckord, dancing student, Archer Institute, Bel Air (*The Aegis & Intelligencer*, 6 Jun 1890)

Reckord, Isabel (O'Connell), 1888-1978 (Mountain Christian Church Cemetery)

Reckord, Jessie, student, Bel Air Academy and Graded School (*The Aegis & Intelligencer*, 23 May 1890); dancing student, Archer Institute, Bel Air (*The Aegis & Intelligencer*, 6 Jun 1890)

Reckord, John Gelder, 1889-1916 (Mountain Christian Church Cemetery)

Reckord, John Henry, 1854-1908 (Mountain Christian Church Cemetery); incorporator, Henry Reckord Manufacturing Company, 1890 (*Havre de Grace Republican*, 21 Feb 1890); member, Mt. Ararat Lodge No. 44, A. F. & A. M., Bel Air (*Havre de Grace Republican*, 11 Jul 1890); patented "a bag holder and truck" (*Havre de Grace Republican*, 22 Aug 1890); see Archie Reckord and Reckord's Mill, q.v.

Reckord, Julia Ann (Lukens) ("the elder"), 1832-1900, resident of Bel Air (Death certificate); incorporator, Henry Reckord Manufacturing Company, 1890 (*Havre de Grace Republican*, 21 Feb 1890); wife of Henry Record, 1825-1888, and mother of Walter P. Record, q.v.

Reckord, Julia Ann, 1873-1966 (Mountain Christian Church Cemetery)

Reckord, Leaman, 1890-1891 (Union Chapel Methodist Church Cemetery)

Reckord, Lillian R. (Chenoweth), 1854-1907 (Jessop Methodist Church Cemetery, Baltimore Co.); wife Walter Paul Reckord, q.v.

Reckord, Lydia A. (Zimmerman), 1856-1945 (Mountain Christian Church Cemetery), wife of John Henry Reckord, q.v.

Reckord, Mabel, born 5 Aug 1885, daughter of John H. Reckord and Lydia A. Zimmerman (Bethel Presbyterian Church Cemetery Records)

Reckord, Milton Atchison, 1879-1975 (Mountain Christian Church Cemetery)

Reckord, Walter Paul, 1857-1943 (Jessop Methodist Church Cemetery, Baltimore Co.); incorporator, Henry Reckord Manufacturing Company, Bel Air (*Havre de Grace Republican*, 21 Feb 1890); librarian, Mountain Christian Church Sunday School (*Havre de Grace Republican*, 7 Feb 1890); secretary, Fallston Road League (*Harford Democrat*, 3 Jan 1890; *The Aegis & Intelligencer*, 17 Jan 1890)

Reckord, William H., 1860-1913 (Mountain Christian Church Cemetery); premium award winner, Class A - Horses, Harford County Fair, 1890 (*The Aegis & Intelligencer*, 24 Oct 1890)

Rector, Albert, 1848-1931 (Mt. Zion Methodist Church Cemetery)

Rector, John H., 1869-1954 (Mt. Zion Methodist Church Cemetery)

Rector, Susan, 1850-1932 (Mt. Zion Methodist Church Cemetery)

Red Cross Packing Co., Havre de Grace (*Havre de Grace Republican*, 20 Jun 1890)

Red Pump Baseball Club [near Frogtown] (*The Aegis & Intelligencer*, 1 Aug 1890)

Redd, Charles D. (colored), 1867-1942, native of Virginia (Death certificate)

Reddick, Martha (colored), wife of William A. Christy, q.v.

Redding, Bridget (Mrs.), 1848-1935 (St. Mary's Catholic Church Cemetery); native of Ireland, resident of Cardiff, Harford Co., born 20 Nov 1848, father unknown, mother ---- Vaughan (Harkins Funeral Home Records)

Redding, Ellen (Kerr), 1872-1953 (St. Ignatius Catholic Church Cemetery)

Redding, John F., 1886-1944 (St. Mary's Catholic Church Cemetery)

Redding, Lucy B., 1884-1968 (St. Mary's Catholic Church Cemetery); native of New York, resident of Street, Harford Co., born 6 Jan 1884, daughter of Timothy Redding and Bridget Vaughan (Harkins Funeral Home Records)

Redding, Martin, 1844-1917 (St. Mary's Catholic Church Cemetery)

Redding, Michael J., 1873-1918 (St. Mary's Catholic Church Cemetery)

Redding, Thomas W., 1872-1945 (St. Ignatius Catholic Church Cemetery)

Redding, Timothy, 1840-1914 (St. Mary's Catholic Church Cemetery); farmer, near Prospect (*The Aegis & Intelligencer*, 9 May 1890); see Lucy B. Redding, q.v.

Redding, Timothy, 1877-1916 (St. Mary's Catholic Church Cemetery)

Reddington, Ellen O'Leary (Young), 1837-1901 (Mt. Erin Cemetery); sold land in November 1890 (*The Aegis & Intelligencer*, 5 Dec 1890)

Reddington, John, 1809-1898, native of Ireland (Mt. Erin Cemetery)

Reddington, John J., 1862-1895 (Mt. Erin Cemetery); hotel proprietor and the "Old Reliable" grocery store merchant at Congress Avenue and Strawberry Alley, Havre de Grace; member, St. Patrick's Catholic Church (*Biographical Dictionary of Harford County, Maryland, 1774-1974*, by Henry C. Peden, Jr. and William O. Carr, 2021, p. 223); businessman (liquor and trader's license), Havre de Grace (*Havre de Grace Republican*, 30 May 1890); city council candidate, Havre de Grace (*Havre de Grace Republican*, 10 Jan 1890); committeeman, Knights of St. Leo, Havre de Grace (*Havre de Grace Republican*, 19 Sep 1890); member, Independent Social Club, Havre de Grace (*Havre de Grace Republican*, 28 Mar 1890); member, Merry Ten Social Club, Havre de Grace (*Havre de Grace Republican*, 25 Jul 1890); delegate, Sixth District, at the Democrat Party Convention (*The Aegis & Intelligencer*, 5 Sep 1890); director, Home Building Association, Havre de Grace (*Havre de Grace Republican*, 22 Aug 1890); organizer and vice president, Havre de Grace Democratic Club (*Havre de Grace Republican*, 31 Oct 1890)

Reed, Andrew (colored), 1844-1915, native of Harford Co. (Death certificate); see Hannah (Whims) Reed, q.v.

Reed, Andrew B., born 12 Aug 1867, son of Josephus Reed and Asenath Ann Denbow (Bethel Presbyterian Church Cemetery Records)

Reed, Annie Laurie (Worthington), 1886-1972, wife of Charles Hopkins Reed, Sr., q.v.

Reed, Annie M. (Gibson) (colored), c1854-1915, native of Perryman, Harford Co. (Death certificate)

Reed, Annie T. (colored), 1878-1931, native of Maryland, born 18 May 1878, daughter of John T. Reed and Elizabeth Williams (Death certificate - married name Dorsey)

Reed, Asenath A., 1824-1906 (North Bend Presbyterian Church Cemetery)

Reed, Azenatha, see Frank Watkins, q.v.

Reed, Charles Hopkins, Sr., 1881-1944 (Darlington Cemetery); born 5th mo. 21st day, 1881, son of H. C. and Rachel H. Reed (Deer Creek Friends Record of Monthly Meeting, First Month, 1883, Register which recorded earlier births)

Reed, Charles M. (Mrs.) (Day), 1872-1957 (Slate Ridge Cemetery, York Co., PA); native of Harford Co., born 11 Jul 1872, daughter of Matthew Day and Sarah Jane Carter (Harkins Funeral Home Records)

Reed, Daniel E. (colored), 1882-1939, native of Perryman, Harford Co., born 16 Aug 1882, son of Isaac H. Reed and Annie Gibson (Death certificate)

Reed, Edward, county out-pensioner [welfare recipient], Fifth District (*Havre de Grace Republican*, 4 Jul 1890); resided at Darlington, blind for 18 years, received his sight again (*Harford Democrat*, 21 Mar 1890)

Reed, Eliza A. (colored), 1869-19-- (Union Methodist Church Cemetery, Aberdeen)

Reed, Ella C. (colored), 1876-1931, native of Maryland, born 21 Apr 1876, daughter of Kailer Reed and Harriett Harris (Death certificate)

Reed, Elwood, born 11th mo., 15th day, 1884, son of H. C. and Rachel H. Reed (Deer Creek Friends Record of Monthly Meeting, First Month, 1883, Register which recorded earlier births)

Reed, Emma, see Charles N. Cantler, Joel H. Cantler, Harry Cantler and Maggie J. Fantom, q.v.

Reed, Ernest Grant, 1871-1956 (Baker Cemetery)

Reed, Grace Mae, 1876-1935, wife of Ernest Grant Reed, q.v.

Reed, Hannah (Whims) (colored), 1839-1899, servant at Mulberry Point, native of Maryland (Death certificate); wife of Andrew Reed, q.v.

Reed, Harriet (colored), see Solomon Benjamin Christy (colored), q.v.

Reed, Isaac H. (colored), 1848-1912 (Death certificate); see Daniel E. Reed and Lillie Eliza Jane Reed, q.v.

Reed, John T., age 22 in 1890 (Marriage License Applications Book ALJ No. 2, 1891)

Reed, John T. (colored), see Anne T. Reed (colored), q.v.

Reed, Josephus, 1824-1901 (North Bend Presbyterian Church Cemetery)

Reed, Kaleb (colored), 1850-1922, native of Maryland (Death certificate)

Reed, Kailer (colored), see Ella C. Reed (colored), q.v.

Reed, Lawrence, born 8th mo., 16th day, 1883, son of H. C. and Rachel H. Reed (Deer Creek Friends Record of Monthly Meeting, First Month, 1883, Register which recorded earlier births)

Reed, Lillie Eliza Jane (colored), 1882-1904, daughter of Isaac H. Reed and Milcah Gibson (Death certificate; Old Union Chapel Cemetery, Michaelsville)

Reed, M. E. (Brown) (colored), 1886-1924 (Union Methodist Church Cemetery, Aberdeen)

Reed, Maggie (Miss), member, Darlington M. E. Church (*The Aegis & Intelligencer*, 10 Jan 1890); actress, musical entertainment, at Darlington (*The Aegis & Intelligencer*, 30 May 1890)

Reed, Maggie B., born 8th mo., 24th day, 1879, daughter of of H. C. and Rachel H. Reed (Deer Creek Friends Record of Monthly Meeting, First Month, 1883, Register which recorded earlier births)

Reed, Mary (Miss), member, Darlington M. E. Church (*The Aegis & Intelligencer*, 10 Jan 1890)

Reed, Mary, wife of George Chenworth and mother of Samuel Thomas Chenworth, q.v.

Reed, Mattie (Miss), member, Norrisville M. P. Church (*The Aegis & Intelligencer*, 7 Mar 1890)

Reed, Rachel (Hopkins), 1847-1934, wife of Thomas H. C. Reed, q.v.; also see Thomas H. C. Reed, Maggie B. Reed, Charles H. Reed, Lawrence Reed and Elwood Reed, q.v.

Reed, Sarah (colored), see Emma Luisa Jackson (colored), q.v.

Reed, Thomas H. C., 1841-1894 (Darlington Cemetery); baker, Darlington (*The Aegis & Intelligencer*, 26 Sep 1890); also see Rachel H. Reed, Maggie B. Reed, Charles H. Reed, Lawrence Reed and Elwood Reed, q.v.

Reed, Thomas H. C., born 12th mo., 25th day, 1877, son of H. C. and Rachel H. Reed (Deer Creek Friends Record of Monthly Meeting, First Month, 1883, Register which recorded earlier births)

Reed, Thomas W., associate judge of elections, Jarrettsville Precinct (*Havre de Grace Republican*, 17 Oct 1890); Civil War veteran, Jarrettsville (*1890 Special Census of the Civil War Veterans of the State of Maryland*, by L. Tilden Moore, Volume III, p. 79); delegate, Fourth District, Republican Party Convention (*The Aegis & Intelligencer*, 26 Sep 1890)

Reed, Walter, student, Oakland School, 1890 (George G. Curtiss Ledger)

Reed, William W., age 24 in 1890 (Marriage License Applications Book ALJ No. 2, 1891)

Rees, Adele (Bailey), 1872-1953 (Slateville Cemetery, York Co., PA); native of Harford Co., born 8 Jul 1872, daughter of Josiah Bailey and Hannah J. Boyle (Harkins Funeral Home Records)

Rees, Benjamin Greene, 1866-1949 (Rock Run Methodist Church Cemetery)

Rees, Clara Elizabeth (Hamby), 1874-1948 (Rock Run Methodist Church Cemetery; Bailey Funeral Home Records); wife of Benjamin Greene Rees, q.v.

Rees, Emmor, 1844-1936 (Rock Run Methodist Church Cemetery)

Rees, Henry Harlan, 1877-1913 (Rock Run Methodist Church Cemetery)

Rees, Isaac N., 1844-1907 (Rock Run Methodist Church Cemetery)

Rees, Mary V. (McGonigal), 1873-1958 (Slateville Cemetery, York Co., PA); native of Forest Hill, Harford Co., born 20 Sep 1873, daughter of Albert McGonigal and Elizabeth Jeffery (Harkins Funeral Home Records)

Rees, Priscilla, 1837-1901 (Rock Run Methodist Church Cemetery); wife of Emmor Rees, q.v.

Rees, Sadie, 1870-1892 (Rock Run Methodist Church Cemetery)

Reese, Frederick, Civil War veteran, Clayton (*1890 Special Census of the Civil War Veterans of the State of Maryland*, by L. Tilden Moore, Volume III, p. 62)

Reese, Lewis, and wife, sold land in May 1890 (*The Aegis & Intelligencer*, 6 Jun 1890)

Reese, Maria Louise (Gilbert), 1843-1911 (Old Brick Baptist Church Cemetery; Death certificate)

Reese (Reaves?), William, 1848-1899 (Death certificate; Alms House Record Book)

Reeside, Dennison, see Johnson's Grist Mill, q.v.

Reeves, Callie M. (colored), 1888-1942 (Clark's Chapel Methodist Church Cemetery); wife of Edward E. Reeves, q.v.

Reeves, Edward E. (colored), 1878-1928 (Clark's Chapel Methodist Church Cemetery)

Reeves, Emma B., born 1870, died ---- (Dublin Methodist Church Cemetery)

Reeves, Mary Griffin (Mrs.), 1843-1926 (Union Chapel Methodist Church Cemetery); native of Maryland, resided at Bel Air (Death certificate)

Reeves, Roland Lee, 1870-1926 (Dublin Methodist Church Cemetery); native of Virginia, resided at Dublin (Death certificate)

Regle, Frederick, 1837-1899, farmer at Clayton, native of Maryland (Death certificate); see F. L. Reigle, q.v.

Reid, Grace (colored), see George A. Pitt (colored), q.v.

Reid, Jennie (colored), died 15 May 1895, no age given (Alms House Record Book)

Reid, William G., 1860-1933 (Christ Episcopal Church Cemetery)

Reidy, Mary, see Joseph A. Shea, q.v.

Reier, Antone, premium award winner, Class I - Agricultural Productions, Harford County Fair (*The Aegis & Intelligencer*, 24 Oct 1890)

Reigle, Annie, student, Bel Air Graded School (*The Aegis & Intelligencer*, 11 Apr 1890)

Reigle, Dora, age 19 in 1890 (Marriage License Applications Book ALJ No. 2, 1891)

Reigle, F. L., engineer and machinist, Bel Air Machine and Boiler Works (*The Aegis & Intelligencer*, 24 Jan 1890); gatekeeper, Bel Air Turnpike Company (*The Aegis & Intelligencer*, 17 Jan 1890); see Frederick Regle, q.v.

Reis (Rice), William, 1836-1898, native of Germany, resident of Churchville or Fountain Green (two death certificates)

Relief Association, Havre de Grace (*Havre de Grace: Its Historic Past, Its Charming Present and Its Promising Future: Harford County's Rural Heritage.* by Jack L. Shagena, Jr. and Henry C. Peden, Jr., 2018, p. 273)

Rembold, A. Matilda, 1861-1933 (Cokesbury Memorial Methodist Church Cemetery)

Rembold, Bessie B., 1887-1973 (Union Chapel Methodist Church Cemetery)

Rembold, Charles, 1869-1939 (Cokesbury Memorial Methodist Church Cemetery); farmer, near Magnolia (*The Aegis & Intelligencer*, 19 Sep 1890)

Rembold, Charles, 1885-1959 (Mt. Zion Methodist Church Cemetery)

Rembold, Fredericka, 1823-1896 (Trinity Evangelical Lutheran Church Cemetery)

Rembold, John, 1855-1932 (Cokesbury Memorial Methodist Church Cemetery)

Rembold, Lula B., 1886-1977 (Mt. Zion Methodist Church Cemetery)

Rembold, Mamie, died 9 Jul 1890, age 8 months (*The Aegis & Intelligencer*, 25 Jul 1890, misspelled her name Rimbold); daughter of Charles Rembold, q.v.

Renner, Mary A., 1838-1901, native of Germany, resided in Havre de Grace, wife of John Renner (Death certificate)

Revell, Eliza J. (colored), 1879-1941 (Tabernacle Mt. Zion Methodist Church Cemetery)

Revell, James H. (colored), 1866-1922 (Tabernacle Mt. Zion Methodist Church Cemetery)

Reynolds' General Store, Fallston, George Reynolds, prop. (*Country Stores: Harford County's Rural Heritage*, by Henry C. Peden, Jr. and Jack L. Shagena, Jr., 2015, p. 204)

Reynolds' General Store, Garland, William L. Reynolds, prop. (*Country Stores: Harford County's Rural Heritage*, by Henry C. Peden, Jr. and Jack L. Shagena, Jr., 2015, pp. 204-205)

Reynolds, Anastatia, 1841-1927 (Angel Hill Cemetery)

Reynolds, Anna D., 1877-1956 (St. George's Episcopal Church Cemetery)

Reynolds, Bertie (Reese), 1868-1967 (William Watters Memorial Methodist Church Cemetery, Cooptown)

Reynolds, Clara E., age 16 in 1889 (Marriage License Applications Book ALJ No. 2)

Reynolds, David A., age 25 in 1889 (Marriage License Applications Book ALJ No. 2)

Reynolds, David H., juror, Fifth District (*Havre de Grace Republican*, 31 Oct 1890)

Reynolds, Diana (Hunsdon), 1875-1958 (Rock Run Methodist Church Cemetery)

Reynolds, Dora M., 1890-1984 (Fallston Methodist Church Cemetery)

Reynolds, Elijah, new name on the voter registration list in the Sixth District (*Havre de Grace Republican*, 17 Oct 1890)

Reynolds, Ella E., age 21 in 1890 (Marriage License Applications Book ALJ No. 2, 1891)

Reynolds, Ellis Truman, 1886-1946 (William Watters Memorial Methodist Church Cemetery, Cooptown)

Reynolds, Emmaline S., born 7 Jul 1884, daughter of John P. and Martha E. Reynolds (John H. Stokes Bible, *Maryland Bible Records, Volume 2*, by Henry C. Peden, Jr., 2003, pp. 142-145)

Reynolds, Esther J., 1841-1913 (Centre Methodist Church Cemetery)

Reynolds, Frank M., 1880-1961 (Rock Run Methodist Church Cemetery)

Reynolds, George, 1867-1958 (Fallston Methodist Church Cemetery); age 23 in 1890 (Marriage License Applications Book ALJ No. 2), married Ida Bell Knight on 19 Nov 1890 at the bride's parents home (*The Aegis & Intelligencer*, 28 Nov 1890)

Reynolds, George, county school book depository manager, Garland (*Havre de Grace Republican*, 13 Jun 1890); transferred from the voter registration list at Hopewell, Second District (*Havre de Grace Republican*, 17 Oct 1890)

Reynolds, Grace D. (Rouse), 1882-1957 (Angel Hill Cemetery)

Reynolds, Hannah (Harlan), 1858-1951 (Holy Trinity Episcopal Church Cemetery); native of Baltimore (Bailey Funeral Home Records)

Reynolds, Hannah Rebecca, born 22nd of 8th month 1879, daughter of John P. and Martha E. Reynolds (John H. Stokes Bible, *Maryland Bible Records, Volume 2*, by Henry C. Peden, Jr., 2003, pp. 142-145)

Reynolds, Harmon Ira, 1851-1915 (William Watters Memorial Methodist Church Cemetery, Cooptown)

Reynolds, Harriet A., 1841-1910 (Holy Trinity Episcopal Church Cemetery)

Reynolds, Harrison, resided near Prospect and Deep Run (*Harford Democrat*, 21 Feb 1890 and 4 Apr 1890)

Reynolds, Hugh, son of Thomas Reynolds, near Mitchell's Mill, died 29 Jul 1890, age 15 (*The Aegis & Intelligencer*, 1 Aug 1890); "Hue Rennels" died 30 Jul 1890, no age given, and "Tom Rennels" died 27 Aug 1890, no age given (Alms House Record Book)

Reynolds, Ida Bell, 1869-1917 (Fallston Methodist Church Cemetery)

Reynolds, James F., 1869-1892, son of L. F. and Johann Reynolds (Rock Run Methodist Church Cemetery); carriage maker at Level and then at Churchville (*Carriages Back in the Day: Harford County's Rural Heritage*, by Jack L. Shagena, Jr. and Henry C. Peden, Jr., 2016, pp. 87-88); son of Lewis F. Reynolds, q.v.

Reynolds, James M., 1836-1908 (Christ Episcopal Church Cemetery); census taker, Bel Air Precinct (*Havre de Grace Republican*, 23 May 1890), reported population of the precinct as 4,091; houses 743; families 764; farms 140; Union soldiers 60; Confederate soldiers 15; inmates at Almshouse 55; population of Bel Air 1,430 (*The Aegis & Intelligencer*, 8 Aug and 5 Sep 1890); senior vice commander, Wann Post No. 49, G. A. R., of Forest Hill (*Havre de Grace Republican*, 25 Jul 1890); superintendent of amusements, Harford County Fair (*The Aegis & Intelligencer*, 5 Sep 1890)

Reynolds, Johanna, 1843-1892, wife of Lewis F. Reynolds (Rock Run Methodist Church Cemetery); also see James F. Reynolds, q.v.

Reynolds, John P., see Rebecca H. Reynolds, q.v.

Reynolds, Joseph Jerome, 1881-1949 (Tabernacle Cemetery); native of Whiteford, Harford Co., born 8 Apr 1881, son of Reuben C. Reynolds and Martha Cunningham (Bailey Funeral Home Records)

Reynolds, Lewis F., 1833-1919 (Rock Run Methodist Church Cemetery); wheelwright and carriage maker at Level (*Carriages Back in the Day: Harford County's Rural Heritage*, by Jack L. Shagena, Jr. and Henry C. Peden, Jr., 2016, p. 87); see Raymond Reynolds, q.v.

Reynolds, Lillian V., 1888-1958 (Mountain Christian Church Cemetery)

Reynolds, Louisa (Cook), 1852-1936 (Darlington Cemetery); native of Pennsylvania (Bailey Funeral Home Records)

Reynolds, M. Van, 1872-1957 (St. George's Episcopal Church Cemetery)

Reynolds, Margaret, see Dora B. Judd, Louis S. Thompson and James Harry Thompson, q.v.

Reynolds, Margaret W., 1889-1978 (Fallston Methodist Church Cemetery)

Reynolds, Martha J, 1838-1893 (Mt. Vernon Methodist Church Cemetery)

Reynolds, Mary Ann, see Mary E. (Wilson) Heaps, q.v.

Reynolds, Mary E., born 26th of 10th month 1875, daughter of John P. and Martha E. Reynolds (John H. Stokes Bible, *Maryland Bible Records, Volume 2*, by Henry C. Peden, Jr., 2003, pp. 142-145)

Reynolds, Mary E. (Truman), 1856-1914 (William Watters Memorial Methodist Church Cemetery, Cooptown)

Reynolds, Mary L., widow of Stephen Reynolds, of Cecil Co., MD, died at the home of her brother Robert Love near Castleton (*The Aegis & Intelligencer*, 28 Feb 1890)

Reynolds, Matthew, 1836-1912 (Angel Hill Cemetery); city council candidate, Havre de Grace (*Havre de Grace Republican*, 10 Jan 1890); sink boat duck hunter (*Havre de Grace Republican*, 7 Nov 1890)

Reynolds, Norman W., 1890-1956 (Angel Hill Cemetery)

Reynolds, Raymond, son of L. F. Reynolds, of Level (*The Aegis & Intelligencer*, 15 Aug 1890)

Reynolds, Rebecca H., 1880-1944 (Broad Creek Friends Cemetery); native of Harford Co., born 22 Aug 1880, daughter of John P. Reynolds and Martha E. Stokes (Bailey Funeral Home Records)

Reynolds, Reuben C., see Joseph Jerome Reynolds, q.v.

Reynolds, Reuben Ellsworth, 1863-1948, native of Harford Co. (Bailey Funeral Home Records)

Reynolds, Sara E. (Mahan), 1882-1978 (Angel Hill Cemetery)

Reynolds, Silas V., 1875-1901 (Rock Run Methodist Church Cemetery)

Reynolds, Stephen, see Mary L. Reynolds, q.v.

Reynolds, Susan C., age 20 in 1889 (Marriage License Applications Book ALJ No. 2, 1889)

Reynolds, Thomas, 1842-1908 (Angel Hill Cemetery); Thomas, and family, resided near Mitchell's Mill (*The Aegis & Intelligencer*, 1 Aug 1890); see Hugh Reynolds, q.v.

Reynolds, Thomas W., 1885-1960 (Angel Hill Cemetery)

Reynolds, Vandiver, charter member, Havre de Grace Gunning Club (*Havre de Grace Republican*, 14 Nov 1890)

Reynolds, Virgil, age 21 in 1889 (Marriage License Applications Book ALJ No. 2, 1889)

Reynolds, William L., 1863-1958, native of Harford Co. (Bailey Funeral Home Records)

Reynolds, Winfield S., new name on the voter registration list in the Sixth District (*Havre de Grace Republican*, 17 Oct 1890); treasurer, The Advance Benevolent Society, Havre de Grace (*Havre de Grace Republican*, 12 Dec 1890)

Rhoades, Anna (Bouffard), 1889-1957 (Darlington Cemetery)

Rhoades, Conrad, 1863-1931 (Death certificate; Heavenly Waters Cemetery)

Rhoades, John Francis, 1882-1947 (Darlington Cemetery)

Rhoades, Ruth Alice, 1869-1925 (Centre Methodist Church Cemetery)

Rhoades, Wilburn E., 1870-1920 (Centre Methodist Church Cemetery)

Rhodes, Daniel A., 1870-1933 (Centre Methodist Church Cemetery)

Rhodes, Emma Shiver, 1882-1963 (Angel Hill Cemetery)

Rhodes, Harry, 1872-1949 (Death certificate; Alms House Record Book)

Rhodes, Maud E., 1889-1963 (Ebenezer Methodist Church Cemetery)

Rhodes, William J., born 1872, died ---- (Centre Methodist Church Cemetery)

Rice, Alexander "Alick" (colored), 1827-1894 (*The Aegis & Intelligencer*, 23 Nov 1894); Civil War veteran, Chrome Hill (*1890 Special Census of the Civil War Veterans of the State of Maryland*, by L. Tilden Moore, Volume III, p. 78)

Rice, Alice (Chancey) (colored), 1852-1928 (Hendon Hill Cemetery); native of Maryland, resided in Bel Air (Death certificate)

Rice, Annie (colored), age 18 in 1889 (Marriage License Applications Book ALJ No. 2, 1889)

Rice, Annie (colored), 1889-1909, native of Maryland, daughter of Edward Rice and Charlotte McComas (Death certificate - married name Hall)

Rice, Annie E. (Preston) (colored), 1848-1920, native of Maryland (Death certificate)

Rice, Arthur M. (colored), 1884-1946 (Union Methodist Church Cemetery, Aberdeen)

Rice, Cassie (colored), see George Dorsey (colored) and Lloyd Rice (colored), q.v.

Rice, Catherine (colored), see Alfred Monk (colored) and Thaddeus Monk (colored), q.v.

Rice, Charles L. (colored), 1890-1952 (Union Methodist Church Cemetery, Aberdeen)

Rice, Charlotte (McComas) (colored), c1856-1903, native of Harford Co., resident of Michaelsville (Death certificate); wife of Edward Rice; also see Annie Rice, Hattie C. Rice, Emma A. Rice, q.v.

Rice, Cordelia (colored), see Edward Rigney, q.v.

Rice, Edith (Garrettson), 1872-1941 (Fallston Methodist Church Cemetery)

Rice, Edward (colored), county out-pensioner [welfare recipients], Second District, 1890 (*Havre de Grace Republican*, 4 Jul 1890); see Charlotte Rice, Annie Rice, Hattie C. Rice, and Emma A. Rice, q.v.

Rice, Eliza (colored), 1817-1903, of Harford Furnace (Death certificate)

Rice, Emma A. (colored), 1885-1922, native of Maryland, born 14 Feb 1885, daughter of Edward Rice and Charlotte McComas (Death certificate - married name Black)

Rice, Enos (colored), mail carrier from Darlington to Havre de Grace, 1890 (*The Aegis & Intelligencer*, 7 Mar 1890); county out-pensioner [welfare recipient], Third District (*Havre de Grace Republican*, 4 Jul 1890); see James Frank Rice, q.v.

Rice, Fannie (colored), see Laura Maxfield (colored), q.v.

Rice, George (colored), c1842-1912, of Castleton, Harford Co. (Death certificate); see John Ernest Rice and Josie L. Rice, q.v.

Rice, Georgeanna (Tinson) (colored), 1867-1926 (Death certificate states born 1867, but Union Methodist Church Cemetery, Aberdeen, tombstone inscribed 1869)

Rice, Gilpin (colored), 1884-1959 (Mt. Zion AME Church Cemetery); native of Harford Co., born 1 Aug 1884, son of William Rice and Elizabeth Wallace (Harkins Funeral Home Records)

Rice, Harriet J. (Stansbury) (colored), 1863-1931 (Death certificate)

Rice, Hattie C. (colored), 1878-1923, native of Harford Co., born 7 Apr 1878, daughter of Edward Rice and Charlotte ---- [McComas] (Death certificate - married name Monk)

Rice, Hattie V. (colored), 1852-1931 (Union Methodist Church Cemetery, Aberdeen)

Rice, Hester (colored), 1860-1912 (Death certificate; St. James United Cemetery)

Rice, James Frank (colored), 1888-1928 (Hendon Hill Cemetery); native of Maryland, born 1 Mar 1888, son of

Enos Rice and Alice A. Chancey (Death certificate)

Rice, Jane R. (Willis) (colored), 1855-1906, native of Maryland, resided at Rocks, wife of Moses Rice (Death certificate)

Rice, Jerome Ridgley (colored), 1859-1928, resided at Pylesville (Death certificate)

Rice, John (colored), prisoner in the county jail, 1890 (*Harford Democrat*, 3 Jan 1890); also see Irene Belle Clark (colored), q.v.

Rice John Ernest (colored), 1881-1903, native of Harford Co., resided at Rocks, son of George Rice and Annie Simms (Death certificate)

Rice, John Henry ("Tony") (colored), c1834-1912 (Death certificate); Civil War veteran, Darlington (*1890 Special Census of the Civil War Veterans of the State of Maryland*, by L. Tilden Moore, Volume III, p. 86)

Rice, John Henry (colored), 1851-1936 (Death certificate)

Rice, John Paca (colored), 1869-1912, of Perryman (Death certificate)

Rice, Josie L.(colored), 1889-1905, native of Pylesville, daughter of George Rice and Annie Barton (Death certificate)

Rice, Laura Rebecca (colored), 1872-1951 (Chestnut Grove Cemetery; *The Aegis*, 30 Nov 1951); wife of William E. Rice, q.v.

Rice, Levin (colored), see William B. Rice (colored), q.v.

Rice, Lloyd [Jr.] (colored), 1869-1929, native of Maryland, born 14 Apr 1869, son of Lloyd Rice and Cassie Rice (Death certificate)

Rice, Lydia (colored), see Ivory Hall, q.v.

Rice, Maria (colored), 1842-1912. native of Maryland, resided at Cherry Hill, parents unknown (Death certificate)

Rice, Mary (colored), see Mary Olivia Kell (colored), q.v.

Rice, Mary V. (Nye) (colored), 1857-1906, native of Maryland, resided at Street (Death certificate)

Rice, Moses (colored), 1834-1907 (Death certificate); Civil War veteran, Chrome Hill (*1890 Special Census of the Civil War Veterans of the State of Maryland*, by L. Tilden Moore, Volume III, p. 78); trustee, LaGrange Colored School No. 2, Fourth District, 1890 (*Havre de Grace Republican*, 30 May 1890); see Jane R. Rice and Sarah Jane Rice, q.v.

Rice, Sarah Jane (colored), 1874-1949, native of Rocks, Harford Co., born 28 Feb 1874, daughter of Moses Rice and Jane Willis (Death certificate)

Rice, Stillie C. (Mr.) (colored), 1880-1962 (St. James Church, Federal Hill, William C. Rice Memorial Cemetery)

Rice, Vallee (colored), 1887-1983 (Clark's Chapel Methodist Church Cemetery)

Rice, W. Edward (colored), c1852-1918, native of Maryland, resident of Havre de Grace (Death certificate)

Rice, Walter Jackson, 1858-1938 (Fallston Methodist Church Cemetery)

Rice, William (colored), age 25 in 1889 (Marriage License Applications Book ALJ No. 2, 1889); see Gilpin Rice, q.v.

Rice, William B. (colored), 1886-1911, native of Perryman, Harford Co., born 31 Jul 1886, son of Levin Rice and ---- (Death certificate; Union Methodist Church Cemetery, Aberdeen)

Rice, William Emerson (colored), 1867-1946 (Death certificate)

Rich, Irena (Miss), uncalled for letter in Bel Air P. O. (*The Aegis & Intelligencer*, 14 Nov 1890)

Richards, John E., 1880-1962 (Mountain Christian Church Cemetery)

Richards, John W., 1889-1982 (Baker Cemetery)

Richards, Jonett P., 1857-1916, of Havre de Grace (Death certificate)

Richards, Lena M., 1888-1947 (Baker Cemetery)

Richards, Lula May, 1882-1955 (Mountain Christian Church Cemetery)

Richards, Michael H., 1848-1917 (Emory Methodist Church Cemetery)

Richardson's General Store, Churchville, Robert C. Richardson, prop. (*Country Stores: Harford County's Rural Heritage*, by Henry C. Peden, Jr. and Jack L. Shagena, Jr., 2015, p. 207)

Richardson's General Store, Paradise, near Aberdeen, William B. Richardson, prop. (*Country Stores: Harford County's Rural Heritage*, by Henry C. Peden, Jr. and Jack L. Shagena, Jr., 2015, p. 207; *Harford Democrat*, 21 Mar 1890)

Richardson's Pharmacy, Bel Air, William S. Richardson, prop. (*Bel Air: An Architectural and Cultural History, 1782-1945*, by Marilynn M. Larew, 1995, p. 170)

Richardson's Private School, near Reckord, Third District (*Harford County, Maryland Teachers and the Schools They Served, 1774-1900*, by Henry C. Peden, Jr., 2022, p. 371)

Richardson, ---- (Miss), member, Lapidum Debating Society (*Havre de Grace Republican*, 7 Feb 1890)

Richardson, ----, catcher, Bel Air Victors Baseball Club (*The Aegis & Intelligencer*, 25 Jul 1890)

Richardson, A. Oliver, 1855-1922 (St. Ignatius Catholic Church Cemetery)

Richardson, Agnes W. (Mrs.) (colored), 1889-1978 (St. James Church, Gravel Hill Cemetery)

Richardson, Alexander K., 1845-1922 (Angel Hill Cemetery)

Richardson, Alfred, jousting tournament herald (*Havre de Grace Republican*, 19 Sep 1890)

Richardson, Alfred Raymond, 1886-1856, native of Havre de Grace, son of James and Lavenia Richardson (Pennington Funeral Home Records)

Richardson, Alice Ann, 1825-1911 (Churchville Presbyterian Church Cemetery), wife of Dr. Elihu Hall Richardson, q.v.

Richardson, Annie E., born 1884, daughter of George O. Richardson and Sarah E. Bull (Bethel Presbyterian Church Cemetery Records); see Annie W. (Richardson) Wilson, q.v.

Richardson, Annie Elizabeth (Miss), 1860-1926 (St. George's Episcopal Church Cemetery tombstone inscribed 1860, but her death certificate states 1861)

Richardson, Benjamin, fox hunter, Bush River Neck (*The Aegis & Intelligencer*, 7 Feb 1890)

Richardson, Benjamin F., 1861-1922 (St. George's Episcopal Church Cemetery); married Blanche Nelson on 30 Apr 1890 at the Aberdeen Southern Methodist Parsonage (*The Aegis & Intelligencer*, 9 May 1890)

Richardson, Bertha, 1882-1961 (William Watters Memorial Methodist Church Cemetery Cooptown)

Richardson, Bessie May, 1876-1945 (Churchville Presbyterian Church Cemetery); born 8 Apr 1876, daughter of William and Elizabeth Richardson (William R. Bissell Bible, *Maryland Bible Records, Volume 1*, by Henry C. Peden, Jr., 2003, p. 34)

Richardson, Blanche N., 1867-1955 (St. George's Episcopal Church Cemetery)

Richardson, Carrie (Mrs.), died 10 Feb 1900, age not given (Death certificate incomplete)

Richardson, Carrie G., 1870-1955, daughter of Benjamin Vincent Richardson and Martha Richardson of Baltimore Co. (*Harford County, Maryland Teachers and the Schools They Served*, by Henry C. Peden, Jr., 2021, p. 262); teacher, Rock Run School No. 14, Second District (*The Aegis & Intelligencer*, 29 Aug 1890)

Richardson, Cassie (colored), see George W. Banks (colored) and Malvina Dorsey (colored), q.v.

Richardson, Charles, 1876-1963 (St. Mary's Episcopal Church Cemetery)

Richardson, Charles (colored), born -- Feb 1872, native of Maryland (1900 Aberdeen Census); see Charles Augustus Richardson (colored) and Murel Richardson (colored), q.v.

Richardson, Charles A., 1880-1967 (Angel Hill Cemetery)

Richardson, Charles Augustus (colored), c1878-1937, native of Oakington, Harford Co., son of Charles

Richardson and ---- [Susanna] (Death certificate)

Richardson, Charles B., 1879-1961 (Highland Presbyterian Church Cemetery)

Richardson, Charles S., 1859-1899 (St. Ignatius Catholic Church Cemetery); resided near Bel Air, son of Henry Williams *(sic)* and ---- (Death certificate)

Richardson, Christopher Chapman, 1866-1932 (Union Chapel Methodist Church Cemetery); of Darlington in 1890 (*The Aegis & Intelligencer*, 13 Jun 1890); jousting tournament rider, Knight of Woodlawn (*Havre de Grace Republican*, 19 Sep 1890); member, Division No. 1, Bel Air Fire and Salvage Corps (*The Aegis & Intelligencer*, 10 Oct 1890)

Richardson, Cornelia T. (Munnikhuysen), 1884-1948 (St. Mary's Episcopal Church Cemetery), wife of Dr. Charles Richardson, q.v.

Richardson, Daisy (Rouse), 1872-1949 (Churchville Presbyterian Church Cemetery)

Richardson, Dora E. (Mrs.), daughter of Prof. Ascherfeld, of Havre de Grace (*The Aegis & Intelligencer*, 8 Aug 1890)

Richardson, E. Maude (Kernan), 1888-1967 (Slate Ridge Cemetery, York Co., PA); native of Harford Co., born 1 Jan 1888, daughter of Eugene and Ruth Kernan (Harkins Funeral Home Records)

Richardson, Edward Dorsey, 1810-1893 (Christ Episcopal Church Cemetery)

Richardson, Elihu Hall, 1849-1917 (St. Ignatius Catholic Church Cemetery)

Richardson, Elihu Hall (Dr.), 1825-1893, son of William Richardson (Churchville Presbyterian Church Cemetery); physician and Civil War veteran; former Board of Education member; member of Mt. Ararat Lodge No. 44, A. F. & A. M., and First Presbyterian Church of Bel Air (*Biographical Dictionary of Harford County, Maryland, 1774-1974*, by Henry C. Peden, Jr. and William O. Carr, 2021, p. 225); executive committee, Bel Air Tennis Club (*The Aegis & Intelligencer*, 16 May 1890); executive committee, Bel Air Academy Association (*Havre de Grace Republican*, 11 Jul 1890)

Richardson, Elihu Hall (Dr.), 1867-1908 (Churchville Presbyterian Church Cemetery); born 5 Nov 1867, son of William Richardson and Elizabeth Bissell (William R. Bissell Bible, *Maryland Bible Records, Volume 1*, by Henry C. Peden, Jr., 2003, p. 34)

Richardson, Elizabeth Ann (Macatee), 1811-1902 (St. Ignatius Catholic Church Cemetery); wife of Henry Richardson, q.v.

Richardson, Elizabeth K., wife of John Samuel Richardson, Jr., q.v.

Richardson, Elizabeth Morris (Bond), 1886-1918 (Fallston Methodist Church Cemetery)

Richardson, Elizabeth Rombough (Bissell), 1835-1890 (Churchville Presbyterian Church Cemetery); wife of William Speed Richardson, q.v.

Richardson, Ellen J. (colored), 1854-1913 (Death certificate; St. James United Cemetery)

Richardson, Emma J. (colored), 1880-1945 (Death certificate; St. James United Cemetery)

Richardson, Ethel, 1880-1924 (St. George's Episcopal Church Cemetery), see Ethel Mitchell, q.v.

Richardson, Etta (Miss), member, Bel Air Tennis Club (*The Aegis & Intelligencer*, 18 Jul 1890); premium award winner, Class K - Household and Domestic Manufactures, Harford County Fair (*The Aegis & Intelligencer*, 24 Oct 1890)

Richardson, Eva Virginia (colored), 1878-1929 (Death certificate; St. James United Cemetery)

Richardson, Ezekiel, trustee, Summit Hill School No. 12, Fourth District (*Havre de Grace Republican*, 30 May 1890)

Richardson, Florence (Hackney), 1882-1950 (Angel Hill Cemetery)

Richardson, Frances (colored), 1839-1904 (Death certificate; St. James United Cemetery)

Richardson, Frances (Sheridan) (colored), 1866-1945, native of Maryland, born 30 Dec 1866, daughter of Daniel Sheridan and Sarah ---- (Pennington Funeral Home Records' St. James A.M.E, Church Cemetery)

Richardson, George G., 1853-1910 (Bethel Presbyterian Church Cemetery Records)

Richardson, George O., born 29 Apr 1887, son of George O. and Sarah C. (Bull) Richardson (Bethel Presbyterian Church Cemetery Records)

Richardson, George Washington, 1844-1930 (St. Ignatius Catholic Church Cemetery); attorney and Democrat member of the House of Delegates (*Biographical Dictionary of Harford County, Maryland, 1774-1974*, by Henry C. Peden, Jr. and William O. Carr, 2021, p. 225); justice of the peace, Third District (*Havre de Grace Republican*, 21 Feb 1890)

Richardson, George Washington, delegate, of Havre de Grace (*Havre de Grace Republican*, 21 Feb 1890); delegate, Sixth District, Republican Party Convention (*The Aegis & Intelligencer*, 26 Sep 1890)

Richardson, George Washington (colored), 1865-1946, born 9 Apr 1865, son of George Washington Richardson and Margaret Tower, all natives of Maryland (Pennington Funeral Home Records)

Richardson, Grace R., 1886-1969 (Highland Presbyterian Church Cemetery)

Richardson, Hannah (Hemore) (colored), 1865-1949, native of Oakington, Harford Co., born 2 Apr 1865, daughter of ---- Hemore and Hazzai or Haggai Richardson (Pennington Funeral Home Records; Death certificate); wife of John H. Richardson, q.v.

Richardson, Harriett Ann (colored), 1861-1946 (Death certificate; St. James United Cemetery)

Richardson, Harriett E. (colored), 1885-1941 (Death certificate; St. James United Cemetery)

Richardson, Hattie E. (Mrs.), c1864-1951, native of Harford Co., parents unknown (Pennington Funeral Home Records)

Richardson, Hazzai or Haggai (colored), see Hannah Richardson (colored), q.v.

Richardson, Henry, 1814-1894 (St. Ignatius Catholic Church Cemetery)

Richardson, Henry (colored), c1854-1924, native of Maryland, resided near Aberdeen, son of ---- Richardson and Mary Brown (Death certificate)

Richardson, Henry Hall, baptized 23 Jul 1882, son of Elihu Hall Richardson, of Harford County, and Virginia Row, of Louisiana (St. Ignatius Catholic Church Baptism Register, p. 61)

Richardson, Howard (colored), 1889-1934, native of Havre de Grace, born 28 Feb 1889, son of Robert Richardson and Florence Sheridan, natives of Havre de Grace (Death certificate; St. James United Cemetery)

Richardson, Howard, son of J. L. Richardson, manager of *Romney Farm* near Michaelsville (*The Aegis & Intelligencer*, 28 Mar 1890)

Richardson, Isabel (Emory), 1869-1949 (Cokesbury Memorial Methodist Church Cemetery)

Richardson, J. L., see Howard Richardson, q.v.

Richardson, J. Marion, 1875-1960 (William Watters Memorial Methodist Church Cemetery Cooptown)

Richardson, J. Wiley, 1863-1914 (Norrisville Methodist Church Cemetery); see Edward Burkins, q.v.

Richardson, J. Wilson, member, Bel Air Tennis Club (*The Aegis & Intelligencer*, 18 Jul 1890); jousting tournament rider, Knight of Indian Hill (*Havre de Grace Republican*, 19 Sep 1890); premium award winner, Class B - Cattle, Harford County Fair (*The Aegis & Intelligencer*, 24 Oct 1890)

Richardson, J. Woodley, 1870-1941 (Cokesbury Memorial Methodist Church Cemetery)

Richardson, James, 1869-1947 (Cokesbury Memorial Methodist Church Cemetery); see Alfred R. Richardson, q.v.

Richardson, James L., corn packer at Old Baltimore on Bush River Neck (*Havre de Grace Republican*, 5 Sep 1890); trustee, Boden School No. 8, Second District (*Havre de Grace Republican*, 30 May 1890)

Richardson, James M., 1840-1920 (Angel Hill Cemetery)

Richardson, James N., 1856-1928 (Fellowship Cemetery)

Richardson, James S., 1827-1907 (St. George's Episcopal Church Cemetery)

Richardson, Japhet or Japheth, 1838-1924, native of Harford Co., resided at Aberdeen, single, son of Richard

Green and ----, and adopted son of Benjamin and Sophia Richardson (Death certificate; Cokesbury Memorial Methodist Church Cemetery tombstones)

Richardson, Jessie Deborah (Irvin), 1842-1916 (Angel Hill Cemetery), wife of Lake H. Richardson, q.v.

Richardson, Jessie P. O., 1877-1957 (Churchville Presbyterian Church Cemetery)

Richardson, John, see Olivia Richardson, q.v.

Richardson, John, 1879-1940 (William Watters Memorial Methodist Church Cemetery Cooptown)

Richardson, John A., 1851-1893 (Fellowship Cemetery)

Richardson, John A. W., 1866-1942 (Churchville Presbyterian Church Cemetery); resident of Bel Air, son of Dr. William S. Richardson, graduated from law school, 1890 (*The Aegis & Intelligencer*, 6 Jun 1890 and 27 Jun 1890); assistant marshal, Bel Air jousting tournament (*Havre de Grace Republican*, 19 Sep 1890); admitted to practice law before the Circuit Court for Harford County (*Harford Democrat*, 14 Nov 1890)

Richardson, John F. (colored), 1875-1934, native of Havre de Grace, born 4 Feb 1875, son of Lloyd Richardson and Elizabeth Bowser [Bodser?] (Death certificate; St. James United Cemetery)

Richardson, John H. (colored), 1865-1957, native of Richmond, VA., resident of Havre de Grace (St. James A.M.E. Church Cemetery; Pennington Funeral Home Records)

Richardson, John Lawrence, born 1879, son of George O. Richardson and Sarah C. Bull (Bethel Presbyterian Church Cemetery Records)

Richardson, John Monroe, 1890-1954 (St. Mary's Episcopal Church Cemetery)

Richardson, John Samuel, Jr., 1864-1927 (Christ Episcopal Church Cemetery); deputy postmaster, Bel Air, 1890 (*The Aegis & Intelligencer*, 27 Jun 1890); postmaster, Bel Air (*The Aegis & Intelligencer*, 4 Jul 1890; *Havre de Grace Republican*, 26 Dec 1890)

Richardson, John Samuel, Sr., 1830-1908 (Cokesbury Memorial Church Cemetery)

Richardson, John T., age 27 in 1890 (Marriage License Applications Book ALJ No. 2, 1891)

Richardson, Joshua Wilson, 1870-1949 (Churchville Presbyterian Church Cemetery)

Richardson, Katherine (Holmes) (colored), 1877-1912 (Death certificate; St. James United Cemetery)

Richardson, Katherine B., 1875-1932 (William Watters Memorial Methodist Church Cemetery Cooptown)

Richardson, Kemp A. K., Civil War veteran, Havre de Grace (*1890 Special Census of the Civil War Veterans of the State of Maryland*, by L. Tilden Moore, Volume III, p. 91)

Richardson, Lake H., 1837-1893 (Angel Hill Cemetery); Civil War veteran, Havre de Grace (*1890 Special Census of the Civil War Veterans of the State of Maryland*, by L. Tilden Moore, Volume III, p. 90); government pensioner, Havre de Grace (*The Aegis & Intelligencer*, 26 Dec 1890), formerly of Dorchester Co, MD, and former city bailiff in Havre de Grace (*Biographical Dictionary of Harford County, Maryland, 1774-1974*, by Henry C. Peden, Jr. and William O. Carr, 2021, p. 226)

Richardson, Laura Elva (Ayres), 1887-1976 (Bethel Presbyterian Church Cemetery)

Richardson, Lavinia, see Alfred R. Richardson, q.v.

Richardson, Lawrence, 1879-1960 (Bethel Presbyterian Church Cemetery); fourth grade student, Mount Horeb School (*The Aegis & Intelligencer*, 14 Feb 1890)

Richardson, Lillian, 1885-1961 (Bethel Presbyterian Church Cemetery)

Richardson, Lloyd (colored), see John F. Richardson (colored), q.v.

Richardson, Lloyd N. (colored), 1856-1912 (Death certificate; St. James United Cemetery)

Richardson, Lotta (Robinson), 1875-1936 (Union Chapel Methodist Church Cemetery)

Richardson, Louis (colored), 1847-1914 (St. James United Cemetery tombstone, but death certificate states age about 59)

Richardson, M. Clara (Crevenston), 1829-1894 (Cranberry Methodist Church Cemetery)

Richardson, Mabel G., 1888-1954 (Holy Trinity Church Cemetery)

Richardson, Margaret (McClung), 1861-1934 (Norrisville Methodist Church Cemetery)

Richardson, Marion, student, LaGrange School No. 14, Fourth District, 1890 (*The Aegis & Intelligencer*, 25 Apr 1890)

Richardson, Martha E. (Mrs.) (colored), 1839-1906 (St. James United Cemetery)

Richardson, Martha W. (Mrs.), 1825-1900 (Death certificate incomplete)

Richardson, Mary A. (Downs), 1859-1914 (Fellowship Cemetery)

Richardson, Mary C., 1864-1930 (Churchville Presbyterian Church Cemetery); premium award winner, Class E - Poultry, and Class N - Floral Decorations, Harford County Fair 1890 (*The Aegis & Intelligencer*, 24 Oct 1890)

Richardson, Mary E., 1835-1907 (St. George's Episcopal Church Cemetery)

Richardson, Mary E., 1866-1961 (Angel Hill Cemetery)

Richardson, Mary Elizabeth (Rouse), 1835-1917 (Cokesbury Memorial Methodist Church Cemetery); wife of John S. Richardson, Sr., q.v.

Richardson, Mary Ellen (Kent), 1884-1966 (Slate Ridge Cemetery, York Co., PA); native of Pylesville, Harford Co., born 2 Apr 1884, daughter of Greer Kent and Alice Whiteford (Harkins Funeral Home Records)

Richardson, Mary O., 1849-1918 (Angel Hill Cemetery)

Richardson, Mary R., born 20 Nov 1888, daughter of Nelson and Margaret (McClung) Richardson (Bethel Presbyterian Church Cemetery Records); see Mary R. Jackson, q.v.

Richardson, Martha "Mattie" S., teacher, Darlington School No. 15, Fifth District (*The Aegis & Intelligencer*, 15 Jul 1881 and 29 Aug 1890)

Richardson, Mary T, 1853-1925 (St. Ignatius Catholic Church Cemetery)

Richardson, Murel (colored), born -- Mar 1889, native of Maryland, son of Charles and Susanna Richardson (1900 Aberdeen Census)

Richardson, Nancy, 1824-1894 (Fellowship Cemetery)

Richardson, Nannie Elizabeth, 1857-1941 (St. Ignatius Catholic Church Cemetery)

Richardson, Oliver, fox hunter, near Bel Air (*The Aegis & Intelligencer*, 14 Feb 1890)

Richardson, Olivia, 1876-1951, native of Havre de Grace, born 9 Apr 1876, daughter of John Richardson and --- - (Pennington Funeral Home Records - married name Durbin)

Richardson, P., pitcher, Havre de Grace Ash Alleys Baseball Club (*The Aegis & Intelligencer*, 27 Jun 1890)

Richardson, Robert (colored), see Howard Richardson (colored), q.v.

Richardson, Robert Christopher, 1862-1919 (Cokesbury Memorial Methodist Church Cemetery); resided near Bel Air (*The Aegis & Intelligencer*, 11 Apr 1890); juror, Third District (*Havre de Grace Republican*, 31 Jan 1890); premium award winner, Class A - Horses, Harford County Fair (*The Aegis & Intelligencer*, 24 Oct 1890)

Richardson, Robert H. (colored), 1862-1916 (Death certificate; St. James United Cemetery)

Richardson, Sabe A., 1884-1964 (Mt. Zion Methodist Church Cemetery)

Richardson, Samuel, Civil War veteran, Upper Cross Roads (*1890 Special Census of the Civil War Veterans of the State of Maryland*, by L. Tilden Moore, Volume III, p. 77)

Richardson, Sandie (colored), see Cassie A. Banks (colored), q.v.

Richardson, Sarah (colored), see Annie E. Brown (colored), q.v.

Richardson, Sarah A., 1860-1933 (Norrisville Methodist Church Cemetery)

Richardson, Sarah C. (Bull), 1850-1906, son of George O. and Sarah C. (Bull) Richardson (Bethel Presbyterian Church Cemetery Records); wife of George O. Richardson, q.v.

Richardson, Stephen J., 1868-1941 (Angel Hill Cemetery)

Richardson, Susanna (colored), born -- Feb 1874, native of Maryland (1900 Aberdeen Census); wife of Charles

Richardson (colored) and Murel Richardson (colored), q.v.

Richardson, Susie, age 31 in 1890 (Marriage License Applications Book ALJ No. 2, 1891)

Richardson, Theodora Emilie, age 27 in 1890 (Marriage License Applications Book ALJ No. 2, 1890)

Richardson, Theodora Emilie, married Cornelius H. Bunting on 31 Dec 1890 (marriage certificate)

Richardson, W., catcher, Bel Air Victors Baseball Club (*The Aegis & Intelligencer*, 30 May 1890); catcher, Creswell Baseball Club (*The Aegis & Intelligencer*, 18 Jul 1890)

Richardson, William Bissell, 1864-1894 (Churchville Presbyterian Church Cemetery); corporal, Jackson Guards [Co. D, 1st Regiment, Maryland National Guard] (*The Aegis & Intelligencer*, 11 Jan 1889 and 28 Nov 1890); member, Division No. 2, Bel Air Fire and Salvage Corps (*The Aegis & Intelligencer*, 10 Oct 1890)

Richardson, William Edward, 1847-1908 (Angel Hill Cemetery)

Richardson, William Nelson, 1856-1908 (Norrisville Methodist Church Cemetery)

Richardson, William Speed, 1830-1894 (Churchville Presbyterian Church Cemetery), physician and Civil War veteran, of Bel Air; former Register of Wills and past master, Mt. Ararat Lodge No. 44, A. F. & A. M. (*Biographical Dictionary of Harford County, Maryland, 1774-1974*, by Henry C. Peden, Jr. and William O. Carr, 2021, p. 227; *The Aegis & Intelligencer*, 27 Jun 1890); juror, Third District (*Havre de Grace Republican*, 2 May 1890); also see John A. W. Richardson, q.v.

Richey, Lizzie (Miss), member, Darlington M. E. Church (*The Aegis & Intelligencer*, 10 Jan 1890); actress, musical entertainment, at Darlington (*The Aegis & Intelligencer*, 30 May 1890)

Richie, Theodore, banjo player, Darlington Orchestra (*Havre de Grace Republican*, 7 Mar 1890)

Rickard, Abbie (Miss), member, Women's Christian Temperance Union, of Havre de Grace (*Havre de Grace Republican*, 19 Sep 1890)

Ricketts, Belinda (Bowen), 1838-1900, native of Maryland, resident of Havre de Grace Angel Hill Cemetery; Death certificate); wife of Samuel J. Ricketts, q.v.

Ricketts, Beulah Delany, 1883-1979, native of Havre de Grace, born 17 Dec 1883, daughter of Thomas Ricketts and Oneida Davis (Pennington Funeral Home Records - married name Myers - also mistakenly stated her father was Thomas Samuel Ricketts; *Maryland Bible Records, Volume 1*, by Henry C. Peden, Jr., 2003, p. 210)

Ricketts, Dora Elizabeth (Ford), 1874-1941 (St. George's Episcopal Church Cemetery)

Ricketts, Effie E., 1871-1940 (Baker Cemeetery)

Ricketts, John Edward, 1873-1952 (St. George's Episcopal Church Cemetery)

Ricketts, Louis Clifton, 1867-1952 (Baker Cemetery); sink boat and sneak boat duck hunter, 1890 (*Havre de Grace Republican*, 7 Nov 1890); age 23 in 1890 (Marriage License Applications Book ALJ No. 2, 1891); brother of John Edward Ricketts, q.v.

Ricketts, Oneida L. (Davis), 1864-1948, native of Havre d Grace, born 14 Sep 1864, daughter of Thomas Davis, of Cecil Co., MD, and Catherine Hayden, Hayder, or Hater, of Germany (Pennington Funeral Home Records); wife of Thomas W. Ricketts, q.v.

Ricketts, Samuel Davis, 1885-1944 (Angel Hill Cemetery); born 19 Jan 1885, son of Thomas Ricketts and Oneida Davis (Thomas W. Ricketts Bible, *Maryland Bible Records, Volume 1*, by Henry C. Peden, Jr., 2003, p. 210)

Ricketts, Samuel J., 1825-1911 (Angel Hill Cemetery; Thomas M. Ricketts Bible and Thomas W. Ricketts Bible, *Maryland Bible Records, Volume 1*, by Henry C. Peden, Jr., 2003, pp. 208-210)

Ricketts, Thomas, see Beulah D. Ricketts and Samuel D. Ricketts, q.v.

Ricketts, Thomas William, 1858-1948 (Angel Hill Cemetery); born 28 Oct 1858, son of Samuel J. and Belinda Ricketts (Thomas W. Ricketts Bible, *Maryland Bible Records, Volume 1*, by Henry C. Peden, Jr., 2003, pp. 209-210)

Rider, Martha, wife of Benjamin F. Minnick, q.v.; see Florence M. Minnick, q.v.

Ridgely's Grocery Store, Main St. near the depot, Bel Air, W. B. Ridgely, prop. (*Harford Democrat*, 14 Feb 1890)

Ridgely, Adelia (colored), born 31 Aug 1884, daughter of George and Mary (Garrett) Ridgely (Death certificate of Adelia Garrett in 1936)

Ridgely, Emma Nelson, see Emma Nelson Ridgely, q.v.

Ridgely, Frank (colored), 1876-1958 (St. James United Cemetery)

Ridgely, George (colored), see Emma Nelson Harris (colored), q.v.

Ridgely, John, of H., premium award winner, Class E - Poultry, Harford County Fair (*The Aegis & Intelligencer*, 24 Oct 1890)

Ridgely, W. B., storekeeper, Main Street near the railroad station, Bel Air (*The Aegis & Intelligencer*, 13 Jun 1890)

Ridgely, Walter, member, Division No. 1, Bel Air Fire and Salvage Corps (*The Aegis & Intelligencer*, 10 Oct 1890)

Ridgley, Charles (colored), see Noah Ridgley (colored), q.v.

Ridgley, Mary R. (Garrett) (colored), 1858-1935 (Death certificate)

Ridgley, Noah (colored), 1879-1951, native of Harford Co., born 15 Jun 1879, son of Charles Ridgley and Harriett ---- (Death certificate)

Ridgley, Sarah E. (Faison) (colored), 1880-1950 (Death certificate states born 1880; St. James United Cemetery tombstone inscribed Ridgeley, born 1883)

Ridgley, William B., age 26 in 1890 (Marriage License Applications Book ALJ No. 2, 1891)

Ridout, Annie E., acquired land in April 1890 (*The Aegis & Intelligencer*, 9 May 1890)

Ridout, Frank A., juror, Fifth District, 1890 (*Havre de Grace Republican*, 31 Jan 1890); resided at Glenville, uncle of Samuel Ridout, of Anne Arundel Co. (*Harford Democrat*, 11 Apr 1890)

Ridout, Franklin, sold land in April 1890 (*The Aegis & Intelligencer*, 9 May 1890)

Ridout, L. Winchester, of Glenville, moved to Macon, GA (*Harford Democrat*, 3 Oct 1890)

Ridout, Mary (Miss), teacher, Glenville School No. 17, Second District, and teacher, Glenville Union Sunday School (*The Aegis & Intelligencer*, 22 Aug and 29 Aug 1890)

Rigby, Annie (colored), see Elinor Turner, Harriett Turner and Phillip Turner, q.v.

Rigdon's General Store, Cambria, Oliver F. Rigdon, prop. (*Country Stores: Harford County's Rural Heritage*, by Henry C. Peden, Jr. and Jack L. Shagena, Jr., 2015, p. 209)

Rigdon's General Store, Chestnut Hill, Charles Rigdon, prop. (*Country Stores: Harford County's Rural Heritage*, by Henry C. Peden, Jr. and Jack L. Shagena, Jr., 2015, p. 208)

Rigdon's General Store, Deep Run, William B. Rigdon, prop. (*Country Stores: Harford County's Rural Heritage*, by Henry C. Peden, Jr. and Jack L. Shagena, Jr., 2015, p. 209)

Rigdon, Alexander, 1823-1892 (Emory Methodist Church Cemetery)

Rigdon, Benjamin, 1820-1908 (Emory Methodist Church Cemetery); see Sarah E. Kennedy, q.v.

Rigdon, Birdenia McC. (Mrs.), 1869-1956 (Emory Methodist Church Cemetery); native of Maryland, born 5 Apr 1869, parents unknown (Harkins Funeral Home Records)

Rigdon, Carene (Mrs.), resident of Chestnut Hill, and daughter of James Johnson (*The Aegis & Intelligencer*, 17 Oct 1890)

Rigdon, Caroline Esther, 1890-1930 (William Watters Memorial Church Cemetery, Cooptown)

Rigdon, Charles, storekeeper, Chestnut Hill (*The Aegis & Intelligencer*, 25 Apr 1890)

Rigdon, Clara E. (Rigdon), 1863-1943 (Bailey Funeral Home Records), married William B. Rigdon. a distant relation, in 1891 (Marriage License Applications Book ALJ No. 2, 1891)

Rigdon, Claude L., born 1887, died ---- (Grove Presbyterian Church Cemetery)

Rigdon, E. Lucinda, 1857-1893 (Broad Creek Friends Cemetery)

Rigdon, Edward L., 1870-1955, native of Maryland, born 10 May 1870, son of Benjamin Rigdon and Nancy Stuart (Pennington Funeral Home Records stated his father was James Rigdon, but Emory Methodist Cemetery indicates his mother Nancy was buried beside Benjamin Rigdon)

Rigdon, Eli S., 1819-1905 (Emory Methodist Church Cemetery); Eli Rigdon, farmer at Mill Green (*The Aegis & Intelligencer*, 3 Jan 1890); also see Lousanna (Rigdon) Famous, q.v.

Rigdon, Evaline "Eva" H. (Miss), 1871-1965 (Emory Methodist Church Cemetery); resided at Mill Green (*The Aegis & Intelligencer*, 29 Aug 1890); wife of Howard Rigdon, q.v.

Rigdon, Frank B., 1867-1941 (Emory Methodist Church Cemetery)

Rigdon, Franklin, 1827-1900 (Emory Methodist Church Cemetery); F. Rigdon, trustee, Mine Branch School No. 10, Fifth District (*Havre de Grace Republican*, 30 May 1890)

Rigdon, George B., 1848-1915 (William Watters Memorial Church Cemetery, Cooptown)

Rigdon, Grace G., born 1889, died ---- (Grove Presbyterian Church Cemetery)

Rigdon, Hannah E., see Lillie Stewart and Sarah E. Stewart, q.v.

Rigdon, Henry, 1863-1909 (Grove Presbyterian Church Cemetery)

Rigdon, Howard, 1871-1935 (Emory Methodist Church Cemetery); son of Franklin Rigdon and Priscilla Harkins; teacher, Boyle's School No. 5, Broad Creek, Fifth District (*Havre de Grace Republican*, 7 Nov and 14 Nov 1890; *Harford County, Maryland Teachers and the Schools They Served*, by Henry C. Peden, Jr., 2021, p. 265)

Rigdon, John A., 1867-1927 (Emory Methodist Church Cemetery), married Myra S. Carr on 17 Apr 1890 at the Dublin P. E. Parsonage (*The Aegis & Intelligencer*, 9 May 1890)

Rigdon, Josephine B. (Beall), 1886-1967 (Slateville Cemetery, York Co., PA); native of Jarrettsville, MD, born 23 Jun 1886, daughter of Lemuel Beall and Charlotte Wilgis (Harkins Funeral Home Records)

Rigdon, L. Virginia, 1838-1909 (Broad Creek Friends Cemetery)

Rigdon, Laura V. (Miss), 1858-1929 (Broad Creek Friends Cemetery)

Rigdon, LeRoy, 1888-1969 (Slateville Cemetery, York Co., PA); native of Harford Co., born 11 Feb 1888, son of Summerfield Rigdon and Martha L. Jones (Harkins Funeral Home Records)

Rigdon, Lillie M., 1867-1937 (Grove Presbyterian Church Cemetery)

Rigdon, Louanna, age 19 in 1889 (Marriage License Applications Book ALJ No. 2, 1889)

Rigdon, Margaret ("Maggie"), age 26 in 1890 (Marriage License Applications Book ALJ No. 2, 1890), married Charles W. Burkins on 28 May 1890 (*The Aegis & Intelligencer*, 6 Jun 1890)

Rigdon, Margaret (Kenly), 1871-1930, native of Maryland, daughter of Charles B. Kenly and Alice Mecklin (Death certificate)

Rigdon, Martha, see Mary Neal, q.v.

Rigdon, Martha L., 1864-1923 (Emory Methodist Church Cemetery)

Rigdon, Mary, 1819-1916 (Emory Methodist Church Cemetery)

Rigdon, Mary, 1834-1913 (Emory Methodist Church Cemetery)

Rigdon, Mary, wife of William W. Healy, q.v.; also see Margaret F. Chamberlain, q.v.

Rigdon, Mary M., 1816-1893 (Emory Methodist Church Cemetery)

Rigdon, Mary M., of Cambria, married Thomas F. Smithson, of Cambria, on 23 Jul 1890 in Towson, MD (*The Aegis & Intelligencer*, 8 Aug 1890)

Rigdon, Mary Y., 1813-1896 (William Watters Memorial Church Cemetery, Cooptown)

Rigdon, Millard F., 1890-1891 (Emory Methodist Church Cemetery)

Rigdon, Myra (Carr), 1870-1942 (Emory Methodist Church Cemetery)

Rigdon, Nancy, 1830-1907 (Emory Methodist Church Cemetery)

Rigdon, Nathan, superintendent, Union Cross Roads Methodist Church Sunday School (*The Aegis & Intelligencer*, 5 Sep 1890); tax collector, Fifth District (*Havre de Grace Republican*, 4 Jul 1890)

Rigdon, Oliver F., 1858-1897 (Emory Methodist Church Cemetery); see Rigdon's General Store, q.v.

Rigdon, Priscilla (Harkins), 1829-1907 (Emory Methodist Church Cemetery); wife of Franklin Rigdon, q.v.

Rigdon, Rosa B., honor student, Norrisville Graded School (*The Aegis & Intelligencer*, 4 Jul 1890); member, Norrisville M. E. Church Sunday School (*The Aegis & Intelligencer*, 20 Jun 1890)

Rigdon, Ross, member, Norrisville Silver Cornet Band (*The Aegis & Intelligencer*, 30 May 1890)

Rigdon, Sallie S., 1864-1940 (William Watters Memorial Church Cemetery, Cooptown)

Rigdon, Sarah E., see Sarah E. Kennedy, q.v.

Rigdon, Stephen, 1849-1926 (Cherry Hill aka Rock Ridge Baptist Church Cemetery)

Rigdon, Summerfield, 1860-1941 (Emory Methodist Church Cemetery); see LeRoy Rigdon, q.v.

Rigdon, William, blacksmith, Norrisville (*Havre de Grace Republican*, 15 Aug 1890)

Rigdon, William B., 1863-1940, native of Harford Co. (Bailey Funeral Home Records); age 27 in 1890, married Clara E. Rigdon, a distant relation, in 1891 (Marriage License Applications Book ALJ No. 2, 1891)

Rigdon, William H., 1865-1891 (Emory Methodist Church Cemetery)

Rigney, Charles H. (colored), 1846-1934, native of Virginia (*Bel Air Times*, 14 Sep 1934, stated he was a nonagenerian, born in slavery; Death certificate stated he died at age 77, parents unknown); delegate, First District, Republican Party Convention, 1890 (*The Aegis & Intelligencer*, 26 Sep 1890)

Rigney, Cordelia (Mrs.) (colored), 1826-1924 (Union Methodist Church Cemetery, Aberdeen); native of Harford Co, resided at Perryman (Death certificate stated parents unknown per Charles Rigney); see Edward Rigney, q.v.

Rigney, Delia (colored), 1850-1926 (Union Methodist Church Cemetery, Aberdeen); wife of Charles H. Rigney, q.v.

Rigney, Edward (colored), 1874-1926 (Union Methodist Church Cemetery, Aberdeen); native of Maryland, resided in Havreed Grace, born 16 Feb 1874, son of ---- Rigney and Cordelia Rice (Death certificate)

Riley, Annie H., 1848-1896 (Angel Hill Cemetery)

Riley, Annie L., age 23 in 1889 (Marriage License Applications Book ALJ No. 2)

Riley, Charles, 1855-1915 (Mt. Erin Cemetery); native of Brooklyn, NY, single, resident of Havre de Grace (Death certificate)

Riley, David (M.D.), 1837-1901 (Dublin Southern Cemetery); physician and trustee, Dublin School No. 13, Fifth District (*Havre de Grace Republican*, 30 May 1890); served on a petit jury in 1890 (*Havre de Grace Republican*, 14 Feb 1890)

Riley, David H., 1866-1927 (Rock Run Methodist Church Cemetery); native of Maryland (Bailey Funeral Home Records)

Riley, Drucilla (Scarborough), 1840-1926 (Dublin Southern Cemetery), wife of David Riley, q.v.

Riley, Elizabeth (Mrs.), c1816-1896 (Wesleyan Chapel Methodist Church Cemetery)

Riley, Florence, 1858-1916, daughter of John and Mary Riley (Rock Run Methodist Church Cemetery)

Riley, Florence A. (Ewing), 1867-1904, wife of David H. Riley (Rock Run Methodist Church Cemetery; *Deaths and Marriages in Harford County, Maryland, and Vicinity, 1873-1904, from the Diaries of Albert Peter Silver*, transcribed by Glenn Randers-Pehrson, 1995, p. 20)

Riley, Frank, member, Cleveland Junior Baseball Club, at Pleasantville (*The Aegis & Intelligencer*, 22 Aug 1890)

Riley, Frank P., 1875-1932 (Dublin Southern Cemetery)

Riley, Harriett (Simpson), 1880-1961 (Angel Hill Cemetery)

Riley, Harry S., 1869-1920 (Grove Presbyterian Church Cemetery)

Riley, Henry, 1872-1924 (St. John's Catholic Church Cemetery, Long Green, Baltimore Co.); native of Maryland, resident of Pleasantville, Harford Co., born 15 Feb 1872, son of James Riley and Bridget Moran, both natives of Ireland (Death certificate); member, Cleveland Junior Baseball Club, at Pleasantville, 1890 (*The Aegis & Intelligencer*, 22 Aug 1890)

Riley, James, see Henry Riley, q.v.

Riley, James, 1885-1948 (Heavenly Waters Cemetery; Alms House Register)

Riley, James Russell, 1888-1952, native of Darlington, Harford Co., born 8 Sep 1888, son of John T. Riley and Annie H. Moore (Pennington Funeral Home Records)

Riley, John, 1829-1891 (Rock Run Methodist Church Cemetery; *Deaths and Marriages in Harford County, Maryland, and Vicinity, 1873-1904, from the Diaries of Albert Peter Silver*, transcribed by Glenn Randers-Pehrson, 1995, p. 20)

Riley, John Francis, 1879-1957 (Angel Hill Cemetery)

Riley, John M., 1867-1950 (Fallston Methodist Church Cemetery)

Riley, John T., 1841-1924, native of Maryland, storekeeper in Havre de Grace (Death certificate); see James Russell Riley, q.v.

Riley, L. Maud (Miss), of Churchville, sister of Mrs. Jesse C. Lukens, of West Grove, PA (*The Aegis & Intelligencer*, 31 Jan 1890 and 31 Oct 1890)

Riley, Lillian M., 1879-1948 (Grove Presbyterian Church Cemetery)

Riley, Margaret (Wiggers), 1821-1902, native of Maryland, resided at Upper Cross Roads (Death certificate; Fallston Methodist Church Cemetery)

Riley, Marian E., 1886-1917 (Fallston Methodist Church Cemetery)

Riley, Mary A. (Ross), 1831-1901 (Rock Run Methodist Church Cemetery); native of Maryland, resided at Churchville (Death certificate)

Riley, Mary Catherine (Amos), 1834-1909 (Ebenezer Methodist Church Cemetery)

Riley, Mary L., 1871-1901 (Fallston Methodist Church Cemetery)

Riley, Metta M., 1885-1920 (Fallston Methodist Church Cemetery)

Riley, Ozella G., 1855-1915 (Fallston Methodist Church Cemetery); see Jones Davidson, q.v.

Riley, William T., 1858-1927 (Fallston Methodist Church Cemetery); trustee, Youth's Benefit School No. 6, Fourth District, 1890 (*Havre de Grace Republican*, 30 May 1890); see Jones Davidson, q.v.

Riley, Wilmer, 1888-1976 (Fallston Methodist Church Cemetery)

Rimmey, Abbie (Miss), 1828-1899, assistant housekeeper in Havre de Grace, native of Baltimore (Death certificate)

Rimmey, Eliza Jane, 1851-1923 (Angel Hill Cemetery); wife of Samuel M. Rimmey, q.v.

Rimmey, Georgia E., 1885-1967, native of Maryland, born 28 Dec 1885, daughter of Samuel Rimmey and Elizabeth Harn (Pennington Funeral Home Records)

Rimmey, Mary Jane (Miss), 1832-1926 (Angel Hill Cemetery); native of Maryland, resided in Havre de Grace (Death certificate)

Rimmey, Raymond E., 1877-1954, native of Maryland, born 7 Apr 1877, son of Samuel Rimmey and Eliza Harn (Pennington Funeral Home Records; Angel Hill Cemetery)

Rimmey, Samuel M., 1847-1916 (Angel Hill Cemetery); see Georgia E. Rimmey, q.v.

Rinehart, E. John, acquired land in April 1890 (*The Aegis & Intelligencer*, 9 May 1890)

Rinehart, Frederick, widower, age 50 in 1890 (Marriage License Applications Book ALJ No. 2, 1891)

Ringgold's General Store, Perryman, George J. Ringgold (colored), prop. (*Country Stores: Harford County's Rural Heritage*, by Henry C. Peden, Jr. and Jack L. Shagena, Jr., 2015, p. 209)

Ringgold, E. A. (Miss), uncalled for letter in Bel Air P. O., 1890 (*The Aegis & Intelligencer*, 14 Nov 1890)

Ringgold, Emma (colored), born -- Feb 1869, native of Maryland (1900 Aberdeen Census); daughter of Lewis Bowser, q.v.

Ringgold, Emory, 1842-1921 (Alms House Record Book)

Ringgold, George J. (colored), c1860-1924, native of Maryland, resided at Perryman, parents unknown (Death certificate); see Ringgold's General Store, q.v.

Ringgold, Hatumale (colored), see Marian V. Tucker (colored), q.v.

Ringgold, Jessie, born -- Jan 1890, native of Maryland (1900 Aberdeen Census); grandson of Lewis Ringgold, q.v.

Ringgold, John (colored), father of Lucy C. Ringgold (colored), q.v.

Ringgold, John (colored), 1863-1917, native of Harford Co., resided at Joppa (Death certificate); see Nathan Ringgold, q.v.

Ringgold, Lotta (colored), see Mary Martha Monk (colored), q.v.

Ringgold, Lucy C. (colored), 1872-1930, native of Maryland, born 21 Sep 1872, daughter of John Ringgold and Susie Parson (Death certificate - married name Lee)

Ringgold, Marion (colored), see Lulu M. Stansbury (colored), q.v.

Ringgold, Mary (colored), see Gran Thompson (colored), q.v.

Ringgold, Nathan (colored), 1886-1901, native of Harford Co., resided at Bel Air, son of John Ringgold and Mary Holmes (Death certificate - name spelled Ringold)

Ringgold, Sarah (colored), see Sadie V. Banks (colored) and Sarah A.Winchester (colored), q.v.

Ringgold, Sarah J. (Rumsey) (colored) c1867-1922 (Death certificate)

Ringgold, Walter (colored), born -- Dec 1887 native of Maryland (1900 Aberdeen Census); grandson of Lewis Bowser, q.v.

Ringgold, William (colored), 1798-1890, resident near Michaelsville, former "body servant"of the late Dr. John A. Preston (*The Aegis & Intelligencer*, 20 Jun 1890)

Ringgold, William F. (colored), 1864-1959 (Mt. Calvary Methodist Church Cemetery)

Ripken's General Store, Ripken's Corner in Stepney, Frederick P. Ripken, prop. (*Country Stores: Harford County's Rural Heritage*, by Henry C. Peden, Jr. and Jack L. Shagena, Jr., 2015, p. 209)

Ripken, Affena Lubina (Wychgram), 1857-1939, wife of Frederick Peter Ripken, q.v.

Ripken, Frederick Peter, 1857-1908 (Baker Cemetery)

Rishel, A. Cook (Clark?), 1852-1925 (St. George's Episcopal Church Cemetery); also see Warren Keen Rishel, q.v.

Rishel, Mary Keen, 1856-1929 (St. George's Episcopal Church Cemetery); also see Warren Keen Rishel, q.v.

Rishel, Warren Keen, 1881-1961 (St. George's Episcopal Church Cemetery); born 8 Jul 1881, son of A. C. and M. K. Rishel (St. George's Episcopal Church Register of Baptisms, pp. 2-3)

Ristau, Herman, 1849-1929, native of Germany, baker in Aberdeen (Baker Cemetery)

Risteau, John Howard, 1890-1908 (William Watters Memorial Methodist Church Cemetery, Cooptown)

Risteau, Mary E., 1850-1935 (William Watters Memorial Methodist Church Cemetery, Cooptown)

Risteau, Mary E. W., 1890-1978 (William Watters Memorial Methodist Church Cemetery, Cooptown)

Risteau, William M., 1945-1910 (William Watters Memorial Methodist Church Cemetery, Cooptown)

Risteau, William M., Jr., 1885-1910 (William Watters Memorial Methodist Church Cemetery, Cooptown)

Riston, Charlotte, 1804-1891 (Norrisville Methodist Church Cemetery)

Riston, Jesse, 1816-1890 (Norrisville Methodist Church Cemetery); Jessie Riston, and Charlotte (1804-1891), sold land in 1890 (*The Aegis & Intelligencer*, 12 Sep 1890)

Ritchie, Amanda, see George T. Cantler, q.v.

Ritchie, Anna W. (Smith), 1868-1951 (Bel Air Memorial Gardens); native of Harford Co., born 13 Feb 1868, daughter of George Smith and ---- [blank] (Harkins Funeral Home Records)

Ritchie, Annie, see Florence Smith, q.v.

Ritchie, Isabella, wife of Wakeman H. Ritchie, q.v.

Ritchie, John, leader, Norrisville Silver Cornet Band (*The Aegis & Intelligencer*, 23 May and 30 May 1890)

Ritchie, Robert, member, Norrisville Silver Cornet Band (*The Aegis & Intelligencer*, 30 May 1890)

Ritchie, Theodore, singer and jig dancer, Darlington Minstrels (*The Aegis & Intelligencer*, 21 Feb 1890)

Ritchie, Wakeman H., 1831-1901, native of Maryland, blacksmith near Berkley (Death certificate)

Ritter, Fannie May (Vandiver), 1859-1933, native of Philadelphia, resided in Havre de Grace (Death certificate; Angel Hill Cemetery)

Ritter, Millard Fillmore, 1857-1939 (Death certificate)

Robb, John A., see Thomas H. Streett, q.v.

Robert, John H. (colored), 1882-1951 (Berkley Memorial Cemetery)

Robert, Ruth W. (colored), born 1886, died 19-- (Berkley Memorial Cemetery); wife of John H. Robert, q.v.

Roberts, A. Alcade (colored), 1873-1951 (Berkley Memorial Cemetery)

Roberts, Andrew "Andy" F., 1884-1968 (Angel Hill Cemetery)

Roberts, Charles Wakeman, 1831-1907 (Little Falls Quaker Cemetery); resided near Emmorton (*The Aegis & Intelligencer*, 21 Mar 1890); trustee, School No. 8, First District (*Havre de Grace Republican*, 30 May 1890); delegate, First District, Republican Party Convention (*The Aegis & Intelligencer*, 26 Sep 1890); also see Lizzie Pine, q.v.

Roberts, David W., see Robert D. Roberts, q.v.

Roberts, Edward Hicks, 1837-1915 (Little Falls Quaker Cemetery)

Roberts, Edward M., 1889-1939 (Mountain Christian Church Cemetery)

Roberts, Elizabeth, 1880-1950 (Holy Cross Church Cemetery)

Roberts, Elizabeth T., 1831-1912 (Little Falls Quaker Cemetery)

Roberts, Ellen Jane (Parry), 1881-1962 (Slate Ridge Cemetery, York Co., PA); native of Cardiff, Harford Co., born 2 Oct 1881, daughter of Thomas Parry and Carrie Stull (Harkins Funeral Home Records)

Roberts, Emory (colored), 1866-1915, native of Maryland (Death certificate)

Roberts, Florence R., 1884-1938 (Highland Presbyterian Church Cemetery)

Roberts, Frances "Fannie," born 7 Nov 1871 daughter of William G. and Mary F. Roberts (Mary Butler Roberts Bible, *Maryland Bible Records, Volume 5*, by Henry C. Peden, Jr., 2004, p. 171); Fannie Roberts, young lady of near Pylesville (*The Aegis & Intelligencer*, 7 Feb 1890)

Roberts, George, 1865-1928 (Christ Episcopal Church Cemetery); born 11 Jan 1865, son of William G. and Mary F. Roberts (Mary Butler Roberts Bible, *Maryland Bible Records, Volume 5*, by Henry C. Peden, Jr., 2004, p. 171); assistant marshal, Bel Air jousting tournament (*Havre de Grace Republican*, 17 Oct 1890); jousting tournament rider, Knight of Aberdeen (*Havre de Grace Republican*, 19 Sep 1890); member, Guy Social Club, Aberdeen (*Havre de Grace Republican*, 31 Oct 1890)

Roberts, Henry, testified in an assault case in 1890 (*Harford Democrat*, 21 Feb 1890)

Roberts, John William, 1874-1950 (Holy Cross Church Cemetery); born 16 Sep 1874, son of William G. and Mary F. Roberts (Mary Butler Roberts Bible, *Maryland Bible Records, Volume 5*, by Henry C. Peden, Jr., 2004, p. 171); young man, of near Pylesville (*The Aegis & Intelligencer*, 7 Feb 1890)

Roberts, M. A. (Mrs.), see Mamie Wheeler, q.v.

Roberts, M. L., vice president, Harford County School Teachers' Association (*Havre de Grace Republican*, 19 Sep 1890)

Roberts, Martin W., 1881-1954 (Highland Presbyterian Church Cemetery)

Roberts, Mary, see Thomas Pearce and William W. Pearce, q.v.

Roberts, Mary, 1870-1948 (Holy Cross Church Cemetery); daughter of William Glasgow Roberts and Mary Frances Butler; teacher, Baptist School No. 7, Fourth District (*The Aegis & Intelligencer*, 29 Aug 1890; *Harford County, Maryland Teachers and the Schools They Served*, by Henry C. Peden, Jr., 2021, p. 267)

Roberts, Mary E., 1867-1891 (Little Falls Quaker Cemetery)

Roberts, Mary Frances (Butler), 1837-1911 (Holy Cross Church Cemetery); wife of William Glasgow Roberts, q.v.

Roberts, Minnie P. (colored), born 1873, died ---- (Berkley Memorial Cemetery); wife of A. Alcade Roberts, q.v.

Roberts, Richard, 1846-1922 (Slateville Cemetery, York Co., PA); machinist, native of Wales, resident of Cardiff, Harford Co., MD (Death certificate); acquired land in May 1890 (*The Aegis & Intelligencer*, 6 Jun 1890)

Roberts, Robert D., 1864-1935 (Slateville Cemetery, York Co., PA); native of Harford Co., born 15 Mar 1864, son of David W. Roberts and Ann Owens (Harkins Funeral Home Records)

Roberts, Susan "Sue" Cordelia, born 22 Dec 1876, daughter of William G. and Mary F. Roberts (Mary Butler Roberts Bible, *Maryland Bible Records, Volume 5*, by Henry C. Peden, Jr., 2004, p. 171)

Roberts, Susanna (Davis), 1835-1915 Churchville Presbyterian Church Cemetery)

Roberts, Thomas H. (Dr.), 1840-1927 (Churchville Presbyterian Church Cemetery; resident of Churchville, and half-brother of Miss Sallie Streett, of Mill Green (*The Aegis & Intelligencer*, 24 Oct 1890)

Roberts, Wilmina "Will," born 13 May 1878, daughter of William G. and Mary F. Roberts (Mary Butler Roberts Bible, *Maryland Bible Records, Volume 5*, by Henry C. Peden, Jr., 2004, p. 171)

Roberts, William Glasgow, 1833-1906 (Holy Cross Church Cemetery); dairyman, (*Harford Democrat*, 14 Feb 1890); see Susanna R. Wilson, q.v.

Roberts, William Jones, 1879-1945 (Darlington Cemetery)

Robertson, Morris L., teacher, Aberdeen School No. 1, Second District (*The Aegis & Intelligencer*, 29 Aug 1890)

Robey, Anna R. (Knight), 1864-1929 (Bailey Funeral Home Records)

Robey, Charles H., 1857-1911 (Darlington Cemetery)

Robin Hood Public School No. 18, Second District (*Harford County, Maryland Teachers and the Schools They Served, 1774-1900*, by Henry C. Peden, Jr., 2022, p. 372)

Robinson's General Store, Dry Branch, John C. and Sarah Robinson, prop. (*Country Stores: Harford County's Rural Heritage*, by Henry C. Peden, Jr. and Jack L. Shagena, Jr., 2015, pp. 210-211)

Robinson's Mill (aka Bell's Mill), on Broad Creek near Macton, Nicholas R. Bell, prop. (*Mills: Grist, Saw, Bone, Flint, Fulling ... & More*, by Jack L. Shagena, Jr., Henry C. Peden, Jr. and John W. McGrain, 2009, p. 240)

Robinson, A. Laura, age 22 in 1890 (Marriage License Applications Book ALJ No. 2, 1891)

Robinson, Abigail (Murphy), 1839-1911 (Bethel Presbyterian Church Cemetery Records); wife of Robert Kirkwood Robinson, q.v.

Robinson, Alice (Barwick), 1858-1949 (Angel Hill Cemetery); wife of L. Walter Robinson; also see Bertie May Robinson and Martin S. Robinson, q.v.

Robinson, Alphonso, 1830-1907 (Union Chapel Methodist Church Cemetery); member, Fallston Road League (*The Aegis & Intelligencer*, 17 Jan 1890); owner, Robinson Can Company of Harford County [Alphonso Robinson &Sons, tin can factory], at Fallston (*Havre de Grace Republican*, 24 Oct 1890; *The Aegis &*

Intelligencer, 19 Sep 1890); trustee, Union Chapel School No. 1, Third District (*Havre de Grace Republican*, 30 May 1890); also see Fannie H. Robinson and B. W. Kindley, q.v.

Robinson, Alphonso Pitts, 1886-1933 (Union Chapel Methodist Church Cemetery)

Robinson, Alverta (Coe), 1874-1964 (Deer Creek Methodist Church Cemetery)

Robinson, Anna Clarkson, born 16 Jan 1869, daughter of Robert Kirkwood and Abigal (Murphy) Robinson (*Kirkwoods and Their Kin, 1731-1971*, by Anna Lee Kirkwood Smith, 1972, p. 129)

Robinson, Anna Laura, see Susan (Robinson) Neville, q.v.

Robinson, Anna M., 1841-1913 (Centre Methodist Church Cemetery)

Robinson, Arlena M., 1867-1927 (Deer Creek Methodist Church Cemetery)

Robinson, Barnes (colored), see Charles Barnes Robinson (colored), q.v.

Robinson, Belle, born 1885, daughter of John C. and Emma (Robinson) Robinson (Bethel Presbyterian Church Cemetery Records); see Belle Anderson, q.v.

Robinson, Bertha, born 29 Jun 1882, daughter of John Calvin and Emma (Robinson) Robinson (Bethel Presbyterian Church Cemetery Records; *Kirkwoods and Their Kin, 1731-1971*, by Anna Lee Kirkwood Smith, 1972, p. 145); see Bertha R. White, q.v.

Robinson, Bertie May, 1888-1958, native of Cambridge,MD, born 19 Jun 1888, daughter of Levin Walrter Robinson and Alice Borwick (Pennington Funeral Home Records - married name Myers)

Robinson, Caroline (colored), c1848-1918 (Death certificate; St. James United Cemetery)

Robinson, Charles, 1862-1950 (William Watters Memorial Methodist Church Cemetery, Cooptown)

Robinson, Charles ("Charlie"), young son of Mr. & Mrs. L. B. Robinson, near Wilna (*The Aegis & Intelligencer*, 3 Jan 1890 and 24 Oct 1890)

Robinson, Charles Barnes (colored), c1871-1943, native of Harford Co., son of Barnes Robinson and Mary Holland (Kurtz Funeral Home Records)

Robinson, Charles Carroll, 1883-1969 (Union Chapel Methodist Church Cemetery); see Lewis Bolivar Robinson, q.v.

Robinson, Charles D., age 25 in 1889 (Marriage License Applications Book ALJ No. 2)

Robinson, Charles Evans, 1865-1942 (Jarrettsville Cemetery)

Robinson, Charles Littleton, 1857-1942 (Deer Creek Methodist Church Cemetery); born 28 Sep 1857, son of Thomas and Elizabeth Robinson (Harkins-Robinson Bible, *Maryland Bible Records, Volume 1*, by Henry C. Peden, Jr., 2003, pp. 103-104)

Robinson, Charlotte (colored), see Matilda Gilbert (colored), q.v.

Robinson, Clara C. (Cain), 1857-1947 (St. Ignatius Catholic Church Cemetery); soprano singer and choir member, St. Ignatius Catholic Church, at Hickory, 1890 (*The Aegis & Intelligencer*, 11 Apr 1890); wife of Thomas Hall Robinson, q.v.

Robinson, Clara M., 1883-1959 (Cokesbury Methodist Church Cemetery)

Robinson, Clarence E., 1879-1927, son of John Thomas and Ellen Melissa (Harkins) Robinson (Christ Episcopal Church Cemetery; *Harkins and Related Families of Harford County, Maryland*, by Henry C. Peden, Jr., 2003, p. 39)

Robinson, Cora A. (Famous), 1876-1964 (Emory Methodist Church Cemetery); native of Mill Green, Harford Co., born 5 Jun 1876, daughter of Andrew J. Famous and Mary A. Carr (Harkins Funeral Home Records)

Robinson, Daniel (colored), see Harry Pearl Robinson (colored), q.v.

Robinson, Edith F., 1882-1934 (Deer Creek Methodist Church Cemetery)

Robinson, Edward Hamilton, 1884-1972 (Deer Creek Methodist Church Cemetery)

Robinson, Edward L. (colored), 1887-1956 (St. James United Cemetery)

Robinson, Elizabeth, 1817-1892 (Deer Creek Methodist Church Cemetery)

Robinson, Elizabeth Eveline, born 5 May 1889, daughter of John Thomas and Ellen Meliss (Harkins) Robinson (*Harkins and Related Families of Harford County, Maryland*, by Henry C. Peden, Jr., 2003, p. 39)

Robinson, Ellen, see Thomas H. Dick, q.v.

Robinson, Ellen Melissa (Harkins), 1851-1925 (Emory Methodist Church Cemetery); wife of John Thomas Robinson, q.v.; also see Elmer E. Robinson, q.v.

Robinson, Elmer E., 1887-1964 (Emory Methodist Church Cemetery); son of John Thomas and Ellen Melissa (Harkins) Robinson (*Harkins and Related Families of Harford County, Maryland*, by Henry C. Peden, Jr., 2003, p. 39); native of Street, Harford Co., born 26 Jan 1887 (Harkins Funeral Home Records)

Robinson, Elwood (Master), of Chestnut Hill (*The Aegis & Intelligencer*, 11 Jul 1890)

Robinson, Emily (colored), c1870-1920, born in Maryland, daughter of Israel Robinson and ---- (Death certificate - married name Lee)

Robinson, Emma (Robinson), 1852-1930 (Bethel Presbyterian Church Cemetery Records); wife of John Calvin Robinson, q.v.

Robinson, Emma L. (Middendorf), 1863-1946 (Mountain Christian Church Cemetery)

Robinson, Emma Maude, born 15 Oct 1888, daughter of John Calvin and Emma (Robinson) Robinson (Bethel Presbyterian Church Cemetery Records; *Kirkwoods and Their Kin, 1731-1971*, by Anna Lee Kirkwood Smith, 1972, p. 145)

Robinson, Elizabeth Eveline, born 5 May 1889, daughter of John Thomas and Ellen Melissa (Harkins) Robinson (*Harkins and Related Families of Harford County, Maryland*, by Henry C. Peden, Jr., 2003, p. 39)

Robinson, Ernest B., 1876-1945 (Darlington Cemetery)

Robinson, Fannie H., age 22, daughter of Mr. & Mrs. Alphonso Robinson, of Fallston, married Rev. B. W. Kindley, age 27, of Frederick Co., on 27 May 1890 in Bel Air (*The Aegis & Intelligencer*, 23 May 1890; Marriage License Applications Book ALJ No. 2, 1890)

Robinson, Florence, born 19 Dec 1879, daughter of John Calvin and Emma (Robinson) Robinson (*Kirkwoods and Their Kin, 1731-1971*, by Anna Lee Kirkwood Smith, 1972, p. 145)

Robinson, Frank H., 1869-1947 (Cokesbury Methodist Church Cemetery)

Robinson, Frankanna (colored), 1868-1928, native of Maryland, born 28 May 1868, daughter of Israel Robinson and Eliza Stansbury (Death certificate - married name Wise)

Robinson, George, c1832-1900, resided at Upper Cross Roads (Death certificate incomplete)

Robinson, George W., groceries and provisions dealer, Havre de Grace (*Havre de Grace Republican*, 4 Jul 1890); Civil War veteran, Havre de Grace (*1890 Special Census of the Civil War Veterans of the State of Maryland*, by L. Tilden Moore, Volume III, p. 89)

Robinson, George W., 1858-1941 (Darlington Cemetery)

Robinson, Georgetta, 1849-1895 (Broad Creek Friends Cemetery)

Robinson, Grace, born c1874, daughter of Robert Kirkwood and Abigal (Murphy) Robinson (*Kirkwoods and Their Kin, 1731-1971*, by Anna Lee Kirkwood Smith, 1972, p. 129)

Robinson, H. S., member, Robinson Can Company of Harford County, at Fallston (*Havre de Grace Republican*, 24 Oct 1890)

Robinson, Hannah J., 1831-1904 (Christ Episcopal Church Cemetery)

Robinson, Harry Pearl (colored), 1890-1914, native of Maryland, born 1 Sep 1890, son of Daniel Robinson and Sadie Jimerson (Death certificate)

Robinson, Howard, 1876-1949, native of Harford Co., parents unknown (Bailey Funeral Home Records)

Robinson, Howard, born c1890, son of John Thomas Robinson and Ellen Melissa Harkins (*Harkins and Related Families of Harford County, Maryland*, by Henry C. Peden, Jr., 2003, p. 39)

Robinson, Huldah, 1868-1942 (William Watters Memorial Methodist Church Cemetery, Cooptown)(William Watters Memorial Methodist Church Cemetery, Cooptown)

Robinson, Ida (Glenn) (colored), 1887-1957 (St. James Church, Federal Hill, William C. Rice Memorial Cemetery); wife of J. Clarence Robinson, q.v.

Robinson, Ida (Jackson) (colored), 1873-1899, house servant at Cooptown, native of Harford Co., wife of Walter Robinson (Death certificate)

Robinson, Israel (colored), see Emily Robinson (colored) and Frankanna Robinson (colored), q.v.

Robinson, Isaac, 1865-1938 (Broad Creek Friends Cemetery); canned goods dealer, of Mill Green (*Havre de Grace Republican*, 10 Jan 1890)

Robinson, J. Clarence (colored), 1887-1966 (St. James Church, Federal Hill, William C. Rice Memorial Cemetery)

Robinson, James C., resident of Third District (*The Aegis & Intelligencer*, 16 May 1890); member, Farmers' Club of Fallston (*Havre de Grace Republican*, 14 Mar 1890)

Robinson, Jennie, secretary, Magnolia M. E. Church Sunday School (*Havre de Grace Republican*, 2 May 1890)

Robinson Jerry R. (colored), c1844-1922 (Death certificate; St. James United Cemetery)

Robinson, Jessie, child of L. B. Robinson (*The Aegis & Intelligencer*, 3 Jan 1890); Jesse Levering Robinson, see Lewis Bolivar Robinson, q.v.

Robinson, John (colored), born -- 1865, baptized 18 Oct 1891, son of John and Cissie Robinson (St. Ignatius Catholic Church Baptism Register, p. 121)

Robinson, John Andrew, born 14 Feb 1872, son of Robert Kirkwood and Abigal (Murphy) Robinson (*Kirkwoods and Their Kin, 1731-1971*, by Anna Lee Kirkwood Smith, 1972, p. 129)

Robinson, John Calvin, 1841-1904 (Bethel Presbyterian Church Cemetery Records); Civil War veteran, of Bradenbaugh (*1890 Special Census of the Civil War Veterans of the State of Maryland*, by L. Tilden Moore, Volume III, p. 82)

Robinson, John Cameron, 1859-1932 (Deer Creek Methodist Church Cemetery); born 28 Sep 1857, son of Thomas and Elizabeth Robinson (Harkins-Robinson Bible, *Maryland Bible Records, Volume 1*, by Henry C. Peden, Jr., 2003, pp. 103-104); delegate, Fourth District, Republican Party Convention (*The Aegis & Intelligencer*, 26 Sep 1890); juror, Fourth District (*Havre de Grace Republican*, 31 Jan 1890)

Robinson, John K., 1831-1915 (Christ Episcopal Church Cemetery)

Robinson, John Thomas, 1844-1925 (Emory Methodist Church Cemetery); see William J. Robinson, q.v.

Robinson, Joseph (colored), Civil War veteran, of Magnolia (*1890 Special Census of the Civil War Veterans of the State of Maryland*, by L. Tilden Moore, Volume III, p. 62); see Mary Jane Robinson, q.v.

Robinson, Joseph Evans, 1817-1891 (Ebenezer Methodist Church Cemetery)

Robinson, Joseph M., 1863-1913 (Emory Methodist Church Cemetery)

Robinson, Julia (Miss), uncalled for letter in Bel Air P. O. (*The Aegis & Intelligencer*, 14 Nov 1890)

Robinson, Katherine "Katie" (Wright) (colored), c1869-1942, native of Havre de Grace, daughter of George Wright and Rachael Harvey, both of Virginia (Pennington Funeral Home Records)

Robinson, Keziah, county out-pensioner [welfare recipient], Third District (*Havre de Grace Republican*, 4 Jul 1890)

Robinson, L. Walter, 1861-1936, native of Cambridge, MD, tailor, resident of Havre de Grace (Death certificate; Angel Hill Cemetery)

Robinson, Laura B. (colored), 1884-1962 (St. James United Cemetery)

Robinson, Lewis Bolivar, 1825-1890 (Union Chapel Methodist Church Cemetery); farmer, near Jerusalem Mills and Wilna (*The Aegis & Intelligencer*, 3 Jan 1890 and 16 May 1890); died testate and his named heirs were wife Marion J. Robinson, daughters Adda Archer and Olivia Smith, and sons Jesse Levering Robinson and Charles

Carroll Robinson (Harford County Will Book JMM 11:102-103)

Robinson, Levin Walter, see Bertie May Robinson, q.v.

Robinson, Lotta R. ("Lottie"), age 15, student, Oakland School, 1890 (George G. Curtiss Ledger); student, Union Chapel Public School (*The Aegis & Intelligencer*, 14 Mar 1890)

Robinson, Lydia, student, Oakland School, 1890 (George G. Curtiss Ledger); student, Union Chapel Public School (*The Aegis & Intelligencer*, 14 Mar 1890); see Lydia Ann Robinson, q.v.

Robinson, M. Katharine (colored), 1872-1942 (St. James United Cemetery); wife of Robert Robinson, q.v.

Robinson, Margaret Minerva, 1857-1945 (Union Chapel Methodist Church Cemetery)

Robinson, Marion J., see Lewis Bolivar Robinson, q.v.

Robinson, Martha J., 1875-1934 (Baker Cemetery)

Robinson, Martha W., 1825-1900 (Broad Creek Friends Cemetery)

Robinson, Martin S., 1885-1940 (Angel Hill Cemetery); born 18 Jun 1885, native of Cambridge, MD, son of L. Walter Robinson, of Cambridge, MD, and Alice B. Barwick, of Easton, MD, resided in Havre de Grace (Death certificate)

Robinson, Mary, born c1878, daughter of Robert Kirkwood Robinson and Abigal Murphy (*Kirkwoods and Their Kin, 1731-1971*, by Anna Lee Kirkwood Smith, 1972, p. 129)

Robinson, Mary Bell (Kirkwood), 1805-1890 (Bethel Presbyterian Church Cemetery Records); wife of William Robinson, q.v.

Robinson, Mary C. (Prigg), 1832-1902 (St. Ignatius Catholic Church Cemetery)

Robinson, Mary Elizabeth, born -- Sep 1890, baptized 1 Nov 1890, daughter of Thomas H. and Clara (Cain) Robinson (St. Ignatius Catholic Church Baptism Register, p. 115)

Robinson, Mary Elizabeth, 1834-1906 (Cokesbury Methodist Church Cemetery)

Robinson, Mary Esabella, see Susan (Robinson) Neville, q.v.

Rovinson, Martha J., 1860-1948 (Deer Creek Methodist Church Cemetery)

Robinson, Mary J. (colored), 1874-1935 (Death certificate; St. James United Cemetery)

Robinson, Mary Jane (colored), 1881-1945 (Community Baptist Church Cemetery); native of Harford Co., born 9 Apr 1881, daughter of Joseph Robinson and Tamer Evans, born natives of Maryland (Death certificate - married name Demby)

Robinson, Mary Lucile, born 14 Jan 1886, baptized 7 Feb 1886, daughter of Thomas H. and Clara (Cain) Robinson (St. Ignatius Catholic Church Baptism Register, p. 85)

Robinson, Mary Lydia, 21 Oct 1890 - 13 Nov 1890 (Union Chapel Methodist Church Cemetery)

Robinson, Mary Magdalen, born -- Mar 1888, born 22 Apr 1888, daughter of Thomas H. and Clara (Cain) Robinson (St. Ignatius Catholic Church Baptism Register, p. 98)

Robinson, Mary Martha (colored), born -- Apr 1890, baptized 18 May 1890, daughter of Scott and Virginia (Green) Robinson (St. Ignatius Catholic Church Baptism Register, p. 113)

Robinson, Mary Rebecca (Stockham), 1840-1928 (St. George's Episcopal Church Cemetery); native and resident of Perryman (Death certificate)

Robinson, Martha S., 1859-1894 (Deer Creek Methodist Church Cemetery)

Robinson, Oliver F., 1883-1917 (Emory Methodist Church Cemetery), son of John Thomas and Ellen Melissa (Harkins) Robinson (*Harkins and Related Families of Harford County, Maryland*, by Henry C. Peden, Jr., 2003, pp. 18-19)

Robinson, R. Louise, wife of George W. Robinson, q.v.

Robinson, Rebecca, see Nellie (Wiley) Day, q.v.

Robinson, Rebecca Bell, born 23 Apr 1885, daughter of John Calvin and Emma (Robinson) Robinson

(*Kirkwoods and Their Kin, 1731-1971*, by Anna Lee Kirkwood Smith, 1972, p. 145)

Robinson, Richard B., 1820-1900, resided at Magnolia (Death certificate incomplete)

Robinson, Richarda L., businesswoman (trader's license), Havre de Grace (*Havre de Grace Republican*, 30 May 1890)

Robinson, Robert, resident of Havre de Grace (*The Aegis & Intelligencer*, 15 Aug 1890)

Robinson, Robert, child at Chestnut Hill (*The Aegis & Intelligencer*, 11 Jul 1890)

Robinson, Robert (colored), 1878-1939 (Death certificate; St. James United Cemetery)

Robinson, Robert Kirkwood (Dr.), 1833-1920 (Bethel Presbyterian Church Cemetery Records); surgeon and Civil War veteran (*Kirkwoods and Their Kin, 1731-1971*, by Anna Lee Kirkwood Smith, 1972, pp. 129-130)

Robinson, Ruby P. (Gibson), 1885-1928 (Slateville Cemetery, York Co., PA); native of Harford Co., born 29 Sep 1885, daughter of William Gibson and Elizabeth Fletcher (Harkins Funeral Home Records)

Robinson, Scott, student, Oakland School, 1890 (George G. Curtiss Ledger); resident near Fallston (*The Aegis & Intelligencer*, 11 Apr 1890)

Robinson (Robison), Selena Guss, see John Varnes, q.v.

Robinson, Susan (colored), see Josephine Gilbert (colored), q.v.

Robinson, Susanna, see Hannah J. Watkins, q.v.

Robinson, Tamer (Evans) (colored), see Mary Jane Robinson (colored), q.v.

Robinson, Thomas, 1811-1900 (Deer Creek Methodist Church Cemetery); resided at Chestnut Hill (Death certificate incomplete)

Robinson, Thomas, Civil War veteran, Aberdeen (*1890 Special Census of the Civil War Veterans of the State of Maryland*, by L. Tilden Moore, Volume III, p. 63)

Robinson, Thomas, farmer at Mill Green (*The Aegis & Intelligencer*, 3 Jan 1890)

Robinson, Thomas Calvin, 1890-1935 (Bethel Presbyterian Church Cemetery Records); born 5 Nov 1890, son of John Calvin Robinson and Emma Robinson (*Kirkwoods and Their Kin, 1731-1971*, by Anna Lee Kirkwood Smith, 1972, p. 145)

Robinson, Thomas Hall, 1860-1930 (St. Ignatius Catholic Church Cemetery); property owner adjacent to Broadway in Bel Air (*The Aegis & Intelligencer*, 16 May 1890); delegate, Third District, Democrat Party Convention (*The Aegis & Intelligencer*, 5 Sep 1890); incorporator, Bel Air Fire and Salvage Corps (*The Aegis & Intelligencer*, 19 Sep 1890); incorporator, Bel Air Water and Light Company (*Havre de Grace Republican*, 14 Feb 1890); incorporator, The Loan, Trust, Security and Insurance Company of Harford County (*Havre de Grace Republican*, 28 Feb 1890); judge, Bel Air jousting tournament (*Havre de Grace Republican*, 19 Sep 1890); member, Bel Air Fire Brigade and Salvage Corps (*Havre de Grace Republican*, 17 Oct 1890); member, Division No. 1, Bel Air Fire and Salvage Corps (*The Aegis & Intelligencer*, 10 Oct 1890); notary public, Third District (*Havre de Grace Republican*, 21 Feb 1890); member, Board of Town Commissioners, Bel Air, 1884-1892 (*Biographical Dictionary of Harford County, Maryland, 1774-1974*, by Henry C. Peden, Jr. and William O. Carr, 2021, pp. 230, 337)

Robinson, Thomas J., 1826-1908 (Cokesbury Methodist Church Cemetery)

Robinson, Thomas J., 1872-1922 (Cokesbury Methodist Church Cemetery)

Robinson, Thomas Jefferson, 1846-1929 (Deer Creek Methodist Church Cemetery); born 11 May 1846, son of Thomas and Elizabeth Robinson (Harkins-Robinson Bible, *Maryland Bible Records, Volume 1*, by Henry C. Peden, Jr., 2003, p. 103); resident of Chestnut Hill, and father of Mrs. Margaret Wheeler, of Baltimore (*The Aegis & Intelligencer*, 11 Jul 1890 and 22 Aug 1890)

Robinson, Walter (colored), see Ida Jackson (colored), q.v.

Robinson, Walter B., 1875-1957 (Baker Cemetery)

Robinson, Walter B., 1888-1963, son of William Harvey Robinson and Anna Mary ---- (Bethel Presbyterian Church Cemetery Records)

Robinson, William E., 1860-1935 (Union Chapel Methodist Church Cemetery); member, Fallston Road League (*The Aegis & Intelligencer*, 17 Jan 1890); member, Robinson Can Company of Harford County, at Fallston (*Havre de Grace Republican*, 24 Oct 1890); transferred from the voter registration list at Hopewell, Second District (*Havre de Grace Republican*, 17 Oct 1890); vice president of the Third Annual Convention, Farmers' Club of Harford County (*Havre de Grace Republican*, 5 Dec 1890)

Robinson, William J., 1881-1949 (Emory Methodist Church Cemetery); son of John Thomas and Ellen Melissa (Harkins) Robinson (*Harkins and Related Families of Harford County, Maryland*, by Henry C. Peden, Jr., 2003, p. 18); native of Harford Co., born 1 Mar 1881 (Harkins Funeral Home Records)

Robinson, William Kirkwood, born c1870, son of Robert Kirkwood and Abigal (Murphy) Robinson (*Kirkwoods and Their Kin, 1731-1971*, by Anna Lee Kirkwood Smith, 1972, p. 129)

Robinson, William L., name stricken off the voter registration list at Abingdon, First District (*Havre de Grace Republican*, 17 Oct 1890)

Robinson, William Thomas, 1839-1919 (Bethel Presbyterian Church Cemetery Records); trustee, Kirkwood School No. 20, Fourth District (*Havre de Grace Republican*, 30 May 1890)

Robinson, Mary E., age 35 in 1890 (Marriage License Applications Book ALJ No. 2, 1891)

Rock Run Methodist Church and cemetery (Craig's Corner Road, near Rock Run)

Rock Run Mill, on Susquehanna River at Rock Run, Clement G. Butler, prop. (*Mills: Grist, Saw, Bone, Flint, Fulling ... & More*, by Jack L. Shagena, Jr., Henry C. Peden, Jr. and John W. McGrain, 2009, p. 245-247)

Rock Run Public School No. 14, Second District (*Harford County, Maryland Teachers and the Schools They Served, 1774-1900*, by Henry C. Peden, Jr., 2022, p. 372)

Rockdale Mills, on Winter's Run near Fallston, Clement Butler, miller, and H. K. and N. L. Mitchell, prop. (*Mills: Grist, Saw, Bone, Flint, Fulling ... & More*, by Jack L. Shagena, Jr., Henry C. Peden, Jr. and John W. McGrain, 2009, pp. 242-243)

Rockey, Charles F., 1866-1940 (Dublin Methodist Church Cemetery); native of Harford Co. (Bailey Funeral Home Records)

Rockey, Lydia Lavinia (Foard), 1875-1945 (Dublin Methodist Church Cemetery); native of Harford Co., born 11 Mar 1875, daughter of Oliver S. Foard and Mary R. Harkins (Bailey Funeral Home Records)

Rockey, Sarah A., 1825-1913 (Fallston Methodist Church Cemetery)

Rockey, William H., 1872-1911 (Fallston Methodist Church Cemetery); Civil War veteran, Pleasantville (*1890 Special Census of the Civil War Veterans of the State of Maryland*, by L. Tilden Moore, Volume III, p. 77)

Rockhold, Annie E., 1847-1928 (Ebenezer Methodist Church Cemetery); wife of Isaac Rockhold, q.v.

Rockhold, Charles M., 1876-1934 (Ebenezer Methodist Church Cemetery)

Rockhold, Elijah, 1826-1901, native of Maryland, farmer at Madonna (Death certificate)

Rockhold, Elizabeth, 1830-1920 (Ebenezer Methodist Church Cemetery)

Rockhold, Isaac, 1836-1900 (Ebenezer Methodist Church Cemetery; Death certificate stated he was born in 1825 and married Anne Elmer); served on a grand jury in 1890 (*The Aegis & Intelligencer*, 14 Nov 1890)

Rockhold, Jemine, 1820-1900 (Ebenezer Methodist Church Cemetery)

Rockhold, Lysias, 1821-1899 (Ebenezer Methodist Church Cemetery); trustee, Sarah Furnace Corner School No. 22, Fourth District (*Havre de Grace Republican*, 30 May 1890); resided at Sarah Furnace near Jarrettsville (Death certificate; *The Aegis & Intelligencer*, 9 May 1890)

Rockhold, Margaret, wife of Elijah Rockhold, q.v.

Rockhold, Margaret M., 1826-1899, resided at Sarah Furnace near Jarrettsville (Death certificate; Ebenezer Methodist Church Cemetery)

Rockhold, Sarah R. (Brierly), 1818-1903 (Bethel Presbyterian Church Cemetery Records)

Rocks of Deer Creek Colored Public School No. 3, near Rocks, Fourth District (*Harford County, Maryland*

Teachers and the Schools They Served, 1774-1900, by Henry C. Peden, Jr., 2022, p. 372)

Rodgers, James, see John D. Grafton, q.v.

Rodgers, Martha A., see John D. Grafton, q.v.

Rodgers, Robert Smith (colonel), 1809-1891 (Rock Creek Cemetery, Washington, DC); vestryman, St. John's Episcopal Church, Havre de Grace (*Havre de Grace Republican*, 11 Apr 1890); Civil War veteran, Havre de Grace (*1890 Special Census of the Civil War Veterans of the State of Maryland*, by L. Tilden Moore, Volume III, p. 68)

Rodgers, William F., new name on the voter registration list at Hopewell in Second District, 1890 (*Havre de Grace Republican*, 17 Oct 1890)

Roe & Tucker's General Store, Forest Hill, John B. Roe and Eli Tucker, prop. (*Country Stores: Harford County's Rural Heritage*, by Henry C. Peden, Jr. and Jack L. Shagena, Jr., 2015, pp. 212-214, 251-253; *1953 Harford County Directory*, p. 320)

Roe, Charles A., see John B. Roe, q.v.

Roe, Charles F., 1881-1914, native of Harford Co., born 19 Feb 1881, son of William D. Roe and Isabel R. Curry (Centre Methodist Church Cemetery tombstone inscribed 1880, but death certificate states 1881)

Roe, John B., 1822-1891 (Centre Methodist Church Cemetery); postmaster [and store proprietor], Forest Hill (*The Aegis & Intelligencer*, 14 Feb 1890); wrote his will in 1878 and died in 1891, naming his wife Mary J. Roe as his only heir, but upon her death everything passed to their children John D. Roe, Sarah Tucker, William Roe, Mary A. Foard, and Charles A. Roe (Harford County Will Book JMM 11:184-185)

Roe, John D., 1850-1916 (Mountain Christian Church Cemetery); see John B. Roe, q.v.

Roe, Lillian (Cooper), 1863-1922 (Mountain Christian Church Cemetery)

Roe, Mary A., 1882-1967 (Centre Methodist Church Cemetery)

Roe, Mary E., 1876-1953 (Centre Methodist Church Cemetery); Mary Roe, student, Forest Hill School, 1890 (*The Aegis*, 2 Jul 1965, school picture)

Roe, Mary J. (Dickinson), 1824-1910 (Centre Methodist Church Cemetery); see John B. Roe, q.v.

Roe, Pearl Estella (McCommons), 1887-1948 (Deer Creek Methodist Church Cemetery)

Roe, Walter Curtis, 1885-1944 (Deer Creek Methodist Church Cemetery); student, Forest Hill School, 1890 (*The Aegis*, 2 Jul 1965, school picture)

Roe, William, 1852-1929 (Centre Methodist Church Cemetery); postmaster, Forest Hill (*Havre de Grace Republican*, 14 Feb 1890); see John B. Roe and Charles E. Hornberger, q.v.

Roe, William D., see Charles F. Roe, q.v.

Rogers' General Store, at Level, Reuben P. Rogers, prop. (*Country Stores: Harford County's Rural Heritage*, by Henry C. Peden, Jr. and Jack L. Shagena, Jr., 2015, p. 214)

Rogers, Almira Jane, 1850-1923 (Mt. Zion Methodist Church Cemetery)

Rogers, Ann (Pennock), 1818-1901, widow of Elisha Harsthorn Rogers (Rock Run Methodist Church Cemetery); native of Maryland, resided at Level (Death certificate)

Rogers, Ann Eliza (Prcotor), 1848-1898 (Mt. Carmel Methodist Church Cemetery; Elisha Johnson Rogers Bible, *Maryland Bible Records, Volume 5*, by Henry C. Peden, Jr., 2004, p. 156); wife of Elisha J. Johnson, q.v.

Rogers, Annette, 1881-1930 (Centre Methodist Church Cemetery)

Rogers, Blanch May, born 21 Mar 1890, daughter of John Owen and Eliza (Stuart) Rogers (John Owen Rogers Bible, *Maryland Bible Records, Volume 2*, by Henry C. Peden, Jr., 2003, pp. 115-116)

Rogers, C. F., musician, Bayside Cornet Band, Havre de Grace (*Havre de Grace Republican*, 31 Jan 1890); delegate, Sixth District, Republican Party Convention (*The Aegis & Intelligencer*, 26 Sep 1890)

Rogers, Calvin Ambrose, 1871-1907 (Rock Run Methodist Church Cemetery); native and resident of Level, Harford Co., son of Solomon Rogers and Dorleskia D. Wiles (Death certificate)

Rogers, Caroline (Metzger), 1833-1926 (Angel Hill Cemetery); businesswoman (trader's license), Havre de Grace, 1890 (*Havre de Grace Republican*, 30 May 1890); see Clara L. Rogers, q.v.

Rogers, Charles F., 1865-1896 (Angel Hill Cemetery); Charles Rogers, cigar and candy store, Havre de Grace, 1890 (*Havre de Grace Republican*, 19 Dec 1890)

Rogers, Charlotte (Miss), honor student, Archer Institute, Bel Air (*The Aegis & Intelligencer*, 20 Jun 1890)

Rogers, Chattie (Miss), dancing teacher, Archer Institute, Bel Air (*The Aegis & Intelligencer*, 6 Jun 1890); singer and member, Emmanuel Episcopal Church, Bel Air (*The Aegis & Intelligencer*, 11 Apr 1890)

Rogers, Clara L., 1868-1946, native and resident of Havre de Grace, born 3 Aug 1868, daughter of George Washington Rogers and Caroline Metzger (Death certificate; Angel Hill Cemetery)

Rogers, Dorleskia D. (Wiles), 1842-1902 (Death certificate incomplete; Rock Run Methodist Church Cemetery); wife of Solomon T. Rogers, q.v.

Rogers, Elisha Johnson, 1851-1932 (Mt. Carmel Methodist Church Cemetery; Elisha Johnson Bible, *Maryland Bible Records, Volume 5*, by Henry C. Peden, Jr., 2004, p. 156); steward, Mt. Carmel M. P. Church (*Havre de Grace Republican*, 28 Feb 1890)

Rogers, Eliza (Stuart), 1860-1947 (Mt. Zion Methodist Church Cemetery); wife of John Owen Rogers, q.v., also see Raymond Lee Rogers and Stuart Owen Rogers, q.v.

Rogers, Elizabeth M., 1809-1899 (Mt. Zion Methodist Church Cemetery)

Rogers, Fillmore, crop thresher, near Bel Air (*The Aegis & Intelligencer*, 15 Aug 1890); see Mary Ellen Rogers, q.v.

Rogers, George, see Mabel V. Keene, q.v.

Rogers, George Washington, 1823-1904, native of Cecil Co., MD, resident of Havre de Grace (Death certificate; Angel Hill Cemetery); see Clara L. Rogers, q.v.

Rogers, Gover, second grade student, School No. 1, Third District (*The Aegis & Intelligencer*, 11 Jul 1890)

Rogers, Howell E., 1875-1958 (Rock Run Methodist Church Cemetery)

Rogers, James M., 1834-1901, native of Maryland, farmer at Forest Hill (Death certificate; Centre Methodist Church Cemetery)

Rogers, John Owen, 1855-1932 (Mt. Zion Methodist Church Cemetery); see Stuart Owen Rogers, Margaret Estella Rogers, and Raymond Lee Rogers, q.v.

Rogers, Joseph, farmer, near Aberdeen (*Havre de Grace Republican*, 28 Feb 1890)

Rogers, Joseph Thomas, 1874-1956 (Mt. Carmel Methodist Church Cemetery); born 24 Nov 1874, son of Elisha J. and Ann E. Rogers (Elisha Johnson Rogers Bible, *Maryland Bible Records, Volume 5*, by Henry C. Peden, Jr., 2004, p. 156); student, Oakland School, 1890 (George G. Curtiss Ledger)

Rogers, L. Gertrude, 1874-1950 (Angel Hill Cemetery)

Rogers, Luella (Donahoo), 1883-1961 (Rock Run Methodist Church Cemetery); wife of Calvin A. Rogers, q.v.

Rogers, Lydia A. (Whitaker), 1870-1945 (Centre Methodist Church Cemetery); native of Harford Co., born 18 Sep 1870, daughter of Wesley Whitaker and Josephine Black (Bailey Funeral Home Records)

Rogers, M. Estelle, 1882-1972 (Mt. Zion Methodist Church Cemetery)

Rogers, Mabel, student, Fallston School (*The Aegis & Intelligencer*, 9 May 1890)

Rogers, Maggie, 1860-1891 (Union Chapel Methodist Church Cemetery)

Rogers, Margaret (Grafton), 1819-1894 (Old Brick Baptist Church Cemetery); wife of John Owen Rogers, q.v.

Rogers, Margaret Estella, born 29 Dec 1882, daughter of John Owen and Eliza (Stuart) Rogers (John Owen Rogers Bible, *Maryland Bible Records, Volume 2*, by Henry C. Peden, Jr., 2003, p. 110)

Rogers, Martha G., 1847-1906 (Centre Methodist Church Cemetery); wife of James M. Rogers, q.v.

Rogers, Mary Ann, 1825-1898 (Mt. Carmel Methodist Church Cemetery)

Rogers, Mary E. (Curley), 1842-1928 (Centre Methodist Church Cemetery); native of Maryland, resided at Prospect (Death certificate)

Rogers, Mary Elizabeth, 1866-1946 (Mt. Carmel Methodist Church Cemetery)

Rogers, Mary Ellen, died 18 Oct 1890, age not stated, wife of Fillmore Rogers (*The Aegis & Intelligencer*, 24 Oct 1890; Mt. Carmel Methodist Church Cemetery)

Rogers, Millard Fillmore, born 11 Apr 1886, son of John Owen and Eliza (Stuart) Rogers (John Owen Rogers Bible, *Maryland Bible Records, Volume 2*, by Henry C. Peden, Jr., 2003, pp. 115-116); see Mary Ellen Rogers, q.v.

Rogers, Oliver Thomas, 1859-1922 (Angel Hill Cemetery); vice president, Republican Club, 1890 (*Havre de Grace Republican*, 7 Nov 1890)

Rogers, Olivia, student, Fallston School (*The Aegis & Intelligencer*, 9 May 1890)

Rogers, R. John, vice president, Harford County Agricultural and Mechanical Society (*The Aegis & Intelligencer*, 10 Jan 1890); steward, Bel Air M. P. Church (*Havre de Grace Republican*, 28 Feb 1890)

Rogers, Rachel Leetta (Hopkins), 1855-1920 (Rock Run Methodist Church Cemetery); wife of John E. Hopkins, q.v.

Rogers, Raymond Lee, 1880-1964 (Mt. Carmel Methodist Church Cemetery); born 23 Feb 1880, son of John Owen and Eliza (Stuart) Rogers (John Owen Rogers Bible, *Maryland Bible Records, Volume 2*, by Henry C. Peden, Jr., 2003, p. 115)

Rogers, Reuben P., 1852-1912 (Rock Run Methodist Church Cemetery); see Rogers' General Store, q.v.

Rogers, Solomon T., farmer, near Level (*Havre de Grace Republican*, 4 Jul 1890); husband of Dorleskia D. Rogers, q.v.

Rogers, Stuart Owen, 1884-1890 (Mt. Zion Methodist Church Cemetery); son of John O. and Eliza Rogers, of Emmorton (*The Aegis & Intelligencer*, 11 Jul 1890; John Owen Rogers Bible, *Maryland Bible Records, Volume 2*, by Henry C. Peden, Jr., 2003, pp. 115-117)

Rogers, Virginia L. (Magowan), 1860-1921 (Angel Hill Cemetery)

Rogers, Wallis O., 1876-1939 (Smith Chapel Methodist Church Cemetery)

Rogers, William, 1827-1892 (Mt. Carmel Methodist Church Cemetery)

Rogers, William E., musician, Bayside Cornet Band, Havre de Grace (*Havre de Grace Republican*, 31 Jan 1890); inside guard, Harford Lodge No. 54, Knight of Pythias, Havre de Grace (*Havre de Grace Republican*, 11 Jul 1890)

Rogers, William F., born -- Jan 1869 (1900 Aberdeen Census)

Rogers, William Gover, born 12 Jul 1880, son of Elisha J. and Ann E. Rogers (Elisha Johnson Rogers Bible, *Maryland Bible Records, Volume 5*, by Henry C. Peden, Jr., 2004, p. 156)

Rogers, William H., resident near Abingdon (*The Aegis & Intelligencer*, 18 Apr 1890)

Rogers, William Henry, 1849-1931, native of Harford Co., famer at Aberdeen (Death certificate; Mt. Zion Methodist Church Cemetery)

Rogge, Emma P., 1859-1924 (William Watters Memorial Church Cemetery, Cooptown)

Rogge, Jesse A., 1860-1926 (William Watters Memorial Church Cemetery, Cooptown)

Rollins, J. Edward, 1874-1954 (Cokesbury Memorial Methodist Church Cemetery)

Rollins, Lillian May, 1878-1951 (Cokesbury Memorial Methodist Church Cemetery)

Romer, B. F., photographic art studio, Main Street adjoining the M. P. Church, Bel Air (*The Aegis & Intelligencer*, 24 Jan 1890)

Romer, B. S., ice cream parlor, Whitaker Building, Main Street, Bel Air (*The Aegis & Intelligencer*, 20 Jun 1890)

Romer, Sallie (Mrs.), premium award winner, Class K - Household and Domestic Manufactures, Harford

County Fair (*The Aegis & Intelligencer*, 24 Oct 1890)

Roney, Anna, appointed administratrix of John Roney, deceased (*Harford Democrat*, 11 Apr 1890)

Roney, James, see Maggie Roney, q.v.

Roney, John, farmer, Fallston (*Havre de Grace Republican*, 4 Apr 1890); sneak boat duck hunter (*Havre de Grace Republican*, 7 Nov 1890)

Roney, John, native of County Wexford, Ireland and citizen of this country for 42 years, died 24 Mar 1890, at home near Forest Hill, in his 75th year (*The Aegis & Intelligencer*, 28 Mar 1890 and 4 Apr 1890)

Roney, Maggie, died 27 May 1900, age not given, native of Maryland, resided at High Point, wife of James Roney (Death certificate)

Rosan, Clifford Dawson, 1876-1927 (Darlington Cemetery); premium award winner, Class E - Poultry, Harford County Fair, 1890 (*The Aegis & Intelligencer*, 24 Oct 1890)

Rosan, H. P. (Mrs.), premium award winner, Class J - Domestic Products, Harford County Fair (*The Aegis & Intelligencer*, 24 Oct 1890)

Rosan, Margaret ("Maggie") (Miss), singer and member, Emmanuel Episcopal Church, Bel Air (*The Aegis & Intelligencer*, 11 Apr 1890); premium award winner, Class A - Horses, Harford County Fair (*The Aegis & Intelligencer*, 24 Oct 1890)

Rosan, Rena R., see Rena R. Scott, q.v.

Ross, Abram T. (Abraham Taylor Ross), see David Harlan Ross, q.v.

Ross, Ada (Wonders), 1871-1934 (Emory Methodist Church Cemetery)

Ross, Amelia (Miss), resident near Sandy Hook (*The Aegis & Intelligencer*, 19 Dec 1890); sister of Robert Ross. q.v.

Ross, Ann C. (Chapman) (colored), 1825-1900, native of Maryland, resident of Havre de Grace, wife of Daniel J. Ross (Death certificate)

Ross, Anna L. (Mrs. A. T.), resided near Bel Air (*The Aegis & Intelligencer*, 19 Sep 1890); see David Harlan Ross, q.v.

Ross, Annie (colored), see Isaac Benjamin Galloway, Jr. (colored), q.v.

Ross, Benjami A., 1875-1959 (Dublin Southern Cemetery)

Ross, David Harlan, born 18 Sep 1885, son of Abram T. (Abraham Taylor) Ross and Anna L. Ross (Holy Trinity Episcopal Church Register of Baptisms, p. 88)

Ross, Daniel J. (colored), see Ann C. Ross (colored), q.v.

Ross, Elizabeth (Mrs.), 1836-1920, native of Maryland, resided at Dublin (Death certificate)

Ross, Henry, seine fisherman, Rock Run shore and Wood Island in the Susquehanna River (*The Aegis & Intelligencer*, 4 Apr 1890); see William B. Ross, q.v.

Ross, Ida M., 1881-1960 (Dublin Southern Cemetery)

Ross, John H. (colored), 1885-1973 (Mt. Zion Methodist Church Cemetery, at Mountain)

Ross, Joseph, 1815-1891 (Dublin Southern Cemetery)

Ross, L. Eugene, 1869-1931 (Broad Creek Friends Cemetery); native of Harford Co., son of Silas W. Ross, q.v. (Bailey Funeral Home Records)

Ross, Lycurgus L., 1844-1912 (Centre Methodist Church Cemetery); resided at Forest Hill (*Harford Democrat*, 21 Feb 1890)

Ross, Mantie L., 1884-1952 (Baker Cemetery)

Ross, Margaret, 1865-1927 (St. George's Episcopal Church Cemetery)

Ross, Mary, see Walter J. Cantler, q.v.

Ross, Mary Ada (Wonders), 1871-1934 (Bailey Funeral Home Records); wife of S. Lindley Ross, q.v.

Ross, Mary E. (Parry), 1884-1967 (Slate Ridge Cemetery, York Co., PA); native of Cardiff, Harford Co., born 1 Mar 1884, daughter of Thomas Parry and Carrie Stull, q.v.

Ross, Mary E. (Warner), 1841-1921 (Broad Creek Friends Cemetery); wife of Silas W. Ross, q.v.

Ross, Phebe (Gilbert), 1885-1963 (Broad Creek Friends Cemetery)

Ross, Robert, c1828-1890 (Mt. Tabor Methodist Church Cemetery); resident of Allibone (*The Aegis & Intelligencer*, 31 Oct 1890)

Ross, Robert, born 1865, died ---- (St. George's Episcopal Church Cemetery)

Ross, Robert L., 1872-1949 (Baker Cemetery)

Ross, S. Lindley, 1870-1942 (Emory Methodist Church Cemetery); native of Harford Co., born 30 Jul 1870, son of Silas W. Ross and Mary E. Warner (Bailey Funeral Home Records)

Ross, Silas W., 1842-1895 (Broad Creek Friends Cemetery); see Wilburn Ross and L. Eugene Ross, q.v.

Ross, Wilburn, born 8 Dec 1874, son of Silas W. Ross and Mary E. Warner (*The Hughes Genealogy, 1636-1953*, by Joseph Lee Hughes, 1953, p. 122; Death certificate)

Ross, William, c1872-1924 (Death certificate; Baker Cemetery)

Ross, William B., 1887-1929 (Rock Run Methodist Church Cemetery); native of Maryland, born 13 Jan 1887, son of Henry H. Ross, of Maryland, and Pauline Winzer, of Germany (Bailey Funeral Home Records)

Ross, William R., 1874-1924 (Broad Creek Friends Cemetery)

Rough Ashlar Club, a Havre de Grace gentlemen's duck hunting association (*Havre de Grace: Its Historic Past, Its Charming Present and Its Promising Future: Harford County's Rural Heritage*. by Jack L. Shagena, Jr. and Henry C. Peden, Jr., 2018, p. 264)

Rouscher, Rosa, businesswoman (trader's license), Havre de Grace (*Havre de Grace Republican*, 30 May 1890)

Rouse & Richardson, carriage and buggy salesmen. Churchville (*Carriages Back in the Day: Harford County's Rural Heritage*, by Jack L. Shagena, Jr. and Henry C. Peden, Jr., 2016, pp. 88-89

Rouse & Richardson's General Store, Churchville, John G. Rouse and Robert C. Richardson, prop. (*Country Stores: Harford County's Rural Heritage*, by Henry C. Peden, Jr. and Jack L. Shagena, Jr., 2015, p. 217; *The Aegis & Intelligencer*, 7 Nov 1890)

Rouse's General Store, Main Street, Bel Air, John G. Rouse, prop. (*Harford Democrat*, 24 Jan 1890; *Country Stores: Harford County's Rural Heritage*, by Henry C. Peden, Jr. and Jack L. Shagena, Jr., 2015, p. 216)

Rouse, Anna Stump (Webster), 1871-1897 (Calvary Methodist Church Cemetery); wife of Willard G. Rouse, q.v.

Rouse, Birck, third grade student, Prospect Hill School. First District (*The Aegis & Intelligencer*, 21 Feb and 24 Oct 1890)

Rouse, Christopher Chapman, 1868-1928 (Churchville Presbyterian Church Cemetery); son of John G. Rouse, merchant, of Bel Air (*The Aegis & Intelligencer*, 10 Jan 1890); member, Division No. 1, Bel Air Fire and Salvage Corps (*The Aegis & Intelligencer*, 10 Oct 1890; *Havre de Grace Republican*, 17 Oct 1890); jousting tournament rider, Knight of the Temple (*Havre de Grace Republican*, 19 Sep 1890); member, Bel Air Tennis Club (*The Aegis & Intelligencer*, 18 Jul 1890); member, Mt. Ararat Lodge No. 44, A. F. & A. M., Bel Air (*Havre de Grace Republican*, 11 Jul 1890); private, Jackson Guards [Co. D, 1st Regiment, Maryland National Guard], 1889-1890 (*The Aegis & Intelligencer*, 11 Jan 1889)

Rouse, Daisy (Miss), member, Bel Air Tennis Club (*The Aegis & Intelligencer*, 18 Jul 1890)

Rouse, Dora, student, Bel Air Academy and Graded School (*The Aegis & Intelligencer*, 23 May 1890); premium award winner, Class L - Children's Department, Harford County Fair (*The Aegis & Intelligencer*, 24 Oct 1890)

Rouse, Edgar, fourth grade student, Prospect Hill School (*The Aegis & Intelligencer*, 21 Feb 1890)

Rouse, Edna, 1872-1929 (Angel Hill Cemetery - married name Jackson); native of Maryland, born 21 Sep 1872, daughter of Stephen N. Rouse and Phoebe Walker, resided in Havre de Grace (Death certificate)

Rouses, Grace, 1882-1957, native of Havre de Grace, born 20 Apr 1882, daughter of Stephen N. Rouse and ---- (Pennington Funeral Home Records - married name Reynolds)

Rouse, Harriet Bayless (Hanway), 1838-1923 (Cokesbury Memorial Methodist Church Cemetery); premium award winner, Class J - Domestic Products, Harford County Fair (*The Aegis & Intelligencer*, 24 Oct 1890); wife of John Gouldsmith Rouse, q.v.

Rouse, Helen, student and actress, Bel Air Graded School (*The Aegis & Intelligencer*, 26 Dec 1890)

Rouse, Henrietta Gertrude (Richardson), 1866-1955 (Churchville Presbyterian Church Cemetery), wife of Christopher Chapman Rouse, q.v.

Rouse, John Gouldsmith, 1844-1902 (Cokesbury Memorial Methodist Church Cemetery); hotel proprietor, Eagle Hotel [aka Hanna's Hotel and Rouse House], Bond Street, Bel Air (*The Aegis & Intelligencer*, 31 Oct 1890); merchant, Bel Air (*The Aegis & Intelligencer*, 10 Jan 1890); president, Bulett Carriage Factory, Bel Air (*The Aegis & Intelligencer*, 31 Jan 1890); director, Bel Air Water and Light Company (*Havre de Grace Republican*, 14 Feb 1890); member, County Board of School Commissioners (*Havre de Grace Republican*, 13 Jun 1890); superintendent, Bel Air M. P. Church Sunday School (*The Aegis & Intelligencer*, 27 Jun 1890); see Christopher Chapman Rouse, Rouse's General Store, and Trundle & Rouse's General Store, q.v.

Rouse, Lydia Ann (Robinson), 1874-1930 (Cokesbury Memorial Methodist Church Cemetery)

Rouse, Phoebe F., 1841-1930 (Angel Hill Cemetery)

Rouse, Stephen N., 1839-1911 (Angel Hill Cemetery); see Edna Rouse and Grace Rouse, q.v.

Rouse, Willard Gouldsmith, 1867-1930 (Cokesbury Memorial Methodist Church Cemetery); executive committee, Bel Air Academy Association (*Havre de Grace Republican*, 11 Jul 1890); member, Bel Air Tennis Club (*The Aegis & Intelligencer*, 18 Jul 1890); jousting tournament rider, Knight of Swarthmore (*Havre de Grace Republican*, 19 Sep and 17 Oct 1890)

Roussey, Ashton F., 1848-1927 (Darlington Cemetery); see Grafton G. Roussey, q.v.

Roussey, Carroll F., 1884-1950 (Darlington Cemetery)

Roussey, Catherine, see Clarence Sadler, q.v.

Roussey, Clara Jane (McNutt), 1851-1933 (Darlington Cemetery); see Grafton G. Roussey, q.v.

Roussey, Della M. (Herrman), 1889-1972 (Darlington Cemetery)

Roussey, Edwin, 1856-1896 (Darlington Cemetery)

Roussey, Eleanor "Ellen" (Boarman), 1829-1908 (Darlington Cemetery)

Roussey, Grafton Gover, 1885-1949 (Darlington Cemetery); native of Harford Co., born 25 Jul 1885, son of Ashton F. Roussey and Clara Jane McNutt (Bailey Funeral Home Records)

Roussey, John Kenton, 1888-1952 (Darlington Cemetery)

Roussey, John W., c1856-1920, native of Maryland (Oakwood Cemetery, Cecil Co., MD; Death certificate)

Roussey, Marshall K., age 25 in 1890, married Allie M. Bay (Marriage License Applications Book ALJ No. 2, 1891); served on an inquest jury in the Fifth District (*The Aegis & Intelligencer*, 1 Aug 1890); secretary, Franklin Sunday School (*Havre de Grace Republican*, 25 Apr 1890, reported him as Marshall T. Rousey)

Rowe, Ada Elizabeth, 1873-1963 (Cokesbury Memorial Methodist Church Cemetery)

Rowe, Caroline Elizabeth, see Caroline Elizabeth Jobes, Edward C. Jobes and George C. Jobes, q.v.

Rowe, Charlie, student, Forest Hill School, 1890 (*The Aegis*, 2 Jul 1965, school picture)

Rowe, Dorsey F., 1882-1936 (Baker Cemetery); son of Walter K. and Carrie Rowe (1900 Aberdeen Census)

Rowe, Emma (Jacobs), 1887-1958 (Baker Cemetery)

Rowe, George F., 1868-1943 (Baker Cemetery)

Rowe, Grace C., born -- May 1890, daughter of Walter K. and Carrie Rowe (1900 Aberdeen Census)

Rowe, Harry Irving, 1878-1954 (Cokesbury Memorial Methodist Church Cemetery); son of Walter K. and Carrie Rowe (1900 Aberdeen Census reported his name as Henry I. Rowe)

Rowe, Lillie (Wiles), 1871-1944 (Cokesbury Memorial Methodist Church Cemetery)

Rowe, Matilda H., 1867-1947 (Baker Cemetery)

Rowe, Maud L., born -- Apr 1875, daughter of Walter K. and Carrie Rowe (1900 Aberdeen Census)

Rowe, Pearl (Arthur), 1881-1962 (Baker Cemetery)

Rowe, Pery B., born -- Oct 1884, son of Walter K. and Carrie Rowe (1900 Aberdeen Census)

Rowe, Robert G., 1885-1964 (Baker Cemetery); son of Walter K. and Carrie Rowe (1900 Aberdeen Census stated born in Sep 1886)

Rowe, W. B., physician, Aberdeen (*The Aegis & Intelligencer*, 4 Jul 1890 and 22 Aug 1890)

Rowe, Walter, jousting tournament herald (*Havre de Grace Republican*, 17 Oct 1890)

Rowe, Walter W. H., 1876-1944 (Cokesbury Memorial Methodist Church Cemetery); student, Forest Hill School, 1890 (*The Aegis*, 2 Jul 1965, school picture); son of Walter K. and Carrie Rowe (1900 Aberdeen Census stated born in Apr 1877)

Rowlands, Jane, see Jane Burke, q.v.

Royston, Jesse, resided near Black Horse (*Harford Democrat*, 14 Feb 1890)

Ruckman, D. V., stock cattle dealer, at Woolsey's Scales, Fountain Green (*The Aegis & Intelligencer*, 7 Nov 1890)

Ruff, Annie (colored), see Stephen A. Bosley (colored), q.v.

Ruff, Asbury (colored), died 30 Jun 1892, adult, age not given (*The Aegis & (Intelligencer*, 8 Jul 1892)

Ruff, Christian (Mrs.) (colored), 1869-1916, native of Harford Co., daughter of ---- and Kitty Hackett (Death certificate)

Ruff, David (colored), 1887-1956 (Mt. Zion Methodist Church Cemetery, at Mountain)

Ruff, Ella Virginia (Findley), 1856-1900 (William Watters Memorial Church Cemetery, Thomas Run; Henry Ruff Bible, *Maryland Bible Records, Volume 1*, by Henry C. Peden, Jr., 2003, p. 212); wife of James Henry Ruff, q.v.

Ruff, Emily E. (Cottman), 1869-1934, native of Maryland (Death certificate); wife of Stephen B. Ruff, q.v.

Ruff, Helen (Mrs.) (colored), died -- Apr 1924, adult, age not given (*The Aegis*, 2 May 1924)

Ruff, Henry, 1817-1903 (William Watters Memorial Church Cemetery, Thomas Run; Henry Ruff Bible, *Maryland Bible Records, Volume 1*, by Henry C. Peden, Jr., 2003, pp. 211-212); premium award winner, Class B - Cattle, Harford County Fair (*The Aegis & Intelligencer*, 24 Oct 1890)

Ruff, Jacob, Civil War veteran, at Singer (*1890 Special Census of the Civil War Veterans of the State of Maryland*, by L. Tilden Moore, Volume III, p. 61)

Ruff, James Henry, 1847-1925 (William Watters Memorial Church Cemetery, Thomas Run); son of Henry and Elizabeth W. Ruff (Henry Ruff Bible, *Maryland Bible Records, Volume 1*, by Henry C. Peden, Jr., 2003, pp. 211-212)

Ruff, Jennie (Mrs.), uncalled for letter in Bel Air P. O., 1890 (*The Aegis & Intelligencer*, 14 Nov 1890)

Ruff, Jesse Harold (colored), 1853-1941, native of Harford Co., resided near Joppa, parents unknown (Death certificate)

Ruff, Joseph (colored), see Miranda V. Ruff (colored), q.v.

Ruff, Mary Catherine (Barnes) (colored), 1834-1906 (Death certificate); wife of William Asbury Ruff; also see Richard A. Ruff, q.v.

Ruff, Mary Elise (colored), 1890-1980, native of Bel Air, born 2 Feb 1890, daughter of Stephen B. Ruff and Emily ---- (Death certificate; Mt. Zion Methodist Church Cemetery, at Mountain)

Ruff, Miranda V. (colored), 1883-1914, native of Harford Co., born 11 Dec 1883, daughter of Joseph Ruff, of Harford Co., and Ellen Hewitt, of Baltimore Co. (Death certificate - married name Jenkins)

Ruff, Richard A. ("Ham"), 1862-1912. native of Harford Co., born 20 Jul 1862, son of William A. Ruff, native of Harford Co., and Mary Barnes, native of St. Mary's Co., MD (Death certificate); see Sarah Elizabeth Ruff, q.v.

Ruff, Sallie (colored), see Priscilla P. Wilson (colored), q.v.

Ruff, Sarah Elizabeth (Norton), 1867-1929, native of Maryland (Death certificate); wife of Richard A. Ruff, q.v.

Ruff, Sophia (colored), see Sulena M. Maddox (colored), q.v.

Ruff, Stephen B. (colored), 1866-1934 (Mt. Zion Methodist Church Cemetery, at Mountain); see Mary Elise Ruff, q.v.

Ruff, William A. (colored), see Mary Catherine Ruff and Richard A. Ruff, q.v.

Rummage, John, died 21 Oct 1895, no age given (Alms House Record Book)

Rumsey, Catherine (colored), see George Edward Hopkins (colored), q.v.

Rumsey, David W., 1866-1943, native of Chester Co., PA (Bailey Funeral Home Records)

Rumsey, Elizabeth (colored), born -- Mar 1862, native of Maryland (1900 Aberdeen Census); wife of James Rumsey (colored), q.v.

Rumsey, George (colored), 1843-1913, resident of Bel Air (Death certificate; Alms House Register Book, 1909-1949; *The Aegis & Intelligencer*, 30 May 1890)

Rumsey, George E. (colored), 1875-1939, native of Thomas Run, Harford Co., born 19 Oct 1875, son of George H. Rumsey and Hannah Preston (Death certificate)

Rumsey, George H. (colored), see George E. Rumsey (colored), q.v.

Rumsey, James, resident of Michaelsville (*The Aegis & Intelligencer*, 15 Aug 1890)

Rumsey, James (colored), born -- Apr 1860, native of Maryland (1900 Aberdeen Census); see Martha Rumsey (colored) and Robert Rumsey (colored), q.v.

Rumsey, Lena M. (Jones), 1874-1939 (Dublin Methodist Church Cemetery); native of Harford Co., born 9 Dec 1874, daughter of Allan Jones and Christean Logan (Bailey Funeral Home Records)

Rumsey, Margaret (Collins) (colored), 1869-1951, native of Harford Co. (Death certificate)

Rumsey, Martha (colored), 1886-1937, native of Harford Co., born 17 Jan 1886, daughter of James Rumsey and Ellen McGaw (Death certificate - married name Taylor)

Rumsey, Robert (colored), born -- Apr 1890, native of Maryland, son of James and Elizabeth Rumsey (1900 Aberdeen Census)

Runan, John, 1865-1940 (Smith Chapel Methodist Church Cemetery)

Runan, Rachel Elizabeth (Bailey), 1862-1918 (Smith Chapel Methodist Church Cemetery)

Rush, Jacob, and wife, sold land in August 1890 (*The Aegis & Intelligencer*, 12 Sep 1890)

Rusia, Ella (Miss), 1866-1926 (Dublin Methodist Church Cemetery; Death certificate)

Rusk, Harry Wells, of Third District, Democrat candidate for Congress, 1890 (*The Aegis & Intelligencer*, 26 Sep 1890)

Russell, Carrie, age 18 in 1889 (Marriage License Applications Book ALJ No. 2, 1889)

Russell, Catherine C., 1864-1935 (St. George's Episcopal Church Cemetery)

Russell, Charles E. (Mrs.), daughter of Thomas Kemp. q.v.

Russell, Daniel, see Jessie Russell, q.v.

Russell, Daniel Thomas, 1833-1894 (Holy Trinity Episcopal Church Cemetery)

Russell, David, see Mary A. Russell, q.v.

Russell, Elizabeth, see Annie R. Morris and Stephen C. Myers, q.v.

Russell, Elizabeth Jane (Williams), 1925-1901 (Angel Hill Cemetery), mother of John A. Russell, q.v.

Russell, George Thomas, 1852-1916 (Cokesbury Memorial Methodist Church Cemetery)

Russell, George Thomas, 1876-1910 (Trinity Evangelical Lutheran Church Cemetery)

Russell, Harrison "Harry" Simpson, 1888-1952 (St. George's Episcopal Church Cemetery)

Russell, Harvey, 1874-1930 (Cokesbury Memorial Methodist Church Cemetery); native of Harford Co., resided at Creswell, born -- Oct 1874, son of Martin Russell and ---- Keener (Death certificate)

Russell, Ida H., 1857-1935 (Angel Hill Cemetery)

Russell, Ida M., 1871-1953 (Darlington Cemetery)

Russell, James Edward, born 9 Apr 1889, baptized 8 May 1889, son of Daniel T. and Susanna Russell (Holy Trinity Episcopal Church Register of Baptisms, p. 96)

Russell, James S., 1803-1895 (St. Francis de Sales Catholic Church Cemetery)

Russell, Jessie, 1882-1934 (Holy Trinity Episcopal Church Cemetery); native of Harford Co., born 29 Feb 1882, son of Daniel Russell and ---- (Bailey Funeral Home Records)

Russell, John A., 1848-1930 (Angel Hill Cemetery); past master and grand inspector, for the district, Susquehanna Lodge No. 130, A.F. & A. M., Havre de Grace (*Havre de Grace Republican*, 11 Ju 1890 and 26 Dec 1890); delegate, Sixth District, Democrat Party Convention (*The Aegis & Intelligencer*, 5 Sep 1890); director and secretary, First National Bank of Havre de Grace (*Havre de Grace Republican*, 17 Jan 1890); member, Board of Educaton, 1889-1893; incorporator, The Loan, Trust, Security and Insurance Company of Harford County (*Havre de Grace Republican*, 28 Feb 1890); organizer and vice president, Havre de Grace Democratic Club (*Havre de Grace Republican*, 31 Oct 1890)

Russell, John Alfred, 1874-1945 (Angel Hill Cemetery); native of Havre de Grace, born 18 Nov 1875, son of Samuel L. Russell and Julia J. Boyd, both natives of Havre de Grace (Pennington Funeral Home Records)

Russell, John H., 1840-1925 (Darlington Cemetery); Civil War veteran, Darlington (*1890 Special Census of the Civil War Veterans of the State of Maryland*, by L. Tilden Moore, Volume III, p. 86); see Mary R. Price, q.v.

Russell, Julia, see Annie E. Lamb, q.v.

Russell, Julia J. (Boyd), 1852-1929 (Angel Hill Cemetery); wife of Samuel Lewis Russell, q.v.

Russell, Lillie A., age 16 in 1889 (Marriage License Applications Book ALJ No. 2, 1889)

Russell, Margaret, see Mae McCann, Francis C. Thompson and Isaac W. Thompson, q.v.

Russell, Martha E., 1872-1913 (Darlington Cemetery)

Russell, Martin, see Harvey Russell, q.v.

Russell, Mary A., 1860-1949, native of Harford Furnace, Harford Co., born 27 Oct 1860, daughter of David Russell, of Ireland, and Mary Cross (Pennington Funeral Home Records)

Russell, Mary Emma, 1847-1916 (Angel Hill Cemetery)

Russell, Mary R., see Mary R. Price, q.v.

Russell, Raymond, 1875-1918 (Darlington Cemetery)

Russell, Richard, native of Ireland, naturalized on 12 May 1890 Harford County Circuit Court Minute Book ALJ No. 5, p. 243)

Russell, Sallie (Miss), second vice president, Women's Christian Temperance Union, of Havre de Grace (*Havre de Grace Republican*, 19 Sep 1890)

Russell, Sallie E., 1890-1919 (Angel Hill Cemetery)

Russell, Samuel Lewis, 1851-1940 (Angel Hill Cemetery); see John Alfred Russell and Steel Russell, q.v.

Russell, Sarah Susanna "Susie" (Mrs.), 1853-1915 (Angel Hill Cemetery); teacher, Edgewood School No. 7, First District (*The Aegis & Intelligencer*, 29 Aug 1890)

Russell, Steel, 1880-1958, native of Maryland, born 27 Jan 1880, daughter of S. Lewis Russell and Julia J. Boyd (Pennington Funeral Home Records - married name Barnes)

Russell, Susanna (Shade), c1851-1918 (Holy Trinity Episcopal Church Cemetery)

Russell, Thomas, see Valley H. Russell, q.v.

Russell, Valley H., 1888-1947 (Rock Run Methodist Church Cemetery); native of Harford Co., born 10 Jun 1888, son of Thomas Russell and ---- (Bailey Funeral Home Records)

Russell, William T., 1854-1931 (St. George's Episcopal Church Cemetery)

Ruth, Bessie M., 1889-1959 (Centre Methodist Church Cemetery)

Ruth, Charles W., of Churchville, son of the late Mrs. Elizabeth Ruth (*The Aegis & Intelligencer*, 31 Jan 1890 and 7 Feb 1890); see Elizabeth Ruth, q.v.

Ruth, Elizabeth, 1823-1890 (Rock Run Methodist Church Cemetery); widow of J. Wesley Ruth (*The Aegis & Intelligencer*, 31 Jan 1890); died testate and her heirs were sons John A. Ruth, William E. Ruth, Charles W. Ruth and James H. Ruth, and daughters Martha Ann Ruth, Emma Jane Ruth, and Sarah Rosena [Rowena?] Ruth (Harford County Will Book JMM 11:79-80)

Ruth, Emma Jane, daughter of the late Mrs. Elizabeth Ruth (*The Aegis & Intelligencer*, 31 Jan 1890 and 7 Feb 1890); see Elizabeth Ruth, q.v.

Ruth, J. Wesley, see Elizabeth Ruth, q.v.

Ruth, James H., of California, son of the late Mrs. Elizabeth Ruth (*The Aegis & Intelligencer*, 31 Jan 1890 and 7 Feb 1890); see Elizabeth Ruth, q.v.

Ruth, John A., of the Dakotas, son of the late Mrs. Elizabeth Ruth (*The Aegis & Intelligencer*, 31 Jan 1890 and 7 Feb 1890); see Elizabeth Ruth, q.v.

Ruth, Martha Ann ("Mattie"), daughter of the late Mrs. Elizabeth Ruth (*The Aegis & Intelligencer*, 7 Feb 1890); see Elizabeth Ruth, q.v.

Ruth, Sarah Rowena [Rosena?], daughter of the late Mrs. Elizabeth Ruth (*The Aegis & Intelligencer*, 7 Feb 1890); see Elizabeth Ruth, q.v.

Ruth, William E., of Churcvhille, son of the late Mrs. Elizabeth Ruth (*The Aegis & Intelligencer*, 31 Jan 1890 and 7 Feb 1890); see Elizabeth Ruth, q.v.

Rutledge's General Store, at Rocks, Charles A. Rutledge, prop., and Joshua N. Rutledge, mgr. (*Country Stores: Harford County's Rural Heritage*, by Henry C. Peden, Jr. and Jack L. Shagena, Jr., 2015, p. 219)

Rutledge's Grist Mill and Saw Mill, Upper Cross Roads, Charles A. Rutledge, prop. (*Mills: Grist, Saw, Bone, Flint, Fulling ... & More*, by Jack L. Shagena, Jr., Henry C. Peden, Jr. and John W. McGrain, 2009, p. 248)

Rutledge's Public School No. 5, Fourth District (*Harford County, Maryland Teachers and the Schools They Served, 1774-1900*, by Henry C. Peden, Jr., 2022, p. 372)

Rutledge, Abraham, see Ariel Rutledge, q.v.

Rutledge, Alice (Miss), 1857-1930 (Highland Presbyterian Church Cemetery)

Rutledge, Ariel, died 12 Sep 1890, age 75 (Bethel Presbyterian Church Cemetery Records); resident of near Federal Hill, widow of Major Abraham Rutledge (*The Aegis & Intelligencer*, 19 Sep 1890)

Rutledge, Bertha, born 8 Mar 1877, daughter of William and Catherine Rutledge (Jacob Rutledge Bible, *Maryland Bible Records, Volume 2*, by Henry C. Peden, Jr., 2003, p. 120)

Rutledge, Caroline Virginia ("Carrie"), died 18 Sep 1890, age not stated (Christ Episcopal Church Cemetery); daughter of the late Ignatius Rutledge, sister of Joshua Rutledge, of Rocks, and sister-in-law of Robert W. Holland, of Bel Air (*The Aegis & Intelligencer*, 29 Aug 1890 and 19 Sep 1890); died testate and her named heirs were nieces Joanna R. Holland and Mary R. Holland (Harford County Will Book JMM 11:151-152)

Rutledge, Carrie E., age 18 in 1889 (Marriage License Applications Book ALJ No. 2, 1890), of Norrisville, sister of Laban Rutledge, married John Duncan on 8 Jan 1890 (*The Aegis & Intelligencer*, 17 Jan 1890)

Rutledge, Catherine Hope (Nelson), 1831-1899 (Bethel Presbyterian Church Cemetery Records); first wife of William S. Rutledge, q.v.

Rutledge, Charles Abraham (M.D.), 1840-1924 (St. James Episcopal Church Cemetery); native of Harford Co., married, resided at Rutledge (Death certificate); physician and postmaster at The Rocks (*Havre de Grace Republican*, 18 Apr 1890); canner, Chrome Hill (*Havre de Grace Republican*, 5 Sep 1890); vestryman, Christ Church, Rock Spring (*Havre de Grace Republican*, 18 Apr 1890); see Rutledge's General Store and Rutledge's Grist Mill and Saw Mill, q.v.

Rutledge, Cynthia (Miss), 1820-1904 (Bethel Presbyterian Church Cemetery Records)

Rutledge, Edward, born -- Nov 1886, son of William and Catherine Rutledge (Jacob Rutledge Bible, *Maryland Bible Records, Volume 2*, by Henry C. Peden, Jr., 2003, p. 120)

Rutledge, Edward H., 1828-1900 (Providence Methodist Church Cemetery)

Rutledge, Edward R., 1852-1914 (Providence Methodist Church Cemetery); E. R. Rutledge, and wife, sold land in August 1890 (*The Aegis & Intelligencer*, 12 Sep 1890)

Rutledge, Emma, born 18 Dec 1878, daughter of William and Catherine Rutledge (Jacob Rutledge Bible, *Maryland Bible Records, Volume 2*, by Henry C. Peden, Jr., 2003, p. 120); see Emma R. Streett, q.v.

Rutledge, Emma L., see Laban L. Rutledge, q.v.

Rutledge, Ethel, died in 1890, age not stated (Fellowship Church Cemetery)

Rutledge, Ignatius, see Caroline Virginia Rutledge, q.v.

Rutledge, Irene Blanche, 1878-1916 (Norrisville Methodist Church Cemetery)

Rutledge, Jacob, 1816-1895 (Bethel Presbyterian Church Cemetery Records)

Rutledge, Jacob Franklin, born 8 Jul 1881, twin of William Horatio Rutledge, sons of William and Catherine (Nelson) Rutledge (Jacob Rutledge Bible, *Maryland Bible Records, Volume 2*, by Henry C. Peden, Jr., 2003, p. 120)

Rutledge, Jesse Pocock, 1840-1922 (Norrisville Methodist Church Cemetery)

Rutledge, John Joshua, born 29 Oct 1873, son of William and Catherine (Nelson) Rutledge (Jacob Rutledge Bible, *Maryland Bible Records, Volume 2*, by Henry C. Peden, Jr., 2003, p. 120)

Rutledge, John Randolph, 1834-1925 (St. James Episcopal Church Cemetery, Monkton, Baltimore County); delegate, Fourth District, Democrat Party Convention (*The Aegis & Intelligencer*, 5 Sep 1890); farmer in Rutledge area of Upper Cross Roads and Civil War (Confederate) veteran (*Biographical Dictionary of Harford County, Maryland, 1774-1974*, by Henry C. Peden, Jr. and William O. Carr, 2021, p. 235; *1890 Special Census of the Civil War Veterans of the State of Maryland*, by L. Tilden Moore, Volume III, p. 77)

Rutledge, Joshua, 1825-1892 (Christ Episcopal Church Cemetery); dairyman (*Harford Democrat*, 14 Feb 1890); see Caroline Virginia Rutledge, q.v.

Rutledge, Joshua Nelson, 1843-1921, native of Harford Co., single (Death certificate); see Rutledge's General Store, q.v.

Rutledge, Laban L., age 22 in 1890, married Emma L. Rutledge (Marriage License Applications Book ALJ No. 2, 1890); also see Carrie E. Rutledge and John Duncan, q.v.

Rutledge, Lida (St. Clair), 1885-1933 (Bethel Presbyterian Church Cemetery Records)

Rutledge, Lillian, born 1 Mar 1883 or 1885, daughter of William and Catherine Rutledge (Jacob Rutledge Bible, *Maryland Bible Records, Volume 2*, by Henry C. Peden, Jr., 2003, p. 120)

Rutledge, Martha J., acquired land in February 1890 (*The Aegis & Intelligencer*, 7 Mar 1890)

Rutledge, Mary (Bevard), 1860-1943 (Bethel Presbyterian Church Cemetery Records); second wife of William S. Rutledge, q.v.

Rutledge, Mary Elizabeth (Famous), 1869-1945 (Highland Presbyterian Church Cemetery); wife of Nicholas N. Rutledge, q.v.

Rutledge, Mary Virginia ("Mollie"), c1865-1933 (Forest Lawn Cemetery, Norfolk, VA); teacher, Dry Branch School No. 2, Fourth District (*The Aegis & Intelligencer*, 29 Aug 1890)

Rutledge, Mattie R., 1857-1897 (Providence Methodist Church Cemetery)

Rutledge, Melissa A. (Lowe), 1842-1913 (Norrisville Methodist Church Cemetery)

Rutledge, Monica A., sold land in February 1890 (*The Aegis & Intelligencer*, 7 Mar 1890)

Rutledge, Nicholas Nelson, 1852-1938 (Highland Presbyterian Church Cemetery)

Rutledge, Patrick Henry, 1830-1902, attorney-at-law in Bel Air and former State's Attorney (*Biographical Dictionary of Harford County, Maryland, 1774-1974*, by Henry C. Peden, Jr. and William O. Carr, 2021, p. 235)

Rutledge, Pearler, born 22 Aug 1888, son of William and Catherine Rutledge (Jacob Rutledge Bible, *Maryland Bible Records, Volume 2*, by Henry C. Peden, Jr., 2003, p. 120; Bethel Presbyterian Church Cemetery)

Rutledge, Phebe S., 1836-1901 (Christ Episcopal Church Cemetery)

Rutledge, Talbot, 10 Feb 1890 - 3 May 1890, son of William and Catherine Rutledge (Jacob Rutledge Bible, *Maryland Bible Records, Volume 2*, by Henry C. Peden, Jr., 2003, p. 120; Bethel Presbyterian Church Cemetery)

Rutledge, Virginia, born 10 Apr 1875, daughter of William and Catherine (Nelson) Rutledge (Jacob Rutledge Bible, *Maryland Bible Records, Volume 2*, by Henry C. Peden, Jr., 2003, p. 120; Bethel Presbyterian Church Cemetery Records); see Virginia Bevard q.v.

Rutledge, William, see Bertha Rutledge, Edward Rutledge, Emma Rutledge John Joshua Rutledge, Jacob Franklin Rutledge, Lillian Rutledge, Pearler Rutledge and Talbot Rutledge, q.v.

Rutledge, William Horatio, born 8 Jul 1881, twin of Jacob Franklin Rutledge, sons of William and Catherine (Nelson) Rutledge (Jacob Rutledge Bible, *Maryland Bible Records, Volume 2*, by Henry C. Peden, Jr., 2003, p. 120)

Rutledge, William S., 1846-1927 (Bethel Presbyterian Church Cemetery Records); trustee, Madonna School No. 9, Fourth District, 1890 (*Havre de Grace Republican*, 30 May 1890)

Rutter, Jonathan, 1856-1942 (Death certificate; Alms House Record Book)

Ryan, Ann Marie, 1847-1933 (Baker Cemetery)

Ryan, Charles C., 1844-1901 (Baker Cemetery)

Ryan, Florence E., 1870-1942 (Fallston Methodist Church Cemetery)

Ryan, Howard W., 1890-1979 (Fallston Methodist Church Cemetery)

Ryan, John, see Mary Virginia Ryan, q.v.

Ryan, Laura, see Mary Virginia Ryan, q.v.

Ryan, Martin, age 30 in 1889 (Marriage License Applications Book ALJ No. 2, 1890); son of Martin Ryan, married Margaret May "Maggie" Anderson on 11 Feb 1890 (St. Ignatius Catholic Church Marriage Register, p. 18; *The Aegis & Intelligencer*, 7 Mar 1890)

Ryan, Mary Virginia, born 23 Jul 1886, daughter of John and Laura Ryan (St. George's Episcopal Church Register of Baptisms, p. 6)

Ryan, Robert, 1871-1932 (Baker Cemetery)

Ryan, Robert, 1881-1961 (Cokesbury Memorial Methodist Church Cemetery)

Ryland, Elizabeth, 1876-1961 (Ebenezer Methodist Church Cemetery)

Ryland, James L., 1879-1947 (Ebenezer Methodist Church Cemetery)

S. J. Seneca, canned goods, Havre de Grace (*Heavy Industries of Yesteryear; Harford County's Rural Heritage*, by Jack L. Shagena, Jr. and Henry C. Peden, Jr., 2015, pp. 33-37)

Sadlazk, Barbara, see John J. Dudeck, q.v.

Sadler, Caroline "Carrie" (Roussey), 1855-1924 (Bailey Funeral Home Records)

Sadler, Clarence, 1886-1961 (Dublin Cemetery); native of Harford Co., born 9 Jun 1886, son of John H. Sadler and Catherine Roussey (Bailey Funeral Home Records)

Sadler, Elizabeth V. (Bussey), 1870-1924 (Hickory *(sic)* Cemetery); native of Maryland, born 25 Nov 1870, daughter of Benedict Bussey and Martha E. O'Donald (Bailey Funeral Home Records)

Sadler, Evans E., 1865-1945 (Darlington Cemetery)

Sadler, George S., 1882-1964 (Dublin Southern Cemetery)

Sadler, John Henry, 1854-1943 (Dublin Cemetery); see Clarence Sadler, q.v.

Sadler, Margareta (pr Margaret A.), 1851-1921 (Angel Hill Cemetery)

Sadler, Maria P. (Robinson), 1853-1924 (Darlington Cemetery)

Sadler, Sarah, see George T. Creswell, q.v.

Sadler, Thomas, Jr., 1834-1917 (Angel Hill Cemetery); director, First National Bank of Havre de Grace (*Havre de Grace Republican*, 17 Jan 1890); Thomas Sadler, businessman (trader's license), Havre de Grace (*Havre de Grace Republican*, 30 May 1890)

Sadler, William E., born 1890, died ---- (Emory Methodist Church Cemetery)

Sadler, William Edward, age 21 in 1890 (Marriage License Applications Book ALJ No. 2, 1890; Holy Trinity Episcopal Church Register of Marriages, p. 216)

Sadler, William H., Civil War veteran, Allibone (*1890 Special Census of the Civil War Veterans of the State of Maryland*, by L. Tilden Moore, Volume III, p. 86)

Sadtler, C., pitcher, Creswell Baseball Club (*The Aegis & Intelligencer*, 18 Jul 1890)

Salada, Mrs., daughter of James Devlin, q.v.

Salem Church of the Evangelical Association (Norrisville Road, near Jarrettsville)

Salick, Annie E., 1880-1927 (Angel Hill Cemetery)

Salick, Catherine, 1873-1915 (Angel Hill Cemetery)

Salick, Charles, 1881-1932, native of Havre de Grace, son of Conrad Salick and ----, natives of Germany (Death certificate)

Salick, Frederick ("Freddie"), 1876-1902 (Death certificate spelled his name Salix)

Salick, James J., 1868-1930 (Angel Hill Cemetery); James Salicks, sneak boat duck hunter, 1890 (*Havre de Grace Republican*, 7 Nov 1890)

Salik, John C., 1840-1904 (Angel Hill Cemetery)

Sallada, Mary A. (Devlin), 1864-1928 (St. Ignatius Catholic Church Cemetery); native of Maryland, resided at Bel Air (Death certificate)

Salsberry, James T. (colored), widower, age 32 in 1890 (Marriage License Applications Book ALJ No. 2, 1890, incomplete, apparently never issued)

Salvation Army, Havre de Grace Post (*Havre de Grace Republican*, 11 Jul 1890)

Sample, George W., 1883-1918 (Angel Hill Cemetery)

Sample, James B., 1844-1920 (Angel Hill Cemetery); Civil War veteran, Line Bridge (*1890 Special Census of the Civil War Veterans of the State of Maryland*, by L. Tilden Moore, Volume III, p. 87)

Samples, Lucinda B. (Banks) (colored), 1872-1919, native of Churchville, daughter of George Banks and Julia Cooper (Death certificate)

Sampson, Dora B., see Dora B. Judd, q.v.

Sampson, Eliza J. (Cantler), 1869-1947, native of Harford Co. (Bailey Funeral Home Records); wife of Samuel F. Sampson, q.v.

Sampson, Ellen E. (Singleton), 1859-1938 (Rock Run Methodist Church Cemetery)

Sampson, Florence, see Florence Smith, q.v.

Sampson, Frances A., 1886-1960, native of Harford Co., born 30 Sep 1886, daughter of Wesley Sampson and ---- (Pennington Funeral Home Records - married name Cullum)

Sampson, George Oliver, 1877-1940 (Rock Run Methodist Church Cemetery); native of Hopewell, Harford Co., born 2 Mar 1877, son of George Foard and Mary Sampson (Bailey Funeral Home Records)

Sampson, Hannah Elizabeth, see Naomi C. Walstrum, q.v.

Sampson, James, see Dora B. Judd, q.v.

Sampson, JoAnn, see Eva L. Knight, q.v.

Sampson, John A., see Florence Sampson, q.v.

Sampson, Marguerite H., 1889-1974 (Angel Hill Cemetery)

Sampson, Mary, see Sallie Evans, q.v.

Sampson, Mary E., see Howard W. Orr, q.v.

Sampson, Richard W., 1887-1961 (Angel Hill Cemetery)

Sampson, Robert Wesley, 1860-1932 (Rock Run Methodist Church Cemetery)

Sampson, Samuel F., 1861-1953 (Tabernacle Cemetery)

Sampson, Walter C., 1877-1945 (Rock Run Methodist Church Cemetery)

Sampson, Wesley R., 1864-1932 (Rock Run Methodist Church Cemetery); see Frances A. Cullum, q.v.

San Domingo Mill, Glen Cove (*Mills: Grist, Saw, Bone, Flint, Fulling ... & More*, by Jack L. Shagena, Jr., Henry C. Peden, Jr. and John W. McGrain, 2009, p. 249)

Sanders, Carrie S., see Carrie S. Jenness, q.v.

Sanders. Charles H., 1869-1925 (Fellowship Church Cemetery)

Sanders, Clara May, 1873-1960, daughter of Thomas E. Sanders and Mary S. Amos (Bethel Presbyterian Church Cemetery Records)

Sanders, Donald B., 1879-1961 (Angel Hill Cemetery)

Sanders, Edward A., age 21 in 1889 (Marriage License Applications Book ALJ No. 2, 1889)

Sanders, Elmer, 1878-1897 (Rock Run Methodist Church Cemetery)

Sanders, Francis, 1816-1908 (Mountain Christian Church Cemetery)

Sanders, George R., 1852-1938 (Fellowship Church Cemetery)

Sanders, Georgenna (Hamilton), 1850-1891 (Rock Run Methodist Church Cemetery); wife of William Sanders (1829-1915), q.v.

Sanders, Hannah, see Hannah E. Huff, Carrie S. Jenness. Grover C. Snodgrass, Sarah Snodgrass, Edmund Snodgrass and Mary F. Webster, q.v.

Sanders, Hannah Elizabeth, age 18 in 1890 (Marriage License Applications Book ALJ No. 2, 1890), married William R. Loving, of Baltimore County, on 20 May 1890 at Jarrettsville (*The Aegis & Intelligencer*, 30 May 1890)

Sanders, Harry F., 1890-1963 (Centre Methodist Church Cemetery)

Sanders, Henry, 1803-1890 (Centre Methodist Church Cemetery)

Sanders, India E., 1880-1970 (Angel Hill Cemetery)

Sanders, Isaac, 1838-1917 (Death certificate; Alms House Record Book)

Sanders, Lizzie, see William Lovel, q.v.

Sanders, Margaret A., 1874-1941 (Angel Hill Cemetery)

Sanders, Mary J., 1851-1922 (Fellowship Church Cemetery)

Sanders, Mary Susan (Amos), 1849-1903 (Bethel Presbyterian Church Cemetery Records)

Sanders, Rosa M., 1876-1945 (Fellowship Church Cemetery)

Sanders, Thomas C., 1873-1924 (Angel Hill Cemetery)

Sanders, Thomas W., 1845-1923 (Angel Hill Cemetery)

Sanders, William, 1812-1899, resident of Mill Green (Death certificate); county out-pensioner [welfare recipient], Fourth District (*Havre de Grace Republican*, 4 Jul 1890)

Sanders, William, 1829-1915 (Rock Run Methodist Church Cemetery)

Sanders, William Henry, c1870-1943 (Bethel Presbyterian Church Cemetery Records)

Sands, Annie (colored), age 19 in 1890 (Marriage License Applications Book ALJ No. 2, 1891)

Sands, John (colored), see Alice Lucinda Elizabeth Peaco (colored), q.v.

Sands, William (colored), age 31 in 1890 (Marriage License Applications Book ALJ No. 2, 1891)

Sanner, Basil P., 1843-1930 (Baker Cemetery)

Sanner, Cora D. (Owen), 1867-1941 (Baker Cemetery)

Sanner, Mary E., 1865-1947 (Baker Cemetery)

Sanner, George R. (Rev.), pastor of Darlington M. E. Church, Darlington (*The Aegis & Intelligencer*, 26 Sep 1890)

Santmyer, Clifford ("Cliff"), 1889-1967, native of Havre de Grace, born 17 Jun 1889, son of Millard Santmyer and Lydia Thompson (www.findagrave.com)

Santmyer, George W., 1827-1898 (Mt. Tabor Methodist Church Cemetery)

Santmyer, Hannah (Donovan), 1852-1940 (Angel Hill Cemetery); native of Ireland, resident of Havre de Grace (Death certificate); wife of Jefferson M. Santmyer, q.v.

Santmyer, Jefferson Marcella, 1849-1925, native of Maryland, resident of Havre de Grace (Death certificate; www.findagrave.com)

Santmyer, Lydia, see Clifford Santmyer and Neta Santmyer, q.v.

Santmyer, Mary Jane (Walker), 1886-1926 (Angel Hill Cemetery)

Santmyer, Millard, see Clifford Santmyer and Neta Santmyer, q.v.

Santmyer, Neta, 1884-1895, native of Havre de Grace, born -- Dec 1884, daughter of Millard F. Santmyer and Lydia ---- (*Havre de Grace Republican*, 23 Feb 1895)

Sappington, John, 1847-1905 (Darlington Cemetery); physician, Darlington (*The Aegis & Intelligencer*, 26 Sep 1890); trustee of the Darlington Academy (*Havre de Grace Republican*, 26 Sep 1890)

Sappington, Mary P. (Hays), 1851-1900 (Darlington Cemetery), wife of Dr. John Sappington, q.v.

Sappington, Nelson, actor, musical entertainment, at Darlington, 1890 (*The Aegis & Intelligencer*, 30 May 1890)

Sappington, W., jousting tournament herald, 1890 (*Havre de Grace Republican*, 19 Sep 1890)

Sarah Furnace Public School No. 22. Fourth District (*Harford County, Maryland Teachers and the Schools They Served, 1774-1900*, by Henry C. Peden, Jr., 2022, p. 372)

Sargable, Michael, Civil War veteran, Calvary (*1890 Special Census of the Civil War Veterans of the State of Maryland*, by L. Tilden Moore, Volume III, p. 70)

Saricks, Annie, student, Havre de Grace High School (*Havre de Grace Republican*, 31 Oct 1890, spelled her name Sarricks)

Saricks, John H., 1829-1914 (Mt. Erin Cemetery); businessman (liquor license), Havre de Grace (*Havre de Grace Republican*, 30 May 1890); vice president, Republican Club (*Havre de Grace Republican*, 7 Nov 1890); delegate, Sixth District, Republican Party Convention (*The Aegis & Intelligencer*, 26 Sep 1890); sneak boat duck hunter (*Havre de Grace Republican*, 7 Nov 1890)

Saulsbury, James T. (colored), age 33 in 1890 (Marriage License Applications Book ALJ No. 2, 1891)

Saunders Cafe, Bel Air, Theodore Saunders, prop. (*Bel Air: An Architectural and Cultural History, 1782-1945*, by Marilynn M. Larew, 1995, p. 81)

Saunders, Carrie, 1871-1963, native of Havre de Grace, born 5 Oct 1871, daughter of Wysong Saunders and Lourinda Johnson (Pennington Funeral Home Records - married name Poplar)

Saunders, Edward D., 1857-1934 (Angel Hill Cemetery); see Minnie Saunders and Ida Saunders, q.v.

Saunders, Elizabeth C., 1856-1935 (Angel Hill Cemetery)

Saunders, Henry (colored), see Samuel N. Saunders (colored), q.v.

Saunders, Ida, 1889-1972, native of Havre de Grace, born 3 Jun 1889, daughter of Edward D. Saunders and Elizabeth Walker (Pennington Funeral Home Records - married name Trumbo)

Saunders, J. C., assistant watchman, Willard Section No. 58, Cadets of Temperance, Havre de Grace (*Havre de Grace Republican*, 11 Jul 1890)

Saunders, Lillie A., 1873-1932 (Darlington Cemetery)

Saunders, Lorinda (Way), 1846-1901 (Angel Hill Cemetery); Lurinda Saundes, businesswoman (trader's license), Havre de Grace (*Havre de Grace Republican*, 30 May 1890); wife of Thomas Wysong Saunders, q.v.; also see Carrie Saunders, q.v.

Saunders, Margare A., 1874-1941 (Angel Hill Cemetery)

Saunders, Minnie, 1886-1979, native of Lapidum, Harford Co., born 3 Jan 1886, daughter of Edward D. Saunders and Elizabeth Walker (Pennington Funeral Home Records - married name Reyburn)

Saunders, Rosalie, see Violet Whitney, q.v.

Saunders, Samuel N. (Rev.) (colored), 1865-1928, native of Maryland, resident of Aberdeen, born 22 Feb 1865, son of Henry Saunders and ---- (Death certificate)

Saunders, Theodore P., prop., M. C. Restaurant, 317 N. Main St. near the depot, Bel Air (*Harford Democrat*, 31 Jan 1890); barber, Bel Air (*Bel Air: An Architectural and Cultural History, 1782-1945*, by Marilynn M. Larew, 1995, pp. 59, 216)

Saunders, Thomas Wysong, 1845-1923 (Angel Hill Cemetery); see Carrie Saunders, q.v.

Savin, Edward, 1844-1925 (Darlington Cemetery)

Savin, Mary A., see Patrick Chapman Savin, q.v.

Savin, Mary J., 1859-1933 (Darlington Cemetery)

Savin, Patrick Chapman, died testate in 1890 and wife Mary A. Savin was his only named heir (Harford County Will Book JMM 11:75-76)

Savin, Sarah, see Charles H. McNabb (MacNabb), q.v.

Sawyer, A. Octavia (Gilbert), 1854-1921, wife of William T. Sawyer (Mt. Carmel Methodist Church Cemetery); native of Maryland, resided near Bel Air (Death certificate)

Sawyer, Agnes (Miss), 1877-1937 (St. Mary's Episcopal Church Cemetery); honor student, Archer Institute, Bel Air (*The Aegis & Intelligencer*, 20 Jun 1890); premium award winner, Class L - Children's Department, Harford County Fair (*The Aegis & Intelligencer*, 24 Oct 1890)

Sawyer, Benjamin, 1819-1891 (Mt. Carmel Methodist Church Cemetery)

Sawyer, Bessie (Miss), resident of Emmorton (*Havre de Grace Republican*, 4 Jul 1890)

Sawyer, Edwin Lea, 1837-1901, native of Maryland, single, farmer at Benson (Death certificate; Mt. Carmel Methodist Church Cemetery)

Sawyer, Elizabeth C., 1872-1941 (St. Mary's Episcopal Church Cemetery)

Sawyer, Elizabeth E. B., 1839-1925 (St. Mary's Episcopal Church Cemetery)

Sawyer, Harry, 1874-1948 (St. Mary's Episcopal Church Cemetery); premium award winner, Class L - Children's Department, Harford County Fair, 1890 (*The Aegis & Intelligencer*, 24 Oct 1890)

Sawyer, John, 1833-1896 (St. Mary's Episcopal Church Cemetery); resident of Emmorton (*The Aegis & Intelligencer*, 29 Aug 1890); road examiner, First District (*Havre de Grace Republican*, 4 Jul 1890)

Sawyer, Mary M., 1825-1922 (Mt. Carmel Methodist Church Cemetery)

Sawyer, N. E., vice president, Republican Club (*Havre de Grace Republican*, 7 Nov 1890)

Sawyer, William Thomas, 1831-1908 (Mt. Carmel Methodist Church Cemetery); vice president of the Third

Annual Convention, Farmers' Club of Harford County (*Havre de Grace Republican*, 5 Dec 1890); vice president, Harford County Farmers' Association (*The Aegis & Intelligencer*, 17 Jan 1890); Mr. & Mrs. Sawyer, residents of Emmorton (*The Aegis & Intelligencer*, 1 Aug 1890); also see John Winkler, q.v.

Say, Louis, 1852-1930 (Heavenly Waters Cemetery)

Say, Matthew, 1858-1932 (Heavenly Waters Cemetery)

Scarboro (Scarborough), Calvin, farmer, near Prospect and Broad Creek (*The Aegis & Intelligencer*, 15 Aug 1890; *Harford Democrat*, 4 Apr 1890)

Scarboro, Georgia Rebecca, 1868-1941, daughter of Dr. Silas Scarboro (Scarborough) and Catherine Bishop; teacher, Mt. Pleasant School No. 11, Fifth District (*The Aegis & Intelligencer*, 29 Aug 1890; *Harford County, Maryland Teachers and the Schools They Served*, by Henry C. Peden, Jr., 2021, p. 277); age 22 in 1890 (Marriage License Applications Book ALJ No. 2, 1891); see Georgia Scarborough, q.v.

Scarboro, Silas (Dr.), 1827-1907 (Broad Creek Friends Cemetery); Civil War veteran, of Scarborough (*1890 Special Census of the Civil War Veterans of the State of Maryland*, by L. Tilden Moore, Volume III, p. 87)

Scarboro, William Hector, 1880-1905 (Mt. Zion Methodist Church Cemetery)

Scarborough's General Store, Deep Run, Andrew H. Scarborough, prop. (*Country Stores: Harford County's Rural Heritage*, by Henry C. Peden, Jr. and Jack L. Shagena, Jr., 2015, pp. 219-220)

Scarborough's General Store, Hurst's Corner near Cooptown, J. Oscar. Scarborough, prop. (*Country Stores: Harford County's Rural Heritage*, by Henry C. Peden, Jr. and Jack L. Shagena, Jr., 2015, pp. 221-222)

Scarborough's General Store, Magnolia, Josepha and Anna Scarborough, prop. (*Country Stores: Harford County's Rural Heritage*, by Henry C. Peden, Jr. and Jack L. Shagena, Jr., 2015, pp. 220-221)

Scarborough's Store, Prospect, J. Ross Scarborough, prop. (*Country Stores: Harford County's Rural Heritage*, by Henry C. Peden, Jr. and Jack L. Shagena, Jr., 2015, p. 221)

Scarborough's General Store, Scarboro, William J. Scarborough, prop. (*Country Stores: Harford County's Rural Heritage*, by Henry C. Peden, Jr. and Jack L. Shagena, Jr., 2015, p. 222)

Scarborough, A. Agnes, 1857-1896 (Church of the Ascension); Miss A. Scarborough, vice president, Ladies' Guild of Ascension P. E. Church, at Scarborough (*Havre de Grace Republican*, 30 May 1890)

Scarborough, Abigail H., 1819-1897, widow of Edward A. Scarborough (Broad Creek Friends Cemetery); A. H. Scarborough, superintendent, Vernon Methodist Church Sunday School (*The Aegis & Intelligencer*, 5 Sep 1890)

Scarborough, Alice S., 1875-1936 (Highland Presbyterian Church Cemetery)

Scarborough, Alithea, see J. Milton Warner, q.v.

Scarborough, Alverda G., 1846-1923 (Darlington Cemetery)

Scarborough, Amelia, see Elmer Scarborough, q.v.

Scarborough, Andrew, see Emmett L. Scarborough, O. O. Scarborough and Hugh S. Scarborough, q.v.

Scarborough, Ann Jane (Bailey), 1841-1919 (Church of the Ascension Cemetery); wife of Samuel Sedgewick Scarborough, q.v.

Scarborough, Anna, 1830-1910 (Broad Creek Friends Cemetery)

Scarborough, Anna E. (Scarborough), 1839-1925 (Church of the Ascension Cemetery); native of Maryland, resided at Scarboro (Death certificate); wife of Philip J. Scarborough, q.v.; also see Anna Rebecca Scarborough and Melvin Scarborough, q.v.

Scarborough, Anna Rebecca, 1870-1949 (Church of the Ascension Cemetery); native of Harford Co., resided near Street, born 11 Oct 1870, daughter of Philip J. Scarborough and Anna E. Scarborough (Death certificate; Bailey Funeral Home Records)

Scarborough, Annie Eliza, 1871-1903 (Centre Methodist Church Cemetery)

Scarborough, Archer, see Jacob Scarborough and Mary Emma Scarborough, q.v.

Scarborough, Asenath S. (Miss), 1863-1935, native of Scarboro, Harford Co. (Bailey Funeral Home Records);

premium award winner, Class J - Domestic Products, Harford County Fair (*The Aegis & Intelligencer*, 24 Oct 1890)

Scarborough, Aseph, canner, Fifth District (*Havre de Grace Republican*, 30 May 1890)

Scarborough, B. Wilson, see Susan Wallace, q.v.

Scarborough, Belle, 1858-1934 (Slate Ridge Cemetery, York Co., PA); native of Harford Co., born 3 Nov 1858, daughter of Franklin Scarborough, of Harford Co., and Frances Bulette, of York Co., PA (Harkins Funeral Home Records)

Scarborough, Belle Virginia (Heaps), 1847-1929 (Emory Methodist Church Cemetery); wife of Parker F. Scarborough, q.v.

Scarborough, Bertha, 1869-1955 (Darlington Cemetery, married name Shure); daughter of Dr. Silas Scarboro (Scarborough) and Catherine Bishop; teacher, Shure's Landing School No. 19, Fifth District (*The Aegis & Intelligencer*, 29 Aug 1890; (*Harford County, Maryland Teachers and the Schools They Served*, by Henry C. Peden, Jr., 2021, p. 276)

Scarborough, Bessie Belle, born 20 Jan 1879, daughter of John and Viola Scarborough (John May Scarborough Bible, *Maryland Bible Records, Volume 2*, by Henry C. Peden, Jr., 2003, p. 124)

Scarborough, Bessie E. (Kelly), 1881-1959 (Dublin Methodist Church Cemetery); native of Thomas Run, Harford Co., born 14 Aug 1881, daughter of Andrew Kelly and Annie Crowl (Harkins Funeral Home Records)

Scarborough, Carrie Jane (Miss), 1871-1957 (Church of the Ascension Cemetery, married name Thomas); daughter of Samuel Sedgewick Scarborough and Ann Jane Bailey; teacher, Chestnut Hill School (*The Aegis & Intelligencer*, 4 Jul 1890; *Harford County, Maryland Teachers and the Schools They Served*, by Henry C. Peden, Jr., 2021, p. 276); secretary, Ladies' Guild of Ascension P. E. Church, at Scarborough (*Havre de Grace Republican*, 30 May 1890)

Scarborough, Catherine M. (Miss), 1845-1925 (Emory Methodist Church Cemetery)

Scarborough, Celia, see Luella Cunningham, q.v.

Scarborough, Clara (Thomas), 1854-1927 (Slate Ridge Cemetery, York Co., PA); wife of William Dallas Scarborough, q.v.

Scarborough, Clarence P., 888-1966 (Slate Ridge Cemetery, York Co., PA); native of Prospect, Harford Co., born 26 May 1888, son of J. Ross Scarborough and wife Mary Parke (Harkins Funeral Home Records)

Scarborough, Columbus, county out-pensioner [welfare recipient], Fifth District (*Havre de Grace Republican*, 4 Jul 1890); see Mary E. Scarborough, q.v.

Scarborough, Cora (Thomas), 1877-1947 (Church of the Ascension Cemetery); native of Harford Co., born 30 Jan 1877, daughter of Delma Thomas and Sarah England (Bailey Funeral Home Records)

Scarborough, David, see Eldridge E. Scarborough, q.v.

Scarborough, E. Pinkney, 1884-1936 (Mt. Zion Methodist Church Cemetery)

Scarborough, Edith Anna (Fantom), 1868-1959 (Church of the Ascension Cemetery); native of Bucks Co., PA (Bailey Funeral Home Records); wife of Frederick Scarborough, q.v.

Scarborough, Edmund, 1829-1903 (Old Brick Baptist Church Cemetery)

Scarborough, Edwin W., 1856-1939 (Old Brick Baptist Church Cemetery)

Scarborough, Eldridge E., 1873-1935 (Pine Grove Church Cemetery); native of Harford Co., born 3 Aug 1873, son of David Scarborough and Margaret Thompson (Harkins Funeral Home Records)

Scarborough, Elizabeth (Mrs.), 1807-1893 (Dublin Southern Cemetery); resident of Greenstone, age 83 in 1890, born 10 Sep 1807 (*The Aegis & Intelligencer*, 19 Sep 1890)

Scarborough, Elizabeth (Ingham), 1817-1902 (Broad Creek Friends Cemetery)

Scarborough, Elizabeth A., 1840-1894 (Church of the Ascension Cemetery); see Joseph Josiah Scarborough, q.v.

Scarborough, Ellis W., 1862-1944 (Highland Presbyterian Church Cemetery)

Scarborough, Elmer, died 14 Feb 1890, age 22, second son of Samuel J. and Amelia Scarborough, of near Prospect (*The Aegis & Intelligencer*, 21 Feb 1890)

Scarborough, Emma, 1867-1929 (Emory Methodist Church Cemetery)

Scarborough, Emmett L., 1890-1962 (Slate Ridge Cemetery, York Co., PA); native of Whiteford, Harford Co., born 22 Jan 1890, son of Andrew Scarborough and Martha Scarborough (Harkins Funeral Home Records)

Scarborough, Eva O. (Tucker), 1873-1952 (Centre Methodist Church Cemetery)

Scarborough, Flora Elva, born 16 Oct 1876, daughter of John and Viola Scarborough (John May Scarborough Bible, *Maryland Bible Records, Volume 2*, by Henry C. Peden, Jr., 2003, p. 124)

Scarborough, Frances (Bulette), 1824-1916, wife of Franklin C. Scarborough, married second to Elisha England (*Ancestral Charts, Volume 4*, Harford County Genealogical Society, 1988, p. 204); see Hannah Jennie Scarborough and Belle Scarborough, q.v.

Scarborough, Frances E. (Fantom), 1865-1952 (Darlington Cemetery; Bailey Funeral Home Records); wife of Harold Scarborough, q.v.

Scarborough, Franklin, see Hannah Jennie Scarborough and Belle Scarborough, q.v.

Scarborough, Franklin Ross, born 16 Oct 1875, son of John and Viola Scarborough (John May Scarborough Bible, *Maryland Bible Records, Volume 2*, by Henry C. Peden, Jr., 2003, p. 124)

Scarborough, Frederick, 1863-1936 (Church of the Ascension Cemetery); carpenter, native of Harford Co., son of Samuel Scarborough and Jane Bailey (Bailey Funeral Home Records); resident near Scarborough P. O. (*The Aegis & Intelligencer*, 31 Oct 1890); trustee, Union Cross Roads School No. 12, Fifth District (*Havre de Grace Republican*, 30 May 1890)

Scarborough, George Washington, 1834-1908 (Broad Creek Friends Cemetery); trustee, Broad Creek School No. 8, Fifth District (*Havre de Grace Republican*, 30 May 1890)

Scarborough, Georgia (Miss), teacher at Public School No. 11, Mill Green (*Havre de Grace Republican*, 4 Apr 1890); see Georgia Scarboro, q.v.

Scarborough, Goldsbur, 1879-1892, son of H. H. and S. E. Scarborough (Broad Creek Friends Cemetery)

Scarborough, Grace L. (Kelly), 1879-1972 (Darlington Cemetery); native of Harford Co., born 9 Sep 1879, daughter of Robert A. Kelly and Annie C. Crowl (Harkins Funeral Home Records)

Scarborough, Guy Wilson, born 22 Nov 1884, son of John May Scarborough and Viola Cecelia Malone (*Ancestral Charts, Volume 4*, Harford County Genealogical Society, 1988, p. 204; John May Scarborough Bible, *Maryland Bible Records, Volume 2*, by Henry C. Peden, Jr., 2003, p. 124)

Scarborough, H. Clinton, 1876-1964 (Darlington Cemetery); native of Darlington, Harford Co., born 26 Dec 1876, son of Harmon H. Scarborough and Sarah Groscup (Harkins Funeral Home Records)

Scarborough, Hamilton Y., 1880-1946 (Rock Run Methodist Church Cemetery)

Scarborough, Hannah E., 1856-1917 (Broad Creek Friends Cemetery); wife of Milton E. Scarborough, q.v.

Scarborough, Hannah Jennie, 1861-1943 (Slate Ridge Cemetery, York Co., PA, married name McNabb); daughter of Franklin and Frances Scarborough; teacher, Rock Hill School No. 3, Fifth District, 1890 (*The Aegis & Intelligencer*, 29 Aug 1890; *Harford County, Maryland Teachers and the Schools They Served*, by Henry C. Peden, Jr., 2021, p. 278)

Scarborough, Harmon Hezekiah, 1843-1925 (Darlington Cemetery); see H. Clinton Scarborough, q.v.

Scarborough, Harold, 1861-1944 (Darlington Cemetery); sold land in February 1890 (*The Aegis & Intelligencer*, 7 Mar 1890, spelled the name Scarboro)

Scarborough, Harry, student, Macton School (*The Aegis & Intelligencer*, 4 Jul 1890)

Scarborough, Henrietta, see Ella R. Love, q.v.

Scarborough, Henry S., see Joseph Josiah Scarborough, q.v.

Scarborough, Hester (Bailey), 1849-1924 (Broad Creek Friends Cemetery)

Scarborough, Howard W., 1869-1923 (Church of the Ascension Cemetery)

Scarborough, Hugh S., 1877-1924 (Rock Run Methodist Church Cemetery); native of Harford Co., born 13 Jul 1877, son of Andrew H. Scarborough and Martha J. Scarborough (Bailey Funeral Home Records)

Scarborough, Ida M. (Day), 1874-1970 (Slate Ridge Cemetery, York Co., PA); native of Harford Co., born 28 May 1874, daughter of George Washington Day and Mary Louisa Stokes (Harkins Funeral Home Records)

Scarborough, J. Oscar, storekeeper, Chrome Hill (*The Aegis & Intelligencer*, 8 Aug 1890); see Scarborough's General Store, q.v.

Scarborough, Jacob, 1872-1900, farmer, native of Maryland, resided at Scarboro, son of Archer Scarborough and Mary ---- (Death certificate)

Scarborough, James Ross, 1858-1941 (Slate Ridge Cemetery, York Co., PA); trustee, Mt. Vernon School No. 4, Fifth District); see Clarence P. Scarborough. R. Marshall Scarborough and N. Maxwell Scarborough, q.v.

Scarborough, Jason H., 1844-1926 (Church of the Ascension Cemetery); native of Maryland, carpenter, married, resided at Fountain Green (Death certificate)

Scarborough, John Barclay, 1835-1909 (Emory Methodist Church Cemetery); teacher and minister, of Mill Green and Dublin; teacher, Dublin School No. 13, Fifth District; Bible class teacher, Dublin M E. Church Sunday School (*Havre de Grace Republican*, 18 Apr 1890; *The Aegis & Intelligencer*, 9 May 1890 and 29 Aug 1890; *Havre de Grace Republican*, 30 May 1890; *Harford County, Maryland Teachers and the Schools They Served*, by Henry C. Peden, Jr., 2021, pp. 280-281)

Scarborough, John Barclay, Jr., resident of Scarborough (*The Aegis & Intelligencer*, 15 Aug 1890)

Scarborough, John C., see Russell K. Scarborough, q.v.

Scarborough, John May, juror, Fifth District (*Havre de Grace Republican*, 2 May 1890 spelled the name Scarboro); see Guy Wilson Scarborough, q.v.

Scarborough, Joseph, merchant, Magnolia (*Havre de Grace Republican*, 4 Jul 1890); storekeeper, Four Corners, Philadelphia Road, Magnolia Cross Roads (*The Aegis & Intelligencer*, 4 Jul 1890; *Harford Democrat*, 4 Jul 1890)

Scarborough, Joseph, student, School No. 11, Fifth District (*The Aegis & Intelligencer*, 18 Apr 1890)

Scarborough, Joseph Harvey, 1866-1955 (Churchville Presbyterian Cemetery)

Scarborough, Joseph W., 1871-1852 (Church of the Ascension)

Scarborough, Josiah Joseph, 1885-1894 (St. Ignatius Catholic Church Cemetery); born 8 Feb 1885, baptized 27 Feb 1885, son of Henry S. and Elizabeth A. (Sapp) Scarborough (St. Ignatius Catholic Church Baptism Register, p. 77)

Scarborough, Julia A., 1826-1897 (Emory Methodist Church Cemetery)

Scarborough, L. Catherine, 1887-1958 (Rock Run Methodist Church Cemetery)

Scarborough, Lawrence C., Sr., 1877-1950 (Mt. Zion Methodist Church Cemetery)

Scarborough, Lemuel, see Winifred H. Carr, q.v.

Scarborough, Lester Guy, 1888-1982 (Church of the Ascension Cemetery)

Scarborough, Lewis F., resided near Scarborough and Mill Green, house burned down (*The Aegis & Intelligencer*, 4 Apr 1890; *Harford Democrat,* 11 Apr 1890)

Scarborough, Louise, see Julia Ann Wallace, q.v.

Scarborough, Lucy M. (Mrs.), born 1881, died ---- (Mt. Zion Methodist Church Cemetery)

Scarborough, Luella, 1865-1922 (Church of the Ascension Cemetery); daughter of Philip J. Scarborough and Ann Elizabeth Scarborough (Bailey Funeral Home Records); premium award winner, Class J - Domestic Products, Harford County Fair (*The Aegis & Intelligencer*, 24 Oct 1890, spelled the name Scarboro)

Scarborough, Lydia, see Ella Bailey, q.v.

Scarborough, Lydia Forwood (Carr), 1830-1911 (Death certificate; Church of the Ascension Cemetery footstone, no tombstone)

Scarborough, Maggie A., age 25 in 1889 (Marriage License Applications Book ALJ No. 2, 1889)

Scarborough, Mamie (Mrs.), recording secretary, Mill Green Women's Christian Temperance Union (*Havre de Grace Republican*, 28 Mar 1890)

Scarborough, Martha, wife of Andrew Scarborough; see Emmett L. Scarborough and O. O. Scarborough, q.v.

Scarborough, Martha A., 1840-1916 (Emory Methodist Church Cemetery)

Scarborough, Martha A., 1854-1938 (Dublin Methodist Church Cemetery)

Scarborough, Martha J., see Hugh S. Scarborough, q.v.

Scarborough, Mary (Scarborough), 1861-1924 (Church of the Ascension Cemetery); Mrs. William H. Scarborough, treasurer, Ladies' Guild of Ascension P. E. Church, at Scarborough (*Havre de Grace Republican*, 30 May 1890)

Scarborough, Mary (Windsor), 1868-1926 (Woodlawn Cemetery, Baltimore); native of Maryland, resided at Mill Green (Death certificate)

Scarborough, Mary A. (McGonigall), c1868-1935 (Churchville Presbyterian Church Cemetery; The Aegis, 11 Jan 1935); wife of Joseph Havey Scarborough, q.v.

Scarborough, Mary Anna, married Harvey Jones on 2 Dec 1890 (*The Aegis & Intelligencer*, 26 Dec 1890)

Scarborough, Mary E., 1844-1928 (Broad Creek Friends Cemetery)

Scarborough, Mary Emma, 1872-1939 (Emory Methodist Church Cemetery); native of Harford Co., born 7 May 1872, daughter of Archer Scarborough and ---- (Bailey Funeral Home Records); age 18 in 1890 (marriage License Applications Book ALJ No. 2)

Scarborough, Mary Grier (Parke), 1863-1909, wife of James Ross Scarborough, q.v.

Scarborough, Melvin, 1875-1951 (Bel Air Memorial Gardens); native of Harford Co., born 18 May 1875, son of Philip J. Scarborough and Annie E. Scarborough (Bailey Funeral Home Records)

Scarborough, Milton E., 1852-1883 (Broad Creek Friends Cemetery)

Scarborough, Mollie (Miss), actress, musical entertainment, at Darlington (*The Aegis & Intelligencer*, 30 May 1890)

Scarborough, Mordecai S., canner, Fifth District (*Havre de Grace Republican*, 30 May 1890); warden, Grace Memorial Church, Darlington (*Havre de Grace Republican*, 18 Apr 1890)

Scarborough, N. Maxwell, 1887-1948 (Slate Ridge Cemetery, York Co., PA); native of Harford Co., born 26 Feb 1887, son of J. Ross Scarborough and Mary Parke (Harkins Funeral Home Records)

Scarborough, Nannie Hall (Robinson), 1871-1942 (Little Falls Quaker Cemetery); daughter of James C. Robinson and Susan Beeman (Death certificae); wife of Nathan E. Scarborough, q.v.

Scarborough, Nathan E., 1862-1945 (Little Falls Quaker Cemetery)

Scarborough, Nellie Beatrice, born 30 Jul 1881, daughter of John and Viola Scarborough (John May Scarborough Bible, *Maryland Bible Records, Volume 2*, by Henry C. Peden, Jr., 2003, p. 124)

Scarborough, Nelson, 1856-1950 (Emory Methodist Church Cemetery)

Scarborough, O. O., 1873-1946 (Slate Ridge Cemetery, York Co., PA); native of Harford Co., born 5 Mar 1873, son of Andrew Scarborough and Martha Scarborough (Harkins Funeral Home Records)

Scarborough, Parker Forwood, 1840-1904 (Emory Methodist Church Cemetery); trustee, Mt. Pleasant School No. 11, Fifth District (*Havre de Grace Republican*, 30 May 1890); acquired land in August 1890 (*The Aegis & Intelligencer*, 12 Sep 1890)

Scarborough, Phillip J., 1834-1909 (Church of the Ascension Cemetery); trustee, Union Cross Roads School No. 12, Fifth District (*Havre de Grace Republican*, 30 May 1890); juror, Fifth District (*Havre de Grace Republican*, 31 Jan 1890, spelled the name Scarboro); see Anna Rebecca Scarborough and Melvin Scarborough, q.v.

Scarborough, R. Frances (Lewin), 1842-1912 (Emory Methodist Church Cemetery)

Scarborough. R. Marshall, 1890-1959 (Slateville Cemetery, York Co., PA); native of Harford Co., born 28 Sep 1890, son of J. Ross Scarborough and Mary Parke (Harkins Funeral Home Records)

Scarborough, Rachel A., wife of Thomas W. Heaps, q.v.; also see Nettie E. Wallace, Rachel A. Wallace, Nelson A. Heaps and Newton E. Heaps, q.v.

Scarborough, Rachel A. (Scarborough), 1818-1893 (Broad Creek Friends Cemetery)

Scarborough, Rhoda May, born 21 Apr 1887, daughter of John and Viola Scarborough (John May Scarborough Bible, *Maryland Bible Records, Volume 2*, by Henry C. Peden, Jr., 2003, p. 124)

Scarborough, Robert Leonard, 1866-1918 (Old Brick Baptist Church Cemetery); son of Edmund and Sarah E. (Hurst) Scarborough (Death certificate)

Scarborough, Russell Kenneth, 1889-1970 (Darlington Cemetery); native of Whiteford, Harford Co., born 4 Apr 1889, son of John M. Scarborough and Viola C. Malone (Harkins Funeral Home Records; John May Scarborough Bible, *Maryland Bible Records, Volume 2*, by Henry C. Peden, Jr., 2003, p. 124)

Scarborough, Ruth Ann, 1813-1908 (Broad Creek Friends Cemetery)

Scarborough, Samuel, see Frederick Scarborough, q.v.

Scarborough, Samuel J., president, Pleasant Hill Lyceum (*The Aegis & Intelligencer*, 3 Jan 1890); see Elmer Scarborough and Adda S. Walter, q.v.

Scarborough, Samuel Richardson, 1819-1889, unmarried resident near Macton (Death certificate; Church of the Ascension Cemetery)

Scarborough, Samuel Sedgewick, 1835-1903 (Church of th Ascension Cemetery); vestryman, Grace Memorial Church, Darlington (*Havre de Grace Republican*, 18 Apr 1890)

Scarborough, Sarah Elizabeth (Hurst), 1836-1918 (Old Brick Baptist Church Cemetery); wife of Edmund Scarborough, q.v.

Scarborough, Sarah Ellen (Groscup), 1849-1922 (Darlington Cemetery)

Scarborough, Sarah F., born 1885, died ---- (Mt. Zion Methodist Church Cemetery)

Scarborough, Sarah Teresa, born 27 Sep 1883, baptized 6 Nov 1883, daughter of Henry S. and Elizabeth A. (Sapp) Scarborough (St. Ignatius Catholic Church Baptism Register, p. 69)

Scarborough, Susan R. (Waters), 1859-1935 (Old Brick Baptist Church Cemetery); widow of Robert L. Scarborough, q.v.

Scarborough, Susanna, 1818-1891 (Emory Methodist Church Cemetery)

Scarborough, Victorene, 1847-1931 (Emory Methodist Church Cemetery)

Scarborough, Viola Cecilia, 1854-1930, wife of John May Scarborough (*Ancestral Charts, Volume 4*, Harford County Genealogical Society, 1988, p. 204); see Russell K. Scarborough, q.v.

Scarborough, W. Elwood, 1882-1954 (Church of the Ascension)

Scarborough, Willametta (Enfield), 1870-1958 (Emory Methodist Church Cemetery); native of Harford Co., born 2 Sep 1870, daughter of William Enfield and ---- Tracey (Harkins Funeral Home Records)

Scarborough, William, 1842-1912 (Darlington Cemetery); sheep farmer, Fifth District (*Havre de Grace Republican*, 2 May 1890)

Scarborough, William Allen, 1854-1910 (Emory Methodist Church Cemetery)

Scarborough, William Dallas, 1853-1926 (Slate Ridge Cemetery, York Co., PA); county commissioner and dentist, Fifth District (*Havre de Grace Republican*, 14 Feb 1890 and 4 Jul 1890; *Biographical Dictionary of Harford County, Maryland, 1774-1974*, by Henry C. Peden, Jr. and William O. Carr, 2021, p. 238)

Scarborough, William H., 1856-1922 (Church of the Ascension Cemetery)

Scarborough, William M., see Leslie Kinsey, q.v.

Scarborough, William T., 1859-1935 (Centre Methodist Church Cemetery)

Scarff's General Store, at Sarah Furnace, James M. Scarff, prop., Israel A, Scarff, storekeeper (*Harford*

Democrat, 24 Jan 1890; *Country Stores: Harford County's Rural Heritage*, by Henry C. Peden, Jr and Jack L. Shagena, Jr., 2015, p. 223)

Scarff's General Store, Pleasantville, William S. Scarff, prop. (*Country Stores: Harford County's Rural Heritage*, by Henry C. Peden, Jr. and Jack L. Shagena, Jr., 2015, p. 223)

Scarff, Amanda J. (McComas), 1867-1941 (Bethel Presbyterian Church Cemetery Records); wife of Charles Ellsworth Scarff, q.v.

Scarff, Anna Belle (Stansbury), 1871-1899, resident near Taylor, native of Baltimore Co., wife of J. Howard Scarff (Ebenezer Methodist Church Cemetery; Two death certificates: one filed under her maiden name and one filed under her married name)

Scarff, Carl W., 1887-1931 (Fallston Methodist Church Cemetery)

Scarff, Charles Ellsworth, 1866-1917 (Bethel Presbyterian Church Cemetery Records); Ellsworth Scarff, member, Providence M. P. Church Sunday School (*The Aegis & Intelligencer*, 18 Jul 1890)

Scarff, Charles Reed, 1854-1927 (Ebenezer Methodist Church Cemetery)

Scarff, Charles Thomas, 1827-1909 (Ebenezer Methodist Church Cemetery)

Scarff, Elizabeth (Watters), 1859-1945 (Fallston Methodist Church Cemetery)

Scarff, Emma C., age 28 in 1890 (Marriage License Applications Book ALJ No. 2, 1890), married Rev. E. Holmes Lamar, Jr., pastor of West Harford Circuit, on 7 Aug 1890 (*The Aegis & Intelligencer*, 15 Aug 1890)

Scarff, Flora Julia, daughter of the late Joshua Scarff, married Edwin Lawrence Pearce on 18 Feb 1890 (*The Aegis & Intelligencer*, 21 Feb 1890); age 23 in 1890 (Marriage License Applications Book ALJ No. 2, 1890)

Scarff, Florence, 1865-1947 (Centre Methodist Church Cemetery)

Scarff, George Ross, 1890-1973 (Bel Air Memorial Gardens)

Scarff, Georgia (Amoss), 1873-1953 (Fallston Methodist Church Cemetery)

Scarff, Hannah, 1831-1905 (Fallston Methodist Church Cemetery)

Scarff, Hannah Belle, 1865-1919 (Ebenezer Methodist Church Cemetery)

Scarff, Harry Caldwell, 1888-1974 (Ebenezer Methodist Church Cemetery)

Scarff, Israel Atkinson, Jr., 1831-1917 (Ebenezer Methodist Church Cemetery); farmer, near Jarrettsville (*Havre de Grace Republican*, 7 Mar 1890)

Scarff, J. A. (Mrs.), postmistress, Sarah Furnace, Marshall's District (*Havre de Grace Republican*, 25 Jul 1890)

Scarff, J. H. (Dr.), 1851-1908 (Ebenezer Methodist Church Cemetery

Scarff, James Morris, 1852-1924 (Ebenezer Methodist Church Cemetery); storekeeper, at Sarah Furnace (*Havre de Grace Republican*, 7 Feb 1890)

Scarff, Jennie A. (Caldwell), 1853-1911 (Ebenezer Methodist Church Cemetery); wife of James Morris Scarff, q.v.

Scarff, John Henry, 1887-1964 (Ebenezer Methodist Church Cemetery

Scarff, Joshua, see Flora Julia Scarff, q.v.

Scarff, Joshua Howard, 1863-1938 (Ebenezer Methodist Church Cemetery)

Scarff, Katherine E. (McComas), 1859-1933, wife of Israel Atkinson Scarff, q.v.

Scarff, Margaret (White), 1860-1941 (Ebenezer Methodist Church Cemetery)

Scarff, Marguerite D., 1890-1979 (Ebenezer Methodist Church Cemetery)

Scarff, Martha, see John I. Taylor, q.v.

Scarff, Martha R., 1835-1891 (Ebenezer Methodist Church Cemetery)

Scarff, Maye R., 1873-1919 (Darlington Cemetery)

Scarff, Oresse H. (Bavington), 1874-1957 (Mountain Christian Church Cemetery)

Scarff, Philip G., 1859-1918 (Fallston Methodist Church Cemetery)

Scarff, Samuel Garrison, 1816-1906 (Fallston Methodist Church Cemetery); farmer, Upper Cross Roads (*Havre de Grace Republican*, 31 Oct 1890)

Scarff, Sarah Elizabeth (Windle), 1854-1928 (Providence Methodist Church Cemetery)

Scarff, Sarah M., see Florence M. Stubbs. George H. Taylor, William B. Taylor and E. Ross Taylor, q.v.

Scarff, Thomas Emory, 1872-1918 (Darlington Cemetery)

Scarff, Thomas Winfield, 1870-1959 (Fallston Methodist Church Cemetery)

Scarff, W. S. (Master), resident near Fallston (*The Aegis & Intelligencer*, 11 Apr 1890)

Scarff, William, 1816-1891 (Fallston Methodist Church Cemetery); resident of Stockton (*The Aegis & Intelligencer*, 5 Dec 1890); premium award winner, Class E - Poultry, and Class O - Discretionary, Harford County Fair (*The Aegis & Intelligencer*, 24 Oct 1890)

Scarff, William S., 1861-1952 (Centre Methodist Church Cemetery); blacksmith at Watters' Cross Roads and tax collector, Fourth District (*The Aegis & Intelligencer*, 5 Dec 1890; *Havre de Grace Republican*, 4 Jul 1890)

Shaeffer, John, 1866-1926 (Parkwood Cemetery, Baltimore); native of Maryland, resided at Perryman (Death certificate)

Schaffer, Katherine E., 1890-1981 (Bel Air Memorial Gardens)

Schantz, Anna Barbara, 1890-1918, daughter of John George and Mary Fredericka Schantz (St. Paul's Lutheran Church Cemetery)

Schantz, Christian, 1842-1902 (St. Paul's Lutheran Church Cemetery)

Schantz, John George, 1856-1945 (St. Paul's Lutheran Church Cemetery)

Schantz, Magdalene, 1841-1890 (St. Paul's Lutheran Church Cemetery)

Schantz, Mary Fredericka, 1861-1921 (St. Paul's Lutheran Church Cemetery)

Schanz, George, age 23 in 1890 (Marriage License Applications Book ALJ No. 2, 1891)

Schanz, Katie, student, Union School House, near Bush Chapel (*The Aegis & Intelligencer*, 14 Mar 1890)

Schanz, Mary, student, Union School House, near Bush Chapel (*The Aegis & Intelligencer*, 14 Mar 1890)

Scheren, Leonard, new name on the voter registration list at Magnolia, First District, 1890 (*Havre de Grace Republican*, 17 Oct 1890)

Schilling's Woolen Factory and Fulling Mill, Henry C. Schilling, prop. (*Mills: Grist, Saw, Bone, Flint, Fulling ... & More*, by Jack L. Shagena, Jr., Henry C. Peden, Jr. and John W. McGrain, 2009, p. 252)

Schilling, Charity C., 1873-1944 (Ayres Chapel Methodist Church Cemetery)

Schilling, Emma C., 1835-1896 (Ayres Chapel Methodist Church Cemetery)

Schilling, Harry N., 1889-1950 (Ayres Chapel Methodist Church Cemetery)

Schilling, Henry B., trustee, Dry Branch School No. 2, Fourth District (*Havre de Grace Republican*, 30 May 1890)

Schilling, Henry C., 1866-1946 (Ayres Chapel Methodist Church Cemetery); see Schilling's Woolen Factory and Fulling Mill, q.v.

Schilling, Howard L., 1863-1932 (Ayres Chapel Methodist Church Cemetery); juror, Fourth District, 1890 (*Havre de Grace Republican*, 2 May 1890)

Schilling, Janie R., 1875-1943 (Ayres Chapel Methodist Church Cemetery)

Schilling, John W., 1873-1946 (Ayres Chapel Methodist Church Cemetery)

Schilling, Mary R., 1863-1936 (Ayres Chapel Methodist Church Cemetery)

Schillinger, Henry, 1879-1963 (Providence Methodist Church Cemetery)

Schillinger, Ida M., 1881-1950 (Providence Methodist Church Cemetery)

Schimminger, Peter, 1841-1913, native of Germany (Death certificate; Alms House Record Book)

Schlereth, Peter, 1866-1926 (St. Stephen's Catholic Church Cemetery, Bradshaw, Baltimore Co.); native of Maryland, married, laborer, resided at Joppa (Death certificate); age 23 *(sic)* in 1890 (Marriage License Applications Book ALJ No. 2, 1890)

Schmidt, J. Christian, farmer near Carsin's Run, died 14 Jan 1890 age 63 (*The Aegis & Intelligencer*, 7 Feb 1890)

Schoel, Charles, member, Jarrettsville Lodge, Knights of Pythias (*Havre de Grace Republican*, 14 Feb 1890)

Schofield, J. Henry, age 25 in 1889 (Marriage License Applications Book ALJ No. 2, 1889)

Schoke, Hermann, member of the firm of J.Faust & Son, Havre de Grace (*Havre de Grace Republican*, 20 Jun 1890); Hermann Schocke, new name on the voter registration list in the Sixth District (*Havre de Grace Republican*, 17 Oct 1890)

Scholtz, Albert, born 8 Aug 1889, son of Albert and Lizzie Scholtz (St. George's Episcopal Church Register of Baptisms, p. 9)

Schritz, Margaret, see Fannie W. Bristow and Margaret Bristow, q.v.

Schriver, Christian, 1823-1911 (Salem Evangelical Lutheran Church Cemetery)

Schriver, Martha, 1826-1903 (Salem Evangelical Lutheran Church Cemetery)

Schroeder, John William H., new name on the voter registration list at Magnolia, First District (*Havre de Grace Republican*, 26 Sep 1890)

Schuck, Charlotte (Gade), 1815-1893 (Christ Episcopal Church Cemetery)

Schuck, John [undertaker], 1813-1894 (Christ Episcopal Church Cemetery)

Schuck, John Martin, born 9 Nov 1881, son of John M. and Mary L. Schuck (Holy Cross Episcopal Church Register of Baptisms, p. 84)

Schuck, Mary L., see John Martin Schuck, q.v.

Schuck, William H., undertaker and furniture maker, near Churchville (*The Aegis & Intelligencer*, 17 Jan 1890); delegate, Third District, Democrat Party Convention (*The Aegis & Intelligencer*, 5 Sep 1890)

Schultz, Eva, 1866-1920 (St. Franci de Sales Catholic Church Cemetery)

Schultz, John, 1858-1928 (Cokesbury Memorial Memorial Church Cemetery)

Schultz, M. Pearl (Smith), 1884-1911. daughter of Clinton and Mamie B. Smith, and wife of William H. Schultz (Rock Run Methodist Church Cemetery)

Schureman, W. D. W. (Rev.), A.M.E. Church, Havre de Grace (*Havre de Grace Republican*, 2 May 1890)

Schuster, Alice, 1890-1969 (Highland Presbyterian Church Cemetery); native of Jarrettsville, born 1 Dec 1890, daughter of John P. Schuster and Mary E Hildt (Harkins Funeral Home Records - married name Wilson)

Schuster, Catherine, 1823-1906, wife of John Schuster (Salem Evangelical Lutheran Church Cemetery)

Schuster, Charles C., acquired land in February 1890 (*The Aegis & Intelligencer*, 7 Mar 1890)

Schuster, Charles Henry, born 1886, son of John P. and Mary E. (Hildt) Schuster (Bethel Presbyterian Church Cemetery Records)

Schuster, John, 1822-1906 (Salem Evangelical Lutheran Church Cemetery)

Schuster, John P., 1859-1935 (Bethel Presbyterian Church Cemetery Records); see Alice Schuster, q.v.

Schuster, Katherine May, born 18 Dec 1887, daughter of John P. and Mary E. (Hildt) Schuster (Bethel Presbyterian Church Cemetery Records)

Schuster, Mary Ella (Hildt), 1862-1944 (Bethel Presbyterian Church Cemetery Records); wife of John P. Schuster, q.v.

Schuster, Mary (Wallis), 1888-1951 (Bethel Presbyterian Church Cemetery Records); wife of Charles H. Schuster, q.v.

Schwamb, Charles, butcher, Darlington (*The Aegis & Intelligencer*, 26 Sep 1890); canner near Wilson's Mill [near Darlington] (*Havre de Grace Republican*, 28 Mar 1890); age 35 in 1889 (Marriage License Applications Book ALJ No. 2, 1889)

Scobey, Hester (King), 1883-1950 (Angel Hill Cemetery)

Scobey, J. Tylee, 1880-1958 (Angel Hill Cemetery)

Scoot, Maggie (Miss), uncalled for letter in Bel Air P. O., 1890 (*The Aegis & Intelligencer*, 14 Nov 1890)

Scott's General Store ("Fallston Lower Store"), at Wimbledon, Mrs. Anna D. Scott, prop. (*Country Stores: Harford County's Rural Heritage*, by Henry C. Peden, Jr. and Jack L. Shagena, Jr., 2015, pp. 224-225)

Scott, Althea Elizabeth (colored), age 18 in 1890 (Marriage License Applications Book ALJ No. 2, 1890)

Scott, Anna A., 1886-1947 (St. Ignatius Catholic Church Cemetery)

Scott, Anna D. (Price), 1809-1892 (Little Falls Quaker Cemetery)

Scott, Annie (colored), see Andrew F. Henson (colored), q.v.

Scott, Caroline D., 1881-1968 (Union Chapel Methodist Church Cemetery)

Scott, Daniel, 1825-1900 (St. Ignatius Catholic Church Cemetery); lawyer, resided in Bel Air, "native of U.S." (Death certificate); see W. Hinkle Jones, q.v.

Scott, Edward (colored), 1814-1901, native of Maryland, farmer at Dublin, Harford Co. (Death certificate); see Margaret M. Scott, q.v.

Scott, Elija (colored), 1860-1925 (Death certificate)

Scott, Elijah (colored), age 25 in 1890 (Marriage License Applications Book ALJ No. 2, 1891)

Scott, Eliza (colored), 1823-1903 (Death certificate; Alms House Record Book)

Scott, Florrie (Hopkins), 1862-1924 (Darlington Cemetery; Bailey Funeral Home Records); wife of Wakeman H. Scott, q.v.

Scott, George Littig, 1833-1893 (Darlington Cemetery); farmer, near Darlington (*The Aegis & Intelligencer*, 13 Jun 1890); leader of the Orthodox Church, Darlington (*The Aegis & Intelligencer*, 26 Sep 1890) premium award winner, Class A - Horses, Harford County Fair (*The Aegis & Intelligencer*, 24 Oct 1890)

Scott, George W., premium award winner, Class C - Sheep, and Class I - Agricultural Productions, Harford County Fair (*The Aegis & Intelligencer*, 24 Oct 1890)

Scott, Hannah (colored), see Eli Turner (colored), q.v.

Scott, Harriett Anne (Waters) (colored), c1847-1935, native of Harford Co. (Death certificate); wife of Elija Scott, q.v.

Scott, Harrison, 1836-1892 (Darlington Cemetery)

Scott, Helen (colored), died 7 Apr 1900, no age given (Alms House Record Book)

Scott, Henry (colored), c1837-1917 (Death certificate; Alms House Record Book)

Scott, James (colored), died 8 Sep 1894, adult, age not given (*The Aegis & Intelligencer*, 14 Sep 1894)

Scott, James (colored), c1834-1914, native of Harford Co. (Death certificate)

Scott, James R., see Walter Francis Scott, q.v.

Scott, James Ward (Dr.), 1845-1899, resident of Bel Air (Death certificate); member, Bel Air Tennis Club (*The Aegis & Intelligencer*, 18 Jul 1890); see Rena R. Scott, q.v.

Scott, Jane, see George Archer Knight, q.v.

Scott, Jennie V. (colored), 1875-1908 (Tabernacle Mt. Zion Methodist Church Cemetery)

Scott, John (colored), see Ella M. Scott (colored), q.v.

Scott, John H. W. (colored), 1868-1942, native of Harford Co., parents unknown (Death certificate)

Scott, Maggie (colored), age 20 in 1890 (Marriage License Applications Book ALJ No. 2, 1891)

Scott, Margaret (colored), died -- Sep 1899, age not given (Alms House Record Book)

Scott, Margaret (colored), see Grace Virginia Taylor (colored), q.v.

Scott, Margaret M. (Peaco) (colored), 1817-1900, servant, native of Maryland, resided at Poole (Death certificate); wife of Edward Scott, q.v.

Scott, Maria E. (Rose) (colored), 1828-1911, native of Rockbridge, VA (Death certificate)

Scott, Martha (colored), see Annie Gilbert (colored) and William Gilbert (colored), q.v.

Scott, Mary (colored), 1811-1911, native of Baltimore Co. (Death certificate)

Scott, Mary ("Mollie"), see Edith Worthington and Helen Worthington, q.v.

Scott, Mary H., 1834-1904 (Darlington Cemetery)

Scott, Mildred I., 1886-1928 (Darlington Cemetery); native of Maryland, born 7 Oct 1886, daughter of W. H. Scott and Florrie Hopkins (Bailey Funeral Home Records)

Scott, Rena R. (Rosan), c1845-1896 (Christ Episcopal Church Cemetery); Mrs. James Ward Scott, resident of Bel Air, 1890 (*The Aegis &2 Intelligencer*, 13 Jun 1890)

Scott, Susan (colored), see Levinia Holland (colored), q.v.

Scott, Wakeman H., 1861-1941 (Darlington Cemetery); see William H. Scott, q.v.

Scott, Walter Francis, 1883-1948, native of Harford Co., born 13 Jul 1883, son of James R. Scott, native of Scotland, and Jane A. Mooney, native of Ireland (Death certificate; St. Ignatius Catholic Church Cemetery)

Scott, William, alias William Johnson, Civil War veteran, Norrisville (*1890 Special Census of the Civil War Veterans of the State of Maryland*, by L. Tilden Moore, Volume III, p. 81)

Scott, William Franklyn (colored), 1879-1932, native of Virginia, resided in Havre d Grace, parents unknown (Death certificate)

Scott, William H., 1890-1949 (Darlington Cemetery); native of Harford Co., born 18 Nov 1890, son of Wakeman Scott and Florrie Hopkins (Bailey Funeral Home Records)

Scott, William L., 1877-1936 (Union Chapel Methodist Church Cemetery)

Scott, Winfield, 1851-1935 (Death certificate; Alms House Record Book)

Scotten, Amy, see Amy Glasgow, q.v.

Scotten, Emma J. (Jones), 1887-1967 (Slate Ridge Cemetery, York Co., PA); native of Cardiff, Harford Co., born 29 Sep 1887, daughter of Hugh W. Jones and Margaret Kirk (Harkins Funeral Home Records)

Scotten, Etta E. S., 1880-1940 (Emory Methodist Church Cemetery)

Scotten, Frederick H., born 1877, died ---- (Christ Episcopal Church Cemetery)

Scotten, Hugh J., 1880-1940 (Emory Methodist Church Cemetery); native of Harford Co., born 5 May 1880, son of Joshua Scotten and Mary McGibney (Harkins Funeral Home Records)

Scotten, J. J., see Mary E. McFadden, q.v.

Scotten, Joshua, see Amy Glasgow, Bessie J. Wiley and Hugh J. Scotten, q.v.

Scotten, Mary (Bull), 1880-1959 (Christ Episcopal Church Cemetery)

Scotten, Mary E., see Mary E. McFadden, q.v.

Scully, John (Mrs.), resident near Magnolia (*The Aegis & Intelligencer*, 3 Jan 1890)

Seagle, Elmira Agnes (Doak), 1867-1917 (Centre Methodist Church Cemetery)

Seagle, Eugene C., 1887-1946 (Centre Methodist Church Cemetery)

Seagle, Walter Terry, 1864-1925 (Centre Methodist Church Cemetery)

Sealor, Hannah, see Harry H. Morrison, q.v.

Sechrist, Pleasant, member, Norrisville Silver Cornet Band (*The Aegis & Intelligencer*, 30 May 1890)

Sechrist, Wesley, member, Norrisville Silver Cornet Band (*The Aegis & Intelligencer*, 30 May 1890); moved to

Kansas City, MO (*Harford Democrat*, 24 Oct 1890)

Second National Bank, 30 Office St., Bel Air (*Bel Air: An Architectural and Cultural History, 1782-1945*, by Marilynn M. Larew, 1995, pp. 72, 209)

Second Presbyterian Church of Bel Air (Pennsylvania Avenue, Bel Air)

Sedlecki, Barbara, see Frank Joseph Dudeck (Dudek), q.v.

Seibert, Herman Charles, 1885-1960 (St. Paul's Lutheran Church Cemetery)

Seibert, Herman R., 1842-1926 (Baker Cemetery)

Seiglar, Nicholas, resident near Clayton, died 3 Jul 1890, in his 78th year (*The Aegis & Intelligencer*, 11 Jul 1890); Nicholas Seichler, deceased and removed from the voter registration list at Abingdon, First District (*Havre de Grace Republican*, 17 Oct 1890)

Seitz, Carrie H., 1888-1966 (Norrisville Methodist Church Cemetery)

Seitz, Elenora, 1882-1933 (Norrisville Methodist Church Cemetery)

Seitz, Harry V., 1879-1945 (Norrisville Methodist Church Cemetery)

Seitz, William E., 1857-1945 (Norrisville Methodist Church Cemetery)

Selfe's General Store and Hardware Store, Darlington, William B. Self, prop. (*Country Stores: Harford County's Rural Heritage*, by Henry C. Peden, Jr. and Jack L. Shagena, Jr., 2015, p. 225)

Selfe, Edith B., 1889-1958 (Darlington Cemetery); native of Harford Co, born 6 Aug 1889, daughter of Henry E. Selfe and Sarah Burton (Bailey Funeral Home Records)

Selfe, Henry Ellsworth, 1861-1933 (Darlington Cemetery); resident of Darlington (*The Aegis & Intelligencer*, 26 Sep 1890)

Selfe, Louise (Webster), 1857-1903 (Darlington Cemetery)

Selfe Sarah A. "Sadie" (Burton), 1860-1929 (Darlington Cemetery), wife of Henry E. Selfe, q.v.

Selfe, William B., 1857-1934 (Darlington Cemetery); blacksmith, Darlington (*The Aegis & Intelligencer*, 26 Sep 1890); warden, Grace Memorial Church, Darlington (*Havre de Grace Republican*, 18 Apr 1890); see Harford Carriage and Wagon Works, q.v.

Sellers, Annie W. (Miss), premium award winner, Class J - Domestic Products, Harford County Fair (*The Aegis & Intelligencer*, 24 Oct 1890)

Sellers, Emma R., 1830-1891 (Mt. Carmel Methodist Church Cemetery)

Sellers, Lilla M. (Nagle), 1875-1942 (Churchville Presbyterian Church Cemetery)

Sellers, Momnia Belle, 1860-1932 (Mountain Christian Church Cemetery)

Sellers, Robert B., 1828-1909 (Mt. Carmel Methodist Church Cemetery)

Sellers, Walter Scott, 1866-1944 (Mountain Christian Church Cemetery) age 25 in 1891 (Marriage License Applications Book ALJ No. 2)

Seneca & Mahan, ice houses, Havre de Grace (*Heavy Industries of Yesteryear; Harford County's Rural Heritage*, by Jack L. Shagena, Jr. and Henry C. Peden, Jr., 2015, p. 94)

Seneca's Cannery, Havre de Grace (*1953 Harford County Directory*, p. 276)

Seneca's General Store and Grocery Store, Havre de Grace, Stephen J. Seneca and Robert Seneca, prop. (*Country Stores: Harford County's Rural Heritage*, by Henry C. Peden, Jr. and Jack L. Shagena, Jr., 2015, p. 226)

Seneca, Annie E. (Mitchell), 1840-1923 (Angel Hill Cemetery), wife of Stephen John Seneca, q.v.

Seneca, Caroline E. (Lawder), 1846-1918 (Angel Hill Cemetery, wife of Robert Seneca, q.v.

Seneca, Catherine A., see Robert Walker Greenleaf, q.v.

Seneca, Dorus, 1811-1890 (Angel Hill Cemetery); native of Switzerland, immigrated in 1815 to Chester, PA, moved to Havre de Grace circa 1840 (*The Aegis & Intelligencer*, 19 Dec 1890); see Robert Seneca and Stephen

J. Seneca, q.v.

Seneca, Robert, 1846-1931, son of Dorus Seneca and Mary A. Teeny (Death certificate; Angel Hill Cemetery; (*Biographical Dictionary of Harford County, Maryland, 1774-1974*, by Henry C. Peden, Jr. and William O. Carr, 2021, pp. 241-242); merchant and mayor of Havre de Grace (*Havre de Grace Republican*, 10 Jan 1890); delegate, Sixth District, Democrat Party Convention (*The Aegis & Intelligencer*, 5 Sep 1890); organizer and vice president, Havre de Grace Democratic Club (*Havre de Grace Republican*, 31 Oct 1890); treasurer, Susquehanna Lodge No. 130, A. F. & A. M. (*Havre de Grace Republican*, 26 Dec 1890); vice president, The Seneca Hosiery Company of Havre de Grace (*Havre de Grace Republican*, 21 Mar 1890)

Seneca, Stephen John, 1837-1918, son of Dorus Seneca and Mary A. Teeny (Death certificate; Angel Hill Cemetery; (*Biographical Dictionary of Harford County, Maryland, 1774-1974*, by Henry C. Peden, Jr. and William O. Carr, 2021, p. 242); tomato packer and can manufacturer, Havre de Grace (*Havre de Grace Republican*, 14 Feb 1890; *1953 Harford County Directory*, p. 276); delegate, Sixth District, Republican Party Convention (*The Aegis & Intelligencer*, 26 Sep 1890); director, Havre de Grace Improvement Company (*Havre de Grace Republican*, 7 Feb 1890); president of The Seneca Hosiery Company of Havre de Grace (*Havre de Grace Republican*, 21 Mar 1890); vice president, Republican Club (*Havre de Grace Republican*, 7 Nov 1890)

Senner, Charles, name removed from the voter registration list in the Sixth District (*Havre de Grace Republican*, 17 Oct 1890)

Senthz, ----, miller, Bush Mills (*Havre de Grace Republican*, 5 Dec 1890)

Severs, Viola A. (Law), 1880-1967 (Chestnut Grove Church Cemetery); native of Harford Co., born 16 Oct 1880, daughter of Robert C. Law and Elizabeth Chenworth (Harkins Funeral Home Records)

Seward, Mamie, student, Macton School (*The Aegis & Intelligencer*, 4 Jul 1890)

Seward, Timothy, of Macton, quarry land owner, Greenstone Serpentine Marble Works Company (*Havre de Grace Republican*, 6 Jun 1890); Civil War veteran, Macton P. O. (*1890 Special Census of the Civil War Veterans of the State of Maryland*, by L. Tilden Moore, Volume III, p. 88)

Sewell, C. K. & Bro., premium award winner, Class A - Horses, Harford County Fair (*The Aegis & Intelligencer*, 24 Oct 1890)

Sewell, Cassie E., 1890-1957 (Mountain Christian Church Cemetery)

Sewell, Clement, delegate, First District, Democrat Party Convention (*The Aegis & Intelligencer*, 5 Sep 1890); trustee, Abingdon School No. 1, First District (*Havre de Grace Republican*, 30 May 1890)

Sewell, Hattie (Kimble), 1884-1957, wife of William Hyde Sewell, q.v.

Sewell, John (colored), see Rosa Sewell (colored), q.v.

Sewell, Joseph, captain of the bug-eye *Puritan*, of Havre de Grace (*Havre de Grace Republican*, 25 Apr 1890)

Sewell, Levi (colored), 1870-1900, native of Harford Co., resided at Forest Hill (Death certificate)

Sewell, Loulie (Miss), resident of Abingdon (*The Aegis & Intelligencer*, 23 May 1890)

Sewell, M. L. (Mrs.), resident at *Rose Hill*, near Abingdon, and grandmother of Miss Lelia Munder, of Baltimore, and Miss Nellie Wilson, Miss Nona Wilson and Master Judson Wilson, of Carroll Co., MD (*The Aegis & Intelligencer*, 15 Aug 1890)

Sewell, Rosa (Miss) (colored), 1872-1920, native of Maryland, daughter of John Sewell and ---- Thompson (Death certificate)

Sewell, Walter Eugene, born 6 Jul 1888, son of William R. and Mary R. Sewell (Pennington Family Records, *Maryland Bible Records, Volume 2*, by Henry C. Peden, Jr., 2003, pp. 108, 110)

Sewell, William Hyde, 1864-1922 (Cokesbury Memorial Methodist Church Cemetery)

Sewell, William Lambert, born 14 Oct 1886, son of William R. and Mary R. Sewell (Pennington Family Records, *Maryland Bible Records, Volume 2*, by Henry C. Peden, Jr., 2003, pp. 108, 110)

Seyfriet, Catherine "Kate" (Thorpy), 1863-1911 (Mt. Erin Cemetery); wife of Joseph Seyfriet, q.v.

Seyfriet, Joseph, 1854-1922 (Mt. Erin Cemetery)

Seyfriet, Joseph Barry, 1888-1948, native of Havre de Grace, born 9 Dec 1888, son of Joseph Seyfriet, of Germany, and Catherine Thorpy, of Ireland (Pennington Funeral Home Records; Mt. Erin Cemetery)

Shade, David, second grade student, Mount Horeb School (*The Aegis & Intelligencer*, 14 Feb 1890)

Shadinger, David, member, Cleveland Junior Baseball Club, at Pleasantville (*The Aegis & Intelligencer*, 22 Aug 1890)

Shadinger, Hannah R., 1848-1891 (Little Falls Quaker Cemetery)

Shadinger, Willie W., 1879-1897 (Little Falls Quaker Cemetery)

Shanahan, Catherine (Kennedy), 1826-1892, mother of Denis John Shanahan, q.v.

Shanahan, Denis John, 1854-1923 (Green Mount Cemetery, Baltimore), architect and master builder, Bel Air; son of John M. Shanahan, 1825-1892, and Catherine Kennedy, 1826-1892, of County Tipperary, Ireland (*Biographical Dictionary of Harford County, Maryland, 1774-1974*, by Henry C. Peden, Jr. and William O. Carr, 2021, p. 243)

Shanahan, John M., 1825-1892, father of Denis John Shanahan, q.v.

Shanahan, Margaret C. (Smith), 1858-1893, mother of William J. Shanahan, q.v.

Shanahan, Richard J., 1850-1899, farmer near Fallston (Death certificate); father of William J. Shanahan, q.v.

Shanahan, William J., 1879-1934 (Cathedral Cemetery, Baltimore), of Bel Air; son of Richard J. Shanahan, 1850-1899, and Margaret C. Smith, 1858-1893 (*Biographical Dictionary of Harford County, Maryland, 1774-1974*, by Henry C. Peden, Jr. and William O. Carr, 2021, p. 243)

Shanbarger, Annie P., age 23 in 1889 (Marriage License Applications Book ALJ No. 2)

Shanbarger, Augusta N., 1843-1922 (Fellowship Cemetery)

Shanbarger, Emma L., age 18, of Federal Hill, Harford County, married Edwin B. Thompson, of Philadelphia, on 30 Apr 1890 in Baltimore (Marriage License Applications Book ALJ No. 2; *The Aegis & Intelligencer*, 2 May 1890)

Shanbarger, Henry, trustee, Enterprise School No. 19, Fourth District (*Havre de Grace Republican*, 30 May 1890, spelled his name Shanberger)

Shanbarger, James N., age 23 in 1890 (Marriage License Applications Book ALJ No. 2, 1891, spelled his name Shanberger)

Shanbarger, John, road contractor (*Havre de Grace Republican*, 7 Mar 1890, spelled his name Shamburger)

Shanbarger, Maggie B., age 22 in 1890 (Marriage License Applications Book ALJ No. 2, 1891)

Shanbarger, William, 1832-1918 (Fellowship Cemetery); member of the Almshouse Committee, Bel Air (*The Aegis & Intelligencer*, 28 Feb 1890); juror, Fourth District (*Havre de Grace Republican*, 31 Jan 1890, spelled his name Shanberger); widower, age 57 in 1890 (Marriage License Applications Book ALJ No. 2, 1890)

Shanck, Granville T., Civil War veteran, Castleton (*1890 Special Census of the Civil War Veterans of the State of Maryland*, by L. Tilden Moore, Volume III, p. 87)

Shane, Annabel, 1875-1971 (Angel Hill Cemetery)

Shane, Annie Mary, 1874-1921, native of Maryland, born 18 Sep 1874, daughter of George H. Shane and Nancy J. Heaps (Death certificate); student, Fourth District (*The Aegis & Intelligencer*, 24 Oct 1890)

Shane, George H., see Annie Mary Shane, q.v.

Shane, Ida May, 1871-1955 (St. George's Episcopal Church Cemetery, married name Ford); teacher, School No. 8, First District (*The Aegis & Intelligencer*, 29 Aug 1890)

Shane, Lewis, 1877-1941 (Angel Hill Cemetery)

Shane, Nancy J. (Heaps), see Annie Mary Shane, q.v.

Shane, Sarah B. (Mrs.), 1838-1903 (St. George's Episcopal Church Cemetery tombstone, but death certificate stated she died at age 35); mother of Ida May Shane, q.v.

Shannon, Adeline F., 1826-1911 (Angel Hill Cemetery)

Shannon, Annie Mary, 1855-1922 (Christ Episcopal Church Cemetery)

Shannon, Edward, of Vale, competitive bicycle rider, Harford County Fair (*Havre de Grace Republican*, 26 Sep 1890; *The Aegis & Intelligencer*, 19 Sep 1890)

Shannon, George Edward, 1873-1895 (Christ Episcopal Church Cemetery)

Shannon, George T., 1843-1910 (Christ Episcopal Church Cemetery)

Shannon, Harry, 1876-1958 (Mountain Christian Church Cemetery)

Shannon, J. Harry, 1875-1948 (Christ Episcopal Church Cemetery)

Shannon, M. Grace, 1876-1969 (Christ Episcopal Church Cemetery)

Shanz, George F., 1868-1943 (Baker Cemetery)

Shanz, Matilda H., 1867-1947 (Baker Cemetery)

Sharon, John T., 1872-1947 (Tabernacle Cemetery); native of Harford Co., born 4 Apr 1872, son of John Sharon and Elizabeth Way (Harkins Funeral Home Records)

Sharon, William S., 1877-1950 (Slate Ridge Cemetery, York Co., PA); native of Harford Co., born 1 Oct 1877, son of William Sharon and Elizabeth Way (Harkins Funeral Home Records)

Sharp, Cyrus Clifford, 1890-1967 (Angel Hill Cemetery)

Shauck, Sarah R., see Mary V. Wilson, q.v.

Shaw, Carrie (Gordon), 1882-1918 (Norrisville Methodist Church Cemetery)

Shaw, Charles Wesley, 1881-1962 (St. Mary's Episcopal Church Cemetery)

Shaw, Charlie H., 1876-1951 (Norrisville Methodist Church Cemetery)

Shaw, Fannie (Bissell), 1883-1948, daughter of Benjamin and Elizabeth H. Bissell (St. Mary's Episcopal Church Cemetery); wife of Charles W. Shaw, q.v.

Shay, Alice, 1812-1895 (St. George's Episcopal Church Cemetery)

Shay, Emma V., see Howard Chapman Shay, Ida Isabel Shay abs William Wallace Shay, q.v.

Shay, George, 1857-1934 (Wesleyan Chapel Methodist Church Cemetery)

Shay, Howard Chapman, born 2 Nov 1880, son of William T. and Emma V. Shay (St. George's Episcopal Church Register of Baptisms, pp. 2-3)

Shay, Ida Isabel, born 8 May 1876, daughter of William T. and Emma V. Shay (St. George's Episcopal Church Register of Baptisms, pp. 2-3)

Shay, James, 1829-1907 (Christ Episcopal Church Cemetery)

Shay, Joseph A., 1863-1925 (St. Francis de Sales Catholic Church Cemetery)

Shay, P. D., 1860-1896 (St. Francis de Sales Catholic Church Cemetery)

Shay, Patrick, Civil War veteran, Havre de Grace (*1890 Special Census of the Civil War Veterans of the State of Maryland*, by L. Tilden Moore, Volume III, p. 89)

Shay, William T., resided at Perryman, reported in Dec 1889 that his wife Ella M. [Emma?] had left him (*Harford Democrat*, 31 Jan 1890); see Howard Chapman Shay, Ida Isabel Shay abs William Wallace Shay, q.v.

Shay, William Wallace, born 4 Jul 1878, son of William T. and Emma V. Shay (St. George's Episcopal Church Register of Baptisms, pp. 2-3)

Shea, Elizabeth, 1816-1891 (Christ Episcopal Church Cemetery)

Shea, Joseph A., 1863-1925 (St. Francis de Sales Catholic Church Cemetery); native of Maryland, farm laborer near Bel Air, son of Joseph Shea and Mary Reidy, of Ireland (Death certificate)

Shea, P. D., 1860-1896, son of Joseph and Mary Shea (St. Francis de Sales Catholic Church Cemetery)

Shears, Amanda, 1838-1906 (St. Francis de Sales Catholic Church Cemetery)

Shears, Charles H., 1868-1910 (St. Francis de Sales Catholic Church Cemetery)

Shears, George, resident of Michaelsville (*Havre de Grace Republican*, 27 Jun 1890)

Shears, Julia A., 1872-1952 (St. Francis de Sales Catholic Church Cemetery)

Shears, Rhoda M. 1872-1891 (Calvary Methodist Church Cemetery)

Shelton, J. W., feather bed and pillow renovator, Bel Air (*The Aegis & Intelligencer*, 21 Mar 1890)

Shelton, Thomas, died 22 Apr 1892, no age given (Alms House Monthly Register); Tom Shelton, of Havre de Grace, was committed to jail for violating a town ordinance in regard to fires (*Harford Democrat*, 28 Feb 1890)

Shepherd, John, executive committeeman, Bel Air Tennis Club (*The Aegis & Intelligencer*, 16 May 1890)

Shepherd, S. M. (Mrs.), premium award winner, Class K - Household and Domestic Manufactures, Harford County Fair (*The Aegis & Intelligencer*, 24 Oct 1890)

Sheppard, Emma, see Violet S. Knight and John H. Gallion, q.v.

Sheppard, Garrow (colored), see Madie Pauline Warfield, q.v.

Sheridan, Alfred Fillmore, 1884-1954 (Rock Run Methodist Church Cemetery); son of Richard and Rebecca Sheridan (Rebecca Sheridan Bible, *Maryland Bible Records, Volume 1*, by Henry C. Peden, Jr., 2003, p. 218)

Sheridan, Belle J., 1875-1975 (Baker Cemetery)

Sheridan, Cora Roberts, 1887-1957, native of Glenville, Harford Co., born 4 Jan 1887, daughter of Richard Sheridan and Rebecca Gallion (Rebecca Sheridan Bible, *Maryland Bible Records, Volume 1*, by Henry C. Peden, Jr., 2003, p. 218; Pennington Funeral Home Records - married name McFadden)

Sheridan, Daniel (colored), see Frances Richardson (colored), q.v.

Sheridan Ella E. (Miss), 1846-1926 (Mt. Zion Methodist Church Cemetery); premium award winner, Class N - Floral Decorations, Harford County Fair, 1890 (*The Aegis & Intelligencer*, 24 Oct 1890)

Sheridan, Emma (Miss), premium award winner, Class J - Domestic Products, Harford County Fair (*The Aegis & Intelligencer*, 24 Oct 1890); Emma A. Sheridan acquired land in April 1890 (*The Aegis & Intelligencer*, 9 May 1890)

Sheridan (Sherdon), Florence (colored), see Howard Richardson (colored), q.v.

Sheridan, Frances (colored), see Frances Richardson (colored), q.v.

Sheridan, George, 1848-1902 (*Deaths and Marriages in Harford County, Maryland, and Vicinity, 1873-1904, from the Diaries of Albert Peter Silver*, transcribed by Glenn Randers-Pehrson, 1995, p. 21); treated by unidentified doctor in 1890 ("Medical Account Book – 1890," Historical Society of Harford County Archives Folder)

Sheridan, Harry E., 1874-1947 (Smith Chapel Methodist Church Cemetery)

Sheridan, Hattie P., 1889-1924 (Smith Chapel Methodist Church Cemetery)

Sheridan, Ida A. (Briney), 1867-1934 (Rock Run Methodist Church Cemetery; Bailey Funeral Home Records)

Sheridan, J. Frank, 1872-1940 (Baker Cemetery)

Sheridan, James, 18365-1897 (Smith Chapel Methodist Church Cemetery); treated by unidentified doctor in 1890 ("Medical Account Book – 1890," Historical Society of Harford County Archives Folder)

Sheridan, John, 1840-1903 (Rock Run Methodist Church Cemetery)

Sheridan, Katherine A. (Esley), 1861-1922 (Holy Trinity Episcopal Church Cemetery)

Sheridan, Letta Booth, 1889-1910 (Rock Run Methodist Church Cemetery); wife of Alfred P. Sheridan, q.v.

Sheridan, Lillian S., 1888-1977 (Rock Run Methodist Church Cemetery)

Sheridan, Lucy Gertrude, born 7 Nov 1881, daughter of Richard and Rebecca Sheridan (Rebecca Sheridan Bible, *Maryland Bible Records, Volume 1*, by Henry C. Peden, Jr., 2003, p. 218)

Sheridan, Luther, treated by unidentified doctor in 1890 ("Medical Account Book – 1890," Historical Society of Harford County Archives Folder); see Mary R. Forwood, q.v.

Sheridan, M., Katherine, 1835-1908 (Smith Chapel Methodist Church Cemetery)

Sheridan, Margaret (Walker), 1821-1904 (Mt. Zion Methodist Church Cemetery)

Sheridan, Mary S., see Mary S. Hughes, q.v.

Sheridan, Rebecca, see Alfred F. Sheridan, q.v.

Sheridan, Rebecca A. (Gallion), 1844-1893 (Rock Run Methodist Church Cemetery)

Sheridan, Richard, 1817-1891 (Mt. Zion Methodist Church Cemetery); janitor for the courthouse and jail (*Havre de Grace Republican*, 4 Jul 1890); Rich Sheridan, treated by unidentified doctor in 1890 ("Medical Account Book – 1890," Historical Society of Harford County Archives Folder)

Sheridan, Richard, 1842-1920 (Rock Run Methodist Church Cemetery); see Alfred F. Sheridan, Cora R. Sheridan and Mary S. Hughes, q.v.

Sheridan, Richard (Mrs.), premium award winner, Class J - Domestic Products, and Class K - Household and Domestic Manufactures, Harford County Fair (*The Aegis & Intelligencer*, 24 Oct 1890)

Sheridan, Richard Coleman, 1860-1934 (Mt. Zion Methodist Church Cemetery); served on a grand jury in 1890 (*Havre de Grace Republican*, 16 May 1890)

Sheridan, Richard Dallas, 1890-1972 (Rock Run Methodist Church Cemetery); born 7 Oct 1890, son of Richard and Rebecca Sheridan (Rebecca Sheridan Bible, *Maryland Bible Records, Volume 1*, by Henry C. Peden, Jr., 2003, p. 218)

Sheridan (Sherdan), Samuel (colored), 1849-1925 (Death certificate)

Sheridan, Sarah (colored), see Frances Richardson (colored), q.v.

Sheridan, Sarah C., 1873-1970 (Rock Run Methodist Church Cemetery)

Sheridan, William Parker, 1878-1963 (Rock Run Methodist Church Cemetery), born 14 Apr 1878, son of Richard and Rebecca Sheridan (Rebecca Sheridan Bible, *Maryland Bible Records, Volume 1*, by Henry C. Peden, Jr., 2003, p. 218)

Sherman, George T., 1868-1947 (Mt. Zion Methodist Church Cemetery)

Sherman, Joanna L., 1870-1933 (Mt. Zion Methodist Church Cemetery)

Sherman, Mabel B., 1881-1962 (Baker Cemetery)

Sherman, Richard L., 1879-1965 (Baker Cemetery)

Sherrer, George Washington, 1877-1930 (Bethel Presbyterian Church Cemetery Records)

Sherrer, Mary Elizabeth (Stansbury), 1883-1956 (Bethel Presbyterian Church Cemetery Records); wife of George W. Sherrer, q.v.

Sherron, William E. and Elizabeth, see Emma E. Kellum, q.v.

Shertzer, Abraham, 1828-1894 (Mt. Zion Methodist Church Cemetery); treated by unidentified doctor in 1890 ("Medical Account Book – 1890," Historical Society of Harford County Archives Folder)

Shertzer, David William, born 20 Feb 1850, son of Jacob and Mary Shertzer (Jacob Shertzer Bible, *Maryland Bible Records, Volume 1*, by Henry C. Peden, Jr., 2003, pp. 219-220); stock cattle dealer, Churchville (*The Aegis & Intelligencer*, 19 Dec 1890); treated by unidentified doctor in 1890 ("Medical Account Book – 1890," Historical Society of Harford County Archives Folder)

Shertzer, Elijah, see Mary (Trego) Shertzer, q.v.

Shertzer, Elizabeth, 1833-1908 (Mt. Zion Methodist Church Cemetery)

Shertzer, Fannie Priscilla, 1860-1897 (Churchville Presbyterian Church Cemetery); daughter of Jacob and Mary Shertzer (Jacob Shertzer Bible, *Maryland Bible Records, Volume 1*, by Henry C. Peden, Jr., 2003, pp. 219-220); Miss Fanny Shertzer, of Bel Air, corresponding secretary, Women's Christian Temperance Union (*Havre de Grace Republican*, 5 Sep 1890)

Shertzer, Harry R., 1866-1950 (Churchville Presbyterian Church Cemetery)

Shertzer, Isaac, treated by unidentified doctor in 1890 ("Medical Account Book – 1890," Historical Society of Harford County Archives Folder)

Shertzer, Jacob, 1820-1901 (Churchville Presbyterian Church Cemetery); treated by unidentified doctor in 1890 ("Medical Account Book – 1890," Historical Society of Harford County Archives Folder)

Shertzer, Jacob, Jr., born 17 Dec 1846, son of Jacob and Mary Shertzer (Jacob Shertzer Bible, *Maryland Bible Records, Volume 1*, by Henry C. Peden, Jr., 2003, p. 219); farmer and clay pigeon shooter near Churchville (*The Aegis & Intelligencer*, 7 Feb 1890)

Shertzer, Louise (Kissell), 1863-1910 (Mt. Zion Methodist Church Cemetery)

Shertzer, Mary, see Jacob Shertzer, Jr., and Mary Ann Shertzer, q.v.

Shertzer, Mary (Trego), 1822-1901, native of Maryland, resided at Churchville, wife of Elijah Shertzer (Churchville Presbyterian Church Cemetery; Jacob Shertzer Bible, *Maryland Bible Records, Volume 1*, by Henry C. Peden, Jr., 2003, pp. 219-220)

Shertzer, Mary Ann, 1842-1910 (Churchville Presbyterian Church Cemetery); born 14 Apr 1842, daughter of Jacob and Mary Shertzer (Jacob Shertzer Bible, *Maryland Bible Records, Volume 1*, by Henry C. Peden, Jr., 2003, pp. 219-220)

Sherwood, Sarah (Mrs.) (colored), 1868-1942, native of Harford Co. (Death certificate)

Shew, Joseph M., age 20 in 1890 (Marriage License Applications Book ALJ No. 2, 1891)

Shillman, Daniel F., 1854-1923 (Trinity Evangelical Lutheran Church Cemetery)

Shillman, Franklin George, 1877-1928 (Trinity Evangelical Lutheran Church Cemetery); native of Maryland, resided at Magnolia, born 30 Sep 1877, son of Daniel F. Shillman, of Germany, and Mary Meyers, of Maryland (Death certificate)

Shillman, Mary, died 10 Dec 1892, age not stated (Trinity Evangelical Lutheran Church Cemetery); see Franklin George Shillman, q.v.

Shimburger, Catherine, died 19 Jul 1926, age about 76 or 96 (Death certificate stated age 76, but the Alms House Record Book stated "Kate Shinbuger" was age 92 in 1922)

Shipley, Alexander, 1866-1943 (Grove Presbyterian Church Cemetery)

Shipley, John A., 1864-1910 (St. Francis de Sales Catholic Church); resided at Harford Furnace, married Mary Agnes Martin, daughter of Thomas Martin, on 24 Dec 1889 at St. Francis de Sales Catholic Church in Abingdon (*The Aegis & Intelligencer*, 3 Jan 1890); age 24 in 1889 (Marriage License Applications Book ALJ No. 2, 1889)

Shipley, Mary (Geary), 1875-1952 (Grove Presbyterian Church Cemetery)

Shipley, Mary A., 1866-1939 (St. Francis de Sales Catholic Church)

Shirley, Charles C., 1878-1945 (Baker Cemetery)

Shirley, Hester, wife of Herman T. Cullison, q.v.; also see Hilda Virginia Cullison, q.v.

Shirley, Lottie M., 1876-1944 (Baker Cemetery)

Shirley, N. H. (Mr.), resident of Upper Cross Roads (*The Aegis & Intelligencer*, 11 Apr 1890)

Shoff, William, died 6 Jun 1900, age not given, husband of Louisa Shoff, "native of U.S.," resided at Castleton, son of Zacharia and Rosa N. Shoff (Death certificate)

Shoney, Nathan R., Civil War veteran, Upper Cross Roads (*1890 Special Census of the Civil War Veterans of the State of Maryland*, by L. Tilden Moore, Volume III, p. 76)

Short, William H., Civil War veteran, Havre de Grace (*1890 Special Census of the Civil War Veterans of the State of Maryland*, by L. Tilden Moore, Volume III, p. 89)

Showell, Mary (colored), 1871-1922 (St. James Church, Gravel Hill Cemetery)

Shriver, Carrie Hanson, born 29 Sep 1874, daughter of Charle and Mary Catherine Shriver (Charles Shriver Bible, *Maryland Bible Records, Volume 2*, by Henry C. Peden, Jr., 2003, p. 132)

Shriver, Charles, 1844-1928 (Charles Shriver Bible, *Maryland Bible Records, Volume 2*, by Henry C. Peden, Jr., 2003, p. 132)

Shriver, Christian, assistant superintendent, Salem Sunday School, Fourth District (*Havre de Grace Republican*,

4 Apr 1890)

Shriver, Harriet L. (VanBibber), 1873-1957 (St. Mary's Episcopal Church Cemetery); wife of Joseph Alexis Shriver, q.v.

Shriver, Joseph Alexis, 1872-1951 (St. Mary's Episcopal Church Cemetery)

Shriver, Mark O. and Katherine D., residents of Harford Furnace (*Havre de Grace Republican*, 27 Jun 1890)

Shriver, Mary Catherine (Sellman), 1848-1897 (Charles Shriver Bible, *Maryland Bible Records, Volume 2*, by Henry C. Peden, Jr., 2003, p. 132); wife of Charles Shriver, q.v.

Shrodes, C. Worth, 1848-1905 (St. Mary's Catholic Church Cemetery)

Shrodes, Charles, resident near Wiley's Mill, Fourth District, age about 90 (*The Aegis & Intelligencer*, 21 Feb 1890)

Shrodes, Margaret C., 1858-1916 (St. Mary's Catholic Church Cemetery)

Shultz, Edward (Mrs.), county out-pensioner [welfare recipient], Third District (*Havre de Grace Republican*, 4 Jul 1890)

Shure's General Store, Berkleyville, George W. Shure, prop. (*Country Stores: Harford County's Rural Heritage*, by Henry C. Peden, Jr. and Jack L. Shagena, Jr., 2015, pp. 228-229)

Shure's General Store, Shure's Landing near Darlington, Daniel F. Shure, propr., and Edward S. Shure, mgr. (*Country Stores: Harford County's Rural Heritage*, by Henry C. Peden, Jr. and Jack L. Shagena, Jr., 2015, pp. 228-229)

Shure's Landing Public School No. 19, near Darlington (*Harford County, Maryland Teachers and the Schools They Served, 1774-1900*, by Henry C. Peden, Jr., 2022, p. 372)

Shure, Bertha M. (Scarborough), 1865-1955 (Darlington Cemetery)

Shure, Catharine, 1810-1895 (Dublin Southern Cemetery)

Shure, Daniel Ferree, 1817-1891 (Darlington Cemetery); superintendent, Tidewater Canal at Shure's Landing, near Darlington, 1842 to 1890 (*Havre de Grace Republican*, 17 Jan and 20 Jun 1890); trustee, Shure's Landing School No. 19, Fifth District (*Havre de Grace Republican*, 30 May 1890); trustee, Darlington Academy (*Havre de Grace Republican*, 26 Sep 1890); first violin in the Darlington Orchestra (*Havre de Grace Republican*, 7 Mar 1890); musical director of the Darlington Minstrels (*The Aegis & Intelligencer*, 21 Feb 1890); wrote his will in 1889 and died in 1891, naming only his wife Jane Shure (Harford County Will Book JMM 11:192-193)

Shure, Edward Savage, 1863-1936 (Darlington Cemetery); drug store proprietor, Darlington (*The Aegis & Intelligencer*, 26 Sep 1890)

Shure, George W., storekeeper, Berkleyville (*Havre de Grace Republican*, 14 Feb 1890)

Shure, Georgeanna R. (Wahl), 1841-1934 (Darlington Cemetery)

Shure, Harry Walters, 1844-1919 (Darlington Cemetery); organizer and secretary, Havre de Grace Democratic Club (*Havre de Grace Republican*, 31 Oct 1890)

Shure, James Buchanan, 1856-1944 (Darlington Cemetery)

Shure, Jane, see Daniel Ferree Shure, q.v.

Shure, John Michael, 1852-1937 (Darlington Cemetery)

Shure, John P., 1833-1903 (Dublin Southern Cemetery)

Shure, Lee, actor, musical entertainment, at Darlington (*The Aegis & Intelligencer*, 30 May 1890)

Shure, Mary Jane (McDarrah), 1824-1907 (Darlington Cemetery)

Shure, Maud (Miss), amateur soprano singer, of Havre de Grace (*Havre de Grace Republican*, 3 Oct 1890)

Shure, Robert Lee, 1867-1894 (Darlington Cemetery)

Shure, Stella (Dinan), 1857-1935 (Darlington Cemetery); wife of James B. Shure, q.v.

Shure, Virginia Stonewall Jackson (Knight), 1863-1911 (Darlington Cemetery)

Shure, Walter H., 1865-1906 (Darlington Cemetery)

Shure, William J., 1861-1932 (Darlington Cemetery)

Sidwell's Tubular Well Drilling Contractor, Macton, C.W. Sidwell, prop. (*Harford Democrat*, 17 Jan 1890)

Sidwell, Charles, uncalled for letter in Bel Air P. O., 1890 (*The Aegis & Intelligencer*, 4 Jul 1890)

Sidwell, Clara, student, Macton School (*The Aegis & Intelligencer*, 4 Jul 1890)

Sidwell, Owen, student, Macton School (*The Aegis & Intelligencer*, 4 Jul 1890)

Siford, Matthew, age 21 in 1890 (Marriage License Applications Book ALJ No. 2, 1891)

Sills, Harry, 1874-1963, native of Harford Furnace, Harford Co., son of William T. Sills and Priscilla Barnaby (Pennington Funeral Home Records)

Sills, Jacob H., 1837-1909 (Cokesbury Memorial Methodist Church Cemetery)

Sills, James Elias, 1870-1948, native of Harford Furnace, Harford Co, born 15 Sep 1870, son of William T. Sills, native of Harford Furnace, and ---- [Priscilla Barnaby], native of Kent Co., MD (Pennington Funeral Home Records)

Sills, John Willard, 1870-1926 (Angel Hill Cemetery)

Sills, Josephine W., 1841-1927 (Cokesbury Memorial Methodist Church Cemetery)

Sills, Oletia Lizzie, 1876-1925 (Angel Hill Cemetery)

Sills, Sadie E., 1873-1960, native of Maryland, born 8 Apr 1873, daughter of William T. Sills and Priscilla Barnaby (Pennington Funeral Home Records - married name Dye)

Sills, Viola (Gordon), 1877-1960 (Angel Hill Cemetery)

Sills, William T., 1840-1906 (Angel Hill Cemetery); see Harry Sills, James Elias Sills and Sadie E. Sills, q.v.

Silver & Son Packing Co., Havre de Grace (*1953 Harford County Directory*, p. 155)

Silver, A. Louise, 1878-1920 (Grove Presbyterian Church Cemetery)

Silver, Albert P., 1852-1905 (Deer Creek Harmony Presbyterian Church Cemetery); road commissioner and surveyor, Second District (*Havre de Grace Republican*, 7 Feb 1890 and 4 Jul 1890)

Silver, Alden R., 1885-1967 (Rock Run Methodist Church Cemetery)

Silver, Anna (Burnsworth), 1860-1924 (Deer Creek Harmony Presbyterian Church Cemetery)

Silver, Anna M., 1864-1952 (Deer Creek Harmony Presbyterian Church Cemetery)

Silver, Anna W. (Whiteford), 1874-1959 (Slateville Cemetery, York Co., PA); native of Flintville, Harford Co., born 20 Dec 1874, daughter of James R. Whiteford and Mary E. Gladden, q.v.

Silver, Annie P., 1822-1891 (Deer Creek Harmony Presbyterian Church Cemetery)

Silver, Benjamin, 1810-1894 (Deer Creek Harmony Presbyterian Church Cemetery); also see Mary Warnock Silver, q.v.

Silver, Benjamin Hoopman, 1857-1937 (Death certificate; Deer Creek Harmony Presbyterian Church Cemetery); superintendent, Glenville Union Sunday School, 1890 (*The Aegis & Intelligencer*, 22 Aug 1890)

Silver, Benjamin, Jr., 1857-1890 (Deer Creek Harmony Presbyterian Church Cemetery); married Frances Howard Archer (*Our Silver Heritage*, by Benjamin Stump Silver and Frances Aylette (Bowen) Silver, 1976, p. 3051); State Senator (*Havre de Grace Republican*, 28 Feb 1890); juror, Second District (*Havre de Grace Republican*, 2 May 1890); deceased and removed from the voter registration list at Hopewell, Second District (*Havre de Grace Republican*, 26 Sep 1890); died testate and his only named heir was his wife Fannie H. Silver (Harford County Will Book JMM 11:123-124)

Silver, Carrie G., 1871-1924 (Deer Creek Harmony Presbyterian Church Cemetery)

Silver, Charles Bartol, 1867-1947 (Rock Run Methodist Church Cemetery); born 17 Nov 1867, son of George B. and Charlotte C. (Hughes) Silver (*The Hughes Genealogy, 1636-1953*, by Joseph Lee Hughes, 1953, p. 106)

Silver, Charlotte Catherine "Kate" (Hughes), 1842-1911 (Rock Run Methodist Church Cemetery), wife of

George Bartol Silver, q.v.

Silver, David H., 1832-1894 (*Deaths and Marriages in Harford County, Maryland, and Vicinity, 1873-1904, from the Diaries of Albert Peter Silver*, transcribed by Glenn Randers-Pehrson, 1995, p. 22)

Silver, David H., 1872-1926 (*Our Silver Heritage*, by Benjamin Stump Silver and Frances Aylette (Bowen) Silver, 1976, p. 3055); actor, musical entertainment, at Darlington (*The Aegis & Intelligencer*, 30 May 1890)

Silver, E. Pamela, 1865-1952 (Deer Creek Harmony Presbyterian Church Cemetery)

Silver, Edith Wistar (Stokes), 1872-1949 (Darlington Cemetery)

Silver, Eliza Jane, 1836-1907 (Deer Creek Harmony Presbyterian Church Cemetery)

Silver, Emily M., see Mary Warnock Silver, q.v.

Silver, Emily R., 1879-1918, married John Z. Bayless (*Our Silver Heritage*, by Benjamin Stump Silver and Frances Aylette (Bowen) Silver, 1976, p. 3051)

Silver, Florence (Small), 1874-1964 (Deer Creek Harmony Presbyterian Church Cemetery), second wife of William Scott Silver, q.v.

Silver, Francina Christie (Hopkins), 1872-1952 (Deer Creek Harmony Presbyterian Church Cemetery), wife of Charles Bartol Silver, q.v.

Silver, Frances H. "Fannie" (Archer), wife of Benjamin Silver, Jr., q.v.

Silver, George Bartol, 1838-1902 (Rock Run Methodist Church Cemetery); county commissioner, Second District (*Havre de Grace Republican*, 4 Jul 1890); George and Charlotte Catherine "Kate" (Hughes) Silver resided near Lapidum (*The Aegis & Intelligencer*, 5 Dec 1890; *Our Silver Heritage*, by Benjamin Stump Silver and Frances Aylette (Bowen) Silver, 1976, p. 3056); partner, Silver, Spencer & Co., fishing floats (*Heavy Industries of Yesteryear; Harford County's Rural Heritage*, by Jack L. Shagena, Jr. and Henry C. Peden, Jr., 2015, p. 62)

Silver, George E., 1854-1924 (Deer Creek Harmony Presbyterian Church Cemetery); president of the Third Annual Convention, Farmers' Club of Harford County (*Havre de Grace Republican*, 28 Nov 1890); president, Harford County Farmers' Association (*The Aegis & Intelligencer*, 17 Jan 1890); trustee, Trappe School No. 14, Fifth District (*Havre de Grace Republican*, 30 May 1890)

Silver, George Osborn, 1859-1920 (Angel Hill Cemetery)

Silver, Harry, 1864-1929 (Deer Creek Harmony Presbyterian Church Cemetery states he was born in 1865, but his death certificate and *Our Silver Heritage*, by Benjamin Stump Silver and Frances Aylette (Bowen) Silver, 1976, p. 3055, both state it was 1864)

Silver, Henrietta, 1833-1890 (Deer Creek Harmony Presbyterian Church Cemetery), daughter of the late William Silver (*The Aegis & Intelligencer*, 18 Apr 1890)

Silver, Henrietta, 1870-1948 (Deer Creek Harmony Presbyterian Church Cemetery)

Silver, Henry Zephaniah, 1840-1910 (Grove Presbyterian Church Cemetery); general road supervisor, Second District (*The Aegis & Intelligencer*, 28 Mar 1890); road mender, near Avondale (*The Aegis & Intelligencer*, 5 Sep 1890); road supervisor, Bush River Neck (*The Aegis & Intelligencer*, 11 Jul 1890); member, Order of the Golden Chain, at Aberdeen (*Havre de Grace Republican*, 14 Mar 1890); delegate, Second District, Democrat Party Convention (*The Aegis & Intelligencer*, 5 Sep 1890); also see Mary Ellen Silver, q.v.

Silver, Ida Mary (Osborn), 1859-1948 (Rock Run Methodist Church Cemetery); second wife of Joel W. Silver, q.v.

Silver, Indiana "India" Pearl (Smith), 1872-1896 (Rock Run Methodist Church Cemetery); first wife of William Scott Silver, q.v.; also see India P. Smith, q.v.

Silver, Isabel Pannell, see George Taylor Milton, q.v.

Silver, Jeremiah P., 1826-1897 (Deer Creek Harmony Presbyterian Church Cemetery); farmer in Glenville (*The Aegis & Intelligencer*, 17 Jan 1890); trustee of the Maryland Agricultural College (*Havre de Grace Republican*, 21 Feb 1890); director, Mutual Fire Insurance Company in Harford County (*The Aegis & Intelligencer*, 10 Jan

1890); J. P. Silver was awarded a diploma from the Paris Exposition of 1889 for his "Silver Yellow" corn measuring fifteen inches long (*Harford Democrat*, 17 Jan 1890)

Silver, Joel W., 1863-1944 (Rock Run Methodist Church Cemetery); farmer and native of Piedmont, WV (Bailey Funeral Home Records); see and Ida Mary Silver and Mary Iola Silver, q.v.

Silver, Joseph, canner, Deer Creek (*Havre de Grace Republican*, 4 Apr 1890); treated by unidentified doctor in 1890 ("Medical Account Book – 1890," Historical Society of Harford County Archives Folder)

Silver, John A., 1863-1916 (Deer Creek Harmony Presbyterian Church Cemetery)

Silver, John E., 1866-1935 (Deer Creek Harmony Presbyterian Church Cemetery)

Silver, Lillian B., born 15 Jan 1888 (John R. Spencer Bible, *Maryland Bible Records, Volume 2*, by Henry C. Peden, Jr., 2003, p. 137)

Silver, Lillie May (Hopkins), 1864-1901 (Deer Creek Harmony Presbyterian Church Cemetery); wife of Benjamin Hoopma Silver, q.v.

Silver, Lydia Corinne, 1879-1963 (Angel Hill Cemetery)

Silver, Margaret A., 1835-1897 (Deer Creek Harmony Presbyterian Church); wife of William Silver, of David (*Our Silver Heritage*, by Benjamin Stump Silver and Frances Aylette (Bowen) Silver, 1976, p. 3053)

Silver, Mary, 1834-1897 (Darlington Cemetery)

Silver, Mary C., 1824-1897 (Deer Creek Harmony Presbyterian Church Cemetery)

Silver, Mary Cordelia, 1842-1928 (Deer Creek Harmony Presbyterian Church Cemetery)

Silver, Mary E., 1827-1903 (Deer Creek Harmony Presbyterian Church Cemetery)

Silver, Mary Ellen (Fletcher), 1839-1929 (Grove Presbyterian Church Cemetery), wife of Henry Zephaniah Silver, q.v.

Silver, Mary Iola, 1854-1931 (Deer Creek Harmony Presbyterian Church Cemetery)

Silver, Mary Iola, 1862-1890 (Rock Run Methodist Church Cemetery); first wife of Joel W. Silver, of near Garland, youngest daughter of Mr. & Mrs. John R. Spencer, and sister-in-law of Charles W. Proctor, of Bel Air (*The Aegis & Intelligencer*, 17 Oct 1890)

Silver, Mary Warnock, 1849-1907, daughter of Benjamin and Emily M. Silver (*Our Silver Heritage*, by Benjamin Stump Silver and Frances Aylette (Bowen) Silver, 1976, p. 3051; Deer Creek Harmony Presbyterian Church Cemetery)

Silver, Mercy, see George Howard Osborne, q.v.

Silver, Moses, Civil War veteran, Stearns Precinct (*1890 Special Census of the Civil War Veterans of the State of Maryland*, by L. Tilden Moore, Volume III, p. 83)

Silver, Rosa Gertrude (Stifler), 1874-1953 (Deer Creek Harmony Presbyterian Church Cemetery)

Silver, Sarah A. (Osmond), 1827-1900 (Death certificate; Deer Creek Harmony Presbyterian Church Cemetery); wife of William Z. Silver, q.v.

Silver, Sarah H., born 2 Nov 1886 (John R. Spencer Bible, *Maryland Bible Records, Volume 2*, by Henry C. Peden, Jr., 2003, p. 137)

Silver, Silas B., 1852-1919 (Deer Creek Harmony Presbyterian Church Cemetery); sold land in April 1890 (*The Aegis & Intelligencer*, 9 May 1890)

Silver, Spencer & Co., float fisherman, below Lapidum in the Susquehanna River (*The Aegis & Intelligencer*, 4 Apr 1890)

Silver, Susan S. (Pannell), 1827-1896 (Deer Creek Harmony Presbyterian Church Cemetery)

Silver, Susanna "Susan" (Kirk), 1839-1901 (Deer Creek Harmony Presbyterian Church Cemetery)

Silver, Susie E. (Miss), 1858-1928 (Deer Creek Harmony Presbyterian Church Cemetery); native of Maryland, resided in Aberdeen (Death certificate)

Silver, Sylvester A., 1828-1916 (Deer Creek Harmony Presbyterian Church Cemetery); resident near Glenville

(*The Aegis & Intelligencer*, 14 Feb 1890); treated by unidentified doctor in 1890 ("Medical Account Book – 1890," Historical Society of Harford County Archives Folder)

Silver, W. F. & Bro., tomato farmers, Chapel Road, near Havre de Grace (*Havre de Grace Republican*, 16 May 1890)

Silver, William, 1866-1923 (Angel Hill Cemetery); trustee, Prospect School No. 15, Second District (*Havre de Grace Republican*, 30 May 1890)

Silver, William, 1870-1934 (Darlington Cemetery)

Silver, William Finney (Rev.), 1859-1944 (Deer Creek Harmony Presbyterian Church Cemetery; Pennington Funeral Home Records); pastor of Hopewell M. P. Church (*Havre de Grace Republican*, 25 Apr 1890)

Silver, William Scott, 1871-1942 (Rock Run Methodist Church Cemetery); actor, Darlington Company, 1890 (*Havre de Grace Republican*, 7 Mar 1890); born 21 Dec 1871, son of George B. and Charlotte C. (Hughes) Silver (*The Hughes Genealogy, 1636-1953*, by Joseph Lee Hughes, 1953, p. 106)

Silver, William Z., 1825-1901 (Deer Creek Harmony Presbyterian Church Cemetery)

Simmonds, George E., 1877-1952 (St. Mary's Episcopal Church Cemetery)

Simmonds, Rina G., 1877-1952 (St. Mary's Episcopal Church Cemetery)

Simmons, Alice (Ford), 1871-1945 (St. George's Episcopal Church Cemetery)

Simmons, Andrew M., 1866-1949 (Grace Chapel Cemetery)

Simmons, C. E. (Rev.), pastor of Jarrettsville Methodist Episcopal Church South (*The Aegis & Intelligencer*, 10 Oct 1890)

Simmons, Carrie Naudine, baptized 6 Nov 1892, age 6, daughter of Joseph M. and Mary V. Simmons (St. George's Episcopal Church Register of Baptisms, pp. 10-11)

Simmons, Charles H., 1866-1956 (St. George's Episcopal Church Cemetery)

Simmons, Ellen (colored), 1852-1911 (Death certificate; St. James United Cemetery)

Simmons, Essie (colored), 1890-1955 (St. James United Cemetery)

Simmons, Henry, 1854-1925 (Mt. Zion Methodist Church Cemetery)

Simmons, James M., 1880-1961 (Mt. Zion Methodist Church Cemetery)

Simmons, Joanne M., 1876-1942 (Grace Chapel Cemetery)

Simmons, Joseph M., 1824-1902 (Angel Hill Cemetery); owner of Poe's Point Fishery at the mouth of the Susquehanna River and former Havre de Grace town commissioner (*Biographical Dictionary of Harford County, Maryland, 1774-1974*, by Henry C. Peden, Jr. and William O. Carr, 2021, p. 249); resident of Spesutia Island by 1890 (*Havre de Grace Republican*, 27 Jun 1890); also see Carrie Naudine Simmons, q.v.

Simmons, Mary Virginia (Morgan), 1848-1936 (Angel Hill Cemetery), second wife of Joseph M. Simmons, q.v.

Simmons, Rieman R., age 26 in 1890 (Marriage License Applications Book ALJ No. 2, 1891)

Simmons, Sarah Ellen, 1858-1933 (Mt. Zion Methodist Church Cemetery)

Simmons, Sarah S., 1882-1956 (Mt. Zion Methodist Church Cemetery)

Simms, Annie (colored), see John Ernest Rice (colored), q.v.

Simms (Sims) Annie S. (colored), see Ada Nickenson (colored), q.v.

Simms, Charles W. (colored), c1864-1914, native of Michaelsville, Harford Co. (*The Aegis*, 6 Nov 1914); trustee, Michaelsville Colored School No. 2, Second District, 1890 (*Havre de Grace Republican*, 30 May 1890)

Simms, Elizabeth, see George Swift, q.v.

Simms, Henrietta (Johnson) (colored), 1819-1901 (Union Methodist Church Cemetery, Aberdeen); native of Michaelsville, Harford Co., wife of Jacob Simms, Sr. (Death certificate)

Simms, Irene (colored), see Howard Johnson (colored), q.v.

Simms, Jacob (colored), 1840-1899 (Union Methodist Church Cemetery, Aberdeen)

Simms. Jacob, Sr. (colored), see Henrietta Simms (colored), q.v.

Simms, Louisa (colored), 1876-1903 (Asbury Church Cemetery)

Simms, Margaret (Mrs.) (colored), c1842-1932, native of Frederick Co., MD, resided at Pylesville, parents unknown (Death certificate); wife of Samuel Simms, q.v.

Simms, Martha (oolored), see Charles Peaker (colored) and Isaiah Peaco (colored), q.v.

Simms, Mary (colored), see Irene Belle Clark (colored), q.v.

Simms, Robert H. (colored), 1873-1929, parents unknown (Death certificate)

Simms, Samuel (colored), 1842-1919, native of Harford Co., resided at Pylesville (Death certificate)

Simonds, Homer L., 1886-1919 (Angel Hill Cemetery)

Simonds, Laura (Miss), 1856-1924 (Cokesbury Memorial Methodist Church Cemetery); native of Harford Co., resided at Emmorton (Death certificate)

Simone, Mary, 1876-1946 (Mt. Erin Cemetery)

Simone, Nunzio, 1869-1925 (Mt. Erin Cemetery)

Simons, Emma (Polk), 1851-1907, native of Maryland, resided in Abingdon, wife of Sidney A. Simons (Death certificate; St. Mary's Episcopal Church Cemetery)

Simpers, ----, left fielder, A. R. Walker Baseball Club, Havre de Grace (*Havre de Grace Republican*, 4 Jul 1890)

Simpers, Francis ("Frank"), Civil War veteran, Havre de Grace (*1890 Special Census of the Civil War Veterans of the State of Maryland*, by L. Tilden Moore, Volume III, p. 91); see Harry W. Simpers and Lewis Simpers, q.v.

Simpers, Harry W., 1870-1928 (Angel Hill Cemetery); native of Maryland, resident of Havre de Grace, born 24 Dec 1870, son of Frank Simpers and ---- (Death certificate)

Simpers, John A., new name on the voter registration list in Sixth District, 1890 (*Havre de Grace Republican*, 17 Oct 1890)

Simpers, Lewis, 1875-1932 (Angel Hill Cemetery); native of Maryland, born 3 Oct 1875, son of Francis Simpers and Nellie McCall (Death certificate)

Simpson, Noah Franklin, 1850-1921 (Baker Cemetery)

Simpson, William H., 1855-1903 (Baker Cemetery)

Singer's General Store and Post Office, at Singer, between Abingdon and Mountain, Catherine Singer, proprietor and post mistress (*Country Stores: Harford County's Rural Heritage*, by Henry C. Peden, Jr. and Jack L. Shagena, Jr., 2015, p. 230)

Singer, Catherine, 1828-1898 (St. Mary's Episcopal Church Cemetery)

Singleton's Singing School, Upper Cross Roads, Fourth District (*Harford County, Maryland Teachers and the Schools They Served, 1774-1900*, by Henry C. Peden, Jr., 2022, p. 372)

Singleton, Acel, 1874-1900, native of Harford Co., resided at Level, son of Acel Singleton and Grace ---- (Death certificate)

Singleton, Amelia A., 1884-1944 (Mt. Tabor Methodist Church Cemetery; Bailey Funeral Home Records stated born in 1885 in Baltimore, daughter of John Steube)

Singleton, Aresice E., see Arisice E. Hutton, q.v.

Singleton, Asel, resident near Glenville, charged with larceny in 1890, found guilty, and sent to the House of Corrections for 6 months (Harford County Criminal Docket, 1888-1892, p. 92; *The Aegis & Intelligencer*, 18 Jul 1890. listed him as Jr.)

Singleton, Charles, 1859-1927 (Mt. Tabor Methodist Church Cemetery); former employee of Robert B. Hopkins, near Churchville (*The Aegis & Intelligencer*, 15 Aug 1890)

Singleton, Charles Henry, 1884-1897 (Holy Trinity Episcopal Church Cemetery), but he was actually born on 29 Jul 1883, son of James P. and Harriet Singleton (Holy Trinity Episcopal Church Register of Baptisms, p. 86)

Singleton, David, born -- May 1879, son of James P. and Harriet A. Singleton (Holy Trinity Episcopal Church Register of Baptisms, p. 82)

Singleton, Elijah Thomas, 1867-1933 (Holy Trinity Episcopal Church Cemetery)

Singleton, Elizabeth (Griffith), 1876-1934 (Mt. Tabor Methodist Church Cemetery); native of Harford Co., born 14 Jan 1876, daughter of William Griffith and Pinie Singleton (Bailey Funeral Home Records)

Singleton, Elizabeth A., 1849-1935 (Tabernacle Cemetery); native of Pilot Town, Cecil Co., MD (Bailey Funeral Home Records); wife of Robert J. Singleton, q.v.

Singleton, Elizabeth J. (Richie), 1843-1931 (Mt. Tabor Methodist Church Cemetery); wife of William T. Singleton, q.v.

Singleton, Emily May, born 17 Feb 1877, daughter of James P. and Harriet A. Singleton (Holy Trinity Episcopal Church Register of Baptisms, p. 82)

Singleton, Florida, see Florida White, q.v.

Singleton, Francis Thomas, born 2 May 1889, baptized 22 Aug 1889, son of James P. and Harriet A. Singleton (Holy Trinity Episcopal Church Register of Baptisms, p. 96)

Singleton, Frederick, 1867-1900 (Holy Trinity Episcopal Church Cemetery)

Singleton, Grace "Gracie" Ann, 1849-1924 (Bailey Funeral Home Records); see Acel Singleton, q.v.

Singleton, Hannah Jane, 1840-1908 (Holy Trinity Episcopal Church Cemetery); wife of Elijah Thomas Singleton; also see Thomas Elsworth Singleton, John Wesley Singleton, William James Singleton and Mary Elizabeth Singleton, q.v.

Singleton, Harriet A., 1842-1917 (Holy Trinity Episcopal Church Cemetery); wife of James P. Singleton, q.v.; also see David Singleton and Elizabeth May Singleton, q.v.

Singleton, Henry, 1830-1912 (Dublin Methodist Church Cemetery)

Singleton, Henry M., see Aresice E. Hutton, q.v.

Singleton, Ida (Cullum), 1880-1922 (Bailey Funeral Home Records)

Singleton, J. Marion, treasurer, Venus Council No. 44, O. U. A. M., Havre de Grace (*Havre de Grace Republican*, 11 Jul 1890)

Singleton, James, see Sarah E. Singleton, q.v.

Singleton, James P., 1845-1917 (Holy Trinity Episcopal Church Cemetery); see Charles Henry Singleton, Sarah Singleton, Frances Thomas Singleton, David Singleton and Elizabeth May Singleton, q.v.

Singleton, John, see John Henry Singleton, q.v.

Singleton, John H., 1828-1923 (Death certificate); Civil War veteran, at Level (*1890 Special Census of the Civil War Veterans of the State of Maryland*, by L. Tilden Moore, Volume III, p. 67); charged with rape, but found not guilty (Harford County Criminal Docket, 1888-1892, p. 88)

Singleton, John H., 1886-1918 (Rock Run Methodist Church Cemetery)

Singleton, John Henry, 1852-1948 (Slate Ridge Cemetery, York Co., PA); native of Harford Co., born 10 Oct 1852, son of John Singleton and Mary Mubury (Harkins Funeral Home Records; Death certificate)

Singleton, John Wesley, born 11 May 1874, son of Elijah Thomas and Hannah Jane Singleton (Holy Trinity Episcopal Church Register of Baptisms, p. 88)

Singleton, Katie E., near Glenville, married Joseph Baldwin on 12 Feb 1890 (*The Aegis & Intelligencer*, 7 Mar 1890); age 21 in 1889 (Marriage License Applications Book ALJ No. 2, 1890)

Singleton, Laura, 1882-1907 (Holy Trinity Episcopal Church Cemetery)

Singleton, Lizzie Jane, age 22 in 1890 (Marriage License Applications Book ALJ No. 2, 1890)

Singleton, Mary (Mrs), died 12 Jan 1896 (Angel Hill Cemetery)

Singleton, Mary Elizabeth, born 17 Aug 1878, daghter of Elijah Thomas and Hannah Jane Simgleton (Holy Trinity Episcopal Church Register of Baptisms, p. 88)

Singleton, Melissa, see Samuel John Norris, q.v.

Singleton, Mollie, student, Macton School (*The Aegis & Intelligencer*, 4 Jul 1890)

Singleton, Pinie, see Elizabeth (Griffth) Singleton, q.v.

Singleton, Robert J., Civil War veteran, Macton P. O. (*1890 Special Census of the Civil War Veterans of the State of Maryland*, by L. Tilden Moore, Volume III, p. 88; Tabernacle Cemetery - no dates on marker)

Singleton, Sarah, born 6 May 1881, daughter of James Polk and Harriet A. Singleton (Holy Cross Episcopal Church Register of Baptisms, p. 84)

Singleton, Sarah E., 1884-1961 (Dublin Cemetery); native of Harford Co., born 11 May 1884, daughter of James Singleton and Harriett Morris (Bailey Funeral Home Records)

Singleton, Theodore, born 25 Aug 1885, son of James Polk and Harriet A. Singleton (Holy Trinity Episcopal Church Register of Baptisms, p. 88)

Singleton, Thomas Elsworth, born 30 Jan 1870, son of Elijah Thomas and Hannah Jane Simgleton (Death certificate and Holy Trinity Episcopal Church Register of Baptisms, p. 88; Holy Trinity Episcopal Church Cemetery tombstone incorrectly inscribed 1868)

Singleton, William, treated by unidentified doctor in 1890 ("Medical Account Book – 1890," Historical Society of Harford County Archives Folder)

Singleton, William James, born 17 May 1880, son of Elijah Thomas and Hannah Jane Singleton (Holy Trinity Episcopal Church Register of Baptisms, p. 88)

Singleton, William Milton, 1886-1968 (Mt. Tabor Methodist Church Cemetery); native of Dublin, Harford Co., born 24 Oct 1886 (Harkins Funeral Home Records)

Singleton, William T., 1833-1914 (Mt. Tabor Methodist Church Cemetery)

Singleton, William Tecomtion, 1864-1931 (Holy Trinity Episcopal Church Cemetery)

Sitzler's General Store and Grocery Store, Havre de Grace, Leonard F. Sitzler, prop. (*Country Stores: Harford County's Rural Heritage*, by Henry C. Peden, Jr. and Jack L. Shagena, Jr., 2015, p. 230; *Havre de Grace Republican*, 19 Dec 1890)

Sitzler, Emma Regina, 1875-1923 (Angel Hill Cemetery)

Sitzler, J. Albert, 1882-1964, native of Havre de Grace, born 15 Nov 1882, son of Leonard Sitzler and ---- (Pennington Funeral Home Records)

Sitzler, L. Franklin, 1879-1928 (Angel Hill Cemetery)

Sitzler, Leonard F., 1843-1927, native of Pennsylvania, Civil War veteran (Angel Hill Cemetery); grocery store merchant, Stokes Street, Havre de Grace (*Havre de Grace Republican*, 19 Dec 1890); officer of the day, John Rodgers Post, G. A. R., Havre de Grace (*Havre de Grace Republican*, 12 Dec 1890); see J. Albert Sitzler, q.v.

Sitzler, Medora Helen, 1855-1923 (Angel Hill Cemetery)

Sitzler, Nola E. (Devine), 1887-1957 (Angel Hill Cemetery)

Skelley, John M., 1861-1923 (Angel Hill Cemetery)

Skelley, Mary A., 1837-1916 (Angel Hill Cemetery)

Skelley, Michael, 1837-1903 (Angel Hill Cemetery); noble grand, Morning Star Lodge No. 20, I. O. O. F., Havre de Grace (*Havre de Grace Republican*, 11 Jul 1890)

Skelley, Nellie F., 1869-1957 (Angel Hill Cemetery)

Skillman, Arthur Albert, 1869-1927 (St. Francis de Sales Catholic Church Cemetery)

Skillman, Blanche (Leone), 1869-1951 (Cokesbury Memorial Methodist Church Cemetery)

Skillman, Elizabeth, 1877-1920 (St. Francis de Sales Catholic Church Cemetery)

Skillman, Emma Alverta, 1874-1900 (St. Francis de Sales Catholic Church Cemetery); native of Harford Co., resided at Edgwood, daughter of Joseph Francis Skillman and Lucretia Ray (Death certificate)

Skillman, Harry, 1883-1952 (Cokesbury Memorial Methodist Church Cemetery)

Skillman, John Lloyd, 1860-1927 (Cokesbury Memorial Methodist Church Cemetery)

Skillman, Joseph Francis, 1855-1926 (St. Francis de Sales Catholic Church Cemetery); native of Maryland, farmer, single, resided at Joppa (Death certificate); see Emma Alverta Skillman, q.v.

Skillman, Lottie, 1887-1946 (Cokesbury Memorial Methodist Church Cemetery)

Skillman, Mary C., 1869-1952 (St. Francis de Sales Catholic Church Cemetery)

Skillman, Thomas, road surveying chain man, First District (*Havre de Grace Republican*, 4 Jul 1890)

Skillman, William N., 1868-1932 (St. Francis de Sales Catholic Church Cemetery); new name on the voter registration list at Magnolia, First District, 1890 (*Havre de Grace Republican*, 17 Oct 1890)

Skinner, Elizabeth (Sorrell) (colored), c1885-1920, native of Maryland (Death certificate)

Skinner, Emma (colored), 1878-1946, native of Havre de Grace, born 16 Jul 1878, daughter of John Skinner and Frances(?) Skinner, both natives of Havre de Grace (Death certificate; Pennington Funeral Home Records - married name Summons)

Skinner, Emma Frances (Willis) (colored), 1883-1973, native of Centeville, MD, resident of Havre de Grace (St. James United Cemetery; *The Aegis*, 18 Oct 1973)

Skinner, Fannie (colored), see William Sorrell (colored), q.v.

Skinner, Frances J. (Legar) (colored), c1842-1920, native of Maryland (Death certificate)

Skinner, Henry, name removed from the voter registration list in Sixth District, 1890 (*Havre de Grace Republican*, 17 Oct 1890)

Skinner, Henry (colored), 1850-1918, native of Maryland (Death certificate)

Skinner, Horace S. (colored), 1867-1934 (St. James United Cemetery); age 23 in 1890 (Marriage License Applications Book ALJ No. 2, 1890)

Skinner, John (colored), see Emma Skinner (colored), q.v.

Skinner, John Tobias "Tobe" (colored), c1863-1930, fish hauling contractor, Havre de Grace, 1890 (Death certificate; *Bel Air Times*, 23 May 1930; *Havre de Grace Republican*, 5 Dec 1890); see William Skinner, q.v.

Skinner, Lewis (colored), 1859-1904 (Death certificate)

Skinner, Mary (colored), born -- Jun 1850, native of Maryland (1900 Aberdeen Census)

Skinner, Mary Ellen (colored), see I. Henry Wise (colored), q.v.

Skinner, Rosa G. (Boydton) (colored), 1871-1936, native of Virginia, resident of Havre de Grace, parents unknown (St. James United Cemetery tombstone inscribed 1871, but death certificate states born 1872)

Skinner, Sadie (colored), 1882?-1901 (Skinner Cemetery, Havre de Grace)

Skinner, Sidney H. (colored), see Thomas G. Skinner (colored), q.v.

Skinner, Thomas G. (colored), 1874-1912, native of Maryland, born 3 Dec 1874, son of Sidney H. Skinner, native of Havre de Grace, and Frances Leger, native of Baltimore (Death certificate)

Skinner, William "Willie" (colored), 1884-1907, son of J. T. Skinner and Lizzie Sorrell (Death certificate; Skinner Cemetery, Havre de Grace)

Slack, Henry, died 14 Jan 1904, adult, no age given (Alms House Record Book)

Slade's General Store and Post Office, Castleton, George Slade, proprietor and postmaster (*Country Stores: Harford County's Rural Heritage*, by Henry C. Peden, Jr. and Jack L. Shagena, Jr., 2015, p. 231)

Slade, Asbury, 1861-1936 (Bethel Presbyterian Church Cemetery Records); resided near Norrisville (*The Aegis & Intelligencer*, 21 Mar 1890); see Caroline Slade, q.v.

Slade, Bertha C. (Mechem), 1883-1918 (St. Ignatius Catholic Church Cemetery)

Slade, Bessie, V., 1885-1959 (Jarrettsville Cemetery)

Slade, Caroline, died testate between 14 Feb 1890 and 12 Feb 1891 and her named heirs were husband Asbury

Slade and grandsons John R. Wiley, Asbury B. Wiley and William R. Wiley (Harford County Will Book JMM 11:165-166)

Slade, Catherine (Lochary), 1830-1907 (St. Ignatius Catholic Church Cemetery)

Slade, Charles, born -- Apr 1884, baptized 22 May 1884, son of William and Frances (Boarman) Slade (St. Ignatius Catholic Church Baptism Register, p. 73)

Slade, Charles Howard, 1887-1974 (St. Mary's Catholic Church Cemetery; born -- Sep 1887, baptized 16 Oct 1887, son of John S. and Rose (Wheeler) Slade (St. Ignatius Catholic Church Baptism Register, p. 95)

Slade, David S., 1882-1966 (Jarrettsville Cemetery)

Slade, Elizabeth A. (Wiley), 1871-1947 (Bethel Presbyterian Church Cemetery Records); wife of Asbury Slade, q.v.

Slade, Elizabeth J., 1877-1937 (Mt. Erin Cemetery)

Slade, Ethel, student, Forest Hill School, 1890 (*The Aegis*, 2 Jul 1965, school picture)

Slade, Ezekiel, see Mary Slade, q.v.

Slade, George, baptized 12 Mar 1882, son of John and Rose (Wheeler) Slade (St. Ignatius Catholic Church Baptism Register, p. 59)

Slade, George W., 1860-1933 (St. Ignatius Catholic Church Cemetery); George W. Slade & Co., cash store, Castleton (*The Aegis & Intelligencer*, 19 Dec 1890)

Slade, Grover C., 1884-1930 (Jarrettsville Cemetery)

Slade, Hannah, see Florence D. Barton and Walter Morris, q.v.

Slade, Hannah (Miss), 1828-1899 (Bethel Presbyterian Church Cemetery Records)

Slade, J. Randolph, 1865-1939 (Bethel Presbyterian Church Cemetery Records)

Slade, James A., 1825-1911 (Bethel Presbyterian Church Cemetery Records)

Slade, James Isaac, 1880-1957 (Jarrettsville Cemetery)

Slade, James J., 1850-1939 (Bethel Presbyterian Church Cemetery Records)

Slade, John S., 1854-1928 (St. Ignatius Catholic Church Cemetery); native of Maryland, farmer, married, resided at Hickory (Death certificate)

Slade, Katherine Mary, baptized 18 Sep 1880, daughter of William Slade and Mary Frances Boarman (St. Ignatius Catholic Church Baptism Register, p. 49)

Slade, L. Sydney (Lynch), 1884-1947 (Jarrettsville Cemetery)

Slade, Laura Regina, born -- Aug 1889, baptized 6 Sep 1889, daughter of William Slade and Mary Frances Boarman (St. Ignatius Catholic Church Baptism Register, p. 107)

Slade, Lawrence, baptized 15 Nov 1882, son of William T. Slade and Mary Frances Boarman, of near Kalmia (St. Ignatius Catholic Church Baptism Register, p. 62; *The Aegis & Intelligencer*, 29 Aug 1890)

Slade, Lida S. (Hunter), 1872-1931 (Bethel Presbyterian Church Cemetery Records); wife of J. Randolph Slade, q.v.

Slade, Louisa B. (Wright), 1829-1909 (Bethel Presbyterian Church Cemetery Records); wife of James A. Slade, q.v.

Slade, M. Elizabeth, 1890-1969 (St. Mary's Catholic Church Cemetery)

Slade, M. Rebecca (Martin), 1863-1947 (St. Ignatius Catholic Church Cemetery)

Slade, Martin, born -- Nov 1885, baptized 20 May 1893, son of Walter Slade, native of Harford Co., and Mary R. Martin, native of York, PA (St. Ignatius Catholic Church Baptism Register, p. 132)

Slade, Mary, widow of Ezekiel Slade, of Norrisville, now in her 95th year, saw a doctor for the first time in her life on 25 Jul 1890 (*The Aegis & Intelligencer*, 1 Aug 1890); died testate and her named heirs were daughters Rachel M. Strong and Alice P. Murphy, granddaughter Emma E. Strong and friend Joshua G. Luckey, executor

(Harford County Will Book JMM 11:132-133)

Slade, Mary Elizabeth, born -- Jul 1883, baptized 10 Aug 1883, daughter of John S. Slade and Rose Wheeler (St. Ignatius Catholic Church Baptism Register, p. 67)

Slade, Mary L. (Miss), 1863-1917 (Bethel Presbyterian Church Cemetery Records)

Slade, Mary Lillian, born -- Feb 1884, baptized 20 May 1893, daughter of Walter Slade, native of Harford Co., and Mary R. Martin, native of York, PA (St. Ignatius Catholic Church Baptism Register, p. 132)

Slade, Mary Susan (Fletcher) 1854-1928 (North Bend Presbyterian Church Cemetery); native of Harford Co., resided at Federal Hill (Death certificate)

Slade, Mary T., 1876-1948, daughter of James J. Slade and ---- Watkins (Bethel Presbyterian Church Cemetery Records)

Slade, Morgan S., 1886-1893 (North Bend Presbyterian Church Cemetery)

Slade, Pauline, born -- Sep 1889, baptized 6 Oct 1889, daughter of John Slade and Rose Wheeler (St. Ignatius Catholic Church Baptism Register, p. 108)

Slade, Rose (Wheeler), 1856-1935 (St. Ignatius Catholic Church Cemetery); wife of John S. Slade, q.v.

Slade, Rosa A., born -- Sep 1886, baptized 2 Nov 1886, daughter of William Slade and Mary Frances Boarman (St. Ignatius Catholic Church Baptism Register, p. 89)

Slade, Sallie J., 1877-1893 (North Bend Presbyterian Church Cemetery)

Slade, Stella, fifth grade student, Mount Horeb School (*The Aegis & Intelligencer*, 14 Feb 1890)

Slade, Tommy, 1890-1893 (North Bend Presbyterian Church Cemetery)

Slade, Walter B., 1889-1948 (St. Ignatius Catholic Church Cemetery)

Slade, Walter R., 1862-1940 (St. Ignatius Catholic Church Cemetery); born -- Feb 1862, baptized 12 Mar 1893 (ex-Methodist), son of Benjamin Slade, native of Washington, and Catharine Lochary, native of Harford Co. (St. Ignatius Catholic Church Baptism Register, p. 121)

Slade, William B., 1875-1950 (Salem Evangelical Lutheran Church Cemetery)

Slade, William R., 1853-1893 (North Bend Presbyterian Church Cemetery)

Slade, William T., farmer, near Kalmia (*The Aegis & Intelligencer*, 29 Aug 1890); see Lawrence Slade, q.v.

Slarrow, J. M. (Rev.), pastor, Bel Air M. E. Church (*Havre de Grace Republican*, 1 Aug 1890; *The Aegis & Intelligencer*, 14 Mar 1890); Rev. & Mrs. Slarrow, members, Loyal Temperance Legion of Bel Air (*The Aegis & Intelligencer*, 2 May 1890)

Slater, John H., milling business at Rockdale Mills on Winter's Run (*The Aegis & Intelligencer*, 20 Jun 1890); steward, Bel Air M. P. Church (*Havre de Grace Republican*, 28 Feb 1890)

Slaterman, Adam, Civil War veteran, Aberdeen (*1890 Special Census of the Civil War Veterans of the State of Maryland*, by L. Tilden Moore, Volume III, p. 64)

Slattery, William, clerk, Emmord's Store, Perryman (*Havre de Grace Republican*, 17 Oct 1890)

Slattery, William J., age 28 in 1890 (Marriage License Applications Book ALJ No. 2, 1891)

Slaymaker, Bertie J. (Miss), premium award winner, Class K - Household and Domestic Manufactures, Harford County Fair (*The Aegis & Intelligencer*, 24 Oct 1890)

Slee & Kenly's General Store, Aberdeen, George Slee and ---- Kenley, prop. (*Country Stores: Harford County's Rural Heritage*, by Henry C. Peden, Jr. and Jack L. Shagena, Jr., 2015, p. 231; *Havre de Grace Republican*, 9 May 1890)

Slee, Albert W., 1848-1909 (St. George's Episcopal Church Cemetery)

Slee, Annie Latty (Martin), 1848-1926 (St. George's Episcopal Church Cemetery; Death certificate)

Slee, Annie May, born 11 Jan 1874, daughter of Cicero C. and Annie L. Slee (Martin-Slee Bible, *Maryland Bible Records, Volume 1*, by Henry C. Peden, Jr., 2003, p. 162); student, Union School House, near Bush Chapel (*The Aegis & Intelligencer*, 14 Mar 1890)

Slee, Cicero Columbus, 1846-1937 (St. George's Episcopal Church Cemetery; Martin-Slee Bible, *Maryland Bible Records, Volume 1*, by Henry C. Peden, Jr., 2003, p. 162)

Slee, Coleman, 1847-1892 (St. George's Episcopal Church Cemetery; Martin-Slee Bible, *Maryland Bible Records, Volume 1*, by Henry C. Peden, Jr., 2003, p. 162)

Slee, George, 1862-1951 (St. George's Episcopal Church Cemetery); sneak boat duck hunter (*Havre de Grace Republican*, 7 Nov 1890)

Slee, George Henry, born 3 May 1881, son of Cicero C. and Annie L. Slee (Martin-Slee Bible, *Maryland Bible Records, Volume 1*, by Henry C. Peden, Jr., 2003, p. 162); student, Union School House, near Bush Chapel (*The Aegis & Intelligencer*, 14 Mar 1890)

Slee, Harold Martin, 1879-1906 (St. George's Episcopal Church Cemetery); born 23 Nov 1879, son of Cicero C. and Annie L. Slee (Martin-Slee Bible, *Maryland Bible Records, Volume 1*, by Henry C. Peden, Jr., 2003, p. 162); student, Union School House, near Bush Chapel (*The Aegis & Intelligencer*, 14 Mar 1890)

Slee, Jessie M., born 20 Jul 1886, died ---- (St. George's Episcopal Church Cemetery)

Slee, John Bay, born 16 Jun 1875, son of Cicero C. and Annie L. Slee (Martin-Slee Bible, *Maryland Bible Records, Volume 1*, by Henry C. Peden, Jr., 2003, p. 162); student, Union School House, near Bush Chapel (*The Aegis & Intelligencer*, 14 Mar 1890)

Slee, Laura F. (Torrance), 1875-1926 (St. George's Episcopal Church Cemetery; native of England, daughter of Dr. ---- Torrence and ---- Courtright (Death certificate)

Slee, Letitia, born 20 Jul 1884, daughter of Cicero C. and Annie L. Slee (Martin-Slee Bible, *Maryland Bible Records, Volume 1*, by Henry C. Peden, Jr., 2003, p. 162)

Slee, Martha Lourinda (Gallup), 1867-1941 (St. George's Episcopal Church Cemetery); wife of George Slee, q.v.

Slee, Mary, 1828-1905 (Churchville Presbyterian Church Cemetery)

Slee, N. Lipton, 1857-1945 (St. George's Episcopal Church Cemetery)

Slee, Sadie L. (Price), 1855-1952 (St. George's Episcopal Church Cemetery)

Slee, Susie Frost, born 21 May 1877, daughter of Cicero C. and Annie L. Slee (Martin-Slee Bible, *Maryland Bible Records, Volume 1*, by Henry C. Peden, Jr., 2003, p. 162); student, Union School House, near Bush Chapel (*The Aegis & Intelligencer*, 14 Mar 1890)

Slee, Warren Hudson, 1886-1950 (St. George's Episcopal Church Cemetery), born 2 Apr 1886, son of Cicero C. and Annie L. Slee (Martin-Slee Bible, *Maryland Bible Records, Volume 1*, by Henry C. Peden, Jr., 2003, p. 162)

Slee, William H., 1844-1924 (St. George's Episcopal Church Cemetery)

Sleek, Essie M., 1890-1965 (Church of the Ascension Church Cemetery)

Sleek, Harry B., 1865-1925 (Church of the Ascension Church Cemetery; Death certificate)

Slirka, Peter, acquired land in November 1890 (*The Aegis & Intelligencer*, 5 Dec 1890)

Sliver, Sarah (Combs), 1882-1961 (Mt. Olivet Cemetery); native of Pylesville, Harford Co., born 22 Aug 1881, daughter of George H. Combs and Mary Tarbert (Harkins Funeral Home Records)

Sloan, Mary (Wiley), 1885-1946, wife of Charles Sloan, of Ohio (Bethel Presbyterian Church Cemetery Records)

Slymer, A. F. (Mrs.), groceries and meats, Stokes Street, Havre de Grace (*Havre de Grace Republican*, 19 Dec 1890)

Slymer, Andrew F., government pensioner, Havre de Grace (*The Aegis & Intelligencer*, 14 Nov 1890); commander, John Rodgers Post, G. A. R., Havre de Grace (*Havre de Grace Republican*, 12 Dec 1890)

Slymer, Katie, married James L. Baker on 22 Oct 1890 (marriage certificate); age 23 in 1890 (Marriage License Applications Book ALJ No. 2, 1890)

Slymer, Mary F., businesswoman (trader's license), Havre de Grace (*Havre de Grace Republican*, 30 May 1890)

Slymer, Mary J., acquired land in February 1890 (*The Aegis & Intelligencer*, 7 Mar 1890)

Small, Florence, born 7 Dec 1874, daughter of Joseph D. and Mary (Pritchard) Small (*The Hughes Genealogy, 1636-1953*, by Joseph Lee Hughes, 1953, p. 117)

Small, George, sold land in February 1890 (*The Aegis & Intelligencer*, 7 Mar 1890)

Small, James Ruff, born 19 Dec 1872, son of Noah and Mary C. Small (Holy Trinity Episcopal Church Register of Baptisms, p. 84)

Small, John Billingsley, born 9 Sep 1877, son of Noah and Mary C. Small (Holy Trinity Episcopal Church Register of Baptisms, p. 84)

Small, Mary C. (Billingsley), 1849-1915, wife of Noah Small, q.v.

Small, Noah, 1844-1916 (Holy Trinity Episcopal Church Cemetery); constable, Third District (*Havre de Grace Republican*, 4 Jul 1890); town bailiff and lamp lighter, Bel Air (*The Aegis & Intelligencer*, 20 Jun 1890); also see John Billingsley Small, Adella Finney Small and James Ruff Small q.v.

Smallsbeck, Alice, premium award winner, Class L - Children's Department, Harford County Fair (*The Aegis & Intelligencer*, 24 Oct 1890)

Smallsbeck, Andrew, 1845-1911 (Wesleyan Chapel Methodist Church Cemetery)

Smallsbeck, Anna A., 1843-1915 (Wesleyan Chapel Methodist Church Cemetery)

Smallsbeck, Ette E., 1884-1957 (Wesleyan Chapel Methodist Church Cemetery)

Smallsbeck, Mary, student, Third District (*The Aegis & Intelligencer*, 24 Oct 1890)

Smart, Ann Mariah (Bradford) (colored), 1853-1917 (Death certificate); see Walter H. Smart, q.v.

Smart, George (colored), charged with disorderly conduct at allston in 1890, but no verdict was recorded in the docket book (*Harford Democrat*, 21 Feb 1890; Harford County Criminal Docket, 1888-1892, p. 82); also see George Guy, q.v.

Smart, Joseph (colored), 1846-1933, native of Baltimore Co. (Death certificate); see Walter H. Smart (colored) and William A. Smart (colored), q.v.

Smart, Marie (colored), see John Wesley Smith (colored), q.v.

Smart, Walter Howard (colored), 1887-1913, native of Harford Co., born 8 Aug 1887, son of Joseph Smart, of Baltimore Co., and Mariah Bradford, of Harford Co. (Death certificate)

Smart, William A. (colored), 1889-1901, native of Harford Co., resided at Clayton, son of Joseph Smart and Maria Bradford (Death certificate)

Smeltzer, Elizabeth, see Henrietta Harman, q.v.

Smeltzer, Mary, see William T. Walte, q.v.

Smeltzer, Philip, transferred from the voter registration list in the Sixth District (*Havre de Grace Republican*, 17 Oct 1890)

Smeltzer, William, superintendent, Tidewater Canal (*Havre de Grace Republican*, 4 Jul 1890)

Smick, Lewis, deceased and removed from the voter registration list at Hopewell, Second District (*Havre de Grace Republican*, 26 Sep 1890)

Smith Chapel Methodist Church and Cemetery (Churchville Road, Churchville)

Smith's General Store, Greenstone, John W. Smith, prop. (*Country Stores: Harford County's Rural Heritage*, by Henry C. Peden, Jr. and Jack L. Shagena, Jr., 2015, p. 234)

Smith's General Store, Lapidum, W. F. Smith, prop. (*Country Stores: Harford County's Rural Heritage*, by Henry C. Peden, Jr. and Jack L. Shagena, Jr., 2015, p. 234)

Smith's Singing School, Bel Air District (*Harford County, Maryland Teachers and the Schools They Served, 1774-1900*, by Henry C. Peden, Jr., 2022, p. 372)

Smith's Tanbark Mill and Feed Mill, Peddler's Run, Glen Cove, B. G. Smith & Sons, prop. (*Mills: Grist, Saw, Bone, Flint, Fulling ... & More*, by Jack L. Shagena, Jr., Henry C. Peden, Jr. and John W. McGrain, 2009, pp.

253-254)

Smith, A., left fielder, Baptist Baseball Club, of Fourth District (*Havre de Grace Republican*, 8 Aug 1890)

Smith, A. Josephine, 1877-1952 (St. Ignatius Catholic Church Cemetery)

Smith, Abigail (colored), 1881-1939, native of Lancaster Co., PA, born 5 Feb 1881, daughter of George Smith and Eliza Green (Death certificate - married name Maddox)

Smith, Abraham (colored), born -- Mar 1870, native of Maryland (1900 Aberdeen Census)

Smith, Adelia, acquired land in April 1890 (*The Aegis & Intelligencer*, 9 May 1890)

Smith, Agnes Lilia, born -- Aug 1886, baptized 21 Sep 1886, daughter of John Smith, native of Harford Co., and Ann Jamison, native of Pennsylvania (St. Ignatius Catholic Church Baptism Register, p. 88)

Smith, Albert (colored), 1885-1972 (St. James United Cemetery)

Smith, Alexander, 1857-1918 (St. Paul's Lutheran Church Cemetery); stockholder, Aberdeen Can Factory (*Havre de Grace Republican*, 19 Dec 1890)

Smith, Alexander, resident at Calvary (*The Aegis & Intelligencer*, 29 Aug 1890); juror, Third District (*Havre de Grace Republican*, 31 Oct 1890); see Mary Elizabeth Smith, q.v.

Smith, Alfred George Victor Clinton, born 10 Jan 1880, son of Robert C. and Mary E. R. Smith (Holy Trinity Episcopal Church Register of Baptisms, p. 84)

Smith, Alfred W., 1881-1952 (Darlington Cemetery)

Smith, Alice (Miller), 1886-1962 (Darlington Cemetery)

Smith, Alice B., age 25 in 1889 (Marriage License Applications Book ALJ No. 2, 1890); daughter of R. Stump Smith, of Darlington, married Joseph E. Ely, of Philadelphia, on 4 Feb 1890 (*The Aegis & Intelligencer*, 7 Feb 1890; marriage record)

Smith, Alice Hall (Patterson), 1851-1933 (Angel Hill Cemetery), wife of Dr. Richard Henry Smith, q.v.

Smith, Amelia (Pennington) (colored), 1859-1935 (Death certificate); wife of Barney Smith, q.v.

Smith, Andrew C., 1872-1932 (Darlington Cemetery); native of Darlington, MD, born 18 Sep 1872, son of William H. Smith and Margaret Kirk (Bailey Funeral Home Records)

Smith, Ann, county out-pensioner [welfare recipient], Third District (*Havre de Grace Republican*, 4 Jul 1890)

Smith, Ann (Tate), 1850-1900, native of Maryland, resident of Prospect, wife of Daniel Smith (Death certificate)

Smith, Anna A. (Jamison), 1851-1898, wife of John Smith, of Bel Air (Death certificate filed under Jamison and noted as Mrs. Smith)

Smith, Anna Lulu, see Anna L. Walker, q.v.

Smith, Anna May, 1873-1902 (Darlington Cemetery)

Smith, Anna W., see Anna W. Ritchie, q.v.

Smith, Annie, age 22 in 1890 (Marriage License Applications Book ALJ No. 2, 1890)

Smith, Annie, student, Fallston School (*The Aegis & Intelligencer*, 21 Feb 1890)

Smith, Annie B., married William A. Creswell on 31 Dec 1890 (marriage certificate)

Smith, Annie H., 1839-1890 (Holy Trinity Episcopal Church Cemetery); native of Culpeper Co., VA, and wife of Herman Smith, of Bel Air (*The Aegis & Intelligencer*, 20 Jun 1890)

Smith, Annie J., 1878-1963 (Darlington Cemetery); see Mary Drucilla Smith, q.v.

Smith, Annie Jane (Miss), 1850-1900 (Churchville Presbyterian Church Cemetery); resided at Darlington (Death certificate)

Smith, Annie M. (James), 1878-1963 (Darlington Cemetery); native of Castleton, Harford Co., born 22 Jan 1878, daughter of William H. James and Alverta Forwood (Harkins Funeral Home Records)

Smith, Augustus, 1856-1902 (Rock Run Methodist Church Cemetery)

Smith, Barbara A., 1847-1919 (Good Will Church Cemetery); B. A. Smith, premium award winner, Class O -

Discretionary, Harford County Fair, 1890 (*The Aegis & Intelligencer*, 24 Oct 1890)

Smith, Barney (colored), resident near Michaelsville, former slave of the late Henry E. Michael, of Gravelly, died 13 Jun 1890, nearly 70 years old (*The Aegis & Intelligencer*, 20 Jun 1890); removed from the voter registration list at Hall's Cross Roads, Second District (*Havre de Grace Republican*, 17 Oct 1890); husband of Amelia Smith, q.v.

Smith, Benjamin (colored), 30th U.S.C.T. (St. James United Cemetery - no dates on marker); see Willis Charles Smith, q.v.

Smith, Benjamin J. (D.D.S), 1835-1918 (Mt. Zion Methodist Church Cemetery); dentist, Main Street, next to Presbyterian parsonage (*Harford Democrat*, 14 Mar 1890); judge of elections, Bel Air, 1890 (*Havre de Grace Republican*, 2 May 1890); secretary, Harford County Temperance Alliance (*Havre de Grace Republican*, 18 Apr 1890)

Smith, Bernard Gilpin, 1835-1925 (Darlington Cemetery); superintendent, Franklin Sunday School (*Havre de Grace Republican*, 25 Apr 1890); see Dorothy Cowgil Smith, Stanton Gould Smith, Smith's Tanbark Mill and Feed Mill, and Stafford Flint Mill, q.v.

Smith, Bertie, premium award winner, Class L - Children's Department, Harford County Fair (*The Aegis & Intelligencer*, 24 Oct 1890)

Smith, Bessie (Miss), member, Darlington M. E. Church (*The Aegis & Intelligencer*, 10 Jan 1890)

Smith, Bessie J., 1875-1930 (Christ Episcopal Church Cemetery)

Smith, Bettye (Hughes), 1880-1963 (Norrisville Methodist Church Cemetery)

Smith, Blanche B., 1859-1915 (Churchville Presbyterian Church Cemetery); see George Dallas Smith and Lena Sophia Smith, q.v.

Smith, C. Elizabeth, see Mary Elizabeth Smith, q.v.

Smith, C. Louanna, teacher, Zion School No. 12, Third District (*The Aegis & Intelligencer*, 29 Aug 1890)

Smith, C. W., member, Darlington Road League (*Havre de Grace Republican*, 6 Jun 1890); member, Deer Creek Farmers' Club (*Havre de Grace Republican*, 3 Oct 1890)

Smith, Caroline (Stansbury) (colored), 1838-1919 (Death certificate); see Charles W. Smith and Solomon J. Smith, q.v.

Smith, Carrie (Hooper) (colored), 1874-1930, native of Maryland, daughter of George W. Hooper and Rebecca Cooper (Death certificate)

Smith, Carrie M. (Courtney), 1864-1924 (Rock Run Methodist Church Cemetery; Bailey Funeral Home Records; *The Hughes Genealogy, 1636-1953*, by Joseph Lee Hughes, 1953, p. 115); wife of Stevenson A. Smith, q.v.

Smith, Carrie (Wilson), 1856-1912 (Rock Run Methodist Church Cemetery); wife of Livingston Smith, q.v.

Smith, Carroll (colored), see Richard Johnson (colored), q.v.

Smith, Casper, 1867-1943 (Angel Hill Cemetery); native of Havre de Grace, born 17 Mar 1867, son of Casper Smith and Elizabeth Mars); brother of Louis H. Smith, q.v.

Smith, Cassandra (Bird), 1841-1922 (Darlington Cemetery; Bailey Funeral Home Records); George and Cassie Smith, treated by unidentified doctor in 1890 ("Medical Account Book – 1890," Historical Society of Harford County Archives Folder)

Smith, Charles (colored), testified in an assault case in 1890 (*Harford Democrat*, 21 Feb 1890)

Smith, Charles C., 1838-1890 (Rock Run Methodist Church Cemetery); portable saw mill manager, Havre de Grace (*Havre de Grace Republican*, 10 Jan 1890); removed from voter registration list at Hopewell, Second District (*Havre de Grace Republican*, 26 Sep 1890); Charles Smith, juror, Second District (*Havre de Grace Republican*, 31 Jan 1890)

Smith, Charles Coleman, 1851-1931 (Darlington Cemetery; Bailey Funeral Home Records)

Smith, Charles Jennings, 1880-1938 (Darlington Cemetery); native of Baltimore, born 6 Jan 1880, son of C. C.

Smith and Fannie H. Jennings (Bailey Funeral Home Records)

Smith, Charles W. (colored), 1874-1944, native of Maryland, born 7 Mar 1874, son of Daniel Smith and Caroline Stansbury (Death certificate)

Smith, Charlotte Ann (Wilson) (colored), 1870-1946 (Berkley Memorial Cemetery; Death certificate states born 1872, daughter of Stephen H. Wilson and Hannah Presbury); see Charlotte Ann Wilson, q.v.

Smith, Christian, Jr., 1859-1918 (St. Paul's Lutheran Church Cemetery); tomato canner, Abingdon District (*The Aegis & Intelligencer*, 15 Aug 1890); director and stockholder, Aberdeen Can Factory (*Havre de Grace Republican*, 19 Dec 1890)

Smith, Christine, 1838-1927 (Deer Creek Methodist Church Cemetery)

Smith, Clara Adelle, see Robert B. McC. Stifler, q.v.

Smith, Clara H., student, Fifth District (*The Aegis & Intelligencer*, 24 Oct 1890)

Smith, Clara H., 1841-1928 (Darlington Cemetery)

Smith, Clara J., age 18 in 1890 (Marriage License Applications Book ALJ No. 2, 1891)

Smith, Clarence B. (colored), 1887-1963 (Fairvew AME Church Cemetery)

Smith, Clarice Lorine, 1866-1958, daughter of Richard Smith and Eliza Ann Hanna, of Churchville (Grove Presbyterian Church Cemetery, married name Cronin); teacher, Fountain Green School (*The Aegis & Intelligencer*, 11 Apr 1890; *Harford County, Maryland Teachers and the Schools They Served*, by Henry C. Peden, Jr., 2021, p. 291)

Snith, Claude K., 1888-1958 (Angel Hill Cemetery)

Smith, Clinton, 1853-1914 (Rock Run Methodist Church Cemetery); carpenter and building contractor, Bel Air (*The Aegis & Intelligencer*, 18 Apr 1890; *Havre de Grace Republican*, 5 Sep 1890); builder of Harford National Bank in Bel Air (*Harford Democrat*, 28 Mar 1890); see M. Pearl Schultz, q.v.

Smith, Clinton A., 1867-1895 (Rock Run Methodist Church Cemetery)

Smith, Cora (Miss), member, Darlington M. E. Church (*The Aegis & Intelligencer*, 10 Jan 1890)

Smith, Cornelia (Copper) (colored), 1862-1926 (Union Methodist Church Cemetery, Aberdeen); native of South Carolina, married, resided in Aberdeen (Death certificate)

Smith, Courtauld Wharton, 1865-1917 (Darlington Cemetery)

Smith, Daniel, see Ann (Tate) Smith and Solomn J. Smith, q.v.

Smith, Daniel (colored), 1833-1906 (Old Union Chapel Cemetery, Michaelsville); see Charles W. Smith, q.v.

Smith, Daniel Clark Wharton, 1834-1925 (Darlington Cemetery); member, Deer Creek Farmers' Club (*Havre de Grace Republican*, 3 Oct 1890); vestryman, Grace Memorial Church, Darlington (*Havre de Grace Republican*, 18 Apr 1890; *Country Stores: Harford County's Rura Heritage*, by Henry C. Peden, Jr. and Jack L. Shagena, Jr., 2015, p. 43)

Smith, Daniel Clark Wharton, Jr., 1889-1979 (Darlington Cemetery)

Smith, Della (Martin), 1867-1948, native of Harford Furnace, resided at Havre de Grace (Death certificate; Angel Hill Cemetery); wife of Casper Smith, q.v.

Smith, Della (colored), 1882-1976, native of Harford Co., daughter of William Smith and Rachel ---- (Death certificate - married name Prigg); wife of Jarrett Prigg, q.v.; also see Della Webster, q.v.

Smith, Dorothy Cowgil, born 8th mo, 24th day, 1887, daughter of B. Gilpin Smith and Rebecca W. ---- [Cowgil] (Deer Creek Friends Record of Monthly Meeting, First Month, 1883, Register which recorded earlier births)

Smith, E. Howard, born 3 Jan 1880, son of George A. and Severna (Fowble) Smith (Bethel Presbyterian Church Cemetery Records)

Smith, Edith (Mason), 1857-1944 (Darlington Cemetery)

Smith, Edith A. (colored), 1874-1909 (Berkley Memorial Cemetery); wife of William T. Smith, q.v.

Smith, Edith Roberta (Gardiner), 1879-1954 (Bethel Presbyterian Church Cemetery Records); wife of E.

Howard Smith, q.v.

Smith, Edward, born 1872, died ---- (Darlington Cemetery)

Smith, Edward, secretary, Black Horse Singing School, 1890, and treasurer, Shawsville Glee Club, 1890 (*Havre de Grace Republican*, 7 Mar 1890 and 28 Mar 1890)

Smith, Edward, born -- Aug 1884, baptized 7 Sep 1884, son of James Smith, of "Fallston, Baltimore County," and Catherine Bradley, native of County Derry, Ireland (St. Ignatius Catholic Church Baptism Register, p. 74)

Smith, Eleanor (Mitchell), 1851-1933 (Rock Run Methodist Church Cemetery); wife of Thomas Ogden Smith, q.v.

Smith, Eliza (Wells) (colored), 1838-1903 (Death certificate)

Smith, Eliza Elizabeth (colored), 1875-1928, native of Harford Co., born 12 Aug 1875, daughter of John Smith and Kate Jamison (Death certificate - married name Lee)

Smith, Elizabeth, 1832-1898, born in Wurtamburg, Germany, widow of Christian Smith (St. Paul's Lutheran Church Cemetery)

Smith, Elizabeth, 1860-1954 (St. Paul's Lutheran Church Cemetery); wife of Alexander Smith (1857-1918), q.v.

Smith, Elizabeth (Mars), see Casper Smith q.v.

Smith, Elizabeth (McDowell), 1863-1926 (Darlington Cemetery)

Smith, Elizabeth (Willey), 1823-1903, widow of Thomas Smith (Rock Run Methodist Church Cemetery)

Smith, Elizabeth (colored), see Ella Stansbury and Charles Jacob Franklyn Stansbury, q.v.

Smith, Elizabeth Alberta, 1843-1934 (Angel Hill Cemetery)

Smith, Elizabeth C., 1845-1900 (Darlington Cemetery)

Smith, Elizabeth Hollis, born 8 Jul 1888, baptized 20 Apr 1891, daughter of Rev. William H. and Mary P. Smith (Holy Trinity Episcopal Church Register of Baptisms, p. 100)

Smith, Elizabeth Newlin, born 9th mo., 15 day, 1884, daughter of Joshua C. and Edith M. Smith (Deer Creek Friends Record of Monthly Meeting, First Month, 1883, Register which recorded earlier births)

Smith, Elizah (Elijah?) (colored), 1881-1968 (Berkley Memorial Cemetery); husband of Lillie P. Smith, q.v.

Smith, Ella R., 1856-1943 (St. Paul's Lutheran Church Cemetery)

Smith, Ellen, 1833-1917 (St. Ignatius Catholic Church Cemetery)

Smith, Elsie Susan, 1884-1948, native of Harford Co, born 11 Feb 1884, daughter of Samuel T. Smith and Elizabeth McDowell (Harkins Funeral Home Records - married name Knight; Darlington Cemetery)

Smith, Emily (Mrs.) (colored), 1854-1912, native of Maryland (Death certificate); wife of Joseph Smith, q.v.

Smith, Emma (colored), born -- May 1882 native of Maryland (1900 Aberdeen Census); also see Mary K. Akins (colored), q.v.

Smith, Emma L. (Miss), secretary, Mite Society of the Norrisville [Methodist] Church (*Havre de Grace Republican*, 18 Apr 1890)

Smith, Esther, 1889-1911 (Darlington Cemetery)

Smith, Ethel (Clinton), 1876-1950 (Darlington Cemetery)

Smith, Ethel Catharine, born -- Sep 1999, baptized 24 Oct 1888, daughter of John Smith native of Harford Co., and Ann A. Jamison, native of Pennsylvania (St. Ignatius Catholic Church Baptism Register, p. 100)

Smith, Eva, second grade honor student and actress, Bel Air Graded School (*The Aegis & Intelligencer*, 4 Jul and 26 Dec 1890)

Smith Eva (Norton) (colored), 1869-1939, native of Harford Co., daughter of Thomas and Eva Norton (Death certificate); wife of George W. Smith, q.v.

Smith, Ezekiel (colored), age 26 in 1890 (Marriage License Applications Book ALJ No. 2, 1891)

Smith, F. Bowie (Mrs.), of Jarrettsville, died 23 Mar 1890 in her 63rd year, mother of Dr. W. L.Smith (*The Aegis*

& Intelligencer, 28 Mar 1890)

Smith, F. Penrose, 1856-1919 (Norrisville Methodist Church Cemetery)

Smith, Fannie (colored), 1841-1905 (Death certificate; Alms House Record Book)

Smith, Fannie H. (Jennings) 1849-1935 (Darlington Cemetery)

Smith, Florence (Sampson), 1882-1947 (Angel Hill Cemetery)

Smith, Florence A. (Miss), 1841-1928 (Norrisville Methodist Church Cemetery); native of Maryland, resided at Norrisville (Death certificate)

Smith, Frank (colored), 1872-1942 (Death certificate; St. James United Cemetery)

Smith, Franklin "Frank" M., 1848-1916 (Cokesbury Memorial Methodist Church Cemetery)

Smith, Frederick, student, Oakland School, 1890 (George G. Curtiss Ledger)

Smith, Frederick "Fred" K., 1879-1965 (Slate Ridge Cemetery, York Co., PA); native of Darlington, Harford Co., born 4 Aug 1879, son of John W. Smith and Annie Klair (Harkins Funeral Home Records)

Smith, G. Harry, 1860-1939 (Cokesbury Memorial Methodist Church Cemetery)

Smith, Georganna (colored), 1873-1936, native of Federal Hill, Harford Co., born 12 Feb 1873, daughter of John Smith and Catherine E. Jamison (Death certificate - married name Swann)

Smith, George (colored), resident of Bel Air, charged with assault and confessed his guilt (Harford County Criminal Docket, 1888-1892, p. 94; *The Aegis & Intelligencer*, 7 Nov 1890)

Smith, George (colored), 1876-1914 (St. James United Cemetery)

Smith, George (colored), see Abigail Smith (colored), q.v.

Smith, George, 1822-1907 (William Watters Memorial Methodist Church Cemetery, Thomas Run)

Smith, George, Civil War veteran, at Level (*1890 Special Census of the Civil War Veterans of the State of Maryland*, by L. Tilden Moore, Volume III, p. 66); also see Anna W. Ritchie, q.v.

Smith, George, and Cassie, treated by unidentified doctor in 1890 ("Medical Account Book – 1890," Historical Society of Harford County Archives Folder)

Smith, George, Jr. (colored), resident of Bel Air, fined for disorderly conduct (*Harford Democrat*, 21 Mar 1890)

Smith, George Clinton, 1880-1944 (Darlington Cemetery)

Smith, George Dallas, 1890-1892 (Churchville Presbyterian Church Cemetery); born 27 Apr 1890, baptized 25 Jan 1892, son of John R. and Blanche B. Smith (Holy Trinity Episcopal Church Register of Baptisms, p. 102)

Smith, George Thomas, see Florence Sampson, q.v.

Smith, George W. (colored), c1860-1931, born in Maryland (Death certificate); age 32 in 1890 (Marriage License Applications Book ALJ No. 2, 1890)

Smith, George W., Civil War veteran, at Cooptown (*1890 Special Census of the Civil War Veterans of the State of Maryland*, by L. Tilden Moore, Volume III, p. 79)

Smith, Georgia (colored), see Georgia Ashton (colored), q.v.

Smith, Georgia A. (colored), 1890-1954 (Union Methodist Church Cemetery, Aberdeen)

Smith, Georgianna (colored), age 20 in 1889 (Marriage License Applications Book ALJ No. 2, 1890), married Walter Swann on 6 Feb 1890 (marriage certificate)

Smith, Gerlinde (Miss), resident of Havre de Grace (*The Aegis & Intelligencer*, 7 Nov 1890)

Smith, Gretta H., 1878-1947 (Deer Creek Methodist Church Cemetery)

Smith, Griffin Milton (colored), 1880-1937 (Berkley Memorial Cemetery tombstone inscribed G. Milton Smith); born in Harford Co., son of Henry Smith and Mary Spriggs (Death certificate)

Smith, H. Clay (Rev.), pastor of Rock Run M. E. Church (*The Aegis & Intelligencer*, 7 Feb 1890); Bush Chapel, East Harford Circuit (*Havre de Grace Republican*, 28 Feb and 14 Mar 1890); tent holder, Carsins Run Camp Meeting of the East Harford Circuit, P. E. Church (*The Aegis & Intelligencer*, 1 Aug and 8 Aug 1890); member,

Mt. Ararat Lodge No. 44, A. F. & A. M., Bel Air (*Havre de Grace Republican*, 11 Jul 1890)

Smith, Hannah, county out-pensioner [welfare recipient], Third District 1890 (*Havre de Grace Republican*, 4 Jul 1890)

Smith Hannah (colored), see Mary E. Morgan (colored) and Mary E. Hewitt (colored), q.v.

Smith, Hannah C. (Hayes), 1844-1922 (Darlington Cemetery; Bailey Funeral Home Records)

Smith, Hannah E., 1864-1940 (Rock Run Methodist Church Cemetery)

Smith, Hanson (colored), born -- May 1873, native of Maryland (1900 Aberdeen Census)

Smith, Harry (colored), age 21 in 1890 (Marriage License Applications Book ALJ No. 2, 1891)

Smith, Harry E., 1870-1946 (Darlington Cemetery)

Smith, Hebb, student, Bel Air Graded School (*The Aegis & Intelligencer*, 11 Apr 1890)

Smith, Helen Anna, 1886-1934 (Mt. Zion Methodist Church Cemetery)

Smith, Helen Field, 1890-1909 (Norrisville Methodist Church Cemetery)

Smith, Helen T., 1884-1957 (Angel Hill Cemetery); native of Havre de Grace, born 22 Sep 1884, daughter of Dr. Richard H. Smith and Alice Patterson (Pennington Funeral Home Records)

Smith, Henrietta M., graduate of State Normal School (*Havre de Grace Republican*, 6 Jun 1890)

Smith, Henry (colored), 1845-1924, native of Maryland, resided at Perryman (Death certificate); see Martha J. Smith, Henson Smith, Robert E. Smith and John C. Smith, q.v.

Smith, Henry (colored), 1846-1900, resided at Edgewood (Death certificate); Civil War veteran, Edgewood (*1890 Special Census of the Civil War Veterans of the State of Maryland*, by L. Tilden Moore, Volume III, p. 62)

Smith, Henry (colored), 1853-1917, native of Maryland (Death certificate); age 36 in 1890 (Marriage License Applications Book ALJ No. 2); see Griffin Milton Smith and Stewart Donald Smith, q.v.

Smith, Henry (colored), see Maggie Smith (colored), q.v.

Smith, Henry (Mrs.), 1869-1899 (Death certificate)

Smith, Henry M., 1854-1935 (Mt. Zion Methodist Church Cemetery)

Smith, Henry Melville, 1849-1891 (Norrisville Methodist Church Cemetery)

Smith, Henson (colored), 1874-1937, native of Perryman, born 10 Jun 1874, son of Henry Smith and Martha Williams (Death certificate)

Smith, Herman, professor, Bel Air (*Havre de Grace Republican*, 20 Jun 1890); also see Annie H. Smith, q.v.

Smith, Horace (colored), 1855-1945, native of Fallston, parents unknown (Death certificate; Alms House Record Book)

Smith, Hosetta, 1864-1935 (Angel Hill Cemetery)

Smith, Hugh, 1834-1904 (Dublin Southern Cemetery); juror, Fifth District, 1890 (*Havre de Grace Republican*, 2 May 1890); see Ella R. Love, q.v.

Smith, India P., born 4 Mar 1872 (*The Hughes Genealogy, 1636-1953*, by Joseph Lee Hughes, 1953, p. 117, listed her as India W. Smith); singer and member, Lapidum M. P. Church (*The Aegis & Intelligencer*, 13 Jun 1890); choral member, Darlington Orchestra (*Havre de Grace Republican*, 7 Mar 1890); see Indiana P. Silver, q.v.

Smith, Isaac (colored), see Vincent H. Smith (colored), q.v.

Smith, Isaac J. (colored), age 32 in 1890 (Marriage License Applications Book ALJ No. 2, 1891)

Smith, Isabel, see William Thomas Taylor, q.v.

Smith, J. George, 1870-1893 (St. Paul's Lutheran Church Cemetery); brother of Christian Smith, Jr., q.v.

Smith, J. Leyburn, fishery proprietor, Roberts' Island, near Lapidum (*Havre de Grace Republican*, 7 Mar 1890)

Smith, J. Orem, 1860-1907 (Mt. Erin Cemetery)

Smith, J. S. (Mrs.) (colored), ladies hairdressing salon, Bel Air (*Bel Air: An Architectural and Cultural History, 1782-1945*, by Marilynn M. Larew, 1995, p. 59)

Smith, Jacob (colored), see John Wesley Smith (colored), q.v.

Smith, Jacob H., name removed from the voter registration list in the Sixth District, 1890 (*Havre de Grace Republican*, 17 Oct 1890)

Smith, James, treated by unidentified doctor in 1890 ("Medical Account Book – 1890," Historical Society of Harford County Archives Folder)

Smith, James, 1817-1905 (Grove Presbyterian Church Cemetery)

Smith, James (colored), 1837-1913 (Death certificate; Alms House Record Book); see John Westley Smith, Mary Smith, William T. Smith and Georgia Ashton, q.v.

Smith, James, Civil War veteran, Aberdeen (*1890 Special Census of the Civil War Veterans of the State of Maryland*, by L. Tilden Moore, Volume III, p. 65)

Smith, James Henry (colored), 1853-1935 (Mt. Joy Church Cemetery, PA); native of Bel Air, resided at Black Horse (Death certificate)

Smith, James Jacob (colored), 1827-1899, laborer, resided at The Cedars, native of Maryland (Death certificate)

Smith, James R., 1844-1915 (Darlington Cemetery); served on an inquest jury in the Fifth District, 1890 (*The Aegis & Intelligencer*, 1 Aug 1890)

Smith, James S., sold land in April 1890 (*The Aegis & Intelligencer*, 9 May 1890)

Smith, James W. (Dr.), 1852-1899, resided in Bel Air, native of Utah (Death certificate; Cokesbury Memorial Methodist Church Cemetery)

Smith, James Warren, 1888-1962 (Mt. Zion Methodist Church Cemetery)

Smith, Jane, see Aresice E. Hutton, q.v.

Smith, Jane (McDougal), 1836-1929, native of Ireland, resident of Havre de Grace (Death certificate)

Smith, Jane (Miss), resident of Chestnut Hill (*The Aegis & Intelligencer*, 22 Aug 1890)

Smith, Jane E. (Johnson) (colored), 1841-1914, native of Churchville (Death certificate)

Smith, Jean (Mason), 1883-1966 (Darlington Cemetery)

Smith, Jennie, age 36 in 1890 (Marriage License Applications Book ALJ No. 2, 1891)

Smith, Jesse (colored), see Frances Ann Teel (colored), q.v.

Smith, Jim, treated by unidentified doctor in 1890 ("Medical Account Book – 1890," Historical Society of Harford County Archives Folder)

Smith, JoAnn, see Elizabeth R. Jones, q.v.

Smith, John, see Mary Ann Thalman, q.v.

Smith, John, carriage maker, Bel Air (*The Aegis & Intelligencer*, 30 May 1890); premium award winner, Class G - Carriages and Leather Manufactures, Harford County Fair (*The Aegis & Intelligencer*, 24 Oct 1890)

Smith, John, treated by unidentified doctor in 1890 ("Medical Account Book – 1890," Historical Society of Harford County Archives Folder)

Smith, John (colored), husband of Kate Smith, q.v.; also see Eliza E. Smith (colored) and Georganna Smith (colored), q.v.

Smith, John B., 1842-1894 (Angel Hill Cemetery)

Smith, John C. (colored), 1886-1935, native of Maryland, born 15 Apr 1886, son of Henry Smith and Martha Williams (Death certificate)

Smith, John Christopher, 1853-1926 (Mt. Zion Methodist Church Cemetery); native of Germany, carpenter, resided at Bynum (Death certificate)

Smith, John Gordon, 1888-1918 (Angel Hill Cemetery)

Smith, John H., 1868-1927 (Deer Creek Methodist Church Cemetery)

Smith, John Henry, 1873-1957 (St. Paul's Lutheran Church Cemetery)

Smith, John Henry, of A., 1874-1965 (St. Paul's Lutheran Church Cemetery)

Smith, John Levi, 1839-1910 (Good Will Church Cemetery)

Smith, John R., 1860-1952 (Churchville Presbyterian Church Cemetery); farmer, near Churchville (*The Aegis & Intelligencer*, 13 Jun 1890); see George Dallas Smith and Lena Sophia Smith, q.v.

Smith, John S., 1839-1911 (Deer Creek Methodist Church Cemetery)

Smith, John T., 1840-1922 (Darlington Cemetery)

Smith, John W., see Frederick K. Smith, Anna L. Walker and Martha L. Wise, q.v.

Smith, John Wesley (colored), 1874-1905, native of Harford Co., son of Jacob Smith and Marie Smart (Death certificate)

Smith, John Westley (colored), 1890-1941, native of Maryland, born 16 Jan 1890, son of James Smith and Ella Black, natives of Maryland (Death certificate)

Smith, Joseph, county out-pensioner [welfare recipient], Second District (*Havre de Grace Republican*, 4 Jul 1890)

Smith, Joseph (colored), 1834-1909, native of Maryland (Death certificate); farm hand at Bel Air (*The Aegis & Intelligencer*, 14 Mar 1890); see Joseph Henry Smith, q.v.

Smith, Joseph Henry (colored), 1872-1925, native of Maryland, son of Joseph Smith and Emily James (Death certificate)

Smith, Joseph L., 1875-1942 (Mt. Erin Cemetery);

Smith, Joseph L., see Mary Drucilla Smith, q.v.

Smith, Joshua (colored), 1856-1921, native of Harford Co., resided at Pylesville, parents unknown (Death certificate)

Smith, Joshua Cowgill, 1857-1911 (Darlington Cemetery); see Stafford Flint Mill, q.v.

Smith, Julia, student, Forest Hill School, 1890 (*The Aegis*, 2 Jul 1965, school picture)

Smith, Kate, see Sara B. Elliott, q.v.

Smith, Kate (colored), 1846-1900, parents unknown (Death certificate); see Catherine E. Jamison, q.v.

Smith, Kate (Dorsey), wife of Dr. James W. Smith, q.v.

Smith, Katherine H. (Donnelly), 1880-1962 (Mt. Erin Cemetery)

Smith, Kathryn E., 1871-1940 (Mt. Zion Methodist Church Cemetery)

Smith, Laura M. (colored), age 21 in 1890 (Marriage License Applications Book ALJ No. 2, 1891)

Smith, Laura V., 1870-1891 (Mt Vernon Methodist Church Cemetery)

Smith, Lawrence, born -- Jun 1885, baptized 11 Aug 1885, son of John and Ann Amelia (Grafton) Smith (St. Ignatius Catholic Church Baptism Register, p. 81)

Smith, Lee, served on an inquest jury in the Fifth District (*The Aegis & Intelligencer*, 1 Aug 1890)

Smith, Lena Sophia, 1885-1952, native of Harford Co., born 27 Jun 1885, baptized 25 Jan 1892, daughter of John R.Smith and Blanche B. Gorrell (Holy Trinity Episcopal Church Register of Baptisms, p. 100; Harkins Funeral Home Records - married name Harry)

Smith, Lewis, Civil War veteran, Upper Cross Roads (*1890 Special Census of the Civil War Veterans of the State of Maryland*, by L. Tilden Moore, Volume III, p. 77); Lewis Smith, alias Lewis Pentz, resident of Upper Cross Roads (*The Aegis & Intelligencer*, 14 Mar 1890)

Smith, Lillie P. (colored), 1885-1967 (Berkley Memorial Cemetery); wife of Elizah (Elijah?) Smith, q.v.

Smith, Lily (Presbury) (colored), 1889-1913 (Berkley Memorial Cemetery); native of Maryland daughter of George Presberry *(sic)* and Susan Wilson (Death certificate); wife of Stewart D. Smith, q.v.

Smith, Livingston, 1855-1935 (Rock Run Methodist Church Cemetery)

Smith, Lizzie (coloed), see Jennie Stansbury, q.v.

Smith, Lloyd A. (colored), 1858-1922 (Death certificate; St. James United Cemetery)

Smith, Louis or Lewis H., 1876-1927 (Angel Hill Cemetery); native of Maryland, born 4 Aug 1876, son of Casper Smith and Elizabeth Myers, of Havre de Grace (Death certificate)

Smith, Lucy (Wilson), 1849-1919 (Mt. Zion Methodist Church Cemetery); wife of Benjamin Smith, q.v.

Smith, Lydia Ann (Holloway), 1821-1904 (Rock Run Methodist Church Cemetery)

Smith, Maggie (colored), 1868-1943, native of Maryland, born 1 Apr 1868, parents unknown; wife of Henry Smith (Death certificate; Pennington Funeral Home Records)

Smith, Mamie B., wife of Clinton Smith, q.v.; also see M. Pearl Schultz, q.v.

Smith, Margaret, see Margaret E. Caulford, Walter C. Caulford and William H. Smith, q.v.

Smith, Margaret (colored), see Margaret Giddings (colored), q.v.

Smith, Margaret A., 1837-1918 (Darlington Cemetery)

Smith, Margaret C., 1884-1911 (Angel Hill Cemetery)

Smith, Margaret (Baldwin), see Robert Hall Smith, q.v.

Smith, Mark (colored), age 25 in 1889 (Marriage License Applications Book ALJ No. 2, 1889), married Mary Priscilla Bond on 1 Jan 1890 (marriage certificate)

Smith, Martha, see Martha J. Jones, Hugh R. Knight and William Wilson Knight, q.v.

Smith, Martha (Miss), 1856-1914, native of Perryman, Harford Co. (Death certificate)

Smith, Martha C., 1847-1918 (Darlington Cemetery)

Smith, Martha E. (Carr), 1875-1943 (Darlington Cemetery); native of Harford Co., born 13 Jul 1875, daughter of Marion Carr and Martha Morris (Bailey Funeral Home Records); wife of Harry E. Smith, q.v.

Smith, Martha J., see Hugh Rufus Knight, q.v.

Smith, Martha J. (Williams), 1854-1922, native of Harford Co. (Death ceritificate); wife of Henry Smith (1845-1924), q.v.

Smith, Martin L., 1874-1915 (Goodwill Church Cemetery)

Smith, Mary, age 18 in 1890 (Marriage License Applications Book ALJ No. 2, 1891)

Smith, Mary, student, Fallston School (*The Aegis & Intelligencer*, 9 May 1890)

Smith, Mary (Mrs.) (colored), 1862-1925, native of Maryland (Death certificate)

Smith, Mary (colored), c1857-1937 (Death certificate; St. James United Cemetery)

Smith, Mary (colored), 1885-1942, native of Harford Co., born 10 Feb 1885, daughter of James Smith and Mary Hollins (Death certificate - married name Harris)

Smith, Mary (Sprigg), wife of Henry Smith, q.v.

Smith, Mary (Stansbury) (colored), 1870-1949 (Death certificate); wife of Vincent Smith, q.v.

Smith, Mary A. (colored), born -- May 1868, native of Maryland (1900 Aberdeen Census)

Smith, Mary A. (colored), widow, age 44 in 1890 (Marriage License Applications Book ALJ No. 2, 1891)

Smith, Mary Ann, see Mary Ann Thalman and John H. Ansalvich, q.v.

Smith, Mary B., 1866-1942 (Rock Run Methodist Church Cemetery)

Smith, Mary Drucilla, born 28 Apr 1875, baptized 3 Dec 1889, daughter of Joseph L. Smith and Annie J. ---- (Holy Trinity Episcopal Church Register of Baptisms, p. 98)

Smith, Mary E., 1857-1890 (Bethel Presbyterian Church Cemetery)

Smith, Mary E. (Johnson) (colored), 1842-1912 (Death certificate; St. James United Cemetery)

Smith, Mary E. (Rhoads), 1847-1922 (Darlington Cemetery; Bailey Funeral Home Records)

Smith, Mary Elizabeth, born 27 Nov 1882, daughter of Alexander and C. Elizabeth Smith (Holy Trinity Episcopal Church Register of Baptisms, p. 86)

Smith, Mary F., see Philip F. McGibney, q.v.

Smith, Mary H. (Mrs.), property owner adjacent to Broadway in Bel Air (*The Aegis & Intelligencer*, 16 May 1890)

Smith, Mary Hooper (Stump), widow of Rev. T. S. C. Smith, died 10 Jun 1902, age 65 (*Deaths and Marriages in Harford County, Maryland, and Vicinity, 1873-1904, from the Diaries of Albert Peter Silver*, transcribed by Glenn Randers-Pehrson, 1995, p. 25)

Smith, Mary J. (Kurtz), 1865-1958 (Norrisville Methodist Church Cemetery)

Smith, Mary J. (Sear) (colored), wife of James Jacob Smith, q.v.

Smith, Mary Jane (colored), widow, age 40 in 1889 (Marriage License Applications Book ALJ No. 2, 1889)

Smith, Mary Jane (Lee) (colored), 1827-1911 (Cedars Chapel Cemetery)

Smith, Mary L., premium award winner, Class L - Children's Department, Harford County Fair (*The Aegis & Intelligencer*, 24 Oct 1890)

Smith, Mary L. "Mollie" (Kammerer), 1860-1925 (St. Paul's Lutheran Church Cemetery); wife of Christian Smith, Jr., q.v.

Smith, Mary M. (Shields) (colored), 1830-1900, native of Maryland, resided at Poole (Death certificate)

Smith, Mary N., 1849-1902 (Darlington Cemetery)

Smith, Mary P., see Richard Hendon Smith, q.v.

Smith, Mary Virginia, 1871-1936 (Angel Hill Cemetery)

Smith, Matilda (Bodt), 1870-1949 (St. Paul's Lutheran Church Cemetery); wife of John Henry Smith (1873-1957), q.v.

Smith, Miranda A., 1858-1899, resident of Magnolia, native of Maryland (Death certificate); wife of Franklin M. Smith, q.v.

Smith, Milton E., 1853-1938 (Norrisville Methodist Church Cemetery); attorney-at-law, Norrisville (*Havre de Grace Republican*, 6 Jun 1890; *The Aegis & Intelligencer*, 6 Jun and 17 Oct 1890)

Smith, Minnie E. (Kohlbus), 1880-1951 (Slate Ridge Cemetery, York Co., PA); native of Harford Co., born 12 Sep 1880, daughter of William H. Kohlbus and Mary Nichol (Harkins Funeral Home Records)

Smith, Nellie E., 1877-1923 (St. Ignatius Catholic Church Cemetery)

Smith, Nicholas, widower, age 34 in 1890 (Marriage License Applications Book ALJ No. 2, 1891)

Smith, O. H., private, Jackson Guards [Co. D, 1st Regiment, Maryland National Guard], 1889-1890 (*The Aegis & Intelligencer*, 11 Jan 1889)

Smith, Olena V., 1878-1950 (Darlington Cemetery)

Smith, Oliver, c1842-1903, native of Baltmore Co., resided at Bel Air (Death certificate)

Smith, Olivia, see Lewis Bolivar Robinson, q.v.

Smith, Olivia Jane (Hanna), c1850-1931 (Rock Run Methodist Church Cemetery; Bailey Funeral Home Records)

Smith, Otho, 1861-1917 (Rock Run Methodist Church Cemetery)

Smith, P., shortstop, Baptist Baseball Club, of Fourth District (*Havre de Grace Republican*, 8 Aug 1890)

Smith, R. Burton, 1869-1951 (Darlington Cemetery); librarian, Franklin Sunday School (*Havre de Grace Republican*, 25 Apr 1890)

Smith, R. C. (Mrs.), teacher, Glenville Union Sunday School (*The Aegis & Intelligencer*, 22 Aug 1890)

Smith, R. Stump, 1833-1890 (Darlington Cemetery); also see Alice B. Smith, q.v.

Smith, R. T., cigar manufacturer in Bel Air, moved his family to Red Lion, York Co., PA in June 1890 (*Havre de*

Grace Republican, 4 Jul 1890; *Harford Democrat*, 27 Jun 1890)

Smith, Rachael A. (colored), 1877-1979 (Berkley Memorial Cemetery)

Smith, Rachel (colored), see Charles Webster (colored), q.v.

Smith, Rebecca (colored), age 33 in 1890 (Marriage License Applications Book ALJ No. 2, 1891)

Smith, Rebecca or Rebecka (Wright), 1855-1938 (Darlington Cemetery), wife of B. Gilpin Smith, q.v.; also see Dorothy Gilpin Smith, q.v.

Smith, Richard, superintendent, Franklin Methodist Church Sunday School (*The Aegis & Intelligencer*, 5 Sep 1890); see Clarice Lorine Smith, q.v.

Smith, Richard G. (colored), born 15 Oct 1873, indentured to William N. Glenn in 1883 (Harford County Indentures Book WSB No. 1)

Smith, Richard G., trustee, Franklin School No. 9, Fifth District (*Havre de Grace Republican*, 30 May 1890)

Smith, Richard Hendon, born 19 Sep 1882, son of Rev. William H. and Mary P. Smith (Holy Trinity Episcopal Church Register of Baptisms, p. 86)

Smith, Richard Henry, 1848-1926 (Angel Hill Cemetery); native of Maryland, physician, resided in Havre de Grace (Death certificate; *Havre de Grace Republican*, 21 Mar 1890); see Helen T. Smith, q.v.

Smith, Robert, farmer, Bush River Neck, overlooking the Chesapeake Bay (*The Aegis & Intelligencer*, 1 Aug 1890)

Smith, Robert Clinton, 1838-1907 (Darlington Cemetery); Civil War veteran, Hopewell (*1890 Special Census of the Civil War Veterans of the State of Maryland*, by L. Tilden Moore, Volume III, p. 69)

Smith, Robert E. (colored), 1882-1931, native of Maryland, born 30 Nov 1882, son of J. Henry Smith and Martha J. Williams (Death certificate)

Smith, Robert H., Jr., vestryman, Spesutia Church, St. George's Parish, Perryman (*Havre de Grace Republican*, 11 Apr 1890); also see Robert Hall Smith, q.v.

Smith, Robert Hall, born 10 Mar 1888, son of Robert Hall, Jr. and Margaret Baldwin Smith (St. George's Episcopal Church Register of Baptisms, p. 7)

Smith, Robert M., 1877-1937 (Angel Hill Cemetery)

Smith, Robert T. (colored), 1856-1929 (Death certificate)

Smith, Roberta (Gardiner), 1880-1954 (Bethel Presbyterian Church Cemetery)

Smith, Rudolph B. 1865-1934 (Mt. Zion Methodist Church Cemetery)

Smith, S. K. (Miss), resident near Fallston (*The Aegis & Intelligencer*, 11 Apr 1890)

Smith, Sallie C. (Miss), singer and member, Emmanuel Episcopal Church, Bel Air (*The Aegis & Intelligencer*, 11 Apr 1890)

Smith, Samuel (colored), see Samuel Durbin Smith (colored), q.v.

Smith, Samuel Durbin (colored), c1884-1922, son of Samuel Smith and Mary Durbin all natives of Maryland (Death certificate; St. James United Cemetery)

Smith, Samuel M., librarian, Mountain Christian Church Sunday School (*Havre de Grace Republican*, 7 Feb 1890)

Smith, Samuel T., 1851-1927 (Darlington Cemetery); also see Elsie Susan Smith, q.v.

Smith, Sarah (Field), 1817-1898 (Norrisville Methodist Church Cemetery)

Smith, Sarah (Mrs.), resident of Norrisville (*The Aegis & Intelligencer*, 15 Aug 1890)

Smith, Sarah C., 1840-1924 (Bethel Presbyterian Church Cemetery)

Smith, Sarah C., 1843-1890 (Rock Run Methodist Church Cemetery)

Smith, Sarah E., 1863-1943 (Baker Cemetery)

Smith, Sarah E. (colored), born -- Jan 1868, native of Maryland (1900 Aberdeen Census); wife of Abraham

Smith, q.v.

Smith, Sarah E. (McDowell), 1863-1926 (Darlington Cemetery; Bailey Funeral Home Records)

Smith, Sarah Elizabeth, born -- Jan 1887, baptized 19 Feb 1887, daughter of James Smith, native of Anne Arundel Co., MD, and Katharine Bradley, native of County Derry, Ireland (St. Ignatius Catholic Church Baptism Register, p. 90)

Smith, Sarah Elizabeth (McCall), 1869-1925 (Angel Hill Cemetery)

Smith, Sarah J. (Moulton) (colored), c1868-1923 (Death certificate; St. James United Cemetery)

Smith, Seth, c1830-1903 (Death certificate ncomplete); farmer, of Oakington (*Havre de Grace Republican*, 28 Feb 1890)

Smith, Silas Brosius, 1878-1926 (Mt. Zion Methodist Church Cemetery)

Smith, Solomon J. (colored), 1871-1922, native of Maryland, born 12 Jul 1871, son of Daniel Smith and Caroline Stansbury (Death certificate)

Smith, Sophia (colored), born -- Mar 1854 native of Maryland (1900 Aberdeen Census)

Smith, Stevenson Archer, 1864-1926 (Rock Run Methodist Church Cemetery tombstone states 1865, but death certificate states 1864); actor, Darlington Company (*Havre de Grace Republican*, 7 Mar 1890); member, Lapidum Debating Society (*Havre de Grace Republican*, 7 Feb 1890); secretary, Lapidum Sunday School (*Havre de Grace Republican*, 30 May 1890); married Carrie M. Courtney on 12 Nov 1890 at Lapidum M. P. Church (Marriage License Applications Book ALJ No. 2, 1890; *The Aegis & Intelligencer*, 28 Nov 1890)

Smith, Stanton Gould, 1882-1959 (Darlington Cemetery); native of Berkley, Harford Co, son of Bernard Gilpin Smith and Rebekah Wright Gould (Bailey Funeral Home Records)

Smith, Stewart Donald (colored), 1890-1925, native of Maryland, son of Henry Smith and Mary E. Spriggs (Death certificate; Berkley Memorial Cemetery tombstone mistakenly inscribed 1924)

Smith, Sue, student, Bel Air Graded School, daughter of Dr. Benjamin Smith (*The Aegis & Intelligencer*, 11 Apr and 26 Dec 1890); premium award winner, Class L - Children's Department, Harford County Fair (*The Aegis & Intelligencer*, 24 Oct 1890)

Smith, Susan, see Delia Hope, q.v.

Smith, Susan B. (Mrs.), 1826-1890 (William Watters Church Cemetery, Thomas Run)

Smith, T. S. C. (Rev), see Mary Hooper (Stump) Smith, q.v.

Smith, Thomas (colored), 1835-1915 (Death certificate; Alms House Record Book)

Smith, Thomas (colored), died 8 Oct 1896, adult, age not given (*The Aegis & Intelligencer*, 16 Oct 1896)

Smith, Thomas Nathaniel, 1845-1902, son of Nathaniel and Lydia Smith (Rock Run Methodist Church Cemetery; Death certificate misfiled with the 1901 certificates)

Smith, Thomas Ogden, 1856-1916 (Rock Run Methodist Church Cemetery)

Smith, Tu Ri V. (Miss), age 19 in 1890 (Marriage License Applications Book ALJ No. 2, 1891); organist, Franklin Sunday School (*Havre de Grace Republican*, 25 Apr 1890)

Smith, Vincent H. (colored), 1870-1927, native of Maryland, born 10 May 1870, son of Isaac Smith and ---- (Death certificate; 1900 Aberdeen Census stated "Vinsent" was born in April 1866)

Smith, W., conductor, Venus Council No. 44, O. U. A. M., Havre de Grace (*Havre de Grace Republican*, 11 Jul 1890)

Smith, W. F. (colored), 1869-1943 (Berkley Memorial Cemetery)

Smith, W. L. (Dr.), assistant superintendent, Jarrettsville M. E. Church Sunday School (*The Aegis & Intelligencer*, 28 Mar 1890); director, Jarrettsville Land, Loan and Building Association (*Havre de Grace Republican*, 18 Apr 1890)

Smith, Walter McC., 1860-1925 (Angel Hill Cemetery)

Smith, Walter T., 1875-1934 (Darlington Cemetery); native of Maryland, born 15 Sep 1875, son of Richard G.

Smith and Cassandra Bird (Bailey Funeral Home Records); Walter Smith, student, Aberdeen Public School (*The Aegis & Intelligencer*, 23 May 1890)

Smith, Willard A., 1867-1948 (Darlington Cemetery)

Smith, William (colored), 1839-1919 (Death certificate); see Margaret Giddings, Della Webster and Della Smith, q.v.

Smith, William, Jr. (colored), age 21 in 1890 (Marriage License Applications Book ALJ No. 2, 1891)

Smith, William A., resided near Aberdeen (*The Aegis & Intelligencer*, 23 May 1890); treated by unidentified doctor in 1890 ("Medical Account Book – 1890," Historical Society of Harford County Archives Folder)

Smith, William A., 1859-1928 (William Watters Memorial Methodist Church Cemetery, Cooptown); native of Harford Co., resided at Upper Cross Roads (Death certificate)

Smith, William Brundage, 1816-1906 (Norrisville Methodist Church Cemetery)

Smith, William E., 1890-1937 (Holy Cross Church Cemetery)

Smith, William H., 1825-1900 (Darlington Cemetery); native of Maryland, farmer at Darlington, husband of Margaret Smith (Death certificate); see Andrew C. Smith, q.v.

Smith, William H., 1867-1945 (Dublin Southern Cemetery)

Smith, William H. (colored), born -- Apr 1890, native of Maryland, son of Vincent and Mary A. Smith (1900 Aberdeen Census)

Smith, William H. (Rev.), see Richard Hendon Smith, q.v.

Smith, William S., 1849-1900, architect and resident of Garland; husband of Jennie Hanna (Death certificate); trustee, Lapidum School No. 13, Second District (*Havre de Grace Republican*, 30 May 1890); treasurer, Lapidum Sunday School (*Havre de Grace Republican*, 30 May 1890); also see Mary Margaret Morrison, q.v.

Smith, William S., 1863-1934 (Rock Run Methodist Church Cemetery)

Smith, William T. (colored), 1873-1942, native of Harford Co., son of James Smith and ---- (Berkley Memorial Cemetery tombstone inscribed 1873, but death certificate states born 1874)

Smith, William V. (colored), 1869-1943, son of William W. and Charlotte L. (Lee) Smith (Death certificate)

Smith, William W. (colored), 1852-1926 (Cokesbury Memorial Methodist Church Cemetery); native of Maryland, laborer, resided at Poole (Death certificate)

Smith, Willis Charles (colored), 1883-1944, native of Perryman, Harford Co., born 7 Mar 1883, son of Benjamin Smith and ---- (Death certificate)

Smithson, Alice, young lady, resided near Pylesville, 1890 (*The Aegis & Intelligencer*, 7 Feb 1890)

Smithson's General Store, at Taylor, William L. Smithson, prop. (*Country Stores: Harford County's Rural Heritage*, by Henry C. Peden, Jr. and Jack L. Shagena, Jr., 2015, p. 235)

Smithson's General Store and Post Office, Federal Hill, James T. Smithson, prop. (*Country Stores: Harford County's Rural Heritage*, by Henry C. Peden, Jr. and Jack L. Shagena, Jr., 2015, p. 235)

Smithson, Anna Louisa, born 6 May 1880, daughter of William Smithson, Jr. and Sophia ---- (John Forwood Bible, *Maryland Bible Records, Volume 1*, by Henry C. Peden, Jr., 2003, p. 83)

Smithson, Bessie, 1881-1958 (Christ Episcopal Church Cemetery)

Smithson, Cassandra, see Grace Hall Patterson, q.v.

Smithson, Clara Eva, 1880-1967 (Centre Methodist Church Cemetery); Clara Smithson, student, Fallston School (*The Aegis & Intelligencer*, 21 Feb 1890)

Smithson, Crissie, 1868-1935 (St. Paul's Methodist Church Cemetery)

Smithson, Elijah Alexander, born 21 Jun 1884, son of Parker F. Smithson and Sally C. ---- (Holy Trinity Episcopal Church Register of Baptisms, p. 86)

Smithson, Elizabeth F., 1849-1918 (St. Paul's Methodist Church Cemetery)

Smithson, Emma Julia, born 25 Mar 1882, daughter of William Smithson, Jr. and Sophia ---- (John Forwood Bible, *Maryland Bible Records, Volume 1*, by Henry C. Peden, Jr., 2003, p. 83)

Smithson, Emory T., 1880-1961 (Slateville Cemetery, York Co., PA); native of Harford Co., born 6 Jan 1880, son of Thomas Smithson and ---- [blank] (Harkins Funeral Home Records)

Smithson, Frank Pierce (Dr.), 1852-1921 (Christ Episcopal Church Cemetery)

Smithson, George Amos, 1849-1922 (St. Paul's Methodist Church Cemetery); see George B. Smithson and Mary Slade, q.v.

Smithson, George B., c1882-1952 (St. Paul's Methodist Church Cemetery); native of Harford Co., son of George A. Smithson and Elizabeth Beall (Bailey Funeral Home Records); George Smithson, second grade student, Mount Horeb School (*The Aegis & Intelligencer*, 14 Feb 1890)

Smithson, Giles W., 1876-1935 (Slate Ridge Cemetery, York Co., PA); native of Harford Co., born 21 Apr 1876, son of James L. Smithson and Virginia Daughton (Harkins Funeral Home Records)

Smithson, Hallie M., age 30 in 1890 (Marriage License Applications Book ALJ No. 2, 1891)

Smithson, Harold G., 1880-1930, son of James T. and Orpah A. (Glenn) Smithson (Bethel Presbyterian Church Cemetery Records)

Smithson, J. Clifton, 1890-1941 (Centre Methodist Church Cemetery)

Smithson, James L., 1853-1926 (St. Paul's Methodist Church Cemetery; Death certificate); see Giles W. Smithson, q.v.

Smithson, James Lee, 1817-1896 (Watters Memorial Church Cemetery, Thomas Run)

Smithson, James Thomas, 1854-1920 (Bethel Presbyterian Church Cemetery Records)

Smithson, Johanna (Johnson), 1855-1908 (Centre Methodist Church Cemetery)

Smithson, John Fletcher, 1853-1932 (Centre Methodist Church Cemetery)

Smithson, John Franklin, 1828-1900 (Centre Presbyterian Church Cemetery, PA)

Smithson, John P., 1820-1900, resided at Cambria (Death certificate incomplete)

Smithson, Josephine, 1854-1932 (Centre Methodist Church Cemetery)

Smithson, Julia, wife of Parker L. Forwood, q.v.; also see Morris O. Forwood and Helena L. West, q.v.

Smithson, Lydia E. (Knight), 1845-1901, native of Harford Co., resided at Churchville (Fallston Methodist Church Cemetery); wife of William Lee Smithson, q.v.

Smithson, M. Myrtle, 1885-1964 (Norrisville Methodist Church Cemetery)

Smithson, Madelene E., 1883-1931 (Norrisville Methodist Church Cemetery)

Smithson, Margaret E., 1882-1904 (Centre Methodist Church Cemetery); student, Forest Hill School, 1890 (*The Aegis*, 2 Jul 1965, school picture)

Smithson, Mary (Amos), 1818-1897, widow of George A. Smithson (Bethel Presbyterian Church Cemetery Records)

Smithson, Mary, see Samuel Oscar Martin, q.v.

Smithson, Mary Alverda (Galloway), 1845-1915 (Holy Cross Church Cemetery)

Smithson, Mary E., 1857-1890, daughter of George A. Smithson and Mary Amos (Bethel Presbyterian Church Cemetery Records); died testate and the only named heir was her brother George A. Smithson (Harford County Will Book JMM 11:92)

Smithson, Mary Elizabeth (Gilbert), 1859-1942 (Mt. Zion Methodist Church Cemetery)

Smithson, Mary Kezia (Barton), 1884-1969 (Bethel Presbyterian Church Cemetery Records); wife of Harold G. Smithson, q.v.

Smithson, Mattie, student, Forest Hill School, 1890 (*The Aegis*, 2 Jul 1965, school picture)

Smithson, Mergy, 9 Dec 1890 - 27 Aug 1891 (Christ Episcopal Church Cemetery)

Smithson, Michael Whiteford, born 28 Nov 1885, son of Parker F. Smithson and Sallie C. ---- (Holy Trinity Episcopal Church Register of Baptisms, p. 88)

Smithson, Milcha E., 1863-1898 (St. Paul's Methodist Church Cemetery)

Smithson, Nettie S., 1888-1971 (Norrisville Methodist Church Cemetery)

Smithson, Olevia, 1867-1904 (St. Paul's Methodist Church Cemetery)

Smithson, Orpah Ann (Glenn), 1850-1936 (Bethel Presbyterian Church Cemetery Records); wife of James T. Smithson, q.v.

Smithson, Parker F., see Elijah Alexander Smithson and Michael Whiyeford Smithson, q.v.

Smithson, Priscilla Frances, 1860-1936 (Christ Episcopal Church Cemetery); wife of Frank Pierce Smithson, q.v.

Smithson, Rumsey E., 1872-1951 (St. Paul's Methodist Church Cemetery)

Smithson, Sally C., see Elijah Alexander Smithson and Michael Whiteford Smithson, q.v.

Smithson, Sarah Ann, 1875-1900, daughter of Thomas P. Smithson and Mary E. ---- resided near Harkins P. O. (Death certificate)

Smithson, Sarah L., sold land in April 1890 (*The Aegis & Intelligencer*, 9 May 1890)

Smithson, Sophia, 1838-1912 (Centre Methodist Church Cemetery); acquired land in April 1890 (*The Aegis & Intelligencer*, 9 May 1890); see Anna Louisa Smithson, Emma Julia Smithson and William Preston Smithson, q.v.

Smithson, Susan G., 1833-1927, wife of John Franklin Smithson, q.v.

Smithson, Thomas, see Emory T. Smithson, q.v.

Smithson, Thomas Edward, 1825-1895 (Centre Methodist Church Cemetery)

Smithson, Thomas F., of Cambria, married Mary M. Rigdon, of Cambria, on 23 Jul 1890 in Towson, MD (*The Aegis & Intelligencer*, 8 Aug 1890)

Smithson, Thomas P., 1861-1940 (Norrisville Methodist Church Cemetery); see Sarah Ann Smihtson, q.v.

Smithson, Wilbur, 1874-1949 (St. Paul's Methodist Church Cemetery)

Smithson, William, 1836-1916 (Centre Methodist Church Cemetery)

Smithson, William, Jr., see Anna Louisa Smithson, Emma Julia Smithson and William Preston Smithson, q.v.

Smithson, William Bull, 1851-1904 (Centre Methodist Church Cemetery)

Smithson, William H., 1878-1942 (Holy Cross Church Cemetery)

Smithson, William Henry, 1843-1923 (Holy Cross Church Cemetery); see Fannie S. Bay, q.v.

Smithson, William L., 1890-1936 (St. Paul's Methodist Church Cemetery)

Smithson, William Lee, 1819-1902 (Fallston Methodist Church Cemetery); husband of Lydia E. Smithson, q.v.

Smithson, William Preston, 1884-1960 (St. George's Episcopal Church Cemetery); native of Harford Co, born 25 Mar 1884, son of William Smithson and Sophia ---- (John Forwood Bible, *Maryland Bible Records, Volume 1*, by Henry C. Peden, Jr., 2003, p. 83; Bailey Funeral Home Records)

Smithson, Willie, student, Forest Hill School, 1890 (*The Aegis*, 2 Jul 1965, school picture)

Smoot, Walter, 1890-1952 (Mt. Zion Methodist Church Cemetery)

Smothers, David H., Civil War veteran, at Level (*1890 Special Census of the Civil War Veterans of the State of Maryland*, by L. Tilden Moore, Volume III, p. 67)

Smothers, Emily (colored), see Olie Smothers (colored) and William Smothers (colored), q.v.

Smothers, Emma (colored), c1828-1928 (Death certificate; Alms House Record Book)

Smothers, James, county out-pensioner [welfare recipient], Fifth District, 1890 (*Havre de Grace Republican*, 4 Jul 1890)

Smothers, James Parker (colored), 1852-1939, native of Calvert Co., MD (Death certificate)

Smothers, Louisa (Dutton) (colored), 1861-1917 (Death certificate)

Smothers, Margaret C. (Collins) (colored), 1873-1942, native of Maryland, born 6 May 1873, daughter of Tobias Collins and ---- (Death certificate)

Smothers, Martha (colored), see Sallie Jones (colored), q.v.

Smothers, Mary (Mrs.) (colored), c1848-1923, native of Harford Co., parents unknown (Death certificate; St. James United Cemetery)

Smothers, Mary Eliza (colored), 1833-1897 (Green Spring Methodist Church Cemetery)

Smothers, Mary Jane, 1883-1945 (Smith Chapel Methodist Church Cemetery)

Smothers, Olie (Miss) (colored), c1890-1926 (St. James United Cemetery); native of Maryland, resided in Havre de Grace, daughter of William Smothers and Emily Wallace (Death certificate)

Smothers, William (colored), c1851-1901, native of Maryland, laborer in Havre de Grace; husband of Emily Smothers (Death certificate); see Olie Smothers, q.v.

Smothers, William M., born 1884, died 19-- (Smith Chapel Methodist Church Cemetery)

Snodgrass' General Store, Mill Green, John I. Snodgrass, prop. (*Country Stores: Harford County's Rural Heritage*, by Henry C. Peden, Jr. and Jack L. Shagena, Jr., 2015, p. 235)

Snodgrass, Alvania (Mrs.), 1868-1951 (Highland Presbyterian Church Cemetery); born 11 Feb 1868, resided at Street, parents not indicated (Harkins Funeral Home Records)

Snodgrass, Catherine A., 1855-1922 (Emory Methodist Church Cemetery)

Snodgrass, Edmund, 1878-1963 (Emory Methodist Church Cemetery); native of Street, Harford Co., born 4 May 1878, son of John I. Snodgrass and Hannah Sanders (Harkins Funeral Home Records); see Jennie Snodgrass, q.v.

Snodgrass, Grover C., 1883-1963 (Slate Ridge Cemetery, York Co., PA); native of Street, Harford Co., born 24 Oct 1883, son of John I. Snodgrass and Hannah Sanders (Harkins Funeral Home Records)

Snodgrass, Hannah (Sanders), 1854-1927 (Emory Methodist Church Cemetery); wife of John I.Snodgrass, q.v., also see Hannah E. Huff, Edmund Snodgrass and Mary F. Webster, q.v.

Snodgrass, James F., 1874-1929 (Deer Creek Methodist Church Cemetery)

Snodgrass, Jennie (Treakle), 1879-1965 (Emory Methodist Church Cemetery); native of Street, Harford Co., born 19 Oct 1879, daughter of Edwin T. Treakle and Martha S. Huff (Harkins Funeral Home Records); wife of Edmund Snodgrass, q.v.

Snodgrass, Jessie L., 1874-1948 (Deer Creek Methodist Church Cemetery)

Snodgrass, John I., 1844-1920 (Emory Methodist Church Cemetery); tomato canner, Mill Green (*The Aegis & Intelligencer*, 5 Sep 1890); see Hannah E. Huff, Carrie S. Jenness, Grover C. Snodgrass, Sarah Snodgrass, Edmund Snodgrass, Mary F. Webster, and Snodgrass' General Store, q.v.

Snodgrass, Mary F., see Mary F. Webster, q.v.

Snodgrass, Nora, 1869-1933 (Mt. Zion Methodist Church Cemetery)

Snodgrass, Paris M., 1871-1919 (Mt. Zion Methodist Church Cemetery)

Snodgrass, Sarah, 1876-1954 (Emory Methodist Church Cemetery); native of Street, Harford Co., born 28 Jan 1876, daughter of John I. Snodgrass and Hannah Sanders (Harkins Funeral Home Records)

Snodgrass, William E., 1848-1911 (Emory Methodist Church Cemetery); native of Maryland, resided at Mill Green (Death certificate); served on a petit jury, of Fifth District, 1890 (*The Aegis & Intelligencer*, 14 Nov 1890); William E.Snodgrass, and wife, sold land in August 1890 (*The Aegis & Intelligencer*, 12 Sep 1890)

Snodgrass, William Ira, 1879-1902 (Emory Methodist Church Cemetery)

Snook, William G., premium award winner, Class B - Cattle, and Class D - Swine, Harford County Fair, 1890 (*The Aegis & Intelligencer*, 24 Oct 1890)

Snow, Elizabeth T. (Bailey), 1848-1917 (Angel Hill Cemetery)

Snow, Henry Bailey (D.D.S.), 1870-1896 (Angel Hill Cemetery); usher, Willard Section No. 58, Order of the Cadets of Temperance, of Havre de Grace, 1890 (*Havre de Grace Republican*, 7 Feb 1890)

Snow, James H., 1842-1928 (Angel Hill Cemetery); native of Massachusetts, stone mason, married, resident of Havre de Grace (Death certificate)

Snow, Martha Elizabeth, born 10 Aug 1883, daughter of James H. Snow and Elizabeth T. Bailey (*Barnes-Bailey Genealogy*, by Walter D. Barnes, 1939, p. H-81)

Snow, Susie, born 11 Mar 1873, daughter of James H. Smow and Elizabeth T. Bailey (*Barnes-Bailey Genealogy*, by Walter D. Barnes, 1939, p. H-81)

Snowden, Anna E. (colored), 1877-1927, native of Maryland, born 15 May 1877, daughter of Jessie Snowden and Caroline Gibson (Death certificate - married name Gwynn)

Snowden, Benjamin Harrison (colored), 1878-1944, native of Maryland, son of Mary Snowden and ---- (Death certificate; 1900 Aberdeen Census stated he was born in April 1874)

Snowden, Chapman (colored), 1871-1931 (Mt. Calvary Methodist Church Cemetery)

Snowden, George (colored), see Gilphin Snowden (colored), q.v.

Snowden, Gilphin (colored), 1868-1940, native of Harford Co., born 15 Oct 1868, son of George Snowden and Mary ----, natives of Maryland (Death certificate; 1900 Aberdeen Census stated "Gilpin" was born in June 1860)

Snowden, Hannah (Smith) (colored), 1859-1912, native of Maryland (Death certificate)

Snowden, Jessie (colored), see Anna E. Snowden (colored), q.v.

Snowden, Louisa (Mrs.) (colored), 1845-1926 (Death certificate; St. James United Cemetery)

Snowden, Lydia A. (Dorsey) (colored), 1867-1929, native of Maryland (Death certificate)

Snowden, Mary (colored), born -- May 1850, native of Maryland (1900 Aberdeen Census)

Snowden, Mary A. (Webster) (colored), 1888-1927, native of Maryland, daughter of George H. Webster and Mary J. Kenly (Death certificate)

Snowden, Mary Jane (Mrs.) (colored), c1841-1919, native of Maryland, resided at Harford Furnace (Death certificate)

Snowden, Mealia (colored), born -- May 1860, native of Maryland (1900 Aberdeen Census); wife of Gilphin Snowden, q.v.

Snowden, Thomas H. (colored), 1850-1932, native of Maryland (Death certificate)

Snyder, Margaret E., age 20 in 1890 (Marriage License Applications Book ALJ No. 2, 1891)

Soelkey, Margaret E. (Mrs.), 1835-1901, resided at Carsins, Harford Co. (Death certificate incomplete)

Somerville, Henry Clay, 1844-1927 (Mountain Christian Church Cemetery)

Somerville, Laura A. (Magness), 1842-1918 (Mountain Christian Church Cemetery), wife of Henry Clay Somerville, q.v.

Somerville, Viola Elizabeth (Pitcock), 1876-1966 (Mountain Christian Church Cemetery), wife of Walter E. Somerville, q.v.

Somerville, Walter Elijah, 1868-1951 (Mountain Christian Church Cemetery); age 21, student, Oakland School, 1890 (George G. Curtiss Ledger)

Sommer, Carl Henry, see George C. Breuninger, q.v.

Sommerfield, Walter E., new name on the voter registration list at Abingdon, First District (*Havre de Grace Republican*, 17 Oct 1890)

Sonbiron, Emily M., see George C. Colder, q.v.

Sonbiron, Mary, see Amelia Elizabeth Power, q.v.

Sons of Temperance, Havre de Grace (*Havre de Grace: Its Historic Past, Its Charming Present and Its*

Promising Future: Harford County's Rural Heritage. by Jack L. Shagena, Jr. and Henry C. Peden, Jr., 2018, p. 274)

Sorrell, Edward (colored), see William Sorrell (colored), q.v.

Sorrell, Elizabeth (colored), c1885-1920, native of Maryland, daughter of James Sorrell and Rachel Armistead (Death certificate - married name Martin)

Sorrell, James (colored), see Elizabeth Sorrell (colored), q.v.

Sorrell, Lizzie (colored), see William Skinner (colored), q.v.

Sorrell, Walter (colored), name removed from the voter registration list in Sixth District, 1890 (*Havre de Grace Republican*, 17 Oct 1890)

Sorrell, William (colored), 1879-1916, native of Harford Co., born 1 Aug 1879, son of Edward Sorrell and Fannie Skinner, natives of Harford Co. (Death certificate)

Sothoron, Flossie, student, Forest Hill School, 1890 (*The Aegis*, 2 Jul 1965, school picture)

Sothoron, Grace, student, Forest Hill School, 1890 (*The Aegis*, 2 Jul 1965, school picture)

Sothoron, Locke student, Forest Hill School, 1890 (*The Aegis*, 2 Jul 1965, school picture)

Sothoron, Margaret, student, Forest Hill School, 1890 (*The Aegis*, 2 Jul 1965, school picture)

Sothoron, Pinkney, student, Forest Hill School, 1890 (*The Aegis*, 2 Jul 1965, school picture)

South Delta Public School No. 20, near Cardiff, Fifth District (*Harford County, Maryland Teachers and the Schools They Served, 1774-1900*, by Henry C. Peden, Jr., 2022, p. 372)

Spalding, Basil Dennis, born 13 Jul 1890, baptized 4 Oct 1890, son of Hargraves and Martha W. Spalding (Holy Trinity Episcopal Church Register of Baptisms, p. 98; William R. Bissell Bible, *Maryland Bible Records, Volume 1*, by Henry C. Peden, Jr., 2003, p. 35)

Spalding, Dennis, resident of Darlington (*The Aegis & Intelligencer*, 13 Jun 1890)

Spalding, Hargraves, 1857-1926 (Holy Trinity Episcopal Church Cemetery); native of Charles Co., married, resided at Churchville (Death certificate); warden, Holy Trinity Episcopal Church (*Havre de Grace Republican*, 18 Apr 1890); served on a petit jury (*The Aegis & Intelligencer*, 14 Nov 1890); see William Hargraves Spalding, q.v.

Spalding, Martha W., 1859-1931 (Holy Trinity Episcopal Church Cemetery); wife of Hargraves Spalding, q.v.

Spalding, William Hargraves, born 12 Mar 1887, son of Hargraves and Martha W. Spalding (Holy Trinity Episcopal Church Register of Baptisms, p. 92; William R. Bissell Bible, *Maryland Bible Records, Volume 1*, by Henry C. Peden, Jr., 2003, p. 35)

Spangler, Margaret, 1829-1911 (Alms House Record Book)

Speake, William F. (Rev.), Havre de Grace M. E Church (*Havre de Grace Republican*, 13 Jun 1890); tent holder, Carsins Run Camp Meeting of the East Harford Circuit, P. E. Church (*The Aegis & Intelligencer*, 1 Aug 1890)

Spencer & McGonigall, lumber and building materials, Lapidum (*Havre de Grace Republican*, 19 Sep 1890)

Spencer's General Store, Washington St., Havre de Grace, John N Spencer, prop. (*Country Stores: Harford County's Rural Heritage*, by Henry C. Peden, Jr. and Jack L. Shagena, Jr., 2015, p. 236)

Spencer House, Havre de Grace, L. W. Williams, prop. (*Harford Democrat*, 14 Feb 1890)

Spencer, Amelia W. (Donahoo), 1859-1923 (Bailey Funeral Home Records)

Spencer, Amos, see Rose Spencer, q.v.

Spencer, Amos D., 1816-1899 (Death certificate; Rock Run Methodist Church Cemetery); proprietor of The Mammoth Store in Havre de Grace (*Havre de Grace Republican*, 4 Apr 1890); businessman (trader's license), Havre de Grace (*Havre de Grace Republican*, 30 May 1890); member, Susquehanna Lodge No. 130, A.F. & A. M., Havre de Grace (*Havre de Grace Republican*, 11 Jul 1890)

Spencer, Annie (Lisby) (colored), 1865-1914 (Death certificate)

Spencer, Annie M., 1879-1963 (William Watters Memorial Methodist Church Cemetery, Cooptown)

Spencer, Benjamin Franklin, 1844-1923 (Old Brick Baptist Church Cemetery; Death certificate)

Spencer, Bessie M. Courtney, born 23 May 1885, daughter of Joseph E. and Hannah (Courtney) Spencer (*The Hughes Genealogy, 1636-1953*, by Joseph Lee Hughes, 1953, pp. 115, 136)

Spencer, Beulah (Lyon), 1875-1955 (Angel Hill Cemetery)

Spencer, Cecil Clyde, 1881-1941 (Mt. Zion Methodist Church Cemetery); son of John Walter Spencer, q.v.

Spencer, Charles (colored), 1865-1930 (Death certificate)

Spencer, Charles Hollingsworth, born 22 Apr 1883, son of Silas L. Spencer and Mary Eliza Mitchell (Silas L. Spencer Bible, *Maryland Bible Records, Volume 2*, by Henry C. Peden, Jr., 2003, pp. 139-140)

Spencer, Clayton Augustus, 1850-1917 (Bethel Presbyterian Church Cemetery Records)

Spencer, Daniel (colored), 1839-1900, farmer, native of Maryland, resided at Benson (Death certificate); member, Ames Chapel M. E. Church, Bel Air, 1890 (*The Aegis & Intelligencer*, 15 Aug 1890); see Eliza Spencer, q.v.

Spencer, Delia (colored), see Joseph A. Spencer (colored), q.v.

Spencer, Eliza (colored), 1872-1910, native of Harford Co., daughter of Daniel Spencer and Mary Johnson (Death certificate - married name Brown)

Spencer, Elizabeth Cole (Herbert), 1822-1910 (Rock Run Methodist Church Cemetery); wife of Jarrett Spencer, q.v.

Spencer, Ella W., 1873-1944 (William Watters Memorial Methodist Church Cemetery, Cooptown)

Spencer, Emma (Whitelock), died 15 Feb 1904, age 51, at Garland (Death certificate)

Spencer, Estelle (Mechem), 1880-1926 (St. Ignatius Catholic Church Cemetery)

Spencer, Ethel, infant daughter of Philip G. Streett, resided at Chrome Hill (*Harford Democrat*, 24 Jan 1890)

Spencer, Hannah Elizabeth (Courtney), 1853-1933 (Rock Run Methodist Church Cemetery; Death certificate); wife of Joseph E. Spencer, q.v.

Spencer, Harry Zehring, 1874-1933 (Angel Hill Cemetery); student, Havre de Grace High School (*Havre de Grace Republican*, 31 Oct 1890)

Spencer, Henrietta H., 1852-1925 (Rock Run Methodist Church Cemetery)

Spencer, Herman, trustee, Lapidum School No. 13, Second District (*Havre de Grace Republican*, 30 May 1890)

Spencer, Jarrett, 1822-1900 (Death certificate; Rock Run Methodist Church Cemetery); fisherman and farmer, near Lapidum and Level (*Havre de Grace Republican*, 21 Feb and 4 Apr 1890); member, Lapidum Debating Society (*Havre de Grace Republican*, 7 Mar 1890); see Jarrett Spencer & Son, q.v.

Spencer, John Herman, 1845-1930 (Rock Run Methodist Church Cemetery; Bailey Funeral Home Records); partner, Silver, Spencer & Co., fishing floats (*Heavy Industries of Yesteryear; Harford County's Rural Heritage*, by Jack L. Shagena, Jr. and Henry C. Peden, Jr., 2015, p. 62); see Mary Elizabeth Spencer, q.v.

Spencer, John N., 1845-1916 (Angel Hill Cemetery); businessman (trader's license), Havre de Grace (*Havre de Grace Republican*, 30 May 1890)

Spencer, John Richard, 1825-1908 (Rock Run Methodist Church Cemetery); fisherman, Havre de Grace (*Havre de Grace Republican*, 14 Feb 1890); also see Mary Iola Silver, q.v.

Spencer, John Walter, 1851-1934 (Mt. Zion Methodist Church Cemetery); acquired land in February 1890 (*The Aegis & Intelligencer*, 7 Mar 1890); librarian, Rock Run Sunday School (*Havre de Grace Republican*, 2 May 1890)

Spencer, Joseph, see Bessie S. Taylor, q.v.

Spencer, Joseph A. (colored), 1874-1929, native of Maryland, son of Delia Spencer and Thomas Osborn (Death certificate)

Spencer, Joseph Ely, 1849-1928 (Rock Run Methodist Church Cemetery); native of Maryland, farmer, near Rock Run Church (Death certificate; *Havre de Grace Republican*, 14 Feb 1890); stone quarry, Lapidum, 1890

(*Havre de Grace Republican*, 28 Nov 1890); Spencer, J. E. (Mr.), member, Lapidum Debating Society (*Havre de Grace Republican*, 7 Feb 1890); assistant superintendent, Lapidum Sunday School (*Havre de Grace Republican*, 30 May 1890); Joseph E. Spencer, and wife, sold land in May 1890 (*The Aegis & Intelligencer*, 6 Jun 1890)

Spencer, Julia (colored), see George Edward Pugh (colored), q.v.

Spencer, Laura P. (Courtney), 1885-1976 (Rock Run Methodist Church Cemetery); wife of John Herman Spencer, q.v.; also see Mary Elizabeth Spencer, q.v.

Spencer, Lavinia (Gross), 1877-1955 (Bethel Presbyterian Church Cemetery Records); wife of Walter Sappington Spencer, q.v.

Spencer, Libbie (Miss), actress, Darlington Company (*Havre de Grace Republican*, 7 Mar 1890); singer and member, Lapidum M. P. Church (*The Aegis & Intelligencer*, 13 Jun 1890)

Spencer, M. Cassandra (Cain), 1848-1936 (Mt. Zion Methodist Church Cemetery); wife of Cecil Clyde Spencer, q.v.

Spencer, Margaret R. (Kelchner), 1849-1919 (Angel Hill Cemetery); wife of John N. Spencer, q.v.

Spencer, Mary (Ruff) (colored), 1861-1926 (Tabernacle Mt. Zion Methodist Church Cemetery); native of Harford Co.. resided at Fallston (Death certificate)

Spencer, Mary A. (Johnson) (colored), 1840-1910, native of Maryland (Death certificate); wife of Daniel Spencer, q.v.; also see Eliza Spencer, q.v.

Spencer, Mary E. (Miss), 1829-1914 (Old Brick Baptist Church Cemetery)

Spencer, Mary Eliza (Mitchell), 1838-1908 (Silas L. Spencer Bible, *Maryland Bible Records, Volume 2*, by Henry C. Peden, Jr., 2003, pp. 139-140), wife of Silas L. Spencer, q.v.

Spencer, Mary Elizabeth, 1872-1941, native of Lapidum, Harford Co., daughter of John Herman Spencer and Laura Courtney (Death certificate - married name Donahoo)

Spencer, Mary Elizabeth, born 14 Jun 1882, daughter of Richard L. and Sarah E. (Cooper) Spencer (Richard Litteton Spencer Bible, *Maryland Bible Records, Volume 5*, by Henry C. Peden, Jr., 2004, p. 188)

Spencer, Mary Estella (Mechem), 1880-1926 (St. Ignatius Catholic Church Cemetery)

Spencer, Mary Iola, 1862-1890, daughter of John Richard and Sarah Spencer (John R. Spencer Bible, *Maryland Bible Records, Volume 2*, by Henry C. Peden, Jr., 2003, pp. 137-138)

Spencer, Maud (Miss), actress, Darlington Company (*Havre de Grace Republican*, 7 Mar 1890); member, Lapidum M. P. Church (*The Aegis & Intelligencer*, 13 Jun 1890)

Spencer, Morgan Sylvester, 1841-1932 (Old Brick Baptist Church Cemetery; *Children of Mt. Soma*, by Gertrude J. Stephens, 1992, p. 454)

Spencer, Oliver R., 1836-1914 (Old Brick Baptist Church Cemetery)

Spencer, P., third baseman, Webster Baseball Club, of Webster (*Havre de Grace Republican*, 25 Jul 1890)

Spencer, P. M. (Mr.), member, Lapidum Debating Society (*Havre de Grace Republican*, 7 Feb 1890)

Spencer, Philip Gover, 1865-1941 (William Watters Memorial Methodist Church Cemetery, Cooptown); son of Silas L. Spencer and Mary Eliza Mitchell (Silas L. Spencer Bible, *Maryland Bible Records, Volume 2*, by Henry C. Peden, Jr., 2003, pp. 139-140); assistant superintendent, Cooptown Sunday School (*Havre de Grace Republican*, 18 Apr 1890)

Spencer, Rachel E., 1866-1922 (William Watters Memorial Methodist Church Cemetery, Cooptown)

Spencer, Richard Littleton, 1858-1898, son of Silas L. Spencer and Mary Eliza Mitchell (Silas L. Spencer Bible, *Maryland Bible Records, Volume 2*, by Henry C. Peden, Jr., 2003, pp. 139-140; Richard Litteton Spencer Bible, *Maryland Bible Records, Volume 5*, by Henry C. Peden, Jr., 2004, p. 188)

Spencer, Robert Walker, 1874-1933 (William Watters Memorial Methodist Church Cemetery, Cooptown); born 3 Dec 1874, son of Silas L. Spencer and Mary Eliza Mitchell (Silas L. Spencer Bible, *Maryland Bible Records, Volume 2*, by Henry C. Peden, Jr., 2003, pp. 139-140)

Spencer, Robertine (Wilkinson), 1853-1932 (Mt. Zion Methodist Church Cemetery); wife of John Walter Spencer, q.v.

Spencer, Rosanna (Tipton), 1866-1950 (Bethel Presbyterian Church Cemetery Records); wife of Clayton A. Spencer, q.v.

Spencer, Rose, native of Havre de Grace, born 16 Oct 1874, daughter of Amos Spencer and ---- (Pennington Funeral Home Records, 1955 - married name Lynd)

Spencer, Rose Ann, 1813-1883 (Rock Run Methodist Church Cemetery); wife of Amos D. Spencer, q.v.

Spencer, Sallie A., 1847-1908, daughter of Hugh E. and Sarah Ann (Way) Spencer (Old Brick Baptist Church Cemetery; Death certificate)

Spencer, Sarah (Bailey), 1827-1912 (John R. Spencer Bible, *Maryland Bible Records, Volume 2*, by Henry C. Peden, Jr., 2003, p. 137); wife of John Richard Spencer, q.v.

Spencer, Sarah Elizabeth (Cooper), 1865-1898 (Richard Litteton Spencer Bible, *Maryland Bible Records, Volume 5*, by Henry C. Peden, Jr., 2004, p. 188)

Spencer, Silas L., 1830-1918 (Rock Run Methodist Church Cemetery; Silas L. Spencer Bible, *Maryland Bible Records, Volume 2*, by Henry C. Peden, Jr., 2003, pp. 139-140); tent holder, Carsins Run Camp Meeting of the East Harford Circuit, P. E. Church (*The Aegis & Intelligencer*, 1 Aug 1890)

Spencer, Silas McLaren, 1871-1918 (William Watters Memorial Methodist Church Cemetery, Cooptown); canner, Chrome Hill (*Havre de Grace Republican*, 5 Sep 1890); librarian, Cooptown Sunday School (*Havre de Grace Republican*, 18 Apr 1890); born 7 May 1871, son of Silas L. Spencer and Mary Eliza Mitchell (Silas L. Spencer Bible, *Maryland Bible Records, Volume 2*, by Henry C. Peden, Jr., 2003, pp. 139-140)

Spencer, Stanley S., 1887-1965 (Mt. Zion Methodist Church Cemetery); son of John Walter Spencer, q.v.

Spencer, W. (Master), actor, Darlington Company (*Havre de Grace Republican*, 7 Mar 1890)

Spencer, Walter Sappington, 1877-1938 (Bethel Presbyterian Church Cemetery Recprds); born 3 Nov 1877, son of Silas L. Spencer and Mary Eliza Mitchell (Silas L. Spencer Bible, *Maryland Bible Records, Volume 2*, by Henry C. Peden, Jr., 2003, pp. 139-140)

Spencer, William Vandiver, 1880-1950 (Rock Run Methodist Church Cemetery; *The Hughes Genealogy, 1636-1953*, by Joseph Lee Hughes, 1953, pp. 115, 136); born 6 Mar 1880, son of Joseph Ely Spencer, q.v.

Spering's General Store and Grocery Store ("Mountan House"), near Clayton and Mountain, Ridgeway T. and Sallie E. Spering, prop. (*Country Stores: Harford County's Rural Heritage*, by Henry C. Peden, Jr. and Jack L. Shagena, Jr., 2015, p. 237)

Spering, Ridgeway T., 1853-1899 (Mountain Christian Church Cemetery; Death certificate); resident of *Mountain View* and merchant at the Mountain, First District (*The Aegis & Intelligencer*, 21 Feb 1890; Mr. & Mrs. R. T. Spering, members of Mountain Reading Circle (*The Aegis & Intelligencer*, 21 Feb 1890)

Spering, Sallie E., 1848-1913 (Mountain Christian Church Cemetery); member, Mountain Reading Circle (*The Aegis & Intelligencer*, 12 Sep 1890)

Spesutia Church, aka St. George's Episcopal Church, and Cemetery (Perryman)

Spesutia Colored Public School No. 3, Spesutia Island, Second District (*Harford County, Maryland Teachers and the Schools They Served, 1774-1900*, by Henry C. Peden, Jr., 2022, p. 372)

Spicer Building Association, Bel Air (*Havre de Grace Republican*, 16 May 1890)

Spicer's General Store, Fallston Station, Ma & Pa Railroad, Holliday H. Spicer, prop. (*Country Stores: Harford County's Rural Heritage*, by Henry C. Peden, Jr. and Jack L. Shagena, Jr., 2015, p. 237)

Spicer, Adeline D. (Guyton), 1840-1925 (Little Falls Quaker Cemetery), wife of Simeon Spicer, q.v.

Spicer, Arabella ("Nellie"), 1873-1975 (Little Falls Quaker Cemetery); age 17, student, Oakland School, 1890 (George G. Curtiss Ledger listed her as Abraella "Nellie" Spicer); daughter of Simeon Spicer, q.v.

Spicer, Abram Augustus, 1858-1892 (Fallston Methodist Church Cemetery)

Spicer, Ariel Sibella, 1857-1937 (Fallston Methodist Church Cemetery)

Spicer, Bessie, student, Oakland School, 1890 (George G. Curtiss Ledger)

Spicer, Daniel Reese, 1870-1945 (Fallston Methodist Church Cemetery)

Spicer, Elizabeth Sibella (Lee), 1835-1920 (Fallston Methodist Church Cemetery)

Spicer, Ella Mae, 1884-1955 (Mountain Christian Church Cemetery)

Spicer, Ella Marion, 1862-1943 (Fallston Methodist Church Cemetery)

Spicer, Ella May, 1886-1947 (Mountain Christian Church Cemetery)

Spicer, Essie, student, Oakland School, 1890 (George G. Curtiss Ledger)

Spicer, Esther Eliza, 1871-1958 (Little Falls Quaker Cemetery); student, Oakland School, 1890 (George G. Curtiss Ledger); daughter of Simeon Spicer, q.v.

Spicer, Frank, age 7, student, Oakland School, 1890 (George G. Curtiss Ledger)

Spicer, George B., 1864-1938 (Mountain Christian Church Cemetery)

Spicer, Holliday Hicks, 1861-1943 (Fallston Methodist Church Cemetery); census taker, Fallston Precinct, 1890 (*Havre de Grace Republican*, 23 May 1890)

Spicer, Ida (Miss), resident of Bel Air (*The Aegis & Intelligencer*, 31 Oct 1890)

Spicer, James Augustus, 1825-1897 (Fallston Methodist Church Cemetery)

Spicer, James Wallace, 1868-1923 (Fallston Methodist Church Cemetery)

Spicer, Jessie Franklin, 1857-1943 (Fallston Methodist Church Cemetery)

Spicer, John T., 1822-1899 (Churchville Presbyterian Church Cemetery)

Spicer, Louisa M. (Turner), 1865-1940 (Mountain Christian Church Cemetery)

Spicer, Margaret (Jones), 1875-1952 (Little Falls Quaker Cemetery)

Spicer, Mary A. 1871-1923 (Fallston Methodist Church Cemetery)

Spicer, Mary E., 1874-1956 (Fallston Methodist Church Cemetery)

Spicer, Naomi (Lee), born 1875, died ---- (Fallston Methodist Church Cemetery)

Spicer, Robert Barclay 1869-1924 (Little Falls Quaker Cemetery); native of Harford Co., resided at Fallston (Death certificate); son of Simeon Spicer, q.v.

Spicer, Samuel A., 1880-1946 (Mountain Christian Church Cemetery)

Spicer, Simeon, 1836-1908 (Little Falls Quaker Cemetery); Civil War veteran, Fallston (*1890 Special Census of the Civil War Veterans of the State of Maryland*, by L. Tilden Moore, Volume III, p. 76)

Spicer, Walter M., died 1896, age not stated (Mountain Christian Church Cemetery)

Spies, Barbara A., 1865-1921 (St. Francis de Sales Catholic Church Cemetery)

Spies, Frederick Charles, 1850-1928 (St. Francis de Sales Catholic Church Cemetery); native of Germany, farmer at Belcamp (Death certificate)

Spies, George Frederick, 1885-1971 (St. Francis de Sales Catholic Church Cemetery)

Spink, Bertrand ("Bert"), 1873-1929 (Angel Hill Cemetery)

Spink, Clara D. (Poplar), 1869-1941 (Angel Hill Cemetery); wife of Bertrand Spink, q.v.

Spink, Harriet E., 1836-1912 (Angel Hill Cemetery)

Sponsaler, Victor, stage manager, Bel Air Specialty Company, an entertainment group mostly connected to the young men of the Bulett Carriage Factory (*The Aegis & Intelligencer*, 13 Jun 1890)

Sprigg, Grace Elizabeth (Duryea), 1870-1949, wife of James Cresap Sprigg, daughter of Edgar E. and Julia Carpenter Duryea, of Glen Cove, Long Island (St. Mary's Episcopal Church Cemetery)

Sprigg, James Cresap, 1858-1957, son of James Cresap and Lucy Addison Sprigg, of Petersburg, VA (St. Mary's Episcopal Church Cemetery)

Spriggs, Amelia (colored), age 21 in 1890 (Marriage License Applications Book ALJ No. 2, 1891)

Spriggs, Augusta (colored), see Cordelia A. Westcott, Ella M. Westcott and Henrietta Westcott, q.v.

Spriggs, Eliza (colored), wife of Joseph E. Bradford, q.v.

Spriggs, Jane (colored), see Katie Moore (colored), q.v.

Spriggs, Joseph H. (colored), 1858-1900 (Asbury Church Cemetery)

Spriggs, Louis (colored), see Nellie Spriggs, q.v.

Spriggs, Louisa (colored), see Lawrence S. Prigg (colored) and Oscar Prigg (colored), q.v.

Spriggs, Mary (colored), see Griffin Milton Smith (colored) and Stewart Donald Smith (colored), q.v.

Spriggs, Nellie (colored), 1871-1912, native of Harford Co., daughter of Louis Spriggs and Christina Sciler, natives of Baltimore Co. (Death certificate)

Spriggs, William Henry (colored), 1853-1912 (Death certificate)

Springer's General Store, at Clayton, Mrs. C. Springer, prop. (*Country Stores: Harford County's Rural Heritage*, by Henry C. Peden, Jr. and Jack L. Shagena, Jr., 2015, p. 238)

Springer, Charles E., 1879-1891 (Rock Run Methodist Church Cemetery)

Springer, Charles L., 1850-1936 (Rock Run Methodist Church Cemetery)

Springer, Eliza S. (Bowman), 1831-1911 (Rock Run Methodist Church Cemetery); wife of William T. Springe, q.v.

Springer, R. Hewgein, 1875-1957 (Norrisville Methodist Church Cemetery)

Springer, Rebecca, 1814-1921 (Norrisville Methodist Church Cemetery)

Springer, Rosala (Spencer), 1857-1943 (Rock Run Methodist Church Cemetery); wife of Charles L. Springer, q.v.

Springer, William T., 1831-1922 (Rock Run Methodist Church Cemetery)

Sprink (Spink), Kitty, wife of William S. Burns, q.v.

Spritehoof, Mary A., see Hannah S. England, q.v.

St. Andrew's Society of St. John's Church, Havre de Grace (*Havre de Grace: Its Historic Past, Its Charming Present and Its Promising Future: Harford County's Rural Heritage*. by Jack L. Shagena, Jr. and Henry C. Peden, Jr., 2018, p. 275)

St. Clair, Bailey, 1825-1907 (Bethel Presbyterian Church Cemetery)

St. Clair, Benjamin F., 1820-1892 (Old Brick Baptist Church Cemetery)

St. Clair, Charles R., 1851-1937 (Bethel Presbyterian Church Cemetery)

St. Claire, Daniel, age 35 in 1890 (Marriage License Applications Book ALJ No. 2, 1890, spelled his name St. Claire)

St. Clair, David Vernay, 1853-1933 (Bethel Presbyterian Church Cemetery Records)

St. Clair, Emma E., 1858-1890 (Bethel Presbyterian Church Cemetery Records); wife of Charles R. St. Clair, of near Rocks (*The Aegis & Intelligencer*, 28 Feb 1890)

St. Clair, H. Allen, born 6 Dec 1888, son of David Vernay and Lavinia (Grafton) St. Clair

St. Clair, Lavinia (Grafton), 1859-1919 (Bethel Presbyterian Church Cemetery); wife of David V. St. Clair, q.v.

St. Clair, Martha L. (Irvin), 1857-1931 (Bethel Presbyterian Church Cemetery Records); third wife of Charles R. St. Clair, q.v.

St. Clair, Mary A., 1861-1910 (Bethel Presbyterian Church Cemetery Records); second wife of Charles R. St. Clair, q.v.

St. Francis de Sales Catholic Church and Cemetery (Abingdon Road, Abingdon)

St. George's Episcopal Church [aka Old Spesutia Church] and Cemetery (Perryman)

St. Ignatius Catholic Church and Cemetery (Conowingo Road, Hickory)

St. James AME Church and Cemetery (Cedar Church Road, near Dublin)

St. James AME Church (Green Street, Havre de Grace)

St. James AME Church and Cemetery (Gravel Hill Road, near Havre de Grace)

St. John the Baptist Beneficial Association, of the Catholic Church, Havre de Grace (*Havre de Grace Republican*, 11 Jul 1890; (*Havre de Grace: Its Historic Past, Its Charming Present and Its Promising Future: Harford County's Rural Heritage.* by Jack L. Shagena, Jr. and Henry C. Peden, Jr., 2018, p. 275)

St. John's Episcopal Church (Union Avenue, Havre de Grace)

St. Mark's Catholic Church (Reckord Road, Fallston)

St. Mary's Catholic Church and Cemetery (St. Mary's Church Road, near Pylesville)

St. Mary's Episcopal Church and Cemetery (St. Mary's Church Road, Emmorton)

St. Patrick's Beneficial Association. Havre de Grace (*Havre de Grace: Its Historic Past, Its Charming Present and Its Promising Future: Harford County's Rural Heritage.* by Jack L. Shagena, Jr. and Henry C. Peden, Jr., 2018, p. 272)

St. Patrick's Catholic Church (Congress Avenue, Havre de Grace); see St. Patrick's Beneficial Association, Independent Social Club, St. John the Baptist Beneficial Association, and Women's Total Abstinence Society, q.v.

St. Paul's Lutheran Church and Cemetery (Spesutia Road, Perryman)

St. Paul's Methodist Church and Cemetery (Telegraph Road, north of Eden Mill)

St. Paul's Public School No. 17, Fourth District (*Harford County, Maryland Teachers and the Schools They Served, 1774-1900*, by Henry C. Peden, Jr., 2022, p. 372)

Staderman, Adam, resident, near Aberdeen (*Havre de Grace Republican*, 6 Jun 1890); surgeon, John Rodgers Post, G. A. R., Havre de Grace (*Havre de Grace Republican*, 12 Dec 1890)

Stafford Flint Mill, on Deer Creek at Stafford Bridge, B. G. and J. C. Smith, prop. (*Mills: Grist, Saw, Bone, Flint, Fulling ... & More*, by Jack L. Shagena, Jr., Henry C. Peden, Jr. and John W. McGrain, 2009, p. 256)

Stafford Mills (Grist, Flour, Bone and Plaster), mouth of Deer Creek near Susquehanna River (*Mills: Grist, Saw, Bone, Flint, Fulling ... & More*, by Jack L. Shagena, Jr., Henry C. Peden, Jr. and John W. McGrain, 2009, pp. 256-258)

Stafford Soapstone Mill (and Quarry), near Dublin, E. M. Allen, Jr., prop. (*Mills: Grist, Saw, Bone, Flint, Fulling ... & More*, by Jack L. Shagena, Jr., Henry C. Peden, Jr. and John W. McGrain, 2009, p. 258)

Stagmer's Hotel, 100 S.Main St., Bel Air, William Stagmer, prop. (*Bel Air: An Architectural and Cultural History, 1782-1945*, by Marilynn M. Larew, 1995, pp. 75, 205)

Stahl, George W., 1860-1927 (Bethel Presbyterian Church Cemetery Records)

Stahl, Julius, 1889-1944 (Wesleyan Chapel Methodist Church Cemetery)

Staley, Harry, student, Bel Air Graded School (*The Aegis & Intelligencer*, 11 Apr 1890)

Staley, Lester B., 1890-1964 (Mt. Zion Methodist Church Cemetery)

Stanberger, Sallie (Miss), teacher at Kirkwood (*Havre de Grace Republican*, 14 Feb 1890)

Standiford, Adaline V., 1863-1896 (Mountain Christian Church Cemetery)

Standiford, Alice, student, Union Chapel Public School (*The Aegis & Intelligencer*, 14 Mar 1890)

Standiford, Anne Eliza (Geatty), 1868-1950 (Bethel Presbyterian Church Cemetery Records); wife of Harry E. Standiford, q.v.

Standiford, Annie P. (Miss), 1865-1904 (Rock Run Methodist Church Cemetery)

Standiford, Austin, 1836-1903, resided at Watervale (Death certificate)

Standiford, Austin (Mrs.), died 31 Oct 1890, age 16 [sic] (*The Aegis & Intelligencer*, 7 Nov 1890, stated she was the youngest daughter of John H. Price and was buried in Mountain Christian Church Cemetery)

Standiford, Benjamin, see Georgianna M. Standiford and Jane Standiford, q.v.

Standiford, Bertie, 1871-1961 (Centre Methodist Church Cemetery)

Stansiford, C. H., 1843-1918 (Darlington Cemetery)

Standiford, Carrie E., 1888-1909 (St. Paul's Methodist Church Cemetery)

Standiford, Charles, see Laura Standiford and Ramsey Standiford, q.v.

Stansiford, Charles H., 1843-1918, resided at Darlington (Death certificate)

Standiford, Charles Richardson, 1839-1927 (Ebenezer Methodist Church Cemetery; Death certificate); treasurer, Ebenezer M. E. Church Sunday School (*Havre de Grace Republican*, 25 Apr 1890); trustee, Sarah Furnace School No. 22, Fourth District (*Havre de Grace Republican*, 30 May 1890)

Standiford, Claudius, 1880-1978 (Ebenezer Methodist Church Cemetery)

Standiford, Dennis H., 1818-1898 (Good Will Church Cemetery); trustee, Rutledge's School No. 5, Fourth District (*Havre de Grace Republican*, 30 May 1890)

Standiford, Eliza (Clark), 1863-1948 (Mountain Christian Church Cemetery)

Standiford, Elizabeth (Beatty), 1868-1950 (Bethel Presbyterian Church Cemetery)

Standiford, Elizabeth B., 1880-1909 (Ebenezer Methodist Church Cemetery)

Standiford, Ella, 1866-1912 (Ebenezer Methodist Church Cemetery)

Standiford, Ethel M., 1889-1956, daughter of William A. Standiford and Elizabeth Carty (Rock Run Methodist Church Cemetery; Bailey Funeral Home Records - married name Starr)

Standiford, Euphemia (Whitelock), 1849-1909 (Darlington Cemetery)

Standiford, Frances M., see Isaac Standiford, q.v.

Standiford, Franklin Whitaker, 1877-1945 (Union Chapel Methodist Church Cemetery); son of Joseph Maltier Standiford, q.v.

Standiford, George M., 1881-1944 (Rock Run Methodist Church Cemetery)

Standiford, George W., age 14, student, Oakland School, 1890 (George G. Curtiss Ledger)

Standiford, Georgianna M. ("Georgie"), daughter of Benjamin Standiford, near Clayton, and proud owner of a three-legged duckling (*The Aegis & Intelligencer*, 20 Jun 1890); member, Mountain Reading Circle (*The Aegis & Intelligencer*, 21 Feb 1890)

Standiford, H. Wilson, 1890-1965 (Mt. Zion Methodist Church Cemetery)

Standiford, Harriet Jane, age 23 in 1890 (Marriage License Applications Book ALJ No. 2, 1891)

Standiford, Harry E., 1864-1959 (Bethel Presbyterian Church Cemetery); wheelwright and carriage maker, Bond Street, Bel Air, 1890 (*Harford Democrat*, 10 Jan 1890; *Carriages Back in the Day: Harford County's Rural Heritage*, by Jack L. Shagena, Jr. and Henry C. Peden, Jr., 2016, p. 127)

Standiford, Harry W., 1887-1976 (St. Paul's Methodist Church Cemetery)

Standiford, Hester A. (Smith), 1835-1923 (Rock Run Methodist Church Cemetery; Death certificate)

Standiford, Isaac, wrote his will in 1889 and died in 1891, naming sons John F. Standiford and George A. Standiford, and daughters Frances M. Standiford, Monemia B. Standiford and Martha W. Hanna (Harford County Will Book JMM 11:193-194)

Standiford, James B., 1818-1898 (Rock Run Methodist Church Cemetery); member, Helping Hand Society of Avondale Christian Church (*Havre de Grace Republican*, 7 Feb 1890)

Standiford, James R., 1873-1933 (Centre Methodist Church Cemetery)

Standiford, Jane, 1818-1900, resided at Long Corner, Harford Co., wife of Benjamin Standiford (Death certificate incomplete)

Standiford, Jessie F. (Bowman), wife of King Standiford, q.v.

Standiford, John Filmore, 1856-1929 (Mountain Christian Church Cemetery); see Isaac Standiford, q.v.

Standiford, John T., charged with damaging and breaking open car *(sic)* in 1890, but no verdict was recorded in the docket book (Harford County Criminal Docket, 1888-1892, p. 94)

Standiford, Joseph Maltier, 1845-1911 (Union Chapel Methodist Church Cemetery)

Standiford, King, 1883-1965 (Rock Run Methodist Church Cemetery)

Standiford, Kinsey A., 1889-1976 (Ebenezer Methodist Church Cemetery)

Standiford, Laura, born 1881, daughter of Charles Standiford and ---- (Bethel Presbyterian Church Cemetery Records); see Laura Lemmon, q.v.

Standiford, Laura Virginia (Bramble), 1847-1925 (Union Chapel Methodist Church Cemetery); wife of Joseph M. Standiford, q.v.

Standiford, Louisa, 1853-1929 (Ebenezer Methodist Church Cemetery)

Standiford, M. (Mr.), resident at Wilna (*The Aegis & Intelligencer*, 4 Apr 1890)

Standiford, Mary E. (Miss), 1846-1934, native of Baltimore (Bailey Funeral Home Records)

Standiford, M. Emma, age 28 in 1890, daughter of William C. Standiford, of Marshall's District, and sister of Wesley Standiford, and cousin of Albert Standiford, married Robert J. Hamrick, of Page Co., VA, age 27, on 10 Jun 1890 (*The Aegis & Intelligencer*, 13 Jun 1890; Marriage License Applications Book ALJ No. 2, 1890)

Standiford, Marian (Miss), actress, musical entertainment, at Darlington (*The Aegis & Intelligencer*, 30 May 1890)

Standiford, Mary Leota, 1881-1973 (Mountain Christian Church Cemetery)

Standiford, Monemia Belle, age 30 in 1890 (Marriage License Applications Book ALJ No. 2, 1891); see Isaac Standiford, q.v.

Standiford, Naomi Blanche (Wilson), 1879-1946 (Union Chapel Methodist Church Cemetery); wife of Franklin W. Standiford, q.v.

Standiford, Nellie, see Nellie Starr, q.v.

Standiford, Philip Lee, 1858-1932 (Mountain Christian Church Cemetery); assistant superintendent, Mountain Christian Church Sunday School (*Havre de Grace Republican*, 7 Feb 1890)

Standiford, Ramsay, 1873-1932 (Darlington Cemetery); native of Harford Co., born 13 Dec 1873, son of Charles Standiford and Euphemia Whitelock (Bailey Funeral Home Records)

Standiford, Ruth Anita (Thompson), 1882-1914 (Darlington Cemetery; Death certificate)

Standiford, Sarah E., 1853-1918 (Rock Run Methodist Church Cemetery); wife of William A. Standiford, q.v.

Standiford, Sarah J. (Knight), 1839-1914 (Ebenezer Methodist Church Cemetery); native of Baltimore Co., resided near Taylor (Death certificate); wife of William C. Standiford, q.v.

Standiford, Stanley R., 1889-1907 (Ebenezer Methodist Church Cemetery)

Standiford, Susanna B., 1828-1918 (Good Will Church Cemetery)

Standiford, Wesley, see M. Emma Standiford, q.v.

Standiford, William A., 1859-1912 (Rock Run Methodist Church Cemetery); see Ethel M. Standiford, q.v.

Standiford, William Claudius, 1836-1928 (Ebenezer Methodist Church Cemetery); native of Harford Co., wheelwright, resided at Rutledge (Death certificate); secretary, Ebenezer M. E. Church Sunday School (*Havre de Grace Republican*, 25 Apr 1890); associate judge of elections, Upper Cross Roads Precinct (*Havre de Grace Republican*, 17 Oct 1890); member, Taylor Fox Hunting Club (*Havre de Grace Republican*, 24 Jan 1890); also see M. Emma Standiford and Robert J. Hamrick, q.v.

Standiford, William R., 1863-1933 (Ebenezer Methodist Church Cemetery)

Staniford, Bessie K., 1878-1951 (Union Chapel Methodist Church Cemetery)

Staniford, George W., 1876-1948 (Union Chapel Methodist Church Cemetery)

Stanley, Agnes May, 1889-1963 (Angel Hill Cemetery)

Stanley, Annie H., 1867-1952 (William Watters Methodist Church Cemetery)

Stanley, Howard, premium award winner, Class O - Discretionary, Harford County Fair (*The Aegis & Intelligencer*, 24 Oct 1890)

Stanley, J. Harry, 1884-1985 (Fallston Methodist Church Cemetery)

Stanley, J. W. (Mr.), superintendent, M P. Church Sunday School, at Cambria (*Havre de Grace Republican*, 23 May 1890)

Stanley, Larking, 1870-1952 (Rock Run Methodist Church Cemetery)

Stanley, Leonard, premium award winner, Class E - Poultry, Harford County Fair (*The Aegis & Intelligencer*, 24 Oct 1890)

Stanley, Lily (Miss), member, Bel Air M. P. Church Sunday School (*The Aegis & Intelligencer*, 27 Jun 1890)

Stanley, Russell, 1886-1955 (William Watters Methodist Church Cemetery)

Stansbury, Abram (colored), see John Z. Stansbury (colored), q.v.

Stansbury, Abraham Rutledge, 1856-1932 (Bethel Presbyterian Church Cemetery Records); see Marian R. Stansbury and Mary E. Stansbury, q.v.

Stansbury, Amanda J., born 26 Jun 1879, daughter of Abraham R. Stansbury and Cordelia McComas (Bethel Presbyterian Church Cemetery Records)

Stansbury, Amanda Rebecca (Miss), 1866-1924 (William Watters Memorial Methodist Church Cemetery, Cooptown); native of Harford Co., nurse, resided at Federal Hill (Death certificate)

Stansbury, Caroline (colored), see Caroline Smith (colored) and Solomon J. Smith (colored), q.v.

Stansbury, Carrie V. (colored), see Carrie V. Thigpen (colored), q.v.

Stansbury, Charles Henry (colored), 1885-1948, native of Aberdeen, Harford Co., born 8 Jan 1885, son of Solomon Stansbury and ---- (Death certificate)

Stansbury, Charles Jacob Franklyn (colored), 1870-1937, native of Maryland, born 20 Feb 1870, son of Philip S. Stansbury and Elizabeth A. Smith (Death certificate)

Stansbury, Charles S. (colored), 1882-1947, native of Perryman, Harford Co., born 13 Dec 1882, son of William H. Stansbury and Delia Tilden (Death certificate)

Stansbury, Clara (colored), see Alice Thompson (colored), q.v.

Stansbury, Cordelia (McComas), 1856-1936 (Bethel Presbyterian Church Cemetery Records); wife of Abraham Rutledge Stansbury, q.v.

Stansbury, Daniel Reese (colored), 1874-1915, native of Harford Co., born 5 Jul 1874, son of John Quincy Stansbury and Eliza Jane Lisby (Death certificate)

Stansbury, Delia S. (Tildon), 1839-1907 (Death certificate)

Stansbury, Eliza (colored), 1842-1902, wife of Isaac Stansbury (Death certificate)

Stansbury, Eliza (colored), mother of Myrtle E. Christy, q.v.; also see Frankanna Robinson, q.v.

Stansbury, Eliza (Livezey) (colored), 1846-1927 (Death certificate)

Stansbury, Elizabeth "Eliza" (colored), wife of Henry Hilton, q.v.; also see Evelyn G. Hilton and Martha Hilton, q.v.

Stansbury, Elizabeth, see Walter L. Iley, q.v.

Stansbury, Ella (colored), 1880-1938, native of Perryman, Harford Co., born 15 Dec 1880. daughter of Philip Stansbury and Elizabeth Smith (Death certificate - married name Williams)

Stansbury, Elsie (colored), see James H. Stansbury (colored), q.v.

Stansbury, Emma (colored), age 17 in 1889 (Marriage License Applications Book ALJ No. 2, 1890), married William H. Johnson on 23 Feb 1890 (marriage certificate)

Stansbury, Emma C. (colored), 1876-1925, native of Maryland, born 8 Feb 1876, daughter of Prince Stansbury and Mary Harris (Death certificate - married name Presbury)

Stansbury, Florence M. (colored), 1884-1952 (Union Methodist Church Cemetery, Aberdeen)

Stansbury, Florence V. (colored), 1883-1972 (Berkley Memorial Cemetery)

Stansbury, Frances (colored), see Mary Williams (colored), q.v.

Stansbury, George H. (colored), 1864-1925 (Death certificate)

Stansbury, Harriet (colored), 1871-1916, native of Maryland, born 17 Mar 1871, daughter of William H. Stansbury and Rebecca Warfield (Death certificate)

Stansbury, Harriet M., 1861-1851 (St. James United Cemetery tombstone inscribed 1861, but death certicicate states Harriet Marie Stanbsury was born in 1868)

Stansbury, Isaac (colored), see Eliza Stansbury (colored) and John H. Stansbury (colored), q.v.

Stansbury, Isaac (colored), 1853-1923 (Death certificate)

Stansbury, J. Grover, 1886-1892, son of Abraham R. Stansbury and Cordelia McComas (Bethel Presbyterian Church Cemetery Records)

Stansbury, James, trustee, Clermont School No. 13, Fourth District, 1890 (*Havre de Grace Republican*, 30 May 1890); see Mary Stansbury, q.v.

Stansbury, James (colored), see Lulu M. Stansbury, (colored) q.v.

Stansbury, James H. (colored), 1875-1931, native of Harford Co., born 7 Feb 1875, son of James Michael and Elsie Stansbury (Death certificate)

Stansbury, Jane (colored), see Josephine Bond (colored), q.v.

Stansbury, Jennie (colored), 1885-1945, native of Perryman, Harford Co., born 8 Sep 1885, daughter of Philip Stansbury and Lizzie Smith (Death certificate - married name Tildon)

Stansbury, John H. (colored), age 20 in 1889, son of Isaac C. Stansbury (Marriage License Applications Book ALJ No. 2, 1889)

Stansbury, John Q. (colored), father of Daniel Reese Stansbry and Mary (Stansbury) Smith, q.v.

Stansbury, John W. (colored), 1868-1948 (Union Methodist Church Cemetery, Aberdeen); husband of Mary J. Stansbury, q.v.

Stansbury, John Z. (colored), 1868-1927, native of Harford Co., born 1 Aug 1868, son of Abram Stansbury and Mary Brown (Death certificate; Union Methodist Church Cemetery, Aberdeen)

Stansbury, Lucinda D., resided at Chrome Hill (*Harford Democrat*, 24 Jan 1890); sold land in February 1890 (*The Aegis & Intelligencer*, 7 Mar 1890)

Stansbury, Lulu M. (colored), 1885-1925, native of Maryland, born 23 Mar 1885, daughter of James Stansbury and Marion Ringgold (Death certificate - married name Tildon)

Stansbury, Maria J. (Jenkins), 1888-1968 (Holy Cross Church Cemetery); native of Pylesville, Harford Co., born 1 Jun 1888, daughter of Henry I. Jenkins and Catherine L. Jenkins (Harkins Funeral Home Records)

Stansbury, Marian Cordelia, born 31 May 1882, daughter of Abraham R. Stansbury and Cordelia McComas (Bethel Presbyterian Church Cemetery Records)

Stansbury, Mary, 1818-1900, wife of James Stansbury (Death certificate)

Stansbury, Mary (Mrs.) (colored), 1834-1904 (Death certificate)

Stansbury, Mary (Mrs.) (colored), 1871-1933, native of Wilmington, DE, parents unknown (Death certificate)

Stansbury, Mary C. (colored), see James Albert Pitt (colored) and Gertie Cordelia Pitt (colored), q.v.

Stansbury, Mary Eliza (Bull), 1858-1903 (Bethel Presbyterian Church Cemetery Records); wife of William Stansbury, q.v.

Stansbury, Mary Elizabeth, born 12 Jul 1883, daughter of Abraham R. Stansbury and Cordelia McComas (Bethel Presbyterian Church Cemetery Records)

Stansbury, Mary J. (colored), 1872-1955 (Union Methodist Church Cemetery, Aberdeen); wife of John W. Stansbury, q.v.

Stansbury, Mary P. (colored), see Susie A. Stansbury (colored), q.v.

Stansbury, Mary Susanna (Smithson), 1824-1900 (Stansbury Family Cemetery at Eden Mill)

Stansbury, Peter (colored), 1854-1917 (Death certificate)

Stansbury, Philip (colored), c1849-1913 (Death certificate); see Charles Jacob Franklyn Stansbury, Ella Stansbury, and Jennie Stansbury, q.v.

Stansbury, Prince (colored), see Emma C. Stansbury (colored), q.v.

Stansbury, Robert A. (colored), 1854-1913 (Death certificate)

Stansbury, S., second baseman, Creswell Baseball Club (*The Aegis & Intelligencer*, 18 Jul 1890)

Stansbury, Sarah "Sallie" A. (Streett), 1848-1896 (Holy Cross Church Cemetery; Sallie A. Stansbury Bible, *Maryland Bible Records, Volume 2*, by Henry C. Peden, Jr., 2003, p. 142)

Stansbury (Stansberry), Sarah (colored), mother of Lottie Carry and King D. Nickenson, Jr., q.v.

Stansbury, Solomon (colored), 1853-1939 (Death certificate); see Charles Henry Stansbury, q.v.

Stansbury, Susie A. (colored), 1887-1982, native of Michaelsville, Harford Co., daughter of Mary P. Stansbury and ---- (*The Aegis*, 20 May 1982 - married name Warfield)

Stansbury, Tobias E., Civil War veteran, Chrome Hill (*1890 Special Census of the Civil War Veterans of the State of Maryland*, by L. Tilden Moore, Volume III, p. 78)

Stansbury, Walter William, 1887-1941, son of William and Sarah Stansbury (Sallie A. Stansbury Bible, *Maryland Bible Records, Volume 2*, by Henry C. Peden, Jr., 2003, p. 142, and Merryman Streett Bible, p. 147)

Stansbury, William, c1855-1929 (Bethel Presbyterian Church Cemetery Records and Register of Deaths)

Stansbury, William (colored), trustee, Sydney Park Colored School No. 3, Second District, 1890 (*Havre de Grace Republican*, 30 May 1890); see Carrie V. Thigpen, q.v.

Stansbury, William (colored), 1870-1950 (Death certificate; Alms House Record Book)

Stansbury, William H. (colored), see Charles S. Stansbury (colored) and Harriet Stansbury (colored), q.v.

Stanton, Eugene, c1844-1930, parents unknown (Death certificate; Alms House Record Book)

Starks, Irene (Thompson) (colored), 1862-1926 (Skinner Cemetery); native of Virginia, resident of Havre de Grace (Death certificate)

Starr's General Store, Glenville, William H. Starr, prop. (*Country Stores: Harford County's Rural Heritage*, by Henry C. Peden, Jr. and Jack L. Shagena, Jr., 2015, p. 239)

Starr, Annie, see Frances Helen Elliott, q.v.

Starr, Ansel, 1882-1956 (Mountain Christian Church Cemetery)

Starr, C. Catherine, 1882-1961 (Norrisville Methodist Church Cemetery)

Starr, Elizabeth F., 1878-1974 (Mountain Christian Church Cemetery)

Starr, Ethel M. (Standiford), 1889-1956 (Rock Run Methodist Church Cemetery); native of Harford Co. (Bailey Funeral Home Records); wife of Walter D. Starr, q.v.

Starr, Frank, chair factory, Aberdeen (*The Aegis & Intelligencer*, 17 Oct 1890)

Starr, Georgeanna, 1856-1914 (Rock Run Methodist Church Cemetery)

Starr, Helen Jean Paul (Mitchell), 1877-1961 (Christ Episcopal Church Cemetery)

Starr, John, see Abbie O. Burkins and Nellie Standiford, q.v.

Starr, John M., c1854-1892 (*Deaths and Marriages in Harford County, Maryland, and Vicinity, 1873-1904, from the Diaries of Albert Peter Silver*, transcribed by Glenn Randers-Pehrson, 1995, p. 26)

Starr, Nellie, 1883-1934 (Rock Run Methodist Church Cemetery - married name Standiford); native of Harford Co., born 14 Jun 1883, daughter of John Starr and Georgina Osborne (Bailey Funeral Home Records); wife of

George M. Standiford, q.v.

Starr, Walter D., 1888-1965 (Rock Run Methodist Church Cemetery)

Starr, William, member, Beattie Post, G. A. R., of Forest Hill (*Havre de Grace Republican*, 15 Aug 1890)

Starr, William H., trustee, Glenville School No. 17, Second District (*Havre de Grace Republican*, 30 May 1890); treated by unidentified doctor in 1890 ("Medical Account Book – 1890," Historical Society of Harford County Archives Folder)

Starr, William H. (Mrs.), teacher, Glenville Union Sunday School (*The Aegis & Intelligencer*, 22 Aug 1890); resided at Glenville (*Harford Democrat*, 19 Sep 1890)

Statzenbach, Herman, member, Bel Air Cornet Band (*The Aegis & Intelligencer*, 1 Aug 1890); member, Division No. 2, Bel Air Fire and Salvage Corps (*The Aegis & Intelligencer*, 10 Oct 1890)

Staufenberg, George, Civil War veteran, Joppa (*1890 Special Census of the Civil War Veterans of the State of Maryland*, by L. Tilden Moore, Volume III, p. 62)

Stauffer, Sallie A. (Reist), wife of John H. Stauffer, died 23 May 1893, age 38 (*Deaths and Marriages in Harford County, Maryland, and Vicinity, 1873-1904, from the Diaries of Albert Peter Silver*, transcribed by Glenn Randers-Pehrson, 1995, p. 26)

Stearns, John A., justice of the peace, Fifth District (*Havre de Grace Republican*, 21 Feb 1890)

Stearns, John Oscar, 1838-1910 (Slate Ridge Cemetery, York Co., PA); justice of the peace, Pylesville (*Harford Democrat*, 28 Feb 1890); magistrate, Fifth District (*Havre de Grace Republican*, 4 Jul 1890); delegate, Fifth District, Democrat Party Convention (*The Aegis & Intelligencer*, 5 Sep 1890); member, Democrat Party, and representative, Harford County Tariff Reform Club (*The Aegis & Intelligencer*, 5 Sep 1890); trustee, Rock Hill School No. 3, Fifth District (*Havre de Grace Republican*, 30 May 1890); son of John L. Stearns and Mary A. Gibbons, q.v.; also see Mary A. Barton, q.v.

Stearns, John, see M. A. Stearns, q.v.

Stearns, Mary A. (Gibbons), 1815-1891, widow of John L. Stearns, of Pylesville (*The Aegis & Intelligencer*, 30 May 1890; North Bend Presbyterian Church Cemetery); Mrs. Mary Stearn (*sic*), uncalled for letter in Bel Air P. O., 1890 (*The Aegis & Intelligencer*, 14 Nov 1890)

Steelberg, John (Mrs.), died 20 Aug 1894, age about 70 (*Deaths and Marriages in Harford County, Maryland, and Vicinity, 1873-1904, from the Diaries of Albert Peter Silver*, transcribed by Glenn Randers-Pehrson, 1995, p. 26)

Steelberg, John, died 13 Jul 1890, age 65, at Stafford (*The Aegis & Intelligencer*, 18 Jul 1890); deceased and removed from the voter registration list at Hopewell, Second District (*Havre de Grace Republican*, 26 Sep 1890)

Steele, Amanda Ann (Everett), 1843-1922 (Mountain Christian Church Cemetery)

Steele, Angie B., 1860-1932 (Deer Creek Harmony Presbyterian Church Cemetery)

Steele, Chattie, fifth grade student, Prospect Hill School, 1890 (*The Aegis & Intelligencer*, 21 Feb 1890)

Steele, Gilbert Victor, 1887-1950 (Deer Creek Harmony Presbyterian Church Cemetery)

Steele, Gilbert W., 1852-1917 (Deer Creek Harmony Presbyterian Church Cemetery)

Steelberg, John, 1825-1890 (*The Aegis & Intelligencer*, 18 Jul 1890)

Steen, Ellen Elizabeth, 1857-1899 (Cokesbury Memorial Methodist Church Cemetery)

Steigler, George, farmer, *Willow Grove Farm*, near Fallston (*The Aegis & Intelligencer*, 2 May 1890)

Steigler, Louisa A., fifth grade student, Fallston School (*The Aegis & Intelligencer*, 21 Feb 1890); student, Oakland School, 1890 (George G. Curtiss Ledger)

Steigler, Minnie, student, Fallston School (*The Aegis & Intelligencer*, 21 Feb 1890)

Stein, Amy May, 1888-1949 (Norrisville Methodist Church Cemetery)

Stein, C. Grafton, 1890-1957 (Norrisvile Methodist Church Cemetery)

Stein, Ernest, 1880-1958 (Baker Cemetery)

Stein, George, 1850-1910 (Salem Evangelical Lutheran Church Cemetery); resided at Madonna (Death certificate)

Stein, James F., 1861-1937 (St. Ignatius Catholic Church Cemetery); native of Harford Co., born 30 Sep 1861, son of John Stein and Mary A. Hoover, natives of Germany (Harkins Funeral Home Records)

Stein, John, see James F. Stein, q.v.

Stein, Mammie D., 1888-1969 (Baker Cemetery)

Steinbach, Edna May, 1888-1983 (Mountain Christian Church Cemetery)

Steinbach, Rozier L., 1888-1962 (Mountain Christian Church Cemetery)

Steiner, Frederick W., 1878-1943 (Angel Hill Cemetery)

Steiner, Grace Estelle (Maynadier), 1885-1974 (Angel Hill Cemetery)

Stengle, Marcus, 1813-1901 (Salem Evangelical Lutheran Church Cemetery)

Stengle, Mary, 1824-1899 (Salem Evangelical Lutheran Church Cemetery)

Stephens, Charles Theodore, 1890-1971 (Bel Air Memorial Gardens)

Stephens, Grace O. (Lilly), 1895-1971 (Churchville Presbyterian Church Cemetery)

Stephens, Herbert, 1880-1944 (Trinity Evangelical Lutheran Cemetery)

Stephens, Hugh Ross, 1890-1976 (Wesleyan Chapel Methodist Church Cemetery)

Stephens, Jeremiah S., 1846-1928 (Deer Creek Harmony Presbyterian Church Cemetery); native of Maryland, stone mason, resided at Level (Death certificate; Bailey Funeral Home Records)

Stephens, Joseph E., sold land in February 1890 (*The Aegis & Intelligencer*, 7 Mar 1890)

Stephens, Martin A., 1880-1965 (Churchville Presbyterian Church Cemetery)

Stephens, Mary E. (Jones), 1851-1921 (Deer Creek Harmony Presbyterian Church Cemetery; Bailey Funeral Home Records); native of Maryland, resided at Level (Death certificate)

Stephenson Lodge No. 128, A. F. & A. M., Lapidum (*Havre de Grace Republican*, 11 Jul 1890)

Stephenson, Ann P., 1810-1892 (Parker Family Cemetery)

Stephenson, Annie M. (Hanna), 1860-1930 (Rock Run Methodist Church Cemetery; Bailey Funeral Home Records); wife of George R. Stephenson, q.v.

Stephenson, Augustus, and wife, sold land in May 1890 (*The Aegis & Intelligencer*, 6 Jun 1890)

Stephenson, Beulah (Palmatary), 1868-1904 (Darlington Cemetery)

Stephenson, Charles (colored), died 23 Jan 1919, age unknown, widower, parents unknown (Death certificate; Alms House Record Book)

Stephenson, D. Murray, 1872-1937 (Rock Run Methodist Church Cemetery)

Stephenson, Elizabeth, 1835-1928 (Angel Hill Cemetery)

Stephenson, Elizabeth S, 1849-1936 (Rock Run Methodist Church Cemetery); wife of William Baines Hopkins, q.v.

Stephenson, George R., 1851-1893 (Rock Run Methodist Church Cemetery); vice president of the Third Annual Convention, Farmers' Club of Harford County (*Havre de Grace Republican*, 5 Dec 1890); chief judge of elections, Hopewell Precinct (*Havre de Grace Republican*, 17 Oct 1890); member, Lapidum Debating Society (*Havre de Grace Republican*, 7 Feb 1890); president, Deer Creek Farmers' Club (*Havre de Grace Republican*, 9 May 1890)

Stephenson, Hettie G. (or Hetty G.), resident near Garland, died 9 Jul 1890 in her 89th year, daughter of the late William Stephenson (*The Aegis & Intelligencer*, 11 Jul 1890); died testate and her named heirs were her sisters Elizabeth ----, Hannah G. ----, and Sarah Parker (and Sarah's daughters, unnamed), and William S. Parker, executor (Harford County Will Book JMM 11:134-135)

Stephenson, Jacob R., age 25 in 1890 (Marriage License Applications Book ALJ No. 2)

Stephenson, James, see Margaret S. Stephenson, q.v.

Stephenson, James F., 1838-1915 (Rock Run Methodist Church Cemetery)

Stephenson, John S., 1883-1937 (Angel Hill Cemetery)

Stephenson, Margaret S., 1816-1899 (Rock Run Methodist Church Cemetery); resided at Rock Run, native of Harford Co., daughter of James and Susan Stephenson (Death certificate; *The Aegis & Intelligencer*, 5 Jan 1900)

Stephenson, Margaret S. (Wilson), 1849-1935 (Death certificate states 1849, but Rock Run Methodist Church Cemetery tombstone was inscribed 1850); born near Havre de Grace, resided at Rock Run (Bailey Funeral Home Records); wife of James F. Stephenson, q.v.

Stephenson, Martha Eulalia (Sale), 1875-1950 (Baker Cemetery; www.findagrave.com)

Stephenson, Mary, 1886-1909, daughter of George R. and Annie M. Stephenson (Rock Run Methodist Church Cemetery)

Stephenson, Mary E., 1854-1907 (Rock Run Methodist Church Cemetery)

Stephenson, Mary E., 1890-1958 (Angel Hill Cemetery)

Stephenson, Mary Priscilla, 1833-1897 (Rock Run Methodist Church Cemetery)

Stephenson, Nellie (Miss), member of the Lapidum Debating Society (*Havre de Grace Republican*, 7 Feb 1890)

Stephenson, Robert, 1847-1916 (Rock Run Methodist Church Cemetery)

Stephenson, Sarah (Wright), 1883-1973 (St. Mary's Episcopal Church Cemetery)

Stephenson, Susan, see Margaret S. Stephenson, q.v.

Stephenson, Susan May, 1879-1968 (Rock Run Methodist Church Cemetery)

Stephenson, William (Rev.), 1828-1899 (Parker Family Cemetery)

Stephenson, William, 1834-1895 (Rock Run Methodist Church Cemetery); road examiner, Second District, 1890 (*Havre de Grace Republican*, 4 Jul 1890); also see George Hanna and Hettie G. Stephenson, q.v.

Stephensoon, William Washington, 1857-1939 (Baker Cemetery)

Stepney Public School No. 10. at Stepney, Second District (*Harford County, Maryland Teachers and the Schools They Served, 1774-1900*, by Henry C. Peden, Jr., 2022, p. 372)

Stepney, John (colored), age 22 in 1890 (Marriage License Applications Book ALJ No. 2, 1891)

Sterrett, Arthur A. (colored), 1876-1962, husband of Fannie A. Sterrett (Asbury Church Cemetery)

Stevens, Arthur T., 1858-1946 (Baker Cemetery)

Stevens, Charles E., 1874-1946 (Baker Cemetery)

Stevens, Ellen C., 1833-1898 (Forest Hill Friends Cemetery)

Stevens, F. (Mr.), former B & O Railroad agent at Joppa (*Havre de Grace Republican*, 26 Dec 1890)

Stevens, Harry Alfred, born 24 May 1882, son of Arthur T. and Mary A. Stevens (Holy Trinity Episcopal Church Register of Baptisms, p. 86)

Stevens, Josephine E., sold land in November 1890 (*The Aegis & Intelligencer*, 5 Dec 1890)

Stevens, Mary (Famous), born 1890, died ---- (Emory Methodist Church Cemetery)

Stevens, Mary A. (Mallack), 1862-1941 (Baker Cemetery; Bailey Funeral Home Records state born in 1861 in Harford Co.); wife of Arthur T. Stevens, q.v.

Stevens, Mary Ann, age 25 in 1890 (Marriage License Applications Book ALJ No. 2, 1890)

Stevens, Mary E., 1876-1936 (Baker Cemetery)

Stevens, Mazy, third grade honor student, Bel Air Graded School (*The Aegis & Intelligencer*, 4 Jul 1890)

Stevens, William F., former agent for B & O Railroad at Joppa (*The Aegis & Intelligencer*, 19 Dec 1890); patented a railroad car telegraph (*Havre de Grace Republican*, 18 Apr 1890)

Stevenson, Augustus, 1819-1901 (Asbury Church Cemetery)

Stevenson, Elizabeth, 1835-1928 (Angel Hill Cemetery)

Stevenson, Minerva Miner, 1840-1900 (Deer Creek Harmony Presbyterian Church Cemetery); wife of Samuel Stevenson, q.v.

Stevenson, Samuel, 1841-1917 (Deer Creek Harmony Presbyterian Church Cemetery)

Stever's General Store, Allibone (aka Sandy Hook), William A. Stever, prop. (*Country Stores: Harford County's Rural Heritage*, by Henry C. Peden, Jr. and Jack L. Shagena, Jr., 2015, p. 240)

Stever, Lillie, see Lillie Walter, q.v.

Stever, William A., see Lillie Walter, q.v.

Stewardsville Colore Public School No. 4, at Gravel Hill, Second District (*Harford County, Maryland Teachers and the Schools They Served, 1774-1900*, by Henry C. Peden, Jr., 2022, p. 372)

Stewart, Alexander, charged with obtaining goods under false pretences, but it was withdrawn (Harford County Criminal Docket, 1888-1892, p. 98)

Stewart, Ann M., see Ruth Elizabeth Stewart and Emma Beeman Stewart, q.v.

Stewart, Clay, see James W. Stewart, q.v.

Stewart, Daisy (Bradford) (colored), 1887-1945, native of Maryland, born 19 Apr 1887, daughter of Jacob Bradford, of Harford Co., and Mary J. Bond, of Germantown, PA (Death certificate)

Stewart, Ellijah (colored), father of William Edward Stewart, q.v.

Stewart, Elizabeth H. (Harry), 1874-1963 (Slate Ridge Cemetery, York Co., PA); native of Pylesville, Harford Co., born 4 Jun 1874, daughter of David Harry and Maria Warner (Harkins Funeral Home Records)

Stewart, Ella M. (colored), see Ella M. Washington (colored), q.v.

Stewart, Emily (colored), 1871-1927, native of Maryland, daughter of John Stewart and Eliza Carroll (Death certificate)

Stewart, Emma Beeman, born 18 Apr 1874, daughter of Samuel E. and Anna M. Stewart (Holy Trinity Episcopal Church Register of Baptisms, p. 84)

Stewart, Eugene, acquired land in May 1890 (*The Aegis & Intelligencer*, 6 Jun 1890)

Stewart, Frisbie (colored), c1853-1928 (Mt. Calvary Methodist Church Cemetery); native of Maryland, farm laborer at Fountain Green (Death certificate)

Stewart, Frisby Brown (colored), age 29 in 1890 (Marriage License Applications Book ALJ No. 2, 1890)

Stewart, Hannah (Dorsey) (colored), county out-pensioner [welfare recipient], Third District, 1890 (*Havre de Grace Republican*, 4 Jul 1890); mother of William Edward Stewart, q.v.

Stewart, Ida R., age 25 in 1889 (Marriage License Applications Book ALJ No. 2, 1889)

Stewart, Isaac, 1858-1945, carpenter, born in Kent Co., MD (Bailey Funeral Home Records)

Stewart, James W., 1872-1953 (Highland Presbyterian Church Cemetery); native of Harford Co., born 27 Aug 1882, son of Clay Stewart and Mary A. Baldwin (Harkins Funeral Home Records)

Stewart, Jane (colored), see Maggie Jackson (colored), q.v.

Stewart, John (colored), see Emily Stewart (colored) and Zachariah Stewart (colored), q.v.

Stewart, John H. (colored), 1856-1903 (Death certificate)

Stewart, Katie (coloed), wife of William Edward Stewart, q.v.

Stewart, Laura J., 1870-1934, daughter of James and Sally E. Stewart, of Baltimore Co. (Baltimore Cemetery, married name Wiegman); teacher, School No. 20, Fifth District (*The Aegis & Intelligencer*, 29 Aug 1890)

Stewart, Lillie (Iley), 1871-1956 (Highland Presbyterian Church Cemetery); native of Harford Co., born 10 Dec 1871, daughter of James Iley and Hannah Rigdon (Harkins Funeral Home Records)

Stewart, Lloyd (colored), see Ella M. Washington (colored), q.v.

Stewart, Margaret, see Thomas T. Drennen, q.v.

Stewart, Mary A., see Chester Cooper, q.v.

Stewart, Mary A. (Baldwin), 1851-1923 (Highland Presbyterian Church Cemetery); wife of Clay Stewart; see James W. Stewart, q.v.

Stewart, Mary Emma, see Nellie Mae Stone, q.v.

Stewart, Mary M., see Emma C. Bennington, q.v.

Stewart, Mary Rebecca (colored), 1881-1977 (Fairvew AME Church Cemetery)

Stewart, Rachel (colored), see Charles H. Stewart (colored) and Eliza M. Taylor (colored), q.v.

Stewart, Ruth Elizabeth, born 15 Apr 1876, daughter of Samuel E. and Anna M. Stewart (Holy Trinity Episcopal Church Register of Baptisms, p. 84)

Stewart, Samuel E., see Ruth Elizabeth Stewart and Emma Beeman Stewart, q.v.

Stewart, Sarah E., 1878-1962 (Highland Presbyterian Church Cemetery); native of Street, Harford Co., born 26 Mar 1878, daughter of James W. Iley and Hannah E. Rigdon (Harkins Funeral Home Records)

Stewart, William, 1854-1923 (Death certificate; Heavenly Waters Cemetery)

Stewart, William Edward (colored), 1847-1901, native of Harford Co., thresher and resident of Forest Hill (Death certificate); sexton, Christ Church, Rock Spring, 1890 (*Havre de Grace Republican*, 18 Apr 1890); trustee, Fairview Colored School No. 1, Fourth District (*Havre de Grace Republican*, 30 May 1890)

Stewart, William H., 1864-1929 (Darlington Cemetery); laborer, born in Pennsylvania (Bailey Funeral Home Records)

Stewart, Zachariah (colored), 1882-1917, native of Maryland, born 10 May 1882, son of John Stewart and ---- (Death certificate; St. James United Cemetery)

Stiegler, Catharine R., age 26 in 1890 (Marriage License Applications Book ALJ No. 2, 1890), married William W. Heuer on 12 Nov 1890 in Bel Air (*The Aegis & Intelligencer*, 21 Nov 1890)

Stiegler, Tressie (Miss), resident of Willow Grove [Fourth District] (*The Aegis & Intelligencer*, 13 Jun 1890)

Stier, J. H. (Dr.), assistant commander, Perryman Lodge, Order of the Golden Chain (*Havre de Grace Republican*, 5 Dec 1890)

Stifler, A. Louisa, 1861-1949 (Norrisville Methodist Church Cemetery)

Stifler, Aaron, 1859-1903 (Norrisville Methodist Church Cemetery); Aaron F. Stifler, farmer, near Norrisville (*Harford Democrat*, 28 Mar 1890); Aaron C. Stifler acquired land in April 1890 (*The Aegis & Intelligencer*, 9 May 1890)

Stifler, Bertha L., 1871-1910, daughter of William Hunter Stifler and Rachel Belle Gailey (Norrisville Methodist Church Cemetery, married name Butler); teacher, Norrisville School No. 1, Fourth District (*The Aegis & Intelligencer*, 29 Aug 1890)

Stifler, Clara Adelle (Smith), 1860-1890 (Norrisville Methodist Church Cemetery)

Stifler, Curtis H., 1826-1896 (Norrisville Methodist Church Cemetery); delegate, Fourth District, Democrat Party Convention (*The Aegis & Intelligencer*, 5 Sep 1890); member, Norrisville Singing School (*The Aegis & Intelligencer*, 30 May 1890)

Stifler, Dora Mabel (Miss), 1881-1905 (Norrisville Methodist Church Cemetery); member, Norrisville M. E. Church Sunday School (*The Aegis & Intelligencer*, 20 Jun 1890)

Stifler, H. C., see Robert B. McC. Sitfler, q.v.

Stifler, Jennie W., 1879-1942 (Norrisville Methodist Church Cemetery)

Stifler, John Royston, 1862-1921 (Norrisville Methodist Church Cemetery); notary public, Third District (*Havre de Grace Republican*, 21 Feb 1890); married Mrs. Wella Broumel on 17 Apr 1890 in Baltimore (*Harford Democrat*, 25 Apr 1890); member, Division No. 1, Bel Air Fire and Salvage Corps (*The Aegis & Intelligencer*, 10 Oct 1890)

Stifler, Katharine R., 1879-1956 (Good Will Church Cemetery)

Stifler, M. Elizabeth, 1882-1953 (Good Will Church Cemetery)

Stifler, Margaret A., 1825-1895 (Norrisville Methodist Church Cemetery)

Stifler, Rachel Belle (Gailey), 1845-1914 (Norrisville Methodist Church Cemetery)

Stifler, Robert B. McC., 1854-1891 (Norrisville Methodist Church Cemetery), son of H. C. Stifler and brother of John Royston Stifler; traveling salesman, married Clara Adelle Smith (*Havre de Grace Republican*, 14 Aug 1891); Robert Stifler was a member of the Norrisville Silver Cornet Band (*The Aegis & Intelligencer*, 30 May 1890)

Stifler, Rosa G., honor student, Norrisville Graded School (*The Aegis & Intelligencer*, 4 Jul 1890); Miss Rosa Stifler, member, Norrisville M. E. Church Sunday School (*The Aegis & Intelligencer*, 20 Jun 1890)

Stifler, Rosa G. ("Rose"), president, Mite Society of the Norrisville [Methodist] Church (*Havre de Grace Republican*, 18 Apr 1890); recording secretary, Norrisville Branch, Young People's Society of Christian Endeavor (*Havre de Grace Republican*, 24 Oct 1890)

Stifler, Silas Hunter, 1875-1964 (Norrisville Methodist Church Cemetery)

Stifler, Welzetta "Wella" (Broumel) McCurley, 1863-1929 (Christ Episcopal Church Cemetery); wife of John Royston Stifler, q.v.

Stifler, William A., superintendent, Norrisville M. E. Church Sunday School (*The Aegis & Intelligencer*, 25 Apr 1890); treasurer, Norrisville Branch, Young People's Society of Christian Endeavor (*Havre de Grace Republican*, 24 Oct 1890)

Stifler, William Curtis, 1871-1942, son of William Hunter Stifler and Rachel Belle Gailey, of Norrisville (*Harford County, Maryland Teachers and the Schools They Served*, by Henry C. Peden, Jr., 2021, p. 307); assistant secretary, Norrisville M. E. Church Sunday School (*The Aegis & Intelligencer*, 25 Apr 1890); cornetist, Norrisville M. E. Church Sunday School (*The Aegis & Intelligencer*, 20 Jun 1890)

Stifler, William Hunter, 1850-1890 (Norrisville Methodist Church Cemetery); foundry owner near Norrisville (*The Aegis & Intelligencer*, 21 Mar 1890); incorporator, Norrisville Methodist Protestant Church (*Havre de Grace Republican*, 4 Apr 1890); member, Norrisville Silver Cornet Band (*The Aegis & Intelligencer*, 30 May 1890); trustee, Norrisville School No. 1, Fourth District (*Havre de Grace Republican*, 30 May 1890)

Stilwood, Henry, 1835-1901, native of Rochester, NY, single, farmer at Clermont Mills (Death certificate)

Stinchcomb. Mary Elizabeth (Unger), 1835-1899 (Cokesbury Memorial Methodist Church Cemetery); resident of Joppa, wife of Noah S. Stinchcomb (Death certificate)

Stinchcomb, Noah Samuel, 1827-1904 (Cokesbury Memorial Methodist Church Cemetery); see Esther Jane Terry, q.v.

Stinchcomb, Samuel, sixth grade student, Prospect Hill School (*The Aegis & Intelligencer*, 21 Feb 1890)

Stine, Agnes Loretta, born -- Oct 1885, baptized 1 Nov 1885, daughter of John P. Stine, native of Harford Co., and M. Margaret Doyle, native of Baltimore Co. (St. Ignatius Catholic Church Baptism Register, p. 84)

Stine, Ann Mary, born -- Jan 1890, baptized 9 Feb 1890, daughter of John P. Stine, native of Harford Co., and Margaret Doyle, native of Baltimore (St. Ignatius Catholic Church Baptism Register, p. 111)

Stine, Anna May, 1820-1908 (St. Ignatius Catholic Church Cemetery)

Stine, Barbara, witnessed an indenture in 1882 (Harford County Indentures Book WSB No. 1)

Stine, Cecelia, born -- Feb 1884, baptized 6 Apr 1884, daughter of John P. Stine, native of Harford Co., and Margaret Doyle, native of Baltimore Co. (St. Ignatius Catholic Church Baptism Register, p. 71)

Stine, Curtis, 1878-1934 (Deer Creek Harmony Presbyterian Church Cemetery tombstone states born in 1880); native of Maryland, born 28 Oct 1878, son of Theodore Stine and Mary C. Traver (Bailey Funeral Home Records)

Stine, Ellen, born -- Sep 1887, baptized 2 Oct 1887, daughter of of John P. Stine, native of Harford Co., and Margaret Doyle, native of Baltimore Co. (St. Ignatius Catholic Church Baptism Register, p. 95)

Stine, Elsie V. (Tyson), 1887-1966 (Darlington Cemetery); native of Harford Co., born 8 Jul 1887, daughter of James Tyson and ---- (Harkins Funeral Home Records)

Stine, Esther Frances, 1873-1928 (Death certificate - married name Sapp); daughter of George S. Stine and Mary A Jordan, born 21 Mar 1873, and indentured to John Stine in 1882 (Harford County Indentures Book WSB No. 1)

Stine, George S., see Esther Frances Stine, John Laurance Stine, Joseph Franklin Stine, Mary Oleita Stine, and William Martin Stine, q.v.

Stine, James F., 1861-1937 (St. Ignatius Catholic Church Cemetery)

Stine, John, husband of Anna Mary Stine, died in 1894 (Harford County Indentures Book WSB No. 1)

Stine, John Laurance, son of George S. Stine, born 21 Apr 1870 and indentured to John Stine in 1882 (Harford County Indentures Book WSB No. 1)

Stine, John P., see Agnes Loretta Stine, Ann P. Stine and Cecelia Stine, q.v.

Stine, John Paul, Sr., 1818-1894 (St. Ignatius Catholic Church Cemetery); resident near Hickory (*The Aegis & Intelligencer*, 25 Apr 1890)

Stine, Joseph Franklin, son of George S. Stine, born 8 Feb 1878 and indentured to John Stine in 1882 (Harford County Indentures Book WSB No. 1)

Stine, Margaret (Doyle), see Agnes Loretta Stine, Ann Mary Stine, Cecelia Stine and Ellen Stine, q.v.

Stine, Mary Oleita, daughter of George S. Stine, born 8 Jan 1876 and indentured to John Stine in 1882 (Harford County Indentures Book WSB No. 1)

Stine, Orville Matthew, born -- Jun 1890, baptized 6 Sep 1891, son of James Stine, native of Harford Co., and Dora Mack, native of Chesterfield Co., VA (St. Ignatius Catholic Church Baptism Register, p. 119)

Stine, Theodore, see Curtis E. Stine and William W. Stine, q.v.

Stine, William, 1877-1956 (Darlington Cemetery)

Stine, William Martin, son of George S. Stine, born on 13 Sep 1880 and indentured to John Stine in 1882 (Harford County Indentures Book WSB No. 1); William Martin Stein, baptized 9 Oct 1880, son of George Stein *(sic)* and Mary Jordan (St. Ignatius Catholic Church Baptismal Register, p. 49)

Stine, William W., 1877-1956 (Darlington Cemetery); native of Martinsburg, WV, born 21 Jul 1877, son of Theodore Stine and Mary C. Traver (Bailey Funeral Home Records)

Stinks, Thomas, acquired land in August 1890 (*The Aegis & Intelligencer*, 12 Sep 1890)

Stirling, Harriet (Almony), 1824-1894, wife of William Stirling (Bethel Presbyterian Church Cemetery Records)

Stirling, John, executive committee, Harford Fire Insurance Company (*Havre de Grace Republican*, 14 Mar 1890)

Stockham, Alice, resident of Perryman (*The Aegis & Intelligencer*, 9 May 1890)

Stockham, Margaret (Miss), resident of *Woodley Cottage Farm* near Perryman (*The Aegis & Intelligencer*, 24 Jan 1890)

Stockham, Mary, resident of Perryman (*The Aegis & Intelligencer*, 9 May 1890)

Stokes' Grist Mill and Saw Mill (aka Chrome Valley Mill), Nathan O. Stokes, prop. (*Mills: Grist, Saw, Bone, Flint, Fulling ... & More*, by Jack L. Shagena, Jr., Henry C. Peden, Jr. and John W. McGrain, 2009, p. 259)

Stokes, Albert (colored), see Sydney Stokes (colored), q.v.

Stokes, Albert W., 1885-1968 (Slateville Cemetery, York Co., PA); native of Whiteford, Harford Co., son of Hugh M. Stokes and Cora Warner (Harkins Funeral Home Records)

Stokes, Carrie C., wife of Alpha L. Payne, q.v.; also see Carrie C. Payne, q.v.

Stokes, Emma V., 1887-1892, daughter of Nathan Oscar and H. Elizabeth (Hughes) Stokes (Bethel Presbyterian Church Cemetery Records)

Stokes, Emmaline, 1805-1891 (Broad Creek Friends Cemetery)

Stokes, H. Elizabeth (Hughes), 1856-1937 (Bethel Presbyterian Church Cemetery Records); wife of Nathan Oscar Stokes, q.v.

Stokes, Harold, flint mill operator, Stafford (*Havre de Grace Republican*, 14 Nov 1890)

Stokes, Harvey, see J. Harold Stokes, q.v.

Stokes, Harvey S., see Carrie C. Payne, q.v.

Stokes, Henry C., farmer and juror, Fifth District (*Havre de Grace Republican*, 31 Jan and 28 Feb 1890)

Stokes, Horace, former postmaster at Stafford (*Havre de Grace Republican*, 7 Mar 1890)

Stokes, Hugh Marion, 1845-1926 (Slateville Cemetery, York Co., PA); native of Harford Co., farmer, married, resided near Whiteford (Death certificate); sold land in April 1890 (*The Aegis & Intelligencer*, 9 May 1890); see Albert W. Stokes and Rigby W. Stokes, q.v.

Stokes, J. Harold, 1873-1962 (Slate Ridge Cemetery, York Co., PA); native of Whiteford, Harford Co., born 16 Apr 1873, son of Harvey Stokes and Mary Streett (Harkins Funeral Home Records)

Stokes, John, see Sarah R. Stokes, q.v.

Stokes, John H., 1798-1890 (Broad Creek Friends Cemetery)

Stokes, John Harvey, 1866-1946 (Broad Creek Friends Cemetery); farmer, Fifth District (*Havre de Grace Republican*, 28 Feb 1890)

Stokes, Julia O. (Devoe), 1878-1959 (Bethel Presbyterian Church Cemetery Records); wife of Marion Marshall Stokes, q.v.

Stokes, Marion Hugh, 1845-1926, native of Harford Co., farmer, resided near Whiteford (Death certificate)

Stokes, Marion Marshall, 1880-1954, born 28 Oct 1880, son of Hugh M. and Cora (Warner) Stokes (Bethel Presbyterian Church Cemetery Records)

Stokes, Martha E., see Rebecca H. Reynolds, q.v.

Stokes, Mary, see Myrtle D. Ellis, q.v.

Stokes, Mary Louisa, see Ida M. Scarborough, q.v.

Stokes, Nathan Oscar, 1847-1933 (Bethel Presbyterian Church Cemetery Records); miller between Jarrettsville and Cooptown (*The Aegis & Intelligencer*, 28 Mar 1890); trustee, Jarrettsville School No. 8, Fourth District (*Havre de Grace Republican*, 30 May 1890); trustee, School No. 8, Fourth District (*Havre de Grace Republican*, 9 May 1890)

Stokes, Rebecca J. (Scarborough), 1822-1901, native of Harford Co., resided at Scarboro (Death certificate; Broad Creek Friends Cemetery); wife of John H. Stokes, q.v.

Stokes, Rigby W., 1887-1963 (Slateville Cemetery, York Co., PA); native of Whiteford, Harford Co., born 28 Dec 1887, son of Hugh M. Stokes and Cora V. Warner (Harkins Funeral Home Records)

Stokes, Sarah "Sallie" R., age 25 in 1890 (Marriage License Applications Book ALJ No. 2, 1890), daughter of John Stokes, married John R. Moore on 13 Mar 1890 (St. Ignatius Catholic Church Marriage Register, p. 18)

Stokes, Susanna L. (Miss), 1859-1923 (Broad Creek Friends Cemetery)

Stokes, Sydney (colored), c1879-1917, native of Maryland, son of Albert Stokes and Rachael Gibson (Death certificate)

Stokes William H., 1877-1930 (Emory Methodist Church Cemetery)

Stokes, William R., age 30 in 1890 (Marriage License Applications Book ALJ No. 2, 1891)

Stokes, William Raymond, 1885-1900, native of Maryland, resided at Jarrettsville, born 5 May 1885, son of Nathan Oscar Stokes and H. Elizabeth Hughes (Death certificate; Bethel Presbyterian Church Cemetery Records)

Stone, Edward A., 1888-1928 (Angel Hill Cemetery); native of Maryland, resided at Havre de Grace, son of John Stone and Mary Johnson (Death certificate)

Stone, Emma, 1858-1924 (Angel Hill Cemetery)

Stone, Hannah J., 1872-1938 (Angel Hill Cemetery)

Stone, John, see Edward A. Stone and Nellie Mae Stone, q.v.

Stone, John H., 1855-1919 (Angel Hill Cemetery)

Stone, Joseph I., 1824-1907 (Angel Hill Cemetery); Civil War veteran, Havre de Grace (*1890 Special Census of the Civil War Veterans of the State of Maryland*, by L. Tilden Moore, Volume III, p. 90); government pensioner, Havre de Grace (*Havre de Grace Republican*, 14 Nov 1890); quartermaster, John Rodgers Post, G. A. R., Havre de Grace (*Havre de Grace Republican*, 12 Dec 1890); see Mary E. Stone, q.v.

Stone, Marion J., 1862-1948 (Angel Hill Cemetery); sneak boat duck hunter (*Havre de Grace Republican*, 7 Nov 1890)

Stone, Mary E., 1834-1900, native of New Orleans, resident of Havre de Grace, wife of Joseph I. Stone, q.v. (Death certificate; Angel Hill Cemetery); businesswoman (trader's license), Havre de Grace (*Havre de Grace Republican*, 30 May 1890)

Stone, Mary E. (Johnson), 1858-1924 (Angel Hill Cemetery; Death certificate); see Edward A. Stone, q.v.

Stone, Mary Emma (Stewart), see Nellie Mae Stone, q.v.

Stone, Nellie, see Mable Elizabeth Forsythe, q.v.

Stone, Nellie Mae, 1890-1971, native of Havre de Grace, born 3 Sep 1890, daughter of John Stone and Mary Emma Stewart (Pennington Funeral Home Records - married name Baker)

Stonebraker, Belle S.(Miss), 1837-1922 (Mt. Zion Methodist Church Cemetery); premium award winner, Class K - Household and Domestic Manufactures, Harford County Fair (*The Aegis & Intelligencer*, 24 Oct 1890)

Stonebraker, Clara Virginia, 1869-1940, daughter of John Stonebraker and Ellen E. Blake (St. Ignatius Catholic Church Cemetery; *Harford County, Maryland Teachers and the Schools They Served*, by Henry C. Peden, Jr., 2021, p. 309); teacher, Frogtown School No. 15, Third District (*The Aegis & Intelligencer*, 11 Jul and 29 Aug 1890)

Stonebraker, Ellen E. (Blake), 1925-1911 (St. Ignatius Catholic Church Cemetery); see Clara Virginia Stonebraker and Laura M. Stronebraker, q.v.

Stonebraker, Isabel A. (Tucker), 1863-1947 (St. Ignatius Catholic Church Cemetery); wife of John C. Stonebraker, q.v.

Stonebraker, John C., 1836-1901, native of Harford Co., carpenter at Hickory (Mt. Zion Methodist Church Cemetery)

Stonebraker, Laura M., 1860-1936, daughter of John Stonebraker and Ellen E. Blake (St. Ignatius Catholic Church Cemetery, married name Gleason; *Harford County, Maryland Teachers and the Schools They Served*, by Henry C. Peden, Jr., 2021, p. 309)

Stonebraker, Sallie A., age 31 in 1890 (Marriage License Applications Book ALJ No. 2, 1891)

Stoner, Amanda E. (Tipton), 1852-1923 (Bethel Presbyterian Church Cemetery Records); wife of Samuel Stoner, q.v.

Stoner, Samuel, 1841-1904 (Bethel Presbyterian Church Cemetery Records)

Stooff, J. W., uncalled for letter in Bel Air P. O. (*The Aegis & Intelligencer*, 14 Nov 1890)

Stoppel, Christianna, 1850-1917 (Rock Run Methodist Church Cemetery); native of Germany, resided at Lapidum (Death certificate spelled her name Stopple)

Stoppel, John Adam, 1854-1906 (Rock Run Methodist Church Cemetery)

Stotzenbach, Herman, clay pigeon shooter, Churchville (*The Aegis & Intelligencer*, 7 Feb 1890)

Stovall, John, married Olivia G. --- on 23 Dec 1889 in Havre de Grace and lived there until 18 Nov 1890 when they moved to Baltimore. (*Harford County Divorces and Separations, 1823-1923*, by Henry C. Peden, Jr., 2016, p. 187)

Stover, Jacob E., c1878-1938, parents unknown (Death certificate; Alms House Record Book)

Strasbaugh's General Store and Post Office, Creswell (near Harford Furnace), Amos H. and Harry P. Strasbaugh, prop. (*Country Stores: Harford County's Rural Heritage*, by Henry C. Peden, Jr. and Jack L. Shagena, Jr., 2015, p. 241)

Strasbaugh, A. B., Mr. & Mrs., of *Slee Farm* near Perryman (*The Aegis & Intelligencer*, 13 Jun 1890; *Havre de Grace Republican*, 14 Mar 1890)

Strasbaugh, Amos Henry, 1834-1919 (Churchville Presbyterian Church Cemetery)

Strasbaugh, Frances Howard (Archer) (Silver), 1864-1942 (Churchville Presbyterian Church Cemetery), second wife of Amos Henry Strasbaugh, q.v.

Strasbaugh, Harry Pannell, 1867-1936 (Churchville Presbyterian Church Cemetery)

Strasbaugh, Isabella Williamson (Pannell), 1834-1901 (Churchville Presbyterian Church Cemetery), first wife of Amos Henry Strasbaugh, q.v.

Strasbaugh, Sadie Virginia, 1868-1899 (Churchville Presbyterian Church Cemetery), first wife of Harry Pannell Strasbaugh, q.v.

Strawbridge, Anna M., 1875-1940 (Norrisville Methodist Church Cemetery)

Strawbridge Bertha V., 1884-1965 (St. Paul's Methodist Church Cemetery)

Strawbridge, Elizabeth (Almoney), 1826-1914

Strawbridge, Blanche (Miss), organist, Norrisville M. E. Church Sunday School (*The Aegis & Intelligencer*, 20 Jun 1890)

Strawbridge, Elizabeth (Almoney), 1828-1914 (Norrisville Methodist Church Cemetery)

Strawbridge, Emma E. (Mrs.), 1857-1897 (Norrisville Methodist Church Cemetery); member, Norrisville M. P. Church (*The Aegis & Intelligencer*, 7 Mar 1890)

Strawbridge, George W., 1868-1936 (Norrisville Methodist Church Cemetery)

Strawbridge, Henry M., 1831-1904 (Norrisville Methodist Church Cemetery); Civil War veteran, Shawsville (*1890 Special Census of the Civil War Veterans of the State of Maryland*, by L. Tilden Moore, Volume III, p. 82)

Strawbridge, Ida H., 1872-1961 (Norrisville Methodist Church Cemetery)

Strawbridge, Isaac Israel, 1824-1899 (Norrisville Methodist Church Cemetery)

Strawbridge, J. Royston, 1858-1928 (Norrisville Metodist Church Cemetery); assistant superintendent, Norrisville M. E. Church Sunday School (*The Aegis & Intelligencer*, 25 Apr 1890); incorporator, Norrisville Methodist Protestant Church (*Havre de Grace Republican*, 4 Apr 1890); trustee, School No. 1, Fourth District (*The Aegis & Intelligencer*, 8 Aug 1890)

Strawbridge, Jeremiah, 1870-1943 (Norrisville Methodist Church Cemetery)

Strawbridge, John E., name stricken off the voter registration list at Abingdon, First District (*Havre de Grace Republican*, 17 Oct 1890)

Strawbridge, John Wesley, 1851-1917 (Fawn Grove Methodist Church Cemetery, York Co., PA); postmaster, Norrisville (*The Aegis & Intelligencer*, 31 Jan 1890); president, Norrisville Branch, Young People's Society of Christian Endeavor (*Havre de Grace Republican*, 24 Oct 1890); postmaster and storekeeper at Norrisville; recently married, wife died last week (*Havre de Grace Republican*, 14 Feb 1890); see Cora Garrett and Louisa J. Strawbridge, q.v.

Strawbridge, Joseph, resident of Mt. Pleasant, near the Long Corner (*The Aegis & Intelligencer*, 31 Jan 1890)

Strawbridge, Lindley V., 1890-1937 (St. Paul's Methodist Church Cemetery)

Strawbridge, Louisa J. (Schilling), 1861-1890 (Ayres Chapel Methodist Church Cemetery); wife of J. Wesley Strawbridge, q.v., of Norrisville (*The Aegis & Intelligencer*, 31 Jan 1890)

Strawbridge, Mary Cecilia (McClung), 1833-1916 (Norrisville Methodist Church Cemetery)

Strawbridge, Rebecca, see Cleveland Heaps and N. Winfield Heaps, q.v.

Strawbridge, Robert B., of Norrisville, moved to California (*The Aegis & Intelligencer*, 1 Aug 1890)

Strawbridge, Sallie (Miss), postmistress, Norrisville (*The Aegis & Intelligencer*, 1 Aug 1890)

Strawbridge, Sarah E., acquired land in February 1890 (*The Aegis & Intelligencer*, 7 Mar 1890)

Strawbridge, Walter, member, Norrisville Silver Cornet Band (*The Aegis & Intelligencer*, 30 May 1890)

Strawbridge, William T., 1860-1950 (Norrisville Methodist Church Cemetery); member, Norrisville Silver Cornet Band (*The Aegis & Intelligencer*, 30 May 1890); age 30 in 1890 (Marriage License Applications Book ALJ No. 2, 1891)

Street, Blanche W., 1890-1968 (Angel Hill Cemetery)

Street, Charles H., vice president of the Third Annual Convention, Farmers' Club of Harford County (*Havre de Grace Republican*, 5 Dec 1890)

Street, E. G., member, Bel Air Fire Brigade and Salvage Corps (*Havre de Grace Republican*, 17 Oct 1890)

Street, J. Polk, director, Maryland Central Dairymen's Association (*Havre de Grace Republican*, 14 Mar 1890)

Street, John, corresponding secretary, Harford County Agricultural and Mechanical Society (*Havre de Grace Republican*, 31 Jan 1890)

Street, John A., member, Maryland Central Dairymen's Association (*Havre de Grace Republican*, 14 Mar 1890)

Street, Laura, see Martha Cushing, q.v.

Street, Louisa, 1829-1899, of North Bend, widow of Roger Street (Death certificate)

Street, Lucy Ann, see Lucy Ann Thoene and Mary Elizabeth Thoene, q.v.

Street, Mary E., 1833-1891 (Bethel Presbyterian Church Cemetery)

Street, Maud, 1885-1891 (North Bend Presbyterian Church Cemetery)

Street, Roger, see Louisa Street, q.v.

Streett, ----, pitcher, Baptist Baseball Club, Fourth District, 1890 (*Havre de Grace Republican*, 8 Aug 1890)

Streett, A. J., 1869-1949 (Old Brick Baptist Church Cemetery; *The Aegis*, 7 Oct 1949)

Streett, A. Smith, resident of Jarrettsville (*The Aegis & Intelligencer*, 18 Apr 1890)

Streett, Albert, 1844-1930 (William Watters Memorial Methodist Church Cemetery, Cooptown); resided at Chrome Hill (*Harford Democrat*, 24 Jan 1890)

Streett, Alverta R. (Rampley), 1877-1965 (Highland Presbyterian Church Cemetery); native of Street, Harford Co., born 3 Jul 1877, daughter of James Rampley and Mary Streett (Harkins Funeral Home Records)

Streett, Ann Priscilla, see Thomas H. Streett, q.v.

Streett, Anna Adaline, born 16 Oct 1886, daughter of John A. Streett and Flora Mitchell (John A. Streett Bible, *Maryland Bible Records, Volume 2*, by Henry C. Peden, Jr., 2003, p. 146); see Anna A. Chester, q.v.

Streett, Annie E., age 23, married Harry C. Hart, ae 28, of Baltimore, on 28 Jul 1890 (Marriage License Applications Book ALJ No. 2, 1890, and marriage certificate)

Streett, Annie, young lady of near Pylesville (*The Aegis & Intelligencer*, 7 Feb 1890)

Streett, Ariel, see Elizabeth H. Streett, q.v.

Streett, Augustus A., 1872-1946, son of Abraham and ---- (McCurdy) Streett (Bethel Presbyterian Church Cemetery Records)

Streett, Bertha A., member, Asbury M. E. Church, Jarrettsville (*The Aegis & Intelligencer*, 28 Feb 1890); resided at Chrome Hill (*Harford Democrat*, 24 Jan 1890)

Streett, Bessie, young lady of Bel Air (*The Aegis & Intelligencer*, 7 Feb 1890)

Streett, Catharine Armitage, born 18 Dec 1888, daughter of John A. Streett and Flora Mitchell (John A. Streett Bible, *Maryland Bible Records, Volume 2*, by Henry C. Peden, Jr., 2003, p. 146)

Streett, Catherine Elizabeth, see Thomas H. Streett, q.v.

Streett, Charles (Mrs.), uncalled for letter in Bel Air P. O. (*The Aegis & Intelligencer*, 4 Jul 1890)

Streett, Charles H., cattle farmer, near Taylor (*The Aegis & Intelligencer*, 12 Dec 1890); vice president, Harford County Farmers' Association (*The Aegis & Intelligencer*, 17 Jan 1890); president, Taylor Baseball Club (*Havre de Grace Republican*, 7 Feb 1890); see Elizabeth H. Streett, q.v.

Streett, Clarice E. (Miss), resided at Chrome Hill (*Harford Democrat*, 24 Jan 1890)

Streett, David, 1819-1907 (North Bend Presbyterian Church Cemetery)

Streett, Edward O., member, Division No. 1, Bel Air Fire and Salvage Corps (*The Aegis & Intelligencer*, 10 Oct 1890)

Streett, Elizabeth (Miss), singer and member, Emmanuel Episcopal Church, Bel Air (*The Aegis & Intelligencer*, 11 Apr 1890)

Streett, Elizabeth (Mrs.), mother-in-law of W. Lloyd Bell, of Emmorton (*The Aegis & Intelligencer*, 24 Jan 1890)

Streett, Elizabeth H., died testate in 1890 and her named heirs were daughtera Martha Bell, Ariel Streett, and Susan C. Streett, and sons Charles H. Streett and St. Clair Streett (Harford County Will Book JMM 11:90-91)

Streett, Elizabeth J. (Wright), 1856-1899, resided at Chrome Hill, native of Maryland, wife of Lawrenc Streett (Death certificate)

Streett, Ella Virginia, born 12 Dec 1879, died in 1890 (Holy Cross Church Cemetery); daughter of John A. Streett and Flora Mitchell (John A. Streett Bible, *Maryland Bible Records, Volume 2*, by Henry C. Peden, Jr., 2003, p. 146)

Streett, Emma M. (Miss), 1864-1956 (Bethel Presbyterian Church Cemetery Records)

Streett, Emma R. (Rutledge), 1878-1953 (Bethel Presbyterian Church Cemetery Records)

Streett, George, see Ida Streett, q.v.

Streett, George Gover, 1867-1920 (Christ Episcopal Church Cemetery); clerk, Bel Air (*Havre de Grace Republican*, 10 Jan 1890 and 17 Jan 1890); executive committee, Bel Air Tennis Club (*Havre de Grace Republican*, 23 May 1890); private, Jackson Guards [Co. D, 1st Regiment, Maryland National Guard], 1889-1890 (*The Aegis & Intelligencer*, 11 Jan 1889)

Streett, George W., juror, Fourth District (*Havre de Grace Republican*, 31 Jan 1890)

Streett, Gover, of Havre de Grace, clerk of the Maryland House of Delegates (*Havre de Grace Republican*, 21 Feb 1890)

Streett, Grace, entered the Episcopal Institute, Winchester, VA (*Harford Democrat*, 19 Sep 1890)

Streett, Howard, see Nettie S. Streett, q.v.

Streett, Ida, born 1 Jun 1872, daughter of George Streett and Ella Mason (Bethel Presbyterian Church Cemetery Records); librarian, Jarrettsville M. E. Church Sunday School (*The Aegis & Intelligencer*, 28 Mar 1890); see Ida Bay, q.v.

Streett, Ignatius, farmer, near Pylesville (*The Aegis & Intelligencer*, 26 Sep 1890)

Streett, J. B., librarian, Salem Sunday School, Fourth District (*Havre de Grace Republican*, 4 Apr 1890)

Streett, J. R., premium award winner, Class A - Horses, Harford County Fair (*The Aegis & Intelligencer*, 24 Oct 1890)

Streett, James Polk, 1846-1932 (Woodlawn Cemetery, Baltimore Co.); dairyman, (*Harford Democrat*, 14 Feb 1890); trustee, Sylvan Retreat School No. 6, Fifth District (*Havre de Grace Republican*, 30 May 1890); see Howard Johnson (colored), q.v.

Streett, James Ruff, age 37 in 1890 (Marriage License Applications Book ALJ No. 2, 1891)

Streett, Jane, died 2 May 1900, age not given, resided at Chrome Hill, wife of Thomas Streett (Death certificate incomplete)

Streett, John, road examiner, Third District (*Havre de Grace Republican*, 4 Jul 1890); premium award winner, Class B - Cattle, and Class I - Agricultural Productions, Harford County Fair (*The Aegis & Intelligencer*, 24 Oct

1890)

Streett, John Abraham, 1854-1924 (Holy Cross Church Cemetery); native of Harford Co., farmer and dairyman, resided near Rocks (Death certificate; *Harford Democrat*, 14 Feb 1890); trustee, Clermont School No. 13, Fourth District (*Havre de Grace Republican*, 30 May 1890); see Anna A. Chester, Catherine A. Streett, Ella V. Streett and Joseph McC. Streett, q.v.

Streett, John D., 1855-1911 (Bethel Presbyterian Church Cemetery Records)

Streett, John Morgan, 1854-1919 (Old Brick Baptist Church Cemetery); John M. and Richard Streett, insolvent canners, 1889-1890 (*Havre de Grace Republican*, 27 Jun 1890)

Streett, Joseph Malcolm, 1838-1921 (Christ Episcopal Church Cemetery); owner of the *Harford Democrat*, Bel Air (*Havre de Grace Republican*, 17 Jan 1890); incorporator, Bel Air Water and Light Company (*Havre de Grace Republican*, 14 Feb 1890); member, Agricultural and Mechanical Society (*Havre de Grace Republican*, 23 May 1890); trustee, Bel Air School No. 14, Third District (*Havre de Grace Republican*, 30 May 1890); vestryman, Emmanuel Church, Bel Air (*Havre de Grace Republican*, 18 Apr 1890); also see Juliet Streett, q.v.

Streett, Joseph McClellan, 1882-1959 (Holy Cross Church Cemetery); native of Rocks, Harford Co., born 16 Sep 1882, son of John A. Streett and Flora Mitchell (Harkins Funeral Home Records; John A. Streett Bible, *Maryland Bible Records, Volume 2*, by Henry C. Peden, Jr., 2003, p. 146)

Streett, Juliet, daughter of Mr. & Mrs. Joseph M. Streett, of Bel Air (*The Aegis & Intelligencer*, 18 Jul 1890)

Streett, Juliet Evans (Gover), 1840-1908, wife of Joseph Malcolm Streett, q.v.

Streett, Laura, born 6 May 1873, daughter of Shadrack Streett and Julia Ann Wright (Bethel Presbyterian Church Cemetery Records); see Laura (Streett) Gluck, q.v.

Streett, Lawrence, trustee, Chrome Hill School No. 16, Fourth District (*Havre de Grace Republican*, 30 May 1890); see Elizabeth J. Streett, q.v.

Streett, Mabel M. (Miss), dancing student, Archer Institute, Bel Air (*The Aegis & Intelligencer*, 6 Jun 1890); student and actress, Bel Air Graded School (*The Aegis & Intelligencer*, 26 Dec 1890); premium award winner, Class L - Children's Department, Harford County Fair (*The Aegis & Intelligencer*, 24 Oct 1890)

Streett, Madonna S. (McCurdy), 1875-1951 (Bethel Presbyterian Church Cemetery Records); wife of Augustus A. Streett, q.v.

Streett, Margaret, 1881-1970 (www.findagrave.com - married name Michael)

Streett, Margaret ("Margie"), young lady of Bel Air (*The Aegis & Intelligencer*, 7 Feb 1890); student and pianist, Bel Air Academy and Graded School (*The Aegis & Intelligencer*, 23 May and 26 Dec1890)

Streett, Marion, bridge builder, near Chrome Hill (*The Aegis & Intelligencer*, 26 Sep 1890)

Streett, Martha C., 1860-1917, daughter of Merryman and Priscilla Streett (Merryman Streett Bible, *Maryland Bible Records, Volume 2*, by Henry C. Peden, Jr., 2003, p. 147)

Streett, Mary, see J. Harold Stokes, q.v.

Streett, Mary A., see Carrie C. Payne, q.v.

Streett, Mary Ellen (Miller), 1833-1891, widow of Samuel Streett, 1825-1889 (Bethel Presbyterian Church Cemetery Records)

Streett, Mary Isabell (Beatty), 1852-1924 (Death certificate; Bethel Presbyterian Church Cemetery Records states she was born in 1851 and married Samuel Streett)

Streett, Mary V., age 24 in 1890 (Marriage License Applications Book ALJ No. 2, 1890)

Streett, Mattie (Mrs.), farm owner, near Clermont Mills (*The Aegis & Intelligencer*, 4 Jul 1890)

Streett, Merryman, see Martha C. Streett, q.v.

Streett, Minna B. (Cairnes), born 2 Jan 1872, daughter of George A. and Cornelia (Haile) Streett (Bethel Presbyterian Church Cemetery Records)

Streett, Nancy, widow of Shadrach Streett, near Federal Hill, born 28 Dec 1791 (*The Aegis & Intelligencer*, 10

Jan 1890)

Streett, Nannie T., age 20 in 1889 (Marriage License Applications Book ALJ No. 2, 1890), married John T. Ensor on 15 Jan 1890 (*The Aegis & Intelligencer*, 24 Jan 1890)

Streett, Nettie S., resided at Chrome Hill, daughter of Howard Streett (*Harford Democrat*, 24 Jan 1890)

Streett, Priscilla, see Thomas H. Streett and Martha C. Streett, q.v.

Streett, Rachel J. (Ensor), 1829-1905 (Bethel Presbyterian Church Cemetery Records); widow of Shadrack Streett (1823-1876)

Streett, Richard A., 1839-1917 (Old Brick Baptist Church Cemetery); see John M. Streett, q.v.

Streett, Sallie (Miss), 1848-1939 (Slateville Cemetery, York Co., P); native of Harford Co, born 13 Jan 1848, daughter of Shade Streett, of Harford Co, and Margaret Hudson, of Baltimore (Harkins Funeral Home Records)

Streett, Sallie (Miss), resident of Mill Green, and half-sister of Dr. Thomas H. Roberts, of Churchville (*The Aegis & Intelligencer*, 24 Oct 1890)

Streett, Samuel, 1868-1953 (Bethel Presbyterian Church Cemetery Records)

Streett, Samuel Owens, 1876-1950, son of James and Ada V. (Ramsay) Streett (Bethel Presbyterian Church Cemetery Records)

Streett, Samuel Whiteford born 11 Oct 1878, son of Charles W. and Roseanne (Beatty) Streett (Bethel Presbyterian Church Cemetery Records; Death certificate)

Streett, Sarah Ann, wife of Thomas H. Streett, q.v.

Streett, Sarah E., 1839-1917 (Old Brick Baptist Church Cemetery); wife of Richard A. Streett, q.v.

Streett, Shade, see Sallie Streett, q.v.

Streett, Shadrach, see Nancy Streett, q.v.

Streett, Shadrack, 1850-1904 (Bethel Presbyterian Church Cemetery Records)

Streett, Sidney H., resided at Chrome Hill (*Harford Democrat*, 24 Jan 1890)

Streett, St. Clair, see Elizabeth H. Streett, q.v.

Streett, Stanley R., 1869-1929 (Bethel Presbyterian Church Cemetery Records)

Streett, Susan, see Elizabeth H. Streett, q.v.

Streett, Thomas, see Jane Streett, q.v.

Streett, Thomas H., of The Rocks of Deer Creek, brother-in-law of John A. Robb, City Register of Baltimore (*The Aegis & Intelligencer*, 19 Dec 1890); T. H. Streett, trustee, Sylvan Retreat School No. 6, Fifth District (*Havre de Grace Republican*, 30 May 1890); died testate and his named heirs were wife Sarah Ann Streett, son Thomas H. Streett and daughters Mary V. Gladden, Catherine Elizabeth Streett and Ann Priscilla Streett (Harford County Will Book JMM 11:166-167)

Streett, Thomas H., Jr., 1873-1891 (Holy Cross Church Cemetery); Tom Streett, young man, resident near Pylesville (*The Aegis & Intelligencer*, 7 Feb 1890)

Streett, William I., served on a grand jury, Fourth District (*The Aegis & Intelligencer*, 14 Nov 1890); acquired land in November 1890 (*The Aegis & Intelligencer*, 5 Dec 1890); *Havre de Grace Republican*, 31 Oct 1890)

Strehl, Catherine, see Elizabeth Fresch, q.v.

Strekham, Mary C. (Rodgers), 1828-1899, widow, resided at Perryman, native of New Jersey (Death certificate)

Stricklen, Ethel Odessa (McCommons), 1889-1944 (Deer Creek Methodist Church Cemetery)

Stricklen, Glenn G., born 1889, died ---- [after 1944] (Deer Creek Methodist Church Cemetery)

Stricklen, Joseph M., 1850-1932 (Calvary Methodist Church Cemetery)

Stricklen, Martha "Mattie" Lyons (Gorrell), 1851-1915 (Calvary Methodist Church Cemetery)

Stricklen, Nessie Elma, 1878-1894 (Calvary Methodist Church Cemetery)

Stritehoff, Bessie (Miss), member, Asbury M. E. Church, Jarrettsville (*Havre de Grace Republican*, 28 Feb

1890)

Stritehoff, Carrie (Miss), member, Asbury M. E. Church, Jarrettsville (*Havre de Grace Republican*, 28 Feb 1890)

Stritehoff, Ella M. (Miss), teacher, Ward's School No. 6, Third District (*The Aegis & Intelligencer*, 29 Aug 1890); principal, Chestnut Hill School (*Havre de Grace Republican*, 18 Jul 1890); member, Asbury M. E. Church, Jarrettsville (*Havre de Grace Republican*, 28 Feb 1890); uncalled for letter in Bel Air P. O., 1890 (*The Aegis & Intelligencer*, 14 Nov 1890)

Stritehoff, Franklin "Frank" Butler, 1839-1912, native of Harford Co., farmer, resided at Jarrettsville (Death certificate; Bethel Presbyterian Church Cemetery Records)

Stritehoff, Frank Price, 1874-1901, native of Maryland, resided at Jarrettsville, born 3 Sep 1874, son of Frank B. and Louisa C. (Smith) Stritehoff (Death certificate; Bethel Presbyterian Church Cemetery Records)

Stritehoff, Joel "Holly" Hollingsworth, born 16 Feb 1878, son of John Wagoner and Mary Ann (Tucker) Stritehoff (Bethel Presbyterian Church Cemetery Records)

Stritehoff, John Wagoner, 1831-1902 (Bethel Presbyterian Church Cemetery Records)

Stritehoff, Louisa Christine (Smith), 1838-1900, native of Mayrland, resident of Jarrettsville (Death certificate; Bethel Presbyterian Church Cemetery Records); wife of Frank B. Stritehoff, q.v.

Stritehoff, Mary Ann (Tucker), 1839-1912 (Bethel Presbyterian Church Cemetery Records); wife of John W. Stritehoff, q.v.

Stritehoff, Nelson Howard, 1868-1930 (Bethel Presbyterian Church Cemetery Records; also see www.findagrave.com)

Stritehoff, Peter, resident of Jarrettsville (*The Aegis & Intelligencer*, 18 Apr 1890)

Strong, Andrew, born -- Apr 1879, native of Maryland, son of Thomas H. and Talitha E. Strong (1900 Aberdeen Census)

Strong, Anna Hill, 1886-1977 (Wesleyan Chapel Methodist Church Cemetery)

Strong, Carrie M. (Case), 1876-1955 (Angel Hill Cemetery)

Strong, Charles S., see William Henry Strong, q.v.

Strong, Ella B., 1880-1942 (Wesleyan Chapel Methodist Church Cemetery); wife of William Henry Strong, q.v.

Strong, Ella F. (Miss), 1862-1928 (Wesleyan Chapel Methodist Church Cemetery); native of Harford Co., resided in Aberdeen, daughter of Thomas H. Strong and Talitha Gilbert (Death certificate)

Strong, Emma E., see Mary Slade, q.v.

Strong, George H., 1870-1947, native of Abingdon, Harford Co., born 25 Dec 1870, son of Thomas H. Strong and Talitha E. Gilbert (Death certificate; Wesleyan Chapel Cemetery; 1900 Aberdeen Census)

Strong, Helen M. (Lieske), 1869-1925 (St. Paul's Lutheran Church Cemetery)

Strong, Horatio D., 1874-1952 (Wesleyan Chapel Methodist Church Cemetery)

Strong, John Mitchell, 1867-1947 (Wesleyan Chapel Methodist Church Cemetery); native of Maryland, born -- Apr 1867, son of Thomas H. and Talitha E. Strong (1900 Aberdeen Census)

Strong, Joseph W., see Rachel M. Strong, q.v.

Strong, Rachel M., widow of Joseph W. Strong, Civil War veteran, Norrisville (*1890 Special Census of the Civil War Veterans of the State of Maryland*, by L. Tilden Moore, Volume III, p. 82); Mrs. Rachel Strong, of Norrisville, daughter of Mrs. Mary Slade (*The Aegis & Intelligencer*, 4 Jul 1890); see Mary Slade, q.v.

Strong, Talitha E. (Gilbert), 1842-1920 (Wesleyan Chapel Methodist Church Cemetery); native of Harford Co., resided on Swan Creek near Aberdeen (Death certificate); wife of Thomas Henry Strong, q.v.; also see Ella F. Strong, q.v.

Strong, Thomas Henry, 1839-1906 (Wesleyan Chapel Methodist Church Cemetery); native of Harford Co., farmer, resided on Swan Creek near Aberdeen (Death certificate; 1900 Aberdeen Census); see George H. Strong,

Ella F. Strong, and Talitha E. Strong, q.v.

Strong, Wilbur D., born -- Oct 1875, native of Maryland, son of Thomas H. and Talitha E. Strong (1900 Aberdeen Census)

Strong, William E., 1861-1941 (St. Paul's Lutheran Church Cemetery); married Mary A. Hill on 22 Oct 1890 (Marriage License Applications Book ALJ No. 2, 1890; *The Aegis & Intelligencer*, 24 Oct 1890)

Strong, William Henry, 1880-1944 (Wesleyan Chapel Methodist Church Cemetery); native of Maryland, born 27 Nov 1880, son of Charles S. Strong and Sarah E. Blackburn, both natives of Maryland (Pennington Funeral Home Records)

Strott, Philip, inner guard, Marshall's Lodge No. 99, Knights of Pythias, at Jarrettsville (*The Aegis & Intelligencer*, 18 Jul 1890)

Struble, Conrad, 1832-1911, native of Germany (Death certificate; Alms House Record Book)

Strubler (Strauber), Charles c1867-1937 (Death certificate; Alms House Record Book)

Stuart, Lillie M., 1871-1892 (Emory Methodist Church Cemetery)

Stuart, Mehetible J., 1803-1891 (Emory Methodist Church Cemetery)

Stuart, Nancy, see Edward L. Rigdon, q.v.

Stubbs, Clarence G. (Mrs), 1886-1969 (Slateville Cemetery, York Co., PA); native of Macton, Harford Co., born 14 Dec 1886, daughter of Clarence C. Galbreath and Sarah Hays (Harkins Funeral Home Records)

Stubbs, Florence M. (Taylor), 1871-1954 (Highland Presbyterian Church Cemetery); native of Harford Co, born 24 Jul 1871, daughter of Richard Taylor and Sarah M. Scarff (Bailey Funeral Home Records)

Stubbs, Maggie B., 1866-1950 (Slateville Cemetery, York Co., PA); native of Harford Co., born 7 Oct 1866, daughter of Joel C. Hollingsworth and Hannah Carter (Harkins Funeral Home Records)

Stubbs, V. G. & Son, slate quarry, Cambria (*The Aegis & Intelligencer*, 17 Oct 1890)

Stuffer, Harry, 1860-1933 (Death certificate; Alms House Record Book)

Stull, Anna, see Thomas J. Parry, q.v.

Stull, Carrie, see Margaret Kauffman, Ellen Jane Roberts, Mary E. Ross and Anna Parry, q.v.

Stull, Catherine, see John H. Frasch, q.v.

Stull, Florence A. (Mellor), 1884-1952 (Bethel Presbyterian Church Cemetery Records); wife of Franklin G. Stull, q.v.

Stull, Franklin G. ("Frank"), 1882-920, son of Rev. William C. and Rose B. Stull (Bethel Presbyterian Church Cemetery Records); student, Jarrettsville Graded School (*The Aegis & Intelligencer*, 25 Apr 1890)

Stull, Julia Ann (Mrs.), 1816-1901, resided near Bel Air, wife of Joseph Stull (Death certificate)

Stull, Rose B., died 1841, widow of Rev. William C. Stull, q.v.

Stull, William Clark (Rev.), 1850-1897, pastor of Bethel Presbyterian Church (*The Aegis & Intelligencer*, 10 Jan 1890; (Bethel Presbyterian Church Cemetery Records state he was Bethel pastor, 1886-1892, and he and were Rosa buried in Belvedere, NJ)

Stull, William, student, Jarrettsville Graded School (*The Aegis & Intelligencer*, 25 Apr 1890)

Stump, Alice (Miss), resident of Darlington (*The Aegis & Intelligencer*, 13 Jun 1890)

Stump, Bertram N., 1856-1929 (St. Mary's Episcopal Cemetery); jousting tournament rider, Knight of Waverly (*Havre de Grace Republican*, 19 Sep 1890); member, Bel Air Tennis Club (*The Aegis & Intelligencer*, 18 Jul 1890)

Stump, Carrie T. (Riegel), 1863-1935 (Stump Family Cemetery)

Stump, Frederick (Judge), 1837-1901 (Stump Family Cemetery)

Stump, George C., husband of Susan (Reese) Stump, q.v.

Stump, Harriet (colored), see Mary Bishop (colored), q.v.

Stump, Henry Archer, 1889-1945 (Churchville Presbyterian Church Cemetery)

Stump, Henry Arthur, 1857-1934 (Stump Family Cemetery)

Stump, Herman, 1836-1917 (St. Mary's Episcopal Church Cemetery), US Congressman, of Second District, Democrat (*The Aegis & Intelligencer*, 26 Sep 1890); vestryman, Emmanuel Church, Bel Air (*Havre de Grace Republican*, 18 Apr 1890)

Stump, James, see Mary Jane Stump, q.v.

Stump, John W. (colored), age 21 in 1889 (Marriage License Applications Book ALJ No. 2, 1889)

Stump, Margaret (Bell), 1863-1934 (St. Mary's Episcopal Cemetery)

Stump, Mary Bartram, 1888-1912 (St. Mary's Episcopal Church Cemetery - married name Leroy)

Stump, Mary Jane ("Mallie") (colored), c1851-1898, wife of James Stump and daughter of Herman Stump (Death certificate); resident of Bel Air (*The Aegis & Intelligencer*, 18 Apr 1890)

Stump, Pauline, 1824-1907 (Stump Family Cemetery)

Stump, Sarah E. (colored), age 28 in 1890 (Marriage License Applications Book ALJ No. 2, 1891)

Stump, Susan (Reese), 1848-1928 (Friends Cemetery, Homestead, Baltimore City; *The Aegis*, 9 Mar 1928); native of Harford Co., resided at Fallston (Death certificate)

Stump, T. B. Coleman, 1831-1912 (St. Mary's Episcopal Cemetery)

Stump, Theresa J. (Ashton) (colored), 1876-1929, native of Maryland, daughter of Thomas Ashton and Annie M. Cornish (Death certificate)

Stump, William, 1869-1926 (St. Mary's Episcopal Cemetery); member, Bel Air Tennis Club, 1890 (*The Aegis & Intelligencer*, 18 Jul 1890)

Stump, William Henry (colored), age 30 in 1890 (Marriage License Applications Book ALJ No. 2, 1891)

Sturden, Peter, treated by unidentified doctor in 1890 ("Medical Account Book – 1890," Historical Society of Harford County Archives Folder)

Sturtz, Caroline (Roach), 1832-1899, resident at Taylor, native of Maryland (Death certificate; (Ebenezer Methodist Church Cemetery)

Sturtz, Jacob, owned a vacant house near Sarah Furnace in 1890 (*Harford Democrat*, 14 Feb 1890)

Sturtz, Jesse, born 1858, died ---- (Ebenezer Methodist Church Cemetery); acquired land in February 1890 (*The Aegis & Intelligencer*, 7 Mar 1890)

Sturtz, Mary L., 1860-1924 (Ebenezer Methodist Church Cemetery)

Sugar, Abraham J., native of Russia, naturalized 18 Aug 1890 in Bel Air (*The Aegis & Intelligencer*, 22 Aug 1890); on 25 Jul 1890 it was reported, "The wife of Abraham Sugar of Baltimore, formerly of this city [Havre de Grace], came over from Russia, last week, bringing their eleven-year-old son with her, but Mr. Sugar refused to receive her, and has entered suit for divorce, in the Circuit Court of that city. Certainly a cool reception, after traveling some thousands of miles to see the husband and father." (Ref: *Havre de Grace Republican*, 25 Jul 1890)

Sullivan, ----, center fielder, Nonpareil Baseball Club, Aberdeen (*Havre de Grace Republican*, 6 Jun 1890)

Sullivan, Catherine, 1830-1906 (St. Francis de Sales Catholic Church); wife of Jeremiah Sullivan, q.v.

Sullivan, Daniel F., 1858-1909 (St. Francis de Sales Catholic Church)

Sullivan, Daniel F. (Mrs.), resident of VanBibber near Abingdon (*The Aegis & Intelligencer*, 26 Sep and 17 Oct 1890)

Sullivan, Deborah, see Jeremiah Joseph Murphy, q.v.

Sullivan, Dennis, see Thomas Sullivan, q.v.

Sullivan, Elizabeth A. (Linsenmeyer), 1876-1957 (St. Francis de Sales Catholic Church Cemetery); wife of Fleury F. Sullivan, q.v.

Sullivan, Ella, student, Harford Furnace School (*The Aegis & Intelligencer*, 14 Feb 1890)

Sullivan, Ellen, 1822-1897 (St. Ignatius Catholic Church Cemetery); also see Thomas J. Sullivan, q.v.

Sullivan, Ellen T., 1877-1948, native of Belcamp, Harford Co., born 28 Jul 1877, daughter of John Sullivan and ----, both of Ireland (Pennington Funeral Home Records - married name Quirk)

Sullivan, Etta (Moran) 1867-1942 (St. Francis de Sales Catholic Church)

Sullivan, F. F., relief railroad agent at VanBibber (*The Aegis & Intelligencer*, 17 Oct 1890)

Sullivan, Fannie, age 35 in 1890 (Marriage License Applications Book ALJ No. 2, 1890), married Robert Hill on 15 Apr 1890 (marriage certificate)

Sullivan, Fleury F., 1870-1951 (St. Francis de Sales Catholic Church Cemetery)

Sullivan, James P., 1859-1929 (St. Francis de Sales Catholic Church)

Sullivan, Jeremiah ("Jerry"), 1835-1911 (St. Francis de Sales Catholic Church); resident of Harford Furnace (*The Aegis & Intelligencer*, 3 Jan 1890); also see Thomas J. Sullivan, q.v.

Sullivan, Jeremiah J., 1864-1954 (St. Francis de Sales Catholic Church); road surveying chain man, First District (*Havre de Grace Republican*, 4 Jul 1890)

Sullivan, John, Civil War veteran, Delta P. O. (*1890 Special Census of the Civil War Veterans of the State of Maryland*, by L. Tilden Moore, Volume III, p. 83)

Sullivan, John, resident near Harford Furnace (*The Aegis & Intelligencer*, 9 May 1890); see Ellen T. Sullivan, q.v.

Sullivan, John J., 1856-1936 (St. Francis de Sales Catholic Church); assistant B & O railroad station agent at VanBibber, and then station agent at Joppa (*The Aegis & Intelligencer*, 17 Oct 1890; *Havre de Grace Republican*, 24 Oct 1890)

Sullivan, John J., 1872-1900 (St. Francis de Sales Catholic Church)

Sullivan, Lizzie, student, Harford Furnace School (*The Aegis & Intelligencer*, 14 Feb 1890)

Sullivan, Margaret (Lynch), 1830-1902 (St. Francis de Sales Catholic Church Cemetery); wife of Thomas J. Sullivan, q.v.

Sullivan, Mary (Miss), resident of Abingdon (*The Aegis & Intelligencer*, 3 Jan 1890); daughter of Thomas J. Sullivan, of near VanBibber (*Harford Democrat*, 14 Nov 1890)

Sullivan, Mary A., 1843-1908 (Mt. Erin Cemetery)

Sullivan, Mary Frances, 1874-1923 (Cokesbury Memorial Methodist Church Cemetery)

Sullivan, Mary M., 1879-1964 (St. Francis de Sales Catholic Church)

Sullivan, Matthew Francis, 1874-1935 (Cokesbury Memorial Methodist Church Cemetery)

Sullivan, Michael, 1859-1907 (St. Francis de Sales Catholic Church)

Sullivan, Minnie A., 1876-1902 (St. Francis de Sales Catholic Church)

Sullivan, Sarah A. (Mrs), c1870-1914 (Death certificate; Alms House Record Book)

Sullivan, Thomas, 1879-1899, resided at Harford Furnace, son of Dennis Sullivan (Death certificate); student, Harford Furnace School (*The Aegis & Intelligencer*, 14 Feb 1890)

Sullivan, Thomas C., 1836-1920 (Mt. Erin Cemetery)

Sullivan, Thomas J., 1827-1912 (St. Francis de Sales Catholic Church Cemetery), of Rock Hall, Abingdon District, son of Jerry [Jeremiah] and Ellen Sullivan of Ireland near the Lakes of Killarney (*The Aegis & Intelligencer*, 9 May 1890)

Sullivan, Thomas Leo, 1884-1933 (St. Francis de Sales Catholic Church)

Summers, Mary A. (Jones), 1822-1899, resident of Havre de Grace, native of Maryland (Death certificate; Angel Hill Cemetery); wife of Peter Summers, q.v.

Summers, Peter, 1824-1916, resident of Havre de Grace, native of Baltimore Co. (Death certificate; Angel Hill

Cemetery)

Summers, Peter A., 1858-1907 (Angel Hill Cemetery); organizer and vice president, Havre de Grace Democratic Club (*Havre de Grace Republican*, 31 Oct 1890); sneak boat duck hunter (*Havre de Grace Republican*, 7 Nov 1890; Death certificate showed his name as Peter Summers, Jr.)

Summerville, Edna (Miss), member, Mountain Reading Circle (*The Aegis & Intelligencer*, 21 Feb 1890)

Summerville, Elijah, member, Mountain Reading Circle (*The Aegis & Intelligencer*, 21 Feb 1890)

Summons, Henry (colored), c1865-1928 (Union Methodist Church Cemetery, Aberdeen); native of Maryland, laborer, resident of Havre de Grace (Death certificate misfiled as Simmons)

Summons, William F. (colored), husband of Emma Skinner, q.v.

Sumption, Rose F., 1845-1930 (Angel Hill Cemetery); corresponding secretary, Women's Christian Temperance Union, of Havre de Grace (*Havre de Grace Republican*, 19 Sep 1890); wife of Thomas M. Sumption, q.v.

Sumption, Thomas Macaral, 1832-1897 (Angel Hill Cemetery); city bailiff, Havre de Grace (*Havre de Grace Republican*, 7 Feb 1890); city council candidate, Havre de Grace (*Havre de Grace Republican*, 10 Jan 1890); Civil War veteran, Havre de Grace (*1890 Special Census of the Civil War Veterans of the State of Maryland*, by L. Tilden Moore, Volume III, p. 89; *Biographical Dictionary of Harford County, Maryland, 1774-1974*, by Henry C. Peden, Jr. and William O. Carr, 2021, p. 266); juror, Sixth District (*Havre de Grace Republican*, 2 May 1890)

Sunderland, Margaret, died 11 Jan 1892, age not given (Alms House Monthly Register)

Supik, Albert [Vojteh], 1844-1933 (St. Francis de Sales Catholic Church Cemetery); see Elizabeth Dudeck, q.v.

Supik, Elizabeth, see Elizabeth Dudeck, q.v.

Supik, Josephine, 1858-1945 (St. Francis de Sales Catholic Church Cemetery)

Susquehanna and Tidewater Canal Office, Canal Basin, Havre de Grace (*1953 Harford County Directory*, p. 324)

Susquehanna Fertilizer Company (*Harford Democrat*, 14 Feb 1890)

Susquehanna Hall Public School No. 6, near Flintville, Fifth District (*Harford County, Maryland Teachers and the Schools They Served, 1774-1900*, by Henry C. Peden, Jr., 2022, p. 373)

Susquehanna Lodge No. 130, A.F. & A. M., Havre de Grace (*Havre de Grace Republican*, 11 Jul 1890)

Susquehanna Log Company, Havre de Grace (*Havre de Grace Republican*, 4 Apr 1890)

Susquehanna Power and Paper Company Mills, near Darlington, Joshua C. Smith and B. Gilpin Smith, prop. (*Mills: Grist, Saw, Bone, Flint, Fulling ... & More*, by Jack L. Shagena, Jr., Henry C. Peden, Jr. and John W. McGrain, 2009, pp. 261-263)

Susquehanna Reynard Club, Havre de Grace (*Havre de Grace: Its Historic Past, Its Charming Present and Its Promising Future: Harford County's Rural Heritage.* by Jack L. Shagena, Jr. and Henry C. Peden, Jr., 2018, p. 276)

Susquehanna Slate Company, Harford County quarry (*Heavy Industries of Yesteryear; Harford County's Rural Heritage*, by Jack L. Shagena, Jr. and Henry C. Peden, Jr., 2015, p. 212)

Sutor, Albert Franklin, 1888-1972, native of Havre de Grace, born 7 Jun 1888, son of Nicholas Sutor and Jennuy Clayman (Pennington Funeral Home Records)

Sutor, Anna B., 1876-1954 (St. George's Episcopal Church Cemetery)

Sutor, Edith M., 1883-1967 (Angel Hill Cemetery)

Sutor, Jennie L. (Clayman), 1861-1930 (Angel Hill Cemetery); wife of Nicholas Albert Sutor, q.v.

Sutor, John F., 1842-1911 (Angel Hill Cemetery)

Sutor, John F., 1873-1948 (Angel Hill Cemetery)

Sutor, John Franklin, 1847-1924 (Angel Hill Cemetery); sneak boat duck hunter, 1890 (*Havre de Grace Republican*, 7 Nov 1890)

Sutor, Margaret (Beecher), 1835-1907 (St. George's Episcopal Church Cemetery)

Sutor, Mary, see Hattie Z. Crawford, q.v.

Sutor, Nicholas Albert, 1844-1932, Civil War veteran (Angel Hill Cemetery); see lbert Franklin Sutor, q.v.

Sutor, Oliver Ergood, 1853-1931, blacksmith (Angel Hill Cemetery)

Sutor, Paul L., 1853-1930 (St. George's Episcopal Church Cemetery)

Sutor, Rebecca, 1842-1911 (Angel Hill Cemetery)

Sutton, A. Luther, 1838-1921 (McKendree Methodist Church Cemetery); see Horace S. Sutton, q.v.

Sutton, Alleretta Jeannette (Troyer), 1849-1909, native of Manor, Baltimore Co., resided near Monkton (Death certificate; McKendree Methodist Church Cemetery); see Horace S. Sutton, q.v.

Sutton, Annie (Gallup), 1876-1952 (St. George's Episcopal Church Cemetery)

Sutton, Bettie (King), 1851-1926 (Bethel Presbyterian Church Cemetery Records); wife of Samuel M. Sutton, q.v.

Sutton, Fannie E., 1877-1896 (McKendree Methodist Church Cemetery)

Sutton, Florence M., 1869-1894 (McKendree Methodist Church Cemetery)

Sutton, Horace S., 1875-1901, native of Maryland, resided at Black Horse, son of A. L. Sutton and Alleretta ---- [Troyer] (Death certificate)

Sutton, Ida (Miss), resident of Perryman (*The Aegis & Intelligencer*, 9 May 1890)

Sutton, Ida S., 1871-1893 (McKendree Methodist Church Cemetery)

Sutton, Janie, born 22 Nov 1885, daughter of Melvin and Bettie (King) Sutton (Bethel Presbyterian Church Cemetery Records); see Janie Burkins, q.v.

Sutton, Jonathan H., died 12 Dec 1890 in his 70th year (*The Aegis & Intelligencer*, 19Dec 1890); John H. Sutton resided at Perryman (*The Aegis & Intelligencer*, 5 Dec 1890); also see William McDonald Sutton, q.v.

Sutton, Margaret, 1844-1917 (Angel Hill Cemetery)

Sutton, Mary E., see William McDonald Sutton, q.v.

Sutton, Milkie, 1828-1912 (St. George's Episcopal Church Cemetery)

Sutton, Nellie I., 1880-1896 (McKendree Methodist Church Cemetery)

Sutton, Ruth A., 1812-1897 (St. George's Episcopal Church Cemetery)

Sutton, Samuel, 1872-1952 (St. George's Episcopal Church Cemetery)

Sutton, Samuel Melville, 1862-1937 (Bethel Presbyterian Church Cemetery Records); jousting tournament rider, Knight of I Will If I Can (*Havre de Grace Republican*, 15 Aug 1890)

Sutton, Susan Jane (Boyd), 1834-1898 (St. Francis de Sales Catholic Church Cemetery); native of Maryland, resident of Boothby Hill, widow of William T. Sutton (Death certificate)

Sutton, Thomas, 1836-1909 (William Watters Memorial Methodist Church Cemetery, Cooptown); Civil War veteran, Jarrettsville (*1890 Special Census of the Civil War Veterans of the State of Maryland*, by L. Tilden Moore, Volume III, p. 80); delegate, Fourth District, Republican Party Convention (*The Aegis & Intelligencer*, 26 Sep 1890)

Sutton, William, 1876-1910 (St. George's Episcopal Church Cemetery)

Sutton, William McDonald, born 8 Apr 1877, son of J. H. and Mary E. Sutton (St. George's Episcopal Church Register of Baptisms, pp. 4-5)

Sutton, William T., 1828-1897 (St. Francis de Sales Catholic Church Cemetery)

Swan Creek Colored Public School No. 3, near Aberdeen (*Harford County, Maryland Teachers and the Schools They Served, 1774-1900*, by Henry C. Peden, Jr., 2022, p. 373)

Swann, Kesiah (colored), age 34 in 1889 (Marriage License Applications Book ALJ No. 2, 1889)

Swann, Walter (colored), age 23 in 1889 (Marriage License Applications Book ALJ No. 2, 1890), married

Georgianna Smith on 6 Feb 1890 (marriage certificate)

Swann, William W. (colored), 1870-1929 (St. James Church, Federal Hill, William C. Rice Memorial Cemetery)

Swansbury Mills (aka Swan Creek Merchant Mills), near Aberdeen, Millard F. Wright, prop. (*Mills: Grist, Saw, Bone, Flint, Fulling ... & More*, by Jack L. Shagena, Jr., Henry C. Peden, Jr. and John W. McGrain, 2009, pp. 263-264)

Swartz, Adolphus O., 1870-1920 (Calvary Methodist Church Cemetery)

Swartz, Annie, student, Union Chapel Public School (*The Aegis & Intelligencer*, 14 Mar 1890)

Swartz, Benjamin, 1818-1902 (Cokesbury Memorial Methodist Church Cemetery)

Swartz, Bessie, student, Public School No. 1, First District (*The Aegis & Intelligencer*, 10 Jan 1890)

Swartz, Cassandra Mary (Ady), 1863-1902 (St. Ignatius Catholic Church Cemetery)

Swartz, David E., 1818-1909 (Rock Run Methodist Church Cemetery)

Swartz, Eddie (Mrs.), choir member, Bel Air M. P. Church (*The Aegis & Intelligencer*, 27 Jun 1890)

Swartz, Elizabeth T., 1842-1924 (Cokesbury Memorial Methodist Church Cemetery); see William J. Price, q.v.

Swartz, Ella, student, Public School No. 1, First District (*The Aegis & Intelligencer*, 10 Jan 1890)

Swartz, Florence Oleita, 1868-1835, wife of Edwin Webster Mitchell (*Ancestral Charts, Volume 2*, Harford County Genealogical Society, 1986, p. 76)

Swartz, Frances Emily, 1820-1905 (Cokesbury Memorial Methodist Church Cemetery)

Swartz, James H., 1832-1892 (Calvary Methodist Church Cemetery); juror, Third District (*Havre de Grace Republican*, 31 Oct 1890)

Swartz, Leonard, 1890-1945 (Cokesbury Memorial Methodist Church Cemetery)

Swartz, Mary J. (Matthews), 1836-1890 (Calvary Methodist Church Cemetery)

Swartz, Nannie C., 1859-1932 (Mt. Zion Methodist Church Cemetery)

Swartz, Roland (Master), member, Bel Air M. P. Church Sunday School (*The Aegis & Intelligencer*, 27 Jun 1890)

Swartz, Rosa May, 1866-1952, daughter of John Wesley Swartz and Elizabeth T. Price (Cokesbury Memorial Methodist Church Cemetery, married name VanHise); May Swartz, teacher, Boden School, Bush River Neck (*The Aegis & Intelligencer*, 25 Apr 1890; *Harford County, Maryland Teachers and the Schools They Served*, by Henry C. Peden, Jr., 2021, p. 314)

Swartz, Sophia W., 1856-1896 (Cokesbury Memorial Methodist Church Cemetery)

Swartz, Thomas B., 1810-1892 (Cokesbury Memorial Methodist Church Cemetery)

Swartz, Thomas E., 1853-1896 (Mt. Zion Methodist Church Cemetery)

Swartz, Wesley (Mrs.), resident of Abingdon (*The Aegis & Intelligencer*, 29 Aug 1890)

Swayne, Sarah E., 1872-1960 (Cokesbury Memorial Methodist Church Cemetery)

Swayne, William W., 1869-1948 (Cokesbury Memorial Methodist Church Cemetery)

Sweeney, Ann, 1818-1891 (St. Ignatius Catholic Church Cemetery)

Sweeney, Caroline R., see Charles A. Glackin, James R. Glackin, Joseph F. Glackin, Florence L. Glackin and Florence L. Kelly, q.v.

Sweeney, Patrick, 1800-1895, native of County Donegal, Ireland (St. Ignatius Catholic Church Cemetery)

Sweet, William H., former proprietor, Eagle Hotel, on Bond Street, Bel Air (*The Aegis & Intelligencer*, 31 Oct 1890)

Sweeting, Benjamin, husband of Margaret Sweeting (1817-1899), q.v.

Sweeting, Charles W., 1857-1952 (Emory Methodist Church Cemetery); transferred from the voter registration list at Hopewell, Second District (*Havre de Grace Republican*, 17 Oct 1890)

Sweeting, Eugenia A., 1867-1956 (William Watters Memorial Methodist Church Cemetery, Cooptown)

Sweeting, George W., 1853-1931 (William Watters Memorial Methodist Church Cemetery, Cooptown); husband of Margaret Tuston Sweeting, q.v.

Sweeting, George W., Jr., 1887-1949 (William Watters Memorial Methodist Church Cemetery, Cooptown)

Sweeting, John R., 1883-1942 (Cokesbury Memorial Methodist Church Cemetery)

Sweeting, John T., 1848-1917 (Cokesbury Memorial Methodist Church Cemetery)

Sweeting, Leon, 1875-1926 (Cokesbury Memorial Methodist Church Cemetery)

Sweeting, Margaret, 1817-1899, resided near Chrome Hill (Death certificate)

Sweeting, Margaret "Maggie" Tuston (Pennypacker), 1853-1900, native of Pennsylvania, resided at Rocks, Harford Co. (Death certificate misspelled her name as Sweeten; William Watters Memorial Methodist Church Cemetery, Cooptown)

Sweeting, Martha Ella, 1852-1890 (Cokesbury Memorial Methodist Church Cemetery)

Sweeting, Ruth A., 1827-1902 (Cokesbury Memorial Methodist Church Cemetery); uncalled for letter for Ruth Sweeting in Bel Air P. O. (*The Aegis & Intelligencer*, 14 Nov 1890)

Sweetman, Frank, student, Union School House, near Bush Chapel (*The Aegis & Intelligencer*, 14 Mar 1890)

Swift, Addie M., wife of Alexander D. Lee, q.v.; also see Addie M. Lee and Beulah B. Orr, q.v.

Swift, Ann R., born 30 Jan 1880, daughter of F. Millard Swift and Anna Reed (Bethel Presbyterian Church Cemetery Records)

Swift, Benjamin F., 1866-1928 (Dublin Southern Cemetery); native of Maryland, resided at Pylesville (Death certificate); served on an inquest jury in Fifth District, 1890 (*The Aegis & Intelligencer*, 1 Aug 1890)

Swift, Catharine Gazette (Ford), wife of James W. Swift, q.v.

Swift, Charles Albert, 1881-1958, son of Robert E. Swift and Margaret Dailey (Darlington Cemetery)

Swift, David, see George Swift, q.v.

Swift, Elizabeth A. (Reed), 1868-1912 (Bethel Presbyterian Church Cemetery Records); first wife of Millard F. Swift, q.v.

Swift, Ethalmi Sophia (Hunter), 1845-1899, resided on Deer Creek, native of Harford Co., wife of Robert E. Swift (Death certificate)

Swift, Ethlyn H., 1849-1899 (Cokesbury Memorial Methodist Church Cemetery)

Swift, F. O., operator at Perryman tower (*Harford Democrat*, 2 May 1890)

Swift, George, 1872-1950 (Slate Ridge Cemetery, York Co., PA); native of Harford Co., born 6 Nov 1872, son of David Swift and Elizabeth Simms (Harkins Funeral Home Records)

Swift, George Edward, 1881-1956 (Dublin Southern Cemetery); native of Dublin, Harford Co., son of ---- and Marilla Swift (Harkins Funeral Home Records)

Swift, Harrison, 1841-1909 (Baker Cemetery)

Swift, Harry R., 1883-1936 (Baker Cemetery)

Swift, Ida Mae (Anderson), 1857-1936 (Dublin Southern Cemetery; Bailey Funeral Home Records); wife of William H. Swift, q.v.

Swift, James W., 1832-1900, native of Maryland, laborer, resided at Dublin, Harford Co. (Death certificate)

Swift, Jerri Dean, 1866-1960 (Highland Presbyterian Church Cemetery)

Swift, John J., 1861-1944 (Highland Presbyterian Church Cemetery)

Swift, Margaret E. (Daily), 1854-1893 (St. Ignatius Catholic Church Cemetery); wife of Robert W. Swift, q.v.

Swift, Marilla or Marrilla, see Katie S. Temple and G. Edward Swift, q.v.

Swift, Martha J. (Robinson), 1875-1934 (Baker Cemetery)

Swift, Mary Louisa (Calary), 1862-1915 (William Watters Memorial Church, Cooptown; Death certificate)

Swift, Millard F., 1856-1925 (Wiseburg Cemetery, Baltimore County)

Swift, Nathan, 1831-1906 (Loudon Park Cemetery, Baltimore); creamery proprietor, Perryman, Harford Co., 1890 (*The Aegis & Intelligencer*, 2 May 1890 and 4 May 1906)

Swift, Pauline B., 1879-1905 (Darlington Cemetery)

Swift, Robert E., 1853-1920 (Darlington Cemetery)

Swift, Sarah E. (Griffith), 1863-1948 (Bailey Funeral Home Records)

Swift. Sarah M. (Baldwin), 1863-1924 (Mt. Olivet Cemetery, York Co., PA); native of Harford Co., resided at Whiteford (Death certificate)

Swift, Sarah V., 1889-1919 (Baker Cemetery)

Swift, Tacy B. (Matthews), 1862-1955 (Bailey Funeral Home Records)

Swift, Thomas O., 1869-1931 (Baker Cemetery); resident of Magnolia, "operator at Perryman block" and general freight agent, P. W. & B. Railroad, at Perryman (*The Aegis & Intelligencer*, 9 May 1890; *Havre de Grace Republican*, 9 May 1890)

Swift, W. Winifred, 1880-1920 (Darlington Cemetery)

Swift, William, see Maude Haslach, q.v.

Swift, William H., 1858-1938 (Dublin Southern Cemetery); resident of Dublin [Fifth District] (*The Aegis & Intelligencer*, 27 Jun 1890); see William McCleary, q.v.

Swift, William R., 1834-1906 (William Watters Memorial Church, Cooptown)

Swift, William Thomas, 1858-1918 (William Watters Memorial Church, Cooptown; Death certificate)

Swingley, Grace, 1878-1959, native of Aberdeen, Harford Co., born 3 Jul 1878, daughter of James A. Swingley and Eliza Hartman (Pennington Funeral Home Records - married name Carver)

Swope, Annie (Feltman), c1842-1892 (St. Paul's Lutheran Church Cemetery)

Swope, Charles Frederick, 1880-1893 (St. Francis de Sales Catholic Church Cemetery); baptized 26 Sep 1880, son of John and Johanna (Tobin) Swope (St. Ignatius Catholic Church Baptism Register, p. 49)

Swope, Frederick, 1841-1912 (St. Paul's Lutheran Church Cemetery)

Swope, George, 1878-1941 (St. Francis de Sales Catholic Church Cemetery)

Swope, Johanna (Tobin), 1844-1910 (St. Francis de Sales Catholic Church Cemetery)

Swope, John, Civil War veteran, Emmorton (*1890 Special Census of the Civil War Veterans of the State of Maryland*, by L. Tilden Moore, Volume III, p. 72)

Swope, Margaret, see Frank Lay (Laye) and George E. Lay, q.v.

Swope, Mary G., 1880-1973 (Mt. Zion Methodist Church Cemetery)

Sylvan Retreat Public School No. 6, near Pylesville (*Harford County, Maryland Teachers and the Schools They Served, 1774-1900*, by Henry C. Peden, Jr., 2022, p. 373)

Sylvester, Mary, 1809-1892, born at Denton, MD, died at Findowrey, Harford Co. (St. Mary's Episcopal Church Cemetery)

Symington, Caroline, see Philip Hopkins Janney and Stuart Symington Janney, q.v.

Tabernacle Colored Public School No. 2, at Benson, Third District (*Harford County, Maryland Teachers and the Schools They Served, 1774-1900*, by Henry C. Peden, Jr., 2022, p. 373)

Tabernacle Evangelical Church and Cemetery (Tabernacle Road, near Whiteford)

Tabernacle Mt. Zion Methodist Church and Cemetery (Connolly Road, Benson)

Tabor, Ariel (Rutledge), 1858-1930 (Highland Presbyterian Church Cemetery)

Tabor, Freeman A., 1841-1910, Civil War veteran (Highland Presbyterian Church Cemetery)

Tabor, Mary A. (Taylor), 1844-1929 (Highland Presbyterian Church Cemetery)

Tabor, Sophia D. (Rutledge), 1842-1937 (Highland Presbyterian Church Cemetery); native of Harford Co. (Bailey Funeral Home Records spelled the name Taber); wife of Freeman A. Tabor, q.v.

Taddy, John, uncalled for letter in Bel Air P. O. (*The Aegis & Intelligencer*, 4 Jul 1890)

Tahaney, Catherine (Corrigan), 1814-1899, of Bel Air, native of Ireland, widow of Hugh Tahaney (Death certificate)

Talbot, Annie (colored), of Abingdon District near McComas Institute, stepmother of Catharine Webster (*The Aegis & Intelligencer*, 21 Feb 1890)

Talbot, Benjamin F. (colored), 1866-1928 (Mountain Colored Cemetery); native of Baltimore Co., laborer, resided at Mountain, Harford Co. (Death certificate)

Talbot, George (colored), see Matilda Talbot (colored), q.v.

Talbot, Mary Jane (Banks) (colored), 1874-1907, daughter of Isaac Banks and ---- (Death certificate)

Talbot, Matilda (colored), 1876-1930, native of Maryland, born 15 Feb 1876, daughter of George Talbot and Jebe(?) Anderson (Death certificate - married name Armstrong)

Talbot, Winfield (colored), husband of Mary Jane (Banks) Talbot, q.v.

Talbott, Gertie (colored), resident of Bel Air (*The Aegis & Intelligencer*, 27 Jun 1890)

Talbott, Helen (Lamb) (Cathcart), 1889-1948 (Bethel Presbyterian Church Cemetery Records); wife of Seth Talbott, q.v.

Talbott, Samuel W. (colored), age 20 in 1890 (Marriage License Applications Book ALJ No. 2, 1891)

Talbott, Seth, 1879-1964 (Bethel Presbyterian Church Cemetery Records)

Taliaferro, Warner Throckmorton Langbourne, 1856-1941, native of Gloucester Co, VA (Ware Episcopal Church Cemetery, VA; *Harford County, Maryland Teachers and the Schools They Served*, by Henry C. Peden, Jr., 2021, pp. 315-316); former principal of Bel Air Academy (*Havre de Grace Republican*, 18 Apr 1890); assistant marshal, Bel Air jousting tournament (*Havre de Grace Republican*, 19 Sep 1890); incorporator and secretary, Bel Air Fire and Salvage Corps (*The Aegis & Intelligencer*, 19 Sep 1890); member, Bel Air Fire Brigade and Salvage Corps (*Havre de Grace Republican*, 17 Oct 1890); member, Division No. 2, Bel Air Fire and Salvage Corps (*The Aegis & Intelligencer*, 10 Oct 1890); member, Mt. Ararat Lodge No. 44, A. F. & A. M., Bel Air (*Havre de Grace Republican*, 11 Jul 1890); orderly sergeant, Jackson Guards [Co. D, 1st Regiment, Maryland National Guard] (*The Aegis & Intelligencer*, 11 Jan 1889 and 28 Nov 1890)

Tally, Hannah (colored), see J. Ann Preston (colored), q.v.

Tammany, Laura B., 1861-1922, daughter of Samuel James Tammany and Laura J. Lort (Angel Hill Cemetery; *Harford County, Maryland Teachers and the Schools They Served*, by Henry C. Peden, Jr., 2021, pp. 316-317); teacher, Havre de Grace High School, Sixth District (*The Aegis & Intelligencer*, 29 Aug 1890); member, Havre de Grace M. E Church (*Havre de Grace Republican*, 13 Jun 1890); assistant treasurer, Willard Section No. 58, Cadets of Temperance, Havre de Grace (*Havre de Grace Republican*, 11 Jul 1890)

Tammany, Samuel James, 1835-1910, native of Cecil Co, MD, teacher and principal, Havre de Grace High School (Angel Hill Cemetery; *Biographical Dictionary of Harford County, Maryland, 1774-1974*, by Henry C. Peden, Jr. and William O. Carr, 2021, p. 267); delegate from the Sixth District, Republican Party Convention (*The Aegis & Intelligencer*, 26 Sep 1890); vice president, Republican Club (*Havre de Grace Republican*, 7 Nov 1890)

Tanner, Belle B., 1863-1922 (Union Chapel Methodist Church Cemetery)

Tanner, Mary Stockham (Taylor), 1878-1956 (St. George's Episcopal Church Cemetery)

Tansen, Harriet (colored), wife of Jacob J. Dallam, q.v.; also see Benjamin W. Dallam, q.v.

Tarbert's General Store, Pylesville, J. A.Tarbert, prop. (*Country Stores: Harford County's Rural Heritage*, by Henry C. Peden, Jr. and Jack L. Shagena, Jr., 2015, p. 245)

Tarbert, Amelia, 1816-1900 (Fellowship Cemetery tombstone, but death certificate stated she died 5 Oct 1900, age 80 years and 8 months, and spelled her name Torbert); wife of Andrew Tarbert, q.v.

Tarbert, Andrew, 1830-1892 (Fellowship Cemetery); Andrew Tarbert, and wife [Amelia], sold land in April 1890 (*The Aegis & Intelligencer*, 9 May 1890)

Tarbert, George, sold land in May 1890 (*The Aegis & Intelligencer*, 6 Jun 1890)

Tarbert, Kate Anna, see Kate Anna Fickus, q.v.

Tarbert, John, resided at Cambria (*Harford Democrat*, 5 Sep 1890)

Tarbert, Louis, 1885-1938 (Mt. Zion Methodist Church Cemetery)

Tarbert, Mary, see Sarah Sliver, q.v.

Tarbert, Mary V., 1857-1932, daughter of Andrew Tarbert and Amelia Burgess; teacher, Sylvan Retreat School No. 6, Fifth District (*The Aegis & Intelligencer*, 29 Aug 1890; *Harford County, Maryland Teachers and the Schools They Served*, by Henry C. Peden, Jr., 2021, p. 319)

Tarbert, Robert, see Florence J. Bennington, q.v.

Tarbert, Sarah E., see Sarah E. Lloyd, q.v.

Tarbert, William, see Sarah E. Lloyd, q.v.

Tariff Reform Club of Harford County, organized 2 Sep 1890, G. Smith Norris, chairman (*Harford Democrat*, 5 Sep 1890)

Tarrant, Henry (Rev.), record of P. E. Church at Rocks of Deer Creek (*Havre de Grace Republican*, 30 May 1890); stockholder, Aberdeen Can Factory (*Havre de Grace Republican*, 19 Dec 1890)

Tarring Funeral Home (Aberdeen)

Tarring, Alice A., 1855-1898 (Grove Presbyterian Church Cemetery)

Tarring, Bertha (Ivins), 1883-1966 (Harford Memorial Gardens)

Tarring, Edward H., 1860-1901 (Grove Presbyterian Church Cemetery)

Tarring, Edward T., 1881-1920 (Grove Presbyterian Church Cemetery); son of Henry and Hannah E. Tarring (1900 Aberdeen Census)

Tarring, Elizabeth B., born 1885, died ---- (Grove Presbyterian Church Cemetery)

Tarring, Hannah Elizabeth (Greenland), 1853-1926 (Grove Presbyterian Church Cemetery); native of Maryland, resided in Aberdeen (Death certificate); wife of Henry Tarring, q.v.

Tarring, Henry, 1852-1927 (Grove Presbyterian Church Cemetery); carriage maker and undertaker, Aberdeen (*Carriages Back in the Day: Harford County's Rural Heritage*, by Jack L. Shagena, Jr. and Henry C. Peden, Jr., 2016, p. 87) see Edward T. Tarring, John G. Tarring, Mabel F. Tarring, Oscar R. Tarring, Roy B. Tarring, Willard H. Tarring, and Fletcher & Tarring, q.v.

Tarring, John G., 1888-1970 (Harford Memorial Gardens); son of Henry and Hannah E. Tarring (1900 Aberdeen Census)

Tarring, Leroy B., 1885-1953 (Grove Presbyterian Church Cemetery)

Tarring, Mabel F., born -- Oct 1878, daughter of Henry and Hannah E. Tarring (1900 Aberdeen Census); member, Aberdeen M. E. Church (*Havre de Grace Republican*, 21 Feb 1890)

Tarring, Oscar R., born -- Feb 1890, son of Henry and Hannah E. Tarring (1900 Aberdeen Census)

Tarring, Roy B., born -- Mar 1884, son of Henry and Hannah E. Tarring (1900 Aberdeen Census)

Tarring, Willard H., born -- Dec 1879, son of Henry and Hannah E. Tarring (1900 Aberdeen Census)

Tasco, Rebecca (colored), 1845-1910 (St. James United Cemetery)

Tasker (Taskey?), Georgeanna (Scott) (colored), 1854-1922 (Death certificate)

Tasker, Ella Jane (colored), see Ella Jane Whittington (colored), q.v.

Tasker, Joseph (colored), trustee, Clark's Chapel Colored School No. 4, Third District (*Havre de Grace Republican*, 30 May 1890)

Tasker, Philip Henry "Harry" (colored), 1868-1957 (*The Democratic Ledger*, 4 Jul 1957)

Tasker, Mrs. (colored), enumerated as age 109 in the 1890 census, near Kalmia, Third District (*Havre de Grace Republican*, 22 Aug 1890, listed a handful of names from the actual 1890 census and she was one of them)

Tasker, Sarah Jane (Young) (colored), 1839-1917, native of Calvert Co., MD (Death certificate)

Tasker, William H. (colored), 1821-1896 (St. James United Cemetery)

Tate, Eliza J., see Carvil Treadway, q.v.

Tate, James, see Martha Ellen Tate and Sara B. Elliott, q.v.

Tate, Laura, see Osborne H. Heaps, q.v.

Tate, Martha Ellen, 1858-1938 (Slate Ridge Cemetery, York Co., PA); native of Harford Co., born 4 Nov 1858, resident of Pylesville, daughter of James and Martha Tate (Harkins Funeral Home Records)

Tate, Mary, see Rebecca Heaps, q.v.

Tatem, George W., Jr., committeeman, Knights of St. Leo, Havre de Grace (*Havre de Grace Republican*, 19 Sep 1890); member, Young Men's Pleasure Club, Havre de Grace (*Havre de Grace Republican*, 21 Nov 1890)

Tatum, George, city council candidate, Havre de Grace (*Havre de Grace Republican*, 10 Jan 1890); inquest jury, Havre de Grace (*Havre de Grace Republican*, 6 Jun 1890)

Taylor's General Store, at Webster, Mr. & Mrs. James R. Taylor, prop. (*Country Stores: Harford County's Rural Heritage*, by Henry C. Peden, Jr. and Jack L. Shagena, Jr., 2015, p. 246)

Taylor Baseball Club, at Taylor (*The Aegis & Intelligencer*, 18 Apr 1890)

Taylor Public School No. 25, at Taylor, Fourth District (*Harford County, Maryland Teachers and the Schools They Served, 1774-1900*, by Henry C. Peden, Jr., 2022, p. 373)

Taylor, ---- first baseman, A. R. Walker Baseball Club, Havre de Grace (*Havre de Grace Republican*, 6 Jun 1890)

Taylor, Adela (colored), 1880-1956 (Hendon Hill Cemetery)

Taylor, Alice, student, Public School No. 1, First District (*The Aegis & Intelligencer*, 10 Jan 1890)

Taylor, Amelia T., see Annie Taylor, q.v.

Taylor, Anna E., see Mary Stockham Taylor, John Howard Taylor and Helen Woolman Taylor, q.v.

Taylor, Annie, born 23 Oct 1882, daughter of D. W. and Amelia T. Taylor (St. George's Episcopal Church Register of Baptisms, pp. 2-3)

Taylor, Annie Jane (colored), see Jane or Annie Jane Taylor (colored), q.v.

Taylor, Asa Alexander, baptized 13 Aug 1882, son of William M. and Isabel Taylor (St. George's Episcopal Church Register of Baptisms, pp. 2-3, did not record his age)

Taylor, B. F. (Mr.), uncalled for letter in Bel Air P. O. (*The Aegis & Intelligencer*, 14 Nov 1890)

Taylor, Bessie S. (Spencer), 1885-1951 (Rock Run Methodist Church Cemetery); native of Harford Co., born 17 May 1885, daughter of Joseph Spencer and Hannah Courtney (Death certificate)

Taylor, Carrie Lillian, see George Hiram Cobourn, q.v.

Taylor, Catherine, 1837-1926 (Cranberry Methodist Church Cemetery); native of Pennsylvania, married, resided at Perryman, parents unknown (Death certificate)

Taylor, Charles (colored), see George A. Taylor (colored), q.v.

Taylor, Charles A. (colored), 1868-1919 (Death certificate; St James United Cemetery)

Taylor, Charles Henry (colored), 1862-1928 (Mt. Calvary Methodist Church Cemetery); native of Maryland, born 14 Dec 1862, son of James Taylor and Rachel Stewart, resided in Havre de Grace (Death certificate)

Taylor, Charles W., county out-pensioner [welfare recipient], Fourth District (*The Aegis & Intelligencer*, 14 Feb 1890)

Taylor, Charlotte (Jenkins) (colored), 1849-1909, native of Virginia, resident of Bel Air, daughter of Moses

Jenkins and ---- (Death certificate)

Taylor, Corbin J., resided in the upper part of Harford Co. near New Park, PA (*Harford Democrat*, 21 Nov 1890); associate judge of elections, Norrisville Precinct (*Havre de Grace Republican*, 17 Oct 1890)

Taylor, Daniel J., juror, Third District (*Havre de Grace Republican*, 31 Oct 1890)

Taylor, Daniel Wesley, resident of Perryman (*The Aegis & Intelligencer*, 7 Nov 1890); director, Mutual Fire Insurance Company in Harford County (*The Aegis & Intelligencer*, 10 Jan 1890); see Annie Taylor and Lillie Taylor, q.v.

Taylor, E. Ross, 1885-1954 (Highland Presbyterian Church Cemetery); native of Maryland, born 2 Oct 1885, daughter of Richard Taylor and Sarah M. Scarff (Harkins Funeral Home Records)

Taylor, Edward, 1880-1953 (Mt. Carmel Methodist Church Cemetery)

Taylor, Edward (colored), see Grace Virginia Taylor (colored), q.v.

Taylor, Eleanor ("Ellen"), see Eleanor Barnard, Charles Nelson Barnard, John James Barnard and Joseph Cochran Barnard, q.v.

Taylor, Eliza (colored), c1832-1931 (Death certificate; St James United Cemetery)

Taylor, Eliza (colored), born -- Mar 1871, native of Maryland (1900 Aberdeen Census)

Taylor, Eliza M. (colored), 1871-1923, native of Maryland, born 15 Aug 1871, daughter of James Taylor and Rachel Stewart (Death certificate - married name Saunders)

Taylor, Elizabeth J., 1827-1891 (Cokesbury Memorial Methodist Church Cemetery)

Taylor, Elizabeth Porter, see George Amos Courtney, q.v.

Taylor, Ella Scott (colored), 1889-1892 (Asbury Church Cemetery)

Taylor, Elsie E., wife of E. Ross Taylor, q.v.

Taylor, Emma (Laport), 1849-1942, wife of James J. W. Taylor, q.v.

Taylor, Emma M., age 18 in 1890 (Marriage License Applications Book ALJ No. 2, 1891)

Taylor, Frances Rosabelle, married William Henry Bernshouse on 29 May 1890 (marriage certificate)

Taylor, Frank, 1847-1899, resided near Dublin (Death certificate); trustee, Dublin School No. 13, Fifth District (*Havre de Grace Republican*, 30 May 1890); Frank Taylor, and family, residents at Dublin (*The Aegis & Intelligencer*, 8 Aug 1890)

Taylor, G. Lillian, 1871-1890 (St. George's Episcopal Church Cemetery)

Taylor, George, member, Norrisville Silver Cornet Band (*The Aegis & Intelligencer*, 30 May 1890)

Taylor, George A. (colored), 1890-1914, native of Havre de Grace, born 12 Mar 1890, son of Charles Taylor and Sarah Brown (Death certificate; St James United Cemetery)

Taylor, George H., 1872-1940 (Highland Presbyterian Church Cemetery); native of Harford Co., born 16 Dec 1872, son of Richard Taylor and Sarah M.Scarff (Harkins Funeral Home Records)

Taylor, Gilder G., 1839-1897 (Highland Presbyterian Church Cemetery); see Harry B. Taylor, Louisa G. Taylor and William Taylor, q.v.

Taylor, Grace Virginia (colored), 1887-1928 (Fairview Church Cemetery); native of Maryland, born 12 Feb 1887, daughter of Edward Taylor and Margaret Scott (Death certificate - married name Turner)

Taylor, Harry (colored), resident near Gravelly Hill (*The Aegis & Intelligencer*, 30 May 1890)

Taylor, Harry B., 1878-1947 (Highland Presbyterian Church Cemetery); native of Harford Co., born 5 Jan 1878, son of Gilder Taylor, of England, and Mary Adams, of Harford Co. (Harkins Funeral Home Records)

Taylor, Harry C. (colored), 1888-1924, native of Maryland, son of William Taylor and Susan Hopkins (Death certificate)

Taylor, Helen Woolman, born 4 Jan 1889, daughter of Joseph W. and Anna E. Taylor (St. George's Episcopal Church Register of Baptisms, pp. 12-13)

Taylor, Henry, charged and found guilty of violating the local option laws in 1890 (Harford County Criminal Docket, 1888-1892, p. 88)

Taylor, Howard, jousting tournament herald (*The Aegis & Intelligencer*, 8 Aug 1890)

Taylor, Isabel, see Willie Thomas Taylor, Ida May Taylor, Asa Alexander Taylor and Lawrence Matthew Taylor, q.v.

Taylor, J. (colored), see Samuel Taylor (colored), q.v.

Taylor, J. C. (Master), member, Asbury M. E. Church, Jarrettsville, 1890 (*Havre de Grace Republican*, 28 Feb 1890)

Taylor, J. Edward "Ned" (colored), 1838-1915, son of ---- Taylor and Charity Foreman (Death certificate); chief hostler at Eagle Hotel in Bel Air for 60 years (*The Aegis & Intelligencer*, 8 Jan 1915; *The Aegis*, 5 Jan 1940); brother of Jarrett Taylor, q.v.

Taylor, J. W., and family, moved from Perryman to Camden, NJ (*Harford Democrat*, 14 Feb 1890)

Taylor, J. W., proprietor, Havre de Grace Marble Works (*Havre de Grace Republican*, 14 Mar 1890)

Taylor, James, student, Public School No. 1, First District (*The Aegis & Intelligencer*, 10 Jan 1890)

Taylor, James (colored), see Charles H. Taylor, John R. Taylor and Eliza M. Taylor, q.v.

Taylor, James J. W., 1831-1911 (prob. Loudon Park Cemetery, Baltimore); mercantile and drug store at Bush, First District, 1890 (*Havre de Grace Republican*, 19 Dec 1890)

Taylor, James R., delegate, Second District, Democrat Party Convention (*The Aegis & Intelligencer*, 5 Sep 1890); member, Stephenson Lodge No. 128, A. F. & A. M., Lapidum (*Havre de Grace Republican*, 11 Jul 1890); see Taylor's General Store, q.v.

Taylor, Jane or Annie Jane (colored), 1826-1935, born in Havre de Grace, parents unknown; employed by the Evans family for many years (Death certificate; *The Aegis*, 11 Oct 1935; *Havre de Grace Republican*, 12 Oct 1935); wife of Japhet C. Taylor, q.v.

Taylor, Japhet C., alias Jabez Taylor, 1838-1904, Civil War veteran (Death certificate; Military pension application of widow Jane or Annie Jane Taylor filed in 1909)

Taylor, Jarrett, age 47, married Sophia Buchanan on 25 Feb 1890 (Marriage License Applications Book ALJ No. 2, and marriage certificate; *The Aegis & Intelligencer*, 7 Mar 1890; member, Maryland Central Dairymen's Association (*Havre de Grace Republican*, 28 Feb 1890)

Taylor, Jarrett (colored), 1837-1900 (Hendon Hill Cemetery; *The Aegis & Intelligencer*, 23 Mar 1900); brother of J. Edward "Ned" Taylor, q.v.

Taylor, Jesse C., trustee, Jarrettsville School No. 8, Fourth District (*Havre de Grace Republican*, 30 May 1890)

Taylor, John (colored), see William Henry Taylor (colored), q.v.

Taylor, John H. (colored), 1856-1916, native of Baltimore, resided at Gravel Hill near Havre de Grace (Death certificate)

Taylor, John Howard, born 10 Nov 1879, son of Joseph W. and Anna E. Taylor (St. George's Episcopal Church Register of Baptisms, pp. 12-13; *The Hughes Genealogy, 1636-1953*, by Joseph Lee Hughes, 1953, p. 136)

Taylor, John I., 1879-1959 (Highland Presbyterian Church Cemetery); native of Street, Harford Co., born 16 Nov 1879, son of Richard Taylor and Martha Scarff (Harkins Funeral Home Records)

Taylor, John R. (colored), born -- Jan 1863, native of Maryland (1900 Aberdeen Census)

Taylor, John R. (colored), 1871-1915, native of Harford Co., born 1 Jan 1871, son of James E. Taylor and ---- (Death certificate)

Taylor, John R. (colored), born -- Nov 1889, native of Maryland, son of John R. and Martha S. Taylor (1900 Aberdeen Census)

Taylor, Joseph E., 1862-1891 (St. George's Episcopal Church Cemetery)

Taylor, Joseph W., see Mary Stockham Taylor, John Howard Taylor and Helen Woolman Taylor, q.v.

Taylor, Latetia (colored), age 23 in 1890 (Marriage License Applications Book ALJ No. 2, 1891)

Taylor, Laura B., born -- Aug 1870, native of Baltimore, daughter of George W. Taylor, of Virginia, and Isabella A. Sisco, of Baltimore; teacher, Glenville, 1890 (*Harford County, Maryland Teachers and the Schools They Served*, by Henry C. Peden, Jr., 2021, p. 320; *Havre de Grace Republican*, 14 Feb 1890); teacher, Jefferson School No. 3, Second District (*The Aegis & Intelligencer*, 29 Aug 1890)

Taylor, Lawrence Matthew, baptized 13 Aug 1882, son of William M. and Isabel Taylor (St. George's Episcopal Church Register of Baptisms, pp. 2-3, did not record his age)

Taylor, Lillie, eldest daughter of Mr. & Mrs. D. W. Taylor, of Perryman, died 5 Jan 1890 (*The Aegis & Intelligencer*, 17 Jan 1890)

Taylor, Louisa G. (Mrs.), 1865-1961 (Highland Presbyterian Church Cemetery); native of Maryland, born 6 Sep 1856, daughter of William Gilder Taylor and Mary Ann Adams (Harkins Funeral Home Records)

Taylor, Margaret, died in 1890 and her named heirs were grandson George Aseph, daughters Walberga Kennett and Mary E. Doyle (wife of Thomas Doyle), with William T. Clark and William T. Walter, executors (Harford County Will Book JMM 11:142-143)

Taylor, Margaret A., 1863-1927 (Fawn Grove Friends Cemetery, York Co., PA); wife of Laban Lowe, q.v.; also see Clayton Lowe, q.v.

Taylor, Margaret A. (Mrs.) (colored), 1845-1915, native of Harford Co., daughter of ---- and Amelia Brown (Death certificate)

Taylor, Marion, see T. Marion Taylor, q.v.

Taylor, Martha S. (colored), born -- Jan 1864, native of Maryland (1900 Aberdeen Census); wife of John R. Taylor (colored), born 1863, q.v.

Taylor, Mary E., see Mary E. McCann, q.v.

Taylor, Mary Jane (Monk) (colored), 1861-1915 (Death certificate)

Taylor, Mary Stockham, born 2 Apr 1878, daughter of Joseph W. and Anna E. Taylor (St. George's Episcopal Church Register of Baptisms, pp. 12-13)

Taylor, Ned (colored), see J. Edward Taylor (colored), q.v.

Taylor, Perline (colored), born -- Jan 1885, native of Maryland, daughter of John R. and Martha S. Taylor (1900 Aberdeen Census)

Taylor, Preston D. P., local preacher of the M. E. Church in Dublin, former principal of Bel Air and Darlington Academies (*Havre de Grace Republican*, 7 Mar 1890)

Taylor, R. Emory, associate judge of elections, Hall's Cross Roads Precinct (*Havre de Grace Republican*, 17 Oct 1890); delegate, Second District, Democrat Party Convention (*The Aegis & Intelligencer*, 5 Sep 1890)

Taylor, Rachel (colored), born -- Apr 1888, native of Maryland, daughter of ---- and Eliza Taylor (1900 Aberdeen Census)

Taylor, Rachel A., see John H. Wheeler and Thomas H. Wheeler, q.v.

Taylor, Rebecca (colored), see Elmira James (colored) and James T. Parker (colored), q.v.

Taylor, Richard, see Florence M. Stubbs, George H. Taylor, John I. Taylor, William B. Taylor and E. Ross Taylor, q.v.

Taylor, Richard M., of Perryman, father of Mrs. Rosa Bernshouse, of New Jersey (*The Aegis & Intelligencer*, 26 Dec 1890); juror, Second District (*Havre de Grace Republican*, 31 Oct 1890); trustee, Perryman School No. 5, Second District (*Havre de Grace Republican*, 30 May 1890)

Taylor, Robert (colored), 1890-1916, native of Maryland, son of William Taylor and Susan Hopkins (Death certificate)

Taylor, Rosa (colored), born -- Feb 1888, native of Maryland, daughter of John R. and Martha S. Taylor (1900 Aberdeen Census)

Taylor, Rosa Belle Frances, age 25 in 1890 (Marriage License Applications Book ALJ No. 2); resided at Perryman (*Harford Democrat,* 14 Mar 1890)

Taylor, Samuel (colored), 1877-1926 (Hendon Hill Cemetery); native of Maryland, son of J. Taylor and Jane Preston, resided in Bel Air (Death certificate)

Taylor, Sarah Ann (Miss), 1858-1926 (Centre Presbyterian Church Cemetery, York Co., PA); native of Maryland, resided near Carea (Death certificate)

Taylor, Sarah M. (Scarff), 1847-1928 (Bailey Funeral Home Records); wife of Richard Taylor; also see Florence M. Stubbs, George H. Taylor, John I. Taylor, William B. Taylor and E. Ross Taylor, q.v.

Taylor, Seth B., age 25 in 1890 (Marriage License Applications Book ALJ No. 2, 1891); resident at the Forest, near Webster (*Havre de Grace Republican,* 7 Feb and 20 Jun 1890); treated by unidentified doctor in 1890 ("Medical Account Book – 1890," Historical Society of Harford County Archives Folder)

Taylor, Sue L. (Huff), 1882-1944 (Highland Presbyterian Church Cemetery); native of Harford Co., born 25 Jul 1882, daughter of Alonzo Huff, of Harford Co., and Alice L. Wilson, of Lancaster Co., PA (Bailey Funeral Home Records)

Taylor, T. Marion, second baseman, Perryman Baseball Club (*The Aegis & Intelligencer,* 18 Jul 1890); jousting tournament rider, Knight of Fairview (*The Aegis & Intelligencer,* 29 Aug 1890); operator at Bush River, better known as take-a-nap-in-the-middle-of-the-night, applied for freight agent at Perryman (*Harford Democrat,* 25 Apr 1890)

Taylor, Virginia (Miss), resident of Jarrettsville (*The Aegis & Intelligencer,* 11 Apr 1890)

Taylor, W. T., jousting tournament rider, Knight of Lone Star, 1890 (*Havre de Grace Republican,* 15 Aug 1890); windmill agent, Perryman (*Havre de Grace Republican,* 30 May 1890)

Taylor, Wilhelmina, native of Havre de Grace, born 28 Feb 1870, daughter of William Taylor and Margaret ---- (Pennington Funeral Home Records, 1956 - married name Weber)

Taylor, William, died 16 Nov 1890, age 18 (Slate Ridge Presbyterian Church Cemetery, York Co., PA); son of Gilder Taylor (*The Aegis & Intelligencer,* 21 Nov 1890 and 19 Dec 1890)

Taylor, William (colored), see Adeline Brown, Robert Taylor, Harry C. Taylor and William H. Taylor, q.v.

Taylor, William B., 1882-1964 (Highland Presbyterian Church Cemetery); native of Street, Harford Co., born 26 Aug 1882, son of Richard Taylor and Sarah Scarff (Harkins Funeral Home Records)

Taylor, William G., 1870-1890 (Highland Presbyterian Church Cemetery)

Taylor, William Gilder, see Gilder Taylor and Louisa G. Taylor, q.v.

Taylor, William H. (colored), c1871-1927, native of Maryland, son of William Taylor and F. Jeannette ---- (Death certificate)

Taylor, William Henry (colored), 1878-1949, native of Harford Co., born 8 Aug 1878, son of John Taylor and Harriett Wells (Death certificate)

Taylor, William M., see William Thomas Taylor, Ida May Taylor, Asa Alexander Taylor and Lawrence Matthew Taylor, q.v.

Taylor, William "Willie" Thomas, 1871-1945 (St. George's Episcopal Church Cemetery); native of Harford Co., born 8 Mar 1871, son of William M. Taylor and Isabel Smith (Bailey Funeral Home Records); Willie Thomas Taylor, baptized 13 Aug 1882 (St. George's Episcopal Church Register of Baptisms, pp. 2-3, did not record his age)

Taylor, Wilson, resident of Havre de Grace (*The Aegis & Intelligencer,* 26 Sep 1890)

Tayson, Charles Edward, 1870-1895 (Smith Chapel Methodist Church Cemetery); born 15 Dec 1870, son of George W. and Rebecca Tayson (Holy Trinity Episcopal Church Register of Baptisms, p. 82)

Tayson, Charlotte Agnes, born 29 Aug 1881, daughter of James A. and Eliza H. Tayson (Holy Cross Episcopal Church Register of Baptisms, p. 84)

Tayson, Clinton M., 1890-1934 (Mt. Tabor Methodist Church Cemetery); native of Harford Co., born 22 Jan

1890, son of George Tayson and Rebecca Morris (Bailey Funeral Home Records)

Tayson, Daniel Jones, age 23 in 1889, maried Etta Duff on 22 Jan 1890 (Marriage License Applications Book ALJ No. 2, 1890, and Marriage Record; Holy Trinity Episcopal Church Register of Marriages, p. 216); served on a grand jury (*The Aegis & Intelligencer*, 14 Nov 1890)

Tayson, David Clifton, born 23 Aug 1877, son of ---- and Martha Tayson (Holy Trinity Episcopal Church Register of Baptisms, p. 82)

Tayson, Elizabeth Harriet "Lizzie" (Humphreys), 1862-1917 (Holy Trinity Episcopal Church Cemetery); see Myrtle Edith Tayson, George Wonders Tayson, Howard Andrew Tayson, James Herbert Tayson, Charlotte Agnes Tayson, and Laura Bessie Tayson, q.v.

Tayson, Elsie Virginia, born 8 Jul 1885, baptized 3 Feb 1892, son of James Anthony and Eliza H. Tayson (Holy Trinity Episcopal Church Register of Baptisms, p. 102)

Tayson, George W., see Charles Edward Tayson, James Burrell Tayson, Lawrence Tayson. Clinton M. Tayson and Philip Colburn Tayson, q.v.

Tayson, George Wonders, born 8 Dec 1883, baptized 3 Feb 1892, son of James Anthony and Elizabeth H. Tayson (Holy Trinity Episcopal Church Register of Baptisms, p. 102)

Tayson, Howard Andrew, born 18 Mar 1889, baptized 10 Oct 1889, son of James Anthony and Elizabeth H. Tayson (Holy Trinity Episcopal Church Register of Baptisms, p. 96)

Tayson, Howard Finney, born 31 Oct 1874, son of John and Rebecca Tayson (Holy Trinity Episcopal Church Register of Baptisms, p. 82)

Tayson, Jackson, Civil War veteran, Cburchville (*1890 Special Census of the Civil War Veterans of the State of Maryland*, by L. Tilden Moore, Volume III, p. 66)

Tayson, James, treated by unidentified doctor in 1890 ("Medical Account Book – 1890," Historical Society of Harford County Archives Folder)

Tayson, James Anthony, 1857-1940 (Holy Trinity Episcopal Church Cemetery); also see Myrtle Edith Smith, George Wonders Tayson, Howard Andrew Tayson, James Herbert Tayson, Charlotte Agnes Tayson, and Laura Bessie Tayson, q.v.

Tayson, James Burrell, born 20 Apr 1883, son of George W. and Rebecca Tayson (Holy Trinity Episcopal Church Register of Baptisms, p. 86)

Tayson, James Herbert, 1890-1891 (Holy Trinity Episcopal Church Cemetery); born 1 Jul 1890, baptized 15 Jul 1891, son of James Anthony and Elizabeth H. Tayson (Holy Trinity Episcopal Church Register of Baptisms, p. 98)

Tayson, John, 1822-1898 (Holy Trinity Episcopal Church Cemetery)

Tayson, John, 1832-1902 (Holy Trinity Episcopal Church Cemetery); farmed the land of Dr. Harlan at Churchville for 14 years (*The Aegis & Intelligencer*, 7 Feb 1890); also see Mary Martha Coale, q.v.

Tayson, John, 1850-1935 (Holy Trinity Episcopal Church Cemetery); also see Howard Finney Tayson, q.v.

Tayson, John, Jr., treated by unidentified doctor in 1890 ("Medical Account Book – 1890," Historical Society of Harford County Archives Folder)

Tayson, John, Sr., treated by unidentified doctor in 1890 ("Medical Account Book – 1890," Historical Society of Harford County Archives Folder)

Tayson, John W., age 27 in 1889 (Marriage License Applications Book ALJ No. 2, 1889)

Tayson, Laura Bessie, born 7 Jan 1887, baptized 3 Feb 1892, daughter of James Anthony and Eliza H. Tayson (Holy Trinity Episcopal Church Register of Baptisms, p. 102)

Tayson, Laura V., age 20 in 1889 (Marriage License Applications Book ALJ No. 2, 1890)

Tayson, Lawrence, 1874-1896 (Smith Chapel Methodist Church Cemetery); born 3 Jan 1874, son of George W. and Rebecca Tayson (Holy Trinity Episcopal Church Register of Baptisms, p. 82)

Tayson, Martha, see David Clifton Tayson, q.v.

Tayson, Martha S. (Ward), 1884-1964 (Deer Creek Methodist Church Cemetery); native of Chestnut Hill, Harford Co., born 1 Jul 1884, daughter of Henry Ward and Ida Gambrill (Harkins Funeral Home Records)

Tayson, Mary, treated by unidentified doctor in 1890 ("Medical Account Book – 1890," Historical Society of Harford County Archives Folder)

Tayson, Myrtle Edith, born 11 Dec 1882, daughter of James A. and Elizabeth H. Tayson (Holy Trinity Episcopal Church Register of Baptisms, p. 86)

Tayson, Philip Colburn, born 20 Aug 1879, native of Harford Co., son of George W. Tyson and Rebecca Morris (Holy Trinity Episcopal Church Register of Baptisms, p. 84; Bailey Funeral Home Records)

Tayson, Rebecca, see Charles Edward Tayson, Howard Finney Tayson, Lawrence Tayson and Philip Colburn Tayson, q.v.

Tayson, Rebecca Charlotte, 1830-1910 (Holy Trinity Episcopal Church Cemetery); also see James Burrell Tayson and Philip Colburn Tayson, q.v.

Tazwell, Mary F. (Mrs.) (colored), 1886-1956 (Union Methodist Church Cemetery, Aberdeen)

Teale, May, student, Havre de Grace High School (*Havre de Grace Republican*, 31 Oct 1890)

Teel, Florine Burch (colored), 1888-1924, native of Maryland, born 5 Sep 1888, daughter of Louis or Lewis Teel, of North Carolina, and Frances Evans, of Maryland (Death certificate); see Frances Ann Teel, q.v.

Teel, Frances Ann (colored), 1846-1927, native of Maryland, daughter of Jesse Smith and Rebecca Evans, and wife of Lewis Teel (Death certificate)

Temple Restaurant, in Masonic Temple, Bel Air, George Lyle, prop. (*Harford Democrat*, 17 Jan 1890)

Temple, ----, right fielder, Baptist Baseball Club, of Fourth District (*Havre de Grace Republican*, 8 Aug 1890)

Temple, Amos Harvey, 1831-1917 (Rock Run Methodist Church Cemetery); son of Joseph S. and Thirza Jane Temple (Joseph S. Temple Bible, *Maryland Bible Records, Volume 2*, by Henry C. Peden, Jr., 2003, p. 154, states he was born 7 Feb 1832;) farmer, Webster (*Havre de Grace Republican*, 6 Jun 1890); Civil War veteran, Havre de Grace (*1890 Special Census of the Civil War Veterans of the State of Maryland*, by L. Tilden Moore, Volume III, p. 68); granted a government pensioner in 1890 (*Havre de Grace Republican*, 26 Dec 1890)

Temple, Benjamin F., 1834-1890, Civil War veteran (Mountain Christian Church Cemetery); son of Joseph S. and Thirza Jane Temple (Joseph S. Temple Bible, *Maryland Bible Records, Volume 2*, by Henry C. Peden, Jr., 2003, pp. 154-155)

Temple, Benjamin F. (Jr.), 1877-1948 (Dublin Southern Cemetery); native of Baltimore Co., born 22 Mar 1877, son of Benjamin F. Temple and ---- (Bailey Funeral Home Records)

Temple, Bessie, third grade student, Bynum School (*The Aegis & Intelligencer*, 11 Jul 1890)

Temple, Charles W., 1884-1944 (Mountain Christian Church Cemetery)

Temple, Edwin O., 1869-1926 (Mt. Tabor Methodist Church Cemetery)

Temple, Eliza J., 1822-1899 (Mt. Tabor Methodist Church Cemetery); married Christian Bavington on 3 Dec 1890 (*The Aegis & Intelligencer*, 5 Dec 1890; Marriage License Applications Book ALJ No. 2; Bel Air Methodist Charge Marriage Records, p. 238)

Temple, Flora L., 1878-1940 (Mt. Carmel Methodist Church Cemetery)

Temple, Harriet Ann, 1847-1930 (Rock Run Methodist Church Cemetery); wife of Amos H. Temple, q.v.

Temple, Harriet R., see Harriet R. House, q.v.

Temple, Isaac D., 1829-1910 (Mountain Christian Church Cemetery)

Temple, James, resident near Red Pump (*The Aegis & Intelligencer*, 2 May 1890); see Harriet R. House and Bessie Lee Walter, q.v.

Temple, James Garfield, 1886-1960 (Mountain Christian Church Cemetery)

Temple, Josie, student, Bynum School (*The Aegis & Intelligencer*, 11 Jul 1890)

Temple, Katie S. (Lee), 1889-1957 (Dublin Cemetery); native of Harford Co., born 17 Sep 1889, daughter of

Alexander Lee and Marrilla Swift (Bailey Funeral Home Records)

Temple, Leona G., 1874-1959 (Rock Run Methodist Church Cemetery)

Temple, Mary A., 1842-1915 (Mt. Carmel Methodist Church Cemetery)

Temple, Samuel A., 1821-1896 (Mt. Carmel Methodist Church Cemetery)

Temple, Samuel O., 1876-1954 (Mt. Carmel Methodist Church Cemetery)

Temple, Susan Ann, 1840-1891 (Mountain Christian Church Cemetery)

Temple, W., left fielder, Havre de Grace Ash Alleys Baseball Club (*The Aegis & Intelligencer*, 27 Jun 1890); left fielder, Webster Baseball Club, of Webster (*Havre de Grace Republican*, 8 Aug 1890)

Temple, William C., 1871-1940 (Mt. Tabor Methodist Church Cemetery); native of Harford Co., born 26 Mar 1871, son of William J. Temple and Abarilla Whitaker (Bailey Funeral Home Records)

Temple, William H., 1874-1944 (Rock Run Methodist Church Cemetery)

Temple, William J., see William C. Temple, q.v.

Temple, William Taylor, 1880-1957 (Mt. Carmel Methodist Church Cemetery)

Templeton, Alexander M., widower, age 54 in 1889 (Marriage License Applications Book ALJ No. 2, 1890); council past president and supreme deputy, Beneficial Order of Equity, Havre de Grace (*Havre de Grace Republican*, 21 Nov 1890)

Tenley, Annie Hill, 1850-1940, of Forest Hill, daughter of Henry and Mary Ellen (Curry) Tenley (Fallston Methodist Church Cemetery tomsbtone states born 1851; Death certificate states born 1850)

Tenley, Catharine Ellen, born 29 Sep 1888, baptized -- Nov 1888, daughter of George and Ann (Kelly) Tenley (St. Ignatius Catholic Church Baptism Register, p. 101)

Tenley, George, baptized 3 Jan 1886, [adult] son of Henry and Mary (Curry) Tenley (St. Ignatius Catholic Church Baptism Register, p. 85)

Tenley, Julia A., 1862-1921 (St. Ignatius Catholic Church Cemetery tombstone spelled the name Tenly)

Tenley, Julia Mary, born -- Oct 1889, baptized 10 Nov 1889, daughter of George and Ann (Kelly) Tenley (St. Ignatius Catholic Church Baptism Register, p. 109)

Tenley, Lydia W., 1858-1923, of Havre de Grace, daughter of Henry Tenley, native of Virginia, and Mary Curry, native of Harford Co. (Fallston Methodist Church Cemetery; Death certificate)

Tenley, William Henry, 1857-1900, son of Henry and Mary E. Tenley (Fallston Methodist Church Cemetery)

Tennant, Annie F. (Jones), 1859-1929, native of Maryland (Bailey Funeral Home Records)

Tennant, David B., 1859-1943, native of Harford Co. (Death certificate)

Tennant, Ella E. (Glasgow), 1868-1930, native of Maryland (Bailey Funeral Home Records)

Tennant, Roxie (Kerr), 1876-1942 (Dublin Southern Cemetery); native of Harford Co., born 26 Oct 1876, daughter of James Kerr and Elizabeth Proctor (Bailey Funeral Home Records)

Tennison, Jessie Mayfield (Pocock), 1881-1974, wife of William B. Tennison (Bethel Presbyterian Church Cemetery Records)

Terkeldson, Peter, 1870-1939, native of Denmark, unmarried, resided near Aberdeen (Death certificate; Alms House Record Book)

Terrell, Alice G. (Gorrell), 1876-1962 (Broad Creek Friends Cemetery); native of Harford Co., born 22 Feb 1976, daughter of Henry Gorrell and Susanna Brannan (Harkins Funeral Home Records); wife of Walton M. Terrell, q.v.

Terrell, Walton M., 1870-1952 (Broad Creek Friends Cemetery); resident of Mill Green, Harford Co., parents not indicated (Harkins Funeral Home Records)

Terry, Ada B., age 23 in 1890 (Marriage License Applications Book ALJ No. 2, 1890), daughter of Mr. & Mrs. G. Frank Terry, married Leonard R. Towson, of Baltimore, on 2 Jul 1890 at her parents' home near Edgewood (*The Aegis & Intelligencer*, 4 Jul 1890)

Terry, Amanda V., 1869-1935 (Christ Episcopal Church Cemetery)

Terry, Charles Henry, 1850-1926 (Death certificate; Alms House Record Book)

Terry, Edith W., 1832-1908 (Fallston Methodist Church Cemetery)

Terry, Esther Jane (Stinchcomb), 1868-1928, native of Harford Co., born 18 Nov 1868, daughter of Noah Stinchcomb, of Baltimore City, and Mary Unger, of Maryland (Death certificate; Jacob L. Terry Bible, *Maryland Bible Records, Volume 2*, by Henry C. Peden, Jr., 2003, pp. 154-155)

Terry, George Frank, resident of Edgewood (*Havre de Grace Republican*, 27 Jun 1890); served on a petit jury (*Havre de Grace Republican*, 14 Feb 1890); also see Ada B. Terry, q.v.

Terry, Jacob Livezey, 1865-1951 (Fallston Methodist Church Cemetery; Jacob L. Terry Bible, *Maryland Bible Records, Volume 2*, by Henry C. Peden, Jr., 2003, pp. 155-156)

Terry, John R., 1860-1899, farmer near Bel Air, husband of Jennie Bull (Death certificate; Christ Episcopal Church Cemetery)

Terry, Joseph R., 1848-1890 (Fallston Methodist Church Cemetery; Alms House Record Book); see Sarah Terry, q.v.

Terry, Rose (colored), see Frances Effie Gore (colored), q.v.

Terry, Sarah Ann, born -- Jan 1862, baptized 11 May 1889 (ex-Baptist), daughter of Joseph R. Terry, native of Harford Co., and Edith W. Livezey, native of Philadephia (St. Ignatius Catholic Church Baptism Register, p. 105); age 21 *(sic)* in 1890 (Marriage License Applications Book ALJ No. 2, 1890), daughter of Joseph Terry, married John S. Lagan on 8 Oct 1890 (St. Ignatius Catholic Church Marriage Register, p. 19)

Thalman, Bertha Iola, born 15 Nov 1889, daughter of George Thalman and Ida Ola Bradfield (*The Hughes Genealogy, 1636-1953*, by Joseph Lee Hughes, 1953, p. 129)

Thalman, George, born 23 Jan 1865, died ---- (Cedar Hill, Havre de Grace City Cemetery)

Thalman, Mary Ann (Smith), 1870-1943, native of Havre de Grace, born 20 Nov 1870, daughter of John Smith and Elizabeth Green, natives of Harford Co. (Pennington Funeral Home Records)

The Aegis & Intelligencer newspaper, 119 S. Main St., Bel Air (*Bel Air: An Architectural and Cultural History, 1782-1945*, by Marilynn M. Larew, 1995, p. 205; *1953 Harford County Directory*, p. 229)

Thigpen, Carrie V. (Stansbury) (colored) 1875-1950 (Union Methodist Church Cemetery, Aberdeen, tombstone inscription, but death certificate stated she was born 18 Oct 1881 at Perryman, daughter of William Stansbury and Delia Tildon)

Thithe, Luther, county out-pensioner [welfare recipient], Fourth District (*Havre de Grace Republican*, 4 Jul 1890)

Thoene, Lucy Ann (Street), 1838-1934 (Mt. Erin Cemetery); wife of William Thoene, q.v.

Thoene, Mary Elizabeth, 1871-1948, native of Perryman, Harford Co., born 29 Oct 1871, daughter of William Thoene, of Germany, and Lucy A. Street, of London, England (Pennington Funeral Home Records - married name Tully)

Thoene, Philip J., 1878-1923 (Mt. Erin Cemetery)

Thoene, William, 1837-1923 (Mt. Erin Cemetery)

Thomas' General Store and Post Office, McIntyre P. O., Minefield Station, Ma & Pa Railroad, W. A. Thomas, prop. (*Country Stores: Harford County's Rural Heritage*, by Henry C. Peden, Jr. and Jack L. Shagena, Jr., 2015, p. 247)

Thomas Run Colored Public School, near Bel Air (*Harford County, Maryland Teachers and the Schools They Served, 1774-1900*, by Henry C. Peden, Jr., 2022, p. 373)

Thomas Run Public School No. 9, near Bel Air (*Harford County, Maryland Teachers and the Schools They Served, 1774-1900*, by Henry C. Peden, Jr., 2022, p. 373)

Thomas, Albert, 1873-1953 (Grove Presbyterian Church Cemetery); see William Thomas, q.v.

Thomas, Alice, wife of William Thomas, q.v.

Thomas, Allen, see Annie Thomas, q.v.

Thomas, Amentis, 1829-1915 (Churchville Presbyterian Church Cemetery)

Thomas, Andrew E., 1878-1955 (Angel Hill Cemetery)

Thomas, Anna E., see Luella M. Grafton, q.v.

Thomas, Annie, 1876-1941, native of Maryland resided at Street, born 30 Sep 1876, daughter of Allen Thomas and Sarah ---- (Death certificate - married name Knight)

Thomas, Annie (colored), born -- Apr 1865, native of Maryland, sister-in-law of John and Georgiana Butler (1900 Aberdeen Census)

Thomas, Arthur, resident near Prospect (*Havre de Grace Republican*, 27 Jun 1890); see Benny Thomas, David Thomas, Maggie Thomas, Mattie Thomas, Oliver Thomas, Robert Thomas, and Sallie Thomas, q.v.

Thomas, Asbury (colored), 1884-1957 (Mt. Calvary Methodist Church Cemetery; 1900 Aberdeen Census stated he was born in Maryland in April 1880, nephew of John and Georgiana Butler)

Thomas, Augusta, 1853-1937, wife of Herman Thomas, 1846-1927 (St. Paul's Lutheran Church Cemetery)

Thomas, B. F. (Mrs.), see L. M. Wheeler, q.v.

Thomas, Belle N., 1866-1928 (Jarrettsville Cemetery)

Thomas, Benny, son of Mr. & Mrs. Arthur Thomas, of Prospect, died 8 Jul 1890, age 6 (*The Aegis & Intelligencer*, 11 Jul 1890)

Thomas, Carrie, age 23 in 1890 (Marriage License Applications Book ALJ No. 2, 1890)

Thomas, Carrie (colored), see Rachel Lynn (colored), q.v.

Thomas, Carrie E., 1872-1958 (Darlington Cemetery)

Thomas, Carrie Jane, 1871-1957 (Church of the Ascension Cemetery)

Thomas, Catherine, wife of Daniel Thomas, residents of Kirkwood, died 8 Jan 1890, age about 66 (*The Aegis & Intelligencer*, 17 Jan 1890)

Thomas, Charles D., 1868-1929 (Church of the Ascension Cemetery)

Thomas, Charles Edgar, 1888-1963 (Darlington Cemetery); native of Darlington, Harford Co., born 13 Jan 1888, son of Charles Y. Thomas and Rebecca S. Edge (Harkins Funeral Home Records); born 1st mo., 13th day, 1888, son of Charles Y. and Rebecca E. Thomas (Deer Creek Friends Record of Monthly Meeting, First Month, 1883, Register which recorded earlier births)

Thomas, Charles Y., 1851-1925 (Darlington Cemetery); census taker, Dublin Precinct (*Havre de Grace Republican*, 23 May 1890); sold land in April 1890 (*The Aegis & Intelligencer*, 9 May 1890); see Rebecca S. Thomas, Richard H. Thomas, Jr., Charles Edgar Thomas, Joseph Edge Thomas and Elizabeth (Smith) Thomas, q.v.

Thomas, Clara B., 1870-1937 (Grove Presbyterian Church Cemetery)

Thomas, Daniel, see Catherine Thomas, q.v.

Thomas, Daniel N., 1864-1927 (Jarrettsville Cemetery)

Thomas, Daniel P., associate judge of elections, Stearns Precinct (*Havre de Grace Republican*, 17 Oct 1890); trustee, Rock Hill School No. 3, Fifth District (*Havre de Grace Republican*, 30 May 1890)

Thomas, David, young son of Mr. & Mrs. Arthur Thomas, of Prospect (*The Aegis & Intelligencer*, 11 Jul 1890)

Thomas, David Edward III, 1869-1928 (Darlington Cemetery)

Thomas, Elizabeth (Smith), 1882-1947, daughter of Charles Y. Thomas and Rebecca S. Edge (Darlington Cemetery; Deer Creek Friends Record of Monthly Meeting, First Month, 1883, Register which recorded earlier births)

Thomas, Delma, see Cora Scarborough, q.v.

Thomas, Edward, 1867-1927 (Mt. Erin Cemetery)

Thomas, Ella, see Levi Gates, q.v.

Thomas, Ella (Wright), 1876-1961 (Hendon Hill Cemetery)

Thomas, Emma G., teacher, Calvary School No. 11, Third District (*The Aegis & Intelligencer*, 29 Aug 1890)

Thomas, Florence Elizabeth (colored), 1888-1948, native of Federal Hill, Harford Co., born 9 Jul 1888, daughter of George Edgar Thomas and Margaret Ann Jones (Kurtz Funeral Home Records - married name Clark)

Thomas, George (colored), charged with assault in 1890, was found not guilty (Harford County Criminal Docket, 1888-1892, p. 84); died 28 Feb 1904, age not given (Alms House Record Book)

Thomas, George Edgar (colored), see Florence E. Thomas (colored), q.v.

Thomas, George Edward (colored), 1844-1923 (Death certificate)

Thomas, Haddie E. (Cavender), 1867-1934 (Bailey Funeral Home Records); wife of Henderson G. Thomas, q.v.

Thomas, Hannah Ellen, 1830-1904 (Churchville Presbyterian Church Cemetery)

Thomas, Hattie N., 1890-1954 (Angel Hill Cemetery)

Thomas, Helen B., 1878-1961 (Jarrettsville Cemetery)

Thomas, Henderson G., 1855-1922 (Emory Methodist Church Cemetery)

Thomas, Henry (colored), 1821-1901, resident of Cole, Harford Co. (Death certificate)

Thomas, Herman, 1837-1903 (Fallston Methodist Church Cemetery)

Thomas, Herman, 1846-1927 (St. Paul's Lutheran Church Cemetery); resided at Calvary (*The Aegis & Intelligencer*, 29 Aug 1890)

Thomas, Ida, see Graceton Heaps, q.v.

Thomas, Ida P., 1874-1958 (Highland Presbyterian Church Cemetery)

Thomas, James H., 1865-1935 (Dublin Southern Cemetery)

Thomas, Jane W. (Williams), 1884-1966 (Bel Air Memorial Gardens); native of Cardiff, Harford Co., born 11 Jun 1884, daughter of Thomas J. Williams and Eleanor Parry (Harkins Funeral Home Records)

Thomas, John, 1824-1894 (Deer Creek Methodist Church Cemetery)

Thomas, John, Civil War veteran, Fountain Green (*1890 Special Census of the Civil War Veterans of the State of Maryland*, by L. Tilden Moore, Volume III, p. 70); clay pigeon shooter, Churchville (*The Aegis & Intelligencer*, 7 Feb 1890); treated by unidentified doctor in 1890 ("Medical Account Book – 1890," Historical Society of Harford County Archives Folder)

Thomas, John, 1864-1890 (Mt. Vernon Methodist Church Cemetery); son of Arthur Thomas, of Prospect (*The Aegis & Intelligencer*, 5 Sep 1890)

Thomas, John (colored), 1884-1918 (Death certificate; Heavenly Waters Cemetery)

Thomas, John Carroll, 1855-1923 (*The Hughes Genealogy, 1636-1953*, by Joseph Lee Hughes, 1953, p. 125)

Thomas, John D., 1852-1917 (Jarrettsville Cemetery)

Thomas, John H., died 6 Sep 1901, age not given (Alms House Record Book); veteran of the Mexican War, pension granted in 1890 retroactive to 1887, resided at Perryman (*Harford Democrat*, 21 Mar 1890)

Thomas, John W., 1876-1964 (Jarrettsville Cemetery)

Thomas, John W., Sr., 1882-1954 (Bel Air Memorial Gardens)

Thomas, Joseph Edge, born 9th mo., 3rd day, 1884, son of Charles Y. and Rebecca E. Thomas (Deer Creek Friends Record of Monthly Meeting, First Month, 1883, Register which recorded earlier births)

Thomas, Julia J. (colored), 1890-1971 (*The Aegis*, 19 Nov 1971 - married name Swann)

Thomas, Laura Bay (McFadden), 1847-1916, resident of Whiteford (Death certificate)

Thomas, Lida V. (Amos), 1871-1951 (Deer Creek Methodist Church Cemetery)

Thomas, Lillie E., 1882-1936 (Dublin Southern Cemetery)

Thomas, Maggie, daughter of Mr. & Mrs. Arthur Thomas, of Prospect, died 7 Jul 1890 (*The Aegis & Intelligencer*, 11 Jul 1890)

Thomas, Margaret A., born 1888, died ---- (Grove Presbyterian Church Cemetery)

Thomas, Mary (colored), born -- Apr 1886 native of Maryland (1900 Aberdeen Census)

Thomas, Mary (Hill) (colored), 1851-1915 (Death certificate)

Thomas, Mary M., see W. Stanley Amos, q.v.

Thomas, Martha T. (Keith), 1843-1918 (Vernon Cemetery)

Thomas, Mattie, eldest unmarried daughter of Mr. & Mrs. Arthur Thomas, of Prospect, died 23 Jun 1890, ag 15 (*The Aegis & Intelligencer*, 11 Jul 1890; *Harford Democrat*, 27 Jun 1890)

Thomas, Nathan W., Civil War veteran, Line Bridge (*1890 Special Census of the Civil War Veterans of the State of Maryland*, by L. Tilden Moore, Volume III, p. 84)

Thomas, Oliver, young son of Mr. & Mrs. Arthur Thomas, of Prospect (*The Aegis & Intelligencer*, 11 Jul 1890)

Thomas, Phoebe Grace, 26 Dec 1889 - 6 Feb 1890 (Emory Methodist Church Cemetery)

Thomas, Robert Oliver, 1866-1933 (Darlington Cemetery); blacksmith and carriage and wagon maker, Berkley, 1890 (*Carriages Back in the Day: Harford County's Rural Heritage*, by Jack L. Shagena, Jr. and Henry C. Peden, Jr., 2016, p. 127)

Thomas, Ralph H., 1834-1897 (Deer Creek Methodist Church Cemetery)

Thomas, Rebecca S. (Edge), 1851-1926 (Darlington Cemetery); wife of Charles Y. Thomas, q.v.; also see Richard H. Thomas, Jr., Joseph Edge Thomas and Elizabeth (Smith) Thomas, q.v.

Thomas, Richard H., 1881-1939 (Darlington Cemetery); born 2nd mo., 18th day, 1881, son of Charles Y. and Rebecca E. Thomas (Deer Creek Friends Record of Monthly Meeting, First Month, 1883, Register which recorded earlier births)

Thomas, Robert, son of Mr. & Mrs. Arthur Thomas, of Prospect, died 8 Jul 1890, age 9 (*The Aegis & Intelligencer*, 11 Jul 1890)

Thomas, Roy J., 1888-1968 (Angel Hill Cemetery)

Thomas, Ruth Virginia, 1890-1958 (Jarrettsville Cemetery)

Thomas, Sallie, daughter of Mr. & Mrs. Arthur Thomas, of Prospect, died 29 Jun 1890, age 15 (*The Aegis & Intelligencer*, 4 Jul 1890)

Thomas, Sarah A. (England), 1830-1916, resident of Forest Hill (Death certificate)

Thomas, Sarah M., 1862-1925 (Jarrettsville Cemetery)

Thomas, Susan (colored), see J. Alfred Whittington (colored), q.v.

Thomas, Susan J., see James Edward Huff, q.v.

Thomas, Virginia P., 1833-1906 (Darlington Cemetery)

Thomas, W. F., member, inquest jury, Havre de Grace, 1890 (*Havre de Grace Republican*, 6 Jun 1890)

Thomas, Walter E., 1888-1966 (Jarrettsville Cemetery)

Thomas, Walter E., 1888-1968 (Churchville Presbyterian Church Cemetery)

Thomas, Walter T., see William Thomas, q.v.

Thomas, William, 1828-1890 (Cokesbury Memorial Methodist Church Cemetery); keeper of boats at Gunpowder Bridge, P. W. & B. Railroad (*The Aegis & Intelligencer*, 12 Dec 1890); died testate and his named heirs were wife Alice Thomas and sons Albert C. Thomas, Walter T. Thomas and Willie H. Thomas (Harford County Will Book JMM 11:155-156)

Thomas, William A., 1862-1925 (Deer Creek Methodist Church Cemetery); married Lida V. "Liddie" Amos, 1871-1951, on 27 Feb 1890 in Bel Air M. E. Parsonage (*The Aegis & Intelligencer*, 7 Mar 1890; Marriage

License Applications Book ALJ No. 2)

Thomas, William H., 1881-1942 (Grove Presbyterian Church Cemetery)

Thomas, William Henry (colored), 1861-1933, native of Richmond, VA, parents unknown (Death certificate)

Thomas, Willie H., see William Thomas, q.v.

Thompkins, Andrew, 1867-1941, age not given (Death certificate; Alms House Record Book)

Thompson's General Store and Post Office, High Point, Isaac W. Thompson, prop. and postmaster (*Country Stores: Harford County's Rural Heritage*, by Henry C. Peden, Jr. and Jack L. Shagena, Jr., 2015, p. 248)

Thompson's General Store, Boothby Hill, W. E. Thompson, prop. (*Country Stores: Harford County's Rural Heritage*, by Henry C. Peden, Jr. and Jack L. Shagena, Jr., 2015, p. 248)

Thompson, Ada (Treadway), 1853-1932 (Wesleyan Chapel Methodist Church Cemetery); wife of Amos Thompson, q.v.

Thompson, Agnes C., 1883-1943 (Rock Run Methodist Church Cemetery); wife of Irving J. Thompson, q.v.

Thompson, Albert Harold, 1878-1947, native of Harford Co., born 24 Nov 1878, son of Charles F. Thompson and Emily E. Baker (Death certificate)

Thompson, Albert L., born 3rd mo., 25th day, 1873, son of Isaac H. and Annie W. Thompson (Deer Creek Friends Record of Monthly Meeting, First Month, 1883, Register which recorded earlier births)

Thompson, Alfred, 1850-1923 (Wesleyan Chapel Methodist Church Cemetery)

Thompson, Alice (colored), 1882-1915, native of Harford Co., born 2 Mar 1882, daughter of Henry Thompson and Clara Stansbury (Death certificate - married name Stephenson)

Thompson, Alice Maud (Payne), 1872-1939 (Christ Episcopal Church Cemetery); wife of Isaac W. Thompson, q.v.

Thompson, Alice R. (Ward), 1852-1902 (Wesleyan Chapel Methodist Church Cemetery); wife of John Wesley Thompson, q.v.

Thompson, Amos, 1847-1910 (Wesleyan Chapel Methodist Church Cemetery); farmer, near Swan Creek (*Havre de Grace Republican*, 7 Feb 1890)

Thompson, Angeline (Whitaker), 1829-1892 (Christ Episcopal Church Cemetery)

Thompson, Anna E., see Ethel Evans Thompson, q.v.

Thompson, Anna Elizabeth (Parker), 1867-1950 (Ebenezer Methodist Church Cemetery)

Thompson, Annie G., 1872-1913 (Calvary Methodist Church Cemetery)

Thompson, Annie L., 1876-1951 (Dublin Southern Cemetery)

Thompson, Annie M., 1861-1935 (Angel Hill Cemetery)

Thompson, Annie W., see Albert L. Thompson, Stanley C. Thompson, Arthur B. Thompson and Benjamin Hayes Thompson, q.v.

Thompson, Arthur B., born 10th mo., 4th day, 1878, son of Isaac H. and Annie W. Thompson (Deer Creek Friends Record of Monthly Meeting, First Month, 1883, Register which recorded earlier births)

Thompson, Arthur Baker, 1881-1952 (Baker Cemetery)

Thompson, Augustus Bradford, 1865-1940 (Wesleyan Chapel Methodist Church Cemetery); native of Harford Co. (Bailey Funeral Home Records); treated by unidentified doctor in 1890 ("Medical Account Book – 1890," Historical Society of Harford County Archives Folder)

Thompson, B. Amos, 1846-1909 (Fellowship Cemetery)

Thompson, Benjamin Hayes, 1882-1905 (Darlington Cemetery); born 6th mo., 4th day, 1882 son of Isaac H. and Annie W. Thompson (Deer Creek Friends Record of Monthly Meeting, First Month, 1883, Register which recorded earlier births)

Thompson, Bennett Yost, 1883-1956 (Mt. Zion Methodist Church Cemetery)

Thompson, Bess (Stuart), 1884-1970 (Mt. Zion Methodist Church Cemetery)

Thompson, Birdie E., 1879-1945 (Cokesbury Memorial Methodist Church Cemetery)

Thompson, C. B., sneak boat duck hunter (*Havre de Grace Republican*, 7 Nov 1890)

Thompson, Carrell J. (colored), born -- Jul 1883, native of Maryland, son of George Thompson and ---- (1900 Aberdeen Census)

Thompson, Carrie Virginia (Johnson), 1881-1978, native of Churchville, daughter of William H. and Mary Elizabeth Johnson (*The Aegis*, 6 Jul 1978); wife of James Carroll Thompson, q.v.

Thompson, Catherine "Kate" (Calary), 1862-1925 (Bethel Presbyterian Church Cemetery Records; Death certificate); wife of Joseph Hopkins Thompson, q.v.

Thompson, Charles, 1870-1942 (Death certificate; Alms House Record Book)

Thompson, Charles, charter member, Havre de Grace Gunning Club (*Havre de Grace Republican*, 14 Nov 1890)

Thompson, Charles D., 1880-1952 (Mt. Zion Methodist Church Cemetery)

Thompson (Thomson), Charles, died 29 Nov 1900, age not given (Death certificate; Alms House Record Book)

Thompson, Charles F., see Albert H.Thompson, q.v.

Thompson, Charles J., postmaster, Churchville (*Havre de Grace Republican*, 18 Apr 1890); Civil War veteran, Churchville (*1890 Special Census of the Civil War Veterans of the State of Maryland*, by L. Tilden Moore, Volume III, p. 70); transferred from the voter registration list at Hall's Cross Roads, Second District (*Havre de Grace Republican*, 17 Oct 1890)

Thompson, Charles Sumner (colored), born 3 Mar 1883, son of George H. and Mary C. Thompson (St. George's Episcopal Church Register of Baptisms, pp. 2-3; 1900 Aberdeen Census stated he was born in Maryland in March 1881)

Thompson, Charles W., transferred from the voter registration list at Hopewell, Second District (*Havre de Grace Republican*, 17 Oct 1890)

Thompson, Charley H., 1883-1922 (Centre Methodist Church Cemetery)

Thompson, Divis, 1875-1955 (Dublin Southern Cemetery); born 4 May 1875, son of William H. Thompson and Margaret M. Russell (Bailey Funeral Home Records; William H. Thompson Bible, *Maryland Bible Records, Volume 5*, by Henry C. Peden, Jr., 2004, pp. 196-197, mistakenly called it the William F. Bible Record)

Thompson, Dollie, 1870-19-- (Fellowship Cemetery)

Thompson, Edith A. (Jones), 1862-1953 (Darlington Cemetery); native of Harford Co. (Bailey Funeral Home Records)

Thompson, Edwin R., 1868-1935 (Darlington Cemetery); native of Harford Co. (Bailey Funeral Home Records)

Thompson, Elizabeth, see George F. Moulsdale, q.v.

Thompson, Elizabeth C., 1812-1893 (Mt. Zion Methodist Church Cemetery)

Thompson, Ella, age 19 in 1890 (Marriage License Applications Book ALJ No. 2, 1891)

Thompson, Ella (Bailey), 1867-1920 (Joseph Thompson Bible, *Maryland Bible Records, Volume 2*, by Henry C. Peden, Jr., 2003, pp. 156-157; Death certificate); see Ella Bailey, q.v.

Thompson, Ella Mindwell (Olcott), 1885-1964 (Christ Episcopal Church Cemetery)

Thompson, Emily H. (Gilliss), 1837-1916, resident of Havre de Grace, native of Worcester Co., MD (Death certificate)

Thompson, Emma, businesswoman (trader's license), Havre de Grace (*Havre de Grace Republican*, 30 May 1890)

Thompson, Emma (colored), see Mary A. Hopkins (colored), q.v.

Thompson, Ethel Evans, born 15 Nov 1885, daughter of George J. and Anna E. Thompson (St. George's Episcopal Church Register of Baptisms, pp. 4-5)

Thompson, Eugene L., 1871-1956, native of Maryland, born 12 May 1872, son of Goldsmith Thompson and Elizabeth Wilson (Pennington Funeral Home Records; Cokesbury Memorial Methodist Church Cemetery); see Lonnie W. Woods, q.v.

Thompson, Evan, 1835-1920 (Wesleyan Chapel Methodist Church Cemetery); miller, near Webster *(Havre de Grace Republican,* 10 Jan 1890)

Thompson, Everett W., 1830-1891 (Wesleyan Chapel Methodist Church Cemetery)

Thompson, Florence S. (Beale), 1882-1967 (Mt. Zion Methodist Church Cemetery)

Thompson, Frances, see Margaret Lay and H. Elwood Thompson, q.v.

Thompson, Francis C., 1861-1934 (Slateville Cemetery, York Co., PA); native of Harford Co., born 8 Feb 1861, son of William Thompson and Margaret Russell (Harkins Funeral Home Records)

Thompson, Frank Elmer, born 8 Nov 1888, son of Joseph Hopkins Thompson and Catherine Callery (Bethel Presbyterian Church Cemetery Records)

Thompson, G., pitcher, Kennedy Baseball Club, of Havre de Grace, 1890 *(Havre de Grace Republican*, 25 Jul 1890)

Thompson, George, born 1859, died ---- (Calvary Methodist Church Cemetery)

Thompson, George (colored), born -- Oct 1837, native of Virginia (1900 Aberdeen Census); see Carrell J. Thompson (colored) and Grace Thompson (colored), q.v.

Thompson, George (colored), born -- Mar 1879, native of Maryland (1900 Aberdeen Census)

Thompson, George J., widower, age 34 in 1890 (Marriage License Applications Book ALJ No. 2, 1890); also see Ethel Evans Thompson, q.v.

Thompson, George W., 1857-1922 (Angel Hill Cemetery); see Hollis Thompson, q.v.

Thompson, Goldsmith, 1835-1906 (Cokesbury Memorial Methodist Church Cemetery); see Eugene L. Thompson, q.v.

Thompson, Grace G. (Miss), treasurer, Young Men's Christian Endeavor Society at Wesleyan Chapel *(Havre de Grace Republican*, 7 Feb 1890); vice president, Forest Literary Society, of Wesleyan Chapel *(Havre de Grace Republican*, 21 Nov and 19 Dec 1890)

Thompson, Grace (colored), 1888-1911, native of Mt. Calvary, Harford Co., born 7 Apr 1888, daughter of George H. Thompson, of Virginia, and Mary Ringgold, of Baltimore (Death certificate; 1900 Aberdeen Census stated Gracey was born in April 1886)

Thompson, Guy N., 1888-1930 (Bethel Presbyterian Church Cemetery Records)

Thompson, H. Elwood, 1887-1939, native of Harford Co., born 26 Feb 1887, son of Henry and Frances Thompson (Death certificate; Dublin Southern Cemetery)

Thompson, H. R., sneak boat duck hunter *(Havre de Grace Republican*, 7 Nov 1890)

Thompson, Hannah (Bond) (colored), 1851-1915, native of Harford Co. (Death certificate)

Thompson, Hannah (Morgan) (colored), c1874-1944, native of Harford Co., daughter of William Morgan and Amelia Miller (Death certificate)

Thompson, Hannah C. (Botts), 1851-1926 (Death certificate; St. George's Episcopal Church Cemetery)

Thompson, Hannah E. (Harvey), 1872-1964 (Highland Presbyterian Church Cemetery); native of Whiteford, Harford Co., born 25 Aug 1872, daughter of Thomas Harvey and Jane Hughes (Harkins Funeral Home Records)

Thompson, Harry J., 1869-1952 (Highland Presbyterian Church Cemetery)

Thompson, Harvey, charter member, Havre de Grace Gunning Club *(Havre de Grace Republican*, 14 Nov 1890)

Thompson, Helen W., 1884-1955 (Baker Cemetery)

Thompson, Henry, see Margaret Lay and H. Elwood Thompson, q.v.

Thompson, Henry (colored), see Alice Thompson (colored), q.v.

Thompson, Hester A., 1839-1927 (Wesleyan Chapel Methodist Church Cemetery); wife of John Crawford Thompson, q.v.; also see Hugh Crawford Thompson, q.v.

Thompson, Hollis, 1890-1971 (Angel Hil Cemetery); native of Street, Harford Co., born 23 Mar 1890, son of George Washington Thompson and Susan Elizabeth Thompson (Pennington Funeral Home Records)

Thompson, Hugh Crawford, 1868-1900 (Wesleyan Chapel Methodist Church Cemetery); born 27 Jan 1868, son of John Crawford Thompson and Hester Ann Gilbert (*The Hughes Genealogy, 1636-1953*, by Joseph Lee Hughes, 1953, p. 119); musician, Forest Literary Society, of Wesleyan Chapel (*Havre de Grace Republican*, 19 Dec 1890); farmer near Hoopman's Chapel [Wesleyan Chapel] and husband of Marian Cooley (Death certificate)

Thompson, Ida Florence (Deckman), 1866-1943 (Wesleyan Chapel Methodist Church Cemetery); native of Harford Co. (Bailey Funeral Home Records); wife of Augustus Bradford Thompson, q.v.

Thompson, Irving Joseph, 1874-1952 (Rock Run Methodist Church Cemetery)

Thompson, Isaac, storekeeper at High Point (*The Aegis & Intelligencer*, 4 Jul 1890) prelate, Marshall's Lodge No. 99, Knights of Pythias, at Jarrettsville (*The Aegis & Intelligencer*, 18 Jul 1890); recorder, Marshall's Lodge, Knights of Pythias, of Jarrettsville (*Havre de Grace Republican*, 25 Jul 1890)

Thompson, Isaac H., 1831-1892 (Darlington Cemetery); trustee, Shure's Landing School No. 19, Fifth District (*Havre de Grace Republican*, 30 May 1890); also see Albert L. Thompson, Stanley C. Thompson, Arthur B. Thompson and Benjamin Hayes Thompson, q.v.

Thompson, Isaac W., 1873-1927 (Dublin Southern Cemetery); native of Maryland, born 22 Mar 1873, son of William H. Thompson and Margaret Russell (Bailey Funeral Home Records)

Thompson, Isaac Whitaker, 1855-1927 (Christ Episcopal Church Cemetery); assistant officer of [voter] registration, Third District (*The Aegis & Intelligencer*, 12 Sep 1890)

Thompson, J. Frank, 1844-1926 (Wesleyan Chapel Methodist Church Cemetery); native of Maryland, merchant, married, resided near Havre de Grace (Death certificate)

Thompson, J. Nelson, 1872-1948 (Wesleyan Chapel Methodist Church Cemetery)

Thompson, James, 1842-1919 (Emory Methodist Church Cemetery); Civil War veteran, Stearns Precinct (*1890 Special Census of the Civil War Veterans of the State of Maryland*, by L. Tilden Moore, Volume III, p. 85); farmer, at the Cedars, Dublin District (*The Aegis & Intelligencer*, 4 Jul 1890); see James Harry Thmpson and Louis S. Thompson, q.v.

Thompson, James Carroll, 1882-1937, native of Maryland, son of George Thompson and ---- (Death certificate gave his name as Carol Thompson, but 1978 obituary of his widow Carrie gave his full name)

Thompson, James H., 1826-1898 (Providence Methodist Church Cemetery)

Thompson, James Harry, 1869-1952 (Highland Presbyterian Church Cemetery); native of Harford Co., born 20 Sep 1869, son of James Thompson and Margaret Reynolds (Harkins Funeral Home Records)

Thompson, James W., 1845-1913 (Baker Cemetery)

Thompson, Jane, 1842-1908 (Calvary Methodist Church Cemetery)

Thompson, Jemima, 1832-1900 (Providence Methodist Church Cemetery)

Thompson, John Crawford, 1841-1913 (Wesleyan Chapel Cemetery; *The Hughes Genealogy, 1636-1953*, by Joseph Lee Hughes, 1953, p. 119); trustee, Forest Institute, School No. 10, Second District (*Havre de Grace Republican*, 30 May 1890); see Ray Eldo Thompson, q.v.

Thompson, John Emory, 1876-1963 (Church of the Ascension Cemetery); native of Scarboro, Harford Co., born 18 Aug 1876, son of John W. Thompson and Sarah Huff (Harkins Funeral Home Records); son of William John Thompson and Sarah Rachel Huff (Joseph Thompson Bible, *Maryland Bible Records, Volume 2*, by Henry C. Peden, Jr., 2003, pp. 156-157)

Thompson, John G., 1831-1897 (*Barnes-Bailey Genealogy*, by Walter D. Barnes, 1939, p. G-8)

Thompson, John Gillis, 1870-1950 (Angel Hill Cemetery)

Thompson, John H., 1866-1933, native of Dublin, Harford Co. (Death certificate)

Thompson, John W., age 23 in 1890 (Marriage License Applications Book ALJ No. 2, 1891)

Thompson, John W., 1887-1957 (Calvary Methodist Church Cemetery)

Thompson, John Wesley, 1841-1900 (Wesleyan Chapel Methodist Church Cemetery); trustee, Paradise School No. 2, Second District (*Havre de Grace Republican*, 30 May 1890); Civil War veteran, Havre de Grace (*1890 Special Census of the Civil War Veterans of the State of Maryland*, by L. Tilden Moore, Volume III, p. 68)

Thompson, Joseph Edmund, 1886-1966 (Christ Episcopal Church Cemetery)

Thompson, Joseph Hopkins, 1857-1913 (Bethel Presbyterian Church Cemetery Records)

Thompson, Josiah Ross, 1853-1923 (Centre Methodist Church Cemetery)

Thompson, Lida "Lidie" E., 1853-1935 (Wesleyan Chapel Methodist Church Cemetery); wife of J. Frank Thompson, q.v.

Thompson, Lidia, see Clifford Santmyer, q.v.

Thompson, Lonnie W. (Woods), 1876-1950 (Cokesbury Memorial Methodist Church Cemetery)

Thompson, Louella A., 1872-1920 (Wesleyan Chapel Methodist Church Cemetery)

Thompson, Louis G., 1885-1956 (Emory Methodist Church Cemetery); native of Street, Harford Co., born 23 Feb 1885, son of James Thompson and Margaret Reynolds (Harkins Funeral Home Records)

Thompson, Lydia A., 1838-1907 (Broad Creek Friends Cemetery)

Thompson, Lydia Elmira, born 7 Feb 1874, daughter of William John and Sarah Rachel Thompson (Joseph Thompson Bible, *Maryland Bible Records, Volume 2*, by Henry C. Peden, Jr., 2003, pp. 156-157)

Thompson, M. L. (Miss), secretary, High Point Lyceum (*Havre de Grace Republican*, 21 Feb 1890)

Thompson, M. Margaret, 1864-1954 (Wesleyan Chapel Methodist Church Cemetery)

Thompson, Mahlon, 1819-1891 (Cokesbury Memorial Methodist Church Cemetery)

Thompson, Malvina J. (Jones), 1869-1954 (Bailey Funeral Home Records)

Thompson, Margaret, see Margaret Lay and Eldridge E. Scarborough, q.v.

Thompson, Margaret J., 1842-1919 (Emory Methodist Church Cemetery)

Thompson, Margaret M. (Russell), see Divis Thompson, q.v.

Thompson, Martha E., see Mary R. Price, q.v.

Thompson, Martha J. (Forsythe), 1819-1894 (Wesleyan Chapel Methodist Church Cemetery)

Thompson, Martha J. (Howard) (colored), 1853-1900, native of Maryland, resided at Dublin, Harford Co. (Death certificate)

Thompson, Mary, born 25 Aug 1888, daughter of Joseph Hopkins Thompson and Catherine Calary (Bethel Presbyterian Church Cemetery Records); see Mary Bosley, q.v.

Thompson, Mary (colored), see David Hill (colored), q.v.

Thompson, Mary A. (colored), see Mary A. Hopkins (colored), q.v.

Thompson, Mary E., see Chester Ellwood Deckman, q.v.

Thompson, Mary E., 1872-1949 (Rock Run Methodist Church Cemetery)

Thompson, Mary Fannie, 1862-1938 (Centre Methodist Church Cemetery)

Thompson, Mary Jane (Miss), 1879-1954 (Broad Creek Friends Cemetery); native of Harford Co. (Bailey Funeral Home Records)

Thompson, Mattie R., 1877-1934 (Wesleyan Chapel Methodist Church Cemetery)

Thompson, Minnie E. (Wells), 1884-1909 (Baker Cemetery)

Thompson, Myrtle (Armstrong), 1883-1950 (Baker Cemetery)

Thompson, Noah, 1861-1944 (Rock Run Methodist Church Cemetery)

Thompson, Norvel R., 1879-1923 (Baker Cemetery)

Thompson, Oliver E., 1850-1901 (Wesleyan Chapel Methodist Church Cemetery)

Thompson, Otto Lynn, 1888-1897 (Bethel Presbyterian Church Cemetery Records); born 18 Nov 1888, son of Joseph Hopkins Thompson and Catherine Calary, q.v.

Thompson, Pearl C., see H. Elwood Thompson, q.v.

Thompson, R. Leonard, 1873-1936 (Cokesbury Memorial Methodist Church Cemetery)

Thompson, Ray Eldo, 1876-1932 (Wesleyan Chapel Methodist Church Cemetery); native of Harford Co., born 27 Jan 1876, son of John Crawford Thompson and Hester Ann Gilbert (Death certificate)

Thompson, Rebecca, see John G. Devoe, q.v.

Thompson, Robert H., 1850-1929 (Providence Methodist Church Cemetery)

Thompson, Sadie Kate (Cross), 1877-1938 (Angel Hill Cemetery), wife of John Gillis Thompson, q.v.

Thompson, Samuel E., Jr., 1885-1952 (St. Mary's Episcopal Church Cemetery); native of Harford Co., born 5 Sep 1885, son of Samuel E. Thompson and Capitola B. Nelson (Pennington Funeral Home Records)

Thompson, Samuel J., 1877-1970 (Pine Grove Church Cemetery); native of Pylesville, Harford Co., born 30 Sep 1877, son of Samuel S. Thompson and Clara K. Denbow (Harkins Funeral Home Records)

Thompson, Samuel S., see Samuel J. Thompson, q.v.

Thompson, Samuel W., 1859-1924 (Ebenezer Methodist Church Cemetery); assistant superintendent, Ebenezer M. E. Church Sunday School (*Havre de Grace Republican*, 25 Apr 1890)

Thompson, Sarah (Barnes), 1832-1916 (*Barnes-Bailey Genealogy,* by Walter D. Barnes, 1939, p. G-8)

Thompson, Sarah E., 1840-1896 (Wesleyan Chapel Methodist Church Cemetery); wife of Evan Tbompson, q.v.

Thompson, Sarah Elizabeth, see Hollis Thompson, q.v.

Thompson, Sarah Rachel (Huff), 1845-1923 (Broad Creek Friends Cemetery)

Thompson, Solomon (colored), see Mary A. Hopkins (colored), q.v.

Thompson, Stanley C., born 1st mo., 13th day, 1876, son of Isaac H. and Annie W. Thompson (Deer Creek Friends Record of Monthly Meeting, First Month, 1883, Register which recorded earlier births)

Thompson, Susan "Susie" E. (Cullum), 1862-1930 (Calvary Methodist Church Cemetery)

Thompson, Susan G. (Moore), 1812-1893 (Wesleyan Chapel Methodist Church Cemetery)

Thompson, Thomas H., 1862-1924 (Darlington Cemetery)

Thompson, Whitaker, mercantile business, High Point (*The Aegis & Intelligencer*, 14 Feb 1890)

Thompson, Wilborn Gilmore, 1875-1950 (Smith Chapel Methodist Church Cemetery)

Thompson, William D., served on a grand jury, Fifth District, 1890 (*Havre de Grace Republican*, 31 Oct 1890; *The Aegis & Intelligencer*, 14 Nov 1890)

Thompson, William E., 1889-1960 (Wesleyan Chapel Methodist Church Cemetery)

Thompson, William H., 1829-1907 (Dublin Southern Cemetery; William H. Thompson Bible, *Maryland Bible Records, Volume 5*, by Henry C. Peden, Jr., 2004, pp. 196-197, mistakenly called it the William F. Bible Record); see Isaac W. Thompson, Mae McCann and Francis C. Thompson, q.v.

Thompson, William H., 1853-1916 (Wesleyan Chapel Methodist Church Cemetery)

Thompson, William H., 1858-1930 (Calvary Methodist Church Cemetery)

Thompson, William J., 1840-1903 (Broad Creek Friends Cemetery)

Thompson, William John, see Alvira T. McFadden, q.v.

Thompson, William Oscar, 1870-1955 (Broad Creek Friends Cemetery); born 19 Nov 1870, son of William John and Sarah Rachel Thompson (Joseph Thompson Bible, *Maryland Bible Records, Volume 2*, by Henry C. Peden, Jr., 2003, pp. 156-157); 1870-1955, native of Harford Co. (Bailey Funeral Home Records)

Thompson, William T., 1859-1935 (Darlington Cemetery); native of Dublin, Harford Co. (Bailey Funeral Home Records)

Thorne, Alfred, native of England, filed for naturalized on 10 Sep 1890 Harford County Circuit Court Minute Book ALJ No. 5, p. 201)

Thorpe, Mary Murdock, see Mary Murdock Carver, q.v.

Thorpy, Catherine (Hallahan), 1870-1937 (Mt. Erin Cemetery), second wife of John J. Thorpy, q.v.

Thorpy, Frank J., 1884-1920 (Mt. Erin Cemetery)

Thorpy, Hannah B., 1871-1917 (Mt. Erin Cemetery)

Thorpy, John J., 1872-1932 (Mt. Erin Cemetery)

Thorpy, Margaret, 1846-1929 (Mt. Erin Cemetery)

Thorpy, Mary (Miss), member, St. Patrick's Women's Total Abstinence Society, Havre de Grace (*Havre de Grace Republican*, 31 Jan 1890, misspelled her name Torpey)

Thorpy, Mary F. (Salick), 1872-1911 (Mt. Erin Cemetery), first wife of John J. Thorpy, q.v.

Thorpy, Thomas M., 1877-1903 (Mt. Erin Cemetery)

Thurston, Zephaniah, 1885-1939 (Wesleyan Chapel Methodist Church Cemetery)

Tibbit (Tibbett), William, died -- Oct 1899, age not given (Alms House Record Book)

Tighe, Cecilia, born 8 Sep 1886, daughter of James Tighe and Annie Carroll, natives of Balluia, County Mayo, Ireland (*The Hughes Genealogy, 1636-1953*, by Joseph Lee Hughes, 1953, p. 129)

Tignor, Margaret, see Leila Barnes, q.v.

Tignor (Tigner), Mary, see John Robert Keen and Bennett Aquila Keen, q.v.

Tildon, Annie (Whims) (colored), 1869-1934 (Death certificate)

Tildon, Annie M. (colored), born -- Jun 1875, native of Maryland (1900 Aberdeen Census); wife of Frank Tildon (colored), q.v.

Tildon, Benjamin W. (colored), c1840-1900 (Union Methodist Church Cemetery, Aberdeen); 39th U.S.C. I., Civil War veteran, Michaelsville (*1890 Special Census of the Civil War Veterans of the State of Maryland*, by L. Tilden Moore, Volume III, p. 63)

Tildon, Cecelia (Dallam) (colored), 1832-1918, native of Harford Co. (Death certificate)

Tildon, Cecelia E. (colored), see George Michael Moore (colored), q.v.

Tildon, Delia (colored), see Charles S. Stansbury (colored) and Carrie V. Thigpen (colored), q.v.

Tildon, Frank (colored), born -- Apr 1877, native of Maryland (1900 Aberdeen Census)

Tildon, Frederick (colored), see Mary Tildon, q.v.

Tildon, Frederick D. (colored), resident of Michaelsville, graduate of Lincoln College (*Havre de Grace Republican*, 6 Jun 1890)

Tildon, Harriet Anne (Garrettson) (colored), 1844-1901 (Death certificate)

Tildon, Henry E. (colored), 1842-1901, "native of America" (Death certificate)

Tildon, Hester (colored), see John Thomas Dennison (colored), q.v.

Tildon, John (colored), see Sarah Tildon (colored), q.v.

Tildon, John C. (colored), see William Russell Tildon (colored), q.v.

Tildon, Mary (colored), 1885-1913, native of Harford Co., born 23 Aug 1885, daughter of Frederick Tildon and Hattie Ransom, natives of Harford Co. (Death certificate - married name Freeman; Union Methodist Church Cemetery, Aberdeen tombstone inscribed Mary P. P. Freeman, wife of Alexander Freeman)

Tildon, Sarah (colored), 1888-1914, native of near Aberdeen, Harford Co., born 10 May 1888, daughter of John Tildon and Mary Field (Death certificate - married name Hall)

Tildon, William Russell (colored), 1868-1900, resided at Michaelsville, Harford Co., son of John C. Tildon and Hattie S. Brown (Death certificate)

Tildon, William S. (colored), 1840-1931 (Union Methodist Church Cemetery, Aberdeen); trustee, Michaelsville Colored School No. 2, Second District (*Havre de Grace Republican*, 30 May 1890); executive committeeman, State Republican League (*Havre de Grace Republican*, 9 May 1890)

Tilghman, William H. (colored), c1862-1924 (St. James AME Church Cemetery); native of Maryland, local preacher, resided in Havre de Grace, son of William H. Tilghman and ---- (Death certificate)

Tillman, Ellanora (colored), 1871-1911, native of Harford Co., born 18 Mar 1871, daughter of Lewis Tillman, native of Maryland's Eastern Shore, and Delia Wilson, of Harford Co. (Death certificate - married name Bond)

Tillson, Rachel (colored), see Rachel Lynn (colored), q.v.

Tilson, Mandie (colored), see Isaac Williams (colored), q.v.

Timbers, David (colored), 1846-1923 (Union Methodist Church Cemetery, Aberdeen)

Timbers, Lizzie (colored), see Ida M. Christy (colored), q.v.

Timbers, Olivia A. (colored), 1847-1914 (Union Methodist Church Cemetery, Aberdeen)

Timblick, Henry C., 1876-1900, native of Harford Co., resident of Dublin, son of William Timblick and Lizzie ---- (Death certificate)

Timmons, Alice L., 1854-1930 (Cokesbury Memorial Methodist Church Cemetery); acquired land in April 1890 (*The Aegis & Intelligencer*, 9 May 1890)

Timmons John E., 1846-1919 (Mountain Christian Church Cemetery)

Timmons, John Oscar, 1882-1960 (Mountain Christian Church Cemetery)

Timmons, Joseph R., 1852-1929 (Cokesbury Memorial Methodist Church Cemetery)

Timmons, Kathryn L., 1888-1914 (Cokesbury Memorial Methodist Church Cemetery)

Timmons, Martha Priscilla, 1882-1966 (Mountain Christian Church Cemetery)

Timmons, Mary L., 1848-1923 (Mountain Christian Church Cemetery)

Timmons, Matilda F., 1883-19-- (Cokesbury Memorial Methodist Church Cemetery)

Timmons, Walter S., 1887-1932 (Cokesbury Memorial Methodist Church Cemetery)

Timmons, William W., 1878-1839 (Centre Methodist Church Cemetery)

Tindall, Hannah, age 21 in 1890 (Marriage License Applications Book ALJ No. 2, 1891)

Tinges, Albert Howard, 1852-1900, railroad worker, native of Maryland, resided near Havre de Grace (Death certificate)

Tinker, David (colored), see Eliza Christy (colored), q.v.

Tinsley, Mack (colored), 1883-1953 (Clark's Chapel Methodist Church Cemetery)

Tinson, Charles (colored), father of George Anna Rice (colored), q.v.

Tinson, Estelle (colored), see Ella Christy (colored), q.v.

Tinson, Ethel (colored), 1884-1920 (Union Methodist Church Cemetery, Aberdeen)

Tinson, Frances E. (colored), see Raymond S. Buchanan (colored), q.v.

Tinson, Ida A. (colored), 1886-1919 (Union Methodist Church Cemetery, Aberdeen)

Tinson, Jacob A. (colored, 1860-1937 (Union Methodist Church Cemetery, Aberdeen)

Tinson, Margaret (colored), see George Francis Tinson (colored), q.v.

Tipman, Edward, c1882-1937, resident of Forest Hill, parents unknown (Death certificate)

Tipton, Alfred Slade, 1850-1919 (Jarrettsville Cemetery); farmer, near Jarrettsville (*The Aegis & Intelligencer*, 11 Jul 1890); justice of the peace, Fourth District (*Havre de Grace Republican*, 21 Feb 1890); director, Jarrettsville Land, Loan and Building Association (*Havre de Grace Republican*, 18 Apr 1890)

Tipton, Catherine B. (Deets), 1823-1896 (Bethel Presbyterian Church Cemetery Records); widow of William B. Tipton (1821-1880)

Tipton, John F., 1853-1944 (Bethel Presbyterian Church Cemetery Records); resident of Jarrettsville (*The Aegis & Intelligencer*, 18 Apr 1890)

Tipton, Mina Jemima (Duncan), 1859-1940 (Jarrettsville Cemetery); treasurer, Jarrettsville M. E. Church Sunday School (*The Aegis & Intelligencer*, 28 Mar 1890); wife of Alfred S. Tipton, q.v.

Tittle, Alice (colored), wife of Nelson Tittle, q.v.

Tittle, Amos (colored), Civil War veteran, Black Horse (*1890 Special Census of the Civil War Veterans of the State of Maryland*, by L. Tilden Moore, Volume III, p. 79); died testate in 1890 and his only named heir was his wife Sarah A. Tittle (Harford County Will Book JMM 11:149)

Tittle, Nelson (colored), 1809-1899, farmer at Madonna, native of Maryland (Death certificate)

Tittle, Oliver (colored), age 27 in 1890 (Marriage License Applications Book ALJ No. 2, 1891)

Tittle, Sarah A., wife of Amos Tittle, q.v.

Toal (Tole), Sarah, see Henry Ignatius Kehoe, Irene Celeste Kehoe and Pauline Angela Kahoe, q.v.

Tobias, Isaac Herbert, 1875-1836 (Darlington Cemetery)

Tobias, Maud (Ramsay), 1877-1933 (Darlington Cemetery)

Tobin, Alfred F., 1884-1969 (Baker Cemetery)

Tobin, Dena C., 1890-1955 (Baker Cemetery)

Tobin, Edward, son of James H. Tobin, near Hickory (*The Aegis & Intelligencer*, 28 Feb 1890)

Tobin, Edward I., 1890-1960 (Baker Cemetery)

Tobin, Edward T., acquired land in February 1890 (*The Aegis & Intelligencer*, 7 Mar 1890)

Tobin, Ellen, 1834-1903 (St. Francis de Sales Catholic Church Cemetery); wife of Martin Tobin, q.v.

Tobin, Frank J., 1866-1892 (St. Ignatius Catholic Church Cemetery)

Tobin, Ida M. (Preston), 1882-1978 (Wesleyan Chapel Methodist Church Cemetery)

Tobin, J. Spaulding, 1872-1894, son of Martin and Ellen Tobin (St. Francis de Sales Catholic Church Cemetery)

Tobin, James, clay pigeon shooter, Churchville (*The Aegis & Intelligencer*, 7 Feb 1890)

Tobin, James H., resident near Hickory (*The Aegis & Intelligencer*, 28 Feb 1890); see Edward Tobin and William Tobin, q.v.

Tobin, James H. (Mrs.), daughter of Alice Ann Lingan, q.v.

Tobin, Jeremiah, see Maggie Tobin, q.v.

Tobin, John T., c1870-1921, resided in Havre de Grace, native of Maryland (Death certificate)

Tobin, Maggie, died 3 Feb 1900, age not stated, single, resided in Havre de Grace, daughter of Jeremiah Tobin (Death certificate incomplete)

Tobin, Marie J., born 1889, died ---- (St. Ignatius Catholic Church Cemetery)

Tobin, Martha A. (Mrs.), c1856-1914 (Mt. Erin Cemetery; Death certificate)

Tobin, Martha Ann, 1862-1898 (St. Ignatius Catholic Church Cemetery)

Tobin, Martin, 1832-1911 (St. Francis de Sales Catholic Church Cemetery); resident near Harford Furnace (*The Aegis & Intelligencer*, 9 May 1890)

Tobin, Mary, 1814-1892 (St. Ignatius Catholic Church Cemetery)

Tobin, Mollie E., age 20, married Oliver C. Bowman on 20 Nov 1890 at St. Ignatius Catholic Church at Hickory (Marriage License Applications Book ALJ No. 2, 1890; *The Aegis & Intelligencer*, 12 Dec 1890, mistakenly gave his name as Boarman)

Tobin, William, son of James H. Tobin, near Hickory (*The Aegis & Intelligencer*, 28 Feb 1890)

Tobin, William M., 1963-1953 (Wesleyan Chapel Methodist Church Cemetery); acquired land in February 1890 (*The Aegis & Intelligencer*, 7 Mar 1890)

Todd, ----, pitcher, Nonpareil Baseball Club, Aberdeen (*Havre de Grace Republican*, 6 Jun 1890)

Todd, Frank F., sneak boat duck hunter (*Havre de Grace Republican*, 7 Nov 1890)

Todd, James R., uncalled for letter in Bel Air P. O., 1890 (*The Aegis & Intelligencer*, 14 Nov 1890)

Todd, John E., sneak boat duck hunter (*Havre de Grace Republican*, 7 Nov 1890)

Todd, William, sneak boat duck hunter (*Havre de Grace Republican*, 7 Nov 1890)

Tolan, Hugh, 1860-1935 (Alms House Record Book)

Tollenger, Alice C., 1854-1904 (Rock Run Methodist Church Cemetery); acquired land in April 1890 (*The Aegis & Intelligencer*, 9 May 1890, spelled her name Tollinger)

Tollenger, Asel, 1837-1918 (Rock Run Methodist Church Cemetery); farmer and owner of *Friendship Farm*, Second District, near Rock Run Church (*Havre de Grace Republican*, 14 Feb 1890 and 28 Mar 1890 spelled his name Tollinger; *The Aegis & Intelligencer*, 7 Feb 1890 and 21 Mar 1890); also see Mrs. Alonzo Deaver, q.v.

Tollenger, Clara Jane (Gallion), 1863-1940, native of Harford Co. (Bailey Funeral Home Records)

Tollenger, George W., 1885-1927 (Rock Run Methodist Church Cemetery)

Tollenger, Hannah E. (Craig), 1868-1904 (Rock Run Methodist Church Cemetery)

Tollenger, Mary R., 1886-1966 (Rock Run Methodist Church Cemetery)

Tollenger, Otis, 1858-1932 (Bailey Funeral Home Records spelled the name Tollinger); age 31 in 1890 (Marriage License Applications Book ALJ No. 2); road surveying chain man, Second District (*Havre de Grace Republican*, 4 Jul 1890); seine fisherman, at Snake Island in the Susquehanna River (*The Aegis & Intelligencer*, 4 Apr 1890)

Tollenger, Robert J., new name on the voter registration list at Hopewell, Second District (*Havre de Grace Republican*, 17 Oct 1890)

Tolley, Anna E (Barton), 1862-1921 (Old Brick Baptist Church Cemetery); wife of Joseph A. Tolley, q.v.

Tolley, Anna Mary (Moore), 1845-1903 (St. James Episcopal Church Cemetery, Monkton; wife of Edward Carvill Tolley, q.v.

Tolley, Charles (colored), resident of Fourth District (*The Aegis & Intelligencer*, 21 Feb 1890); charged with larceny in 1890, found guilty, and sent to the House of Corrections for 6 months (Harford County Criminal Docket, 1888-1892, p. 82)

Tolley, Edward Carvill, 1843-1921 (St. James Episcopal Church Cemetery, Monkton)

Tolley, Joseph A., 1852-1930 (Old Brick Baptist Church Cemetery)

Tolley, May (Miss), resident of Taylor (*The Aegis & Intelligencer*, 26 Dec 1890)

Tolley, Octavius H., juror, Fourth District (*Havre de Grace Republican*, 31 Oct 1890); Civil War veteran (Confederate), at Taylor (*1890 Special Census of the Civil War Veterans of the State of Maryland*, by L. Tilden Moore, Volume III, p. 77)

Tollinger, C., shortstop, Webster Baseball Club, of Webster (*Havre de Grace Republican*, 25 Jul 1890)

Tollinger, Clemency, see James Webster Trago, q.v.

Tollinger, Francina or Francisca, age 44 in 1890 (Marriage License Applications Book ALJ No. 2; married D. A. Dever on 4 Mar 1890 (*The Aegis & Intelligencer*, 7 Mar 1890)

Toner, James, charged with asssault in 1890, but no verdict was recorded in the docket book (Harford County Criminal Docket, 1888-1892, p. 98; *The Aegis & Intelligencer*, 14 Nov 1890)

Toney, Bessie J. (colored), 1885-1923, native of Maryland, born 22 Apr 1885, daughter of George Toney and Georganna White (Death certificate)

Toney, David M. (colored), 1875-1921, native of Maryland, born 25 Dec 1875, son of Joseph Toney and Urith F. "Fannie" Guy (Death certificate); see Joseph Edward Toney, q.v.

Toney, George (colored), see Bessie J. Toney (colored), q.v.

Toney, Hannah (colored), 1883-1928 (Tabernacle Mt. Zion Church Cemetery); native of Maryland, resided at Bel Air, born -- Feb 1883, daughter of Joseph Toney and Hannah Guy, natives of Maryland (Death certificate - married name Cox)

Toney, Hannah (Rice) (colored), 1888-1961 (*The Aegis*, 2 Feb 1971); wife of Joseph E. Toney, q.v.

Toney, Joseph (colored), father of Hannah Toney, q.v.; also see Joseph Edward Toney, q.v.

Toney, Joseph Edward ("Ned"), 1874-1949, native of Harford Co., born 17 Sep 1874, son of Joseph Toney and Fannie Guy (Death certificate)

Toney, Joseph M. (colored), 1847-1927, native of Maryland, parents unknown (Death certificate)

Toney, Lloyd (colored), acquired land in November 1890 (*The Aegis & Intelligencer*, 5 Dec 1890); see Martha Jane Toney, q.v.

Toney, Martha Jane (colored), 1853-1909, wife of Lloyd Toney, Sr. (Tabernacle Mt. Zion Methodist Church Cemetery)

Toney, William E. (colored), age 23 in 1889 (Marriage License Applications Book ALJ No. 2, 1889); resident of Third District (*The Aegis & Intelligencer*, 7 Nov 1890)

Torrence, Laura F., see Laura F. Slee, q.v.

Touchstone, Cornelia, see Fred C. Jones and James T. Jones, q.v.

Touchstone, S., acquired land in April 1890 (*The Aegis & Intelligencer*, 9 May 1890)

Touchton, Alfred M., 1848-1918 (Wesleyan Chapel Methodist Church Cemetery)

Touchton, Anna G., 1875-1964, native of Maryland, born 13 Mar 1875, daughter of John L Touchton and Mary G. Moulton (Pennington Funeral Home Records); student, Havre de Grace High School (*Havre de Grace Republican*, 31 Oct 1890, spelled the name Touchstone)

Touchton, Annie R., 1850-1930 (Wesleyan Chapel Methodist Church Cemetery); wife of Alfred M. Touchton, q.v.

Touchton, Edgar E., examiner on the Forest Road (*Havre de Grace Republican*, 14 Feb 1890, spelled hs name Touchton); assistant superintendent, Mt. Carmel M. P. Church, at Emmorton (*The Aegis & Intelligencer*, 27 Jun 1890, spelled the name Touchstone)

Touchton, Herman, 1822-1897, member of the Oddfellows (Wesleyan Chapel Methodist Church Cemetery)

Touchton, John L., 1842-1917 (Wesleyan Chapel Methodist Church Cemetery); see Anna G. Touchton, q.v.

Touchton, Lillian Jane, born 1873, daughter of Alfred M. and Annie E. Touchton (Bethel Presbyterian Church Cemetery Records)

Touchton, Mary G. (Moulton), 1844-1937 (Wesleyan Chapel Methodist Church Cemetery); Mrs. Tuchton, *(sic)* resident near Abingdon (*The Aegis & Intelligencer*, 8 Aug 1890); wife of John L. Touchton, q.v.

Touchton, Pamelia A., 1821-1903 (Wesleyan Chapel Methodist Church Cemetery); wife of Herman Touchton, q.v.

Touchton, Rachel, 1819-1903 (Wesleyan Chapel Methodist Church Cemetery)

Touchton, Walter M., 1885-1912, son of Alfred M. and Annie R. Touchton (Wesleyan Chapel Methodist Church Cemetery)

Tower, Margaret (colored), see George Washington Richardson (colored), q.v.

Towner, Gertrude Bonn, c1859-1922 (St. George's Episcopal Church Cemetery; *The Aegis & Intelligencer*, 28 Jul 1922); also see Jay Ferdindand Towner, Rena Towner, Joseph Bond Towner and Leonard Fair Towner, q.v.

Towner, Jay Ferdinand, 1857-1935 (St. George's Episcopal Church Cemetery); peach farmer, near Perryman (*The Aegis & Intelligencer*, 29 Aug 1890); commander-in-chief, Perryman Lodge No. 88, Order of the Golden Chain (*Havre de Grace Republican*, 27 Jun 1890); husband of Gertrude Bonn Towner; also see Rena Towner and Leonard Fair Towner and Joseph Bond Towner, q.v.

Towner, Jay Ferdinand, Jr., 1883-1947 (St. George's Episcopal Church Cemetery)

Towner, Joseph Bond, born 27 Jan 1886, son of Jay F. and Gertrude Towner (St. George's Episcopal Church Register of Baptisms, pp. 4-5)

Towner, Leonard Fair, 1888-1915 (St. George's Episcopal Church Cemetery); son of Jay F. and Gertrude Towner (St. George's Episcopal Church Register of Baptisms, p. 7, did not record the date of birth, but his death certificate states 10 Oct 1888)

Towner, Rena, born 24 Nov 1884, daughter of Jay F. and Gertrude B. Towner (St. George's Episcopal Church Register of Baptisms, pp. 4-5)

Townsley, Frank, resident near Upper Cross Roads (*The Aegis & Intelligencer*, 14 Mar 1890)

Townsley, George W., 1856-1895 (Rock Run Methodist Church Cemetery); property owner adjacent to Broadway in Bel Air (*The Aegis & Intelligencer*, 16 May 1890); also see Nellie Townsley, q.v.

Townsley, James, see James M. Townsley, q.v.

Townsley, James M., 1887-1967 (Emory Methodist Church Cemetery); native of Harford Co., born 22 May 1887, son of James Townsley and Anna Coe (Harkins Funeral Home Records)

Townsley, Lizzie (Miss), resident near Upper Cross Roads (*The Aegis & Intelligencer*, 14 Mar 1890)

Townsley, Louis E., 1890-1982 (Mountain Christian Church Cemetery)

Townsley, Margaret E., 1890-1955 (Jarrettsville Cemetery)

Townsley, Martha (Miss), resident near Upper Cross Roads (*The Aegis & Intelligencer*, 14 Mar 1890)

Townsley, Martha S., age 19 in 1890 (Marriage License Applications Book ALJ No. 2, 1890), married William Gunther on 24 Dec 1890 (marriage certificate)

Townsley, Mary A, 1890-1954 (Mountain Christian Church Cemetery)

Townsley, Mary E., see Mary E. Bradley, q.v.

Townsley, Myrtle I., 1888-1958 (Jarrettsville Cemetery)

Townsley, Nellie, age 7, eldest daughter of George Townsley, of Bel Air (*The Aegis & Intelligencer*, 16 May 1890)

Townsley, Nora Grace, 1888-1941 (Ebenezer Methodist Church Cemetery)

Townsley, Samuel A., 1835-1915 (Ebenezer Methodist Church Cemetery); resident near Upper Cross Roads (*The Aegis & Intelligencer*, 14 Mar 1890); see Mary E. Bradley, q.v.

Townsley, Wesley, farmer, near Upper Cross Roads (*Havre de Grace Republican*, 4 Apr 1890; *The Aegis & Intelligencer*, 14 Mar 1890)

Townsley, William H., 1859-1917 (Mountain Christian Church Cemetery)

Towson, Mary E. (Weaver), 1855-1944, native of Harford Co. (Bailey Funeral Home Records)

Towson, William, see William Michael Towson, q.v.

Towson, William Michael, 1881-1960 (Darlington Cemetery); native of Harford Co., born 21 Sep 1881, son of William Towson and Mary Weaver (Bailey Funeral Home Records)

Tracy, Florence V., age 18 in 1890 (Marriage License Applications Book ALJ No. 2, 1891)

Tracy, Ida E., age 21 in 1890 (Marriage License Applications Book ALJ No. 2, 1891)

Tracy (Tracey), Joshua, 1839-1915 (Norrisville Methodist Church Cemetery); Civil War veteran, Clermont Mills (*1890 Special Census of the Civil War Veterans of the State of Maryland*, by L. Tilden Moore, Volume III, p. 80, gave his name as Joshua H. Tracy); U.S. Navy veteran and government pensioner, Clermont Mills (*Havre de Grace Republican*, 22 Aug 1890, gave his name as Joshua W. Tracey)

Tracy (Tracey), Laura Virginia, 1884-1935, native of Maryland, born 22 Jun 1884, daughter of Joshua Tracey and Katherine Smith (Death certificate - married name Duncan)

Tracy, Mary M., see Mary A. Kenny, q.v.

Tracy, Starrett, 1810-1900 (Death certificate incomplete; name spelled Tracey)

Trago, Alice E., 1855-1941 (Churchville Presbyterian Church Cemetery)

Trago, Arthur, treated by unidentified doctor in 1890 ("Medical Account Book – 1890," Historical Society of Harford County Archives Folder)

Trago, Arthur Linn, 1877-1959 (Churchville Presbyterian Church Cemetery); born 19 Oct 1877, son of William Arthur Trago and Alice Eugenia Coale (Churchville Presbyterian Church Register Roll of Infant Church Members or Baptized Children, No. 294)

Trago, Charles A., 1871-1902 (Mt. Zion Methodist Church Cemetery)

Trago, Clemency (Tollinger), 1831-1907 (Rock Run Methodist Church Cemetery)

Trago, George W., 1853-1901 (Churchville Presbyterian Church Cemetery)

Trago, Harris Archer, 1879-1940 (Churchville Presbyterian Church Cemetery); born 30 Mar 1879, son of William Arthur Trago and Alice Eugenia Coale (Churchville Presbyterian Church Register Roll of Infant Church Members or Baptized Children, No. 307)

Trago, Henry Altemus, 1890-1980 (Baker Cemetery); born 26 Apr 1890 (Churchville Presbyterian Church Chronological Roll of Communicants, No. 680)

Trago, James Webster, 1866-1944 (Churchville Presbyterian Church Cemetery); native of Harford Co., born 16 Feb 1866, son of John Trago and Clemency Tollinger, both natives of Maryland (Pennington Funeral Home Records)

Trago, John, 1817-1899 (Rock Run Methodist Church Cemetery); see James Webster Trago, q.v.

Trago, John H., 1859-1901 (Churchville Presbyterian Church Cemetery); justice of the peace, Third District (*Havre de Grace Republican*, 21 Feb 1890); trustee, Zion School No. 12, Third District (*Havre de Grace Republican*, 30 May 1890); glass ball shooting champion (*Harford Democrat*, 24 Jan 1890)

Trago, L. Josephine, 1874-1927 (Churchville Presbyterian Church Cemetery)

Trago, Lillia May, born 21 Apr 1875, daughter of William Arthur Trago and Alice Eugenia Coale (Churchville Presbyterian Church Register Roll of Infant Church Members or Baptized Children, No. 285)

Trago, Mary Ann (Miss), 1815-1890, died at home near Michaelsville, buried in Walnut Tree graveyard, a private burial ground on the farm occupied by Ellsworth Ivins (*The Aegis & Intelligencer*, 6 Jun 1890, spelled her name Trager)

Trago, Oliver Coale, born 28 Mar 1882, son of William Arthur Trago and Alice Eugenia Coale (Churchville Presbyterian Church Register Roll of Infant Church Members or Baptized Children, No. 314)

Trago, Rebecca M., 1871-1941 (Churchville Presbyterian Church Cemetery)

Trago, Susan F., 1821-1894, daughter of William and Ellenor Trago (Rock Run Methodist Church Cemetery)

Trago, William Arthur, 1852-1933 (Churchville Presbyterian Church Cemetery); see Arthur Trago, Harris Archer Trago, Oliver Coale Trago, and Lillian May Trago, q.v.

Trail, James O., 1854-1895 (Centre Methodist Church Cemetery)

Trail, Laura M., 1866-1926 (Centre Methodist Church Cemetery)

Trail, William Joseph, 1872-1942 (Angel Hill Cemetery); native of Virgina, resided in Havre de Grace (Death certificate)

Trainor, D. T., steward, Union Cbapel M. P. Church (*Havre de Grace Republican*, 28 Feb 1890)

Trappe Church and Cemetery (north of Priestford, Fifth District)

Trasch, J. M., road surveying chain man, First District (*Havre de Grace Republican*, 4 Jul 1890)

Traver, Mary C., see Curtis E. Stine and William W. Stine, q.v.

Travers, Cora M., 1880-1976 (Baker Cemetery)

Travers, Ellia (Ellis?), prisoner in the county jail (*Harford Democrat*, 3 Jan 1890)

Travers, Emma M., 1855-1943 (Baker Cemetery)

Travers, George C., 1883-1959 (Baker Cemetery)

Travers, George F., 1868-1943 (Baker Cemetery)

Travers, Harold V., 1886-1964 (Baker Cemetery)

Travers, J. Wesley, 1850-1930 (Baker Cemetery)

Travers, John M., 1875-1918 (Baker Cemetery)

Travers, Katherine M., 1885-1927 (Baker Cemetery)

Travers, Matilda H., 1867-1947 (Baker Cemetery)

Travers, Nellie (Miss), resided in Aberdeen (*Harford Democrat,* 14 Mar 1890)

Traverse, Lewis H. (colored), 1886-1965 (Union Methodist Church Cemetery, Aberdeen)

Trayer, Jacob H., age 27 in 1890 (Marriage License Applications Book ALJ No. 2, 1891)

Treadway, Aquila E., husband of Sarah Ann Treadway, q.v.; also see Ellen B. Treadway, q.v.

Treadway, Carvil, died testate in 1890 and his named heirs were wife Eliza E. Treadway, brother James Treadway, sister Mary A.Monks, and also Frank T. Bull, James H. Monks and Eliza J. Tate (Harford County Will Book JMM 11:116-118)

Treadway, Ellen B. (Miss), 1860-1906 (Barnes Family Cemetery); daughter of Aquila E. Treadway and Sarah Ann Barnes (*Barnes-Bailey Genealogy,* by Walter D. Barnes, 1939, p. H-19)

Treadway, Elsie, 1856-1928 (Wesleyan Chapel Methodist Church Cemetery); native of Maryland, married, resided at Havre de Grace (Death certificate)

Treadway, James, see Carvil Treadway, q.v.

Treadway, Margaret Jane (Carroll), 1826-1909 (Wesleyan Chapel Methodist Church Cemetery)

Treadway, Otis A., 1860-1944 (Wesleyan Chapel Methodist Church Cemetery); insolvent who sold land in November 1890 (*The Aegis & Intelligencer*, 21 Nov 1890 and 5 Dec 1890)

Treadway, Sarah Ann (Barnes), 1832-1901, native of Maryland, resided at Havre de Grace (Death certificate misfiled as Meadway; Barnes Family Cemetery)

Treadway, Thomas, county out-pensioner [welfare recipient], Third District (*Havre de Grace Republican*, 4 Jul 1890)

Treadway, Victoria B., 1878-1956 (Wesleyan Chapel Methodist Church Cemetery)

Treadwell, Bertha W. (Temple), 1876-1950 (Mountain Christian Church Cemetery)

Treadwell, Clarence E., 1984-1932 (Centre Methodist Church Cemetery)

Treadwell, Cordelia, 1866-1943 (Centre Methodist Church Cemetery)

Treadwell, J. B., trustee, School No. 3, Third District (*Havre de Grace Republican*, 9 May 1890)

Treadwell, J. Howard, 1884-1890 (St. Francis de Sales Catholic Church Cemetery); son of James T. Treadwell, of Hall's Shops, Abingdon (*The Aegis & Intelligencer*, 3 Oct 1890)

Treadwell, James T., 1857-1921 (St. Francis de Sales Catholic Church Cemetery); see J. Howard Treadwell, q.v.

Treadwell, Joseph Baker, 1829-1914 (St. Ignatius Catholic Church Cemetery)

Treadwell, Katie E., age 19 in 1890 (Marriage License Applications Book ALJ No. 2, 1891, spelled her name Tredwell)

Treadwell, Mary Alice, 1872-1971 (Fallston Methodist Church Cemetery)

Treadwell, Rebecca R., 1867-1944 (Fallston Methodist Church Cemetery)

Treadwell, Robert, student, Oakland School, 1890 (George G. Curtiss Ledger)

Treadwell, Robert L., 1868-1929 (St. Ignatius Catholic Church Cemetery)

Treadwell, S. Olivia, 1864-1953 (St. Francis de Sales Catholic Church Cemetery)

Treadwell, William B., 1870-1897 (Fallston Methodist Church Cemetery)

Treakle & Huff, undertakers, Mill Green (*Harford Democrat*, 11 Apr 1890)

Treakle, Basil G., 1850-1903 (Emory Methodist Church Cemetery); trustee, Mill Green School No. 7, Fifth District (*Havre de Grace Republican*, 30 May 1890); Mrs. Basil Treakle (Bessie Huff) died in 1889; see John S. Huff and Edith R. Treakle, q.v.

Treakle, Edith R., 1883-1967 (Emory Methodist Church Cemetery); native of Street, Harford Co., born 14 Oct 1883, daughter of Basil Treakle and Sarah E. Huff (Harkins Funeral Home Records)

Treakle, Edwin Thomas, 1847-1921 (Emory Methodist Church Cemetery); carriage maker, Mill Green (*Carriages Back in the Day: Harford County's Rural Heritage*, by Jack L. Shagena, Jr. and Henry C. Peden, Jr., 2016, p. 88); Thomas Treakle, associate judge of elections, Dublin Precinct (*Havre de Grace Republican*, 17 Oct 1890); superintendent, Emory Methodist Church Sunday School (*The Aegis & Intelligencer*, 5 Sep 1890); see Jennie Snodgrass, q.v.

Treakle, Martha S. (Huff), 1847-1935, native of Mill Green, Harford Co. (Bailey Funeral Home Records; Emory Methodist Church Cemetery); daughter of John S. Huff, q.v., and wife of Edwin T. Treakle, q.v.

Treakle, Sarah E., 1854-1955 (Emory Methodist Church Cemetery); daughter of John S. Huff, q.v., and wife of Basil G. Treakle, q.v.

Tredick, Trafton ("Toffy"), 1874-1926 (Harleigh Cemetery, Camden, NJ; www.findagrave.com; *Harford Democrat*, 25 Apr 1890, mistakenly reported his name as Grafton); jousting tournament herald, 1890 (*The Aegis & Intelligencer*, 8 Aug 1890); third baseman, Perryman Baseball Club (*The Aegis & Intelligencer*, 18 Jul 1890)

Tredway, Alice L., 1867-1931 (Mt. Tabor Methodist Church Cemetery)

Tredway, Clarence F., 1872-1961 (William Watters Memorial Methodist Church Cemetery, Cooptown)

Tredway, Dora M., 1880-1960 (Norrisville Methodist Church Cemetery)

Tredway, Eliza A., 1837-1892 (McKendree Methodist Church Cemetery)

Tredway, James B., 1841-1914 (McKendree Methodist Church Cemetery)

Tredway, James W., 1887-1962 (Norrisville Methodist Church Cemetery)

Tredway, Jemima J., 1844-1898 (Norrisville Methodist Church Cemetery)

Tredway, John Norris, 1834-1925 (Norrisville Methodist Church Cemetery)

Tredway, Martha L., 1828-1908 (Mt. Tabor Methodist Church Cemetery)

Tredway, Martha R., 1833-1903 (Mt. Tabor Methodist Church Cemetery)

Tredway, Martha Viola, 1879-1966 (William Watters Memorial Methodist Church Cemetery, Cooptown)

Tredway, Mary E., 1852-1930 (McKendree Methodist Church Cemetery)

Tredway, Mary F., 1870-1928 (Norrisville Methodist Church Cemetery)

Tredway, Mary S., born 1864, died ---- (Mt. Tabor Methodist Church Cemetery)

Tredway, Oliver T., 1854-1934 (Mt. Tabor Methodist Church Cemetery)

Tredway, Rebecca J., 1885-1964 (Norrisville Methodist Church Cemetery)

Tredway, Thomas, 1868-1953 (Norrisville Methodist Church Cemetery)

Tredway, Thomas M., 1831-1905 (Mt. Tabor Methodist Church Cemetery)

Tredway, Walter T., 1872-1907 (Mt. Tabor Methodist Church Cemetery)

Trench, Theodosia (Kelly), 1871-1959 (Angel Hill Cemetery)

Trench, William, 1881-1958 (Angel Hill Cemetery)

Trenton Flint and Spar Company, Broad Creek, near Flintville (*Havre de Grace Republican*, 4 Jul 1890)

Trimble, Annie L., see George Marbury Trimble, Harry Walter Trimble and Susanna Silver Trimble, q.v.

Trimble, Charles H., see George Marbury Trimble, Harry Walter Trimble and Susanna Silver Trimble, q.v.

Trimble, Elizabeth R., c1840-1902, wife of William P. Trimble, q.v. (St. Mary's Episcopal Church Cemetery)

Trimble, George Marbury, 29 Feb 1884, son of Charles H. and Annie L. Trimble (St. George's Episcopal Church Register of Baptisms, pp. 4-5)

Trimble, Harry Walter, born 26 Feb 1881, son of Charles H. and Annie L. Trimble (St. George's Episcopal Church Register of Baptisms, pp. 4-5)

Trimble, Phoebe Dyer (Carr), 1841-1914 , native of Harford Co., resided at Perryman (Death certificate; Loudon Park Cemetery, Baltimore)

Trimble, Susanna Silver, born 20 Oct 1886, daughter of Charles and Annie Trimble (St. George's Episcopal Church Register of Baptisms, p. 8)

Trimble, William Presstman, 1837-1913 (St. Mary's Episcopal Church Cemetery); vestryman, St. Mary's Church, Emmorton (*Havre de Grace Republican*, 18 Apr 1890); vice president of the Third Annual Convention, Farmers' Club of Harford County (*Havre de Grace Republican*, 5 Dec 1890); vice president, Harford County Farmers' Association (*The Aegis & Intelligencer*, 17 Jan 1890); see Elizabeth R. Trimble, q.v.

Trinity Evangelical Lutheran Church and Cemetery (Philadelphia Road, near Joppa)

Trost, Charles, 1853-1923 (Alms House Record Book)

Trott, Emily, 1844-1927 (St. George's Episcopal Church Cemetery)

Trott, James E., 1839-1913 (St. George's Episcopal Church Cemetery)

Trounce, Edward (colored), see Edward Wilson (colored), q.v.

Trout, Abraham, 1840-1900, resided near Clermont Mill (Death certificate); see Mary Catherine Trout, q.v.

Trout, Florence, 1857-1938 (Broad Creek Friends Cemetery)

Trout, Mary Catherine, native of Maryland, daughter of Abraham Trout, q.v. (Pennington Funeral Home Records, 1950, age not given - married name Kelly)

Trout, Michael D., Civil War veteran, Norrisville (*1890 Special Census of the Civil War Veterans of the State of Maryland*, by L. Tilden Moore, Volume III, p. 82); resident of Norrisville (*The Aegis & Intelligencer*, 17 Oct 1890); died 10 Aug 1900, age not stated (Death certificate)

Trout, Nancy, wife of Abraham Trout, q.v.

Trout, Rose M., born 2 Dec 1878, daughter of Abram and Nancy Jane (Morris) Trout (Bethel Presbyterian Church Cemetery Records)

Trout, Thomas, resident at Clermont (*Harford Democrat*, 14 Mar 1890)

Troutner, Amanda, see Nelson McCann, q.v.

Troutner David, 1835-1910 (Dublin Southern Cemetery)

Troutner, James F., 1863-1938 (Dublin Southern Cemetery)

Troutner, Jane (Jones), 1861-1944, native of Maryland (Bailey Funeral Home Records)

Troutner, Jane J., 1841-1923 (Dublin Southern Cemetery)

Troutner, Mary, see Mary J. Poff, q.v.

Troutner, Mary Ellen (Murphy), 1867-1933, native of Darlington, MD (Bailey Funeral Home Records)

Troutner, Sarah J., see Staton W. Knight, q.v.

Troutner, William A., 1865-1945, native of Harford Co. (Dublin Southern Cemetery; Bailey Funeral Home Records)

Troyer's General Store, Black Horse, Howard Troyer, prop. (*Country Stores: Harford County's Rural Heritage*, by Henry C. Peden, Jr. and Jack L. Shagena, Jr., 2015, p. 251)

Troyer, Charles O., 1858-1927 (McKendree Methodist Church Cemetery)

Troyer, Luella May, born 12 Aug 1887, daughter of Lewis and Jennie Troyer (Bethel Presbyterian Church Cemetery Records); see Luella May Gross, q.v.

Troyer, Mary E., 1859-1923 (McKendree Methodist Church Cemetery)

Troyer, Maud Ethel, 1889-1914 (McKendree Methodist Church Cemetery)

Troyer, Susan Alverda, born 26 Apr 1885, daughter of Charles C. and Mary (Miles) Troyer (Bethel Presbyterian Church Cemetery Records)

Trundle & Rouse's General Store, Joppa, James C. Trundle and John G. Rouse, prop. (*Country Stores: Harford County's Rural Heritage*, by Henry C. Peden, Jr. and Jack L. Shagena, Jr., 2015, p. 251)

Trundle, James C., storekeeper and postmaster, Joppa (*Havre de Grace Republican*, 4 Apr and 11 Jul 1890); jousting tournament rider, Knight of Joppa (*Havre de Grace Republican*, 19 Sep 1890)

Tucker, Aaron H., 1817-1893 (Centre Methodist Church Cemetery); see Emory Tucker, q.v.

Tucker, Agnes (Miss), 1880-1900, resided at Emmorton (Mt. Carmel Methodist Church; Death certificate incomplete); premium award winner, Class L - Children's Department, Harford County Fair, 1890 (*The Aegis & Intelligencer*, 24 Oct 1890)

Tucker, Alfred, born 7 Jan 1879, son of Eli Tucker and Sarah Roe (Eli Tucker Bible, *Maryland Bible Records, Volume 2*, by Henry C. Peden, Jr., 2003, p. 163; *Harkins and Related Families of Harford County, Maryland*, by Henry C. Peden, Jr., 2003, p. 17)

Tucker, Allen, student, Forest Hill School, 1890 (*The Aegis*, 2 Jul 1965, school picture)

Tucker, Alva J., 1861-1899 (Darlington Cemetery)

Tucker, Barclay D., 1878-1956 (Centre Methodist Church Cemetery); student, Forest Hill School, 1890 (*The Aegis*, 2 Jul 1965, school picture)

Tucker, Charles Edwin, 1872-1934 (Centre Methodist Church Cemetery); born 29 Oct 1872, son of Eli Tucker and Sarah Roe (Eli Tucker Bible, *Maryland Bible Records, Volume 2*, by Henry C. Peden, Jr., 2003, p. 163; *Harkins and Related Families of Harford County, Maryland*, by Henry C. Peden, Jr., 2003, p. 17); Edwin Tucker, student, Bel Air Academy and Graded School (*The Aegis & Intelligencer*, 23 May 1890)

Tucker, Carrie A., 1887-1984 (Centre Methodist Church Cemetery)

Tucker, Cassie (colored), 1810-1899, native of Harford Co., servant at Muttonsburg (Death certificate); wife of Joshua Tucker, q.v.

Tucker, Clara A., 1876-1916 (Centre Methodist Church Cemetery)

Tucker, Clarence C., 1890-1919 (Darlington Cemetery)

Tucker, David L., 1844-1917 (Centre Methodist Church Cemetery); tax collector, Third District (*Havre de Grace Republican*, 16 May 1890); trustee, Forest Hill School No. 5, Third District (*Havre de Grace Republican*, 30 May 1890)

Tucker, Delia, student, Forest Hill School, 1890 (*The Aegis*, 2 Jul 1965, school picture)

Tucker, E. C., secretary, Forest Hill Republican Club (*Havre de Grace Republican*, 21 Mar 1890)

Tucker, E. Julia (Smithson), 1882-1973 (Centre Methodist Church Cemetery)

Tucker, E. May, 1879-1933 (Centre Methodist Church Cemetery)

Tucker, Edwin, see C. Edwin Tucker, q.v.

Tucker, Eli, 1839-1911 (Centre Methodist Church Cemetery); born 25 Nov 1839, son of Aaron and Hannah Jane (Harkins) Tucker (Eli Tucker Bible, *Maryland Bible Records, Volume 2*, by Henry C. Peden, Jr., 2003, p. 163; *Harkins and Related Families of Harford County, Maryland*, by Henry C. Peden, Jr., 2003, p. 17); Civil War veteran, Third District (*1890 Special Census of the Civil War Veterans of the State of Maryland*, by L. Tilden Moore, Volume III, p. 73); see Alfred Tucker, Charles E. Tucker, Ella May Tucker, Emma Adelia Tucker, Eugene Tucker, Fred Roe Tucker, Mary Grace, W. Irwin Tucker, Walter Eli Tucker, and Roe & Tucker's General Store, q.v.

Tucker, Elisha R., 1834-1899 (Centre Methodist Church Cemetery); tax collector, Third District (*Havre de Grace Republican*, 4 Jul 1890)

Tucker, Elizabeth (Berry) (colored), 1855-1900, native of Maryland, resident of Berkley, daughter of Alexander and Ann Berry, and wife of James Tucker (Death certificate)

Tucker, Ella May, born 31 Dec 1890, daughter of Eli Tucker and Sarah Roe (Eli Tucker Bible, *Maryland Bible Records, Volume 2*, by Henry C. Peden, Jr., 2003, p. 163; *Harkins and Related Families of Harford County, Maryland*, by Henry C. Peden, Jr., 2003, p. 17)

Tucker, Ellis Joel, 1831-1911 (Darlington Cemetery)

Tucker, Ellis R., born 2nd mo., 5th day, 1872, son of Ellis J. and Melissa E. Tucker (Deer Creek Friends Monthy Meeting Record)

Tucker, Elsie M., 1877-1946 (Centre Methodist Church Cemetery)

Tucker, Emma Adelia, born 5 May 1884, daughter of Eli Tucker and Sarah Roe (Eli Tucker Bible, *Maryland Bible Records, Volume 2*, by Henry C. Peden, Jr., 2003, p. 163; *Harkins and Related Families of Harford County, Maryland*, by Henry C. Peden, Jr., 2003, p. 17)

Tucker, Emma L., 1839-1920 (Centre Methodist Church Cemetery)

Tucker, Emory, 1842-1905 (Centre Methodist Church Cemetery); born 22 Aug 1842, son of Aaron and Hannah Tucker (Eli Tucker Bible, *Maryland Bible Records, Volume 2*, by Henry C. Peden, Jr., 2003, p. 163); see Gertrude Maude Tucker, q.v.

Tucker, Esther J., 1888-1891 (Centre Methodist Church Cemetery)

Tucker, Eugene, of Forest Hill, member of the Council of Maryland Division, Sons of [Confederate] Veterans (*Havre de Grace Republican*, 27 Jun 1890); delegate to division encampment, Warren Camp, Sons of [Confederate] Veterans, Forest Hill (*Havre de Grace Republican*, 19 Dec 1890)

Tucker, Eugene, 1871-1925 (Centre Methodist Church Cemetery); born 7 Jan 1871, son of Eli Tucker and Sarah Roe (Eli Tucker Bible, *Maryland Bible Records, Volume 2*, by Henry C. Peden, Jr., 2003, p. 163; *Harkins and Related Families of Harford County, Maryland*, by Henry C. Peden, Jr., 2003, p. 17)

Tucker, Florence E., age 20 in 1890 (Marriage License Applications Book ALJ No. 2, 1891)

Tucker, Fred Roe, 1885-1973 (Centre Methodist Church Cemetery); born 9 Nov 1885, son of Eli Tucker and Sarah Roe (Eli Tucker Bible, *Maryland Bible Records, Volume 2*, by Henry C. Peden, Jr., 2003, p. 163; *Harkins and Related Families of Harford County, Maryland*, by Henry C. Peden, Jr., 2003, p. 17); student, Forest Hill School, 1890 (*The Aegis*, 2 Jul 1965, school picture)

Tucker, Georgia A., 1855-1928 (Centre Methodist Church Cemetery)

Tucker, Gertrude Maude, 1881-1899, of Forest Hill, daughter of Emory Tucker (Death certificate; Centre Methodist Church Cemetery)

Tucker, Grace, student, Forest Hill School, 1890 (*The Aegis*, 2 Jul 1965, school picture)

Tucker, Hannah (Ecoff), 1833-1921 (Centre Methodist Church Cemetery), wife of Elisha R. Tucker, q.v.

Tucker, Hannah Jane (Harkins), 1821-1892 (Centre Methodist Church Cemetery); wife of Aaron H. Tucker, q.v.

Tucker, Herbert, student, Forest Hill School, 1890 (*The Aegis*, 2 Jul 1965, school picture)

Tucker, Howard, student, Forest Hill School, 1890 (*The Aegis*, 2 Jul 1965, school picture)

Tucker, James (colored), see Elizabeth Tucker (colored) and Marian V. Tucker (colored), q.v.

Tucker, John C., 1835-1918 (Centre Methodist Church Cemetery)

Tucker, Joshua (colored), died 4 Oct 1901, age not given (Alms House Record Book); see Cassie Tucker, q.v.

Tucker, Laura Virginia, 1868-1939 (Centre Methodist Church Cemetery)

Tucker, Lester W., 1889-1953 (Centre Methodist Church Cemetery)

Tucker, Lulu G., 1880-1920 (Centre Methodist Church Cemetery)

Tucker, Mabel Viola, 1886-1902 (Darlington Cemetery)

Tucker, Margaret C., 1850-1931 (Centre Methodist Church Cemetery)

Tucker, Marion V. (colored), 1873-1941, native of Perryman, Harford Co., born 16 Apr 1873, daughter of James Tucker and Hatumale Ringgold (Death certificate)

Tucker, Mary (Rigdon), 1887-1944 (William Watters Memorial Church Cemetery, Cooptown)

Tucker, Mary Grace, born 20 Jul 1881, daughter of Eli Tucker and Sarah Roe (Eli Tucker Bible, *Maryland Bible Records, Volume 2*, by Henry C. Peden, Jr., 2003, p. 163; *Harkins and Related Families of Harford County, Maryland*, by Henry C. Peden, Jr., 2003, p. 17)

Tucker, Mattie D., 1874-1936 (Centre Methodist Church Cemetery)

Tucker, Melissa E., 1837-1926 (Darlington Cemetery); wife of Ellis J. Tucker, q.v.

Tucker, Millard R., 1875-1927 (Centre Methodist Church Cemetery)

Tucker, Milton C., officer of the guard, John Rodgers Post, G. A. R., Havre de Grace (*Havre de Grace Republican*, 12 Dec 1890)

Tucker, Samuel W., 1881-1920 (Centre Methodist Church Cemetery)

Tucker, Sarah, see John B. Roe, q.v.

Tucker, Sarah A., 1830-1890 (Centre Methodist Church Cemetery); widow of William Tucker, 1824-1889, and mother of William H. Tucker, of near Fallston (*The Aegis & Intelligencer*, 28 Nov 1890)

Tucker, Sarah E., 1845-1918 (Centre Methodist Church Cemetery)

Tucker, Sarah R., 1850-1925 (Centre Methodist Church Cemetery)

Tucker, Virginia, 1860-1930 (St. Paul's Methodist Church Cemetery)

Tucker, W. Irwin, 1874-1922 (Centre Methodist Church Cemetery); born 4 Oct 1874, son of Eli Tucker and Sarah Roe (Eli Tucker Bible, *Maryland Bible Records, Volume 2*, by Henry C. Peden, Jr., 2003, p. 163; *Harkins and Related Families of Harford County, Maryland*, by Henry C. Peden, Jr., 2003, p. 17)

Tucker, W. Roy, 1885-1961 (Centre Methodist Church Cemetery)

Tucker, Walter, student, Forest Hill School, 1890 (*The Aegis*, 2 Jul 1965, school picture)

Tucker, Walter Eli, 1887-1965 (William Watters Memorial Church Cemetery, Cooptown); born 4 Nov 1887, son of Eli Tucker and Sarah Roe (Eli Tucker Bible, *Maryland Bible Records, Volume 2*, by Henry C. Peden, Jr., 2003, p. 163; *Harkins and Related Families of Harford County, Maryland*, by Henry C. Peden, Jr., 2003, p. 17)

Tucker, William H., 1854-1941 (Centre Methodist Church Cemetery); farmer, of near Fallston (*The Aegis & Intelligencer*, 21 Feb 1890) served on a grand jury, Third District (*The Aegis & Intelligencer*, 14 Nov 1890); see Sarah A. Tucker, q.v.

Tucker, Wilson, student, Forest Hill School, 1890 (*The Aegis*, 2 Jul 1965, school picture)

Tully, Hugh F., new name on the voter registration list at Hall's Cross Road, Second District, 1890 (*Havre de Grace Republican*, 26 Sep 1890)

Turnbaugh, Margaret, see Charles A. Cochran, Sarah E. Parlett and Ozella V. Gross, q.v.

Turnbaugh, William, see Margaret Cochran, q.v.

Turnbull, Daniel, farmer, near Taylor (*Havre de Grace Republican*, 10 Jan 1890)

Turnbull, George M., age 37 in 1890 (Marriage License Applications Book ALJ No. 2, 1891)

Turner, Alice (colored), 1890-1964 (St. James Church, Gravel Hill Cemetery)

Turner, Alice Lee (Stauffer), 1863-1916 (Union Chapel Methodist Church Cemetery)

Turner, Andrew, 1816-1892 (Bethel Presbyterian Church Cemetery Records)

Turner, Annie M. (colored), 1866-1864 (Fairview AME Church Cemetery)

Turner, Avarilla A. (Botts), 1842-1902 (Wesleyan Chapel Methodist Church Cemetery); wife of Byard Turner, q.v.

Turner, Byard, 1834-1892, Civil War veteran (Angel Hill Cemetery; www.findagrave.com); officer of the guard, Rodgers Post, G. A. R., Havre de Grace, 1890 (*Havre de Grace Republican*, 11 Jul 1890, spelled his name

Bayard)

Turner, Catherine (Bahr), 1853-1927 (Bethel Presbyterian Church Cemetery Records); second wife of Thomas Turner, q.v.

Turner, Charles E., see Thomas T. Turner, q.v.

Turner, Charles Smith, 1886-1949 (Angel Hill Cemetery)

Turner, Clara (colored), 1879-1952 (Mt. Zion Methodist Church Cemetery, at Mountain); wife of Henry Turner, q.v.

Turner, Clara Augustus (Lee), 1862-1940 (Death certificate); wife of Samuel Turner, q.v.; also see William R. Turner, q.v.

Turner, Cornelia (colored) (Mrs.), 1869-1901, native of Harford Co., resided at Fulford (Death certificate incomplete)

Turner, David, Civil War veteran, Upper Cross Roads (*1890 Special Census of the Civil War Veterans of the State of Maryland*, by L. Tilden Moore, Volume III, p. 77)

Turner, Edward (colored), 1889-1940, native of Havre de Grace, son of Henry Turner and Elizabeth Brown, natives of Harford Co. (Death certificate)

Turner, Eli, 1826-1894 (Bethel Presbyterian Church Cemetery Records)

Turner, Eli (colored), died testate between 13 Dec 1890 and 11 Feb 1891 and his named heirs were sons John Turner and Henry E. Turner and daughters Hannah Scott and Harriet W. Turner (Harford County Will Book JMM 11:164)

Turner, Eli (colored), see Elinor Turner, Harriett Turner, and Phillip Turner, q.v.

Turner, Elinor (colored), 1861-1926 (Asbury Church Cemeteryt); native of Maryland, daughter of Eli Turner and Annie Rigby (Death certificate)

Turner, Ella M., 1870-1951 (Highland Presbyterian Church Cemetery)

Turner, Ellen (colored), see Eliza Bond (colored), q.v.

Turner, Emanuel (colored), see Emma J. Turner (colored), q   .v.

Turner, Emma J. (colored), 1890-1913, native of Harford Co., born 2 Sep 1890, daughter of Emanuel Turner and Elizabeth Banks, natives of Harford Co. (Death certificate)

Turner, Fannie (colored), see Charles H. Jenkins (colored) and Lucy Jane Bond (colored), q.v.

Turner, Florence (colored) age 22 in 1889 (Marriage License Applications Book ALJ No. 2, 1889)

Turner, Frances Olivia, born 17 Sep 1872, daughter of Thomas and Lizzie (Bahr) Turner (Bethel Presbyterian Church Cemetery Records); see Frances Olivia Kinhart, q.v.

Turner, Frank C., 1871-1941 (Rock Run Methodist Church Cemetery)

Turner, Frank T., 1855-1927 (Bethel Presbyterian Church Cemetery Records)

Turner, Frederick, 1869-1941 (Mountain Christian Church Cemetery)

Turner, George A., 1888-1965, son of Robert C. and Louise (Vanhart) Turner (Bethel Presbyterian Church Cemetery Records)

Turner, Georgeann or Georgianna (colored), see Bertha Murray and Ellis Murray, q.v.

Turner, Harriett (colored), mother of William Christy, q.v.

Turner, Harriett (Miss) (colored), c1861-1935, native of Harford Co., daughter of Eli Turner and Harriett Norris, natives of Harford Co. (Death certificate)

Turner, Harry, 1873-1946 (Mountain Christian Church Cemetery)

Turner, Hattie (Peevey) (colored), 1887-1949, native of Maryland, daughter of John Peevey and Rachel McCormick (Death certificate)

Turner, Henry (colored), resident of Bel Air (*The Aegis & Intelligencer*, 12 Sep 1890)

Turner, Henry (colored), see Edward Turner (colored), q.v.

Turner, Henry (colored), 1869-1926 (Mt. Zion Methodist Church Cemetery, at Mountain); native of Maryland, resided at Van Bibber, son of ---- and Louisa Turner (Death certificate)

Turner, Henry (colored), c1881-1941, native of Harford Co., parents unknown (Death certificate; St. James United Cemetery)

Turner, Henry E. (colored), 1866-1923 (Fariview AME Church Cemetery); see Eli Turner (colored), q.v.

Turner, Henry M., 1817-1891 (Cokesbury Memorial Methodist Church Cemetery)

Turner, J. Frank, 1886-1940, son of Robert C. and Louise (Vanhart) Turner (Bethel Presbyterian Church Cemetery Records)

Turner, James, county out-pensioner [welfare recipient], First District (*Havre de Grace Republican*, 4 Jul 1890)

Turner, James, 1832-1906 (Bethel Presbyterian Church Cemetery Records); resident at Black Horse (*The Aegis & Intelligencer*, 3 Jan 1890); trustee, Madonna School No. 9, Fourth District (*Havre de Grace Republican*, 30 May 1890)

Turner, James Leslie, 1863-1950 (Bethel Presbyterian Church Cemetery Records)

Turne, Jane Maria (Armstrong) (colored), 1815-1900, native of St. Mary's Co., MD, resided at Edgewood, Harford Co. (Death certificate)

Turner, John (colored), see Eli Turner (colored), q.v.

Turner, John H., 1851-1925 (Union Chapel Methodist Church Cemetery)

Turner, Julia A. (Whiteford), 1833-1905 (Bethel Presbyterian Church Cemetery Records); wife of Andrew Turner, q.v.

Turner, Lee, 1888-1943 (Baptist View Cemetery)

Turner, Louisa S. (Vanhart), 1853-1941 (Bethel Presbyterian Church Cemetery Records); wife of Robert C. Turner, q.v.

Turner, Lucinda, 1821-1897 (Cokesbury Memorial Methodist Church Cemetery)

Turner, Mamie A. (colored), 1890-1956 (Clark's Chapel Methodist Church Cemetery); wife of William W. Turner, q.v.

Turner, Martha (colored), c1855-1939, native of the Big Woods near Bel Air, Harford Co., daughter of ----and Betsy Chancy (Death certificate); wife of Philip Turner, q.v.

Turner, Martha (Whittington) (colored), 1843-1915, native of Texas, Baltimore Co., MD, resident of Bel Air (Death certificate)

Turner, Marvia, see George W. Broadwater, q.v.

Turner, Mary (colored), see Phillip A.Turner (colored), q.v.

Turner, Mary (Ensor), 1834-1895 (Bethel Presbyterian Church Cemetery Records); wife of Eli Turner, q.v.

Turner, Mary A., 1857-1930 (Cokesbury Memorial Methodist Church Cemetery)

Turner, Mary A. (colored), see Susan V. Presberry (colored), q.v.

Turner, Mary G. (Bowman), 1871-1953, native of Harford Co. (Bailey Funeral Home Records)

Turner, Mary Jane, 1832-1907 (Deer Creek Quaker Cemetery)

Turner, Mary Laura, 1851-1916 (Cokesbury Memorial Methodist Church Cemetery)

Turner, Morgan, resident of Norrisville (*The Aegis & Intelligencer*, 17 Oct 1890)

Turner, Nancy (Miskimons), 1861-1938 (Bethel Presbyterian Church Cemetery Records); wife of James L. Turner, q.v.

Turner, Phillip (colored), 1847-1928 (Asbury Church Cemetery); native of Maryland, laborer at Bel Air, son of Eli Turner and Annie Rigby (Death certificate)

Turner, Phillip A. (colored), 1871-1934, native of Harford Co., son of Mary Turner and ---- (Death certificate)

Turner, Rebecca A., 1885-1920 (Cranberry Methodist Church Cemetery)

Turner, Robert, Civil War veteran, at Level (*1890 Special Census of the Civil War Veterans of the State of Maryland*, by L. Tilden Moore, Volume III, p. 67)

Turner, Robert, resident near Black Horse (*The Aegis & Intelligencer*, 8 Aug 1890); Civil War veteran, Madonna (*1890 Special Census of the Civil War Veterans of the State of Maryland*, by L. Tilden Moore, Volume III, p. 79)

Turner, Robert C., 1851-1896 (Bethel Presbyterian Church Cemetery Records)

Turner, Robert Calhoun, born 24 May 1881, son of Thomas Turner and Catherine Bahr (Bethel Presbyterian Church Cemetery Records)

Turner, Robert J. (colored), see William B. Turner (colored), q.v.

Turner, Samuel (colored), c1832-1917, native of Maryland, parents unknown (Death certificate); see Abraham Bond and Eliza Bond, q.v.

Turner, Samuel (colored), 1860-1906 (Death certificate); see Clara A. Turner and William R. Turner, q.v.

Turner, Samuel B., 1856-1941 (Cokesbury Memorial Methodist Church Cemetery)

Turner, Samuel W., 1860-1909 (Bethel Presbyterian Church Cemetery Records)

Turner, Sarah Ellen (Miss), 1828-1912 (Bethel Presbyterian Church Cemetery Records)

Turner, Talitha, widow of Hannon Miller, Civil War veteran, at Level (*1890 Special Census of the Civil War Veterans of the State of Maryland*, by L. Tilden Moore, Volume III, p. 67); treated by unidentified doctor in 1890 ("Medical Account Book – 1890," Historical Society of Harford County Archives Folder)

Turner, Thomas, 1846-1916 (Bethel Presbyterian Church Cemetery Records); see Robert Calhoun Turner, q.v.

Turner, Thomas E., 1848-1919 (Cokesbury Memorial Methodist Church Cemetery)

Turner, Thomas T., 1866-1950 (Highland Presbyterian Church Cemetery); native of Harford Co., born 30 Aug 1866, son of Charles E. Turner and Mary Way (Harkins Funeral Home Records)

Turner, Virginia, born 1885, died ---- (Baptist View Church Cemetery)

Turner, Virginia (Pitts), 1886-1964 (Angel Hill Cemetery)

Turner, Warren H., 1889-1948 (Union Chapel Methodist Church Cemetery)

Turner, Willanna, 1869-1941 (Mountain Christian Church Cemetery)

Turner, William B. (colored), 1867-1921, native of Maryland, born 6 May 1867, son of Robert J. Turner and Theodosia Washington, natives of Maryland (Death certificate)

Turner, William Raymond (colored), 1884-1951, native of Gravel Hill, Harford Co., son of Samuel Turner and Clara Lee (*Democratic Ledger*, 23 Mar 1951)

Turner, William W. (colored), 1888-1976, native of Thomas Run, Harford Co., born 2 Feb 1888, parents not mentioned (*The Aegis*, 8 Apr 1976; Clark's Chapel Methodist Church Cemetery)

Turner, Zay Wesley (colored), 1879-1931 (St. James Church, Gravel Hill Cemetery)

Turner, Zora (Wilson), 1874-1938 (Bethel Presbyterian Church Cemetery Records); wife of Samuel Turner, q.v.

Twining, Albert Binney, 1878-1918, native of Harford Co., resided at Fores Hill, born 10 Jan 1878, son of Horace B. Twining, of Bucks Co., PA, and Sarah F. Ashton, of Harford Co. (Death certificate; Christ Episcopal Church Cemetery)

Twining, Horace B., 1832-1895 (Little Falls Quaker Cemetery); resident, near Forest Hill (*Havre de Grace Republican*, 13 Jun 1890); member, Maryland Association of California Pioneers (*The Aegis & Intelligencer*, 22 Aug 1890); see Albert B. Twining, q.v.

Twining, Joseph, farmer, Upper Cross Roads (*The Aegis & Intelligencer*, 4 Apr 1890)

Twining, Mamie (Miss), resident near High Point (*The Aegis & Intelligencer*, 8 Aug 1890)

Twining, Martha Elma (Miss), 1830-1901, native of Pennsylvania, resided at Scarff, Harford Co. (Death certificate; Little Falls Quaker Cemetery)

Twining, Susan Frances (Ashton), 1852-1924 (Centre Methodist Church Cemetery); wife of Horace B. Twining, q.v.; also see Albert B. Twining, q.v.

Tydings, Mary Bond (O'Neill), 1864-1936 (Angel Hill Cemetery); wife of Millard Fillmore Tydings, q.v.

Tydings, Millard Evelyn, 1890-1961, native of Havre de Grace, born 6 Apr 1890, son of Millard F. Tydings and Mary O'Neill (Pennington Funeral Home Records); US Senator, 1926-1951 (Angel Hill Cemetery)

Tydings, Millard Fillmore, 1859-1941, native of Calvert Co., MD, born 26 Sep 1859, son of Samuel Tydings and Sarah Dixon, also of Calvert Co.; resident of Havre de Grace (Pennington Funeral Home Records; Angel Hill Cemetery); see Millard E. Tydings, q.v.

Tydings, Samuel, see Millard Fillmore Tydings, q.v.

Tydings, Thomas J., 1845-1906 (Cokesbury Memorial Methodist Church Cemetery); agent, P. W. & B. Railroad, at Edgewood (*The Aegis & Intelligencer*, 23 May 1890); delegate, First District, Democrat Party Convention (*The Aegis & Intelligencer*, 5 Sep 1890); juror, First District (*Havre de Grace Republican*, 2 May 1890); trustee, Edgewood School, First District (*Havre de Grace Republican*, 30 May 1890)

Tyler, Mary Rosa ("Rose"), 1870-1960, native of Virginia (Edge Hill Cemetery, Accomack Co, VA, married name Bell; *The Aegis & Intelligencer*, 4 Jul 1890); teacher, Harford Seminary School No. 12, near Webster (*Havre de Grace Republican*, 25 Apr and 5 Sep 1890; *The Aegis & Intelligencer*, 18 Apr 1890 and 29 Aug 1890); actress, Darlington Company (*Havre de Grace Republican*, 7 Mar 1890)

Tyrrell, Joseph B., Civil War veteran, Norrisville (*1890 Special Census of the Civil War Veterans of the State of Maryland*, by L. Tilden Moore, Volume III, p. 81)

Tyson, Elsie V., see Elsie V. Stine, q.v.

Tyson, James, see Else V. Stine, q.v.

Tyson, Roland A., of Havre de Grace, 1890-1959 (Arlington National Cemetery)

Ulrich, Jacob Frederick, native of Germany, applied for naturalization on 5 Sep 1890 Harford County Circuit Court Minute Book ALJ No. 5, p. 255; (*The Aegis & Intelligencer*, 12 Sep 1890)

Umbarger, George C., 1869-1953 (Baker Cemetery)

Umbarger, Joseph N., 1861-1937 (Mt. Zion Methodist Church Cemetery)

Umbarger, Louisa J., 1872-1939 (Baker Cemetery)

Underwood, James O., 1865-1937 (Churchville Presbyterian Church Cemetery)

Underwood, Mary J, 1867-1948 (Churchville Presbyterian Church Cemetery)

Unger, Catherine (Miss), 1838-1899, of Joppa (Death certificate)

Unger, Mary, see Esther Jane Terry, q.v.

Union Chapel Colored Public School No. 2, at Perryman (*Harford County, Maryland Teachers and the Schools They Served, 1774-1900*, by Henry C. Peden, Jr., 2022, p. 373)

Union Chapel Methodist Church and Cemetery (Old Joppa Road, near Wilna)

Union Chapel Methodist Episcopal Church (African American) (Michaelsville)

Union Cbapel Public School No. 1, Third District (*Harford County, Maryland Teachers and the Schools They Served, 1774-1900*, by Henry C. Peden, Jr., 2022, p. 373)

Union Public School No.10, near Aberdeen (*Harford County, Maryland Teachers and the Schools They Served, 1774-1900*, by Henry C. Peden, Jr., 2022, p. 373)

United American Mechanics, Venus Council No. 44, Havre de Grace (*Havre de Grace: Its Historic Past, Its Charming Present and Its Promising Future: Harford County's Rural Heritage.* by Jack L. Shagena, Jr. and Henry C. Peden, Jr., 2018, p. 277)

United States Benevolent Fraternity, Chesapeake Council No. 26, Havre de Grace (*Havre de Grace: Its Historic Past, Its Charming Present and Its Promising Future: Harford County's Rural Heritage.* by Jack L. Shagena, Jr. and Henry C. Peden, Jr., 2018, p. 277)

United Workmen, Eureka Lodge No. 22, Havre de Grace (*Havre de Grace: Its Historic Past, Its Charming Present and Its Promising Future: Harford County's Rural Heritage.* by Jack L. Shagena, Jr. and Henry C. Peden, Jr., 2018, pp. 277-278)

Unkle, Clarence G., born -- Mar 1871 (1900 Aberdeen Census); jousting tournament rider, Knight of Harford, 1890 (*The Aegis & Intelligencer*, 29 Aug 1890)

Unkle, Elizabeth E., 1843-1917, widow of George Unkle, 1821-1879 (St. George's Episcopal Church Cemetery)

Upper Cross Roads Colored Public School No. 2, Fourth District (*Harford County, Maryland Teachers and the Schools They Served, 1774-1900*, by Henry C. Peden, Jr., 2022, p. 373)

Upper Cross Roads Public School No. 23, Fourth District (*Harford County, Maryland Teachers and the Schools They Served, 1774-1900*, by Henry C. Peden, Jr., 2022, p. 373)

Vail, Charles Lindley, 1851-1940 (Forest Hill Friends Cemetery); member, Maryland Central Dairymen's Association (*Havre de Grace Republican*, 28 Feb 1890); trustee, Forest Hill School No. 5, Third District (*Havre de Grace Republican*, 30 May 1890); vice president of the Third Annual Convention, Farmers' Club of Harford County (*Havre de Grace Republican*, 5 Dec 1890); vice president, Harford County Farmers' Association (*The Aegis & Intelligencer*, 17 Jan 1890); premium award winner, Class I - Agricultural Productions, Harford County Fair (*The Aegis & Intelligencer*, 24 Oct 1890)

Vail, Cornelia (Hilton), 1851-1941 (Forest Hill Friends Cemetery)

Vail, Georgie S., 1852-1923? (Forest Hill Friends Cemetery)

Vail, James H., 1847-1920 (Forest Hill Friends Cemetery)

Vail, Rachel H., 1812-1892 (Forest Hill Friends Cemetery)

Valentine, A. D. (Rev.) (colored), pastor of Ames Chapel M. E. Church, Bel Air (*The Aegis & Intelligencer*, 15 Aug 1890; *Havre de Grace Republican*, 21 Mar 1890)

Valentine, Georgia (colored), wife of Moses E. Webster; see Carroll M. Webster and Eva V. Webster, q.v.

Valentine, Harriet Augusta (colored), age 23 in 1890 (Marriage License Applications Book ALJ No. 2, 1891)

Valentine, Henry or Harry, see Henry or Harry Wooden, q.v.

VanBibber Public School No. 11, at VanBibber, First District (*Harford County, Maryland Teachers and the Schools They Served, 1774-1900*, by Henry C. Peden, Jr., 2022, p. 373)

VanBibber, Adele Franklin, 1845-1921 (Churchville Presbyterian Church Cemetery); wife of George L. VanBibber, q.v.

VanBibber, Armfield Franklin, 1872-1953 (St. George's P. E. Church Cemetery)

VanBibber, George Lindenberger, Jr., 1845-1911 (Churchville Presbyterian Church Cemetery), of Bel Air, and uncle of Parker Doane, of Jacksonville, IL (*The Aegis & Intelligencer*, 3 Oct 1890); insolvent, 1890 (*The Aegis & Intelligencer*, 21 Apr 1890); incorporator, The Old Peach Bottom Slate Company of Harford County (*Havre de Grace Republican*, 27 Jun 1890) director, Bel Air Turnpike Company (*The Aegis & Intelligencer*, 17 Jan 1890); director, Bel Air Trust Company (*Havre de Grace Republican*, 14 Mar 1890); member, Bel Air Social, Literary, Musical and Dramatic Club (*Havre de Grace Republican*, 27 Jun 1890)

VanBibber, Hannah Catherine, 1815-1906 (Churchville Presbyterian Church Cemetery)

VanBibber, Lena Chew (Miss), 1875-1962 (Churchville Presbyterian Church Cemetery); honor student, Archer Institute, Bel Air, 1890 (*The Aegis & Intelligencer*, 20 Jun 1890)

VanBibber, Susanna Rebecca (Michael), 1877-1955, wife of Armfield VanBibber, q.v.

Vance, Cecilia M., 1834-1915 (Bethel Presbyterian Church Cemetery Records)

Vance, Mary Ellen, 1839-1924 (Bethel Presbyterian Church Cemetery Records)

Vancourt, Ann ("Annie"), age 27, married Cornelius Barrow on 12 Nov 1890 at the Bel Air Parsonage (Marriage License Applications Book ALJ No. 2; Bel Air Methodist Charge Marriage Records, p. 238)

Vanderpool, Gilbert, prisoner in the county jail (*Harford Democrat*, 3 Jan 1890)

Vandever, Mitterbert, 1861-1925 (Angel Hill Cemetery); see Marshall H. Vandiver, q.v.

Vandiver, Annie (Clayton), 1858-1939 (Angel Hill Cemetery), wife of J. Murray Vandiver, q.v.; also see Robert M. Vandiver, q.v.

Vandiver, J. Murray, 1845-1916 (Angel Hill Cemetery); director, First National Bank of Havre de Grace (*Havre de Grace Republican*, 17 Jan 1890; delegate, Sixth District, Democrat Party Convention (*The Aegis & Intelligencer*, 5 Sep 1890); member, Democrat Party; representative, Harford County Tariff Reform Club (*The Aegis & Intelligencer*, 5 Sep 1890); member, Susquehanna Lodge No. 130, A.F. & A. M., Havre de Grace (*Havre de Grace Republican*, 11 Jul 1890); secretary-treasurer, Democratic State Central Committee (*Havre de Grace Republican*, 4 Jul 1890); see Robert M. Vandiver, q.v.

Vandiver, Marshall Herbert, 1861-1925, native of Pomeroy, PA, resident of Havre de Grace (Death certificate information, but Angel Hill Cemetery tombstone is inscribed Mitterbert Vandever)

Vandiver, Robert Murray, 1888-1970, native of Havre de Grace, born 17 Oct 1888, son of Murray Vandiver and Annie Clayton (Pennington Funeral Home Records; Angel Hill Cemetery)

Vanhise, J. H., farmer near Abingdon (*The Aegis & Intelligencer*, 15 Aug 1890)

Vanhise, J. R. (Mrs.), resident of Abingdon, and sister of Mrs. James Day, of New Jersey (*The Aegis & Intelligencer*, 11 Jul 1890)

VanHorn, Isaac, Jr., 1830-1896 (Providence Methodist Church Cemetery)

VanHorn, Luvenia, sold land in May 1890 (*The Aegis & Intelligencer*, 6 Jun 1890)

Vanneman, Caroline Isador "Carrie" (Kerr), 1829-1899, resident of Havre de Grace, native of Maryland, widow of Daniel Vanneman (Death certificate; Hopewell Methodist Church, Port Deposit, MD); member, Havre de Grace M. E Church (*Havre de Grace Republican*, 13 Jun 1890); treasurer, Women's Christian Temperance Union, of Havre de Grace (*Havre de Grace Republican*, 19 Sep 1890); C. I. Vanneman & Co., trader's license, Havre de Grace (*Havre de Grace Republican*, 30 May 1890); mother of Robert Kerr Vanneman, q.v.

Vanneman, Laura Virginia (Nesbitt), 1856-1930, wife of Robert Kerr Vanneman, q.v.

Vanneman, Reeve (Master), member, Havre de Grace M. E Church (*Havre de Grace Republican*, 13 Jun 1890)

Vanneman, Robert Kerr, 1854-1912 (Hopewell Methodist Church, Port Deposit, MD); director, First National Bank of Havre de Grace (*Havre de Grace Republican*, 17 Jan 1890); secretary-treasurer, Havre de Grace Improvement Company (*Havre de Grace Republican*, 7 Feb 1890); vice president, Republican Club (*Havre de Grace Republican*, 7 Nov 1890; member, Susquehanna Lodge No. 130, A.F. & A. M., Havre de Grace (*Havre de Grace Republican*, 11 Jul 1890); Mrs. R. K. Vanneman was superintendent of Sunday School work, Women's Christian Temperance Union, of Havre de Grace (*Havre de Grace Republican*, 19 Sep 1890)

Vansant's Public School No, 19, Fourth District (*Harford County, Maryland Teachers and the Schools They Served, 1774-1900*, by Henry C. Peden, Jr., 2022, p. 373)

VanTrump, Samuel, residence and store, West Liberty (*Harford Democrat*, 4 Apr 1890); secretary, Charity Lodge No. 134, A. F. & A. M., Norrisville (*The Aegis & Intelligencer*, 26 Dec 1890)

Varnes, John, 1818-1890 (Old Brick Baptist Church Cemetery and Records); died testate on 29 Jan 1890 and his named heirs were wife Sarah Varnes, daughter Elmira Jane Patterson and Selina Guss Robison, son John Berlin Varnes and son-in-law John W. Patterson (Harford County Will Book JMM 11:80-82)

Varnes, John Berlin, see John Varnes, q.v.

Varnes, Mary Jane, see Hannah Jane Grafton, q.v.

Varnes, Sarah, 1806-1890 (Old Brick Baptist Church Cemetery and Records; Harford County Will Book JMM 11:83-85); second wife of John Varnes, q.v.

Vaughan, Bridget, see Lucy B. Redding, q.v.

Vaught, Fred Thomas, 1890-1970 (Baker Cemetery)

Vaught, Nancy, see Eliza Jane Catron, q.v.

Veasey, Essa Maude "Essie" (Bonneville), 1881-1950 (Angel Hill Cemetery); wife of William Edward Veasey, q.v.

Veasey, William Edward, 1883-1958 (Angel Hill Cemetery)

Venus Council No. 44, O. U. A. M., Havre de Grace (*Havre de Grace Republican*, 11 Jul 1890)

Venzke, Anna E., 1884-1964 (Trinity Evangelical Lutheran Church Cemetery)

Venzke, Charles, 1850-1924 (Trinity Evangelical Lutheran Church Cemetery)

Venzke, Charles G., 1890-1977 (Trinity Evangelical Lutheran Church Cemetery)

Venzke, Susanna, 1850-1903 (Trinity Evangelical Lutheran Church Cemetery)

Venzke, William E., 1877-1965 (Trinity Evangelical Lutheran Church Cemetery)

Venzke. Dorothy E. (Gunther), 1881-1977 (Trinity Evangelical Lutheran Church Cemetery)

Vernay, Martha (Miss), 1810-1891 (Bethel Presbyterian Church Cemetery Records)

Vernon, Stephen (colored), c1848-1913 (Death certificate)

Vickers, Archibald Edwards, 1883-1909 (Deer Creek Methodist Church Cemetery)

Vickers, Charles Andrew, born 1886, son of Mr. & Mrs. W. J. Vickers, of Bel Air (*Harford Democrat*, 11 Jul 1890)

Vickers, Charles W., 1890-1948 (Deer Creek Methodist Church Cemetery)

Vickers, Daisy May (Mrs.), 1881-1925 (Deer Creek Methodist Church Cemetery)

Vickers, Evan K., 1858-1910 (Deer Creek Methodist Church Cemetery)

Vickers, George W., 1854-1918 (Deer Creek Methodist Church Cemetery)

Vickers, Katherine B., 1884-1955 (Angel Hill Cemetery)

Vickers, Margaret M., 1864-1948 (Christ Episcopal Church Cemetery)

Vickers, Rebecca, 1866-1937 (Deer Creek Methodist Church Cemetery)

Vickers, Sarah Ann (Otto), 1828-1891 (Deer Creek Methodist Church Cemetery)

Vickers, Solon E., 1885-1953 (Angel Hill Cemetery)

Vickers, William J., resident of Bel Air (*The Aegis & Intelligencer*, 11 Jul 1890)

Victors Baseball Club, Bel Air (*Harford Democrat*, 30 May 1890)

Vidleman, Townson, resident of Havre de Grace (*The Aegis & Intelligencer*, 26 Sep 1890)

Vincent, Annie (Hughes), 1850-1942 (*The Hughes Genealogy, 1636-1953*, by Joseph Lee Hughes, 1953, p. 108) ; wife of Thomas Vincent, q.v.

Vincent, Ella Jillard, born 17 Jan 1877, daughter of Thomas and Annie (Hughes) Vincent (*The Hughes Genealogy, 1636-1953*, by Joseph Lee Hughes, 1953, pp. 108, 121)

Vincent, Thomas, 1850-1938 (*The Hughes Genealogy, 1636-1953*, by Joseph Lee Hughes, 1953, p. 108)

Virdin, Catherine Emily Lewis (Dunn), 1839-1908, wife of William W. Virdin, Jr., q.v.

Virdin, Elizabeth Baltimore, wife of Silas Wright Barnes, q.v.

Virdin, John Williamson, born 27 Nov 1869, son of Dr. William Ward Virdin and Catherine Emily Lewis (Churchville Presbyterian Church Register Roll of Infant Church Members or Baptized Children, No. 272)

Virdin, Joseph Dunn, born 2 Feb 1872, son of Dr. William Ward Virdin and Catherine Emily Lewis (Churchville Presbyterian Church Register Roll of Infant Church Members or Baptized Children, No. 273)

Virdin, Martha Lee, born 2 Feb 1873, daughter of Dr. William Ward Virdin and Catherine Emily Lewis (Churchville Presbyterian Church Register Roll of Infant Church Members or Baptized Children, No. 269)

Virdin, William Ward, Jr., 1829-1897 (Churchville Presbyterian Church Cemetery); physician, of Lapidum (*Havre de Grace Republican*, 10 Jan 1890); delegate, Democrat Convention, and secretary, Harford Co. Tariff Reform Club (*The Aegis & Intelligencer*, 5 Sep 1890); juror, Second District (*Havre de Grace Republican*, 31 Oct 1890); member, Harford County Medical Society (*Havre de Grace Republican*, 16 May 1890); secretary,

Democratic Club (*Havre de Grace Republican*, 5 Sep 1890); member, Stephenson Lodge No. 128, A. F. & A. M., Lapidum (*Havre de Grace Republican*, 11 Jul 1890); secretary, Tariff Reform Club of Harford County (*Harford Democrat*, 5 Sep 1890); also see Joseph Dunn Virdin, q.v.

Vogts, Anton Henry, 1869-1936 (St. George's Episcopal Church Cemetery); A. Vogts, wheelwright, son of William N. Vogts, of Kellville (*The Aegis & Intelligencer*, 6 Jun 1890, but death certificate stated he was born at Franklinville. Baltimore Co., son of John M. Vogts, of Germany, and Harriett Corbus, of Holland)

Vogts, Ellen V. "Nellie" (Creswell), 1858-1944 (Union Chapel Methodist Church Cemetery)

Vogts, Henry A., 1853-1907 (Union Chapel Methodist Church Cemetery)

Vogts, James Frank, 1869-1899, blacksmith at Kellville, native of Harford Co., son of William Vogts and ---- (Death certificate; Mountain Christian Church Cemetery)

Vogts, Jennie H., born -- Jun 1871, native of Maryland (1900 Aberdeen Census); wife of Willliam A. Vogts, q.v.

Vogts, John M., see Anton Henry Vogts, q.v.

Vogts, Maggie M., 1880-1891 (Union Chapel Methodist Church Cemetery)

Vogts, Mary E., born -- Feb 1890, native of Maryland, daughter of William A. and Jennie H. Vogts (1900 Aberdeen Census)

Vogts, Nora, student, Union Chapel Public School (*The Aegis & Intelligencer*, 14 Mar 1890); member, Mountain Reading Circle (*The Aegis & Intelligencer*, 21 Feb 1890)

Vogts, William A., born -- Nov 1867, native of Maryland (1900 Aberdeen Census)

Vogts, William N., 1843-1893, blacksmith and carriage maker, Kellville (Union Chapel Cemetery; *The Aegis & Intelligencer*, 6 Jun 1890; *Carriages Back in the Day: Harford County's Rural Heritage*, by Jack L. Shagena, Jr. and Henry C. Peden, Jr., 2016, p. 88); see Anton Henry Vogts and James Frank Vogts, q.v.

Volkart, Edna (Ripken), 1884-1984 (Baker Cemetery)

Volkart, Ernest, 1884-1969 (Baker Cemetery)

Volz, Cathran (Scotten), 1884-1958 (St. Paul's Lutheran Church Cemetery)

Volz, Charles Alexander, 1856-1914 (St. Paul's Lutheran Church Cemetery); Charles Voltz was naturalized on 14 Jan 1890 Harford County Circuit Court Minute Book ALJ No. 5, p. 218)

Von, Charles S., 1860-1891 (Angel Hill Cemetery)

Vosbury, Johanna (Hopkins), 1833-1912 (Angel Hill Cemetery)

Vosbury, Louis Arthur, 1865-1926 (Mount Meta Burial Park, San Benito, TX); junior warden, Susquehanna Lodge No. 130, A. F. & A. M. (*Havre de Grace Republican*, 26 Dec 1890); treasurer, Harford Bicycle Club, of Havre de Grace (*Havre de Grace Republican*, 1 Aug 1890)

Vosbury, Nettie, see Mary Carver, q.v.

W. R. Evans & Co., drugs, patent medicines, mineral water, tobacco products, Main Street and Hickory Avenue, Bel Air (*Harford Democrat*, 17 Jan 1890)

Waddell, Allen C., 1886-1953 (Rock Run Methodist Church Cemetery)

Waddell, Polly Anna, 1890-1966 (Mt. Zion Methodist Church Cemetery)

Waddell, Walter G., 1879-1936 (Fallston Methodist Church Cemetery)

Wade, Charity (colored), c1839-1899, mother of Hannah Ann Perry (Hendon Hill Cemetery tombstone inscribed Wades)

Wade, Orange (colored), see Ramsey Wade (colored), q.v.

Wade, Ramsey (colored), c1857-1935, born in Bel Air, son of Orange Wade and Harriett Hall (Death certificate; Alms House Record Book; Heavenly Waters Cemetery)

Wade, Stewart K. (colored), 1869-1901, brother of Hannah Ann Perry (Hendon Hill Cemetery tombstone inscribed Wades, but death certificate stated Stuart Wade)

Wadlow, Elizabeth, 1800-1898 (Christ Episcopal Church Cemetery)

Wagner, Anna M., 1866-1934 (St. Paul's Lutheran Church Cemetery)

Wagner, Celia M., 1865-1947 (Upper Cross Roads Baptist Church)

Wagner, Charles, 1872-1960 (Cokesbury Memorial Methodist Church Cemetery)

Wagner, Charles H., 1878-1949 (St. George's Episcopal Church Cemetery)

Wagner, Charles J., 1856-1927 (St. Paul's Lutheran Church Cemetery)

Wagner, Christina, 125-1902 (Providence Methodist Church Cemetery)

Wagner, David, 1865-1947 (North Bend Presbyterian Church Cemetery)

Wagner, Estella B., 1882-1962 (St. Paul's Methodist Church Cemetery)

Wagner, Frederick, 1856-1933 (North Bend Presbyterian Church Cemetery)

Wagner, Gus W., 1884-1969 (Churchville Presbyterian Church Cemetery)

Wagner, Gustave J., Civil War veteran, Bynum (*1890 Special Census of the Civil War Veterans of the State of Maryland*, by L. Tilden Moore, Volume III, p. 73)

Wagner, James T., 1863-1950 (Upper Cross Roads Baptist Church)

Wagner, Margaret, 1827-1911 (North Bend Presbyterian Church Cemetery)

Wagner, Mary A., 1871-1951 (Calvary Methodist Church Cemetery)

Wagner, Philip, 1819-1897 (Providence Methodist Church Cemetery); uncalled for letter in Bel Air P. O., 1890 (*The Aegis & Intelligencer*, 4 Jul 1890)

Wagner, Rebecca J., 1874-1955 (Churchville Presbyterian Church Cemetery)

Wagner, Stella K., born 1874, died ---- (St. George's Episcopal Church Cemetery)

Wagonhoffer, Peter, 1859-1932, native of New York (Death certificate; Alms House Record Book)

Wainwright, Ernest B. (colored), 1884-1950, native of Maryland (Death certificate)

Wakefield, Jean "Nanna" (Cohn), 1889-1971 (Rock Run Methodist Church Cemetery)

Wakeland, Alonza, 1853-1891 (Smith Chapel Methodist Church Cemetery); treated by unidentified doctor in 1890 ("Medical Account Book – 1890," Historical Society of Harford County Archives Folder)

Wakeland, Benedict Hanson, see Eliza Kennedy Wakeland, q.v.

Wakeland, Benjamin R., 1874-1933 (Rock Run Methodist Church Cemetery)

Wakeland, Carrie E., 1874-1954 (Smith Chapel Methodist Church Cemetery)

Wakeland, Dora, 1873-1949 (Rock Run Methodist Church Cemetery); wife of Benjamin R. Wakeland, q.v.

Wakeland, Edward Sherman, 1876-1905 (Smith Chapel Methodist Church Cemetery)

Wakeland, Eliza Kennedy, born 6 Sep 1874, daughter of Benedict Hanson Wakeland and Sarah Ann McVey (Churchville Presbyterian Church Register Roll of Infant Church Members or Baptized Children, No. 279)

Wakeland, George, died 28 Dec 1892, age not stated (Churchville Presbyterian Church Cemetery Register of Deaths, Non-Member)

Wakeland, George Polk, born 14 Dec 1878, son of John A. and Sarah A. Wakeland (Holy Cross Episcopal Church Register of Baptisms, p. 84)

Wakeland, Harry A., 1889-1958 (Smith Chapel Methodist Church Cemetery)

Wakeland, Harry Butler, 1890-1892 (Mt. Zion Methodist Church Cemetery)

Wakeland, J. Finney, 1850-1918 (Smith Chapel Methodist Church Cemetery); trustee, School No. 10, Third District (*The Aegis & Intelligencer*, 4 Jul 1890); tent holder, Carsins Run Camp Meeting of the East Harford Circuit, P. E. Church (*The Aegis & Intelligencer*, 1 Aug 1890)

Wakeland, J. Howard, 1872-1931 (Smith Chapel Methodist Church Cemetery)

Wakeland, James B., see Mary A. Wakeland, q.v.

Wakeland, John A., see George Polk Wakeland and John Oliver Wakeland, q.v.

Wakeland, John Oliver, born 4 Jan 1877, son of John A. and Sarah A. Wakeland (Holy Trinity Episcopal Church Register of Baptisms, p. 84)

Wakeland, John T., acquired land in May 1890 (*The Aegis & Intelligencer*, 6 Jun 1890)

Wakeland, John Wesley, 1837-1917 (Churchville Presbyterian Church Cemetery)

Wakeland, Lynn Rush, born 14 Jun 1874, child of John Finney Wakeland and Rachel Catherine Keithley (Churchville Presbyterian Church Register Roll of Infant Church Members or Baptized Children, No. 261)

Wakeland, Margaret, see Margaret S. Boyle, q.v.

Wakeland, Mary A., 1857-1937, native of Harford Co., born 7 May 1857, daughter of James B. Wakeland and Mary Sarah Greenland, resided near Churchville (Death certificate; Churchville Presbyterian Church Cemetery)

Wakeland, Mary Susan (Greenland), 1834-1908 (Churchville Presbyterian Church Cemetery)

Wakeland, Rachel A., 1853-1924 (Smith Chapel Methodist Church Cemetery)

Wakeland, Sarah A., see George Polk Wakeland and John Oliver Wakeland, q.v.

Wakeland, Sarah Elizabeth, 1850-1928 (Smith Chapel Methodist Church Cemetery)

Walbeck, Catharine, 1842-1920 (Salem Evangelical Lutheran Church Cemetery); wife of Herman Walbeck, q.v.

Walbeck, Charles H., age 24 in 1889 (Marriage License Applications Book ALJ No. 2)

Walbeck, Herman, 1838-1916 (Salem Evangelical Lutheran Church Cemetery)

Waldenberg, Nellie (Miss), teacher, Jarrettsville School No. 8, Fourth District (*The Aegis & Intelligencer*, 29 Aug 1890)

Waldman, John, 1852-1891 (Cokesbury Memorial Methodist Church Cemetery)

Walker's General Store, Aberdeen, George F. Walker, prop. (*Country Stores: Harford County's Rural Heritage*, by Henry C. Peden, Jr. and Jack L. Shagena, Jr., 2015, p. 255)

Walker's General Store, Hall's Cross Roads [Aberdeen], George W. Walker, prop. (*Country Stores: Harford County's Rural Heritage*, by Henry C. Peden, Jr. and Jack L. Shagena, Jr., 2015, p. 256)

Walker, ----, third baseman, Aberdeen Baseball Club (*The Aegis & Intelligencer*, 25 Jul 1890); third baseman, Baptist Baseball Club, of Fourth District (*Havre de Grace Republican*, 8 Aug 1890)

Walker, A. W., 1838-1923 (Wesleyan Chapel Methodist Church Cemetery)

Walker, Abraham B., 1856-1942 (Good Will Church Cemetery); member, Taylor Fox Hunting Club (*Havre de Grace Republican*, 24 Jan 1890)

Walker, Ada Jane, 1865-1944 (Churchville Presbyterian Church Cemetery)

Walker, Albert Raymond, 1873-1906 (Grove Presbyterian Church Cemetery)

Walker, Alice Anna (Smallsbeck), 1877-1950 (Wesleyan Chapel Methodist Church Cemetery)

Walker, Alonzo Robert, 1859-1942 (Angel Hill Cemetery); extra policeman, Havre de Grace (*Havre de Grace Republican*, 5 Sep 1890); member, Guiding Star Council No. 9, Jr. O. U. A. M. (*Havre de Grace Republican*, 11 Jul 1890); inside guard, Venus Council No. 44, O. U. A. M., Havre de Grace (*Havre de Grace Republican*, 11 Jul 1890); A. R. Walker Baseball Club, of Havre de Grace (*Havte de Grace Republican*, 6 Jun 1890)

Walker, Amy (McCourtney), 1876-1954 (Deer Creek Methodist Church Cemetery)

Walker, Andrew K., 1847-1927 (Angel Hill Cemetery)

Walker, Anna Lulu (Smith), 1876-1951 (Slate Ridge Cemetery, York Co., PA); native of Harford Co., born 15 Feb 1876, daughter of John W. Smith and Annie Klair (Harkins Funeral Home Records)

Walker, Annie E., born -- Jun 1849, wife of George Walker (1900 Aberdeen Census); Mrs. George Walker, choir member, Grove Presbyterian Church, Aberdeen (*The Aegis & Intelligencer*, 10 Jan 1890)

Walker, Annie E. M., 1834-1905 (Wesleyan Chapel Methodist Church Cemetery); wife of J. Reese Walker, q.v.

Walker, Augustus, trustee, Avondale School No. 11, Second District (*Havre de Grace Republican*, 30 May 1890)

Walker, Bertha H., 1889-1966 (Fallston Methodist Church Cemetery)

Walker, Birdie (Keen), 1867-1958 (Fallston Methodist Church Cemetery)

Walker, Carrie Mabel (North), 1872-1924 (Angel Hill Cemetery); native of Dorchester Co., MD, resided in Havre de Grace (Death certificate)

Walker, Catherine, 1872-1934 (St. Ignatius Catholic Church Cemetery)

Walker, Cecil T., 1887-1973 (Mt. Zion Methodist Church Cemetery)

Walker, Charles (colored), see Henrietta Walker (colored), q.v.

Walker, Charles K., 1880-1953 (Deer Creek Methodist Church Cemetery)

Walker, Charles W., 1885-1965 (Fallston Methodist Church Cemetery)

Walker, Charles W., 1852-1910 (Fallston Methodist Church Cemetery)

Walker, Charles Wesley, 1848-1917 (Wesleyan Chapel Methodist Church Cemetery); resided near Level, married Ella Deckman on 29 Jan 1890 (*The Aegis & Intelligencer*, 7 Mar 1890)

Walker, Christian Hoopman, 1827-1912 (Wesleyan Chapel Methodist Church Cemetery); canner, near Wesleyan Chapel (*Havre de Grace Republican*, 6 Jun 1890)

Walker, Clara R. (Hunt), 1861-1902 (Fallston Methodist Church Cemetery)

Walker, Clarence W., 1889-1966 (Mt. Zion Methodist Church Cemetery)

Walker, Cornelia A. (Ewing), 1840-1892, wife of J. P. Walker (Rock Run Methodist Church Cemetery)

Walker, Cornelia Ann (Coale), 1836-1916 (Wesleyan Chapel Methodist Church Cemetery); wife of Christian Hoopman Walker, q.v.

Walker, Cornelia K., 1886-1962 (Fallston Methodist Church Cemetery)

Walker, Dorothy Mildred (Whyte), 1889-1945 (Angel Hill Cemetery)

Walker, Edna L., 1890-1968 (Mt. Zion Methodist Church Cemetery)

Walker, Edward (colored), husband of Sarah (Dougherty) Walker, q.v.

Walker, Elizabeth, born -- Aug 1840, school teacher, daughter of George and Annie E. Walker (1900 Aberdeen Census); sister of George Walker, q.v.; also see Minnie Saunders and Ida Saunders, q.v.

Walker, Elizabeth Keen (Miss), premium award winner, Class J - Domestic Products, Harford County Fair (*The Aegis & Intelligencer*, 24 Oct 1890); daughter of George Frank Walker, q.v.

Walker, Elizabeth Keen, 1811-1897 (Grove Presbyterian Church Cemetery), wife of George Frank Walker, q.v., and second wife of James Walker)

Walker, Ella J., 1869-1929 (Wesleyan Chapel Methodist Church Cemetery)

Walker, Emma Oscena, married Murray Donohoo on 16 Apr 1890 (marriage certificate); age 22 in 1890 (Marriage License Applications Book ALJ No. 2, 1890)

Walker, Estella (Mrs.), uncalled for letter in Bel Air P. O., 1890 (*The Aegis & Intelligencer*, 4 Jul 1890)

Walker, Frances, 1873-1906 (Grove Presbyterian Church Cemetery)

Walker, Frances Eleanora, 1890-1933 (Jarrettsville Cemetery)

Walker, Frances H."Fannie" (Raymond), 1852-1894 (Grove Presbyterian Church Cemetery)

Walker, Frank (Master), resident near Fallston (*The Aegis & Intelligencer*, 11 Apr 1890)

Walker, George, born -- Aug 1848, merchant (1900 Aberdeen Census); director and stockholder, Aberdeen Can Factory (*Havre de Grace Republican*, 19 Dec 1890); tent holder, Carsins Run Camp Meeting of the East Harford Circuit, P. E. Church (*The Aegis & Intelligencer*, 1 Aug 1890); worshipful master, Aberdeen Lodge No. 87, A. F. & A. M. (*Havre de Grace Republican*, 11 Jul 1890); treated by unidentified doctor in 1890 ("Medical Account Book – 1890," Historical Society of Harford County Archives Folder)

Walker, George F., of W., 1888-1961 (St. Mary's Episcopal Church Cemetery)

Walker, George Francis, 1870-1937 (Churchville Presbyterian Church Cemetery); see Catherine A. Elliott, q.v.

Walker, George Francis (Mrs.), choir member, Grove Presbyterian Church, Aberdeen (*Havre de Grace Republican*, 14 Feb 1890); premium award winner, Class J - Domestic Products, Harford County Fair (*The Aegis & Intelligencer*, 24 Oct 1890)

Walker, George Frank, 1837-1903 (St. Mary's Episcopal Church Cemetery); ex-sheriff, of *Auburn Heights*, near Bel Air (*The Aegis & Intelligencer*, 19 Sep 1890); member, Mt. Ararat Lodge No. 44, A. F. & A. M., Bel Air (*Havre de Grace Republican*, 11 Jul 1890); private, Jackson Guards [Co. D, 1st Regiment, Maryland National Guard], 1889-1890 (*The Aegis & Intelligencer*, 11 Jan 1889)

Walker, George H., 1875-1964 (Angel Hill Cemetery)

Walker, George Robert, 1878-1954 (Wesleyan Chapel Methodist Church Cemetery); native of Harford Co., born 9 Sep 1878, son of George W. Walker and Sarah A. Hopkins (Bailey Funeral Home Records)

Walker, George W., 1845-1914 (Wesleyan Chapel Methodist Church Cemetery); see George Robert Walker, q.v.

Walker, George W., 1852-1897 (Angel Hill Cemetery)

Walker, Gussye A., 1889-1959 (St. Mary's Episcopal Church Cemetery)

Walker, H. B., employee of Archer and Howard's Mill on Winter's Run, near Bel Air, moved to Jacksonville, FL in 1890 (*The Aegis & Intelligencer*, 26 Dec 1890)

Walker, Hannah E. (Hopkins), 1844-1932 (Bailey Funeral Home Records)

Walker, Harriett E., married William J. Barrett on 12 Nov 1890 (marriage certificate)

Walker, Harry E., 1890-1977 (Fallston Methodist Church Cemetery)

Walker, Harvey J., 1886-1950 (Fallston Methodist Church Cemetery)

Walker, Henrietta (colored), died 1891, wife of Charles Walker (Mt. Zion Methodist Church Cemetery, at Mountain)

Walker, Henry G., 1856-1938 (Fallston Methodist Church Cemetery); incorporator and trustee, Friendship M. E. Church, Third District (*The Aegis & Intelligencer*, 14 Nov 1890); carriage maker, Pleasantville (*Carriages Back in the Day: Harford County's Rural Heritage*, by Jack L. Shagena, Jr. and Henry C. Peden, Jr., 2016, p. 127)

Walker, Hiram B., 1852-1891 (Ebenezer Methodist Church Cemetery)

Walker, Hiram Ball, 1875-1923, native of Harford Co., born 8 Nov 1875, son of Hiram B. Walker, of Harford Co., and Elizabeth Chilcote, of Baltimore Co. (Death certificate; Wesleyan Chapel Cemetery)

Walker, J. Crawford, see Mary Frances Walker, q.v.

Walker, J. P., see Cornelia A. Walker, q.v.

Walker, J. Harry, 1856-1934 (Mt. Zion Methodist Church Cemetery)

Walker, J. Reese, 1834-1915 (Wesleyan Chapel Methodist Church Cemetery)

Walker, Jacob P., 1840-1934 (Wesleyan Chapel Methodist Church Cemetery); see M. Barrett Walker, q.v.

Walker, James T., 1844-1896 (Grove Presbyterian Church Cemetery); canner and horse breeder, *Romney Stock Farm*, Second District (*The Aegis & Intelligencer*, 29 Aug 1890; *Havre de Grace Republican*, 4 Apr 1890); delegate, Second District, Democrat Party Convention (*The Aegis & Intelligencer*, 5 Sep 1890); jousting tournament timer (*The Aegis & Intelligencer*, 8 Aug 1890); owner, *Brick House Farm*, near Michaelsville (*The Aegis & Intelligencer*, 18 Apr 1890); trustee, Bush River Neck School No. 9, Second District (*Havre de Grace Republican*, 30 May 1890)

Walker, Jesse, member, Taylor Fox Hunting Club (*Havre de Grace Republican*, 24 Jan 1890)

Walker, Jesse, 1862-1922 (St. Ignatius Catholic Church Cemetery); age 27 in 1890 (Marriage License Applications Book ALJ No. 2)

Walker, John, Civil War veteran, Aberdeen (*1890 Special Census of the Civil War Veterans of the State of Maryland*, by L. Tilden Moore, Volume III, p. 64); see Mary J. Walker, q.v.

Walker, John C., 1829-1915 (Angel Hill Cemetery)

Walker, John L., premium award winner, Class E - Poultry, Harford County Fair, 1890 (*The Aegis &*

Intelligencer, 24 Oct 1890)

Walker, John R., Mr. & Mrs., residents of Level and members of the Mite Society of Level M. P. Church (*The Aegis & Intelligencer*, 7 Nov 1890)

Walker, John W., 1858-1916 (Fallston Methodist Church Cemetery); trustee, Angleside School No. 3, Third District (*Havre de Grace Republican*, 30 May 1890)

Walker, Laura E., 1840-1921 (St. Mary's Episcopal Church Cemetery)

Walker, Lillian, 1889-1907 (Wesleyan Chapel Methodist Church Cemetery)

Walker, Lillie B., 1862-1895 (Fallston Methodist Church Cemetery)

Walker, Lizzie (Miss), first maid of honor, Bel Air jousting tournament, 1890 (*Havre de Grace Republican*, 19 Sep 1890)

Walker, Lucy, 1856-1929 (Angel Hill Cemetery)

Walker, M. Barrett, 1873-1966, native of Harford Co., born 27 Jun 1873, son of Jacob P. Walker and Cornelia Ewing (Pennington Funeral Home Records); Barrett Walker, student, Third District, 1890 (*The Aegis & Intelligencer*, 24 Oct 1890)

Walker, Mabel, 1887-1946 (Fallston Methodist Church Cemetery)

Walker, Mabel Monroe, born 1 Aug 1883, daughter of James T. and Fannie H. Walker (St. George's Episcopal Church Register of Baptisms, pp. 2-3)

Walker, Marianne L., born -- Sep 1889, daughter of George and Annie E. Walker (1900 Aberdeen Census)

Walker, Martha J., of Havre de Grace, married Samuel L. Forsythe, of Havre de Grace, on 13 Jul 1890 in Dublin, Fifth District (*The Aegis & Intelligencer*, 18 Jul 1890); age 22 in 1890 (Marriage License Applications Book ALJ No. 2, 1890)

Walker, Martha Susan, 1879-1961 (Angel Hill Cemetery)

Walker, Mary (Mrs.) (colored), 1880-1923 (Death certificate); wife of Thomas E. Walker, q.v.

Walker, Mary E. (Brookhart), 1863-1938 (Good Will Church Cemetery); wife of Abraham B. Walker, q.v.

Walker, Mary Ella, 1855-1935 (Fallston Methodist Church Cemetery)

Walker, Mary Frances (Sutor), 1842-1899, native of Havre de Grace, wife of J. Crawford Walker (Death certificate; Angel Hill Cemetery)

Walker, Mary J., 1856-1937 (Mt. Zion Methodist Church Cemetery)

Walker, Mary J., 1886-1926 (Angel Hill Cemetery - married name Santmyer), native of Maryland, born 22 Sep 1886, daughter of John Walker and Cora Murphy, both natives of Pennsylvania (Death certificate; Pennington Funeral Home Records)

Walker, Mary J. (Spencer), 1865-1945 (St. Mary's Episcopal Church Cemetery)

Walker, Mary R. (Hopkins), 1843-1916 (Rock Run Methodist Church Cemetery)

Walker, May T. (Easterday), 1881-1953 (Fallston Methodist Church Cemetery)

Walker, Milford, 1883-1936 (William Watters Memorial Methodist Church Cemetery, Cooptown)

Walker, Minnie M., 1890-1969 (Mt. Zion Methodist Church Cemetery)

Walker, Myrtle Mae (Alan), 1880-1953 (Angel Hill Cemetery); wife of Alonzo Robert Walker, q.v.

Walker, Nellie B., 1889-1975 (Good Will Church Cemetery)

Walker, Oleita Harlan (Donahoo), 1865-1938 (Wesleyan Chapel Methodist Church Cemetery), wife of Winfield Scott Walker, q.v.

Walker, Percival L., born -- Jul 1886, son of George and Annie E. Walker (1900 Aberdeen Census)

Walker, Phoebe, see Edna Rouse, q.v.

Walker, Rebecca Louise (Hoopman), 1856-1946 (Wesleyan Chapel Methodist Church Cemetery); wife of Jacob P. Walker, q.v.

Walker, Robert J., 1831-1913 (Rock Run Methodist Church Cemetery); road examiner, Second District (*Havre de Grace Republican*, 4 Jul 1890); farmer near Garland and former county commissioner (*Biographical Dictionary of Harford County, Maryland, 1774-1974*, by Henry C. Peden, Jr. and William O. Carr, 2021, pp. 280-281)

Walker, Russell (master), resided in Aberdeen (*Harford Democrat*, 3 Jan 1890)

Walker, Samuel Edwin, 1871-1943 (Wesleyan Chapel Methodist Church Cemetery)

Walker, Samuel T., 1859-1950 (Fallston Methodist Church Cemetery)

Walker, Sarah A., 1851-1910 (Angel Hill Cemetery)

Walker, Sarah (Dougherty) (colored), 1869-1944, native of Maryland, daughter of George Samuel Dougherty and Sallie McLean (Death certificate)

Walker, Sarah A. (Hopkins), 1846-1910 (Wesleyan Chapel Methodist Church Cemetery); wife of George W. Walker, q.v.

Walker, Sarah R. (Spencer), 1835-1904 (Rock Run Methodist Church Cemetery), first wife of Robert J. Walker, q.v.

Walker, Thomas, 1817-1894 (Ebenezer Methodist Church Cemetery)

Walker, Thomas E. (colored), 1867-1920, native of Maryland (Death certificate)

Walker, Victorine D., 1826-1897 (Ebenezer Methodist Church Cemetery)

Walker, Wilhelmina, age 20 in 1889 (Marriage License Applications Book ALJ No. 2, 1889)

Walker, William, hauling contractor, Havre de Grace (*Havre de Grace Republican*, 20 Jun 1890)

Walker, William E., businessman (liquor license), Havre de Grace (*Havre de Grace Republican*, 30 May 1890)

Walker, William E., 1863-1894 (St. Mary's Episcopal Church Cemetery); brakeman, PW&B Railroad, married son of George F. Walker, of Baltimore; husband of the former ---- Adams, of Havre de Grace (*The Aegis*, 17 Aug 1894s)

Walker, William H., 1884-1955 (Fallston Methodist Church Cemetery)

Walker, Winfield Scott, 1860-1924, native of WV, farmer near Havre de Grace (Death certificate; Wesleyan Chapel Cemetery; Bailey Funeral Home Records); trustee, Forest Institute, School No. 10, Second District, 1890 (*Havre de Grace Republican*, 30 May 1890)

Walker, William W., 1872-1960 (Angel Hill Cemetery)

Wall, Bridget, see Michael Henry Quirk, q.v.

Wall, Julia, see Katherine J. Hollahan, q.v.

Wallace, Benjamin (colored), c1878-1930, native of Maryland, parents unknown (Death certificate; Union Methodist Church Cemetery, Aberdeen)

Wallace, Eliza Louisa (Scarborough), 1854-1924 (Highland Presbyterian Church Cemetery); native of Harford Co., resided at Street (Death certificate)

Wallace, Elizabeth (colored), see Gilpin Rice (colored), q.v.

Wallace, Elizabeth E. (Mrs.) (colored), 1879-1966 (Cedars Chapel Cemetery); wife of Joseph H. Wallace, q.v.

Wallace, Emily (colored), see Olie Smothers (colored), q.v.

Wallace, John, Mr. & Mrs., near Highland Station, celebrated their 10th anniversary on 28 Jan 1890 (*The Aegis & Intelligencer*, 7 Feb 1890); see John D. Wallace, q.v.

Wallace, John D., 1890-1962 (St. Ignatius Catholic Church Cemetery); native of Nikep(?), MD, born 25 Jun 1890, son of Johm Wallace and ---- [blank] (Harkins Funeral Home Records)

Wallace, John N., see Julia Ann Wallace, q.v.

Wallace, Joseph Henry (colored), 1870-1949, native of Harford Co., born 10 May 1870, son of William Wallace and Margaret Hopkins (Death certificate; Cedars Chapel Cemetery)

Wallace, Julia Ann, 1883-1971 (Highland Presbyterian Church Cemetery); native of Street, Harford Co., born 18 Feb 1882, daughter of John N. Wallace and Louise Scarborough (Harkins Funeral Home Records)

Wallace, Maggie (colored), wife of William H. Wallace, q.v.

Wallace, Martha, see Nellie G. Enfield, q.v.

Wallace, Nettie E. (Heaps), 1876-1937 (Slate Ridge Cemetery, York Co., PA); native of Harford Co., born 3 Apr 1876, daughter of Thomas W. Heaps and Rachel A. Scarborough (Harkins Funeral Home Records)

Wallace, Susan (Scarborough), 1878-1968 (Slate Ridge Cemetery, York Co., PA); native of Whiteford, Harford Co., born 8 Oct 1878, daughter of B. Wilson Scarborough and Jane Beard (Harkins Funeral Home Records)

Wallace, William (colored), see Joseph Henry Wallace (colored), q.v.

Wallace, William H. (colored), 1839-1900, laborer, native of Maryland, resided at Darlington (Death certificate)

Wallace, William T. (colored), c1864-1930 (Death certificate)

Wallis, Adelaide W., see Joseph W. Wallis, q.v.

Wallis, Amanda D., 1836-1915 (Centre Methodist Church Cemetery)

Wallis, Ann Eliza, 1834-1910 (Centre Methodist Church Cemetery)

Wallis, Columbus, student, Forest Hill School, 1890 (*The Aegis*, 2 Jul 1965, school picture)

Wallis, Elizabeth (Arnold), c1843-1921, native of Tennessee (Bailey Funeral Home Records)

Wallis, Elkanah, c1837-1921, native of Tennessee (Bailey Funeral Home Records)

Wallis, Frances Ann, 1859-1932 (Mt. Zion Methodist Church Cemetery)

Wallis, Grace W., 1875-1930 (Centre Methodist Church Cemetery)

Wallis, Hannah Elizabeth, 1855-1931, wife of Charles Edward Gross (*Ancestral Charts, Volume 2*, Harford County Genealogical Society, 1986, p. 76)

Wallis, Harriett S., 1852-1918 (Christ Episcopal Church Cemetery); see Joseph W. Wallis, q.v.

Wallis, Howard Elmer, 1879-1901, native of Harford Co., farmer at Forest Hill, son of William Wallis and Sarah Kellogg (Death certificate; Centre Methodist Church Cemetery)

Wallis, Ida, student, Forest Hill School, 1890 (*The Aegis*, 2 Jul 1965, school picture)

Wallis, John N., trustee, School No. 17, Fifth District (*Havre de Grace Republican*, 30 May 1890)

Wallis, John S., 1848-1908 (Christ Episcopal Church Cemetery); see Joseph W. Wallis, q.v.

Wallis, Joseph W., 1806-1890 (Christ Episcopal Church Cemetery); farmer, of Forest Hill, near Rock Spring Church (*The Aegis & Intelligencer*, 27 Jun 1890); died testate and his named heirs were son John S. Wallis, daughters Harriett S. Wallis, Adelaide W. Wallis, Josephine Whitaker, and grandson Charles Whitaker (Harford County Will Book JMM 11:121-122)

Wallis, Lilly D., 1863-1949 (Christ Episcopal Church Cemetery)

Wallis, Lizzie E. (colored), age 22 in 1889 (Marriage License Applications Book ALJ No. 2)

Wallis, Lulu (Miss), organist, Deer Creek Methodist Church (*The Aegis & Intelligencer*, 11 Jul 1890)

Wallis, Maria Isabella (Mrs.), 1844-1933 (St. George's Episcopal Church Cemetery)

Wallis, Mary, botrn 28 Sep 1888, daughter of William R. and Sallie (Kellogg) Wallis (Bethel Presbyterian Church Cemetery Records); see Mary (Wallis) Schuster, q.v.

Wallis, Preston M., 1877-1964 (Centre Methodist Church Cemetery)

Wallis, Robert Orman, 1858-1906 (Mt. Zion Methodist Church Cemetery); mail carrier for Wheel P. O., 1890 (*The Aegis & Intelligencer*, 11 Jul 1890)

Wallis, Rose Ida, 1850-1927 (Centre Methodist Church Cemetery)

Wallis, S. Cornelia, 1878-1958 (Centre Methodist Church Cemetery)

Wallis, Sallie S., 1844-1930 (Centre Methodist Church Cemetery)

Wallis, Thomas (colored), age 29 in 1890 (Marriage License Applications Book ALJ No. 2, 1891)

Wallis, Wilbur F., 1847-1925 (Centre Methodist Church Cemetery); resident near Forest Hill (*The Aegis & Intelligencer*, 7 Mar 1890)

Wallis, William H., 1850-1915 (Christ Episcopal Church Cemetery)

Wallis, William Hawkins, 1846-1916 (St. George's Episcopal Church Cemetery)

Wallis, William R., 1839-1928 (Centre Methodist Church Cemetery); native of Ohio, farmer near Jarrettsville (Death certificate); Civil War veteran, Forest Hill (*1890 Special Census of the Civil War Veterans of the State of Maryland*, by L. Tilden Moore, Volume III, p. 79); see Howard E. Wallis, q.v.

Wallis, William Stanley, 1890-1952 (Mt. Zion Methodist Church Cemetery)

Walsh, Edward J., 1888-1920 (St. Francis de Sales Catholic Church Cemetery)

Walsh, J. L. (Rev.), pastor of Aberdeen M. E. Church (*Havre de Grace Republican*, 14 Mar 1890); tent holder, Carsins Run Camp Meeting of the East Harford Circuit, P. E. Church (*The Aegis & Intelligencer*, 1 Aug 1890)

Walsh, James, proprietor, Harford Furnace Iron Works (*Havre de Grace Republican*, 11 Apr 1890)

Walsh, John Carroll (colonel), 1816-1904 (Green Mount Cemetery, Baltimore); director of the Female House of Refuge (*Havre de Grace Republican*, 21 Feb 1890); director, executive committee [and president], Harford Fire Insurance Company (*Havre de Grace Republican*, 10 Jan 1890 and 14 Mar 1890); former State Senator; resided at *The Mound* in Harford County (*Biographical Dictionary of Harford County, Maryland, 1774-1974*, by Henry C. Peden, Jr. and William O. Carr, 2021, p. 282) also see Charles Waters, q.v.

Walsh, Sarah Amanda (Lee), 1817-1908, wife of John Carroll Walsh, q.v.

Walstrum, John R., age 24 in 1890 (Marriage License Applications Book ALJ No. 2, 1891)

Walstrum, Naomi Cornelia (Mitchell), 1886-1950 (Rock Run Methodist Church Cemetery); native of Harford Co., born 20 Jul 1886, daughter of William Robert Mitchell and Hannah Elizabeth Sampson (Bailey Funeral Home Records)

Waltemyer, Walter W., age 22 in 1890 (Marriage License Applications Book ALJ No. 2, 1890)

Walter's Grist Mill, Walters Mill Road at Stout Bottle Branch, John O. Smith, prop. (*Mills: Grist, Saw, Bone, Flint, Fulling ... & More*, by Jack L. Shagena, Jr., Henry C. Peden, Jr. and John W. McGrain, 2009, pp. 270-271)

Walter, Ada E., 1861-1893 (Providence Methodist Church Cemetery); acquired land in May 1890 (*The Aegis & Intelligencer*, 6 Jun 1890)

Walter, Adda S. (Scarborough), 1870-1960 (Slateville Cemetery, York Co., PA); native of Harford Co., born 26 Jul 1870, daughter of S. J. Scarborough and Amelia Miller (Harkins Funeral Home Records)

Walter (Walters), Albert L., see Charles William Walter and Allan G. Walters, q.v.

Walter, Andrew T., 1879-1952 (Mt. Tabor Methodist Church Cemetery)

Walter, Annie H., see Thurman C. Walter, q.v.

Walter, Bessie Lee (Temple), 1880-1961 (Mt. Tabor Methodist Church Cemetery); native of Harford Co., born 3 Jan 1880, daughter of James Temple and Averilla Whitaker (Bailey Funeral Home Records spelled the name Walters)

Walter, Catherine, 1823-1893 (Ebenezer Methodist Church Cemetery)

Walter, Catherine M., 1860-1905 (Mt. Tabor Methodist Church); wife of Lewis Albert Walter, q.v.

Walter, Charles, seine fisherman, mouth of Deer Creek in the Susquehanna River (*The Aegis & Intelligencer*, 4 Apr 1890)

Walter, Charles E., 1885-1962 (Mt. Tabor Methodist Church Cemetery)

Walter, Charles S., 1860-1920 (Mt. Tabor Methodist Church Cemetery); see Walters General Store, q.v.

Walter, Charles William, 1887-1958 (Mt. Tabor Methodist Church Cemetery); native of Harford Co., born 10 Apr 1887, son of Albert L. Walter and Anna H. Grimes (Bailey Funeral Home Records)

Walter, Edward H., 1841-1908 (Christ Episcopal Church Cemetery)

Walter, Ethel M., 1890-1945 (Mt. Tabor Methodist Church Cemetery)

Walter, Hannah, 1844-1932 (Rock Run Methodist Church Cemetery); county out-pensioner [welfare recipient], Third District (*Havre de Grace Republican*, 4 Jul 1890)

Walter, Harry A., 1865-1928 (Mt. Tabor Methodist Church Cemetery)

Walter, Henry P., 1879-1918 (Centre Methodist Church Cemetery)

Walter, Joan (Lee), 1876-1943 (Highland Presbyterian Church Cemetery)

Walter, Joseph E., 1876-1949 (Mt. Tabor Methodist Church Cemetery)

Walter, Lafemia (Miles), 1827-1897 (Mt. Tabor Methodist Church Cemetery)

Walter, Lewis Albert, 1858-1920 (Mt. Tabor Methodist Church Cemetery); see Thurman C. Walter, q.v.

Walter, Lillie (Stever), 1878-1962 (Slateville Cemetery, York Co, PA); native of Sandy Hook, Harford Co., born 8 Nov 1878, daughter of William A. Stever and Octavia Cunningham (Harkins Funeral Home Records)

Walter, Maggie E., 1873-1947 (Highland Presbyterian Church Cemetery)

Walter, Mary A., 1841-1913 (Centre Methodist Church Cemetery)

Walter, Robert L., 1874-1951 (Highland Presbyterian Church Cemetery)

Walter, Samuel, new name on the voter registration list at Abingdon, First District (*Havre de Grace Republican*, 17 Oct 1890)

Walter, Theodore, see William T. Walter, q.v.

Walter, Thurman C., 18 Feb 1890 - 20 Apr 1890 (Mt. Tabor Methodist Church Cemetery); son of Lewis Albert Walter and Annie H. Walter, of near Forest Hill (*The Aegis & Intelligencer*, 25 Apr 1890)

Walter, William Oliver, 1857-1922 (Mt. Tabor Methodist Church Cemetery)

Walter, William T., 1827-1913 (Centre Methodist Church Cemetery); trustee, School No. 10, Fifth District (*The Aegis & Intelligencer*, 5 Dec 1890); see Margaret Taylor, q.v.

Walter, William T., 1868-1959 (Slateville Cemetery, York Co., PA); native of Harford Co., born 20 Dec 1868, son of Theodore Walter and Mary Smeltzer (Harkins Funeral Home Records)

Waltermyer, Jennie, wife of Abraham Waltemyer, of near Shawsville, and daughter of the late Samuel Garrett, died 7 Aug 1890 in her 34th year (*The Aegis & Intelligencer*, 15 Aug 1890)

Walters General Store, Mechanicsville, C. S. Walters, prop. (*Country Stores: Harford County's Rural Heritage*, by Henry C. Peden, Jr. and Jack L. Shagena, Jr., 2015, p. 256)

Walters, Allan G., 1889-1969, native of Harford Co., born 25 Sep 1889, son of Albert Lewis Walters and ---- (Pennington Fnneral Home Records)

Walters, Callie Jane, 1868-1948 (Mt. Zion Methodist Church Cemetery)

Walters, George W., assistant librarian, Ebenezer M. E. Church Sunday School (*Havre de Grace Republican*, 25 Apr 1890)

Walters, Hannah (Creswell), 1853-1943 (Cokesbury Memorial Methodist Church Cemetery)

Walters, Hattie (colored), age 24 in 1890 (Marriage License Applications Book ALJ No. 2, 1891)

Walters, Lloyd (colored), age 34 in 1890 (Marriage License Applications Book ALJ No. 2, 1890)

Walters, Robert Le, 1864-1950 (Mt. Zion Methodist Church Cemetery)

Walters, Smith, student, School No. 1, Third District (*The Aegis & Intelligencer*, 11 Jul 1890)

Walters, Walter (colored), see Charles McLain (colored), q.v.

Waltham, Amanda, 1874-1954 (Trinity Evangelical Lutheran Church Cemetery)

Waltham, Augustus, 1827-1897 (Cokesbury Memorial Methodist Church Cemetery)

Waltham, Charlton S., see Eliza Billingslea, q.v.

Waltham, Georgeana, see Eliza Billingslea, q.v.

Waltham, Maria B., see Eliza Billingslea, q.v.

Walther, Frank A., Civil War veteran, near Reckord P. O. (*1890 Special Census of the Civil War Veterans of the State of Maryland*, by L. Tilden Moore, Volume III, p. 75)

Waltier, Richard (colored), trustee, Havre de Grace Colored School, Sixth District (*Havre de Grace Republican*, 30 May 1890)

Waltimyer, Jacob, resident of Norrisville (*The Aegis & Intelligencer*, 20 Jun 1890)

Walton, David (colored), 1860-1910 (John Wesley Methodist Church Cemetery, Abingdon)

Walton, Elizabeth H. (Moore), 182-1903 (Little Falls Quaker Cemetery); E. H. Walton, corresponding secretary, Wilna Women's Christian Temperance Union (*The Aegis & Intelligencer*, 30 May 1890)

Walton, Frank Anna (colored), 1852-1905 (John Wesley Methodist Church Cemetery, Abingdon)

Walton, Graham W., 1890-1956 (Bel Air Memorial Gardens)

Walton, Maggie C., age 21 in 1889 (Marriage License Applications Book ALJ No. 2, 1889)

Walton, Martha M. (colored), see George Willis James (colored), q.v.

Walton, Mary L. (colored), age 18 in 1890 (Marriage License Applications Book ALJ No. 2, 1890)

Walton, Robert K. (colored), 1890-1973 (St. James Church, Federal Hill, William C. Rice Memorial Cemetery)

Walton, William (colored), member, Ames Chapel M. E. Church, Bel Air (*The Aegis & Intelligencer*, 15 Aug 1890)

Walton, William Upton (colored), 1852-1918, native of Harford Co. (Death certificate)

Wane, Maggie, 1850-1930 (Heavenly Waters Cemetery)

Wann's General Store, Emmorton, James H. Wann, prop. (*Country Stores: Harford County's Rural Heritage*, by Henry C. Peden, Jr. and Jack L. Shagena, Jr., 2015, p. 257)

Wann Post No. 49, G. A. R., near Forest Hill (*The Aegis & Intelligencer*, 29 Aug 1890)

Wann, Annie L., 1858-1935 (Mountain Christian Church Cemetery)

Wann, Archibald H., 1846-1915 (Mountain Christian Church Cemetery); native of Harford Co., resided at Wilna (Death certificate)

Wann, Augustus Jerome, 1842-1918 (Centre Methodist Church Cemetery); Gus J. Wann, farmer, near Forest Hill (*The Aegis & Intelligencer*, 12 Sep 1890)

Wann, Benjamin, 1876-1938 (Mountain Christian Church Cemetery)

Wann, Bertha A., 1874-1957 (Mt. Carmel Methodist Church Cemetery)

Wann, Bessie Emmaline, born 25 Sep 1880, daughter of Archibald H. and Rebecca Emmaline (Pearce) Wann (Bethel Presbyterian Church Cemetery Records); see Bessie Archer, q.v.

Wann, Charles David, 1855-1913 (Centre Methodist Church Cemetery); Charles Wann, clay pigeon shooter, Forest Hill, 1890 (*The Aegis & Intelligencer*, 7 Feb 1890); shooting champion, Forest Hill Gun Club, 1890 (*Harford Democrat*, 21 Feb 1890)

Wann, Eliza J., 1830-1902 (Mt. Tabor Methodist Church Cemetery); native of Maryland, resided at Hickory, wife of John A. Wann (Death certificate incomplete)

Wann, Elizabeth H. (O'Donnell), 1846-1911 (St. Ignatius Catholic Church Cemetery); native of Harford Co., seamstress, resided at Bynum (Death certificate)

Wann, Evelyn, 1871-1938 (Mountain Christian Church Cemetery)

Wann, Frances Jane, 1834-1919 (Christ Episcopal Church Cemetery)

Wann, Grace Olivia, 1889-1984 (Mountain Christian Church Cemetery)

Wann, Jacob F., 1856-1948 (Mountain Christian Church Cemetery)

Wann, James, 1809-1891 (Christ Episcopal Church Cemetery)

Wann, James Henry, 1832-1913 (Mt. Carmel Methodist Church Cemetery); James Wann, trustee, Emmorton

School No. 3, First District (*Havre de Grace Republican*, 30 May 1890)

Wann, James Henry, 1850-1894 (Mountain Christian Church Cemetery); member, Mt. Ararat Lodge No. 44, A. F. & A. M., Bel Air (*Havre de Grace Republican*, 11 Jul 1890)

Wann, Jessie, 1838-1922 (Alms House Record Book; Heavenly Waters Cemetery)

Wann, John, 1832-1908, native of Harford Co., resided at Kalmia (Death certificate)

Wann, John A., 1829-1910 (Death certificate; Mt. Tabor Methodist Church Cemetery); house and sign painter, grainer and kalsomimer, Bel Air (*Harford Democrat*, 7 Mar 1890)

Wann, Joshua, 1833-1903 (Christ Episcopal Church Cemetery); delegate, Third District, Republican Party Convention (*The Aegis & Intelligencer*, 26 Sep 1890); warden, Christ Church, Rock Spring (*Havre de Grace Republican*, 18 Apr 1890)

Wann, Mary Ann, 1842-1924 (Mountain Christian Church Cemetery)

Wann, Mary Caroline (Vogts), 1858-1894 (Mountain Christian Church Cemetery)

Wann, Minerva, wife of John Wann, q.v.

Wann, Olevia Anna, 1851-1934 (Centre Methodist Church Cemetery)

Wann, Sarah C. (colored), 1856-1907 (Mt. Zion Methodist Church Cemetery, at Mountain)

Wann, Sarah H., 1828-1910 (Mountain Christian Church Cemetery)

Wann, Sarah J. (Miss), 1825-1909, native of Maryland, resided at Hickory (Death certificate)

Wann, Sarah Rebecca, 1828-1910, resided near Benson (Death certificate)

Wann, William J., 1811-1901, native of Maryland, wood turner, resided at Churchvile (Death certificate)

Wannamacher (Rev.), pastor, German [St. Paul's] Lutheran Church, near Perryman (*Havre de Grace Republican*, 28 Nov 1890)

Waples, L. Virginia (Miss), teacher, Bel Air School No. 14, Third District (*The Aegis & Intelligencer*, 11 Apr and 29 Aug 1890)

Ward's Chapel School, Jarrettsville (*Harford County, Maryland Teachers and the Schools They Served, 1774-1900*, by Henry C. Peden, Jr., 2022, p. 373)

Ward's General Store, Black Horse, John T. Ward, prop. (*Country Stores: Harford County's Rural Heritage*, by Henry C. Peden, Jr. and Jack L. Shagena, Jr., 2015, p. 257)

Ward's General Store, Pylesville, William M. Ward, prop. (*Country Stores: Harford County's Rural Heritage*, by Henry C. Peden, Jr. and Jack L. Shagena, Jr., 2015, p. 257)

Ward's Grist Mill and Saw Mill, at Webster, Joseph E. Ward, prop. (*Mills: Grist, Saw, Bone, Flint, Fulling ... & More*, by Jack L. Shagena, Jr., Henry C. Peden, Jr. and John W. McGrain, 2009, p. 257)

Ward, Albert Norman, 1871-1935, son of John Thomas Ward and Elizabeth A. Mellor (Westminster Cemetery, Carroll Co., MD); teacher, Rutledge's School No. 5, Fourth District (*The Aegis & Intelligencer*, 29 Aug 1890; *Harford County, Maryland Teachers and the Schools They Served*, by Henry C. Peden, Jr., 2021, p. 332)

Ward, Annie M., 1878-1917 (Christ Episcopal Church Cemetery)

Ward, Bertha M., born 11 Nov 1882, daughter of William H. and Ida V. Ward (William H. Ward Bible, *Maryland Bible Records, Volume 2*, by Henry C. Peden, Jr., 2003, p. 167)

Ward, Bessie (Miss), member, Asbury M. E. Church, Jarrettsville (*Havre de Grace Republican*, 28 Feb 1890)

Ward, Catherine, 1830-1898 (St. Ignatius Catholic Church Cemetery)

Ward, Charles H., 1862-1915 (Union Chapel Methodist Church Cemetery)

Ward, Clara H. (Kurtz), 1868-1953 (Jarrettsville Cemetery)

Ward, Edward, 1854-1935 (Deer Creek Methodist Church Cemetery)

Ward, Eleanor F., 1886-1957 (Deer Creek Methodist Church Cemetery)

Ward, Elizabeth (Barnes), 1823-1902 (Wesleyan Chapel Methodist Church Cemetery); wife of Jarrett E. Ward, q.v.

Ward, Elizabeth (Robinson), 1853-1935 (Deer Creek Methodist Church Cemetery)

Ward, Elizabeth Ann (Mellor), 1839-1911 (Deer Creek Methodist Church Cemetery), native of England, wife of John T. Ward, q.v.

Ward, Ella B. (Bernard), 1889-1968 (Angel Hill Cemetery)

Ward, Ella G., 1866-1922 (Union Chapel Methodist Church Cemetery)

Ward, Ella M., 1863-1942, married J. Stewart Lowe, 1849-1933, on 26 Feb 1890 (marriage certificate)

Ward, Ellen W., age 22 in 1890 (Marriage License Applications Book ALJ No. 2, 1890)

Ward, Emery Ellis, 1869-1909 (Angel Hill Cemetery)

Ward, Emma (Miss), 1846-1912, daughter of Jarrett E. and Elizabeth (Barnes) Ward (*Barnes-Bailey Genealogy*, by Walter D. Barnes, 1939, p. H-21)

Ward, Estelle (Grier), 1874-1951 (Deer Creek Methodist Church Cemetery)

Ward, Ethel (Bayless), 1888-1981 (Wesleyan Chapel Methodist Church Cemetery); wife of H. Gilbert Ward, q.v.

Ward, Ethel Blanche (Murchison), 1876-1938, wife of Albert Norman Ward, q.v.

Ward, Frederick M., 1868-1929 (Deer Creek Methodist Church Cemetery)

Ward, George E., 1880-1945 (Angel Hill Cemetery)

Ward, George P., 1825-1893 (St. Ignatius Catholic Church Cemetery)

Ward, Goven R., 1873-1960 (Deer Creek Methodist Church Cemetery)

Ward, Grace C., 12 Dec 1886 - 18 Jan 1891, daughter of William H. and Ida V Ward (William H. Ward Bible, *Maryland Bible Records, Volume 2*, by Henry C. Peden, Jr., 2003, p. 167)

Ward, H. Gilbert, 1887-1950 (Wesleyan Chapel Methodist Church Cemetery)

Ward, H. Janie, 1879-1950 (Deer Creek Methodist Church Cemetery)

Ward, Harriett A., 1848-1933 (Wesleyan Chapel Methodist Church Cemetery)

Ward, Harry E., 1890-1973 (Old Brick Baptist Church Cemetery)

Ward, Harry Oscar, 1871-1895, son of Joseph E. Ward and Mary E. Thompson (Wesleyan Chapel Methodist Church Cemetery)

Ward, Hattie V., born 1876, daughter of John T. and Elizabeth (Mellor) Ward (Bethel Presbyterian Church Cemetery Records); member, Asbury M. E. Church, Jarrettsville (*The Aegis & Intelligencer*, 28 Feb 1890); treasurer, Co. D., Loyal Temperance League, of Jarrettsville (*Havre de Grace Republican*, 21 Mar 1890)

Ward, Henry, see Martha S. Tayson, q.v.

Ward, Hester Jane (Harkins), 1847-1916 (Deer Creek Methodist Church Cemetery); wife of John T. Ward, q.v.; also see Nannie M. Ward, q.v.

Ward, Hugh, 1871-1928 (St. Ignatius Catholic Church Cemetery), native of Harford Co., born 3 Aug 1871, son of John Ward and Jennie McGaw (Death certificate)

Ward, Ida C., 1859-1950 (Wesleyan Chapel Methodist Church Cemetery)

Ward, Ida V., 1860-1919 (Deer Creek Methodist Church Cemetery); wife of William H. Ward, q.v.

Ward, J. B., chancellor, Marshall's Lodge No. 99, Knights of Pythias, at Jarrettsville (*The Aegis & Intelligencer*, 18 Jul 1890)

Ward, James A., 1831-1913 (Deer Creek Methodist Church Cemetery); James and Virginia Ward, residents of Chestnut Hill (*The Aegis & Intelligencer*, 12 Dec 1890)

Ward, Jarrett E., 1802-1898 (Wesleyan Chapel Methodist Church Cemetery)

Ward, Jarrett Lewis, 1861-1936, son of Jarrett E. and Elizabeth (Barnes) Ward (*Barnes-Bailey Genealogy*, by Walter D. Barnes, 1939, p. H-21)

Ward, Jennie (McGaw), see Hugh Ward, q.v.

Ward, John, see Hugh Ward, q.v.

Ward, John H., 1880-1901 (Deer Creek Methodist Church Cemetery)

Ward, John S., 1859-1903 (Wesleyan Chapel Methodist Church Cemetery); sold land in November 1890 (*The Aegis & Intelligencer*, 5 Dec 1890)

Ward, John T., 1839-1894 (Deer Creek Methodist Church Cemetery)

Ward, John Thomas, 1833-1907 (Deer Creek Methodist Church Cemetery); tobacco farmer, near Chestnut Hill (*The Aegis & Intelligencer*, 7 Nov 1890); see Albert Norman Ward, q.v.

Ward, John Thomas, 1860-1934 (Mt. Erin Cemetery)

Ward, Joseph Edward, born 1842, died ---- (Wesleyan Chapel Methodist Church Cemetery); see Ward's Grist Mill and Saw Mill, q.v.

Ward, Joseph Henry, 1884-1951 (Angel Hill Cemetery)

Ward, Joshua B., 1865-1926 (Jarrettsville Cemetery); member, Asbury M. E. Church, Jarrettsville (*Havre de Grace Republican*, 28 Feb 1890); brother of T. H. Ward, married Clara H. Kurtz on 6 Mar 1890 (*The Aegis & Intelligencer*, 14 Mar 1890); age 24 in 1890 (Marriage License Applications Book ALJ No. 2, 1890)

Ward, Juliet Ellen (Jarrett), 1867-1933, native of Jarrettsville (Death certificate; Bethel Presbyterian Church Cemetery Records); wife of Thomas Henry Ward, q.v.

Ward, Kate, 1853-1911 (Deer Creek Methodist Church Cemetery)

Ward, Laney M., 1876-1948 (Deer Creek Methodist Church Cemetery)

Ward, Laura F. (Carlin), 1863-1920 (McKendree Methodist Church Cemetery)

Ward, Lydia Lucinda, 1854-1899 (Wesleyan Chapel Methodist Church Cemetery); dressmaker, resided near Havre de Grace, daughter of Jarrett E. Ward and Elizabeth Barnes (Death certificate; *Barnes-Bailey Genealogy*, by Walter D. Barnes, 1939, p. H-21)

Ward, Maggie (Miss), member, St. Patrick's Women's Total Abstinence Society, Havre de Grace (*Havre de Grace Republican*, 31 Jan 1890)

Ward, Maggie A., age 27 in 1890 (Marriage License Applications Book ALJ No. 2, 1890), married A. A. Hergenrother on 26 Nov 1890 (marriage certificate)

Ward, Margaret, 1835-1895 (Mt. Erin Cemetery)

Ward, Martha, see Benjamin Johnson, q.v.

Ward, Martha P., 1856-1940 (Wesleyan Chapel Methodist Church Cemetery)

Ward, Martha S., born 1 Jul 1884, daughter of William H. and Ida V. Ward (William H. Ward Bible, *Maryland Bible Records, Volume 2*, by Henry C. Peden, Jr., 2003, p. 167); see Martha S. Tayson, q.v.

Ward, Mary E., 1858-1941 (Mt. Erin Cemetery)

Ward, Mary E. (Thompson), born 1839, died ---- (Wesleyan Chapel Methodist Church Cemetery); wife of Joseph E. Ward, q.v.

Ward, Mary Eliza, 1859-1890 (Deer Creek Methodist Church Cemetery)

Ward, Mary Elizabeth "Lizzie" (Smith), 1859-1923 (Angel Hill Cemetery)

Ward, Maud (Miss), member, Asbury M. E. Church, Jarrettsville (*Havre de Grace Republican*, 28 Feb 1890)

Ward, Maud B. (Gallion), 1888-1974 (Wesleyan Chapel Methodist Church Cemetery); wife of William C. Ward, q.v.

Ward, Millie F., age 26 in 1890 (Marriage License Applications Book ALJ No. 2, 1890); see James W. Wood, q.v.

Ward, Minnie M., 1890-1975 (Jarrettsville Cemetery)

Ward, Myrtle (Jamison), 1883-1941 (Deer Creek Harmony Presbyterian Church Cemetery)

Ward, Nannie M., 1873-1928 (Deer Creek Methodist Church Cemetery); native of Maryland, born 9 Jun 1873, daughter of John T. Ward and Hester J. Hawkins (Death certificate - married name McCommons); resided at Chestnut Hill, 1890 (*The Aegis & Intelligencer*, 22 Aug 1890)

Ward, Nattie (Miss), member, Asbury M. E. Church, Jarrettsville (*Havre de Grace Republican*, 28 Feb 1890)

Ward, Nellie B., 1886-1941 (Ebenezer Methodist Church Cemetery)

Ward, Noble (colored), c1880-1948 (Death certificate; Heavenly Waters Cemetery)

Ward, Oleita, 1885-1968 (Centre Methodist Church Cemetery)

Ward, Phoebe (Gilbert), 1853-1898 (Wesleyan Chapel Methodist Church Cemetery); wife of Jarrett L. Ward, q.v.

Ward, Roland, 1882-1958 (Centre Methodist Church Cemetery)

Ward, Samuel J., 1886-1962 (Angel Hill Cemetery)

Ward, Samuel W., 1874-1953 (Christ Episcopal Church Cemetery)

Ward, Sophie E., 1889-1972 (Angel Hill Cemetery)

Ward, Thomas Henry (or Harry), 1867-1951 (Bethel Presbyterian Church Cemetery); master at arms, Marshall's Lodge No. 99, Knights of Pythias, at Jarrettsville (*The Aegis & Intelligencer*, 18 Jul 1890; *Havre de Grace Republican*, 25 Jul 1890); member, Asbury M. E. Church, Jarrettsville (*The Aegis & Intelligencer*, 28 Feb 1890)

Ward, Vannie (Miss), resided at Chestnut Hill (*The Aegis & Intelligencer*, 22 Aug 1890)

Ward, Virginia J., 1839-1927 (Deer Creek Methodist Church Cemetery); wife of James A. Ward, q.v.

Ward, W. Henry, 1859-1935 (Deer Creek Methodist Church Cemetery)

Ward, Walter R., born 10 Jul 1890, son of William H. and Ida V. Ward (William H. Ward Bible, *Maryland Bible Records, Volume 2*, by Henry C. Peden, Jr., 2003, p. 167)

Ward, William, 1804-1893 (Deer Creek Methodist Church Cemetery)

Ward, William A., 13 Apr 1888 - 12 Jan 1891, son of William H. and Ida V. Ward (William H. Ward Bible, *Maryland Bible Records, Volume 2*, by Henry C. Peden, Jr., 2003, p. 167)

Ward, William B. S., 1890-1982 (Angel Hill Cemetery)

Ward, William Cairnes, 1883-1954 (Wesleyan Chapel Methodist Church Cemetery)

Ward, William Hall, 1850-1908, native of Maryland, resided at Chestnut Hill (Deer Creek Methodist Church Cemetery; Death certificate)

Ward, William M., 1861-1914 (McKendree Methodist Church Cemetery)

Ward, William R., 1879-1961 (Ebenezer Methodist Church Cemetery)

Wardenburg, Annie (Miss), assistant teacher, Jarrettsville School (*The Aegis & Intelligencer*, 31 Jan 1890)

Ware, Eliza A., 1845-1907, daughter of John B. and Mary Ware (Christ Episcopal Church Cemetery)

Ware, John B., 1822-1891, daughter of John B. and Mary Ware (Christ Episcopal Church Cemetery)

Ware, Laura L., 1847-1890 (Christ Episcopal Church Cemetery)

Waream, Anne Elizabeth, 1884-1954 (Baker Cemetery)

Waream, Sarah S., 1852-1923 (Grove Presbyterian Church Cemetery)

Waream, Walter W., 1882-1963 (Baker Cemetery)

Wareham, Sarah E., 1838-1916 (Angel Hill Cemetery)

Warfel, Henry C., 1881-1926 (Angel Hill Cemetery); native of Pennsylvania, resident of Havre de Grace (Death certificate)

Warfel, Mary (Lawder), 1887-1976 (Angel Hill Cemetery)

Warfield, Aaron (colored), 1865-1913, native of Harford Co., born 31 Aug 1865, son of Joseph Warfield and ---- (Death certificate)

Warfield, Addie (colored), mother of Walter L. Warfield and William O. Warfield, q.v.

Warfield, Amanda (Hill) (colored), 1852-1917, native of Harford Co. (Death certificate)

Warfield, Effie (colored), born -- Aug 1867, servant (1900 Aberdeen Census)

Warfield, Garrow (Mrs.) (colored), 1870-1963 (Union Methodist Church Cemetery, Aberdeen); wife of James Henry Warfield, q.v.; also see Madie Pauline Warfield, q.v.

Warfield, George (colored), see Sarah Holland (colored), q.v.

Warfield, George A. (colored), born Mar 1845, native of Maryland (1900 Aberdeen Census)

Warfield, George A. (colored), 1867-1923, native of Maryland (Death certificate)

Warfield, George H. (colored), 1843-1920, native of Maryland (Death certificate)

Warfield, Henry (colored), see Sarah V. Warfield (colored), q.v.

Warfield. James (colored), 1844-1912, native of Maryland (Death certificate)

Warfield, James Henry (colored), 1867-1948, son of Moses Warfield and Schalett [Charlotte] Monk (Death certificate); age 24 in 1891 (Marriage License Applications Book ALJ No. 2); see Madie Pauline Warfield, q.v.

Warfield, Joseph (colored), see Aaron Warfield (colored), q.v.

Warfield, Madie Pauline (colored), 1888-1977, native of Harford Co., born 28 Apr 1888, daughter of James Henry Warfield and Garrow Sheppard (*The Aegis*, 3 Mar 1977)

Warfield, Mary (colored), see Georgia Ashton (colored) and Charles H. Prigg (colored), q.v.

Warfield, Mary A. (colored), born -- Apr 1846, native of Maryland, wife of George A. Warfield (1900 Aberdeen Census)

Warfield, Moses (colored), see James Henry Warfield (colored), q.v.

Warfield, Rebecca (colored), see Harriet Stansbury (colored), q.v.

Warfield, Sabina (colored), see Azenier Johnson (colored), q.v.

Warfield, Sarah V. (colored), 1872-1930, native of Maryland, born 5 Apr 1872, daughter of Henry Warfield and Susan Johnson (Death certificate)

Warfield, Susie (colored), see John W. Christy (colored), q.v.

Warfield, Walter L. (colored), 1878-1940, son of Addie Warfield and ---- (Death certificate)

Warfield, William A. (colored), born -- Feb 1870, native of Maryland, son of George A. and Mary A. Warfield (1900 Aberdeen Census)

Warfield, William O. (colored), c1880-1935, son of Addie Warfield and ---- (Death certificate)

Warner, Brinton F., associate judge of elections, Fallston Precinct (*Havre de Grace Republican*, 17 Oct 1890; trustee, Davis' Corner School No. 21, Fourth District (*Havre de Grace Republican*, 30 May 1890)

Warner, Charles Smith, 1884-1940 (Centre Methodist Church Cemetery)

Warner, Cora, see Albert W. Stokes and Rigby W. Stokes, q.v.

Warner, D. Riley, c1867-1935, native of Harford Co. (Bailey Funeral Home Records)

Warner, Hannah, wife of David H. House, q.v., also see Martha C. House, q.v.

Warner, J. B. (Rev.) (colored), pastor of the African M. E. Church in Havre de Grace (*The Aegis & Intelligencer*, 2 May 1890; *Havre de Grace Republican*, 2 May 1890)

Warner, J. Milton, 1870-1932 (Darlington Cemetery); native of Maryland, born 6 Jun 1870, son of Joseph J. Warner and Alithea Scarborough (Bailey Funeral Home Records)

Warner, John, acquired land in May 1890 (*The Aegis & Intelligencer*, 6 Jun 1890)

Warner, Joseph, Jr., sneak boat duck hunter (*Havre de Grace Republican*, 7 Nov 1890)

Warner, Joseph James, 1829-1901 (Trappe Church Cemetery); see J. Milton Warner, q.v.

Warner, Mallie (Miss), actress, musical entertainment, at Darlington (*The Aegis & Intelligencer*, 30 May 1890)

Warner, Marcelean (Scarborough), 1849-1895, wife of Silas Warner, q.v.

Warner, Margaret (Mrs.), 1861-1953, native of Scotland, resident of Havre de Grace, born 17 Mar 1861, parents unknown (Pennington Funeral Home Records)

Warner, Maria Jane, wife of David G. Harry, q.v.; also see Margaret G. Harry and Elizabeth H. Stewart, q.v.

Warner, Martha F. (Carr), 1825-1890 (Broad Creek Friends Cemetery)

Warner, Mary A. (colored), age 24 in 1890 (Marriage License Applications Book ALJ No. 2, 1891)

Warner, Mary E., see Amy R. Lackey, Wilburn Ross and S. Lindley Ross, q.v.

Warner, Philip, 1811-1891 (Deer Creek Quaker Cemetery)

Warner, Sarah, see Purlie W. Carr, q.v.

Warner, Sarah, student, Bel Air Graded School (*The Aegis & Intelligencer*, 11 Apr 1890)

Warner, Sarah Jane (Craig), 1871-1941 (Darlington Cemetery); native of Harford Co., born 18 Oct 1871, daughter of John Craig, of Ireland, and Alitha Mitchell, of Harford Co. (Bailey Funeral Home Records); wife of J. Milton Warner, q.v.

Warner, Silas, 1857-1928 (Centre Methodist Church Cemetery); native of Harford Co., dentist, resided at Forest Hill (Death certificate)

Warner, William, 1831-1908, native of Pennsylvania, resided at Street, Harford Co. (Death certificate)

Warner, William, 1890-1891 (Deer Creek Quaker Cemetery)

Warner, William, member, Norrisville Silver Cornet Band (*The Aegis & Intelligencer*, 30 May 1890)

Warner, William B., 1820-1893 (Little Falls Quaker Cemetery)

Warren, Henry (colored), see John H. Warren (colored), q.v.

Warren, Isaac S., proprietor, brick yard near Bel Air (*The Aegis & Intelligencer*, 24 Oct 1890); Bel Air Brick & Tile Yard, Isaac S. Warren, prop. (*Harford Democrat*, 10 Jan 1890); Civil War veteran, Bel Air (*1890 Special Census of the Civil War Veterans of the State of Maryland*, by L. Tilden Moore, Volume III, p. 71); member, Bel Air Methodist Church (*The Aegis & Intelligencer*, 8 Aug 1890); judge of elections, Bel Air (*The Aegis & Intelligencer*, 9 May 1890)

Warren, John H. (colored), c1872-1915, native of Harford Co., son of Henry Warren and ---- (Death certificate)

Warren, Mary (Miss), pianist and student, Archer Institute, Bel Air (*The Aegis & Intelligencer*, 20 Jun 1890); student and pianist, Bel Air Graded School (*The Aegis & Intelligencer*, 26 Dec 1890)

Warren, Mary A. (Mrs.) (colored), 1841-1927, native of Maryland (Death certificate)

Warren, Mary Elizabeth (colored), see Mary Elizabeth Hemore (colored), q.v.

Warren, Mary L. (colored), age 19 in 1890 (Marriage License Applications Book ALJ No. 2, 1891)

Warren, Noble, member, Loyal Temperance Legion of Bel Air (*The Aegis & Intelligencer*, 2 May 1890)

Warren, Thompson Noble, student, Bel Air Graded School (*The Aegis & Intelligencer*, 11 Apr 1890)

Warren, William (colored), 1839-1918, native of Virginia, resided in Havre de Grace (Death certificate spelled his name Worin); see Mary Elizabeth Hemore, q.v.

Washington, Albert (colored), 1885-1910, native of Maryland, son of William Washington, native of Virginia, and Edith ---- (Death certificate)

Washington, Amos N. (colored), resident near Level (*The Aegis & Intelligencer*, 19 Dec 1890); insolvent, 1890 (*The Aegis & Intelligencer*, 14 Mar 1890); treated by unidentified doctor in 1890 ("Medical Account Book – 1890," Historical Society of Harford County Archives Folder)

Washington, Anna Marie (Smith) (colored), 1817-1892 (Green Spring Methodist Church Cemetery); wife of Isaac Washington, q.v.

Washington, Clara (colored), see Clara Hopkins (colored), q.v.

Washington, Cleo (colored), see Edith Hopkins (colored), q.v.

Washington, Elisha (colored), 1853-1929, native of Maryland (Death certificate); trustee, Hosanna Colored School No. 1, Fifth District (*Havre de Grace Republican*, 30 May 1890)

Washington, Eliza (colored), age 17 in 1890 (Marriage License Applications Book ALJ No. 2, 1891)

Washington, Eliza (Harris) (colored), 1882-1950, native of Maryland, daughter of Hazzard Harris and ---- (Death certificate)

Washington, Ella M. (Stewart) (colored), 1874-1929, native of Maryland, daughter of Lloyd Stewart and ---- (Death certificate)

Washington, Frances L. (colored), age 20 in 1890 (Marriage License Applications Book ALJ No. 2, 1891)

Washington, George (colored), died 26 Jul 1894 (*Havre de Grace Republican*, 27 Jul 1894)

Washington, George R., delegate, First District, Republican Party Convention, 1890 (*The Aegis & Intelligencer*, 26 Sep 1890)

Washington, Hampton (colored), see Rachael E. Washington (colored), q.v.

Washington, Hannah (Con) "Mammy" (colored), 1830-1915, native of Shepherdstown, VA [now WV], servant to the J. Abell Hunter family of Bel Air for over 30 years (Hendon Hill Cemetery; *The Aegis & Intelligencer*, 15 Jan 1915)

Washington, Harriet (colored), see Gertrude Hardy (colored) and Alba Moulton, Jr. (colored), q.v.

Washington, Henry (colored), 1880-1923, native of Maryland, born 23 May 1880, son of William Washington and Elsie Henson (Death certificate)

Washington, Howard M., new name on the voter registration list at Hopewell, Second District, 1890 (*Havre de Grace Republican*, 17 Oct 1890)

Washington, Isaac (colored), 1812-1893 (Green Spring Methodist Church Cemetery); treated by unidentified doctor in 1890 ("Medical Account Book – 1890," Historical Society of Harford County Archives Folder); husband of Annie M.Washington, q.v.

Washington, John (colored), 1872-1929, native of Harford Co., born 15 Mar 1872, son of John H. Washington and Jannette Bowser (Death certificate)

Washington, John H. (colored), manager of the ferry at Spesutia Narrows, died 1890, age not stated (*The Aegis & Intelligencer*, 7 Mar 1890); deceased and removed from the voter registration list at Hall's Cross Roads, Second District, 1890 (*Havre de Grace Republican*, 17 Oct 1890); se John Washington and Pauline Washington, q.v.

Washington, Lloyd Alexander (colored), age 21 in 1890 (Marriage License Applications Book ALJ No. 2, 1890)

Washington, Maria (colored), 1839-1919 (Death certificate)

Washington, Mary (colored), see Addison Jones, Hattie V. Jones and Isaac O. Jones, q.v.

Washington, Mary E. (Hill) (colored), 1837-1901, wife of Sylvester Washington, resided at Castleton, "native of U.S." (Death certificate)

Washington, Mary J. (colored), see Mary E. Banks, William Banks and William Lee, q.v.

Washington, Pauline (colored), c1888-1957, native of Harford Co., daughter of John Washington and Jennetta Hoke (Pennington Funeral Home Records - married name Giles)

Washington, Rachael E. (Haines) (colored), 1830-1899, resided in Berkley, Harford Co., native of Maryland, wife of Hampton Washington (Death certificate; Berkley Memorial Cemetery)

Washington, Susan (colored), see Susan Presberry (colored), q.v.

Washington, Sylvester (colored), see Mary E. Washington (colored) and Susan Presberry (colored), q.v.

Washington, Theodosia (colored), see William B. Turner (colored), q.v.

Washington, Wesley (colored), see Clara Hopkins (colored), q.v.

Washington, William (colored), see Albert Washington (colored) and Henry Washington (colored), q.v.

Waterman, ----, Civil War veteran, Hopewell (*1890 Special Census of the Civil War Veterans of the State of*

Maryland, by L. Tilden Moore, Volume III, p. 69)

Waterman, Amy, age 20 in 1889 (Marriage License Applications Book ALJ No. 2, 1889)

Waters & Wetherill (Misses), millinery goods store, Main St., Bel Air (*The Aegis & Intelligencer*, 28 Mar 1890); Waters & Wetherill's Dressmaking Shop, 116 S. Main St., Bel Air, Elizabeth A. Waters and Rebecca H. Wetherill, prop. (*Bel Air: An Architectural and Cultural History, 1782-1945*, by Marilynn M. Larew, 1995, p. 204)

Waters' General Store, Vale, William H. Waters and A. Streett Waters, prop. (*Country Stores: Harford County's Rural Heritage*, by Henry C. Peden, Jr. and Jack L. Shagena, Jr., 2015, pp. 258-259)

Waters' General Store, at Wimbledon in south Fallston, George D. Waters, prop. (*Country Stores: Harford County's Rural Heritage*, by Henry C. Peden, Jr. and Jack L. Shagena, Jr., 2015, p. 258)

Waters, Abraham Streett, 1866-1905 (Christ Episcopal Church Cemetery); see Waters' General Store, Vale, q.v.

Waters, Cassandra, 1823-1893 (Old Brick Baptist Church Cemetery); wife of William Waters, q.v.

Waters, Charles (colored), died 22 Apr 1890, in his 86th year; employed many years on Col. John Carroll Walsh's farm *The Mound* near Jerusalem Mills; "buried at the colored M. E. Church on the Mountain" (*The Aegis & Intelligencer*, 2 May 1890)

Waters, Elizabeth Ann (Miss), 1850-1930 (Old Brick Baptist Church Cemetery); see Waters & Wetherill, q.v.

Waters, Elizabeth Green (Streett), 1868-1954 (Christ Episcopal Church Cemetery)

Waters, Georganna (colored), 1877-1930, native of Maryland, born 20 Oct 1877, daughter of Shirley Waters and Mary Dallam (Death certificate - married name McDaniels)

Waters, George Denbow, 1853-1909 (Old Brick Baptist Church Cemetery)

Waters, Harriet Henrietta (Pinkney((colored), 1852-1934, native of Maryland (Death certificate)

Waters, J. Edward (colored), 1842-1925 (Death certificate)

Waters, Jacob (colored), 1883-1975, native of Harford Co. (*The Aegis*, 19 Sep 1975)

Waters, John W., delegate, First District, Republican Party Convention, 1890 (*The Aegis & Intelligencer*, 26 Sep 1890)

Waters, John W. (colored), 1851-1927, native of Harford Co. (Death certificate)

Waters, John William, 1889-1953 (Christ Episcopal Church Cemetery); born 30 Jun 1889 at Watervale, son of Abraham Streett and Green Waters (Green Streett Waters Bible, *Maryland Bible Records, Volume 5*, by Henry C. Peden, Jr., 2004, pp. 202-203)

Waters, Joseph (colored), resident of Bel Air (*The Aegis & Intelligencer*, 7 Nov 1890)

Waters, Lloyd (colored), c1852-1937, native of Maryland (Death certificate)

Waters, Mary Ida, 1872-1953, daughter of Edmund and Sarah E. (Hurst) Scarborough (Old Brick Baptist Church Cemetery; *The Aegis*, 16 Jan 1953); widow of George D. Waters, q.v.

Waters, Priscilla (Miss) (colored), died 6 Apr 1918, adult, age unknown (Death certificate; St. James United Cemetery)

Waters, Samuel E. (colored), 1879-1963 (Asbury Church Cemetery)

Waters, Sarah (colored), 1843-1899 (Mt. Zion Methodist Church Cemetery, at Mountain)

Waters, Sarah Maynadier, 1809-1890 (Christ Episcopal Church Cemetery)

Waters, Sbirley (Mr.) (colored), see Georganna Waters (colored), q.v.

Waters, Viola M. (Henry), 1886-1959 (Slateville Cemetery, York Co., PA); native of Harford Co., born 2 Aug 1886, daughter of Thomas Henry and Molly Cooper (Harkins Funeral Home Records)

Waters, William, 1824-1909 (Old Brick Baptist Church Cemetery); charged with forgery in 1890, but found not guilty (Harford County Criminal Docket, 1888-1892, p. 90)

Waters, William H., 1833-1916 (Christ Episcopal Church Cemetery); vestryman, Christ Church, Rock Spring

(*Havre de Grace Republican*, 18 Apr 1890); see Waters' General Store, Vale, and Watervale Mills, q.v.

Watervale Mills, on Winter's Run at Vale, or Watervale, William H. Waters, prop. (*Mills: Grist, Saw, Bone, Flint, Fulling ... & More*, by Jack L. Shagena, Jr., Henry C. Peden, Jr. and John W. McGrain, 2009, pp. 272-274)

Watkins, David, see Frank Watkins and William M. Watkins, q.v.

Watkins, Eliza (Grafton), 1821-1931, wife of John Watkins (Old Brick Baptist Church Cemetery)

Watkins, Frank, 1884-1963 (Slate Ridge Cemetery, York Co., PA); native of Cardiff, Harford Co., born 27 Jul 1884, son of David Watkins and Azenatha Reed (Harkins Funeral Home Records)

Watkins, Hanna J. (Amoss), 1868-1952 (Highland Presbyterian Church Cemetery); native of Harford Co., born 6 Feb 1868, daughter of Benjamin Amoss and Susanna Robinson (Harkins Funeral Home Records)

Watkins, John, see Eliza Watkins, q.v.

Watkins, Raymond, student, LaGrange School No. 14, Fourth District (*The Aegis & Intelligencer*, 25 Apr 1890)

Watkins, Temperance, student, LaGrange School No. 14, Fourth District (*The Aegis & Intelligencer*, 25 Apr 1890)

Watkins, William, chief judge of elections, Jarrettsville Precinct, 1890 (*Havre de Grace Republican*, 17 Oct 1890); resided at Chrome Hill (*Harford Democrat*, 24 Jan 1890)

Watkins, William Newton, 1878-1950 (Slate Ridge Cemetery, York Co., PA); native of Cardiff, Harford Co., born 17 Nov 1878, son of David Watkins and Jennie Herman (Harkins Funeral Home Records)

Watkins, William T., trustee, LaGrange School No. 14, Fourth District (*Havre de Grace Republican*, 30 May 1890)

Watslach, Joseph, born -- Aug 1889, baptized 1 Sep 1889, son of John and Catharine (Mocher) Watslach, both natives of Germany (St. Ignatius Catholic Church Baptism Register, p. 107)

Watson, Annie G., see Annie G. Jones, q.v.

Watson, Annie J., student, Oakland School, 1890 (George G. Curtiss Ledger); premium award winner, Class L - Children's Department, Harford County Fair (*The Aegis & Intelligencer*, 24 Oct 1890)

Watson, Berkie N., premium award winner, Class L - Children's Department, Harford County Fair (*The Aegis & Intelligencer*, 24 Oct 1890)

Watson, Eva J., see Eva J. Mitzel, q.v.

Watson, James, c1840-1908 (Death certificate; Alms House Record Book); county out-pensioner [welfare recipient], Third District (*Havre de Grace Republican*, 4 Jul 1890)

Watson, James A., premium award winner, Class L - Children's Department, Harford County Fair (*The Aegis & Intelligencer*, 24 Oct 1890)

Watson, John, see Lillie T. Butler, Eva J. Mitzel and John E. Watson, q.v.

Watson, John Edward, 1869-1954 (Slate Ridge Cemetery, York Co., PA); native of Harford Co., born 29 Mar 1869, son of John Watson and Mary E. Connolly (Harkins Funeral Home Records)

Watson, Martha, student, Oakland School, 1890 (George G. Curtiss Ledger); premium award winner, Class J - Domestic Products, Harford County Fair (*The Aegis & Intelligencer*, 24 Oct 1890)

Watson, Lourena, see H. Raymond Morris and John C. Morris, q.v.

Watson, William T., director, Bel Air Turnpike Company (*The Aegis & Intelligencer*, 17 Jan 1890); premium award winner, Class I - Agricultural Productions, Harford County Fair (*The Aegis & Intelligencer*, 24 Oct 1890)

Watt, Carrie J., born 1871, daughter of Nicholas and Rebecca J. (Cairnes) Watt (Bethel Presbyterian Church Cemetery Records); see Carrie J. Wiley, q.v.

Watt, Nicholas, 1836-1910 (Bethel Presbyterian Church Cemetery Records)

Watt, Rebecca J. (Cairnes) (Bay), 1835-1910 (Bethel Presbyterian Church Cemetery Records); wife of Nicholas Watt, q.v.

Watters' General Store, Cooptown, J. Howard Watters, prop. (*Country Stores: Harford County's Rural Heritage*,

by Henry C. Peden, Jr. and Jack L. Shagena, Jr., 2015, p. 259)

Watters' Memorial Methodist Church (Cooptown)

Watters' Memorial Methodist Church (Thomas Run)

Watters, Alexander "Alex" Y., 1876-1958 (Jarrettsville Cemetery)

Watters, Anna Mary, see Anna Mary McNeal, q.v.

Watters, Annie (Miss), premium award winner, Class K - Household and Domestic Manufactures, Harford County Fair (*The Aegis & Intelligencer*, 24 Oct 1890)

Watters, Annie Anderson (Dance), 1856-1944 (Fallston Methodist Church Cemetery)

Watters, Annie M., 1854-1935 (Fallston Methodist Church Cemetery)

Watters, Annie Maria, 1826-1909 (William Watters Memorial Church Cemetery, Thomas Run)

Watters, C. Archer, 1866-1930 (Fallston Methodist Church Cemetery)

Watters, Edward, Civil War veteran, Hickory (*1890 Special Census of the Civil War Veterans of the State of Maryland*, by L. Tilden Moore, Volume III, p. 72)

Watters, Edwin Dorsey, 1829-1892 (William Watters Memorial Church Cemetery, Thomas Run)

Watters, Eleanor Gorsuch, 1874-1954, daughter of James A. Watters and Annie M. Walker (Fallston Methodist Church Cemetery, married name Amoss)

Watters, Elizabeth G., 1825-1906 (William Watters Memorial Church Cemetery, Cooptown)

Watters, Esther Y., 1819-1907 (William Watters Memorial Church Cemetery, Cooptown)

Watters, Fanny Howard (Munnikhuysen), 1834-1916 (Watters Memorial Methodist Church, Thomas Run); wife of James David Watters, q.v.

Watters, Grace (Miss), 1854-1939, native of Harford Co. (Bailey Funeral Home Records)

Watters, Grace Irene (Bay), 1875-1958 (Bethel Presbyterian Church Cemetery Records); wife of Alexander Bay, q.v.; also see Grace Irene Bay, q.v.

Watters, H. Eliza, 1830-1913 (William Watters Memorial Church Cemetery, Thomas Run)

Watters, Hattie V. (Wisnom), 1875-1942 (Jarrettsville Cemetery)

Watters, Henry (colored), see George Henry Bond (colored), q.v.

Watters, Henry, Civil War veteran, Hickory (*1890 Special Census of the Civil War Veterans of the State of Maryland*, by L. Tilden Moore, Volume III, p. 72)

Watters, Henry R., 1822-1910 (Watters Memorial Methodist Church, Thomas Run); "squire" and justice of the peace, Darlington (*The Aegis & Intelligencer*, 11 Jul 1890 and 26 Sep 1890); delegate from Fifth District to Democrat Party Convention (*The Aegis & Intelligencer*, 5 Sep 1890)

Watters, Ida (colored), c1873-1923, native of Maryland, daughter of John Watters and Henrietta Bond (Death certificate - married name Durban)

Watters, J. Howard, 1823-1906 (William Watters Memorial Church Cemetery, Cooptown)

Watters, James, 1824-1902 (William Watters Memorial Church Cemetery, Thomas Run)

Watters, James A., 1845-1909 (Fallston Methodist Church Cemetery); juror, Third District (*Havre de Grace Republican*, 31 Jan 1890); trustee, Angleside School No. 3, Third District (*Havre de Grace Republican*, 30 May 1890)

Watters, James David, 1834-1908 (Watters Memorial Methodist Church, Thomas Run); judge of the circuit court, Bel Air (*Havre de Grace Republican*, 10 Jan 1890); Civil War (Confederate Army) veteran (*Havre de Grace Republican*, 20 Jun 1890); member, Mt. Ararat Lodge No. 44, A. F. & A. M.; resided at *Ruff's Chance* in Thomas Run Valley (*Biographical Dictionary of Harford County, Maryland, 1774-1974*, by Henry C. Peden, Jr. and William O. Carr, 2021, p. 284); see Anna Mary McNeal, q.v.

Watters (Waters), James S. (colored), c1867-1912, native of Harford Co. (Death certificate)

Watters, John C. (colored), 1840-1918, native of Maryland (Death certificate); trustee, McComas Institute, Colored School No. 2, First District, 1890 (*Havre de Grace Republican*, 30 May 1890); see Ida Watters, q.v.

Watters, Joshua (colored), see William H. Watters (colored), q.v.

Watters, Julia (Goings), 1840-1909, native of Gunpowder Neck, Harford Co. (Death certificate)

Watters, Letenore (colored), see Bertie Wescott Dorsey (colored), q.v.

Watters, Levin (colored), widower, age 51 in 1890 (Marriage License Applications Book ALJ No. 2, 1891)

Watters, Margaret C., see John Doyle Denham, q.v.

Watters, Mary E. (Peaco) (colored), 1864-1932, native of Harford Co. (Death certificate)

Watters, Mary F., 1827-1912 (William Watters Memorial Church Cemetery, Cooptown); treasurer, Cooptown Sunday School (*Havre de Grace Republican*, 18 Apr 1890)

Watters, Miriam L., 1886-1902 (Fallston Methodist Church Cemetery)

Watters, Robert, resided at Rocks (*Harford Democrat*, 25 Aug 1890)

Watters, Robert A., see John Doyle Denham, q.v.

Watters, Sarah E. (Miss), 1826-1899 (William Watters Memorial Church Cemetery, Cooptown); "lady" at Cooptown, native of Maryland (Death certificate)

Watters, Sarah S. ("Sallie"), former teacher at Kirkwood (*Havre de Grace Republican*, 14 Feb 1890), married Charles Garrett on 12 Feb 1890 (*The Aegis & Intelligencer*, 21 Feb 1890)

Watters, T. Walker, 1884-1955 (Fallston Methodist Church Cemetery)

Watters, Walter, 1808-1891 (William Watters Memorial Church Cemetery, Cooptown)

Watters, Walter (colored), 1869-1939, native of Harford Co. (Death certificate)

Watters, William (colored), age 21 in 1890 (Marriage License Applications Book ALJ No. 2, 1891)

Watters, William (Mrs.), premium award winner, Class J - Domestic Products, Harford County Fair (*The Aegis & Intelligencer*, 24 Oct 1890)

Watters, William H. (colored), 1883-1934, native of Harford Co., born 3 May 1883, son of Joshua Watters and Lettie Peters (Death certificate)

Watts Chapel (Branch Church) (Federal Hill Road, near Jarrettsville)

Watts, Edward, 1890-1962 (Mt. Erin Cemetery)

Watts, J. H. C., judge in Bel Air jousting tournament (*Havre de Grace Republican*, 19 Sep 1890); premium award winner, Class A - Horses, Harford County Fair (*The Aegis & Intelligencer*, 24 Oct 1890)

Watts, Kennedy, honor student, Bel Air Graded School (*The Aegis & Intelligencer*, 4 Jul 1890)

Watts, Mary (Saunders), 1857-1925, native of Maryland (Death certificate)

Watts, Theodore, 1855-1890 (Mt. Erin Cemetery)

Waxwood, Judia (colored), c1830-1920, native of Maryland (Death certificate)

Way, Andrew J., 1865-1928 (Angel Hill Cemetery); native of Maryland, fisherman, married, resided in Havre de Grace (Death certificate); A. J. Way, sneak boat duck hunter, 1890 (*Havre de Grace Republican*, 7 Nov 1890)

Way, Bessie M. (Clark) (colored), 1878-1944, native of Harford Co., born 12 Mar 1878, daughter of Sam Way and Annie Wilson (Death certificate)

Way, Elizabeth, see John T. Sharon and William S. Sharon, q.v.

Way, Emma (Bachtel), 1876-1948 (Angel Hill Cemetery)

Way, James C., 1829-1891 (Forest Hill Friends Cemetery)

Way, Laura V., 1844-1931 (Vernon Cemetery)

Way, Mary, see Thomas T. Turner, q.v.

Way, Rebecca Jane (Davis), 1869-1924 (Angel Hill Cemetery); wife of Ulysses Grant Way, q.v.

Way, Sam (colored), see Bessie M. Way (colored), q.v.

Way, Ulysses Grant, 1863-1946 (Angel Hill Cemetery); member, Young Men's Pleasure Club, Havre de Grace (*Havre de Grace Republican*, 21 Nov 1890)

Wayman, Christy (colored), 1883-1936 (St. James United Cemetery)

Wayne, Margaret (Miss), c1850-1930 (Death certificate; Alms House Record Book)

Wayne, Sarah, see Mary Elizabeth Clark, q.v.

Weaver, Alice C., 1878-1905 (Smith Chapel Methodist Church Cemetery)

Weaver, Cloyd S., 1885-1972 (Churchville Presbyterian Church Cemetery)

Weaver, Ellen (Lewis), 1874-1929 (Darlington Cemetery)

Weaver, Elsie, student, Macton School (*The Aegis & Intelligencer*, 4 Jul 1890)

Weaver, Granville, 1870-1948 (Darlington Cemetery)

Weaver, Henry, 1841-1896 (Dublin Southern Cemetery)

Weaver, Laura, see John E. Beale and E. Rebecca Jones, q.v.

Weaver, Mary, see William Michael Towson, q.v.

Weaver, Mary Jane (White), 1847-1926 (Dublin Southern Cemetery); native of Maryland, resided at Castleton (Death certificate)

Weaver, Michael, and, county out-pensioners [welfare recipients], Fifth District (*Havre de Grace Republican*, 4 Jul 1890)

Weaver, Mortimer B., 1874-1919 (Dublin Southern Cemetery)

Weaver, Nathan L., 1890-1986 (Deer Creek Harmony Presbyterian Church Cemetery)

Weaver, Rebecca (Combs), 1882-1922 (Bailey Funeral Home Records)

Weaver, Sallie, student, Macton School (*The Aegis & Intelligencer*, 4 Jul 1890)

Weaver, Willie, student, Macton School (*The Aegis & Intelligencer*, 4 Jul 1890)

Webb, Addie H., 1878-1965 (Baker Cemetery)

Webb, Charles, farmer at Big Branch (*The Aegis & Intelligencer*, 28 Nov 1890)

Webb, Eliza (Walker), 1827-1910 (Ebenezer Methodist Church Cemetery)

Webb, George (colored), 1878-1929, native of North Carolina (Death certificate)

Webb, Harriet Ellen (Barnes), 1848-1928 (*Barnes-Bailey Genealogy,* by Walter D. Barnes, 1939, p. G-14)

Webb, Harry Silver, 1869-1933 (Grove Presbyterian Church Cemetery); employed with Hanway & Jacobs, at Perryman (*The Aegis & Intelligencer*, 22 Aug 1890); new name on the voter registration list at Hall's Cross Roads, Second District (*Havre de Grace Republican*, 17 Oct 1890)

Webb, John D., 1843-1922 (*Barnes-Bailey Genealogy,* by Walter D. Barnes, 1939, p. G-14)

Webb, Martin Luther, 1888-1970 (Rock Run Methodist Church Cemetery)

Webb, Mary E., 1841-1899 (Churchville Presbyterian Church Cemetery)

Webb, Sarah E. (F.?), 1863-1925 (Angel Hill Cemetery)

Weber, Charles A., 1873-1968 (Churchville Presbyterian Church Cemetery)

Weber, Elizabeth, 1832-1905 (Trinity Evangelical Lutheran Church Cemetery)

Weber, Elizabeth, see Aloysius Hergenrother, q.v.

Weber, Ella Louise (Harris), 1879-1974 (Churchville Presbyterian Church Cemetery)

Weber, Harry LeRoy, 1878-1936 (Centre Methodist Church Cemetery)

Weber, John, 1832-1904 (Trinity Evangelical Lutheran Church Cemetery)

Weber, Kate Estelle (Myers), 1855-1930 (Angel Hill Cemetery)

Weber, Lydia Ann, 1874-1949 (Centre Methodist Church Cemetery)

Weber, Walter H., 1869-1941 (Angel Hill Cemetery); florist, Havre de Grace (*Havre de Grace Republican*, 22 Aug 1890); greenhouse plants, N. Union Ave., Havre de Grace (*Havre de Grace Republican*, 24 Jan 1890); new name on the voter registration list in the Sixth District (*Havre de Grace Republican*, 17 Oct 1890)

Weber, Wilhelmina (Taylor), 1870-1956 (Angel Hill Cemetery), wife of Walter H. Weber, q.v.

Webster Baseball Club, near Havre de Grace (*Havre de Grace Republican*, 8 Aug 1890)

Webster Colored School No. 4, at Webster, Second District (*Harford County, Maryland Teachers and the Schools They Served, 1774-1900*, by Henry C. Peden, Jr., 2022, p. 373)

Websters Grist Mill, on James Run at Calvary, James Webster, prop. (*Mills: Grist, Saw, Bone, Flint, Fulling ... & More*, by Jack L. Shagena, Jr., Henry C. Peden, Jr. and John W. McGrain, 2009, pp. 274-275)

Webster, Abraham (colored), see Mary Martha Webster (colored) and Sarah Jane Webster (colored), q.v.

Webster, Adaline B., 1830-1911 (Calvary Methodist Church Cemetery)

Webster, Alfonso (colored), 1890-1978, World War I veteran (Union Methodist Church Cemetery, Aberdeen)

Webster. Alfred (colored), see William Webster (colored), q.v.

Webster, Anna Jane (Stump), 1840-1911 (Calvary Methodist Church Cemetery)

Webster, Annie (Presberry) (colored), c1872-1940, see Annie Presberry (colored), q.v.

Webster, Annie E. (colored), 1888-1981 (Berkley Memorial Cemetery)

Webster, Annie E. (Bradford) (colored), 1847-1915, native of Maryland, daughter of Benedict Bradford and Jane James, also of Maryland (Death certificate)

Webster, Annie Eliza Cornelia (colored), born 20 Nov 1881, daughter of Milkie Ann Webster and Isaac Dennison (St. George's Episcopal Church Register of Baptisms, pp. 2-3)

Webster, Annie Lester, born 13 Feb 1872, daughter of John Thomas and Susanna (Mitchell) Webster (Churchville Presbyterian Church Register Roll of Infant Church Members or Baptized Children, No. 250)

Webster, Augusta (Moore), 1875-1958 (St. Mary's Catholic Church Cemetery)

Webster, Benjamin (colored), 1889-1917, native of Berkley, Harford Co., son of Elisha and Jane Webster (Death certificate)

Webster, Benjamin Franklin, 1862-1947 (Emory Methodist Church Cemetery)

Webster, Benjamin Franklin, Jr., 1887-1958 (St. Ignatius Catholic Church Cemetery)

Webster, Caroline Henderson (McCormick), 1821-1907, wife of Edwin Hanson Webster, of Henry, q.v.

Webster, Caroline Henderson, born 6 Jan 1876, daughter of William and Anna Jane (Webster) Stump (Churchville Presbyterian Church Register Roll of Infant Church Members or Baptized Children, No. 302)

Webster, Caroline M., 1870-1950 (Calvary Methodist Church Cemetery)

Webster, Carroll M. (colored), 1888-1945 (Berkley Memorial Cemetery); native of Harford Co., son of Moses C. Webster and Georgia C. Valentine, also of Harford Co. (Death certificate)

Webster, Catharine (colored), student, McComas Institute in the Abingdon District, and stepdaughter of Annie Talbot (*The Aegis & Intelligencer*, 21 Feb 1890)

Webster, Celeste (Wright), 1888-1982 (St. Mary's Catholic Church Cemetery)

Webster, Charles (colored), 1859-1938, son of Thomas Webster and Rachel Smith, all natives of Darlington, Harford Co. (Death certificate); see Edward Webster and Logan A. Webster, q.v.

Webster, Clara J. (colored), 1878-1930, native of Maryland, born 1 Sep 1878, daughter of Edwin Webster and Alice Bond (Death certificate)

Webster, Daniel (colored), 1865-1933 (Death certificate); husband of Mary Williams, q.v.

Webster, Daniel Robert (colored), 1889-1966, son of Phillip W. Webster and Mary Aikins (*The Aegis*, 9 Jun 1966)

Webster, Della (Smith) (colored), 1865-1951, native of Harford Co., daughter of William Smith and Rachel Corn (Death certificate - married name Densby)

Webster, Dora C. (Rouse), 1874-1930, wife of James Edwin Webster, q.v., and daughter of John Gouldsmith Rouse, q.v.

Webster, Dora (colored), 1890-1915, native of Maryland, daughter of Moses Webster and Georgia Presberry (Death certificate)

Webster, Edward (colored), 1882-1919, native of Maryland, son of Charles H. Webster and Sarah A. Berry (Death certificate)

Webster, Edwin (colored), see Clara J. Webster (colored), q.v.

Webster, Edwin Hanson, of Henry, 1829-1893 (Calvary Methodist Church Cemetery); president, Harford National Bank (*The Aegis & Intelligencer*, 2 May 1890); colonel, US Army, Civil War veteran, Bel Air (*1890 Special Census of the Civil War Veterans of the State of Maryland*, by L. Tilden Moore, Volume III, p. 72)

Webster, Edwin Hanson, of John, 1859-1929 (Calvary Methodist Church Cemetery); attorney-at-law (*Havre de Grace Republican*, 25 Apr 1890); jousting tournament rider, Knight of the Creek (*Havre de Grace Republican*, 19 Sep 1890)

Webster, Elinore Rice (colored), 1876-1930, native of Maryland, born 16 Nov 1876, daughter of George Webster and Eliza Gibson (Death certificate - married name Taylor)

Webster, Elisha (colored), 1865-1931, native of Castleton, Harford Co., son of William Webster and Annie Prigg (Death certificate); see Benjamin Webster, q.v.

Webster, Eliza (colored), see Charles W. Dennison, Jr. (colored) and Mary M. Dennison (colored), q.v.

Webster, Eliza (Gibson) (colored), c1837-1917, native of Harford Co. (Death certificate)

Webster, Eva Virginia (colored), 1885-1900, servant, native of Maryland, resided at Poole, daughter of Moses E. Webster and Georgia Valentine (Death certificate)

Webster, George (colored), 1868-1916, native of Harford Co. (Death certificate)

Webster, George (coloed), see Elinore Rice Webster (colored), q.v.

Webster, George H. (colored), see Mary A. Snowden (colored), q.v.

Webster, George Smith, 1825-1902 (Calvary Methodist Church Cemetery)

Webster, Georgia (Presberry) (colored), 1862-1908, native of Pennsylvania, resided at Castleton, Harford Co. (Death certificate)

Webster, Georgianna C. (Heuisler), 1856-192 (St. Mary's Catholic Church Cemetery)

Webster, Harriet Susanna, born 14 Jun 1874, daughter of John Thomas Webster and Susanna Mitchell (Churchville Presbyterian Church Register Roll of Infant Church Members or Baptized Children, No. 260); Hattie Webster, student, Bel Air Academy and Graded School (*The Aegis & Intelligencer*, 23 May 1890)

Webster, Hattie P., 1880-1969 (St. Mary's Episcopal Church Cemetery)

Webster, Helen B. (colored), 1876-1916, native of Harford Co., born 11 Jul 1876, daughter of M. N. Webster and Sarah Bessicks, natives of Harford Co. (Death certificate - married name Hawkins)

Webster, Henrietta M. (Ady), 1859-1915 (St. Ignatius Catholic Church Cemetery); first wife of Benjamin Franklin Webster, q.v.

Webster, Henry, 1855-1939 (Calvary Methodist Church Cemetery)

Webster, Ida, wife of John Abell Hunter, q.v.; also see Martha Abell Hunter, q.v.

Webster, J., center fielder, Creswell Baseball Club (*The Aegis & Intelligencer*, 18 Jul 1890)

Webster, J. Thomas, resident near Harford Furnace (*The Aegis & Intelligencer*, 9 May 1890); superintendent, Churchville Presbyterian Church Sunday School (*The Aegis & Intelligencer*, 13 Jun 1890); trustee, Harford Furnace School No. 2, First District (*Havre de Grace Republican*, 30 May 1890)

Webster, Jacob, husband of Rose Webster, q.v.

Webster, Jacob Brown, 1840-1899 (Calvary Methodist Church Cemetery; Death certificate); member, Calvary Road League (*The Aegis & Intelligencer*, 17 Jan 1890); trustee, Calvary School No. 11, Third District (*Havre de Grace Republican*, 30 May 1890)

Webster, Jacob W. (colored), 1855-1921 (Union Methodist Church Cemetery, Aberdeen)

Webster, James, 1814-1902 (Calvary Methodist Church Cemetery)

Webster, James (colored), see Nellie (Garrison) Webster (colored), q.v.

Webster, James Byas (Dr.), 1828-1890 (Webster Family Cemetery); Civil War veteran, (*1890 Special Census of the Civil War Veterans of the State of Maryland*, by L. Tilden Moore, Volume III, p. 61); removed from the voter registration list at Abingdon, First District (*Havre de Grace Republican*, 17 Oct 1890); son of Capt. John Adams Webster, died at *Mount Adams* near Creswell (*The Aegis & Intelligencer*, 15 Aug 1890)

Webster, James E. (colored), 1853-1921 (Union Methodist Church Cemetery, Aberdeen)

Webster, James Edwin, 1857-1928 (Christ Episcopal Church Cemetery); State's Attorney for Harford County (*Havre de Grace Republican*, 24 Jan 1890 and 14 Feb 1890); director, Bel Air Trust Company (*Havre de Grace Republican*, 14 Mar 1890)

Webster, Jane (colored), see Benjamin Webster (colored), q.v.

Webster, John, trustee, Clermont School No. 13, Fourth District (*Havre de Grace Republican*, 30 May 1890); also see Edwin H. Webster, q.v.

Webster, John A. (colored), 1882-1960 (Berkley Memorial Cemetery)

Webster, John Adams, see James Byas Webster and Charles Boston q.v.

Webster, John Stump, 1873-1948 (Churchville Presbyterian Church); born 17 Jun 1873, son of William Webster and Anna Jane Stump (Churchville Presbyterian Church Register Roll of Infant Church Members or Baptized Children, No. 254)

Webster, John T. (colored), 1855-1927, native of Maryland (Death certificate)

Webster, John Thomas, 1842-1912 (Calvary Methodist Church Cemetery)

Webster, John W., 1857-1916 (St. Mary's Catholic Church Cemetery); see Mary E. Webster, q.v.

Webster, Joseph Ignatius, 1890-1962 (St. Ignatius Catholic Church Cemetery)

Webster, Logan A., 1884-1919, native of Maryland, son of Charles H. Webster and Sarah Berry (Death certificate)

Webster, M. E. (Mrs.), premium award winner, Class E - Poultry, Harford County Fair (*The Aegis & Intelligencer*, 24 Oct 1890)

Webster, M. N. (colored), see Helen B. Webster (colored), q.v.

Webster, Mabel P. (Presberry) (colored), 1876-1948, native of Harford Co., daughter of Robert Presberry and Jane Howard (Death certificate)

Webster, Marie Elizabeth, 1833-1909 (Calvary Methodist Church Cemetery)

Webster, Martha L. (Mrs.) (colored), 1876-1956 (St. James United Cemetery)

Webster, Mary A., age 21 in 1889 (Marriage License Applications Book ALJ No. 2, 1889)

Webster, Mary A. (colored), see Mary A. Snowden (colored), q.v.

Webster, Mary E., 1885-1971 (St. Mary's Catholic Church Cemetery); native of Rocks, Harford Co., born 24 Jun 1885, daughter of John W. Webster and Georgianna Heuisler (Harkins Funeral Home Records)

Webster, Mary F. (Snodgrass), 1886-1968 (Emory Methodist Church Cemetery); native of Street, Harford Co., born 9 Sep 1886, daughter of John Snodgrass and Hannah Sanders (Harkins Funeral Home Records)

Webster, Mary J. (Kenley) (colored), 1858-1923, native of Maryland, daughter of William Kenley and Mary Aikens (Death certificate); see Mary A. Snowden, q.v.

Webster, Mary M. (colored), age 20 in 1890 (Marriage License Applications Book ALJ No. 2, 1890)

Webster, Mary Martha (colored), 1882-1944, native of Maryland, born 17 Oct 1882, daughter of Abraham Webster and Mary Prigg (Death certificate - married name Hawkins)

Webster, Mary Olivia (Christie) (colored), c1848-1908, native of Harford Co., resided near Perryman (Death certificate)

Webster, Mary W. (colored), born 1868, died ---- (Berkley Memorial Cemetery)

Webster, Matilda, or Matilda Peck *(sic)*, c1849-1911, native of Lancaster Co., PA, resided at Dublin, Harford Co. (Death certificate)

Webster, Milkie Ann (colored), see Annie Eliza Cornelia Webster (colored), q.v.

Webster, Nellie (Garrison) (colored), 1846-1901, native of Maryland, resided at Perryman, wife of James Webster (Death certificate)

Webster, Moses (colored), see Carroll M. Webster, Dora Webster and Eva V. Webster, q.v.

Webster, Nellie (Garrison) (colored), c1856-1901, native of Maryland (Death certificate)

Webster, Phillip (colored), 1839-1915 (Berkley Memorial Cemetery; Death certificate); Civil War veteran, at Stafford (*1890 Special Census of the Civil War Veterans of the State of Maryland*, by L. Tilden Moore, Volume III, p. 86); see Daniel Robert Webster, q.v.

Webster, Priscilla Frances (Smithson), 1821-1919 (Calvary Methodist Church Cemetery), mother of Benjamin F. Webster, q.v.

Webster, Richard E., 1833-1923 (Calvary Methodist Church Cemetery)

Webster, Richard Henry, born 18 Jul 1870, son of William Webster and Anna Jane Stump (Churchville Presbyterian Church Register Roll of Infant Church Members or Baptized Children, No. 243); premium award winner, Class E - Poultry, Harford County Fair (*The Aegis & Intelligencer*, 24 Oct 1890)

Webster, Rose (Thompson), 1863-1900, native of Harford Co., resident of Havre de Grace, wife of Jacon Webster (Death certificate)

Webster, Sabina (colored), 1828-1913, native of Maryland (Death certificate)

Webster, Sallie (Brown), 1850-1922 (Calvary Methodist Church Cemetery)

Webster, Sarah (colored), see Margaret Bessex (colored), q.v.

Webster, Sarah A. (Berry) (colored), 1860-1935, native of Harford Co., daughter of Alexander Berry and Ann Peaco (Death certificate)

Webster, Sarah Jane (Fletcher), 1838-1910 (Calvary Methodist Church Cemetery); confirmed 1 Nov 1890 (Churchville Presbyterian Church Chronological Roll of Communicants, No. 553);wife of Jacob B. Webster, q.v.

Webster, Sarah Jane (Webster) (colored), 1872-1941, native of Harford Co., daughter of Abraham Webster and Mary Prigg, both natives of Harford Co. (Death certificate)

Webster, Sophia C., 1836-1906 (Calvary Methodist Church Cemetery)

Webster, Sophie (Miss), honor student, Archer Institute, Bel Air (*The Aegis & Intelligencer*, 20 Jun 1890)

Webster, Susanna (Mitchell), 1839-1925 (Calvary Methodist Church Cemetery)

Webster, Thomas (colored), see Charles Webster (colored), q.v.

Webster, William, 1831-1914 (Calvary Methodist Church Cemetery); vice president of the Third Annual Convention, Farmers' Club of Harford County (*Havre de Grace Republican*, 5 Dec 1890); vice president, Harford County Farmers' Association (*The Aegis & Intelligencer*, 17 Jan 1890); director, Harford County Agricultural and Mechanical Society (*The Aegis & Intelligencer*, 10 Jan 1890); served on a grand jury foreman, Third District (*Havre de Grace Republican*, 31 Jan and 14 Feb 1890); insurance company board of directors (*Havre de Grace Republican*, 10 Jan 1890); trustee, Calvary School No. 11, Third District (*Havre de Grace Republican*, 30 May 1890); premium award winner, Class C - Sheep, Harford County Fair (*The Aegis & Intelligencer*, 24 Oct 1890)

Webster, William, 1865-1923 (St. Mary's Catholic Church Cemetery)

Webster, William (colored), see Annie Presberry (colored) and Elisha Webster (colored), q.v.

Webster, William (colored), c1829-1914, native of Maryland (Death certificate)

Webster, William (colored), 1873-1912, native of Maryland, son of Alfred Webster and Ann James (Death certificate)

Webster, William E. (Mrs.), premium award winner, Class O - Discretionary, Harford County Fair (*The Aegis & Intelligencer*, 24 Oct 1890); premium award winner, Class J - Domestic Products, Harford County Fair (*The Aegis & Intelligencer*, 24 Oct 1890)

Wechter, Arthur Wayne, 1857-1926 (Neffsville Lutheran Cemetery, PA); native of Pennsylvania, farmer, resided near Churchville (Death certificate); W. Wechter, treated by unidentified doctor, 1890 ("Medical Account Book – 1890," Historical Society of Harford County Archives Folder)

Wechter, Mary C., wife of Arthur W. Wechter, q.v.

Weedly, Emma H. (Mrs.), premium award winner, Class K - Household and Domestic Manufactures, Harford County Fair (*The Aegis & Intelligencer*, 24 Oct 1890)

Weeks, Bertha (Frieze) (colored), 1873-1941 (Death certificate)

Weeks, George, premium award winner, Class A - Horses, Harford County Fair (*The Aegis & Intelligencer*, 24 Oct 1890)

Weeks, Harriet Ann (colored), 1855-1942 (Death certificate)

Weeks, John T., butcher, resident of S. J. Whiteford's farm at Line Bridge (*The Aegis & Intelligencer*, 24 Jan 1890)

Weeks, Susan, 1824-1899 (St. Mary's Catholic Church Cemetery)

Weeks, Tacy, see Lyda Cox and Harry Enfield, q.v.

Weeks, William T. (colored), 1880-1939 (Death certificate)

Weems, Robert (colored), born -- Apr 1882, native of Maryland (1900 Aberdeen Census)

Wehrman, Joseph, prelate, Harford Lodge No. 54, Knights of Pythias, Havre de Grace (*The Aegis & Intelligencer*, 11 Jul 1890)

Weikert, Elizabeth (Bailey), 1833-1915 (Rock Run Methodist Church Cemetery; *Barnes-Bailey Genealogy*, by Walter D. Barnes, 1939, p. G-19)

Weikert, John, 1866-1951, son of ---- and Elizabeth B. Weikert (Rock Run Methodist Church Cemetery)

Weiser, Frederick, 1883-1940 (Death certificate; Heavenly Waters Cemetery)

Welch, Ann Teresa, 1826-1901 (St. Mary's Catholic Church Cemetery)

Welch, Ellen E., 1886-1965 (St. Mary's Catholic Church Cemetery)

Welch, Ella J., 1884-1965 (St. Mary's Catholic Church Cemetery); born 1 Nov 1884, daughter of Thomas Welch and Rebecca Dick (Harkins Funeral Home Records)

Welch, Emma F. (Miss), graduate of State Normal School (*Havre de Grace Republican*, 6 Jun 1890)

Welch, Frank James, 1886-1959 (Angel Hill Cemetery)

Welch, Isaac (colored), 1839-1907 (Death certificate)

Welch, James E., 1849-1924 (St. Mary's Catholic Church Cemetery)

Welch, Jane C., 1850-1931 (St. Mary's Catholic Church Cemetery)

Welch, Joseph E., new name on the Havre de Grace voter registration list (*Havre de Grace Republican*, 19 Sep 1890)

Welch, Joseph E. (colored), 1871-1911 (Union Methodist Church Cemetery, Aberdeen)

Welch, Lucy F. A., 1888-1957 (Angel Hill Cemetery)

Welch, Mary Ann, see Alice J. Glackin, q.v.

Welch, Mary R., 1860-1931 (St. Mary's Catholic Church Cemetery)

Welch, Susanna "Susan" (colored), c1852-1917 (Death certificate; Alms House Record Book)

Welch, Teresa C., see Teresa C. Kulp, q.v.

Welch, Thomas, see Ella J. Welch and Teresa C. Kulp, q.v.

Welch, Thomas M., 1854-1927 (St. Mary's Catholic Church Cemetery)

Welch, William H., 1887-1956 (St. Mary's Catholic Church Cemetery)

Wells & Cronin Saw Mill, Aberdeen (*Harford Democrat*, 28 Feb 1890)

Wells, ---- (Mr.), mail carrier from Dublin to Aberdeen (*The Aegis & Intelligencer*, 28 Feb 1890)

Wells, ----, left fielder, Nonpareil Baseball Club, Aberdeen (*Havre de Grace Republican*, 6 Jun 1890)

Wells, ----, shortstop, Aberdeen Baseball Club (*The Aegis & Intelligencer*, 25 Jul 1890)

Wells, Ada H. (Osborn), 1865-1950 (Baker Cemetery), wife of Robert Wildey Wells, q.v.

Wells, Annie C. (Enswiler), 1861-1951 (North East Methodist Church Cemetery, Cecil Co., MD), wife of Ira Wells, q.v.

Wells, C. Elmer, 1866-1891 (St. George's Episcopal Church Cemetery)

Wells, Carrie (Miss), resident of Perryman (*The Aegis & Intelligencer*, 2 May 1890)

Wells, Carvel (colored), see Henry Wells (colored), q.v.

Wells, Charlotte (Connor), c1830-1924 (Angel Hill Cemetery), wife of James B. Wells, q.v.

Wells, Edward Asels, born 3 Sep 1872, son of Joseph and Matilda C. Wells (St. George's Episcopal Church Register of Baptisms, pp. 4-5)

Wells, Edward C., 1871-1948 (Grove Presbyterian Church Cemetery)

Wells, Eli J., 1881-1931 (Baker Cemetery)

Wells, Elizabeth (Cole), 1824-1896 (Baker Cemetery), mother of Robert Wildey Wells, q.v.

Wells, Eugene D., 1862-1929 (Angel Hill Cemetery)

Wells, Florence (colored), see Ellen Wells Daugherty (colored), q.v.

Wells, Fritz, 1878-1946 (Heavenly Waters Cemetery; Alms House Record Book)

Wells, George B., 1850-1901 (Union Chapel Methodist Church Cemetery); George Wells, and family, resided at Fallston (*The Aegis & Intelligencer*, 3 Jan 1890)

Wells, George (colored), see Mary E. Dorsey (colored) and Laura Wells (colored), q.v.

Wells, Harriett (colored), see William Henry Taylor (colored), q.v.

Wells, Henry (colored), c1875-1933, native of Maryland, son of Carvel Wells and Mary Williams (Death certificate)

Wells, Henry Lee, 1852-1928 (Angel Hill Cemetery)

Wells, Ira, 1851-1932 (North East Methodist Church Cemetery, Cecil Co., MD); hotel proprietor, Central Hotel, St. John and Green Streets, Havre de Grace (*Havre de Grace Republican*, 24 Jan 1890); delegate, Sixth District, Republican Party Convention (*The Aegis & Intelligencer*, 26 Sep 1890); juror, Sixth District (*Havre de Grace Republican*, 31 Oct 1890)

Wells, J., sneak boat duck hunter (*Havre de Grace Republican*, 7 Nov 1890)

Wells, James, 1837-1908 (Union Chapel Methodist Church Cemetery)

Wells, James Bayard, c1830-1921 (Angel Hill Cemetery)

Wells, Jams Frank, 1869-1944 (Cokesbury Memorial Methodist Church Cemetery)

Wells, James M., 1884-1951 (Mt. Zion Methodist Church Cemetery)

Wells, James W., 1842-1906 (St. George's Episcopal Church Cemetery); J. W. Wells, farmer, at Spirngdale near Perryman (*Havre de Grace Republican*, 4 Apr 1890; *Harford Democrat*, 28 Mar 1890)

Wells, John B., age 21 in 1890 (Marriage License Applications Book ALJ No. 2, 1891)

Wells, John Finney, 1854-1933 (Baker Cemetery); chief manager, Carsins Run Camp Meeting of the East Harford Circuit, P. E. Church (*The Aegis & Intelligencer*, 1 Aug 1890); acquired land in February 1890 (*The Aegis & Intelligencer*, 7 Mar 1890)

Wells, Joseph, see Edward Asels Wells, q.v.

Wells, L. Amelia, 1889-1951 (Mt. Zion Methodist Church Cemetery)

Wells, Laura (colored), 1863-1923, born in Maryland, daughter of George Wells and Amanda Presco (Death certificate states born 1863, but Asbury Church Cemetery tombstone states 1865)

Wells, Laura A., 1872-1945 (Cokesbury Memorial Methodist Church Cemetery)

Wells, Margaret R., 1886-1971 (Baker Cemetery)

Wells, Martha J. (Snowden) (colored), 1864-1927, native of Maryland (Death certificate)

Wells, Mary A., 1809-1898 (Wells-Cole Family Cemetery, Aberdeen, now gone)

Wells, Mary E. (colored), see Mary E. Dorsey (colored), q.v.

Wells, Matilda C., see Edward Asels Wells, q.v.

Wells, Minnie L. (Gerting), 1878-1938 (Grove Presbyterian Church Cemetery), wife of Edward C. Wells, q.v.

Wells, Mollie Richardson (Herring), 1860-1917 (St. George's Episcopal Church Cemetery); wife of John Finney Wells, q.v.

Wells, R. K., storekeeper, St. John Street, Havre de Grace (*Havre de Grace Republican*, 16 May 1890)

Wells, Richard G., 1854-1901 (Baker Cemetery)

Wells, Robert E., 1890-1959 (Cokesbury Memorial Methodist Church Cemetery)

Wells, Robert Wildey, 1866-1909 (Baker Cemetery)

Wells, Sarah M., 1852-1935 (Angel Hill Cemetery)

Wells, Sarah R., 1840-1920 (St. George's Episcopal Church Cemetery); see Effie M. Arthur, q.v.

Wells, Semelia A., sold land in February 1890 (*The Aegis & Intelligencer*, 7 Mar 1890)

Wells, Susie L (McMaster), 1855-1934 (Angel Hill Cemetery)

Wells, Telitha (colored), see Agnes J. Corns (colored), q.v.

Wells, William Alfred, 1856-1924 (Mt. Olivet Cemetery, Baltimore Co.); native of Harford Co., single, carpenter, resided at Aberdeen (Death certificate)

Welsh, Alice C. (colored), daughter of Isaac A. and Harriet A. Welsh, born 29 May 1876 and indentured to Thomas J. Tydings in October 1888 (Harford County Indentures Book WSB No. 1)

Welsh, Alice R. (colored), 1887-1906 (Asbury Church Cemetery)

Welsh, Anna R., 1890-1985 (Mt. Erin Cemetery)

Welsh, Augusta "Gussie Minnie, 1860-1953 (Baker Cemetery)

Welsh, Catherine J., 1865-1944 (Mt. Erin Cemetery)

Welsh, Daniel K. (colored), 1888-1975 (Union Methodist Church Cemetery, Aberdeen)

Welsh, Elizabeth, wife of Theodore Henderson Welsh, q.v.

Welsh, Garrett, see William Nathaniel Welsh, q.v.

Welsh, Harriet (colored), see Alice C. Welsh (colored), q.v.

Welsh, Harry W., 1880-1909 (Baker Cemetery)

Welsh, Isaac (colored), trustee, Gunpowder Neck Colored School No. 3, First District (*Havre de Grace Republican*, 30 May 1890); also see Alice C. Welsh, q.v.

Welsh, Johanna, wife of Martin Flavin, q.v.; also see Katherine V. Flavin, q.v.

Welsh, John, 1854-1937 (Mt. Erin Cemetery); sold land in November 1890 (*The Aegis & Intelligencer*, 5 Dec 1890); see Katherine Welsh, q.v.

Welsh, John W. (colored), 1866-1951, native of Edgewood, Harford Co. (Death certificate)

Welsh, Joseph C., 1885-1949 (Baker Cemetery)

Welsh, Julia A., 1859-1918 (Mt. Erin Cemetery)

Welsh, Katherine, 1885-1963, native of Havre de Grace, born 15 Jul 1885, daughter of John Welsh and Mary McGee (Pennington Funeral Home Records)

Welsh, Margaret (Fahey), 1836-1901, native of Ireland, resided at Havre de Grace (Death certificate states 1829, but Mt. Erin Cemetery tombstone states 1836); wife of Patrick Welsh, q.v.

Welsh, Mary (colored), age 21 in 1890 (Marriage License Applications Book ALJ No. 2, 1891)

Welsh, Mary (colored), wife of Leven Henry Collins, Sr.., q.v.

Welsh, Myrtle V., born 1890, died ---- (Baker Cemetery)

Welsh, Patrick, 1834-1911 (Mt. Erin Cemetery)

Welsh, Theodore Henderson, 1820-1901, native of Harford Co., veterinarian at Chestnut Hill (Death certificate)

Welsh, Thomas P., 1860-1917 (Baker Cemetery)

Welsh, Warner W., 1884-1973 (Darlington Cemetery)

Welsh, William Nathaniel (colored), born 22 Jul 1884, son of Garrett and Sedonia Welsh (Holy Trinity Episcopal Church Register of Baptisms, p. 86, spelled his father's surname Walsh)

Welsh, William T., 1870-1907 (Norrisville Methodist Church Cemetery)

Wendt, Charles W. J., 1860-1890 (Broad Creek Friends Cemetery); native of Germany, resided near Dublin, married, but no children (*The Aegis & Intelligencer*, 5 Dec 1890 and 19 Dec 1890)

Wendt, Ernest A., 1878-1957 (Emory Methodist Church Cemetery)

Wene, Charles, 1808-1891 (Alms House Record Book)

Werner, John, sneak boat duck hunter (*Havre de Grace Republican*, 7 Nov 1890)

Wesley Colored Public School No. 2, Upper Cross Roads, Fourth District (*Harford County, Maryland Teachers and the Schools They Served, 1774-1900*, by Henry C. Peden, Jr., 2022, p. 373)

Wesley, Stephen, Civil War veteran, Delta P. O. (*1890 Special Census of the Civil War Veterans of the State of Maryland*, by L. Tilden Moore, Volume III, p. 84)

Wesleyan Chapel Methodist Church and Cemetery (Paradise Road, near Aberdeen)

West Liberty AME Church and Cemetery (Fallston Road near Nelson Lane)

West Liberty Colored Public School No. 2, Upper Cross Roads, Fourth District (*Harford County, Maryland Teachers and the Schools They Served, 1774-1900*, by Henry C. Peden, Jr., 2022, p. 373)

West, Clarkson H., 1815-1899, resident near High Point (Death certificate; Fallston Methodist Church Cemetery; *The Aegis & Intelligencer*, 24 Jan 1890)

West, Frank Hanway, 1862-1944 (Fallston Methodist Church Cemetery); resident near Fallston (*The Aegis & Intelligencer*, 15 Aug 1890)

West, Helen (Edel), 1883-1977 (Fallston Methodist Church Cemetery)

West, Helena L. (Forwood), 1883-1968 (Deer Creek Methodist Church Cemetery); native of Forest Hill, Harford Co., daughter of Parker L. Forwood and Julia Smithson (Harkins Funeral Home Records)

West, Isabella (Blair), 1824-1914, native of Pennsylvania, resident near Forest Hill (Death certificate; Fallston Methodist Church Cemetery); widow of Clarkson H. West, q.v.

West, James Alexander, 1866-1936 (Fallston Methodist Church Cemetery)

West, Louisa W. (Ewing), 1836-1908, native of Dublin, Harford Co., resided at Chrome Hill (Death certificate; William Watters Memorial Methodist Church Cemetery, Cooptown)

West, Mary (Dallam), 1809-1907 (William Watters Memorial Methodist Church Cemetery, Cooptown)

West, Wilson Dallam, 1836-1908 (William Watters Memorial Church Cemetery, Cooptown); trustee, Chrome

Hill School No. 16, Fourth District (*Havre de Grace Republican*, 30 May 1890); Civil War veteran, Chrome Hill (*1890 Special Census of the Civil War Veterans of the State of Maryland*, by L. Tilden Moore, Volume III, p. 78); quartermaster, Wann Post No. 49, G. A. R., of Forest Hill (*Havre de Grace Republican*, 25 Jul 1890); delegate, Fourth District, Republican Party Convention (*The Aegis & Intelligencer*, 26 Sep 1890)

Westcott, Augusta (colored), 1851-1909, native of Maryland, servant in Bel Air, wife of Noah Westcott (Death certificate states her maiden name was Prigg; other records state it was Spriggs)

Westcott (Wescott), Bertha J. (colored), 1886-1960 (Mt. Zion Methodist Church Cemetery, at Mountain); wife of Carvel A. Westcott (Wescott), q.v.

Westcott (Wescott), Carvel A. (colored), 1890-1962 (Mt. Zion Methodist Church Cemetery, at Mountain)

Westcott (Wastcoat), Cordelia A. (colored), 1885-1912, native of Harford Co., born 10 De 1885, daughter of Noah Wastcoat and Agusta Prigg [Augusta Spriggs] (Death certificate - married name Hill); see Henrietta Wastcoat, q.v.

Westcott (Westcoat), Ella M., 1876-1929, native of Maryland, born 6 Mar 1876, daughter of Noah Westcott and Augusta Spriggs (Death certificate - married name Waters)

Westcott (Wescott), Henrietta, 1881-1928 (Hendon Hill Cemetery); native of Maryland, resided near Bel Air, born 7 Aug 1881, daughter of Noah Wescott, of North Carolina, and Augusta Spriggs, of Maryland (Death certificate - married name Lisby); see Cordelia A. Wastcoat, q.v.

Westcott (Wescott, Wastcoat), Noah (colored), see Augusta Westcott, Cordelia A. Westcott, Ella M. Westcott and Henrietta Westcott, q.v.

Westerall, Jeremiah Alexander, 1857-1926 (Cokesbury Memorial Methodist Church Cemetery); native of Maryland, married, farmer, resided at Joppa (Death certificate)

Westerblad, Ruth E. (Jourdan), 1881-1951 (Darlington Cemetery); native of Harford Co., born 11 Jul 1881, daughter of C. Reed Jourdan and Martha J. Hopkins (Bailey Funeral Home Records)

Westerman, John L., new name on the voter registration list in Sixth District, 1890 (*Havre de Grace Republican*, 17 Oct 1890)

Westphal, Catherine (Myers), 1830-1901, native of Germany, resided at Gibson (Death certificate)

Wetherall, Benener Knight, 1840-1896 (Cokesbury Memorial Methodist Church Cemetery)

Wetherall, J., road surveying chain man, First District (*Havre de Grace Republican*, 4 Jul 1890)

Wetherall, Jeremiah Alexander, 1838-1926, native of Maryland, farmer, near Joppa (Cokesbury Memorial Methodist Church Cemetery tombstone inscribed 1840, but death certificate states 1838); Civil War veteran, Clayton (*1890 Special Census of the Civil War Veterans of the State of Maryland*, by L. Tilden Moore, Volume III, p. 61); trustee, Prospect Hill School No. 5, First District (*Havre de Grace Republican*, 30 May 1890)

Wetherall, Mary A., 1841-1925 (Cokesbury Memorial Methodist Church Cemetery)

Wetherill's General Store, at The Rocks, Joseph R. Wetherill, prop. (*Country Stores: Harford County's Rural Heritage*, by Henry C. Peden, Jr. and Jack L. Shagena, Jr., 2015, p. 261)

Wetherill, B. (Mrs.), treasurer, Magnolia M. E. Church Sunday School (*Havre de Grace Republican*, 2 May 1890)

Wetherill, Eliza Mirza, see Mary Ellen Gladden q.v.

Wetherill, James O. E., Civil War veteran, Magnolia (*1890 Special Census of the Civil War Veterans of the State of Maryland*, by L. Tilden Moore, Volume III, p. 62); government pensioner, of Magnolia (*The Aegis & Intelligencer*, 25 Apr 1890); superintendent, Magnolia M. E. Church Sunday School (*Havre de Grace Republican*, 2 May 1890); trustee, Magnolia School No. 6, First District (*Havre de Grace Republican*, 30 May 1890)

Wetherill, Joseph R., 1837-1926 (Immanuel Episcopal Church Cemetery, Sparks, Baltimore Co.); resided at Rocks, Harford Co.; see Watters' General Store, q.v.

Wetherill, Mary W., 1849-1931 (William Watters Memorial Church Cemetery, Cooptown)

Wetherill, Rebecca H. (Miss), 1844-1918 (William Watters Memorial Church Cemetery; Samuel Wetherill Bible, *Maryland Bible Records, Volume 2*, by Henry C. Peden, Jr., 2003, p. 177); see Waters & Wetherill, q.v.

Wetherill, Solomon S., 1824-1895 (William Watters Memorial Church Cemetery, Cooptown; Samuel Wetherill Bible, *Maryland Bible Records, Volume 2*, by Henry C. Peden, Jr., 2003, p. 177)

Wetherill, William Philemon, 1839-1924 (William Watters Memorial Church Cemetery, Cooptown; Samuel Wetherill Bible, *Maryland Bible Records, Volume 2*, by Henry C. Peden, Jr., 2003, p. 177)

Whaland, Bridget (Carroll), 1820-1894 (St. Ignatius Catholic Church Cemetery)

Whaland, Ellen Catherine, born 6 Aug 1885, baptized 23 Aug 1885, daughter of James and Johanna (Hartigan) Whaland (St. Ignatius Catholic Church Baptism Register, p. 82)

Whaland, J. Maurice, 1889-1946 (St. Ignatius Catholic Church Cemetery)

Whaland, James P., 1856-1930 (St. Ignatius Catholic Church Cemetery)

Whaland, Johanna (Hartigan), 1860-1946 (St. Ignatius Catholic Church Cemetery)

Whaland (Whalen), Lawrence, enumerated as age 87 in the 1890 census, First District (*Havre de Grace Republican*, 22 Aug 1890, listed a handful of names from the actual 1890 census and he was one of them); county out-pensioner [welfare recipient], First District (*Havre de Grace Republican*, 4 Jul 1890, reported his name as Larry Whalan); Larance Whalen, of Clayton, Harford Co., wrote his will in 1890 and died in 1891, naming son Thomas Whalen as his only heir (Harford County Will Book JMM 11:183-184)

Whaland, Michael, 1824-1907 (St. Ignatius Catholic Church Cemetery)

Whalen, Barry, 1890-1970 (Mt. Erin Cemetery)

Whalen, James P., 1852-1920 (Mt. Erin Cemetery)

Whalen, John T., 1860-1937 (Mt. Erin Cemetery)

Whalen, Julia, see Edward Ellsworth Hollahan, q.v.

Whalen, Margaret F., 1866-1948 (Mt. Erin Cemetery)

Whalen, Mary R., 1868-1919 (Angel Hill Cemetery)

Whalen, Thomas, see Lawrence Whaland (Whalen), q.v.

Whaling, Frederick C., 1867-1946 (Deer Creek Methodist Church Cemetery)

Whaling, Juliet Shannon, 1872-1949 (Deer Creek Methodist Church Cemetery)

Wheatley, George, first grade student, School No. 1, Third District (*The Aegis & Intelligencer*, 11 Jul 1890)

Wheatley, Nellie, student, School No. 1, Third District (*The Aegis & Intelligencer*, 11 Jul 1890)

Wheel Factory and Grist Mill, on Wheel Road, J. C. Hollingsworth & Sons, prop. (*Mills: Grist, Saw, Bone, Flint, Fulling ... & More*, by Jack L. Shagena, Jr., Henry C. Peden, Jr. and John W. McGrain, 2009, p. 277)

Wheeler & Wilson's General Store, at Rocks near Ma & Pa Station, William A. Wheeler and W. F. Wilson, prop. (*Country Stores: Harford County's Rural Heritage*, by Henry C. Peden, Jr. and Jack L. Shagena, Jr., 2015, p. 262)

Wheeler's Public School No. 1, near Pylesville, Fifth District (*Harford County, Maryland Teachers and the Schools They Served, 1774-1900*, by Henry C. Peden, Jr., 2022, p. 373)

Wheeler, Caroline "Carrie" Theresa, 1870-1947, daughter of Sylvester Wheeler and Martha Ann Glacken (St. Mary's Catholic Church Cemetery, married name Harry); teacher, LaGrange School No. 14, Fourth District (*The Aegis & Intelligencer*, 25 Apr 1890)

Wheeler, Harriett S., see Augustus Freeborn Brown, Jr., q.v.

Wheeler, Henry Green, 1833-1907 (Bethel Presbyterian Church Cemetery Records); farmer, near Black Horse (*The Aegis & Intelligencer*, 4 Jul 1890); trustee, Black Horse School No. 3, Fourth District (*Havre de Grace Republican*, 30 May 1890); see James A. Wheeler, q.v.

Wheeler, Ignatius M., of Harford County, guard at the Maryland House of Corrections (*Havre de Grace Republican*, 13 Jun 1890)

Wheeler, Israel M., 1851-1891 (St. Ignatius Catholic Church Cemetery)

Wheeler, James A., 1874-1965 (Bethel Presbyterian Church Cemetery Records); born 23 May 1874, son of Henry Green and Mary Ann (Cairnes) Wheeler, q.v.

Wheeler, John B., 1844-1901, "native of America," resided at Swan Creek (Death certificate incomplete)

Wheeler, John H., 1865-1940 (Slate Ridge Cemetery, York Co., PA); native of Harford Co., born 19 Sep 1865, son of Joseph H. Wheeler and Rachel A. Taylor (Harkins Funeral Home Records); resident of Delta, PA, age 25, married Mary E. Wiley, age 27, of Harford Co., 1890 (Marriage License Applications Book ALJ No. 2)

Wheeler, Joseph, see John H. Wheeler and Thomas H. Wheeler, q.v.

Wheeler, L. M. (Mrs.), of Thomas Run, aunt of Mrs. B. F. Thomas, of Baltimore (*The Aegis & Intelligencer*, 29 Aug 1890)

Wheeler, Leonard W., general road supervisor, Bel Air and Churchville Precincts (*The Aegis & Intelligencer*, 11 Apr 1890)

Wheeler, Lillian E. (Parrish), 1877-1941, daughter of Edward Moore Parrish and Sabra Ellen Henderson (Bethel Presbyterian Church Cemetery Records); first wife of James A. Wheeler, q.v.

Wheeler, Malissa (Brookhart) (Devoe), 1887-1964 (Bethel Presbyterian Church Cemetery Records); third wife of James A. Wheeler, q.v.

Wheeler, Mamie (Miss), of Thomas Run, sister of Mrs. M. A. Roberts, of Wilmington, DE (*The Aegis & Intelligencer*, 29 Aug 1890)

Wheeler, Margaret (Robinson), 1843-1917 (Bethel Presbyterian Church Cemetery Records); wife of Samuel W. Wheeler, q.v.

Wheeler, Mary Ann (Cairnes), 1833-1913 (Bethel Presbyterian Church Cemetery Records); wife of Henry Green Wheeler, q.v.

Wheeler, Mary E. (Tarbert), 1857-1932, wife of William Augustus Wheeler, q.v.

Wheeler, Mary Rose, born -- May 1889, baptized 2 Jun 1889, daughter of Bernard and Agnes (Bradley) Wheeler (St. Ignatius Catholic Church Baptism Register, p. 106)

Wheeler, Mattie (Miss), resident near the Rocks of Deer Creek (*Havre de Grace Republican*, 4 Jul 1890)

Wheeler, Pauline (Miss), resident of Thomas Run (*The Aegis & Intelligencer*, 24 Oct 1890)

Wheeler, Samuel W., 1839-1901, native of Maryland, painter at Forest Hill (Death certificate)

Wheeler, Thomas H., 1869-1950 (Slate Ridge Cemetery, York Co., PA); native of Harford Co., born 23 Nov 1869, son of Joseph Wheeler and Rachel Ann Taylor (Harkins Funeral Home Records)

Wheeler, William Augustus, 1856-1933 (Highland Presbyterian Church Cemetery); ruling elder, Highland Presbyterian Church (*The Aegis & Intelligencer*, 10 Jan 1890); W. A. Wheeler, former postmaster, The Rocks (*Havre de Grace Republican*, 18 Apr 1890); see Wheeler & Wilson's General Store, q.v.

Whims [Weems], Charles (colored), see Howard Whims (colored), q.v.

Whims [Wheems], Elizabeth (colored), see Stephen Preston (colored), q.v.

Whims, Ella (colored), 1872-1946, native of Harford Co., born 1 Apr 1872, daughter of Trilus Whymms [Whims] and ---- (Death certificate - married name Pitt)

Whims, Frances S. (colored), born -- Mar 1881, native of Maryland (1900 Aberdeen Census)

Whims, Frank (colored), 1879-1949, born in Maryland, born 21 Jun 1879, son of T. Whims and ---- (Death certificate)

Whims, Hattie C. (Webster) (colored), 1861-1930 (Death certificate)

Whims, Hetty (colored), 1828-1913, born in Maryland (Death certificate)

Whims, Howard (colored), 1870-1935, native of Maryland, born 7 Oct 1870, son of Charles Weems [Whims] and Anna Griffin (Death certificate informant was Maggie Whims]

Whims, Isaac W. (colored), age 23 in 1890 (Marriage License Applications Book ALJ No. 2; Holy Trinity

Episcopal Church Register of Marriages, p. 216)

Whims, Lydia "Lidie" (colored), 1888-1943, native of Harford Co.,. born -- Feb 1888, daughter of Snapp Whims and Mary McGaw, natives of Harford Co. (Death certificate - married name Monk; 1900 Aberdeen census stated her parents were Isaac and Mamie Whimms)

Whims, Lloyd (colored), born -- Jul 1889, native of Maryland, so of Isaac and Mamie Whims (1900 Aberdeen Census)

Whims, Louis (colored), 1860-1923, native of Harford Co., son of Trilus Whims and ---- (Death certificate)

Whims, Maggie (colored), see Howard Whims (colored), q.v.

Whims, Mamie, born -- Dec 1868, native of Pennsylvania, wife of Isaac Whims (1900 Aberdeen Census spelled the name Whimms)

Whims, Mary (colored), see Hannah Ellen Hall (colored), q.v.

Whims, Snapp (colored), see Lidie Whims (colored), q.v.

Whims, Trilus (colored) see Ella Whims, Frank Whims and Louis Whims, q.v.

Whistler, Elijah B., 1842-1935 (Mt. Zion Methodist Church Cemetery); resided near Fountain Green (*Harford Democrat*, 30 May 1890)

Whistler, Harry W., 1856-1928 (Mt. Zion Methodist Church Cemetery); native of Maryland, fertilizer salesman, married, resided at Fountain Green (Death certificate)

Whistler, Oleita, 1858-1935 (Mt. Zion Methodist Church Cemetery); Mrs. H. W. Whistler, premium award winner, Class K - Household and Domestic Manufactures, Harford County Fair, 1890 (*The Aegis & Intelligencer*, 24 Oct 1890)

Whistler, Sarah E., 1859-1953 (Mt. Zion Methodist Church Cemetery); Mrs. Sallie Whistler, of the Christian Church, vice president and corresponding secretary, Fountain Green Women's Christian Temperance Union (*Havre de Grace Republican*, 2 May 1890; *The Aegis & Intelligencer*, 25 Apr 1890)

Whistler, Samuel E., 1802-1891 (Mountain Christian Church Cemetery)

Whitaker's General Store, Upper Cross Roads, Marion S. Whitaker, prop. (*Country Stores: Harford County's Rural Heritage*, by Henry C. Peden, Jr. and Jack L. Shagena, Jr., 2015, p. 262)

Whitaker Mill (aka Duncale Mill), on Whitaker Mill Road at Winter's Run, Franklin Whitaker, prop. (*Mills: Grist, Saw, Bone, Flint, Fulling ... & More*, by Jack L. Shagena, Jr., Henry C. Peden, Jr. and John W. McGrain, 2009, pp. 277-278)

Whitaker, A. B. & Brother, property owners adjacent to Broadway in Bel Air (*The Aegis & Intelligencer*, 16 May 1890)

Whitaker, Abarilla, see William C. Temple, q.v.

Whitaker, Alethia, 1878-1943 (Centre Methodist Church Cemetery); native of Harford Co., born 28 Apr 1878, daughter of Wesley Whitaker and Josephine Black (Bailey Funeral Home Records)

Whitaker, Anna Ruff, 1828-1911 (William Watters Memorial Methodist Church Cemetery, Cooptown)

Whitaker, Aquilla B., 1845-1920 (Christ Episcopal Church Cemetery); resident of Bel Air, brother of Octavian M. Whitaker, of Bel Air, and Price Whitaker, of Delta, PA (*The Aegis & Intelligencer*, 31 Oct 1890)

Whitaker, Averilla, see Harriet R. House and Bessie Lee Walter, q.v.

Whitaker, C., catcher, Havre de Grace Ash Alleys Baseball Club (*The Aegis & Intelligencer*, 27 Jun 1890)

Whitaker, Charles, 1830-1896 (Old Brick Baptist Church Cemetery); entered the milking business at Forest Hill, 1890 (*Havre de Grace Republican*, 17 Oct 1890); also see Harry Whitaker, q.v.

Whitaker, Charles, student, Bel Air Academy and Graded School, 1890 (*The Aegis & Intelligencer*, 23 May 1890); see Joseph W. Wallis, q.v.

Whitaker, Charles O., 1871-1918 (Christ Episcopal Church Cemetery)

Whitaker, Ellen Ramsay (Miss), 1846-1927, native of Maryland, resident of Havre de Grace (Death certificate;

Angel Hill Cemetery)

Whitaker, Franklin, 1818-1891 (St. Mary's Episcopal Church Cemetery); resided near Bel Air (*The Aegis & Intelligencer*, 4 Apr 1890); see Whitaker Mill, q.v.

Whitaker, Grace A., 1848-1921 (Angel Hill Cemetery)

Whitaker, Hannah, see Hannah Way Ely, q.v.

Whitaker, Hannah F., 1858-1935 (William Watters Memorial Methodist Church Cemetery, Cooptown)

Whitaker, Harry, son of Charles Whitaker, of Pleasantville; class valedictorian and ninth grade honor student, Bel Air Academy and Graded School (*The Aegis & Intelligencer*, 23 May and 4 Jul 1890)

Whitaker, Henry A., 1874-1957 (Christ Episcopal Church Cemetery)

Whitaker, Howard, 1790-1879 (William Watters Memorial Methodist Church Cemetery, Cooptown)

Whitaker, Howard (master), resided near Fallston (*The Aegis & Intelligencer*, 11 Apr 1890)

Whitaker, Ida Jane, 1871-1923, native of Harford Co., born 2 Jun 1871, daughter of Joshua Whitaker, of Harford Co., and Virginia H. Walker, of Baltimore City (Death certificate - married name Onion)

Whitaker, J. Richard, 1852-1941, native of Harford Co. (Bailey Funeral Home Records)

Whitaker, John A., trustee, Cooptown School No. 18, Fourth District (*Havre de Grace Republican*, 30 May 1890)

Whitaker, Josephine E., 1843-1903 (Centre Methodist Church Cemetery)

Whitaker, Josephine M. (Wallis), 1854-1922 (Christ Episcopal Church Cemetery); see Joseph W. Wallis, q.v.

Whitaker, Joshua R., constable, Third District (*Havre de Grace Republican*, 4 Jul 1890); see Ida Jane Whitaker, q.v.

Whitaker, L. G. (Miss), member, Havre de Grace Reading Circle (*Havre de Grace Republican*, 7 Feb 1890)

Whitaker, Lamar, husband of Lillie Ella Monks, q.v.

Whitaker, Lane R., 1884-1956 (Slate Ridge Cemetery, York Co., PA); native of Bel Air, Harford Co., born 19 Mar 1884, son of Price Whitaker and Florence Flowers (Harkins Funeral Home Records)

Whitaker, Leila G., 1855-1914 (Angel Hill Cemetery)

Whitaker, Lottie M., 1884-1901, native of Maryland, resided near Scarff P. O., born 15 Apr 1884, daughter of Wesley Whitaker and Josephine Black (Death certificate)

Whitaker, Lydia A., 1856-1906 (Rock Run Methodist Church Cemetery)

Whitaker, Marion S., 1857-1948 (William Watters Memorial Methodist Church Cemetery, Cooptown); see Whitaker's General Store, q.v.

Whitaker, Mary (Ramsay), 1824-1892 (Angel Hill Cemetery)

Whitaker, Mary Ashton (Twining), 1873-1916 (Christ Episcopal Church Cemetery)

Whitaker, Mary E., age 38 in 1889 (Marriage License Applications Book ALJ No. 2, 1889)

Whitaker, Mary F., 1852-1930 (Old Brick Baptist Church Cemetery); widow of Charles Whitaker, q.v.

Whitaker, Mary V., 1890-1954 (William Watters Memorial Methodist Church, Cooptown)

Whitaker, Nora, 1877-1899, daughter of James Whitaker (Death certificate)

Whitaker, Octavian M., 1849-1908 (Christ Episcopal Church Cemetery); resident of Bel Air, brother of Aquilla B. Whitaker, of Bel Air, and Price Whitaker, of Delta, PA (*The Aegis & Intelligencer*, 31 Oct 1890); director, Bel Air Water and Light Company (*Havre de Grace Republican*, 14 Feb 1890); register of voters, Third District (*Havre de Grace Republican*, 21 Feb 1890)

Whitaker, Price, see Octavian M. Whitaker and Lane R. Whitaker, q.v.

Whitaker, Virginia H., 1836-1907 (William Watters Memorial Methodist Church Cemetery, Cooptown)

Whitaker, Wesley, see Lottie M. Whitaker, Lydia A. Rogers and Alethia Whitaker, q.v.

Whitcomb, Samuel, proprietor, Cranberry Mill, near Perryman (*Havre de Grace Republican*, 28 Mar 1890)

Whitcomb, William, age 26 in 1890 (Marriage License Applications Book ALJ No. 2, 1890)

White, Alice R., see Henry B. Ellis, q.v.

White, Annie (Ruff) (colored), 1855-1915, native of Maryland, resident of Bel Air (Death certificate)

White, Bertha (Robinson), 1882-1963 (Bethel Presbyterian Church Cemetery Records); wife of William White, q.v.

White, C. Oliver, 1890-1910 (Angel Hill Cemetery)

White, Charles, 1835-1926 (Cokesbury Memorial Methodist Church Cemetery); native of Germany, married, laborer, resided at Joppa (Death certificate)

White, Charles, c1855-1937 (Death certificate); wheelwright near Bel Air, native of Harford Co., parents unknown (Bailey Funeral Home Records)

White, Elijah (colored), 1871-1957 (Clark's Chapel Methodist Church Cemetery)

White, Eliza, widow of Jesse White, Civil War veteran, Havre de Grace (*1890 Special Census of the Civil War Veterans of the State of Maryland*, by L. Tilden Moore, Volume III, p. 91)

White, Eliza (colored), 1841-1927 (Death certificate)

White, Ella V., age 17 in 1890 (Marriage License Applications Book ALJ No. 2, 1890), married Edward Forwood on 18 Jun 1890 (marriage certificate)

White, Florence E. (colored), 1887-1912, native of Harford Co., born 20 May 1887, daughter of George White and Emily Poole (Death certificate)

White, Florida, 1880-1924, native of Maryland, born 25 Jun 1880, daughter of Henry White and Elizabeth Miller (Death certificate - married name Singleton)

White, Frank, 1878-1969 (Bethel Presbyterian Church Cemetery Records)

White, Frank (colored), 1880-1923 (St. James United Cemetery)

White, George, see Joseph A. White, q.v.

White, George (colored), 1857-1922, native of Maryland (Death certificate); see Florence E. White, q.v.

White, George Pinkney, 1890-1911 (Darlington Cemetery)

White, Georgeanna (colored), see Bessie J. Toney (colored), q.v.

White, Hannah, age 28 in 1890 (Marriage License Applications Book ALJ No. 2, 1890), married J. William Johnson on 28 Apr 1890 at a private residence near Forest Hill (*The Aegis & Intelligencer*, 9 May 1890)

White, Henry, county out-pensioner [welfare recipient], Fifth District, 1890 (*Havre de Grace Republican*, 4 Jul 1890); see Florida White, q.v.

White, James, Civil War veteran, Third District (*1890 Special Census of the Civil War Veterans of the State of Maryland*, by L. Tilden Moore, Volume III, p. 73)

White, James Silas, 1883-1945 (Dublin Cemetery); native of Harford Co., born 19 Nov 1883, son of Samuel White and Mary Lilly (Bailey Funeral Home Records; Death certificate)

White, Jasper (colored), c1830-1900, laborer, resided at Fountain Green, Harford Co (Death certificate)

White, Jesse, see Eliza White, q.v.

White, Jesse (colored), 1857-1926 (St. James United Cemetery); native of Maryland, married, laborer, resided in Havre de Grace (Death certificate)

White, John, seine fisherman, at Omits Island in the Susquehanna River (*The Aegis & Intelligencer*, 4 Apr 1890)

White, Joseph A., 1886-1943 (Darlington Cemetery); native of Harford Co., born 20 Oct 1886, son of George White and Sarah Gates (Bailey Funeral Home Records)

White, Laura (colored), see Sarah Frances Bond (colored), q.v.

White, Margaret Anna (Taylor), 1856-1936, wife of Thomas Michael White, q.v.

White, Nannie (Miss), resided at Forest Hill (*Harford Democrat*, 21 Feb 1890)

White, Patrick, died 5 Aug 1901, adult, age not given, native of Ireland, resided at Perryman (Death certificate)

White, Robert, 1879-1928 (Darlington Cemetery); native of Maryland, born 14 Mar 1879, son of Samuel R. White and Susan Lilly (Death certificate; Bailey Funeral Home Records)

White, Rosetta or Rosita (colored), 1826-1912 (Death certificate); see Samuel White, q.v.

White, Samuel (colored), 1831-1899, laborer at Havre de Grace, native of Harford Co., husband of Rosetta White (Death certificate)

White, Samuel, 1851-1930 (Dublin Cemetery); stone mason, native of Maryland (Bailey Funeral Home Records); see James Silas White, q.v.

White, Samuel, manager of *Bayside Farm* near Michaelsville (*The Aegis & Intelligencer*, 12 Dec 1890)

White, Samuel, Jr. (colored), 1867-1898, native of Maryland, married, barber in Havre de Grace, son of Samuel and Nettie White (Death certificate); trustee, Havre de Grace Colored School, Sixth District (*Havre de Grace Republican*, 30 May 1890)

White, Samuel R., see Robert White, q.v.

White, Sarah E. (Gates), 1858-1923 (Darlington Cemetery); nurse, native of Maryland (Bailey Funeral Home Records); see Joseph A. White, q.v.

White, Susan A., 1855-1940 (Bailey Funeral Home Records); see Robert White, q.v.

White, T. May, county out-pensioner [welfare recipient], Fifth District, 1890 (*Havre de Grace Republican*, 4 Jul 1890)

White, Thomas Michael, 1851-1934 (Angel Hill Cemetery); Havre de Grace city councilman, 1889, candidate, 1890 (*Havre de Grace Republican*, 10 Jan 1890) see McVey & White;s Carriage Shops, q.v.

White, Wesley (colored), 1886-1954 (Clark's Chapel Methodist Church Cemetery)

White, William, 1817-1900, cooper, native of Germany, resided at Dublin, Harford Co (Death certificate)

White, William (colored), 1855-1945, native of Maryland (Death certificate)

White, William E., resident of Havre de Grace (*The Aegis & Intelligencer*, 26 Sep 1890)

Whiteford Brothers Flint Works (aka Whiteford's Flint Mill), near the mouth of Broad Creek, H. C. and S. J. Whiteford, prop. (*Mills: Grist, Saw, Bone, Flint, Fulling ... & More*, by Jack L. Shagena, Jr., Henry C. Peden, Jr. and John W. McGrain, 2009, p. 279; *Havre de Grace Republican*, 11 Apr 1890)

Whiteford, ----, center fielder, Baptist Baseball Club, of Fourth District (*Havre de Grace Republican*, 8 Aug 1890)

Whiteford, Ada Belle (Kennedy), 1879-1971 (Baker Cemetery); wife of Clarence William Whiteford, q.v.

Whiteford, Alice, see Mary Ellen Richardson, q.v.

Whiteford, Ann (Beatty), 1804-1891 (Bethel Presbyterian Church Cemetery Records); wife of James Whiteford, q.v.

Whiteford, Anna Catherine (Streett), 1856-1920 (Highland Presbyterian Church Cemetery), wife of John Streett Whiteford, q.v.

Whiteford, Anna Elizabeth (Silver), 1844-1922 (Darlington Cemetery), wife of William H. H. Whiteford, q.v.

Whiteford, Anna W., see Anna W. Silver, q.v.

Whiteford, Augustine Biddle (Streett), 1822-1913 (Slate Ridge Presbyterian Church Cemetery), wife of Michael C. Whiteford, q.v.

Whiteford, Bessie Nelson (Stokes), 1878-1961 (Bethel Presbyterian Church Cemetery Records), wife of William M. Whiteford, q.v.

Whiteford, Calvin, 1865-1931 (Slate Ridge Presbyterian Church Cemetery; James Ross Whiteford Bible, *Maryland Bible Records, Volume 5*, by Henry C. Peden, Jr., 2004, pp. 212-213)

Whiteford, Clarence William, 1884-1952 (Baker Cemetery)

Whiteford, Clay P., 1884-1948 (Slateville Cemetery, York Co., PA); native of Whiteford, Harford Co., born 14 Jan 1884, son of W. Scott Whiteford, of Harford Co., and Marian J. McConkey, of York Co., PA (Harkins Funeral Home Records)

Whiteford, Daniel, see Grover Cleveland Whiteford and William M. Whiteford, q.v.

Whiteford, Elizabeth J., age 46 in 1890 (Marriage License Applications Book ALJ No. 2, 1890)

Whiteford, Elizabeth S., died 16 Jun 1890, age not stated (Cokesbury Memorial Church Cemetery)

Whiteford, Elizabeth Virginia (Bennington), 1860-1931, wife of Stevenson Archer Whiteford, q.v.

Whiteford, Elmer Martin, 1876-1965; youngest son of Samuel Martin and second wife Sarah Jane (Heaps) Whiteford (Old Brick Baptist Church Cemetery; *The Whiteford Genealogy*, by Hazel W. Baldwin, 1992, pp.95-96)

Whiteford, Grover Cleveland, 1885-1971 (Slateville Cemetery, York Co., PA); native of Harford Co., born 5 Jul 1885, son of Daniel Whiteford and Mary E. Bavington (Harkins Funeral Home Records)

Whiteford, H. Kenton, 1877-1954 (Darlington Cemetery); native of Harford Co., born 16 Jun 1877, son of Hugh Clay Whiteford and D, Sallie Prigg (Bailey Funeral Home Records)

Whiteford, Henry C., 1880-1946 (Slateville Cemetery, York Co., PA); resident of Whiteford, Harford Co., son of Scott Whiteford and Marian McConkey (Harkins Funeral Home Records)

Whiteford, Hugh C., of Michael, died 6 Mar 1896, age 89 (*Deaths and Marriages in Harford County, Maryland, and Vicinity, 1873-1904, from the Diaries of Albert Peter Silver*, transcribed by Glenn Randers-Pehrson, 1995, p. 31)

Whiteford, Hugh Campbell, 1806-1894 (Slate Ridge Cemetery); former member, House of Delegates (*Biographical Dictionary of Harford County, Maryland, 1774-1974*, by Henry C. Peden, Jr. and William O. Carr, 2021, p. 292)

Whiteford, Hugh Clay (Dr.), of S., 1845-1892 (Darlington Cemetery); physician and postmaster, Darlington (*The Aegis & Intelligencer*, 26 Sep 1890); member, Harford County Medical Society (*Havre de Grace Republican*, 16 May 1890); manager of the old Semple fish battery at the mouth of Broad Creek on the Susquehanna River (*The Aegis & Intelligencer*, 9 May 1890); trustee, Boyle's School No. 5, Fifth District (*Havre de Grace Republican*, 30 May 1890); see H. Kenton Whiteford and W. Morgan Whiteford, q.v.

Whiteford, James R., see Anna W. Silver and S. Marshall Whiteford, q.v.

Whiteford, James Ramsey (colonel), 1843-1906 (*The Whiteford Genealogy*, by Hazel Whiteford Baldwin, 1992, p. 116); brickyard, Cambria Station, at Whiteford (*The Aegis & Intelligencer*, 24 Jan 1890); juror, Fifth District (*Havre de Grace Republican*, 31 Oct 1890); John R. Whiteford, and wife, sold land in November 1890 (*The Aegis & Intelligencer*, 5 Dec 1890)

Whiteford, James Ross, 1833-1908 (James Ross Whiteford Bible, *Maryland Bible Records, Volume 5*, by Henry C. Peden, Jr., 2004, pp. 212-213)

Whiteford, John Streett, 1852-1926, father of Clarence William Whiteford, q.v.

Whiteford, Joseph, 1841-1908, native of Maryland, resided at Abingdon (Death certificate)

Whiteford, Joseph Silver, 1859-1923 (Slateville Cemetery); trustee, Whiteford's School No. 2, Fifth District (*Havre de Grace Republican*, 30 May 1890)

Whiteford, Letitia M., age 23 in 1890 (Marriage License Applications Book ALJ No. 2, 1891)

Whiteford, Katheryn May, 1885-1937 (Old Brick Baptist Church Cemetery); wife of Elmer M. Whiteford, q.v.

Whiteford, M. Janita, student, Fifth District (*The Aegis & Intelligencer*, 24 Oct 1890)

Whiteford, M. Nelson, trustee, Fairview School No. 1, Fifth District (*Havre de Grace Republican*, 30 May 1890); juror, Fifth District (*Havre de Grace Republican*, 2 May 1890); see Nelson Whiteford, q.v.

Whiteford, Margaret Jane (Jones), 1862-1932 (Slateville Cemetery); wife of Joseph Silver Whiteford, q.v.

Whiteford, Margaret L. (Streett), 1842-1916 (Bethel Presbyterian Church Cemetery Records); wife of William W. Whiteford, q.v.

Whiteford, Marion, young man of near Pylesville (*The Aegis & Intelligencer*, 7 Feb 1890)

Whiteford, Mary Alice, see Irene C. Pennington, q.v.

Whiteford, Mary E., age 24 in 1890 (Marriage License Applications Book ALJ No. 2, 1891)

Whiteford, Mary Elizabeth (Streett), 1846-1891, wife of James Ramsey Whiteford, q.v.

Whiteford, Mary J., see William J. Barton, q.v.

Whiteford, Michael Crook, 1822-1891 (Slate Ridge Presbyterian Church Cemetery); former county commissioner, near Pylesville (*The Aegis & Intelligencer*, 11 Jul 1890)

Whiteford, Nannie (Miss), young lady, of Bel Air (*The Aegis & Intelligencer*, 7 Feb 1890); honor student, Archer Institute, Bel Air (*The Aegis & Intelligencer*, 20 Jun 1890)

Whiteford, Nelson, see Edward Proctor and M. Nelson Whiteford, q.v.

Whiteford, Rachael (Mrs.), c1835-1900 (Death certificate)

Whiteford, Rachel E. (McConkey), 1838-1900 (James Ross Whiteford Bible, *Maryland Bible Records, Volume 5*, by Henry C. Peden, Jr., 2004, pp. 212-213)

Whiteford, Rachel L., age 43 in 1890 (Marriage License Applications Book ALJ No. 2, 1891)

Whiteford, S. J., see John T. Weeks, q.v.

Whiteford, S. Marshall, 1872-1954 (Slate Ridge Cemetery, York Co., PA); native of Harford Co, born 29 Aug 1872, son of James R. Whiteford and Mary E. Gladden (Harkins Funeral Home Records)

Whiteford, Sallie F., married Albert Gorrell on 11 Apr 1890 (marriage certificate)

Whiteford, Samuel, road examiner, Fourth District (*Havre de Grace Republican*, 4 Jul 1890)

Whiteford, Samuel J., of Samuel, died 28 Sep 1900, age 53 (*Deaths and Marriages in Harford County, Maryland, and Vicinity, 1873-1904, from the Diaries of Albert Peter Silver*, transcribed by Glenn Randers-Pehrson, 1995, p. 31)

Whiteford, Sarah Jane (Heaps), 1833-1909, second wife of Samuel Martin Whiteford, 1809-1889 (*Biographical Dictionary of Harford County, Maryland, 1774-1974*, by Henry C. Peden, Jr. and William O. Carr, 2021, p. 293)

Whiteford, Scott, see Henry C. Whiteford, q.v.

Whiteford, Stevenson Archer, 1859-1934 (Slate Ridge Presbyterian Church Cemetery)

Whiteford, W. Morgan, 1872-1935 (Slateville Cemetery, York Co., PA); native of Whiteford, Harford Co., born 12 Jan 1872, son of H. Clay Whiteford and Anna C. Morgan (Harkins Funeral Home Records)

Whiteford, W. Scott, see Clay P. Whiteford and S. Marshall Whiteford, q.v.

Whiteford, Will, young man, resident near Pylesville (*The Aegis & Intelligencer*, 7 Feb 1890)

Whiteford, William Ebenezer, 1834-1894 (Bethel Presbyterian Church Cemetery Records); road examiner, Fourth District, and former sheriff (*Havre de Grace Republican*, 4 Jul 1890; *Biographical Dictionary of Harford County, Maryland, 1774-1974*, by Henry C. Peden, Jr. and William O. Carr, 2021, p. 293)

Whiteford, William Henry Harrison, 1840-1911 (Darlington Cemetery); cabinet maker, undertaker, and fire department chief, Darlington (*The Aegis & Intelligencer*, 26 Sep 1890); road commissioner, Fifth District (*Havre de Grace Republican*, 7 Feb 1890); member, Darlington Road League (*Havre de Grace Republican*, 7 Mar 1890); general manager, Darlington Minstrels (*The Aegis & Intelligencer*, 21 Feb 1890); delegate, Fifth District, Democrat Party Convention (*The Aegis & Intelligencer*, 5 Sep 1890); member, Board of Education (*Biographical Dictionary of Harford County, Maryland, 1774-1974*, by Henry C. Peden, Jr. and William O. Carr, 2021, pp. 293-294, 327)

Whiteford, William M., 1874-1945 (Slateville Cemetery, York Co., PA); native of Harford Co., born 14 Sep 1874, son of Daniel Whiteford and Mary E. Bavington (Harkins Funeral Home Records)

Whiteford, William Martin, 1874-1949 (Bethel Presbyterian Church Cemetery Records); jousting tournament rider, Knight of Cambria (*Havre de Grace Republican*, 15 Aug 1890 and 17 Oct 1890)

Whiteford, William S., member, Maryland Central Dairymen's Association (*Havre de Grace Republican*, 28 Feb 1890)

Whiteley, ----, secretary, Green Serpentine Marble Company, Fifth District (*Havre de Grace Republican*, 2 May 1890)

Whiteley, Charles E., secretary-treasurer, Greenstone Serpentine Company, on Broad Creek (*Havre de Grace Republican*, 25 Jul 1890)

Whitelock's General Stores, one in Darlington and one in Dublin, George D. Whitelock, prop. (*Country Stores: Harford County's Rural Heritage*, by Henry C. Peden, Jr. and Jack L. Shagena, Jr., 2015, pp. 262-263

Whitelock, Annie (Hopkins), 1854-1943 (Darlington Cemetery); wife of George D. Whitelock, q.v.

Whitelock, Annie L., 1845-1924 (Angel Hill Cemetery)

Whitelock, Bertha M. "Bertie" (Miss), 1872-1967, daughter of Mrs. Mary Bowman, of Webster (*The Aegis & Intelligencer*, 11 Jul 1890; Angel Hill Cemetery)

Whitelock, Caroline (Bowman), 1823-1899, resided at Darlington, native of Maryland, wife of James Whitelock, q.v. (Death certificate)

Whitelock, Caroline C., 1861-1954 (Rock Run Methodist Church Cemetery)

Whitelock, Edward W., of James, died 8 Feb 1899, age 54 (*Deaths and Marriages in Harford County, Maryland, and Vicinity, 1873-1904, from the Diaries of Albert Peter Silver*, transcribed by Glenn Randers-Pehrson, 1995, p. 31); farmer, near Level (*Havre de Grace Republican*, 21 Feb 1890)

Whitelock, Euphemia, see Ramsey Standiford, q.v.

Whitelock, Frededick C., 1844-1923 (Angel Hill Cemetery)

Whitelock, George Dallas, 1845-1899, general store, Darlington, native of Harford Co. (Death certificate; Darlington Cemetery; *The Aegis & Intelligencer*, 26 Sep 1890); see Whitelock's General Stores, q.v.

Whitelock, James, of John, 1822-1897 (*Deaths and Marriages in Harford County, Maryland, and Vicinity, 1873-1904, from the Diaries of Albert Peter Silver*, transcribed by Glenn Randers-Pehrson, 1995, p. 31); farmer, near Level (*Havre de Grace Republican*, 21 Feb 1890)

Whitelock, Lilia V., widow, age 39 in 1889 (Marriage License Applications Book ALJ No. 2, 1889)

Whitelock, Mary (Hopkins), 1886-1938 (Darlington Cemetery)

Whitelock, Mary R. (Prigg), 1848-1926 (Darlington Cemetery); native of Maryland, resided at Darlington (Bailey Funeral Home Records)

Whitfield, Loretta (colored), 1870-1933 (Death certificate)

Whiting, Carrie (Coldwell), 1863-1932 (Ebenezer Methodist Church Cemetery)

Whitney, Harry Clay, 1879-1949, native of Havre de Grace, born 12 Oct 1879, son of William G. Whitney and Elizabeth Harward (Pennington Funeral Home Records spelled his mother's name Harwood)

Whitney, Sadie L. (Edmondson), 1885-1975 (Angel Hill Cemetery), wife of Harry Clay Whitney, q.v.

Whitney, Sarah Elizabeth (Harward), 1852-1933 (Angel Hill Cemetery); wife of William G. Whitney, q.v.

Whitney, Sherman, hauling contractor, Havre de Grace (*Havre de Grace Republican*, 6 Jun 1890); see Violet Whitney, q.v.

Whitney, Violet, 1885-1952, native of Maryland, born 20 Aug 1885, daughter of Sherman Whitney and Rosalie Saunders (Pennington Funeral Home Records - married name Mackin)

Whitney, William G., 1848-1915 (Angel Hill Cemetery); ice house owner, Havre de Grace (*Havre de Grace Republican*, 4 Apr 1890); see Harry Clay Whitney, q.v.

Whitney, William G., Jr., 1889-1947, native of Havre de Grace, born 9 Aug 1889, son of William G. Whitney and Sarah E. Harward (Pennington Funeral Home Records spelled mother's name Harwood; Angel Hill Cemetery)

Whitson, Daniel A., 1817-1902 (Fallston Methodist Church Cemetery); incorporator and trustee, Friendship M. E. Church, Third District (*Havre de Grace Republican*, 21 Nov 1890)

Whitson, Edwin W., 1862-1928 (Fallston Methodist Church Cemetery)

Whitson, Joseph B., 1829-1896 (Fallston Methodist Church Cemetery)

Whitson, Lydia Elizabeth, 1825-1903 (Fallston Methodist Church Cemetery)

Whitson, Sallie, see Kate L. Miller, q.v.

Whitson, Sarah A., 1845-1927 (Fallston Methodist Church Cemetery)

Whitten, Elijah, treated by unidentified doctor in 1890 ("Medical Account Book – 1890," Historical Society of Harford County Archives Folder)

Whittington, Betsy J. (Christy) (colored), died 9 May 1918, widow, age not given, native of Maryland (Death certificate)

Whittington, Ella Jane (Tasker) (colored), 1869-1931, native of Maryland (Death certificate)

Whittington, Ida Elizabeth (Wilson) (colored), 1880-1926, native of Maryland, daughter of Samuel Wilson and Elizabeth Banks (Death certificate)

Whittington, J. Alfred (colored), 1869/1875-1931, native of Maryland, born 17 Mar 1869 or 1875, son of James E. Whittington and Susan Thomas (Death certificate has two different birth years)

Whittington, James (colored), widower, age 63 in 1890 (Marriage License Applications Book ALJ No. 2, 1890); see J. Alfred Whittington, q.v.

Whittington, James, sold land in May 1890 (*The Aegis & Intelligencer*, 6 Jun 1890)

Whittington Ora H. (Tasker) (colored), 1872-1934, native of Calvert Co., MD (Death certificate)

Whittington, Thomas Andrew (colored), 1889-1985 (*The Aegis*, 5 Sep 1985)

Whittle, G. S. (Miss), resident and property owner adjacent to Broadway in Bel Air (*The Aegis & Intelligencer*, 16 May and 18 Jul 1890)

Whyte, John E., 1868-1923 (Wesleyan Chapel Methodist Church Cemetery)

Whyte, Kate E., 1868-1944 (Wesleyan Chapel Methodist Church Cemetery)

Wiers, Laura (Miss), teacher, Union School House, near Bush Chapel (*The Aegis & Intelligencer*, 14 Mar 1890); E. Laura Wiers, teacher, School No. 10, First District (*The Aegis & Intelligencer*, 29 Aug 1890)

Wiggers, John H., married Hattie Ehrhart on 11 Dec 1890 at Jarrettsville M. E Parsonage (*The Aegis & Intelligencer*, 19 Dec 1890)

Wiggers, Sarah Ann, 1817-1890 (Fallston Methodist Church Cemetery)

Wiggins, Annie (Hooper) (colored), 1865-1901, native of Maryland, domestic, resided at Churchville, wife of July Wiggins (Death certificate)

Wiggins, Harriet (colored), see James Alfred Wiggins (colored), q.v.

Wiggins, Isaac (colored), died 12 Dec 1903, age not given (Alms House Record Book)

Wiggins, James Alfred (colored), 1867-1964, born near Emmorton, Harford Co., son of Jesse and Harriet Wiggins (*The Aegis*, 20 Feb 1964)

Wiggins, Jesse (colored), widower, age 64, in 1890 (Marriage License Applications Book ALJ No. 2, 1890); Jesse Wiggans *(sic)* sold land in August 1890 (*The Aegis & Intelligencer*, 12 Sep 1890); delegate, First District, Republican Party Convention (*The Aegis & Intelligencer*, 26 Sep 1890); see James Alfred Wiggins, q.v.

Wiggins, John H. (colored), age 27 in 1890 (Marriage License Applications Book ALJ No. 2, 1890)

Wiggins, July (colored), see Annie Wiggins (colored), q.v.

Wiggins, Samuel (colored), c1878-1897 (*The Aegis & Intelligencer*, 15 Jan 1897)

Wiker, Charles H., 1847-1928 (Fork Christian Church Cemetery, Baltimore Co.); native of Harford Co., mailman, married, resided at Bel Air (Death certificate)

Wiker, Margaret (Herr), 1823-1901, resided at Fountain Green (Death certificate)

Wildason, Ambrose, 1842-1912 (Mt. Zion Methodist Church Cemetery); see Susanna Wildason, q.v.

Wildason, Amelia, see Susanna Wildason, q.v.

Wildason, Charles C., 1881-1949 (Mt. Zion Methodist Church Cemetery)

Wildason, Claude S., 1884-1937 (Mt. Zion Methodist Church Cemetery)

Wildason, Ella, see Susanna Wildason, q.v.

Wildason, Ellen R., 1866-1948 (Mt. Zion Methodist Church Cemetery)

Wildason, Emma K., 1889-1935 (Mt. Zion Methodist Church Cemetery)

Wildason, George W., 1879-1953 (Mt. Zion Methodist Church Cemetery)

Wildason, John T., 1864-1931 (Mt. Zion Methodist Church Cemetery)

Wildason, Martha E., 1884-1969 (Mt. Zion Methodist Church Cemetery)

Wildason, Mary A., 1884-1962 (Mt. Zion Methodist Church Cemetery)

Wildason, Mary Catherine (Williams), 1865-1942 (Mt. Zion Methodist Church Cemetery)

Wildason, Susanna ("Susan"), 1843-1899, resident of Bel Air, native of Pennsylvania, wife of Ambrose Wildason, q.v. (Mt. Zion Methodist Church Cemetery; Death certificate; "In Memoriam" in *The Aegis & Intelligencer*, 10 Nov 1899, by daughters Ella and Amelia Wildason who spelled the name Wilderson)

Wildason, Theodore Ambrose, 1874-1923 (Mt. Zion Methodist Church Cemetery)

Wilde, Annie E., student, Bel Air Academy and Graded School (*The Aegis & Intelligencer*, 23 May and 24 Oct 1890)

Wilde, Mark, painting room foreman, Bulett Carriage Factory, Bel Air (*The Aegis & Intelligencer*, 31 Jan 1890); dealer in cigars, tobacco, paper and stationery (*The Aegis & Intelligencer*, 7 Nov 1890); member, Mt. Ararat Lodge No. 44, A. F. & A. M., Bel Air (*Havre de Grace Republican*, 11 Jul 1890)

Wilds, Mary Emma (Bartol), 1884-1910, wife of Louis C. Wilds (Angel Hill Cemetery; *Havre de Grace Republican*, 28 May 1910)

Wileman, Isamiah K. (Felty), 1857-1961, wife of Thomas William Wileman, Jr., q.v.

Wileman, Joseph Henry, 1864-1949 (Angel Hill Cemetery); prelate, Harford Lodge No. 54, Knight of Pythias, Havre de Grace (*Havre de Grace Republican*, 11 Jul 1890)

Wileman, Lillie Kate (Walker), 1864-1941, native of Havre de Grace (Angel Hill Cemetery; Pennington Funeral Home Records); wife of Joseph Henry Wileman, q.v.

Wileman, Thomas William, Jr., 1850-1916 (Bardsdale Cemetery, Ventura Co., CA); butcher and grocery store merchant on Stokes Street and city council candidate, Havre de Grace (*Havre de Grace Republican*, 10 Jan 1890 and 17 Jan 1890)

Wiles, Blanche W. (Davis), 1817-1898 (Rock Run Methodist Church Cemetery)

Wiles, Elizabeth (colored), see Laura Britton (colored), q.v.

Wiles, James A., 1845-1908 (Cokesbury Memorial Methodist Church Cemetery); carriage and wagon maker, Aberdeen (*Carriages Back in the Day: Harford County's Rural Heritage*, by Jack L. Shagena, Jr. and Henry C. Peden, Jr., 2016, p. 90); assistant commander, Harford Lodge No. 54, of Aberdeen, Order of the Golden Chain, 1890 (*Havre de Grace Republican*, 28 Nov 1890)

Wiles, James, 1818-1891 (Deer Creek Harmony Presbyterian Church)

Wiles, Lillie M. C., bor -- Jul 1872, daughter of James A. and Mary E. Wiles (1900 Aberdeen Census); student, Aberdeen Public School (*The Aegis & Intelligencer*, 23 May 1890); member, Aberdeen M. E. Church (*The Aegis & Intelligencer*, 21 Feb 1890)

Wiles, Mary Elizabeth (Hawkins) (Wood), 1835-1902, wife of James A. Wiles, q.v.

Wiley's Grist Mill (Upper Mill), on Deer Creek near Norrisville, George Norris Wiley, prop. (*Mills: Grist, Saw,*

Bone, Flint, Fulling ... & More, by Jack L. Shagena, Jr., Henry C. Peden, Jr. and John W. McGrain, 2009, pp. 280-281)

Wiley, Andrew Jackson, 1825-1906 (Bethel Presbyterian Church Cemetery Records)

Wiley, Asbury B., see Caroline Slade, q.v.

Wiley, Asbury S. ("Buck"), 1860-1927 (Bethel Presbyterian Church Cemetery Records)

Wiley, Anna Blanche ("Annie"), 1868-1941, orphaned daughter of William Nelson Wiley and Rebecca Jane Robinson (West Liberty Cemetery, White Hall, Baltimore Co., married name Gemmill)

Wiley, Bertram Bradford, 1884-1929, son of Thomas and Elizabeth (Wheeler) Wiley (Bethel Presbyterian Church Cemetery Records)

Wiley, Bessie J. (Scotten), 1882-1938 (Slateville Cemetery, York Co., PA); native of Harford Co., born 14 May 1882, daughter of Joshua Scotten, of York Co., PA, and Mary McGibney, of Ireland (Harkins Funeral Home Records)

Wiley, Betty M. (Slade), 1867-1955 (Bethel Presbyterian Church Cemetery Records); wife of Richard H. Wiley, q.v.

Wiley, Caroline (Bradford), 1805-1891 (Bethel Presbyterian Church Cemetery Records); wife of William Wiley, q.v.

Wiley, Carrie J. (Watt), 1871-1948 (Bethel Presbyterian Church Cemetery Records); wife of Robert L. Wiley, q.v.

Wiley, Charles Lewis, 1863-1917 (Bethel Presbyterian Church Cemetery Records)

Wiley, David A., trustee, Mt. Pleasant School No. 11, Fourth District (*Havre de Grace Republican*, 30 May 1890); David A. Wiley, and wife, sold land in April 1890 (*The Aegis & Intelligencer*, 9 May 1890)

Wiley, Elizabeth A., born 14 Oct 1871, daughter of Thomas Hutchins and Rebecca Ann (Wiley) Wiley (Bethel Presbyterian Church Cemetery Records); see Elizabeth A. Slade, q.v.

Wiley, George, resident near Five Forks (*The Aegis & Intelligencer*, 21 Feb 1890)

Wiley, George Norris, 1837-1912 (Bethel Presbyterian Church Cemetery Records); see Wiley's Grist Mill, q.v.

Wiley, Hannah Catherine "Dolly" (Pennington), 1868-1948 (Bethel Presbyterian Church Cemetery Records);wifeof John Franklin Wiley, q.v.

Wiley, Harry Fields, 1862-1951 (Bethel Presbyterian Church Cemetery Records); vice president, Black Horse Singing School (*Havre de Grace Republican*, 28 Mar 1890); vice president, Shawsville Glee Club (*Havre de Grace Republican*, 7 Mar 1890)

Wiley, Henrietta Elizabeth (Wheeler), 1858-1928 (Bethel Presbyterian Church Cemetery Records); wife of Thomas Hope Wiley, q.v.

Wiley, Ida, see Chester A. McLaughlin, q.v.

Wiley, Ida Nelson, born 4 May 1870, daughter of Nelson and Rebecca (Robinson) Wiley (*Kirkwoods and Their Kin, 1731-1971*, by Anna Lee Kirkwood Smith, 1972, p. 139)

Wiley, Isabella, see Sarah M. Davis and W. Harry Galbreath, q.v.

Wiley, J. Ross, born 8 Feb 1874, son of William O. and Rachel A. (Strawbridge) Wiley (Bethel Presbyterian Church Cemetery Records)

Wiley, James A., chief judge of elections, Norrisville Precinct (*Havre de Grace Republican*, 17 Oct 1890)

Wiley, Jane Robinson, born 18 Feb 1875, daughter of Nelson and Rebecca (Robinson) Wiley (*Kirkwoods and Their Kin, 1731-1971*, by Anna Lee Kirkwood Smith, 1972, p. 144)

Wiley, Jessie B., 1890-1891 (Norrisville Methodist Church Cemetery)

Wiley, John Franklin, 1869-1936 (Bethel Presbyterian Church Cemetery Records); president, Shawsville Glee Club (*Havre de Grace Republican*, 7 Mar 1890); president, Black Horse Singing School (*Havre de Grace Republican*, 28 Mar 1890); age 21 in 1890 (Marriage License Applications Book ALJ No. 2, 1891)

Wiley, John R., see Caroline Slade, q.v.

Wiley, M. Blanche, born 6 Feb 1879, daughter of Andrew Jackson and Margaret Emma (Astin) Wiley (Bethel Presbyterian Church Cemetery Records)

Wiley, Margaret Emma (Astin), 1838-1901 (Bethel Presbyterian Church Cemetery Records); wife of Andrew Jackson Wiley, q.v.

Wiley, Mary (Amos), 1811-1899, resident near Norrisville, wife of Joseph Wiley, 1809-1887 (Death certificate; Norrisville Methodist Church Cemetery)

Wiley, Mary Alberta (Anderson), 1882-1967 (Bethel Presbyterian Church Cemetery Records); wife of J. Ross Wiley, q.v.

Wiley, Mary Amanda (Wiley), 1838-1910 (Bethel Presbyterian Church Cemetery); widow of David Wiley (1824-1886)

Wiley, Mary Elizabeth, 1862-1891, of Harford County, married John H. Wheeler, of Delta, PA, on 27 Nov 1890 at Bethel Parsonage near Jarrettsville (*The Aegis & Intelligencer*, 5 Dec 1890)

Wiley, Mary Edith (McComas), 1876-1917 (Bethel Presbyterian Church Cemetery Records); wife of Charles Lewis. Wiley, q.v.

Wiley, Mary E., see John H. Wheele, q.v.

Wiley, Mary L. (Holland), 1885-1971 (Bethel Presbyterian Church Cemetery Records); wife of Bertram Bradford Wiley, q.v.

Wiley, Maude B., born in 1890 (Bethel Presbyterian Church Cemetery)

Wiley, Maude (Nelson), 1871-1950 (Bethel Presbyterian Church Cemetery Records); wife of Harry Fields Wiley, q.v.

Wiley, Nellie (Miss), teacher, Chestnut Hill School (*The Aegis & Intelligencer*, 4 Jul 1890); teacher, Kirkwood School No. 20, Fourth District (*The Aegis & Intelligencer*, 29 Aug 1890)

Wiley, R. Nicholas, trustee, Dry Branch School No. 2, Fourth District (*Havre de Grace Republican*, 30 May 1890)

Wiley, Rebecca Ann (Wiley), 1829-1890 (Bethel Presbyterian Church Cemetery); wife of Thomas H. Wiley, of Shawsville, q.v. (*The Aegis & Intelligencer*, 7 Mar 1890)

Wiley, Rebecca Jane, born 5 Feb 1874, daughter of Thomas H. and Rebecca Ann (Wiley) Wiley (Bethel Presbyterian Church Cemetery Records)

Wiley, Richard Hutchins, 1858-1939 (Bethel Presbyterian Church Cemetery Records)

Wiley, Robert L., 1867-1938 (Bethel Presbyterian Church Cemetery Records)

Wiley, Thomas H., 1828-1905 (Bethel Presbyterian Church Cemetery); delegate, Fourth District, Democrat Party Convention (*The Aegis & Intelligencer*, 5 Sep 1890); road examiner and commissioner, Fourth District (*Havre de Grace Republican*, 7 Feb 1890 and 4 Jul 1890); also see Rebecca A. Wiley, q.v.

Wiley, Thomas Hope, 1857-1928 (Bethel Presbyterian Church Cemetery Records); native of Harford Co., farmer, married, resided near Jarrettsville (Death certificate)

Wiley, Thomas Hutchins, 1828-1905 (Bethel Presbyterian Church Cemetery Records)

Wiley, William, see Nellie (Wiley) Day, q.v.

Wiley, William, member, Division No. 1, Bel Air Fire and Salvage Corps (*The Aegis & Intelligencer*, 10 Oct 1890)

Wiley, William A., resident near Norrisville (*The Aegis & Intelligencer*, 21 Mar 1890); drum major, Norrisville Silver Cornet Band (*The Aegis & Intelligencer*, 30 May 1890)

Wiley, William R., see Caroline Slade, q.v.

Wiley, William Randolph, 1877-1911, son of William Owen and Rachel Ann (Strawbridge) Wiley (Bethel Presbyterian Church Cemetery Records)

Wiley, William Richard, 1887-1959, son of Thoma Hope and Elizabeth (Wheeler) Wiley (Bethel Presbyterian Church Cemetery Records)

Wiley, Zana Idalett (Wiley), 1842-1923 (Bethel Presbyterian Church Cemetery Records); wife of George Norris Wiley, q.v.

Wilfong, Cora M., 1877-1948 (Baker Cemetery)

Wilfong, Luzetta Wallace, 1878-1957 (Baker Cemetery)

Wilgis, Anna Elizabeth, born -- Mar 1883, baptized 12 Jun 1883, daughter of John and Margaret (O'Donnell) Wilgis (St. Ignatius Catholic Church Baptism Register, p. 66)

Wilgis, Anna Rebecca (Winkler), 1857-1895 (Mt. Carmel Methodist Church Cemetery)

Wilgis, Catherine Rebecca, born -- Jun 1885, baptized 25 Sep 1885, daughter of John and Margaret (O'Donnell) Wilgis (St. Ignatius Catholic Church Baptism Register, p. 83, spelled his name Wilgus)

Wilgis Charlotte, see Lemuel Beall and Josephine B. Rigdon, q.v.

Wilgis, Elijah R., 1856-1931 (Mt. Zion Methodist Church Cemetery); farmer, Thomas Run (*The Aegis & Intelligencer*, 11 Jul 1890)

Wilgis, Elizabeth (Watters), 1822-1902 (Mt. Tabor Methodist Church Cemetery)

Wilgis, Florence (Doxen), 1868-1943 (Mt. Zion Methodist Church Cemetery)

Wilgis, Florence Cecelia, baptized 27 Jul 1881, daughter of John and Margaret (O'Donnell) Wilgis (St. Ignatius Catholic Church Baptismal Register, p. 56)

Wilgis, Florence Virginia (Watters), 1854-1947 (Mt. Zion Methodist Church Cemetery)

Wilgis, George W., 1818-1890 (Mt. Tabor Methodist Church Cemetery); county out-pensioner [welfare recipient], Third District (*Havre de Grace Republican*, 4 Jul 1890); resided near Hickory (*The Aegis & Intelligencer*, 1 Aug 1890)

Wilgis, Herman Stump, 1880-1950 (Mt. Zion Methodist Church Cemetery)

Wilgis, Ida E., 1860-1933 (Mt. Zion Methodist Church Cemetery)

Wilgis, James, 1812-1893 (Mt. Zion Methodist Church Cemetery)

Wilgis, John T., 1852-1932 (Mt. Tabor Methodist Church Cemetery); member, Division No. 1, Bel Air Fire and Salvage Corps (*The Aegis & Intelligencer*, 10 Oct 1890); property owner adjacent to Broadway in Bel Air (*The Aegis & Intelligencer*, 16 May 1890 and 1 Aug 1890); son of George W. Wilgis, q.v.

Wilgis, John Wesley, 1851-1939 (Mt. Zion Methodist Church Cemetery)

Wilgis, Joseph Charles, born -- Mar 1890, baptized 18 May 1890, son of John and Margaret (O'Donnell) Wilgis (St. Ignatius Catholic Church Baptism Register, p. 113, spelled his name Wilgus)

Wilgis, Mabel E., 1887-1937 (Mt. Zion Methodist Church Cemetery)

Wilgis, Margaret Elizabeth (O'Donnell), 1852-1926 (Mt. Tabor Methodist Church Cemetery); wife of John T. Wilgis, q.v.

Wilgis, William J., 1867-1947 (Mt. Zion Methodist Church Cemetery)

Wilkes, Robert L., 1874-1944 (Trinity Evangelical Lutheran Church Cemetery)

Wilkinson, ----, first baseman, Nonpareil Baseball Club, Aberdeen (*Havre de Grace Republican*, 6 Jun 1890)

Wilkinson, Amelia E., 1835-1907, wife of Joseph H. Wilkinson (Wesleyan Chapel Methodist Church Cemetery)

Wilkinson, Arthur C., 1873-1963 (Mt. Zion Methodist Church Cemetery)

Wilkinson, Catherine Rebecca (Walker), 1864-1960 (Rock Run Methodist Church Cemetery); wife of Edmund L. Wilkinson, q.v.

Wilkinson, Clara (Mrs.), of the Presbyterian Church, vice president, Fountain Green Women's Christian Temperance Union (*Havre de Grace Republican*, 2 May 1890; *The Aegis & Intelligencer*, 25 Apr 1890)

Wilkinson, Edmund L., 1858-1904 (Rock Run Methodist Church Cemetery)

419

Wilkinson, Elizabeth (Osborn), 1830-1914 (Mt. Zion Methodist Church Cemetery), wife of Thomas M. Wilkinson, q.v.

Wilkinson, Ella, 17 Sep 1890 - 29 Oct 1890 (Mt. Zion Methodist Church Cemetery)

Wilkinson, George A., 1851-1925 (Rock Run Methodist Church Cemetery); expressman, Havre de Grace (*Havre de Grace Republican*, 7 Feb 1890); tomato canner, near Level (*The Aegis & Intelligencer*, 15 Aug 1890); trustee, School No. 14, Second District (*The Aegis & Intelligencer*, 8 Aug 1890)

Wilkinson, Hannah Jane (Pyle), 1844-1904 (Emory Methodist Church Cemetery)

Wilkinson, Harvey M., 1861-1894 (Mt. Zion Methodist Church Cemetery; resident of Fountain Green (*The Aegis & Intelligencer*, 31 Oct 1890); shortstop, Creswell Baseball Club (*The Aegis & Intelligencer*, 18 Jul 1890)

Wilkinson, John Nicholas, 1889-1965 (Churchville Presbyterian Church Cemetery); born 4 Jun 1889, son of John N. and Mary J. Wilkinson (William R. Bissell Bible, *Maryland Bible Records, Volume 1*, by Henry C. Peden, Jr., 2003, p. 35)

Wilkinson, Laura M., 1876-1941 (Baker Cemetery)

Wilkinson, Louisa Mary "Lulu" (Walker), 1858-1933 (Rock Run Methodist Church Cemetery); wife of George A. Wilkinson, q.v.

Wilkinson, Mary Archer, 1885-1972 (Churchville Presbyterian Church Cemetery); born 17 Sep 1885, daughter of John N. and Mary J. Wilkinson (William R. Bissell Bible, *Maryland Bible Records, Volume 1*, by Henry C. Peden, Jr., 2003, p. 35)

Wilkinson, Mary Bissell, 1861-1924 (Churchville Presbyterian Church Cemetery)

Wilkinson, Maude Evelyn (McGibney), 1887-1958 (Darlington Cemetery); native of Harford Co., born 12 Aug 1887, daughter of Philip F. McGibney and Mary F. Smith (Bailey Funeral Home Records)

Wilkinson, Nannie, 1893-1896 (Mt. Zion Methodist Church Cemetery)

Wilkinson, R. Walker, 1879-1918 (Rock Run Methodist Church Cemetery)

Wilkinson, Rebecca (Raysor), 1845-1928 (Cemetery, West Conshohocken, PA); native of Pennsylvania, married, resided in Aberdeen (Death certificate)

Wilkinson, Thomas M., 1825-1900, farmer, native of Maryland, resided at Fountain Green, Harford Co. (Death certificate; Mt. Zion Methodist Church Cemetery); property committeeman, Mt. Zion Methodist Church (*The Aegis & Intelligencer*, 25 Apr 1890)

Wilkinson, Vernon Stephens, 1887-1937 (Rock Run Methodist Church Cemetery)

Wilkinson, Walter, see Wilfred W. Wilkinson and William Walter Wilkinson, q.v.

Wilkinson, Walter, high school student, Second District (*Havre de Grace Republican*, 31 Oct 1890)

Wilkinson, Wilfred W., 1888-1953 (Darlington Cemetery tombstone inscribed 1889); native of Harford Co., born 6 Feb 1888, son of Walter Wilkinson and Ida M. Carr (Bailey Funeral Home Records)

Wilkinson, William Walter, 1862-1926 (Broad Creek Friends Cemetery; Bailey Funeral Home Records); age 28 in 1890 (Marriage License Applications Book ALJ No. 2)

Willan, Mary H., 1878-1955 (Angel Hill Cemetery)

Willard Section No. 58, Cadets of Temperance, Havre de Grace (*Havre de Grace Republican*, 11 Jul 1890)

Willard, Lamar H., 1826-1900, native of Retreat, NJ, resided near Cambria, Harford Co., husband [widower in 1900] of Sarah Ann Willard (Death certificate)

Willey, Alice, see Lesley Hopper Galloway, q.v.

William Watters' Memorial Methodist Church (Cooptown)

William Watters' Memorial Methodist Church (Thomas Run)

Williams' General Store, Darlington, Benjamin J. Williams, prop. (*Country Stores: Harford County's Rural Heritage*, by Henry C. Peden, Jr. and Jack L. Shagena, Jr., 2015, p. 264)

Williams' General Store, at Ludwig, David J. Williams, prop. (*Country Stores: Harford County's Rural Heritage*,

by Henry C. Peden, Jr. and Jack L. Shagena, Jr., 2015, p. 264)

Williams, ----, right fielder, A. R. Walker Baseball Club, Havre de Grace (*Havre de Grace Republican*, 6 Jun 1890)

Williams, Ada (colored), 1883-1919, native of Maryland, born 9 Jun 1883, daughter of Harrison Williams and Annie S. Sims (Death certificate - married named Nickenson)

Williams, Adeline (Pevey) (colored), 1890-1925, native of Maryland, daughter of John Pevey and Rachel McComas (Death certificate)

Williams, Amanda S., sold land in April 1890 (*The Aegis & Intelligencer*, 9 May 1890)

Williams, Annie, age 18 in 1890 (Marriage License Applications Book ALJ No. 2); wife of William J. Williams, q.v.

Williams, Annie Elizabeth (Johnston), 1861-1944, native of Havre de Grace, born 5 Jan 1861, daughter of John L. Johnston, of Pennsylvania, and Mary Cameron, of Maryland (Pennington Funeral Home Records)

Williams, Annie G. (colored), 1871-1949, native of Maryland, born 19 Mar 1871, daughter of John W. Williams and Susie Ann Kenly (Death certificate - married name Wilmore)

Williams, Annie M. (Mrs.), 1886-1961 (Slateville Cemetery, York Co., PA); native of Dublin, Harford Co., born 23 Nov 1886, parents not indicated (Harkins Funeral Home Records)

Williams, Annie Sophin (Simms), 1838-1915 (Death certificate)

Williams, Ariel Elizabeth (Streett), 1850-1940, wife of Stevenson Archer Williams, q.v.

Williams, Belle (Miss), member of the Guy Social Club in Aberdeen (*Havre de Grace Republican*, 31 Oct 1890)

Williams, Ben (colored), c1860-1934 (Death certificate; Heavenly Waters Cemetery)

Williams, Benjamin J., 1849-1925 (Darlington Cemetery; Bailey Funeral Home Records); general store, Darlington (*The Aegis & Intelligencer*, 18 Apr and 26 Sep 1890); delegate, Democrat Convention, and vice president, Harford County Tariff Reform Club (*The Aegis & Intelligencer*, 5 Sep 1890); vice president, Democratic Club (*Havre de Grace Republican*, 5 Sep 1890, listed him as B. G. Williams); member, Deer Creek Farmers' Club (*Havre de Grace Republican*, 3 Oct 1890); vestryman, Grace Memorial Church, Darlington (*Havre de Grace Republican*, 18 Apr 1890); trustee, Darlington Academy (*Havre de Grace Republican*, 26 Sep 1890); also see Edgar Williams, q.v.

Williams, Burley J. (Mrs.) (Norris), 1888-1969 (Slate Ridge Cemetery, York Co., PA); native of Whiteford, Harford Co., born 21 Oct 1888, daughter of Reuben Norris and Amanda Duncan (Harkins Funeral Home Records)

Williams, Caleb E., age 20 in 1890 (Marriage License Applications Book ALJ No. 2, 1891); see Mary Williams, q.v.

Williams, Catharine, businesswoman (trader's license), Havre de Grace (*Havre de Grace Republican*, 30 May 1890)

Williams, Catharine (Collins) (colored), 1834-1912 (Death certificate)

Williams, Charles (colored), see Mary Williams (colored), q.v.

Williams, Charles T. (colored), 1820-1905 (Death certificate)

Williams, Clarence Howard (colored), baptized 7 Oct 1890, age 5, son of Henry and Levantia Williams (St. George's Episcopal Church Register of Baptisms, pp. 10-11)

Williams, Daniel T. (colored), 1877-1919, native of Maryland, son of Edward Williams and Katharine Colline (Death certificate)

Williams, David J., 1864-1939 (Slateville Cemetery, York Co., PA); native of Harford Co., born 18 Nov 1864, son of James J. Williams and Mary Jones (Harkins Funeral Home Records); postmaster at Ludwig, Dublin District (*The Aegis & Intelligencer*, 14 Nov 1890); Civil War veteran, Delta P. O. (*1890 Special Census of the Civil War Veterans of the State of Maryland*, by L. Tilden Moore, Volume III, p. 85); resident of Brookville (*The Aegis & Intelligencer*, 12 Sep 1890)

Williams, Edgar, age 12 in 1890, son of B. J. Williams, of Darlington (*The Aegis & Intelligencer*, 5 Dec 1890)

Williams, Edward (colored), 1840-1935, native of Harford Co. (Death certificate); see Daniel T. Williams and George E Williams, q.v.

Williams, Elise, pianist and honor student, Archer Institute, Bel Air (*The Aegis & Intelligencer*, 20 Jun 1890); student and pianist, Bel Air Graded School (*The Aegis & Intelligencer*, 26 Dec 1890); premium award winner, Class L - Children's Department, Harford County Fair (*The Aegis & Intelligencer*, 24 Oct 1890)

Williams, Eliza (colored), see Eleanor Brown Chambers (colored), q.v.

Williams, Eliza (Anderson) (colored), 1843-1920, native of Maryland (Death certificate)

Williams, Elizabeth (colored), see Annie T. Reed (colored), q.v.

Williams, Elizabeth (Lisby) (colored), 1855-1914, native of Maryland (Death certificate)

Williams, Elizabeth Cooke (Forwood), 1864-1933 (Darlington Cemetery; www.findagrave.com); wife of Benjamin J. Williams, q.v.

Williams, Ellen (Gibson) (colored), 1870-1936 (Death certificate)

Williams, Elsie (colored), see Caroline K. Monk (colored) and William S. Monk (colored), q.v.

Williams, Emanuel, tent holder, Carsins Run Camp Meeting of the East Harford Circuit, P. E. Church (*The Aegis & Intelligencer*, 1 Aug 1890)

Williams, Frances G. (colored), 1879-1918, native of Maryland, born 11 Feb 1879, daughter of L. Williams and Lizzie Brown (Death certificate - married name Christ)

Williams, Franklin, Civil War veteran, Norrisville (*1890 Special Census of the Civil War Veterans of the State of Maryland*, by L. Tilden Moore, Volume III, p. 82)

Williams, Frederick Rodgers, 1861-1937 (Churchville Presbyterian Church Cemetery); incorporator, The Loan, Trust, Security and Insurance Company of Harford County (*Havre de Grace Republican*, 28 Feb 1890); incorporator, The Old Peach Bottom Slate Company of Harford County (*Havre de Grace Republican*, 27 Jun 1890); secretary-treasurer, Maryland Central Dairymen's Association (*Havre de Grace Republican*, 14 Mar 1890); treasurer, Spicer Building Association, of Bel Air (*Havre de Grace Republican*, 13 Jun 1890)

Williams, George, 1880-1940 (Death certificate; Alms House Record Book)

Williams, George E. (colored), 1872-1938, born at West River, MD on 12 Sep 1872, son of Edward Williams and Catherine Collins, both natives of Harford Co. (Death certificate)

Williams, Hallie, pianist and student, Archer Institute, Bel Air (*The Aegis & Intelligencer*, 20 Jun 1890); student and pianist, Bel Air Graded School (*The Aegis & Intelligencer*, 26 Dec 1890)

Williams, Harriet (Brown) (colored), 1888-1954 (Union M. E. Church Cemetery), wife of Vandellia Armatage Williams, q.v.

Williams, Harriet (colored), 1872-1950 (Clark's Chapel Methodist Church Cemetery)

Williams, Harriet A., premium award winner, Class L - Children's Department, Harford County Fair (*The Aegis & Intelligencer*, 24 Oct 1890)

Williams, Harrison (colored), see Ada Williams (colored), q.v.

Williams, Harry A., 1878-1890 (Baker Cemetery)

Williams, Harry J., 1870-1952 (Hanover Green Cemetery, PA); native of Harford Co., born 4 Mar 1870, parents not indicated (Harkins Funeral Home Records)

Williams, Hattie E. (colored), 1888-1954 (Union Methodist Church Cemetery, Aberdeen)

Williams, Hattie J. (colored), age 19 in 1890 (Marriage License Applications Book ALJ No. 2, 1891)

Williams, Henrietta (Miss) (colored), 1852-1917 (Death certificate)

Williams, Henry (colored), 1844-1915 (Death certificate); see Joseph Sovis Williams, Clarence Howard Williams, William Sidney Williams and Mary Margaret Williams, q.v.

Williams, Hiram N., 1844-1937 (Baker Cemetery); government pensioner, Aberdeen (*The Aegis & Intelligencer*,

28 Nov 1890)

Williams, Isaac (colored), 1859-1945, native of Maryland, son of Norman Williams and Mandie Tilson (Pennington Funeral Home Records)

Williams, Isaac Clay (colored), 1841-1912 (Union Methodist Church Cemetery, Aberdeen)

Williams, J. Oliver, tomato farmer on Isaac Amos' farm near Emmorton (*The Aegis & Intelligencer*, 15 Aug 1890)

Williams, J. Wesley (colored), trustee, Abingdon Colored School No. 1, First District (*Havre de Grace Republican*, 30 May 1890)

Williams, James (colored), 1861-1928 (St. James United Cemetery); native of Alabama, married, fisherman and gunner, resided in Havre de Grace (Death certificate)

Williams, James J., see David J. Williams, q.v.

Williams, Jane Nettie (colored), 1872-1913, native of Maryland, born 30 May 1872, daughter of Isaac Williams and Rachael Christy (Death certificate - married name Lisby)

Williams, John (colored), 1861-1928 (Death certificate)

Williams, John (colored), 1875-1920, native of Maryland, born 27 Jun 1875, son of John and Lizzie Williams (Death certificate)

Williams, John Richard (colored), 1861-1939, native of Harford Co. (Death certificate)

Williams, John Savage, see Lillian Williams, q.v.

Williams, John Thomas (colored), 1857-1923, native of Maryland (Death certificate)

Williams, John W., 1876-1953 (Slate Ridge Cemetery, York Co., PA); resident of Cardiff, MD, born 12 Sep 1876, parents not indicated (Harkins Funeral Home Records)

Williams, John W. (colored), see Annie G. Williams (colored), q.v.

Williams, Joseph Sovis (colored), baptized 7 Oct 1890, age 6, son of Henry and Levantia Williams (St. George's Episcopal Church Register of Baptisms, pp. 10-11)

Williams, Katherine, 1886-1966, native of Havre de Grace, born 11 Sep 1886, daughter of William Williams and Anna Johnson (Pennington Funeral Home Records - married name McCommons)

Williams, L. (colored), see Frances G. Williams (colored), q.v.

Williams, Levantia (colored), see Joseph Sovis Williams, Clarence Howard Williams, William Sidney Williams and Mary Margaret Williams, q.v.

Williams, Lewis W., hotel proprietor, Spencer House, Havre de Grace (*Havre de Grace Republican*, 24 Jan and 30 May 1890)

Williams, Lillian, daughter of John Savage Williams, Esq., near Abingdon, their summer home (*The Aegis & Intelligencer*, 25 Jul 1890)

Williams, Lizzie (colored), see John Williams, q.v.

Williams, Margrett Elnora (Hickey), 1884-1908, native of Slate Hill, PA, resided at Ludwig, Harford Co. (Death certificate)

Williams, Martha (colored), see Martha J. Smith, Henson Smith, Robert E. Smith and John C. Smith, q.v.

Williams, Martha V. (Brown) (colored), 1858-1900, native of Maryland, resident of Perryman, wife of Solomon W. Williams (Death certificate)

Williams, Mary, 1851-1891 (Ayres Chapel M. P. Church Cemetery)

Williams, Mary (colored), see Henry Wells (colored), q.v.

Williams, Mary (colored), 1872-1901, native of Maryland, daughter of Charles Williams and Frances Stansbury (Death certificate - married name Webster)

Williams, Mary (Mrs.), 1826-1908, native of Wales, resided at Ludwig, Harford Co. (Death certificate)

Williams, Mary (Williams), 1872-1960 (Slate Ridge Cemetery, York Co., PA); native of Cardiff, Harford Co., born 12 Mar 1872, daughter of William L. Williams and Margaret Jones (Harkins Funeral Home Records); age 18 in 1890 (Marriage License Applications Book ALJ No. 2, in 1891); wife of Caleb E. Williams, q.v.

Williams, Mary F. (Mrs.) (colored), 1864-1904, native of Harford Co. (Death certificate)

Williams, Mary J., sold land in April 1890 (*The Aegis & Intelligencer*, 9 May 1890)

Williams, Mary Margaret (colored), baptized 7 Oct 1890, age 1 year 5 months, daughter of Henry and Levantia Williams (St. George's Episcopal Church Register of Baptisms, pp. 10-11)

Williams, Mary Zew (colored), 1872-1932 (Death certificate); wife of William R. Williams, q.v.

Williams, Maud, 1876-1890 (Darlington Cemetery); daughter of B. J. and Susy Williams (*Harford Democrat,* 18 Apr 1890)

Williams, May (Miss), premium award winner, Class C - Sheep, and Class J - Domestic Products, Harford County Fair (*The Aegis & Intelligencer*, 24 Oct 1890)

Williams, Minerva, age 22 in 1890 (Marriage License Applications Book ALJ No. 2, 1891)

Williams, Mollie (Whims) (colored), 1863-1937 (Death certificate)

Williams, Morgan, 1835-1918, native of Wales (Bethel Presbyterian Church Cemetery Records); Civil War veteran, resident of Madonna (*1890 Special Census of the Civil War Veterans of the State of Maryland*, by L. Tilden Moore, Volume III, p. 79)

Williams, Norman (colored), see Isaac Williams (colored), q.v.

Williams, Philip I. (colored), 1858-1905 (St. James United Cemetery)

Williams, R. Jane (Benson), 1885-1905, native of Maryland (Death certificate)

Williams, Rachel (Collins) (colored), 1862-1937, native of Harford Co. (Death certificate)

Williams, Richard, young son of Richard Williams, of Hickory (*The Aegis & Intelligencer*, 19 Dec 1890)

Williams, Richard (colored), resided near Clark's Chapel (*Harford Democrat*, 21 Nov 1890)

Williams, Rush, youngest daughter of Mr. & Mrs. S. A. Williams, of Bel Air (*The Aegis & Intelligencer*, 8 Aug 1890)

Williams, Ruth Eliza (Wilson), 1815-1921 (Darlington Cemetery); native of Harford Co. (Bailey Funeral Home Records)

Williams, Sarah E., sold land in April 1890 (*The Aegis & Intelligencer*, 9 May 1890)

Williams, Solomon (colored), see Hattie C. Christy (colored) and Vandellia A. Williams (colored), q.v.

Williams, Solomon W. (colored), 1857-1915 (Death certificate); see Martha V. Williams, q.v.

Williams, Stevenson Archer, 1851-1932 (Churchville Presbyterian Church Cemetery); director, Bel Air Turnpike Company (*The Aegis & Intelligencer*, 17 Jan 1890); director, Harford National Bank (*The Aegis & Intelligencer*, 2 May 1890); incorporator, Bel Air Water and Light Company (*Havre de Grace Republican*, 14 Feb 1890); solicitor, Jarrettsville Land, Loan and Building Association (*Havre de Grace Republican*, 18 Apr 1890); vestryman, St. Mary's Church, Emmorton (*Havre de Grace Republican*, 18 Apr 1890); Confederate Army veteran (*Havre de Grace Republican*, 30 May 1890); incorporator, Henry Reckord Manufacturing Company (*Havre de Grace Republican*, 21 Feb 1890); incorporator, The Loan, Trust, Security and Insurance Company of Harford County (*Havre de Grace Republican*, 28 Feb 1890); also see Rush Williams, q.v.

Williams, Sydney A. (Miller) (colored), 1854-1916 (Death certificate)

Williams, Thomas J., Civil War veteran, Delta P. O. (*1890 Special Census of the Civil War Veterans of the State of Maryland*, by L. Tilden Moore, Volume III, p. 85); see Jane W. Thomas and Margaret W. Wilson, q.v.

Williams, Vandellia Armatage (colored), 1887-1988, born in Perryman, Harford Co., son of Solomon Williams and ---- (Union M. E. Church Cemetery; *Havre de Grace Record*, 6 Jan 1988)

Williams, Viola J. (Hamilton), 1881-1960 (Slate Ridge Cemetery, York Co., PA); native of Flintville, Harford Co., born 17 Apr 1881, daughter of William Hamilton and Margaret McFadden (Harkins Funeral Home

Records)

Williams, Virgie (colored), mother of Hattie C. Christy, q.v.

Williams, W., member, Guiding Star Council No. 9, Jr. O. U. A. M., Havre de Grace (*Havre de Grace Republican*, 11 Jul 1890)

Williams, William, sneak boat duck hunter (*Havre de Grace Republican*, 7 Nov 1890); see Katherine Williams, q.v.

Williams, William (colored), c1867-1932 (Death certificate; Heavenly Waters Cemetery)

Williams, William (colored), 1868-1927 (Death certificate)

Williams, William H., see Annie Elizabeth Williams, q.v.

Williams, William J., age 21, married Miss Annie Williams, of South Delta, on 4 Aug 1890 at the Bel Air Parsonage (Marriage License Applications Book ALJ No. 2; Bel Air Methodist Charge Marriage Records, p. 238; *The Aegis & Intelligencer*, 8 Aug 1890)

Williams, William L., Civil War veteran, Delta P. O. (*1890 Special Census of the Civil War Veterans of the State of Maryland*, by L. Tilden Moore, Volume III, p. 85); see Mary Williams, q.v.

Williams, William M., 1819-1896 (Angel Hill Cemetery)

Williams, William M., 1871-1935 (Slateville Cemetery, York Co., PA); native of Whiteford, Harford Co., born 2 Dec 1871, son of William M. Williams and Mary Lewis, both of Wales (Harkins Funeral Home Records)

Williams, William R. (colored), 1871-1926 (Clark's Chapel Methodist Church Cemetery); native of Maryland, born 4 Apr 1871, son of Edward Williams and Katherine Collins (Death certificate)

Williams, William Sidney (colored), baptized 7 Oct 1890, age 2 1/2 years, son of Henry and Levantia Williams (St. George's Episcopal Church Register of Baptisms, pp. 10-11)

Williamson, A. A. (Rev.), First Baptist Church (*Havre de Grace Republican*, 25 Jul 1890)

Williamson, Catherine (colored), see Mary Gray (colored), q.v.

Williamson, Henry (colored), 1867-1945, native of Calvert Co., MD (Death certificate)

Williamson, Lizzie (colored), age 26 in 1890 (Marriage License Applications Book ALJ No. 2)

Williamson, Louisa (Butler) (colored), 1854-1931, native of Maryland (Death certificate)

Williamson, Mary (Turner) (colored), 1867-1921, native of Maryland (Death certificate)

Williamson, Mary E. (Smith) (colored), 1859-1921, native of Maryland (Death certificate)

Williamson, Sarah E. (colored), see George D. Ray (colored) and Sarah E. Ray (colored), q.v.

Willis, B., uncalled for letter in Bel Air P. O. (*The Aegis & Intelligencer*, 14 Nov 1890)

Willis, Cass (colored), county out-pensioner [welfare recipient], Fourth District (*Havre de Grace Republican*, 20 Jun 1890)

Willis, Kirby S., age 21 in 1890 (Marriage License Applications Book ALJ No. 2, 1891)

Willis, Jane (colored), see Sarah Jane Rice (colored), q.v.

Willow Grove Grist Mill, E. E. Phillips, prop. (*Mills: Grist, Saw, Bone, Flint, Fulling ... & More*, by Jack L. Shagena, Jr., Henry C. Peden, Jr. and John W. McGrain, 2009, pp. 281-282)

Wills, Laura Jane, 1878-1949 (Angel Hill Cemetery)

Wills, Lotta (Jackson), wife of Richard Wills, q.v.

Wills, Richard, died 21 Apr 1901, adult, age not given, native of Maryland, farmer at Aberdeen (Death certificate)

Wills, Sherwood O., 1871-1940 (Bethel Presbyterian Church Cemetery Records)

Willson, Ann (colored), died 15 Dec 1894 (Alms House Monthly Record)

Wilmore, Alice (colored), 1890-1918, native of Maryland, born 10 Aug 1890, daughter of Isaac Wilmore and Ida Jones (Death certificate - married name Preston)

Wilmore, Isaac (colored), age 35 in 1890 (Marriage License Applications Book ALJ No. 2); see Alice Wilmore, q.v.

Wilmore, James A. (colored), 1840-1915 (Death certificate); see Sara Wilmore, q.v.

Wilmore, James L. (colored), see William P. Wilmore (colored), q.v.

Wilmore, Mary E. (Hamilton) (colored), 1878-1924 (Union Methodist Church Cemetery, Aberdeen); native of Harford Co., resided near Swan Creek, daughter of Isaac Hamilton and Melinda Cooper (Death certificate stated buried in Asbury Church Cemetery, but her husband William was buried in Union Methodist Church Cemetery)

Wilmore, Sara (colored), 1841-1921 (Union Methodist Church Cemetery, Aberdeen); wife of James A. Wilmore, q.v.

Wilmore, William P. (colored), 1871-1924 (Union Methodist Church Cemetery, Aberdeen); native of Maryland, resided near Swan Creek, born 5 Sep 1871, son of James L. Wilmore and Sarah L. Lewis (Death certifiicate)

Wilna Farmers' Club (*Harford Democrat*, 21 Feb 1890)

Wilna Women's Christian Temperance Union (*Harford Democrat*, 28 Mar 1890)

Wilson's General Store, Abingdon, James W. Wilson, prop. (*Country Stores: Harford County's Rural Heritage*, by Henry C. Peden, Jr. and Jack L. Shagena, Jr., 2015, pp. 265-266)

Wilson's Mills, on Deer Creek at Darlington Road, David E. Wilson, prop. (*Mills: Grist, Saw, Bone, Flint, Fulling ... & More*, by Jack L. Shagena, Jr., Henry C. Peden, Jr. and John W. McGrain, 2009, pp. 282-284)

Wilson's Public School No. 6, near Pylesville (*Harford County, Maryland Teachers and the Schools They Served, 1774-1900*, by Henry C. Peden, Jr., 2022, p. 373)

Wilson, Abel D., 1846-1930 (Christ Episcopal Church Cemetery); associate judge of elections, Bel Air Precinct (*Havre de Grace Republican*, 17 Oct 1890); delegate, Democrat Convention, and vice president, Harford County Tariff Reform Club (*The Aegis & Intelligencer*, 5 Sep 1890); vice president, Democratic Club (*Havre de Grace Republican*, 5 Sep 1890)

Wilson, Abram J., 1883-1949, born 11 Feb 1883, son of David Wilson and Rachel Slade (Bethel Presbyterian Church Cemetery Records)

Wilson, Addison Streett, 1869-1901 (Centre Methodist Church Cemetery)

Wilson, Agnes, 1889-1963, native of Havre de Grace, born 3 Nov 1889, daughter of Louis Wilson and Emma Green (Pennington Funeral Home Records - married name Stanley)

Wilson, Albert H., 1882-1927 (Angel Hill Cemetery)

Wilson, Alfred H., 1871-1950 (St. George's Episcopal Church Cemetery)

Wilson, Alice, see Sue L. Taylor and Mercy Huff, q.v.

Wilson, Alice (Schuster), 1890-1969 (Highland Presbyterian Church Cemetery)

Wilson, Alice Helena, 1879-1970, daughter of Henry Clay Wilson and Delia A. ---- (St. Mary's Episcopal Church Cemetery)

Wilson, Alonzo, 1876-1965 (Bel Air Memorial Gardens); native of Pylesville, Harford Co., born 3 May 1876, son of Samuel Wilson and Mary McCallister (Harkins Funeral Home Records)

Wilson, Amy H., 1885-1961 (Angel Hill Cemetery)

Wilson, Ann Eliza (Foard), 1857-1938, wife of John Curtis Wilson (*Ancestral Charts, Volume 4*, Harford County Genealogical Society, 1988, p. 204)

Wilson, Anna Lee, 1877-1963 (Holy Trinity Episcopal Church Cemetery)

Wilson, Annabel, student, Sixth District (*The Aegis & Intelligencer*, 24 Oct 1890)

Wilson, Anne (Hopkins), 1885-1970, wife of Thomas Archer Wilson, q.v. (St. Mary's Episcopal Church Cemetery)

Wilson, Annie (colored), see Bessie M. Way (colored), q.v.

Wilson, Annie E. (Ferguson), 1826-1900 (Deer Creek Harmony Presbyterian Church Cemetery); widow of

William W. Wilson; died 1 Aug 1900, age 75 *(sic)* (*Deaths and Marriages in Harford County, Maryland, and Vicinity, 1873-1904, from the Diaries of Albert Peter Silver*, transcribed by Glenn Randers-Pehrson, 1995, p. 32)

Wilson, Annie E. (Richardson), 1884-1966 (Bethel Presbyterian Church Cemetery Records); wife of David Hutchins Wilson, q.v.

Wilson, Annie H. (Wheeler), 1853-1934 (Darlington Cemetery)

Wilson, Annie T., age 7 in 1890, student, Oakland School (George G. Curtiss Ledger); premium award winner, Class L - Children's Department, Harford County Fair (*The Aegis & Intelligencer*, 24 Oct 1890); resident of Darlington, sister of James W. Wilson (*The Aegis & Intelligencer*, 12 Dec 1890)

Wilson, Annie V., see Jeremiah Lowe, q.v.

Wilson, Annie W. (Wallace), 1855-1926 (Highland Presbyterian Church Cemetery); native of Maryland, resided at Whiteford (Death certificate)

Wilson, Archibald, 1830-1912 (Highland Presbyterian Church Cemetery); farmer near Pylesville (*Havre de Grace Republican*, 14 Mar 1890); member, Maryland Central Dairymen's Association (*Havre de Grace Republican*, 14 Mar 1890); vice president, Harford County Farmers' Association (*The Aegis & Intelligencer*, 17 Jan 1890); register of voters, Fifth District (*Havre de Grace Republican*, 21 Feb 1890); vice president, Third Annual Convention, Farmers' Club of Harford Co. (*Havre de Grace Republican*, 5 Dec 1890); see Harry S. Wilson and Edward A. Wilson, q.v.

Wilson, Benjamin F., age 28 in 1890 (Marriage License Applications Book ALJ No. 2, 1890)

Wilson, Benjamin W., 1851-1914 (St. Ignatius Catholic Church Cemetery)

Wilson, Benjamin W., Jr., 1888-1910, born -- Sep 1888, baptized 13 Oct 1888, son of Benjamin W. Wilson and Florence Smithson (St. Ignatius Catholic Church Baptism Register, p. 99)

Wilson, Blanche R., 1890-1920 (Mt. Zion Methodist Church Cemetery)

Wilson, C., member, Darlington Road League, 1890 (*Havre de Grace Republican*, 7 Mar 1890)

Wilson, Calvin D. (Rev.), pastor of Churchville Presbyterian Church, and brother of Rev. Dr. Maurice Wilson, of Dayton, OH (*The Aegis & Intelligencer*, 29 Aug 1890; *Havre de Grace Republican*, 20 Jun 1890); age 32 in 1889 (Marriage License Applications Book ALJ No. 2, 1889)

Wilson, Carrie B., 1874-1965 (Angel Hill Cemetery)

Wilson, Carrie Dever (Ivins), 1890-1958 (Baker Cemetery)

Wilson, Carrie N., 1873-1937 (St. George's Episcopal Church Cemetery)

Wilson, Cassie (Hill) (colored), c1861-1918, native of Maryland (Death certificate)

Wilson, Charles, student, Forest Hill School, 1890 (*The Aegis*, 2 Jul 1965, school picture)

Wilson, Charles A., 1869-1908 (Highland Presbyterian Church Cemetery)

Wilson, Charles H., 1882-1973 (Christ Episcopal Church Cemetery)

Wilson, Charles R., transferred from the voter registration list at Hopewell, Second District, 1890 (*Havre de Grace Republican*, 17 Oct 1890)

Wilson, Charles T., actor, musical entertainment, at Darlington (*The Aegis & Intelligencer*, 30 May 1890 and 13 Jun 1890)

Wilson, Charles Taylor, 1848-1921 (Angel Hill Cemetery); teacher and vice principal, Havre de Grace High School (*Havre de Grace Republican*, 11 Apr 1890); member, Havre de Grace M. E Church (*Havre de Grace Republican*, 13 Jun 1890); secretary, Republican Club (*Havre de Grace Republican*, 7 Nov 1890); sneak boat duck hunter (*Havre de Grace Republican*, 7 Nov 1890); Prof. CharlesWilson, choir member, Grove Presbyterian Church, Aberdeen (*Havre de Grace Republican*, 14 Feb 1890)

Wilson, Charles Wesley, 1874-1950 (Angel Hill Cemetery)

Wilson, Charlotte Ann (colored), age 20 in 1890 (Marriage License Applications Book ALJ No. 2, 1891); see Charotte Ann Smith, q.v.

Wilson, Christopher, 1827-1906 (Darlington Cemetery); juror, Fifth District (*Havre de Grace Republican*, 2 May 1890); trustee, Darlington School No. 15, Fifth District (*Havre de Grace Republican*, 30 May 1890); Christopher Wilson, and wife, residents of Darlington (*The Aegis & Intelligencer*, 26 Dec 1890)

Wilson, Clara, born -- Jul 1885, baptized 20 Aug 1885, daughter of Benjamin and Florence (Smithson) Wilson (St. Ignatius Catholic Church Baptism Register, p. 82)

Wilson, Clinton A, 1886-1954 (Angel Hill Cemetery)

Wilson, Cynthia Jane, 1858-1932 (Angel Hill Cemetery)

Wilson, Cyrena (Bateman), 1851-1938 (Angel Hill Cemetery), wife of Charles Taylor Wilson, q.v.

Wilson, David E., 1870-1941 (Darlington Cemetery); native of Harford Co., born 20 Jun 1870, son of David E. Wilson and Mary Wilson (Bailey Funeral Home Records)

Wilson, David Elisha, 1822-1901 (Darlington Cemetery; native of Maryland, merchant in Darlington, husband of Mary S. Wilson (Death certificate stated he was born in 1823); trustee, Darlington Academy (*Havre de Grace Republican*, 26 Sep 1890); resident of Darlington (*The Aegis & Intelligencer*, 13 Jun 1890); see Wilson's Mills, q.v.

Wilson, David Gilpin, 1867-1935 (Darlington Cemetery); native of Darlington, MD (Bailey Funeral Home Records)

Wilson, David Hutchins, 1868-1936 (Bethel Presbyterian Church Cemetery)

Wilson, David Joshua, 1846-1927 (Mt. Carmel Methodist Church Cemetery); attorney-at-law, Bel Air (*Harford Democrat*, 14 Feb 1890)

Wilson, Delia (colored), see Ellanora Tillman (colored), q.v.

Wilson, Delia Lee (Archer), 1849-1924 (St. Mary's Episcopal Church Cemetery); wife of Henry Clay Wilson, q.v.; also see Deliverance Hannah Lee, q.v.

Wilson, E. Estelle, 1843-1908 (St. Mary's Episcopal Church Cemetery)

Wilson, Edith, born 1879, daughter of David Wilson and Rachel Slade (Bethel Presbyterian Church Cemetery Records)

Wilson, Edward (colored), see Susan V. Presberry (colored), q.v.

Wilson, Edward (colored), alias Edward Trounce, age 12 in 1890 (*The Aegis & Intelligencer*, 28 Feb 1890); prisoner in the county jail (*Harford Democrat*, 3 Jan 1890); charged with destroying property in Albert S. Holloway's barn and stealing a horse from William Hopkins, was found guilty, and sent to the House of Reformation for Colored Children (*Harford Democrat*, 21 Feb 1890; Harford County Criminal Docket, 1888-1892, p. 80)

Wilson, Edward A., 1865-1938 (Slate Ridge Cemetery, York Co., PA); born 12 Mar 1865, son of Archibald Wilson and Hannah Gladden (Harkins Funeral Home Records); farmer, near Pylesville (*Havre de Grace Republican*, 14 Mar 1890); premium award winner, Class A - Horses, and Class C - Sheep, Harford County Fair (*The Aegis & Intelligencer*, 24 Oct 1890)

Wilson, Edward Charles, 1873-1948 (Darlington Cemetery); native of Harford Co., born 11 Dec 1873, son of Isaac Wilson and Jenney Dermitt, of Pittsburgh, PA (Bailey Funeral Home Records)

Wilson, Elizabeth, see Eugene L. Thompson, q.v.

Wilson, Elizabeth, 1821-1891 (Smith Chapel Methodist Church Cemetery)

Wilson, Elizabeth, 1882-1963 (Angel Hill Cemetery)

Wilson, Elizabeth, student, Forest Hill School, 1890 (*The Aegis*, 2 Jul 1965, school picture)

Wilson, Ella (Ruppert), 1857-1939 (Highland Presbyterian Church Cemetery)

Wilson, Ella (Tarbert), 1862-1935 (Highland Presbyterian Church Cemetery)

Wilson, Ellen (Armstrong), 1829-1900, native of Baltimore Co., resided at Fallston, Harford Co., wife of Henry Wilson (Death certificate)

Wilson, Emma A., 1869-1961 (Cokesbury Memorial Methodist Church Cemetery)

Wilson, Emma A. (Green), 1861-1916 (Angel Hill Cemetery); wife of Louis O. Wilson, q.v.; also see William H. Wilson, q.v.

Wilson, Ethel, 1888-1973, native of Havre de Grace, born 22 Apr 1888, daughter of Summerfield Wilson and Cynthia Conley (Pennington Funeral Home Records - married name Cloak)

Wilson, Ethel (Neale), 1883-1960 (Darlington Cemetery)

Wilson, Fanny (Kennard), 1872-1956 (St. Mary's Episcopal Church Cemetery)

Wilson, Florence (Smithson), 1853-1923 (St. Ignatius Catholic Church Cemetery); wife of Benjamin W. Wilson, q.v.

Wilson, Forrester, see Mary E. (Wilson) Heaps, q.v.

Wilson, Frances, born -- Nov 1886, baptized 19 May 1887, daughter of Benjamin and Florence (Smithson) Wilson (St. Ignatius Catholic Church Baptism Register, p. 93)

Wilson, Frances (Davis), wife of Dr. Henry B. Wilson, q.v.

Wilson, Frances Jane (colored), 1848-1893, wife of William H. Wilson (St. James Church, Gravel Hill Cemetery)

Wilson, Frank, died 16 May 1900, adult, age not given, worked at the Franklinville [Cotton] Mills, oldest son of Mr. & Mrs. Thomas Wilson, resided at Joppa (Death certificate incomplete; *The Aegis & Intelligencer*, 18 May 1900)

Wilson, G. O., premium award winner, Class A - Horses, and Class B - Cattle, Harford County Fair (*The Aegis & Intelligencer*, 24 Oct 1890)

Wilson, Garfield M., 1882-1946 (Mt. Zion Methodist Church Cemetery)

Wilson, Gilpin, resident of Darlington (*The Aegis & Intelligencer*, 13 Jun 1890)

Wilson, Gretta (Miss), resident of Darlington (*The Aegis & Intelligencer*, 13 Jun 1890)

Wilson, Hannah (Mrs.) (colored), 1863-1933, parents unknown, wife of Levi Wilson (Death certificate); see Henrietta Wilson, q.v.

Wilson, Hannah Elizabeth, 1845-1925 (Christ Episcopal Church Cemetery)

Wilson, Hannah J. (Presbury) (colored), 1849-1919, native of Harford Co., daughter of George and Ann Presbury [Presberry], also natives of Harford Co. (Death certificate)

Wilson, Hannah Jane (Gladden), 1836-1923 (Highland Presbyterian Church Cemetery); wife of Archibald Wilson, q.v., and mother of Harry S. Wilson, q.v.

Wilson, Harris Archer, 1878-1939, son of Henry Clay Wilson and Delia A. ---- (St. Mary's Episcopal Church Cemetery)

Wilson, Harry, see R. Blanche Wilson, q.v.

Wilson, Harry Anderson, 1888-1983, native of Perryman. Harford Co. (Berkley Memorial Cemetery; World War I military records; *The Aegis*, 24 Feb 1983)

Wilson, Harry S., 1870-1890 (Highland Presbyterian Church Cemetery); son of Archibald and Hannah J. Wilson, of near Clermont Mills (*The Aegis & Intelligencer*, 12 Sep 1890 and 19 Sep 1890)

Wilson, Helen (Miss), actress, musical entertainment, at Darlington (*The Aegis & Intelligencer*, 30 May 1890)

Wilson, Henrietta (colored), 1885-1911, daughter of Levi Wilson and Hannah Barrett, of Bel Air (Death certificate)

Wilson, Henry, see Ellen Wilson and Mary Louisa Wilson, q.v.

Wilson, Henry II, 1885-1914 (Holy Trinity Episcopal Church Cemetery)

Wilson, Henry (colored), 1854-1928 (Green Spring Methodist Church Cemetery)

Wilson, Henry B. (Dr.), 1863-1900 (St. George's Episcopal Church Cemetery); native of Maryland, resided at

Aberdeen, Harford Co. (Death certificate)

Wilson, Henry Clay, 1831-1925 (St. Mary's Episcopal Church Cemetery); road examiner in the First District (*Havre de Grace Republican*, 4 Jul 1890); vestryman, St. Mary's Episcopal Church, Emmorton (*Havre de Grace Republican*, 18 Apr 1890)

Wilson, Herbert, student, Union School House, near Bush Chapel (*The Aegis & Intelligencer*, 14 Mar 1890)

Wilson, Howard (colored), 1871-1906 (Mt. Zion Methodist Church Cemetery, at Mountain)

Wilson, Humphrey, 1817-1905 (Christ Episcopal Church Cemetery); justice of the peace, Third District (*Havre de Grace Republican*, 21 Feb 1890); father of Joseph Pearl Wilson, q.v.

Wilson, Ida Elizabeth (colored), see Ida Elizabeth Whittington (colored), q.v.

Wilson, Isaac, 1835-1896 (Darlington Cemetery); trustee, Darlington Academy (*Havre de Grace Republican*, 26 Sep 1890); see Edward C. Wilson, q.v.

Wilson, J. S. (Mrs.), superintendent of literature, Women's Christian Temperance Union, of Havre de Grace (*Havre de Grace Republican*, 19 Sep 1890)

Wilson, James, Civil War veteran, Perryman (*1890 Special Census of the Civil War Veterans of the State of Maryland*, by L. Tilden Moore, Volume III, p. 63)

Wilson, James H., 1852-1917 (Rock Run Methodist Church Cemetery); son of William C. Wilson, q.v.

Wilson, James J., 1856-1925 (Highland Presbyterian Church Cemetery); ruling elder, Highland Presbyterian Church (*The Aegis & Intelligencer*, 10 Jan 1890)

Wilson, James S., 1880-1952 (St. Ignatius Catholic Church Cemetery); baptized 3 Jul 1881, son of Benjamin W. and Florence (Smithson) Wilson (St. Ignatius Catholic Church Baptismal Register, p. 56)

Wilson, James W., see Annie T. Wilson, q.v.

Wilson, James W., 1859-1931 (Bailey Funeral Home Records)

Wilson, Jane Mary (Dorus), 1869-1940, wife of Samuel W. Wilson (Death certificate; Highland Presbyterian Church Cemetery)

Wilson, Jenny (Dermitt), wife of Isaac Wilson, q.v.

Wilson, Jessie O. (Huff), 1871-1947 (St. George's Episcopal Church Cemetery); wife of Alfred H. Wilson, q.v.

Wilson, John, tramp, arrested for robbing a store and post office in Perryman sent to Baltimore for trial (*Harford Democrat*, 18 Jul 1890)

Wilson, John (colored), see Virginia L. Hill (colored), q.v.

Wilson, John Archer (colored), 1870-1935, native of Harford Co., son of John L. Wilson, of Towson, Baltimore Co., and Emiline Green, of Harford Co. (Death certificate)

Wilson, John B., Civil War veteran, Forest Hill (*1890 Special Census of the Civil War Veterans of the State of Maryland*, by L. Tilden Moore, Volume III, p. 74)

Wilson, John Curtis, 1848-1930 (*Ancestral Charts, Volume 4*, Harford County Genealogical Society, 1988, p. 204)

Wilson, John D., 1854-1891 (Old Brick Baptist Church Cemetery)

Wilson, John E., 1860-1944 (Angel Hill Cemetery); librarian, Lapidum Sunday School, 1890 (*Havre de Grace Republican*, 30 May 1890)

Wilson, John F., see Jeremiah Lowe, q.v.

Wilson, John L. (colored), see John Archer Wilson (colored), q.v.

Wilson, John R., age 27 in 1890 (Marriage License Applications Book ALJ No. 2)

Wilson, John S. (captain), 1821-1892 (Angel Hill Cemetery); father of Charles Taylor Wilson, q.v.

Wilson, John T., delegate, First District, Democrat Party Convention (*The Aegis & Intelligencer*, 5 Sep 1890)

Wilson, John T., 1830-1895 (Darlington Cemetery)

Wilson, John T., c1856-1925 (Fellowship Church Cemetery)

Wilson, Joseph Pearl, 1865-1934 (Death certificate stated J. Purlington Wilson; Mt. Zion Methodist Church Cemetery)

Wilson, Josephine, student, Havre de Grace High School (*Havre de Grace Republican*, 31 Oct 1890)

Wilson, Josephine S., 1873-1936 (Holy Cross Church Cemetery)

Wilson, Josephine S., 1880-1968 (Angel Hill Cemetery)

Wilson, Josias, 1883-1940 (St. Ignatius Catholic Church Cemetery); born 11 Jul(?), 1883, baptized 7 Nov 1883, son of Benjamin W. and Florence (Smithson) Wilson (St. Ignatius Catholic Church Baptism Register, p. 70)

Wilson, Judson, see Mrs. M. L. Sewell, q.v.

Wilson, Julia, see Edwin T. McNutt and Richard S.McNutt, q.v.

Wilson, Julia G. (Billingslea), 1870-1948 (Mt. Zion Methodist Church Cemetery); wife of Joseph Pearl Wilson, q.v.

Wilson, Kate E., 1866-1945 (Mt. Zion Methodist Church Cemetery)

Wilson, Katie (Miss), member, Lapidum M. P. Church (*The Aegis & Intelligencer*, 13 Jun 1890)

Wilson, L. Maude, 1886-1983 (Angel Hill Cemetery)

Wilson, Laura Gray, 1883-1957, native of Havre de Grace, born 8 Aug 1883, daughter of Lewis O. Wilson and Emma Green (Pennington Funeral Home Records - married name Jobes)

Wilson, Laura M., 1838-1914 (Darlington Cemetery)

Wilson, Laura M, 1873-1942 (Holy Trinity Episcopal Church Cemetery)

Wilson, Lena S., 1866-1954 (Fallston Methodist Church Cemetery)

Wilson, Leroy, 1887-1918 (Highland Presbyterian Church Cemetery)

Wilson, Levi (colored), see Hannah Wilson (colored) and Henrietta Wilson (colored), q.v.

Wilson, Lewis (colored), and family, resided near Ruff's Mill (*The Aegis & Intelligencer*, 12 Sep 1890)

Wilson, Lida, 1879-1963 (Angel Hill Cemetery - married name Broadwater); native of Havre de Grace, born 15 Jan 1879, daughter of Summerfield Wilson and Cynthia Connelly (Pennington Funeral Home Records state 1882, but tombstone states 1879)

Wilson, Lillian S., 1858-1939 (Darlington Cemetery)

Wilson, Lillie (Mrs.), treasurer, Abingdon M. E. Church Sunday School (*Havre de Grace Republican*, 2 May 1890)

Wilson, Louis O., 1855-1910 (Angel Hill Cemetery); charter member, Havre de Grace Gunning Club (*Havre de Grace Republican*, 14 Nov 1890); member, Guiding Star Council No. 9, Jr. O. U. A. M., Havre de Grace (*Havre de Grace Republican*, 11 Jul 1890); extra policeman, Havre de Grace (*Havre de Grace Republican*, 5 Sep 1890); sink boat duck hunter (*Havre de Grace Republican*, 7 Nov 1890); see Laura Gray Wilson and Agnes Wilson, q.v.

Wilson, Louis O. (Jr.), 1885-1934 (Angel Hill Cemetery)

Wilson, Lucy S., 1889-1946 (Highland Presbyterian Church Cemetery)

Wilson, Lydia A.(Shanberger), 1873-1950 (Angel Hill Cemetery)

Wilson, M. Louises, 1876-1902 (Holy Trinity Episcopal Church Cemetery)

Wilson, Malinda Jane (Cullison), 1831-1913, wife of William H. Wilson, q.v.

Wilson, Margaret, 1886-1918, daughter of William J. and Sarah Belle Wilson (Christ Episcopal Church Cemetery)

Wilson, Margaret J. (Miss), 1833-1918, native of Maryland, resided at Pylesville (Death certificate; Slate Ridge Cemetery, York Co., PA)

Wilson, Margaret W. (Williams), 1880-1972 (Highland Presbyterian Church Cemetery); native of Cardiff, Harford Co., born 16 Apr 1880, daughter of Thomas J. Williams and Mary Parry (Harkins Funeral Home

Records)

Wilson, Margaretta M., age 24 in 1890 (Marriage License Applications Book ALJ No. 2, 1891)

Wilson, Marie Berrie, 1878-1947 (Angel Hill Cemetery)

Wilson, Martha E. (Mrs.), 1836-1917, native of Port Deposit, Cecil Co., resident of Havre de Grace (Death certificate; Angel Hill Cemetery)

Wilson, Mary, county out-pensioner [welfare recipient], Second District, 1890 (*Havre de Grace Republican*, 4 Jul 1890)

Wilson, Mary (Miss), resident of Darlington (*The Aegis & Intelligencer*, 13 Jun 1890)

Wilson, Mary (Miss) (colored), 1869-1936, resident of Havre de Grace (St. James United Cemetery; Death certificate)

Wilson, Mary (Runley), see William J. Wilson, q.v.

Wilson, Mary A, 1845-1914 (Highland Presbyterian Church Cemetery)

Wilson, Mary Alicia (Webster), 1868-1930 (Churchville Presbyterian Church Cemetery)

Wilson, Mary Ann (Irwin), 1825-1906, native of Cecil Co., MD (Death certificate; Angel Hill Cemetery); businesswoman (trader's license), Havre de Grace (*Havre de Grace Republican*, 30 May 1890); mother of Charles Taylor Wilson, q.v.

Wilson, Mary Emma (Green), 1860-1917, native of Delaware, resident of Havre de Grace (Angel Hill Cemetery)

Wilson, Mary Frances, see Theodore Gover, q.v.

Wilson, Mary K., 1821-1911 (Angel Hill Cemetery)

Wilson, Mary Louisa, 1875-1902, born 17 Aug 1875, daughter of Henry and Priscilla Wilson (Holy Trinity Episcopal Church Cemetery, and Register of Baptisms, p. 82)

Wilson, Mary S. (Wilson), 1826-1902 (Darlington Cemetery); wife of David Elisha Wilson and mother of Charles Taylor Wilson and David E. Wilson, q.v.

Wilson, Mary V., 1879-1965 (Hopewell Cemetery, York Co., PA); native of Darlington, Harford Co., born 17 Apr 1877, daughter of Samuel Wilson and Sarah R. Shauck (Harkins Funeral Home Records)

Wilson, Nellie, student, Union School House, near Bush Chapel (*The Aegis & Intelligencer*, 14 Mar 1890); also see Mrs. M. L. Sewell, q.v.

Wilson, Nona, see Mrs. M. L. Sewell, q.v.

Wilson, Olivia Ann, see Jeremiah Lowe, q.v.

Wilson, Omelia, see William T. Wright, q.v.

Wilson, Patricia (Parke), 1872-1954, wife of Edward A. Wilson, q.v.

Wilson, Pauline C., 1849-1903 (Highland Presbyterian Church Cemetery)

Wilson, Pearl (Mr.), choir member, Bel Air M. P. Church (*The Aegis & Intelligencer*, 27 Jun 1890); member, Bel Air Cornet Band (*The Aegis & Intelligencer*, 1 Aug 1890); member, Division No. 2, Bel Air Fire and Salvage Corps (*The Aegis & Intelligencer*, 10 Oct 1890); "an aged negro impersonator," Bel Air Specialty Company, an entertainment group mostly connected to the young men of the Bulett Carriage Factory (*The Aegis & Intelligencer*, 13 Jun 1890)

Wilson, Priscilla, see Mary Louisa Wilson, q.v.

Wilson, Priscilla Gover (Lee), 1845-1905 (Holy Trinity Episcopal Church Cemetery); see R. Blanche Wilson, q.v.

Wilson, Priscilla P. (Presberry) (colored), 1865-1911, native of Harford Co., daughter of George Presbury [Presberry] and Sallie Ruff, also natives of Harford Co. (Death certificate)

Wilson, R. Blanche, 1880-1947, native of Bel Air, born 13 Feb 1880, daughter of Henry ("Harry") Wilson and Priscilla G. Lee (Death certificate)

Wilson, Rachael (Slade), 1837-1908, native of White Hall, resided at Jarrettsville (Death certificate)

Wilson, Ralph Lee, 1833-1911, son of Joshua Wilson and Rebecca Lee ---- (St. Mary's Episcopal Church Cemetery)

Wilson, Rebecca Barbara (Miss), 1843-1927, native of Harford Co., resided at Emmorton (Death certificate; Mt. Carmel Methodist Church Cemetery)

Wilson, Richard B., Civil War veteran, Cooptown (*1890 Special Census of the Civil War Veterans of the State of Maryland*, by L. Tilden Moore, Volume III, p. 79); officer of the day, Wann Post No. 49, G. A. R., of Forest Hill (*Havre de Grace Republican*, 25 Jul 1890)

Wilson, Robert Lee, 1871-1957 (St. Mary's Episcopal Church Cemetery), born 29 Jan 1871, son of William G. and Frances Anna (Wilson) Lee (William G. Wilson Bible, *Maryland Bible Records, Volume 2*, by Henry C. Peden, Jr., 2003, p. 186); R. L. Wilson, farmer, Emmorton (*The Aegis & Intelligencer*, 25 Apr 1890)

Wilson, Rose W., born 1889, died ---- (St. Ignatius Catholic Church Cemetery)

Wilson, Sadie L., student, Third District (*The Aegis & Intelligencer*, 24 Oct 1890)

Wilson, Sallie E., 1842-1912 (Cokesbury Memorial Methodist Church Cemetery)

Wilson, Samuel, 1845-1933 (Highland Presbyterian Church Cemetery); also see Alonzo Wilson and Mary V. Wilson, q.v.

Wilson, Samuel (colored), 1835-1913, native of Harford Co. (Death certificate); see Harriet W. Berry and Ida Elizabeth Whittington, q.v.

Wilson, Samuel J., of South Delta, married Miss Lottie J. Burns, of Fawn Grove, on 2 Jan 1890 at Grangers' Hotel in Bel Air (*Harford Democrat*, 3 Jan 1890; *The Aegis & Intelligencer*, 3 Jan 1890)

Wilson, Samuel T., Civil War veteran, Greenstone (*1890 Special Census of the Civil War Veterans of the State of Maryland*, by L. Tilden Moore, Volume III, p. 87)

Wilson, Samuel W., 1864-1952 (Highland Presbyterian Church Cemetery)

Wilson, Sarah Ann (Durham), 1821-1899, resident of Forest Hill, "native of America," wife of Humphrey Wilson, q.v. (Death certificate; Old Brick Baptist Church Cemetery)

Wilson, Sarah Belle, 1849-1920. wife of William J. Wilson (Christ Episcopal Church Cemetery); see Margaret Wilson and Walter Wilson, q.v.

Wilson, Sarah Jane (Parrott) (colored), 1868-1934 (Death certificate)

Wilson, Sarah Lucinda, 1876-1957 (Christ Episcopal Church Cemetery)

Wilson, Stanley, register of voters, Fourth District, 1890 (*The Aegis & Intelligencer*, 27 Jun 1890)

Wilson, Stephen, Civil War veteran, Dublin (*1890 Special Census of the Civil War Veterans of the State of Maryland*, by L. Tilden Moore, Volume III, p. 88)

Wilson, Stephen H. (colored), 1843-1924, native of Maryland (Death certificate); see Sarah W. Johnson and Charlotte A. Smith, q.v.

Wilson, Summefield, 1855-1940 (Angel Holl Cemetery); see Ethel Wilson and Lida Wilson, q.v.

Wilson, Summefield, Jr., 1877-1915 (Angel Hill Cemetery)

Wilson, Susan (colored), see Lily (Presbury) Smith (colored), q.v.

Wilson, Susan G. (Adams), 1825-1893 (Rock Run Methodist Church Cemetery); wife of William C. Wilson, q.v.

Wilson, Susan V., see Susan V. Presberry, q.v.

Wilson, Susanna R. (Lyon), 1834-1914 (Darlington Cemetery)

Wilson, Susanna "Susie" (Roberts), 1876-1935 (Darlington Cemetery); native of Harford Co., born 12 Dec 1876, daughter of William G. Roberts, of Norfolk, VA, and Mary F. Butler (Bailey Funeral Home Records); wife of David Gilpin Wilson, q.v.

Wilson, Thomas (colonel), of Havre de Grace (*Havre de Grace Republican*, 21 Feb 1890); juror, Sixth District (*Havre de Grace Republican*, 31 Oct 1890); secretary, Republican Club (*Havre de Grace Republican*, 7 Nov

1890); also see Rebecca A. McCall, q.v.

Wilson, Thomas Archer, 1883-1961 (St. Mary's Episcopal Church Cemetery)

Wilson, Thomas B., 1886-1949 (Angel Hill Cemetery)

Wilson, Verna L., 1887-1975 (Mt. Zion Methodist Church Cemetery)

Wilson, Virginia (Jones), 1879-1967 (Darlington Cemetery)

Wilson, Virginia L. (colored), see Virginia L. Hill (colored), q.v.

Wilson, W. H., trustee, Union School No. 10, First District, 1890 (*Havre de Grace Republican*, 30 May 1890)

Wilson, Walter, student, Forest Hill School, 1890 (*The Aegis*, 2 Jul 1965, school picture)

Wilson, Walter, 1885-1917, son of William J. and Sarah Belle Wilson (Christ Episcopal Church Cemetery)

Wilson, Walter E., 1877-1936, native of Havre de Grace, born 27 Jun 1877, son of William Wilson and Sarah Hyland (Death certificate; Angel Hill Cemetery)

Wilson, Wesley D., 1873-1944 (Darlington Cemetery)

Wilson, William, 1819-1895 (Smith Chapel Methodist Church Cemetery); Civil War veteran, Churchville (*1890 Special Census of the Civil War Veterans of the State of Maryland*, by L. Tilden Moore, Volume III, p. 70); died 21 Oct 1895 (Alms House Record Book)

Wilson, William A., associate judge of elections, Stearns Precinct [Fifth District] (*Havre de Grace Republican*, 17 Oct 1890); delegate, Democrat Party Convention (*The Aegis & Intelligencer*, 5 Sep 1890)

Wilson, William A., miller, Jerusalem Mills (*The Aegis & Intelligencer*, 7 Feb 1890), and his wife was a daughter of Jeremiah Lowe, q.v.; also see Jerusalem Mills, q.v.

Wilson, William A., 1886-1929, native of Maryland, born 25 Jun 1886, son of William H. Wilson and Mary Knight (Death certificate; Angel Hill Cemetery)

Wilson, William C., 1825-1916 (Rock Run Methodist Church Cemetery)

Wilson, William F., 1861-1939 (Highland Presbyterian Church Cemetery); farmer near Pylesville (*Havre de Grace Republican*, 14 Mar 1890); son of Archibald Wilson, q.v.

Wilson, William H., 1825-1915 (Highland Presbyterian Church Cemetery); dairyman (*Harford Democrat*, 14 Feb 1890)

Wilson, William H., 1826-1902 (St. George's Episcopal Church Cemetery); Civil War veteran, Havre de Grace (*1890 Special Census of the Civil War Veterans of the State of Maryland*, by L. Tilden Moore, Volume III, p. 91); director, Maryland Central Dairymen's Association (*Havre de Grace Republican*, 14 Mar 1890)

Wilson, William H., 1829-1897, captain (Angel Hill Cemetery)

Wilson, William H., 1877-1936, native of Havre de Grace, born 10 Dec 1877, son of Lewis O. Wilson and Emma Green (Death certificate; Angel Hill Cemetery)

Wilson, William H., see William A. Wilson, q.v.

Wilson, William H. (colored), see Frances Jane Wilson (colored), q.v.

Wilson, William J., husband of Sarah Belle Wilson, q.v.; also see Margaret Wilson and Walter Wilson, q.v.

Wilson, William J., 1858-1930 (Old Brick Baptist Church Cemetery)

Wilson, William J., 1870-1940, native of Lapidum, Harford Co., born 27 Feb 1870, son of William K. Wilson, of Pennsylvania, and Mary Runley, of Germany (Death certificate; Angel Hill Cemetery)

Wilson, William K., see William J. Wilson and Katie A. (Wilson) Johnson, q.v.

Wilson, William Lee, 1890-1981 (Holy Trinity Episcopal Church Cemetery)

Wilson, William W., Civil War veteran, Forest Hill (*1890 Special Census of the Civil War Veterans of the State of Maryland*, by L. Tilden Moore, Volume III, p. 74)

Wilson, William W., 1856-1937 (Darlington Cemetery)

Wilson, William W., 1884-1921 (Darlington Cemetery)

Wilson, Zora, born 1874, daughter of David and Racahel (Slade) Wilson (Bethel Presbyterian Church Cemetery Records); see Zora (Wilson) Turner, q.v.

Wilsy, Mary E., age 27 in 1890 (Marriage License Applications Book ALJ No. 2, 1890)

Wilton, James, 15 Mar - 14 Jul 1890 (St. George's Episcopal Church Cemetery)

Wilton's Grist Mill and Merchant Mill, on Winter's Run near Bel Air, Thomas Wilton, prop. (*Country Stores: Harford County's Rural Heritage*, by Henry C. Peden, Jr. and Jack L. Shagena, Jr., 2015, p. 285)

Wimbledon Public School, Fallston (*Harford County, Maryland Teachers and the Schools They Served, 1774-1900*, by Henry C. Peden, Jr., 2022, p. 373)

Winchester, Elizabeth (Mrs.), resident on corner of Broadway and Franklin Street, Bel Air (*The Aegis & Intelligencer*, 19 Sep 1890)

Winchester, Harriet, see Helen A. Evans, q.v.

Winchester, Louis (colored), see Susan A. Winchester (colored), q.v.

Winchester, Susan A. (colored), c1872-1922, daughter of Louis Winchester and Sarah Ringgold, natives of Maryland (Death certificate - married name Peters)

Windolph, Augustian J., 1832-1910 (Darlington Cemetery)

Windolph, George, actor, musical entertainment, at Darlington (*The Aegis & Intelligencer*, 30 May 1890)

Windolph, John Lauzalier (Dr.), 1848-1896 (Darlington Cemetery); veterinarian, Darlington (*The Aegis & Intelligencer*, 26 Sep 1890); owner, Deer Creek Stock Farm, Darlington (*The Aegis & Intelligencer*, 30 May 1890); member, Harford County Agricultural and Mechanical Society (*The Aegis & Intelligencer*, 10 Jan 1890); Civil War veteran, Darlington (*1890 Special Census of the Civil War Veterans of the State of Maryland*, by L. Tilden Moore, Volume III, p. 87)

Winemiller, Clarence C., 1888-1975 (Norrisville Methodist Church Cemetery)

Winemiller, Joseph, resident near Norrisville (*The Aegis & Intelligencer*, 9 May 1890); see Milton Winemiller, q.v.

Winemiller, Milton, 1876-1955 (Stewartstown Cemetery, York Co., PA); native of Baltimore Co., born 11 Oct 1876, son of Joseph B. Miller and Sopha Bowman (Bailey Funeral Home Records)

Winfield, George Francis (colored), 1877-1944, native of Perryman, Harford Co., born 15 Jun 1877, son of Peter Winfield and Margaret Tinson (Death certificate)

Wing, Abe, deceased and removed from the Havre de Grace voter registration list (*Havre de Grace Republican*, 19 Sep 1890)

Wing, Rufus (colored), 1883-1958 (St. James United Cemetery)

Wing, Verle (colored), 1882-1968 (St. James United Cemetery); wife of Rufus Wing, q.v.

Winkler, John, 1826-1901, native of Germany, farmer on William T. Sawyer's farm near Emmorton (Death certificate incomplete; *The Aegis & Intelligencer*, 19 Sep 1890)

Winkler, John S., 1871-1897 (Mt. Carmel Methodist Church Cemetery)

Winters, William, commander, E. B. Morrison Post No. 387, G. A. R., at Norrisville (*The Aegis & Intelligencer*, 6 Jun 1890)

Winzer, Pauline, see William B. Ross, q.v.

Wirsing, Charles E., 1890-1953 (Baker Cemetery)

Wirsing, Elizabeth F., 1861-1929 (Smith Chapel Methodist Church Cemetery)

Wirsing, Emma A., 1874-1942 (St. Paul's Lutheran Church Cemetery)

Wirsing, Frederick J., 1860-1926 (Smith Chapel Methodist Church Cemetery); native of Maryland, farmer, married, resided near Aberdeen (Death certificate gave name as John F. Wirsing)

Wirsing, Peter G., 1860-1921 (St. Paul's Lutheran Church Cemetery)

Wise, Daniel (colored), see I. Henry Wise (colored) and Mary Ellen Wise (colored), q.v.

Wise, Davis Winslow (colored), c1888-1950 (Death certificate)

Wise, Frankanna (Robinson) (colored), 1868-1928 (Union Methodist Church Cemetery, Aberdeen); native of Maryland, resided in Havre de Grace (Death certificate)

Wise, I. Henry (colored), 1876-1924, native of Maryland, born 29 Oct 1876, son of Daniel Wise and Mary Ellen Skinner (Death certificate)

Wise, Martha L. (Smith), 1887-1958 (Bryansville Cemetery, York Co., PA); native of Harford Co., born 7 Apr 1887, daughter of John W. Smith and Annie K. Klair (Harkins Funeral Home Records)

Wise, Mary Ellen (Skinner) (colored), 1858-1926 (Skinner Cemetery, Havre de Grace; Death certificate states age circa 60); wife of Daniel Wise, q.v.

Wise, Teresa, age 19 in 1890 (Marriage License Applications Book ALJ No. 2, 1891)

Wisher, Rosa Margaret (Shubert), 1842-1928 (Trinity Evangelical Lutheran Church Cemetery); native of Germany, resided at Joppa (Death certificate)

Wiseman, Samuel, c1881-1933, of Norrisville (Alms House Record Book)

Wisotzky, Mary Anna, 1867-1911 (Salem Evangelical Lutheran Church Cemetery)

Wisotzkey, William Craig, 1861-1939 (Salem Evangelical Lutheran Church Cemetery); age 29 in 1890 (Marriage License Applications Book ALJ No. 2, 1891)

Withers, J. M., see Hannah A. Pennell, q.v.

Wittkowsky, August, 1853-1926 (St. Paul's Lutheran Church Cemetery); native of Germany, day laborer, married, resident of Perryman (Death certificate)

Wittkowsky, Anna, wife of August Wittkowsky, q.v.

Witts, Dora, 1880-1918, native of Harford Co., born 26 Apr 1880, daughter of William Witts, of Virginia, and Sallie A. Clark, of Harford Co. (Death certificate - married name Ward)

Wolan, Anna Maria (Pyle), 1851-1926 (Mt. Carmel Methodist Church Cemetery); native of Maryland, resided at Emmorton (Death certificate)

Wolfe, Carl A., 1835-1910 (St. Paul's Lutheran Church Cemetery); Charles August Wolfe, native of Germany, farmer, married, resided at Carsins Run (Death certificate)

Wolfe, Bertha L., age 26 in 1889 (Marriage License Applications Book ALJ No. 2)

Wolfe, Dorthea, 1845-1918 (St. Paul's Lutheran Church Cemetery); Mary Dorthea (Thom) Wolfe, native of Germany, wife of Carl A. Wolfe (Death certificate)

Wolfe, Edward F., 1880-1940, son of Carl A. and Dorthea M. Wolfe (St. Paul's Lutheran Church Cemetery)

Wollas, Mary (colored), died 3 Jan 1890, of old age (Alms House Record Book)

Women's Christian Temperance Union, Havre de Grace (*Havre de Grace: Its Historic Past, Its Charming Present and Its Promising Future: Harford County's Rural Heritage.* by Jack L. Shagena, Jr. and Henry C. Peden, Jr., 2018, p. 278)

Women's Foreign Missionary Society of Churchville Presbyterian Church (*The Aegis & Intelligencer*, 25 Jul 1890)

Women's Total Abstinence Society, St. Patrick's Catholic Church, Havre de Grace (*Havre de Grace: Its Historic Past, Its Charming Present and Its Promising Future: Harford County's Rural Heritage.* by Jack L. Shagena, Jr. and Henry C. Peden, Jr., 2018, p. 279)

Wonders, Elma S., 1837-1902 (Bailey Funeral Home Records); Mrs. George Wonders, sister of Robert Ross, q.v.

Wonders, George, 1835-1922 (Deer Creek Methodist Church Cemetery); native of Germany (Bailey Funeral Home Records); farmer, near Mill Green (*The Aegis & Intelligencer*, 31 Jan 1890)

Wood, Albert H., 1873-1955 (Angel Hill Cemetery); son of James W. Wood, q.v.

Wood, Annie, student, Union Chapel Public School (*The Aegis & Intelligencer*, 14 Mar 1890)

Wood, Charles H., assistant superintendent, Magnolia M. E. Church Sunday School (*Havre de Grace Republican*, 2 May 1890)

Wood, Hutson, farmer, near Edgewood (*The Aegis & Intelligencer*, 10 Oct 1890)

Wood, J. W. (Mr.), assistant superintendent, Union Chapel M. P. Church (*The Aegis & Intelligencer*, 10 Jan 1890)

Wood, James W., 1842-1926 (Angel Hill Cemetery); father of Albert H. Wood, q.v.

Wood, James W., widower, age 42, married Millie F. Ward on 22 Apr 1890 ath the Bel Air Parsonage (Marriage License Applications Book ALJ No. 2, Bel Air Methodist Charge Marriage Records, p. 238)

Wood, Lida, student, Union Chapel Public School (*The Aegis & Intelligencer*, 14 Mar 1890)

Wood, Mary Ann, see Bertha Barnes, q.v.

Wood, Minnie Heisler (Smith), 1869-1940, native of Reisterstown, Baltimore Co., resided in Havre de Grace (Death certificate; Angel Hill Cemetery); wife of Albert H. Wood, q.v.

Wood, Olivia, see Susan (Robinson) Neville, q.v.

Wood, Thomas (Rev.), pastor of Bel Air M. E. Church, Harford Circuit (*The Aegis & Intelligencer*, 24 Jan 1890; *Havre de Grace Republican*, 14 Mar 1890)

Woodall, Lillian A., teacher, Black Horse School No. 3, Fourth District (*The Aegis & Intelligencer*, 29 Aug 1890)

Wooden, Clifton, student, Union School House, near Bush Chapel (*The Aegis & Intelligencer*, 14 Mar 1890)

Wooden, Henry or Harry, alias Valentine, charged with stealing a horse and wagon, found guilty, and sent to the Maryland Penitentiary for 6 years (Harford County Criminal Docket, 1888-1892, p. 92; *Harford Democrat*, 10 Oct 1890 and 28 Nov 1890; *The Aegis & Intelligencer*, 14 Nov 1890)

Wooden, J. Frederick (Rev.), pastor, Deer Creek M. P. Church (*Havre de Grace Republican*, 31 Oct 1890)

Wooden, Mary, student, Union School House, near Bush Chapel (*The Aegis & Intelligencer*, 14 Mar 1890)

Wooden, Osborn, student, Union School House, near Bush Chapel (*The Aegis & Intelligencer*, 14 Mar 1890)

Woodhouse, Elizabeth, 1808-1899, resident of Havre de Grace, wife of William Woodhouse (Death certificate; Angel Hill Cemetery)

Woodhouse, Elnathan N., 1833-1902 (St. Mary's Episcopal Church Cemetery); Confederate Army veteran, Havre de Grace (*Havre de Grace Republican*, 30 May 1890)

Woodland, Cassandra D., 1804-1895 (Mountain Christian Church Cemetery)

Woodmancy, Stella H., born 1874, died ---- (Mt. Erin Cemetery)

Woodrow, Edwin Everist ("Eddie"), 1881-1890 (Angel Hill Cemetery), only child of Mr. & Mrs. J. Frank Woodrow, of Havre de Grace (*Havre de Grace Republican*, 12 Dec 1890)

Woodrow, Estelle (Lemmon), 1874-1944 (Bethel Presbyterian Church Cemetery Records)

Woodrow, Eva R., 1862-1938 (Norrisville Methodist Church Cemetery)

Woodrow, Henrietta Thomas (Irwin), 1836-1907 (Angel Hill Cemetery; Death certificate); Mrs. J. Frank, of Havre de Grace, superintendent of press work, Women's Christian Temperance Union (*Havre de Grace Republican*, 5 Sep 1890); organist, Havre de Grace M. E Church (*Havre de Grace Republican*, 13 Jun 1890); recording secretary and superintendent of press work, Women's Christian Temperance Union, of Havre de Grace (*Havre de Grace Republican*, 19 Sep 1890)

Woodrow, John, 1837-1912 (Norrisville Methodist Church Cemetery); Civil War veteran, Norrisville (*1890 Special Census of the Civil War Veterans of the State of Maryland*, by L. Tilden Moore, Volume III, p. 81); government pensioner, Norrisville (*Havre de Grace Republican*, 20 Jun 1890)

Woodrow, John T., 1883-1951 (Norrisville Methodist Church Cemetery)

Woodrow, Joseph Francis ("J. Frank"), 1845-1895 (Angel Hill Cemetery), master builder, Havre de Grace

(*Havre de Grace Republican*, 23 May 1890); member, Susquehanna Lodge No. 130, A.F. & A. M., Havre de Grace (*Havre de Grace Republican*, 11 Jul 1890); also see Edwin Everist Woodrow, q.v.

Woodrow, Lydia, 1839--1928 (Norrisville Methodist Church Cemetery)

Woodrow, Lysander W., 1859-1934 (Norrisville Methodist Church Cemetery); farmer, *Greenbriar Farm*, near Norrisville (*Harford Democrat*, 28 Mar 1890)

Woodrow, Mary (Miss), member, Norrisville M. P. Church (*The Aegis & Intelligencer*, 7 Mar 1890)

Woodrow, William H. R., 1877-1956 (Bethel Presbyterian Church Cemetery Records)

Woods, Albert S., 1873-1955, native of Harford Co., born 2 May 1873, son of James W. Woods and Susan Grimes (Pennington Funeral Home Records)

Woods, Annie (Miss), member, Mountain Reading Circle (*The Aegis & Intelligencer*, 21 Feb 1890)

Woods, David Langley, c1877-1951 (Mt. Erin Cemetery); resided in Havre de Grace, parents unknown (Bailey Funeral Home Records)

Woods, Edith, premium award winner, Class J - Domestic Products, Harford County Fair (*The Aegis & Intelligencer*, 24 Oct 1890)

Woods, Esther (Mrs.), resident near Fallston (*The Aegis & Intelligencer*, 15 Aug 1890)

Woods, James W., trustee, Union Chapel School No. 1, Third District (*Havre de Grace Republican*, 30 May 1890); see Lonnie W. Woods and Albert S. Woods, q.v.

Woods, John, died 6 Aug 1905, age not given (Alms House Record Book)

Woods, Lida (Miss), member, Mountain Reading Circle (*The Aegis & Intelligencer*, 21 Feb 1890)

Woods, Lonnie W., 1876-1950, native of Baltimore Co., born 9 Nov 1876, daughter of James W. Woods and Mary J. Parker (Cokesbury Memorial Methodist Church Cemetery; Pennington Funeral Home Records and Death certificate gave her name as Mrs. Eugene L. Thompson)

Woods, Susie (colored), see Jane Rebecca Amos (colored), q.v.

Woods, William, and wife, sold land in May 1890 (*The Aegis & Intelligencer*, 6 Jun 1890)

Woods, William, farmer, near The Rocks (*Havre de Grace Republican*, 4 Jul 1890)

Woodward, Nelson, served on a petit jury, Fourth District (*The Aegis & Intelligencer*, 16 May 1890; *Havre de Grace Republican*, 16 May 1890)

Woolfman, John C., farmer, near Edgewood (*Havre de Grace Republican*, 14 Nov 1890)

Woolford, Emily, see Orion G. Coale, q.v.

Woolsey, Rebecca (Miss), 1823-1901, native of Harford Co., resided near Churchville (Death certificate; Churchville Presbyterian Church Cemetery)

Worthington, Annie, 1854-1904 (Darlington Cemetery)

Worthington, Annie Elizabeth (Laughinghouse), 1886-1967 (Darlington Cemetery)

Worthington, Bell, 1886-1958 (Churchville Presbyterian Church Cemetery)

Worthington, Blanche (Mrs.), 1853-1925 (Angel Hill Cemetery)

Worthington, Blanche Hall (Lee), 1822-1897 (Darlington Cemetery); resided near Darlington; mother-in-law of C. Bosley Littig, of Baltimore, who had married Hannah Pamela Worthington (*The Aegis & Intelligencer*, 29 Aug 1890); also see James Moores Worthington, q.v.

Worthington, Charles Hammond, 1846-1903 (Darlington Cemetery)

Worthington, Clarence, 1875-1970 (Angel Hill Cemetery)

Worthington, Drucilla Taylor, 1860-1897, daughter of Mr. & Mrs. Joseph E. Worthington (*The Aegis*, 15 Oct 1897; Trappe Church Cemetery)

Worthington, Edith, 1881-1948 (Darlington Cemetery); native of Harford Co., daughter of Moores Worthington and Mollie Scott (Bailey Funeral Home Records)

Worthington, Elizabeth, 1845-1916 (Angel Hill Cemetery)

Worthington, Elizabeth (Green), 1857-1943 (Angel Hill Cemetery)

Worthington, Elizabeth Viola, 1886-1963 (Churchville Presbyterian Church Cemetery)

Worthington, Ezekiel (colored), born -- Apr 1845, whitewasher, native of Maryland (1900 Aberdeen Census)

Worthington, Fannie J., 1866-1953. native of Darlington, Harford Co., born 8 Apr 1866, daughter of Joseph E. Worthington and Olivia Johnson (Pennington Funeral Home Records - married name Gorrell); see Stanley Worthington Gorrell, q.v.

Worthington, George M., 1882-1955 (Angel Hill Cemetery)

Worthington, Helen Lee, 1879-1931 (Darlington Cemetery); native of Maryland, born 23 Nov 1879, daughter of James M. Worthington and Mary E. Scott (Bailey Funeral Home Records)

Worthington, James, 1851-1930 (Angel Hill Cemetery)

Worthington, James, see Virginia L. Frieze, q.v.

Worthington, James Moores, 1847-1890 (Darlington Cemetery); son of James C. Worthington, 1819-1884, and Blanche Hall (Lee) Worthington, 1822-1897, q.v. (*The Aegis & Intelligencer*, 18 Apr 1890)

Worthington, John Dallam, 1856-1922 (Darlington Cemetery); son of William Worthington Dallam and Mary Wilson; former teacher and school principal (*Biographical Dictionary of Harford County, Maryland, 1774-1974*, by Henry C. Peden, Jr. and William O. Carr, 2021, p. 303); County School Examiner, of Bel Air (*Havre de Grace Republican*, 14 Feb 1890; member of the State Board of Education (*Havre de Grace Republican*, 21 Feb 1890; secretary, Harford School Board (*Havre de Grace Republican*, 11 Apr 1890; member, Loyal Temperance Legion of Bel Air (*The Aegis & Intelligencer*, 2 May 1890); premium award winner, Class B - Cattle, Harford County Fair (*The Aegis & Intelligencer*, 24 Oct 1890)

Worthington, John S., 1854-1918 (Angel Hill Cemetery)

Worthington, John Thomas Chew, 1843-1922 (Darlington Cemetery)

Worthington, John W., 1839-1918, native of Maryland, farmer near Have de Grace (Death certificate; Angel Hill Cemetery)

Worthington, Joseph E., juror, Fifth District, 1890 (*Havre de Grace Republican*, 2 May 1890); see Fannie J. Worthington and Drucilla Taylor Worthington, q.v.

Worthington, Joseph F., 1803-1896 (Churchville Presbyterian Church Cemetery)

Worthington, Joseph Kent, 1854-1896 (Darlington Cemetery); also see John Keating, q.v.

Worthington, Joseph Kent, 1882-1923 (Darlington Cemetery)

Worthington, Josephine G. (Harlan), 1857-1957 (Darlington Cemetery)

Worthington, Littleton Green, 1884-1945, native of Havre de Grace, born 1 Dec 1884, son of William E. Worthington and Louisa Green (Pennington Funeral Home Records)

Worthington, Lottie M., 1883-1967 (Angel Hill Cemetery)

Worthington, Louisa (Green), 1859-1939 (Churchville Presbyterian Church Cemetery); wife of Joseph E. Worthngton, q.v.

Worthington, Louise H., 1885-1979 (Angel Hill Cemetery)

Worthington, Malcolm McLean, 1882-1933 (Darlington Cemetery); second grade honor student and actor, Bel Air Graded School, 1890 (*The Aegis & Intelligencer*, 4 Jul 1890 and 26 Dec 1890)

Worthington, Margaret H., died 12 Aug 1896, age 76 (*Deaths and Marriages in Harford County, Maryland, and Vicinity, 1873-1904, from the Diaries of Albert Peter Silver*, transcribed by Glenn Randers-Pehrson, 1995, p. 33)

Worthington, Mary (Chapman), 1854-1933 (Darlington Cemetery)

Worthington, Mary (Spencer), 1880-1972 (Darlington Cemetery)

Worthington, Mary Eliza (Scott), 1845-1904 (Darlington Cemetery); wife of James Moores Worthington, q.v.

Worthington, Mary S., 1858-1913 (Churchville Presbyterian Church Cemetery)

Worthington, Mary Theresa (McCormick), 1855-1951 (Darlington Cemetery); premium award winner, Class J - Domestic Products, Harford County Fair (*The Aegis & Intelligencer*, 24 Oct 1890); wife of John Dallam Worthington, q.v.

Worthington, Moores, see Edith Worthington and James Moores Worthington, q.v.

Worthington, Oleita, 1883-1962, native of Havre de Grace, born 9 Mar 1883, daughter of William Worthington and Louisa Green (Pennington Funeral Home Records - married name Osborn)

Worthington, Rebecca, 1828-1905 (Churchville Presbyterian Church Cemetery)

Worthington, Roberta Parker (Miss), 1858-1934 (Bailey Funeral Home Record; Darlington Cemetery)

Worthington, Sarah C., 1854-1926 (Angel Hill Cemetery)

Worthington, William, see Oleita Worthington, q.v.

Worthington, William E., 1855-1940 (Churchville Presbyterian Church Cemetery); served on a petit jury, Sixth District, 1890 (*Havre de Grace Republican*, 31 Oct 1890; *The Aegis & Intelligencer*, 14 Nov 1890); see Littleton Green Worthington, q.v.

Worthington, William Evans, 1881-1918 (Angel Hill Cemetery)

Wren, Belvia S., wife of Oliver W. Wren, q.v.

Wren, Oliver W., 1842-1901, native of England, actor, resided in Havre de Grace (Death certificate)

Wright's School, Franklin St. and Broadway, Bel Air, Prof. Wright, vocal and instrumental music and French teacher (*Harford Democrcat*, 3 Jan 1890)

Wright, Almira Elizabeth, 1888-1977 (Bethel Presbyterian Church Cemetery); second daughter of Charles Thomas Wright, q.v.

Wright, Alverta H., 1882-1928, native of Maryland, born 18 Aug 1882, daughter of John Wright and Clara Hamilton (Death certificate - married name Wilson; *Havre de Grace Republican*, 8 Apr 1927)

Wright, Camilla B., c1878-1928 (Mountain Christian Church Cemetery); native of Maryland, resided at Wilna, daughter of Thomas Wright and Sallie Bond (Death certificate)

Wright, Charles Milton, 1881-1976 (Bel Air Memorial Gardens); born 22 Sep 1881, son of William B. and Laura Jane (Jackson) Wright (Caleb Wright Bible, *Maryland Bible Records, Volume 2*, by Henry C. Peden, Jr., 2003, p. 188)

Wright, Charles Thomas, 1850-1922 (Bethel Presbyterian Church Cemetery); principal, Bel Air Graded School (*The Aegis & Intelligencer*, 11 Apr 1890)

Wright, Clara (Hamilton), 1859-1911 (St. George's Episcopal Church Cemetery)

Wright, Clarence Leslie, 1871-1969, native of Havre de Grace, born 17 Nov 1871, son of John Wright and Martha Irvin (Pennington Fnneral Home Records; Angel Hill Cemetery); assistant secretary, Willard Section No. 58, Cadets of Temperance, Havre de Grace, 1890 (*Havre de Grace Republican*, 11 Jul 1890)

Wright, Cora (Garrett), 1880-1956 (Ayres Chapel Methodist Church Cemetery)

Wright, D. Yingling, 1888-1960 (St. Paul's Methodist Church Cemetery)

Wright, Eliza, see Walter Streett Morris, q.v.

Wright, Elizabeth, see Carrie Blanche Hamby and George Henry Wright, q.v.

Wright, Elizabeth J., 1856-1953 (Bethel Presbyterian Church Cemetery)

Wright, Emma Elizabeth, 1864-1942 (St. George's Episcopal Church Cemetery)

Wright, Fannie W. (Bristow), 1874-1956 (Angel Hill Cemetery)

Wright, Frances A., 1885-1960 (Rock Run Methodist Church Cemetery)

Wright, George (colored), see Katherine Robinson (colored), q.v.

Wright, George Edward, 1865-1935 (St. George's Episcopal Church Cemetery)

Wright, George Edward, Jr., 1887-1930 (St. George's Episcopal Church Cemetery)

Wright, H. Blanche, 1885-1970 (Ayres Chapel Methodist Church Cemetery)

Wright, Hannah, 1819-1902 (St. Paul's Methodist Church Cemetery)

Wright, Hannah (Wright), 1830-1911 (Bethel Presbyterian Church Cemetery Records); widow of J. Franklin Wright (1829-1860)

Wright, Hannah Elizabeth, born 21 Jun 1887, daughter of William B. and Laura Jane (Jackson), Wright (Caleb Wright Bible, *Maryland Bible Records, Volume 2*, by Henry C. Peden, Jr., 2003, p. 188)

Wright, Hannah Elizabeth (Jackson), 1856-1953 (Bethel Presbyterian Church Cemetery Records); wife of Charles Thomas Wright, q.v.

Wright, James Thomas, 1833-1905 (Mountain Christian Church Cemetery)

Wright, Jeff, age 24 in 1889 (Marriage License Applications Book ALJ No. 2, 1889)

Wright, John, see Clarence L. Wright, William H. Wright and Taylor M. Wright, q.v.

Wright, John, resident of Norrisville (*The Aegis & Intelligencer*, 17 Oct 1890)

Wright, John, seine fisherman, Rock Run shore and Wood Island in the Susquehanna River (*The Aegis & Intelligencer*, 4 Apr 1890); see Alverta H. Wright, q.v.

Wright, John C., employee of DuBois Saw Mill, Havre de Grace (*The Aegis & Intelligencer*, 5 Sep 1890)

Wright, John C. B., 1860-1930 (Bethel Presbyterian Church Cemetery Records); acquired land in November 1890 (*The Aegis & Intelligencer*, 5 Dec 1890)

Wright, John Geyer, 1860-1928 (Angel Hill Cemetery)

Wright, John W., see William T. Wright, q.v.

Wright, Josephine (colored), 1889-1926 (St. James United Cemetery)

Wright, Joshua W., 1825-1899, resided at Wright's Corner near Carea (Death certificate; *The Aegis & Intelligencer*, 31 Mar 1899; St. Paul's Methodist Church Cemetery); see Sallie R. Wright and Benjamin Franklin Lowe, q.v.

Wright, Katherine (colored), see Katherine Robinson (colored), q.v.

Wright, Laura E. (Oliver), 1865-1928 (St. Mary's Episcopal Church Cemetery)

Wright, Laura Jane (Jackson), 1855-1943 (Ayres Chapel Methodist Church Cemetery), wife of William Benton Wright, q.v.

Wright, Leslie Floyd, 1879-1959 (Ayres Chapel Methodist Church Cemetery)

Wright, M., third baseman, Creswell Baseball Club (*The Aegis & Intelligencer*, 18 Jul 1890)

Wright, Margaret, see Rebecca J. Barrett, Caroline P. Jones and Americus I. Jones q.v.

Wright, Margaret A., 1855-1921 (St. Paul's Methodist Church Cemetery)

Wright, Marion, 1883-1961, native of Havre de Grace, born 30 Mar 1883, daughter of William H. Wright and Mary C. Curry (Pennington Funeral Home Records - maiden name Vicari)

Wright, Martha Jane, 1830-1910 (Angel Hill Cemetery)

Wright, Mary Ellen (Reed), 1850-1938 (Ayres Chapel Methodist Church Cemetery)

Wright, Mary Susan, see Thomas Emory Cathcart, q.v.

Wright, Maude, see George Walter Jordan, q.v.

Wright, Millard F., 1863-1957 (St. Mary's Episcopal Church Cemetery); miller, at Swansbury, near Aberdeen, and also near Calvary (*The Aegis & Intelligencer*, 8 Aug 1890); *Havre de Grace Republican*, 7 Mar and 1 Aug 1890)

Wright, Nellie B., 1883-1928 (Ayres Chapel Methodist Church Cemetery)

Wright, R. Virginia (Bull), 1852-1920 (St. Paul's Methodist Church Cemetery)

Wright, Rachel, county out-pensioner [welfare recipient], Fifth District (*Havre de Grace Republican*, 4 Jul 1890); see Robert A. Jones, q.v.

Wright, Sallie R., age 28 in 1890 (Marriage License Applications Book ALJ No. 2, 1890), married Benjamin Franklin Lowe on 19 Feb 1890 at the home of Joshua W. Wright (marriage certificate)

Wright, Sarah, see Ella Norris, q.v.

Wright, Sarah (Stephenson), 1883-1973 (St. Mary's Episcopal Church Cemetery)

Wright, Sidney (Mrs.), premium award winner, Class J - Domestic Products, Harford County Fair (*The Aegis & Intelligencer*, 24 Oct 1890)

Wright, Taylor M., 1888-1963, native of Havre de Grace, born 29 Dec 1888, son of John Wright and Clara Hamilton (Pennington Funeral Home Records; Angel Hill Cemetery)

Wright. Thomas Chapman, 1876-1891 (Mountain Christian Church Cemetery)

Wright, William A., 1852-1925 (St. Paul's Methodist Church Cemetery)

Wright, William Benton, 1848-1918 (Ayres Chapel Methodist Church Cemetery); justice of the peace, Fourth District (*Havre de Grace Republican*, 21 Feb 1890); magistrate, Fourth District (*Havre de Grace Republican*, 4 Jul 1890); trustee, Dry Branch School No. 2, Fourth District (*Havre de Grace Republican*, 30 May 1890); see Charles Milton Wright, q.v.

Wright, William H., 1880-1939 (Rock Run Methodist Church Cemetery); native of Harford Co., born 19 Feb 1880, son of John Wright and Mary Crew (Bailey Funeral Home Records)

Wright, William H., see Marion Wright, q.v.

Wright, William Perdue, 1883-1963 (Ayres Chapel Methodist Church Cemetery); born 22 May 1883, son of William B. and Laura Jane (Jackson) Wright (Caleb Wright Bible, *Maryland Bible Records, Volume 2*, by Henry C. Peden, Jr., 2003, p. 188)

Wright, William T., 1869-1921, native of Aberdeen, MD, buried in Wilmington, DE; son of John W. Wright and Omelia Wilson (Bailey Funeral Home Records)

Wright, William V., age 45 in 1890 (Marriage License Applications Book ALJ No. 2, 1891)

Wroth, E. Pinkney, 1889-1946 (Darlington Cemetery)

Wroth, Edward Worrell (Rev.), 1851-1924 (Darlington Cemetery); pastor of Grace Memorial P. E. Church, Darlington (*The Aegis & Intelligencer*, 26 Sep 1890)

Wroth, John, student, Fifth District (*The Aegis & Intelligencer*, 24 Oct 1890)

Wroth, Margaret G. {Price), 1858-1924 (Darlington Cemetery); native of Maryland, born 20 Jan 1858, daughter of John Price and Mary R. Parker (Bailey Funeral Home Records); Mrs. E. W. Wroth, organist, Grace Memorial P. E. Church, Darlington (*The Aegis & Intelligencer*, 26 Sep 1890); wife of Rev. Edward W. Wroth, q.v.

Wyatt, D. P. (Prof.), director, musical entertainment, at Darlington (*The Aegis & Intelligencer*, 30 May 1890)

Wyatt, J. Thomas, 1890-1967 (Jarrettsville Cemetery)

Wye, James Henry, born 1871, died ---- (St. Mary's Catholic Church Cemetery)

Wye, Lewis W. (colored), age 34 in 1890 (Marriage License Applications Book ALJ No. 2, 1891)

Wynde, William, merchant tailor and clothing store, Darlington (*The Aegis & Intelligencer*, 3 Jan 1890 and 26 Sep 1890; *Country Stores: Harford County's Rural Heritage*, by Henry C. Peden, Jr. and Jack L. Shagena, Jr., 2015, p. 268); actor, musical entertainment, at Darlington (*The Aegis & Intelligencer*, 30 May 1890)

Wysong, Annie P., 1850-1922 (Christ Episcopal Church Cemetery)

Wysong, D. Preston (Dr.), home owner on corner of Broadway and Franklin Street, Bel Air (*The Aegis & Intelligencer*, 16 May 1890 and 19 Sep 1890)

Wysong, Ella J. (Grimes), 1874-1905 (Christ Episcopal Church Cemetery), wife of John; Bond Wysong, q.v.

Wysong, Frank, 1856-1926 (Christ Episcopal Church Cemetery)

Wysong, John Bond, 1847-1918 (Christ Episcopal Church Cemetery); vestryman and register, Christ Church,

Rock Spring (*Havre de Grace Republican*, 18 Apr 1890); served on a grand jury (*The Aegis & Intelligencer*, 14 Nov 1890); juror, Third District (*Havre de Grace Republican*, 31 Oct 1890); member, Deer Creek Farmers' Club (*Havre de Grace Republican*, 16 May 1890); son of Thomas Turner Wysong, q.v.

Wysong, Sarah Frances (Preston), 1825-1898 (Christ Episcopal Church Cemetery); wife of Thomas Turner Wysong, q.v.

Wysong, Thomas Turner, 1816-1899, resided in Bel Air, native of West Virginia (Death certificate; Christ Episcopal Church Cemetery)

Yarnell, Harriet Ellen, born 24 Mar 1890, daughter of Jacob P. and Harriet E. Yarnell (St. George's Episcopal Church Register of Baptisms, pp. 10-11)

Yarnell, Jacob P., see Harriet Ellen Yarnell and Robert Bruce Yarnell, q.v.

Yarnell, Robert Bruce, born 15 Aug 1887, son of Jacob P. and Harriet E. Yarnell (St. George's Episcopal Church Register of Baptisms, pp. 10-11)

Yarrish, Agnes, student, Union School House, near Bush Chapel (*The Aegis & Intelligencer*, 14 Mar 1890)

Yeager, Annie, 1862-1933 (Union Chapel Methodist Church Cemetery)

Yeager, Catherine, died 16 Aug 1892, of old age (Alms House Monthly Register)

Yellott, George T., 1819-1902 (Trinity Episcopal Church Cemetery, Baltimore County)

Yellott, Howard, 1879-1954, son of George W. and Nannie Yellott (St. Mary's Episcopal Church Cemetery)

Yellott, Richard, student, Oakland School, 1890 (George G. Curtiss Ledger)

Yerkes, Jacob E., miller, Deep Run Mills (*Harford Democrat*, 12 Sep 1890); see Deep Run Mills, q.v.

Yewell, Richard W., 1888-1949 (Mountain Christian Church Cemetery)

Yingling, Jacob M. (Rev.), pastor of St. Paul's M. P. Church, near the Long Corner (*The Aegis & Intelligencer*, 31 Jan 1890); incorporator, Norrisville Methodist Protestant Church (*Havre de Grace Republican*, 7 Feb and 4 Apr 1890); also see John Yost, q.v.

York and Peach Bottom Slate Manufacturing Company, Harford County quarry (*Heavy Industries of Yesteryear; Harford County's Rural Heritage*, by Jack L. Shagena, Jr. and Henry C. Peden, Jr., 2015, p. 212)

York, Harriet (Stewart) (colored), 1848-1917, native of Maryland (Death certificate)

York, John W. (colored), 1829-1892 (Old Union Chapel Cemetery, Michaelsville)

Yost, John, young son of Jacob Yost, of Norrisville (*The Aegis & Intelligencer*, 9 May 1890)

Young Muffer Baseball Club, of Bel Air (*The Aegis & Intelligencer*, 14 Mar 1890)

Young Sluggers Baseball Club, of Bel Air (*The Aegis & Intelligencer*, 4 Jul 1890)

Young's General Store, Bel Air, James C. Young, prop. (*Country Stores: Harford County's Rural Heritage*, by Henry C. Peden, Jr. and Jack L. Shagena, Jr., 2015, p. 268)

Young, Adam (Mrs.), actress, musical entertainment, at Darlington (*The Aegis & Intelligencer*, 30 May 1890)

Young, Albert (colored), 1847-1934, resident of Emmorton (Death certificate)

Young, Alexander (colored), c1868-1938, native of Harford Co., parents unknown (Death certificate)

Young, Andrew Jackson, Jr., 1888-1965 (St. Mary's Episcopal Church Cemetery)

Young, Annie (Miss), singer and member, Emmanuel Episcopal Church, Bel Air (*The Aegis & Intelligencer*, 11 Apr 1890)

Young, Caroline (Johnson) (colored), 1858-1901, native of Harford Co. (Death certificate)

Young, Christian, 1825-1909, native of Germany, resided at Cooptown (Death certificate; *The Aegis & Intelligencer*, 22 Jan 1909)

Young, Esther, 1834-1908 (Angel Hill Cemetery)

Young, Florence (Miss), premium award winner, Class K - Household and Domestic Manufactures, Harford County Fair (*The Aegis & Intelligencer*, 24 Oct 1890)

Young, Fred H., 1882-1962 (Angel Hill Cemetery)

Young, Gertrude S., 1881-1961 (Rock Run Methodist Church Cemetery); wife of William A. Young, q.v.

Young, Henry, see Raymond C. Young, q.v.

Young, Henry [Harry] Lee, 1860-1944 (St. Mary's Episcopal Church Cemetery); son of William S. Young, q.v.

Young, J. Henry, see Mary A. Young, q.v.

Young, James C., 1859-1930 (St. Mary's Episcopal Church Cemetery); chief marshal, Bel Air jousting tournament, 1890 (*Havre de Grace Republican*, 19 Sep 1890); member, Division No. 2, Bel Air Fire and Salvage Corps (*The Aegis & Intelligencer*, 10 Oct 1890); son of William S. Young, q.v.; also see Young's General Store, and Cochran & Young's General Store, q.v.

Young, John, 1862-1934 (Old Brick Baptist Church Cemetery)

Young, John A., 1853-1929 (Mt. Zion Methodist Church Cemetery); watchmaker, jeweler, engraver and optician, Main St., Bel Air (*Harford Democrat*, 10 Jan 1890; *Biographical Dictionary of Harford County, Maryland, 1774-1974*, by Henry C. Peden, Jr. and William O. Carr, 2021, p. 307); junior warden, Mt. Ararat Lodge, A. F. & A. M., Bel Air (*Havre de Grace Republican*, 19 Dec 1890)

Young, John Scott, 1855-1939 (St. Mary's Episocpal Church Cemetery; incorporator and director, Bel Air Trust Company (*Havre de Grace Republican*, 14 Mar 1890); son of William S. Young, q.v.

Young, Kate E. (Brandt), 1861-1933 (Mt. Zion Methodist Church Cemetery); resident near Harford Furnace (*The Aegis & Intelligencer*, 9 May 1890); soprano singer and choir member, St. Ignatius Catholic Church, at Hickory (*The Aegis & Intelligencer*, 11 Apr 1890); wife of John A. Young, q.v.

Young, Lillie B., 1880-1963 (Angel Hill Cemetery)

Young, Mary A., filed for a divorce from her husband J. Henry Young on 6 Jul 1888 and it was granted on 19 Jun 1890 (*Harford County Divorces and Separations, 1823-1923*, by Henry C. Peden, Jr., 2016, p. 220)

Young, Mary A. (Fulton), 1835-1905 (St. Ignatius Catholic Church Cemetery)

Young, Mary Alice (Durham), 1872-1945 (Old Brick Baptist Church Cemetery); widow of John Young and daughter of Mr. & Mrs. William Durham (*The Aegis*, 30 Mar 1945)

Young, Mary Elizabeth (Cochran) (Bowers), 1828-1915 (St. Mary's Episcopal Church Cemetery); premium award winner, Class B - Cattle, and Class K - Household and Domestic Manufactures, and Class O - Discretionary, Harford County Fair (*The Aegis & Intelligencer*, 24 Oct 1890); wife of William S. Young, q.v.

Young, Mary Ella, see Josephine Burk, q.v.

Young, Mary V., 1872-1932 (Mt. Erin Cemetery)

Young, Millicent Linn "Millie" (Miss), 1866-1938, daughter of William and Mary E. Young (St. Mary's Episcopal Church Cemetery); singer and member, Emmanuel Episcopal Church, Bel Air (*The Aegis & Intelligencer*, 11 Apr 1890)

Young, Mr., blacksmith, uncalled for letter in Bel Air P. O., 1890 (*The Aegis & Intelligencer*, 4 Jul 1890)

Young, R. A., merchant in Bel Air, moved his family to Mt. Vernon in Somerset Co., MD (*Harford Democrat*, 21 Mar 1890)

Young, Rachel (colored), see Lillie Jeanette Harris (colored), q.v.

Young, Raymond C., 1889-1957 (William Watters Memorial Methodist Church, Cooptown); native of Harford Co., born 5 Nov 1889, son of Henry Young and Elizabeth F. Durham (Bailey Funeral Home Records)

Young, Robert (colored), husband of Caroline Young (colored), q.v.

Young, Thomas J., 1866-1938 (Mt. Erin Cemetery); sneak boat duck hunter (*Havre de Grace Republican*, 7 Nov 1890)

Young, Walter B., 1881-1951 (Mt. Zion Methodist Church Cemetery); student and actor, Bel Air Graded School (*The Aegis & Intelligencer*, 26 Dec 1890)

Young, Walter C., 1886-1965 (Fallston Methodist Church Cemetery)

Young, William A., 1882-1974 (Rock Run Methodist Church Cemetery)

Young, William C., 1880-1906 (Old Brick Baptist Church Cemetery)

Young, William R., 1828-1909 (Angel Hill Cemetery)

Young, William S., 1828-1892, Baltimore (St. Mary's Episcopal Church Cemetery); attorney-at-law and probable Civil War (Confederate Army) veteran; former county surveyor and sheriff (*Biographical Dictionary of Harford County, Maryland, 1774-1974*, by Henry C. Peden, Jr. and William O. Carr, 2021, p. 307)

Youse, Alice (Miss), 1863-1938, ntrive of Baltimore (Loudon Park Cemetery); teacher, Bel Air Graded School (*The Aegis & Intelligencer*, 11 Apr 1890)

Youth's Benefit Public School No. 6, near Fallston (*Harford County, Maryland Teachers and the Schools They Served, 1774-1900*, by Henry C. Peden, Jr., 2022, p. 373)

Zacharias, George, 1851-1931, resident of Bel Air (Death certificate; Alms House Record Book)

Zealor, Dilla C., 1880-1959 (William Watters Memorial Methodist Church Cemetery, Cooptown)

Zealor, Ormsby Mitchell, 1870-1947 (William Watters Memorial Methodist Church Cemetery, Cooptown)

Zech, Isaac, 1820-1896, resided near Pylesville (Slate Ridge Cemetery; *The Aegis & Intelligencer*, 22 May 1896)

Zeigler, Dora, 1871-1926, wife of Valentine Zeigler (Union Chapel Methodist Church Cemetery)

Zeitler, Charles J., 1827-1913 (Mt. Erin Cemetery); jeweler and city councilman, Havre de Grace (*Havre de Grace Republican*, 10 Jan 1890); businessman (trader's license), Havre de Grace (*Havre de Grace Republican*, 30 May 1890); director, Havre de Grace Improvement Company (*Havre de Grace Republican*, 7 Feb 1890); organizer and vice president, Havre de Grace Democratic Club (*Havre de Grace Republican*, 31 Oct 1890)

Zeitler, Edward A., 1858-1931 (Angel Hill Cemetery); pharmacist, Havre de Grace (Death Certificate); council vice president, Beneficial Order of Equity, Havre de Grace (*Havre de Grace Republican*, 21 Nov 1890); juror, Sixth District (*Havre de Grace Republican*, 31 Jan 1890); businessman (trader's license), Havre de Grace (*Havre de Grace Republican*, 30 May 1890)

Zeitler, Mary Margarum, 1832-1910 (Mt. Erin Cemetery); wife of Charles J. Zeitler, q.v.

Zeitler, Susan "Sue" (Charshee), 1850-1950 (Angel Hill Cemetery); native and resident of Havre de Grace (Death certificate), wife of Edward A. Zeitler, q.v.

Zellman, Amelia (Whicker), 1855-1931 (Holy Trinity Episcopal Church Cemetery)

Zellman, John, 1890-1956 (Bailey Funeral Home Records); native of Harford Co., born 4 Feb 1890, baptized 17 Oct 1890, son of John and Amelia Zellman (Holy Trinity Episcopal Church Register of Baptisms, pp. 98-99, misspelled the name as Zellmar; Deer Creek Harmony Presbyterian Church Cemetery tombstone inscribed 1891)

Zellman, John D., 1852-1921 (Holy Trinity Episcopal Church Cemetery); farmer and native of Germany (Bailey Funeral Home Records)

Zellman, Mary, 1871-1921 (Holy Trinity Episcopal Church Cemetery)

Zellman, Mary A., 1881-1969 (Death certificate - married name Thomas); daughter of John D. Zellman and Amelia A. Whicker (www.findagrave.com)

Zimmerman, Charles K., see Axer & Zimmerman's General Store, q.v.

Zimmerman, John A., 1874-1952 (Darlington Cemetery); parents unknown (Bailey Funeral Home Records)

Zimmerman, Mary A., 1811-1897 (Union Chapel Methodist Church Cemetery)

Zimmerman, Mary J., 1826-1910 (Union Chapel Methodist Church Cemetery)

Zinkham, Sarah Ethel, 1890-1965 (William Watters Memorial Methodist Church Cemetery, Cooptown)

Zinkham, Sophia M. (Shriver), 1861-1946 (William Watters Memorial Methodist Church Cemetery, Cooptown)

Zinkham, William Casper, 1961-1947 (William Watters Memorial Methodist Church Cemetery, Cooptown)

Zirl, August F., new name on the voter registration list in Sixth District, 1890 (*Havre de Grace Republican*, 17 Oct 1890)

Heritage Books by Henry C. Peden, Jr.:

1890 Reconstructed Census of Harford County, Maryland, Volume 1: A-J

1890 Reconstructed Census of Harford County, Maryland, Volume 2: K-Z

A Closer Look at St. John's Parish Registers [Baltimore County, Maryland], 1701–1801

A Collection of Maryland Church Records

A Guide to Genealogical Research in Maryland: 5th Edition, Revised and Enlarged

Abstracts of Marriages and Deaths in Harford County, Maryland, Newspapers, 1837–1871

Abstracts of the Ledgers and Accounts of the Bush Store and Rock Run Store, 1759–1771

Abstracts of the Orphans Court Proceedings of Harford County, 1778–1800

Abstracts of Wills, Harford County, Maryland, 1800–1805

African American Cemeteries in Harford County, Maryland

Anne Arundel County, Maryland, Marriage References 1658–1800
Henry C. Peden, Jr. and Veronica Clarke Peden

Baltimore City [Maryland] Deaths and Burials, 1834–1840

Baltimore County, Maryland, Overseers of Roads, 1693–1793

Bastardy Cases in Baltimore County, Maryland, 1673–1783

Bastardy Cases in Harford County, Maryland, 1774–1844

More Bastardy Cases in Harford County, Maryland, 1773–1893

Bible and Family Records of Harford County, Maryland, Families: Volume V

Biographical Dictionary of Harford County, Maryland, 1774–1974:
Over 1,200 Sketches of Prominent Citizens during the First 200 years of the County's
History with Seventeen Appendices Listing Public Officials from 1774 to 2020
Henry C. Peden, Jr. and William O. Carr

Cecil County, Maryland Marriage References, 1674–1824
Henry C. Peden, Jr. and Veronica Clarke Peden

Children of Harford County: Indentures and Guardianships, 1801–1830

Colonial Delaware Soldiers and Sailors, 1638–1776

Colonial Families of the Eastern Shore of Maryland
Volumes 5, 6, 7, 8, 9, 11, 12, 13, 14, 16, and 19
Henry C. Peden, Jr. and F. Edward Wright

Colonial Families of the Eastern Shore of Maryland: Volume 21 and Volume 23

Colonial Maryland Soldiers and Sailors, 1634–1734

Colonial Tavern Keepers of Maryland and Delaware, 1634–1776

Dorchester County, Maryland, Marriage References, 1669–1800
Henry C. Peden, Jr. and Veronica Clarke Peden

Dr. John Archer's First Medical Ledger, 1767–1769, Annotated Abstracts

Early Anglican Records of Cecil County

Early Harford Countians, Individuals Living in Harford County, Maryland in Its Formative Years
Volume 1: A to K, Volume 2: L to Z, and Volume 3: Supplement

Family Cemeteries and Grave Sites in Harford County, Maryland, (Revised Edition)

First Presbyterian Church Records, Baltimore, Maryland, 1840–1879

Frederick County, Maryland, Marriage References and Family Relationships, 1748–1800
Henry C. Peden, Jr. and Veronica Clarke Peden

Genealogical Gleanings from Harford County, Maryland, Medical Records, 1772–1852
Winner of the Norris Harris Prize from MHS for the best genealogical reference book in 2016!

Harford County Taxpayers in 1870, 1872 and 1883

Harford County, Maryland Death Records, 1849–1899

Harford County, Maryland Deponents, 1775–1835

Harford County, Maryland Divorces and Separations, 1823–1923

Harford County, Maryland, Death Certificates, 1898–1918: An Annotated Index

Harford County, Maryland, Divorce Cases, 1827–1912: An Annotated Index

Harford County, Maryland, Inventories, 1774–1804

Harford County, Maryland, Marriage References and Family Relationships, 1774–1824
Henry C. Peden, Jr. and Veronica Clarke Peden

Harford County, Maryland, Marriage References and Family Relationships, 1825–1850

Harford County, Maryland, Marriage References and Family Relationships, 1851–1860
Henry C. Peden, Jr. and Veronica Clarke Peden

Harford County, Maryland, Marriage References and Family Relationships, 1861–1870
Henry C. Peden, Jr. and Veronica Clarke Peden

Harford County, Maryland, Marriage References and Family Relationships, 1871–1875

Harford County, Maryland, Marriage References and Family Relationships, 1876–1880

*Harford (Maryland) Homicides: Cases of Murder and Attempted Murder:
Committed by Men and Women Who Were "Seduced by the Instigation of the Devil"
in Harford County, Maryland During the 18th and 19th Centuries*

*Harford (Maryland) Suicides: Cases of Self-killings and Attempted Suicides Committed by Men and
Women Who Suffered from an "Aberration of the Mind" in Harford County, Maryland, 1817–1947*

*Harford (Old Brick Baptist) Church, Harford County, Maryland, Records and Members (1742–1974),
Tombstones, Burials (1775–2009) and Family Relationships*

Heirs and Legatees of Harford County, Maryland, 1774–1802

Heirs and Legatees of Harford County, Maryland, 1802–1846

Inhabitants of Baltimore County, Maryland, 1763–1774

Inhabitants of Cecil County, Maryland 1774–1800

Inhabitants of Cecil County, Maryland, 1649–1774

Inhabitants of Harford County, Maryland, 1791–1800

Inhabitants of Kent County, Maryland, 1637–1787

Insolvent Debtors in 19th Century Harford County, Maryland: A Legal and Genealogical Digest

*Joseph A. Pennington & Co., Havre De Grace, Maryland, Funeral Home Records:
Volume II, 1877–1882, 1893–1900*

Kent County, Maryland Marriage References, 1642–1800
Henry C. Peden, Jr. and Veronica Clarke Peden

Marriages and Deaths from Baltimore Newspapers, 1817–1824

Maryland Bible Records, Volume 1: Baltimore and Harford Counties

Maryland Bible Records, Volume 2: Baltimore and Harford Counties

Maryland Bible Records, Volume 3: Carroll County

Maryland Bible Records, Volume 4: Eastern Shore

Maryland Bible Records, Volume 5: Harford, Baltimore and Carroll Counties

Maryland Bible Records, Volume 7: Baltimore, Harford and Frederick Counties

Maryland Deponents, 1634–1799

Maryland Deponents: Volume 3, 1634–1776

Maryland Prisoners Languishing in Goal, Volume 1: 1635–1765

Maryland Prisoners Languishing in Goal, Volume 2: 1766–1800

*Maryland Public Service Records, 1775–1783: A Compendium of Men and Women of Maryland
Who Rendered Aid in Support of the American Cause against Great Britain during the Revolutionary War*

Marylanders and Delawareans in the French and Indian War, 1756–1763

Marylanders to Carolina: Migration of Marylanders to North Carolina and South Carolina prior to 1800

Marylanders to Kentucky, 1775–1825

Marylanders to Ohio and Indiana, Migration Prior to 1835

Marylanders to Tennessee

Methodist Records of Baltimore City, Maryland: Volume 1, 1799–1829

Methodist Records of Baltimore City, Maryland: Volume 2, 1830–1839

*Methodist Records of Baltimore City, Maryland: Volume 3, 1840–1850
(East City Station)*

More Maryland Deponents, 1716–1799

More Marylanders to Carolina: Migration of Marylanders to North Carolina and South Carolina prior to 1800

More Marylanders to Kentucky, 1778–1828

More Marylanders to Ohio and Indiana: Migrations Prior to 1835

Orphans and Indentured Children of Baltimore County, Maryland, 1777–1797

www.ingramcontent.com/pod-product-compliance
Lightning Source LLC
Chambersburg PA
CBHW080603270326
41928CB00016B/2904